FOREWORD

I've been playing video games too long to admit. Years ago, I was blessed with my first job as a game designer. And then I was blessed again to be employed at Bethesda Game Studios to finish up *TES IV: Oblivion* and then move on to our take on the iconic *Fallout* universe with *Fallout 3*.

The *Fallout* franchise is one of legend. A world set in an alternative timeline, full of both horror and humor. A world where nearly anything goes, where solving problems is not a straight line, a world in which nothing is black and white.

The move into three dimensions, a first-person perspective and real time forever changed the way the game would be perceived. And now, with *Fallout 76*, we are moving into another dimension. One in which every other human you interact with is another player, experiencing their own story, in their own way, in their own home.

I'm excited to explore this vision with you, our amazing fans. The thrill of participating in events with your friends. The fear of stumbling on someone deep in the forest when on your own, wounded and low on ammo. The discovery of creatures of local legend. The thrill of hunting down a wanted murderer.

This game will tell you stories like none other. Set out into Appalachia and lose yourself in your new home, which you now share with others. And if you stumble across a vault dweller playing a banjo in their camp on the side of an irradiated river, wave at them—that's probably me.

Jeff Gardiner

Project Leader

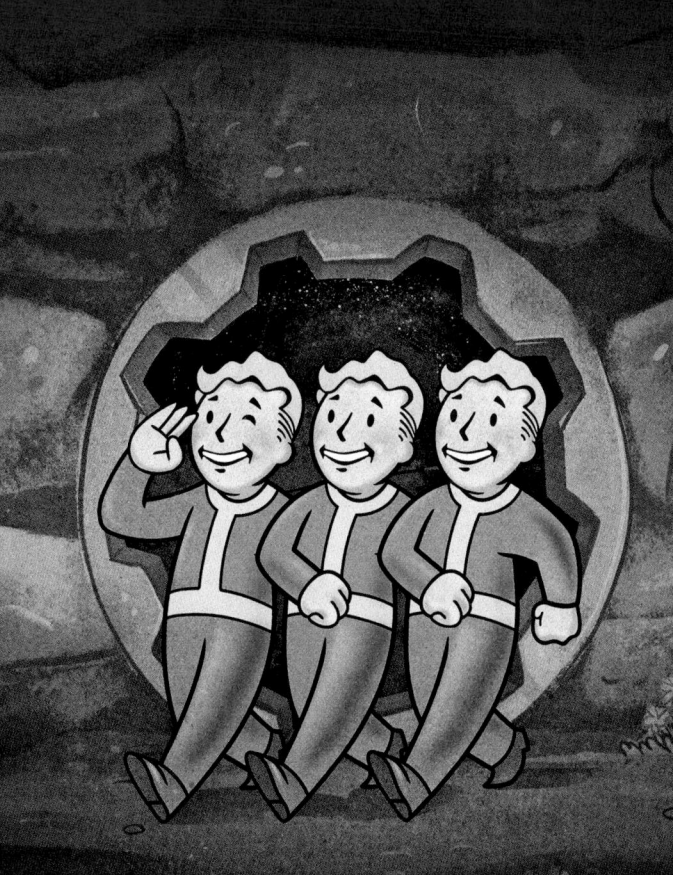

Reclamation Begins!

WELCOME TO WEST VIRGINIA!

VAULT 76 WAS BUILT TO SAVE THE BEST AND THE BRIGHTEST IN THE EVENT OF A NUCLEAR HOLOCAUST. ON RECLAMATION DAY, THEY WOULD EMERGE AND BEGIN TO REBUILD AMERICA. TODAY IS THAT DAY....

APPALACHIA: THE REGIONS OF WEST VIRGINIA

REGION 1: THE FOREST

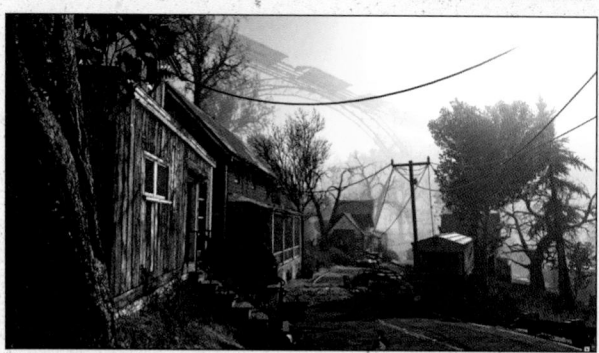

The region surrounding Vault 76 was known as "the Forest" to the survivors of Appalachia. Still rich in plant and animal life, it is an ideal place to scrounge for food and water. Although relatively untouched by the bombs, the Forest is still home to the mutated beasts that now roam the countryside. Survivors even reported finding mutated plants with unusual properties...Near the Vault 76 construction site is the small town of Flatwoods, which was home to a local motel, tavern, and church. Vault-Tec projections for the survivability of the area's residents were not optimistic. Farther to the northeast is the larger settlement of Morgantown, which was home to Vault-Tec University and experienced something of a revitalization before the war. The townspeople all knew the harsh truth: that Vault entrance was not guaranteed. To the south is the old West Virginia capital of Charleston, one of the largest cities in the area. Prior to the Great War, it was a hotbed of political dissent and saw countless protests for workers' rights.

REGION 2: TOXIC VALLEY

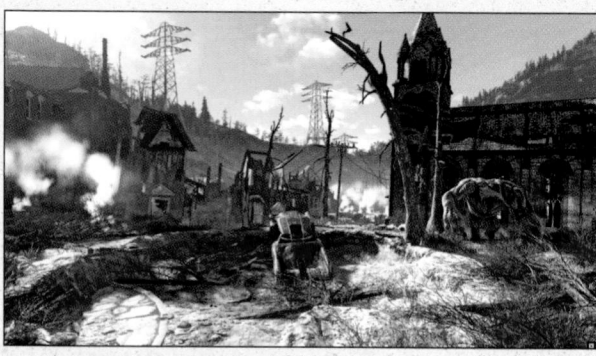

The region known to survivors as "Toxic Valley" is covered by industrial white powder and polluted water sources. The lake and other deadly waters of the Toxic Valley region are home to all manner of mutated, aquatic beasts. Above the fetid lake, Grafton Steel Mill was the center of economic development for the town of Grafton, and its large, industrial machines remain relatively intact. Grafton was built on the shores of the Tygart Valley River. It was a hub for shipping prior to the Great War, thanks to having both water and railroad access. Now it seems deserted and inhospitable. Straddling the boundary between Toxic Valley and the Forest is Grafton Dam. Built to provide power to the Steel Mill, the dam is now filled with the polluted waters of Toxic Valley.

REGION 3: THE ASH HEAP

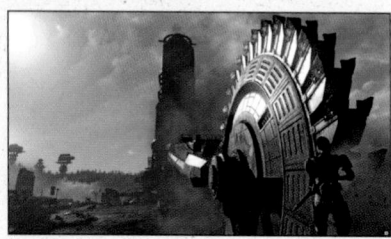

Smoke and cinders constantly bellow up from the mines in the Ash Heap. Survivors believed this was caused by fires in the tunnels below, raging unceasingly for some unknown reason. As the winds blow and the wind changes, it is common for thick layers of filthy smoke to blanket the area, providing cover for friend and foe alike. But there are reasons to venture into this choking nightmare; the mines deep within Appalachia's mountains still hold riches for those brave enough to venture below....Top of the Heap, Mount Blair, was a large-scale coal mining site before the War, where gigantic digging machines removed entire portions of the mountaintop at once. The Garrahans and Hornwrights were the two major families in charge of Appalachia's mining industry. They owned lavish estates in the mountains overlooking their precious mines.

REGION 4: SAVAGE DIVIDE

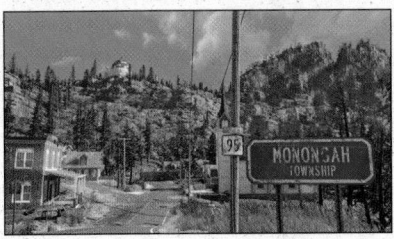

The region of Appalachia known to survivors as the "Savage Divide" is a mountainous area whose rocky landscape is difficult to cross and easy to get lost in. Before the Great War, these high mountains of Appalachia were home to ski resorts, bed-and-breakfasts, and cabins available to rent by eager tourists. Among the most popular was Top of the World, originally an enormous ski lift station, complete with shops and restaurants at its peak. Farther north and nestled in the mountains is a spiritual retreat center known as the Palace of the Winding Path. Its unique architecture stands in stark contrast to the rest of Appalachia. Elsewhere, government facilities dot the landscape of Appalachia's mountains. Trading rumors of the goings-on inside those fenced-in walls was a popular prewar pastime.

REGION 5: THE MIRE

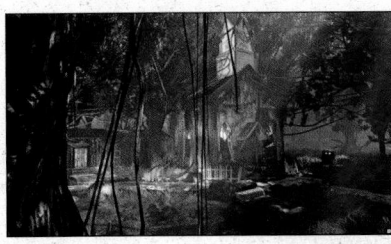

Known as the "Mire" by the survivors of Appalachia, this swampy region is home to twisting vines, large tree canopies, and tall grass. All easy places for things to hide...Tread deeper into the dark swamp, and you may find mutated plants known as "strangler vines" that infest the Mire. They attach to living things, notably the large trees in the area. The Mire is also home to the Dyer Chemical plant, which originally produced animal feed and other phosphates used for nearby farms. Another place to check for signs of life is Harpers Ferry, a small town that depended on tourism: This put them at odds with the growing "Free States" movement, whose conspiracy theories put off patriotic visitors. Don't leave the Mire without visiting the Survival Training Center, a survival skills training facility, open to tourists who want to learn how to rough it out in the wilderness. Hopefully, those lessons came in handy.

REGION 6: CRANBERRY BOG

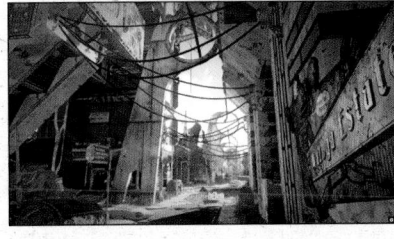

The colorful red floras of Cranberry Bog were originally West Virginia's naturally occurring cranberry, pitcher, and sundew plants. The survivors of Appalachia avoided the Cranberry Bog more than any other region, and only the most well-equipped dared to travel here, not least because of the stories told about the Allegheny Asylum, which was originally built in the mid-1800s as a treatment facility for the mentally ill. Farther into the Bog, Watoga was built as a joint effort between the federal government, RobCo, and Atomic Mining Services to build a "city of the future." All public services in Watoga were designed to be completely automated, including a full staff of security robots.

THE FACTIONS OF WEST VIRGINIA

BROTHERHOOD OF STEEL

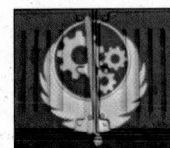

Taggerdy's Thunder was a US Army Ranger unit led by Lieutenant Elizabeth Taggerdy. She continued to lead her troops—as a Paladin—after they all joined the Brotherhood of Steel. Paladin Taggerdy was known for only recruiting from those who had military experience and found it difficult to coordinate with the other, more "civilian" factions in Appalachia. Fort Defiance served as headquarters for the newly established Appalachian branch of the Brotherhood of Steel.

THE FREE STATES

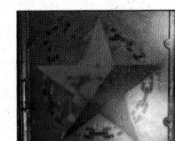

The Free States were a group of Appalachian anarchists who seceded from the United States shortly before the bombs fell. Paranoid that the government was lying to its people about the Vault program, the Free States movement built their own concrete bunkers to survive in case of nuclear devastation. While Raleigh Clay was the public face of the Free States, his arrest would reveal US Senator Sam Blackwell to also be a driving force behind the movement. Most of Appalachia considered the Free States movement to be nothing but political agitators and traitors. After the war, many of these same people would turn to the Free States for help.

RAIDERS

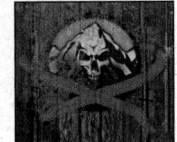

The Raider groups of Appalachia were bloodthirsty psychopaths who terrorized the other survivors, taking whatever they wanted from them. Expert scavengers, the Raider groups of Appalachia were surprisingly ingenuous when it came to salvaging old world technology. After the bombs fell, several wealthy tourists on Appalachian ski holidays reverted to their baser instincts. Selfishness turned to violence, and these entitled elitists became vicious Raiders.

THE RESPONDERS

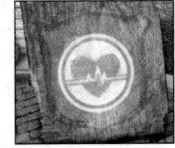

After the Great War, Appalachia's emergency personnel mobilized to help their fellow citizens. These Responders became part government, part crisis relief. The Responders provided automated survival training to anyone in need. And it was needed quite a bit. Survival and security became paramount after the devastation of the Great War, and the Responders desperately tried to help as many of their neighbors as they could.

THE WHITESPRING RESORT

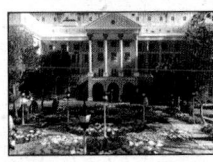

Built in 1858, The Whitespring was famous for its southern style and sulfur springs. The Whitespring Resort had a long history of business with the federal government and counted sitting US presidents among its guests. Under great financial strain before the war, The Whitespring was forced to sell much of its surrounding land and replace the resort staff with more cost-effective robots.

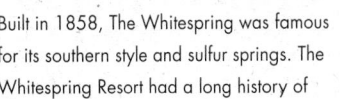

STATUS: YOU WILL EMERGE!

INITIAL PREPARATIONS FOR LIFE OUTSIDE VAULT 76

Your Pip-Boy, Your Friend

INVENTORY MANAGEMENT!

RADIO RECEIVER!

HEALTH MONITORING...

AND MORE!

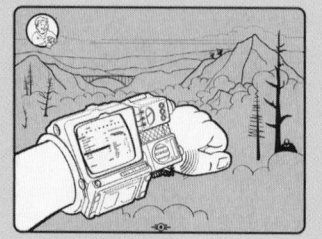

WELCOME TO WEST VIRGINIA! AS YOU PREPARE TO LEAVE VAULT 76, WE SUGGEST READING THIS INITIAL SECTION OF THE "TRAINING" CHAPTER TO FAMILIARIZE YOURSELF WITH MENU AND HEAD'S-UP DISPLAY (HUD) INFORMATION. YOU WILL THEN LEARN THE BASIC MANEUVERS (BOTH PASSIVE AND VIOLENT) THAT WILL SAVE YOUR LIFE AFTER RECLAMATION DAY. YOUR APPALACHIAN EXPERIENCE AWAITS!

Helpful Hint from Vault-Boy!

READ THIS FIRST!

You may be initially overwhelmed with the new life that awaits you outside of the safety of Vault 76. Before seeking calming chemical stimulants, it is worth familiarizing yourself with the Main Menu (accessed via the map) and the "Help" option: This provides a complete basic training in the arts of survival and is worth digesting before you seek deeper meaning about your emergence throughout this guide.

LOOKING GOOD: CHARACTER CREATION

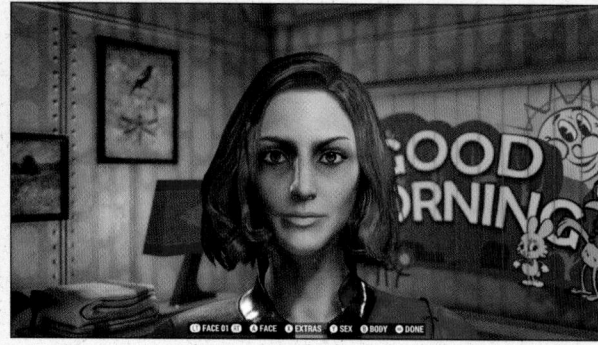

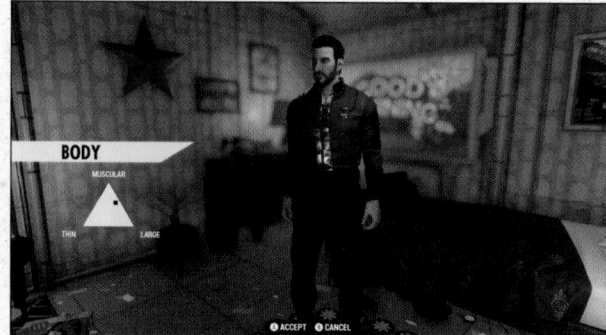

You begin in Vault 76 with some adjustments to your appearance. Spend as long as you like changing your gender, face, and body. Then name your character, and take a photo for your Vault 76 Resident Card. Don't worry! This image (and your entire look) can be changed later.

THE PIP-BOY 2000

Once you leave your Vault chamber, you'll have attached a RobCo Industries technological wonder to your wrist; the Pip-Boy 2000! This grants you a variety of useful information and a HUD (Heads-Up Display) to augment your normal sight, but getting to know where all of this information is, and what it means, may take a few moments.

OPTIMIZED VIEWING PORTAL

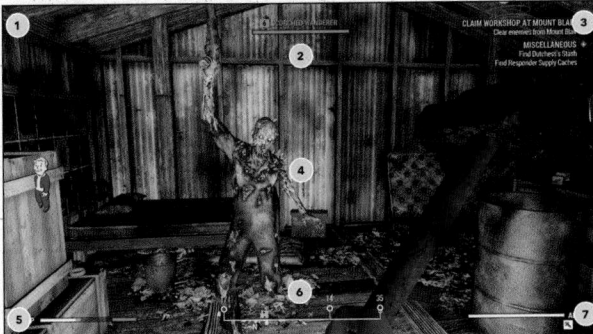

Optimized Viewing Portal (Normal view).

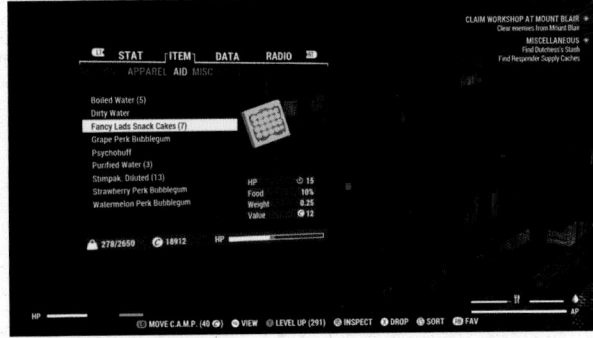

"Quick-Boy": Streamlined Viewing Portal (Normal view).

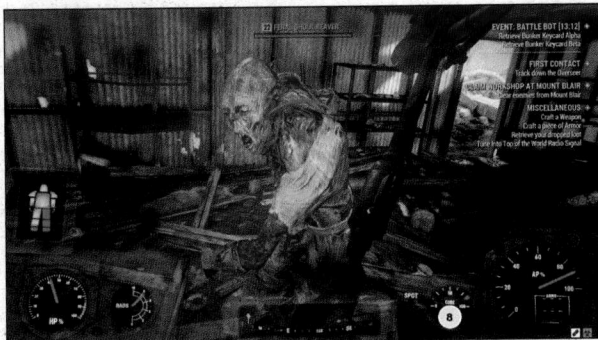

Optimized Viewing Portal (Power Armor view).

This is your optimized viewing portal, or "view". Pip-Boy functionality helps you navigate the hostile environment, whether you're wearing Power Armor or not.

1 TOP LEFT CORNER SECTION

Information from Vault-Tec: When you encounter something, Vault-Tec sends a helpful note.

Item Pick-up: When an item is gathered and stored, the name (and amount) is noted.

Radio: If a radio station becomes available, you are informed here.

New Effect: If your well-being changes, a Vault-Boy icon appears (such as when you're crippled, famished or parched, or receive a disease).

2 TOP MIDDLE SECTION

Quest Start and Completion: If a new quest becomes available, its name and Vault-Boy animation appear here. Completion rewards are also shown here.

Entity Information: When an entity is in visual range, its health, level, and sub-type are shown. Sub-types include: Boss (Crown), Legendary (Star), Radioactive (Radiation), Toxic (Poison Drip), Weak, Extra Difficulty (Stars), or too-powerful to handle yourself (Skull).

Sneaking Level: If you're Sneaking, your Level of Detection is indicated.

3 TOP RIGHT SECTION

Quest Objectives: With one or more active quests (for you and your teammates), the latest objectives are listed here, with the compass showing the checkpoint or area to explore.

4 CENTRAL SECTION

Target and Damage Taken: This changes from a dot to a target of varying dimensions depending on the weapon or action you're undertaking. Use this to target a foe when firing from the hip, and the curved red marks to determine where you're being wounded from.

Context Sensitive Information: When interacting with an object, be it a door, fallen foe, trader, container, or anything else, the button required is shown here, along with your Carry Weight if you're gathering an item.

5 BOTTOM LEFT CORNER SECTION

Health Bar: This shows your Health as a percentage. The right side indicates how many of the 1,000 Rads you can take, as after receiving Rad damage, the right side of the bar fills up red. Take Rad-X (and protective clothing) before entering radioactive areas, and take RadAway after contracting radiation to restore your Health Bar.

Damage Type: This indicates the type of damage. Normal damage isn't flagged, but there are icons for Explosive, EMP/Pulse, Radiation, Energy, and Poison damage.

Reward Information: If you've completed a Challenge or other feat, information is briefly displayed here.

Teammate Information: If you're partnered with friends, their icon and health bar are shown here.

6 BOTTOM MIDDLE SECTION

Compass: This displays pertinent information including: nearby locations, enemies, quest checkpoints, checkpoint areas, events, CAMPs, your last death, other players, your Team Leader, Hostile Players, and the Custom Marker.

Other Information: Also expect this area to show location names, your Caps Total when you gain or lose Caps, your Critical Hit Meter (in V.A.T.S.), Experience Points (XP) rewards, when you level up, and you or another's Wanted Level (if you or they have slain other players).

7 BOTTOM RIGHT SECTION

Server-Related Information: When you enter the game world, join a team, or the server has information to impart, it is listed here.

Ammo and Projectiles: The current ranged weapon ordnance you're carrying, along with your currently-equipped projectile, are flagged here.

Hunger and Thirst: This indicates how much food and drink you need to consume to gain bonuses and avoid penalties. If you don't see either meter, you're usually okay. Both meters drain over time (Thirst more rapidly).

Action Points (APs) and Current Conditions: APs are used up by sprinting, Power Attacks, V.A.T.S., and steadying your aim. If your AP meter is too low, these actions may be blocked or canceled. AP constantly regenerates unless you're hungry, thirsty, or over-encumbered. Agility (total AP) and Endurance (Sprinting and AP) grant you a higher AP. Under the AP bar are any effects (penalties or buffs) you are suffering from, like being Well-Rested or Mutated.

8 CORE (POWER ARMOR ONLY)

This measures the remaining energy in your Power Armor's Fusion Core. Once the Fusion Core drains, movement and AP actions are impossible for your Power Armor. Fusion Cores are automatically swapped, so always carry a spare. Or eight.

TRAINING

CRAFTING AND C.A.M.P.ing

INVENTORY

QUESTS

ATLAS

BESTIARY

APPENDICES

PIP-BOY 2000: MENU ACCESS ACTIVATED!

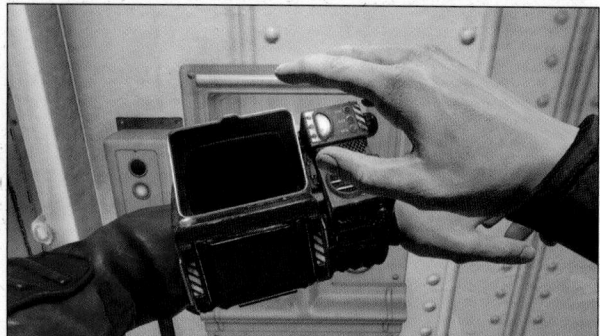

RobCo Industries has constructed a tough wrist-mounted device with analog counters for the Date and Time, as well as a Rad-Meter. Here is how to read all four of the menus, vitally important to your well-being, on your Pip-Boy:

Active Menu: This menu allows you to bring up your C.A.M.P., switch between regular and "Quick-Boy" views, and access your Perks.

STAT: Stimpak and RadAway: Immediately access these Chems for faster narcotic delivery!

ITEM: Fav, Inspect, Drop and Sort, Play: Favorite the 12 items, weapons, apparel, and aid you use the most. Inspect anything you pick up for additional data, drop items you don't want to carry any more, and play Holotapes.

DATA: Toggle Active, Hide, Show on Map: Toggle quest information, turn it on your off if your HUD is getting cluttered, as well as showing Quests on your map.

STAT Tab (Status): Maintain your health and well-being as well as your SPECIAL abilities from this tab.

ITEM Tab: Check your arsenal, outfits, chems, collection, and auxiliary objects in your collection from this tab. Access information for your Weapons, Apparel, Aid, Misc (items that don't fit into other categories), Holo (your Holotapes), Notes (clues you've picked up as well as Recipes and Plans), Junk ("useless" items you break down into useful crafting, modding, or building components), Mods (for advanced weaponry or armor), and Ammo.

DATA Tab: Access and highlight all the various quest-related activities you are undertaking from this tab.

RADIO Tab: Highlight and tune in to any available music or transmitting station within a specific radius.

PIP-BOY FLASHLIGHT

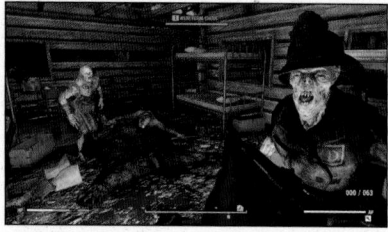

Remember that your Pip-Boy, certain mining helmets, and Power Armor helmets all have flashlight capabilities for exploring in dark places. Though the green-tinged hue you give off attracts both enemies and Vault-Dwellers alike (making this a non-starter for a stealthy infiltration of an area), you're far less likely to get lost, miss loot or enemies, or lose your footing. To turn on your Pip-Boy's (or Power Armor's) flashlight (or headlamp), hold down the button you used to access the Pip-Boy, and again to turn it off again.

Helpful Hint from Vault Boy!

Any items you carry have pertinent data displayed in the STAT area of the screen, as follows:

Level (Weapons, Apparel): The level of an item (some items are higher than your current level, and are grayed out. It's impossible to equip these until you reach the correct level). When you craft an item, you can choose its level depending on your own (for every five Levels you raise, you can unlock another).

CND (Condition) (Weapons, Apparel): This shows the current condition of the item. The item's condition will decrease through use and combat damage until the item breaks and can no longer be used without repairing it at an appropriate workbench.

Damage (Weapons): This is the damage, in Hit Points, that the weapon inflicts with a single bullet, shotgun blast, or beam strike.

DMG Resist (Damage Resistance) (Apparel): This value does not indicate the Hit Points of damage your armor absorbs from an enemy attack, but rather a percentage of the potential damage. Basically, if your DMG Resist is the same as your enemy's weapon damage, expect to absorb around half of the attack's damage. The higher the rating, the better the resistance.

Speed (Weapons): The swiftness of a melee-range weapon is listed here.

Ammo Type (Weapons): This is the type of ammunition the weapon uses. Scavenge, purchase, or craft more of this to keep yourself from running out of ammo. Receiver mods can change the ammo type.

Fire Rate (Weapons): The number of shots you're likely to get off within a 10 second span of time, not including reloading. The higher, the better.

Range (Weapons): The distance the weapon can fire before the projectile fired from it begins to loose its potency. The higher, the better.

Accuracy (Weapons): Unsurprisingly, this is how precise each shot from the weapon can be, within the parameters of the weapon's range. The higher, the better.

Information (Aid): This indicates the SPECIAL attribute the Aid will affect, the HP or AP the item grants you, whether you'll receive Rads, the chance at Disease, and whether the item is Water or Food; basically all helpful information to know before a consumable is used.

Components (Junk): This extremely helpful information shows what components a piece of Junk breaks down into when scrapped at a workbench.

Weight (Weapons, Aid, Misc, Holo, Notes, Junk, Mods, Ammo): This is how heavy the item is. Every single item has a weight, and once the total of all your Inventory items is higher than your Carry Weight, you start to suffer penalties.

Value (Weapons, Aid, Misc, Holo, Notes, Junk, Mods, Ammo): This is how many Caps you can expect to receive when you sell this item to a Vendor. Use this value if you're selling to other players too.

INITIAL INTERACTIONS

With basic functionality out of the way (and other menus of interest covered later into this Training chapter), it is worth learning some basic passive techniques to help overcome your initial trepidations.

ACTIVE EFFECTS

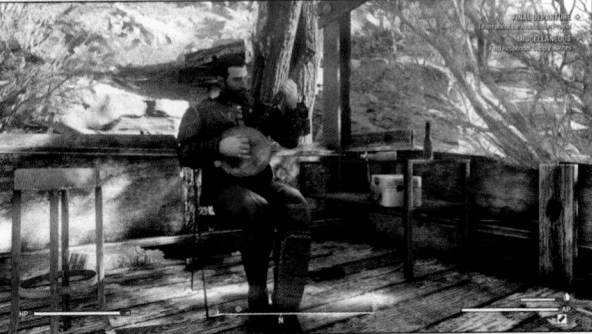

Whether you're twanging a banjo or tinkling the ivories on the ol' Joanna, bring music to the wilderness.

As previously discussed, it is worth adding as many bonuses to your statistics as possible. This is primarily achieved through the use of Perk Cards, but there are temporary effects too. Aside from eating and drinking, using chems, gathering collectibles like Bobbleheads and Magazines, wearing outfits and armor, or using weapons, there are a couple simple effects you can add, essentially for free, such as the Well Tuned bonus (for playing a musical instrument). Gain the Rested or Well Rested bonuses by sleeping on a nice bed, but avoid any mattress or sleeping bag on the ground (not in your Camp or Workshop), which may give you a disease if you attempt to sleep in filthier conditions. Conversely, there are diseases to worry about, too, and these are discussed in their own section of this Training chapter, along with mutations.

OBJECT INTERACTIONS

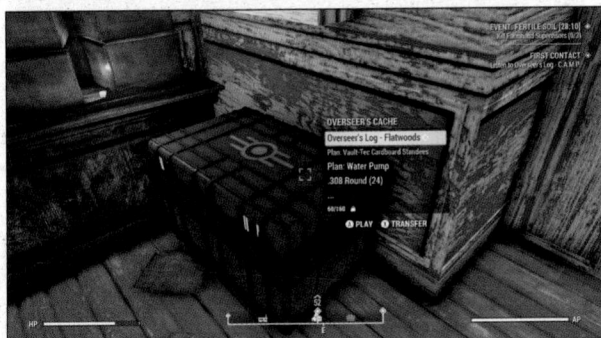

Activate: Whether you're inspecting the contents of a desk (or a Mole Rat's innards), unlocking a door, activating a terminal, or disarming a trap, use this function.

Transfer: If you wish to transfer a large amount of loot into or out of inventory, then complete this function.

ENTITY INTERACTIONS: FRIEND OR FOE?

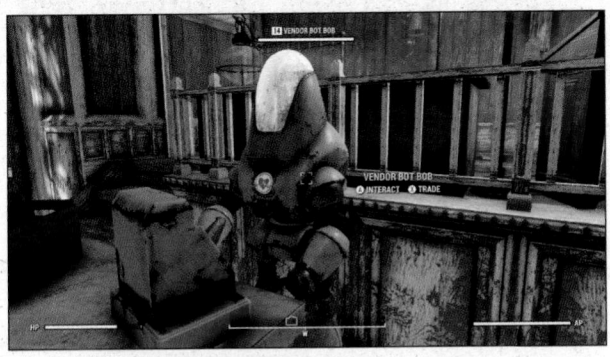

This faceless automaton may be seen as cold, unfeeling, and untrustworthy, but it belongs to a friendly sort. Appearances can sometimes be deceptive.

The survivors in Appalachia, along with your previous Vault-dwelling community, are likely to be eking out a subsistent existence. Friendly or neutral entities appear with a pale yellow Health bar; usually they won't attack unless provoked. Hostile entities appear with a red Health bar, so you must either engage them or tactically withdraw from combat. Interact with such nonhuman entities and receive information from them, including getting possible quests. If talking to another human, exercise the etiquette discussed later in the Training chapter.

TRAINING

CRAFTING AND C.A.M.P.ING

INVENTORY

QUESTS

ATLAS

BESTIARY

APPENDICES

POSSIBLE CHECKPOINT INTERACTIONS: ARE WE THERE YET?

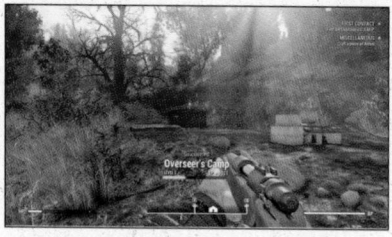

If you're in doubt about where you're going and what you're doing, then visit a checkpoint (aka a "waypoint"). Switch these yellow diamond icons off and on in your Data > Quests Pip-Boy menu, and read your quest descriptions to get a clue about what you might find or get up to when you reach one. Sometimes, if you need to reach an unknown location, there will be a search area to navigate, which is represented by a circle on your compass. Also remember that not all quests trigger a checkpoint after each objective, so don't rely on them constantly.

FIRST- AND THIRD-PERSON PERSPECTIVES

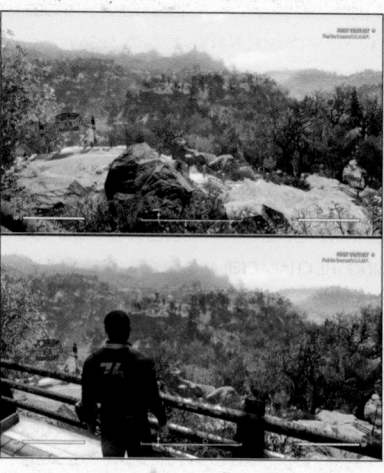

Toggling your POV (point of view) is an important asset. Need to see behind you? That's a good idea, as the adjacent pictures demonstrate; you're able to enhance your peripheral vision considerably, but at the expense of completing more complex and pinpoint-accurate maneuvers, especially jumping.

JUMPING

Leaping over low walls and across gaps, or ascending steep or rocky slopes is made possible if you jump! It also prevents a tiny amount of Rad damage if you clear a small patch of irradiated materials, like a puddle of toxic water. It also makes you a bit more difficult to hit with a weapon.

RUNNING AND SPRINTING

Need to quicken the pace? Then run, which allows faster movement, and doesn't consume AP. Need an even faster option? Press and hold the Sprint action, and move at the maximum speed your attributes and perks allow. This consumes AP (shown in the bottom-right bar), and is useful if you're closing in on a target, attempting to flee from combat, or needing to explore at speed. Due to the AP usage, be very careful sprinting while low on health, while you're being attacked, or if you're over-encumbered (your pace will slow anyway if you're carrying too much). You can easily run out of AP and be exhausted, then overwhelmed if enemies are in pursuit. Need to sprint for longer? Increase your AP and how fast those points regenerate by using chems and, more importantly, AP-increasing perks like the Agility perk Action Boy/Girl.

WORD OF WARNING FROM VAULT-BOY!

NO REST FOR THE COMMITTED

REMEMBER THAT YOU CANNOT PAUSE YOUR TIME IN THE APPALACHIAN WILDERNESS OR "WAIT" FOR TIME TO PASS (EXCEPT IN REAL-TIME, OBVIOUSLY). WITH THIS IN MIND, IT'S WORTH UTILIZING YOUR QUICK-BOY TRANSPARENT PIP-BOY VIEW (SO YOU CAN SEE PROBLEMS AS WELL AS YOUR MENUS) AND MOVING TO A SAFER LOCATION: TAKE REFUGE WITH A ROBOTIC VENDOR INSIDE A STRUCTURE OR AT YOUR CAMP, OR FAST-TRAVEL TO THE ENTRANCE OF VAULT 76 TO LESSEN THE CHANCES OF BEING ATTACKED WHILE YOUR FOCUS IS ELSEWHERE.

AGGRESSIVE INTERACTIONS

Now that you have more control of your actions, it is time to learn how to react if you're faced with situations that may turn violent. If diplomacy fails or you're encountering an entity that you can't reason with, prove your point with aggression.

ATTACKING

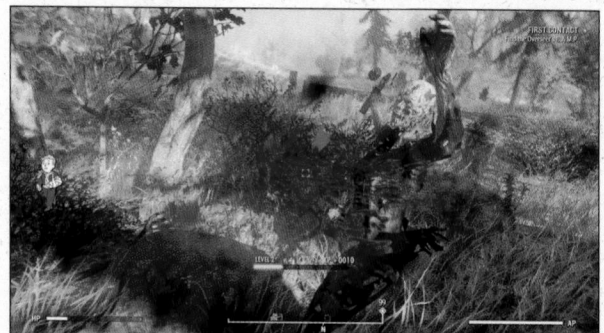

There is little doubt that this revolting specimen isn't here to sell you Stimpaks: A more offensive posture is therefore mandatory.

Enemies are easy to spot, from their red Health bars to the wild glints in their eyes, or for the more base creatures, a leap and a chew in your general direction. You should have prepared an offensive tool to remedy this situation. Early into your outing, experiment with the available weaponry, ideally a ranged weapon from the initial selection you scavenge, as well as a melee implement.

Then as you progress, choose bigger or better weapons, pick Perk Cards that help you make the most of the weapons you've chosen to specialize in, and craft better-quality or modified versions of the weapons. For your first few battles, though, scramble to use what you can and place at least two weapons in your Favorites Menu Wheel so you're not fumbling around on your Pip-Boy after your pitchfork breaks and you didn't assign another weapon to quickly swap to!

FISTS (OR PITCHFORKS) OF FURY: MELEE COMBAT

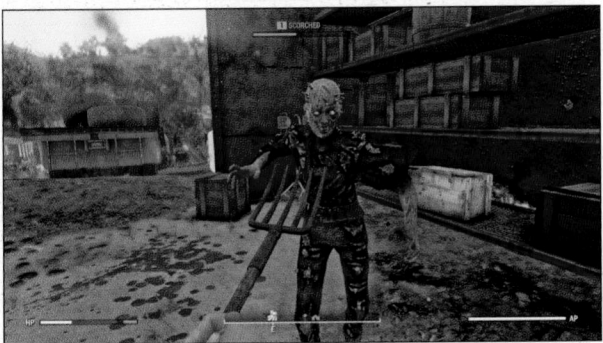

Close-range combat isn't for the squeamish and involves a "dance of death"!

If you're using a fist or a one- or two-handed melee weapon, you must close the gap to the enemy as soon as possible. Then comes a "dance of death"—countering your foe if they employ similar weapons or quickly cutting or bludgeoning them if they're carrying a ranged weapon. Remember you have some techniques at your disposal:

- **BASH:** ATTACK NORMALLY TO INFLICT THE REGULAR DAMAGE FOR THE MELEE WEAPON YOU'RE USING AND TO QUICKLY HIT YOUR FOE IF THEY'RE ATTEMPTING A SLOWER "POWER" ATTACK WITH A MELEE WEAPON; TIME THIS CORRECTLY AND YOU CAN STAGGER THEM, ALLOWING YOU TO PRESS FORWARD AND STRIKE AGAIN.
- **POWER ATTACK:** BREAK A FOE'S BLOCK WITH A POWER ATTACK (AND HOPEFULLY STAGGER THEM, TOO!). THIS STRIKE TAKES A LONG TIME TO BUILD (BY TAPPING THE POWER ATTACK BUTTON IN QUESTION), DURING WHICH TIME YOU CAN BE STRUCK AND STAGGERED YOURSELF, BUT THIS ATTACK PROVIDES MORE DEVASTATING DAMAGE. TIMING IS KEY HERE, AND YOU CAN ALWAYS BEGIN A BATTLE BY STARTING A POWER ATTACK AS YOU CHARGE IN TO MEET YOUR FOE, RELEASING IT JUST AS YOU REACH MELEE RANGE.
- **BLOCK:** IF A FOE SWINGS AT YOU USING A MELEE STRIKE (YOU CAN'T BLOCK PROJECTILES), QUICKLY BLOCK JUST BEFORE THE SWING CONNECTS. THIS GREATLY REDUCES, AND SOMETIMES NULLIFIES ALL, DAMAGE, MAY STAGGER YOUR FOE, AND ALLOWS YOU TO QUICKLY COUNTERATTACK.
- **CHARGE:** SPRINT INTO THE FRAY IF YOUR OPPONENT IS RELOADING, CONFUSED, HASN'T SEEN YOU, IS PREOCCUPIED, OR HAS BEEN STAGGERED. THEN BRING THEM TO HEEL WITH A BUMP IF YOU HAVE POWER ARMOR AND THE PAIN TRAIN PERK, OR STRIKE WITH A MELEE WEAPON BEFORE THEY CAN REACT.

Helpful Hint from Vault Boy!

SILENCE... IS VIOLENCE!

Unless you're brandishing a ranged weapon with a silencer (check into suppressor mods if you want one!), melee weapons are much quieter to use and are excellent for those wishing to sneak. The potency of such weapons is increased with additional Strength Points and by wearing Power Armor. Augment your melee damge by increasing your Strength attribute and adding Perk Cards that give bonuses to melee attacks (check the Perks section for all recommendations).

THE LONG AND THE SHORT OF IT: RANGED COMBAT

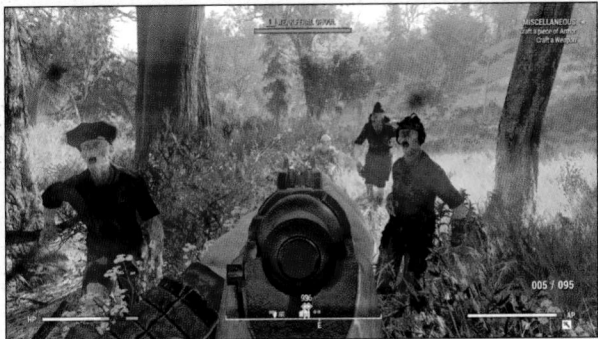

Pick just how far away you want to be when taking out enemies by the type of ranged weapon you select.

If you don't want to see the reds of your opponents' eyes when you drop them, use a ranged weapon. Any gun will do, though the various types have their own strengths and weaknesses (detailed meticulously in the Inventory chapter). Just be aware of the different techniques you can muster when you pull the trigger:

- **HIP FIRE AND AIMING:** HIP-FIRING IS ANY SHOOTING DONE WITHOUT PRESSING THE AIM BUTTON. YOUR ONSCREEN CROSSHAIRS ARE WIDE WHEN HIP-FIRING AND NARROWER WHEN AIMING. FIRE FROM THE HIP DURING NORMAL COMBAT CONDITIONS OR WHEN NEUTRALIZING A CHAOTIC SITUATION AND YOUR MANUAL DEXTERITY, COPIOUS BULLETS, AND A WEAPON DESIGNED FOR SUCH PURPOSES (E.G., AN AUTOMATIC RIFLE) ARE NEEDED, LIKE MASS COMBAT. LOOK FOR THE MOST DANGEROUS THREATS AND NEUTRALIZE THEM. FOCUS ON ATTRIBUTES AND PERKS THAT HELP IN THIS REGARD, USING THE CHARACTER ARCHETYPES LATER IN THIS TRAINING CHAPTER AS A GUIDE.
- **AIMING:** AIMING IS ANY SHOOTING DONE BY AIMING DOWN THE BARREL OR THROUGH A SIGHT. AIMING IS FOR SITUATIONS WHERE YOU HAVE A LITTLE MORE TIME, PERHAPS WITH A WEAPON DESIGNED FOR SUCH A SHOT (LIKE A SNIPER RIFLE). LOOKING OR ZOOMING DOWN THE SIGHTS OF A WEAPON, OR EVEN LINING UP A BARREL, GIVES A MORE ACCURATE SHOT BUT AT THE COST OF SPEED. REMEMBER THIS IS COMPOUNDED BY THE WEIGHT OF YOUR WEAPON; THE LARGER IT IS, THE SLOWER YOU ARE TO REACT.
- **CROUCH-FIRING:** HIP-FIRING AND AIMING CAN BE DONE WHILE CROUCHING, IN ORDER TO ADD ACCURACY TO YOUR SHOTS, ESPECIALLY IF YOU'RE AIMING. THIS COMES AT ADDITIONAL COST TO YOUR MANEUVERABILITY AND SPEED; YOU'RE ESSENTIALLY A SITTING DUCK UNLESS YOU'RE BEHIND COVER. YOU ALSO CANNOT RUN OR SPRINT (UNLESS PERKS ARE USED), SO USE CROUCH MORE FREQUENTLY DURING SNEAKING MOVEMENTS.
- **DAMAGE TYPES:** BOTH YOU AND YOUR ENEMIES INFLICT DIFFERENT TYPES OF DAMAGE:

  - **Ballistic:** Bullets, shells, or normal projectile damage: By far the most common damage type.
  - **Energy:** Powerful blasts of electricity, laser, or plasma fire, usually inflicted by robots.
  - **Radiation:** Damage with a radioactive element, usually environmental or inflicted by radioactive enemies or a camp defense trap.
  - **Poison:** Usually attacks from certain types of unclean claws or projectile spittle.

TRAINING

CRAFTING AND C.A.M.P.ING

INVENTORY

QUESTS

ATLAS

BESTIARY

APPENDICES

- **FIRING:** SHOOT AT YOUR FOES UNTIL ONLY ONE OF YOU IS STANDING.
  LET'S HOPE IT'S YOU. IS THE FOE RUNNING? AIM FOR THE LEGS; BETTER TO
  EARN SOME XP FOR EXPENDING YOUR BULLETS BY KILLING YOUR TARGET.

- **RELOADING:** THIS RELOADS THE AMMUNITION YOU'RE EXPENDING,
  REFILLING THE CHAMBER OF THE GUN, AT THE EXPENSE OF YOUR AMMO
  RESERVES. SCAVENGE TO FIND MORE AMMUNITION, OR CRAFT IT AT A
  TINKER'S WORKBENCH. NOTE THE SPEED IN WHICH YOU RELOAD AND TRY
  TO TIME IT DURING A LULL IN THE ACTION. YOU AUTOMATICALLY RELOAD
  IF YOUR CHAMBER IS EMPTY, BUT YOU GAIN A LITTLE MORE CONTROL BY
  RELOADING MANUALLY, WHEN IT IS SAFE TO DO SO. SOMETIMES IT IS SAFER
  TO SWITCH TO A SECONDARY WEAPON TO KILL A FOE RATHER THAN RISK
  DAMAGE WHILE RELOADING, ESPECIALLY IF YOU ARE BEING OVERRUN, HAVE
  LOW AP, OR YOUR PREFERRED WEAPON IS LOW ON AMMUNITION. ALSO
  CONSULT THE PERKS SECTION TO LEARN ABOUT SEVERAL PERK CARDS THAT
  SIGNIFICANTLY IMPROVE YOUR RELOADING.

- **WEAPON BASH:** REMEMBER, YOU CAN USE THE WEAPON (EVEN A
  RANGED ONE) YOU'RE CARRYING TO HIT FOES THAT ARE TOO CLOSE FOR
  COMFORT! THIS IS USUALLY FOLLOWED BY YOU STEPPING BACK AFTERWARD
  AND FIRING. USE THIS IN PLACE OF A RELOAD OR TO FINISH OFF A BADLY
  WOUNDED FOE INSTEAD OF (OR IN ADDITION TO) USING BULLET FIRE.
  CHECK THE STRENGTH PERK BASHER IF YOU WANT TO INFLICT MORE
  BASHING (AND POSSIBLY CRIPPLING) DAMAGE.

AREA EFFECT: PROJECTILE (AND EXPLOSIVE) COMBAT

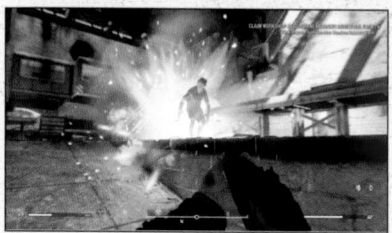

Grenades and
mines are a great
way to damage
foes within a
large area or to
create a diversion.

Grenades: Don't forget the third main method of foe disposal—using and
throwing projectile weaponry, like grenades. Utilize them to soften up the
enemy as you close in; hold down to throw and aim the arc of the throw so
the projectile lands just in front of an enemy who is moving toward you; this
means the attack detonates on them, not behind them. As ever, there are
perks to increase the potency of these attacks.

Mines: Placing static, explosive charges on the ground, floor, or roof is
more of a stealth-based option. Also drop them on enemy patrol paths,
at chokepoints, or in thoroughfares or through doorways in your camps
or workshops.

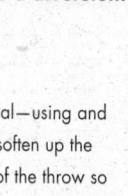
V.A.T.S.: VAULT-TEC ASSISTED TARGETING SYSTEM COMBAT

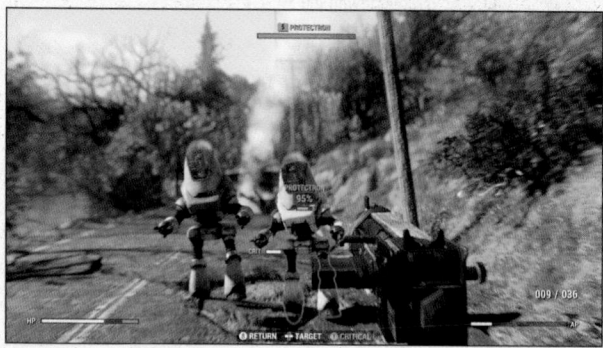

Augmented targeting courtesy of V.A.T.S, with additional
information visible due to active Perk Cards: Learn your
enemy's weakness, and defeat them with a stylish Critical Hit!

Overview: Augmented by your Perception (hit chance), your Agility
(Action Points), and your Luck (the refill of your Critical Hits meter), V.A.T.S.
combat allows you to utilize an HUD targeting system that easily flags
multiple enemies in your vision field, allowing you to aim and shoot them
with a percentage chance of a successful hit indicated on your HUD. It offers
increased combat precision and tactical awareness at the cost of AP, speed,
and instant peripheral vision.

Recommended Situations: V.A.T.S. is preferable over firing from the hip
or aiming, in the following types of situations:

- IF YOU HAVE A TARGET IN AN AREA THAT'S DIFFICULT TO MANUALLY HIT (SUCH
  AS UNDERGROWTH) AND CAN'T EASILY SEE THE ENEMY TO AIM AT THEM.

- IF THE TARGET IS MOVING MORE QUICKLY THAN YOU CAN MANUALLY AIM
  AND SHOOT AT THEM.

- IF THE TARGET IS FAR AWAY, AND YOUR LONG-RANGE AIMING IS LESS
  PROFICIENT THAN THE PINPOINT ACCURACY OF V.A.T.S.

- IF YOU'RE EXECUTING STEALTH COMBAT AND THE SITUATION IS
  ADVANTAGEOUS TO USE IT.

- IF YOU'VE PICKED A NUMBER OF PERK CARDS THAT MORE FULLY AUGMENT
  V.A.T.S., ADDING FEATURES LIKE ENEMY INFORMATION, THE ABILITY TO
  TARGET LIMBS, AP BONUSES, AND MORE. THE PERKS SECTION HAS THE PERKS
  TO LOOK FOR.

Circumventing Drawbacks: The biggest drawback is the increased use
of AP. Need to maximize your V.A.T.S. potential? Then augment your AP by
using chems, Bobbleheads, and Magazines; increasing your agility; and
most importantly, using perks. Due to increased AP use, limit your sprinting
just before entering V.A.T.S.

Other Advantages: V.A.T.S. is helpful in tracking foes and noting other
dangers such as mines, which are automatically spotted if nearby.

Critical Hits: Note the Critical Hit Meter in the adjacent picture. This is
a key advantage in V.A.T.S.; each successful hit fills this Meter (and how
quickly this occurs, or refills afterwards, can be augmented with Perks).
When the Meter is full, you can execute a Critical Hit; a devastating, higher-
than-normal attack that inflicts far more damage than normal, and it always
hits! If you want the additional XP, and a better damage-per-bullet ratio, pick
V.A.T.S. and use Critical Hits to remove threats.

Maximizing Critical Hit: Aside from chem and perk use, if you want to maximize the frequency of your Critical Hits, start your attack with a weapon that uses a small amount of APs (like a pistol). Build your meter up with that weapon before quickly swapping it for a weapon with a much larger base Damage value, and execute the Critical with the second weapon: The resulting hit will be far more damaging!

If your foe is in the distance or difficult to hit, build up your Critical Meter on easy-to-hit targets (usually closer to your location, including stationary hostile targets like turrets); then unleash a critical on the far target, as criticals always hit!

SHADOWY STEALTH: CROUCHING AND SNEAKING

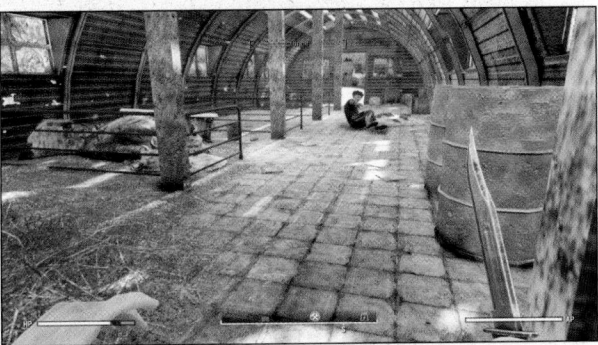

Hide in the shadows, waiting to strike after obtaining all the Sneak-based perks you can gather. The results can be both silent and spectacular!

Crouching: Simply crouch when you wish to sneak, reduce your physical size to the enemy, remove your location from the world map, hide behind lower defensive structures during a battle, or check a menu.

Stealth: Those placing points in their Agility attribute, and even those who don't, should still think about sneaking to avoid detection by enemies (usually nonhuman, though crouching removes your map location). To sneak, simply crouch: Your current level of detection will be displayed onscreen. There are four levels of detection:

- **HIDDEN:** NO NEARBY CHARACTERS DETECT YOU. THE BRACKETS AROUND THE WORD "HIDDEN" INDICATE HOW CLOSE YOU ARE TO BEING DETECTED. THE FARTHER APART THE BRACKETS, THE MORE SUCCESSFUL YOUR SNEAKING. WHILE HIDDEN, ANY ATTACKS YOU MAKE ARE CONSIDERED "SNEAK ATTACKS" AND DEAL INCREASED DAMAGE (WHICH CAN BE FURTHER AUGMENTED BY PERKS AND YOUR WEAPON'S DAMAGE VALUE), BUT ATTACKING RISKS EXPOSING YOUR POSITION. YOU MAY WISH TO TRY LONG-RANGE TAKEDOWNS WITH SILENCED WEAPONRY AS WELL.
- **DETECTED:** NONHOSTILE CHARACTERS NEARBY HAVE BEEN ALERTED TO YOUR PRESENCE. THE ONLY IMMEDIATE DANGER YOU FACE IS POSSIBLE EMBARRASSMENT.
- **CAUTION:** ENEMIES HAVE DETECTED YOU AND ARE ACTIVELY SEARCHING FOR YOU. THE FARTHER APART THE BRACKETS AROUND "CAUTION," THE CLOSER YOU ARE TO RETURNING TO "HIDDEN." EVADE FOES BY WATCHING THE BRACKETS AROUND THE WORD "CAUTION" EXPAND AND RETURN TO HIDDEN STATUS. SNEAK ATTACKS ARE STILL COUNTED. IF YOU CAN EVADE THEM FOR LONG ENOUGH, ENEMIES RETURN TO THEIR PREVIOUS ACTIVITY.
- **DANGER:** ENEMIES HAVE SPOTTED YOU AND WILL BEGIN ATTACKING. ANOTHER TYPE OF COMBAT IS NOW PREFERABLE, AS IS RUNNING AWAY.

Sneaking Successfully: Sneaking is affected by several factors:

- **LIGHT LEVEL:** THE DARKER THE SPOT YOU'RE SNEAKING IN, THE HARDER IT IS FOR ENEMIES TO SPOT YOU. IF YOU'RE CLOSE TO BEING DETECTED, TRY DUCKING INTO THE SHADOWS TO REMAIN HIDDEN. STAY IN THE SHADOWS AND TURN OFF THE PIP-BOY'S FLASHLIGHT, YOU MUPPET!
- **LINE OF SIGHT:** IF ENEMIES DON'T HAVE LINE OF SIGHT TO YOU, THEY'RE MUCH LESS LIKELY TO DETECT YOU.
- **MOVEMENT:** YOU'RE HARDEST TO DETECT WHILE MOTIONLESS AND EASIER TO SPOT WHILE MOVING. IT'S SIGNIFICANTLY HARDER TO SNEAK WHILE MOVING QUICKLY (ALTHOUGH THIS CAN BE IMPROVED WITH PERKS). SLOW DOWN.
- **SOUND:** ATTACKING WITH NONSILENCED OR HEAVY WEAPONS MAKES NOISE, WHICH MAY ALERT ENEMIES TO YOUR PRESENCE.
- **ARMOR:** THE HIGHER YOUR ARMOR'S WEIGHT, THE MORE NOISE IT MAKES WHILE MOVING. SNEAKING IS EXTREMELY CHALLENGING IN POWER ARMOR. ALSO CHOOSE ARMOR THAT INCREASES YOUR AGILITY OR YOUR SNEAKING, AND ALSO FIND, PURCHASE, OR CRAFT STEALTH BOYS OR PHANTOM DEVICES (ENHANCED STEALTH BOYS), WHICH FURTHER ADD TO YOUR STEALTH.
- **ENVIRONMENTAL DISTRACTIONS:** ENEMIES WILL ALSO REACT TO LOUD NOISES IN THE ENVIRONMENT. IF YOU CAN TRIGGER AN EXPLOSION OR TRAP WITHOUT BEING DETECTED, YOU CAN LURE AWAY UNSUSPECTING ENEMIES.
- **BRACKET WATCHING:** CHECK THE BRACKETS AROUND YOUR DETECTION LEVEL; IF THEY BEGIN TO MOVE, YOU CAN BE ALERTED BEFORE YOU EVEN SEE AN ENEMY.
- **HUMAN WATCHING:** SNEAK ATTACKS, AND BEING STEALTHY IS STILL POSSIBLE WHEN FACING A HUMAN OPPONENT, THOUGH THEY ARE OBVIOUSLY GOVERNED WITH THE SAME VISION AS YOU. CROUCH AND CREEP IN BEHIND YOUR FOE AFTER LEARNING WHERE THEY LIKE TO STAND OR REST, AND POUNCE WHEN THEY ARE STATIONARY OR LOOKING AT THEIR PIP-BOY.

Check the Appalachian Archetypes section for an example of what abilities and perks it takes to become a successful stealth operative.

TRAINING

CRAFTING AND C.A.M.P.ING

INVENTORY

QUESTS

ATLAS

BESTIARY

APPENDICES

STATUS: YOU HAVE EMERGED!

NOW WHAT?

Adapting to Life Outside

ACCEPT YOUR NEWER, HARSHER SURROUNDINGS	SCAVENGE WEAPONS AND ITEMS TO HELP YOU SURVIVE.	SEEK SAFETY IN NUMBERS!	ALWAYS ASK...WHAT CAN I DO TO BUILD A BETTER AMERICA?

INITIAL EXPLORATIONS AFTER EMERGENCE

The first few hours after Vault 76's door seals behind you are critical to your survival. This chapter charts the progress you should be making, including securing armaments, dealing with your impending Thirst and Hunger, learning the basics of quest management, and learning how to meet and greet your fellow survivors. Your Appalachian experience starts now!

The First 76 Seconds...Minutes...and Hours

NEED HELP OR REASSURANCE? SURE YOU DO! THERE'S NO HARM IN LEARNING SOME KEY ELEMENTS FOR SURVIVING AND THRIVING. IF YOU DON'T HAVE THE TIME FOR A DEEPER DIVE INTO WHAT TO EXPECT AS YOU EXPLORE THE INITIAL WOODLAND AND VALLEYS OF THE FOREST, JUST FOLLOW THE SEVEN SETS OF SURVIVAL SKILLS YOU'LL NEED TO MUSTER:

SURVIVAL SKILL #1: STAY HYDRATED!

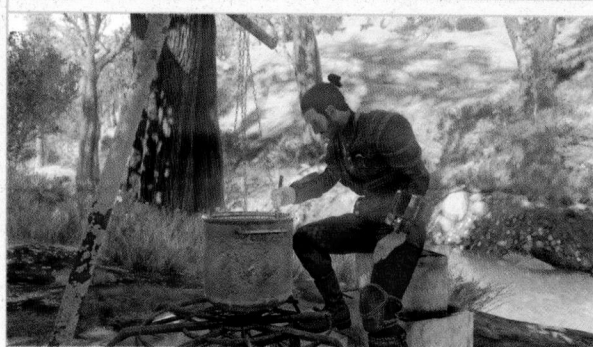

Obtain Water > Find Campfire > Boil Water > Enjoy!

Drinks prevent Dehydration. Open your Pip-Boy and go to Items > Aid.

Keep your Thirst and Hunger bars over 75% for bonus active effects.

Thirst: Find Dirty Water at a pump or river. Boil it at a cooking station. Purify it at Flatwoods, a chemistry Station, or your camp (with the correct equipment). Consume, and enjoy!

Thirst: Harvest wild flora and find recipes for more beneficial drinks that remove Thirst and offer other bonuses.

Hunger: Find uncooked meat, harvest some wild flora, then cook immediately so you aren't as likely to receive a disease from it. Consume immediately or very soon, or the food spoils.

Hunger: In addition, scavenge canned or processed food that can be stored in your inventory and eaten whenever you like; it does not spoil.

Hunger: Cooked food takes longer to spoil. You have to eat the same amount of food regardless of when you eat, so feast early to stay above your 75% range for the benefits.

Hunger: You can sort the Pip-Boy Aid Menu by "Spoil" to check which foods are about to go off; eat those first!

Hunger and Thirst: You need wood to cook stuff; so make sure you gather wood from logs as you explore.

Rad-X: Each time you eat or drink, you receive a small dose of radiation applied to your Health Bar. Consume Rad-X first to reduce or remove that chance for a limited time.

Add your most-often used food and drink to your Favorites menu wheel. Add more drink than food as you become thirsty more often than hungry.

Complete the Responders Quests in Flatwoods to gain step-by-step guidance on food and drink preparation.

SURVIVAL SKILL #2: HEALTH AND MEDICATION!

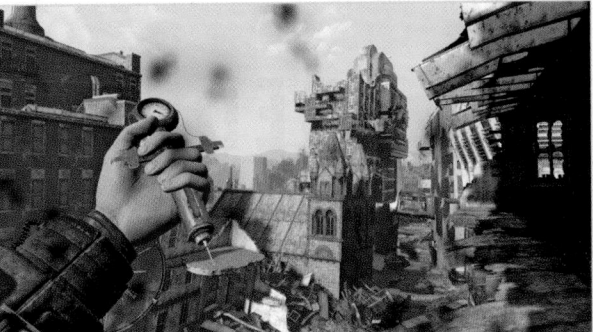

Fight Valiantly > Use Stimpak > Be Healthy > Avoid Radiation!

Stimpaks heal damage over time. Quick-use them instead of flailing in your Pip-Boy menus when you need healing the most.

There is a wealth of other items that can heal you too (including food and drink).

Be aware of the strengths (buffs and boosts) and weaknesses (radiation, thirst, addiction) when using chems.

Learn there are recipes for Super Stimpaks, and there's Diluted Stimpaks if you don't need a full boost of health juice.

Craft more Stimpaks as a matter of priority, as well as Disease Cures and a host of other useful concoctions at any chemistry station.

RadAway removes radiation over time. It is used often, and should be on your Favorite menu wheel. Search or craft these as a matter of priority.

Use Diluted Stimpaks, Rad-X, and RadAway more often. Unlike Stimpaks, they grant their health benefits without the need for you to be badly wounded. Good Health also means protecting yourself; gather a few pistols, find one you enjoy the most, craft ammo for it, and either specialize (adding perks) and/or test out a different weapon type as you gain experience. Find plans and mods for these weapons.

Good Health also means protecting your body; search for armor plans and craft protection at an Armor Workbench.

Repair your armor and weapons at the appropriate workbench. Craft ammo instead of purchasing it. Learn the base components of your weapon and armor, and scavenge more of it so you can easily repair these critical items.

Visit the Overseer's Camp on the road between Vault 76 and Flatwoods to gain guidance on armor and weapon repairing.

SURVIVAL SKILL #3: POWER IS KEY!

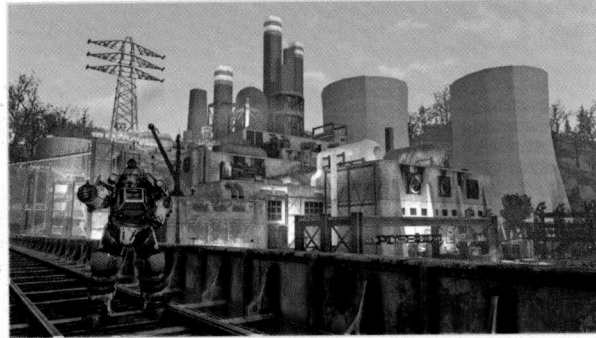

Find New Home > Build Generator > Wire it Up > Power!

Before wiring up your first dwelling (i.e., your camp), start to forage for building supplies.

You leave Vault 76 with a few supplies; add to them by scavenging.

You need to focus on gathering Wood, Concrete, and Steel for the majority of the foundation, walls, and roof of your dwelling.

For this, you need to find objects that either automatically break down into components (like Logs, which break down into Wood Scraps, or small, roadside Gravel Pits, which contain Concrete Scrap).

Scrap junk items you find at different locations. Use your common sense to figure out the type of junk that's available at lumber yards, farmsteads, coffee shops, so you have some idea of what you'll be returning with.

Scrap everything you scavenge at any workbench or Power Armor station, reducing your weight in the process.

Items with components can be used for crafting (cooking, armor, weapons, and ammo) and construction.

Stay in the initial valley and forests, and make a concentric circle of exploration, scavenging each location you find and noting the types of items so you can return there in a day to grab similar items again.

This guide's Atlas provides helpful knowledge on the types of junk at every Primary Location in Appalachia.

Got Junk? Then build generators to power lights, traps, some defenses (like sliding doors) and most importantly; resource generators!

Need more power? Then siphon it from Substations and Power Plants once you bring plants back online.

SURVIVAL SKILL #4: JOIN A TEAM

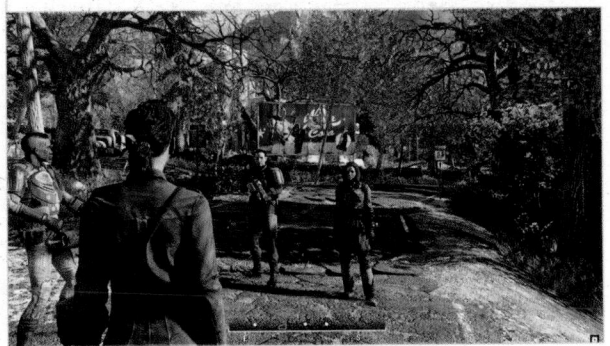

Meet Strangers > Exchange Pleasantries > Share Skillsets > Succeed!

Don't be intimidated or worried about meeting your fellow Vault Dwellers again.

Start off with a wave or other Emote by learning and perfecting the Emote menu wheel and the Social Menu.

Offer to trade and talk to your new neighbors. If you're both friendly sorts, team up.

Teaming up offers some advantages over going it alone; you can share quests, workshop building techniques, and perks (some are tailored to team play). You can also divide responsibilities as you explore.

After reaching Level 5, you become susceptible to damage from hostile humans. But there are easy ways to mitigate this.

TRAINING

CRAFTING AND C.A.M.P.ING

INVENTORY

QUESTS

ATLAS

BESTIARY

APPENDICES

SURVIVAL SKILL #5: CAMPING MADE EASY!

After you leave the Vault, build a C.A.M.P. in the wilderness.

The optimal time is when you're Level 5–10, after you've completed the Responder Quest in the woods north of Morgantown (after investigating the airport).

Find an area of flat ground to make it easier to place your foundations.

If you place an item and need to move or remove it, do not scrap it; this destroys the object and gives you only half the components you used to create it. Move or store it instead.

Utilize the resources you gathered and make a basic construction; err on the side of a small cabin. Do not make a large structure, as you will run out of budget!

Find Plans to unlock more types of construction objects. To begin, place your camp near a workbench you use a lot, so you can quickly scrap items as you build.

Blueprint your camp so you can move and erect it again in seconds, not minutes.

Move your camp close to where you want to explore, so you have somewhere to return to and a free Fast-Travel location.

Later in your exploration, place your Camp in the center of the map to lessen the Caps cost no matter where you Fast Travel to.

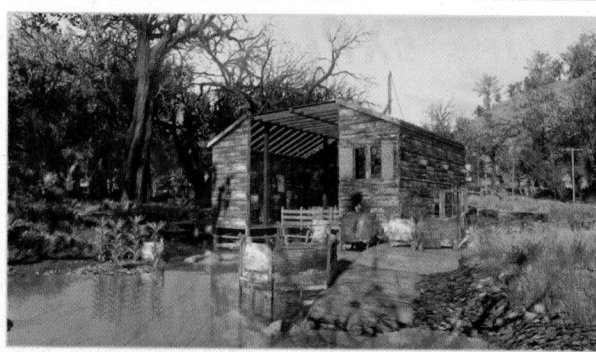

**Find Flat Ground >
Drop Your C.A.M.P. >
Use Resources & Build
> Survive in Style**

SURVIVAL SKILL #6: GET A JOB!

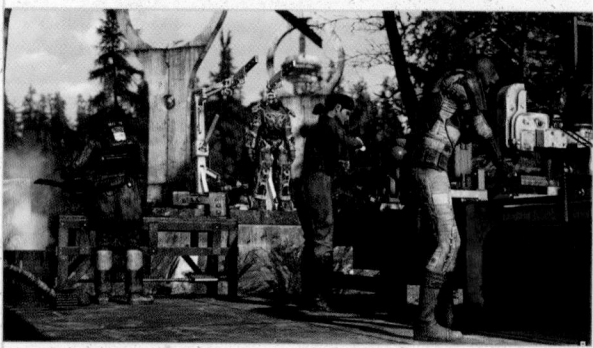

Find Your Calling > Study > Learn > Work!

To begin, learn everything about your SPECIAL attributes and perks so you can more effectively tailor your choices to your play style.

Your calling involves trying out different tasks, which increase as you learn more about Appalachia. To start, try to be the best forager and scavenger possible.

Specialize in weapons crafting and modding, or Tinker's Workbench ammo creation.

Find collectibles; holotapes, Bobbleheads, Magazines, Power Armor frames, and Caps Stashes.

Visit robots, listen to holotapes, follow checkpoints, and complete quests, gathering up some choice rewards.

Set up a workshop with your friends, and mine or grow resources for fun and profit.

Set up a camp with your friends, and bring out the banjos!

Show others how to create a particularly bitchin' cabin, defensive turret tower, or other structure.

Find a specific location, explore it, and regale others with tales of your exploits.

Become a hunter of enemies, both mundane and bizarre, including mythical Appalachian cryptids!

Join others and complete a variety of challenges, events, and team quests.

Find out exactly what happened to the Brotherhood of Steel, the Responders, the Raiders, the Free States, the Mothman Cultists...and dwellers from other Vaults?!

Set about finding every recipe, mod, or plan you can find.

Find some choice spots for a selfie, looking for the best views in West Virginia.

Journey to all four corners of the map and all six regions before you reach Level 20.

Plan on becoming one type of character archetype (like a stealth expert or melee-focused warrior) before changing to another build type. And another.

Band together and attempt to solve some fiendish cryptic passwords in order to get into a secret military base, so you can launch nukes.

Then parlay many of these jobs into profit-making schemes by selling items you made or found, or the knowledge that you acquired on your journeying.

SURVIVAL SKILL #7: WEIGH YOUR OPPORTUNITIES!

**Find Items >
Collect Items
> But Don't
Hoard Items >
Overencumbered
Is Underprepared!**

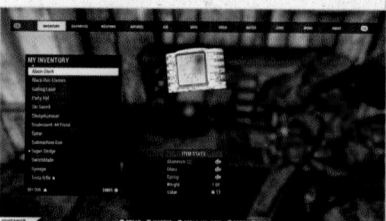

Carry Weight represents how much you can haul in your inventory before it starts to slow you down.

Look for your current/maximum Carry Weight (and icon) in the following places:

- The Items menu of your Pip-Boy (bottom-left corner).
- The bottom-right corner of your world map.
- The bottom-left corner of each menu box when you're about to pick something up.

When the Carry Weight information turns red (in menus aside from your Pip-Boy's), you are overencumbered.

The more Strength you have, the more you can carry.

Each item you pick up has a weight value. If the total weight of all your items exceeds your Carry Weight, you start to suffer penalties:

- You will not be able to Fast Travel.
- Your Action Points (AP) will continuously drain and won't regenerate. You'll still be able to move at full speed, but actions like Sprinting or V.A.T.S. will become unavailable since they cost AP.

Eventually, if you pick up enough items to exceed *double* your Carry Weight, then your movement speed will be reduced to a walk, in addition to draining your AP. Getting around becomes difficult and you'll be vulnerable to any enemy trying to chase you.

The fastest way to reduce your inventory weight is to drop items.

To drop an item, enter the Pip-Boy and navigate to the Items tab, highlight the items you wish to drop, and do so.

Items you drop will appear in the world inside a paper bag. Other players can loot this bag, and the bag will disappear over time or when you log out.

The other way to reduce inventory weight is to scrap junk or unwanted items into components (at a workbench), which usually results in an overall weight reduction. If you want to increase your Carry Weight or reduce the weight of items:

- Choose Strength when you level up to increase your total Carry Weight.
- Wear a suit of Power Armor. The suit will increase your Strength as long as you're in it.
- Equip perks like Thru-Hiker or Packin' Light to reduce the weight of certain items.
- Consume items that temporarily raise Strength, like Buffout.
- Store excess items in a secure container, like your Stash Box.

ONWARD TO FLATWOODS: EIGHT STEPS IN YOUR INITIAL EXPLORATION (LEVELS 2–10)

Survey the wooded valley from the exit of Vault 76. Pick out structures you can see (a lookout tower, the old Wixon property, a rusting lumber yard, and other nearby locations hidden in the forest). Then take your first tentative steps. But only after you read this section, which provides recommendations for your immediate courses of action!

FASCINATING FACT FROM VAULT BOY!

FORAGING TOO:
OTHER ACTIVITIES TO TRY AS YOU GO

AS YOU COMPLETE THE FOLLOWING STEPS, DON'T FORGET TO MULTITASK: LOOT, FORAGE, COLLECT, SCAVENGE, AND BEGIN TO COLLECT CAPS. ALSO, START OR CONTINUE ANY LOCAL QUESTS, PARTICULARLY THE ONES RELATED TO THE OVERSEER AND RESPONDERS OF FLATWOODS.

STEP 1: FINDING A FIREARM:
YOUR FIRST WEAPONS

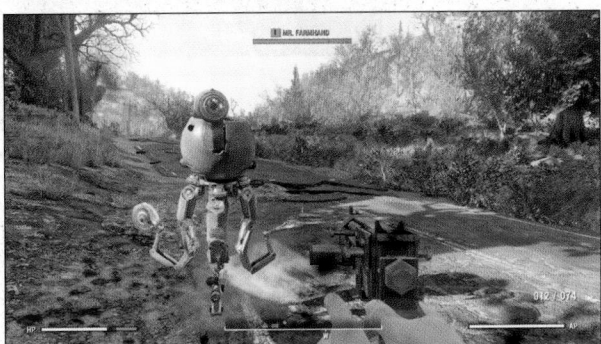

Your first gun—likely to be pistol-sized and made from pipe. Though anything that brings down an enemy at range is worth trying out.

After leaving the Vault, your first priority is to protect yourself. You're inadequately prepared for life outside, so immediately begin searching for two weapons: one you wield in your hands (a melee weapon like a lead pipe, pitchfork, or a machete) and a pistol or rifle with ranged capabilities (like a pipe pistol, 10-mm pistol, or .44 revolver). Simply check the guide's Atlas for nearby locations to check. Or just take the gun from the Responder corpse lying just to the side of the Vault 76 entrance.

Helpful Hint from Vault Boy!

SCORCHED SLAUGHTERING AT SLOCUM'S JOE

Engaging Scorched is an admirable plan, especially as some of them use melee and ranged weapons. While occasionally you'll be greeted by a Scorched with a grenade launcher (whose level may be too high for you to use), most of the time Scorched employ pipe pistols or their variants. As they also carry ammunition for pipe pistols, you can try a few raids against small clusters of Scorched (there's always some at the Wixon Homestead) as you gather some initial supplies, stockpile their ammo, and scrap their weapons for parts, or swap them if they're in better condition or have better statistics.

STEP 2: THIRST:
WHEN IN DOUBT, BOIL IT OUT!

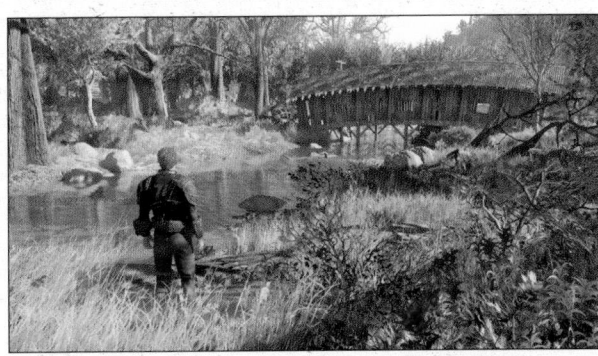

Water, water everywhere, but not a drop to drink...unless you want dysentery, or worse. Boil it all.

To survive in postwar Appalachia, it's important to make sure you're always stocked with food and water. Thirst and hunger can kill you just as sure as any Scorchbeast, and your Thirst (Water) and Hunger (Food) meters are constantly decreasing (though you get thirsty more often). Natural water sources (including water pumps) are irradiated and carry disease, and drinking directly from rivers and streams is perilous. When in doubt, boil it out! This is simply a matter of collecting the water and boiling it at a cooking station (there are two in Flatwoods). Check inside the church at Flatwoods to purify the water, too, which removes the slight radiation damage you take, even from boiled water. Then learn a recipe for Purified Water, and make this your default drink for your first few levels. Then consult the Crafting chapter for more potent drinks.

STEP 3: HUNGER:
IF THE FOOD IS RAW, KEEP A CLOSED JAW!

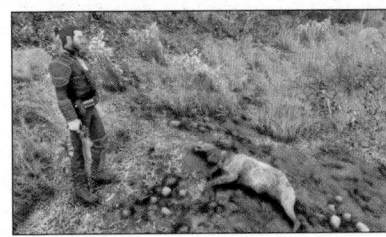

Meat, meat, everywhere, and all of it is about to go rotten.

Receive a boost to your Hunger by harvesting ingredients from the wilderness or killing animals and looting their still-twitching corpses. Though devouring raw meat and plant ingredients may satisfy hunger, cooking them will increase their effectiveness and removes the risk of disease. Basic cooking recipes (for both food and drink) will unlock when you first pick up a new type of raw food. Also be aware that raw plants and meat, as well as food and (some) drink cooked with these ingredients, have a very short shelf life; they spoil quickly, leaving you rotten ingredients that are just as bad for you as raw ones. So scarf down food when you make it (unless you have a perk that lengthens the time before food spoils). The other option? Head to any location and scavenge their boxed or tinned foodstuffs; they offer a slight radiation uptick but satisfy hunger and don't spoil.

TRAINING

CRAFTING AND C.A.M.P.ING

INVENTORY

QUESTS

ATLAS

BESTIARY

APPENDICES

STEP 4: I HAVEN'T GOT A STITCH TO WEAR: YOUR FIRST CLOTHING AND ARMOR

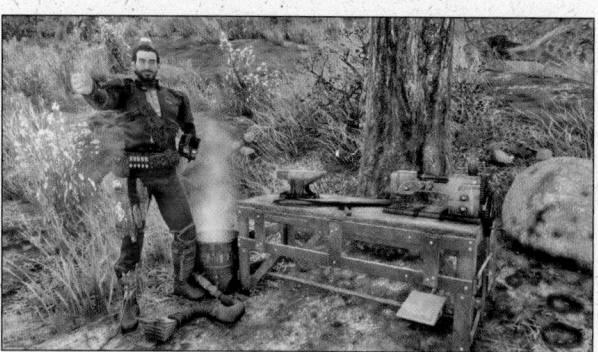

Wear outfits over armor or jumpsuits under it. Whatever your style, leather is your first form of protection.

Where's my Power Armor? We'll get to that in a few levels. For the moment, head down to the Overseer's Camp and attempt to construct your first armor part. Due to the items lying around the camp (especially inside the cache), you should have enough component parts to construct some protective Leather Armor. Wear this by highlighting it in your Pip-Boy's Items > Apparel menu. Note that as you level up, you create "Leveled" versions of these items, which have better statistics. For now, you lack the experience (XP) and Plans to craft better armor (or the Caps to buy it). However, as you progress, other types of armor become available to build, trade, and modify:

- **COMBAT:** DESIGNED TO PROTECT SOLDIERS IN ANY SITUATION, COMBAT ARMOR GIVES THE WEARER EQUAL AMOUNTS OF RESISTANCE TO PHYSICAL AND ENERGY DAMAGE.
- **LEATHER:** THICK LAYERS OF ANIMAL HIDE MAKE LEATHER ARMOR PARTICULARLY SUITED TO PROTECTING AGAINST ENERGY DAMAGE.
- **MARINE COMBAT:** OUTCLASSED ONLY BY POWER ARMOR, EVERY PIECE OF MARINE COMBAT ARMOR PROVIDES EXCEPTIONAL PROTECTION IN NEARLY EVERY BATTLEFIELD SCENARIO.
- **METAL:** CONSTRUCTED OF THICK, HAND-WELDED STEEL OR ALUMINUM, METAL ARMOR OFFERS ADDITIONAL PROTECTION AGAINST PHYSICAL DAMAGE.
- **ROBOT:** CRAFTED FROM DESTROYED ROBOTS, THE HIGH-TECH PLATING OF ROBOT ARMOR OFFERS ADDITIONAL PROTECTION AGAINST ENERGY DAMAGE.
- **UNDERARMOR:** IF YOU'RE WORRIED YOUR VAULT SUIT DOESN'T OFFER ENOUGH PROTECTION, YOU CAN MIX AND MATCH PIECES OF ALL ARMOR TYPES AND WEAR THEM DIRECTLY OVER IT.

In addition, you can wear clothing, headgear, hats, and other items that are aesthetically pleasing, offer a bonus, or provide both. There are functional pieces of clothing, too, like gas masks and hazmat suits, which enable breathing across inhospitable environments (e.g., the Ash Heap).

For more information on armor and the Armor Workbench you'll make these items on, consult the Crafting chapter.

STEP 5: YOU LITTLE TINKER: AMMUNITION ASSISTANCE

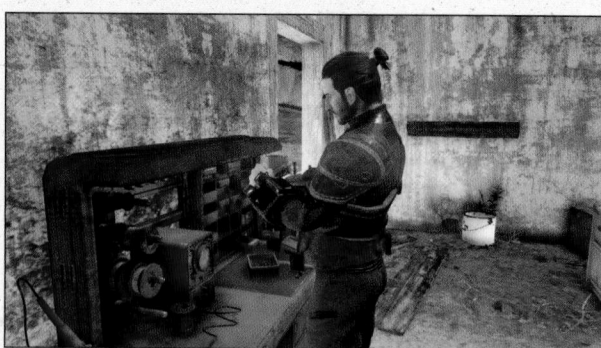

Use these workbenches to craft all your preferred ammunition: Scavenge smarter, not harder!

Although ammo can be bought from Robot Vendors or traded for with other players, your best method of gathering bullets (which nets you the most XP) is by crafting them at the Tinker's Workbench. Find one of your first Tinker's Workbenches at Gilman's Lumber Mill, at the bottom of the valley Vault 76 sits in. Scrap junk items you're scavenging (to lighten your load), and you should start to become self-sufficient regarding your ammunition use.

Assuming you're using ranged weaponry with bullets (and if you're purely melee, make ammo to sell instead, as it's extremely lightweight with few components), scroll down the Workbench menu to see the base components necessary to make more ammo for your favorite (or current) weapon, and then get searching! Need gunpowder? Then craft it at a chemistry station (using its own set of components) instead of searching for it.

STEP 6: FIREARM FORTE: WEAPON CONSTRUCTING

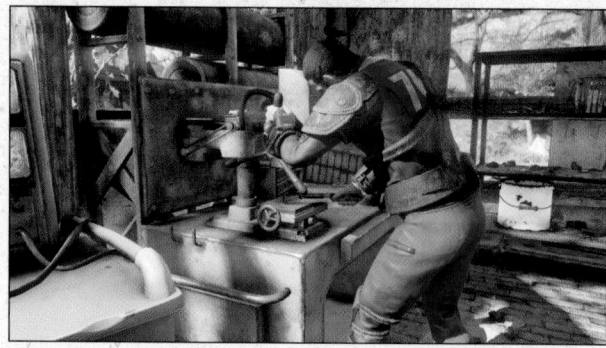

Use these workbenches to scrap, craft, repair, and finally modify your weapons of choice.

Should you visit the Overseer's Camp (and you should), one of your first miscellaneous tasks is to craft a weapon on the workbench there. Fortunately, the Overseer's Cache and other junk lying around should give you enough base components to make your own weapon. If you need more components,

Training – Status: You Have Emerged!

TRAINING

CRAFTING AND C.A.M.P.ING

INVENTORY

QUESTS

ATLAS

BESTIARY

APPENDICES

break down (scrap) weapons you've picked up (usually from fallen Scorched), especially as this sometimes gives you a new weapon plan! Need even more components? Start a scavenge around Wixon Homestead and other nearby locations. Compare the stats between a found and a crafted weapon (and remember you can craft significantly better versions of weapons at Levels 5, 10, 15, 20, etc.), learn to Repair your weapon (and stockpile the components needed so you can repair quickly and frequently), and look for plans to gain more weaponry. Check the Weapons section of the Inventory chapter for a list of weaponry. Don't worry about modding yet; that's what the Crafting chapter of this guide is for!

STEP 7: CHEMICAL INDEPENDENCY: CHEMISTRY STATION CRAFTING

Overlook the benefits of the chemistry station at your peril. Aside from the Caps to be made churning out chems for your friends and robot vendors (they are lucrative, as they don't weigh much, so they have a great weight-to-value ratio), focus on concocting chems to boost your statistics (i.e., "buffs"). Be careful taking too many chems. Not only do you risk addiction, but also many chems increase Hunger and Thirst. Check the Perks section for chem-related perks to offset addiction, allowing you to craft or use additional chems. Note that Chemistry Stations also allow you to craft Flamer Fuel and ingredients like gunpowder or smelted ore.

Below are the dozen best chems to try to concoct, after you find recipes):

- **ADDICTOL:** COMPLETELY CURES ITS USER OF ALL ADDICTIONS.
- **BUFFOUT:** A POWERFUL STEROID GRANTING TEMPORARY BONUSES TO STRENGTH, ENDURANCE, AND MAXIMUM HEALTH.
- **CALMEX:** HIGHLY SOUGHT AFTER BY HUNTERS AND ASSASSINS THROUGHOUT THE WASTELAND, CALMEX GRANTS A TEMPORARY BONUS TO PERCEPTION, AGILITY, AND SNEAK ATTACK DAMAGE.
- **DADDYO:** WHO NEEDS FRIENDS WHEN YOU'RE THIS SMART? USING DADDY-O GRANTS A TEMPORARY BONUS TO INTELLIGENCE AND PERCEPTION, BUT ALSO A TEMPORARY PENALTY TO CHARISMA.
- **DAYTRIPPER:** SOLD AS "HAPPINESS IN A BOTTLE," DAYTRIPPER GRANTS A TEMPORARY BONUS TO CHARISMA AND LUCK, AND A TEMPORARY PENALTY TO STRENGTH.
- **MEDX:** A POWERFUL PAINKILLER, MED-X GRANTS A TEMPORARY BONUS TO DAMAGE RESISTANCE.

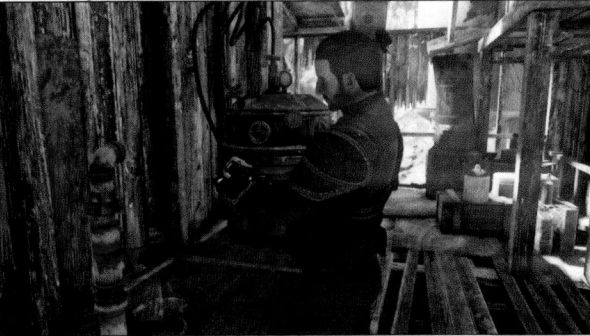

Start a different type of cooking at the chemistry station. There's one at the Moonshiner's Shack near the Vault.

- **MENTATS:** POPULAR WITH STUDENTS AND SCIENTISTS ALIKE, MENTATS GRANT A TEMPORARY BONUS TO PERCEPTION AND INTELLIGENCE.
- **PSYCHO:** DEVELOPED BY THE U.S. MILITARY AS A COMBAT DRUG, PSYCHO GRANTS A TEMPORARY BONUS TO DAMAGE DEALT AND DAMAGE RESISTANCE.
- **RADIATION CHEMS:** TO FIGHT RADIATION, USE THE CHEMS RAD-X AND RADAWAY. TAKE RAD-X TO TEMPORARILY INCREASE YOUR RADIATION RESISTANCE. TAKE RADAWAY IF YOU'VE ALREADY BEEN EXPOSED.
- **STIMPAK:** THE MEDICATION INSIDE A STIMPAK HEALS INJURIES AND CAN EVEN RESTORE DAMAGED LIMBS.
- **X-CELL:** THE EXPERIMENTAL CHEM X-CELL GRANTS A TEMPORARY BONUS TO EVERY SPECIAL ATTRIBUTE.

STEP 8: STAKING A CLAIM: CAMPING AND WORKSHOPS (LEVELS 5–10)

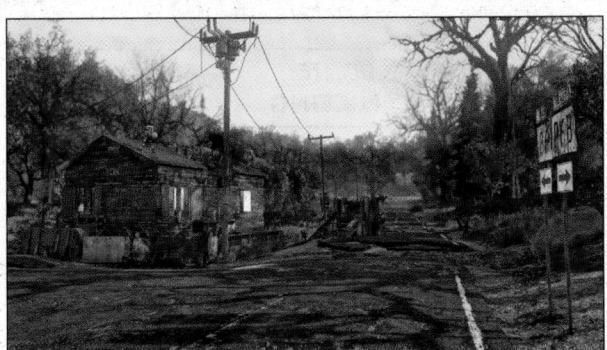

This shack doesn't appear on any known map...because it's a Vault Dweller's Camp.

This is an optional but recommended last course of action, though you should perhaps have ventured a bit farther afield to the woods north of Morgantown to complete a Camp-related Tutorial Quest for the Responders after finishing the related quests in Flatwoods. Find a patch of ground, bring out your C.A.M.P., and create a small but suitably rustic, imaginative, functional, and defensive camp of your own. Initially, this is a movable location that's free to Fast-Travel to, with a My Stash Box you can place to keep your Inventory manageable. Later on, there are numerous enhancements (via perks and plans) you can make to your home.

You can also visit a workshop location; the closest is either Sunshine Meadows near Flatwoods or Gorge Junkyard north of the Overseer's Camp. With some Caps and a modicum of chutzpah, you can stake a claim to a workshop, build up defenses (using the workshop's already-stocked inventory of components), and start to farm the resources these workshop locations are renowned for. Check the Crafting and Workshops chapters for more details.

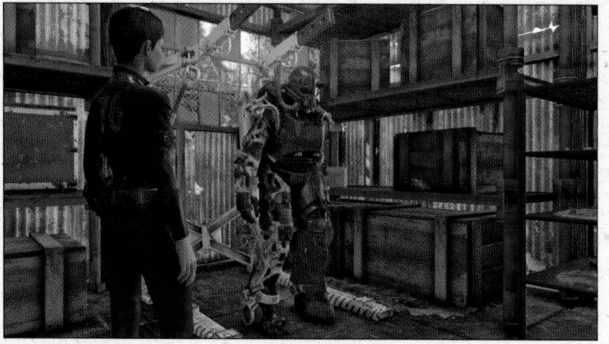

A suit of Power Armor, sitting at a Power Armor Station; be patient as it requires you to level up to access its benefits.

Many Vault Dwellers may be itching to clamber into a variety of impressive-looking exoskeletons known as Power Armor. Unfortunately, the initial area around Vault 76 is bereft of such armor, though the closest frame is located at Morgantown Trainyard, to the north. You can gather Power Armor Frames right now, but you must be Level 15 or higher to start adding armor pieces to the frame (and even then, you're limited to Raider pieces).

But what is Power Armor? Well, it's only the most advanced form of protection you can find! It provides the following benefits:

- SIGNIFICANTLY REDUCES INCOMING DAMAGE.
- INCREASES MELEE DAMAGE.
- INCREASES CARRY WEIGHT.
- PREVENTS ALL DAMAGE FROM FALLING.
- WITH A HELMET EQUIPPED, INCREASES HOW LONG YOU CAN STAY UNDERWATER.

Walk up to a suit of Power Armor and enter it. Hold the Action button to exit it.

CLAIMING POWER ARMOR

You can claim any suit of Power Armor (that another player does not own) by walking up to it and interacting with it. If you are told that you are not high enough level to enter the Power Armor, then you can still claim the Power Armor Frame by stripping the armor pieces from the suit, via the Transfer menu. Then try to enter the suit again.

COLLECTING AND RECALLING

Once you claim a suit of Power Armor, you can place it in your inventory by exiting the suit and collecting the Power Armor. Your suit will be added to your inventory under Items > Apparel with the name Power Armor Chassis. Your Power Armor will also automatically be recalled to your inventory if you exit it and leave the area, disconnect, or after a period of time has passed.

DEPLOYING AND DROPPING

You can deploy your Power Armor from your inventory by opening your Pip-Boy, selecting Power Armor Chassis, then placing it; you need to place it in a valid spot, which will turn the highlight around the armor green. Deployed Power Armor is owned by you, and other players cannot enter it. As you are the owner, the Power Armor will be recalled into your inventory if you do not enter it. If you want to give up ownership of the Power Armor, you can select it from your inventory and drop it. Dropped Power Armor will appear next to you in the world and can be claimed by any other player.

FUSION CORES

Power Armor runs on Fusion Cores. Performing any of the following actions will reduce your Power Armor core's charge: running, sprinting, Power Attacks, and V.A.T.S. Once your Fusion Core has been emptied, you will move at a reduced rate and will be unable to Power Attack or use V.A.T.S. If you have another Fusion Core in your inventory when your current core runs out, it will automatically be installed in your suit. Otherwise, you'll need to find a new core to restore your Power Armor's functionality.

POWER ARMOR PIECES

All Power Armor is made from two major components: a frame and a set of armor pieces.

Each armor piece attached to your frame increases your Damage Resistance, but a Power Armor frame does not require armor pieces to function. A frame without armor pieces will still provide protection against falling, increased melee damage, extra Carry Weight, and some Damage Resistance.

Armor pieces can become damaged over time. The current state of your armor pieces is visible on the suit icon to the screen's left. Pieces in red have taken significant damage and should be repaired. Empty sections mean a piece is either missing or destroyed and must be replaced.

You can view an armor piece's current condition by opening your Pip-Boy and going to Items > Apparel, or by using a Power Armor Station. To add or remove an armor piece from your frame, open your Pip-Boy and go to Items > Apparel, select the piece you want to add or remove, and use it.

You can also equip or unequip armor pieces at a Power Armor Station or by approaching your Power Armor suit and opening the Transfer menu.

POWER ARMOR STATIONS

A Power Armor Station allows you to craft new armor pieces, modify existing pieces, and make repairs to pieces. In order to use a Power Armor Station, first walk into the station while wearing the Power Armor, then exit the armor. Walk over to the Power Armor Station and access it. Otherwise, use Power Armor Stations to scrap junk or other items. The nearest Power Armor Station to Vault 76 is at Wilson Brother's Auto Repair or the Gorge Junkyard.

POWER ARMOR VARIANTS

Power Armor Frame: Even without additional limb armor, a Power Armor frame still provides tactical advantages, like increased Carry Weight, greater melee damage, and the elimination of falling damage. You can access and wear these frames at any Level.

Excavator: Developed by Garrahan Mining Co., the "Excavator" class of Power Armor never saw full production, despite being heavily advertised in Appalachia as the future of mining.

Raider: Scavenged and restored by Appalachia's vicious and anarchistic gangs, Raider Power Armor features crude plating, rusty spikes, and significant battlefield protection.

T45: Built by defense contractor West-Tek, the T-45 series of Power Armor was the first to be successfully deployed on the battlefield. Its introduction changed the nature of modern warfare.

T51: The Battle of Anchorage saw the first deployment of the advanced T-51 series of Power Armor. With advanced servos and composite armor plating, it was a vast improvement over earlier models.

T60: The most advanced suits of Power Armor to see extensive use were the T-60 models. By the time of the Great War, they were a common sight in all U.S. military engagements.

YOU WILL EXPLORE:
GENERAL ACTIVITIES TO UNDERTAKE

TRAINING

CRAFTING AND C.A.M.P.ING

INVENTORY

QUESTS

ATLAS

BESTIARY

APPENDICES

Now that you have a good understanding of the critical activities (your first eight steps), and you've perhaps discovered around 10 to 20 primary locations between or around Vault 76 and Flatwoods, it's time to widen your scope of exploration: Check out the Forest, including trips to the two largest settlements of Morgantown (northeast) and Charleston (south). Do this only when you feel ready, usually between Levels 5 and 10, and after Level 15 if you want to start utilizing Power Armor. During this time, learn the finer points of the following techniques:

COUGHS AND SNEEZES (AND ALMOST EVERYTHING ELSE) SPREAD DISEASES

DISEASES

DISEASES ARE TEMPORARY NEGATIVE EFFECTS. YOU HAVE A CHANCE TO CATCH A DISEASE WHEN YOU DO ANY OF THE FOLLOWING:

- SLEEP ON A BED WITHOUT A FRAME (LIKE A MATTRESS OR SLEEPING BAG), THAT ISN'T IN YOUR CAMP OR WORKSHOP.
- RECEIVE MELEE DAMAGE BY A DISEASED ENEMY.
- DRINK DIRTY WATER.
- MOVE THROUGH ENVIRONMENTAL HAZARDS.
- EAT RAW FOOD.
- SWIM IN DIRTY WATER.
- GET HIT BY A TRAP.
- MOVE THROUGH AN AREA THAT HAS BAD WEATHER.

The chance to catch a disease is based on your Endurance. The higher your Endurance, the lower the chance you'll catch any disease. Also be aware that catching a Disease in a Region of Appalachia with a higher Threat Level causes the duration of the disease to last longer. Prevent catching a disease entirely by:

- SLEEPING ONLY IN BEDS THAT HAVE A FRAME, OR A MATTRESS OR SLEEPING BAG IN YOUR OWN CAMP OR WORKSHOP.
- AVOIDING GETTING CLOSE TO DISEASED ENEMIES, SO THEY CAN'T HIT YOU.
- BOILING DIRTY WATER AT A COOKING STATION BEFORE DRINKING IT.
- WEARING A HAZMAT SUIT OR GAS MASK BEFORE MOVING THROUGH ENVIRONMENTAL HAZARDS, SWIMMING THROUGH WATER, OR EXPLORING OUTSIDE IN BAD WEATHER.
- COOKING RAW FOOD AT A COOKING STATION BEFORE EATING IT.
- WATCHING OUT FOR TRAPS AND DISARMING THEM BEFORE THEY SPRING.

If you catch a disease, you can open your Pip-Boy and go to STAT > Effects to see more information on the penalties you'll face until the disease is cured. Disease cures and antibiotics will remove one disease. Diseases will also expire on their own, given enough time. You can craft remedies for diseases at a cooking station or chemistry station. Without a remedy, a disease will run its course and go away after enough time has passed.

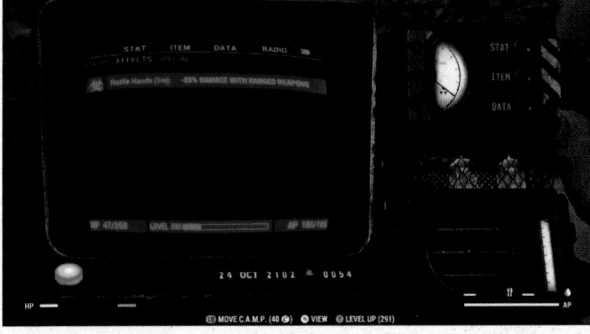

Feeling strange? You may be diseased. Feeling stranger? You may be mutating!

MUTATIONS

Mutations give you a mixture of powerful positive and negative effects. Whenever you take radiation damage (which is also sometimes related to certain diseases), you have a chance to gain a mutation.

You can see the effects of any mutations you have by opening the Pip-Boy and going to STAT > Effects.

Mutations are semi-permanent. Every time you use RadAway, there is a chance it will remove a mutation. You can keep using RadAway for more attempts to remove a mutation (the lower your current rads when RadAway is consumed, the higher the chance the removal, up to 100 percent if you have no rads). Or, you can pick a perk that negates this, if you actually want the mutation! You can actually inject yourself (or others) with mutations by using serums: These are consumable items that will grant a specific mutation as soon as you use it. If you already have that mutation, the serum will temporarily suppress the mutation's negative effects and increase the positive effects.

You're more likely to get mutations if you have high Rads, and cure them with low Rads. Also note there's a cooldown period after receiving one mutation, before you can obtain another.

A complete list of diseases and mutations is listed in the Active Effects section of the "Being a Better You!" chapter.

QUESTS

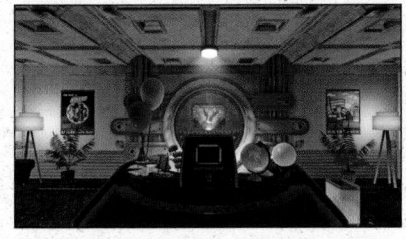

Your very first quest involves tracking your Overseer. Where can she be?

As you gradually progress away from the cradle of Vault 76, you will be called upon to perform certain activities, investigate odd or important happenings, solve disappearances, and handle other quest-related activities. (These are covered, in impressive detail, in other chapters of this guide.) If you're unsure of what to do in your current environment, it is always an excellent idea to complete a nearby quest. Why?

- TO OBTAIN A BOOST OF ITEMS, INCLUDING RECIPES, MODS, AND PLANS, WHICH ARE (RANDOMLY) AWARDED UPON THE COMPLETION OF A QUEST.
- TO GAIN EXPERIENCE POINTS (XP), ALLOWING YOU TO MORE QUICKLY LEVEL UP, CRAFT BETTER ITEMS, AND USE BETTER "LEVELED" EQUIPMENT.
- TO UNCOVER THE SECRETS OF APPALACHIA!

Quests begin in a variety of ways. There are different types (all covered in the Main Quests, Side Quests, Miscellaneous Quests, Events, and Challenges chapters). Here are the main methods of adding a quest to your Pip-Boy:

ANNOUNCEMENTS

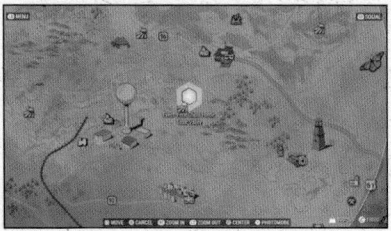

Vault-Tec's automated systems intermittently announce special quests that are available in your area and sometimes far into a different region of Appalachia. These are usually events, and some require multiple players to complete, as enemy forces may be too great to face on your own. These events are indicated by a yellow hexagon; check these sooner rather than later since most are timed (and are repeatable).

HOLOTAPES

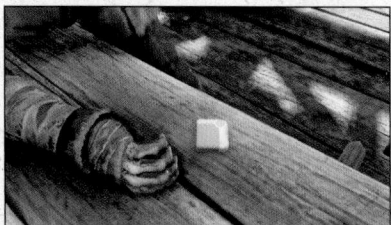

Similar to notes are orange-and-white holotapes, designed to be played on your Pip-Boy and most terminals. The audio information contained on the holotape may prove extremely useful and can further your questing, give hints on a new quest, or offer information on a location you've not yet visited. Or the holotape could contain the ramblings of a madman.

OVERSEER CACHES

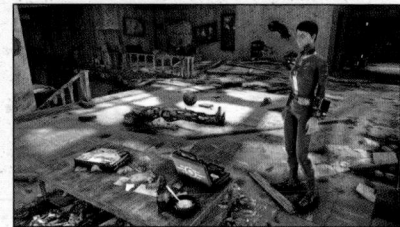

Look for large trunks, about the size of your My Stash Box, with the Vault logo on them. These not only contain a wealth of supplies but also clues to the travels and recent whereabouts of the Vault Overseer. For additional information, look for smaller, dark blue Vault-Tec holotape cases and tapes with audio from the Overseer.

NOTES

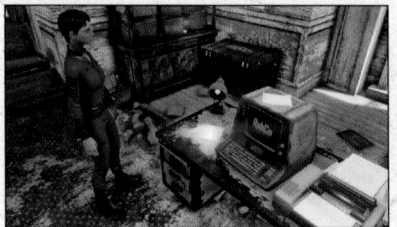

You may find notes along your travels, usually fragments of paper with musings, alarming scribbling, or printed advertisements. Pick up every note you see (the Atlas tracks locations with a high chance of finding one), and follow the instructions, if you wish.

ROBOTS

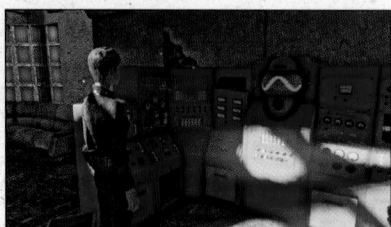

Robots are an excellent source of quest information; you can speak or listen to them, and some of them (usually a Mr. Handy or Protectron variant with a yellow health bar on your screen) have requests they wish you to perform. You may also gain access to a mainframe robot computer, such as the Mayor of Grafton; these sentient supercomputers may also have requirements of you.

SHARING

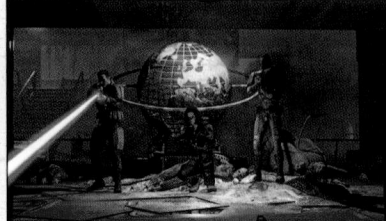

If you are a team member with other friends active, you can help with any of the quests your team leader has activated. Get together and pool your resources, and finish tasks together!

MAPS (MENU) AND MISCELLANEOUS

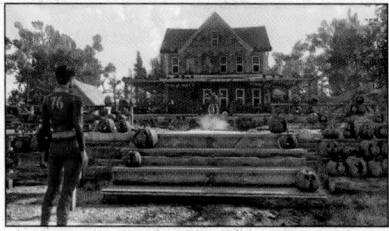

From time to time, you may wander past a location (or dash past it while being savaged by the Scorched) and not realize there was a quest there. Periodically check your world map, as well as your Data > Quests menu on your Pip-Boy to see if there are tasks (particularly in the "Miscellaneous" part of the menu) that require attention.

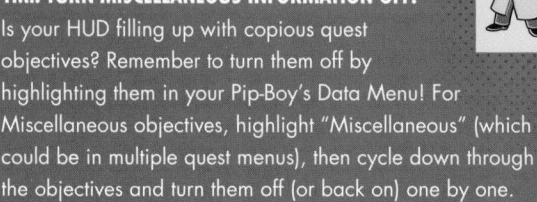

Helpful Hint from Vault Boy!

TMI: TURN MISCELLANEOUS INFORMATION OFF!

Is your HUD filling up with copious quest objectives? Remember to turn them off by highlighting them in your Pip-Boy's Data Menu! For Miscellaneous objectives, highlight "Miscellaneous" (which could be in multiple quest menus), then cycle down through all the objectives and turn them off (or back on) one by one.

THE CRAFTY ART OF FORAGING

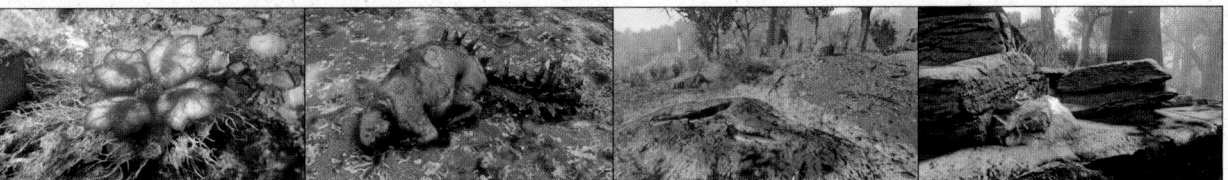

Exploit the natural (and unnatural) flora and deposits across Appalachia; harvest plants (left), loot animal corpses (left-center), farm deposits (right-center), and exploit veins (right).

Components that you need for recipes (food, chems, ammo), as well as mods and plans can be broken down either from natural resources (foraging) or junk items (scavenging or looting). Every region in Appalachia has interesting indigenous plant life to find and utilize, usually for consumables. Also present are large sunken deposits, primarily within a workshop, but also across the wilderness. There are also smaller, naturally occurring veins of certain mineral ores. The latter two types of resources can be mined (without the need of any special equipment—not even an ax!). Deposits, though, can be farmed using collectors you can build, either inside a workshop or as one of your resource objects if you set up a camp nearby. The resulting items can be broken down or crafted into usable base components and/or sold to vendors, teammates, or strangers.

THE FINER ARTS OF LOOTING

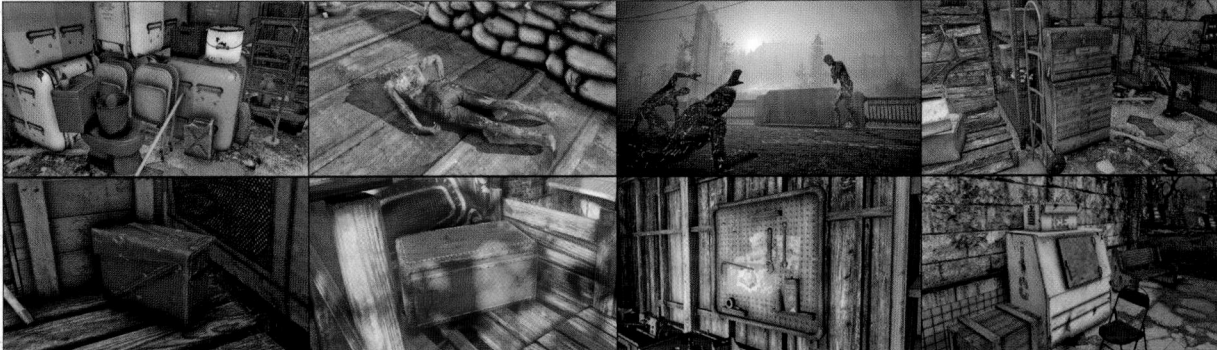

A variety of looting opportunities: Top row (L–R): Items in the environment, corpses, petrified corpses, container selection. Bottom row (L–R): Ammo box, industrial trunk, worker's item board, machine.

Loot man-made items or those belonging to foes you've recently killed. As shown in the adjacent examples, there are numerous containers, ranging from corpses to ice boxes; all of them contain random items. Simply grab what you need! Here are some specific containers to look out for:

USUAL LOOTABLE OBJECTS

* Denotes an item possibly flagged for interest throughout this guide's Atlas.

Items in the Environment*: Every location has a large amount of junk items, detritus, and other abandoned objects and foodstuffs for you to gather. If you can see them (i.e., they're on a table), they are usually not random, but may sometimes be substituted by a different piece of junk. Also make sure you figure out which are valuable to you, and remember to come back for them again in a day, when they reappear.

Corpses: These are arguably the most important of all the "objects" you can loot; after each kill, check what the enemy has on them. Animals give you raw meat, while other species, monsters, and rarer entities may (randomly) give you exceptional or rare loot!

Petrified Corpses: You can also loot the dead that are about to turn into Scorched—usually for a small radioactive addition and a few Caps; this is helpful if you need to clear an area of these. Shoot them from range to avoid the radiation.

Tool Boxes, Lunch Pails, Suitcases, Wood Crates: This is just a small example of all the different containers that hold items. Simply check each one, unlocking them using bobby pins if they are locked at Levels 0 (Normal), 1 (Advanced), 2 (Expert), or 3 (Master).

Ammo Boxes, Duffel Bags*: Find ammunition and more explosive items in these military-style containers.

Industrial Trunks*: These large trunks are usually green or red and sometimes have a star insignia. These often indicate that a location you've explored has concluded, as they are housed in the last chamber, though you can find them anywhere. Expect a reasonably better selection of items from these containers.

Safes*: A free-standing or floor-mounted immovable safe, mostly locked and requiring a picklocking minigame to obtain the interior contents.

Worker's Item Boards: Don't forget to check the walls of garages, basements, and sheds used by mechanics or other working folk; this hanging board usually has a number of handyman items.

Machines: Nuka Cola Machines, Ice Boxes, Fertilizer Storage, Eat-O-Matic machines—all of these could hold items, usually the type the machine used to store before the War.

TRAINING

CRAFTING AND CAMPING

INVENTORY

QUESTS

ATLAS

BESTIARY

APPENDICES

UNUSUAL LOOTABLE OBJECTS

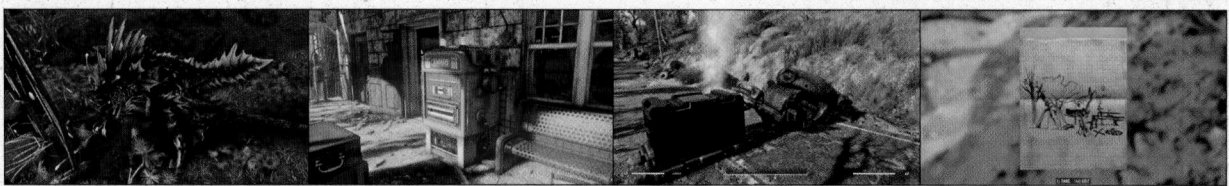

A variety of unusual looting opportunities.
Top row (L–R): Legendary enemy corpse, vending machine, government air drop, treasure chest.

Specific Enemy Corpses: Specific enemies also give you specific loot; Legendary enemies always drop a piece of Legendary equipment, and robots may have Fusion Cores or circuits for your more specific crafting needs.

Vending Machines*: Found at gas stations, train stations, and (once you have the plans) at your camp if you build one, these sell a random selection of items to anyone who's buying. Check these periodically for rare items to purchase. Note there are location-specific vending machines, too, with specific items to obtain (examples include prize-awarding machines after collecting tokens, or U-Mine-It! vending machines offering information on where rare minerals and ores can be farmed).

Government Air Drops: If you see a dropped item or one close to a hovering Vertibot, or if you find a holotape or terminal at one of the many small hilltop relay towers across Appalachia, quickly gather the high-quality military items inside. The air drop case has a brightly colored smoke trail visible to all.

Treasure Maps and Other Oddities and Trinkets: If you chance upon a parchment with a sketch on it (found randomly across Appalachia), compare the picture to a location you've visited; if you can find the same vantage point as the picture indicates, you can find a hidden treasure stash there! You'll also start to discover odd trinkets in the landscape, like souvenir lighthouses at the Landview Lighthouse. What are these for? Perhaps you'll find out later.

THE ADDICTIVE ART OF COLLECTING

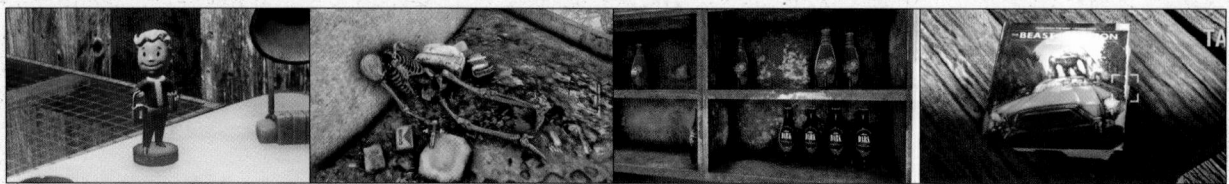

Your collection of more valuable objects includes (L–R): Bobbleheads, Caps Stashes, rare Nuka Cola, and Magazines.

Though there's not a category of items known as "collectibles," this guide has flagged certain high-value items as such. Note that in the case of Bobbleheads, Caps Stashes, holotapes, Magazines, and Nuka Colas (as well as Power Armor frame locations), these items semi-randomly appear. This means they are sometimes at a location, but their appearance is random. They have a set location (e.g., on a picnic table just north of the Landview Lighthouse), but the object may or may not appear. And it definitely won't if another player has just grabbed it! Here are some high-value items to look for:

* Denotes an item possibly flagged for interest throughout this guide's Atlas.

Bobbleheads*: There are 20 different types of Bobbleheads to find, and a random one is found each time you visit a location where one was previously located. Sadly, these have already been taken out of the packaging. But they do bestow a fancy improvement for a limited time period.

Caps Stashes*: These lunch tins contain a good number of Caps and randomly appear in the same location every time.

Holotapes*: These could tell the frightening story of the Mothman, provide knowledge of the Overseer's past, offer clues to solving a quest, or simply be the ravings of a nutcase. Some, found at Magazine locations, have a RobCo Fun! game you can play.

Magazines*: There are 12 different Magazine publications for you to gather, including one set with a free holotape game you simply must attempt! They all have effects related to the Magazine series they are from, and a random one is found each time you visit a location where one was previously located (so you won't get Grognak the Barbarian #4 at the same place twice!).

Nuka Colas*: Sometimes, the locations of a regular Nuka Cola may be replaced by a rarer Nuka Cherry or an even rarer Nuka Cola Quantum (both have more pronounced bonus effects when consumed). There are even rarer Nuka Colas out there too. Now, how do you get into The Whitespring Resort again?

Power Armor Frames*: Appalachia has a large number of Power Armor frames, with attached armor sections on each suit. Each also comes with a Fusion Core. Pick off the armor pieces and store them until you're high enough level to use them.

Note there are a whole host of other items to think about searching for, such as: Arms and Ammo, Health and Chems, Fusion Cores, Harvestables, Notes, Recipes/Mods/Plans, and Trunks. These are all described at the start of the Atlas chapter.

Note the statistical improvements you receive for Bobbleheads and Magazines are detailed in the Active Effects section of the Being a Better You! chapter.

THE IMPRESSIVE ARTS OF HACKING AND LOCKPICKING

TERMINALS

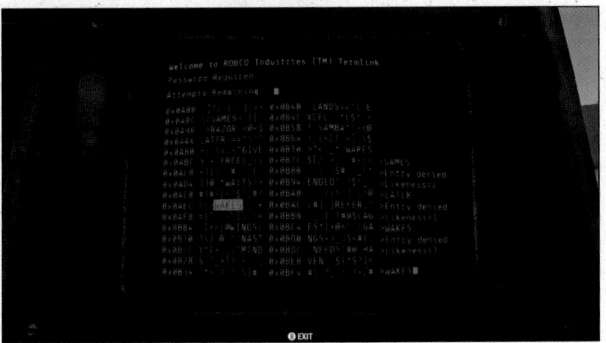

If you're hacking a terminal, prepare for a short minigame where you're prone to attacks.

Terminals are plentiful across Appalachia, whether set into a wall, on a desk, or as part of a vending unit. Some are locked, at various levels of difficulty. Access terminals to uncover useful information; unlock secure doors; take control of linked turrets, bots, and spotlights; or play holotapes. Some terminals can hold (or contain) holotapes. To enter a terminal, approach and access it.

HACKING A TERMINAL

Hacking lets you access terminals locked with a password. Locked terminals have a difficulty level, usually between 0 (Normal) and 3 (Master). A level 0 terminal can always be hacked, but higher-level terminals will require you to equip the perks Hacker, Expert Hacker, and Master Hacker. Each perk you equip increases your Hacking skill by 1. You will need to equip all three perks to hack Level 3 terminals.

When hacking, a terminal will display a list of potential passwords and random characters. Only one word listed is the correct password:

– MOVE THE CURSOR AND SELECT A WORD, AND USE IT AS THE PASSWORD BY CLICKING ON IT.
– IF THE GUESS IS CORRECT, THE TERMINAL WILL UNLOCK.
– IF THE GUESS IS WRONG, A "LIKENESS" NUMBER WILL BE DISPLAYED IN THE CORNER OF THE TERMINAL SCREEN.

The likeness number tells you how many letters, in the correct position, match the actual password. For example, if the password is *BOOK* and you guess *BACK*, the likeness number is 2, because there's a *B* in position 1 and a *K* in position 4. But if you guess *OATS*, the likeness number is 0. Even though both *BOOK* and *OATS* contain the letter *O*, the word *OATS* has an *O* in position 1, and the letter in position 1 of the actual password is *B*, so it's not a match.

Use the likeness number to narrow your search by comparing the letters and letter positions of your guess to the remaining options.

As you move your cursor through the lists of characters, keep an eye out for pairs of matching brackets—for example, (){}. If a matching pair of brackets becomes highlighted, then selecting the brackets might remove a dud word or reset your number of attempts for the hack.

You have four attempts to select the right password. If you fail to find the correct entry after four attempts, you'll be locked out of the terminal for 10 seconds.

You can exit the terminal at any time.

CONTAINER AND DOORS: LOCKPICKING

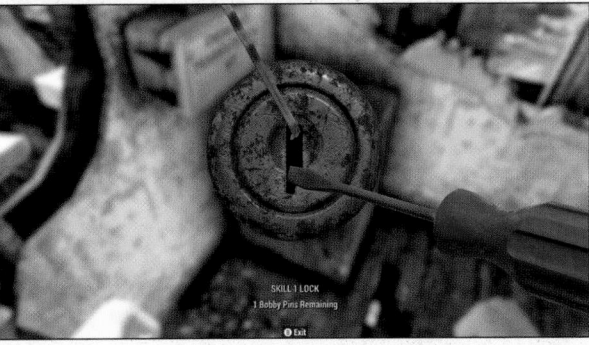

If you're picking a lock, prepare for a short minigame where you're prone to both attacks and the loss of your bobby pins.

Many containers (including safes) and doors across Appalachia are already unlocked or open. But some are locked (and you can add locks to some camp and workshop objects to stop thievery). Picking locks will let you open doors, safes, and containers.

Locks have a difficulty level, usually between 0 (Normal) and 3 (Master). A Level 0 lock can always be picked, but higher-level locks will require you to equip the perks Picklock, Expert Picklock, and Master Picklock. Each perk you equip increases your Picklock skill by 1. You will need to equip all three perks to pick level 3 locks.

To pick a lock, you must have at least one bobby pin in your inventory. To find bobby pins, explore Appalachia, purchase them from robot vendors, or trade for them with other players. Once you have a bobby pin, approach the locked door or container and start to pick it:

– ROTATE THE BOBBY PIN, THEN ROTATE THE SCREWDRIVER.
– IF THE LOCK RESISTS, RELEASE THE SCREWDRIVER AND REPOSITION THE BOBBY PIN BEFORE TRYING AGAIN. THE CLOSER THE BOBBY PIN IS TO THE CORRECT POSITION, THE FARTHER THE LOCK WILL ROTATE BEFORE YOU EITHER ENCOUNTER RESISTANCE OR THE BOBBY PIN BREAKS.
– WHEN THE BOBBY PIN IS IN THE CORRECT POSITION, THE LOCK WILL FULLY ROTATE AND OPEN. MORE DIFFICULT LOCKS REQUIRE MORE PRECISE PLACEMENT OF THE BOBBY PIN.

Some locks require a key and cannot be opened through lockpicking.

TRAINING

CRAFTING AND C.A.M.P.ING

INVENTORY

QUESTS

ATLAS

BESTIARY

APPENDICES

BANKING ON IT: CAPS COLLECTING

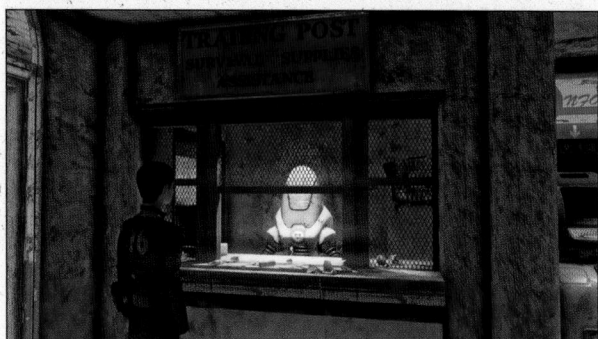

Pre-War Money? That's so pre-apocalyptic!
There's a new currency in town: Caps! Acquire more in
a variety of ways, like selling unwanted wares to your
Protectron pal: a Vendor Bot.

As money no longer has any value, the survivors of Appalachia are utilizing a new type of currency: Caps! The tops of Nuka Cola bottles allow you to gain wealth, and any item with value is measured in Caps. Caps are used up when you Fast-Travel to anywhere you've previously explored or revealed, except your camp or Vault 76. You use them when you start a new camp, claim a workshop, trade, or pay off a bounty (usually with your life).

Find your Caps total in the bottom-right of your world map or the bottom-middle of most of your Pip-Boy menus. But how do you get more Caps?

- **FROM NUKA COLA BOTTLES:** YOU MAY NOT THINK TO DO THIS, BUT DRINKING DOWN ANY NUKA COLA BOTTLE ALLOWS YOU TO KEEP THE BOTTLE CAP, ADDING ONE TO YOUR CAPS TOTAL.
- **FROM THE ENVIRONMENT:** SINGLE CAPS ARE SOMETIMES STREWN ABOUT ON TABLES, FLOORS, OR CHESSBOARDS.
- **FROM CAPS STASHES:** THESE LUNCH BOXES ARE CRAMMED WITH CAPS (OR THEY WILL BE IF YOU HAVE THE LUCK PERK CAP COLLECTOR ACTIVE).
- **FROM CORPSES:** CHECK THE CONTENTS OF THAT MOLE RAT, SUPER MUTANT, OR OTHER EVEN MORE REVOLTING SPECIMEN YOU JUST DEFEATED; THEY MIGHT HAVE CARRIED (OR SWALLOWED) SOME CAPS.
- **FROM PETRIFIED CORPSES:** THE STATIC ASH STATUES THAT FORM THE SCORCHED ALMOST ALWAYS HAVE A CAP IF YOU SEARCH THEM AND CAN WITHSTAND THE SLIGHT RADIATION POISONING WHEN THESE CORPSE STATUES DISINTEGRATE.
- **FROM CONTAINERS:** OPEN ANYTHING AND EVERYTHING YOU CAN INTERACT WITH; THERE COULD BE CAPS INSIDE!
- **FROM VENDORS (ROBOTS):** HEAD TO A VENDOR AND SELL THEM YOUR SCAVENGED OR CRAFTED EQUIPMENT.
- **FROM TRADING (PLAYERS):** BECKON A FELLOW VAULT DWELLER OVER FOR A SPOT OF BARTERING, SELLING THEM YOUR SCAVENGED OR CRAFTED EQUIPMENT.
- **FROM BOUNTIES (PLAYERS):** WE MADE TIME TO TAKE OUT THAT TROUBLESOME "VITO" AND HIS OLDER, SWEATIER BROTHER "PEPPER," KNOWN AS "THE HEAVY-SET BANDITS" WHO'VE BEEN MASSACRING INNOCENT FOLKS NEAR MAMA DOLCE'S FOOD PROCESSING FACTORY FOR A WHILE NOW. THE BOUNTY COMES OUT OF THEIR OWN CAPS TOTALS, MAKING THEIR COMEUPPANCE ALL THE SWEETER!
- **FROM QUESTS:** AFTER COMPLETING A QUEST, EXPECT A JINGLE OF ADDITIONAL CAPS ALONG WITH OTHER REWARDS.

VENDORS

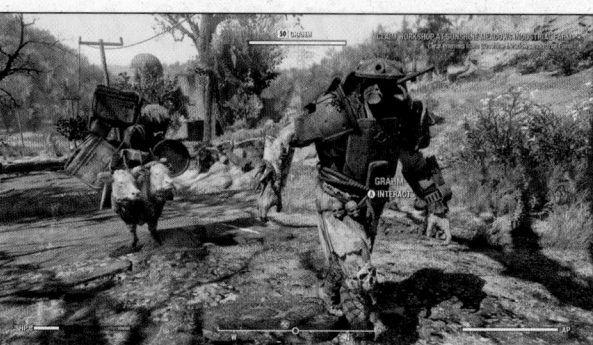

Most vendors are Protectrons, standing in a Responder
Trading Post, ready to buy and sell. There are some other
types of vendor, including Grahm and his pack Brahmin
Moo-Moo. Try not to shoot him!

Vendors are typically robots that have been programmed by the previous survivors of Appalachia to sell goods. They are found in settlements previously occupied by the Responders Faction, as well as every train station in Appalachia. Expect vendors from different regions to have a variety of items specific to that region. Also expect to see "wandering vendors," usually a Protectron with a Brahmin caravan behind them. There's also a friendly Super Mutant vendor who sells some pretty choice wares.

When you find a vendor, a Trade prompt appears. In the Trade menu, the list on the left contains your inventory, and the list on the right contains all the items the vendor is selling. At the bottom of each list are the number of Caps you each have. A vendor that is out of Caps will not be able to purchase your items. You must have enough Caps to purchase the items, or the transaction will fail.

If you're interested in selling items, collect the items that have a good ratio to them: look at the value of an item in your Pip-Boy, and compare it to the item's weight, or the general availability, and decide to focus on items that are light, valuable, and easy to come by.

One of the ways to make Caps is to sell your crafted items to vendors, but due to their limited budgets, you won't make a huge amount at one time. Not so if you try trading with other players instead (see later in this chapter for trading information).

MONTANI SEMPER LIBERI: ADVENTURING ACROSS APPALACHIA

By now you should have studied the entirety of the Appalachian wilderness in map form (and even glanced at the guide's Atlas). When you feel ready, and you've learned the threat level posed in each of the six major regions, you should pluck up the courage to venture farther afield.

YOU WILL EXPLORE: THE ENVIRONMENT OF APPALACHIA

The biggest concern when leaving the (relative) normalcy of the Forest region is the threats that each of the other regions pose. As a quick overview, read the guide's introduction to each region, and study the threat levels, as shown below:

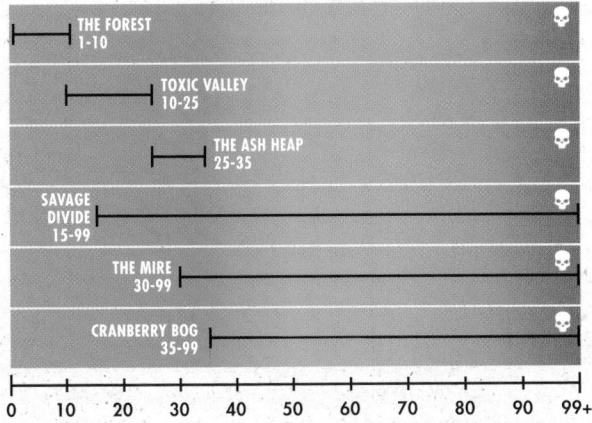

ENEMY THREAT LEVELS

THE FOREST 1-10	💀
TOXIC VALLEY 10-25	💀
THE ASH HEAP 25-35	💀
SAVAGE DIVIDE 15-99	💀
THE MIRE 30-99	💀
CRANBERRY BOG 35-99	💀

0   10   20   30   40   50   60   70   80   90   99+

A threat level indicates the usual level of the enemies within a particular region, though this can change over time. For regions where the threat level peaks at Level 99, expect the highest level enemy to be matched to the highest level player in that region. So if a Level 75 player is wandering around Cranberry Bog, expect the toughest foes to be around that level too.

YOU WILL EXPLORE: MAPPED (PRIMARY) LOCATIONS

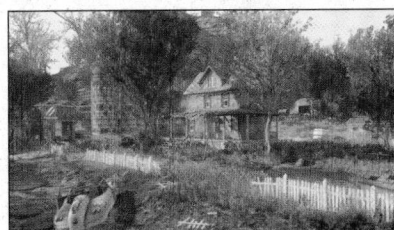

Marked on the map, and varying in size from shacks to cities, this is a primary location.

Start an exploration of a new area you haven't seen before by checking the guide's Atlas (there are around 358 of these!) and locating the nearest primary location. These are marked places on your in-game world map, and your compass, and the main source of scavenging, items, enemies, quest information, and other information. Read the Atlas to learn how big, problematic, or easy each location is to conquer, and then go explore. Feel free to return to each location a day later to clear it out a subsequent time, and repeat the process for more items and XP (e.g., if collectibles didn't appear the first time you checked).

YOU WILL EXPLORE: UNMAPPED (SECONDARY) POI LOCATIONS

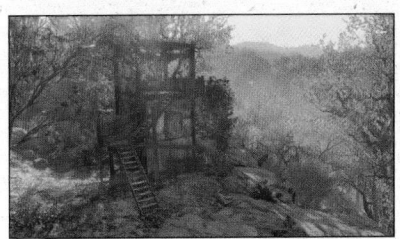

Not usually marked on the map, expect a multitude of smaller locations known as secondary locations.

There are hundreds (literally; this guide tracks 494, but there are sure to be more) of odd, small, and usually out-of-the-way locations across Appalachia too. These are unlikely to have other players near them, and they have their fair share of items to scavenge. They may have a bizarre Mothman totem, an impressive rock formation, or other, more dangerous secrets....

Helpful Hint from Vault Boy!

SITE-SEEING? SIGHT-SEEING!

There's more to life than just scavenging and fighting foes at primary and secondary locations. Build a camp close to these points of interest (especially secondary locations), and record your progress using Photomode, so you can remember the sights...and that time you were taking a selfie and didn't see that Wendigo until it was too late.

YOU WILL EXPLORE: PLAYER LOCATIONS

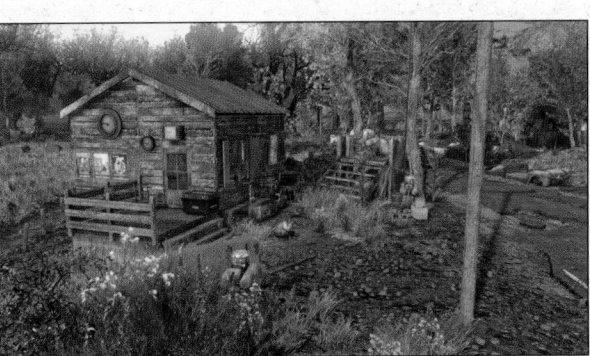

That wooden hut wasn't there yesterday, and looks like it's been built by another Human.

If you see a small dwelling, usually with turrets and a generator, and it doesn't appear as a primary or secondary location on this guide's Atlas map, then we've either made a grave mistake or you've stumbled upon a player location (or camp). Exercise caution (or don't; wreck the place if you're sure you can survive). Inspect the place to see how it was built. Take a photo before and after wrecking it. Or befriend the player and start a new and beautiful friendship....

TRAINING

CRAFTING AND C.A.M.P.ING

INVENTORY

QUESTS

ATLAS

BESTIARY

APPENDICES

YOU WILL EXPLORE: NAVIGATING YOUR PATHS TO SUCCESS

While there's a certain thrill when you try to sprint in a direct path from one location to the next, the difficult terrain, many hazards, and general dangers present in Appalachia means you should think about using the natural geography to your advantage, when you're trekking and ensuring you've explored every nook and cranny of a particular area.

ROADS

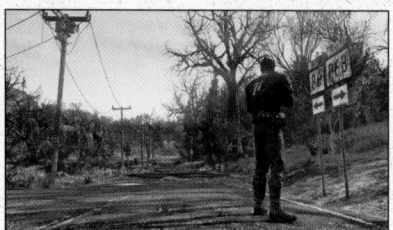

This is obvious, but the clogged arterial interstate, route, and road network is a great way to get about. You're more likely to encounter other players, wandering vendors, quests, and possibly enemies, as well as primary locations along the roadside. Plus, there are gravel pits along the roads if you need to mine concrete. Even if you're wandering in the wilderness, keep yourself within a quick sprint of the road, and segment road, rail, and river sections into quadrants and explore within those boundaries to thoroughly inspect each part of a region.

RIVERS

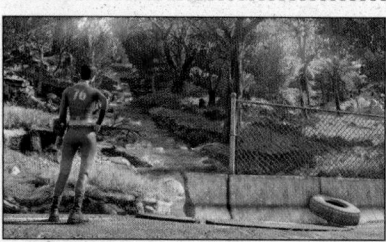

The meandering rivers, including ponds, dried up sludge beds, toxic streams, and other bodies of water, are another natural landmark and boundary to follow.

RAILROADS

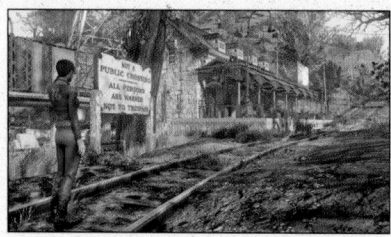

The buckled railroads snaking throughout West Virginia, including the once-impressive but now derelict monorail system to the southeast (in Savage Divide and Cranberry Bog) also allow you to stay within a quadrant and find more areas of interest if you keep close by.

FOOTPATHS AND TRAILS

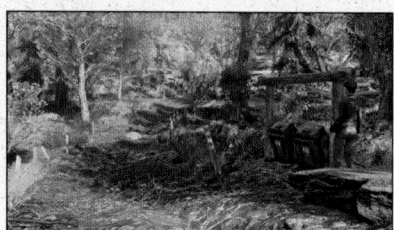

If you're ready for a slightly tougher adventure, set off into the wilderness, but utilize the many footpaths, which are still in relatively good shape. If you want exceptional vistas; smaller, out-of-the-way locations to explore; and more chances of being ambushed, trek along the trails and footpaths that start at the side of most roads and usually lead to another road or a location.

SIGNPOSTS

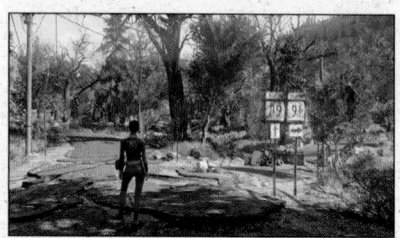

Read (and possibly shoot at) every signpost you spot, so you know which road you're on and what towns are coming up ahead of you. There are a host of smaller signs, too, like trailhead and campsite information, and areas daubed with the logo of a particular faction, so you know who was here before you.

LANDMARKS

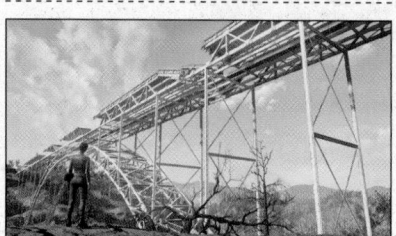

Another fantastic way to navigate around West Virginia is via the landmarks; if you've seen that Landview Lighthouse a few too many times, you know you're wandering in circles! Check your world map for drawings of the largest landmarks, and see if you can spot them from your vantage point. Use the larger and smaller landmarks when navigating.

BOG CHANNELS

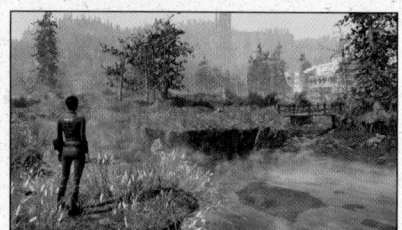

Special mention must be made of the sunken channels that snake through Cranberry Bog. These provide a modicum of cover (and danger, as they're not easy to jump out of), and you can more easily sneak around this region by using the channels. Plus, there's a secret tunnel system from Watoga to the Abandoned Bog Town no one knows about yet!

OFF THE BEATEN PATH

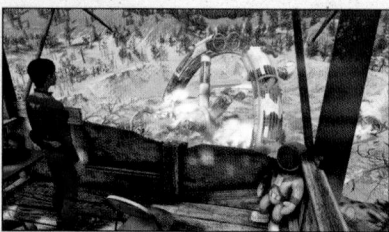

Finally, just throw caution to the wind, pick a point on the map, and journey to it. Find interesting flora and fauna, deadly encounters, majestic vistas, and much, much more along the way. Have you found the tightrope walk yet?

YOU WILL DO MORE: INTERACTIONS IN THE ENVIRONMENT*

While the RobCo Robot Pods (located in most larger towns) have yet to go online (but might be accessible right now!), there are other actions you can undertake during your Appalachian exploration. Here are some of the more helpful and entertaining that haven't yet been mentioned:

PURIFYING THE AIR

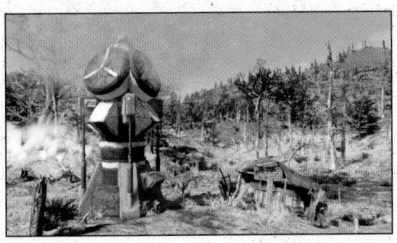

Two of the regions are known for their inhospitable atmosphere, which can cause health problems and diseases if you're not wearing a gas mask, hazmat suit, or Power Armor. However, should you chance upon a large Aerosolizer (Toxic Valley; pictured) or Purifier (the Ash Heap), and it happens to be functional, it creates a pocket of breathable air. These devices are scattered across the two regions and offer a brief respite to the choking weather pervading the northwest and southwest.

POWERING UP POWER PLANTS

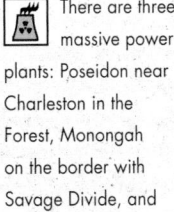 There are three massive power plants: Poseidon near Charleston in the Forest, Monongah on the border with Savage Divide, and Thunder Mountain 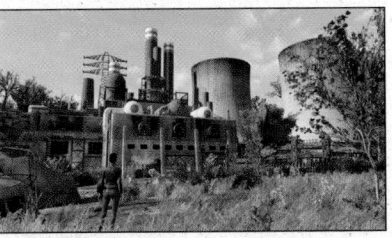 in the Mire. All three of these large plants (with cooling towers) used to provide power to the substations and certain other locations around the map. Complete a quest to restore power, and you can hook up camp or workshop wiring to these power boxes and siphon power without the need for a generator (which can be vandalized). Free power is most helpful. Oh, and don't leave a power plant without switching the Fusion Core collectors; these pump out Fusion Cores on the hour, allowing you to collect them like any other resource.

LOOKOUT TOWERS: SURVEY AREAS

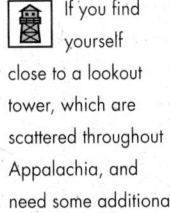 If you find yourself close to a lookout tower, which are scattered throughout Appalachia, and need some additional knowledge of the local 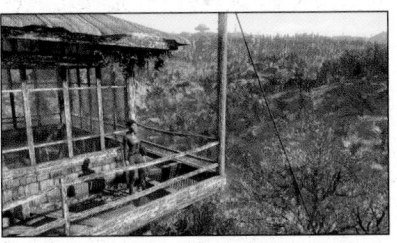 landmarks, climb to the top and onto the lookout's balcony. A "Survey Area" prompt appears, allowing you to immediately spot a few additional primary locations (unless you've already been to them). Now descend, and check them out.

OTHER LOCATION TYPES: VAULTS

 Rumors abound that Vault 76 wasn't the only Vault-Tec-approved subterranean habitat in the Appalachian wilderness! In fact, there are three other 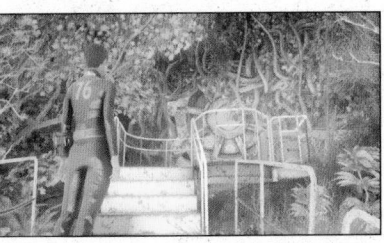 Vaults to discover and a special demonstration vault beneath Vault-Tec University in Morgantown. All but one of these Vaults has a special "cog" map icon instead of the normal, light gray map icon. But where is the last Vault? And why can't you enter yet?

OTHER LOCATION TYPES: WORKSHOPS

 There is a chapter devoted to workshops, which are essentially large, stationary camps you can build with components already stocked at the 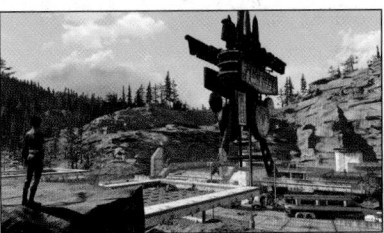 workshop. You gain XP by fending off waves of foes or stop other humans from contesting the workshop, but mainly you just exploit the natural resource hubs these locations provide for you. There are 22 to find.

OTHER LOCATION TYPES: FISSURES

 Should this icon appear on your map, exercise extreme caution! This is a Scorchbeast lair and features this particularly deadly enemy, along with a 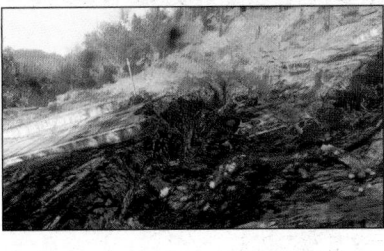 whole horde of Scorched. Unless you're tooled up, and with a competent set of teammates, give these locations a wide berth; even the fissure the Scorchbeast rises from can kill you!

YOU WILL EXPLODE: DANGERS IN THE ENVIRONMENT*

Lose your footing, wade into a toxic pond, get burned alive in a mine... the ways to depart Appalachia are numerous!

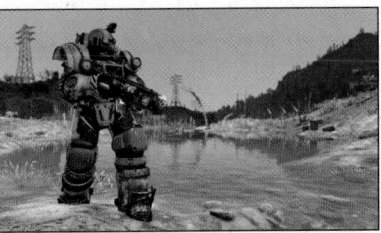

Aside from enemies to worry about, there's other, more environmental areas that are even more than inhospitable; they can be downright deadly! Here are some dangers to be concerned about:

TRAINING

CRAFTING AND C.A.M.P.ING

INVENTORY

QUESTS

ATLAS

BESTIARY

APPENDICES

- **CAN AND BONE CHIMES:** BRUSH AGAINST THESE, AND ENEMIES (OR OTHER PLAYERS) CAN HEAR YOU COMING.
- **EXPLOSIVE CANISTERS:** SHOOT THESE BARRELS AND LONGER CANISTERS, USUALLY COLORED RED, AND EXPECT AN AREA-OF-EFFECT EXPLOSION.
- **FLAMETHROWER TRAPS:** TRIGGER THESE AND RECEIVE HEAT DAMAGE.
- **GRENADE TRAPS:** TRIGGER THESE, AND A "BOUQUET" FALLS TO THE GROUND AND EXPLODES. TRY TO DISARM THESE BEFORE THIS HAPPENS.
- **HEAT:** WEAR SPECIAL PROTECTIVE GEAR (FIREFIGHTER OUTFITS, POWER ARMOR, OR HAZMAT SUITS) WHEN EXPLORING THE EXTREME HEAT OF SOME UNDERGROUND MINES IN THE ASH HEAP.
- **RADTOAD EGG MINES:** WATCH THE SPAWN OF THE RAD-TOAD; THEY EXPLODE WITH THE SAME FEROCITY AS A MINE.
- **TRAPS:** PUNJI BOARDS, SPIKE BOARDS, TENSION TRIGGERS, TRIPWIRES, TESLA ARCS, RADIATION EMITTERS...YOU NAME IT, A LOCATION, CAMP, OR WORKSHOP MAY HAVE ONE OF THESE TRAPS TO EITHER STEP OVER OR DISARM.

- **LONG DROPS:** FALL TOO FAR, AND WITHOUT CERTAIN MUTATIONS OR POWER ARMOR, AND EXPECT TO CRIPPLE YOUR LEGS. FALL EVEN FARTHER AND YOU DIE. SO EXERCISE EXTREME CAUTION ON CLIFFTOPS AND OTHER VERTIGO-INDUCING LOCATIONS.
- **MINES:** PLACED MINES, EASY TO SEE IN V.A.T.S., MAY EXPLODE WITH AREA-OF-EFFECT DAMAGE AT YOUR FEET IF YOU DON'T SHOOT OR DISARM THEM.
- **OIL:** LIGHT THIS ON FIRE AND IT BURNS QUICKLY, IGNITING ANY NEARBY EXPLOSIVE ITEMS LIKE BARRELS.
- **RADIATION:** VERY COMMON, VARYING IN STRENGTH FROM WEAK (DIRTY WATER) TO DEADLY (RADIOACTIVE PONDS). REDUCE RADIATION WITH RAD-X AND RADAWAY, OR USE PERKS THAT BENEFIT YOU WHEN YOU'RE IRRADIATED.
- **TURRETS:** VARIED, PLACED ON THE GROUND OR ROOFTOPS OF CAMPS AND WORKSHOPS, OR SET INTO CEILINGS AND WALLS. SHOOT THEM, AVOID THEM, OR TURN THEM OFF AT A TERMINAL.

* Most interactions and dangers are flagged for interest throughout this guide's Atlas. OTHER DANGERS: Expect health loss when breathing smoke plumes in Ash Heap, the toxic vents in Toxic Valley, and Sundew Spores in Cranberry Bog.

YOU WILL EXPLODE: NUKED!

There may come a time when you're caught off guard by an impromptu nuclear strike. First, check where you are: Are you in the blast radius of the nuke (shown as a giant red circle on your world map)? If so, then panic, unless you're clad in Power Armor. If not, remain outside the blast radius, as the ensuing Rad storms and utterly inhospitable terrain are anathema to your survival! But there is reason to be hopeful:

- **NUCLEAR STRIKES ARE NOTORIOUSLY DIFFICULT TO LAUNCH:** THEY REQUIRE AN EXTREMELY DIFFICULT AND CONVOLUTED METHOD OF LAUNCHING, AND DO NOT OCCUR OFTEN. THIS GUIDE'S QUEST CHAPTER HAS THE MISSION WHERE A STRIKE BECOMES AVAILABLE. PERUSE IT AT YOUR PERIL!
- **NOT EVERYWHERE IS UNSAFE:** YOU WILL RECEIVE A COUNTDOWN AND WARNING IF A NUCLEAR STRIKE IS IMMINENT. THIS ALLOWS YOU TO FLEE TO YOUR CAMP IF IT IS OUTSIDE THE BLAST ZONE OR TO VAULT 76 (WHICH CANNOT BE TARGETED BY A STRIKE, ALONG WITH SOME PARTS OF THE FOREST). THIS ENABLES YOU TO ESCAPE THE ATTACK.
- **STRIKES ARE EPHEMERAL:** THE EXPLOSIVE FORCE OF THE ATTACK IS IMPRESSIVE, BUT THE LANDSCAPE REVERTS BACK TO ITS PREVIOUS STATE AFTER A FEW HOURS. SO WHY LAUNCH AN ATTACK AT ALL? BECAUSE:

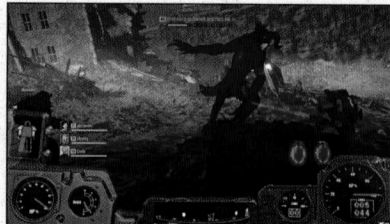

Well, that's going to leave a mark hotter than the devil.

- **BLAST ZONES HAVE LOOT:** EXPECT THE BLAST ZONE TO FEATURE HIGHLY IRRADIATED, GLOWING, AND SPECIFIC TYPES OF MUTATED AND VERY HIGH-LEVEL ENEMIES. WHILE THESE FOES MAY BE HARD TO KILL IF YOU'RE NOT PREPARED, THE ITEMS YOU CAN LOOT FROM THEIR CORPSES ARE AMONG THE BEST YOU'LL EVER FIND!
- **BLAST ZONES HAVE FLORA:** THE FLORA WITHIN THE BLAST ZONE IS REPLACED WITH STRANGE PLANTS KNOWN AS "FLUX," WHICH COMES IN A VARIETY OF COLORS. GATHER THEM ALL AND USE THEM TO CRAFT SOME OF THE MOST HELPFUL AND HIGH-LEVEL ITEMS, SUCH AS FUSION CORES, IF YOU HAVE THE APPROPRIATE PLANS.

ALMOST HEAVEN: DEATH IN APPALACHIA

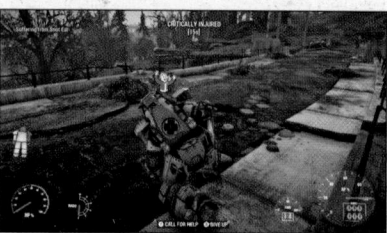

After taking one too many shots to the cranium, this Vault Dweller croaked.

 It's a fact of life in these parts: Death occurs whenever your Health drops to zero.

Plans for Revival: You drop to the ground and a timer begins. If another player revives you before the timer runs out, you will stand back up. Otherwise, you will need to respawn when the timer runs out or if you press the Give Up button.

When you respawn, you need to pick a location on the map. Locations far away from you will cost Caps to respawn there, but you will always be able to respawn at your C.A.M.P. or Vault 76 for free.

Corpses and Dropped Loot: After you respawn, you'll have left behind a corpse. This appears on your map and the compass as a skull and crossbones icon. Your corpse contains any crafting materials you had on you when you died. These are typically objects found in the Items > Junk section of the Pip-Boy. Other players can loot your dropped objects. They will also go away if you die again or disconnect from the game, so get back to your corpse with haste! Or drop your junk in a Stash Box more frequently, so you're not frantically attempting to gather junk you just spent hours foraging for.

Helpful Hint from Vault Boy!

NUKED: LET YOUR TURRETS DO THE TALKING

Is your camp in a possible blast zone? Then ensure it is bristling with turrets and leave the area, only to return once the bomb has dropped (wearing protective gear, naturally). If your camp was close to where enemies appear, your turrets should have destroyed the irradiated monstrosities on your behalf. Now claim all the loot, with none of the ammo and health expenditure!

Training

LET'S WORK WITH OTHERS!

THE ART OF COOPERATION

Work Through No Vault of Your Own

COOPERATION IS THE KEY TO SUCCESS!

THERE'S NO "I" IN NUCLEAR WASTELAND!

TURN MOMENTS INTO MEMORIES!

CATALOG YOUR REBUILDING OF AMERICA!

YOU'RE NOT ALONE: MAKING FIRST CONTACT

During your exit of Vault 76, and in the subsequent stumble down the hill to the south, you may get the feeling you're not alone. This is due to the other members of Vault 76, who are also attempting to rebuild and reclaim America now that Reclamation Day has passed. This chapter gives a brief overview and pointers on how to improve relationships with your fellow Dwellers.

THE SOCIAL MENU

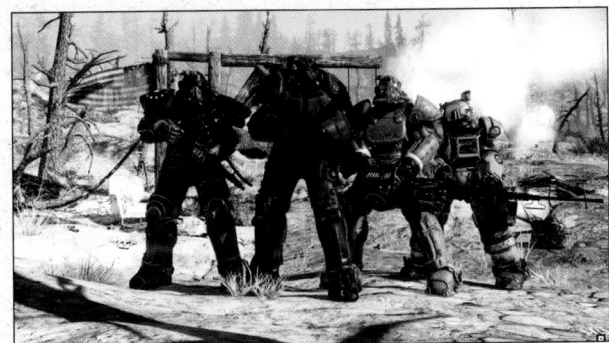

Though you can still wander alone, why not band together with a few other like-minded power armor enthusasts?

The Social menu, accessed as part of your Map menu, allows you to view the Vault Dwellers currently active across Appalachia. The large, gray-box menu allows you to search and add friends, check in with your team (if you allied with anyone), and see who is currently active. With any other player, you can highlight their name or their yellow dot on the map, and learn some basic information about them, such as their icon, name, and level. Highlight a player, and you can:

- **JOIN:** FAST-TRAVEL TO A PREVIOUS FRIEND AND START EXPLORING WITH THEM.
- **INVITE TO TEAM:** ASK A VAULT DWELLER INTO YOUR TEAM, WITH THE INVITEE BEING THE TEAM LEADER.
- **IGNORE:** STOP BEING BOTHERED BY VAULT DWELLERS YOU AREN'T INTERESTED IN.
- **BLOCK:** COMPLETELY IGNORE VAULT DWELLERS WHO MAY BE HASSLING YOU.
- **REMOVE FRIEND:** DELETE A PREVIOUS FRIEND IF YOUR COMPANIONSHIP GOES SOUR.

If you are using a Stealth Boy, if you're crouching, or if you have blocked another player, your yellow circle map icon may not appear.

INITIAL CONTACT

EMOTES AND CHATTER

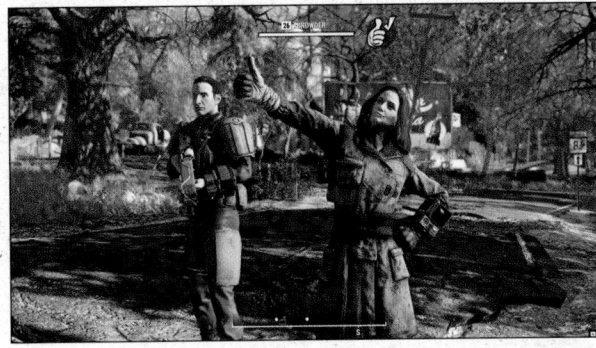

Meet and greet a new or old friend, and use the Emote to pinpoint yourself, too.

Greet your new friend, and folks you might pass in the woods or along the ruined roadways, with a friendly wave. Initial impressions matter, and one of the key ways to begin a conversation is via the use of Emotes. Emotes allow you to communicate with other players. Open the Emotes menu and select an Emote and trigger it. Your character completes the Emote and that same icon appears above your head and next to your Health bar on the other player's screen if you're already a friend. Players who can't see you directly can still see the icon from the Emote, letting other players find you more easily.

SHARING IS CARING

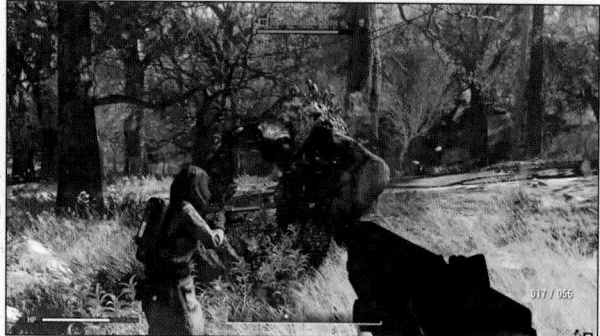

Heading off to face dangers, including quests that require multiple players, is now possible. Have you tried hunting down some particularly deadly cryptids lately?

After agreeing to become a friend with someone, some sharing is immediately enabled: Objectives and quest targets with a star icon next to them (or the word *Sharing*) are being shared by your team leader. You are helping them complete this objective and will receive bonus rewards when they do. In addition, items with a double-diamond icon next to them are quest items for one of your teammates. Your teammate must pick up this item themselves, so let them know where it is!

Teammates helping you on a quest can fight enemies and locate quest items, but they cannot pick up your quest items or activate terminal entries meant for your quest. Also, your own icon and Health bar is shown at the bottom-left corner of your friend's screen, and vice versa.

TRADING IS RECOMMENDED

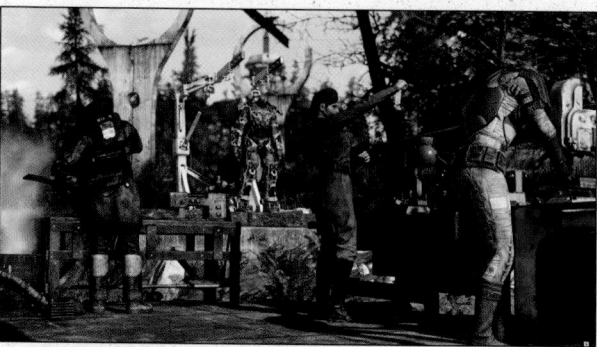

If you spot a fellow Vault Dweller with a fancy outfit, or a friendly wave, try trading with them. Later on, team up and start cranking out high quality goods at team workbenches.

Trading between players allows you to buy and sell items from each other for Caps. Walk up to another player and invite them to trade. The other player will need to look at you and also agree, so you're both in the Trade menu.

From the Trade menu, you can select items to sell and buy. The list on the left contains your inventory, and the list on the right contains any items that the other player has for sale.

When you select an item to sell, you can set the max number of that item the other player can buy.

You will then be asked to set an item price. For example, if you set the item price to 10 Caps, and the other player buys two items, they pay a total of 20 Caps.

MAKING THE DREAM WORK: TEAMS

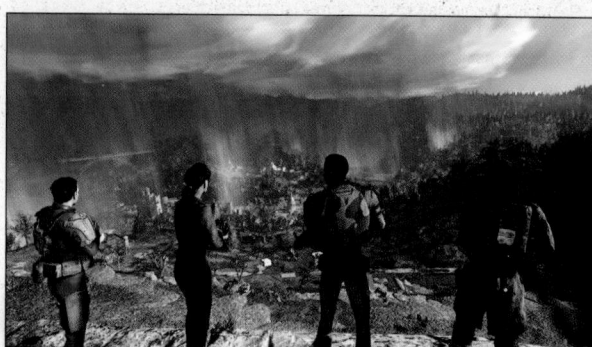

Share resources (and selfies), complete quests, and build camps and workshops together. Make a difference!

Teams are groups of players made up of one team leader and up to three teammates.

You can invite another player to join your team by walking up to them and interacting with them. You can also invite players on your Friends list by using the Social menu or by selecting them on the map. The player you invite will need to open the Social menu and select you in order to accept your request.

TEAM LEADER

The player who initially invites other players to join their team becomes the team leader. The team leader can kick players off the team or promote another player to be team leader instead. The team leader will also automatically share Group Quests. He or she has a star inside the player dot to indicate this status.

GROUP QUESTS

A team leader automatically shares some of their quests with other teammates. They will appear on the team leader's HUD with a "Sharing" tag before the name of the quest. Teammates will see the quest with a "Shared By" tag, including the name of the player sharing the quest. Teammates help the team leader complete quest objectives and will receive bonus rewards as objectives and quests get completed. You will also receive bonus rewards as your other teammates complete objectives in their own quests, although these aren't shown in the HUD in the same way as the team leader's quests.

PERK SHARING

You can select a perk that will be shared with all members of your team. Enter the Perk menu, select an equipped perk that you are currently using, and share it. Now all members of your team share in this bonus! You can share perks that add up to the point value of (or lower than) your Charisma. This is in addition to any personal Charisma perks that are primarily designed to benefit your team (and sometimes everyone in the team except you), though these can be shared too!

FAST-TRAVELING

Finally, you can Fast-Travel to your team leader or teammates for free by selecting them or their camps on the map. This provides key advantages, as it allows far more flexibility regarding where you can travel to and lessens your Caps expenditure for doing so.

THE GOOD NEIGHBOR: PLAYER VS ENEMY (PVE)

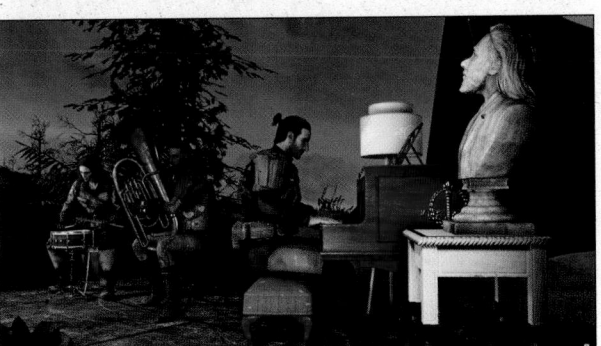

Once you've established an impressive Workshop, pooling the resources and talents of Teammates working together, why not start a band?

What can you do in a team that you can't on your own? A great deal. Aside from helping each other with quest revelations and completions, you can share resources and really start to specialize so that one member of your team is responsible for certain aspects of your team's overall well-being. You can:

- DIVIDE PLAYER ROLES INTO SPECIALIZATIONS BASED ON THE PLAYER ARCHETYPES (AND THEIR ATTRIBUTES AND AVAILABLE PERKS). HAVE A FORAGER, SCAVENGER, CAMP BUILDER, COOK, MEDIC, AMMUNITION-MAKER, WEAPONSMITH, ARMORSMITH, AND A VARIETY OF OTHER ROLES. NEED SOME DOWNTIME? PLAY INSTRUMENTS, HIKE TO VISTAS, MOVE CAMPS, BECOME INFECTED WITH MUTATIONS...ALL TOGETHER!
- BOLSTER YOUR CAMP DEFENSES BY BUILDING CAMPS ADJACENT TO ONE ANOTHER OR ACROSS APPALACHIA SO YOU CAN FAST-TRAVEL FAR DISTANCES FOR FREE.
- AGREE TO ENTER A LARGE-SCALE LOCATION, NEUTRALIZE ANY FOES, GATHER ALL IMPORTANT LOOT, AND THEN TRADE/SHARE IT AFTERWARD.
- AGREE TO CLAIM A WORKSHOP, DURING WHICH TIME ALL FOUR OF YOU CAN BUILD DEFENSIVE STRUCTURES (WITH THE TEAM LEADER BEING ABLE TO ADJUST ANY STRUCTURES DEEMED LESS THAN ADEQUATE). THEN THESE CAN BE DEFENDED MORE EASILY FROM ENTITIES AND OTHER HUMANS.
- YOU CAN TEAM UP WITH ANOTHER TEAM AND SET ABOUT LARGER-SCALE EXPLORATIONS, REMOVING SCORCHBEASTS AND HORDES OF FOES AND EVEN FIGURING OUT HOW TO LAUNCH A NUKE!
- OR, IF YOU'RE IGNORING ALL YOUR PREVIOUS VAULT-TEC ADVICE, YOU CAN TURN INTO A BUNCH OF BANDITS AND CAUSE HAVOC. THE MORE OF YOU THERE ARE, THE LARGER THE ANARCHY YOU CAN CAUSE!

QUICKPLAY PVE MATCHES

Expect to be invited to frantic and entertaining sessions, where you are matched with other players, ready to face the challenges of Appalachia as a team. These are events you and your team are tasked with completing. Work together! Are you already grouped up with your friends? Then the event will match you all together. Perhaps you and your team are entering the Irrational Fear event. This involves helping a struggling Mr. Handy unit retrieve honey. What could go wrong? Look for such events to pop up intermittently.

WORD OF WARNING FROM VAULT BOY!

THE APPALACHIAN ANARCHISTS

REMEMBER: ALL OF THE ADVANTAGES OF BEING ON A TEAM CAN BE NEGATED IF YOU TURN YOURSELF AND YOUR FELLOW PLAYERS INTO ANARCHISTS WHO SPEND THEIR TIME HUNTING HUMAN PREY!

WORD OF WARNING FROM VAULT BOY!

THE ACCIDENTAL ANARCHIST

REMEMBER TO TAKE CARE WITH FIREARMS AND MELEE WEAPONS, AND NOTE THAT DAMAGING PROPERTY THAT DOESN'T BELONG TO YOU (E.G., ANOTHER PLAYER'S/TEAM'S CAMP OR WORKSHOP YOU HAVEN'T CORRECTLY CONTESTED AND CLAIMED FOR YOURSELF) RESULTS IN YOU BEING VIEWED AS HOSTILE — AND POSSIBLY WANTED BY OTHERS.

THE BAD NEIGHBOR: PLAYER VS PLAYER (PVP)

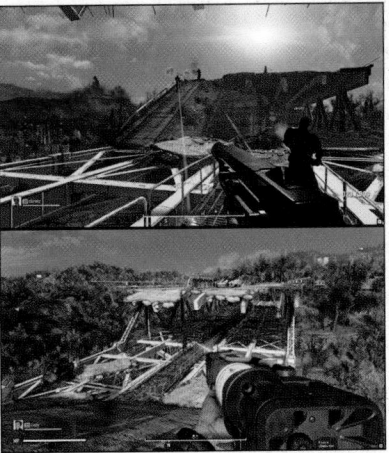

A simple misunderstanding can escalate into blind, ugly violence; in this case on both sides of the New Gorge Bridge.

In the very rare case that a Vault-Tec-raised human ignores all previous teachings, attempts to go rogue, and becomes a common criminal working to undermine America's rebuilding, you and your fellow Vault Dwellers should galvanize yourselves into action and stop this atrocity! This practice is known as "player versus player" and occurs when two or more players exhibit aggressive tendencies toward one another. This won't happen at all before you reach Level 5; you are immune to other player attacks until then.

If a previously neutral or even friendly player attacks you (or you attack them), there is no stern talking-to by the Overseer. Instead, the attacker starts to inflict a very small amount of damage on the other player. If the defending player reciprocates, and both players strike each other (with ranged or melee attacks), then hostilities commence, and the damage dealt rises to normal levels.

However, if the aggressor presses the attack and kills the innocent player, the hostile player becomes Wanted, and a bounty is awarded. The dead player must seek revenge for this to occur, and they also drop their junk, just as if they were killed by an Appalachian entity.

If you're on a team, however, every member of the team counts for the purposes of determining if you hit another player and if they hit you back. So if you shoot another player and that player shoots any member of your team back, then that player is now hostile to your entire team. This means teams can become hostile to other teams if any members trade hits.

Hostile players now show up on your map and compass as red dots.

Wanted players now show up on your map and compass as red dots with a star inside.

TRAINING

CRAFTING AND C.A.M.P.ING

INVENTORY

QUESTS

ATLAS

BESTIARY

APPENDICES

WANTED LEVELS AND BOUNTY HUNTING

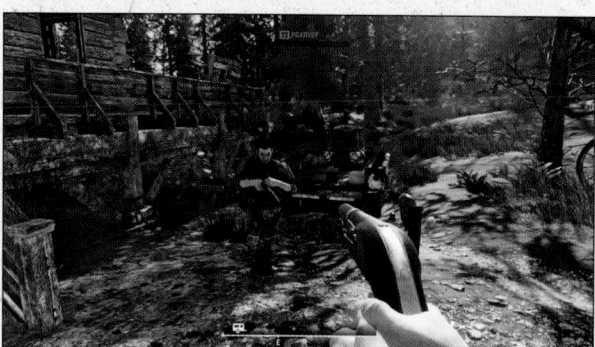

Claim a bounty from a criminal player, using their own Caps as reward!

Killing a player who hasn't hit you back can make you Wanted. If you are Wanted, you are considered hostile to *all other players*, and they can strike you for full damage (as you can to them). You may be able to survive for a while, and the Caps reward (seen on your screen) increases each time you kill another human. The reward is also usually greater if the Wanted foe is a higher level than the hunter who tracks and slays them.

So, wrangle up a posse, track down that varmint, and make them pay—literally, with their own Caps and junk bag you can loot after killing them!

DO IT YOURSELFIE: PHOTO MODE

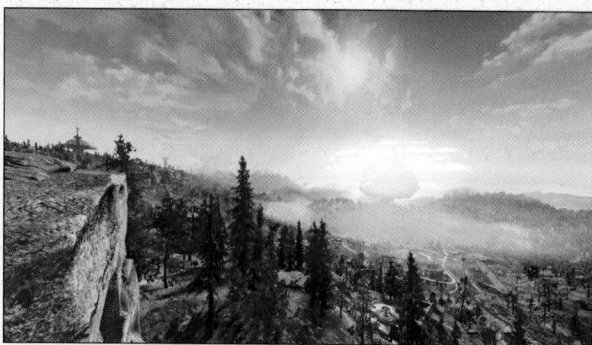

Record your progress from your first steps outside Vault 76 to the time you nuked Morgantown!

Photomode lets you take snapshots of your adventures! You can use Photomode at any time by going to the Main menu (Map). Here, you have several options to tailor the photograph to your liking. Start by finding a place you want to take a photograph, stand so the area of interest is behind you, and bring up your Photo Mode settings:

CAMERA MENU

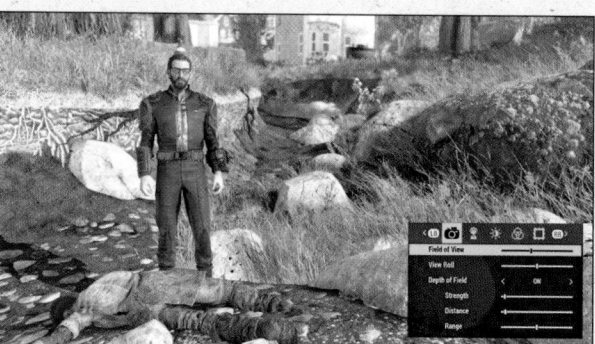

This menu allows you to play with your camera settings, such as Depth of Field (shown).

Field of View: This zooms in and out, creating a tighter or wider shot.

View Roll: This rotates the camera for a rakish angle.

Depth of Field: This blurs the image, usually the background so foreground objects stand out more easily. The Strength is how blurry the background is, and the Distance and Range are how far away the blur is from the foreground and how much of the image is blurred, which can include blurring everything including the foreground!

PLAYER MENU

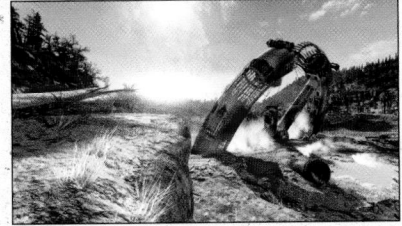

You don't need Vault Dwellers cluttering up your picture when Appalachia is calling!

Show Player: This removes you from the picture if you want a landscape-only image.

Expression: This changes your expression. Show some emotion!

Pose: This changes your pose, from a variety of categories, to add some whimsy (or brutality) to your stance.

IMAGE MANIPULATION (LIGHT LEVELS AND EFFECTS)

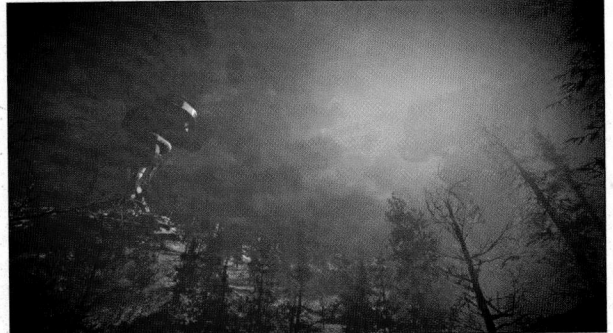

Turn a location visit into an old-timey classic with the correct clothing and camera effects. Or, just wait for a rad storm!

Brightness, Saturation, and Contrast: Fiddle with the light levels and more.

Filter and Texture: This adds a wide variety of colorizing options to your image, as well as scuffs and general texture "noise."

FRAMES

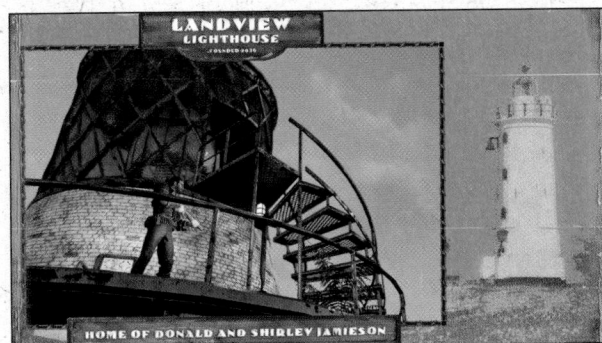

Wish you were here! Claim specific location frames when you visit certain locations.

Frame and Category: This enables you to add a frame around your image in a large variety of styles. Zoom the initial image out a bit so none of your photograph is cut off when you choose the frame. Note that various locations across Appalachia have their own frame, turning your photographs into postcards. You usually receive these when you visit them (they are typically landmarks or settlements). Have you unlocked them all?

GETTING ARTY

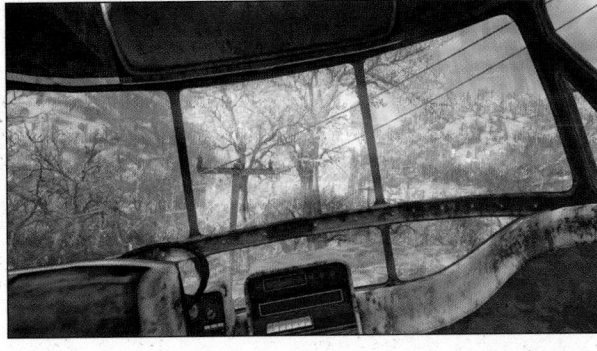

Turn a nondescript junk pile on a patch of ground into a well-lit masterpiece with some professional advice. Here are some tips:

- MANEUVER YOUR CAMERA INTO A VARIETY OF DIFFERENT ANGLES, LOOKING DOWN FROM ABOVE OR FROM THE GROUND UP.
- KEEP YOUR HUMAN SUBJECTS FACING THE SUN, SO THEIR FACES AREN'T SHADED.
- CHOOSE A NATURAL "FRAME" LIKE THE FLAPS OF A TENT OR THE WALL OF AN OLD BARN.
- KEEP A LOOKOUT FOR WEATHER CONDITIONS AND EFFECTS, AS WELL AS TIME OF DAY, AND TAKE PICTURES AT DIFFERENT TIMES FOR DIFFERENT EFFECTS.
- PLAY WITH YOUR DEPTH OF FIELD TO ACCENTUATE THE FOREGROUND AND MINIMIZE BACKGROUND; THIS WORKS PARTICULARLY WELL WHEN SHOWING SOMETHING ON TOP OF A ROOF OR CLIFF.
- APPALACHIA IS DOTTED WITH STRANGE LANDMARKS. TAKE PICTURES OF THEM ALL, FROM ODD ANGLES AND USING DIFFERENT FILTERS.
- THE LANDMARKS DON'T HAVE TO BE BIG; AN OLD ROW BOAT WITH A SKELETON IN IT CAN MAKE FOR AN EERIE PHOTOGRAPH, AS CAN PHOTOGRAPHS FROM INSIDE RUSTING VEHICLES, LOOKING OUT.
- GAIN HEIGHT AND TAKE RISKS TO INCREASE THE QUALITY AND SPECTACULAR NATURE OF YOUR IMAGES.
- LOOK FOR A VIGNETTE THAT ALREADY EXISTS OR DOCUMENT YOUR OWN (BY BUILDING A CAMP ON A VISTA).
- SIGNPOSTS, BRIDGES, RIVERS, CURVED ROADS, AND INTERESTING OBJECTS IN THE FOREGROUND TO THE BACKGROUND ALL HELP MAKE A GREAT PICTURE.
- BRING IN OTHER PLAYERS AND CHART THEIR PROGRESS, SHOW THEM WORKING, FORAGING, AND FIGHTING. HAVE YOU THOUGHT ABOUT A CAREER AS A DOCUMENTARIAN?
- GIVE YOUR EYE SOMETHING TO LOOK AT THROUGHOUT A PICTURE. THE USE OF DIAGONAL LINES TO "POINT" IN THE DIRECTION OF BACKGROUND OBJECTS HELPS MAKE A COHESIVE PICTURE.
- MAKE YOUR FILTER EFFECTS SUBTLE RATHER THAN OVERWHELMING.
- USE LIGHTNING STORMS (ESPECIALLY IN THE MIRE) TO GREAT EFFECT; IF YOU CAN TIME YOUR SHOT TO CAPTURE A FLASH OF LIGHTNING, THE PICTURE CAN LOOK SPECTACULAR!
- YOUR OWN LIFE IS SECONDARY TO A GOOD PICTURE. AS YOU CAN TAKE PHOTOGRAPHS RIGHT UP TO THE POINT OF YOUR DEATH, YOU CAN ACHIEVE GRUESOMELY EPIC PICTURES AS A FOE BEARS DOWN ON YOU!

THE PHOTO GALLERY

Your photos are stored in the Photo Gallery. Access this from the Main menu, and previously taken photos appear on the loading screen. If you don't like the way you looked when you took your profile photo inside Vault 76 and want to change it, go to the Photo Gallery. Find the photo you want to use, and select it.

TRAINING

CRAFTING AND C.A.M.P.ING

INVENTORY

QUESTS

ATLAS

BESTIARY

APPENDICES

STATUS:
BEING A BETTER YOU!

SPECIAL ATTRIBUTES AND PERKS

WHAT MAKES YOU SPECIAL?

Your Strength, Perception, Endurance, Charisma, Intelligence, Agility, and Luck, of course! These primary statistics, also known as attributes, are the bedrock from which you're chiseled. They range in value from 1 (woefully inadequate) to 15 (godlike). Each affects a different aspect of you and allows you to use a specific number of Perk Cards. This chapter provides advice on leveling up, and covers the other active effects that can affect your attributes. We also give a comprehensive tactical analysis of every one of the 211 perks you can acquire.

ATTRIBUTES OVERVIEW

Strength: Measures your raw physical power. It affects how much you can carry and determines the damage of all melee attacks.

Perception: Your sense of environmental awareness. It affects your hit chance in V.A.T.S. and the distance that hostiles will show up on your compass.

Endurance: Measures your overall physical fitness. It affects your total Health, Action Point (AP) drain from sprinting, and chance to get a disease.

Charisma: Your ability to work with others. It affects which perks you can share with your team, the rewards from completing group quests, and the prices you get when buying from and selling to vendors.

Intelligence: Measures your overall mental acuity. It affects the condition and durability of crafted items, the amount of material gained from scrapping, and the difficulty of hacking.

Agility: Measures your overall finesse and reflexes. It determines your AP in V.A.T.S. and your ability to sneak.

Luck: Measures your general good fortune. It affects the recharge rate of Critical Hits and the condition and durability of items you loot.

EXPERIENCE, LEVELING UP, AND PERKS

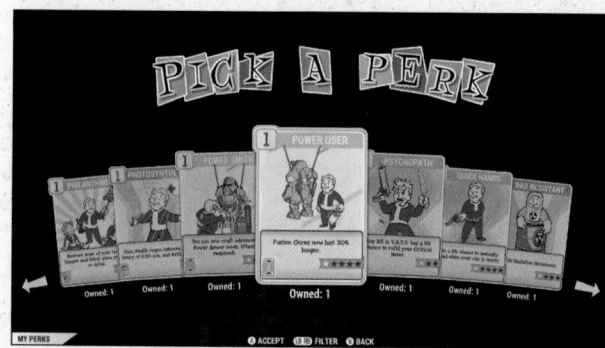

Just leveled up? Opened a new Perk Pack? Want to swap out some Perk Cards? Then Pick a Perk!

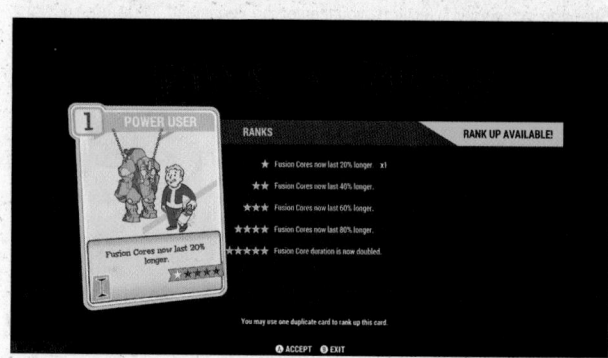

Don't forget: you can inspect every Perk Card you own to see how the perk improves at higher ranks (if applicable).

Leveling up allows you to increase one of your SPECIAL stats, gives you a choice of a new perk (from the Card Packs you've opened), and helps you meet the level requirements for certain equipment.

As you complete quests, defeat enemies, and explore the world, you'll earn Experience Points (XP). Once you've gained sufficient XP, your level will increase.

Open your Pip-Boy and access the Level Up menu. Choose one of your SPECIAL stats to increase. Also choose a new perk associated with the SPECIAL stat you chose.

(Note: You will stop receiving SPECIAL increases once your level is higher than 50, but you will keep receiving new perks).

After selecting a SPECIAL stat to level up, you don't have to choose a perk card related specifically to that attribute: Instead, you can swap to a different Attribute to choose your perk.

PERK UP!

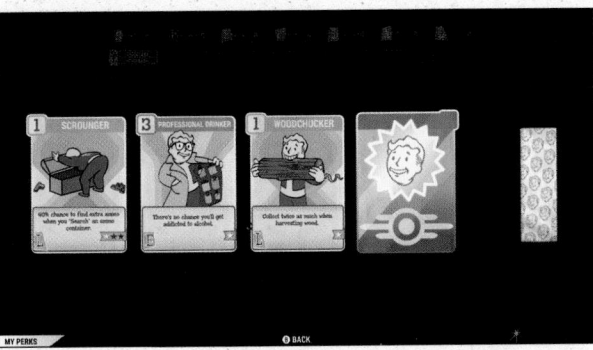

After unwrapping a Perk Pack, you may find a gold card (fancy, but offers no other benefits), and a stick of gum (which fends off hunger and thirst for a little bit).

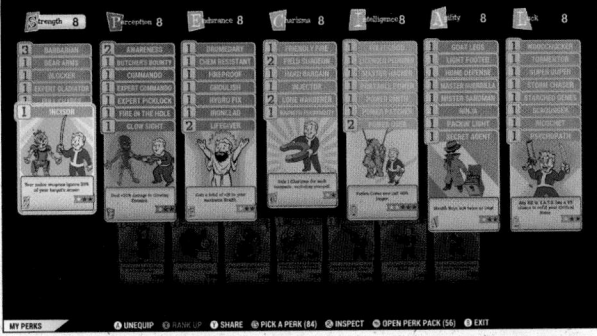

By the time you max out your Attribute Points, you'll have placed numerous cards in every Attribute slot.

After you make your selections, you'll enter the Perk menu. Perks are special abilities that can affect everything form the damage you deal in combat, to your ability to help your teammates, to being able to open locks and hack terminals. You can reassign all your perks from the Perk Menu. The bottom row of cards are your available perks, and the top row of cards are all the perks you have equipped.

When you equip a perk, it is assigned to its associated SPECIAL stat. For example, the Gladiator perk is a Strength perk, and goes into your Strength slot when you equip it.

There is a limit to the number of perks that each SPECIAL stat can hold. Every perk has a number in the upper-left corner. This is how many points the perk is worth. Your total number of perk points can't exceed the associated SPECIAL stat. For example, if your Strength is 3, then you cannot have more than 3 points' worth of Strength perks. Whether you choose to equip several low-point perks or one high-point perk is up to you.

Also make sure you add Perk Cards to every attribute, not just the ones you're interested in. Every one of your attributes should have one or more Perk Cards active, or you're wasting the power of your perks!

LEVEL REQUIREMENTS FOR ITEMS

Some weapons, armor, and Power Armor pieces have a minimum level requirement to use them. You can't equip an item if you aren't the appropriate level or higher. You can see the minimum level of an item by going to the Items category in the Pip-Boy and selecting the item.

PERK RANKS

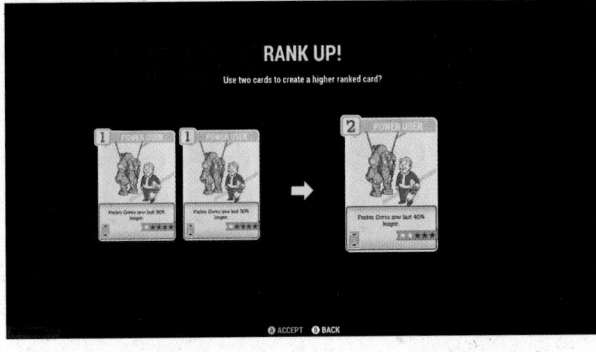

Some perks have multiple ranks. You can rank up a perk by combining it with a duplicate. For example, two Gladiator rank 1 perks can be combined to produce one Gladiator rank 2 perk.

To rank up a perk, first equip the perk and then consume the duplicate perk.

SHARING PERKS

You can elect a perk to share with all members of your team. Enter the Perk Menu, select an equipped perk, and share it. In order to share perks, your Charisma must be greater than or equal to three times the point value of the point card you are trying to share. (for example, 3 CHA for a 1-point card, or 9 CHA for a 3-point card).

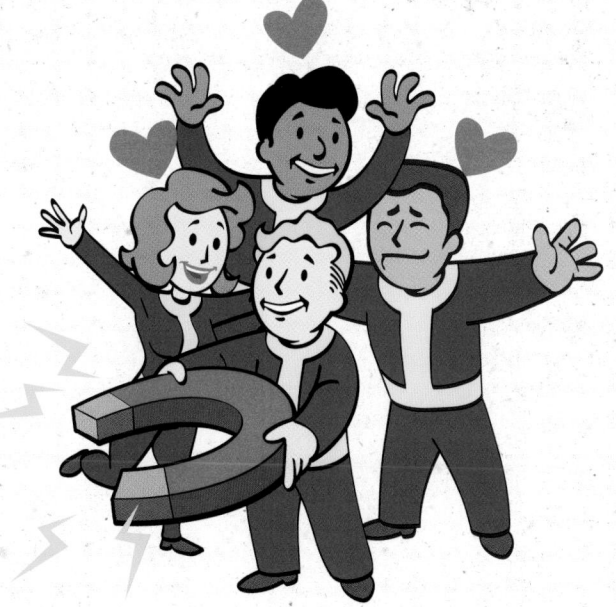

TRAINING

CRAFTING AND C.A.M.P.ING

INVENTORY

QUESTS

ATLAS

BESTIARY

APPENDICES

BUILDING CHARACTER: PERK AVAILABILITY BY LEVEL

As you continue to level up, more potent and additionally interesting perks become available to add to each of your attributes. Remember, Perk Card packs are random, with a selection of Common, Uncommon, and (possible) Rare cards in them. While you can always select a perk card when levelling up, you aren't always guaranteed to receive a Perk Card by the indicated level (you could obtain it much sooner or even later!). The following chart lists all the available perks and the player level at which they become available. Check later in this chapter for detailed descriptions of every Perk card!

PERK CARDS AVAILABLE (COST PER RANK)

LEVEL	STRENGTH	PERCEPTION	ENDURANCE	CHARISMA	INTELLIGENCE	AGILITY	LUCK
Level 2	Iron Fist (1, 2, 3, 4, 5)	Concentrated Fire (1, 2, 3)	Lead Belly (1, 2, 3)	Inspirational (1, 2, 3)	First Aid (1, 2, 3, 4)	Action Boy/Girl (1, 2, 3)	Pharma Farma (1, 2, 3)
Level 3	Traveling Pharmacy (1, 2, 3)	Butcher's Bounty (1, 2, 3)	Dromedary (1, 2, 3)	Happy Camper (1, 2)	Makeshift Warrior (1, 2, 3)	Thru-Hiker (1, 2, 3) / Born Survivor (1, 2, 3)	Scrounger (1, 2, 3)
Level 4	Bandolier (1, 2, 3)	Green Thumb (1)	Iron Stomach (1, 2, 3)	Lone Wanderer (2, 3, 4)	Hacker (1)	Gun Runner (1)	
Level 5	Gladiator (1, 2, 3)	Picklock (1)	Slow Metabolizer (1, 2, 3)	Bodyguards (1, 2, 3, 4)	Licensed Plumber (1, 2, 3)	Moving Target (1, 2, 3)	Serendipity (1, 2, 3)
Level 6	Pack Rat (1, 2, 3)		Thirst Quencher (1, 2, 3)		Pharmacist (1, 2, 3)	Gunslinger (1, 2, 3)	
Level 7	Slugger (1, 2, 4)	Crack Shot (1, 2, 3, 4)		Hard Bargain (1, 2, 3)			Can Do! (1, 2, 3)
Level 8		Rifleman (1)	Good Doggy (1, 2, 3)		Exotic Weapons (1, 2)	Dead Man Sprinting (1, 2)	
Level 9					E.M.T. (1, 2, 3)	Packin' Light (1, 2, 3)	Good With Salt (1, 2, 3)
Level 10	Shotgunner (1, 2, 3)	Skeet Shooter (1, 2, 3, 4)	Natural Resistance (1, 2, 3)		Demolition Expert (1, 2, 3, 4, 5)	Guerrilla (1, 2, 3)	Junk Shield (1, 2, 3)
Level 11	Basher (1, 2)			Bloodsucker (1, 2, 3)			
Level 12		Pannapictagraphist (1)	Hydro Fix (1, 3), Rejuvenated (1, 2)				Mystery Meat (1, 2, 3)
Level 13	Sturdy Frame (1, 2)			Magnetic Personality (1, 2)	Scrapper (1)	Marathoner (1, 2, 3)	
Level 14	Barbarian (1, 2, 3)	Exterminator (1, 2, 3)	Cola Nut (1, 2)				Luck of the Draw (1, 2, 3)
Level 15		Commando (1, 2, 3)		Field Surgeon (2)	Armorer (1, 2, 3)	Ninja (1, 2, 3)	
Level 16	Martial Artist (1, 2, 3)	Percepti-Bobble (1)	Vaccinated (1, 2, 3)		Exotic Weapons Expert (1, 2)		Cap Collector (1, 2, 3, 4)
Level 17			Munchy Resistance (1, 3)	Happy-Go-Lucky (1, 2)		Evasive (1, 2, 3)	Woodchucker (1)
Level 18	Scattershot (1, 2, 3, 4)	Ground Pounder (1, 2, 3, 4)			Contractor (1, 2)	Modern Renegade (1, 2, 3, 4)	
Level 19		Expert Picklock (1)	Homebody (1, 2)	Injector (1, 2, 3)			Curator (1)
Level 20	Expert Gladiator (1, 2, 3)	Expert Rifleman (1, 2, 3)		Team Medic (1, 2, 4)	Science (1, 2)	Sneak (1, 2, 3, 4, 5)	
Level 21	Blocker (1, 2, 3)		Adamantium Skeleton (1, 2, 3, 4, 5)				Psychopath (1, 2, 3)
Level 22		Fortune Finder (1)	Solar Powered (1, 2, 3)	Quack Surgeon (1)	Expert Hacker (1)	Home Defense (1, 2, 3)	
Level 23	Expert Shotgunner (1, 2, 3)		Chem Fiend (1, 2, 3)		Gunsmith (1, 2, 3)		Dry Nurse (1, 2, 3)
Level 24	Expert Slugger (1, 2, 3)	Night Person (1, 2, 3)		Party Boy/Girl (2, 3)		Expert Gunslinger (1, 2, 3)	Lucky Break (1)
Level 25		Expert Commando (1, 2, 3)	Cannibal (1, 2, 3)		Exotic Weapons Master (1, 2)	Expert Guerilla (1, 2, 3)	
Level 26	Strong Back (1, 2, 3, 4)		Aquaboy (1)	Travel Agent (1)			Mysterious Stranger (1, 2, 3)
Level 27		Awareness (2)	Fireproof (1, 2, 3)		Fix It Good (1, 2, 3)	Covert Operative (1, 2, 3)	Last Laugh (1)
Level 28		Sniper (1, 2, 3)		Healing Hands (1, 2, 3)	Batteries Included (1, 2, 3)		
Level 29			Nocturnal Fortitude (1, 2)		Wrecking Ball (1, 2, 3)	Light Footed (1)	Four Leaf Clover (1, 2, 3, 4)
Level 30	Heavy Gunner (1, 2, 3)	Tank Killer (1, 2, 3, 4)	Ironclad (1, 2, 3, 4, 5)	Animal Friend (1, 2, 3)		Enforcer (1, 2, 3, 4)	Starched Genes (1, 2)
Level 31	Ordnance Express (1, 2, 3)				Science Expert (1, 2)		One Gun Army (1, 2, 3, 4)
Level 32		Refractor (1, 2, 3, 4)	Revenant (1, 2)	Overly Generous (1, 2)		Goat Legs (1, 2)	
Level 33	Full Charge (1, 2)	Glow Sight (1, 2, 3)			Grease Monkey (1, 2)		Grim Reaper's Sprint (1, 2, 3)
Level 34	Incisor (1, 2, 3)		Rad Resistant (1, 2, 3, 4)	Anti-Epidemic (1, 2)	Chemist (1, 2)	Ammosmith (1, 2, 3)	
Level 35	Bear Arms (1, 2, 3, 4)	Grenadier (1, 2)				Escape Artist (1)	Storm Chase (1, 2)
Level 36			Ghoulish (1, 2, 3)	Spiritual Healer (1, 2)	Stabilized (1, 2, 3, 4)		

LEVEL	STRENGTH	PERCEPTION	ENDURANCE	CHARISMA	INTELLIGENCE	AGILITY	LUCK
Level 37	Lock and Load (1, 2, 3)	Long Shot (1, 2, 3, 4)		Squad Maneuvers (1, 2)		Mister Sandman (1, 2)	Tormentor (1, 2, 3, 4)
Level 38		Fire in the Hole (1, 2, 3)	Radicool (1)		Master Hacker (1)		Ricochet (1, 2, 3, 4)
Level 39	Bullet Shield (1, 2, 3, 4)		Professional Drinker (3)	Philanthropist (1, 2, 3)		White Knight (1, 2, 3)	
Level 40	Expert Heavy Gunner (1, 2, 3)	Master Picklock (1)		Suppressor (1, 2, 3)	Weapon Artisan (1, 2, 3)		Quick Hands (1, 2, 3, 4, 5)
Level 41	Pain Train (1, 2, 3)		All Night Long (1, 2, 3)		Power Smith (1, 2, 3)	Master Gunslinger (1, 2, 3)	
Level 42		Master Rifleman (1, 2, 3)		Strange in Numbers (1)			Bloody Mess (1, 2, 3)
Level 43	Master Gladiator (1, 2, 3)		Chem Resistant (1, 2)		Science Master (1, 2)	Master Guerrilla (1, 2, 3)	
Level 44				Rad Sponge (1, 2)	Power Patcher (1, 2, 3)		Critical Savvy (1, 2, 3)
Level 45	Master Shotgunner (1, 2, 3)	Master Commando (1, 2, 3)	Sun Kissed (1, 2)			Dodgy (1, 2, 3)	
Level 46				Tenderizer (1,2,3)	Nerd Rage! (1,2,3)		Class Freak (1,2,3)
Level 47		Night Eyes (2)	Photosynthetic (1,2)			Secret Agent (1,2,3)	Better Criticals (1,2,3)
Level 48	Master Slugger (1,2,3)			Friendly Fire (1, 2, 3)	Robotics Expert (1, 2, 3)		
Level 49					Portable Power (1, 2, 3)	Adrenaline (1, 2, 3, 4, 5)	Mysterious Savior (1, 2, 3)
Level 50	Master Heavy Gunner (1, 2, 3)	Penetrator (1 ,2, 3)	Lifegiver (2, 3, 4)	Wasteland Whisperer (1, 2, 3)	Power User (1, 2, 3, 4, 5)	Gun Fu (1, 2, 3)	Super Duper (1, 2, 3, 4)

TIPS: PERTINENT PERK PLANNING AND THE RIGHT ATTRIBUTE ATTITUDE

Effectively using perks with your attribute bonuses and other bonuses bestowed on you by items, weaponry, and other effects is the key to thriving, not just surviving. Make sure you understand how perks can benefit you.

ATTRIBUTES: NO SUBSTITUTES!

You have a maximum of 50 attribute points to allocate. These are much more important than your Perk Card choices, as allocating attribute points is permanent. With each attribute having a theoretical maximum of 15, you'd need 105 attribute points to max all of them out. With only 50 total, you need to specialize, so figure it out early (look to our Archetypes section for quick advice). If you want a "flat" attribute, gradually bring each attribute up to 7, with one at 8 (which equals 50).

ATTRIBUTES: OVER THE MAXIMUM!

As the Archetypes section demonstrates, the example Level 50 characters actually have attribute points that add up to 56. How so? Because Attribute-increasing perks, chems, armor, weapons, Bobbleheads, and Magazines were all used to achieve this (though you can't equip perks with SPECIAL bonuses provided by magic effects). If you need an extra boost, check your inventory for items that can do the job.

EARLY LEARNING

Look at the levels of every perk and single out the ones you can use early, along with the associated items or weapons with those perks. For example, look to specialize your one-handed melee weapons at Level 5 with the Gladiator perk, rather than heavy guns (as Heavy Gunner perk requires you to be Level 30). The same is true for many other items, like Power Armor.

GROUPING PERKS

One of the benefits of the Perk Card system is that you can swap out your active Perk Cards at any time. Have a group of perks for your different styles of play, and only have them active when they are actively benefiting you. For example, remove (or "shelve") the Luck perk Woodchucker until you're focusing only on collecting wood and want higher yields.

STACKING PERKS

Stacking is usually available in most situations, allowing you to add additional benefits in the following ways:

- **UTILIZING MULTIPLES OF THE SAME PERK:** FOR EXAMPLE, GLADIATOR RANKS 1, 2, AND 3, AND EXPERT GLADIATOR RANKS 1, 2, 3.
- **UTILIZING RELATED BONUSES OF TWO DIFFERENT PERKS:** FOR EXAMPLE, USING THE STRENGTH PERK STRONG BACK, WHICH ADDS TO YOUR CARRY WEIGHT; AND USING THE ENDURANCE PERK RADICOOL, WHICH ADDS STRENGTH ATTRIBUTE POINTS IF YOU'RE IRRADIATED, AND MORE STRENGTH ALSO ADDS TO YOUR CARRY WEIGHT.
- **UTILIZING RELATED BONUSES OF A PERK AND OTHER ITEM:** FOR EXAMPLE, THE ENDURANCE PERK RADICOOL, WHICH ADDS STRENGTH ATTRIBUTES IF YOU'RE IRRADIATED, AND THE STRENGTH BOBBLEHEAD, WHICH ADDS STRENGTH ATTRIBUTE POINTS FOR A LIMITED TIME.

WEAPON SPECIALIZATION PERKS ACROSS ATTRIBUTES

You may be focusing on strength and looking to specialize in melee, shotguns, and (eventually) heavy weapons. But there are similar, damage-increasing Perception perks such as Commando (auto rifles) and Rifleman (nonauto rifles), and the Agility perks Guerrilla (auto pistols) and Gunslinger (nonauto pistols). Why are these important? Because you can specialize in, say, auto rifles, freeing your Strength points up for other, non-weapon-related perks.

SUPER-SPECIALIZATION: A WARNING

It really pays not to super-specialize your SPECIALs; if you choose one attribute and go deep with just that, then spread out your level ups evenly, it allows you to choose Perks late into the game that suit the challenges you're facing. But if you (for example) have three SPECIALs at 15, you'll have very little ability to pick up key Perks you decide you need later, related to the other attributes.

TRAINING

CRAFTING AND C.A.M.P.ING

INVENTORY

QUESTS

ATLAS

BESTIARY

APPENDICES

OTHER ACTIVE EFFECTS

Before we delve into the world of Perk Cards, be sure you're aware of other effects that can penalize or increase your statistics and general well-being. While effects that are item-related (like chems) are listed in the Inventory chapter, the following details environmental and collectible effects:

RESTING AND INSTRUMENTS

Rest on a bed away from the ground (or you risk a disease), and/or play a musical instrument to receive the following:

EFFECT	DESCRIPTION	BONUS OR PENALTY
Well Rested	Sleep in a mattress or bed	+10% to your XP (limited time)
Well Tuned	Play a musical instrument	+25 AP Regeneration (limited time)

DISEASES

Diseases are entirely negative penalties to the player. They only last for a specific amount of time. They can be acquired from diseased creatures or from the environment (airborne, waterborne, from traps, and from beds).

DISEASE	PENALTY
Blight	-1 to all SPECIAL stats for 15 minutes
Blood Worms	Take 25% more damage for 15 minutes
Bone Worms	Take 50% more limb damage for 15 minutes
Buzz Brain	-2 Intelligence for 15 minutes
Dysentery	Periodic water loss for 15 minutes
Fever Claw	-25% Damage with Ranged Weapons for 15 minutes
Flap Limb	-2 Strength for 15 minutes
Glowing Pustules	Bleed radiation from wounds for 15 minutes
Heat Flashes	-2 Endurance for 15 minutes
Jelly Fingers	+50% Ranged VATS AP Cost for 15 minutes
Lock Joint	+50% Melee VATS AP Cost for 15 minutes
Needle Spine	-10 Carry Capacity for 15 minutes
Parasites	Periodic food loss for 15 minutes
Rad Worms	Take 50% more Radiation Damage for 15 minutes
Rattle Hands	-25% Damage with Ranged Weapons for 15 minutes
Shell Shock	Action Point drain from wounds for 15 minutes
Sludge Lung	-50% Action Points and AP regeneration for 15 minutes
Snot Ear	-2 Perception for 15 minutes
Swamp Gas	-2 Charisma for 15 minutes
Swamp Itch	-2 Agility for 15 minutes
Weeping Sores	Bleed from wounds for 15 minutes
The Woopsies	-2 Luck for 15 minutes

MUTATIONS

Mutations are permanent effects (though they can be cured). They bring both positive and negative aspects that alter a player's gameplay. Players will consider these desirable or undesirable depending on their chosen build.

Mutations are not related to diseases. Players obtain mutations by being exposed to Radiation. The higher a player's current Rads, the more likely it is that they will gain a mutation. Mutations can be cured with RadAway, Diluted RadAway or decontamination arches found in the world. The lower a players' Rads, the more likely that a mutation will be cured.

The Starched Genes perk can remove the player's chance to mutate and also prevent mutations from being cured, allowing players to lock in the mutations that they may want, and/or not engage further with mutations at all.

MUTATION	POSITIVE EFFECTS	NEGATIVE EFFECTS
Adrenal Reaction	Increased damage output at low health	-50 Health
Bird Bones	+4 Agility, fall more slowly, and take less damage from falling	-4 Strength
Carnivore	Gain double benefits from eating meat with no risk of disease	Gain no benefits from eating vegetables
Chameleon	Invisible in combat if unarmored and stationary	Must be unarmored and stationary for effect to work
Eagle Eyes	+4 Perception and +25% V.A.T.S. Critical Damage	-4 Strength
Egg Head	+6 Intelligence	-3 Strength, -3 Endurance
Electrically Charged	Chance to shock enemies in a radius when you are struck by melee attacks	Small damage to yourself when this occurs
Empath	Your teammates receive 25% less damage	You receive 33% more damage
Grounded	+100 Energy Resistance	-50% Energy Weapon damage
Healing Factor	Permanent health regeneration	Chem effects (including healing) reduced by 55%
Herbivore	Gain double benefits from eating vegetables with no risk of disease	Gain no benefits from eating meat
Herd Mentality	+2 to all SPECIALs when in a group	-2 to all SPECIALs when solo
Marsupial	+20 carry weight, and you can jump much higher	-4 Intelligence
Plague Walker	Gain an aura of poison damage, scaling with the number diseases you are suffering (up to a ceiling of 4)	You must be diseased
Scaly Skin	+50 Damage and Energy Resistance	-50 Action Points
Speed Demon	+20% run and sprint speed, +30% faster reload speed	Gain hunger and thirst 50% more quickly while moving
Talons	+25% Fist Damage, and fist attacks cause 25 additional bleed damage over 5 seconds	-4 Agility
Twisted Muscles	+25% Melee Damage, and a small chance to cripple your opponent	Gun accuracy reduced by 50%
Unstable Isotope	Chance to blast enemies in a radius with radiation when you are struck by melee	Small damage to yourself when this occurs (and many enemies are immune to radiation)

BOBBLEHEADS

Should you acquire a Bobblehead on your travels (which appear in the same places but randomly and not every time you visit), keep it until you wish to utilize it, as it only lasts for a short time (though if you leave and return to the game, the effect still continues). Use the Luck perk Curator to increase the time a Bobblehead lasts.

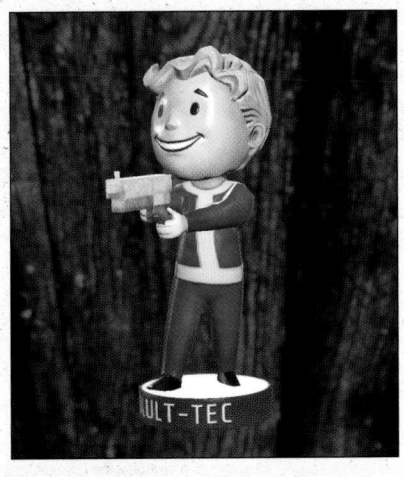

BOBBLEHEAD	DESCRIPTION
Agility	"Never be afraid to dodge the sensitive issues." Gain +2 Agility for 10 hours.
Big Guns	"The best way to win an argument is to be the loudest." Gain +20% damage with heavy guns for 10 hours.
Caps	"Never forget to walk away with more than you've bought." You are twice as likely to find better Caps Stashes for 10 hours.
Charisma	"Nothing says pizzazz like a winning smile." Gain +2 Charisma for 10 hours.
Endurance	"Always be ready to take one for the team." Gain +2 Endurance for 10 hours.
Energy Weapons	"Arrive at peaceful resolutions by using superior firepower." Gain +20% damage with energy guns for 10 hours.
Explosives	"The best way to solve a problem is to make it go away." Gain +30% damage with explosives for 10 hours.
Intelligence	"The smartest individuals realize there's always more to learn." Gain +2 Intelligence for 10 hours.
Leader	"Lead by example." Gain 5% more experience for 10 hours.
Lockpicking	"Always strive for the unobtainable." Gain a 30% wider "sweet spot" when lockpicking for 10 hours.
Luck	"There's only one way to give 110%." Gain +2 Luck for 10 hours.
Medicine	"The smart man knows a bandage only hides his wounds." Heal 30% more with Stimpaks for 10 hours.
Melee Weapons	"It's important to do business up close and personal." Gain +20% damage with melee weapons for 10 hours.
Perception	"Only through observation will you perceive weakness." Gain +2 Perception for 10 hours.
Repair	"Why go down with the ship when you can try to fix it?" Fusion Cores last 30% longer for 10 hours.
Science	"Always be prepared to explain the hows and the whys." For 10 hours get one extra guess when hacking terminals.
Small Guns	"Because it's easier to have courage from a safe distance away." Gain +20% damage with ballistic guns for 10 hours.
Sneak	"The safest distance between two points is a shadowy line." You are 30% harder to detect for 10 hours.
Strength	"It's essential to give your arguments impact." Gain +2 Strength for 10 hours.
Unarmed	"When words fail, there's always fists." Gain +25% damage with unarmed attacks for 10 hours.

MAGAZINES

Also keep a lookout for various reading materials throughout your travels. Like Bobbleheads, these, too, appear in the same places but randomly, and not every time you visit. Keep the Magazine until you wish to utilize it, as it lasts for only a short amount of time (though if you leave and return to the game, the effect still continues). Use the Luck perk Curator to increase the time a Magazine lasts.

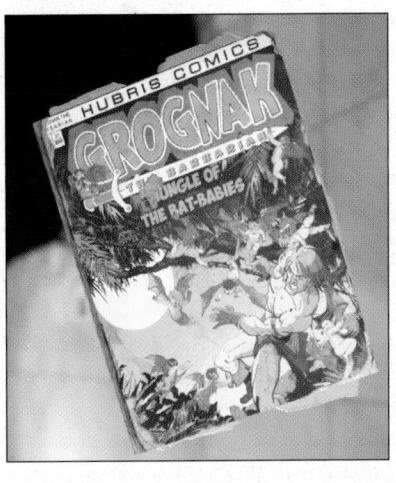

MAGAZINE	DESCRIPTION
Astonishing Tales 1	For 2 hours, do +15% damage against Mothmen.
Astonishing Tales 2	For 2 hours, do +15% damage against the Grafton Monsters.
Astonishing Tales 3	For 2 hours, do +15% damage against the Snallygasters.
Astonishing Tales 4	For 2 hours, do +15% damage against Flatwoods Aliens.
Astonishing Tales 5	For 2 hours, do +15% damage against the Wendigos.
Astoundingly Awesome Tales 1	For 2 hours, do 15% more damage to Mirelurks.
Astoundingly Awesome Tales 2	For 2 hours, do 15% more damage to Super Mutants.
Astoundingly Awesome Tales 3	For 2 hours, swim twice as fast.
Astoundingly Awesome Tales 4	For 2 hours, do 25% more damage with the Alien Blaster.
Astoundingly Awesome Tales 5	For 2 hours, do 25% more damage with the Cryolator.
Astoundingly Awesome Tales 6	For 2 hours, regenerate 20 points of health per minute.
Astoundingly Awesome Tales 7	For 2 hours, gain 5 maximum AP.
Astoundingly Awesome Tales 8	For 2 hours, take 25% less damage from robots.
Astoundingly Awesome Tales 9	For 2 hours, gain 15 Poison Resistance.
Astoundingly Awesome Tales 10	For 2 hours, do +15 more damage with scoped weapons.
Astoundingly Awesome Tales 11	For 2 hours, do +15 more damage to Ghouls.
Astoundingly Awesome Tales 12	For 2 hours, you are 30% less likely to catch a disease.
Astoundingly Awesome Tales 13	For 2 hours, RadAway will heal 30% more radiation damage.
Backwoodsman 1	For 2 hours, collect extra meat when you search dead animals.
Backwoodsman 2	For 2 hours, do 25% more damage with tomahawks.
Backwoodsman 3	For 2 hours, crafting weapons costs fewer materials.
Backwoodsman 4	For 2 hours, gain a 50% chance for double yield when harvesting plants.
Backwoodsman 5	For 2 hours, do 15% more damage to animals.
Backwoodsman 6	For 2 hours, receive 50% more healing from cooked food.
Backwoodsman 7	For 2 hours, you are 50% less likely to become diseased from food and drink.

TRAINING

CRAFTING AND C.A.M.P.ING

INVENTORY

QUESTS

ATLAS

BESTIARY

APPENDICES

MAGAZINE	DESCRIPTION
Backwoodsman 8	For 2 hours, you are 30% more satisfied by eating and drinking.
Backwoodsman 9	For 2 hours, repairs to your camp or workshop cost 50% fewer materials.
Backwoodsman 10	For 2 hours, turrets in your camp or workshop do 50% more damage.
Grognak the Barbarian 1	For 2 hours, do 15% more melee damage.
Grognak the Barbarian 2	For 2 hours, you are 20% harder to detect while sneaking.
Grognak the Barbarian 3	For 2 hours, gain 15 Poison Resistance.
Grognak the Barbarian 4	For 2 hours, do +30% V.A.T.S. crit damage with melee weapons.
Grognak the Barbarian 5	For 2 hours, do 15% more damage to Scorched enemies.
Grognak the Barbarian 6	For 2 hours, melee weapons weigh 75% less.
Grognak the Barbarian 7	For 2 hours, melee weapons lose condition 50% more slowly.
Grognak the Barbarian 8	For 2 hours, gain 2 Damage Resistance for each point of Charisma.
Grognak the Barbarian 9	For 2 hours, gain 10 Carry Capacity.
Grognak the Barbarian 10	For 2 hours, gain 15 Energy Resistance.
Guns and Bullets 1	For 2 hours, do 15% more damage to robots.
Guns and Bullets 2	For 2 hours, do +30% V.A.T.S. crit damage with laser weapons.
Guns and Bullets 3	For 2 hours, do +30% V.A.T.S. crit damage with ballistic guns.
Guns and Bullets 4	For 2 hours, gain 6 AP regeneration.
Guns and Bullets 5	For 2 hours, gain 50% more components when scrapping weapons.
Guns and Bullets 6	For 2 hours, gain 10 Damage Resistance at night.
Guns and Bullets 7	For 2 hours, do 10% more damage with guns without scopes.
Guns and Bullets 8	For 2 hours, do 15% more damage to Yao Guai.
Guns and Bullets 9	For 2 hours, do +30% V.A.T.S. crit damage with plasma weapons.
Guns and Bullets 10	For 2 hours, do 15% more damage to Liberator Bots.
Live and Love 1	For 2 hours, gain 10 maximum health when on a team.
Live and Love 2	For 2 hours, inflict +5 more damage when you are on a team.
Live and Love 3	For 2 hours, heal 50% more from eating vegetables and fruits.
Live and Love 4	For 2 hours, gain 10 AP regeneration when on a team.
Live and Love 5	For 2 hours, gain +2 Luck from drinking alcohol.
Live and Love 6	For 2 hours, gain +10 Damage Resist when on a team.
Live and Love 7	For 2 hours, gain 10 max AP when on a team.
Live and Love 8	For 2 hours, ain 5% more XP while in a team.
Live and Love 9	For 2 hours, take 25% less damage from robots.
Scout's Life 1	For 2 hours, suffer 30% less radiation from eating or drinking.
Scout's Life 2	For 2 hours, take 25% less damage from insects.
Scout's Life 3	For 2 hours, gain 10 Carry Capacity.
Scout's Life 4	For 2 hours, you have twice the normal bleedout time before dying.
Scout's Life 5	For 2 hours, you are 80% less likely to catch diseases from creatures.
Scout's Life 6	For 2 hours, you become hungry and thirsty 30% more slowly.
Scout's Life 7	For 2 hours, take 25% less damage from animals.
Scout's Life 8	For 2 hours, sprinting uses 20% fewer AP.
Scout's Life 9	For 2 hours, placing a camp costs 80% fewer Caps.

MAGAZINE	DESCRIPTION
Scout's Life 10	For 2 hours, equipped items lose condition 30% more slowly.
Tesla Science 1	For 2 hours, take 25% less damage from robots.
Tesla Science 2	For 2 hours, take 25% less damage from plasma weapons, grenades, and mines.
Tesla Science 3	For 2 hours, your explosive attacks have a 30% larger radius.
Tesla Science 4	For 2 hours, your Power Armor consumes Fusion Cores 15% more slowly.
Tesla Science 5	For 2 hours, your heavy guns consume ammo 20% more slowly.
Tesla Science 6	For 2 hours, gain 15 Radiation Resistance vs. the environment.
Tesla Science 7	For 2 hours, do +30% V.A.T.S. crit damage with energy weapons.
Tesla Science 8	For 2 hours, do +15% V.A.T.S. crit damage with all weapons.
Tesla Science 9	For 2 hours, do +30% V.A.T.S. crit damage with heavy guns.
Tumblers Today 1	For 2 hours, gain a 20% wider "sweet spot" while lockpicking.
Tumblers Today 2	For 2 hours, find extra bobby pins when you search bobby pin boxes.
Tumblers Today 3	For 2 hours, gain +1 lockpicking skill.
Tumblers Today 4	For 2 hours, your bobby pins will never break while picking locks.
Tumblers Today 5	For 2 hours, gain a 20% wider "sweet spot" while lockpicking.
The Unstoppables 1	For 2 hours, gain a 5% chance to take no damage from an enemy attack.
The Unstoppables 2	For 2 hours, gain a 20% chance of taking no damage from Scorched enemies.
The Unstoppables 3	For 2 hours, gain a 30% chance of taking no damage from explosions.
The Unstoppables 4	For 2 hours, gain a 30% chance of taking no damage from melee attacks.
The Unstoppables 5	For 2 hours, gain a 30% chance of taking no damage from energy weapon attacks.
U.S. Covert Operations Manual 1	For 2 hours, gain 10 Damage Resistance while sneaking.
U.S. Covert Operations Manual 2	For 2 hours, hide 50% better, even in full light.
U.S. Covert Operations Manual 3	For 2 hours, take 10% less damage from other players.
U.S. Covert Operations Manual 4	For 2 hours, gain 1 Perception.
U.S. Covert Operations Manual 5	For 2 hours, gain 1 Perception.
U.S. Covert Operations Manual 6	For 2 hours, make 50% less noise while sneaking.
U.S. Covert Operations Manual 7	For 2 hours, hostile players' V.A.T.S. accuracy will be reduced by 50% when they target you.
U.S. Covert Operations Manual 8	For 2 hours, do 25% more damage with knives or unarmed attacks.
U.S. Covert Operations Manual 9	For 2 hours, Stealth Boys last 50% longer.
U.S. Covert Operations Manual 10	For 2 hours, gain 1 Agility.
Atomic Command	Magazine and Holotape.
Automatron	Magazine and Holotape.
Grognak & the Ruby Ruins	Magazine and Holotape.
Nuka Tapper	Magazine and Holotape.
Pipfall	Magazine and Holotape.
Red Menace	Magazine and Holotape.
Wastelad	Magazine and Holotape.
Zeta Invaders	Magazine and Holotape.

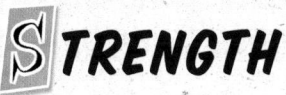TRENGTH

- **MODIFICATIONS: CARRY WEIGHT, MELEE WEAPON DAMAGE**
- **BUFFS: STRENGTH BOBBLEHEAD, SOLAR POWERED (ENDURANCE), RADICOOL PERK (ENDURANCE), MOST POWER ARMOR, FOOD (MOSTLY STEAK-RELATED), X-CELL, MOST ALCOHOL.**

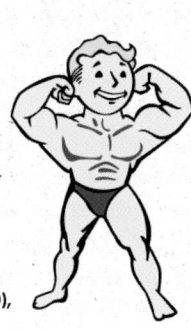

Strength is a measure of your raw physical power. It affects how much you can carry and the damage of all melee attacks. Remember that every item you scavenge has a weight associated with it, so the higher your Strength, the more you can physically carry before becoming over-encumbered. Melee damage is inflicted with weaponry you wield with your hands or that you wear on your hands.

STRENGTH	MAX CARRY WEIGHT	ADDITIONAL MELEE DAMAGE
1	105	+5%
2	110	+10%
3	115	+15%
4	120	+20%
5	125	+25%
6	105	+30%
7	110	+35%
8	115	+40%
9	120	+50%
10	125	+55%
11	130	+60%
12	105	+65%
13	110	+70%
14	115	+75%
15	120	+80%

STRENGTH-RELATED PERKS: OVERVIEW

Strength has the most number of "weapon specialization" perks to consider (Gladiator for one-handed melee, Heavy Gunner for nonexplosive heavy guns, Shotgunner for shotguns, and Slugger for two-handed melee). It is dominated by perks that reduce your item weight (like food, drink, chems, junk items, weapon ammo, armor, Power Armor, melee weapons, and even thrown explosives) and those upping the damage of weapons (as long as those weapons are melee, shotguns, or heavy guns). Expect a Power Armor maneuver perk, extra Carry Weight, and even a bonus to gun-bashing. These are mostly offensive, melee, heavy, shotgun, or weight-offsetting perks.

STRENGTH PERKS (30)

The following table shows all 30 Strength Perk Cards, listed by the earliest level you can obtain them.

PERK NAME	C	U	R	LEVEL	RANKS	DESCRIPTION
Iron Fist	x			2	1, 2, 3, 4, 5	Punching attacks do +20/40/60/80/100% damage with a 5/10/15/20/25% chance to stagger your opponent.
Traveling Pharmacy	x			3	1, 2, 3	Weights of all Chems (including Stimpaks) are reduced by 30/60/90%.
Bandolier	x			4	1, 2, 3	Ballistic weapon ammo weighs 30/60/90% less.
Gladiator			x	5	1, 2, 3	Your one-handed melee weapons now do +10/15/20% damage.
Pack Rat	x			6	1, 2, 3	The weight of all junk items is reduced by 25/50/75%.
Slugger			x	7	1, 2, 3	Your two-handed melee weapons now do +10/15/20% damage.
Shotgunner			x	10	1, 2, 3	Your shotguns now do +10/15/20% damage.
Basher			x	11	1, 2	Gun bashing does +25/50% damage with a 5/10% chance to cripple your opponent.
Sturdy Frame		x		13	1, 2	Armor weighs 25/50% less than normal.
Barbarian			x	14	1, 2, 3	Every point of Strength adds +2/3/4 Damage Resist (max 40/60/80). (No Power Armor).
Martial Artist			x	16	1, 2, 3	Your melee weapons weigh 20/40/60% less, and you can swing them 10/20/30% faster.
Scattershot		x		18	1, 2, 3, 4	Shotguns now weigh 20/40/60/80% less and you reload them 10/20/30/40% faster.
Gladiator (Expert)			x	20	1, 2, 3	Your one-handed melee weapons now do +10/15/20% damage.
Blocker			x	21	1, 2, 3	Take 15/30/45% less damage from your opponents' melee attacks.
Shotgunner (Expert)			x	23	1, 2, 3	Your shotguns now do +10/15/20% damage.
Slugger (Expert)			x	24	1, 2, 3	Your two-handed melee weapons now do +10/15/20% damage.
Strong Back		x		26	1, 2, 3, 4	Gain +10/20/30/40 to carry weight.
Heavy Gunner			x	30	1, 2, 3	Your non-explosive heavy guns now do +10/15/20% damage.
Ordnance Express		x		31	1, 2, 3	Thrown explosives weigh 30/60/90% less.
Full Charge	x			33	1, 2	Sprinting in Power Armor consumes half as much/no extra Fusion Core energy.
Incisor			x	34	1, 2, 3	Your melee weapons ignore 25/50/75% of your target's armor.
Bear Arms		x		35	1, 2, 3, 4	Heavy Guns weigh 20/40/60/80% less.
Lock and Load		x		37	1, 2, 3	Heavy guns reload 10/20/30% faster.
Bullet Shield			x	39	1, 2, 3, 4	Gain 10/20/30/40 Damage Resistance while firing a heavy gun.
Heavy Gunner (Expert)			x	40	1, 2, 3	Your non-explosive heavy guns now do +10/15/20% damage.
Pain Train		x		41	1, 2, 3	Damage/ Smash/ Devastate and stagger enemies by sprinting into them with Power Armor.
Gladiator (Master)			x	43	1, 2, 3	Your one-handed melee weapons now do +10/15/20% damage.
Shotgunner (Master)			x	45	1, 2, 3	Your shotguns now do +10/15/20% damage.
Slugger (Master)			x	48	1, 2, 3	Your two-handed melee weapons now do +10/15/20% damage.
Heavy Gunner (Master)			x	50	1, 2, 3	Your non-explosive heavy guns now do +10/15/20% damage.

TRAINING

CRAFTING AND C.A.M.P.ING

INVENTORY

QUESTS

ATLAS

BESTIARY

APPENDICES

BANDOLIER

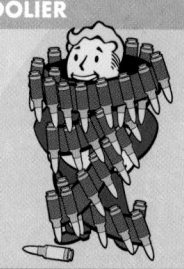

RARITY: COMMON
LEVEL: 4
RANKS: ★★★★★
POINTS: 1, 2, 3

DESCRIPTION: BALLISTIC WEAPON AMMO WEIGHS 30%/60%/90% LESS.

Advice: Do you carry around a lot of ammunition (from normal, ranged weapons that don't fire Energy rounds), and does it weigh a lot? For heavier weapons, the ammunition weight may be problematic, and if you want to negate some (or at the highest rank, almost all) of that weight, then employ this perk. However, some ammunition is extremely light, meaning you may be wise to choose other perks that negate Carry Weight penalties instead. Or just carry less ammo, or choose a weapon with lighter ammunition (unless you're a master Tinker and part of your plan is to trade bullets for Caps or to keep your teammates filled with ballistic ordnance). Note the Energy weapon ammo version of this perk is called Batteries Included.

BARBARIAN

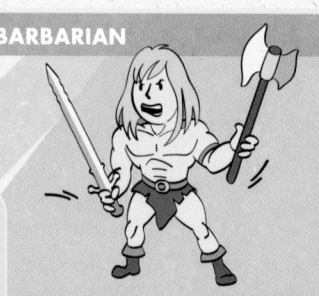

RARITY: RARE
LEVEL: 14
RANKS: ★★★★★
POINTS: 1, 2, 3

DESCRIPTION: EVERY POINT OF STRENGTH ADDS +2/3/4 DAMAGE RESIST (MAX 40/60/80). (NO POWER ARMOR).

Advice: Everyone likes free armor, right? Well, depends on your play-style. This might be better suited to a player who enjoys charging into combat and is always receiving damage, compared to a sniper or long-range specialist who rarely receives damage. This bonus to your Damage Resistance is added to your base value, so if you've already tooled up in some high-value armor and your Damage Resist is, say, 36, this perk would only grant you 4 additional points at Rank 1. Therefore, you may wish to forgo more difficult-to-find or expensive protection in favor of your naturally tough exterior, or (especially at Rank 3) add a great deal to your defensive posture, providing you have the necessary high Strength. Note that wearing no armor won't ever get you to the maximum Resistance rating of 40/60/80—that requires a Strength of 20 (which is 5 more than the 15 you can have...unless you add buffs, of course!). Finally, there are many other perks offering Damage Resistance under other circumstances. Add the following to stack or use instead of Barbarian:

- **Bodyguards (Charisma perk):** up to 36 Damage Resistance with up to three teammates
- **Bullet Shield (Strength perk):** up to +40 Damage Resistance when firing a heavy gun)
- **Refractor (Perception perk):** up to +20 Energy Resistance
- **Ironclad (Endurance perk):** up to +50 Damage and Energy Resistance while wearing armor
- **Evasive (Agility perk):** Agility Points add Damage and Energy Resistance to +45
- **Moving Target:** up to +45 Damage and Energy resistance while Sprinting
- **Junk Shield (Luck perk):** up to 45 Damage and Energy Resistance when carrying more junk.

And that's before any armor is counted!

BASHER

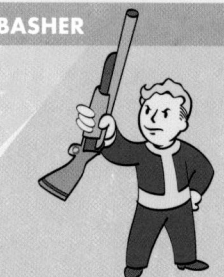

RARITY: RARE
LEVEL: 11
RANKS: ★★★★★
POINTS: 1, 2

DESCRIPTION: GUN BASHING DOES +25/50% DAMAGE WITH A 5/10% CHANCE TO CRIPPLE YOUR OPPONENT.

Advice: First, it's worth learning exactly how to gun-bash, then use it more often, and then time it so you utilize the bash with your weapon's reload. Try staggering foes with a bash, shooting, then bashing them again so you're effectively using far less ammunition and pushing back foes that are swarming you. Also try reloading immediately so you aren't quite as prone to attacks. With this perk you wade in and bash; then the damage and cripple chance is applied. It helps if your weapon has a bayonet or other mod to add some additional damage. However, this usually doesn't inflict as much damage as a melee weapon, which benefits from a far greater range of perks at hand-to-hand combat range: Indeed, this should be seen as extra insurance for those primarily using ranged weapons, in more confined locations or areas where swarms of foes are expected.

BEAR ARMS

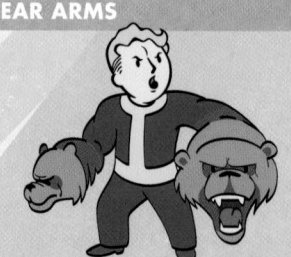

RARITY: UNCOMMON
LEVEL: 35
RANKS: ★★★★★
POINTS: 1, 2, 3, 4

DESCRIPTION: HEAVY GUNS WEIGH 20/40/60/80% LESS.

Advice: Your average Gatling laser weighs around 20, while a minigun is a hefty 35, compared to the positively (and far less powerful) pipe gun, with a weight of around 2. Using your inventory to compare the weights of your available weapons, then figuring out how many of a particular weapon type you use, is key to figuring out if it's worth spending points in this perk. Remember this doesn't help reduce the ammunition of a heavy gun, which is among the heaviest, but the Bandolier Strength perk does. This is already using up Strength Points you may be wanting for other perks. Of course, if you're carrying one of every heavy weapon or multiple miniguns, having more room for "ol' painless and friends" is a good idea. One of the key elements of this perk is the level you can first use it, so it's worth finding and keeping a variety of heavy guns in your collection but not employing them until you're at a high enough level.

BLOCKER

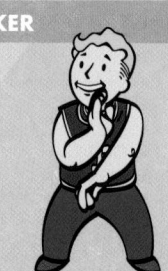

RARITY: RARE
LEVEL: 21
RANKS: ★★★★★
POINTS: 1, 2, 3

DESCRIPTION: TAKE 15%/30%/45% LESS DAMAGE FROM YOUR OPPONENTS' MELEE ATTACKS.

Advice: This perk is extremely situational but is extremely well suited to players favoring an up-close-and-personal method for dispatching foes. It's worth considering with other perks that hinder enemies at close quarters and with mutations, such as Electrically Charged, which zaps enemies as they attack. Perks to consider include the Strength perks Gladiator, Incisor, Martial Artist, and Slugger. Naturally, if your playtest favors enemies never getting anywhere close enough to actually damage you, this is less of a must-have perk. Play around with the stacking capabilities of other perks offering Damage Resistance, such as the Agility perk Evasive, for even less possible damage.

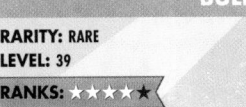

BULLET SHIELD

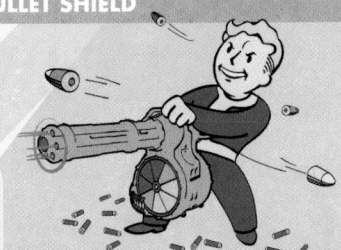

RARITY: RARE
LEVEL: 39
RANKS: ★★★★★
POINTS: 1, 2, 3, 4

DESCRIPTION: GAIN 10/20/30/40 DAMAGE RESISTANCE WHILE FIRING A HEAVY GUN.

Advice: By their very nature, heavy guns are on the cumbersome side, so shrugging off an enemy's gunfire or mauling while firing your favorite minigun or Gatling laser can help you immeasurably, especially as you're likely to already have Power Armor with good defense. Think of this as another coat of free armor; either use this perk in place of up to 40 points of additional armor (adding to your weight) or in addition to it so you become a mobile fortress! Note the related perks, such as the Strength perk Bear Arms and Heavy Gunner, the Intelligence perk Stabilized, and the Luck perk One Gun Army. The Strength perk Lock and Load is perhaps the best one to partner; you can withstand an enemy strike while you reload, before finishing them off without even wincing! You should also cross-reference all the Damage Resistance perks (listed in the entry for Barbarian); add some or all of those to your defenses too.

FULL CHARGE

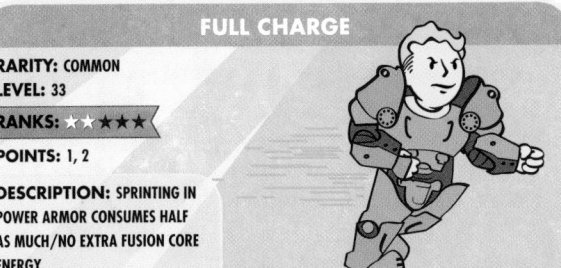

RARITY: COMMON
LEVEL: 33
RANKS: ★★★★
POINTS: 1, 2

DESCRIPTION: SPRINTING IN POWER ARMOR CONSUMES HALF AS MUCH/NO EXTRA FUSION CORE ENERGY.

Advice: This perk is excellent for lengthening the time it takes between Fusion Core swapping, though the fact that Fusion Cores can be manufactured at Power Plants means that with some planning, you can gather a good deal of Fusion Cores and never need this perk. Do you want to lose (up to) 2 Strength Perk Points when there may be more offensive perks out there to utilize? Also figure out how often you sprint while wearing this armor; if it's a lot, consider taking this perk. This perk is advantageous when you explore areas far from a power plant, where you're concentrating on scavenging, and when you need to free up your Carry Weight and want your Fusion Cores to last as long as possible.

GLADIATOR

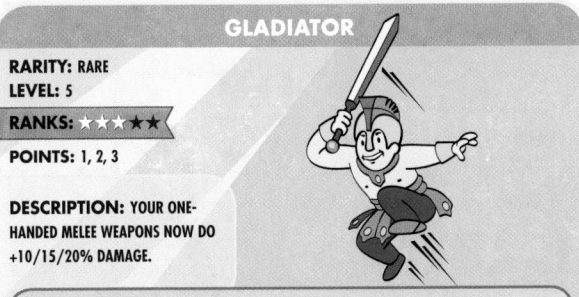

RARITY: RARE
LEVEL: 5
RANKS: ★★★★★
POINTS: 1, 2, 3

DESCRIPTION: YOUR ONE-HANDED MELEE WEAPONS NOW DO +10/15/20% DAMAGE.

Advice: From a common pitchfork to the lethal Shishkebab, the smaller, lightweight (but initially less-damaging) one-handed melee weapons are an excellent choice, and this perk is likely to be one of the first you'll have access to, as many use melee weapons as a backup to a pistol after emerging from Vault 76. You must then decide whether to further specialize in one-handed (compared to fist or two-handed) weaponry. The Slugger trio of cards (offering the same bonuses but for two-handed melee weapons) become accessible a few levels higher than Gladiator. Though this causes you to focus less generally on all melee weapons, this can be beneficial; you can then start light modding your pitchfork or machete in addition to partnering the Gladiator cards with the Strength perks Incisor and Martial Artist, the Charisma perk Overly Generous, and the Intelligence perk Makeshift Warrior.

(EXPERT) GLADIATOR

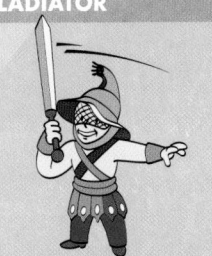

RARITY: RARE
LEVEL: 20
RANKS: ★★★★★
POINTS: 1, 2, 3

DESCRIPTION: YOUR ONE-HANDED MELEE WEAPONS NOW DO +10/15/20% DAMAGE.

Advice: Taking a few Gladiator cards is a great idea, but you need firm commitment to one-handed weaponry before taking this specialization up a notch: Have you checked the "Weapons" chapter of this guide to compare damage values for melee weaponry? Did you compare the damage and the speed of your two-handed weaponry (with damage similarly augmented by the Slugger trio of perks)? Once you're keen on this type of close-assault combat, think about partnering the Gladiator cards with the Strength perks Incisor and Martial Artist, the Charisma perk Overly Generous, and the Intelligence perk Makeshift Warrior.

(MASTER) GLADIATOR

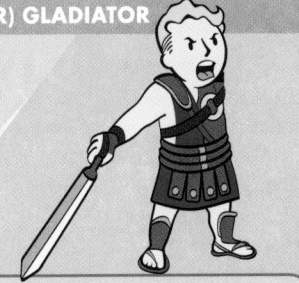

RARITY: RARE
LEVEL: 43
RANKS: ★★★★★
POINTS: 1, 2, 3

DESCRIPTION: YOUR ONE-HANDED MELEE WEAPONS NOW DO +10/15/20% DAMAGE.

Advice: By the time you can utilize this aspect of the Gladiator perk line, you're likely to be close to maximum Strength and have an armory full of modded and/or Legendary one-handed melee weapons, with little time for other damage-causing ordnance (unless you swap out to a different Strength-focused build, of course). Shrug off those ranged attacks (as it's assumed your armor is tough due to your tendency to stand and bludgeon or stab) and do some quick math: If you want your two-handed melee weapons to inflict +100% damage, you need Gladiator Rank 3, Expert Gladiator Rank 3, and Master Gladiator Rank 3, for a total of 9 Strength Points. But add in any bonuses that your Strength attribute and weapon gives you, and you'll see this focus is definitely worthwhile for close-combat professionals or those stealthy types who like to inflict massive damage on unsuspecting foes.

HEAVY GUNNER

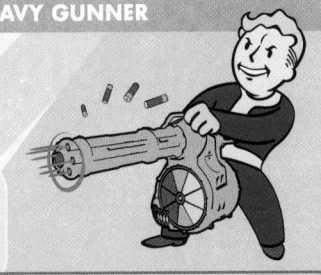

RARITY: RARE
LEVEL: 30
RANKS: ★★★★★
POINTS: 1, 2, 3

DESCRIPTION: YOUR NON-EXPLOSIVE HEAVY GUNS NOW DO +10/15/20% DAMAGE.

Advice: Aside from the small drawback that this perk does not apply to missile launchers, Fat Man launchers, or other heavyweight weapons that cause explosive, area-of-effect damage, this is an excellent choice for an explorer who wishes to concentrate on upping the devastation caused by miniguns, Gatling lasers, and the infamous Broadsider. As with all perks offering a similar benefit, take time to ascertain how much combat you attempt using these types of weapons and the associated cost (and weight) of making them your primary choice of armament (e.g., if you're going to be blasting away with a minigun, it might as well be your go-to weapon). Combine this with Strength perks Bear Arms, Bullet Shield, and Lock and Load. Also check out the Intelligence perk Stabilized and the Luck perk One Gun Army.

TRAINING
CRAFTING AND C.A.M.P.ING
INVENTORY
QUESTS
ATLAS
BESTIARY
APPENDICES

(EXPERT) HEAVY GUNNER

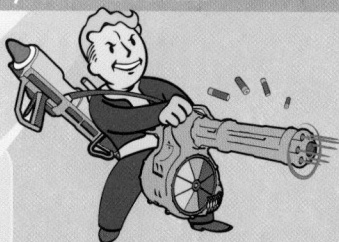

RARITY: RARE
LEVEL: 40
RANKS: ★★★★★
POINTS: 1, 2, 3

DESCRIPTION: YOUR NON-EXPLOSIVE HEAVY GUNS NOW DO +10/15/20% DAMAGE.

Advice: Much like other weapon-specialization perks, the choice of becoming an Expert in heavy guns (of the non-explosive kind) depends on how many points you're pouring into Strength. This is particularly true for Heavy Gunner, as the base advice listed three Strength perks: Bear Arms (four ranks), Bullet Shield (four ranks), and Lock and Load (three ranks). With all the associated points costs (e.g., if you want the highest ranks on all three partner perks, that's 11 Strength Points without even adding Heavy Gunner!), you need to choose what type of damage your heavy guns are going to inflict—the pure "extra damage" of these three perks or the different bonuses of the associated perks. Also remember if you want your heavy guns to inflict +40% more damage, you'll need to play your Heavy Gunner Rank 3 and Expert Heavy Gunner Rank 3 together. Each costs 3 Strength Points to use (so six in total), leaving you little room for other Strength perks.

(MASTER) HEAVY GUNNER

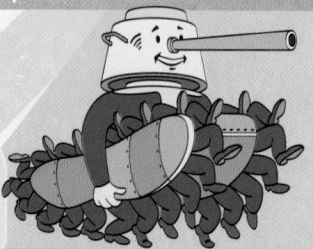

RARITY: RARE
LEVEL: 50
RANKS: ★★★★★
POINTS: 1, 2, 3

DESCRIPTION: YOUR NON-EXPLOSIVE HEAVY GUNS NOW DO +10/15/20% DAMAGE.

Advice: Nine Strength points: That's how much it's going to cost to get +60% additional damage for each heavy gun round that enters an enemy (Heavy Gunner Rank 3, Expert Heavy Gunner Rank 3, and Master Heavy Gunner Rank 3). Are you happy with this specialization? Do you really need to devastate hordes of foes or a Scorchbeast single-handedly? Of course you do! Then add the Intelligence perk Stabilized and the Luck perk One Gun Army, which involve non–Strength Point costs to create the ultimate "human tank"!

INCISOR

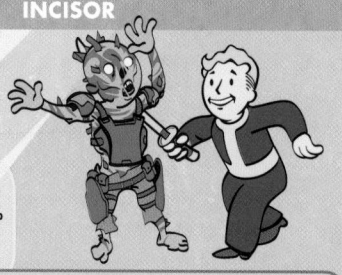

RARITY: RARE
LEVEL: 34
RANKS: ★★★★★
POINTS: 1, 2, 3

DESCRIPTION: YOUR MELEE WEAPONS IGNORE 25%/50%/75% OF YOUR TARGET'S ARMOR.

Advice: Whether you're cajoling your opponent into a fight using boxing gloves, a machete, or a super sledge, anything you're hitting at close range that wears armor deserves to receive additional damage. Check the enemy's stats (in V.A.T.S. or in this guide's Bestiary) to see how much armor they are wearing and its value to gauge the effectiveness of this perk. For example, you may find that simply utilizing Strength perks Gladiator or Slugger gives you a better overall damage rating. However, one benefit Incisor has over the aforementioned perks is that it applies to any melee weapon, rather than just those that are one- or two-handed.

IRON FIST

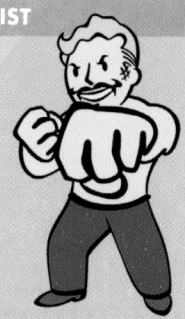

RARITY: COMMON
LEVEL: 2
RANKS: ★★★★★
POINTS: 1, 2, 3, 4, 5

DESCRIPTION: PUNCHING ATTACKS DO +20%/40%/60%/80%/100% DAMAGE WITH A 5%/10%/15%/20%/25% CHANCE TO STAGGER YOUR OPPONENT.

Advice: Fist weapons, including boxing gloves, power fists, and the fabled Deathclaw Gauntlet, aren't particularly numerous, but they are entertaining. Since this becomes available at such a low level, searching out a fist weapon should be a priority for those interested in both damaging and possibly staggering their enemies (after which you can continue the punching punishment or switch to a gun to finish off a staggered foe). Remember that fist weapons are melee weapons, so partner perks like the Strength perk Blocker and, more importantly, Incisor; the Intelligence perk Makeshift Warrior; and the Agility perk Ninja. Finally, note that some weapons (e.g., boxing glove, knuckles, or the infamous Power Fist) are only craftable on Weapons Workbenches with this perk active.

LOCK AND LOAD

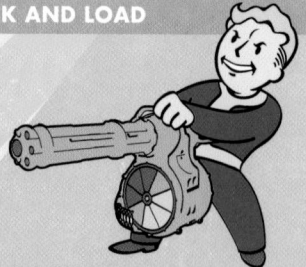

RARITY: UNCOMMON
LEVEL: 37
RANKS: ★★★★★
POINTS: 1, 2, 3

DESCRIPTION: HEAVY GUNS RELOAD 10%/20%/30% FASTER.

Advice: As heavy guns are among the slowest weapons to reload, taking this perk makes perfect sense, as long as your combat routine involves utilizing heavy guns to their fullest extent, rather than wading in with a heavy gun, using it until it needs reloading, and then switching to a different weapon to finish the job. If your heavy gun needs a reload multiple times during a fight, then you should take this perk. However, balance these benefits with perks like the Strength perk Heavy Gunner; though you can have both, you might simply need to increase your damage rating to remove most clusters of threats (using a heavy gun that doesn't launch area-of-effect projectiles), rather than reloading a bit more quickly. Check other related perks, such as the Luck perk One Gun Army; then test out your stagger and cripple chances using a fast-firing weapon like the minigun. Again, does this do the job without the need to reload? If it doesn't, take this perk.

MARTIAL ARTIST

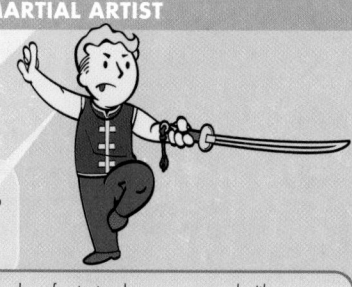

RARITY: RARE
LEVEL: 16
RANKS: ★★★★★
POINTS: 1, 2, 3

DESCRIPTION: YOUR MELEE WEAPONS WEIGH 20%/40%/60% LESS, AND YOU CAN SWING THEM 10%/20%/30% FASTER.

Advice: This affects a large number of potent melee weapons used with one or both hands and is a must-have for a character build that focuses on this type of close-combat carnage. The relatively low level that this becomes available at, and the double benefit (lighter and faster) helps you gather more of these weapons and utilize them with more flexibility and ferocity. In fact, you may wish to grab two identical weapons, break one down into component parts, keep the other intact, and see what the weight disparity is; you may find the intact weapon is now lighter than its component parts (unless of course, you also have the Pack Rat perk active)! Martial Artist lends itself to stealth-based combat, especially when partnered with the Strength perks Incisor, Gladiator, and Slugger; the Intelligence perk Makeshift Warrior; and the Agility perk Ninja.

ORDNANCE EXPRESS

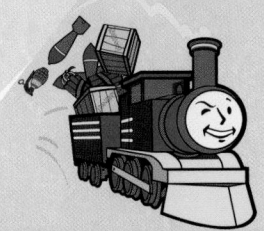

RARITY: UNCOMMON
LEVEL: 31
RANKS: ★★★★★
POINTS: 1, 2, 3

DESCRIPTION:
THROWN EXPLOSIVES WEIGH
30%/60%/90% LESS.

Advice: Usually, a grenade weighs between one-half and one point, which isn't particularly light compared to most ammunition but still isn't overly heavy, unless you're carrying a whole load of grenades (and mines). This is obviously incredibly useful for those whose play style employs grenades to soften up enemies, cause distractions, or defeat clusters of foes in a single explosion, or those who like to lay mine traps for trespassers. For grenade-focused explorers, partner this with the Perception perks Fire in the Hole and Grenadier, and the Intelligence perk Demolition Expert. But if grenades aren't your main focus, you may wish to spend your points on a perk that benefits your Carry Weight, such as the Strength perk Strong Back, which gives you +10, 20, or 30 to your Carry Weight for the same point cost; this translates to 20, 40, or 60 extra 0.5-point weight grenades: Calculate which is more beneficial to you.

PACK RAT

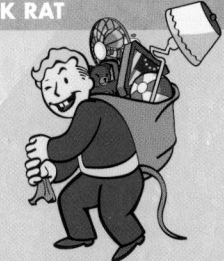

RARITY: COMMON
LEVEL: 6
RANKS: ★★★★★
POINTS: 1, 2, 3

DESCRIPTION: THE WEIGHT
OF ALL JUNK ITEMS IS REDUCED BY
25%/50%/75%.

Advice: This is exceptionally useful throughout your exploration, allowing you to carry a great deal more items that appear in the Junk menu of your Pip-Boy, which includes base components too. You don't need to return to your Stash Box as often, and you can investigate multiple new areas, as you aren't as worried about becoming over-encumbered during explorations of larger locations. However, don't become overconfident, as you can still die and leave your loot behind! However, as you progress, other perks that give a more general bonus to your Carry Weight (e.g., the Strength perk Strong Back) may be a better choice, as Pack Rat applies only to junk. Also check out which junk is the heaviest (and perhaps priciest), and carry that for you or your team. If you're teaming up, use this perk to become the player who carries everything before sharing it at the end of the adventure. Also think about partnering this with the Luck perk Junk Shield to give you some extra defense.

PAIN TRAIN

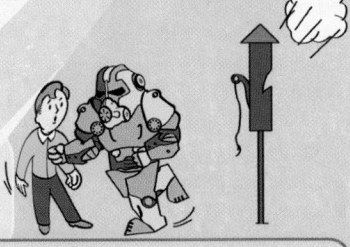

RARITY: UNCOMMON
LEVEL: 41
RANKS: ★★★★★
POINTS: 1, 2, 3

DESCRIPTION: DAMAGE/
SMASH/DEVASTATE AND STAGGER
ENEMIES BY SPRINTING INTO THEM
WITH POWER ARMOR.

Advice: This offers an excellent opening offense in close-combat fighting while using Power Armor; therefore, it's preferable to partner this perk with weapons designed for short-range fighting too (like melee or shotgun weaponry rather than sniper rifles!). Your prowess becomes even more pronounced when you add the Strength perk Full Charge. The Intelligence perks Fit It Good, Power Patcher, and Power User allow you to sprint into foes for longer before your suit needs mending.

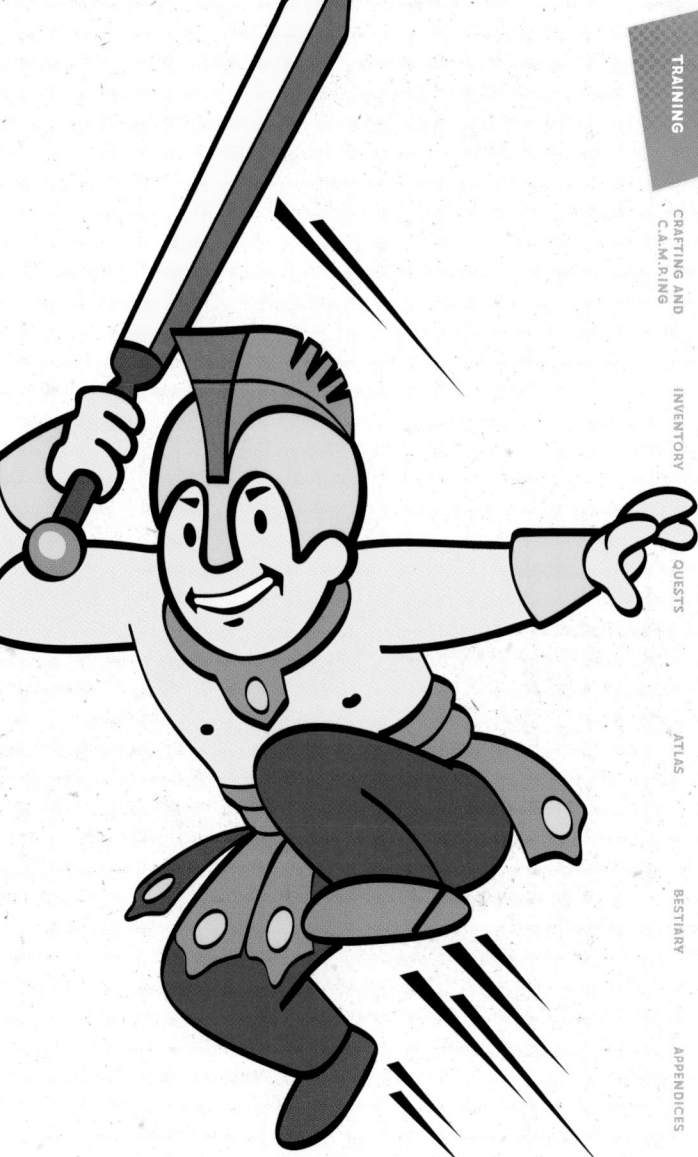

TRAINING

CRAFTING AND C.A.M.P.ING

INVENTORY

QUESTS

ATLAS

BESTIARY

APPENDICES

SCATTERSHOT

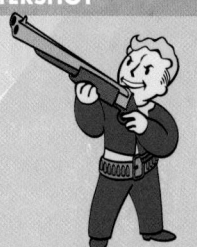

RARITY: UNCOMMON
LEVEL: 18
RANKS: ★★★★★
POINTS: 1, 2, 3, 4

DESCRIPTION: SHOTGUNS NOW WEIGH 20%/40%/60%/80% LESS AND YOU RELOAD THEM 10%/20%/30%/40% FASTER.

Advice: A perfect accompaniment to the Shotgunner perk, this negates the two biggest drawbacks of the shotgun: their relatively heavy weight and slow reload speed. However, you won't be able to equip all the Shotgunner perks (including Expert and Master) and Scattershot, as it costs too many Strength Points (17; your maximum Strength is 15). But prior to reaching the upper levels, wading into combat with this and Shotgunner is an excellent way to dispose of foes, providing shotguns are your preferred method of enemy disposal.

SHOTGUNNER

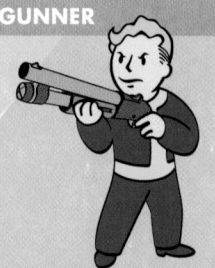

RARITY: RARE
LEVEL: 10
RANKS: ★★★★★
POINTS: 1, 2, 3

DESCRIPTION: YOUR SHOTGUNS NOW DO +10%/20%/30% DAMAGE.

Advice: Do you like a shorter-range, a slightly longer load time, but a wider burst and devastating closer-range damage to your guns? Then consult the "Weapons" chapter and pick a shotgun to find, before searching for better and modded shotguns to make the most of this perk. Also consider partnering other perks with this, such as the Strength perk Scattershot, the Perception perk Skeet Shooter, and the Agility perk Enforcer, and starting your own crazed shotgun shell creation at a Tinker's Workbench (so check the "Crafting" section for associated perks for this workbench).

(EXPERT) SHOTGUNNER

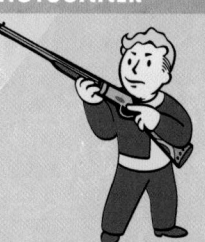

RARITY: RARE
LEVEL: 12
RANKS: ★★★★★
POINTS: 1, 2, 3

DESCRIPTION: YOUR SHOTGUNS NOW DO +10/15/20% DAMAGE.

Advice: Like even more mayhem and damage for your shotguns? Then add even more to the damage they inflict. There isn't some subtle nuance to this perk; it simply makes your enemies melt into pellet-marked goo after a burst from your terrible boomstick! Just remember you're throwing your lot in by spending so many points on stacking this and the Shotgunner perk: So if you want your shotguns to inflict +40% more damage, you'll need to play your Shotgunner Rank 3 and Expert Shotgunner Rank 3 together. Each costs 3 Strength Points to use (so 6 in total), leaving you little room for other Strength perks, but if you positively must spray shotgun death on foes, place all these cards together!

(MASTER) SHOTGUNNER

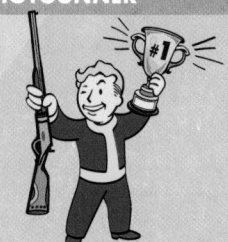

RARITY: RARE
LEVEL: 45
RANKS: ★★★★★
POINTS: 1, 2, 3

DESCRIPTION: YOUR SHOTGUNS NOW DO +10/15/20% DAMAGE.

Advice: Want to melt through enemies with buckshot like butter? Then think about adding even more damage to your shotgun total: Just be sure you need all these ranks, and you can afford all this point expenditure; it's going to cost you nine points for a 60% damage bonus for each shot fired (Shotgunner Rank 3, Expert Shotgunner Rank 3, and Master Shotgunner Rank 3), so check other Strength cards to see if you need to broaden your focus. If not, it's time to gun down anything! Also be mindful that your shotgun may be killing foes too quickly if you're employing lots of stacked damage modifiers, meaning all this extra damage may only be needed for big-ticket behemoths like Scorchbeasts!

SLUGGER

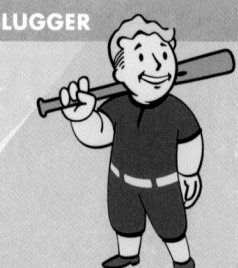

RARITY: RARE
LEVEL: 7
RANKS: ★★★★★
POINTS: 1, 2, 3

DESCRIPTION: YOUR TWO-HANDED MELEE WEAPONS NOW DO +10/15/20% DAMAGE.

Advice: Before you commit to using two-handing melee weapons, take a glance at the "Weapons" chapter to see the variety and damage you can cause with them. Then expect an extremely impressive damage bonus, which has additional bonuses for each point of Strength attribute you have. The similar Gladiator perk (which allows one-handed melee weapons to inflict additional damage) becomes available at a few levels less than this, so consider that too. Once you're committed, think about partnering the Slugger cards with the Strength perks Incisor and Martial Artist, the Charisma perk Overly Generous, and the Intelligence perk Makeshift Warrior. Finally, note that some weapons (such as the baseball bat, golf club, pool cue, sledgehammer, super sledge, and war drum) are only craftable on Weapons Workbenches with this perk active.

(EXPERT) SLUGGER

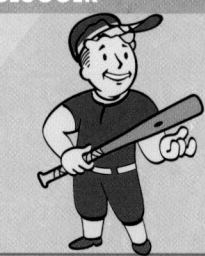

RARITY: RARE
LEVEL: 24
RANKS: ★★★★★
POINTS: 1, 2, 3

DESCRIPTION: YOUR TWO-HANDED MELEE WEAPONS NOW DO +10/15/20% DAMAGE.

Advice: When you reach a higher level, you can add even more damage to your two-handed melee weapons by becoming an Expert in this perk! The damage bonuses stack, but at the expense of using up all your Strength points. So if you want your melee weapons to inflict +40% more damage, you'll need to play your Slugger Rank 3 and Expert Slugger Rank 3 together. Each costs 3 Strength points to use (so 6 in total), leaving you little room for other Strength perks, so you really need to be focusing on Strength as an attribute and two-handed weapons as a favored form of punishment!

(MASTER) SLUGGER

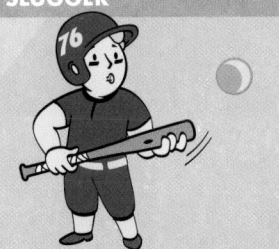

RARITY: RARE
LEVEL: 48
RANKS: ★★★★★
POINTS: 1, 2, 3

DESCRIPTION: YOUR TWO-HANDED MELEE WEAPONS NOW DO +10/15/20% DAMAGE.

Advice: Okay, it's all getting a bit out of hand and "bludgeony" at this point, right? You need to really be keen on using a Legendary, modded two-handed melee weapon, possibly forsaking all other Strength perks in order to receive some truly deranged damage bonuses! Who cares if you're getting peppered at long ranges, right? It's assumed you're using armor and charging in to batter enemies to a pulp. And if you want your two-handed melee weapons to inflict +60% damage, you need Slugger Rank 3, Expert Slugger Rank 3, and Master Slugger Rank 3, for a total of nine Strength Points. But add in any bonuses that your Strength Attribute and weapon give you, and you know this is as entertaining as it is worthwhile!

STRONG BACK

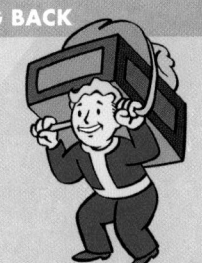

RARITY: UNCOMMON
LEVEL: 26
RANKS: ★★★★★
POINTS: 1, 2, 3, 4

DESCRIPTION: GAIN +10/20/30/40 TO CARRY WEIGHT.

Advice: If you like to go longer between Stash Box visits, want to accrue a huge number of items and objects during a lengthy scavenge, go beyond the normal limits of your Strength Carry Weight bonus, or enjoy employing heavy weapons and armor but still want a good amount of weight left for collecting, then pick this. If you're finding you have to drop items or return to Stash Boxes more frequently than you'd like, take this perk. And if you enjoy complex math, you could always figure out the average weight you're saving by employing perks like Traveling Pharmacy based on the number of chems you carry, compared to the extra Carry Weight you get with this perk and which perk offers better value. Remember, Strong Back allows 10 to 40 extra Carry Weight at any time, though!

STURDY FRAME

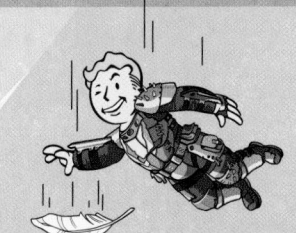

RARITY: UNCOMMON
LEVEL: 13
RANKS: ★★★★★
POINTS: 1, 2

DESCRIPTION: ARMOR WEIGHS 25%/50% LESS THAN NORMAL.

Advice: Depending on how heavy your armor is (with pieces of Power Armor and metal armor weighing more than, say, leather), this becomes a rather useful way to lessen your Carry Weight. Remember this includes armor you aren't wearing, so if you like to craft armor or run around with multiple suits of armor, this perk is a must-have. If you like to stick to one type of armor and keep any spare sets in your Stash Box, this is less useful, as unlike perks that lessen weight for item types you collect a huge number of (e.g., junk or chems), you don't usually have as many armor pieces in your inventory. Partner this with the Intelligence perk Armorer, the Endurance perk Iron Clad, and the Agility perk White Knight.

TRAVELING PHARMACY

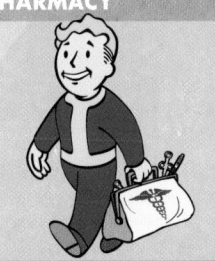

RARITY: COMMON
LEVEL: 4
RANKS: ★★★★★
POINTS: 1, 2, 3

DESCRIPTION: WEIGHTS OF ALL CHEMS (INCLUDING STIMPAKS) ARE REDUCED BY 30%/60%/90%.

Advice: This becomes very useful if you frequently utilize a wide variety of chems, you enjoy crafting and selling chems, and you understand that chems don't usually weigh a massive amount (meaning you can carry a huge number, especially when you get that Chemistry Station cranking!). Also make the most out of this perk by using it with other related chem perks: Endurance perks such as Chem Fiend, Chem Resistant, Hydro Fix and Munchy Resistance; the Intelligence perk Chemist; and the Luck perk Pharma Farma. Also think about being the chem-carrier for your team.

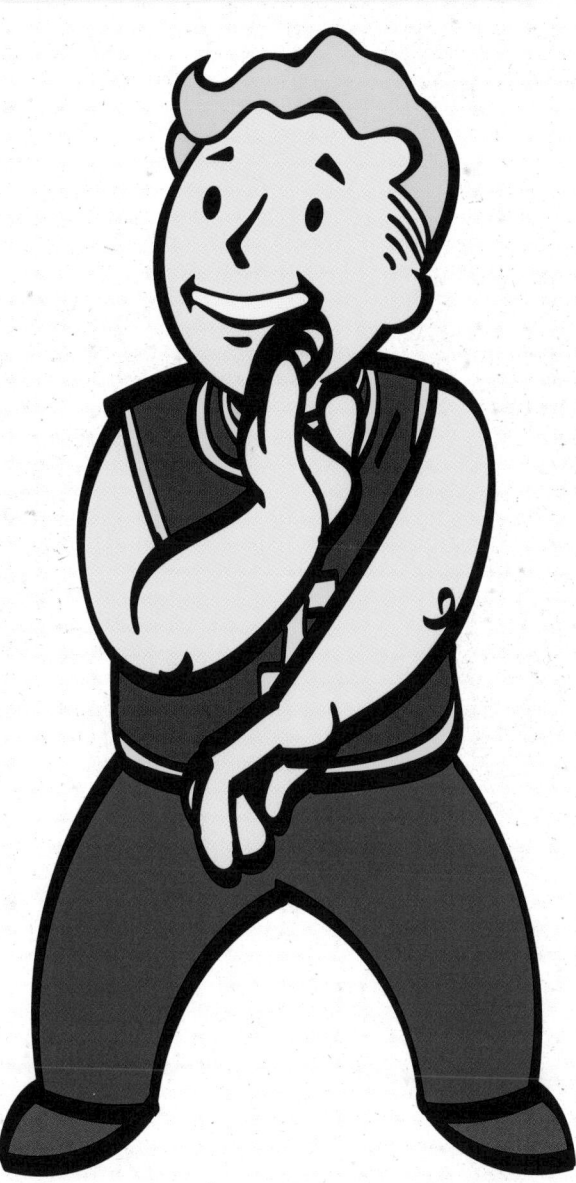

CRAFTING AND C.A.M.P.ING

INVENTORY

QUESTS

ATLAS

BESTIARY

APPENDICES

PERCEPTION

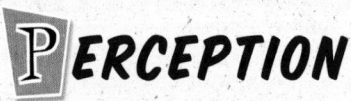

- **MODIFICATIONS: COMPASS RANGE, LOCKPICKING, V.A.T.S. ACCURACY**
- **BUFFS: PERCEPTION BOBBLEHEAD, U.S. COVERT OPERATIONS MANUAL 4 AND 5 MAGAZINES, NIGHT PERSON (PERCEPTION), CERTAIN TYPES OF ARMOR AND CLOTHING, CHEMS (SUCH AS BUFFTATS, CALMEX, DADDY-O, MENTATS, X-CELL)**

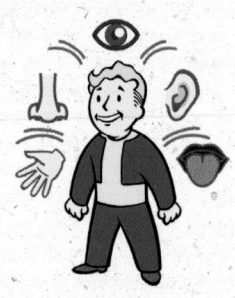

Perception affects your awareness of nearby enemies, your ability to detect stealthy movement, and your weapon accuracy in V.A.T.S. If you employ V.A.T.S. on a regular basis, and you accrue additional Perception Points, there is a much greater chance of hitting your enemies. A higher Perception also reveals detected threats—which appear as red dots on your compass—at a greater distance.

VALUE	V.A.T.S. ACCURACY BONUS	COMPASS DISTANCE IN FEET
1	+0.4%	85
2	+0.8%	97
3	+1.2%	109
4	+1.6%	121
5	+2.0%	133
6	+2.4%	145
7	+2.8%	157
8	+3.2%	169
9	+3.6%	181
10	+4.0%	193
11	+4.4%	205
12	+4.8%	217
13	+5.2%	229
14	+5.6%	241
15	+6.0%	253

PERCEPTION-RELATED PERKS: OVERVIEW

Expect some of these perks to be environmental in nature, giving you additional help with your bobby pin on locked doors, safes, and containers; granting additional foraging bonuses (for animal meat and flora); giving you aquatic mastery; and helping you locate Caps Stashes, Magazines, or Bobbleheads. There are a couple of nighttime perks, one offering energy resistance, a couple to improve your grenade-throwing, attack bonuses on a couple of enemy types, and a trio of V.A.T.S. improvements (one early, one in mid-exploration, and one very late). Come here especially if you want to specialize in rifles, both non-automatic and automatic.

PERCEPTION PERKS (30)

The following table shows all 30 Perception Perk Cards, listed by the earliest level you can obtain them.

PERK NAME	C	U	R	LEVEL	RANKS	DESCRIPTION
Concentrated Fire	x			2	1, 2, 3	V.A.T.S. now targets limbs. Focus fire to gain accuracy and damage/more accuracy and damage/high accuracy and damage per hit.
Butchers Bounty	x			3	1, 2, 3	40/60/80% chance to find extra meat when you search an animal corpse.
Green Thumb	x			4	1	Reap twice as much when harvesting flora.
Picklock	x			5	1	Gain a +1 Lockpicking skill; the Lockpicking "sweet spot" is 10% larger.
Crackshot			x	7	1, 2, 3, 4	All pistols have 5/10/15/20% more range and more/even more/much better/excellent accuracy when sighted.
Rifleman			x	8	1, 2, 3	Your non-automatic rifles now do +10/15/20% damage.
SkeetShooter			x	10	1, 2, 3, 4	Your shotguns have improved/even better/much better/excellent accuracy and spread.
Pannapictagraphist	x			12	1	You hear directional audio when in range of a Magazine.
Exterminator	x			14	1, 2, 3	Your attacks ignore 25/50/75% armor of any insect.
Commando			x	15	1, 2, 3	Basic combat training means automatic rifles do +10/15/20 damage.
PerceptiBobble	x			16	1	You hear directional audio when in range of a Bobblehead.
Ground Pounder			x	18	1, 2, 3, 4	Automatic rifles now reload 10/20/30/40% faster and have better/even better/much better/excellent hip fire accuracy.
Picklock (Expert)	x			19	1	Gain a +1 Lockpicking skill; the Lockpicking "sweet spot" is 10% larger.
Rifleman (Expert)			x	20	1, 2, 3	Your non-automatic rifles now do +10/15/20% damage.
Fortune Finder	x			22	1	You hear directional audio when in range of a Caps Stash.
Night Person		x		24	1, 2, 3	Gain +1/2/3 INT and +1/2/3 PER between the hours of 6:00 p.m. and 6:00 a.m.
Commando (Expert)			x	25	1, 2, 3	Rigorous combat training means automatic rifles do +10/15/20 damage.
Awareness			x	27	2	You can view a target's specific damage resistances in V.A.T.S.
Sniper			x	28	1, 2, 3	Gain improved control and hold your breath 20/40/60% longer while aiming scopes.
Tank Killer			x	30	1, 2, 3, 4	Your rifles ignore 10/20/30/40% armor and have a 2/4/6/8% chance to stagger.
Refractor		x		32	1, 2, 3, 4	Gain +5/10/15/20 Energy Resistance.
Glow Sight		x		33	1, 2, 3	Deal +20/40/60% damage to Glowing Enemies.
Grenadier			x	35	1, 2	Your explosives detonate with a 50% larger radius/twice the radius.
Longshot			x	37	1, 2, 3, 4	Your rifles have 5/10/15/20% more range and more/even more/much better/excellent accuracy when sighted.
Fire in the Hole			x	38	1, 2, 3	See a throwing arc when tossing grenades, and grenades fly 15/30/50% farther.
Picklock (Master)	x			40	1	Gain a +1 Lockpicking skill; the Lockpicking "sweet spot" is 10% larger.
Rifleman (Master)			x	42	1, 2, 3	Your non-automatic rifles now do +10/15/20% damage.
Commando (Master)			x	45	1, 2, 3	Lifelong combat training means automatic rifles do +10/15/20 damage.
Night Eyes			x	47	2	Gain Night Vision while sneaking between 6:00 p.m. and 6:00 a.m.
Penetrator			x	50	1, 2, 3	V.A.T.S. can hit enemy body parts blocked by cover with reduced/improved/normal accuracy.

AWARENESS

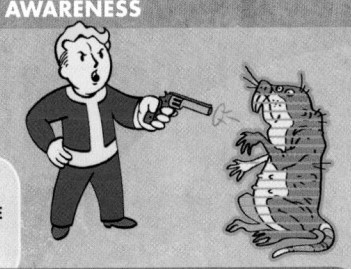

RARITY: RARE
LEVEL: 27
RANKS: ★ ★ ★ ★
POINTS: 2

DESCRIPTION: YOU CAN VIEW A TARGET'S SPECIFIC DAMAGE RESISTANCES IN V.A.T.S.

Advice: Is your enemy shrugging off your best and violent intentions to harm them? Then add a little awareness to your combat. Here's what to expect to see:

Shield: knowing your enemy's resistance to ballistic, explosive, or impact-related damage.

Lightning: Your enemy's resistance to energy weapons.

Radiation: Your enemy's resistance to weapons inflicting radiation damage.

Poison Drip: Your enemy's resistance to weapons inflicting poison damage.

Now you know what the enemy most dislikes getting struck by, and now you're a high enough level so you should be utilizing weaponry that has a variety of effects. Pick a weapon best suited to taking advantage of the enemy's weaknesses. This perk is obviously only useful if you utilize V.A.T.S., but even if you don't, you can flick on V.A.T.S., check the information, and start combat under normal conditions. You may not need this information if you already know what a target's resistances are, but for encountering new and potentially deadly creatures in the more dangerous wild lands of Appalachia, this can be most helpful.

BUTCHER'S BOUNTY

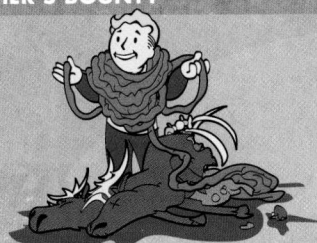

RARITY: COMMON
LEVEL: 3
RANKS: ★ ★ ★ ★
POINTS: 1, 2, 3

DESCRIPTION: 40/60/80% CHANCE TO FIND EXTRA MEAT WHEN YOU SEARCH AN ANIMAL CORPSE.

Advice: An early perk, and one that helps in your hunt for animal meat (Mongrel, Brahmin, Opossum, Mole Rat, and all other animals). It lessens the time it takes to hunt and loot animals, allowing you more time for other types of exploration (e.g., acquiring junk). This also relates to finding meat-based recipes and using a cooking station, which you should have learned how to do by the time you choose this perk. If you're firmly against hunting, or you prefer the taste of Carrot Soup, there are other ways to satiate your Hunger, but this lessens the usefulness of this perk, as you obviously need to focus on killing animals and utilizing their meat afterward. As such, meat needs to be cooked and spoils quickly (unless you've taken the Luck perk Good With Salt). Think about volunteering to be your team's "butcher," crafting hot and delicious meat dishes for immediate consumption by your friends.

COMMANDO

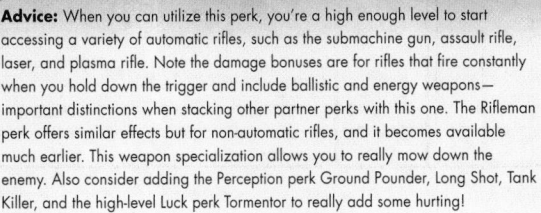

RARITY: RARE
LEVEL: 15
RANKS: ★ ★ ★ ★
POINTS: 1, 2, 3

DESCRIPTION: BASIC COMBAT TRAINING MEANS AUTOMATIC RIFLES DO +10/15/20 DAMAGE.

Advice: When you can utilize this perk, you're a high enough level to start accessing a variety of automatic rifles, such as the submachine gun, assault rifle, laser, and plasma rifle. Note the damage bonuses are for rifles that fire constantly when you hold down the trigger and include ballistic and energy weapons—important distinctions when stacking other partner perks with this one. The Rifleman perk offers similar effects but for non-automatic rifles, and it becomes available much earlier. This weapon specialization allows you to really mow down the enemy. Also consider adding the Perception perk Ground Pounder, Long Shot, Tank Killer, and the high-level Luck perk Tormentor to really add some hurting!

(EXPERT) COMMANDO

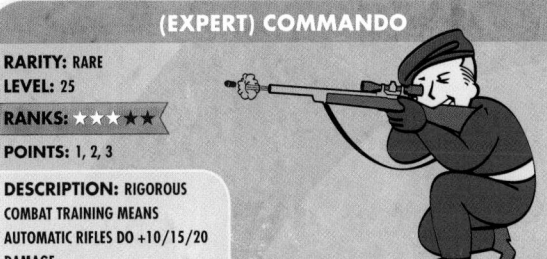

RARITY: RARE
LEVEL: 25
RANKS: ★ ★ ★ ★
POINTS: 1, 2, 3

DESCRIPTION: RIGOROUS COMBAT TRAINING MEANS AUTOMATIC RIFLES DO +10/15/20 DAMAGE.

Advice: Ten more levels later, the second set of Commando perks become available. If you're fully committed to full-automatic takedowns and have the necessary Perception Points to allocate (at the expense of other Perception perks), then start your damage stacking! As a quick calculation, if you want your automatic rifles to inflict +40% more damage, utilize the Commando perk (Rank 3 for 3 points) and the Expert Commando perk (Rank 3 for another 3 points). Also note that it becomes increasingly difficult to utilize other Perception perks that benefit rifles, like Ground Pounder, Long Shot, and Tank Killer: Your maximum Perception won't allow the highest ranks of all these perks to be active, so pick and choose based on what is most potent and effective to your needs.

(MASTER) COMMANDO

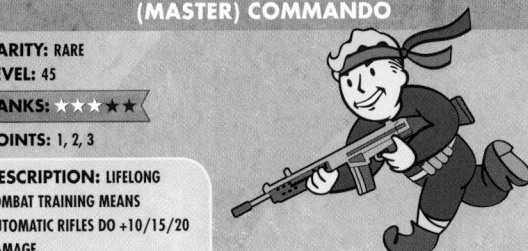

RARITY: RARE
LEVEL: 45
RANKS: ★ ★ ★ ★
POINTS: 1, 2, 3

DESCRIPTION: LIFELONG COMBAT TRAINING MEANS AUTOMATIC RIFLES DO +10/15/20 DAMAGE.

Advice: When you're using automatic rifles to the exception of everything else, and you've found that stacking Commando perks is more beneficial than partnering lower-level Commando perks with other rifle-related Perception perks, then add a final layer of mayhem with Master Commando! It takes nine Perception Points to get +60% additional damage (Commando Rank 3, Expert Commando Rank 3, and Master Commando Rank 3). With so many Perception Points allocated, search the other attributes for partner perks you can use with Commando. Focus on perks that allow even more proficient use of your weapons, like the classic Agility perk Action Boy/Girl or the Strength perks Bandolier and Intelligence Perk. Batteries Included.

CONCENTRATED FIRE

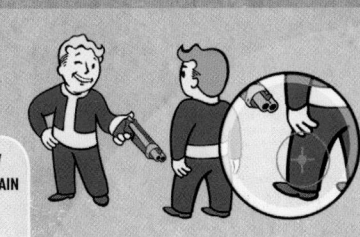

RARITY: COMMON
LEVEL: 2
RANKS: ★ ★ ★ ★
POINTS: 1, 2, 3

DESCRIPTION: V.A.T.S. NOW TARGETS LIMBS. FOCUS FIRE TO GAIN ACCURACY AND DAMAGE/MORE ACCURACY AND DAMAGE/HIGH ACCURACY AND DAMAGE PER HIT.

Advice: There are two separate effects to be aware of once you equip this low-level, must-use perk: First, you have the ability to pick the head, torso, and limbs off any enemy that has them (or specific body parts for foes with more odd forms); this means you can slow foes down by aiming at their legs, prevent them from firing as proficiently by targeting their arms, or just aim for the head, which results in a quicker (and sometimes messier) death. Second, you can "focus fire," which means you receive a small cumulative bonus for aiming at a body part and then hitting it again and again. This is an excellent choice for snipers, those who might later want to partner this perk with damage-bonus perks (as well as benefiting from the accuracy bonuses for each point of Perception you allocate permanently to this attribute). This can lead to exceptionally quick and proficient takedowns. Aim for the head, increase your weapon's damage, and start your V.A.T.S. mastery now!

TRAINING

CRAFTING AND C.A.M.P.ing

INVENTORY

QUESTS

ATLAS

BESTIARY

APPENDICES

CRACK SHOT

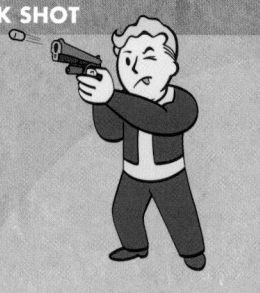

RARITY: RARE
LEVEL: 7
RANKS: ★★★★★
POINTS: 1, 2, 3, 4

DESCRIPTION: ALL PISTOLS HAVE 5/10/15/20% MORE RANGE AND MORE/EVEN MORE/MUCH BETTER/EXCELLENT ACCURACY WHEN SIGHTED.

Advice: Available almost immediately (if you're lucky enough to get one in a Perk Pack!), this grants you more accuracy for sighted pistols, on top of any bonuses a sight might already grant you. This perk gently forces you to try Weapons Workbench modding (e.g., so you can find the components necessary to add to your 10-mm pistol), though there are some sighted pistols out there to pick up at this point in your exploration. Note the twofold advantages—range *and* accuracy—for the weapon. However, it is also worth comparing a sighted pistol with this perk to a nonsighted pistol *without* this perk; if the latter isn't significantly less helpful, or you're finding you can take foes down with or without this perk (as it doesn't grant extra damage, which is a much more helpful perk type), then consider a different perk. The same goes for Vault Dwellers who aren't interested in using pistols.

EXTERMINATOR

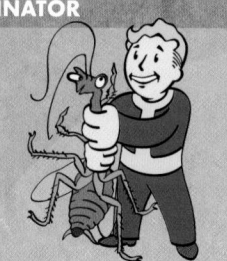

RARITY: COMMON
LEVEL: 14
RANKS: ★★★★★
POINTS: 1, 2, 3

DESCRIPTION: YOUR ATTACKS IGNORE 25%/50%/75% ARMOR OF ANY INSECT.

Advice: Though this perk would have been much more impressive if it wasn't confined to simply insects, it is still an excellent early card to obtain and stack, though it is environmentally situational: That is, you should check to see if irradiated insects have been spotted at a location (listed in this guide's Atlas) before heading into combat. The good news: You can blast Radroaches, Bloodwings, and anything else revolting enough to scuttle about (check this guide's Bestiary for a complete list), and blast them much more easily, with less ammo consumption or weapon damage, and with any weapon you like. The bad news: this is ineffective on any other enemy type.

FIRE IN THE HOLE

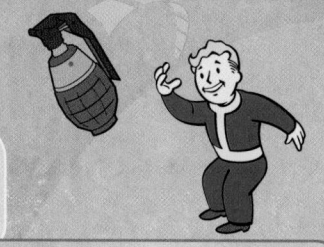

RARITY: RARE
LEVEL: 38
RANKS: ★★★★★
POINTS: 1, 2, 3

DESCRIPTION: SEE A THROWING ARC WHEN TOSSING GRENADES, AND GRENADES FLY 15%/30%/50% FARTHER.

Advice: If you want to cause a disturbance or a distraction, catch a group of foes in an explosion, or add additional offensive capabilities (especially if you're defending a workshop), then having more prowess with grenades can be extremely helpful. Lobbing grenades one-and-a-half times the normal distance (Rank 3), with a trajectory detail to help pinpoint your punting, means you're more likely to hit foes and remove threats (including enemies, human foes trying to assault you or your base, and inanimate objects like fortifications or turrets). Conversely, if you're able to manually throw grenades with expected accuracy more often than not, and you don't need to lob a grenade farther than normal, this isn't a perk to pick; however, you should try it out before making that decision. Think about combining this with the Strength perk Ordnance Express, the Perception perk Grenadier, and the Intelligence perk Demolition Expert.

FORTUNE FINDER

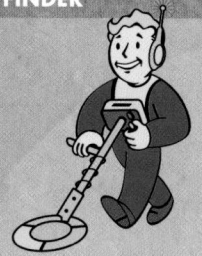

RARITY: COMMON
LEVEL: 22
RANKS: ★★★★★
POINTS: 1

DESCRIPTION: YOU HEAR DIRECTIONAL AUDIO WHEN IN RANGE OF A CAPS STASH.

Advice: This is one of three Perception perks that grant an audible pinging sound (which can occasionally prevent you from hearing important noises like enemies moving) as you close in on a Caps Stash. The other two are Pannapictagraphist (for Magazines) and Percepti-Bobble (for Bobbleheads). This is a low-cost perk, and due to the slightly random nature of how Caps Stashes appear, it's well worth adding if you have a spare slot while exploring (otherwise, refer to the Atlas Chapter of this guide for possible locations). Remember to partner this with the Luck perk Cap Collector, which gives you more Caps for each stash you open.

GLOW SIGHT

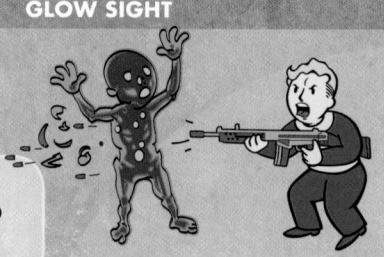

RARITY: UNCOMMON
LEVEL: 33
RANKS: ★★★★★
POINTS: 1, 2, 3

DESCRIPTION: DEAL +20%/40%/60% DAMAGE TO GLOWING ENEMIES.

Advice: When venturing into high-rad zones or entering into combat with especially irradiated enemies (such as the infamous "Glowing One" Ghouls), you may spot certain extra-mutated members of the enemy group that exhibit glowing tendencies. Pick this perk, and you can inflict some pretty substantial additional damage to them! While this perk is highly situational, it's worth taking, especially after a nuclear strike when most of the surviving entities in the blast area are going to be glowing! Otherwise, shelve this perk and quickly bring it out if you see a glowing foe. Partner this with rad-reducing, or damage-increasing perks, at your discretion.

GREEN THUMB

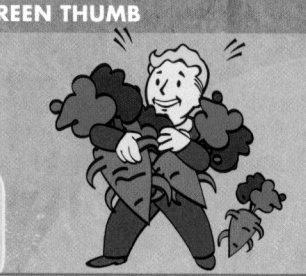

RARITY: COMMON
LEVEL: 4
RANKS: ★★★★★
POINTS: 1

DESCRIPTION: REAP TWICE AS MUCH WHEN HARVESTING FLORA.

Advice: At the start of your explorations outside the Vault, and even during subsequent adventuring when you need to turn to a plant-based recipe at the cooking station, you want to ensure you're getting the most out of the flora dotted throughout Appalachia. This is especially true when you stumble across plants that aren't that common (such as Ash Rose and Aster, and to a lesser extent Melons) or you need to gather crops from a workshop and turn them into tasty beverages or meals for you and your team. You don't have to keep this perk active constantly; just remember to turn it on when foraging. Also check your recipes, decide which food or drink you want to keep making, search for the specific plants needed, and flick the perk on before you start the picking.

GRENADIER

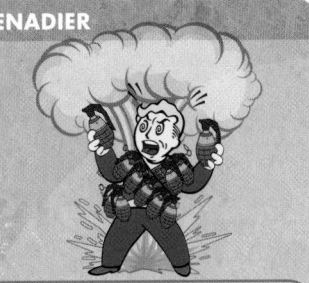

RARITY: RARE
LEVEL: 35
RANKS: ★★★★
POINTS: 1, 2

DESCRIPTION: YOUR EXPLOSIVES DETONATE WITH A 50% LARGER RADIUS/TWICE THE RADIUS.

Advice: If you want to increase the splash damage, also known as area of effect (AoE), of your explosives, then pick this low-cost, reasonably high-level augmentation to your explosives collection. By "collection," remember this applies not just to your projectiles like grenades: Think about the additional radius of your mines and explosive heavy weapons (like the missile launcher and legendary Fat Man), as well as missile turrets and artillery strikes you've made for your camp or workshop. This enables you to place mines farther apart from each other, and changes where you aim your ordnance; you're no longer confined to a specific area. Just be aware of the additional damage this can do in confined spaces! Add additional potency by partnering this with the Strength perk Ordnance Express and the Perception perk Fire in the Hole, but the most help is the Intelligence perk Demolitions Expert, which adds up to 100% extra damage to any type of explosive, bolstering the already-massive damage you can wreak!

GROUND POUNDER

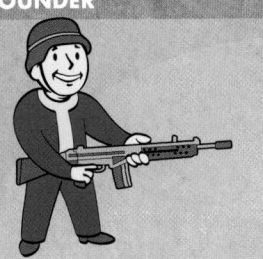

RARITY: RARE
LEVEL: 18
RANKS: ★★★★
POINTS: 1, 2, 3, 4

DESCRIPTION: AUTOMATIC RIFLES NOW RELOAD 10/20/30/40% FASTER AND HAVE BETTER/EVEN BETTER/MUCH BETTER/EXCELLENT HIP FIRE ACCURACY.

Advice: If you're "spraying and praying" with automatic rifles, or you're the kind of sharpshooter who likes to primarily fire your rifle from the hip, then pick this perk that ups your accuracy (when you're not aiming through a sight) and quickens your reload speed (which can really cause havoc as you swap out clips while maintaining an impressive rate of "fire and forget" projectiles). This perk is made to use in situations where covering fire, or mowing down several foes, is required. Just be sure you understand this only affects automatic rifles, not rifles with a bolt action. Now augment this further with rifle-related perks (whether you're focusing on automatic or nonautomatic variants with the Perception perks Commando and Rifleman); pick the Perception perk Long Shot, the Tank Killer, and the Luck perk Tormentor.

LONG SHOT

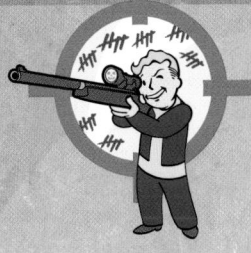

RARITY: RARE
LEVEL: 37
RANKS: ★★★★
POINTS: 1, 2, 3, 4

DESCRIPTION: YOUR RIFLES HAVE 5/10/15/20% MORE RANGE AND MORE/EVEN MORE/MUCH BETTER/EXCELLENT ACCURACY WHEN SIGHTED.

Advice: Though you may immediately think this is an excellent choice for snipers (and it is!), having any weapon in the rifle category that features enhanced range and accuracy (even those that fire automatically, with only a light sighted mod necessary for the perk to work) is an exceptional help to those specializing in rifles. Try out all your rifles with a sight, and this perk, and figure out whether the results fit your play style. Obviously, snipers tend to use sights rather than hip-firing, so this is definitely tailored more to this play style. Whether you're focusing on automatic or nonautomatic variants, add on as many other rifle-related perks as you can, such as the Perception perks Commando and Rifleman; pick the Perception perks Ground Pounder and Tank Killer and the Luck perk Tormentor.

NIGHT EYES

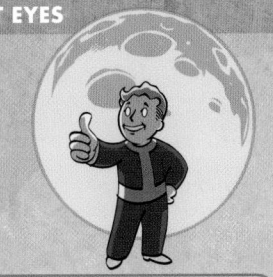

RARITY: RARE
LEVEL: 47
RANKS: ★★★★
POINTS: 2

DESCRIPTION: GAIN NIGHT VISION WHILE SNEAKING BETWEEN 6:00 P.M. AND 6:00 A.M.

Advice: Be completely clear on what this actually does; it gives an enhanced view of your surroundings, not unlike a night vision scope that you can add (as a mod) to some rifles. Dark areas are still there, but shadows are reduced considerably, and you're able to view your surroundings in almost the same detail as during daylight hours. Now be sure you're crouched and sneaking, or Night Vision won't work. Obviously, this adds a great deal to a stealth style of exploration and is usually used as such, though having a better view of an enemy workshop or large location you're about to investigate or overthrow, is always better. Now think about using perks that benefit you during the night (listed in the Night Person perk advice), as well as those V.A.T.S. improving perks, like the Perception perk Concentrated Fire, the Agility perk Gun Fu, and the Luck perks Better Criticals, Critical Savvy, Four Leaf Clover, Grim Reaper's Sprint, and Psychopath.

NIGHT PERSON

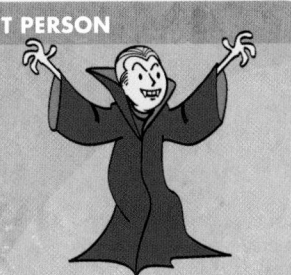

RARITY: UNCOMMON
LEVEL: 24
RANKS: ★★★★
POINTS: 1, 2, 3

DESCRIPTION: GAIN +1/2/3 INT AND +1/2/3 PER BETWEEN THE HOURS OF 6:00 P.M. AND 6:00 A.M.

Advice: First, it's worth figuring out what this additional Intelligence and Perception is going to provide you. Expect better condition and durability of items that you craft; better return from scrapping items (Intelligence); better weapon accuracy in V.A.T.S.; and better situational awareness (Perception). Secondly, figure out the best use of your (night) time, especially if you're utilizing the other perks that work during the night, too. In this case, V.A.T.S. combat in the dark and a whole lot of scrapping and crafting will be in order! If you're after some nighttime combat, add the Perception perk Night Eyes and the Endurance perk Nocturnal Fortitude.

PANNAPICTAGRAPHIST

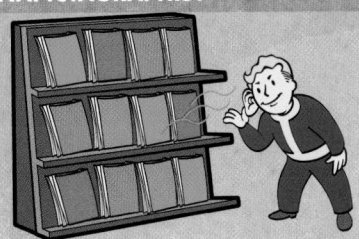

RARITY: COMMON
LEVEL: 12
RANKS: ★★★★
POINTS: 1

DESCRIPTION: YOU HEAR DIRECTIONAL AUDIO WHEN IN RANGE OF A MAGAZINE.

Advice: This is one of three Perception perks that grant an audible pinging sound as you close in on a Magazine. The other two are Fortune Finder (for Caps Stashes) and Percepti-Bobble (for Bobbleheads). This is a low-cost perk, and due to the slightly random nature of how Magazines appear (sometimes they are at a location specified in this guide's atlas, and sometimes not), it's well worth adding if you have a spare slot while exploring (otherwise, refer to the Atlas for possible locations).

TRAINING

CRAFTING AND C.A.M.P.ING

INVENTORY

QUESTS

ATLAS

BESTIARY

APPENDICES

PENETRATOR

RARITY: RARE
LEVEL: 50
RANKS: ★★★★★
POINTS: 1, 2, 3

DESCRIPTION: V.A.T.S. CAN HIT ENEMY BODY PARTS BLOCKED BY COVER WITH REDUCED/IMPROVED/NORMAL ACCURACY.

Advice: This is your ultimate reward if you've been utilizing V.A.T.S. as your go-to combat-planning system of choice, and even if you haven't, it offers something you can't get via regular means—the ability to shoot through cover! Naturally, tufts of grass weren't stopping foes before Penetrator became available, but trees and walls certainly were! Now, nowhere is safe (unless foes are behind two walls!), and at Rank 3, you can dish just as much damage as if you shot them out in the open! Naturally, there are many ways to play with this perk; it's impossible for melee strikes, but it is amazing during a sneak, with a long-range or silenced weapon. Sniper rifles can tag foes at range, and remember, the cover can be near you *or* your victim! This gives you the edge when assaulting an enemy workshop, but also if you're defending one. You can use your own defenses to fire through at foes. Also be sure to partner this with the other V.A.T.S.-improving perks, such as the Perception perk Awareness and Concentrated Fire; the Agility perk Gun Fu; and the Luck perks Better Criticals, Four Leaf Clover, Grim Reaper's Sprint, and Psychopath.

PERCEPTI-BOBBLE

RARITY: COMMON
LEVEL: 16
RANKS: ★★★★★
POINTS: 1

DESCRIPTION: YOU HEAR DIRECTIONAL AUDIO WHEN IN RANGE OF A BOBBLEHEAD.

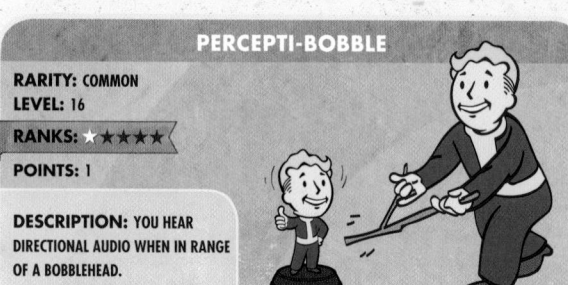

Advice: This is one of three Perception perks that grant an audible pinging sound (which can prevent you from hearing critical noises like adversaries shuffling around) as you close in on a Bobblehead. The other two are Fortune Finder (for Caps Stashes) and Pannapictagraphist (for Magazines). This is a low-cost perk, and due to the slightly random nature of how Bobbleheads appear, it's well worth adding if you have a spare slot while exploring (otherwise, refer to the Atlas for possible locations).

PICKLOCK

RARITY: COMMON
LEVEL: 5
RANKS: ★★★★★
POINTS: 1

DESCRIPTION: GAIN A +1 LOCKPICKING SKILL, AND THE LOCKPICKING "SWEET SPOT" IS 10% LARGER.

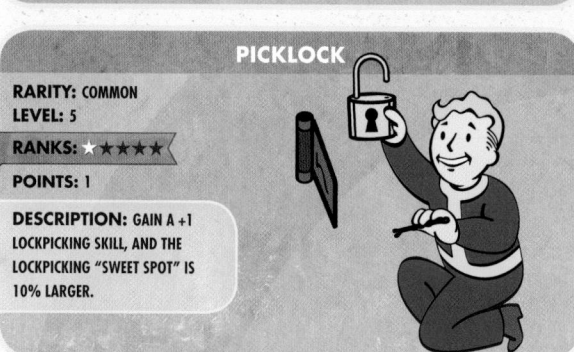

(EXPERT) PICKLOCK

RARITY: COMMON
LEVEL: 19
RANKS: ★★★★★
POINTS: 1

DESCRIPTION: GAIN A +1 LOCKPICKING SKILL, AND THE LOCKPICKING "SWEET SPOT" IS 10% LARGER.

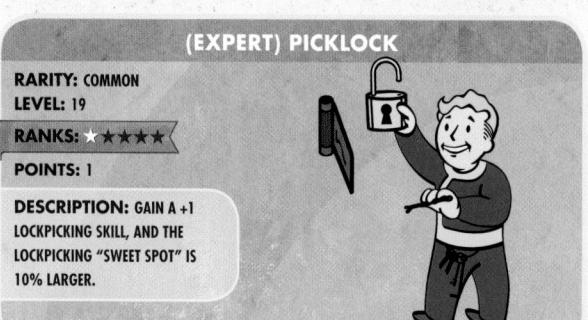

(MASTER) PICKLOCK

RARITY: COMMON
LEVEL: 40
RANKS: ★★★★★
POINTS: 1

DESCRIPTION: GAIN A +1 LOCKPICKING SKILL, AND THE LOCKPICKING "SWEET SPOT" IS 10% LARGER.

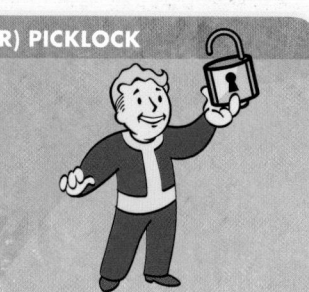

Advice: If you're not activating this perk, whenever you locate a door, container, or safe that requires unlocking (with bobby pins) to open it, only those with a Normal ("0") level of difficulty are accessible, providing you have the bobby pins and solve the minor unlocking puzzle. With the three levels of the Picklock perk, however, the more stubborn locks become accessible, which is important; if you don't have the Picklock perk, you can't even open the higher level doors, safes, and containers. Furthermore, the area where the bobby pin can be rotated to pick the lock successfully widens by 10%, meaning a Master Picklock perk gives you pretty much all of a Normal lock's rotation to open, and bobby pins (which are scavenged) aren't used up nearly as quickly. Picklock allows access of Advanced ("1") locks. Expert Picklock allows access of Expert ("2") locks. And Master Picklock allows access of Master ("3") locks (the toughest). If you only have a few Perception Points, swap these cards out with a Perception perk you run all the time, only swapping back when there's a lock to fiddle with. Remember that you can forgo this perk in favor of the Intelligence perk Hacker, especially as some locations are accessible only via a password-protected terminal. However, most terminals are linked to a door or safe with a lock to pick, so either Picklock or Hacker are viable in around 80% of examples. Note there are far more items hidden behind locked objects than terminals across Appalachia, so between the two perks, choose this one. Just be aware you're missing out on some hidden areas, turret controls, and robot commanding if you do!

REFRACTOR

RARITY: UNCOMMON
LEVEL: 32
RANKS: ★★★★★
POINTS: 1, 2, 3, 4

DESCRIPTION: GAIN +5/10/15/20 ENERGY RESISTANCE.

Advice: Extra protection from certain damage types, without the need for weighty armor, or perks that offer protection but have a negative penalty are always welcome, and Refractor is no exception. Though the protection is relatively light (only 20 points at Rank 4), it does enable you to withstand damage from robots, laser weapons (including the powerful turrets your rivals may be using at their workshop), and plasma weapons (including guns and projectiles such as mines and traps). Pick this perk if you're heading into an environment you know is populated by robots (like Watoga), or when energy-using enemies appear. Otherwise, remember energy damage isn't as common as regular ballistic damage, so you may wish to pick a perk that helps in that regard. Need even more energy resistance? Then partner this with the Charisma perk Bodyguards, the Endurance perk Ironclad, the Agility perks Evasive and Moving Target, and the Luck perk Junk Shield.

RIFLEMAN

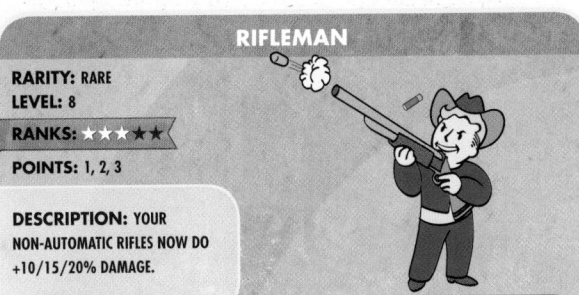

RARITY: RARE
LEVEL: 8
RANKS: ★★★☆☆
POINTS: 1, 2, 3

DESCRIPTION: YOUR NON-AUTOMATIC RIFLES NOW DO +10/15/20% DAMAGE.

Advice: Once activated, which is early in your exploration of Appalachia, you're able to dish out some impressive additional damage with any rifle you've gathered, bought, or crafted, as long as it's nonautomatic. This includes bolt-action based rifles, hunting rifles, and anything you fit a nonautomatic receiver mod onto. Basically, if the weapon is a rifle and doesn't automatically shoot bullets when you hold the trigger down, use this perk! Also think about making one or more of your rifles into an effective, long-distance sniper rifle—one of the keys to using this perk in character builds that benefit from single, high-damage, long-range strikes. Note the Commando perk offers similar effects, but for automatic rifles, and becomes available later in your exploration. This weapon specialization allows you to really dish single, usually well-aimed, and devastating shots (both in and out of V.A.T.S.). Think about adding the Perception perks Ground Pounder, Long Shot, Tank Killer, and the high-level Luck perk Tormentor to heighten your one-shot kill chances!

(EXPERT) RIFLEMAN

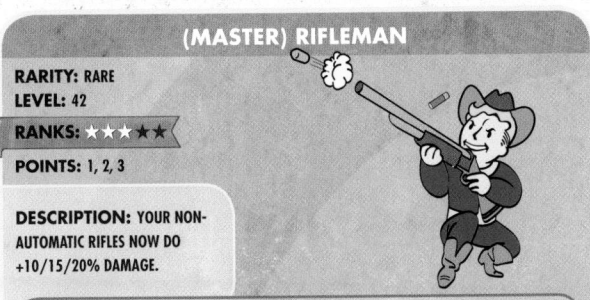

RARITY: RARE
LEVEL: 20
RANKS: ★★★☆☆
POINTS: 1, 2, 3

DESCRIPTION: YOUR NON-AUTOMATIC RIFLES NOW DO +10/15/20% DAMAGE.

Advice: After around 12 more levels of exploration, the next set of Rifleman perks start to show up. If you're single-minded in your single-shot takedown philosophy, and you're enjoying the nonautomatic rifle methods of foe disposal, and you have the necessary Perception Points to allocate (at the expense of other Perception perks), then start your damage stacking! As a quick calculation, if you want your nonautomatic rifles to inflict +40% more damage, utilize the Rifleman perk (Rank 3 for 3 points) and the Expert Rifleman perk (Rank 3 for another 3 points). Also note that it becomes increasingly difficult to utilize other Perception perks that benefit rifles, like Ground Pounder, Long Shot, and Tank Killer: Your maximum Perception won't allow the highest ranks of all these perks to be active, so pick and choose based on what is most potent and effective to your needs.

(MASTER) RIFLEMAN

RARITY: RARE
LEVEL: 42
RANKS: ★★★☆☆
POINTS: 1, 2, 3

DESCRIPTION: YOUR NON-AUTOMATIC RIFLES NOW DO +10/15/20% DAMAGE.

Advice: If you're employing nonautomatic rifles to the exception of everything else, then your Perception attribute is doing all the heavy lifting for this series of perks: If stacking Rifleman perks is more beneficial than partnering lower-level Rifleman perks with other rifle-related Perception perks, then add a final layer of mayhem with Master Rifleman! It takes nine Perception Points to get +60% additional damage (Rifleman Rank 3, Expert Rifleman Rank 3, and Master Rifleman Rank 3). With so many Perception Points allocated, search the other attributes for partner perks you can use with Rifleman. Focus on perks that allow even more proficient use of your weapons, like the classic Agility perk Action Boy/Girl or the Strength perk Bandolier and Intelligence Perk Batteries Included.

SKEET SHOOTER

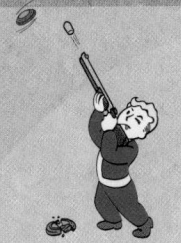

RARITY: RARE
LEVEL: 10
RANKS: ★★★★☆
POINTS: 1, 2, 3, 4

DESCRIPTION: YOUR SHOTGUNS HAVE IMPROVED/EVEN BETTER/MUCH BETTER/EXCELLENT ACCURACY AND SPREAD.

Advice: Make your enemies squirm with more focused shotgun blasts; while this doesn't change the relatively short distance, it really ups the accuracy. Partner perks from the Strength attribute also augment this already-impressive (and quite low-level) offensive perk: Scattershot and Shotgunner are both exceptionally helpful. Then add in the Agility perk Enforcer, and you're able to spread out your points while concentrating on making your boomsticks the very best they can be—and that's before any modifications at your Weapons Workbench!

SNIPER

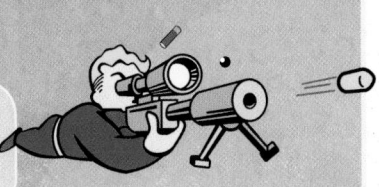

RARITY: RARE
LEVEL: 28
RANKS: ★★★☆☆
POINTS: 1, 2, 3

DESCRIPTION: GAIN IMPROVED CONTROL AND HOLD YOUR BREATH 20/40/60% LONGER WHILE AIMING SCOPES.

Advice: Providing you're actually employing the scope in question and you're using aim-enhancing chems like Jet to aid your targeting, this is an extremely helpful perk for long-distance takedowns. Tagging foes at range, without the "wobble" of normal sniper rifle aiming, allows for more proficient kills, though you want to watch the length of time you need to hold your breath for, as you may simply reload before you run out of breath at higher ranks of this perk, making it less necessary. Add all the beneficial Perception perks, as well as stealth-related perks if your sniping is more clandestine and less about charging in afterward. Don't bother with Long Shot, though; unfortunately the benefits of that perk are related to sights, not scopes.

TANK KILLER

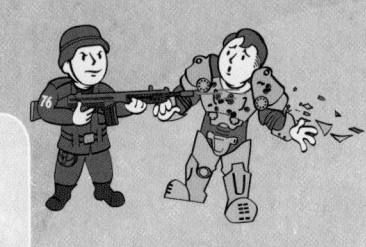

RARITY: RARE
LEVEL: 30
RANKS: ★★★★☆
POINTS: 1, 2, 3, 4

DESCRIPTION: YOUR RIFLES IGNORE 10%/20%/30%/40% ARMOR AND HAVE A 2%/4%/6%/8% CHANCE TO STAGGER.

Advice: Working for both automatic and nonautomatic rifles, this has huge benefits if you're choosing these weapons as the main method of foe disposal. Though you might immediately see the benefits of employing this with a sniper rifle (which is an excellent idea), this perk is just as potent with a submachine gun or auto assault rifle. Note the twofold benefits—ignoring some armor *and* a small stagger chance. Now up the potency by partnering this with the main Perception rifle perks Commando and Rifleman, Ground Pounder, Adrenaline, Evasive, and various other stealth-related or conditional perks (mainly using Agility). And don't forget the Luck card Tormentor.

TRAINING

CRAFTING AND C.A.M.P.ING

INVENTORY

QUESTS

ATLAS

BESTIARY

APPENDICES

ENDURANCE

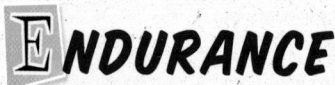

- **MODIFICATIONS: MAXIMUM HIT POINTS, DISEASE RESISTANCE**
- **BUFFS: ENDURANCE BOBBLEHEAD, SOLAR POWERED (ENDURANCE), ARMOR AND CLOTHING BONUSES AND EFFECTS, BUFFJET, BUFFTATS, PSYCHOBUFF, X-CELL, BOURBON**

Endurance is a measure of your overall physical fitness. It affects your total health, the Action Point drain from sprinting, and your resistance to disease. Health is the amount of damage you can take before dying. Obviously a higher Health is more helpful, especially if you enjoy a more reckless fighting style, rather than lurking in the shadows when slaying foes. As Action Points (APs) and sprinting are both incredibly important, a larger AP reserve (and thus the ability to sprint over longer distances) is most helpful. The higher your Endurance, the lower your chance to catch a disease.

VALUE	MAX HEALTH	SPRINTING AP DRAIN REDUCED BY:
1	250	5%
2	255	10%
3	260	15%
4	265	20%
5	270	25%
6	275	30%
7	280	35%
8	285	40%
9	290	45%
10	295	50%
11	300	55%
12	305	60%
13	310	65%
14	315	70%
15	320	75%

ENDURANCE-RELATED PERKS: OVERVIEW

Endurance focuses on your health and well-being; in fact, the first 12 available perks (in level order) feature a bonus to eating, drinking, or taking chems (including extra benefits from Nuka-Cola!). Expect more pronounced bonuses of this nature, with perks enabling limb regeneration and novel (and sometimes disgusting) new ways you can reduce your thirst and hunger. Additional types of resistance (Rads, and to a lesser extent, fire), help with alcohol withdrawal, and toward the higher-level perks, actual regeneration of health or radiation damage, or just a large bonus to your health. Need to tweak your ingestion and consumption? This is the attribute to check out.

ENDURANCE PERKS (31)

The following table shows all 31 Endurance Perk Cards, listed by the earliest level you can obtain them.

PERK NAME	C	U	R	LEVEL	RANKS	DESCRIPTION
Lead Belly	x			2	1, 2, 3	You take 30% less radiation /60% less radiation/no radiation from eating or drinking.
Dromedary	x			3	1, 2, 3	All drinks quench thirst by an additional 25/50/75%.
Iron Stomach		x		4	1, 2, 3	Your chance to catch a disease from food is reduced by 30/60/90%.
Slow Metabolizer	x			5	1, 2, 3	All food satisfies hunger by an additional 25/50/75%.
Thirst Quencher		x		6	1, 2, 3	Drinking any liquid has a 30/60/90% reduced chance to cause disease.
Good Doggy	x			8	1	Eating dog food is now three times as beneficial.
Natural Resistance		x		10	1, 2, 3	You are 30/60/90% less likely to catch a disease from the environment.
Hydro Fix	x			12	1, 3	Chems generate 50% less/no thirst.
Rejuvenated	x			12	1, 2	You gain increased/ much increased benefit from being Well Fed or Well Hydrated.
Cola Nut		x		14	1, 2	Nuka-Cola products are now twice/three times as beneficial.
Vaccinated		x		16	1, 2, 3	Chance of catching a disease from creatures is reduced by 30/60/90%.
Munchy Resistance		x		17	1, 3	Using chems induces 50% less/no hunger.
Homebody Card	x			19	1, 2	Gain gradual health regeneration/improved health and limb regeneration while in your camp or workshop.
Adamantium Skeleton			x	21	1, 2, 3, 4, 5	Your limb damage is now reduced by 20/40/60/80/100%.
Solar-Powered		x		22	1, 2, 3	Gain +1/2/3 to STR and END between the hours of 6:00 a.m. and 6:00 p.m..
Chem Fiend		x		23	1, 2, 3	Any chems you take last 30/60/100% longer.
Cannibal		x		25	1, 2, 3	Eating human, Ghoul, Super Mutant, Scorched, or Mole Miner corpses restores some/more/even more Health and hunger.
Aqua Boy/Girl	x			26	1	You no longer take Rad damage from swimming and can breathe underwater.
Fireproof		x		27	1, 2, 3	Immediately gain +20/40/60 Fire Resistance.
Nocturnal Fortitude			x	29	1, 2	Gain +20/+40 to Max Health between the hours of 6:00 p.m. and 6:00 a.m.
Ironclad			x	30	1, 2, 3, 4, 5	You now gain 10/20/30/40/50 Damage and Energy Resistance while not wearing Power Armor.
Revenant			x	32	1, 2	Gain a +25/50% damage bonus for 2 minutes when a player revives you.
Rad Resistant	x			34	1, 2, 3, 4	Gain +10/20/30/40 Radiation Resistance.
Ghoulish	x			36	1, 2, 3	Radiation now regenerates some/even more/even more of your lost Health.
Radicool			x	38	1	The greater your Rads, the greater your Strength (max +5 STR)!
Professional Drinker	x			39	3	There's no chance you'll get addicted to alcohol.
All Night Long	x			41	1, 2, 3	You suffer 20/40/60% less from hunger and thirst.
Chem Resistant	x			43	1, 2	You're half as likely to get addicted when consuming Chems/you gain complete immunity to chem addiction.
Sun-Kissed	x			45	1, 1	Slowly/quickly regen radiation damage between the hours of 6:00 a.m. and 6:00 p.m.
Photosynthetic			x	47	1, 2	Gain Health regeneration/improved Health regeneration between the hours of 6:00 a.m. and 6:00 p.m.
Lifegiver			x	50	2, 3, 4	Gain a total of +15/30/45 to your maximum Health.

ADAMANTIUM SKELETON

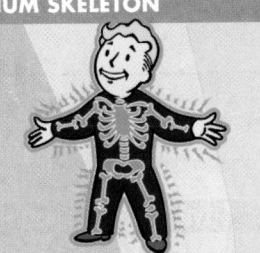

RARITY: RARE
LEVEL: 21
RANKS: ★★★★★
POINTS: 1, 2, 3, 4, 5

DESCRIPTION: YOUR LIMB DAMAGE IS NOW REDUCED BY 20%/40%/60%/80%/100%.

Advice: This effectively lessens and removes (at Rank 5) any chance of your limbs becoming crippled due to enemy attacks or environmental mishaps, such as falling. It stops any rival player from utilizing the bonuses of some weapon-specific and offensive perks like the Agility perk Modern Renegade, as well as V.A.T.S. limb targeting (i.e., a foe needs to target your head or torso) or weaponry with a crippling chance. However, the high point cost means you should weigh whether this perk is a better option than spending 5 Endurance Points on perks offering a more general level of protection. As crippled limbs are healed using a Stimpak, you can easily return from being crippled, so this perk's usefulness is questionable. However, if you want to completely rid yourself of "extremities damage" (including occasional leg-breaking from being overly encumbered or vision loss from a sniper's headshot) and heal using something other than Stimpaks (you're using Rads with the Endurance perks Ghoulish and Sun Kissed together), then this perk becomes essential.

ALL NIGHT LONG

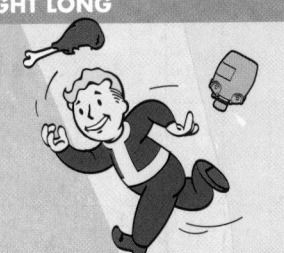

RARITY: COMMON
LEVEL: 41
RANKS: ★★★★★
POINTS: 1, 2, 3

DESCRIPTION: YOU SUFFER 20%/40%/60% LESS FROM HUNGER AND THIRST.

Advice: By the time you reach the level necessary for this perk to become available, you'll have eaten and drunk hundreds of times, so you may be thankful to ignore this aspect of "self maintenance" and go 60% longer (Rank 3) before needing a drink or meal. Though the perk still means you'll need to keep your Hunger and Thirst meters above 75% for the relevant bonuses, not needing to craft recipes or hunt for boxed food or drinks frees you up for other activities. You can add this to the other perks that help stave off hunger and thirst, such as the Endurance perks Hydro Fix/Munchy Resistance and Dromedary/Slow Metabolizer and the Charisma perks Bloodsucker, Happy Camper, and Philanthropist.

AQUA BOY/GIRL

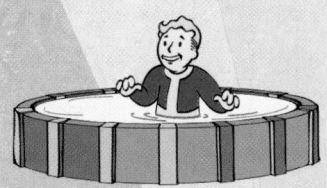

RARITY: COMMON
LEVEL: 26
RANKS: ★★★★★
POINTS: 1

DESCRIPTION: YOU NO LONGER TAKE RAD DAMAGE FROM SWIMMING AND CAN BREATHE UNDERWATER.

Advice: Assuming you're not actively gathering Rads to become a "Ghoulish" character (see perk), being able to more thoroughly search bodies of water without worrying about Rads and health loss means you can grab absolutely everything there is to find in most locations, including in underwater alcoves. Breathing underwater is helpful, as it more easily allows you to search for and gather underwater objects (like junk in the middle of Twin Lakes or the underwater Kerwood Mine and some flooded quarries in Cranberry Bog) without worrying about drowning (especially as retrieving your junk bag can be a real pain). However, underwater activities are minimal across Appalachia, and the small amount of Rad damage (outside of Toxic Valley) can be easily negated using a simple RadAway. Keep this ready in case of submerging, though!

CANNIBAL

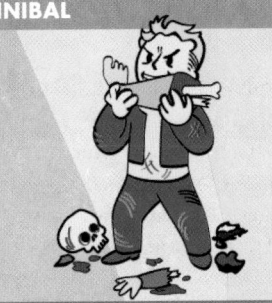

RARITY: UNCOMMON
LEVEL: 25
RANKS: ★★★★★
POINTS: 1, 2, 3

DESCRIPTION: EATING HUMAN, GHOUL, SUPER MUTANT, SCORCHED, OR MOLE MINER CORPSES RESTORES SOME/MORE/EVEN MORE HEALTH AND HUNGER.

Advice: Who needs Stimpaks?! If your answer is "Not me, I've acquired the taste for mutated flesh!" then welcome to your perfect perk, you deviant! While this may not be an etiquette-pleaser, it's a stomach-filler, negating the need for Stimpaks AND food! As you're always close to a dead ghoul, Scorched, or Super-mutant, you have an abundant crop of meals, even if they all taste a bit like mutated chicken. Human flesh is on the menu too—not from other players, but from the corpses of raiders and dwellers from other vaults that you may find rotting across Appalachia. While some deem this revolting and antisocial, others crave this perk, as it allows you to heal without Stimpaks and RadAway. This is key to staying alive while utilizing the benefits that Rads give you, as long as you have the Endurance perks Ghoulish and Sun Kissed working together, Radicool, the Charisma perks Overly Generous and Rad Sponge, and the Luck perk Storm Chaser.

CHEM FIEND

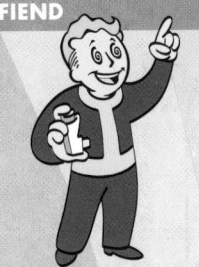

RARITY: UNCOMMON
LEVEL: 23
RANKS: ★★★★★
POINTS: 1, 2, 3

DESCRIPTION: ANY CHEMS YOU TAKE LAST 30%/60%/100% LONGER.

Advice: While you'll need to wait a while for the perfect partner perk to become available (i.e., the Endurance perk Chem Resistant, which removes any addiction problems associated with chems [Rank 2]), you may not need it if you can manage your narcotic intake correctly; taking chems that last twice as long means you'll become addicted around half as often! Expect to become addicted after taking around five of the same type of chem (excluding Stimpaks), and if you don't have Addictol (a rare chem that cures Addiction), using this perk lengthens the time before this occurs. Need additional Strength and Endurance buffs for double the time? Then take Buffout and have Chem Fiend active! Furthermore, the Strength perk Traveling Pharmacy reduces your chem weights, and the Endurance perks Hydro Fix and Munchy Resistance removes some or all of the thirst and hunger problems connected with chem consumption, too.

TRAINING

CRAFTING AND C.A.M.P.ING

INVENTORY

QUESTS

ATLAS

BESTIARY

APPENDICES

CHEM RESISTANT

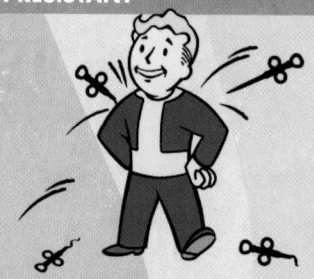

RARITY: COMMON
LEVEL: 43
RANKS: ★★☆☆☆
POINTS: 1, 2

DESCRIPTION: YOU'RE HALF AS LIKELY TO GET ADDICTED WHEN CONSUMING CHEMS OR YOU GAIN COMPLETE IMMUNITY TO CHEM ADDICTION.

Advice: If you haven't acquired a plentiful supply of Addictol by this point in your leveling up (a rare chem that cures you of chem dependency), forgo the entire hassle of negative consequences of chem withdrawal and become immune to everything chem-related, from Psycho to Mentats! By this point, you're usually able to make your own chems (and the Intelligence perk Chemist gives you up to triple the quantity when crafting them) and carry a larger number of them (thanks to the Strength perk Traveling Pharmacy that reduces your chem weights), so you can start popping those Mentats like your life depended on it—because it could! Stack chem effects, carefully check the Chems section of this guide for good combinations of chems to utilize, and never worry about the side effects! Just be sure you have the Endurance perks Hydro Fix and Munchy Resistance (to remove some or all of the Thirst and Hunger) if you don't have a stock of food and drink to take afterward.

DROMEDARY

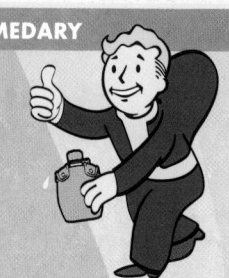

RARITY: COMMON
LEVEL: 3
RANKS: ★★★☆☆
POINTS: 1, 2, 3

DESCRIPTION: ALL DRINKS QUENCH THIRST BY AN ADDITIONAL 25/50/75%.

Advice: As you may be wandering around the initial valley outside Vault 76 when this perk becomes available, it's a great perk to take early on. Thirst is more of a problem than Hunger, so you should aim to keep your thirst meter above 75% to receive the Well Hydrated bonus (AP Regeneration and Disease Resistance), and never adventure when you're below 25% or receive the Parched penalty (AP reduction and less Disease Resistance). How is this achieved? By adding this perk and lengthening the time between drinks. This allows you to utilize less water (or other liquids), and take more consumables (such as chems) that make you thirsty. Increase the hydration bonuses by employing later perks like the Endurance perk All Night Long, Hydro Fix, Lead Belly, Thirst Quencher, the Charisma perk Happy Camper, and Philanthropist. Note the "sister" perk of this is the Endurance perk Slow Metabolizer.

COLA NUT

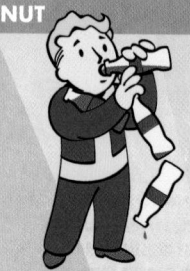

RARITY: UNCOMMON
LEVEL: 14
RANKS: ★★☆☆☆
POINTS: 1, 2

DESCRIPTION: NUKA-COLA PRODUCTS ARE NOW TWICE/THREE TIMES AS BENEFICIAL.

Advice: If you had a Cappy bedspread back in Vault 76, and you've acquired a hankering for that Nuka-Cola taste, there's good news: Appalachia is full of the stuff! Even better news: this perk is available relatively early on, and the benefits—Hit Points and Action Points per Nuka-Cola—are pretty impressive. Relatively common are Nuka-Cherry drinks, which give much-improved HP and AP increases (and more Rads), but finding Nuka-Cherry is relatively random (expect between 1 and 3 in the larger locations). Much more rare is Nuka-Cola Quantum, offering a massive HP and AP gain (and low Rads), and the Kanawha Nuka-Cola Plant (the Forest, Zone D) is the best place to forage for those. While you may not be at a high-enough level to get the full, tripled (Rank 2) benefits of a Nuka-Cola Quantum, having this active every time you take a Nuka-Cola or Cherry is an excellent way to get free health and APs, and quench your thirst. Simply take a RadAway to ward off the Rads. Or, if you plan to use Rads to your benefit (see the Endurance perk Cannibal), this can heal you without using Stimpaks.

FIREPROOF

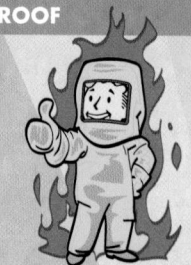

RARITY: UNCOMMON
LEVEL: 27
RANKS: ★★★☆☆
POINTS: 1, 2, 3

DESCRIPTION: IMMEDIATELY GAIN +20/40/60 FIRE RESISTANCE.

Advice: While ostensibly helpful when you're exploring the more "inclement" locations of the Ash Heap that are literally on fire (the aptly named Burning Mine is a great example), having the ability to shrug off over half (Rank 3) of any fire damage you receive is helpful if you find yourself on the receiving end of a Flare Gun or the heavy gun Flamer, if you step near a flamethrower trap (usually at a camp or workshop), if you're struck by a Molotov Cocktail, or if you set oil ablaze. Mr. Handy robots also sometimes like to torch you (or explode in a fiery inferno) too. However, other than these examples, being hurt by fire is a relatively rare occurrence, so you may wish to play this Perk card under specific circumstances rather than all the time, freeing up other Endurance cards in the process. Note that Fireproof is required in order to construct Flamethrowers at your own camp or workshop.

GHOULISH

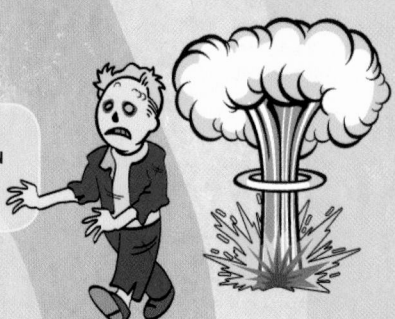

RARITY: COMMON
LEVEL: 36
RANKS: ★★★☆☆
POINTS: 1, 2, 3

DESCRIPTION: RADIATION NOW REGENERATES SOME/EVEN MORE/EVEN MORE OF YOUR LOST HEALTH.

Advice: Radiation damage is eventually going to kill you; once that red bar fills up your HP meter from right to left, even the most mutated and radiation-riddled adventurer is unable to continue. However, if you can correctly manage your Rads, initially using Rad-X and RadAway, you can use radiation to your advantage, especially when the Ghoulish perk becomes available. Here's how Ghoulish works: Step into an irradiated environment, and any missing health is gradually restored, *while at the same time* your radiation damage starts to increase. Eventually, they meet in the middle of your health bar, before the radiation continues to kill you. This has the hidden benefit of making anything radioactive that you ingest (like uncooked food) more "healthy," as the radiation also bolsters health! When health starts to diminish instead of increase, reach for the RadAway, or better yet, have the Endurance perk Sun Kissed, which constantly knocks your radiation back out of danger levels. Add some insurance with the Agility perk Born Survivor, the Charisma perk Field Surgeon, Rad Sponge if you're with a team and a host of other radiation or radiation resistance–related perks.

GOOD DOGGY

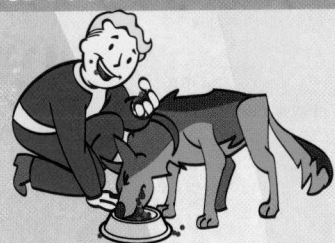

RARITY: COMMON
LEVEL: 8
RANKS: ★★★★
POINTS: 1

DESCRIPTION: EATING DOG FOOD IS NOW THREE TIMES AS BENEFICIAL.

Advice: Not all perks offer amazing benefits. But most offer something a little more impressive than a small Hit Points increase, some light radiation, and the ignominy of gulping down Fido's lunch. If there was a Doghouse Brand Factory right next to the Kanawha Nuka-Cola Plant, then this would be a great perk to take. But Good Doggy isn't anywhere near as useful as Cola Nut, and Canned Dog Food is far less prevalent across the Appalachian wilderness. Sure, you can check with a vendor or your friends, and scavenge every container or home with a blue plastic dog bowl you might spot. And when you find a can, be sure to activate this perk (if you accidentally chose to add it). Eating mongrel dog meat doesn't count either!

HOMEBODY

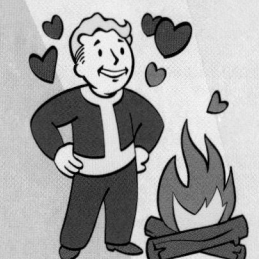

RARITY: COMMON
LEVEL: 19
RANKS: ★★★★
POINTS: 1, 2

DESCRIPTION: GAIN GRADUAL HEALTH REGENERATION/ IMPROVED HEALTH AND LIMB REGENERATION WHILE IN YOUR CAMP OR WORKSHOP.

Advice: This is a particularly excellent "passive" perk to swap in after you limp home from a successful foraging, but with some rather worrying health loss and crippled limbs. By the level at which this perk appears, you should have figured out a proper use of your time, where you're scavenging before returning to your home base (a camp or workshop) to craft, repair, and modify items; add new sections to your structures; and heal yourself. Partner this with the Endurance perk Photosynthetic or Sun Kissed if you're camping during daylight hours; the Charisma perk Happy Camper; and the Luck perk Storm Chaser if the weather is lousy. Now you can save the Stimpaks; just potter around your base of operations and gradually become well again. There's no place like home!

HYDRO FIX

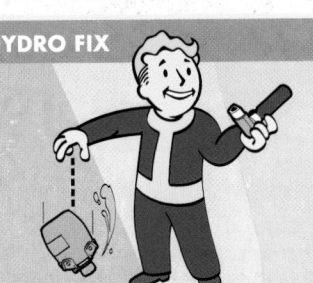

RARITY: COMMON
LEVEL: 12
RANKS: ★★★★
POINTS: 1, 3

DESCRIPTION: CHEMS GENERATE 50% LESS/NO THIRST.

Advice: If you don't wish to gather components in order to make thirst-quenching recipes on your cooking station, and you're a big fan of chems, then this is a helpful perk that's available relatively early in your exploration. While this doesn't negate the addiction aspects of chem dependency, it does reduce or wipe out (Rank 2) the reduction in your Thirst meter, allowing you to keep the Well Hydrated bonus for longer. However, if you've focused on making a quantity of drink, think about satisfying your thirst that way. Obviously, if you're not using chems (and only the chems that make you thirsty), this isn't necessary to utilize at all. You may want to lessen the problems of thirst by also employing the Endurance perks All Night Long and Chem Fiend. There is a Hunger-based variant of this perk called Munchy Resistance.

IRON STOMACH

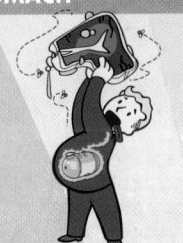

RARITY: UNCOMMON
LEVEL: 4
RANKS: ★★★★
POINTS: 1, 2, 3

DESCRIPTION: YOUR CHANCE TO CATCH A DISEASE FROM FOOD IS REDUCED BY 30%/60%/90%.

Advice: Whether you're gnawing down on a delicious Salisbury Steak, or taking in the broth-based benefits of a warm Carrot Soup, then worry no more; this perk lessens your chances of catching a disease from anything you eat. Now, you'll still receive other negative effects from such conditions (like possible radiation damage), but diseases won't be part of the aftereffects. As it's relatively easy to find or concoct a Cure Disease salve, and diseases (while detrimental) never usually kill you and can lead to more impressive mutations (with both positive and negative effects), you may find this perk to be less helpful, especially as time passes. But if you're overwhelmed by all the ways Appalachia is out to get you, remove one of these problems almost entirely (at Rank 3). If you want to remove disease threats from your drink, environment, and enemies (leaving only sleeping on the ground or being struck by a trap as the ways to become diseased), choose the Endurance perks Natural Resistance (environment), Thirst Quencher (drink), and Vaccinated (enemies).

IRONCLAD

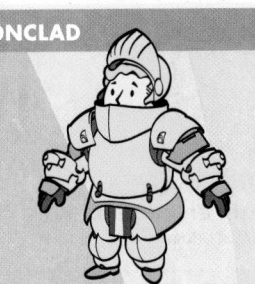

RARITY: RARE
LEVEL: 30
RANKS: ★★★★★
POINTS: 1, 2, 3, 4, 5

DESCRIPTION: YOU NOW GAIN 10/20/30/40/50 DAMAGE AND ENERGY RESISTANCE WHILE NOT WEARING POWER ARMOR.

Advice: This perk is essentially some extra free armor, becoming accessible once you're wearing no armor, or any piece of normal armor (not Power Armor). Though the point cost can be steep (5 points for 50 Damage and Energy Resistance), the protection is from the two most common forms of damage (ballistic and energy). Shrugging off more of your enemies' attacks (without adding to your Carry Weight) is always worth considering. While this is a simple and effective perk, you can use others to "stack" with this one, like the Strength perks Barbarian and Bullet Shield, the Charisma perk Lone Wanderer, and the Intelligence perk Nerd Rage.

LEADBELLY

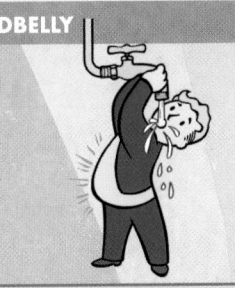

RARITY: COMMON
LEVEL: 2
RANKS: ★★★★★
POINTS: 1, 2, 3

DESCRIPTION: YOU TAKE 30% LESS RADIATION /60% LESS RADIATION/NO RADIATION FROM EATING OR DRINKING.

Advice: Note the level that this perk becomes available and then utilize it; you're likely to obtain this very early in your exploration. Any time you can eat and drink (activities you undertake frequently in order to maintain a Well Fed and Well Hydrated bonus), you are also ingesting a small amount of radiation through these consumables that you can lessen with Rad-X and remove with RadAway. This does away (at Rank 3) with radiation damage from food and drink, essentially giving you the full bonus of the meal or liquid. If you're using RadAways too frequently, take this. If you're fine with your RadAway management, this becomes less vital. Later on, you may want a bit of radiation to help with your mutations, and there are perks that actively reward you when you actually take radiation damage, like Ghoulish, but for the moment, radiation is bad.

TRAINING

CRAFTING AND C.A.M.P.ING

INVENTORY

QUESTS

ATLAS

BESTIARY

APPENDICES

LIFEGIVER

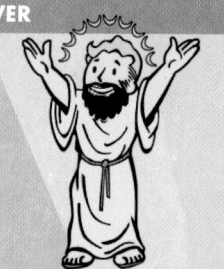

RARITY: UNCOMMON

LEVEL: 50

RANKS: ★★★☆☆

POINTS: 2, 3, 4

DESCRIPTION: GAIN A TOTAL OF +15/30/45 TO YOUR MAXIMUM HEALTH.

Advice: This is a good, old-fashioned, no-nonsense, high-level, easy-to-understand perk that simply increases your maximum health by a maximum of 45 (Rank 3). Unlike other perks that reward you with more health (like the Endurance perk Nocturnal Fortitude), there are no other stipulations; just add this perk, and receive additional Health to help prevent death, allow you to absorb more damage and Rads, and change the timing of when related perks kick in (like those that utilize Stimpaks or grant bonuses when you reach a certain low health threshold). As your Endurance Point score is the arbiter of increasing your Hit Points, this may be a good perk to use to bolster that, if you've not focused on Endurance earlier. Or, you can focus on boosting your armor, damage-resistance, and healing chems so losing Health is less of a threat to your overall well-being.

MUNCHY RESISTANCE

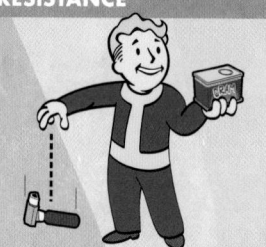

RARITY: UNCOMMON

LEVEL: 17

RANKS: ★★★★★

POINTS: 1, 3

DESCRIPTION: USING CHEMS INDUCES 50% LESS/NO HUNGER.

Advice: If you're not wanting to forage for food components in order to make delicious meals using recipes on your cooking station (or grab Cram, Sugar Bombs, or Salisbury Steaks more frequently) *and* you're a big fan of chems, then this is a helpful perk that's available relatively early in your exploration. While this doesn't negate the addiction aspects of chem dependency, it does reduce or wipe out (Rank 2) the reduction in your Hunger meter, allowing you to keep the Well Fed bonus for longer. However, if you've focused on making a quantity of food (of the non-spoiling kind), or you can easily pause the action and chef up a meal, think about satisfying your hunger that way. Obviously, if you're not using chems (and only the chems that make you hungry), this isn't necessary to utilize at all. You may want to lessen the problems of hunger by also employing the Endurance perks All Night Long and Chem Fiend. There is a Thirst-based variant of this perk called Hydro Fix.

PHOTOSYNTHETIC

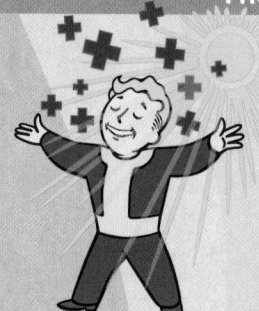

RARITY: RARE

LEVEL: 47

RANKS: ★★★★★

POINTS: 1, 2

DESCRIPTION: GAIN HEALTH REGENERATION/ IMPROVED HEALTH REGENERATION BETWEEN THE HOURS OF 6:00 A.M. AND 6:00 P.M..

NATURAL RESISTANCE

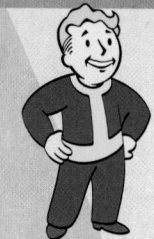

RARITY: UNCOMMON

LEVEL: 10

RANKS: ★★★★★

POINTS: 1, 2, 3

DESCRIPTION: YOU ARE 30%/60%/90% LESS LIKELY TO CATCH A DISEASE FROM THE ENVIRONMENT.

Advice: Whether you're journeying into an environment where Rad storms deluge you with irradiated rain, moving through irradiated ponds, breathing in fetid air in the Ash Heap or Toxic Valley, or otherwise experiencing unpleasant environmental effects (which are usually announced in the top-left corner of your screen), then rest assured, your chances of catching a disease from such inclement conditions is lessened by using this perk. Now, you'll still receive other negative effects from such conditions (like radiation damage and health loss if you're breathing in toxic vapors), but diseases won't be part of the aftereffects. As it's relatively easy to find or concoct a Cure Disease salve, and diseases (while detrimental) never usually kill you and can lead to more impressive mutations (with both positive and negative effects), you may find this perk to be less helpful, especially as time passes. But if you're overwhelmed by all the ways Appalachia is trying to damage you, remove one of these problems almost entirely (at Rank 3). If you want to remove disease threats from your food, drink, and enemies (leaving only sleeping on the ground or being struck by a trap as the ways to become diseased), choose the Endurance perks Iron Stomach (food), Thirst Quencher (drink), and Vaccinated (enemies).

NOCTURNAL FORTITUDE

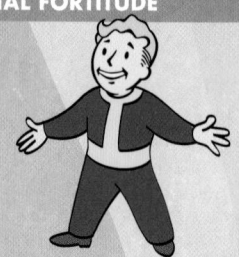

RARITY: RARE

LEVEL: 29

RANKS: ★★★★★

POINTS: 1, 2

DESCRIPTION: GAIN +20/+40 TO MAX HEALTH BETWEEN THE HOURS OF 6:00 P.M. AND 6:00 A.M.

Advice: More health during nighttime prowls? What an excellent idea, especially if you're one to utilize the cover of darkness for clandestine sneaking, which makes you visually a little more difficult to spot, especially if you're trying to get the jump on an enemy human, team, or workshop settlement. Even if you're wandering around, shooting anything with the subtlety of a super mutant, some extra health is obviously extremely handy. If you're tailoring your more violent explorations to the night (meaning you craft, rest, build your camp and workshop, or trade during the day), partner this with the Perception perks Night Eyes and Night Person, as well as the Agility perk Mister Sandman.

Advice: If you don't want to expend items like Nuka-Cola or Stimpaks in order to raise your Hit Points, you could simply bask in the sun all day and not worry too much about your health, as it's always healing back to maximum (minus your Rad damage)! Though not available until later into your exploration, this enables you to ignore damage unless you're almost dead, and instead romp through the Appalachian wilderness like you own the place. Look at your Pip-Boy to determine the correct time and your active effects, or ignore this perk and just use a Stimpak or other healing items; it's up to you. With this perk in effect, you're better able to explore the hardest environments, tackle enemy workshops, and further improve your daytime prowess with the Endurance perks Photosynthetic and Solar Powered, before returning to your camp or workshop to craft, build, trade or relax during the night. Just ensure you're healed before dusk!

PROFESSIONAL DRINKER

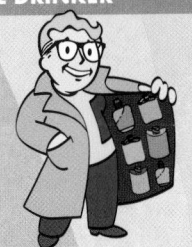

RARITY: COMMON
LEVEL: 39
RANKS: ★☆☆☆
POINTS: 3

DESCRIPTION: THERE'S NO CHANCE YOU'LL GET ADDICTED TO ALCOHOL.

Advice: This is a single, three-point perk but one that does exactly what it says on the tin: It stops the negative effects of alcohol addiction, removing withdrawal problems and essentially allowing you to drink as much as you want! If you utilize the buffs that the different types of alcoholic beverages bring, and you're content to keep searching for them, then this offers a no-nonsense alternative to Addictol (a rare chem curing addiction). Alcohol includes all the beer, moonshine, bourbon, rum, vodka, whiskey, and wine you can find. Then use the partner Charisma perks Happy-Go-Lucky and Party Boy/Girl to heighten the benefits of alcohol, with none of the downsides.

RAD RESISTANT

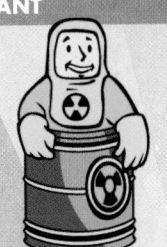

RARITY: COMMON
LEVEL: 34
RANKS: ★★★★
POINTS: 1, 2, 3, 4

DESCRIPTION: GAIN +10/20/30/40 RADIATION RESISTANCE.

Advice: This is an instant and impressive resistance against environmental radiation, as well as the attacks from an enemy that inflicts radiation damage. While it's no substitute for a good frame of Power Armor or a hazmat suit, this resistance is great if you're unable or unwilling to wear such attire (e.g., due to your specialization in stealth). While Rad-X and RadAway should still be in your back pocket, they're used infrequently, while traversing more irradiated landscapes becomes more feasible (though very high Rad zones are to be avoided). Continue your more laissez-faire attitude toward Rads by adding a few additional insurance policies, such as the Agility perk Born Survivor, the Charisma perk Field Surgeon, the Endurance perk Aqua Boy/Girl, Lead Belly, Sun Kissed, the Intelligence perk Pharmacist, and the Luck perk Starched Genes.

RADICOOL

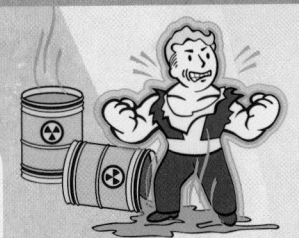

RARITY: RARE
LEVEL: 38
RANKS: ★☆☆☆
POINTS: 1

DESCRIPTION: THE GREATER YOUR RADS, THE GREATER YOUR STRENGTH (MAX +5 STR)!

Advice: Step 1: Figure out exactly what benefits a boost in Strength is going to get you (additional melee damage and an increase in your Carry Weight). Step 2: Figure out exactly what you'll do with your newfound Strength (gather more items, especially from highly irradiated areas, while dropping any Rad-removing chems into your Stash Box and utilizing melee weapons in combat for that extra damage). Step 3: Plan a method of becoming irradiated without actually dying: This final step requires the most forethought, and that starts with the Endurance perk Ghoulish, which you can use to keep from dying (though you need to keep some RadAway since your radiation poisoning still rises; use Sun Kissed or RadAway to negate this). Be sure to bolster your defenses, so enemy damage hits your armor, rather than your mediocre health. Also think about the Agility perk Born Survivor for insurance purposes—you don't die but can still utilize that high Rad damage. Partner Radicool with the Charisma perks Overly Generous and Rad Sponge. This is good if you're with others and are playing the "freak" role!

REJUVENATED

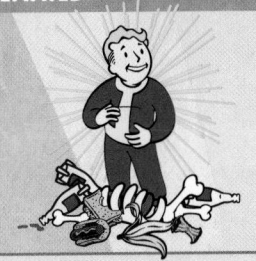

RARITY: COMMON
LEVEL: 12
RANKS: ★★★★
POINTS: 1, 2

DESCRIPTION: YOU GAIN INCREASED/MUCH INCREASED BENEFIT FROM BEING WELL FED OR WELL HYDRATED.

Advice: Some aspects of life in Appalachia are constants: the choking air of the Ash Heap, the penchant for Super Mutants to bludgeon their victims into pulp, and the fact that from time to time, you'll start to feel thirsty and (to a lesser extent) hungry. While foraging for food and water, and then cooking and boiling it so you're not struck down with a disease, is a worthwhile endeavor, you may wish to spend time with other explorations. Lengthen that time with this perk. This also keeps your Well Fed and Well Hydrated bonuses for having 75% or higher Hunger and Thirst meters. Note you need to have eaten and drunk enough for the bonuses to activate in the first place. Partner this with the Charisma perk Happy Camper, as well as all the related Endurance perks: All Night Long, Cannibal, Dromedary, Good Doggy, and Slow Metabolizer.

REVENANT

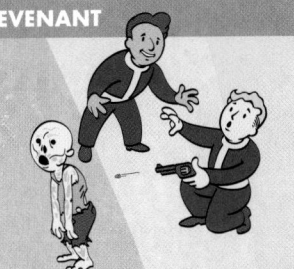

RARITY: UNCOMMON
LEVEL: 32
RANKS: ★★★★
POINTS: 1, 2

DESCRIPTION: GAIN A +25%/50% DAMAGE BONUS FOR 2 MINUTES WHEN A PLAYER REVIVES YOU.

Advice: When adventuring with a group of like-minded Vault Dwellers, whether you're entering hostile territories (guarded by rival humans or Appalachian entities) or defending your own workshop from enemy attacks, it's good to know that if you fall, you can add an impressive 50% (Rank 2) to any attacks for 2 minutes after your return. Naturally, this involves team-play, another individual helping you back into battle, so it's mainly used to get a downed team member to immediately push back previously overly enthusiastic foes who may not be expecting a respawned player to be so vicious. Take back that location! Seek immediate and satisfying revenge! Be sure your team is fully aware of the semi-related "revival" perks, which provide additional and concurrent benefits, though unlike this perk, those must be utilized by the reviver, rather than the fallen player.

SLOW METABOLIZER

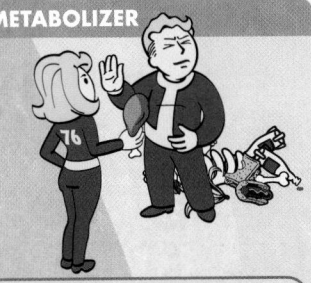

RARITY: COMMON
LEVEL: 5
RANKS: ★★★★☆
POINTS: 1, 2, 3

DESCRIPTION: ALL FOOD SATISFIES HUNGER BY AN ADDITIONAL 25/50/75%.

Advice: As you may be staggering around the Flatwoods when this perk becomes available, it's great to take early on. Though Thirst is more of a problem than Hunger (you need to consume more drinks than meals), you should still aim to keep yourself full of food, with your Hunger meter above 75% to receive the Well Fed bonus (Health and Disease Resistance). Never adventure when you're below 25% or you receive the Famished penalty (AP reduction and less Disease Resistance). How is this achieved? By adding this perk and lengthening the time between meals. This allows you to ignore your cooking station (or opening packaged food) for a longer amount of time and take more chems that induce hunger. Further enhance the food-based bonuses by employing later perks like the Endurance perk All Night Long, Cannibal, Good Doggy, Iron Stomach, Lead Belly, Munchy Resistance, the Charisma perk Happy Camper, and Philanthropist. The "sister" perk of this is the Endurance perk Dromedary.

TRAINING

CRAFTING AND C.A.M.P.ING

INVENTORY

QUESTS

ATLAS

BESTIARY

APPENDICES

SOLAR POWERED

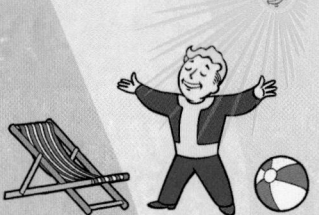

RARITY: UNCOMMON

LEVEL: 22

RANKS: ★★★★★

POINTS: 1, 2, 3

DESCRIPTION: GAIN +1/2/3 TO STR AND END BETWEEN THE HOURS OF 6:00 A.M. AND 6:00 P.M..

Advice: With a small bonus to your Carry Weight and Melee attacks (courtesy of the Strength bonus), and a slight increase in your Hit Points and Disease Resistance (courtesy of the Endurance bonus), use this perk to plan out your days (and nights) more stringently. Look at your Pip-Boy to determine the correct time and your active effects. Then spend the days foraging, fighting, and exploring (using the bonuses this perk grants you to give you the edge), but always be home before sundown! Then, at night, focus on camp building, local foraging, and perhaps crafting, where this bonus isn't necessary to have. Further increase your daytime prowess with the Endurance perks Photosynthetic and Sun Kissed.

SUN KISSED

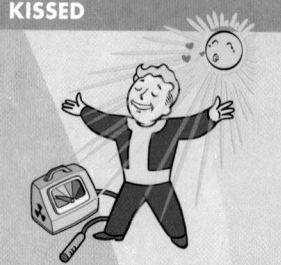

RARITY: COMMON

LEVEL: 45

RANKS: ★★★★★

POINTS: 1, 1

DESCRIPTION: SLOWLY/ QUICKLY REGENERATE RADIATION DAMAGE BETWEEN THE HOURS OF 6:00 A.M. AND 6:00 P.M.

Advice: There's little need for RadAway when you can naturally regenerate lost radiation damage during daylight hours. This allows you to get well, save RadAway, or ignore this chem until you attempt nighttime explorations. Look at your Pip-Boy to determine the correct time and your active effects, and watch the Rads on your Health bar start to melt away! Or, ignore this perk and just use a RadAway; it's up to you. You may wish to spend your convalescence time building a camp or workshop or crafting and trading. Or, you may wish to further your daytime prowess with Endurance perks Photosynthetic and Solar Powered, and spend the days scavenging, slaying, and exploring, using the bonuses of these perks to give you the edge. Just be home by nightfall! Finally, think about using Sun Kissed in conjunction with the Endurance perk Ghoulish; then wander irradiated areas (during daylight hours!), with Ghoulish healing you and Sun Kissed removing the radiation damage as it accumulates!

THIRST QUENCHER

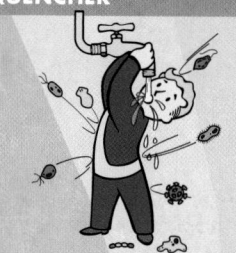

RARITY: UNCOMMON

LEVEL: 6

RANKS: ★★★★★

POINTS: 1, 2, 3

DESCRIPTION: DRINKING ANY LIQUID HAS A 30%/60%/90% REDUCED CHANCE TO CAUSE DISEASE.

Advice: Whether you're sipping on a Firecracker Berry Juice or even grabbing the nearest Boiled Water, you don't have to fret anymore; the chances of catching a disease from anything you're drinking is lessened by using this perk. Now, you'll still receive other negative effects from such conditions (like possible radiation damage), but diseases won't be part of the aftereffects. As it's relatively easy to find or concoct a Cure Disease salve, and diseases (while detrimental) never usually kill you and can lead to more impressive mutations (with both positive and negative effects), you may find this perk to be less helpful, especially as time passes. But if you're overwhelmed by all the ways Appalachia steadfastly refuses to let you live, remove one of these problems almost entirely (at Rank 3). If you want to remove disease threats from your food, environment, and enemies (leaving only sleeping on the ground or being struck by a trap as the ways to become diseased), choose the Endurance perks Iron Stomach (food), Natural Resistance (environment), and Vaccinated (enemies).

VACCINATED

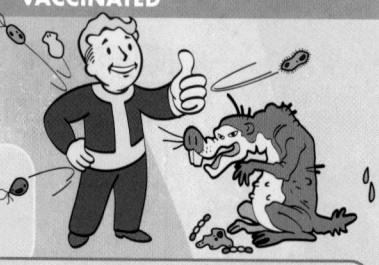

RARITY: UNCOMMON

LEVEL: 16

RANKS: ★★★★★

POINTS: 1, 2, 3

DESCRIPTION: CHANCE OF CATCHING A DISEASE FROM CREATURES IS REDUCED BY 30%/60%/90%.

Advice: Whether you're fending off the fetid fangs of a saggy-skinned Ghoul, nimbly avoiding the darting proboscis of a Bloodwing, or sidestepping the revolting airborne pestilence of a Bloatfly, don't worry about disease damage from these revolting attacks; the chances of catching a disease from a creature's attack is lessened by using this perk. Now, you'll still receive other negative effects from such conditions (like Hit Point damage or crippling blows), but diseases won't be an aftereffect. As it's relatively easy to find or concoct a Cure Disease salve, and diseases (while detrimental) never usually kill you and can lead to more impressive mutations (with both positive and negative effects), you may find this perk to be less helpful, especially as time passes. But if you're overwhelmed by all the times you've caught the Scorched Plague, remove this problem almost entirely (at Rank 3). If you want to remove disease threats from your food, drink, or environment (leaving only sleeping on the ground or being struck by a trap as the ways to become diseased), choose the Endurance perks Iron Stomach (food), Thirst Quencher (drink), and Natural Resistance (environment).

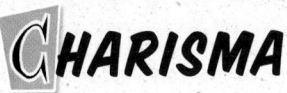

CHARISMA

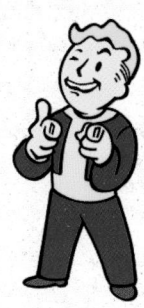

- MODIFICATIONS: TEAM PLAY, BARTER BONUS
- BUFFS: CHARISMA BOBBLEHEAD, MAGNETIC PERSONALITY (CHARISMA; TEAMMATES ONLY), SOME CLOTHING, CHEMS (DAY TRIPPER, GRAPE MENTATS, X-CELL), BEER

Charisma is your ability to lead and help others. It allows you to share higher-point perks and also affects your rewards from Group Quests and prices when you barter. As your Charisma increases, you'll see small discounts to your vendor purchase prices, but greatly increased vendor sale prices. To share a perk card, you need 3 points of CHA per point value of the card you wish to share (for example, 9 CHA to share a 3-point card).

VALUE	XP FROM GROUP QUESTS	CAPS FROM GROUP QUESTS
1	+0%	+0%
2	+5%	+5%
3	+10%	+10%
4	+15%	+15%
5	+25%	+25%
6	+30%	+30%
7	+35%	+35%
8	+40%	+40%
9	+45%	+45%
10	+50%	+50%
11	+55%	+55%
12	+60%	+60%
13	+65%	+65%
14	+70%	+70%
15	+75%	+75%

CHARISMA-RELATED PERKS: OVERVIEW

Aside from a couple of perks tailored to the Lone Wanderer, expect many of these perks to be related to team interaction and play, including "self-sacrificial" perks that do you no good but affect other members of your squad. There are a few perks with bonuses during the revival of others, granting you powers to diminish diseases and Rads and give health to teammates. Other perks augment the power of Stimpaks and alcohol. Also expect a better way to barter, lessen the costs of Fast-Traveling, and a method to pacify animals (and later, all creatures). Mainly, though, this is an attribute that plays well with others.

CHARISMA PERKS (28)

The following table shows all 28 Charisma Perk Cards, listed by the earliest level you can obtain them.

PERK NAME	C	U	R	LEVEL	RANKS	DESCRIPTION
Inspirational		x		2	1, 2, 3	When you are on a team, gain 5/10/15% more XP.
Happy Camper	x			3	1, 2	Hunger and thirst grow 40/80% more slowly when in camp or in a team workshop.
Lone Wanderer			x	4	2, 3, 4	When adventuring alone, take 10/15/20% less damage and gain 10/20/30% AP regen.
Bodyguards		x		5	1, 2, 3, 4	Gain 6/8/10/12 Damage & Energy Resist (max 18/24/30/36) for each teammate, excluding you.
Hard Bargain	x			7	1, 2, 3	Buying and selling prices at vendors are better/even better/much better.
EMT	x			9	1, 2, 3	Players you revive come back with Health regen for 15/30/60 seconds.
Bloodsucker		x		11	1, 2, 3	Bloodpacks now satisfy thirst, no longer irradiate, and heal 50/100/150% more.
Magnetic Personality	x			13	1, 2	Gain 1/2 Charisma for each teammate, excluding yourself.
Field Surgeon			x	15	2	Stimpaks and RadAway will now work much more quickly.
Happy-Go-Lucky	x			17	1, 2	Your Luck is increased by 2/3 while under the influence of alcohol.
Injector	x			19	1, 2, 3	Players you revive have +6/12/18 AP regen for 10 minutes.
Team Medic		x		20	1, 2, 4	Your Stimpaks now also heal nearby teammates for 50/75/100% the normal strength.
Quack Surgeon		x		22	1	Revive other players with liquor!
Party Boy/Girl	x			24	2, 3	The effects of alcohol are doubled/ tripled.
Travel Agent	x			26	1	You pay 30% fewer Caps when Fast Traveling.
Healing Hands	x			28	1	Players you revive are cured of all Rads.
Animal Friend		x		30	1, 2, 3	Aim your gun at any animal below your level for a 25/50/75% chance to pacify it.
Overly Generous			x	32	1, 2	Rads increase your chance to inflict 25/50 Rads with melee attacks!
Anti-Epidemic		x		34	1, 2	Your disease cures have a 50/100% chance to cure a disease on nearby teammates.
Spiritual Healer		x		36	1, 2, 3	You regenerate health for 5/7/10 seconds after reviving another player.
Squad Maneuvers		x		37	1, 2	Run 10/20% faster when part of a team.
Philanthropist		x		39	1, 2, 3	Restore some/more/much more of your team's hunger and thirst when you eat or drink.
Suppressor		x		40	1, 2, 3	Reduce your target's damage output by 10/20/30% for 2 seconds after you attack.
Strange in Numbers		x		42	1	Positive mutation effects are +25% stronger if teammates are mutated too.
Rad Sponge		x		44	1, 2, 3	When affected by Rads, you periodically heal 15/30/50 Rads on nearby teammates.
Tenderizer		x		46	1, 2, 3	Make your target receive 5/6/7% more damage for 5/7/10 seconds after you attack.
Friendly Fire		x		48	1, 2, 3	Teammates hit by your flame weapons regen health briefly/more health briefly/even more health (no Molotovs).
Wasteland Whisperer		x		50	1, 2, 3	Aim your gun at a creature below your level for a 25/50/75% chance to pacify it.

ANIMAL FRIEND

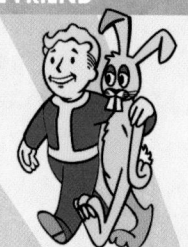

RARITY: UNCOMMON
LEVEL: 30
RANKS: ★★★★★
POINTS: 1, 2, 3

DESCRIPTION: AIM YOUR GUN AT ANY ANIMAL BELOW YOUR LEVEL FOR A 25%/50%/75% CHANCE TO PACIFY IT.

Advice: You need to wait a while to access this perk, but once you have it, anything that's considered an irradiated animal may become docile. Aim down your sight at the animal you want to pacify, and if it works, you can give it simple commands (e.g., pacifying a Mutant Hound and ordering to attack its previous Super Mutant masters). This tends not to work on Legendary animals. Also, if you holster your weapon, use a terminal, sit, or leave and return to the area, a pacified animal becomes hostile again. Expect this to affect Brahmin, Dogs, Mole Rats, Opossums, Mutant Hounds, Radstags, Yao Guais, Wolves. You can then keep it as a temporary "pet" (although it's more of a meat shield) until it dies or you kill it. Then activate the Perception perk Butcher's Bounty. Finally, note there are two variants of this perk, called Wasteland Whisperer (Charisma) and Robotics Expert (Intelligence), which affects creatures and robots rather than creatures. Pick all three for true mastery!

BLOODSUCKER

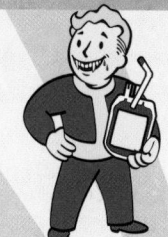

RARITY: UNCOMMON
LEVEL: 11
RANKS: ★★★★★
POINTS: 1, 2, 3

DESCRIPTION: BLOODPACKS NOW SATISFY THIRST, NO LONGER IRRADIATE, AND HEAL 50%/100%/150% MORE.

Advice: The benefits of this perk, which is accessible relatively early into your exploration, become much more pronounced when you accrue a number of these items, either purchased from a Health Supplies Vending Machine or by scouring hospitals, such as the AVR Medical Center in Charleston. But the real bonus comes after acquiring the recipe to make Blood Packs at the Chemistry Station, after which this perk becomes much more helpful. While Blood Packs may not remove the need for Stimpaks entirely, they have a set amount of Hit Points they grant you (plus the bonus of the perk) compared to a Stimpak, which offers a percentage increase; this can be more advantageous depending on the situation, though Stimpaks are much more ubiquitous. Remember to study the Stimpak-related perks (e.g., the Intelligence perk First Aid, the Agility perk Born Survivor, and the Luck perk Mystery Meat), and the low-Health-related perks (e.g., the Intelligence perk Nerd Rage and the Agility perk Dead Man Sprinting). These may be negatively affected by Bloodsucker.

ANTI-EPIDEMIC

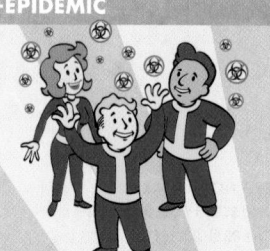

RARITY: UNCOMMON
LEVEL: 34
RANKS: ★★★★★
POINTS: 1, 2

DESCRIPTION: YOUR DISEASE CURES HAVE A 50%/100% CHANCE TO CURE A DISEASE ON NEARBY TEAMMATES.

Advice: Providing your teammates are close enough (it's worth instructing them to move away if they don't want to be cured), this acts as Cure Disease up to 100% of the time by Rank 2. Naturally, if you have three teammates and everyone has a disease, then this is a huge boon to getting rid of a pesky bout of Dysentery, but this isn't a perk you need to have active constantly. Indeed, it's only needed infrequently, especially as diseases won't incapacitate you or your team. There are Endurance perks (e.g., Iron Stomach, Natural Resistance, Thirst Quencher, and Vaccinated) that reduce the chances of catching a disease, making this perk far less effective (or, you can tell your team to ignore those perks, so they can pick other Endurance perks, while you throw out disease cures like candy): In fact, once you acquire a Cure Disease Recipe, you should activate this perk (if you're the team "medic") so you can receive XP from the multiple doses you administer and from making the cures.

BODYGUARDS

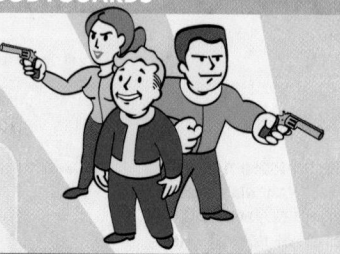

RARITY: UNCOMMON
LEVEL: 5
RANKS: ★★★★★
POINTS: 1, 2, 3, 4

DESCRIPTION: GAIN 6/8/10/12 DAMAGE AND ENERGY RESIST (MAX 18/24/30/36) FOR EACH TEAMMATE, EXCLUDING YOU.

Advice: A good offense is a good defense, said some sports guy before the bombs dropped, and this adage has never been more apt than with the correct use of this perk. It essentially allows you (and teammates if they have this perk or are sharing it) some "free armor" and resistance from the most common enemy damage, and it stacks with your other Damage Resistance perks. So, as a "perk overload" example, with three other teammates, you can receive up to 36 Damage Resistance (Rank 4). Then add one or more of the following: The Strength perk Barbarian and Bullet Shield, the Perception perk Refractor, the Endurance perk Ironclad, the Agility perks Evasive and Moving Target, and the Luck perk Junk Shield. You can maximize your defense with some of these perks active, and that's before any armor is counted!

E.M.T.

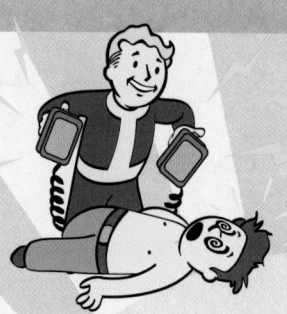

RARITY: COMMON
LEVEL: 9
RANKS: ★★★★★
POINTS: 1, 2, 3

DESCRIPTION: PLAYERS YOU REVIVE COME BACK WITH HEALTH REGEN FOR 15/30/60 SECONDS.

Advice: This perk is available early but is sometimes overlooked: If you're a lone wanderer out to make friends or you overhear a fellow player in distress, utilize this perk to give the revived player some additional chance at survival. Perhaps they'll thank (or pay) you for your gesture? But where this perk truly shines is with a group of like-minded teammates: Volunteer to be the "medic" and then step in and revive your fellow explorers if the feces hits the fan. If you're fighting other humans, this becomes even more important, as you want to combine as many benefits on newly revived teammates as possible. Think about partner perks, such as the Charisma perks Healing Hands, Injector, and Quack Surgeon, and the Luck perk Dry Nurse. These are also useful additions to your battlefield care of duty.

FIELD SURGEON

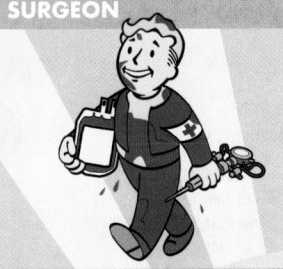

RARITY: RARE
LEVEL: 15
RANKS: ★☆☆☆
POINTS: 2

DESCRIPTION: STIMPAKS AND RADAWAY WILL NOW WORK MUCH MORE QUICKLY.

Advice: Both Stimpaks and RadAway are likely to be your most often-used chems, and both work to heal you or remove radiation from you over a number of seconds. Lessening that offers a small but helpful reduced window of time that can occasionally mean the difference between life and death: For example, take this perk if you're being struck by multiple Ghouls and their Rad attacks and damage are overwhelming the healing/curing powers of the Stimpaks and RadAway you're frantically applying. The perk has no ranks to worry about either; it just works. The main problem with this perk is that it's unnecessary in most other situations—if you're healing in safety, you can wait a few seconds longer to feel better, so there's no need to use this perk. However, you can quickly select it, use your Stimpaks and RadAways, and shelve the perk again. Consider other 2-point Charisma perks that involve combat, where Field Surgeon is most effective; you may have one you prefer over this, or you may want this to give you the edge during frantic combat situations where quick healing is key.

FRIENDLY FIRE

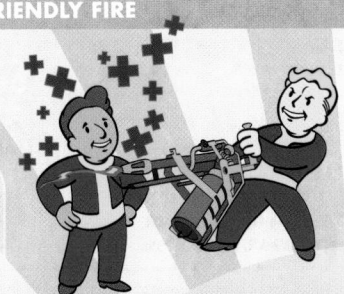

RARITY: UNCOMMON
LEVEL: 48
RANKS: ★★★☆☆
POINTS: 1, 2, 3

DESCRIPTION: TEAMMATES HIT BY YOUR FLAME WEAPONS REGEN HEALTH BRIEFLY/MORE HEALTH BRIEFLY/EVEN MORE HEALTH (NO MOLOTOVS).

Advice: Instead of setting fellow teammates ablaze without any positive (or negative) effects, why not give them a slight health boost for a couple of seconds? Though this perk is highly situational, there are tactical advantages for such a burned offering: First, "flame attacks" can be launched from a flare gun or a Flamer, or if you activate a flamethrower trap in your C.A.M.P. or workshop, or if you set a patch of oil ablaze. Why would you want to do this? If you're defending your C.A.M.P. or workshop from enemies and you've set up flamethrower traps that you are triggering using a switch, or you're lugging about a Flamer. Let your friends charge in, or give them a roasting, and watch as that extra health regeneration bolsters them into defeating the enemy. Don't have a Flamer or flamethrowers? Then you might only want to bring this perk out for occasions when you do. Do you have multiple Flamers? Then everyone set fire to everyone else, intermittently but continuously, as you burn your foes alive! Worried about damage? Consider the Endurance perk Fireproof.

HARD BARGAIN

RARITY: COMMON
LEVEL: 7
RANKS: ★★★★☆
POINTS: 1, 2, 3

DESCRIPTION: BUYING AND SELLING PRICES AT VENDORS ARE BETTER/EVEN BETTER/MUCH BETTER.

HAPPY CAMPER

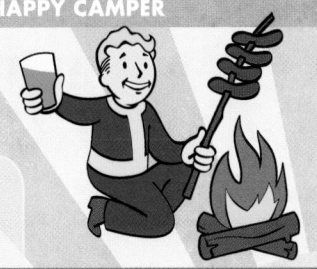

RARITY: COMMON
LEVEL: 3
RANKS: ★★☆☆
POINTS: 1, 2

DESCRIPTION: HUNGER AND THIRST GROW 40%/80% MORE SLOWLY WHEN IN CAMP OR IN A TEAM WORKSHOP.

Advice: It can take some time to build your first (or even your tenth) C.A.M.P. to make it just right, and even longer to construct a defensive, resource-rich workshop that the enemy will trouble attacking. So why not remove most of your hunger pangs and thirst while you're under construction? Basically, any time you enter the C.A.M.P. or workshop build menu modes, this perk is active, so this is the time to activate it. This is a low-level perk, but one that's helpful even as you progress; it prevents you from wasting as much food and drink and enables you to concentrate on building the best base you can muster. You could also play this perk, sit in your C.A.M.P. or workshop, and bring up the Build menu while you ponder your next move, consult this guide, or pause the game, slowing down your metabolism while you take a real-life break without worrying too much about the constant need to eat or drink. Also augment this with all the related Endurance perks All Night Long, Cannibal, Dromedary, Good Doggy, and Slow Metabolizer.

HAPPY-GO-LUCKY

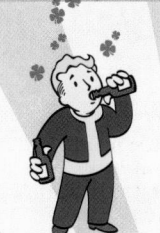

RARITY: COMMON
LEVEL: 17
RANKS: ★★☆☆
POINTS: 1, 2

DESCRIPTION: YOUR LUCK IS INCREASED BY 2/3 WHILE UNDER THE INFLUENCE OF ALCOHOL.

Advice: Increased Luck provides a better Critical Hit recharge rate and finer-quality looted item condition and durability. These can be excellent for those focusing on V.A.T.S. combat or who want better scavenged items. Take this perk and raise your Luck by up to 3 (Rank 2) once you find alcohol to imbibe (do this just before you need the extra Luck, as alcohol effects last only a few minutes). Alcohol includes all the Beer, Moonshine, Bourbon, Run, Vodka, Whiskey, and Wine you can find; though you can't craft alcohol, it is abundant throughout Appalachia. Remember you also receive the effects the alcoholic beverage gives you, on top of the Luck increase! Then use the partner Endurance perk Professional Drinker, and the Charisma perk Party Boy/Girl to lessen the negative effects of being a lush.

Advice: Note that "vendor" in this instance means the robotic vendors, as well as any wandering vendors you might meet. Remember, too, that your Charisma Points affect the vendor's bartering, so increase that by normal means, chemical means (like Grape Mentats), or with another perk (e.g., Magnetic Personality, which adds Charisma for each teammate you're with). This is an excellent perk to take; it's available early on, and it's the foundation of anyone who wants to start a career as a crafter or resource manager. Just be aware that a vendor has a set amount of Caps, and once you've cleaned out the vendor, they cannot purchase any more from you. So, have a good working knowledge of where all the trading posts are in Appalachia (typically at every train station and in most towns). Then figure out what crafting materials give you the best rate of return (think about items that have a high value in your Pip-Boy's Item menu but are easily or cheaply produced). Once you have resource generators at your C.A.M.P. or workshop, you can set and forget them, return and gather the resources, then sell them and accrue Caps quickly and proficiently—and for a much better price if this perk is active. Finally, the Weapons Store, Armor Store, and Clothing Store Vending Machines available for your camp or workshop require Rank 2 of this perk to be constructed.

TRAINING

CRAFTING AND C.A.M.P.ING

INVENTORY

QUESTS

ATLAS

BESTIARY

APPENDICES

HEALING HANDS

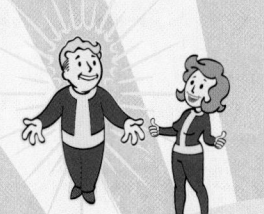

RARITY: COMMON
LEVEL: 28
RANKS: ★★★★★
POINTS: 1

DESCRIPTION: PLAYERS YOU REVIVE ARE CURED OF ALL RADS.

Advice: This perk allows you to revive any player you like; they don't have to be part of your team. While most players are likely to be thankful (though you get the XP for your charitable action), some might not want Rads out of their system—like those using the Endurance perk Radicool and the Charisma perks Overly Generous, Rad Sponge, and, most importantly, Ghoulish. In fact, very occasionally, you actively revive an enemy player with Healing Hands who is relying on high Rads and you cause yourself or your team problems! Once it's determined whether your team actually needs Rad cures at their time of revival, offer to become the team "medic" and think about partner perks, such as the Charisma perks E.M.T., Injector, and Quack Surgeon, and the Luck perk Dry Nurse.

INJECTOR

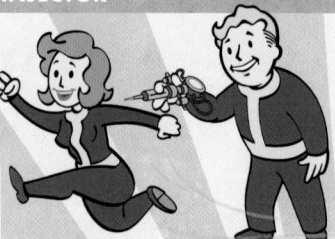

RARITY: COMMON
LEVEL: 19
RANKS: ★★★★★
POINTS: 1, 2, 3

DESCRIPTION: PLAYERS YOU REVIVE HAVE +6/12/18 ACTION POINT REGEN FOR 10 MINUTES.

Advice: Unlike some revival perks that may actually backfire on the revived player (such as using Healing Hands on a player with the Ghoulish perk), there isn't any downside to a revived player getting an enhanced AP regeneration for 10 minutes: Just make sure the revived player is friendly and doesn't turn this gesture into an advantageous battle against you or your team. As with other "Team Medic" Charisma perks, think about partnering this with the Charisma perks E.M.T., Healing Hands, and Quack Surgeon, and the Luck perk Dry Nurse.

INSPIRATIONAL

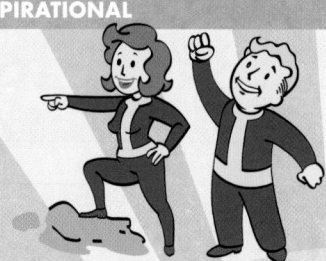

RARITY: UNCOMMON
LEVEL: 2
RANKS: ★★★★★
POINTS: 1, 2, 3

DESCRIPTION: WHEN YOU ARE ON A TEAM, GAIN 5%/10%/15% MORE XP.

Advice: This is an early perk, and taking it too early might not be entirely beneficial; you aren't able to be shot at or enter PvP combat with other humans until Level 5, but you'll reach that level more quickly with this perk active. However, your teammates are likely to help you out, and as you progress and want to reach a pivotal level (such as Levels 10, 15, 20, etc., where you can craft higher-level items or weapons), then this becomes much more helpful. It also gains more importance the higher level you are, as the XP gains are percentage-based. As it takes a lot more XP to get from Level 29 to 30, compared to 2 to 3, reaching that Level 15 percent more quickly (Rank 3) suddenly becomes a much more interesting proposition, providing you can find some friends out there in the wilderness. Also note this is the only perk that actively adds XP bonuses.

LONE WANDERER

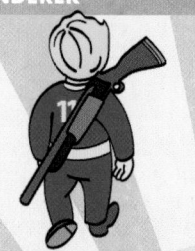

RARITY: RARE
LEVEL: 4
RANKS: ★★★★★
POINTS: 2, 3, 4

DESCRIPTION: WHEN ADVENTURING ALONE, TAKE 10%/15%/20% LESS DAMAGE AND GAIN 10%/20%/30% AP REGEN.

Advice: Who needs friends? Not anyone who wants to take advantage of this damage bonus and quicker AP regeneration! Technically, "adventuring alone" means not being part of a team, so you could conceivably keep this perk active, pal around with some friends, but not become a teammate via the Social menu until you need to, or the perks everyone is sharing are better than this one. If you're lucky enough to get this perk early on, use it immediately, as it's a powerful perk for such an early level. Also compare and stack it with all the other Damage Resistance and AP-related perks from this and other attributes. You also want to compare this to Bodyguards, which is essentially the "team" version of this perk; if you have a team of four, the bonuses are better than wandering by yourself.

MAGNETIC PERSONALITY

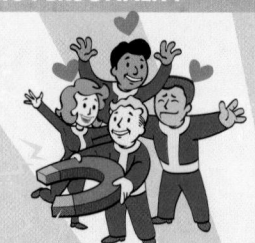

RARITY: COMMON
LEVEL: 13
RANKS: ★★★★★
POINTS: 1, 2

DESCRIPTION: GAIN 1/2 CHARISMA FOR EACH TEAMMATE, EXCLUDING YOURSELF.

Advice: Depending on your team and perk rank, you could have a team-related Charisma modifier of up to +6 (three teammates, Rank 2). You can also stack Charisma bonuses by swigging a Beer, with the fabled Grape Mentats (adding +5 to your Charisma) or other chemical means. Now that you have the Charisma of a cult leader, it's time to put this charm into practice by taking advantage of the main benefits a high Charisma grants you. Get to a trader and start haggling for some of their more valuable items without paying normal prices. Use the Hard Bargain Charisma perk to get a price so low your friends will think you've stolen that Weapon Mod! Finally, make sure you gobble down your Grape Mentats and apply this perk just before you finish any Group Quest; that way you receive the very best rewards the quest has to offer. Need rare goods? This is a great way to get them!

OVERLY GENEROUS

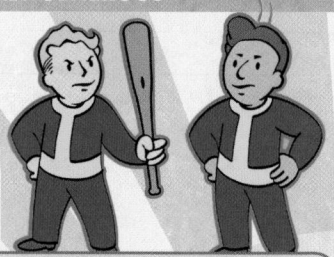

RARITY: RARE
LEVEL: 32
RANKS: ★★★★★
POINTS: 1, 2

DESCRIPTION: RADS INCREASE YOUR CHANCE TO INFLICT 25/50 RADS WITH MELEE ATTACKS!

Advice: This is a dangerous perk, but one with some rewarding benefits as it dishes out a rare damage type (Rads) against anyone you're battering, bludgeoning, or slicing with a melee weapon. This could be a stealth attack or simple, bloody hand-to-hand combat with a human foe you want to irradiate, though your attack won't really affect anyone in Power Armor. Remember that high Rads may also lead to mutations! To keep from dying from radiation poisoning, partner this perk with the Endurance perk Ghoulish to keep you from dying or using up too many RadAways. You may also take Rad Resistance, lessening your radiation increases but still allowing the melee attacks to be irradiated. The Charisma perk Rad Sponge doesn't offer similar effects, but it does rely on you having high Rads, making it useful if you're tagging along in a team.

PARTY BOY/GIRL

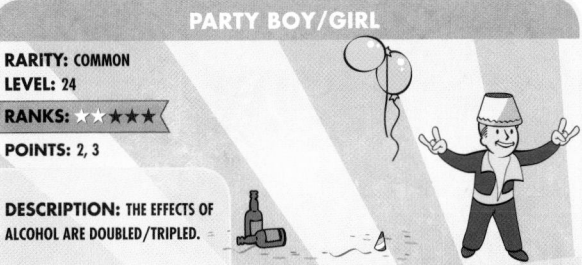

RARITY: COMMON
LEVEL: 24
RANKS: ★★★★★
POINTS: 2, 3

DESCRIPTION: THE EFFECTS OF ALCOHOL ARE DOUBLED/TRIPLED.

Advice: Woohoo! Whether you're taking the Strength and (lack of) Intelligence buff from Whiskey, or the Strength, Charisma, and (lack of) Intelligence buff from Beer, this perk can turn you into a hulking brute or any other combination of buffs and negative effects that alcohol gives you. At Rank 2, think about using alcohol as a cheaper replacement (or addition) to chems, as they offer similar benefits. For example, take Vodka to heal at a much enhanced rate, instead of, or as well as, Buffout. Just ensure you understand the addition penalties and negate them with the Endurance perk Professional Drinker, before thinking about adding the Charisma perk Happy Go Lucky to further play with your various attributes, Health, Carry Weight, and other statistics.

PHILANTHROPIST

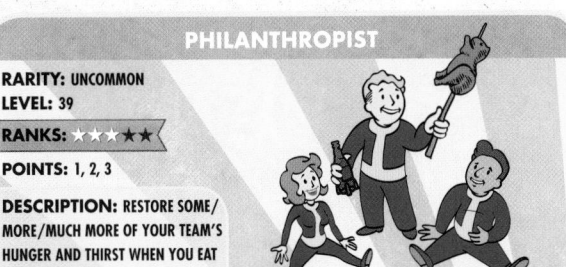

RARITY: UNCOMMON
LEVEL: 39
RANKS: ★★★★★
POINTS: 1, 2, 3

DESCRIPTION: RESTORE SOME/ MORE/MUCH MORE OF YOUR TEAM'S HUNGER AND THIRST WHEN YOU EAT OR DRINK.

Advice: Correctly preparing for an outing in a newly discovered part of the Appalachian wilderness includes prepping for running out of ammunition, gathering items to repair weapons with, and obtaining a good supply of food and drink in order to keep everyone (ideally) Well Fed and Well Hydrated (over 75% Hunger and Thirst meter). With this perk, only you need to concern yourself with the team's culinary needs, effectively quadrupling the effectiveness of food and drink (Rank 3), providing everyone needs to be fed at the same time. Scavenging for food and drink, pooling resources so only around a quarter of the usual food and drink are needed means time spent attempting other activities. Also augment this with all the related Endurance perks All Night Long, Cannibal, Dromedary, Good Doggy, and Slow Metabolizer, as well as the Charisma perk Happy Camper. The last perk is very helpful if you're contending with a drawn-out enemy battle!

QUACK SURGEON

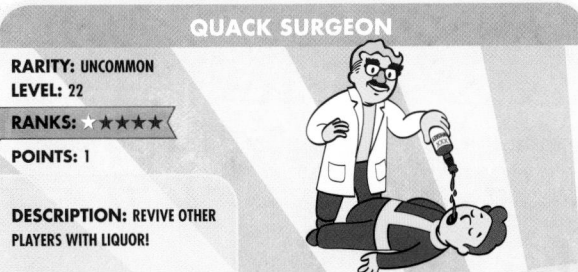

RARITY: UNCOMMON
LEVEL: 22
RANKS: ★★★★★
POINTS: 1

DESCRIPTION: REVIVE OTHER PLAYERS WITH LIQUOR!

Advice: Though this appears to be more of an amusing diversion than a perk to take seriously, it allows you to carry alcohol and Stimpaks and to use liquor (which is a less valuable item) in a revival. It means you have more opportunities to revive, and the revived player usually takes the bonus the liquor grants them along with the chance to live again. Also remember this can be done on any player, including teammates (meaning it can be used in a pinch during a workshop defense or other group battle). This perk is also cheap, only taking up a single point of Charisma. Add it to your "revival" repertoire, employing it with "revival" Charisma perks E.M.T., Healing Hands, and Injector, and the Luck perk Dry Nurse.

RAD SPONGE

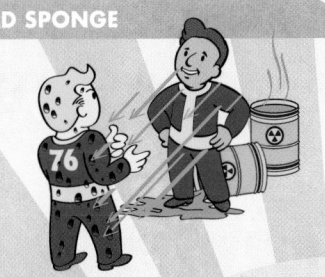

RARITY: UNCOMMON
LEVEL: 44
RANKS: ★★★★★
POINTS: 1, 2, 3

DESCRIPTION: WHEN AFFECTED BY RADS, YOU PERIODICALLY HEAL 15/30/50 RADS ON NEARBY TEAMMATES.

Advice: For this to occur, and for the effects to be particularly potent, you need to be adventuring in extremely hostile environments, such as during a Rad Storm, in a highly irradiated area, and after a nuclear strike. While you take the brunt of the Rad damage, your teammates are content with Rad removal instead. You can heal Rads yourself, though for the perk to be continuously effective, you need to be taking Rad damage (e.g., by testing out less protective clothing). The benefits of this perk can be tentative at best, until you partner this with the Endurance perk Ghoulish, allowing you to absorb all the Rads you could ever wish for, with your teammates staying safe and Rad-free, even under the most oppressive of radioactive conditions!

SPIRITUAL HEALER

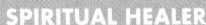
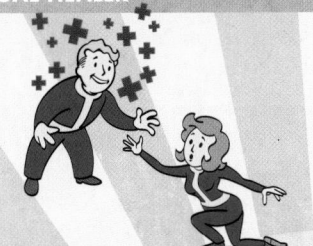

RARITY: UNCOMMON
LEVEL: 36
RANKS: ★★★★★
POINTS: 1, 2, 3

DESCRIPTION: YOU REGENERATE HEALTH FOR 5/7/10 SECONDS AFTER REVIVING ANOTHER PLAYER.

Advice: This doesn't have to be limited to teammates, and technically it isn't one of the "revival" perks, as the perk affects you and not anyone on your team. This perk is highly situational, meaning you'll use it very rarely, so you may wish to simply swap the perk in just before a revival. It's actually more helpful if you're under attack from enemy players, and you need a modicum of health regeneration to protect you while the player is saved and immediately afterward. In addition, increase the potency of every revival by choosing some related Charisma perks like E.M.T., Healing Hands, Injector, and Quack Surgeon, and the Luck perk Dry Nurse.

SQUAD MANEUVERS

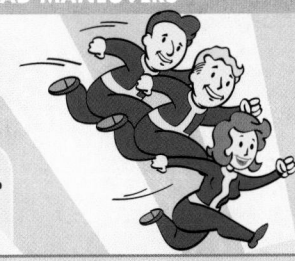

RARITY: UNCOMMON
LEVEL: 37
RANKS: ★★★★★
POINTS: 1, 2

DESCRIPTION: RUN 10%/20% FASTER WHEN PART OF A TEAM.

Advice: This gives your entire team the benefit of enhanced movement, though this is related to running rather than sprinting. Only one of your team needs to activate this perk, and it has no upper range limit. It's great for getting into position before your rivals (whether they're human or not) and can be used in place of sprinting if you don't need to reach a location as early as possible but still fairly quickly (and it saves you AP in the process). It also has benefits to a variety of other perks where running is featured, like the Agility perks Escape Artist and Gun Runner. Escape Artist is particularly interesting, as it allows one or more of your team all the benefits of sneaking, without the usual "crouch speed" slowdown. And if the stealthy members are carrying a silenced pistol with Gun Runner equipped...then you can sneak at almost sprint speeds!

TRAINING

CRAFTING AND C.A.M.P.ING

INVENTORY

QUESTS

ATLAS

BESTIARY

APPENDICES

STRANGE IN NUMBERS

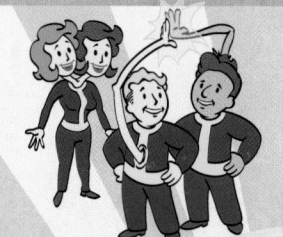

RARITY: UNCOMMON
LEVEL: 42
RANKS: ★★★★
POINTS: 1

DESCRIPTION: POSITIVE MUTATION EFFECTS ARE +25% STRONGER IF TEAMMATES ARE MUTATED TOO.

Advice: Only one of your team needs to have this perk active, and not all your teammates must have mutations active, though only those with mutations will feel the strengthened positive effects. Remember this works with any number of mutations you've managed to catch and cultivate! If you've studied the Mutations section of this guide and found one whose negative effects you can stand, then ensure one of your teammates is looking a bit odd after a disease bout, and mutate beautifully together! Also be sure to look out for the Luck perks Class Freak and Starched Genes to keep your impurities more potent, and for as long as possible!

SUPPRESSOR

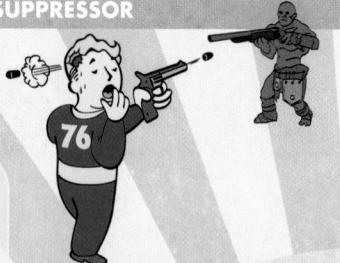

RARITY: UNCOMMON
LEVEL: 40
RANKS: ★★★★
POINTS: 1, 2, 3

DESCRIPTION: REDUCE YOUR TARGET'S DAMAGE OUTPUT BY 10/20/30% FOR 2 SECONDS AFTER YOU ATTACK.

Advice: Battling foes can be extremely difficult, especially when facing down groups, so activate this perk before combat, launch an attack, and add a few seconds of "enforced downtime" for your foe, whose retaliatory attacks are at almost two thirds strength (Rank 3) for a couple of seconds. This gives you time to attack another foe (and repeat the technique), reload, reach for a Stimpak, or finish off your foe while they're weakened. This is also great for using on human foes you're battling, striking them before moving into a different position and shrugging off far less damage from them than normal. The only downside is that the perk halts the effect if you attack again, and sometimes enemies (especially humans) like to heal during that time instead, creating a "shoot, then wait, then shoot" plan for those wise to what is happening to them. You can't really stop that by pressing the attack without interrupting the effects. This is the sister perk to Tenderizer, so think about using both of them together.

TEAM MEDIC

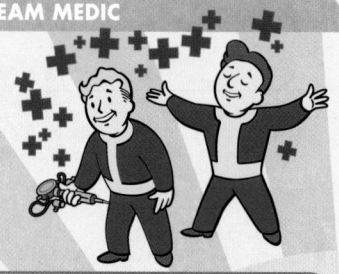

RARITY: UNCOMMON
LEVEL: 20
RANKS: ★★★★
POINTS: 1, 2, 4

DESCRIPTION: YOUR STIMPAKS NOW ALSO HEAL NEARBY TEAMMATES FOR 50%/75%/100% THE NORMAL STRENGTH.

Advice: Some of the previous perks in the Charisma section of this guide recommended you become the team's medic in order for everyone to have a specific role (to employ a wider variety of perks), but this perk really takes that role and runs with it! At Rank 3, your Stimpaks are essentially four times as potent, providing everyone is nearby, everyone needs healing at the same time, and you don't mind using the four Charisma points necessary to have this perk in play (over other, more "selfish" Charisma perks). Think about partnering this with the different revival Charisma perks E.M.T., Healing Hands, Injector, and Quack Surgeon, and the Luck perk Dry Nurse.

TENDERIZER

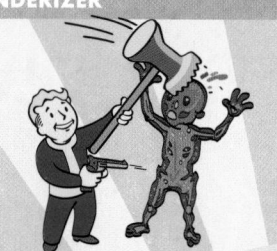

RARITY: UNCOMMON
LEVEL: 46
RANKS: ★★★★
POINTS: 1, 2, 3

DESCRIPTION: MAKE YOUR TARGET RECEIVE 5/6/7% MORE DAMAGE FOR 5/7/10 SECONDS AFTER YOU ATTACK.

Advice: Here's a rather unique method of slaying foes—by almost killing them and then breaking off the attack just prior to their demise and watching them falter and fall remotely. Or, use it when tackling multiple opponents, engaging the first, then switching targets, wounding every foe while your perk carries out the remote attacks. Remember that at Rank 3, expect to inflict a more sizable remote wounding. For example, if you strike a foe for 50 damage, expect another 3.5 damage (7%) for 10 seconds afterward, adding to your damage for free! This is also a great way to finish off a human foe; before they realize it, they've taken additional damage they weren't expecting! The only downside is that the perk halts the damage if you attack again, and sometimes enemies (especially humans) like to heal, and you can't really stop that by pressing the attack without interrupting the effects. This is the sister perk to Suppressor, so think about using them together.

TRAVEL AGENT

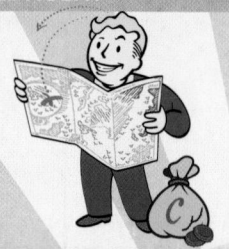

RARITY: COMMON
LEVEL: 26
RANKS: ★★★★
POINTS: 1

DESCRIPTION: YOU PAY 30% FEWER CAPS WHEN FAST TRAVELING.

Advice: A place that used to cost 10 Caps now costs 7? What might be seen as a travel bargain to some could be seen as a perk with little use other than for this very specific need. If you're constantly spending Caps traveling to and from locations, or simply wish to save a few Caps by utilizing the card for Fast-Travel, then give it a go. If you don't mind the extra Caps expenditure (as you can make up the lost Caps through searching for Caps Stashes or trading), or you circumvent paying for Fast-Travel entirely by placing your (or using your teammate's) C.A.M.P. near a location as a staging area, or you Fast-Travel to a train station nearby without the Caps expenditure, then you might want to shuffle this card to the back of your deck.

WASTELAND WHISPERER

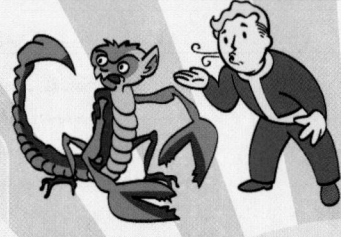

RARITY: UNCOMMON
LEVEL: 50
RANKS: ★★★★
POINTS: 1, 2, 3

DESCRIPTION: AIM YOUR GUN AT A CREATURE BELOW YOUR LEVEL FOR A 25%/50%/75% CHANCE TO PACIFY IT.

Advice: This is a late-level perk, but once it's accessible, anything counted as a creature may become docile. Aim down your sight at the creature you want to pacify, and if it works, you can give it simple commands (e.g., pacifying a Feral Ghoul and then instructing it to attack its fellows). This tends not to work on Legendary variants, and if you holster your weapon, use a terminal, sit, or leave and return to the area, a pacified creature becomes hostile again. Expect Feral Ghouls, Scorched, Super Mutants, Mirelurks, Radtoads, Radroaches, Radscorpions, Deathclaws, Bloatflies, Bloodbugs, Stingwings, Mongrels, Anglers, Gulpers, Hermit Crabs, and other creatures to be affected by this. You can then keep your new pal as a temporary pet (although it's more of a meat shield) until it dies or you kill it. Finally, note there are two variants of this perk: Animal Friend (Charisma) and Robotics Expert (Intelligence), which affects animals and robots rather than creatures. Pick all three to dominate the lesser life-forms of Appalachia!

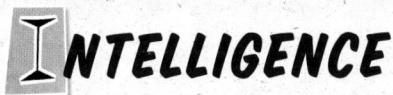 NTELLIGENCE

– MODIFICATIONS:
  ITEM CONDITION AND
  DURABILITY, SCRAPPING
  RETURN
– BUFFS: INTELLIGENCE
  BOBBLEHEAD, NIGHT
  PERSON (PERCEPTION),
  SOME ARMOR AND
  CLOTHING, CHEMS (DADDY-O; BERRY MENTATS,
  MENTATS, X-CELL), ALCOHOL (BEER, BOURBON, RUM)

Intelligence is a measure of your overall mental acuity and affects your ability to hack terminals (raising INT decreases the number of words in the Hacking mini-game), the condition and durability of items that you craft, and the return you get from scrapping items.

VALUE	CRAFTED ITEM CONDITION BONUS	SCRAPPING YIELD
1	+0%	+0%
2	+5%	+20%
3	+10%	+33%
4	+15%	+40%
5	+25%	+46%
6	+30%	+50%
7	+35%	+53%
8	+40%	+56%
9	+45%	+58%
10	+50%	+60%
11	+55%	+61%
12	+60%	+62%
13	+65%	+64%
14	+70%	+65%
15	+75%	+66%

INTELLIGENCE-RELATED PERKS: OVERVIEW

This attribute offers an interesting mixture of perks related largely to crafting, item improvements, and hacking; there are those that increase the durability and lessen the repair costs of specific weapons. You're able to hack increasingly difficult terminals. Stimpaks and RadAway are given boosts. Exotic Weapons, Explosives, Armor, Power Armor, and Energy Guns are all able to be crafted and improved, and weapons are harder to break, as well as being improved over their maximum condition. Scrap items after taking weapons and armor apart are increased. At the highest levels, robots can be pacified, Fusion Cores receive improvements, and you can become a workshop-destroying maelstrom!

INTELLIGENCE PERKS (31)

The following table shows all 31 Intelligence Perk Cards, listed by the earliest level you can obtain them.

PERK NAME	C	U	R	LEVEL	RANKS	DESCRIPTION
First Aid	x			2	1, 2, 3, 4	Stimpaks restore 10/20/30/40% more lost Health.
Makeshift Warrior		x		3	1, 2, 3	Your melee weapons break 30/60/90% more slowly and are cheaper to repair.
Hacker	x			4	1	Gain +1 hacking skill, and terminal lockout time is reduced.
Licensed Plumber	x			5	1, 2, 3	Your pipe weapons break 30/60/90% more slowly and are cheaper to repair.
Pharmacist		x		6	1, 2, 3	RadAway removes 30% more/60% more/twice as much radiation.
Exotic Weapons	x			8	1, 2	You can now craft crossbows, black powder guns, and more! (Plans required). // You can now craft Rank 1 exotic weapon mods (Plans required).
Demolition Expert			x	10	1, 2, 3, 4, 5	Your explosives do +20/40/60/80/100% damage.
Scrapper		x		13	1	Obtain more components when you scrap weapons and armor.
Armorer	x			15	1, 2, 3	You can now craft advanced armor mods (Plans required). / Crafting armor now costs fewer materials. / Your crafted armor has improved durability.
Exotic Weapons (Expert)	x			16	1, 2	You can craft Rank 2 exotic weapon mods (Plans required). / Crafting exotic weapons now costs fewer materials.
Contractor	x			18	1, 2	Crafting workshop items now cost 25/50% fewer materials.
Science	x			20	1, 2	You can now craft energy guns (Plans Required). / You can craft Rank 1 energy gun mods (Plans required).
Hacker (Expert)	x			22	1	Gain +1 Hacking skill, and terminal lockout time is reduced.
Gunsmith		x		23	1, 2, 3	Your guns break 25/50/75% more slowly and are cheaper to repair.
Exotic Weapons (Master)	x			25	1, 2	You can craft Rank 3 exotic weapon mods (Plans required). / Your crafted exotic weapons have improved durability.
Fix It Good	x			27	1, 2, 3	You can repair armor and Power Armor to 130/160/200% of normal maximum condition.
Batteries Included	x			28	1, 2, 3	Energy weapon ammo weighs 30/60/90% less.
Wrecking Ball	x			29	1, 2, 3	You deal +40/80/120% damage to workshop objects.
Science (Expert)	x			31	1, 2	You can now craft Rank 2 energy gun mods (Plans required). / Crafting energy guns now costs fewer materials.
Grease Monkey	x			33	1, 2	Workshop items are 30/60% cheaper to repair.
Chemist	x			34	1, 2	You get double/triple the quantity when you craft Chems!
Stabilized			x	36	1, 2, 3, 4	In Power Armor, heavy guns gain more/even more/much better/excellent accuracy and ignore 10/20/30/40% armor.
Hacker (Master)	x			38	1	Gain +1 Hacking skill, and terminal lockout time is reduced.
Weapon Artisan	x			40	1, 2, 3	You can repair any weapon to 130/160/200% of normal maximum condition.
Power Smith	x			41	1, 2, 3	You can now craft advanced Power Armor mods (Plans required). / Crafting Power Armor now costs fewer materials. / Your crafted Power Armor now has improved durability.
Science (Master)	x			43	1, 2	You can now craft Rank 3 energy gun mods (Plans required). / Crafted energy guns have improved durability.
Power Patcher		x		44	1, 2, 3	Your Power Armor breaks 20/40/60% more slowly and is cheaper to repair.
Nerd Rage			x	46	1, 2, 3	While below 20% Health, gain 20/30/40 Damage Resist, 10/15/20% damage and 15% AP regen.
Robotics Expert		x		48	1, 2, 3	Hack an enemy robot for a 25/50/75% chance to pacify it.
Portable Power	x			49	1, 2, 3	All Power Armor parts and chassis weights are reduced by 25/50/75%
Power User		x		50	1, 2, 3, 4, 5	Fusion Cores now last 20/40/60/80/200% longer.

TRAINING

CRAFTING AND C.A.M.P.ING

INVENTORY

QUESTS

ATLAS

BESTIARY

APPENDICES

ARMORER

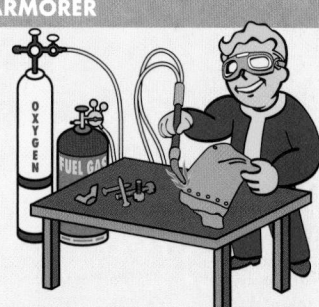

RARITY: COMMON
LEVEL: 15
RANKS: ★★★★★
POINTS: 1, 2, 3

DESCRIPTION: YOU CAN NOW CRAFT ADVANCED ARMOR MODS (PLANS REQUIRED)/CRAFTING ARMOR NOW COSTS FEWER MATERIALS./YOUR CRAFTED ARMOR HAS IMPROVED DURABILITY.

Advice: Whether you're taking your armor crafting (literally) to the next level due to your own requirements or because you're crafting pieces of armor to sell or give to your teammates, or to trade and make Caps, this perk is an obvious and substantially helpful investment. It more fully opens up the Armor Workbench, allowing a full range of Heavy Armor, Helmets, Light Armor, Sturdy Armor, and Under Armor to be crafted and modified. The only potential problem is locating the Plans necessary, due to the random nature of obtaining them. Though this is the basis of creating the very best in protective outfits, there are other perks that specifically help augment armor: the Intelligence perks Fix It Good and Scrapper and the Agility perk White Knight. Finally, look to the Intelligence perk Gunsmith as the Weapons-related version of this perk.

BATTERIES INCLUDED

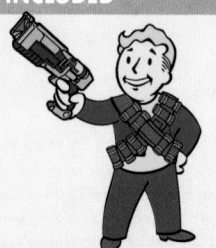

RARITY: COMMON
LEVEL: 28
RANKS: ★★★★★
POINTS: 1, 2, 3

DESCRIPTION: ENERGY WEAPON AMMO WEIGHS 30/60/90% LESS.

Advice: As you progress, you may switch from ballistic to energy weapons. When you do, inspect the weight of the energy weapon ammunition you're carrying. If this has become your primary weapon type or you're collecting (or trading energy ammunition for Caps or keeping your teammates fully loaded with energy ammunition via the Tinker's Workbench), then think about choosing this perk. For heavier weapons, the ammunition weight may be problematic, and if you want to negate some (or at the highest rank, almost all) of that weight, then employ this perk. Add up all the energy ammunition you have, and if the weight you're about to negate is higher than a perk that removes more general Carry Weight penalties, then this is for you. Just be aware of how specific this weight reduction is.

CHEMIST

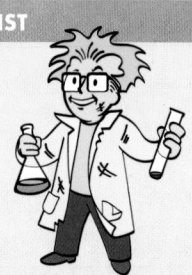

RARITY: COMMON
LEVEL: 34
RANKS: ★★★★★
POINTS: 1, 2

DESCRIPTION: YOU GET DOUBLE/TRIPLE THE QUANTITY WHEN YOU CRAFT CHEMS!

Advice: If you've made a career of crafting all the different items available at a chemistry station, or you're thinking about reaping enhanced benefits as this perk becomes available, obtaining more from your components is a boon to your needs: This affects the Drugs, Healing, and Mutation Serums you can craft at a chemistry station (just Chems, rather than non-ingestible items like Gunpowder). This can keep you in Mentats or Stimpaks for days, and extra chems can be stored, given to your teammates, or sold. Make this perk even better: You may want to reduce the weight of all these chems using the Strength perk Traveling Pharmacy. You can also pick Endurance perks Chem Fiend, Chem Resistant, and Hydro Fix along with Munchy Resistance to add further longevity to your personal stash and reduce the negative effects of the chems.

CONTRACTOR

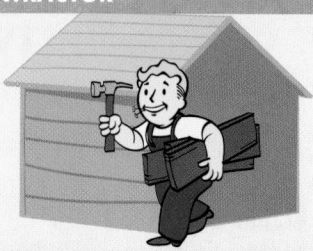

RARITY: COMMON
LEVEL: 18
RANKS: ★★★★
POINTS: 1, 2

DESCRIPTION: CRAFTING WORKSHOP ITEMS NOW COST 25%/50% FEWER MATERIALS.

Advice: Need to make a defensive base at a Public Workshop using roughly half the available materials (at Rank 2)? Then depending on the raw materials already available at the workshop, this becomes a most helpful or marginally helpful perk, due to the reasonably large quantity of components already stocked at a workshop. Remember that your workshop budget is usually the limiting factor regarding how big you can build a structure, though this varies depending on the workshop's location, size, and scope. Where this perk really comes into its own, however, is during the maintenance and defense of a workshop, especially during prolonged battles with rival gangs of humans! Ensure you specify a "Handyman" on your team with this perk, whose responsibility is to repair and reinforce all defensive structures, turrets, and other buildings, while using far fewer materials in the process, so you don't have to dip into any personal materials or (at worst) head off to forage when you should be keeping your workshop free from foes. The Intelligence perk Grease Monkey is the main perk to partner with this, as well as the Endurance perk Homebody, the Charisma perk Happy Camper, and the perks that help craft more powerful turrets and traps.

DEMOLITIONS EXPERT

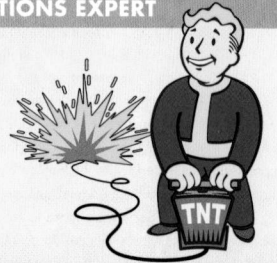

RARITY: RARE
LEVEL: 10
RANKS: ★★★★★
POINTS: 1, 2, 3, 4, 5

DESCRIPTION: YOUR EXPLOSIVES DO +20%/40%/60%/80%/100% DAMAGE.

Advice: If you're not throwing grenades at foes to soften them up or cause distractions, remedy that situation at once! This perk doesn't affect only your projectiles: Think about the additional damage of your grenades, mines, and explosive heavy weapons, as well as the missile turrets and artillery strikes you've made for your camp or workshop. If effectively doubling the damage (at Rank 5) these weapons inflict is appealing, then pick this perk, even though it can eat up your Intelligence points! Add further mayhem to your area-of-effect explosives by partnering this with the Strength perk Ordnance Express and the Perception perks Grenadier and Fire in the Hole to inflict the largest amount of explosive pain that you can, over the widest area!

EXOTIC WEAPONS

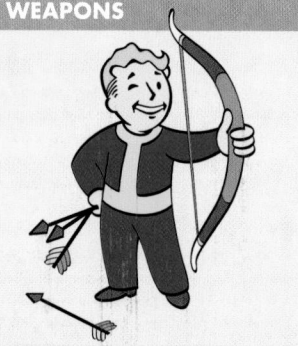

RARITY: COMMON
LEVEL: 8
RANKS: ★★★★
POINTS: 1, 2

DESCRIPTION: YOU CAN NOW CRAFT CROSSBOWS, BLACK POWDER GUNS, AND MORE! (PLANS REQUIRED). // YOU CAN NOW CRAFT RANK 1 EXOTIC WEAPON MODS (PLANS REQUIRED).

(EXPERT) EXOTIC WEAPONS

RARITY: COMMON
LEVEL: 16
RANKS: ★★★★★
POINTS: 1, 2

DESCRIPTION: YOU CAN CRAFT
RANK 2 EXOTIC WEAPON MODS
(PLANS REQUIRED)./CRAFTING
EXOTIC WEAPONS NOW COSTS FEWER
MATERIALS.

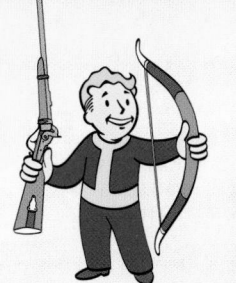

(MASTER) EXOTIC WEAPONS

RARITY: COMMON
LEVEL: 25
RANKS: ★★★★★
POINTS: 1, 2

DESCRIPTION: YOU CAN CRAFT
RANK 3 EXOTIC WEAPON MODS
(PLANS REQUIRED)./YOUR CRAFTED
EXOTIC WEAPONS HAVE IMPROVED
DURABILITY.

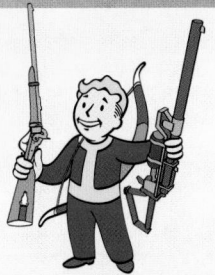

Advice: Everybody in Appalachia enjoys wandering around with an enhanced crossbow or learning the archaic methods of reloading a Black Powder Rifle, so why not become the de facto crafter of such items? This opens up the number of "exotic" weapons available to you and your fellow Vault Dwellers. Furthermore, if you'd previously found a Plan for an exotic weapon but hadn't obtained this perk, the material costs would have been more; this is no longer the case. Unlike most other crafting station/workbench improvements, this splits up exotic weapons into three stages, and the total points can add up! It's going to take six Intelligence points to craft the very best crossbow, or one that has better durability! Also think about partnering these perks with the low-level Strength perk Pack Rat when you're scavenging materials and the high-level Luck perk Super Duper. If you take weapon crafting seriously, or if you craft weapons to sell or give to your teammates, or to trade and make Caps from, this perk is an obvious and substantially helpful investment. It more fully opens up the Weapons Workbench, and at a lower XP level than you might expect. Make this the first foray into the world of weapons crafting!

FIRST AID

RARITY: COMMON
LEVEL: 2
RANKS: ★★★★★
POINTS: 1, 2, 3, 4

DESCRIPTION: STIMPAKS
RESTORE 10%/20%/30%/40%
MORE LOST HEALTH.

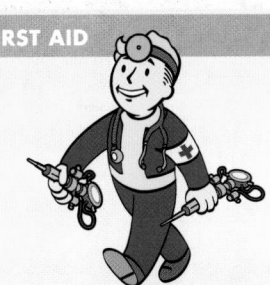

Advice: This perk is essential when you're first stepping out from Vault 76, as anything that prolongs your life span during the time you're adjusting to your new life in the Appalachian wilderness should be seen as a gift. Activate this immediately upon seeing it, and begin to search first aid boxes for more Stimpaks. Learn the base components for crafting Stimpaks (Antiseptic, Blood Pack, and Steel), learn the variants (Diluted and Super variants), and count your blessings; you have a reasonably good supply from the Vault. Switch this out if you're running low on Intelligence points and want a different perk to be active, utilizing First Aid each time you use a Stimpak—if you're not in a frantic combat situation or you're using perks where Stimpaks are automatically administered. As you progress, find more health-related help, such as the Strength perk Traveling Pharmacy, the Agility perk Born Survivor, the Charisma perks Field Surgeon and Team Medic, and the Luck perks Dry Nurse and Mystery Meat. Finally, the Medical Store Vending Machine (Vendors) requires Rank 1 of this perk to be constructed in your camp or workshop.

FIX IT GOOD

RARITY: COMMON
LEVEL: 27
RANKS: ★★★★★
POINTS: 1, 2, 3

DESCRIPTION: YOU CAN REPAIR
ARMOR AND POWER ARMOR TO
130%/160%/200% OF NORMAL
MAXIMUM CONDITION.

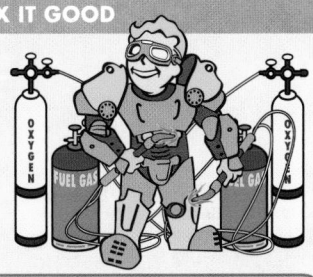

Advice: Shelve this perk for most of your adventuring, but don't forget the vital bonuses it grants you when you reach an Armor Workbench, or Power Armor Station. Start to repair any battle-dented armor or Power Armor you may be wearing. Remember to share this perk with your teammates, so they can take advantage of mending their own armor, or become the "blacksmith" for your team and fix everyone's armor yourself (for the XP). Also consider selling armor and Power Armor that's been improved for a greater number of Caps. Check other perks with similar effects, such as the Intelligence perks Power Patcher and Scrapper and the Agility perk White Knight.

GREASE MONKEY

RARITY: COMMON
LEVEL: 33
RANKS: ★★★★★
POINTS: 1, 2

DESCRIPTION: WORKSHOP
ITEMS ARE 30%/60% CHEAPER TO
REPAIR.

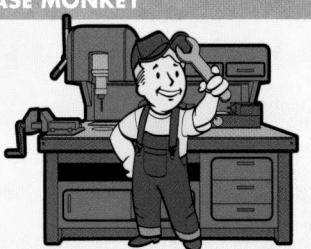

Advice: This perk offers highly situational but extremely helpful effects when you or your team attempt to defend a public workshop against hordes of foes or a persistent rival team of humans. Having fewer components needed when repairing damaged parts of your workshop (usually generators, walls, and defenses like turrets and traps) becomes a boon to your dwindling supplies, so ensure your teammates know about this perk to prevent them from repairing objects at a higher cost! You should also have the Intelligence perk Contractor so your supplies are even healthier, and think about utilizing the Endurance perk Homebody and the Charisma perk Happy Camper so your survival chances and ability to maintain a workshop under siege are greatly improved.

GUNSMITH

RARITY: UNCOMMON
LEVEL: 23
RANKS: ★★★★★
POINTS: 1, 2, 3

DESCRIPTION: YOUR
GUNS BREAK 25%/50%/75%
MORE SLOWLY AND ARE
CHEAPER TO REPAIR.

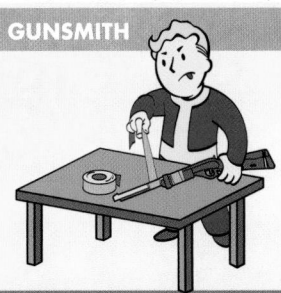

Advice: This takes your Weapons Workbench hammering into professional territory while allowing you to forge best-quality weaponry that doesn't swallow up all your base components as quickly. This essentially gives you time away from junk scavenging or allows you make to far more items with the junk you are breaking down into weapon components. Sell these enhanced weapons to others or give them to teammates. Naturally, this is a solid perk investment (arguably even more so than the Intelligence Armorer perk, which offers the same bonuses but for items you have a narrower variety of), though it affects only guns, not melee weapons (choose Intelligence perk Makeshift Warrior for that). Remember to look for partner perks to help your weapon augmentations even more, such as the Intelligence perk Weapon Artisan.

TRAINING

CRAFTING AND C.A.M.P.ING

INVENTORY

QUESTS

ATLAS

BESTIARY

APPENDICES

HACKER

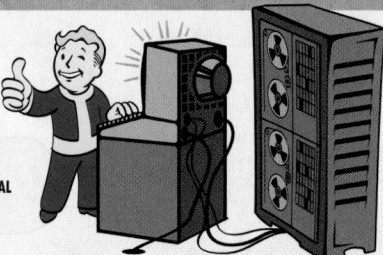

RARITY: COMMON
LEVEL: 4
RANKS: ★☆☆☆
POINTS: 1

DESCRIPTION: GAIN +1 HACKING SKILL, AND TERMINAL LOCK-OUT TIME IS REDUCED.

(EXPERT) HACKER

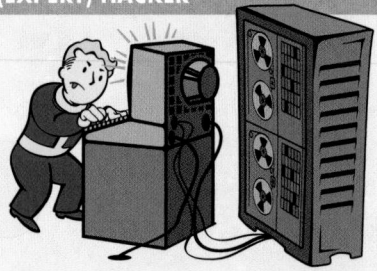

RARITY: COMMON
LEVEL: 22
RANKS: ★☆☆☆
POINTS: 1

DESCRIPTION: GAIN +1 HACKING SKILL, AND TERMINAL LOCKOUT TIME IS REDUCED.

(MASTER) HACKER

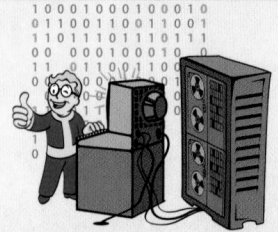

RARITY: COMMON
LEVEL: 38
RANKS: ★☆☆☆
POINTS: 1

DESCRIPTION: GAIN +1 HACKING SKILL, AND TERMINAL LOCKOUT TIME IS REDUCED.

Advice: Without this perk, whenever you locate a terminal that requires hacking to access it, only terminals with a Normal ("0") level of password protection are accessible, and if you fail in your hacking attempt, expect to be locked out of the terminal for around 10 seconds. With the three levels of this Hacker perk, however, the more well-encrypted terminals become accessible; this is important because if you don't have the Hacker perk, you can't even get into higher level terminals, and the lockout time is reduced. Hacker allows access to Advanced ("1") terminals. Expert Hacker allows access to Expert ("2") terminals. And Master Hacker allows access to Master ("3") terminals (the highest encryption). Find the encryption number when you attempt to activate a terminal, and if you only have a few Perception points, swap these cards out with a Perception perk you run all the time, and just swap back when there's a terminal to face. Remember that terminals aren't anywhere nearly as common as locks, so if you only want to unlock one set of environmental objects, the Perception perk Picklock, which enables the easier picking of docks, safes, and containers, will yield more opportunities. Note, though, that Hacker is the only way to get access to some areas of hidden Appalachia, and some terminals allow you to deactivate turrets and control robots (usually Protectrons), which can be most helpful!

LICENSED PLUMBER

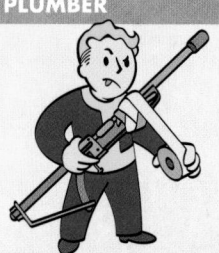

RARITY: COMMON
LEVEL: 5
RANKS: ★★★☆☆
POINTS: 1, 2, 3

DESCRIPTION: YOUR PIPE WEAPONS BREAK 30%/60%/90% MORE SLOWLY AND ARE CHEAPER TO REPAIR.

Advice: This is a very specific weapons-based perk, though it's extremely useful in the initial stages of your Appalachia exploration due to the common number of pipe weapons in the Flatwoods area. Pipe weapons are plentiful and helpful to utilize during the initial stages of play, and you're wise to invest in more robust variations. Note this includes all the different weapons: the revolver, pistol, and automatic variants designed so you can test each out to see which you prefer before "graduating" to better weaponry with similar firing qualities. This also helps with the lead pipe melee weapon! Licensed Plumber allows you to forge best-quality pipe weaponry that doesn't swallow up all your base components as quickly, essentially giving you time away from junk scavenging or allowing you make to far more items with the junk you are breaking down into weapon components. Sell these enhanced weapons to others, or give them to teammates.

MAKESHIFT WARRIOR

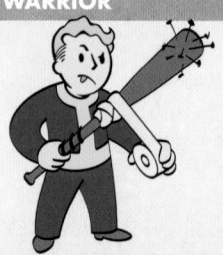

RARITY: UNCOMMON
LEVEL: 3
RANKS: ★★★☆☆
POINTS: 1, 2, 3

DESCRIPTION: YOUR MELEE WEAPONS BREAK 30%/60%/90% MORE SLOWLY AND ARE CHEAPER TO REPAIR.

Advice: Are your blunt, sharp, or striking melee and fist weapons taking a beating? By their very nature they should be, so making them almost twice as tough (Rank 3), with fewer components needed for their eventual repair means you can spend more time exploring, bashing, foraging, and bludgeoning, and less time at the Weapons Workbench. You have more time away from junk scavenging (or allowing you make far more items with the junk you are breaking down into weapon components). Sell these enhanced weapons to others, or give them to teammates. Naturally, this is a solid perk investment, though it only affects melee weapons, not guns (choose the Intelligence perk Gunsmith for that). Look for partner perks to help your weapon augmentations even more, such as the Intelligence perk Weapon Artisan.

NERD RAGE

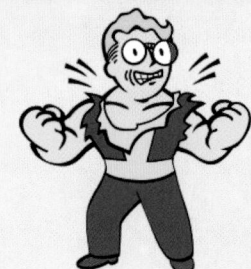

RARITY: RARE
LEVEL: 46
RANKS: ★★★☆☆
POINTS: 1, 2, 3

DESCRIPTION: WHILE BELOW 20% HEALTH, GAIN 20/30/40 DAMAGE RESIST, 10/15/20% DAMAGE AND 15% AP REGEN.

Advice: From initial inspection, this looks like a dangerous way to fight: close to death with low health. However, by the time you can access this perk, you're high enough level to still have a reasonable pool of Hit Points, even at 20% of your full health. Plus, your resistances (and other perks that help stack resistances) should keep you from an early death. Think about partnering this with other "low health" perks that work in tandem with Nerd Rage: the Agility perk Dead Man Sprinting, the Luck perk Serendipity, and possibly the Endurance perk Lifegiver. This also allows you to have a high radiation level, so make the most of Rad-based perks that give you bonuses to your irradiated state, like the Strength perk Radicool, and the Charisma perks Overly Generous and Rad Sponge.

PHARMACIST

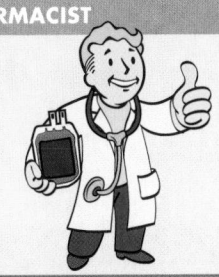

RARITY: UNCOMMON
LEVEL: 6
RANKS: ★★★★★
POINTS: 1, 2, 3

DESCRIPTION: RADAWAY REMOVES 30% MORE/60% MORE/ TWICE AS MUCH RADIATION.

Advice: Initially at least, there are two main chems you'll utilize (so much so that you should be putting them in your Favorites menu wheel for easy access): Stimpaks and RadAway. As you'll begin to take radiation damage even if you actively avoid highly irradiated areas (due to consumption of tainted food and water or the damage some enemies inflict), having your RadAway grant you more radiation removal is helpful. It's not as helpful as, say, First Aid because Stimpaks cure every other type of damage and you don't want to waste RadAway by using a RadAway too early (so it could have removed much more radiation damage than you were affected by). Later on, give your RadAway even more potency with the Charisma perk Field Surgeon and ponder the benefits of the Luck perk Starched Genes.

PORTABLE POWER

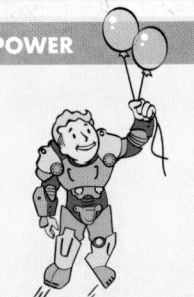

RARITY: COMMON
LEVEL: 49
RANKS: ★★★★★
POINTS: 1, 2, 3

DESCRIPTION: ALL POWER ARMOR PARTS AND CHASSIS WEIGHTS ARE REDUCED BY 25%/50%/75%.

Advice: Your standard T-45 Power Armor weighs around 79 units (Torso: 16; Helmet: 11; Left and Right Arm: 12 each; Left and Right Leg: 14 each), so despite the extra Carry Weight this armor affords you, the weight is still a problem for those who must go longer between managing their inventory. You'll be a very high level by this time, so you may already have figured out a method to circumvent this problem, or you may want to use the 1 to 3 points for other perks. However, Rank 3 drops your armor weight to around around 20 (while clad in T-45 Power Armor) giving you significant additional room to scavenge while on long trips.

POWER PATCHER

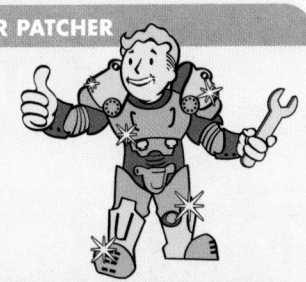

RARITY: UNCOMMON
LEVEL: 44
RANKS: ★★★★★
POINTS: 1, 2, 3

DESCRIPTION: YOUR POWER ARMOR BREAKS 20%/40%/60% MORE SLOWLY AND IS CHEAPER TO REPAIR.

Advice: Much like the Agility perk White Knight (which offers the same bonuses but for regular Armor), this grants you tougher Power Armor and fewer materials necessary to make repairs, which is particularly helpful given the large amount of scrap usually needed. With more robust Power Armor, you can explore more of Appalachia for longer and spend more time before visits to the Power Armor Station. Also be aware that accompanying multiple damage-resistance perks (such as the ones listed in the Agility perk Evasive) also keeps your Power Armor intact for longer. The best partner perks for Power Patcher are within the Intelligence perks deck, such as Fix It Good and Power Smith.

POWER SMITH

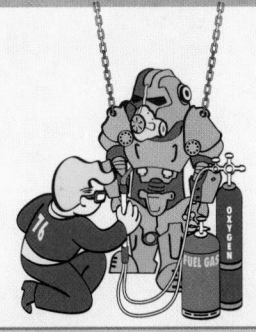

RARITY: COMMON
LEVEL: 41
RANKS: ★★★★★
POINTS: 1, 2, 3

DESCRIPTION: YOU CAN NOW CRAFT ADVANCED POWER ARMOR MODS (PLANS REQUIRED)./ CRAFTING POWER ARMOR NOW COSTS FEWER MATERIALS./YOUR CRAFTED POWER ARMOR NOW HAS IMPROVED DURABILITY.

Advice: This perk should be at the center of your Power Armor upgrade path, as it enables you to expand the quality of mods (plans permitting), lessen the large materials cost associated with Power Armor, and (at Rank 3), improve the durability of the armor pieces you work on. Whether you're working on Excavator, Raider, T-45, T-51b, T-60, Ultracite, X-01, or Enclave Power Armor, this perk enables the creation of the very best in protective exoskeletons! Also invest in the Intelligence perks Fix It Good, Power Patcher, and Power User. Finally, look to the Intelligence perk Armorer Gunsmith as the Armor Workbench and Weapons Workbench-related versions of this perk.

POWER USER

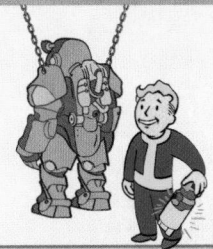

RARITY: UNCOMMON
LEVEL: 50
RANKS: ★★★★★
POINTS: 1, 2, 3, 4, 5

DESCRIPTION: FUSION CORES NOW LAST 20%/40%/60%/80%/200% LONGER.

Advice: Fusion Cores serve two main purposes (one more ubiquitous than the other): powering fusion generators (that you can place in your camp or workshop) or powering your Power Armor. If you need them to last up to three times the longevity as normal (Rank 5), pick this perk. Beware of just how many Intelligence perks this costs and the fact that you need to have the cards constantly active for the perk to be in effect, giving you less flexibility for adding other Intelligence perks. While having additional "juice" in your Fusion Cores is undeniably helpful, by the time you receive this perk, you may already have nuked part of Appalachia, harvested irradiated plants, turned them into "Flux," found the chemistry station plan, and started to craft your own Fusion Core! Or, just go to any large power plant and start the Fusion Core generators outside the plant grounds and gather a large number of them (or scavenge for them). That's not to say this perk isn't useful (it is), but think about alternative methods of gaining the additional Fusion Cores you need to avoid using this perk.

TRAINING

CRAFTING AND C.A.M.P.ING

INVENTORY

QUESTS

ATLAS

BESTIARY

APPENDICES

ROBOTICS EXPERT

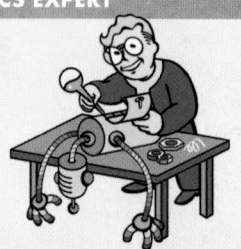

RARITY: UNCOMMON
LEVEL: 48
RANKS: ★★★ ★★
POINTS: 1, 2, 3

DESCRIPTION: HACK AN ENEMY ROBOT FOR A 25%/50%/75% CHANCE TO PACIFY IT.

Advice: You'll need to wait awhile to access this perk, but once you have it, anything that's counted as robot, whether it's an intelligent turret, a lowly Protectron, or a hulking sentry bot, may become docile. Access the robot by aiming or looking at it, either normally or in V.A.T.S. Check for a special icon above the robot's head so you know it's susceptible to this perk. Then quickly hack (as you can't pause the action), and if it works, you can shut the robot down or give it simple commands (e.g., to attack others). This tends not to work on Legendary robots, and if you use a terminal, sit, or leave and return to an area, expect hostilities to resume. Expect this to affect Robotrons, Robobrains, Mr. Gutsys, Mr. Handys, Assaultrons, and Sentry Bots, and other robots. You can then keep one as a temporary "pet" (although it's more of a shield of reinforced metal and circuitry) until it dies or you kill it. Finally, note there are two variants of this perk: Animal Friend (Charisma) and Wasteland Whisperer (Charisma), which affects animals and creatures rather than robots. Pick all three to dominate lowly life-forms!

SCIENCE

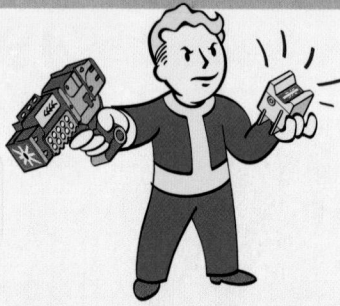

RARITY: COMMON
LEVEL: 20
RANKS: ★ ★★★
POINTS: 1, 2

DESCRIPTION: YOU CAN NOW CRAFT ENERGY GUNS (PLANS REQUIRED)./YOU CAN CRAFT RANK 1 ENERGY GUN MODS (PLANS REQUIRED).

(EXPERT) SCIENCE

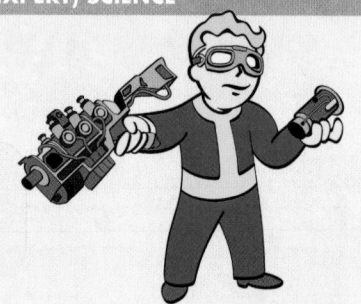

RARITY: COMMON
LEVEL: 31
RANKS: ★★ ★★★
POINTS: 1, 2

DESCRIPTION: YOU CAN NOW CRAFT RANK 2 ENERGY GUN MODS (PLANS REQUIRED)./CRAFTING ENERGY GUNS NOW COSTS FEWER MATERIALS.

(MASTER) SCIENCE

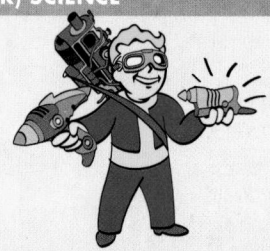

RARITY: COMMON
LEVEL: 43
RANKS: ★★ ★★★
POINTS: 1, 2

DESCRIPTION: YOU CAN NOW CRAFT RANK 3 ENERGY GUN MODS (PLANS REQUIRED)./CRAFTED ENERGY GUNS HAVE IMPROVED DURABILITY.

Advice: Need to build weaponry that relies on energy and inflicts energy damage? Then you've come to the right perk! This essentially turns any Weapons Workbench into a portal for creating laser weapons (including the awesome Gatling laser!), plasma weapons, and guns. At higher ranks, better weapon modifications are available for energy guns, and fewer materials are needed. You can then sell these prized items to vendors or friends, or seek out energy weapon specializations (like Perception perks Commando and Rifleman for rifles, the Agility perks Guerrilla and Gunslinger for pistols and Strength for heavy guns) to further augment your crafted weapons. Don't forget the energy ammunition; pick the Strength perk Batteries Included and the Agility perk Ammosmith. Note that a ranking in Science is required to construct the more powerful turrets and traps in your camp and workshop building menu; along with the Agility perk Home Defense, expect to build laser turrets, tesla arcs, and radiation emitters with appropriate ranks of Science.

SCRAPPER

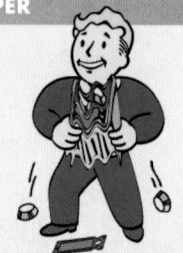

RARITY: UNCOMMON
LEVEL: 13
RANKS: ★ ★★★★
POINTS: 1

DESCRIPTION: OBTAIN MORE COMPONENTS WHEN YOU SCRAP WEAPONS AND ARMOR.

Advice: When you return to an Armor, Power Armor, or Weapons Workbench after a good old-fashioned scavenger hunt, you can turn all your junk into base components. But don't forget to scrap any unwanted armor and weapons too! There is a chance you'll unlock a craftable version of the item (including mods!), but you receive several components to use in crafting items you really want to utilize or sell. With this perk, those components are greatly increased. Need more components for your weapon, armor, and Power Armor creations? Then employ this perk! Also, if you're lucky enough to acquire a copy of Guns and Bullets #5 Magazine, use it with this perk for an absolute pile of helpful scrap!

STABILIZED

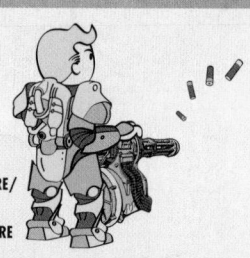

RARITY: RARE
LEVEL: 36
RANKS: ★★★★ ★
POINTS: 1, 2, 3, 4

DESCRIPTION: IN POWER ARMOR, HEAVY GUNS GAIN MORE/ EVEN MORE/MUCH BETTER/ EXCELLENT ACCURACY AND IGNORE 10/20/30/40% ARMOR.

Advice: One aspect of brandishing a minigun, missile launcher, or other weighty weapon is that getting pinpoint accuracy is somewhat tricky. While this perk doesn't give you the accuracy of a sniper rifle, it does offer some excellent stability to your aiming and gives any heavy gun some armor-piercing bonuses, all with the stipulation that you must be wearing Power Armor at the same time. This is another excellent buff-adding perk to a specific type of weapon and should be further augmented by picking perks that help your Power Armor and Heavy Guns abilities. For Power Armor improvements, check any of the Power Intelligence perks. For more Heavy Guns improvements, add the Strength perks Bear Arms, Bullet Shield, Heavy Gunner, Lock and Load, and the Lurk perk One Gun Army.

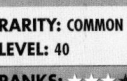

WEAPON ARTISAN

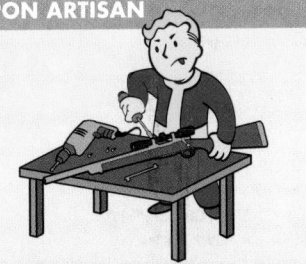

RARITY: COMMON

LEVEL: 40

RANKS: ★★★★★

POINTS: 1, 2, 3

DESCRIPTION: YOU CAN REPAIR ANY WEAPON TO 130%/160%/200% OF NORMAL MAXIMUM CONDITION.

Advice: This is the perk to obtain before you can train yourself to the pinnacle of weapon workmanship! While at a Weapons Workbench, you can double (at Rank 3) the maximum condition of any weapon you like. Remember, this doesn't just apply to guns; any melee, energy, heavy gun, or other offensive object gets a boost to condition, giving you much longer to utilize the weapon before repairs are needed. Naturally, using this in tandem with other Weapon Workbench perks allows the creation of an exceptional arsenal: Look at partnering with the Intelligence perk Exotic Weapons/Science Rank 3; Gunsmith/Licensed Plumber/Makeshift Warrior; and the Luck perk Super Duper.

WRECKING BALL

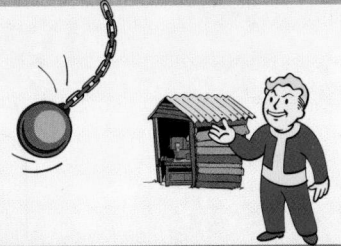

RARITY: COMMON

LEVEL: 29

RANKS: ★★★★★

POINTS: 1, 2, 3

DESCRIPTION: YOU DEAL +40%/80%/120% DAMAGE TO WORKSHOP OBJECTS.

Advice: Has a rival band of humans taken over a high-yielding workshop, perhaps one that you and your team once owned? Or do you just want to wander into a rival workshop without any provocation and start destroying stuff? Then employ the Wrecking Ball perk to ensure your workshop-decimation skills are top-notch! Inflicting almost double damage (Rank 3) on any workshop object? This enables you to snipe turrets from range; blow up defenses with explosives; take a melee weapon to walls, vending machines, and other key objects in an opponent's base; and destroy them in record time! Remember, the damage stacks along with all the weapon bonuses you should be employing too!

Also think about augmenting this already-impressive perk with another workshop-related Charisma perk, such as Happy Camper; it doesn't have to be your workshop that you're in!

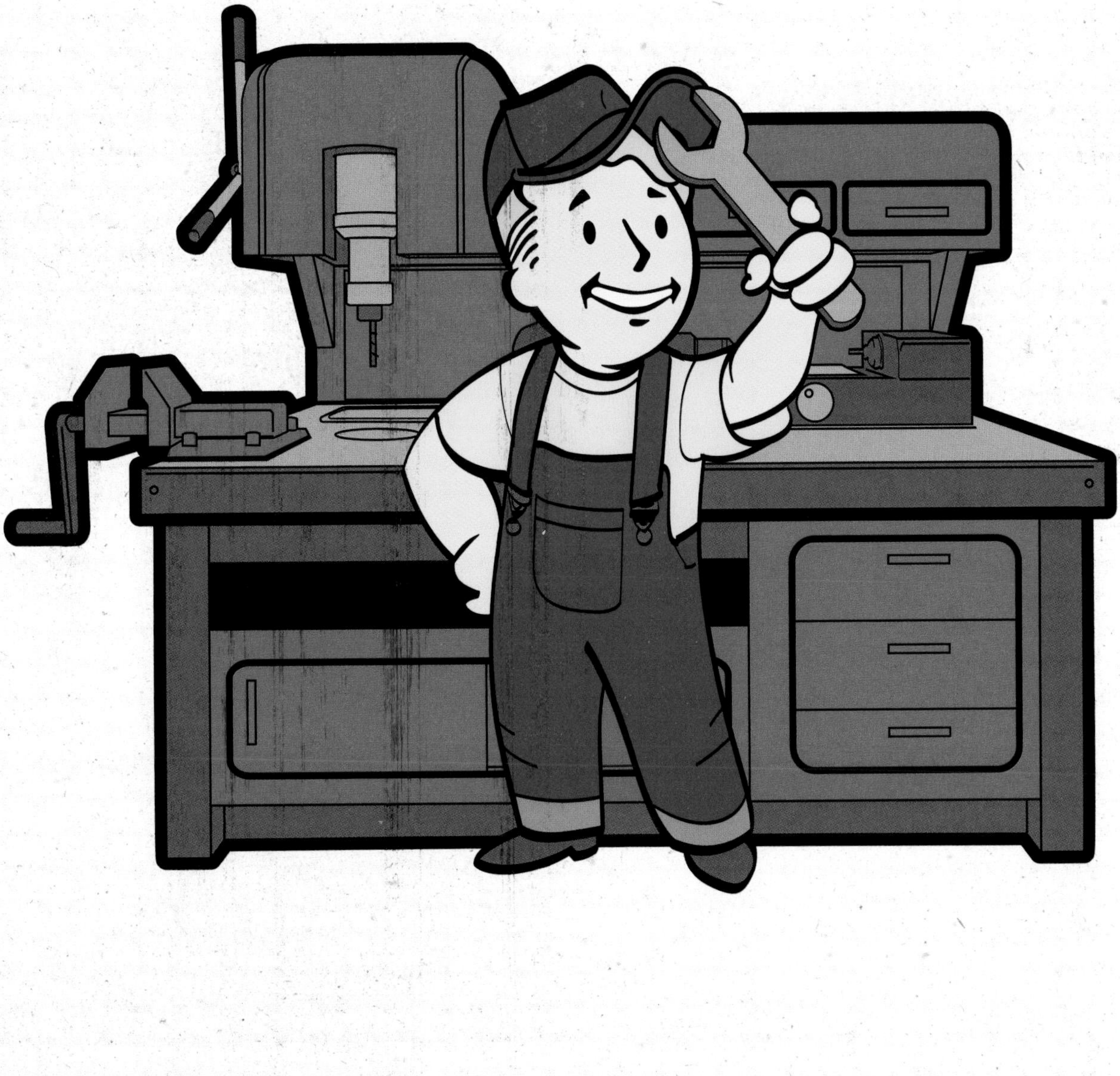

TRAINING

CRAFTING AND C.A.M.P.ING

INVENTORY

QUESTS

ATLAS

BESTIARY

APPENDICES

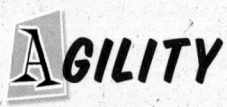

AGILITY

- **MODIFICATIONS:** ACTION POINTS IN V.A.T.S., BONUS TO SNEAK
- **BUFFS:** AGILITY BOBBLEHEAD, U.S. COVERT OPERATIONS MANUAL 10 MAGAZINE, CLOTHING, ARMOR, AND EFFECTS FROM ARMOR, CHEMS (CALMEX, X-CELL), RUM

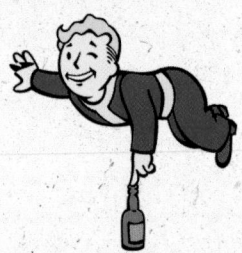

Agility is a measure of your overall finesse and reflexes. If affects the number of Action Points (AP) in V.A.T.S. and your ability to sneak. It is an important attribute to those who use stealth to maneuver around while crouching and remaining unseen. As you need the largest number of AP as possible (if you favor V.A.T.S. combat), this is another reason to never overlook this attribute.

VALUE	MAX ACTION POINTS	SNEAK RATING BONUS
1	105	5
2	115	10
3	125	15
4	135	20
5	145	25
6	155	30
7	165	35
8	175	40
9	185	45
10	195	50
11	205	55
12	215	60
13	225	65
14	235	70
15	245	75

AGILITY-RELATED PERKS: OVERVIEW

As you'd expect, AP improvements, bonuses while sprinting, stealth maneuvering, and reduced damage from falling are a number of bonuses you can take while Sneaking, at night, and with the use of the Stealth Boy (which also has its longevity improved). Central to this attribute are pistols; you can specialize and improve both nonautomatic and automatic variants, and add other augmentations too. There are also some unique perks (increased Well Fed and Hydrated bonuses, shotgun improvements, disarming turrets and traps, and the gaining of damage after kills).

AGILITY PERKS (31)

The following table shows all 31 Agility Perk Cards, listed by the earliest level you can obtain them.

PERK NAME	C	U	R	LEVEL	RANKS	DESCRIPTION
Action Boy/Girl	x			2	1, 2, 3	AP regenerates 15/30/45% faster.
Born Survivor		x		3	1, 2, 3	Falling below 20/30/40% health will automatically use a Stimpak.
Thru Hiker	x			3	1, 2, 3	Food and drink weights are reduced by 30/60/90%.
Gun Runner		x		4	1, 2	Your running speed is increased by 10/20% when you have a pistol equipped.
Moving Target		x		5	1, 2, 3	Gain +15/30/45 Damage and Energy Resistance while sprinting. (No Power Armor).
Gunslinger			x	6	1, 2, 3	Your non-automatic pistols now do +10/15/20% damage.
Dead Man Sprinting		x		8	1, 2	Sprint 10/20% faster at an increased AP cost when your health is below 40/50%.
Packin' Light	x			9	1, 2, 3	Your pistols weigh 25/50/75% less.
Guerrilla			x	10	1, 2, 3	Your automatic pistols now do +10/15/20% damage.
Marathoner	x			13	1, 2, 3	Sprinting consumes 20/30/40% fewer AP.
Ninja			x	15	1, 2, 3	Sneak attacks with melee weapons do 2.3x/2.6x/3x normal damage.
Evasive		x		17	1, 2, 3	Each point of Agility adds +1/2/3 Damage and Energy Resist (max 15/30/45). (No Power Armor).
Modern Renegade			x	18	1, 2, 3, 4	Gain some/more/even more/excellent Pistol hip fire accuracy and a +1/2/3/4% chance to cripple a limb.
Sneak		x		20	1, 2, 3, 4, 5	You are 20/30/40/50/60% harder to detect while sneaking.
Home Defense	x			22	1, 2, 3	You can craft and disarm better/advanced/expert traps and craft better/advanced/expert turrets (Plans required).
Gunslinger (Expert)			x	24	1, 2, 3	Your non-automatic pistols now do +10/15/20% damage.
Guerrilla (Expert)			x	25	1, 2, 3	Your automatic pistols now do +10/15/20% damage.
Covert Operative			x	27	1, 2, 3	Your ranged sneak attacks deal 2.15x/2.3x/2.5x normal damage.
Light Footed	x			29	1	While sneaking, you never trigger mines or floor-based traps.
Enforcer Card			x	30	1, 2, 3, 4	Your shotguns gain a 5/10/15/20% stagger chance and a 3/6/9/12% chance to cripple a limb.
Goat Legs	x			32	1, 2	Take 40/80% less damage from falling.
Ammosmith	x			34	1, 2, 3	Produce 30/60/100% more rounds when crafting ammunition.
Escape Artist			x	35	1	Sneak to lose enemies, and running no longer affects stealth.
Mister Sandman			x	37	1, 2	At night your silenced weapons do additional 25/50% sneak attack damage.
White Knight		x		39	1, 2, 3	Your armor breaks 30/60/90% more slowly and is cheaper to repair.
Gunslinger (Master)			x	41	1, 2, 3	Your non-automatic pistols now do +10/15/20% damage.
Guerrilla (Master)			x	43	1, 2, 3	Your automatic pistols now do +10/15/20% damage.
Dodgy			x	45	1, 2, 3	Avoid 10/20/30% of incoming damage at the cost of 30 APs per hit.
Secret Agent		x		47	1, 2, 3	Stealth Boys last twice/three times/four times as long!
Adrenaline		x		49	1, 2, 3, 4, 5	Gain +6/7/8/9/10% (max 36/42/48/54/60%) damage for 30s per kill. Duration refreshes with kills.
Gun Fu			x	50	1, 2, 3	V.A.T.S. swaps targets on kill with +10% damage/10%, then 20% damage/10%, 20%, then 30% damage to your next target/two targets/three targets.

ACTION BOY/GIRL

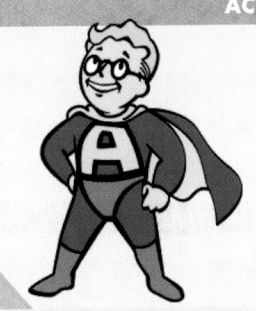

RARITY: COMMON
LEVEL: 2
RANKS: ★★★★★
POINTS: 1, 2, 3

DESCRIPTION: AP REGENERATES 15%/30%/45% FASTER.

Advice: This is arguably the most important perk to pick as you first emerge from Vault 76, and one that's tough to beat as you progress through Appalachia: You constantly need AP—for combat and for sprinting. The ability to move quickly or fight with a smaller resting time is a lifesaving advantage. It's worth considering bolstering this perk by adding more Agility Points (as these increase your AP) and by adding perks related to AP, like the Intelligence perk Nerd Rage, the Agility perks Dead Man Sprinting and Marathoner, and the Luck perk Grim Reaper's Sprint. The only time to possibly shelve this perk is when you're not exploring, when you're crafting or building, and when you have other Agility perks that are more beneficial during those times.

ADRENALINE

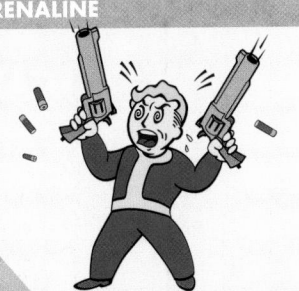

RARITY: UNCOMMON
LEVEL: 49
RANKS: ★★★★★
POINTS: 1, 2, 3, 4, 5

DESCRIPTION: GAIN +6%/7%/8%/9%/10% (MAX 36%/42%/48%/54%/60%) DAMAGE FOR 30S PER KILL. DURATION REFRESHES WITH KILLS.

Advice: This is a high-level perk, so by the time you obtain it, you'll be finessing your devastating killing techniques based on your preferred play style. But this perk's flexibility (use it in both normal and V.A.T.S. combat), the relatively unique bonuses it grants you (up to 60% extra damage for 30 seconds at Rank 5), and the fact that you can continuously "juggle" this combo by killing additional foes and refreshing the duration back to another 30 seconds makes this a perfect perk for crowd-control situations. It is slightly less potent when engaging fewer or "boss" foes with massive health reserves. Bring all your stacked damage-modifying perks with you, like the Agility perk Evasive, and the weapon-enhancing perks (like the Agility perk Guerrilla for pistols or the Strength perk Shotgunner for shotguns), to further the carnage.

BORN SURVIVOR

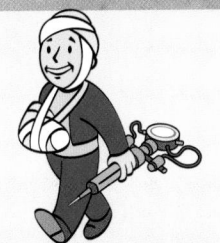

RARITY: UNCOMMON
LEVEL: 3
RANKS: ★★★★★
POINTS: 1, 2, 3

DESCRIPTION: FALLING BELOW 20%/30%/40% HEALTH WILL AUTOMATICALLY USE A STIMPAK.

Advice: For those taking their first steps outside the Vault and are unsure of when to use a Stimpak and why, this can be an automatic lifesaver, as it allows you to concentrate on defeating that group of Ghouls mauling you rather than scrambling for a Stimpak at the Favorites menu. Unlike most other perks, it isn't that necessary to add ranks in Born Survivor, though these keep you away from the "danger zone" of low health. However, there are downsides to automatically taking Stimpaks; you need to have some in your inventory, you can't take other forms of healing, you might want to free up the Agility points for another perk, you're competent enough to manually stab yourself with a Stimpak syringe, and most importantly, you could be utilizing a perk that grants you bonuses at low Health! It's important *not* to use Born Survivor with the following "non-partner" perks, *as their benefits clash with this perk*: the Intelligence perk Nerd Rage, the Agility perk Dead Man Sprinting, and the Luck perk Serendipity.

AMMOSMITH

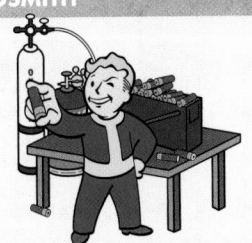

RARITY: COMMON
LEVEL: 34
RANKS: ★★★★★
POINTS: 1, 2, 3

DESCRIPTION: PRODUCE 30%/60%/100% MORE ROUNDS WHEN CRAFTING AMMUNITION.

Advice: You should start crafting your own (ballistic) ammo, energy ammo, explosive ammo, grenades, mines, and traps at a Tinker's Workbench sooner rather than later, so you can utilize the junk in the landscape to provide ammo to use and sell, instead of buying it from vendors and scrabbling around for a few extra rounds in containers. After climbing the levels, it's worth taking this perk when you continue to provide ammunition for you (to use and sell) and your team for the obvious reasons: more killing potential and less time sifting through junk. Think about partnering this with the Strength perks Bandolier and Batteries Included if you need to carry this ammo, while the Strength perk Pack Rat allows you to grab many more components specific to your ammunition needs so you can create one massive ammo dump in one Tinker's Workbench session. Once you become a master at crafting, there's always the Luck perk Super Duper, which gives a 40% chance (Rank 4) at upping your crafting ammo count even more!

COVERT OPERATIVE

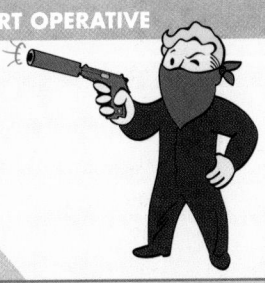

RARITY: RARE
LEVEL: 27
RANKS: ★★★★★
POINTS: 1, 2, 3

DESCRIPTION: YOUR RANGED SNEAK ATTACKS DEAL 2.15X/2.3X/2.5X NORMAL DAMAGE.

Advice: If you're planning on taking advantage of the points you're pouring into Agility (to increase your Sneak bonuses) and want to start shooting at foes, then this is a perk you'll want to utilize on an almost-permanent basis. You can scout ahead, take up a defensive posture near (and usually above) a group of foes, and either tag them before they know what's happening or soften them up before revealing yourself. Imagine if there were four of you with this perk! Remember this works in and out of V.A.T.S., so the damage modifiers you get from V.A.T.S., from your weapon, and those you are using generally all can combine to inflict instant-kill level damage! However, if you're seeking to remain stealthy, partner this with other stealth-related bonuses, from the Perception perk Night Eyes and the Agility perks Escape Artist, Light Footed, Mister Sandman, Ninja, and Sneak.

TRAINING

CRAFTING AND C.A.M.P.ING

INVENTORY

QUESTS

ATLAS

BESTIARY

APPENDICES

DEAD MAN SPRINTING

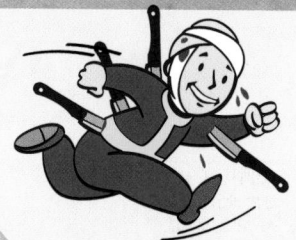

RARITY: UNCOMMON
LEVEL: 8
RANKS: ★★★★
POINTS: 1, 2

DESCRIPTION: SPRINT 10%/20% FASTER AT A INCREASED AP COST WHEN YOUR HEALTH IS BELOW 40%/50%.

Advice: Don't let the name of this perk put you off; this can save your life, especially at lower levels, where you're less likely to know what you're doing and exactly how many foes there are in an area you haven't explored. Use the extra speed to seek defensive positions or to simply flee, as the increased AP cost it takes to dash at faster rates means you have less AP left for combat. It's worth taking perks that increase your AP to make full use of the enhanced Sprinting, such as the Agility perk Action Boy/Girl. Otherwise, look at the Intelligence perk Nerd Rage and the Agility perk Marathoner. Note that some adventurers keep their Health at 50% (Rank 2) so they can sprint and explore more quickly, in which case you need to be wary of perks that clash with this one, and raise your health, such as the Agility perk Born Survivor: However, the two can be used together; if you use Born Survivor at Rank 1 (Stimpaks are used at 20%) and Dead Man Sprinting at Rank 2 (Sprint faster at below 50%), there's a "sweet spot" of 20–50% health, when Dead Man Sprinting works but before Stimpaks automatically stop you from dying.

DODGY

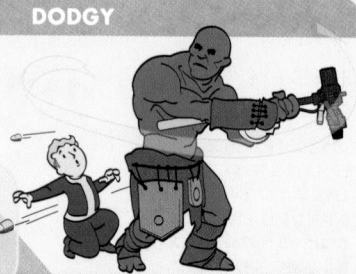

RARITY: RARE
LEVEL: 45
RANKS: ★★★★★
POINTS: 1, 2, 3

DESCRIPTION: AVOID 10%/20%/30% OF INCOMING DAMAGE AT THE COST OF 30 AP PER HIT.

Advice: This is a cool trick, and one you'll need to level up a few dozen times to access, but it does allow you to shrug off incoming damage at the expense of your AP. If you've cultivated your AP and have enough to spare, or if you've used it to shrug off damage in the place of or in addition to armor, then Dodgy is a great perk to take. Basically, Dodgy makes you even more difficult to wound. Worry about enemies that strike you more often, such as Super Mutants with miniguns, as your AP depletion is per hit. If you haven't managed your AP properly, then using this perk can be a problem, as you can reduce your AP too quickly, limiting your combat and sprinting capabilities. Ensure your AP won't be the bottleneck by partnering Dodgy with the Agility perk Action Boy/Girl. Also look at the Intelligence perk Nerd Rage and the Agility perk Marathoner (sprinting consumes fewer APs). Then check the Bestiary and see the damage an enemy inflicts and remove (up to) 30% of it—your Dodgy bonus.

ENFORCER

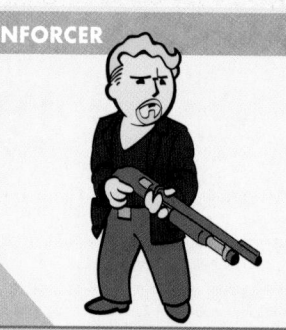

RARITY: RARE
LEVEL: 30
RANKS: ★★★★★
POINTS: 1, 2, 3, 4

DESCRIPTION: YOUR SHOTGUNS GAIN A 5%/10%/15%/20% STAGGER CHANCE AND A 3%/6%/9%/12% CHANCE TO CRIPPLE A LIMB.

Advice: First, ensure you're the sort of sadist who enjoys playing with your foes, waylaying them while you're killing them so they're off-balance and can't return fire (staggered), and they're slower to run or attack (crippled). Second, if you want to stack this perk with others that also offer stagger and/or cripple potential with a shotgun, there aren't any. Not to worry, though: increase the potency of your shotguns by utilizing the Strength perks Scattershot and Shotgunner, and the Perception perk Skeet Shooter. Enforcer is a perk you want to use when shotguns are your bread and butter. Note this is a similar perk to the Strength perk Basher, the Agility perk Modern Renegade, and the Luck perk One Gun Army.

ESCAPE ARTIST

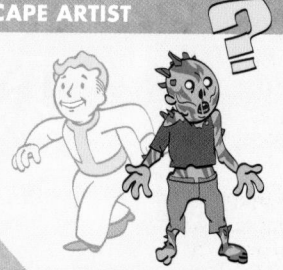

RARITY: RARE
LEVEL: 35
RANKS: ★★★★★
POINTS: 1

DESCRIPTION: SNEAK TO LOSE ENEMIES, AND RUNNING NO LONGER AFFECTS STEALTH.

Advice: This can be a real game-changer, as it enhances a stealth practitioner's maneuvering in almost every circumstance: First, this grants you two helpful methods of upping your stealth techniques. Primary used when facing non-humans, you can crouch, retreat into cover, and stop enemies from investigating when they spot something suspicious; this gives you much more effective (and safe) scouting capabilities. Then you can run (not sprint!), effectively giving you extra speed to move between cover opportunities or behind enemies before attacking or dropping a grenade in their pocket (a classic!). Second, these enhancements cost you only a single perk point! Third, become a real silent assassin and professional reconnoiterer by partnering this with other stealth-related bonuses, from the Perception perk Night Eyes to all the stealth-related Agility perks, such as Covert Operative, Light Footed, Mister Sandman, Ninja, and Sneak.

EVASIVE

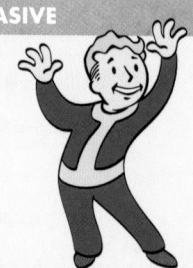

RARITY: UNCOMMON
LEVEL: 17
RANKS: ★★★★★
POINTS: 1, 2, 3

DESCRIPTION: EACH POINT OF AGILITY ADDS +1/2/3 DAMAGE AND ENERGY RESIST (MAX 15/30/45). (NO POWER ARMOR).

Advice: This perk's effectiveness is purely centered around how many points of Agility you have. An Agility of 15, for example, gives you the maximum Damage (+45) and Energy Resistance (+45) at Rank 3, and there's no one wandering the Appalachian wilderness who doesn't like extra damage modifiers and defense against robotic weaponry! Conversely, if you've ignored Agility by the time this becomes available and allocated only 3 points to it (for example), your Rank 3 Evasive perk is only worth +9 Damage and Energy Resistance; at this point, you should scan for other perks that offer a better Perk-to-Attribute Point ratio. This is similar to the Strength perk Barbarian. Having both gives you resistance against most normal damage types. Finally, don't forget to stack this with the numerous perks that increase the damage you inflict. Also stack this with the Endurance perk Ironclad, the Charisma perk Bodyguards, the Agility perk Moving Target, and the Luck perk Junk Shield.

GOAT LEGS

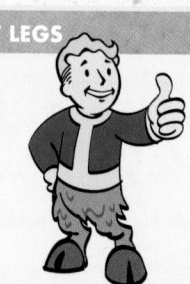

RARITY: COMMON
LEVEL: 32
RANKS: ★★★★★
POINTS: 1, 2

DESCRIPTION: TAKE 40%/80% LESS DAMAGE FROM FALLING.

Advice: If you're at a higher level but don't need to utilize Power Armor for its cushioning effect on falling, or you want extra protection when you take a misstep along a high rooftop or cliff, then consider Goat Legs. It offers very specialized bonuses; for instance, if you're wandering around the flatter areas of Appalachia, you may need this perk infrequently. However, it's great to use as an insurance policy when clambering up cliffs or searching the skyscrapers of Watoga. It's also helpful to further augment the bonuses you receive from Mutation. However, if you're careful where you step, you might swap this perk out for something more helpful in a wider range of situations.

GUERRILLA

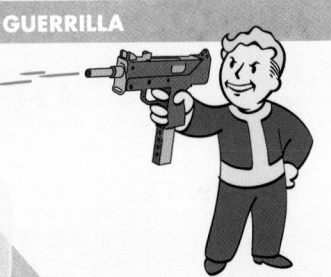

RARITY: RARE
LEVEL: 10
RANKS: ★★★★★
POINTS: 1, 2, 3

DESCRIPTION: YOUR AUTOMATIC PISTOLS NOW DO +10/15/20% DAMAGE.

Advice: As you're becoming familiar with the more complex combat capabilities available to you, and exploration has taken you away from the initial Flatwoods area, this perk should come calling: Your scavenging (and possibly crafting and modding) should have unearthed a variety of auto-pistols. Note the damage bonuses are for pistols that fire constantly when you hold down the trigger and include ballistic and energy weapons—important distinctions when stacking other partner perks with this one. The Gunslinger perk offers similar effects, but for nonautomatic pistols, and becomes available a little earlier. This weapon specialization allows you to take down enemies much more efficiently, while expending fewer bullets. It can also help when dropping foes in V.A.T.S. and during stealthy encounters. Partner this with the Strength perk Packin' Light, the Perception perk Crack Shot, and the Agility perk Modern Renegade to turn what was initially seen as a regular weapon into something much more lethal (and cheap to repair and modify to boot).

(MASTER) GUERRILLA

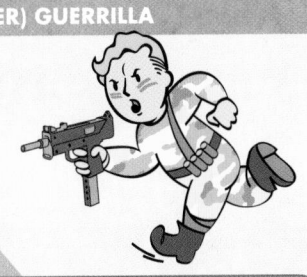

RARITY: RARE
LEVEL: 43
RANKS: ★★★★★
POINTS: 1, 2, 3

DESCRIPTION: YOUR AUTOMATIC PISTOLS NOW DO +10/15/20% DAMAGE.

Advice: If you've committed to using automatic pistols to the exception of everything else, and you've found that stacking Guerrilla perks is more beneficial than partnering lower-level Guerrilla perks with other pistol-related Agility perks, then add a final layer of mayhem with Master Guerrilla! It takes nine Agility Points to get +60% additional damage (Guerrilla Rank 3, Expert Guerrilla Rank 3, and Master Guerrilla Rank 3). With so many Agility Points allocated, search the other attributes for partner perks you can use with Guerrilla. Focus on perks allowing even more proficient use of weapons related to that ability, like rifles in Perception, or shotguns in Strength. A final word of warning: you'll be negating the effects of the classic Agility perk Action Boy/Girl, as you don't have enough Agility Points to run all three Guerrilla perks and Action Boy/Girl at maximum rank. Something's gotta give!

(EXPERT) GUERRILLA

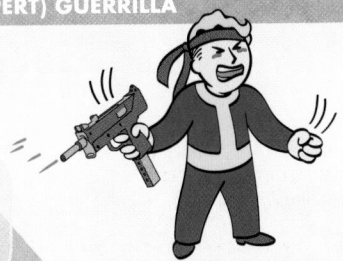

RARITY: RARE
LEVEL: 25
RANKS: ★★★★★
POINTS: 1, 2, 3

DESCRIPTION: YOUR AUTOMATIC PISTOLS NOW DO +10/15/20% DAMAGE.

Advice: Fifteen levels down the (country) road, you can further augment your automatic pistol potency with the second set of Guerrilla perks. If you're committed to fully automatic foe fighting and have the necessary Agility Points to allocate (at the expense of other active Agility perks), then start your damage stacking! As a quick calculation, if you want your automatic pistols to inflict +40% more damage, utilize the Guerrilla perk (Rank 3 for 3 points) and the Expert Guerrilla perk (Rank 3 for another 3 points). Also note that as you're using Agility Points for Guerrilla perks, it becomes increasingly difficult to utilize other Agility perks that benefit pistols, like Gun Runner or Modern Renegade. If you want Guerrilla (Rank 3), Expert Guerrilla (Rank 3), Gun Runner (Rank 2), and Modern Renegade (Rank 4) to be active at once, your Agility needs to be 12! Therefore, more frequent perk-switching becomes necessary, so pick and choose based on what is most potent and effective to your immediate needs.

GUN FU

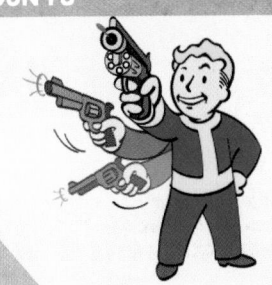

RARITY: UNCOMMON
LEVEL: 50
RANKS: ★★★★★
POINTS: 1, 2, 3

DESCRIPTION: V.A.T.S. SWAPS TARGETS ON KILL WITH +10% DAMAGE/10%, THEN 20% DAMAGE/10%, 20%, THEN 30% DAMAGE TO YOUR NEXT TARGET, TWO TARGETS, THREE TARGETS.

Advice: Do you know Gun Fu? You won't until you reach the last level at which it's possible to obtain Attribute Points (Level 50). This offers a substantial augmentation to your V.A.T.S. combat. Depending on the rank, once you inflict your first kill, Gun Fu automatically targets the next threat(s) for you and gives you a damage bonus to that target(s). Essentially this means a fight gets easier the longer it progresses, as long as there are enemies available to cull. If you're at Rank 3 of Gun Fu, and you're only attacking one or two foes in the vicinity at once, the third rank won't affect combat. But if you're battling a horde (and if this is V.A.T.S., you may be employing stealth tactics!), the additional, stackable damage is impressive, especially when partnered with other V.A.T.S. and damage-increasing perks, which are too numerous to mention. Naturally, this is a perk to use along with high-damage, perk-enhanced weapons from other attributes (e.g., rifles from Perception), rather than those requiring Agility Points (e.g., pistols) because you can't use fully ranked Guerrilla and Gunslinger perks, as the cost takes you over the maximum of 15 Agility Points.

GUN RUNNER

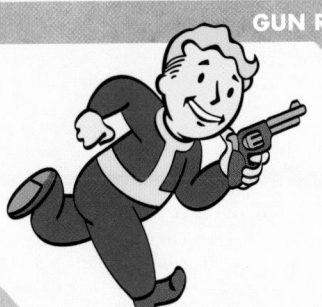

RARITY: UNCOMMON
LEVEL: 4
RANKS: ★★★★★
POINTS: 1, 2

DESCRIPTION: YOUR RUNNING SPEED IS INCREASED BY 10%/20% WHEN YOU HAVE A PISTOL EQUIPPED.

Advice: This starter perk is designed to keep you from getting bogged down in the Flatwoods area of the Forest, but you can use it at any time, even if you don't intend to specialize in pistols. The advantages are obvious—you're able to escape, cover distances, and maneuver more quickly than normal without extra depletion of AP—so it's worth keeping your lightest pistol in both your inventory and your Favorites menu, even if you've moved on to other weapon types; you can equip it as a running companion rather than a firearm for offense! Then simply swap it out for your more potent weapon as necessary. Remember this is your running, rather than your sprinting speed, so compare the quickness of your running with and without a pistol to see if the extra speed is worth it.

TRAINING

CRAFTING AND C.A.M.P.ING

INVENTORY

QUESTS

ATLAS

BESTIARY

APPENDICES

GUNSLINGER

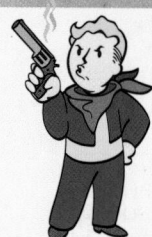

RARITY: RARE
LEVEL: 6
RANKS: ★★★★★
POINTS: 1, 2, 3

DESCRIPTION: YOUR NON-AUTOMATIC PISTOLS NOW DO +10/15/20% DAMAGE.

Advice: Early into your exploration, there's a slim chance you'll uncover your first Gunslinger card. This is likely to be the initial "weapon specialization" card, and one that turns previously unimpressive firearms into weapons you can't live without. By this time, you should have at least one nonautomatic pistol in your inventor; having additional damage for each shot becomes exceptionally useful, reducing the need for constant ammunition foraging or crafting and enabling more proficient foe takedowns. It can also help when dropping foes in V.A.T.S. and during stealthy encounters. Don't forget that "nonautomatic" means the pistol fires only a single shot until you pull the trigger a second time. The .44 pistol is a great weapon to use with this perk. The Guerrilla perk offers similar effects, but for automatic pistols, and is available a little later. Partner this with the Strength perk Packin' Light, the Perception perk Crack Shot, and the Agility perk Modern Renegade to turn a regular weapon into something much more potent (and cheap to repair and modify to boot).

(EXPERT) GUNSLINGER

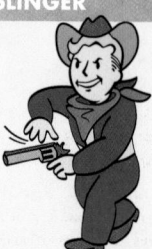

RARITY: RARE
LEVEL: 24
RANKS: ★★★★★
POINTS: 1, 2, 3

DESCRIPTION: YOUR NON-AUTOMATIC PISTOLS NOW DO +10/15/20% DAMAGE.

Advice: Eighteen levels later, you're able to utilize three more levels of potency for your nonautomatic pistols. Think about committing yourself to crafting the best damn revolver or hand cannon you can, with both mods and these cards (at the expense of other active Agility perks). With a quick calculation, if you want your nonautomatic pistols to inflict +40% more damage, utilize the Gunslinger perk (Rank 3 for 3 points) and the Expert Gunslinger perk (Rank 3 for another 3 points). Also note that as you're using Agility Points for Gunslinger perks, it becomes increasingly difficult to utilize other Agility perks that benefit pistols, like Gun Runner or Modern Renegade. If you want Gunslinger (Rank 3), Expert Gunslinger (Rank 3), Gun Runner (Rank 2), and Modern Renegade (Rank 4) to be active at once, your Agility needs to be 12! With all this in mind, perfect your access of the perk menu to switch perks, basing your choice on your immediate needs.

(MASTER) GUNSLINGER

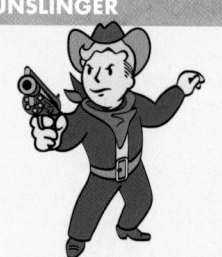

RARITY: RARE
LEVEL: 41
RANKS: ★★★★★
POINTS: 1, 2, 3

DESCRIPTION: YOUR NON-AUTOMATIC PISTOLS NOW DO +10/15/20% DAMAGE.

Advice: If you've come this far with a six-shooter (or other nonautomatic pistol) and you've found that stacking Gunslinger perks is more beneficial than partnering lower-level Gunslinger perks with other pistol-related Agility perks, then add a final layer of perfection with Master Gunslinger! It takes nine Agility Points to get +60% additional damage (Gunslinger Rank 3, Expert Gunslinger Rank 3, and Master Gunslinger Rank 3). With so many Agility Points allocated, search the other attributes for partner perks you can use with Gunslinger. Focus on perks that allow even more proficient use of weapons related to that ability, like rifles in Perception or shotguns in Strength. A final word of warning: you'll be negating the effects of perks like the classic Agility perk Action Boy/Girl (APs regenerate faster), as you don't have enough Agility Points to run all three Gunslinger perks and Action Boy/Girl at maximum rank. But nothing gets in the way of your revolver slaying, right, cowboy?

HOME DEFENSE

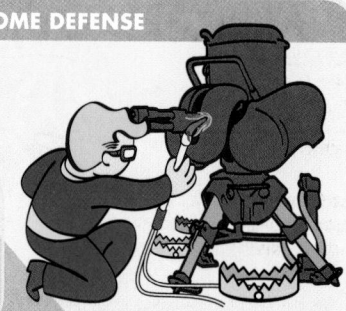

RARITY: COMMON
LEVEL: 22
RANKS: ★★★★★
POINTS: 1, 2, 3

DESCRIPTION: YOU CAN CRAFT AND DISARM BETTER/ADVANCED/EXPERT TRAPS AND CRAFT BETTER/ADVANCED/EXPERT TURRETS (PLANS REQUIRED).

Advice: Available in both the C.A.M.P. and workshop building menus, this is a highly situational but very important and helpful perk to obtain, for the specific purpose of augmenting your C.A.M.P. and to a much more potent extent, you or your team's public workshop. It gets much more helpful once you accrue the necessary plans: With plans, this brings a much larger variety of traps and turrets into the mix. Note that some of the traps and turrets require other perks to become available, as well as the usual components to construct and power to operate. Remember these can be switched on or off (automatically or manually) and cause a variety of different headaches and hurting for enemies who try to intrude on your territory.

TRAP OR TURRET	HOME DEFENSE RANK NEEDED
Heavy Machine Gun Turret	2
Laser Turret	3*
Heavy Laser Turret	3**
Shotgun Turret	1
Missile Turret	3
Spotlight (Turret)	1
Spotlight (Wall)	1
Spike Board Trap (four variants)	1
Spring Trap	1
Powered Spring Trap	2
Sawblade Trap	2
Tesla Arc	2*
Flamethrower Trap	2***
Radiation Emitter	3**

* Intelligence perk Science Rank 1 also needed.
** Intelligence perk Science Rank 2 also needed.
*** Endurance perk Fireproof Rank 1 also needed.

LIGHT FOOTED

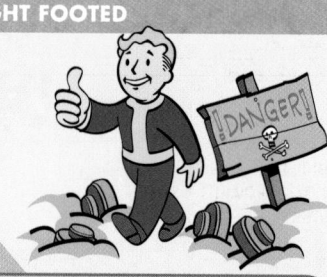

RARITY: COMMON
LEVEL: 29
RANKS: ★★★★★
POINTS: 1

DESCRIPTION: WHILE SNEAKING, YOU NEVER TRIGGER MINES OR FLOOR-BASED TRAPS.

Advice: Though it takes a little time for this perk to become available, it only costs you a point to utilize and completely circumvents particular types of traps without the need to expend any AP or other valuable person assets. Most of the time, you won't need this perk, but there are two main times when it's incredibly helpful: (1) when you're maneuvering through an unknown location where mines or traps have been spotted and (2) when you're assaulting a rival team's C.A.M.P. or workshop. It's also helpful when you're moving around and don't want to walk on your own Punji Board, for example. Remember you need to be crouched for this to work, whether you're building your own trap-filled base or assaulting an enemy stronghold. Further augment all sneaking perks (listed in the entry for the Agility perk Covert Operative) along with this one to become the ultimate silent assassin.

MARATHONER

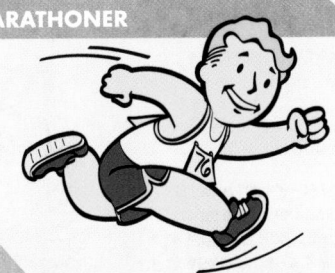

RARITY: COMMON
LEVEL: 13
RANKS: ★★★☆☆
POINTS: 1, 2, 3

DESCRIPTION: SPRINTING CONSUMES 20%/30%/40% FEWER ACTION POINTS.

Advice: This simple, extremely helpful perk is designed to lengthen the time it takes between rests, freeing up AP for things like attacking or during V.A.T.S. combat after a more lengthy sprint. It also allows you to cover longer distances. Aside from the points cost, there's not a single downside (unless your AP level is so impressive that you don't need this perk; you never end up low on AP in most situations, even after a Sprint). To further complement this card, add more Agility Points, as well as the usual AP-modifying perks like the Intelligence perk Nerd Rage, the Agility perks Action Boy/Girl and Dead Man Sprinting, and the Luck perk Grim Reaper's Sprint.

MISTER SANDMAN

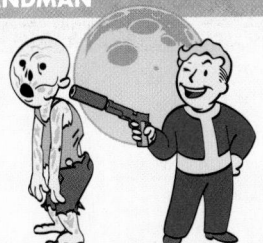

RARITY: RARE
LEVEL: 37
RANKS: ★★★★☆
POINTS: 1, 2

DESCRIPTION: AT NIGHT YOUR SILENCED WEAPONS DO ADDITIONAL 25%/50% SNEAK ATTACK DAMAGE.

Advice: This is a highly situational but highly prized perk for those who must silently take down enemies. The bonus only applies when you make a (usually crouched) sneak attack with a gun. This also allows you to more easily swap between melee and ranged weapon sneak attacks, but only between 6:00 p.m. and 6:00 a.m. (spend the daytime crafting, modding, trading, and building). Take an avid interest in modding weapons, finding suppressor mods, and looking at Pipe, 10 mm, Combat, Assault, Hunting, Submachine, Gauss, and other rifle types as possible weapons. Aside from the additional sneak-based perks to partner with Mister Sandman, which are listed in the Covert Operative advice, also think about taking perks that help you during the night: the Perception perks Night Eyes and Night Person.

MODERN RENEGADE

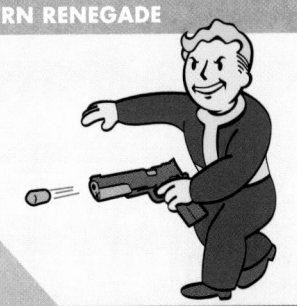

RARITY: RARE
LEVEL: 18
RANKS: ★★★★☆
POINTS: 1, 2, 3, 4

DESCRIPTION: GAIN SOME/ MORE/EVEN MORE/EXCELLENT PISTOL HIP FIRE ACCURACY AND A +1/2/3/4% CHANCE TO CRIPPLE A LIMB.

Advice: If you want to make hip-firing much more accurate, along with a small chance to cripple each time, then use the Modern Renegade perk. There's no AP expenditure, but there's no damage bonus either, so if you feel you're accurate enough already, you use sights predominantly, or you aren't using pistols, then purchase a different perk. Note this is the only perk that allows a cripple chance for a pistol, so if you're already augmenting your handgun with a silencer (Mister Sandman), obtain better damage ratings (Guerrilla or Gunslinger) by trying a variety of pistol, sneak, V.A.T.S., or nighttime perks to partner this with (usually giving your pistol additional buffs, rather than augmenting accuracy and crippling).

MOVING TARGET

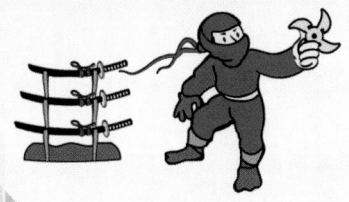

RARITY: UNCOMMON
LEVEL: 5
RANKS: ★★★☆☆
POINTS: 1, 2, 3

DESCRIPTION: GAIN +15/30/45 DAMAGE AND ENERGY RESISTANCE WHILE SPRINTING. (NO POWER ARMOR).

Advice: A classic perk for those pretending to be tanks, this allows you to shrug off all ballistic and energy damage to the amount listed, assuming you're sprinting. As soon as combat starts or you spot an enemy, it's worth charging at or around them, keeping the sprint (and therefore the damage) for as long as possible and hoping your Action Points don't run out. They won't if you've also played the Intelligence perk Nerd Rage, the Agility perks Action Boy/Girl, Dead Man Sprinting, and Marathoner. To a lesser extent, the Luck perk Grim Reaper's Sprint can help, but you need to stop the sprinting, execute a V.A.T.S. kill, and start the sprint again. The Strength perk Pain Train is also a good perk to pair with this. Lastly, stack this with other Damage and Energy Resistance perks, such as those listed with the Agility perk Evasive.

NINJA

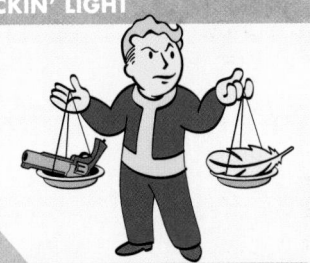

RARITY: RARE
LEVEL: 15
RANKS: ★★★★☆
POINTS: 1, 2, 3

DESCRIPTION: SNEAK ATTACKS WITH MELEE WEAPONS DO 2.3X/2.6X/3X NORMAL DAMAGE.

Advice: The relatively low level at which you can obtain this fantastic damage-multiplying perk, and the amazing damage you can do with it make this a must-have perk for those trying to perfect a stealthy explorer, despite it being relatively tricky to complete this attack on a human foe. "Sneak attack" indicates that the foe must not see you, and you should be crouched. You can use any melee weapon but you'd be wise to ensure it inflicts a single, massive damage strike to take advantage of the first, definite strike. Then you can slink back into the shadows and move to your next foe, or switch tactics if you're discovered. As you'd expect, partner perks are those that augment sneaking and stealth maneuvers and are listed with the Agility perk Secret Agent.

PACKIN' LIGHT

RARITY: COMMON
LEVEL: 9
RANKS: ★★★★☆
POINTS: 1, 2, 3

DESCRIPTION: YOUR PISTOLS WEIGH 25%/50%/75% LESS.

Advice: Consider this perk during the initial stages of your exploration, when pistols are the predominant weapon in Appalachia. If you have a wide variety of pistols or extra pistols to cannibalize for parts, and you don't want to store many (or any) of them, then take this perk. Check the pistol weight against other weapon types, and you may find these aren't adding a colossal amount to your Carry Weight. And if you have this perk activated, check the disassembled weight of the component parts of each pistol you find, compared to the new perk weight; it may cause you to keep normally heavier but now lighter pistols longer before breaking them down at a workbench.

TRAINING

CRAFTING AND C.A.M.P.ING

INVENTORY

QUESTS

ATLAS

BESTIARY

APPENDICES

SECRET AGENT

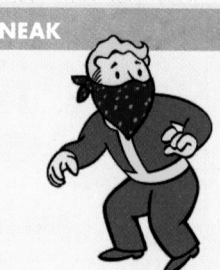

RARITY: UNCOMMON
LEVEL: 47
RANKS: ★★★★★
POINTS: 1, 2, 3

DESCRIPTION: STEALTH BOYS LAST TWICE/THREE TIMES/FOUR TIMES AS LONG!

Advice: Usually a Stealth Boy lasts around 30 seconds and merges your physical presence with the landscape, effectively making you invisible. Take this perk and increase that time to around 2 minutes (Rank 3)! This is a must-have for those who've found, crafted, or otherwise obtained a Stealth Boy and the related Phantom Unit. It's a cornerstone of a stealth-based player and should be partnered with any perk that effectively adds to your stealthiness, such as the Perception perks Night Eyes and the Agility perks Covert Operative, Escape Artist, Light Footed, Mister Sandman, Ninja, and Sneak.

THRU-HIKER

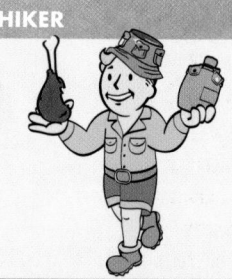

RARITY: COMMON
LEVEL: 3
RANKS: ★★★★★
POINTS: 1, 2, 3

DESCRIPTION: FOOD AND DRINK WEIGHTS ARE REDUCED BY 30%/60%/90%.

Advice: This is an early card to take, and one you should think about carefully: As freshly made food (made at cooking stations, rather than boxed or canned goods) is the one item that spoils with speed (employ the Luck perk Good With Salt to negate this), you won't be able to carry some of the Hunger-related items for very long. But having the ability to gather and carry a multitude of food and water is always helpful, though it isn't usually used as often as chems (e.g., Stimpaks and RadAway). Are you always near your Stash Box? Then ignore this perk. But if you're utilizing related Endurance perks like Good Doggy, consider this before asking yourself, "Do I consume more dog food than chems?" Note that perks like Slow Metabolizer and Philanthropist actually negate the effectiveness of this perk! Also think about being the food and drink carrier for your team.

SNEAK

RARITY: UNCOMMON
LEVEL: 20
RANKS: ★★★★★
POINTS: 1, 2, 3, 4, 5

DESCRIPTION: YOU ARE 20%/30%/40%/50%/60% HARDER TO DETECT WHILE SNEAKING.

Advice: The act of sneaking involves crouching to avoid enemy detection, remaining "hidden" so you can launch sneak attacks, and focusing on Agility, as this is the primary attribute that sneak Perk Cards are played from. While this has little effect on another human player spotting you crouching in a dark corner (though you can still attack them if they have their back to you, as your location disappears from the map when you crouch), it is still a viable method of killing. The Secret Agent perk is a great partner perk with Sneak, along with all the stealth-related perks listed in the Secret Agent advice.

WHITE KNIGHT

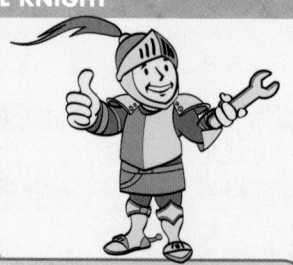

RARITY: UNCOMMON
LEVEL: 39
RANKS: ★★★★★
POINTS: 1, 2, 3

DESCRIPTION: YOUR ARMOR BREAKS 30%/60%/90% MORE SLOWLY AND IS CHEAPER TO REPAIR.

Advice: Granting you two additional benefits for wearing armor, this makes it almost twice as sturdy (Rank 3) and allows you to use fewer materials when repairing armor. The latter may not be of huge benefit, if the armor's components are relatively easy to find, but it's still helpful. With more durable armor, you can explore farther for longer and spend more time before visits to the Armor Workbench. Also be aware that playing multiple Damage Resistance perks (such as the ones listed in the Agility perk Evasive) also keep armor intact longer. The best partner perks for White Knight are the Intelligence perks Armorer and Fix It Good. There's also the Luck perk Lucky Break and the Strength perk Sturdy Frame to think about, too.

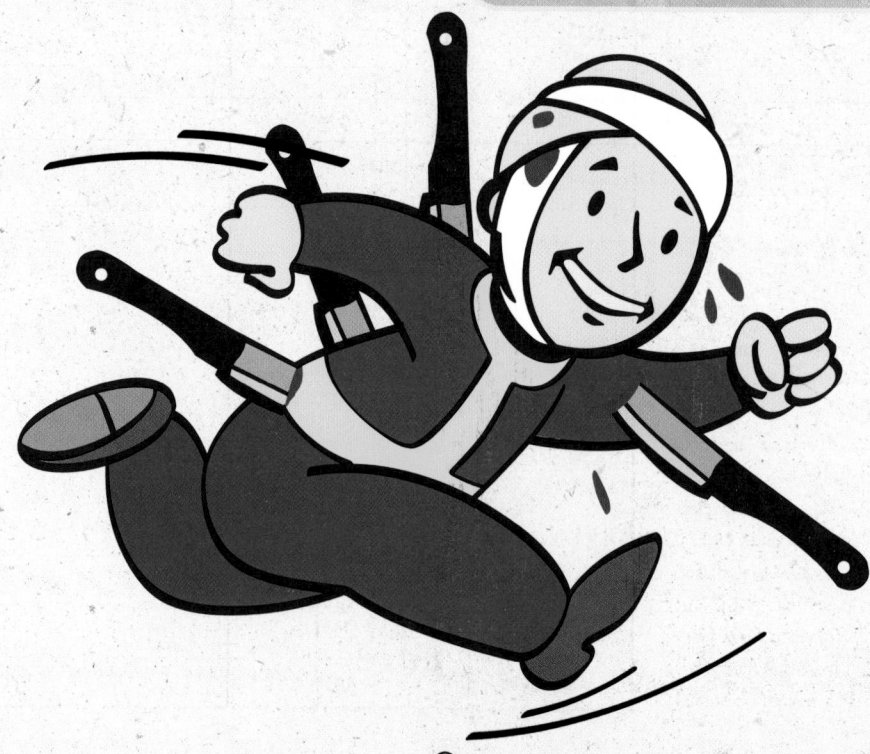

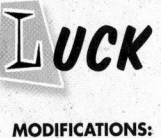

LUCK

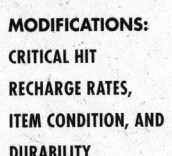
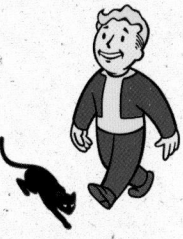

- MODIFICATIONS:
  CRITICAL HIT
  RECHARGE RATES,
  ITEM CONDITION, AND
  DURABILITY
- BUFFS: LUCK BOBBLEHEAD, LIVE, AND LOVE 5
  MAGAZINE, HAPPY-GO-LUCKY (CHARISMA), SOME
  ARMOR AND CLOTHING (AND EFFECTS), CHEMS (DAY
  TRIPPER, X-CELL)

Luck is a measure of your general good fortune and affects the recharge rate of Critical Hits as well as the condition and durability of items that you loot. The condition of looted items (as opposed to crafted ones) is determined by a random dice roll between a min and max condition value. In combat, Luck benefits your Critical Hits, hastening a target's departure in quicker, more violent ways, which is obviously both beneficial and entertaining.

VALUE	LOOTED ITEM MIN CONDITION	LOOTED ITEM MAX CONDITION	V.A.T.S. CRITICAL GAIN PER ATTACK (MAX CRITICAL IS 100)
1	15	65	6.5
2	18.3	68.3	8
3	21.7	71.7	9.5
4	25	75	11
5	37.5	87.5	12.5
6	50	100	14
7	52.5	102.5	15.5
8	55	105	17
9	57.5	107.5	18.5
10	60	110	20
11	67.5	117.5	21.5
12	75	125	23
13	80	130	24.5
14	85	135	26
15	90	140	27.5

LUCK-RELATED PERKS: OVERVIEW

You'll see the word *chance* appear multiple times throughout your Luck card wrangling. This applies to finding extra Chems, ammo, and even canned food, and later on, filling your Critical Meter, the chance to instantly reload, ricochet damage back at a foe, or drop a live grenade as you die! The benefits of collectibles is increased, there are four major V.A.T.S. Improvements to consider, and there are perks that reduce negative effects (like mutations and a Mysterious Savior to revive you when no one else is around). Add to this some oddities (the classic Bloody Mess and Mutation-stabilization), and you have a better than normal chance of survival.

LUCK PERKS (30)

The following table shows all 30 Luck Perk Cards, listed by the earliest level you can obtain them.

PERK NAME	C	U	R	LEVEL	RANKS	DESCRIPTION
Pharma Farma		x		2	1, 2, 3	40/60/80% chance to find extra first aid Chems when you "Search" a chem container.
Scrounger		x		3	1, 2, 3	40/60/80% chance to find extra ammo when you "Search" an ammo container.
Serendipity		x		5	1, 2, 3	While below 30% Health, gain a 15/30/45% chance to avoid damage.
CanDo!	x			7	1, 2, 3	40/60/80% chance to find an extra canned food when you search a food container.
Good with Salt		x		9	1, 2, 3	Food in your inventory will spoil 30/60/90% more slowly.
Junk Shield			x	10	1, 2, 3	Carry junk to gain up to 10/20/30 Damage and Energy Resistance. (No Power Armor).
Mystery Meat		x		12	1, 2, 3	Stimpaks may generate/generate more/generate excessive edible meat tissue. Higher Rads improve the chance.
Luck of the Draw		x		14	1, 2, 3	Slight chance your weapon will repair/chance your weapon will repair/chance your weapon will greatly repair itself when hitting an enemy.
Cap Collector			x	15	1, 2, 3, 4	You have a chance/better chance/excellent chance/almost always to find more bottle caps when opening a Caps Stash.
Woodchucker	x			17	1	Collect twice as much when harvesting wood.
Curator	x			19	1	The benefits of bobbleheads and magazines last twice as long.
Psychopath		x		21	1, 2, 3	Any kill in V.A.T.S. has a 5/10/15% chance to refill your Critical Meter.
Dry Nurse	x			23	1	You have a 50% chance to keep your Stimpak when you revive another player.
Lucky Break		x		24	1, 2, 3	Slight chance your equipped armor will repair/chance your equipped armor will repair/chance your equipped armor will greatly repair itself when struck.
Mysterious Stranger			x	26	1, 2, 3	The Mysterious Stranger will appear occasionally/more often/so frequently he knows your name in V.A.T.S. to lend a hand.
Last Laugh		x		27	1	You drop a live grenade from your inventory when you die.
Four Leaf Clover		x		29	1, 2, 3, 4	Each hit in V.A.T.S. has a chance/better chance/good chance/excellent chance to fill your Critical meter.
Starched Genes	x			30	1, 2	Less/no chance for you to mutate from Rads or for RadAway to cure mutations.
One Gun Army			x	31	1, 2, 3, 4	Heavy guns gain a 2/4/6/8% stagger chance and a 2/4/6/8% chance to cripple a limb.
Grim Reaper's Sprint		x		33	1, 2, 3	Any kill in V.A.T.S. has a 15/25/35% chance to restore all AP.
Storm Chaser	x			35	1, 2	Gain health regeneration/high health regeneration while outside during rain or Rad storms.
Tormentor			x	37	1, 2, 3, 4	Your rifle attacks have a 3/6/9/12% chance of crippling a limb.
Ricochet			x	38	1, 2, 3, 4	Gain a 5/10/15/20% chance to deflect back some of enemies' ranged damage. (No PvP).
Quick Hands		x		40	1, 2, 3, 4, 5	Gain a 5/10/15/20/25% chance to instantly reload when your clip is empty.
Bloody Mess		x		42	1, 2, 3	5/10/15% bonus damage means enemies may explode into a gory red paste.
Critical Savvy		x		44	1, 2, 3	Critical Hits now only consume 85/70/55% of your critical meter.
Class Freak	x			46	1, 2, 3	The negative effects of your mutations are reduced by 25/50/75%.
Better Criticals		x		47	1, 2, 3	V.A.T.S. criticals now do +20/30/40% damage.
Mysterious Savior		x		49	1, 1, 1	A mysterious savior will occasionally/more frequently/regularly appear to revive you when downed.
Super Duper		x		50	1, 2, 3, 4	When you craft anything, there is a 10/20/30/40% chance you'll get double results!

TRAINING

CRAFTING AND C.A.M.P.ING

INVENTORY

QUESTS

ATLAS

BESTIARY

APPENDICES

BETTER CRITICALS

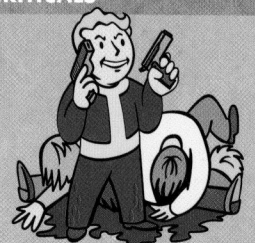

RARITY: UNCOMMON
LEVEL: 47
RANKS: ★★★★★
POINTS: 1, 2, 3

DESCRIPTION:
V.A.T.S. CRITICALS NOW DO +20%/30%/40% DAMAGE.

Advice: Once you learn how critical hits and damage work, and you've accrued enough levels to access this perk, you can use it to really finish off your adversaries in style! Naturally, you have used V.A.T.S. over normal methods of foe disposal, as well as partnering the perk with the Perception perk Concentrated Fire, the Agility perk Gun Fu, and related Luck perks like Critical Savvy, Four Leaf Clover, Grim Reaper's Sprint, and Psychopath. If you're especially keen on V.A.T.S. combat, Better Criticals does exactly what you'd expect it to.

BLOODY MESS

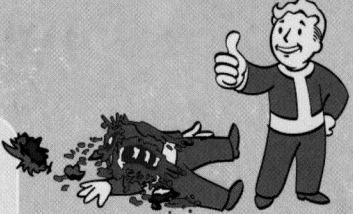

RARITY: UNCOMMON
LEVEL: 42
RANKS: ★★★★★
POINTS: 1, 2, 3

DESCRIPTION:
5%/10%/15% BONUS DAMAGE MEANS ENEMIES MAY EXPLODE INTO A GORY RED PASTE.

Advice: Though you'll need to raise several levels to access this perk, it provides both a revoltingly spectacular end to a fight and additional damage to each hit, without any limitations to the type of weapon you use. Stack these bonuses with other perks, depending on your focused fighting style: For example, consider the Intelligence perks Demolition Expert and Nerd Rage, the Luck perk Junk Shield, and the specific weapon-based bonus perks like Commando for automatic rifles or Heavy Gunner for nonexplosive heavy guns.

CAN DO!

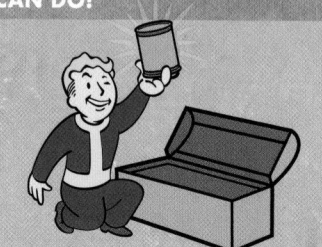

RARITY: COMMON
LEVEL: 7
RANKS: ★★★★★
POINTS: 1, 2, 3

DESCRIPTION: 40/60/80% CHANCE TO FIND AN EXTRA CANNED FOOD WHEN YOU SEARCH A FOOD CONTAINER.

Advice: Aside from the classic Canned Dog Food, there's Cram and Potato Crisps to consider and any other food with a sealed metal container. Since canned food doesn't spoil, meaning you can carry it with you and eat it any time, having more hidden inside containers can be helpful. However, there are drawbacks; you need to scavenge areas to find food containers, and there's not a 100% chance any will have canned food in it. However, any time you're in a cafeteria or kitchen (or other places where a lot of boxed food is lying around), use this perk while opening containers. Alternatively, cook your own food using recipes. Partner this with the questionable Endurance perk Good Doggy, thus granting you more dog food to consume.

CAP COLLECTOR

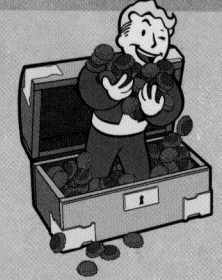

RARITY: RARE
LEVEL: 15
RANKS: ★★★★★
POINTS: 1, 2, 3, 4

DESCRIPTION: YOU HAVE A CHANCE/BETTER CHANCE/EXCELLENT CHANCE/ALMOST ALWAYS TO FIND MORE BOTTLE CAPS WHEN OPENING A CAPS STASH.

Advice: This perk reacts to a specific collectible object: the tins of Caps Stashes hidden around the landscape and tracked throughout the Atlas. Make sure your scavenging yields greater-than-normal dividends by using this perk. Partner this with the Perception perk Fortune Finder to ensure you find every hidden Stash. And check the Atlas to figure out the theoretical maximum stashes a location (both outside and in) may be hiding. Finally, remember there are other ways to make money in Appalachia (like selling Fusion Cores); scrounging for Caps might not be the best use of your time, but it's still worthwhile if it's not your main exploratory focus.

CLASS FREAK

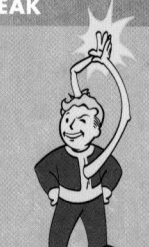

RARITY: COMMON
LEVEL: 46
RANKS: ★★★★★
POINTS: 1, 2, 3

DESCRIPTION: THE NEGATIVE EFFECTS OF YOUR MUTATIONS ARE REDUCED BY 25%/50%/75%.

Advice: Turn mutations you can acquire into much more beneficial, perk-like bonuses, advantages that take a little time to gestate (you need to catch the disease and watch it mutate first). Consult the section of this guide on Diseases and Mutations for a complete list. If you're high enough level to utilize this Perk Card, try to catch the disease from which a mutation is likely to morph and then lessen any problematic effects from it. Then partner this with the Charisma perk Strange in Numbers and the Luck perk Starched Genes.

CRITICAL SAVVY

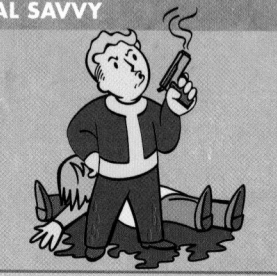

RARITY: UNCOMMON
LEVEL: 44
RANKS: ★★★★★
POINTS: 1, 2, 3

DESCRIPTION: CRITICAL HITS NOW CONSUME ONLY 85%/70%/55% OF YOUR CRITICAL METER.

Advice: When you take down a foe with a particularly satisfying Critical Hit, the only downside is your meter depleting back to zero. Not so with this perk, which keeps at least some of the Critical Meter filled. This can effectively halve the time it takes to refill the meter. Combine this with the Luck perks Better Criticals and Four Leaf Clover to further increase this perk's effectiveness. However, the Luck perk Psychopath certainly isn't detrimental to partner with Critical Savvy, but sometimes lessens its effectiveness.

CURATOR

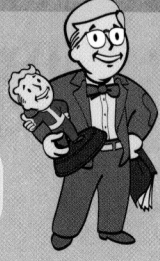

RARITY: COMMON
LEVEL: 19
RANKS: ★★★★
POINTS: 1

DESCRIPTION: THE BENEFITS OF BOBBLEHEADS AND MAGAZINES LAST TWICE AS LONG.

Advice: This is a spectacular perk to obtain, especially if you're using several Bobbleheads and Magazines at once (in fact, it's only worth utilizing while your Bobblehead and Magazine effects are in play). Obviously you can shelve this perk and use other Luck perks until this happens. Due to the random nature of the Bobbleheads and Magazines you acquire, you should calculate whether expending Luck Points to activate Curator gives you better bonuses compared to using up your points to activate a different Luck perk. For example, you have Luck 3 and Charisma 3, and you have the Luck perk Junk Shield Rank 3 (+45 Damage Resistance while carrying Junk), and you pick up Grognak the Barbarian issue #8 (gain +2 Damage Resistance for each point of Charisma; or +6 DR in this example); though the Magazine is still beneficial (and the bonus will stack), the bonuses from your Junk Shield perk far outweighs using Curator to bolster the time you benefit from the Magazine's lesser Damage Resistance bonus.

DRY NURSE

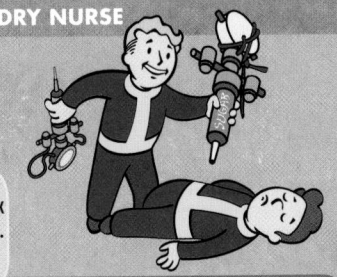

RARITY: COMMON
LEVEL: 23
RANKS: ★★★★
POINTS: 1

DESCRIPTION: YOU HAVE A 50% CHANCE TO KEEP YOUR STIMPAK WHEN YOU REVIVE ANOTHER PLAYER.

Advice: This is a helpful perk if you're playing the informal role of "medic" with fellow teammates, or indeed anyone crying out for help in the Appalachian wilderness. This allows better management of Stimpaks, keeps more of this vital Chem in your inventory before you need to craft or scavenge for more, and the act of saving another can lead to life-long friendships (or indifference)! The only drawback is that you don't usually revive others very often, so this is a card to shelve and bring out just before you need it.

FOUR LEAF CLOVER

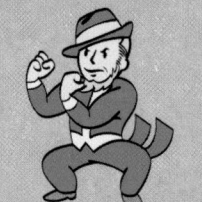

RARITY: UNCOMMON
LEVEL: 29
RANKS: ★★★★
POINTS: 1, 2, 3, 4

DESCRIPTION: EACH HIT IN V.A.T.S. HAS A CHANCE/ BETTER CHANCE/GOOD CHANCE/ EXCELLENT CHANCE TO FILL YOUR CRITICAL METER.

Advice: Normally, successful V.A.T.S.-related strikes gradually fill your Critical meter, after which you can unleash a Critical attack. Now there is a chance your meter could fill after every single hit, which becomes entertaining and means you need to actually launch critical hits much more often to take advantage of this perk; it's no good just sitting on a full meter and never using it. Launch Criticals as soon as the meter fills so this perk becomes as useful as possible. Then ensure your Criticals are further augmented by partnering with Luck perks like Better Criticals and the slightly less potent but very similar Psychopath. Also of note, but to a lesser extent, is Critical Savvy. Critical Savvy isn't problematic when used with Four Leaf Clover, as Four Leaf Clover only has a chance of refilling your Critical meter, but the latter perk negates Critical Savvy's quicker refill ability by offering an instantly full meter.

GOOD WITH SALT

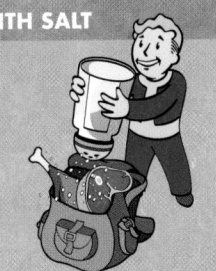

RARITY: UNCOMMON
LEVEL: 9
RANKS: ★★★★★
POINTS: 1, 2, 3

DESCRIPTION: FOOD IN YOUR INVENTORY WILL SPOIL 30%/60%/90% MORE SLOWLY.

Advice: This early perk negates the need to instantly gobble down food you've cooked before it spoils. This adds a great deal more flexibility to when and where you need to use cooking stations, stops you from eating spoiled food (unless you're actively wanting to get a Disease like Dysentery!), and allows you to treat "fresh" food a little more like the boxed foods you would usually be able to wait to eat. This heightens the usefulness of every recipe that uses fresh ingredients and also counts toward food in your My Stash Box. It allows you to forage across the land for a longer time, use crops at workshops, and keep the picked plants instead of them staying on the vine. It allows you to create more recipes without wasting resources. Just make sure to play this Perk Card continuously, or your food soon reverts to its "rotten" state, and accidentally removing this perk can cause mass spoilage!

GRIM REAPER'S SPRINT

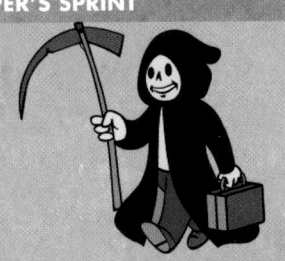

RARITY: UNCOMMON
LEVEL: 33
RANKS: ★★★★
POINTS: 1, 2, 3

DESCRIPTION: ANY KILL IN V.A.T.S. HAS A 15%/25%/35% CHANCE TO RESTORE ALL ACTION POINTS.

Advice: This can turn you into a killing machine if you're attacking larger groups of foes (this perk is useless against single enemies), and you've tried to obtain and modify weapons that can take down lesser foes in one or two shots (and also by employing weapon specialization and other perks that cause greater damage to be inflicted). Think about partnering this with the Perception perk Concentrated Fire, the Agility perk Gun Fu, and your related Luck perks Critical Savvy, Four Leaf Clover, and Psychopath. Combat in a scenario where Grim Reaper's Sprint would be effective would be to engage a main entity (say, a Scorchbeast) until your Action Points are low, then switch to a horde of lesser Scorched foes, killing these until your AP is restored, and then switch back to the Scorchbeast. This effectively gives you continuous offense until you either run out of ammunition or combat concludes.

JUNK SHIELD

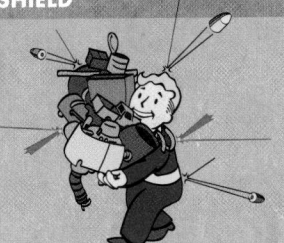

RARITY: RARE
LEVEL: 10
RANKS: ★★★★
POINTS: 1, 2, 3

DESCRIPTION: CARRY JUNK TO GAIN UP TO 10/20/30 DAMAGE AND ENERGY RESISTANCE. (NO POWER ARMOR).

Advice: This is a low-level, high-yield perk with excellent defenses you can use in place of and, once you find the necessary items or Mods, and in addition to armor to gain some additional defense resistance against the two most common forms of damage. You should be gathering junk anyway, so check what you're carrying in the Items > Junk menu and increase it until you start to see those resistance bonuses. Just be aware that scrapping the junk, dropping it, or having another player steal the junk from your corpse negates this perk. This makes Junk Shield a perk you can't completely rely on; it just provides some additional defense. The other problem is that junk obviously adds to your Carry Weight, so augment your capacity: the Strength perk Pack Rat allows you to reach the maximum Resistance much more easily and without dropping or scrapping objects. Also check out all the Strength perks that augment the weight of items or your Carry Weight, such as Strong Back.

LAST LAUGH

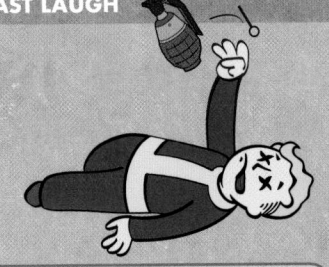

RARITY: UNCOMMON
LEVEL: 27
RANKS: ★★★★★
POINTS: 1

DESCRIPTION: GAIN A YOU DROP A LIVE GRENADE FROM YOUR INVENTORY WHEN YOU DIE.

Advice: This can be more of an annoying amusement (for you) than a bona fide tactic, and it obviously requires you to have grenades in your inventory, or this simply becomes a waste of Perk points. But this does enable you to damage a foe. If you're fighting on a team, using this after a suicidal charge against others can help soften up the enemy at the expense of your own life. It can also (hopefully) cause a previously victorious but wounded human enemy to die from the explosion, allowing you to reach your death location and steal the junk bags you both left behind! Conversely, when defeating an enemy who has used grenades, wait a moment or two after you defeat them for any grenades to detonate, and then inspect anything else that was dropped.

TRAINING

CRAFTING AND C.A.M.P.ING

INVENTORY

QUESTS

ATLAS

BESTIARY

APPENDICES

LUCK OF THE DRAW

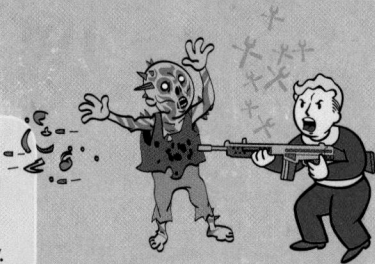

RARITY: UNCOMMON
LEVEL: 14
RANKS: ★★★★★
POINTS: 1, 2, 3

DESCRIPTION: SLIGHT CHANCE YOUR WEAPON WILL REPAIR/CHANCE YOUR WEAPON WILL REPAIR/CHANCE YOUR WEAPON WILL GREATLY REPAIR ITSELF WHEN HITTING AN ENEMY.

Advice: The requires the weapon to physically strike the foe, which is usually the function of melee weapons (of the fist, one-handed, or two-handed variety), but this also works with weapon bashing, so it can become a tactic when using guns too! Forgo that Weapon Workbench hammering by hoping your weapon's contact with an enemy has (approximately) a 1 in 5 chance of improving the weapon (at Rank 3). Obviously, this perk is more helpful to those favoring close combat, and partnering Luck of the Draw with the Strength-related perks that increase the damage of one-handed (Gladiator) and two-handed (Slugger) weapons helps you maintain such a weapon for longer. Also think about partnering this with Intelligence perk Makeshift Warrior. Even if you're using ranged weapons, this perk also works well with Intelligence perks like Gunsmith and Licensed Plumber. Finally, don't overlook the Luck perk Weapon Artisan, which when used with Luck of the Draw allows more attempts to regain the weapon's condition simply because it has such a high condition to begin with.

LUCKY BREAK

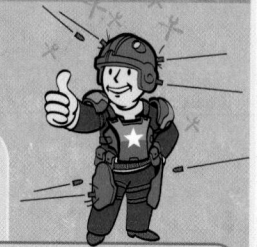

RARITY: UNCOMMON
LEVEL: 24
RANKS: ★★★★★
POINTS: 1, 2, 3

DESCRIPTION: SLIGHT CHANCE YOUR EQUIPPED ARMOR WILL REPAIR/CHANCE YOUR EQUIPPED ARMOR WILL REPAIR/CHANCE YOUR EQUIPPED ARMOR WILL GREATLY REPAIR ITSELF WHEN STRUCK.

Advice: The word *struck* means hit by an enemy's ranged weapon or their melee-range attacks. Obviously, some enemies may strike you more often than not (e.g., a Super Mutant with a minigun compared to a Scorchbeast), making this perk more useful in certain situations (when attacks are fast and weak). This perk's effectiveness depends on how often you're usually hit during combat (e.g., a tank-like character should see more benefits over a sniper). Forgo that Armor Workbench mending by hoping 1 in 5 incoming hits improves your armor (at Rank 3). Think about the benefits of using this with the Intelligence perks Armorer and Fix It Good and the Agility perk White Knight.

MYSTERIOUS SAVIOR

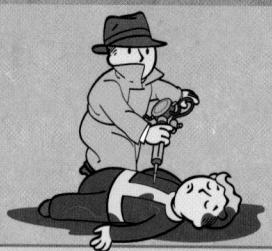

RARITY: UNCOMMON
LEVEL: 49
RANKS: ★★★★★
POINTS: 1, 1, 1

DESCRIPTION: A MYSTERIOUS SAVIOR WILL OCCASIONALLY/MORE FREQUENTLY/REGULARLY APPEAR TO REVIVE YOU WHEN DOWNED.

Advice: Having an unknown friend coaxing you back from the brink doesn't occur until you're a veteran of Appalachian exploration; therefore, you may feel this card is unnecessary due to your prowess against the attacks of others. But there are situations where this becomes incredibly useful, such as when you're maneuvering through a complex and lengthy hostile environment and are far from a Fast-Travel point, and foes are getting the best of you. It also helps when you're in a group event and you're getting overwhelmed, but you're likely to turn the tide if you die and quickly return. This perk is also helpful during Scorchbeast battles, when you're fighting with teammates (they don't need to worry about you as much). Finally, and arguably most importantly, this perks helps when you're dueling with fellow humans! Surprise a previously cocky victor by returning to seek instant revenge! Heck, add the Luck perk Last Laugh so you become almost as lethal during your death as during the previous battle!

MYSTERIOUS STRANGER

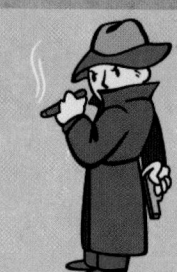

RARITY: RARE
LEVEL: 26
RANKS: ★★★★★
POINTS: 1, 2, 3

DESCRIPTION: THE MYSTERIOUS STRANGER WILL APPEAR OCCASIONALLY/MORE OFTEN/SO FREQUENTLY HE KNOWS YOUR NAME IN V.A.T.S. TO LEND A HAND.

Advice: It seems not all surviving humans in Appalachia are only from Vault 76. This is a free and extra V.A.T.S. attack, accompanied by an announcement chime to let you know the attack (usually a single shot for exceptional damage) is incoming. It usually takes out a foe for you. Remember this only occurs in V.A.T.S., and you need to weigh the entertainment and value of the Mysterious Stranger (and the random nature of his appearance) compared to Luck perks that are guaranteed to help you during V.A.T.S., like Better Criticals, Critical Savvy, Four Leaf Clover, Grim Reaper's Sprint, and Psychopath. While some of these have a chance at occurring, they all rely on your actions, usually occur more frequently, and one or more may be more helpful to use instead, if you've only a few Luck Points allocated.

MYSTERY MEAT

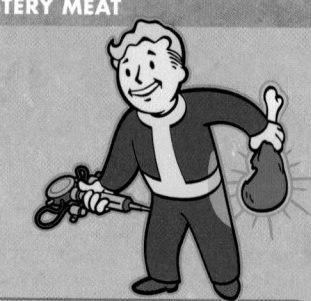

RARITY: UNCOMMON
LEVEL: 12
RANKS: ★★★★★
POINTS: 1, 2, 3

DESCRIPTION: STIMPAKS MAY GENERATE/GENERATE MORE/GENERATE EXCESSIVE EDIBLE MEAT TISSUE. HIGHER RADS IMPROVE THE CHANCE.

Advice: Edible meat tissue: It's what's for dinner! While this might not sound appetizing to those with weak stomachs (in which case, don't read about the Endurance perk Cannibal!), the meat in question is fine to consume and offers another method to satiate your Hunger without the need to scavenge for crops, meat, or canned goods. Remember you can attempt to acquire even more of this meat by partnering this with other perks that help your Stimpak consumption, such as the Strength perk Traveling Pharmacy, the Intelligence perk First Aid, and the Luck perk Dry Nurse. The only potential issue is the high Rads you need to improve mystery meat generation, so adventure with higher Rads due to the Endurance perk Ghoulish and to a lesser extent, Rad Resistant.

ONE GUN ARMY

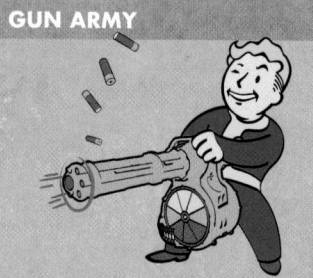

RARITY: RARE
LEVEL: 31
RANKS: ★★★★★
POINTS: 1, 2, 3, 4

DESCRIPTION: HEAVY GUNS GAIN A 2%/4%/6%/8% STAGGER CHANCE AND A 2%/4%/6%/8% CHANCE TO CRIPPLE A LIMB.

Advice: Though this perk is for those specializing in heavy weaponry and affects only those weapon types, this can help augment the already-powerful takedown potential of heavy guns, especially ones like the minigun that fires multiple shots with extreme speed. This is the sort of perk that an explorer focusing on Heavy Guns perks (within the Strength attribute category) should take if they have extra Luck points to spend: Partner it with the Strength perk Bear Arms, Bullet Shield, Heavy Gunner, and especially Lock and Load. If you're a Power Armor fan, try the Intelligence perk Stabilized.

PHARMA FARMA

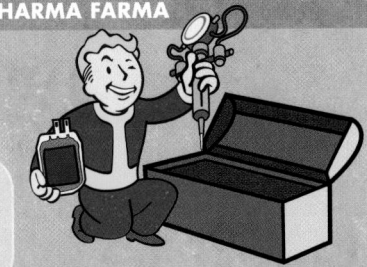

RARITY: UNCOMMON
LEVEL: 2
RANKS: ★★★★★
POINTS: 1, 2, 3

DESCRIPTION: 40/60/80% CHANCE TO FIND EXTRA FIRST AID CHEMS WHEN YOU "SEARCH" A CHEM CONTAINER.

Advice: Chem containers are the white and yellow metal boxes scattered throughout Appalachia. Having the ability to add additional first aid chems (usually a Stimpak or variant thereof) to your inventory (which you can use on yourself or your team) is always helpful. You're likely to obtain this perk in the initial stages of your Appalachian exploration, so use it if you're always running low on Stimpaks, can't afford to purchase them, and don't want to make your own on a Chemistry Station. However, making your own is a worthwhile endeavor, as it's better to be self-sufficient than rely on containers for your continuing health. Partner this with the Strength perk Traveling Pharmacy.

PSYCHOPATH

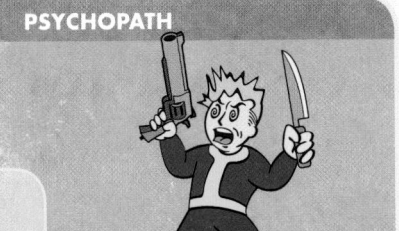

RARITY: UNCOMMON
LEVEL: 21
RANKS: ★★★★★
POINTS: 1, 2, 3

DESCRIPTION: ANY KILL IN V.A.T.S. HAS A 5%/10%/15% CHANCE TO REFILL YOUR CRITICAL METER.

Advice: Once you learn the benefits of unleashing Critical hits on foes, place this perk in with your V.A.T.S.-improvement perks. Though the chance to refill your meter is low, it still usually happens 1 in 6 or 7 chances at Rank 3, each time an enemy is killed in V.A.T.S. The number of enemies you face also determines the effectiveness of Psychopath; if you're only facing one or two foes, this perk isn't really viable, but for events or tackling hordes of foes, it can be a real help. Further augment your Criticals by partnering with Luck perks like Better Criticals and the similar but even more potent Four Leaf Clover. Also of note is Critical Savvy. This perk isn't problematic when used with Psychopath (as Psychopath only has a chance of refilling your Critical meter), but the latter perk may negate Critical Savvy's quicker refill ability by instantly filling the meter instead.

QUICK HANDS

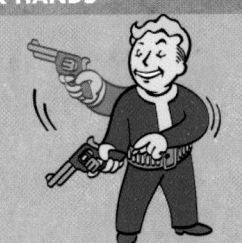

RARITY: UNCOMMON
LEVEL: 40
RANKS: ★★★★★
POINTS: 1, 2, 3, 4, 5

DESCRIPTION: GAIN A 5%/10%/15%/20%/25% CHANCE TO INSTANTLY RELOAD WHEN YOUR CLIP IS EMPTY.

Advice: This is a relatively high-level perk, with five ranks to think about merging together. The highest rank offers a one-in-four chance of an instant reload. Now you need to figure out whether your other Luck perks (as a Rank 5 Quick Hands costs 5 Luck points) are more or less helpful than a relatively small instant reload chance. Instant reloading is obviously helpful and becomes so in many different ways, depending on the type of weapon (e.g., shotguns and heavy guns take longer to reload, so they're helped more by Quick Hands compared to Pistols). Remember your clip needs to be empty, so reloading midway through a clip negates this perk's effectiveness. Also note the Strength perks Lock and Load and Scattershot, as well as the Perception perk Ground Pounder. Quick Hands doesn't help or hinder these similar-sounding perks, but they should be seen as weapon-specific alternatives to Quick Hands if you can't afford the Luck points cost.

RICOCHET

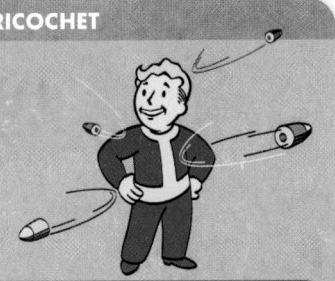

RARITY: RARE
LEVEL: 38
RANKS: ★★★★★
POINTS: 1, 2, 3, 4

DESCRIPTION: GAIN A 5/10/15/20% CHANCE TO DEFLECT BACK SOME OF ENEMIES' RANGED DAMAGE. (NO PVP).

Advice: It is great for tank-like Vault Dwellers who prefer to charge into the fray, leaving foes no alternative but to fire on them, before (possibly) receiving a dose of their own medicine. Think of this as softening up targets you're about to engage without needing to perform any maneuvers except standing there and hoping foes aren't attacking with melee weapons or claws. Naturally, this is proficient against certain types of enemies, like Scorched and Super Mutants who favor ranged attacks, compared to foes who like to maul like Ghouls or most animals. The main drawback with this perk is that it's effective only if you're actively taking damage, so if you favor a hide-and-strike plan of attack, you may want to try a different perk. Finally, there are some similar perks that further negate enemy ordnance, like the Agility perk Dodgy.

SCROUNGER

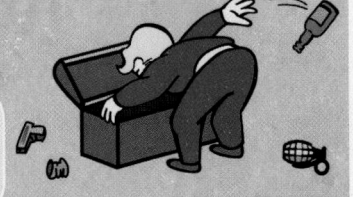

RARITY: UNCOMMON
LEVEL: 3
RANKS: ★★★★★
POINTS: 1, 2, 3

DESCRIPTION: 40/60/80% CHANCE TO FIND EXTRA AMMO WHEN YOU "SEARCH" AN AMMO CONTAINER.

Advice: This is one of the first Luck perks you're likely to come across. It increases your ammunition gathering every time you dip a hand into an ammo container, so focus your foraging on those. This allows you to keep your always-depleting supplies of ammunition higher than normal, after which you can use these in your guns or break them down and employ them at a Tinker's Workbench when you make your own ammo—once you decide on a type of gun that you want to use. The drawback is that the ammo type you find is random; regardless, this is a good perk to have, even if you're using melee weapons and not collecting ammunition at all, as any ammunition can be sold or given to a needy teammate.

SERENDIPITY

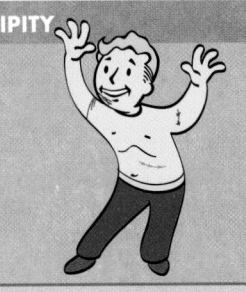

RARITY: UNCOMMON
LEVEL: 5
RANKS: ★★★★★
POINTS: 1, 2, 3

DESCRIPTION: WHILE BELOW 30% HEALTH, GAIN A 15%/30%/45% CHANCE TO AVOID DAMAGE.

Advice: This is ostensibly a perk that you utilize during the initial stages of your Appalachian experience, keeping you alive as you figure out exactly how to survive and before you've crafted or found some better armor and proficient use of health chems. Naturally, being low on health is dangerous, but having a nearly 1 in 2 chance (at Rank 3) of shrugging off any attack is pretty powerful. If you're finding this helpful, partner Serendipity with the high-level Intelligence perk Nerd Rage. At Rank 3, Nerd Rage offers 40% Damage Resistance, and with this, it stacks to 85%!

However, this is one of the few perks that may actively clash with others. The Endurance perk Photosynthetic and the Agility perk Born Survivor affect Serendipity negatively, so pick one over the others. Think about employing this with other perks that also offer bonuses for those low on Health, like the Agility perk Dead Man Sprinting. The Endurance perk Life Giver is another one to think about partnering Serendipity with, as this effectively ups your health even at low levels, allowing you to survive for longer, though it's not available for a long while.

TRAINING

CRAFTING AND C.A.M.P.ING

INVENTORY

QUESTS

ATLAS

BESTIARY

APPENDICES

STARCHED GENES

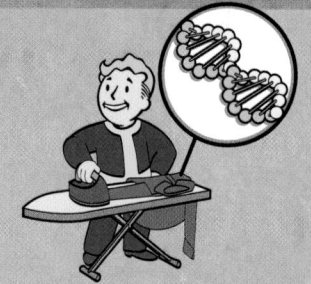

RARITY: COMMON
LEVEL: 30
RANKS: ★★★★★
POINTS: 1, 2

DESCRIPTION: LESS/NO CHANCE FOR YOU TO MUTATE FROM RADS OR FOR RADAWAY TO CURE MUTATIONS.

Advice: This offers a dichotomy of two opposing choices—for the mutation lover or hater! If you dislike mutations, then this keeps you "cleansed" from contracting them and their sometimes wonderful, sometimes problematic effects. However, if you're intrigued by mutations and you've already contracted one you want to keep, pick this; when ridding yourself of radiation poisoning with RadAway, the chem won't get rid of the mutation as it normally does. Now that you're able to permanently "keep" your mutation, why not make it more potent with the Charisma perk Strange in Numbers, as well as the Luck perk Class Freak.

STORM CHASER

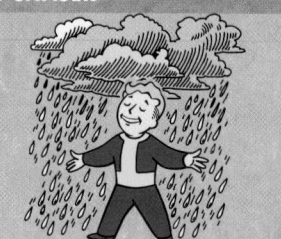

RARITY: COMMON
LEVEL: 35
RANKS: ★★★★★
POINTS: 1, 2

DESCRIPTION: GAIN HEALTH REGENERATION/HIGH HEALTH REGENERATION WHILE OUTSIDE DURING RAIN OR RAD STORMS.

Advice: As long as it's raining "something" down on your head, and you're wanting freedom from Stimpak use with a penchant for reckless behavior, why not investigate areas during inclement weather? There's relatively little else to worry about, though you must shelve the perk when different weather is in effect. If no rainfall is occurring where you are, seek higher ground and look for weather systems in the distance. If you spot clouds (of rain or radiation), then Fast-Travel there to take advantage of the environmental situation. If this investigation is taking place during a Rad Storm, think about using the Endurance perk Ghoulish to keep your cheeks even rosier, even as the conditions worsen.

TORMENTOR

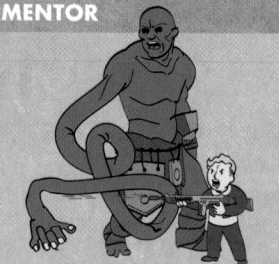

RARITY: RARE
LEVEL: 37
RANKS: ★★★★★
POINTS: 1, 2, 3, 4

DESCRIPTION: YOUR RIFLE ATTACKS HAVE A 3%/6%/9%/12% CHANCE OF CRIPPLING A LIMB.

Advice: Do you need a chance at some specific crippling damage (which is normally only applied during V.A.T.S. once the Perception perk Concentrated Fire is active)? Do you like using rifles (of any type, though this perk seems to be suited to sniper rifles, although automatic rifles with a rapid fire capacity tend to cripple more frequently)? Are you hoping to hobble a foe into reducing their speed (including humans) by crippling a leg or winging them in the arm and preventing them from aiming their weapons as proficiently? Are you concentrating on rifles over other weapon types? If you answered yes to any of these questions, then the Tormentor perk is for you: Not only that, but also a proficiency in rifles (mainly the Perception perks like Commando, Ground Pounder, Long Shot, Rifleman, or Tank Killer) makes the chances of a foe surviving your onslaught even less probable! Finally, remember this also works in V.A.T.S.!

SUPER DUPER

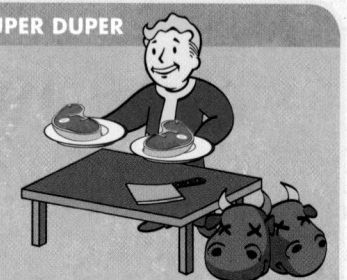

RARITY: UNCOMMON
LEVEL: 50
RANKS: ★★★★★
POINTS: 1, 2, 3, 4

DESCRIPTION: WHEN YOU CRAFT ANYTHING, THERE IS A 10%/20%/30%/40% CHANCE YOU'LL GET DOUBLE RESULTS!

Advice: This perk doesn't become available until you're at a high level, but its positive effects are undeniable: almost a 50/50 chance (at Rank 4) that you'll double your item count when crafting an item. Remember this includes the following:

- **Armor Workbench:** Clothing, Heavy Armor, Helmets, Light Armor, Nuked Flora, Sturdy Armor, and Under Armor.
- **Chemistry Station:** Water, Ammo, Drugs, Energy Ammo, Grenades, Healing, Mutation Serums, Nuked Flora, and Smelting items.
- **Cooking Station:** Drink, Food, Healing, Meat, Plants, Prepared, and Utility items.
- **Power Armor Station:** Enclave, Excavator, Raider, T-45, T51b, T-60, Ultracite, and X-01 Prototype Power Armors.
- **Tinker's Workbench:** Ammo, the Phantom Device, Energy Ammo, Explosive Ammo, Grenades, Mines, and Traps.
- **Weapons Workbench:** Blunt Melee, Edged Melee, Energy Guns, Exotic Weapons, Heavy Guns, Launchers, Machine Guns, Pipe Guns, Throwing Weapons, and Ultracite Weapons.

That's quite a collection! Remember this perk is usually shelved until you're on a workbench or station, and it's well worth using just before crafting something particularly valuable or something that has required some considerable raw-material scavenging to get the components for.

Further this perk's potency (and number of items) by applying other crafting perks to it, such as the Agility perk Ammosmith, Home Defense, the Intelligence perks Armorer, Chemist, Exotic Weapons, Power Smith, and Science. Phew! This is the point where you become the finest crafter in Appalachia!

WOODCHUCKER

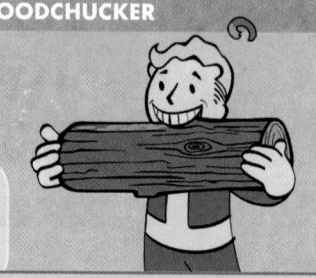

RARITY: COMMON
LEVEL: 17
RANKS: ★★★★★
POINTS: 1, 2, 3

DESCRIPTION: COLLECTING WOOD YIELDS 50%/100%/200% MORE.

Advice: Wood is a staple building block for your C.A.M.P. and to a lesser extent some of your crafting, such as for boiling water. Once you ascertain how much wood you usually use (it can be a lot when building your first C.A.M.P.), and you want to spend less time scavenging for it, then have this perk active. It's much more helpful early on in your exploration when you're searching the woods for logs to utilize as the floors and walls of your abode. Later on, you may have automated resource management at a C.A.M.P. or workshop to take over this scavenging duty (some workshops also allow wood gathering to be accrued as a resource).

APPALACHIAN ARCHETYPES

BUILDING CHARACTER: LEVEL 50 EXAMPLES

If your head is still reeling from the sheer number of possible character combinations, why not take a Calmex and consider emulating one of the following Appalachian archetypes? These level 50 examples show how different a character's path through West Virginia can be. Listed for each type are the perks to aim for, the attributes to increase, and the tactics to attempt. Some of the pictured equipment and outfits may just be for show. Good luck!

COMMANDO

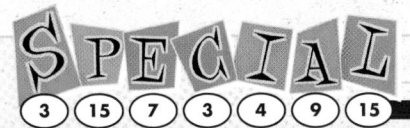

SPECIAL — 3 · 15 · 7 · 3 · 4 · 9 · 15 — Total 56

PERKS EQUIPPED - RANK		SPECIAL/COST	EFFECT
BANDOLIER	3/3	STR/3	BALLISTIC WEAPON AMMO WEIGHS 90% LESS.
COMMANDO	2/3	PER/2	BASIC COMBAT TRAINING MEANS AUTOMATIC RIFLES DO +20% DAMAGE.
GROUNDER POUNDER	4/4	PER/4	AUTOMATIC RIFLE HIP-FIRE ACCURACY AND RELOAD SPEED ARE IMPROVED BY 40%.
EXPERT COMMANDS	2/3	PER/2	RIGOROUS COMBAT TRAINING MEANS AUTOMATIC RIFLES DO +20% DAMAGE.
TANK KILLER	3/3	PER/3	YOUR RIFLES IGNORE 30% ARMOR AND HAVE A 6% CHANCE TO STAGGER.
LONG SHOT	4/4	PER/4	YOUR RIFLES HAVE 20% MORE RANGE AND 40% MORE ACCURACY WHEN SIGHTED.
IRONCLAD	4/5	END/4	YOU NOW GAIN 40 DAMAGE AND ENERGY RESISTANCE WHILE WEARING ARMOR.
LIFEGIVER	2/3	END/3	GAIN A TOTAL OF +30 TO YOUR MAXIMUM HEALTH.
TENDERIZER	3/3	CHA/3	MAKE YOUR TARGET RECEIVE 10% MORE DAMAGE FOR 10 SECONDS AFTER YOU ATTACK.
GUNSMITH	2/3	INT/2	YOUR GUNS BREAK 50% MORE SLOWLY AND ARE CHEAPER TO REPAIR.
WEAPON ARTISAN	2/3	INT/2	YOU CAN REPAIR ANY WEAPON TO 160% OF NORMAL MAXIMUM CONDITION.
ACTION BOY/GIRL	3/3	AGL/3	AP REGENERATES 45% FASTER.
MARATHONER	3/3	AGL/3	SPRINTING CONSUMES 40% FEWER AP.
AMMOSMITH	3/3	AGL/3	PRODUCE 100% MORE ROUNDS WHEN CRAFTING AMMUNITION.
SCROUNGER	3/3	LCK/3	ALWAYS FIND EXTRA AMMO WHEN YOU "SEARCH" AN AMMO CONTAINER.
TORMENTOR	4/4	LCK/4	YOUR RIFLE ATTACKS HAVE A 12% CHANCE OF CRIPPLING A LIMB.
QUICK HANDS	5/5	LCK/5	GAIN A 25% CHANCE TO INSTANTLY RELOAD WHEN YOUR CLIP IS EMPTY.
BLOODY MESS	3/3	LCK/3	15% BONUS DAMAGE MEANS ENEMIES MAY EXPLODE INTO A GORY RED PASTE.

The Commando is simple: Run, shoot, reload, repeat.

With a focus on automatic rifle damage, accuracy, and reload speed, the Commando is a deadly build for players who enjoy fast-paced action. Reduced weapon degradation and the ability to find and craft more ammunition ensures that they reduce their chances of running dry out in the wasteland. Moderate health and armor perks also provide an extra edge.

CRITICAL MASTER

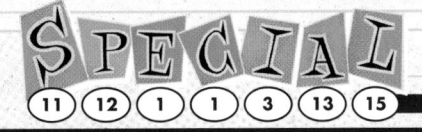

SPECIAL — 11 · 12 · 1 · 1 · 3 · 13 · 15 — Total 56

PERKS EQUIPPED - RANK		SPECIAL/COST	EFFECT
SHOTGUNNER	2/3	STR/2	YOUR SHOTGUNS NOW DO +20% DAMAGE.
EXPERT SHOTGUNNER	2/3	STR/2	YOUR SHOTGUNS NOW DO +20% DAMAGE.
MASTER SHOTGUNNER	3/4	STR/3	YOUR SHOTGUNS NOW DO +30% DAMAGE.
SCATTERSHOT	4/4	STR/4	SHOTGUNS NOW WEIGH 80% LESS AND YOU RELOAD THEM 40% FASTER.
CONCENTRATED FIRE	3/3	PER/3	V.A.T.S. TARGETS LIMBS. FOCUS FIRE TO GAIN HIGH ACCURACY AND DAMAGE PER HIT.
SKEET SHOOTER	4/4	PER/4	YOUR SHOTGUNS HAVE 40% IMPROVED ACCURACY AND SPREAD.
AWARENESS	1/1	PER/2	YOU CAN VIEW A TARGET'S SPECIFIC DAMAGE RESISTANCES IN V.A.T.S.
PENETRATOR	3/3	PER/3	NO V.A.T.S. ACCURACY PENALTY VS. ENEMY BODY PARTS BLOCKED BY COVER.
GUNSMITH	3/3	INT/3	YOUR GUNS BREAK 75% MORE SLOWLY AND ARE CHEAPER TO REPAIR.
MARATHONER	3/3	AGL/3	SPRINTING CONSUMES 40% FEWER AP.
ACTION BOY/GIRL	3/3	AGL/3	AP REGENERATES 45% FASTER.
ENFORCER	4/4	AGL/4	YOUR SHOTGUNS GAIN A 20% STAGGER CHANCE AND A 12% CHANCE TO CRIPPLE A LIMB.
GUN FU	3/3	AGL/3	V.A.T.S. SWAPS TARGETS ON KILL WITH +10%, 20%, THEN 30% DAMAGE TO YOUR NEXT 3 TARGETS.
PSYCHOPATH	3/3	LCK/3	ANY KILL IN V.A.T.S. HAS A 15% CHANCE TO REFILL YOUR CRITICAL METER.
FOUR LEAF CLOVER	3/3	LCK/3	EACH HIT IN V.A.T.S. HAS AN EXCELLENT CHANCE TO FILL YOUR CRITICAL METER.
GRIM REAPER'S SPRINT	3/3	LCK/3	ANY KILL IN V.A.T.S. HAS A 35% CHANCE TO RESTORE ALL AP.
BETTER CRITICALS	3/3	LCK/3	V.A.T.S. CRITICALS NOW DO +40% DAMAGE.
CRITICAL SAVVY	3/3	LCK/3	CRITICAL HITS NOW ONLY CONSUME 55% OF YOUR CRITICAL METER.

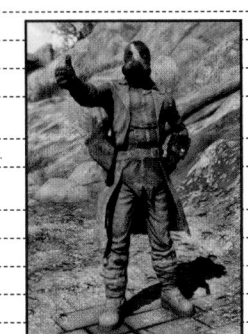

The Crits focus on critical hits for maximum damage over a short period of time.

By focusing on shotgun perks that raise damage and accuracy while reducing weapon degradation, players can sprint in wildly, take several shots with V.A.T.S., and have a high chance to score massive damage with critical hits and also cripple limbs. While the build isn't focused on stealth, the element of surprise can certainly be helpful.

TRAINING
CRAFTING AND C.A.M.P.ING
INVENTORY
QUESTS
ATLAS
BESTIARY
APPENDICES

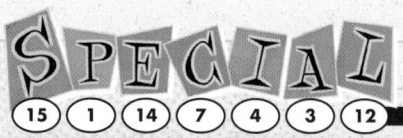
HEAVY GUNNER

PERKS EQUIPPED - RANK		SPECIAL/COST	EFFECT
STURDY FRAME	2/2	STR/2	ARMOR WEIGHS 50% LESS THAN NORMAL.
STRONG BACK	4/4	STR/4	GAIN +40 TO CARRY WEIGHT.
HEAVY GUNNER	2/3	STR/2	YOUR NONEXPLOSIVE HEAVY GUNS NOW DO +20% DAMAGE.
BEAR ARMS	4/4	STR/4	HEAVY GUNS WEIGH 80% LESS.
LOCK AND LOAD	3/3	STR/3	HEAVY GUNS RELOAD 30% FASTER.
ADAMANTIUM SKELETON	5/5	END/5	YOUR LIMB DAMAGE IS COMPLETELY ELIMINATED.
IRONCLAD	5/5	END/5	YOU NOW GAIN 50 DAMAGE AND ENERGY RESISTANCE WHILE WEARING ARMOR.
LIFEGIVER	4/4	END/4	GAIN A TOTAL OF +45 TO YOUR MAXIMUM HEALTH.
BODYGUARDS	4/4	CHA/4	GAIN 12 DAMAGE & ENERGY RESIST (MAX 36) FOR EACH TEAMMATE, EXCLUDING YOU.
TENDERIZER	3/3	CHA/3	MAKE YOUR TARGET RECEIVE 10% MORE DAMAGE FOR 10 SECONDS AFTER YOU ATTACK.
FIRST AID	4/4	INT/4	STIMPAKS RESTORE 40% MORE LOST HEALTH.
WHITE KNIGHT	3/3	AGL/3	YOUR ARMOR BREAKS 90% MORE SLOWLY AND IS CHEAPER TO REPAIR.
QUICK HANDS	5/5	LCK/5	GAIN A 25% CHANCE TO INSTANTLY RELOAD WHEN YOUR CLIP IS EMPTY.
BLOODY MESS	3/3	LCK/3	15% BONUS DAMAGE MEANS ENEMIES MAY EXPLODE INTO A GORY RED PASTE.
ONE GUN ARMY	4/4	LCK/4	HEAVY GUNS GAIN A 8% STAGGER CHANCE AND A 8% CHANCE TO CRIPPLE A LIMB.

The Heavy loves to carry big guns. And shoot them. Often.

This build focuses on maxing out weight-reduction perks and boosting armor effectiveness and damage output. This build is for the player who wants to be a bullet sponge for the team while dealing huge amounts of damage from a vast array of heavy weaponry.

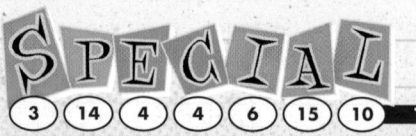
LONE SNIPER

PERKS EQUIPPED - RANK		SPECIAL/COST	EFFECT
BANDOLIER	3/3	STR/3	BALLISTIC WEAPON AMMO WEIGHS 90% LESS.
SNIPER	4/4	PER/4	GAIN IMPROVED CONTROL AND HOLD YOUR BREATH 60% LONGER WHILE AIMING SCOPES.
LONG SHOT	4/4	PER/4	YOUR RIFLES HAVE 20% MORE RANGE AND 40% MORE ACCURACY WHEN SIGHTED.
RIFLEMAN	2/3	PER/2	YOUR NONAUTOMATIC RIFLES NOW DO +20% DAMAGE.
EXPERT RIFLEMAN	2/3	PER/2	YOUR NONAUTOMATIC RIFLES NOW DO +20% DAMAGE.
NIGHT EYES	1/1	PER/2	GAIN NIGHT VISION WHILE SNEAKING BETWEEN 6:00 P.M. AND 6:00 A.M.
NATURAL RESISTANCE	3/3	END/3	YOU ARE 90% LESS LIKELY TO CATCH A DISEASE FROM THE ENVIRONMENT.
AQUA BOY/GIRL	1/1	END/1	YOU NO LONGER TAKE RAD DAMAGE FROM SWIMMING AND CAN BREATHE UNDERWATER.
LONE WANDERER	3/3	CHA/4	WHEN ADVENTURING ALONE, TAKE 20% LESS DAMAGE AND GAIN 30% AP REGEN.
GUNSMITH	3/3	INT/3	YOUR GUNS BREAK 75% MORE SLOWLY AND ARE CHEAPER TO REPAIR.
WEAPON ARTISAN	3/3	INT/3	YOU CAN REPAIR ANY WEAPON TO 200% OF NORMAL MAXIMUM CONDITION.
ACTION BOY/GIRL	3/3	AGL/3	AP REGENERATES 45% FASTER.
MARATHONER	3/3	AGL/3	SPRINTING CONSUMES 40% FEWER AP.
COVERT OPERATIVE	3/3	AGL/3	YOUR RANGED SNEAK ATTACKS DEAL 2.5X NORMAL DAMAGE.
AMMOSMITH	3/3	AGL/3	PRODUCE 100% MORE ROUNDS WHEN CRAFTING AMMUNITION.
ADRENALINE	5/5	AGL/3	GAIN +10% (MAX 48%) DAMAGE FOR 30S PER KILL. DURATION REFRESHES WITH KILLS.
GOOD WITH SALT	3/3	LCK/3	FOOD IN YOUR INVENTORY WILL SPOIL 90% MORE SLOWLY.
LUCK OF THE DRAW	3/3	LCK/3	YOUR WEAPON HAS A 20% CHANCE TO REGAIN CONDITION WHEN HITTING AN ENEMY.
STORM CHASE	2/2	LCK/2	GAIN HIGH HEALTH REGENERATION WHILE OUTSIDE DURING RAIN OR RAD STORMS.
BLOODY MESS	3/3	LCK/2	10% BONUS DAMAGE MEANS ENEMIES MAY EXPLODE INTO A GORY RED PASTE.

The Lone Sniper likes to stay out in the wilderness alone for long periods of time and deal with enemies from afar. The perks max out rifle range and accuracy and increase rifle damage and crits. AP consumption is reduced to allow more shots and quick getaways. Other perks will allow them to stay out in the wilderness for longer and include protection from the elements and Rads, reduced food spoilage, reduced weapon degradation, and lowered ammo carry weight.

POWER ARMOR TANK

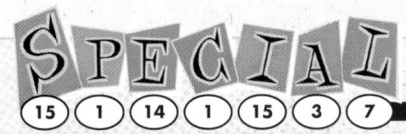

SPECIAL

| 15 | 1 | 14 | 1 | 15 | 3 | 7 | Total → 56 |

TRAINING

CRAFTING AND C.A.M.P.ING

INVENTORY

QUESTS

ATLAS

BESTIARY

APPENDICES

PERKS EQUIPPED - RANK		SPECIAL/COST	EFFECT
BEAR ARMS	4/4	STR/4	HEAVY GUNS WEIGH 80% LESS.
LOCK AND LOAD	3/3	STR/3	HEAVY GUNS RELOAD 30% FASTER.
FULL CHARGE	2/2	STR/2	SPRINTING IN POWER ARMOR CONSUMES NO EXTRA FUSION CORE ENERGY.
PAIN TRAIN	3/3	STR/3	DEVASTATE AND STAGGER ENEMIES BY SPRINTING INTO THEM WITH POWER ARMOR.
PORTABLE POWER	3/3	STR/3	ALL POWER ARMOR PARTS AND CHASSIS WEIGHTS ARE REDUCED BY 75%.
PROFESSIONAL DRINKER	3/3	END/3	THERE'S NO CHANCE YOU'LL GET ADDICTED TO ALCOHOL.
ADAMANTIUM SKELETON	5/5	END/5	YOUR LIMB DAMAGE IS COMPLETELY ELIMINATED.
PHOTOSYNTHETIC	2/2	END/2	GAIN IMPROVED HEALTH REGEN BETWEEN THE HOURS OF 6:00 A.M. AND 6:00 P.M.
LIFEGIVER	3/3	END/4	GAIN A TOTAL OF +45 TO YOUR MAXIMUM HEALTH.
POWER SMITH	3/3	INT/3	YOUR CRAFTED POWER ARMOR NOW HAS IMPROVED DURABILITY.
STABILIZED	4/4	INT/4	IN POWER ARMOR, HEAVY GUNS GAIN 40% ACCURACY AND IGNORE 40% ARMOR.
ROBOTICS EXPERT	3/3	INT/3	YOUR POWER ARMOR BREAKS 60% MORE SLOWLY AND IS CHEAPER TO REPAIR.
POWER USER	5/5	INT/5	FUSION CORE DURATION IS NOW DOUBLED.
ACTION BOY/GIRL	3/3	AGL/3	AP REGENERATES 45% FASTER.
BLOODY MESS	3/3	LCK/3	15% BONUS DAMAGE MEANS ENEMIES MAY EXPLODE INTO A GORY RED PASTE.
ONE GUN ARMY	4/4	LCK/4	HEAVY GUNS GAIN A 8% STAGGER CHANCE AND AN 8% CHANCE TO CRIPPLE A LIMB.

The Tank is all about that Power Armor. While not as versatile as the Heavy, the Tank trades increased damage output for sheer defensive capability. The focus is square on utilizing Power Armor to its maximum potential by increasing its damage resistance and durability. This build also allows Power Armor users to catch enemies off guard by running right into the middle of the fray, allowing the rest of their team to get the jump.

SCAVENGER

SPECIAL

| 11 | 3 | 2 | 6 | 15 | 3 | 15 | Total → 55 |

PERKS EQUIPPED - RANK		SPECIAL/COST	EFFECT
PACK RAT	3/3	STR/3	THE WEIGHT OF ALL JUNK ITEMS IS REDUCED BY 75%.
STRONG BACK	4/4	STR/4	GAIN +40 TO CARRY WEIGHT.
TRAVELING PHARMACY	3/3	STR/2	WEIGHTS OF ALL CHEMS (INCLUDING STIMPAKS) ARE REDUCED BY 90%.
THRU-HIKER	3/3	STR/2	FOOD AND DRINK WEIGHTS ARE REDUCED BY 90%.
PICKLOCK	1/1	PER/1	GAIN +1 LOCKPICKING SKILL, AND THE LOCKPICKING "SWEET SPOT" IS 10% LARGER.
EXPERT PICKLOCK	1/1	PER/1	GAIN +1 LOCKPICKING SKILL, AND THE LOCKPICKING "SWEET SPOT" IS 10% LARGER.
MASTER PICKLOCK	1/1	PER/1	GAIN +1 LOCKPICKING SKILL, AND THE LOCKPICKING "SWEET SPOT" IS 10% LARGER.
HOMEBODY	2/2	END/2	GAIN IMPROVED HEALTH AND LIMB REGENERATION WHILE IN YOUR CAMP OR WORKSHOP.
HAPPY CAMPER	3/3	CHA/3	HUNGER AND THIRST GROW 80% MORE SLOWLY WHEN IN CAMP OR IN A TEAM WORKSHOP.
HARD BARGAIN	3/3	CHA/3	BUYING AND SELLING PRICES AT VENDORS ARE NOW MUCH BETTER.
EXOTIC WEAPONS	2/2	INT/2	YOU CAN NOW CRAFT CROSSBOWS, BLACK POWDER GUNS, THE SYRINGER AND MORE! / YOU CAN NOW CRAFT RANK 1 EXOTIC WEAPON MODS.
SCRAPPER	2/2	INT/2	OBTAIN MANY MORE COMPONENTS WHEN YOU SCRAP WEAPONS AND ARMOR.
EXOTIC WEAPONS EXPERT	1/2	INT/1	YOU CAN NOW CRAFT RANK 2 EXOTIC WEAPON MODS.
CONTRACTOR	2/2	INT/2	CRAFTING WORKSHOP ITEMS NOW COSTS 50% FEWER MATERIALS.
SCIENCE	2/2	INT/2	YOU CAN NOW CRAFT ENERGY GUNS. / YOU CAN CRAFT RANK 1 ENERGY GUN MODS.
SCIENCE EXPERT	1/2	INT/1	YOU CAN CRAFT RANK 2 ENERGY GUN MODS.
GREASE MONKEY	2/2	INT/2	WORKSHOP ITEMS ARE 60% CHEAPER TO REPAIR.
POWER SMITH	1/3	INT/1	YOU CAN NOW CRAFT ADVANCED POWER ARMOR MODS.
SCIENCE MASTER	1/2	INT/1	YOU CAN NOW CRAFT RANK 3 ENERGY GUN MODS.
CHEMIST	1/2	INT/1	YOU GET DOUBLE THE QUANTITY WHEN YOU CRAFT CHEMS!
HOME DEFENSE	3/3	AGL/3	YOU CAN CRAFT AND DISARM EXPERT TRAPS AND CRAFT EXPERT TURRETS.
PHARMA FARMA	3/3	LCK/3	ALWAYS FIND EXTRA FIRST AID CHEMS WHEN YOU "SEARCH" A CHEM CONTAINER.
SCROUNGER	3/3	LCK/3	ALWAYS FIND EXTRA AMMO WHEN YOU "SEARCH" AN AMMO CONTAINER.
CAP COLLECTOR	3/3	LCK/3	YOU ALMOST ALWAYS FIND MORE BOTTLE CAPS WHEN OPENING A CAPS STASH.
WOODCHUCKER	2/3	LCK/2	COLLECTING WOOD YIELDS 100% MORE.
SUPER DUPER	4/4	LCK/4	WHEN YOU CRAFT ANYTHING, THERE IS A 40% CHANCE YOU'LL GET DOUBLE RESULTS!

The Scavenger will take anything and make anything. The player will have to grab many items and find blueprints throughout the world, but this build will allow them to craft just about anything, be it weapons, armor, mods, workshop, or chems.

STEALTH OPERATIVE

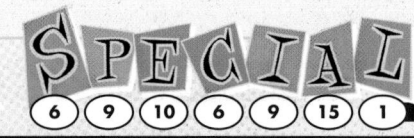

PERKS EQUIPPED - RANK		SPECIAL/COST	EFFECT
BANDOLIER	3/3	STR/3	BALLISTIC WEAPON AMMO WEIGHS 90% LESS.
PACKIN' LIGHT	3/3	STR/3	YOUR PISTOLS WEIGH 75% LESS.
PICKLOCK	1/1	PER/1	GAIN +1 LOCKPICKING SKILL, AND THE LOCKPICKING "SWEET SPOT" IS 10% LARGER.
CRACK SHOT	4/4	PER/4	ALL PISTOLS NOW HAVE 20% MORE RANGE AND 40% MORE ACCURACY WHEN SIGHTED.
EXPERT PICKLOCK	1/1	PER/1	GAIN +1 LOCKPICKING SKILL, AND THE LOCKPICKING "SWEET SPOT" IS 10% LARGER.
MASTER PICKLOCK	1/1	PER/1	GAIN +1 LOCKPICKING SKILL, AND THE LOCKPICKING "SWEET SPOT" IS 10% LARGER.
NIGHT EYES	1/1	PER/2	GAIN NIGHT VISION WHILE SNEAKING BETWEEN 6:00 P.M. AND 6:00 A.M.
AQUA BOY/GIRL	1/1	END/1	YOU NO LONGER TAKE RAD DAMAGE FROM SWIMMING AND CAN BREATHE UNDERWATER.
RAD RESISTANT	3/4	END/3	YOU NOW HAVE +30 RADIATION RESISTANCE.
PROFESSIONAL DRINKER	1/1	END/3	THERE'S NO CHANCE YOU'LL GET ADDICTED TO ALCOHOL.
ALL NIGHT LONG	3/3	END/3	YOU SUFFER 60% LESS FROM HUNGER AND THIRST.
LONE WANDERER	3/3	CHA/4	WHEN ADVENTURING ALONE, TAKE 20% LESS DAMAGE AND GAIN 30% AP REGEN.
CHEM RESISTANT	2/2	CHA/2	YOU GAIN COMPLETE IMMUNITY TO CHEM ADDICTION.
HACKER	1/1	INT/1	GAIN +1 HACKING SKILL, AND TERMINAL LOCKOUT TIME IS REDUCED.
EXPERT HACKER	1/1	INT/1	GAIN +1 HACKING SKILL, AND TERMINAL LOCKOUT TIME IS REDUCED.
MASTER HACKER	1/1	INT/1	GAIN +1 HACKING SKILL, AND TERMINAL LOCKOUT TIME IS REDUCED.
GUNSMITH	3/3	INT/3	YOUR GUNS BREAK 75% MORE SLOWLY AND ARE CHEAPER TO REPAIR.
WEAPON ARTISAN	3/3	INT/3	YOU CAN REPAIR ANY WEAPON TO 200% OF NORMAL MAXIMUM CONDITION.
MASTER GUNSLINGER	2/4	AGL/2	YOUR NONAUTOMATIC PISTOLS NOW DO +20% DAMAGE.
ESCAPE ARTIST	1/1	AGL/1	SNEAK TO LOSE ENEMIES, AND RUNNING NO LONGER AFFECTS STEALTH.
LIGHT FOOTED	1/1	AGL/1	WHILE SNEAKING, YOU NEVER TRIGGER MINES OR FLOOR-BASED TRAPS.
SNEAK	5/5	AGL/5	YOU ARE 60% HARDER TO DETECT WHILE SNEAKING.
COVERT OPERATIVE	3/3	AGL/3	YOUR RANGED SNEAK ATTACKS DEAL 2.5X NORMAL DAMAGE.
SECRET AGENT	3/3	AGL/3	STEALTH BOYS LAST FOUR TIMES AS LONG!

The Stealth Op can sneak, hack, pick, and hide in just about every situation. With a focus on pistols and sneak attacks with chem and alcohol immunity, the player can boost their stats with a variety of drugs to deal a lot of damage without being seen. Hacking and lockpicking allow them to access just about any area, and Rad resistance allows them to make getaways into dangerous areas.

TEAM MEDIC

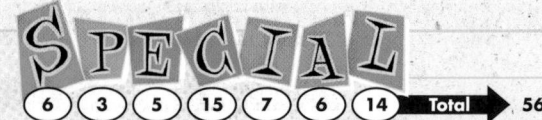

PERKS EQUIPPED - RANK		SPECIAL/COST	EFFECT
TRAVELING PHARMACY	3/3	STR/3	WEIGHTS OF ALL CHEMS (INCLUDING STIMPAKS) ARE REDUCED BY 90%.
THRU-HIKER	3/3	STR/3	FOOD AND DRINK WEIGHTS ARE REDUCED BY 90%.
BUTCHER'S BOUNTY	3/3	PER/3	ALWAYS FIND EXTRA MEAT WHEN YOU "SEARCH" AN ANIMAL CORPSE.
PROFESSIONAL DRINKER	3/3	END/3	THERE'S NO CHANCE YOU'LL GET ADDICTED TO ALCOHOL.
CHEM RESISTANT	2/2	END/2	YOU GAIN COMPLETE IMMUNITY TO CHEM ADDICTION.
ANTI-EPIDEMIC	2/2	CHA/2	YOUR DISEASE CURES ALWAYS CURE A DISEASE FROM NEARBY TEAMMATES TOO.
FIELD SURGEON	1/1	CHA/2	STIMPAKS AND RADAWAY WILL NOW WORK MUCH MORE QUICKLY.
HEALING HANDS	3/3	CHA/3	PLAYERS YOU REVIVE HAVE RADS REDUCED BY 900.
TEAM MEDIC	3/3	CHA/4	YOUR STIMPAKS NOW ALSO HEAL NEARBY TEAMMATES TO THEIR FULL STRENGTH.
QUACK SURGEON	1/1	CHA/1	REVIVE OTHER PLAYERS WITH WHISKEY!
PHILANTHROPIST	3/3	CHA/3	RESTORE MUCH MORE OF YOUR TEAM'S HUNGER AND THIRST WHEN YOU EAT OR DRINK.
FIRST AID	4/4	INT/4	STIMPAKS RESTORE 40% MORE LOST HEALTH.
PHARMACIST	3/3	INT/3	RADAWAY REMOVES TWICE AS MUCH RADIATION.
BORN SURVIVOR	1/3	AGL/1	FALLING BELOW 20% HEALTH WILL AUTOMATICALLY USE A STIMPAK.
REJUVENATED	2/2	AGL/2	YOU GAIN MUCH INCREASED BENEFIT FROM BEING WELL FED OR WELL HYDRATED.
DODGY	3/3	AGL/3	AVOID 30% OF INCOMING DAMAGE AT THE COST OF 30 AP PER HIT.
PHARMA FARMA	3/3	LCK/3	ALWAYS FIND EXTRA FIRST AID CHEMS WHEN YOU "SEARCH" A CHEM CONTAINER.
SERENDIPITY	3/3	LCK/3	WHILE BELOW 30% HEALTH, GAIN A 45% CHANCE TO AVOID DAMAGE.
GOOD WITH SALT	3/3	LCK/3	FOOD IN YOUR INVENTORY WILL SPOIL 90% MORE SLOWLY.
MYSTERY MEAT	3/3	LCK/2	STIMPAKS GENERATE MORE EDIBLE MEAT TISSUE. HIGHER RADS IMPROVE THE CHANCE.
DRY NURSE	3/3	LCK/3	YOU HAVE A 90% CHANCE TO KEEP YOUR STIMPAK WHEN YOU REVIVE ANOTHER PLAYER.

The Medic assumes your teammates are going to die. A lot. It also assumes that because the wasteland is devoid of caring mothers, your teammates won't eat or drink enough, so you should probably do it for them.

This build is for players who want to carry tons of rations and medical supplies to distribute to or revive teammates. It also provides plenty of perks that can be shared with teammates, depending on the need. Additionally, the ability to dodge damage allows the medic to run into the line of fire to help a downed teammate.

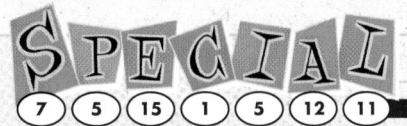

UNHINGED GRENADIER

SPECIAL: 7 5 15 1 5 12 11 — **Total** → 56

PERKS EQUIPPED - RANK		SPECIAL/COST	EFFECT
STRONG BACK	4/4	STR/4	GAIN +40 TO CARRY WEIGHT.
ORDNANCE EXPRESS	3/3	STR/3	THROWN EXPLOSIVES WEIGH 90% LESS.
GRENADIER	2/2	PER/2	YOUR EXPLOSIVES DETONATE WITH TWICE THE RADIUS.
FIRE IN THE HOLE	3/3	PER/3	SEE A THROWING ARC WHEN TOSSING GRENADES, AND GRENADES FLY 50% FARTHER.
SUN KISSED	2/2	END/2	QUICKLY REGEN RADIATION DAMAGE BETWEEN THE HOURS OF 6:00 A.M. AND 6:00 PM.
GHOULISH	2/3	END/2	RADIATION NOW REGENERATES MORE OF YOUR LOST HEALTH!
CANNIBAL	2/3	END/2	EATING HUMAN, GHOUL, SUPER MUTANT, OR SCORCHED CORPSES RESTORES MORE HEALTH AND HUNGER.
LEAD BELLY	3/3	END/3	YOU TAKE NO RADIATION FROM EATING OR DRINKING.
NATURAL RESISTANCE	2/3	END/2	YOU ARE 90% LESS LIKELY TO CATCH A DISEASE FROM THE ENVIRONMENT.
AQUA BOY/GIRL	1/1	END/1	YOU NO LONGER TAKE RAD DAMAGE FROM SWIMMING AND CAN BREATHE UNDERWATER.
IRON STOMACH	3/3	END/3	YOUR CHANCE TO CATCH A DISEASE FROM FOOD IS REDUCED BY 90%.
DEMOLITION EXPERT	5/5	INT/5	YOUR EXPLOSIVES DO +100% DAMAGE.
ACTION BOY/GIRL	3/3	AGL/3	AP REGENERATES 45% FASTER.
MARATHONER	3/3	AGL/3	SPRINTING CONSUMES 40% FEWER AP.
HOME DEFENSE	3/3	AGL/3	YOU CAN CRAFT AND DISARM EXPERT TRAPS AND CRAFT EXPERT TURRETS.
LIGHT FOOTED	1/1	AGL/1	WHILE SNEAKING, YOU NEVER TRIGGER MINES OR FLOOR-BASED TRAPS.
GOAT LEGS	2/2	AGL/2	TAKE 80% LESS DAMAGE FROM FALLING.
LAST LAUGH	2/2	LCK/2	YOU ALWAYS DROP A LIVE GRENADE FROM YOUR INVENTORY WHEN YOU ARE DOWNED.
BLOODY MESS	3/3	LCK/3	15% BONUS DAMAGE MEANS ENEMIES MAY EXPLODE INTO A GORY RED PASTE.
MYSTERIOUS SAVIOR	3/3	LCK/3	THE MYSTERIOUS SAVIOR WILL REGULARLY APPEAR TO REVIVE YOU WHEN DOWNED.
MYSTERY MEAT	3/3	LCK/3	STIMPAKS GENERATE EXCESSIVE, EDIBLE MEAT. HIGHER RADS IMPROVE THE CHANCE.

The Unhinged Grenadier's love of explosives and food found on the ground may make you ask if they're unstable. Yes.

The Unhinged Grenadier focuses on perks that increase explosive damage and radius. The Cannibal perk combined with Rad resistance and disease immunity allows the player to eat or drink anything in the world and not have to worry about carrying much survival gear. This, of course, means they can carry more explosives.

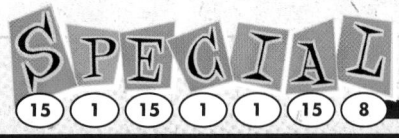

WEAPON MELEE SPECIALIST

SPECIAL: 15 1 15 1 1 15 8 — **Total** → 56

PERKS EQUIPPED - RANK		SPECIAL/COST	EFFECT
BARBARIAN	3/3	STR/3	EVERY POINT OF STRENGTH ADDS +4 DAMAGE RESIST (MAX 80).
INCISOR	3/3	STR/3	YOUR MELEE WEAPONS IGNORE 75% OF YOUR TARGET'S ARMOR.
MARTIAL ARTIST	3/3	STR/3	YOUR MELEE WEAPONS WEIGH 60% LESS, AND YOU CAN SWING THEM 30% FASTER.
SLUGGER	2/3	STR/2	YOUR TWO-HANDED MELEE WEAPONS NOW DO +20% DAMAGE.
EXPERT SLUGGER	2/3	STR/2	YOUR TWO-HANDED MELEE WEAPONS NOW DO +20% DAMAGE.
MASTER SLUGGER	2/4	STR/2	YOUR TWO-HANDED MELEE WEAPONS NOW DO +20% DAMAGE.
LIFE GIVER	3/3	END/4	GAIN A TOTAL OF +45 TO YOUR MAXIMUM HEALTH.
AQUA BOY/GIRL	1/1	END/1	YOU NO LONGER TAKE RAD DAMAGE FROM SWIMMING AND CAN BREATHE UNDERWATER.
COLA NUT	2/2	END/2	NUKA-COLA PRODUCTS ARE NOW THREE TIMES AS BENEFICIAL.
IRONCLAD	5/5	END/5	YOU NOW GAIN 50 DAMAGE AND ENERGY RESISTANCE WHILE WEARING ARMOR.
SOLAR POWERED	3/3	END/3	GAIN +3 TO STR AND END BETWEEN THE HOURS OF 6:00 A.M. AND 6:00 P.M.
ADRENALINE	5/5	AGL/5	GAIN +10% (MAX 60%) DAMAGE FOR 30S PER KILL. DURATION REFRESHES WITH KILLS.
EVASIVE	3/3	AGL/3	WHILE UNARMORED, EACH POINT OF AGI ADDS +3 DAMAGE AND ENERGY RESIST (MAX 45).
ACTION BOY/GIRL	3/3	AGL/3	AP REGENERATES 45% FASTER.
BORN SURVIVOR	1/1	AGL/1	FALLING BELOW 20% HEALTH WILL AUTOMATICALLY USE A STIMPAK.
MARATHONER	3/3	AGL/3	SPRINTING CONSUMES 40% FEWER AP.
RICOCHET	4/4	LCK/4	YOU HAVE A 20% CHANCE TO DEFLECT BACK A PORTION OF ENEMIES' RANGED DAMAGE.
BLOODY MESS	3/3	LCK/3	15% BONUS DAMAGE MEANS ENEMIES MAY EXPLODE INTO A GORY RED PASTE.
STORM CHASE	1/2	LCK/1	GAIN HEALTH REGENERATION WHILE OUTSIDE DURING RAIN OR RAD STORMS.

The Weapon Melee gets up close and personal.

This build allows players to run circles around their opponents and output a high amount of damage in a short period of time. Boosted health and damage resistance and automatic Stimpak usage helps the player outlive their targets and beat them into the dust.

TRAINING

CRAFTING AND C.A.M.P.ING

INVENTORY

QUESTS

ATLAS

BESTIARY

APPENDICES

CRAFTING AND MODIFICATIONS

CRAFTING: DO IT YOURSELF!

SUPPLIES MAY BE SCARCE AFTER THE WAR.

MANY THINGS CAN BE BROKEN DOWN INTO USEFUL CRAFTING MATERIALS!

USE YOUR C.A.M.P. TO ESTABLISH A MOBILE BASE OF OPERATIONS.

FIND AND USE WORKBENCHES TO BUILD IN DESIGNATED AREAS.

If you want something done properly, do it yourself! With the help of scavenging, scrapping, and then crafting at a workbench or station, you can create consumables and objects for yourself and your team, instead of subsisting on found items, or running out of Caps at the hands of unscrupulous crafter players, or losing in bartering with an emotionless and high-priced robotic vendor. What awaits are upgraded items, the finest cuisine, chems, and ammunition, as well as the latest and greatest armor and weaponry, and Power Armor fashioned to your liking, with multitudes of modifications to boot! Now *you* get to be the crafter player, unscrupulous, or otherwise....

PART 1: TYPES OF CRAFTING STATIONS AND WORKBENCHES—THE BASICS

Crafting may looking intimidating, but it's relatively straightforward (at least to begin with). Depending on the type of item you wish to craft, there's a different crafting location—either called workbenches or stations—that allows crafting of that type of item. Below is a quick checklist of them all (listed in the order you're likely to use them). Note that some stations and workbenches have two or more variants, which are aesthetically different but identical in terms of crafting access.

WATER PUMP

Need a plentiful supply of water? This is one place to go.

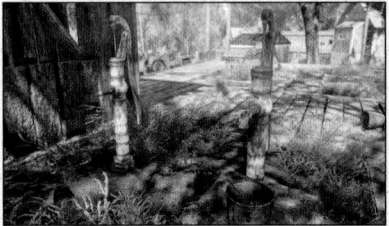

You get thirsty the quickest, so you need a supply of relatively non-revolting (and only lightly irradiated) water. Find one of these pumps, usually in most towns, and you have a source of water. Don't drink it yet, though; you don't want dysentery... or worse!

- – **CAN YOU CRAFT HERE?** NO
- – **CAN YOU SCRAP ITEMS HERE?** NO
- – **CAN YOU MODIFY OR REPAIR ITEMS HERE?** NO
- – **INSTRUCTIONS NEEDED FOR ITEM CRAFTING?** NONE
- – **CAN THIS BE BUILT IN YOUR C.A.M.P. WITH A PLAN?** YES (1 VARIANT)
- – **WHY AM I CRAFTING HERE?** YOU'RE NOT; YOU'RE SIMPLY GATHERING WATER TO BOIL AT A COOKING STATION.

COOKING STATION

Come here to cook up food, drinks, and herbal remedies.

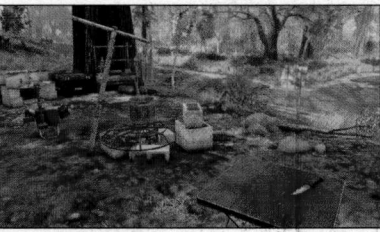

Instead of a water pump, come to one of the hundreds of cooking stations dotted around Appalachia. These usually take the form of a large campfire with a pot and breeze blocks, but there's a small "pot on a fire," a spit roast, and a kitchen stove; all of these provide the same cooking capabilities. Head here to cook up a tasty meal or a beverage (including boiled water).

- – **CAN YOU CRAFT HERE?** YES
- – **CAN YOU SCRAP ITEMS HERE?** NO
- – **CAN YOU MODIFY OR REPAIR ITEMS HERE?** NO
- – **INSTRUCTIONS NEEDED FOR ITEM CRAFTING?** RECIPES
- – **CAN THIS BE BUILT IN YOUR C.A.M.P. WITH A PLAN?** YES (4 VARIANTS)
- – **WHY AM I COOKING HERE?** TO CRAFT FOOD AND DRINK TO LESSEN THE EFFECTS OF HUNGER AND THIRST.

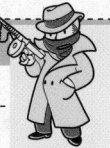

TRAINING

CRAFTING AND C.A.M.P.ING

INVENTORY

QUESTS

ATLAS

BESTIARY

APPENDICES

A WORD OF WARNING FROM VAULT-BOY

CONTAMINATION AND RADIATION IN YOUR BLOATFLY LOAF?

UNLESS YOU'RE USING A PERK TO NEGATE THE EFFECTS OF RADIATION, MOST OF THIS FOOD AND DRINK GIVE YOU A SLIGHT CASE OF RADIATION POISONING — DELICIOUS! WASH THAT DOWN WITH A RADAWAY IF YOUR RAD METER IS GETTING ALARMINGLY HIGH AND IMPEDING YOUR HEALTH BAR.

ARMOR WORKBENCH

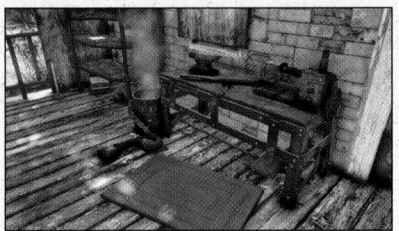

Hammer away at this forge and create armor and armor mods.

- CAN YOU CRAFT HERE? YES
- CAN YOU SCRAP ITEMS HERE? YES
- CAN YOU MODIFY OR REPAIR ITEMS HERE? YES
- INSTRUCTIONS NEEDED FOR ITEM CRAFTING? MODS/PLANS
- CAN THIS BE BUILT IN YOUR C.A.M.P. WITH A PLAN? YES (1 VARIANT)
- WHY AM I CRAFTING HERE? TO CREATE, MAINTAIN, MODIFY, OR REPAIR ARMOR FOR ADDED PROTECTION.

Construct protective armor pieces for your various limbs, torso, and head at this location, gradually increasing in quality and type as you level up. Repair or modify this protection, too, and stitch together a variety of uniforms, outfits, costumes, and regular clothing pieces that you can wear over armor. When you find a style you like, try selling it (to buyers both robotic or human).

WEAPONS WORKBENCH

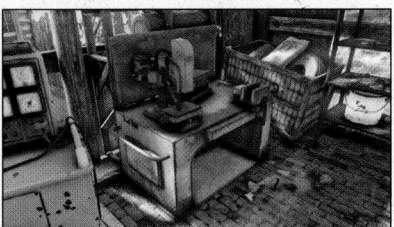

Take apart and rebuild every type of weapon, and add weapon mods.

- CAN YOU CRAFT HERE? YES
- CAN YOU SCRAP ITEMS HERE? YES
- CAN YOU MODIFY OR REPAIR ITEMS HERE? YES
- INSTRUCTIONS NEEDED FOR ITEM CRAFTING? MODS/PLANS
- CAN THIS BE BUILT IN YOUR C.A.M.P. WITH A PLAN? YES (2 VARIANTS)
- WHY AM I CRAFTING HERE? TO CREATE, MAINTAIN, MODIFY, OR REPAIR WEAPONRY FOR COMBAT.

By far the largest collection of items can be crafted and repaired here, namely every type of weapon available to you. Naturally, you'll need to bring the parts, but anything from a baseball bat to a mini-nuke launcher can be constructed here. Furthermore, most weapons have a variety of mods you can apply, leading to an almost limitless array of guns, blades, bats, launchers, and other offensive ordnance.

TINKER'S WORKBENCH

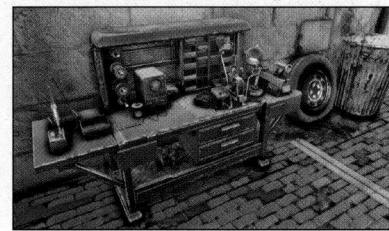

Need to craft your own ammunition, grenades, mines, and more? Head here.

- CAN YOU CRAFT HERE? YES
- CAN YOU SCRAP ITEMS HERE? YES
- CAN YOU MODIFY OR REPAIR ITEMS HERE? YES
- INSTRUCTIONS NEEDED FOR ITEM CRAFTING? AVAILABLE BY DEFAULT
- CAN THIS BE BUILT IN YOUR C.A.M.P. WITH A PLAN? YES (1 VARIANT)
- WHY AM I CRAFTING HERE? TO CREATE AMMUNITION FOR YOUR RANGED WEAPONS AS WELL AS EXPLOSIVES.

Instead of scrambling around for ammunition or paying for it at a vending machine or vendor, it's cheaper to scavenge the component parts and bring it all to this workbench and begin to craft all manner of ammunition; be sure it matches the guns you're using! Later on, with more esoteric ammo on hand, you can create grenades, mines, and other explosives.

CHEMISTRY STATION

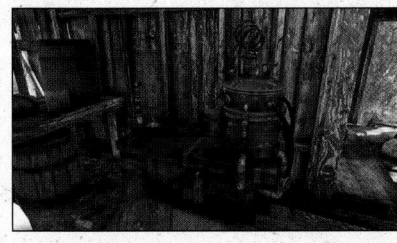

For chems, Flamer fuel, and ingredients like gunpowder (for ammo) and smelted ore (for metal scrap).

- CAN YOU CRAFT HERE? YES
- CAN YOU SCRAP ITEMS HERE? YES
- CAN YOU MODIFY OR REPAIR ITEMS HERE? NO
- INSTRUCTIONS NEEDED FOR ITEM CRAFTING? RECIPES
- CAN THIS BE BUILT IN YOUR C.A.M.P. WITH A PLAN? YES (2 VARIANTS)
- WHY AM I CRAFTING HERE? TO CREATE PURIFIED WATER, CHEMS, AND SOME SPECIFIC IMPORTANT ITEMS.

Think of the Chemistry Station as bridging the gap between craftable items you can consume and those you can utilize; only this station has stuff you can eat, as well as stuff you can smelt down to make raw materials for mods and structures! This is mainly used for crafting chems to bolster and buff you up (before the withdrawal brings you down). You can also make gunpowder, a key component for ammo (used at the Tinker's Workbench).

POWER ARMOR STATION

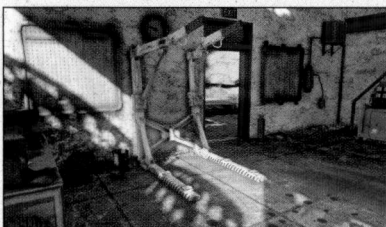

When you're high enough level, come here for Power Armor pieces and mods.

- **CAN YOU CRAFT HERE?** YES
- **CAN YOU SCRAP ITEMS HERE?** YES
- **CAN YOU MODIFY OR REPAIR ITEMS HERE?** YES
- **INSTRUCTIONS NEEDED FOR ITEM CRAFTING?** MODS/PLANS
- **CAN THIS BE BUILT IN YOUR C.A.M.P. WITH A PLAN?** YES (2 VARIANTS)
- **WHY AM I CRAFTING HERE?** TO CREATE, MAINTAIN, MODIFY, OR REPAIR POWER ARMOR FOR ULTIMATE PROTECTION!

Once you present a Power Armor frame (which you must scavenge for, then either wear or place it in your Stash Box until you arrive) at this station, you can add various limb appendages, torso, and helmets, if you're high enough level to use it. Then you can further mod each piece if you have the mods in your inventory. Expect to access this station last.

WORKSHOP WORKBENCH

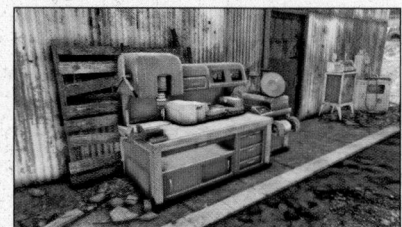

Not strictly a Crafting Workbench, these are found and used to build large-scale structures to defend.

- **CAN YOU CRAFT HERE?** YES*
- **CAN YOU SCRAP ITEMS HERE?** YES*
- **CAN YOU MODIFY OR REPAIR ITEMS HERE?** YES*
- **WHAT INSTRUCTIONS NEEDED FOR ITEM CRAFTING?** PLANS
- **CAN THIS BE BUILT IN YOUR C.A.M.P. WITH A PLAN?** NO (1 VARIANT)*
- **WHY AM I CRAFTING HERE?** TO BUILD A WORKSHOP BASE TO MINE RESOURCES AND DEFEND FROM OTHERS.
- *ACCESSING WORKSHOP WORKBENCHES BEGINS AN ENTIRELY DIFFERENT CONSTRUCTION MENU.

This last red work surface certainly looks like a workbench, and it technically is, but it forms the basis of a self-contained location called a Public Workshop. You pay Caps to claim it (or fight others to contest it), before building sometimes elaborate defenses and mining the rare resources that each Appalachian workshop has within its boundaries. Consult the next section for more information.

CRAFTING STATIONS AND WORKBENCHES: A MENU

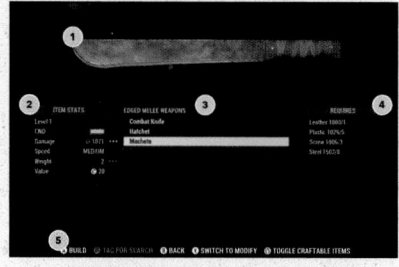

Here's an example of what a workbench menu looks like when you access it. This example shows a Weapon Workbench.

When you interact with a station or workbench, depending on the type (as the table previously listed), you can access some or all of the following:

- **CRAFT:** ACCESS THIS TO REACH THE CRAFT MENU, SHOWING ALL THE ITEMS YOU CAN CRAFT, THE COMPONENTS (OR INGREDIENTS) NEEDED TO CRAFT IT, ALONG WITH ANY PERKS NEEDED.
- **MODIFY:** ACCESS THIS TO REACH THE MODIFY MENU.
- **①** **ITEM NAME AND PICTURE:** THIS IS A HIGH-QUALITY IMAGE OF THE ITEM YOU'VE SELECTED.
- **②** **ITEM STATS:** THIS GIVES YOU THE PIP-BOY INFORMATION OF EACH STATISTIC THE ITEM POSSESSES, INCLUDING ITS LEVEL (THE HIGHER THE BETTER). THE REMAINING STATISTICS ARE THE SAME AS THOSE DISCUSSED IN THE PREVIOUS CHAPTER REGARDING YOUR PIP-BOY'S ITEMS MENU. NOTE THE (---) AND (+++) IN THE RIGHT MARGINS; THESE INDICATE GOOD OR BAD VALUES, AND, FOR MORE COMPLEX ITEMS, WHETHER A PROPOSED MOD MAKES A STATISTIC BETTER OR WORSE.
- **③** **CRAFTABLE OR MODDABLE ITEM:** A LIST OF THE ITEMS OF A PARTICULAR TYPE THAT YOU CAN SELECT TO CRAFT OR MODIFY.
- **④** **MATERIALS, INGREDIENTS, OR AVAILABLE MODS:** THIS LISTS THE MATERIALS (FOR NONCONSUMABLES), INGREDIENTS (FOR FOOD AND DRINK OR ITEMS YOU INGEST), AND THE MODIFICATIONS AVAILABLE (IF ANY).
- **⑤** **SCRAP, REPAIR, MODIFY, EXIT, SWITCH, TAG FOR SEARCH:** THE MENU AT THE SCREEN'S BOTTOM ALLOWS YOU TO SWITCH BETWEEN CRAFTING AND MODDING MENUS AND TO REPAIR THE ITEM (IF THE STATS CND OR ITEM CONDITION IS LESS THAN A FULL BAR).

CRAFTING STATIONS AND WORKBENCHES OVERVIEW: A CHART

Now you know what all the different crafting locations look like, here's a small chart that shows the initial activities you can attempt at them (detailed later in this chapter):

CRAFTING LOCATION	CRAFT	SCRAP	MODIFY/REPAIR	RECIPE/MOD/PLAN	BUILT IN YOUR C.A.M.P. WITH A PLAN?
Water Pump	No	No	No	None	Yes (1 variant)
Cooking Station	Yes	No	No	Recipes	Yes (4 variants)
Armor Workbench	Yes	Yes	Yes	Mods/Plans	Yes (1 variant)
Weapons Workbench	Yes	Yes	Yes	Mods/Plans	Yes (2 variants)
Tinker's Workbench	Yes	Yes	No	Recipe	Yes (1 variant)
Chemistry Station	Yes	Yes	No	Recipe	Yes (2 variants)
Power Armor Station	Yes	Yes	Yes	Mods/Plans	Yes (2 variants)
Workshop Workbench	Yes*	Yes*	Yes*	Plans	No (1 variant)*
*Accessing Workshop Workbenches begins an entirely different construction menu.					

Helpful Hint from Vault-Boy!

WHERE ARE ALL THE WORKBENCHES?

Good news! Aside from building your own stations and workbenches at your C.A.M.P. or workshop, you can utilize any crafting location within the Appalachian wilderness. Even better news! The guide's Atlas tells you where pretty much all of them are (and with the larger locations, they're even plotted on a map for you). And the best news of all? The initial overview of the first zone, the Forest region, lists where the nearest station and workbench of each type is compared to Vault 76. Now it's time for you to build on that information.

PART 2: RECIPES, PLANS, AND MODIFICATIONS, AND OTHER WAYS TO UNLOCK ITEMS

You can create almost anything you like...
if you have the instructions first!

Now that you've seen the various crafting locations available, you may be puzzled that you have few (if any) options when it comes to crafting, especially the first time you visit one: That's because you may be lacking in the instructions necessary to craft, or you haven't found the right item to scrap yet. To begin, let's look at the three main types of instructions:

INSTRUCTION TYPES

RECIPES: BITE-SIZED CONSUMABLES, CHEMS, AND AMMO

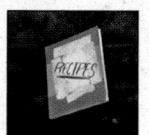

– CRAFTING LOCATIONS THAT USE THIS INSTRUCTION TYPE: COOKING, CHEMISTRY

These look like cookbooks and are most often located in containers or scattered throughout Appalachia. Use your powers of deduction: you're more likely to find recipes for chems at medical locations, while food and drink recipes are more common at cafes.

PLANS: COMBAT CLOTHING, WEAPONRY, AND CONSTRUCTION CAPABILITIES

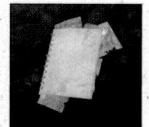

– CRAFTING LOCATIONS THAT USE THIS INSTRUCTION TYPE: ARMOR, WEAPONS, POWER ARMOR, C.A.M.P., WORKSHOP

These look like pages in a variety of styles and are most often located in containers or scattered throughout Appalachia. You can find them anywhere, but military locations, survivalists' bunkers, mechanic's garages, or in and around workshops are good places to start looking.

MODS: ENHANCEMENTS FOR PROTECTION AND OFFENSE, TAILORED TO YOUR LIKING

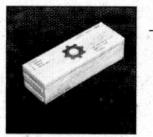

– CRAFTING LOCATIONS THAT USE THIS INSTRUCTION TYPE: ARMOR, WEAPONS, POWER ARMOR

These look like long wooden boxes with a cog insignia on them and are found in containers or scattered throughout Appalachia. Find them close to weapon caches, military locations, mechanic's garages, and other grimy places.

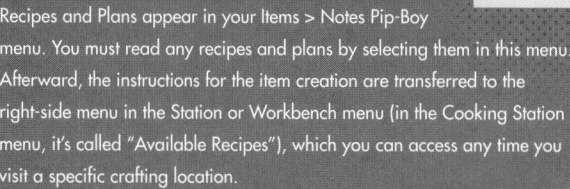

Helpful Hint from Vault-Boy

PIP-BOY POWER: UNLOCKING YOUR INSTRUCTIONS (RECIPES AND PLANS)

Recipes and Plans appear in your Items > Notes Pip-Boy menu. You must read any recipes and plans by selecting them in this menu. Afterward, the instructions for the item creation are transferred to the right-side menu in the Station or Workbench menu (in the Cooking Station menu, it's called "Available Recipes"), which you can access any time you visit a specific crafting location.

FASCINATING FACTS FROM VAULT-BOY

GET A GRIP: AND A BARREL, MUZZLE, SIGHT, AND RECEIVER

MODS ARE SPECIAL ATTACHMENTS OR ALTERATIONS YOU CAN ADD TO ARMOR, POWER ARMOR, AND WEAPONS. THEY AUGMENT THESE ITEMS IN VARIOUS WAYS, FROM CHANGING THE COLOR OF AN ITEM TO AFFECTING RANGE, RECOIL, ACCURACY, WEIGHT, AMMO CAPACITY, DAMAGE RESISTANCE, ENERGY RESISTANCE, AND MANY MORE STATISTICS. FIND OUT MORE ABOUT MODS IN THE INVENTORY CHAPTER OF THIS GUIDE.

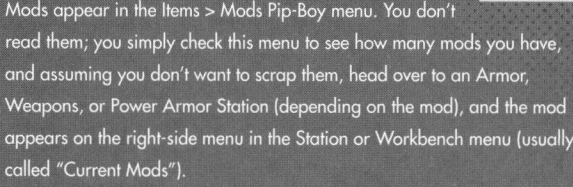

Helpful Hint from Vault-Boy

PIP-BOY POWER: UNLOCKING YOUR INSTRUCTIONS (MODS)

Mods appear in the Items > Mods Pip-Boy menu. You don't read them; you simply check this menu to see how many mods you have, and assuming you don't want to scrap them, head over to an Armor, Weapons, or Power Armor Station (depending on the mod), and the mod appears on the right-side menu in the Station or Workbench menu (usually called "Current Mods").

Helpful Hint from Vault-Boy!

I NEED A COMPLETE LIST OF MODS!

Sorry there, friend; that's not going to happen. Mods are learned from Plans or by scrapping weapons and armor. There are thousands of possible mods, and even more will be added after game launch. Plus, all of the relevant information is detailed in your Workbench menu when you obtain the mod. Rest assured that every piece of armor (powered or not) and weapon has a variety of mods. Hey, we're trying our best, here!

TRAINING

CRAFTING AND C.A.M.P.ing

INVENTORY

QUESTS

ATLAS

BESTIARY

APPENDICES

INSTRUCTIONS FOR SUCCESS: PLANNING AND THE RECIPE FOR SURVIVAL

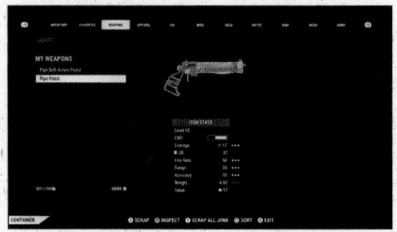

An example of scrapping an item (in this case a weapon at an Armor Workbench); the weapon plan was then learned!

This is generally achieved in one of the following ways:

Obtaining a recipe: You acquire a recipe, plan, or mod by finding it in the landscape or inside a container, buying it from a friend or vendor, or by finishing a quest.

Scrapping an item: If you have a piece of armor, ammo, weapon, or Power Armor or other nonconsumable item and you scrap it into its component material parts, you sometimes receive the recipe or plan for that item. Look for confirmation in your screen's top-left corner.

Picking up an item: This usually occurs with harvestable foodstuffs, like Tatos, Razorgrain, Corn, Mud Fruit, or other naturally occurring foods, including meat from animals you've encountered or killed. Sometimes a recipe is automatically added.

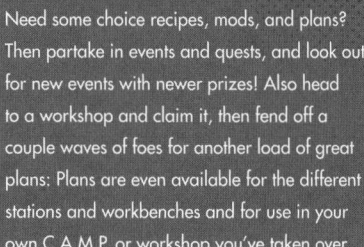

Helpful Hint from Vault-Boy!

MAKING PLANS FOR APPALACHIAN DOMINATION!

Need some choice recipes, mods, and plans? Then partake in events and quests, and look out for new events with newer prizes! Also head to a workshop and claim it, then fend off a couple waves of foes for another load of great plans. Plans are even available for the different stations and workbenches and for use in your own C.A.M.P. or workshop you've taken over.

PART 3: CRAFTING COMPONENTS AND WHERE TO FIND THEM

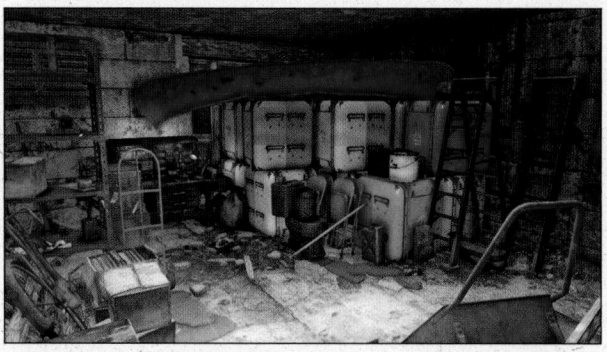

This junk-filled cellar is a scavenger's dream, a paradise crammed with useless detritus you can turn into gold! Or at least, into helpful items you can use or sell for Caps.

ONE MAN'S JUNK IS ANOTHER MAN'S TREASURE

Now you know where to craft and the types of instructions you need to find in order to craft. But what are the items made from? And where do you find all of it? Crafting an item consumes components, and components are found primarily in junk items, non-junk items, harvested items, and deposits or veins.

JUNK ITEMS

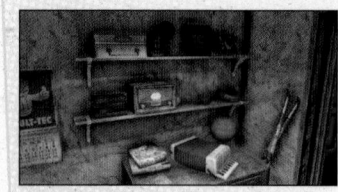

A selection of junk items, sitting there just waiting for you to forage them. And then come back a day later, and forage them again!

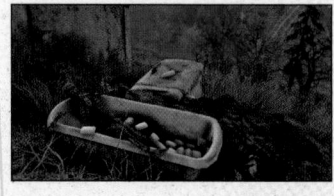

A skeleton sitting in a bathtub full of soap (near Flatwoods). Ordinarily an oddity, but for the junk collector, a huge boon to your oil collecting (the component soap breaks down into)!

Junk items are numerous and contain a large number of disparate components. Did you know, for example, that the Blast Radius Board Game contains Nuclear Material, an otherwise reasonably rare component? If an item is visible to you, it's always there and reappears around a day after your initial scavenge.

To start with, gather junk you can physically see in the environment, and worry about what it contains later. As your foraging mentality matures, if you tag items for searching (see below) or you remember that a certain junk item has components you need, then determine your favorite locations and hone in on those items. The Atlas chapter flags larger quantities of visible junk to help in this regard (though that list is not exhaustive due to the vastness of Appalachia).

NON-JUNK ITEMS

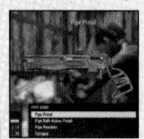

A pipe-pistol. While some see a rudimentary firearm, others see a component-filled item ready to be destroyed and its component parts rebuilt into something even cooler!

The main difference between a junk and non-junk item is that junk items can be group-scrapped at a workbench and serve no other purpose than to be scrapped into component parts. Non-Junk items (found in your other Items menu when gathered) cannot be group-scrapped and may have other uses, which are mostly obvious. For example, a pipe-pistol is a cool gun, as well as a group of components you can use with other components to build better pipe-pistols, other weaponry, or anything you like! If you want to scrap a non-junk item, select these individually at your workbench (which sometimes grants you a plan). Be sure the item isn't too valuable or provides other vital services first!

CONTAINER-LOOTED ITEMS

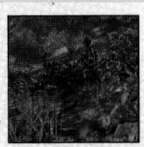

A box of delights, a container allows you to grab a random selection of items, some of which are junk but could also include ammo, weapons, recipes, plans, or mods.

Along with junk and non-junk items you can see, there are those that appear randomly in a large number of different containers. These range from small lunch pails and tool boxes to large industrial trunks and Overseer Caches. Basically, if it's got a door or a lid, check it for goodies! Items inside containers are usually random, so don't bank on finding the same selection of stuff when containers replenish (around a day later).

HARVESTED AND CORPSE-LOOTED ITEMS

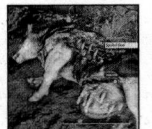

The Soot Flower and Rhododendron: two harvestable plants available immediately.

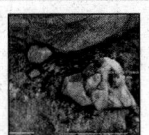

The contents of an animal: a corpse to loot, with meat, hide, and possibly a half-digested Cap.

Crops, fungus, flowers, tree bark, weird carnivorous plant life, and crops still growing in or around farmsteads, these are important components, mainly for cooking recipes but occasionally for other items too. If you have a C.A.M.P. or active workshop, you can plant some of these as crops or order Robotrons to forage for them without having to do it yourself!

It's also important to attempt a spot of hunting, whether you're dropping a large Radstag or battling a Deathclaw, Yao Guai...or worse! Once you stand over the corpse, loot it for crafting components. Like harvested items, these are mainly for cooking recipes. And if you start eating Ghoul meat, think about either reevaluating your mental state or picking the Cannibal perk.

DEPOSITS AND VEINS (AND RESOURCES)

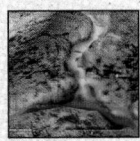

A pit of acid. Not a thrilling location to look at but definitely excellent to find and exploit!

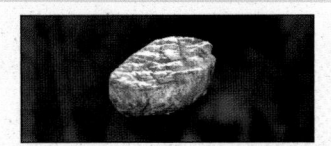

A vein of Black Titanium. If you want lots of a minerals, rather than individual components from certain junk, then dig it up.

Due to its rich mining history, you'd expect Appalachia to be pock-marked with old resource-heavy nodes, and you'd be correct! There are ground depressions called deposits and veins of ore (or acid), all containing larger quantities of specific resources. You can manually clean these veins or deposits out, or construct a resource generator and mine the deposits (but not the veins) continuously. In fact, this forms the basis of why you'd claim a workshop; they all have a number of resources to exploit.

FASCINATING FACT FROM VAULT-BOY!
READING MATERIALS: COMPONENT GUIDANCE

THE INVENTORY CHAPTER OF THIS GUIDE LISTS, BY TYPE, ALL HARVESTED, MINING, AND JUNK ITEMS YOU CAN GATHER. THE ATLAS CHAPTER GIVES A (NON-EXHAUSTIVE) LIST OF EXPECTED HARVESTED, MINING, AND JUNK ITEMS AT EVERY PRIMARY LOCATION IN APPALACHIA. YOU'RE WELCOME!

EXAMPLE 1: MOLE RAT CHUNKS
(CORPSE-LOOTED CONSUMABLE)

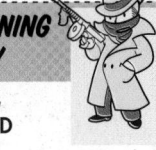

On our exploration, we slaughtered a family of irradiated Mole Rats and looted their still-twitching corpses, securing the component called Mole Rat Chunks. This automatically revealed a recipe called Mole Rat Meat. Because the recipe was revealed (rather than collected), we didn't need to read it; when we reached our cooking station, this was on the menu tonight:

★
MOLE RAT CHUNKS

A sizable chunk of toothy rodent, sizzled to perfection over a wood grill.

Requirements:
Mole Rat Meat (1), Wood (1), Cooking Station

Stats:
Rads +5, Food +10%, HP +25, STR +1, Weight 0.5, Value: 20 Caps

---

We cooked up a few chunks, realizing that it needed to be eaten soon or it would spoil, the meat would rot, and consuming it then would be just asking for a disease. We also had some Soot Flowers and Rhododendron components for a healthy, yet slightly irradiated drink to wash down this rodent.

A WORD OF WARNING FROM VAULT-BOY

A GOOD FORAGING SPOILED: EAT UP, AND FAST!

BE AWARE THAT FOOD YOU COOK HAS THE TENDENCY TO SPOIL QUICKLY, SO CONSUME IT AS SOON AS POSSIBLE. SELECT ANY FOOD ITEM IN YOUR PIP-BOY TO SEE ITS HEALTH AND HOW SOON IT WILL SPOIL. LOOK FOR DIFFERENT MEATS (FROM SLAIN ANIMALS AND INSECTS OR OTHER CREATURES), AND HARVEST THE DIFFERENT FLORA AND FUNGI THROUGHOUT APPALACHIA TO OBTAIN INITIAL RECIPES. ONE ALTERNATIVE TO COOKING FRESH FOOD IS TO EAT PACKAGED FOOD (FOUND IN THE SAME PLACES AS JUNK) INSTEAD; DON'T WORRY ABOUT THE EXPIRY DATE!

TRAINING

CRAFTING AND C.A.M.P.ing

INVENTORY

QUESTS

ATLAS

BESTIARY

APPENDICES

**EXAMPLE 2: ALARM CLOCK
(JUNK BUILDABLE)**

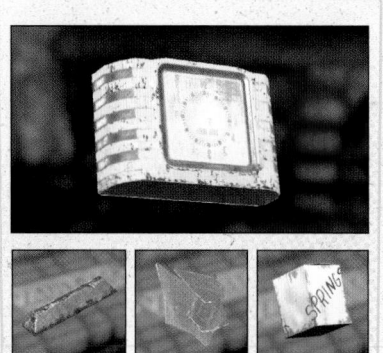

As we continued our exploration of the valley below Vault 76, we removed the revolting residents of the Wixon Homestead and conducted a sweep of the entire farm and outbuildings. This yielded a large amount of junk items, both lying around on floors, shelves, and tables and inside containers. Among the junk was a yellow alarm clock. Nothing fancy.

★

ALARM CLOCK (JUNK ITEM)

A bedside alarm clock, with a light coat of dust and suspicious fluid stains across it.

Stats:
Produces Aluminum (2), Glass, Spring;
Weight: 1.0; Value: 30 Caps

Bring up the alarm clock on the Pip-Boy (Items > Junk menu) or the Scrapping menu of a Tinker's Workbench to see the components that comprise the alarm clock. You can keep the alarm clock intact, or you can break it down into its component parts at a workbench. We scrapped the clock into its separate components Aluminum (2), Glass, and Spring, which weigh less than the clock itself, thus allowing us additional Carry Weight and more room to store additional Junk!

Helpful Hint from Vault-Boy!

COMPONENT SCRAPPING: LIGHTENING YOUR LOAD

Junk is useless scenic items that don't really serve a purpose except to bolster your crafting potential: Grab anything not bolted down. Then go to a workbench (or Chemistry Station) and scrap all of the junk you've collected to lighten your load. You can automatically scrap all junk items at once, making this a very quick and easy experience. If an item isn't categorized as junk (like a beer bottle or pipe-pistol), simply highlight it in the Scrapping menu, check to see the components it generates, and manually scrap these items (you may receive recipes or plans for some of them in the process).

MY STASH BOX: JUNK IN THE TRUNK

Then place all the junk in your My Stash Box so it's still available to you when crafting (My Stash Boxes are linked to your crafting locations). This frees up your Carry Weight for...what else? Foraging for more components!

ITEM ATTENTION: COMPONENT REQUIREMENTS

Whether you scrap junk or not, when you decide to craft a more complex item, its component requirements are listed on the right side of the Crafting menu. The left of the two numbers indicates how many of a component you have, either as a scrapped component item or within a junk item you haven't scrapped, which is automatically destroyed and associated raw components refunded to your collection. This means you don't *have* to scrap all your junk.

TAG FOR SEARCH: MAGNIFYING THE ISSUE

If you're selecting an item to craft, components you don't have (or don't have enough of) are grayed out. Look at the screen's bottom for the "Tag for Search" feature and press it. After tagging the component(s) you desperately need more of, a magnifying glass icon appears next to them. Now when you continue your scavenging, any junk item or container that you find with those tagged components has that same magnifying glass icon; this means you can quickly and easily gather junk with your missing components. "Tag for Search" again at a workbench to remove any tags or add additional components for tagging.

Helpful Hint from Vault-Boy

I NEED A LIST OF ALL THE COMPONENT TYPES. RIGHT NOW!

Easy there, sport! The good news is that a complete list of all base components (sometimes called "materials") can be found in the Inventory chapter of this guide. This covers harvested and aid items, as well as items for all the workbenches and stations and everything else. A list of components for C.A.M.P. and workshop building is provided in the next chapter.

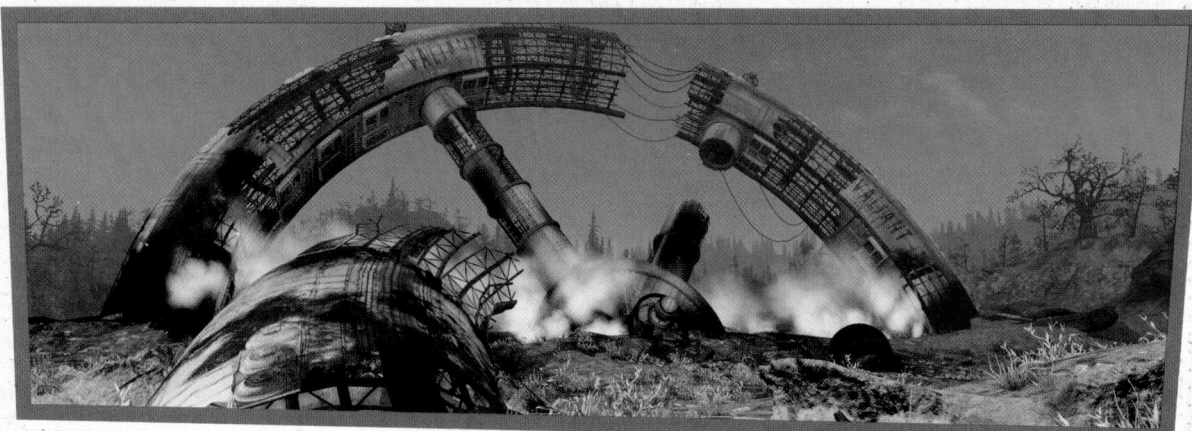

PART 4: ENHANCING YOUR CRAFTING—PERKS AND MORE

Now that you're able to craft at stations and workbenches without fear, it's worth learning a few additional skills to make the most out of your crafting.

Helpful Hint from Vault-Boy!

PERK UP TO GET TO THE GOOD STUFF!

"I don't like reading. What perk should I focus on in order to get the most out of crafting?" Great question there, sport, marred somewhat by your disinterest in hidden knowledge. But the short answer is "Intelligence." The long answer? See below.

BENEFICIAL BUFFS: MAGAZINES

Magazines are always in a particular location, but they randomly appear. However, there are some particularly important Magazines to the crafter, and if you find one of the following, and you've read what the bonus entails, then grab it! Afterward, treasure the reading material and prepare yourself for a "mass crafting session" if necessary beforehand (as Magazine bonuses last only a few hours), *and then use* the Magazine. Don't forget the Luck perk Curator; it appears around Level 19 and gives you Magazine benefits for up to 2/3/4x (Rank 1/2/3) the normal time!

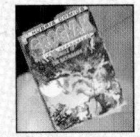

Oh, I've been looking for this copy of *Grognak the Barbarian* everywhere. Aside from the cool articles on loin cloths and axes, it's got some great tips on weapon care!

MAGAZINE NAME	DESCRIPTION OF BONUS	WHY IS THIS USEFUL?
Backwoodsman 1	Collect extra meat when you search dead animals.	More meat equals more cooking recipes for you and your team to nibble on!
Backwoodsman 3	Crafting weapons costs fewer materials.	Craft any weapon you like, but don't use as many components (materials) doing so.
Backwoodsman 4	Gain a 50% chance for double yield when harvesting plants.	Picking a tato fruit (or is it a vegetable)? Need two of them instead of one?
Backwoodsman 6	Receive 50% more healing from cooked food.	Any cooking station Hunger-abating meal gives you more HP.
Backwoodsman 7	You are 50% less likely to become diseased from food and drink.	Lessen the chances of disease, allowing you to even eat uncooked food (though the risk still remains).
Backwoodsman 8	You are 30% more satisfied by eating and drinking.	This fills your Thirst and Hunger meter for longer; fewer stops to eat and drink.
Grognak the Barbarian 6	Melee weapons weigh 75% less.	More Carry Weight equals more scavenging time for junk collecting!
Grognak the Barbarian 7	Melee weapons lose condition 50% more slowly.	Fewer visits to the Weapons Workbench (and using of components) to fix them.
Grognak the Barbarian 9	Gain 10 Carry Capacity.	More Carry Weight equals more scavenging time for junk collecting!

MAGAZINE NAME	DESCRIPTION OF BONUS	WHY IS THIS USEFUL?
Guns and Bullets 5	Gain 50% more components when scrapping weapons.	More components equals more crafting, repairing, or modding opportunities.
Live and Love 3	Heal 50% more from eating vegetables and fruits.	Less need to use them in cooking recipes.
Scout's Life 1	Suffer 30% less radiation from eating or drinking.	Less need for RadAway and a fuller Health Bar.
Scout's Life 3	Gain 10 Carry Capacity.	More Carry Weight equals more scavenging time for junk collecting!
Scout's Life 6	You become hungry and thirsty 30% more slowly.	Your Thirst and Hunger meters are fuller for longer; fewer stops to eat and drink.
Scout's Life 10	Equipped items lose condition 30% more slowly.	Less need to repair them at armor, Power Armor, or Weapons Workbenches.
Tesla Science 4	Your Power Armor consumes Fusion Cores 15% more slowly.	Less need to make your own Fusion Cores, which are high level and require ultra-rare materials; churn out Fusion Cores at Power Plants instead!
Tesla Science 5	Your heavy guns consume ammo 20% more slowly.	Less ammo use means fewer trips to the Tinker's Workbench and a bigger ammo stockpile.

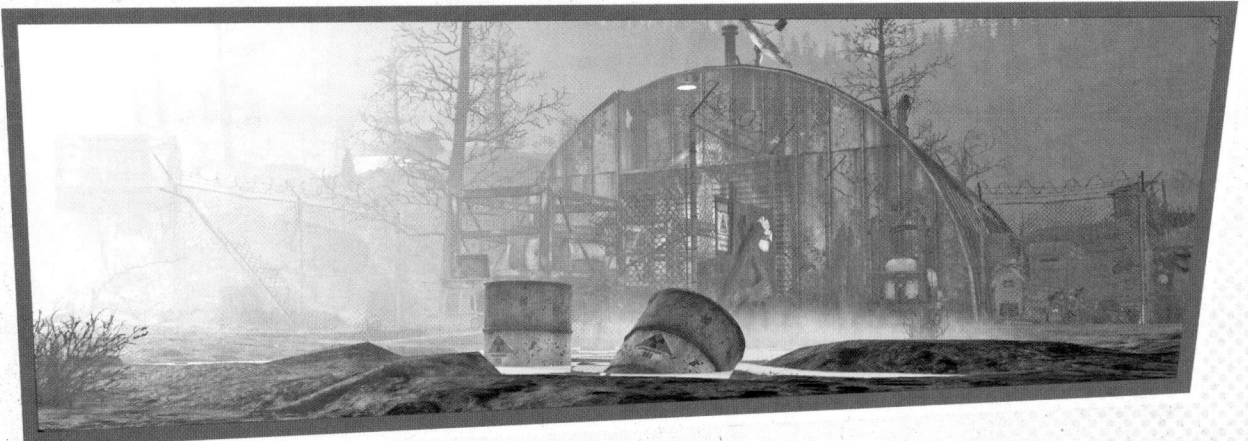

TRAINING

CRAFTING AND C.A.M.P.ING

INVENTORY

QUESTS

ATLAS

BESTIARY

APPENDICES

BENEFICIAL BUFFS: PERKS

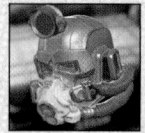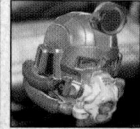

Wait, two Power Armor helmets? I only thought I'd made one! But that was before I added the Super Duper Luck perk to my deck!

The Perk section of this guide gives you an exhaustive run-down of every perk from all seven SPECIAL attributes. But which ones specifically benefit the crafter? Glad you asked! The following lists (in SPECIAL and level order) which perks you should consider using. Remember some can stack with each other and/or a Magazine (if they all have a similar benefit).

STRENGTH PERKS

PERK NAME	LEVEL	RANKS	DESCRIPTION OF BONUS
Traveling Pharmacy	4	1, 2, 3	Weights of all Chems (including Stimpaks) are reduced by 30/60/90%.
Pack Rat	7	1, 2, 3	The weight of all junk items is reduced by 25/50/75%.
Bandolier	8	1, 2, 3	Ballistic weapon ammo weighs 30/60/90% less.
Sturdy Frame	13	1, 2	Armor weighs 25/50% less than normal.
Martial Artist	16	1, 2, 3	Your melee weapons weigh 20/40/60% less, and you can swing them 10/20/30% faster.
Scattershot	18	1, 2, 3, 4	Shotguns now weigh 20/40/60/80% less and you reload them 10/20/30/40% faster.
Strong Back	26	1, 2, 3, 4	Gain +10/20/30/40 to Carry Weight.
Ordnance Express	31	1, 2, 3	Thrown explosives weigh 30/60/90% less.
Bear Arms	35	1, 2, 3, 4	Heavy Guns weigh 20/40/60/80% less.

Strength: These perks all reduce the weight of particular items, meaning you can either carry more of them, or you have more room (Carry Weight) left for scavenging.

PERCEPTION PERKS

PERK NAME	LEVEL	RANKS	DESCRIPTION OF BONUS
Butcher's Bounty	3	1, 2, 3	40/60/80% chance to find extra meat when you search an animal corpse.
Green Thumb	4	1	Reap twice as much when harvesting flora.

Perception: Only two Perception perks directly affect crafting, mainly allowing you to loot and harvest more animal meat and flora. This means you can stockpile these items more quickly (e.g., if you need to make a lot of food and drink for your team).

ENDURANCE PERKS

PERK NAME	LEVEL	RANKS	DESCRIPTION OF BONUS
Lead Belly	2	1, 2, 3	You take 30% less/60% less/no radiation from eating or drinking.
Dromedary	3	1, 2, 3	All drinks quench thirst by an additional 25/50/75%.
Iron Stomach	4	1, 2, 3	Your chance to catch a disease from food is reduced by 30/60/90%.
Slow Metabolizer	5	1, 2, 3	All food satisfies hunger by an additional 25/50/75%.
Thirst Quencher	6	1, 2, 3	Drinking any liquid has a 30/60/90% reduced chance to cause disease.
Hydro Fix	12	1, 3	Chems generate 50% less/no thirst.
Rejuvenated	12	1, 2	You gain increased/much increased benefit from being Well Fed or Well Hydrated.
Munchy Resistance	17	1, 3	Using chems induces 50% less/no hunger.
Chem Fiend	23	1, 2, 3	Any chems you take last 30/60/100% longer.
Cannibal	25	1, 2, 3	Eating human, Ghoul, Super Mutant, Scorched, or Mole Miner corpses restores some/more/even more Health and hunger.
All Night Long	41	1, 2, 3	You suffer 20/40/60% less from hunger and thirst.
Chem Resistant	43	1, 2	You're half as likely to get addicted when consuming chems/You gain complete immunity to chem addiction.

Endurance: While some of these perks are only tangentially connected to crafting (they simply offer bonuses for eating, drinking, taking chems, and reducing disease), this leads to less time at the Cooking and Chemistry Stations.

CHARISMA PERKS

PERK NAME	LEVEL	RANKS	DESCRIPTION OF BONUS
Happy Camper	3	1, 2	Hunger and thirst grow 40/80% more slowly when in camp or in a team workshop.
Bloodsucker	11	1, 2, 3	Bloodpacks now satisfy thirst, no longer irradiate, and heal 50/100/150% more.
Field Surgeon	15	2	Stimpaks and RadAway will now work much more quickly.

Charisma: Though there are additional perks from this attribute that increase chem bonuses and reduce radiation poisoning, these Cooking and Chemistry Station–related perks are most relevant.

INTELLIGENCE PERKS

PERK NAME	LEVEL	RANKS	DESCRIPTION OF BONUS
First Aid	2	1, 2, 3, 4	Stimpaks restore 10/20/30/40% more lost Health.
Makeshift Warrior	3	1, 2, 3	Your melee weapons break 30/60/90% more slowly and are cheaper to repair.
Licensed Plumber	5	1, 2, 3	Your pipe weapons break 30/60/90% more slowly and are cheaper to repair.
Exotic Weapons	8	1, 2	You can now craft crossbows, black powder guns, and more! (Plans required.) // You can now craft Rank 1 exotic weapon mods. (Plans Required.)
Scrapper	13	1, 2	Obtain more components when you scrap weapons and armor.
Batteries Included	28	1	Energy weapon ammo weighs 30/60/90% less.

PERK NAME	LEVEL	RANKS	DESCRIPTION OF BONUS
Armorer	15	1, 2, 3	You can now craft advanced armor mods. (Plans required)./Crafting armor now costs fewer materials./Your crafted armor has improved durability.
Exotic Weapons Expert	16	1, 2	You can craft Rank 2 exotic weapon mods. (Plans required)./Crafting exotic weapons now costs fewer materials.
Contractor	18	1, 2	Crafting workshop items now cost 25/50% fewer materials.
Science	20	1, 2	You can now craft energy guns (Plans Required)/You can craft Rank 1 energy gun mods (Plans required).
Gunsmith	23	1, 2, 3	Your guns break 25/50/75% more slowly and are cheaper to repair.
Exotic Weapons Master	25	1, 2	You can craft Rank 3 exotic weapon mods. (Plans required)./Your crafted exotic weapons have improved durability.
Fix It Good	27	1, 2, 3	You can repair armor and Power Armor to 130/160/200% of normal maximum condition.
Science Expert	31	1, 2	You can now craft Rank 2 energy gun mods (Plans required)./Crafting energy guns now costs fewer materials.
Chemist	34	1, 2	You get double/triple the quantity when you craft chems!
Weapon Artisan	40	1, 2, 3	You can repair any weapon to 130/160/200% of normal maximum condition.
Power Smith	41	1, 2, 3	You can now craft advanced Power Armor mods (Plans required)./Crafting Power Armor now costs fewer materials./Your crafted Power Armor now has improved durability.
Science Master	43	1, 2	You can now craft Rank 3 energy gun mods (Plans required)./Crafted energy guns have improved durability.
Power Patcher	44	1, 2, 3	Your Power Armor breaks 20/40/60% more slowly and is cheaper to repair.

Intelligence: Bingo! You've found the crafter's attribute! Not only is Intelligence the key to crafting specific types of weapons, but it's also the key to getting the most out of your stations and workbenches by crafting advanced mods and higher ranks of armor, Power Armor, and weaponry, as well as crafting more hard-wearing items. Need to open all the crafting menus on your workbench? Need to craft high-level armor, Power Armor, and weapons? Then a high Intelligence (or a crazy amount of Perk Card swapping before each workbench session) is a must!

AGILITY PERKS

PERK NAME	LEVEL	RANKS	DESCRIPTION OF BONUS
Thru Hiker	3	1, 2, 3	Food and drink weights are reduced by 30/60/90%.
Packin' Light	9	1, 2, 3	Your pistols weigh 25/50/75% less.
Home Defense	22	1, 2, 3	You can craft and disarm better/advanced/expert traps and craft better/advanced/expert turrets (Plans required).
Ammosmith	34	1, 2, 3	Produce 30/60/100% more rounds when crafting ammunition.
White Knight	39	1, 2, 3	Your armor breaks 30/60/90% more slowly and is cheaper to repair.

Agility: Though Home Defense is mainly for workshop items (covered in the next section of this guide), Ammosmith is of particular importance to those making ammo at a Tinker's Workbench. Cheaper repair costs at Armor Workbenches is also a help.

LUCK PERKS

PERK NAME	LEVEL	RANKS	DESCRIPTION OF BONUS
Good With Salt	9	1, 2, 3	Food in your inventory will spoil 30/60/90% more slowly.
Junk Shield	10	1, 2, 3	Carry junk to gain up to 10/20/30 Damage and Energy Resistance. (No Power Armor)
Woodchucker	17	1, 2, 3	Collecting wood yields 50/100/200% more.
Curator	19	1	The benefits of Bobbleheads and Magazines last twice as long.
Lucky Break	24	1, 2, 3	Slight chance your equipped armor will repair/chance your equipped armor will repair/chance your equipped armor will greatly repair itself when struck.
Super Duper	50	1, 2, 3, 4	When you craft anything, there is a 10/20/30/40% chance you'll get double results!

Luck: While some of these perks don't affect your workbench hammering directly, they're worth considering in the grand scheme of things. Luck also has the single biggest bonus perk to crafting of all: the high-level but insanely helpful Super Duper, which gives you a 40% chance (Rank 4) at doubling the results of anything you craft!

SPECIFIC STATION AND WORKBENCH ITEM PERKS

ATTRIBUTE	PERK NAME	CRAFTING LOCATION	ITEM NAMES
Strength	Gladiator	Weapon Workbench	Some One-Handed Melee Weapons
Strength	Heavy Gunner	Weapon Workbench	Some Heavy Guns
Strength	Iron Fist	Weapon Workbench	Some Fist and One-Handed Melee Weapons
Strength	Shotgunner	Weapon Workbench	Some Shotguns
Strength	Slugger	Weapon Workbench	Some Two-Handed Melee Weapons
Perception	Commando	Weapon Workbench	Some Automatic Rifles
Perception	Green Thumb	Cooking Station	Disease Cures
Perception	Rifleman	Weapon Workbench	Some Non-Automatic Rifles
Intelligence	Chemist	Chemistry Station	Antibiotics, Disease Cures
Intelligence	Chemist	Cooking Station	Disease Cures
Intelligence	Demolition Expert	Tinker's Workbench	Some Grenades and Mines
Intelligence	Exotic Weapons	Weapon Workbench	All Exotic Weapons (Ballistic, Energy)
Intelligence	Pharmacist	Chemistry Station	Disease Cures, Water Filter
Intelligence	Science	Tinker's Workbench	Some Grenades and Mines
Intelligence	Science	Weapon Workbench	Some Energy Weapons and Energy Heavy Guns
Agility	Action Boy/Girl	Weapon Workbench	Some Repairs
Agility	Guerrilla	Weapon Workbench	Some Automatic Pistols
Agility	Gunslinger	Weapon Workbench	Some Non-Automatic Pistols
Agility	Home Defense	Tinker's Workbench	Some Traps

Advice: This table shows that specific types of weapons need a particular perk to craft them, along with a particular rank. If you want to craft a particular type of item, be sure you have these perks handy! Note this is in addition to perks that unlock the advanced crafting options.

The final part of your crafting knowledge features information on what to expect from a fully unlocked station and workbench, based on collecting the different types of available recipes, plans, and mods, and reaching Level 50. Also shown are some expert crafting examples from a grand master of the crafting arts!

STATISTICAL FORTITUDE: CRAFTING AND RATIOS

So you're about to make a career out of crafting. Or do just enough crafting to get by. Either way, make sure you're working smarter, not harder, at all aspects of this craft: That means using your Item Stats information to your advantage.

The Item Stats menu at your station or workbench has a variety of information. Certain statistics (usually the weight and value of non-damaging items, with Damage, Range, and Accuracy added for weapons) sometimes receive a set of up to three plus (+++) or minus (–) signs. This is to indicate whether the item has a particularly impressive value compared to other items of that type. Here are some examples. Your stats should be generally the same, but the values may be different, depending on active effects:

- **COOKING:** CRANBERRY JAM HAS A HEAVY WEIGHT (1) COMPARED TO OTHER FOOD (---).
- **TINKER:** A MININUKE HAS A HEAVY WEIGHT (12) COMPARED TO OTHER AMMO (---).
- **ARMOR:** A BROTHERHOOD OF STEEL COMBAT ARMOR CHEST PLATE HAS A GREAT DAMAGE RESISTANCE (27) COMPARED TO OTHER COMBAT ARMOR CHEST PIECES (+++).
- **WEAPONS:** A SLEDGEHAMMER HAS A LARGE DAMAGE (63) COMPARED TO OTHER MELEE WEAPONS (+++).

How is this useful? Because you can change the order of the statistics to list every item of a certain type by any of its statistics. And then figure out some particularly beneficial ratios, based on the recipes and plans you've unlocked. Here are some to think about using, if you want to make a load of Caps or use your time scavenging more wisely:

- ITEMS WITH THE BEST **STAT TO COMPONENT REQUIREMENTS** RATIO (FOR VALUABLE ITEMS COMPONENTS THAT ARE EASY TO FORAGE FOR).
- ITEMS WITH THE BEST **STAT TO LIGHTEST WEIGHT** RATIO (FOR ITEMS TO LESSEN OVERENCUMBERANCE).
- ITEMS WITH THE BEST **LEAST COMPONENTS TO HIGHEST VALUE** RATIO (FOR SELLING TO HUMANS OR VENDORS).

COOKING STATIONS

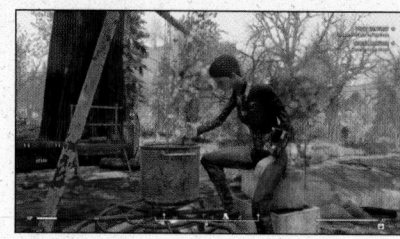

TYPES OF FOOD AND DRINK

All Drinks: Every recipe you know that quenches your thirst (merged from the other menus) is listed here. Aside from boiling water, expect this to be mainly juices and teas.

All Food: Every recipe you know that satisfies your hunger (merged fro

m the other menus) is listed here. Expect ribs, soups, omelettes, steaks, pies, and even jerky!

Healing: Here you'll find Detoxing Salves (for removing rads), Disease Cures, and Healing Salves. Note some disease cures require the Green Thumb (Perception) and Chemist (Intelligence) perks.

Meat: This menu contains items derived from looted creature corpses you've discovered on your travels. Note that these meals usually grant food but can also grant water bonuses too.

Plants: This menu contains items derived from harvested flora and fungi you've picked throughout the landscape. Most give you hydration bonuses, but some offer to satisfy your hunger too.

Prepared: This is food and drink that doesn't spoil too quickly, allowing you to take it with you on short journeys, though food spoils while water-based recipes remain unspoiled for longer.

Utility: Here you can craft Vegetable Starch, which you can turn into the Adhesive crafting component.

EXAMPLE 1 (BEGINNER): SIMPLE BLOODLEAF TEA (HARVESTED CONSUMABLE: DRINK)

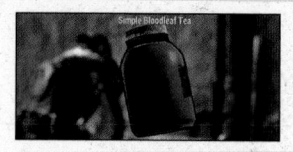

★

SIMPLE BLOODLEAF TEA

An extremely purple tea designed to resist both disease and an easy description of how it tastes.

Requirements:
Bloodleaf, Boiled Water, Wood

Stats:
Rads +5, Water 15%, HP +10, Disease Resist +5, Weight 0.5, Value 11 Caps

---

After boiling some water, wading into some water to pluck a Bloodleaf flower, and gathering some wood, we were back at the cooking station, ready to try out a simple tea:

EXAMPLE 2 (BEGINNER): BRAIN FUNGUS SOUP (HARVESTED CONSUMABLE: FOOD AND DRINK)

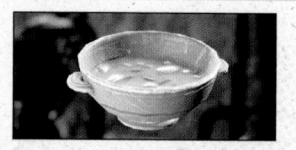

★

BRAIN FUNGUS SOUP

Offering both a little braininess and bitterness, this bowl needs to be consumed before it spoils.

Requirements:
Boiled Water, Brain Fungus, Wood

Stats:
Rads +5, Water 15%, Food +10%, HP +12, INT +2, Weight 0.5, Value 13 Caps

---

We returned from exploring a cave with some fungus; it looks like a brain, but it isn't. It did have some splattered Ghoul cranium on it, but we washed that off before cooking it and suddenly felt a lot more intelligent.

EXAMPLE 3 (EXPERT): SWEETWATER SPECIAL BLEND (HARVESTED CONSUMABLE: DRINK)

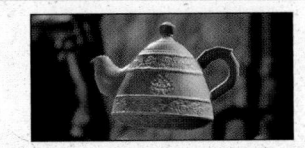

★
SWEETWATER SPECIAL BLEND

A dainty little brew, that comes in its own fancy teapot!

Requirements:
Bloodleaf, Boiled Water, Bourbon, Honey, Wood

Stats:
Rads +1, Water 55%, PER +2, Weight 0.5, Value 32 Caps

Anyone for tea? We braved a band of ferocious woodland bees and brought Bourbon back from Point Pleasant in order to make this Perception-increasing beverage.

EXAMPLE 4 (EXPERT): MEGASLOTH TENDERLOIN (CORPSE-LOOTED CONSUMABLE: FOOD)

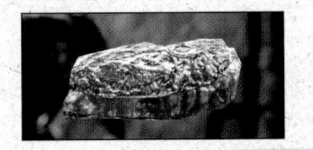

★
MEGASLOTH TENDERLOIN

The best bits of a Megasloth are cut out to make this health-imbibing steak dinner.

Requirements:
Boiled Water, Megasloth Meat, Salt, Silt Bean, Wood

Stats:
Rads +5, Food +25%, HP +90, Energy Resist +35, Weight 1, Value 131 Caps

After a successful hunt in the wilds of the Mire, we returned with the innards of a legendary Mega Sloth. Cutting out the gross bits, we cheffed up a steak that more than satisfies a craving for Health points!

CHEMISTRY STATIONS

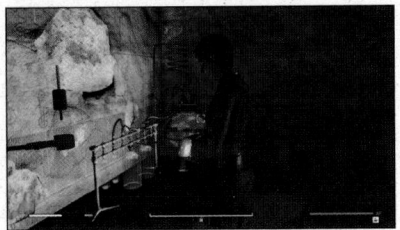

TYPES OF CHEMS AND OTHER ITEMS

All Drinks: This is usually boiled water, but purified water is also available (thirst-quenching without the Rads or need for a C.A.M.P. water purifier).

Ammo: When the recipe is uncovered, you can make gunpowder here, which is a component necessary in Tinker's Workbench ammunition construction.

Drugs: Craft a variety of chems here, from the delicious (and only lightly addictive) Berry Mentats, to Overdrive, Fury, and Psychobuff. If you've found the recipe, you can craft it here.

Energy Ammo: Recipe-permitting, items like Fuel (e.g., for your flamethrower traps) or Fusion Cores are here.

Grenade: If you want to freak out the enemy (they frenzy for 30 seconds), and you've found a recipe for Hallucigen Gas Grenades, you can craft them here.

Healing: A much more comprehensive list of healing chems compared to the cooking station, including Blood Packs, Detoxing Salves, Disease Cures, RadAway, and Stimpaks. Note some Healing items require the Intelligence perks Chemist and Pharmacist.

Mutation Serums: Once certain criteria have been met, and you've collected some pretty dangerous components, you can create a serum that gives you (or a friend) a mutation!

Nuked Flora: After a nuclear missile has decimated an area, only "flux" plants are left. This turns raw flux plants into stable ones, for creating advanced mods and items like Fusion Cores.

Smelting: This is where any raw ore materials you've mined (with your hands or by a resource machine) are turned into scrap, nuclear waste, raw black titanium, fertilizer, for use in mods and construction.

Utility: You can create cutting fluid (which is broken down into oil), and types of solvent.

EXAMPLE 5 (BEGINNER): GUNPOWDER (AMMO)

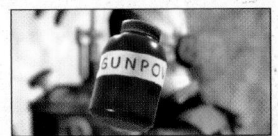

- WHEN YOU'VE ENOUGH ACID AND CLOTH, AND DON'T KNOW WHAT TO DO WITH THEM.
- REQUIREMENTS: ACID, CLOTH
- STATS: WEIGHT 0.1, VALUE 6 CAPS

This fine powder is built in one crafting location and utilized in another. Statistically, it's not that impressive, but that's not the point: Gunpowder is the building block of ammunition, and well used in your Tinker's Workbench.

EXAMPLE 6 (EXPERT): BERRY MENTATS (DRUG)

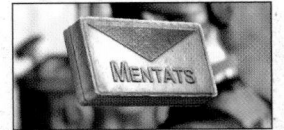

- IF YOU NEED A BOOST OF SMARTS, WITH A HINT OF FIRECRACKER BERRY.
- REQUIREMENTS: BRAIN FUNGUS, FIRECRACKER BERRY, MENTATS, STARLIGHT BERRIES
- STATS: WATER −3%, INT +5, WEIGHT 0.3, VALUE 75

One of the higher-end drugs you can make, mainly due to the three different harvested plants you need to create it.

EXAMPLE 7 (PROFESSIONAL): FUSION CORE (ENERGY AMMO)

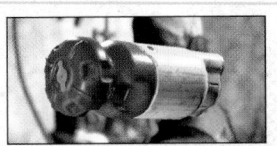

- IF YOU'RE TOO LAZY TO VISIT A POWER PLANT, WHY NOT MAKE YOUR OWN FUSION CORE FROM HIGHLY UNSTABLE MATERIALS?
- REQUIREMENTS: PURE COBALT FLUX, PURE CRIMSON FLUX, FLUORESCENT FLUX, PURE VIOLET FLUX, PURE YELLOWCAKE FLUX.
- STATS: FULL CND, CHARGE 100/100, WEIGHT 3, VALUE 348

After being surprised by a nuclear attack on Morgantown, we scoured the surrounding hills for mutated plant life, refined it, and used it to make our own Power Armor batteries.

TRAINING

CRAFTING AND C.A.M.P.ING

INVENTORY

QUESTS

ATLAS

BESTIARY

APPENDICES

ARMOR WORKBENCHES

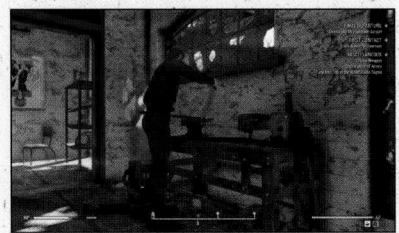

TYPES OF ARMOR AND OTHER CRAFTING RESULTS

Clothing: If you tire of your Vault 76 clothing, you can wear the outfits of the people of West Virginia: the recently dead, the long-dead, and the pretending-to-be-dead for Halloween (vanity clothing like the Civil War–Era Suit, Skiiing Purple and White Outfit, and Halloween Costume Skeleton).

Heavy Armor: Combat, Leather, Metal, Raider, and Robot variants of armor designed to offer excellent protection with some slight weight restrictions.

Headwear: Any masks, glasses, hats, and helmets. Helmets don't provide extra defense and are not required as armor; headwear is purely to add style to your look.

Light Armor: Combat, Leather, Metal, Raider, and Robot variants of armor designed to offer reasonable protection with good maneuverability.

Sturdy Armor: Combat, Leather, Metal, Raider, and Robot variants of armor designed to be the "sweet spot" between heavy and light armor, offering good protection and maneuverability.

Under Armor: Offering some reasonable degree of protection, these are designed to be worn under armor.

EXAMPLE 8 (BEGINNER): HALLOWEEN COSTUME SKELETON (CLOTHING)

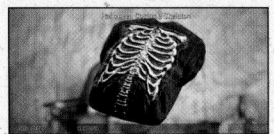

- – SCARE FOLKS BY DRESSING UP AS A SKELETON. DON'T WORRY, THEY'RE MENTALLY PREPARED FOR IT.
- – **REQUIREMENTS:** CLOTH, PLASTIC
- – **STATS:** LEVEL 1, WEIGHT 1, VALUE 25

Plans were acquired near a high school. After returning to an Armor Workbench, the crafting was delightfully simple and the results were suitably terrifying. At least from a distance.

EXAMPLE 9 (EXPERT): HEAVY COMBAT ARMOR CHEST PIECE (HEAVY ARMOR)

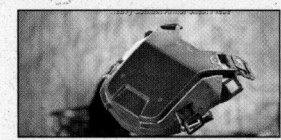

- – OFFERING IMPRESSIVE BALLISTIC AND ENERGY DAMAGE RESISTANCE, AND ONLY MILD CHAFING.
- – **REQUIREMENTS:** LEATHER, PLASTIC, RUBBER, STEEL
- – **STATS:** LEVEL 20, DMG RESIST (BALLISTIC) 20, (ENERGY) 14, WEIGHT 14.5, VALUE 446

We had to wait until Level 20 to be able to craft and wear this chunky piece of torso armor. Then we added the limbs and helmet to complete the look.

EXAMPLE 10 (PROFESSIONAL): HEAVY COMBAT ARMOR CHEST PIECE (MODDED)

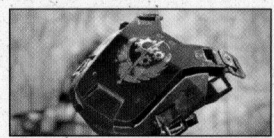

- – ASIDE FROM THE INSIGNIA ON YOUR CHEST, YOU CAN TELL EVERYONE YOU USED TO BE A PALADIN.
- – MODS: BROTHERHOOD OF STEEL
- – **REQUIREMENTS:** ADHESIVE, CLOTH, LEATHER, OIL, STEEL
- – STATS (BEFORE MODDING): LEVEL 50, DMG RESIST (BALLISTIC) 40 (ENERGY) 14, WEIGHT 14.5, VALUE 291.
- – STATS (AFTER MODDING): LEVEL 50, DMG RESIST (BALLISTIC) 67 (ENERGY) 27, RADIATION 1, WEIGHT 14.5, VALUE 291.

One of the first modifications to our Heavy Combat Armor was more than just a paint job; the Brotherhood of Steel mod gave us better damage resistance for the same weight.

TINKER'S WORKBENCHES

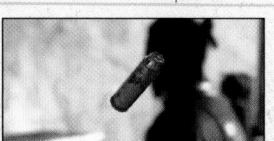

TYPES OF AMMO AND OTHER CRAFTING RESULTS

Ammo: Ranging from the esoteric to the mundane, every type of ammunition you've already found or broken down can be reconstructed providing you have the raw materials.

Buff: If you've received the recipe for this as a reward, you can craft an upgraded Stealth Boy called the Phantom Device here (which renders you invisible while frenzying nearby creatures).

Energy Ammo: If you're short on cryo cells, flares, gamma rounds, plasma cartridges, or other ammunition for energy weapons, craft it from this menu.

Explosive Ammo: There's no need to scrounge around for mininukes; craft them here along with other heavy gun ordnance.

Grenades: From the relatively mundane (Molotov cocktails) to the truly odd (pumpkin grenades), craft all manner of projectiles (like Gryo, Grag MIRV, pulse, and baseball grenades), recipes permitting. Note that some grenades require (Intelligence) Demolitions Expert and Science perks.

Mines: If you need to craft some explosive bait, or the usual bottlecap, frag, cryo, pulse, plasma, or nuke mines, check them out here. Note that some mines require the Intelligence perks Demolitions Expert and Science.

EXAMPLE 11 (BEGINNER): .44 ROUNDS (BALLISTIC AMMO)

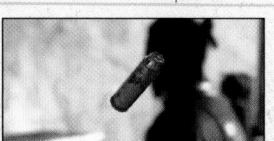

- – EXTREMELY LIGHT, REASONABLY EASY TO MAKE, AND GOOD VALUE TO SELL. BULLETS ARE BIG BUSINESS.
- – **REQUIREMENTS:** GUNPOWDER, LEAD, STEEL
- – **STATS:** WEIGHT 0.004, VALUE 8

Finding a vial of gunpowder in a container helped us craft more (at the Chemistry Station) before gathering other components and creating multiple bullets for our brand-new, stolen-off-a-corpse .44 revolver—the next step up from a pipe pistol!

EXAMPLE 12 (EXPERT): MOLOTOV COCKTAIL (GRENADE)

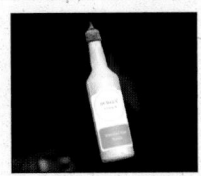

- NEED TO SET THINGS YOU DON'T LIKE ON FIRE WHILE ADVENTURING? CRAFT ONE OR TWO (DOZEN) OF THESE COCKTAILS!
- REQUIREMENTS: ADHESIVE, BEER BOTTLE, CLOTH, OIL
- STATS: DAMAGE 50 (ENERGY DAMAGE 8), FIRE RATE 0, RANGE 94, ACCURACY 0, WEIGHT 0.5, VALUE 20.

We had trouble with a couple of Vault Dwellers running around, hitting our C.A.M.P.'s generator. Aside from some turrets, we crafted a couple of crates of Molotovs to provide some real "suppressing fire."

WEAPONS WORKBENCHES

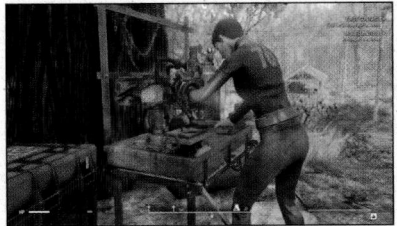

TYPES OF WEAPONS AND OTHER CRAFTING RESULTS

Blunt Melee Weapons: Melee weapons with a blunt edge, like a baseball bat.

Edged Melee Weapons: Melee weapons with a sharp edge, like a machete.

Energy Guns: Weapons that utilize energy ammunition, like a laser pistol.

Exotic Weapons: Odd or esoteric weapons like crossbows and black powder guns.

Heavy Guns: A heavy weapon that's usually slow with massive damage potential, like a minigun.

Launchers: A heavy weapon with an explosive payload, like a missile launcher.

Machined Guns: Pistols, rifles, or small automatic submachine guns and other pistols.

Pipe Guns: Pistols and rifles that are the "pipe" type, along with other rifles.

Throwing Weapons: Weapons that are thrown, but not explosive, like a tomahawk.

Ultracite Weapons: Weapons using the powerful Ultracite ammunition, like the Gatling laser cannon.

EXAMPLE 13 (EXPERT): POWER FIST (BLUNT MELEE WEAPON)

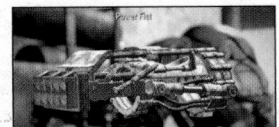

- PUNCH FOES TO DEATH WITH A GIANT YELLOW FIST. AND THAT'S ONE OF THE MORE SUBTLE BLUNT MELEE WEAPONS.
- REQUIREMENTS: ALUMINUM, GEAR, OIL, PLASTIC, RUBBER, SCREW, STEEL, STRENGTH PERK IRON FIST RANK 2
- STATS: LEVEL 30, DAMAGE 48, SPEED MEDIUM, WEIGHT 4, VALUE 203

All that strength training paid dividends as we found plans for a giant mechanical arm we could use to punch foes to death with. Though there were quite a few requirements, the results were worth it!

EXAMPLE 14 (BEGINNER): LEAD PIPE (MODDED)

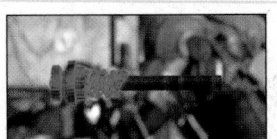

- NEED TO ADD WEIGHT TO YOUR MELEE WEAPONS? NO? WHAT IF YOU COULD CRIPPLE LIMBS? NICE!
- MODS: HEAVY
- REQUIREMENTS: ADHESIVE, CONCRETE, LEAD, STEEL
- STATS (BEFORE MODDING): LEVEL 1, DAMAGE 17, SPEED MEDIUM, WEIGHT 3, VALUE 30
- STATS (BEFORE MODDING): LEVEL 1, DAMAGE 24, SPEED MEDIUM, WEIGHT 5.3, VALUE 53

Though the statistics aren't that different, a heavy lead pipe inflicts superior damage, has a chance to cripple, and inflicts extra limb damage.

EXAMPLE 15 (PROFESSIONAL): ULTRACITE GATLING LASER (ULTRACITE WEAPONS)

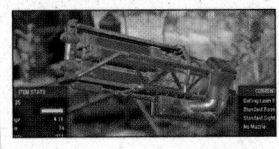

- A GATLING LASER, FOR THOSE WHO ARE USING A MINIGUN AND WANT EVEN MORE CARNAGE.
- REQUIREMENTS: ALUMINUM, CIRCUITRY, CRYSTAL, FIBER OPTICS, PLASTIC, STEEL, ULTRACITE
- STATS: LEVEL 35, DAMAGE (ENERGY) 16, FIRE RATE 273, RANGE 395, ACCURACY 48, WEIGHT 19.4, VALUE 650

Once we discovered the joys of the rare material Ultracite, we were lucky enough to fashion one of the most exceptional weapons of Appalachia: a rapid-fire laser cannon!

EXAMPLE 16 (PROFESSIONAL): ULTRACITE GATLING LASER (MODDED)

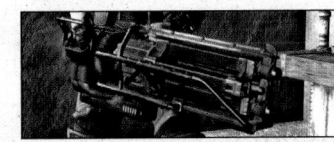

- TAKE A HULKING GREAT LASER CANNON AND MAKE IT BETTER.
- STATS (BEFORE MODDING): LEVEL 50, DAMAGE (ENERGY) 20, CORE 2, FIRE RATE 273, RANGE 204, ACCURACY 48, WEIGHT 19.4, VALUE 492

- MODS: RECEIVER (VICIOUS GATLING LASER), BARREL (ALIGNED LONG BARREL), SIGHTS (STANDARD REFLEX)
- REQUIREMENTS (RECEIVER): ADHESIVE, CIRCUITRY, CRYSTAL, RUBBER, SCREWS, SILVER, STEEL, ULTRACITE, INTELLIGENCE PERK SCIENCE MASTER RANK 1
- REQUIREMENTS (BARREL): ADHESIVE; CIRCUITRY; CRYSTAL; FIBER OPTICS; GEAR; GLASS; OIL; RUBBER; SCREW; SILVER; INTELLIGENCE PERK SCIENCE, MASTER RANK 1

- REQUIREMENTS (SIGHTS): ADHESIVE, ALUMINUM, GLASS, NUCLEAR MATERIAL, SCREW, SILVER
- STATS (AFTER RECEIVER): ACCURACY +4, IMPROVED HIP-FIRE ACCURACY, CRITICAL SHOT DAMAGE
- STATS (AFTER BARREL): ACCURACY +5, IMPROVED RANGE, IMPROVED RECOIL, AND HIP-FIRE ACCURACY
- STATS (AFTER SIGHTS): ACCURACY +5, WEIGHT +1.3

After building a different Ultracite Gatling laser cannon, we added modifications to the three areas of the weapon that had this feature: the receiver, barrel, and sights. The results were improved accuracy, recoil, range, hip-fire accuracy, a slight weight increase, and the removal of many scavenged components.

TRAINING

CRAFTING AND C.A.M.P.ing

INVENTORY

QUESTS

ATLAS

BESTIARY

APPENDICES

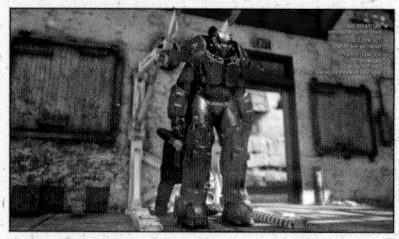

TYPES OF WEAPONS AND OTHER CRAFTING RESULTS

The following types of Power Armor (each with a torso, helmet, left and right arm, left and right leg) are accessible, and these submenus unlock as you gather more raw materials and plans:

– **ENCLAVE POWER ARMOR:** POWER ARMOR DEVELOPED BY THE SECRETIVE NATION STATE OF THE SAME NAME.

– **EXCAVATOR POWER ARMOR:** GARRAHAN MINING CORPORATION'S PROTOTYPE POWER ARMOR.

– **RAIDER POWER ARMOR:** ROUGH AND ARCHAIC ARMOR USED BY RAIDERS; THE FIRST YOU CAN UTILIZE.

– **T-45 POWER ARMOR:** WEST TEK DEFENSE CONTRACTOR MILITARY-GRADE POWER ARMOR.

– **T-51B POWER ARMOR:** THE MOST COMMON OF THE (NOW LOST) A-F MODEL VARIANTS FROM WEST TEK.

– **T-60 POWER ARMOR:** A LARGER, MORE PROTECTIVE AND MODERN VERSION OF WEST TEK'S ARMOR.

– **ULTRACITE POWER ARMOR:** A PROTOTYPE POWER ARMOR UTILIZING THE ULTRACITE META-MATERIAL.

– **X-01 PROTOTYPE ARMOR:** A NUKA-WORLD AND U.S. MILITARY COOPERATIVE PROTOTYPE.

EXAMPLE 17 (EXPERT): T-51B HELMET (T-51B POWER ARMOR)

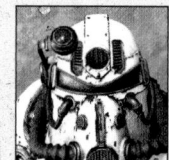

– WHEN YOU'RE READY FOR SOME REAL POWER ARMOR, UPGRADE FROM RAIDER TO OFFICIALLY SANCTIONED EXOSKELETONS.
– **REQUIREMENTS:** ALUMINUM, CIRCUITRY, GEAR, NUCLEAR MATERIAL, RUBBER, SCREW, STEEL
– **STATS:** LEVEL 30, DMG RESIST (BALLISTIC) 52, (ENERGY (52), RADIATION (30), WEIGHT 17, VALUE 365

It took until after Level 30, but we finally got our hands on plans for a T-51b Helmet. After some impressive scavenging, we melded all the raw materials into one iconic helmet!

EXAMPLE 18 (PROFESSIONAL): T-51B POWER ARMOR TORSO (WINTERIZED) (MODS)

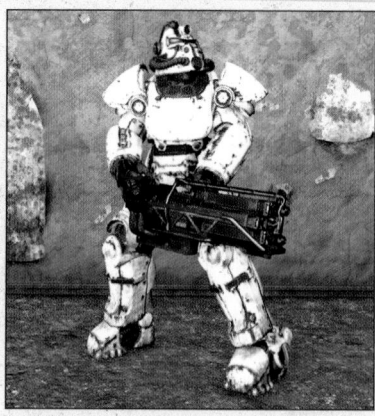

– THOUGH NOT ORIGINALLY INTENTIONAL, THIS COLOR OF ARMOR BLENDS NICELY WHILE WANDERING AROUND TOXIC VALLEY.
– **STATS:** LEVEL 30, DMG RESIST (BALLISTIC) 52, (ENERGY (52), RADIATION (30), WEIGHT 17, VALUE 248.
– **MODS:** WINTERIZED COATING, MOTION-ASSIST SERVOS, MEDIC PUMP, BLOOD CLEANSER, CORE ASSEMBLY, KINETIC DYNAMO, EMERGENCY PROTOCOLS, JET PACK, REACTIVE PLATES, STEALTH BOY, TESLA COILS
– **REQUIREMENTS (WINTERIZED COATING):** ADHESIVE, ALUMINUM, RUBBER
– **STATS (AFTER WINTERIZED COATING):** WEIGHT +0.9
– **REQUIREMENTS (MOTION-ASSIST SERVOS):** ADHESIVE, ALUMINUM, RUBBER, SPRING
– **STATS (AFTER MOTION-ASSIST SERVOS):** STR +2, WEIGHT +1.7, VALUE +56
– **REQUIREMENTS (MEDIC PUMP):** ADHESIVE, ALUMINUM, ANTISEPTIC, CIRCUITRY
– **STATS (AFTER MEDIC PUMP):** WEIGHT +1.7, VALUE +56, DETECTS HITS DURING COMBAT AND AUTOMATICALLY USES A STIMPAK WHEN HEALTH IS LOW.

– **REQUIREMENTS (BLOOD CLEANSER):** ADHESIVE, ALUMINUM, ANTISEPTIC, RUBBER
– **STATS (AFTER BLOOD CLEANSER):** WEIGHT +1.7, VALUE +56, REDUCES CHANCE FOR ADDICTION FROM DRUGS
– **REQUIREMENTS (CORE ASSEMBLY):** ADHESIVE, ALUMINUM, CIRCUITRY, NUCLEAR MATERIAL
– **STATS (AFTER CORE ASSEMBLY):** AP REGENERATION 6, WEIGHT +1.7, VALUE +56, INCREASES ACTION POINT REFRESH SPEED
– **REQUIREMENTS (KINETIC DYNAMO):** ADHESIVE, ALUMINUM, CERAMIC, RUBBER
– **STATS (AFTER KINETIC DYNAMO):** WEIGHT +1.7, VALUE +56, TAKING DAMAGE RECHARGES ACTION POINTS
– **REQUIREMENTS (EMERGENCY PROTOCOLS):** ADHESIVE, ALUMINUM, CIRCUITRY, NUCLEAR MATERIAL
– **STATS (AFTER EMERGENCY PROTOCOLS):** WEIGHT +1.7, VALUE +56, BELOW 20% HEALTH, SPEED INCREASES 25% AND INCOMING DAMAGE IS REDUCED 50%.
– **REQUIREMENTS (JET PACK):** ADHESIVE, ALUMINUM, ASBESTOS, NUCLEAR MATERIAL
– **STATS (AFTER JET PACK):** AP 1, WEIGHT +2.5, VALUE +90, ENABLES JET-ASSISTED BOOST WHILE JUMPING
– **REQUIREMENTS (REACTIVE PLATES):** ADHESIVE, ALUMINUM, ASBESTOS, NUCLEAR MATERIAL
– **STATS (AFTER REACTIVE PLATES):** WEIGHT +1.7, VALUE +56, REFLECTS 50% OF MELEE DAMAGE BACK ON ATTACKER.
– **REQUIREMENTS (STEALTH BOY):** ADHESIVE, ALUMINUM, CIRCUITRY, FIBER OPTICS, GOLD
– **STATS (AFTER STEALTH BOY):** WEIGHT +1.7, VALUE +56, ACTIVATES STEALTH FIELD WHILE CROUCHED
– **REQUIREMENTS (TESLA COILS):** ADHESIVE, ALUMINUM, COPPER, FIBER OPTICS, RUBBER
– **STATS (AFTER TESLA COILS):** WEIGHT +1.7, VALUE +56, DEALS ENERGY DAMAGE TO NEARBY ENEMIES.

This example shows a fully tricked-out T-51b Power Armor torso, winterized, with a variety of improvements. We also tricked out both arms, legs, and the helmet before exhausting ourselves and our team's component supplies. But the results were worth it!

C.A.M.P.ING AND WORKSHOPS

TRAINING

CRAFTING AND C.A.M.P.ING

INVENTORY

QUESTS

ATLAS

BESTIARY

APPENDICES

THIS CHAPTER SHOWS YOU HOW TO CONSTRUCT THE VERY BEST CAMPS AND WORKSHOPS YOU CAN; IT'S A MUST-READ BEFORE YOU STAKE A CLAIM TO A PIECE OF WEST VIRGINIA.

COUNTRY ROADS, TAKE ME HOME: CONSTRUCTION OVERVIEW

One of the key aspects of surviving and thriving in the Appalachian wilderness is to find and return to the safety of your own dwelling. Achieve this by setting up a Construction and Assembly Mobile Platform, or C.A.M.P., in a tactically advantageous location and use it as your base of operations. In addition, and using the same construction menu, are Public Workshops: Larger-scale, immovable bases that are usually part of an existing structure or facility, workshops provide key resources. Some have unique object-creating capabilities, and all are subject to attack from rival humans, teams, and your nonhuman enemies.

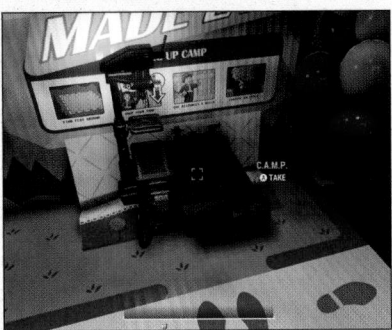

The compact Construction and Assembly Mobile Platform (C.A.M.P.). Use this to build your own personal structure. Small and portable.

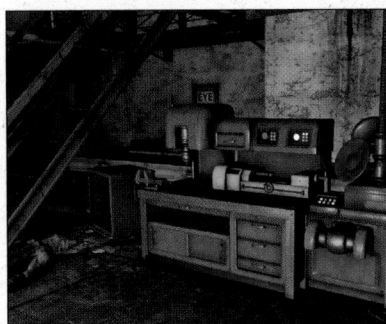

The Workshop Workbench. Claim this, then use it to build increasingly elaborate defenses at a resource-rich location. Large and immovable.

Part 1 details all the pertinent information for creating the very best C.A.M.P. you can, including a step-by-step tutorial on building and examples of different types of camps.

Part 2 reveals the key tactics in building (and defending) workshops across Appalachia, along with examples of different defenses within a workshop.

Part 3 lists the different building structures available when you access the (almost identical) C.A.M.P. and Workshop construction menus. It also lists relevant perks and bonuses to use when building.

CAMPS AND WORKSHOPS: A MENU

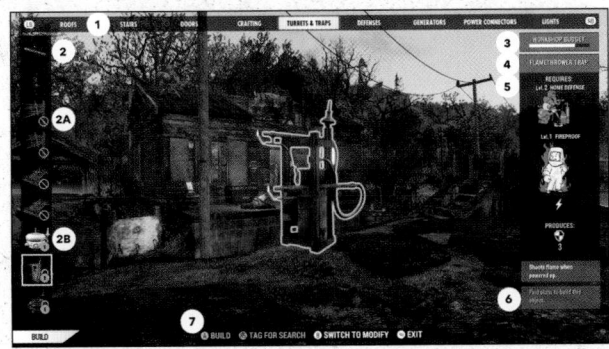

This is what the Construction menu looks like when you access your C.A.M.P. or workshop workbench. This is the Build menu to use when creating your structures.

When you place a C.A.M.P. on the ground or access a workshop after claiming it, you can head to it and interact with the "Build" prompt. However, once you step through the perimeter of the camp or workshop, you can hold down the Build button and access the menu well away from the C.A.M.P. or workshop workbench, which speeds up construction considerably. What you can do at the C.A.M.P. or workshop workbench is "Repair all Structures"; this is a shortcut to fix all damaged objects, broken by creatures or unpleasant humans. The structures are then repaired, if you have the necessary component materials.

1 **Object Tab Menu:** Stretching across the top of the screen are all the different types of objects you can build. At the beginning, the vast majority of them are not accessible, either due to you not placing a foundation yet or you not having the necessary plans to unlock the object. This chapter details the entire list of what each object menu contains.

2 **Objects:** The Object Tab menu shows a variety of objects, all of which you can eventually place within your camp or workshop boundary.

Object and Variant Arrow: Each small box has a type of object in it, which you can place within the boundary if you have the necessary components. The arrow (either on the left or right of an object box) indicates a variant for the type of object selected. Cycle through these to widen your choice of the object type.

2A **Inaccessible Icon:** This indicates the object is available, but it can't currently be placed for some reason. The reason is listed by the object's name, on the right side of the menu. It's usually because you don't have the components, or it needs a foundation, but there are other reasons.

2B **Lock:** The lock indicates that the object's Plan has not been found yet. Obtain the Plan to unlock the object (or object variant) and make it usable.

3 Budget: This ever-increasing bar indicates how much of the camp or workshop's budget you've used. Every time you place an object, the budget creeps up. When it fills, no more objects can be placed. Think about ensuring your camp or workshop has good structural integrity before the budget is exceeded. The one object that uses up the budget compared to everything else? Turrets.

4 Object Name: This shows the name of the object you have highlighted, and what variant number it is (if applicable). This is the same name as the plans you're collecting.

5 Requirements: Most importantly, this shows what components the object requires in order to be made. In addition, if extra requirements are needed (e.g., electricity from a generator or a perk), they are listed here. If the object gives you back components (like a Resource generator), that is also listed here.

6 Warnings: This appears if you're trying to place an object and are unable to. The reason is listed here.

7 Build, Tag for Search, Variant, Switch to Modify, Exit: The menu at the bottom of the screen allows you to build an object you've selected, switch between crafting and modifying menus. With the Modify menu active, you can edit, make a blueprint of it, or switch back to the Build menu.

PART 1: GOING C.A.M.P.ING

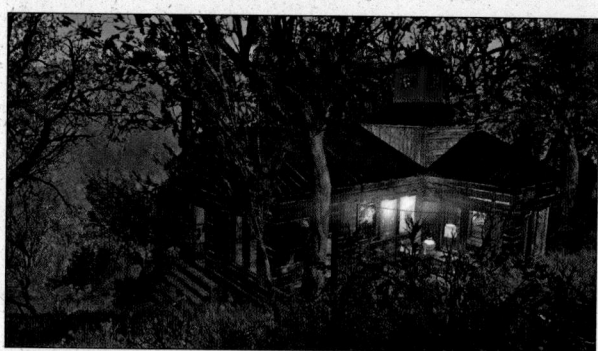

Always wanted your own cabin in the woods? With some simple foraging, now you can!

This section details all the pertinent information for creating the very best C.A.M.P. possible, including a step-by-step tutorial on building and examples of different types of camps.

ACCESSING YOUR C.A.M.P.

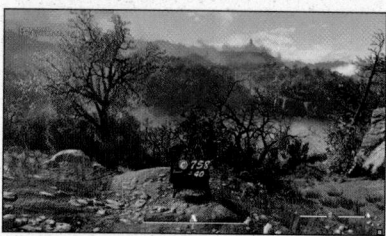

When you've found a patch of ground to call home, drop your C.A.M.P. and start construction.

You receive your C.A.M.P. when you pick it up during your departure from Vault 76. To access it, bring up your Pip-Boy menu, and select the Camp option. Do this in relative safety, as you don't have a weapon handy until the C.A.M.P. is placed or you switch to a weapon. When the C.A.M.P. appears, it hovers above the ground in front of you. Move around normally, and when the C.A.M.P. turns green, you can place it. Don't worry about dropping it in an exact location; you can move it later. If you're moving a C.A.M.P. from a different location, prepare to pay a small Caps fee for this.

When you drop your C.A.M.P., it becomes visible on your world map. Only you and your friends (and teammates) can see where it is (and you can see their camps too). Great news! When you want to return to your camp (or your friend's), you can Fast-Travel from anywhere in Appalachia, and it doesn't cost any Caps! However, you can't if you're overencumbered before you Fast-Travel (normal rules apply), so don't overindulge in the foraging.

PREPARATION: CAMPING COMPONENTS

Before you can do any important construction (even though your camp's budget only allows a cabin-sized structure), you must forage for components. But what do you need to construct a camp? The short answer: wood, steel, and a bit of concrete. The long answer: See below!

WHAT COMPONENTS YOU NEED TO FORAGE

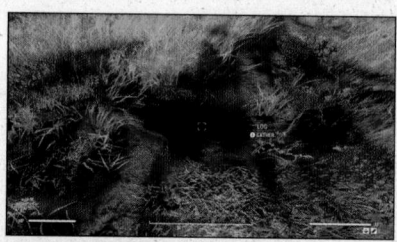

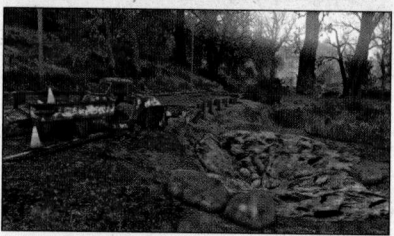

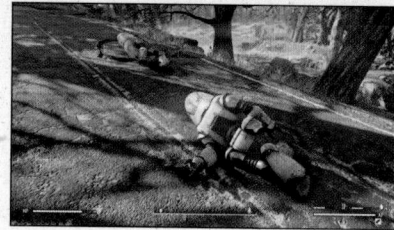

There are three main components to find during initial construction: wood, concrete, and steel.

Just like when you're crafting, there's a large list of components needed for camp construction. In fact, all of the components are the same ones you find in junk, other items you break down into parts, and the other types of materials you use when crafting. The Junk section of the inventory has a complete list of all components for every type of building activity (both crafting and camping/workshops), along with advice on what items the components contain and general advice on locating each component. The following section details just the components needed to build objects in a camp or workshop.

FORAGING TIME

Early in your adventures, you'll want to focus your foraging on the essential components for constructing the plans you've discovered so far. You will always have need for wood, so collect it often and in quantity.

Other components worth foraging for include concrete, steel, copper, oil, screws, and gears.

As you start collecting more plans, you may be glad to have some of the rarer components on hand. Keep an eye out for aluminum, rubber, circuits, cloth, springs, plastic, glass, and ceramic.

Certain materials are pretty rare, so pick these up when you find them: asbestos, fiberglass, fiber optics, lead, and nuclear material.

Later in your game, when you've unlocked most of the available plans and are ready to get really creative with your defenses and decorations, you'll still need an ample supply of wood, steel, and concrete, but will benefit from having spent the time to collect those rarer ingredients. Nothing gets in the way of crafting like discovering you've run out of screws, circuits, or ceramic!

PREPARATION: LOCATION, LOCATION, CREATION

Choose your camp's location. Don't worry, you can move it later if you make a mistake! Base your decision on several factors (some of them are diametrically opposed to one another, so you can't check all the following metaphorical boxes). Note that "Beginner" and "Expert" flags indicate the advice is usually more pertinent for an "initial" (low-level) player or an "expert" (higher level) player.

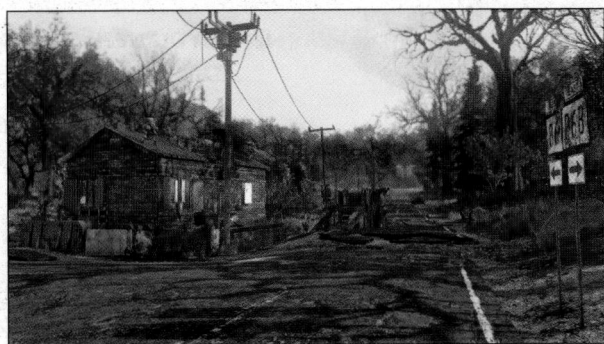

Someone's always building near the Overseer's Camp, aren't they? It's all that easy access to logs and workbenches!

Near Stations and Workbenches (Beginner): You need to scrap items, make food and drink, and tinker with ammunition, and you may not have plans to unlock Crafting Workbenches yet. So why not place your camp within dashing distance of a location with your favorite stations?

Near (Main) Resources (Beginner): To begin with, you need wood to construct walls and concrete to make foundations. You find logs in the forest and concrete in large divots along the main ruined roads (among other places). So you may want to put your camp close to these main sources of building components.

Near Civilization (Beginner): Drop a camp down on the road junction near the covered bridge and Overseer's Camp; you won't be invaded by marauding creatures (too often), and you won't get lost and overwhelmed in the wilderness or savaged by creatures too tough to fend off.

Away from Civilization (Expert): Drop a camp well away from the road junction near the covered bridge and Overseer's Camp. Why? Because it's a high-traffic area, and you can't trust those Vault Dwellers not to start bashing your building! Get away from it all but still find a spot in the valley between Vault 76 and Flatwoods until you get your bearings—just more of a hidey-hole where you won't be bothered.

Helpful Hint from Vault-Boy

WOOD? STEEL? CONCRETE? WHERE IS IT?

Don't know where a component is? Then check the Junk section of the Inventory chapter for a quick overview. Now "Tag for Search" in your camp's Build menu, and make a sweep of the dozen or so primary locations, as well as the forest floor between Vault 76 and Flatwoods; most of the initial components can be found with a thorough forage and junk hunt. Then use any workbench with the "Scrap" feature to turn your junk into components, to lighten your load, and to Fast-Travel back to your camp and start building!

WE'RE ONLY MAKING PLANS FOR SURVIVAL

To unlock the full variety of objects you can construct, you're going to need to find plans. Follow the same search pattern as for the crafting recipes, mods, and plans: They are scattered around locations, in containers (especially Overseer's Caches), on enemies, bought at vendors and vending machines, found in the Atomic Shop, and given as quest rewards. But the largest haul of building plans is likely to be after you complete the quest requiring you to claim a workshop and defend it from enemies. Keep doing those to unlock a load of plans!

TRAINING

CRAFTING AND C.A.M.P.ING

INVENTORY

QUESTS

ATLAS

BESTIARY

APPENDICES

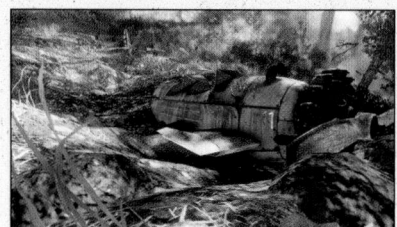

There are hundreds of odd little structures, totems, and gnomes you can build close to.

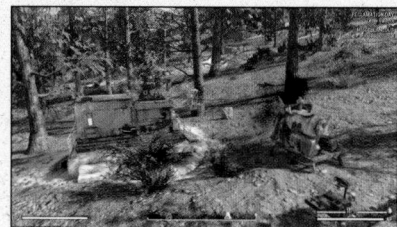

While placing a resource-mining device on a node is usually part of your plan at a workshop, there are remote deposits to suck dry, too!

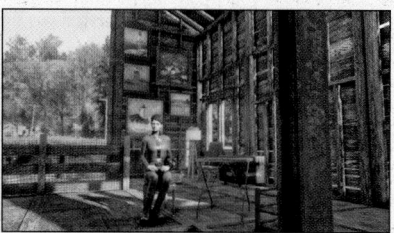

Build a camp on flat ground. You can build taller and faster, leaving more time to enjoy your handiwork!

Near Primary Locations (Expert): This is usually what you should attempt after finishing your first camp—select it (or sections of it), save it as a Blueprint, then move to a location you want to explore (hopefully with teammates), and place the camp nearby. Then you can prepare food, ammo, repair items, and ready yourself properly without needing to spend Caps (or other resources) on Fast-Traveling or manually slogging to and from a location and your far-off camp.

Near Secondary Locations (Expert): There are hundreds of smaller, unmarked locations across Appalachia that you can find by cross-referencing the Atlas. These are usually odd totems, strange shacks, or other remote or abandoned hovels. Check each one; some are near resources or vistas. Build a camp near one, or make the secondary location part of your camp if you can.

Near a Vendor (Beginner): If you're using your camp as a drop point with your Stash Box, or you've started to craft for fun and profit, being close to a vendor (usually at a train station) shortens the distance between selling sessions. While you're at a vendor, you can also check his vending machine (or any you've placed in your camp), as these occasionally give out random rare loot...as long as you pay for it!

Away from Enemies (Beginner): If your camp is always swamped by irradiated wildlife or worse, you may have built it near a location where enemies spawn. Move it to a quieter area. If you want to concentrate on building and haven't got the hang of switching quickly between menus, think about putting your camp well away from where you've seen monsters.

Near Enemies (Expert): If you're out camping for a cryptid or want to accrue some XP or get some great monster loot, then drop your camp close to where you saw a good number of monsters. Ready a turret-filled tower and place it within shooting distance of a fissure (though that's not going to end well unless you have teammates with their own turret towers). Better yet, drop a camp in a zone that's about to be nuked, flee the area, and return after the explosion and see what new foes the camp has killed for you!

Near Power Boxes (Beginner): Some locations, such as electrical substations (listed in the Atlas), have power boxes you can connect to for some free power. While they always have a little power you can draw on, they provide much more power if their power plant is online. If it's broken down, head over to the plant and complete Event: Powering Up to get the current flowing again.

Near Valuable Resources (Expert): Workshops tend to have deposits you can mine; in fact, it's one of the reasons to claim a workshop. But there are remote mineral or rare material deposits throughout Appalachia; situating your camp there can yield impressive numbers, as a Resource Collector is available to build if you place your camp within the deposit. Just be sure the collector is powered, and no one steals the collected components from your device!

Near Friends (Beginner and Expert): While there's safety in numbers when you're first starting out, having a camp near friends is extremely beneficial no matter what level you are. You can't build too close to another camp, but from within walking distance of your friends, you can watch (and copy) their construction, ask them to forage while you build, and strategically place extra defenses, workbenches, and pooled resources!

Away from Friends (Expert): Perhaps you're a loner. Perhaps you want a bit of peace and quiet. Or perhaps you're part of a team, moving to a remote, "forward operations" area of uncharted territory and setting up a camp so your teammates can join you, creating up to four linked team camps you can Fast-Travel between.

Near a Workshop (Expert): Defending any workshop you claim is a lot easier if you (and your team) have all constructed their camps (along with defenses and turrets) on the workshop's perimeter. Now enemies must contend with both your camps and the workshop defenses, and you have another place to retreat to, spawn at, build items at, and, if you've built a camp with numerous turrets, another free workshop turret tower!

Near a Quest Location (Expert): Drop a camp close to a high-traffic (and usually dangerous and large) location that you know has a quest you wish to complete. During a lull in the action, head into the location and complete the quest, Fast-Traveling back if under duress or after claiming some rare loot.

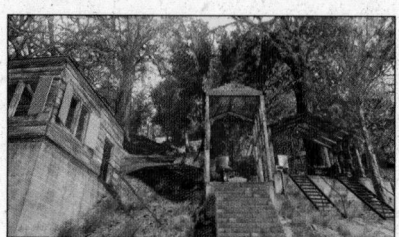

When building on steeper terrain, consider building smaller structures linked by steps.

On Flat and Open Ground (Beginner): If you're having trouble placing foundations, or you're falling when trying to build your structure, you may be on steeper ground than is necessary. Why not seek out a flatter area? Think about areas close to farms, under electrical pylons, or on cliff edges.

On Steep and Unforgiving Ground (Expert): Steeper terrain is still a viable spot for some daring campers; just be prepared to build something a little more vertical, and usually in two, three, four, or more separate areas, all linked (hopefully) by stairs to give the ground a bit of stability. The good news is that you're less likely to be attacked (or found at all) in the more remote area of rougher terrain.

Near a Spectacular View (Expert): If you want to attempt a bit of sightseeing, situate yourself so you know where east and west are, and place your camp atop a promontory with views of the nuclear sunset (or sunrise), weather formations, or large landmarks. Or sit yourself down in a forest where the sunlight dapples through the leaves, near a once-idyllic, now only slightly radioactive lake.

CAMP CONSTRUCTION: MY FIRST CAMP (LEVELS 5–10)

Welcome to the My First Camp tutorial! This takes you through a step-by-step building and decoration of a small cabin, using mostly basic objects that are unlocked from the start of your exploration, with a smattering of objects requiring plans to unlock them. Think about constructing your first camp when you're between Levels 5 and 10. It's also recommended that you've finished the Responder quests in Flatwoods and met the amusingly named Protectron in the woods north of Morgantown and completed the camp-related quest there first. This tutorial assumes you've foraged for enough materials to create a rudimentary camp, though you can always finish some of the camp, go forage, and return to complete the job.

STEP 1: FOUNDATION CREATION

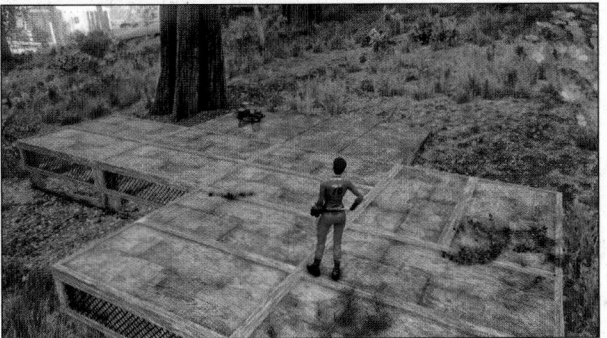

Camps need a good foundation. Or at least, they need to be attached to the ground with one.

Ignore all other objects; you can't construct anything without having to place down either wood or concrete foundations first. Concrete is sometimes preferred, as you'll use most or all of your wood on the walls. For this example, create an eight-block floor; you want this to be manageable, defensible, and within budget (unless you can live without a roof).

Notice in the pictures that the "footprint" of the foundation isn't a simple rectangle (though it could be!); you may want your cabin to have an interesting shape, where furniture can fit into nooks and crannies, rather than a large box. Either option is fine.

If you're building on a slope, place a lower and upper connected foundation and adjust the height before placement so all foundations slot together without becoming hidden (as walls may not snap to the foundations). If you make a mistake, do not scrap the foundation! Instead, edit it and maneuver it until it's in a better position, or store it and use it later.

If you're building on a steep slope, be mindful that you're likely to use more resources and may need to separate different parts of your camp due to the topography. To start with, keep your foundations on lower, shallower slopes or flat areas like farmland or clearings near electrical pylons.

Choose one or two foundations with stairs, or add the short wood stairs, so you have easy access from ground level. Finally, while in Modify mode, pick up your C.A.M.P. and move it onto the middle of the foundation, so it's not in the way. You can make minor adjustments to its position later.

STEP 2: THE WALLS GO IN

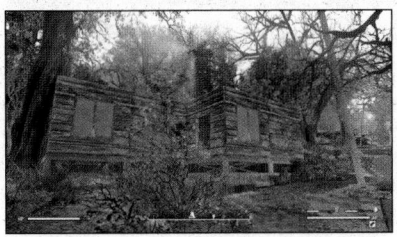

With a few wall sections up, your camp cabin is already looking both rustic and charming!

Though you may wish to add a single staircase now, if you're worried about its position, the best next step is to place the outer walls of your cabin on the foundation. Check the three variants of wall—wall, doorway, and window. Cycle left and right, and think about having at least one door (in case you need to escape!), two or three shutters (which you can open when you quit out of the Build menu), and the rest regular walls.

It's easiest follow the perimeter of the foundation floors with your walls. But you can also leave one (or more) foundation sections outside the walls to act as a porch, or a place behind your cabin wall to set a generator for later. Or, you can add more foundations now (or later) to create the same effect.

STEP 3: THE ROOF AND DOOR GO ON

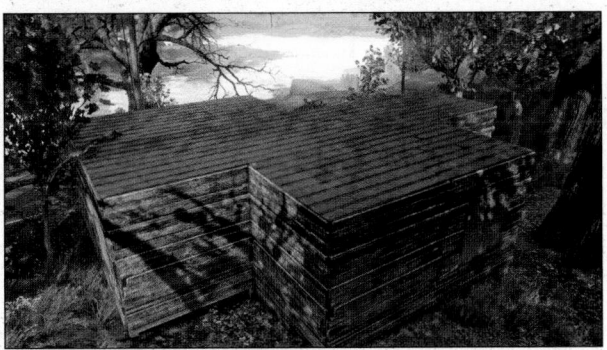

A flat roof may not look quite as rustic but beggars (without necessary roof plans) can't be choosers.

No second level? Not in this example; look to the alternate build for a second floor! As this cabin is limited by the relatively few plans that were available, the roof was a simple flat section of steel and wood, with eight of them placed directly above their foundation section counterparts. The structural skeleton of the cabin is now complete!

Finishing the main structure, we added a door for a bit of security, and opened all the shutters. Though enemies can see inside, you can see out, so it's up to you to determine how much you want outsiders to see! We also moved the C.A.M.P. into a corner of the cabin, as it offers a small amount of free illumination.

TRAINING

CRAFTING AND C.A.M.P.ING

INVENTORY

QUESTS

ATLAS

BESTIARY

APPENDICES

STEP 4: OUTSIDE PERIMETER—CROPS AND A CAMPFIRE

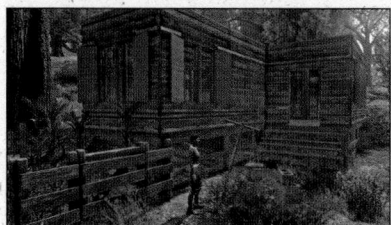

Adding crops, water, and a cooking station puts the "fun" in functionality!

Corn was available for us to plant, so we periodically harvest it to bolster our raw food materials. Of course, the crops are also available for any ne'er-do-well to steal, so we added a scarecrow, which makes no impact whatsoever but looks suitably apropos. Then we added a fence and a gate, which actually helps a little. Continuing with that "farm to table" vibe, we added a cooking station, a water pump, a fold-out table and deck chair, and a radio that plays all your Appalachian favorites. Two plastic flamingos finish the look. And that look is "yokel."

STEP 5: OUTSIDE PERIMETER—DEFENSES AND POWER

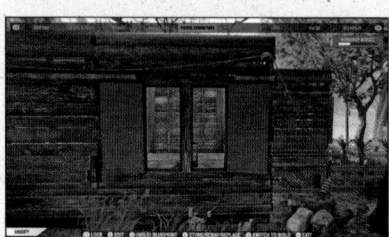

Connect wires from your generator to a series of connectors and easily power your cabin's lights.

There was a method to our madness when choosing this location; the rear of the premises brush up against an old oak tree, and jamming a small power generator in there hides and protects it slightly, keeps the generator fumes out of your cabin, and allows you to string along a power connector in an aesthetically pleasing manner from the generator to the far corner of the cabin. That way, any lights you place will light up (they don't have to be linked; just close to the connector).

STEP 6: INSIDE CABIN—LET THERE BE LIGHTS

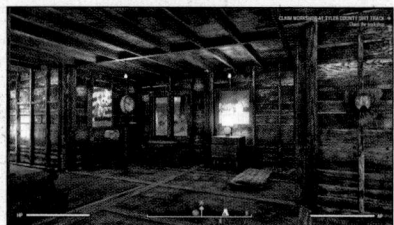

With the lights on, the newly decorated cabin looked a whole less dank and unpleasant.

With limited choices from the Lights menu, we opted for ceiling bulbs, a table and floor lamp, and the C.A.M.P. in a corner, giving off a nice warm glow. What would a cabin be without a backlit poster of Mr. Pebbles (the First Cat in Space)? A dreary shack, that's what!

STEP 7: INSIDE CABIN—FURNITURE AND FINISHING TOUCHES

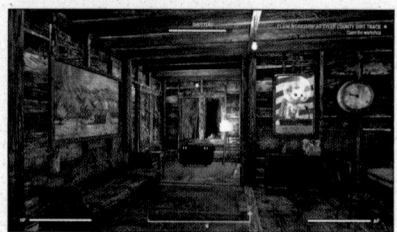

The finished interior, with space to sit, sleep, hammer at workbenches, and grab stashed items. Bliss!

With some working illumination, the rugs and then the heavy furniture were moved in. Next, we moved on to the lighter furniture: shelves, side tables, wall paintings, smaller coolers on those shelves, a wall clock, a mattress, a My Stash Box in the windowed alcove, and a welcome mat at the doorway. With a few object edits, we finished the first cabin and stayed just under budget!

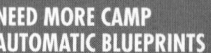

Helpful Hints from Vault-Boy!

NEED MORE CAMP AUTOMATIC BLUEPRINTS

Don't worry about accidentally setting up a new C.A.M.P. and destroying your previous structure. When you move your camp, a Blueprint of your previous structure is saved; just access it from the Blueprints menu! You can choose to delete, store, or place the saved structure.

CAMP EXAMPLE 1: MY FIRST CABIN

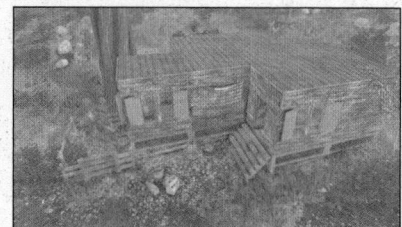

- AESTHETICS: ★★★★☆
- FUNCTIONALITY: ★★★☆☆
- DEFENSE: ★☆☆☆☆

Here's the finished cabin, with this guide's arbitrary rating. Aesthetically, it looks great, especially considering you're able to build something similar to this early on and with only a few unlocked plans. It loses a point due to a smoky Armor Workbench indoors. How gauche!

Functionally, it does the job well, offering good workbench and crops, though a Tinker's or Chemistry workbench would have helped (which is why the cabin is next to Tyler County Dirt Track; there's a small farm adjacent to it that has a Chemistry Station in a barn). The only real issue is the placement of the Stash Box; placing it by the front door would have meant quicker access to your stored loot.

Defense-wise, this is somewhat problematic, but this is an issue for all initial camps; there's no turrets, the crops are easily stolen, and you can break apart most of the structure rather easily. Even adding a sloping roof (so grenades roll off it and down to the ground) would have helped.

Helpful Hints from Vault-Boy!

NEED MORE CAMP CONSTRUCTION TIPS?

If you need more advice on what those odd-shaped wall sections are, how best to use each of the object types in the Build menu, and just what to do with a water purifier, consult Part 3 of this chapter.

CAMP CONSTRUCTION: MY EXPERT CAMPS (LEVEL 10+)

With the basics down, you should now learn the construction techniques necessary for optimal camp creation, as well as moving camps and working with friends.

Helpful Hint from Vault-Boy!

SCRAPPING, STORING, AND POSITIONING

Before you continue, learn the best times to scrap (when you have no use for an object and can afford to destroy it into half the components you used to make it), store (when you made an object, can't use it now, but want to keep it for later), and reposition an object (remember you can rotate it in all directions and move it up and down). When you place an object, highlight and edit it, and reposition it if you don't like where it is: For example, move the C.A.M.P. if it's in the way of your foundation.

GOING OVER (AND UNDER) BUDGET

Be ever mindful of your budget. Depending on your needs, and as a general rule of thumb, think about stopping when your Workshop Budget bar fills to a certain state:

Structure: Try not to have your bar filled more than one-half to two-thirds.

Defenses: Turrets will wipe out your budget almost immediately! Try not to add more than three (unless you're primarily building a turret tower), and augment your defenses with walls, traps, and other objects that aren't so budget-intensive. A well-placed turret behind partial cover can be more effective than three sitting on a mesh floor.

Exterior Decorations: Limit your exterior elements to only a few lights and a scattering of chairs, containers, and other objects. For quick use, have your Stash Box by the main door. You can create a lightshow, but at the expense of other elements. Or as part of a team camp.

Crafting Locations: Only place the workbenches and stations you're sure to use regularly. Share workbenches with teammates across camps. And make workbenches easy to access: for example, close to a main door rather than three floors up in a bedroom (unless you have specific reasons for this placement).

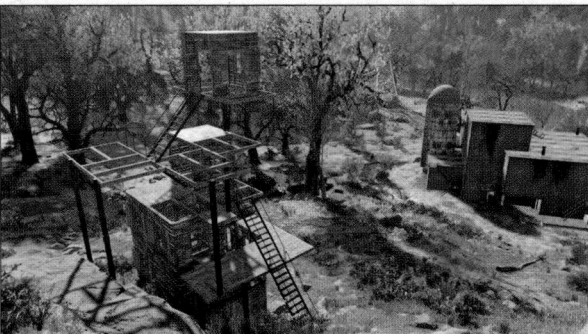

This is a great example of a half-finished camp where the builder ran out of budget.

Interior Decorations: Many builders fall into the trap of constructing a large dwelling but run out of decorations to make it look lived in. Place lights and rugs first, followed by the larger pieces of furniture, then the smaller objects, and finally the smallest objects and containers you can put on shelving. Don't use up every space on a wall, or area in a floor; make it lived in, not cramped!

GOING UP AND GOING OUT

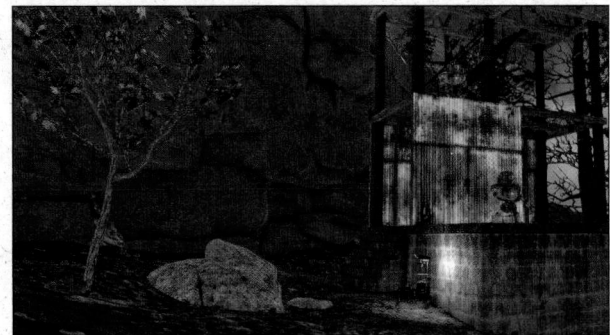

Towers can be built, but don't get too grandiose in your planning; a monument to budget mismanagement is not impressive.

Camp structures can be built upward and outward. Expect to run out of room after around four vertical floors (and build towers rather than wide and tall structures). A particularly flat structure can be around 20 foundation squares in total, though it won't look particularly great. A good, large-scale two-level structure should have around three by five squares in its footprint, as one of our examples demonstrates.

GOING TO THE GARAGE

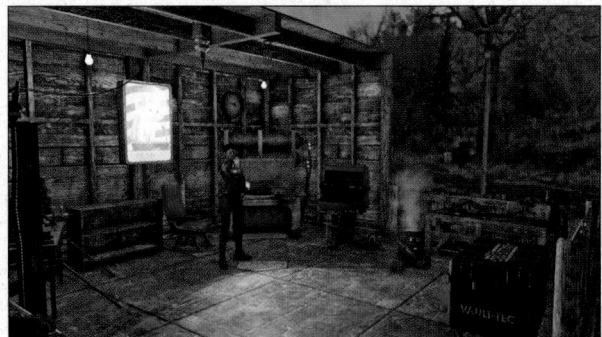

Need a place to rest, as well as a cool mechanic's garage to fiddle with your Power Armor? Build both!

Your camp doesn't have to be one structure. Aesthetically, or for ease of access, you may wish to place all your workbenches in a shed, away from your living structure. This is easily achieved, as long as you make both buildings smaller than normal.

TRAINING

CRAFTING AND C.A.M.P.ing

INVENTORY

QUESTS

ATLAS

BESTIARY

APPENDICES

BALCONIES AND INDESTRUCTIBLE FLOORING

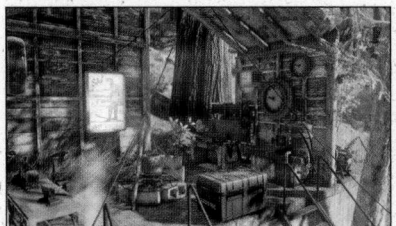

An example of a cozy-looking interior; the den of a tinkerer.

Floors are particularly interesting, as they are indestructible. You can break all other objects (including walls, rooftops, generators, and basically anything else), but not floors. However, mesh floors can be shot through (in both directions), so bear this in mind when placing upper floors in your camp. Shoot down through them to remove enemy threats, using the height to your advantage. Or place wooden floors that completely shield you from anyone stupid enough to fire up or down at them.

Balconies are another aspect of building structures, as they are easy to create, offer places to put turrets or fire down on foes from, and add an extra layer of security; you can look out and spot enemies from a greater height. Think about attaching floors around and outside upper walls, but don't overdo it!

LOOKING GOOD: AESTHETICS

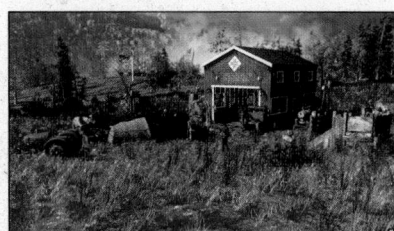

Try mixing the wall types, build and take advantage of foliage and scenery, and don't create big boxes.

Don't worry too much about aesthetics; build a camp using the objects you've unlocked (via plan acquisition), and gradually add to it using foraged components and a whole load of log looting! If you're concerned your camp is looking too "boxy," vary the foundation footprint so it's less rectangular. Lower the foundation so bushes, grass, and trees envelop your camp. Change the roof line and add a dormer window. Swap out wall styles like the picture shows. Add crops and a variety of different objects in places you'd usually expect them to be. Divide the house into living, eating, sleeping, and workbench areas. Study and take photographs of camps whose looks you like. But most importantly, if you're happy with it, that's all that matters!

LOOKING ODD: FREAKISH FUNCTIONALITY

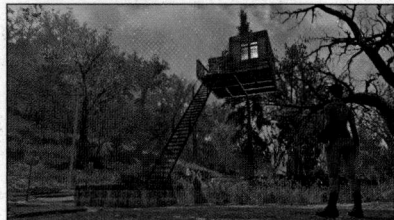

This is technically the smallest amount of ground you need in order to create an "airborne camp"!

There is one overriding rule: Your camp must connect to the ground foundations. Other than that, you're free to move the majority of your camp into the air, ignoring the rules of physics, in favor of supreme defensiveness. If you can block the path from the ground, up into your floating home with only a staircase to access it, then very few enemies will be able to enter. The Escher Lodge example (below) is one to think about attempting in this regard. If you don't like the aesthetic of such a camp, try adding steel posts (in the Stairs menu) to give the illusion the structure is on stilts, though this realism is done at the cost of your budget!

LOOKING GOOD: IMPRESSIVELY DEFENSIBLE

Make your walls out of metal or brick when possible; these types of walls are tougher and may dissuade attackers. Add mesh floors that both attacker and defender can fire through, but hopefully you're up top with the advantage. Add a variety of traps, including just inside doorways or at the tops of dark stairs to wound foes without the traps being spotted. Create distractions, or even a rude message spelled out in neon letters, on a prominent wall to dissuade thieves coming after your resources, and use it as a camp and a workshop.

TURRETS SYNDROME: DEFENSIVE STRUCTURES

Forget those comfy sofas and giant copper lion statues; why not focus on a tower bristling with defenses instead? Learn the reason why there are so many odd-shaped sloped wall sections in your Walls menu; they aren't just there to create dormer windows! Place triangular sections in front of a turret so it can still fire out but is protected from enemy fire or grenades. Add to the protection by setting turrets on a wooden second floor that can't be shot through. Add a roof with sloping sections so grenades roll down and away from the turret.

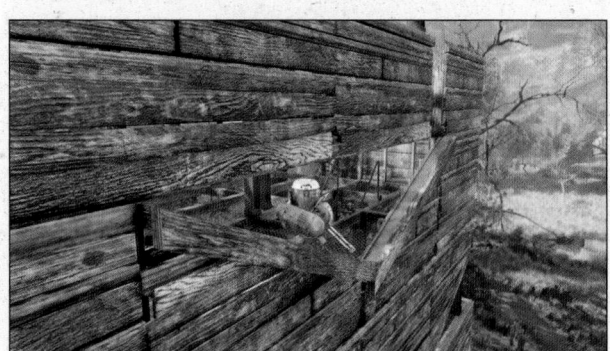

You can place a turret on your camp. But can you keep attackers from destroying it?

MOVING HOUSE: REBUILDING CAMPS

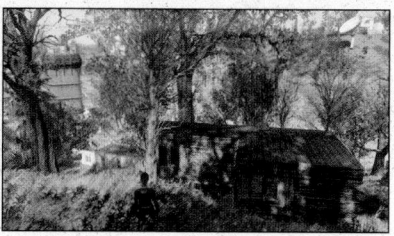

My First Cabin, picked up and moved to a hilltop close to Charleston, with only minor rearrangements.

When it's time to move camps, for whatever reason, simply return to your camp, locate or take a blueprint if you wish to save the camp for later, and head to the new location. Place your C.A.M.P. down again, and don't be startled if your camp budget is almost full; your previous camp is likely to have been placed in the Build > Stored menu. You can now:

– USE THE BLUEPRINT MENU AND PLACE THE CAMP AT THE NEW LOCATION, WITH SOME MINOR ADJUSTMENTS BASED ON TOPOGRAPHY. NOTE THAT YOU CAN BLUEPRINT PIECES OF YOUR CAMP SO SECTIONS (AND PERHAPS IMPROVEMENTS) CAN BE PLACED ONE AT A TIME.

– PLACE THE OLD CAMP FROM THE STORED MENU, BREAK IT UP MANUALLY, AND REUSE THE INDIVIDUAL PARTS.

– OR IF YOU DON'T CARE ABOUT DESTROYING HALF YOUR COMPONENTS, SCRAP EVERYTHING AND START OVER.

Helpful Hint from Vault-Boy!

STRIP-MINING AN AREA: THE FOCUSED LOCUST

When you uproot your camp, move it close to the area where you're going to spend time. Then "strip-mine" the area, clearing out any interior locations and containers. You can also slay foes, complete nearby quests, and utilize all the natural (and post-nuclear) resources. During this time, Fast-Travel (for free) back to your camp, pack up, and move on, or back to a previous location where you gathered good loot.

BUILDING ONE FOR THE TEAM: MULTIPLE CAMPS

Circling Your Wagons: Are you part of a movement? A band of like-minded Vault Dwellers ready to rebuild for America? Then why not come together and build yourselves a series of relatively-close camps along a road or across an expanse of land? Each of you volunteer to create a

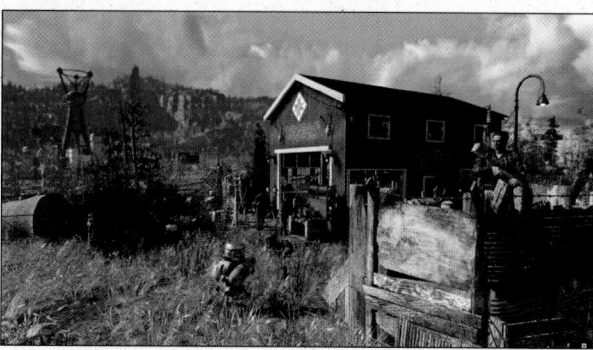

The Devil's Pitchfork. What happens when teammates pool their resources? A large-scale group of camps.

different type of space: Perhaps two of you each work on a defensive tower brimming with turrets, while a third player outfits a garage with workbenches, and a fourth player constructs living quarters with an instrument stage and bunk beds. Bring the same planning to your quartet of camps as you do to creating a workshop base. Pool resources and create four separate dwellings accessible by the team, all looking out for each other. Now imagine if four more players turn up and add their dwellings too!

The Wagon Train: Alternatively, team up and place camps across Appalachia, so you have a free Fast-Travel site wherever you wish to generally get to. Perhaps at each checkpoint of a quest (one camp at the start, one at the end)? Or between two trading locations. As you can freely Fast-Travel to any of your team's camps, this is three times as helpful!

DESTRUCTION, NOT CONSTRUCTION: CAMP ATTACK!

Of course, there's a fair amount of destruction you can attempt on another player's camp, whether they're at the location or (ideally) when they're away exploring. Breaking a few walls or a fence is one thing, but if you really want to do some damage, take out their

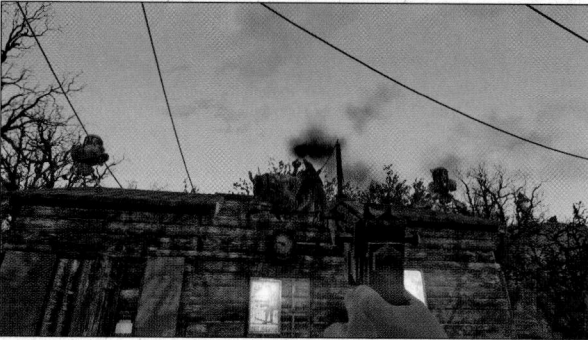

Keen on wanton acts of vandalism? Then be sure to target the right parts of a camp.

generator (as this knocks out anything requiring power in their camp), and ensure you're far enough away before trying to blow up their turret. Or perhaps you want to try a spot of "scrumping": stealing crops, mined resources, or items any Protectrons have collected. Of course, acts of vandalism instantly make you Wanted; continued misbehavior against other players' camps increases your Wanted Level.

How do you stop this damage? With blind, ugly violence, by ensuring your turrets are covering all angles, by moving your generator so it can't easily be seen or struck (hide it on the roof or inside the structure), building a structure around a resource collector, and build locks for your resource containers.

MAINTENANCE, NOT CONSTRUCTION: CAMP REPAIR

Finally, it's worth remembering that your camp requires some light maintenance work. This mainly takes the form of checking (at the C.A.M.P.) each time you return to see if anything has been damaged; use "Repair All" for a quick, overall repair. Of course, if your turrets are smoking and the generator's out, some rapscallion has been by and done a number on your hard work. So always keep an amount of components at the ready, especially those needed for repairing the type(s) of turrets you've chosen, to keep your camp in tip-top shape.

TRAINING

CRAFTING AND C.A.M.P.ING

INVENTORY

QUESTS

ATLAS

BESTIARY

APPENDICES

CAMP EXAMPLES

To conclude the section on camps, we provide a series of examples of what a camp budget and various found and unlocked plans can get you. Note that some of these camps could be rebuilt inside a workshop or as part of a team camp. Also don't forget to check the Build Resources list at the end of this chapter for more construction ideas.

CAMP EXAMPLE 1: THE TURRET TOILET

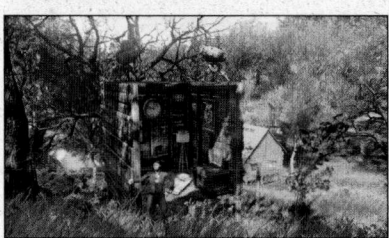

- AESTHETICS: ★★★★☆
- FUNCTIONALITY: ★★★★☆
- DEFENSE: ★★☆☆☆

Here's a camp for someone who hates building camps; it's a low-cost, no-frills, easy-to-erect outhouse-sized dwelling with a turret at the top and a sleeping bag and Stash Box in the "outhouse" living space. A little too compact, but it's easy moving around the map and is quick to repair if attacked. The base functionality allows you to come and go as you please, and its small footprint makes it easy to place almost anywhere.

CAMP EXAMPLE 2: WIXON FIELD QUARTERS

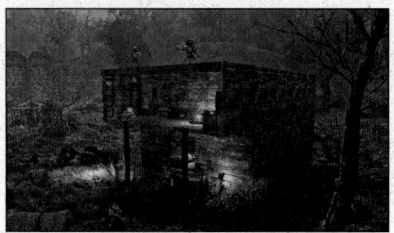

- AESTHETICS: ★★☆☆☆
- FUNCTIONALITY: ★★★★★
- DEFENSE: ★★★★☆

This large, blocky dwelling had to be built on a large area of flat ground. It features two floors and a balcony and was constructed with functionality in mind, as well as the ability to defend the location. There's only one way in and a balcony over the entrance so the owner can see foes coming. The visibility continues inside; there's nowhere to hide, the owner has a balcony to shoot down from, and any lighting is by gas, which doesn't require a generator. This is an early exploration construction, if a large, full budget dwelling that's great to defend and doesn't need generators is what you're wanting.

CAMP EXAMPLE 3: NEW GORGE FORGE

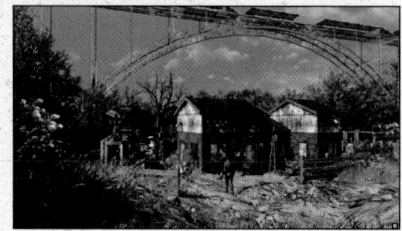

- AESTHETICS: ★★★★☆
- FUNCTIONALITY: ★★★★☆
- DEFENSE: ★★★★☆

When you're able to access the later wall sections (metal and brick in this example), as well as constructing linked sections that connect the two main structures together (and use angled wall sections to join to the sloping roof line), you can create some excellent structures, complete with spotlights, wind-powered generators, and defenses to ensure that the "open" welcome isn't taken as a sign of weakness!

CAMP EXAMPLE 4: A RIVER RUNS THROUGH IT

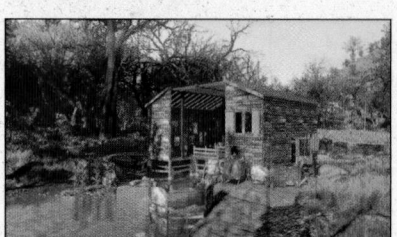

- AESTHETICS: ★★★★☆
- FUNCTIONALITY: ★★★☆☆
- DEFENSE: ★★★☆☆

Who says you need to construct a camp over dry ground? As long as the river is shallow enough, you can enjoy constructing a larger, barn-like structure that fords both sides of the river. You've plenty of water, can take a slightly irradiated dip whenever you want, and there are wonderful views to be had watching the sunlight glint off the water. Also try variants that start on one side of a cliff edge, and end at the other, if you have the building skill!

CAMP EXAMPLE 5: MECHANIC'S DOMAIN

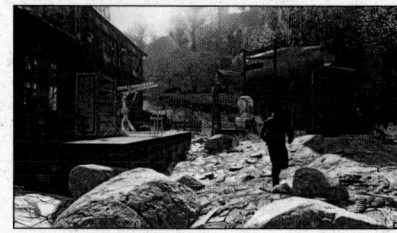

- AESTHETICS: ★★★★☆
- FUNCTIONALITY: ★★★★☆
- DEFENSE: ★★★☆☆

This section of a larger camp features brick and corrugated metal walls, giving the place an authentic and grimy feel, but shows that you don't need to worry about the weather; situate whatever you like outside (worry more about it getting damaged than being rained on). Augment such a place with a whole load of appropriate containers, workbenches, stations, furniture, and in pride of place; a suit of Power Armor. If it's rusting, it's likely to be sitting somewhere around this tinkerer's paradise.

CAMP EXAMPLE 6: NEWLY ARISEN PRISON

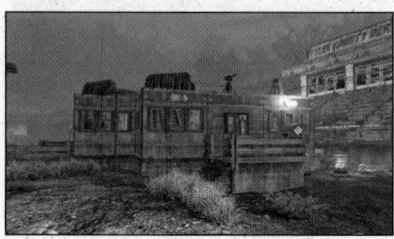

- AESTHETICS: ★★☆☆☆
- FUNCTIONALITY: ★★★★☆
- DEFENSE: ★★☆☆☆

The thick-walled metal sections give this relatively small structure a sheen of imposing protection; everything is blue metal and concrete, with doors and furniture chosen to complement the place's look. Inside, there's a particularly interesting surprise—a stairwell leading to a turret-laden roof, but the real revelation is a resource generator, attached to power, within an inner cell, which the entire structure was built around. This is one way to keep out thieves!

CAMP EXAMPLE 7:
TOWER OF POWER

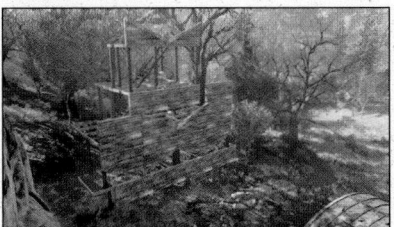

- AESTHETICS: ★★★☆☆
- FUNCTIONALITY: ★★★★★
- DEFENSE: ★★★★★

This is a large example of a "turret camp," which is self-contained; smaller variants are usually placed close to where enemies have been spotted spawning (so you're getting your Caps' worth out of those turrets!). As you get XP from foes the turrets kill, and you can loot the foes' corpses for fun and profit, it's worth moving this type of camp to a dangerous area. These camps are particularly helpful when mopping up terrifying or recently nuked parts of Appalachia, softening up the newly mutated creatures so you can step in, finish them off, and claim some amazing loot. Note the diagonally-shaped wall sections added to protect turrets from attackers.

CAMP EXAMPLE 8:
THE BUCOLIC CABOOSE

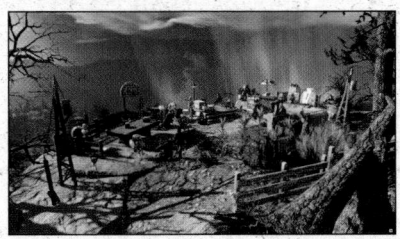

- AESTHETICS: ★★★★★
- FUNCTIONALITY: ★★☆☆☆
- DEFENSE: ★★★☆☆

What a view! Forget for a moment that it was an insanely difficult hike to reach this location, with treacherous cliff drops to contend with. But once you're here, you can Fast-Travel and take in the sunsets and the weather and listen to old-timey songs on the radio. The structure is built to take advantage of the view, with a large expansive deck, a place to twang a banjo, and no real defenses, except the difficulty of getting here in the first place!

CAMP EXAMPLE 9:
BANJO TOWER EXTENSION

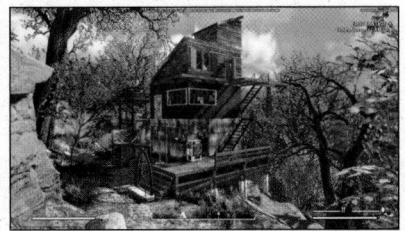

- AESTHETICS: ★★★☆☆
- FUNCTIONALITY: ★★★★☆
- DEFENSE: ★★★★☆

This is a good example of a camp that considers two types of planning; it is built to be attached to a structure already in Appalachia, which is usually impossible. It is also built at a secondary location to take advantage of it, essentially giving you a "second tower" to utilize (mainly for playing the banjo or mouth harp). The structure doesn't technically touch the secondary location, but platforms are close enough for you to get back and forth. It also offers good defense, views, and elements like a sleeping bag that are already in the landscape. Check the Atlas (the Forest Zone A: Secondary Locations) for this tower's location.

CAMP EXAMPLE 10:
THE ESCHER LODGE

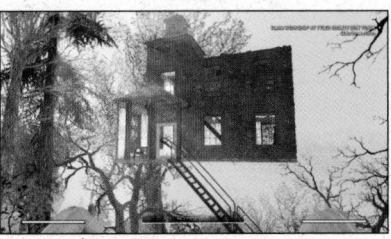

- AESTHETICS: ★☆☆☆☆
- FUNCTIONALITY: ★★★★☆
- DEFENSE: ★★★★★

Placed on a steep slope, this features the most reinforced staircase ever seen (two of them stacked atop each other). It has the minimal foundation necessary, with a floating house atop the staircase, like a mad, gravity-defying hypno-shack! A turret on the front porch puts pay to anything that manages to climb the steps, but larger creatures won't even try. Notice the floor of the floating house is wood and impenetrable; enemies need to be inside the house to even damage most of it! If it all looks too weird, think about adding metal pole stilts to fake some foundations, or make a stilt house, which can have much the same effect.

CAMP EXAMPLE 11:
MOUNT BLAIR BERTH

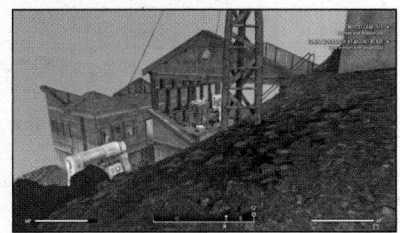

- AESTHETICS: ★★★★☆
- FUNCTIONALITY: ★★★★☆
- DEFENSE: ★★★★☆

Donning Power Armor and working in the choking air of the Ash Heap, near the gigantic excavator arm, this camp demonstrates how to separate different areas into three steeply sloped locations, with a viewing hut at the top. A lucrative quest occurs here, and this is a great place to watch other players move to and from the excavator, before launching an exploration when the coast is clear. Should the quest become overwhelming, it's an easy sprint or Fast-Travel back to this home base, which features resource-collecting robots, an artillery cannon, vending machines (for inquisitive players of if you want to check for randomly appearing Legendary items!), and a lower metal shed with workbenches and a bed.

TRAINING

CRAFTING AND C.A.M.P.ING

INVENTORY

QUESTS

ATLAS

BESTIARY

APPENDICES

PART 2: WORKSHOPS

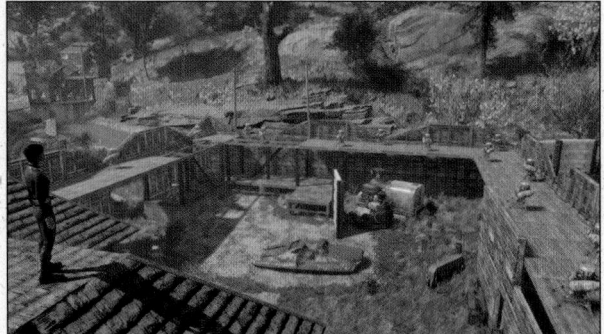

Always wanted your own resource-producing base? With some involved building and defending, now you can!

THIS SECTION DETAILS ALL THE HELPFUL INFORMATION FOR CLAIMING ANY OF THE 22 WORKSHOPS (ALSO CALLED PUBLIC WORKSHOPS) SCATTERED THROUGHOUT APPALACHIA, INCLUDING ADVICE ON CONTESTING AND KEEPING A WORKSHOP FOR AS LONG AS POSSIBLE.

WHAT IS A WORKSHOP?

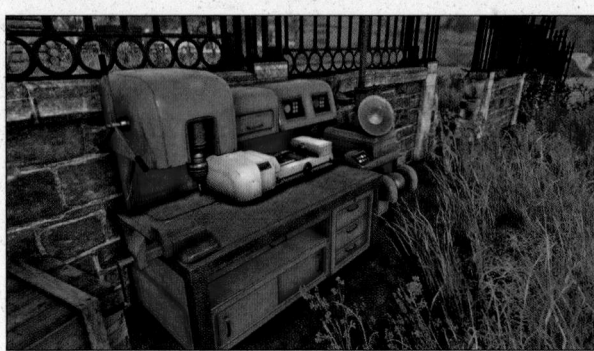

The Workshop Workbench: the key to claiming and keeping a workshop space.

A public workshop is a primary location appearing on your world map (and throughout this guide's Atlas). When you discover a workshop, hover over the map icon to gain some important information, such as whether the workshop has been claimed, who has claimed it, and what resources the workshop has to offer you.

Workshops are usually large, industrial, military, or agricultural in nature. Unlike camps, they are immovable. Think of public workshops as large-scale camps that you or your team can claim, exploit, and own temporarily. Each public workshop has a single large red workbench.

Workshop workbenches are perhaps the most important location within a workshop. They are the hub of the location and act as a "flag" you need to "capture" (or in this case, claim), then defend from others contesting your claim. They also act as large, stationary C.A.M.P.s, offering the same Build and Modify construction menu, allowing you to build exactly the same sort of structures that you did when erecting your camp, albeit on a larger scale. Therefore, it's wise to learn all facets of camp building before staking your claim on a workshop.

WHERE ARE THE WORKSHOPS?

There are 22 different workshops throughout Appalachia. All of them are different in size, location, difficulty, and the types of resources that are available to you once you claim the workshop. For a closer look at each workshop, along with a map showing an "unimproved" workshop with the perimeter boundary of each, consult the Atlas. Below is a list of all available Appalachian workshops, along with their location and expected resources:

APPALACHIAN WORKSHOP LOCATION

#	REGION AND ZONE	# AND NAME	RESOURCES
1	1. The Forest: Zone A	16. Sunshine Meadows Industrial Farm	Food [10], Water [3], Packaged Food [1]*, Fertilizer [3], Junk [1], Aluminum [1], Concrete [1]
2	1. The Forest: Zone B	22. Tyler County Dirt Track	Food [1], Water [3], Fertilizer [1], Junk [1], Silver [3], Aluminum [1], Steel [1]
3	1. The Forest: Zone C	31. Gorge Junkyard	Food [5], Water [3], Junk [1], Titanium [1], Concrete [1], Wood [1]
4	1. The Forest: Zone D	62. Billings Homestead	Food [5], Water [3], Fertilizer [1], Crystal [1], Gold [1], Copper [1]
5	1. The Forest: Zone D	73. Poseidon Energy Plant Yard	Food [9], Water [8], Fusion Core [3], Lead [1], Aluminum [1], Nuclear [1], Concrete [1]
6	1. The Forest: Zone E	77. Charleston Landfill	Food [6], Water [8], Junk [3], Aluminum [1], Copper [1], Steel [1]
7	1. The Forest: Zone E	83. Wade Airport	Food [5], Water [5], Silver [1], Copper [1], Oil [3]
8	1. The Forest: Zone E	86. Lakeside Cabins	Food [6], Water [6], Silver [1], Crystal [1], Lead [1], Wood [1]
9	2. Toxic Valley	6. Hemlock Holes Maintenance	Food [3], Water [3], Crystal [1], Gold [1], Acid [3]
10	2. Toxic Valley	23. Grafton Steel	Food [2], Water [2], Lead [1], Copper [1], Steel [4], Oil [1]
11	3. The Ash Heap: Zone A	9. Beckley Mine Exhibit	Food [6], Water [8], Crystal [1], Gold [1], Oil [3]
12	3. The Ash Heap: Zone A	17. Mount Blair	Food [9], Water [8], Ore [1]
13	4. Savage Divide: Zone A	2. Converted Munitions Factory	Food [7], Water [8], Junk [1], Ammo [1]*, Silver [1], Lead [1], Aluminum [1], Oil [1]
14	4. Savage Divide: Zone A	14. Red Rocket Mega Stop	Food [5], Water [8], Junk [1], Aluminum [3], Nuclear [1], Steel [1]
15	4. Savage Divide: Zone A	20. Monongah Power Plant Yard	Food [8], Water [9], Fusion Core [3], Silver [1], Acid [1], Nuclear [1], Wood [1]
16	4. Savage Divide: Zone C	80. Spruce Knob	Food [4], Water [4], Gold [3], Copper [1], Acid [1]
17	4. Savage Divide: Zone C	87. Federal Disposal Field HZ-21	Food [9], Water [4], Acid [1], Nuclear [3], Oil [1]
18	5. The Mire: Zone A	16. Dolly Sods Campground	Food [9], Water [7]
19	5. The Mire: Zone A	20. Thunder Mountain Power Plant Yard	Food [7], Water [9], Fusion Core [3], Crystal [1], Nuclear [1], Steel [1], Wood [1]
20	5. The Mire: Zone A	25. Berkeley Springs West	Food [1], Water [10], Crystal [1], Lead [1], Aluminum [1]
21	5. The Mire: Zone B	41. Dabney Homestead	Food [6], Water [8], Fertilizer [1], Junk [1], Copper [3], Concrete [1], Wood [1]
22	6. Cranberry Bog: Zone A	17. Abandoned Bog Town	Food [7], Water [3], Silver [1], Gold [1], Acid [1], Concrete [3], Oil [1]

(* Indicates a unique resource requiring a possible small quest to unlock, and generators to power)

Now that you have an overview of where to find each workshop, it's time to drill a bit deeper into what workshops contain and why they are so valuable.

STEP 1: LEARNING YOUR WORKSHOP'S ASSETS

The 22 different workshops are used for extracting food, water, and materials from the ground; ensuring your continued well-being; crafting; and camping. They offer alternatives to gathering components the old-fashioned way (from junk and other items), and resource generating collectors also offer higher quantities of rare minerals and other items, providing you can keep them powered and away from thieves. Here are the various important locations within a workshop:

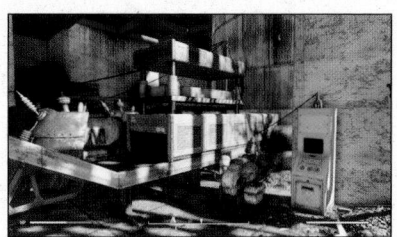

A conveyor belt full of processed foodstuff you can get running? Count me in!

Workshop Workbench: This is like an immobile C.A.M.P., which you claim and use the (identical) Build menu, along with the workshop's stack of components, which you don't need to collect yourself. It's the most important object in the workshop.

Food and Water Resources: If a location lists food or water as a resource, the number indicates the maximum amount produced per cycle. For example, a Water value of 4 means that up to four Water Purifiers will produce each cycle. If you have more than four Water Purifiers, the Workshop will randomly select and produce at four of the available purifiers. Water Purifiers that aren't powered or at full inventory are ignored, so if you had six purifiers but three were full, the other three purifiers would produce.

Resource Deposits (Collectors): If a location has any other listed asset, it's usually a deposit requiring a collector to farm. Access these collectors from the Build > Resources menu. They need power (from power plants or your own generators) in order to work. They produce the listed item, usually in a component format that doesn't need to be smelted or changed; it's immediately usable for crafting. Simply gather produced materials from a collector while it is powered, or steal from it. Beware of thieves gathering your materials; place a lock to prevent this from happening. Collectors have inventory limits, so gather resources frequently to keep them producing.

Unique Resources: Certain workshops may have a small Miscellaneous Quest to complete that unlocks a unique resource at the location. For example, Sunshine Meadows Industrial Farm (the Forest Zone A) has a system inside the main facility structure that churns out boxed food. The Converted Munitions Factory (Savage Divide Zone A) has a system that churns out specialized ammunition (once you power the control terminal)! Check a workshop to see if there are additional assets like this.

Enemies (and Their Loot): Though various types of foes are likely to attack you, certain locations (like the Converted Munitions Factory) tend to spawn a particular type of enemy (Super Mutants in this case) over others. As each enemy drops a particular type of loot, focus on a workshop where you know a certain foe type is likely to be.

Power Boxes: Some workshops have power boxes. These always yield at least some power, but provide much more if their power plant is online. To make the most of your time at the workshop, head to the plant and complete Event: Powering Up, then use the power boxes to run your Resource Collectors and other defenses.

Vertibot Landing Pads: Certain workshops may have one or more landing pads: Wade Airport (the Forest Zone E), Grafton Steel (Toxic Valley), and the Converted Munitions Factory (Savage Divide Zone A), for example. Access the Signal Grenade Box (usually on the edge of the circular landing pad) and lob a grenade to summon the airborne attack (or another if the previous one was destroyed). The Vertibot is an autonomous attack craft that targets enemies on the ground. It's useful in open outdoor areas; it doesn't target foes inside buildings. Use these during times of extended combat!

Also check for existing Military Turret defenses (in Workshops like the Converted Munitions Factory or Grafton Steel Yard). Access, repair, and bring online to defend attacks and reduce the need to make your own turrets.

Perimeter: The exterior boundary of the workshop is delineated by a green line, like the one around your camp. Collect and build all assets inside this area, and optionally add your own camps just outside a workshop for extra defense. Keep enemies away from this line; if they get in, your base could be damaged. This guide's Atlas maps show the perimeter of each workshop. The workshop perimeter may only be a small part of the overall location.

STEP 2: CLAIMING (AND CONTESTING) A WORKSHOP

Unowned: If a workshop is unowned, then expect the location and its immediate surroundings to have a scattering of (random) enemies you must remove as part of the Claim Workshop at [Location] quest. Simply defeat all the foes, move to the red Workshop Workbench, and activate it. If you can't because there are enemies left to kill, they are usually tagged with a diamond icon, allowing you to finish the quest easily.

Contested: If a workshop is owned by a player, then expect the location around the Workshop Workbench to be bristling with complex and dangerous defenses, including walls, turrets, buildings, traps, and rival human forces with little time for your infiltration! Or, you may find a badly defended, completely open workshop that is ripe for the taking! At this point, you can:

- **LEAVE:** IF THE ENEMIES PRESENT TOO MUCH OF A THREAT, SIMPLY FIND A DIFFERENT WORKSHOP TO CLAIM.
- **CONTEST:** IF YOU BELIEVE THE WORKSHOP IS VALUABLE ENOUGH TO RISK TIME, HEALTH, AND RESOURCES TO CONTEST, YOU CAN MANEUVER IN, HEAD TO THE WORKSHOP WORKBENCH, AND CONTEST IT.

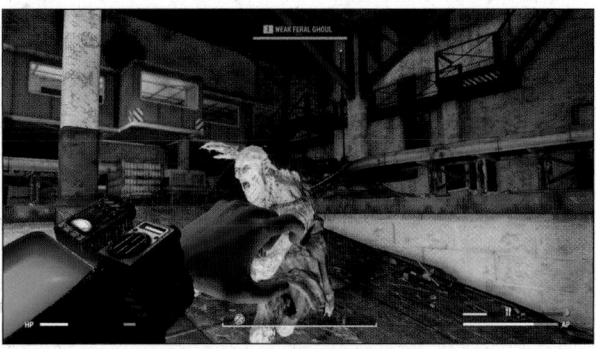

You must remove the collection of unwanted enemies before the construction begins.

If you're contesting a workshop, the human enemy will be informed and a tough battle will follow. If you attack before contesting it, you become Wanted.

STAKING YOUR CLAIM! CLAIMING WORKSHOP WORKBENCHES

The physical act of claiming or contesting a workshop depends on the status of the workbench. Look for a metal pole with a tiny satellite dish cluster at the top:

- **UNOWNED:** IF IT IS RETRACTED INTO THE MAIN BODY OF THE WORKBENCH, THE PLACE IS UNOWNED. STEP UP TO THE WORKBENCH, ACTIVATE IT, AND WAIT IN A SMALL GLOWING GREEN CIRCLE AS THE WORKSHOP CLAIM BAR FILLS. WHEN IT'S FULL, THE WORKSHOP IS OFFICIALLY YOURS! NOTE YOU WILL HAVE TO PAY CAPS FOR THIS PRIVILEGE.
- **CONTESTED:** IF THE POLE IS EXTENDED, THE WORKSHOP MUST BE CONTESTED, AND ANY DEFENSES (SUCH AS TURRETS) WILL BE HOSTILE TO YOU. AFTER YOU PAY A CAPS FEE FOR THE CONTESTING, YOU MUST WAIT IN A SMALL GLOWING GREEN CIRCLE AS THE WORKBENCH METAL POLE RETRACTS DOWN AND IT RESETS. REMAIN IN THE GREEN CIRCLE AS THE WORKSHOP CLAIM BAR REFILLS AS YOU GO FROM CONTESTING TO CLAIMING THE WORKSHOP.

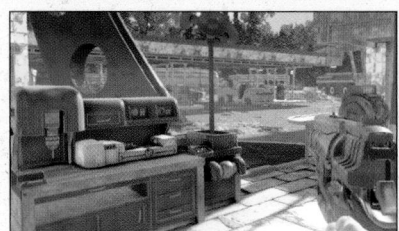

Stand inside a small workbench threshold while you claim or contest: Then the workshop is yours!

Note that contesting a workshop usually takes twice as long as claiming a workshop, and costs more Caps (as you're essentially usurping another human's hard work!). Also, contesting is usually never as cut and dry as standing around, waiting for the workbench pole to retract and extend, as the contesting usually stalls when you have to take cover from enemy fire.

Once you've claimed the workshop, the new claimant (usually you or your team leader) appears on the world map, and you are able to start building.

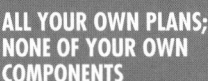

Helpful Hint from Vault-Boy!

ALL YOUR OWN PLANS; NONE OF YOUR OWN COMPONENTS

Great news! The workshop you've claimed has its own collection of resources (shown in green on the menu), meaning you don't have to search for and use your own base components (shown in yellow on the menu)! Set about constructing your defenses knowing you're not siphoning any building materials from your own stock—though you can supplement a workshop with your own components. Any building plans you've unlocked along your travels work for both camps and workshops, but there are no extra plans (until you've completed the Workshop Quest and repelled waves of enemies, which is a great way to randomly obtain more plans).

STEP 3: BUILDING UP YOUR WORKSHOP STRUCTURES

Immediately upon claiming your workshop, you can repair any existing structures and start to build your own, using the same building methods as we described for a camp. You must set about defending your workshop and then exploiting the resources within its green boundary perimeter. To achieve success, there are some simple rules to follow:

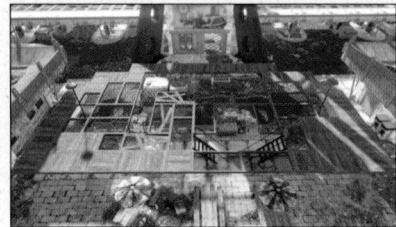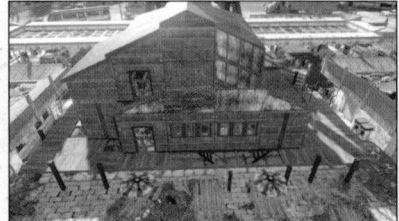

Turn this (picture 1) into this (picture 2) with some rapid defensive structural construction.

RULE 1: DEFEND YOUR WORKSHOP WORKBENCH AT ALL COSTS!

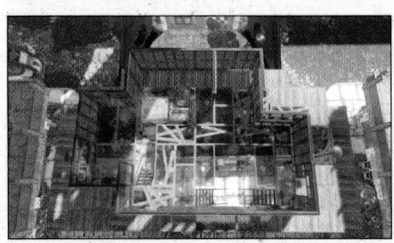

A workshop workbench, inside a turret and trap-filled structure; make this difficult to find, let alone contest!

You've just demonstrated why the Workshop Workbench is the most important part of this location: It's the only object that an enemy player can claim; once claimed, all the workshop defenses and structures revert to the new claimant. Your goal is to make it impossible for the enemy to reach the workbench. Think about the following tactical defenses (efficacy may change with post-launch game changes):

- **TURRETS AND TRAPS:** AS SOON AS YOU CLAIM A BASE, START DROPPING TURRETS FOR SOME INSTANT PROTECTION. FEEL FREE TO ADD TRAPS OF VARIOUS KINDS TOO, ANYTHING TO WOUND A FOE OR CAUSE THEM TO THINK TWICE BEFORE REACHING YOUR WORKBENCH.
- **RAISED TURRETS:** THEN START CREATING RUDIMENTARY TWO- OR THREE-FLOOR DEFENSES AND PLACE TURRETS AT THE TOP.
- **WORKBENCH ENCASEMENT:** BUT THE REAL TRICK IS TO "ENCASE" A WORKBENCH, OR HIDE IT SO IT'S ALMOST IMPOSSIBLE TO REACH, POSSIBLY BY EITHER SIDE. REMEMBER, ONCE THE WORKSHOP IS YOURS, YOU CAN ACCESS THE BUILD MENU ANYWHERE INSIDE THE PERIMETER.

- Jam a wall close to the bench so only a single narrow opening is accessible to the bench, and fill that choke point with traps.

- Wrap an entire structure with walls, doors, floor and wall traps, around a workbench if the location allows it (like the Red Rocket Mega Stop).

- Place defenses directly above the workbench (mesh floor towers with turrets) so you can fire down on foes as they approach.

RULE 2: SCRAP EXISTING TRASH, DEFEND RESOURCE COLLECTORS

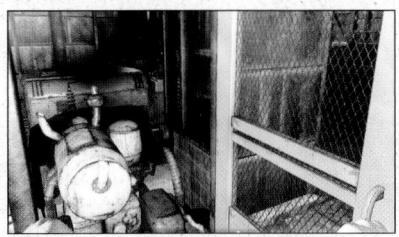

A resource collector (locked), with a generator inside a room, inside a heavily guarded metal cabin; try getting to this, enemy fiends!

With an initial stopgap measure to protect the workbench complete, begin to construct and farm the resources:

Scrapping Scenery: With the workbench now under turret guard, start to remove any trash lying around the location. This doesn't add anything to your raw materials or components; the scenery is lost. Only remove areas you don't aesthetically like the look of or want to build on without any obstacles.

Resource Collector Encasement: Place a resource collector on top of any deposits (ground pits) within the perimeter. Hook each one up to power (ideally a generator you can hide near the collector). Then place defensive walls, access doors, floors, outer walls, defenses, turrets, and whatever else you wish to create an encasement, making it difficult for enemies to reach the collector. With multiple collectors, you may have to leave it out in the open but close to a turret tower. Any player can access resource collectors in a public workshop. To prevent theft, build a lock for the collector or move the collected items into your private Stash Box.

Generator Placement: Alternatively, place generators on rooftops, away from enemy attackers. Or place them well away from a collector but linked with power connectors; this way an enemy can't easily bring a collector offline!

RULE 3: BUILD PROPER DEFENSES

By now, you may have had to fend off some lighter attacks from non-human enemies. While this is occurring, start to build your workshop bases in earnest: Attempt any or all of the following:

Wall Defenses (Type A: Wall Menu): Start with a few foundation pieces, then build stairs and an upper walkway floor running the length of your wall. Next, connect wall sections below the floating upper wall so you don't waste budget building foundations all the way across. A mesh walkway and triangular wall sections between your turrets allow them some protection but can

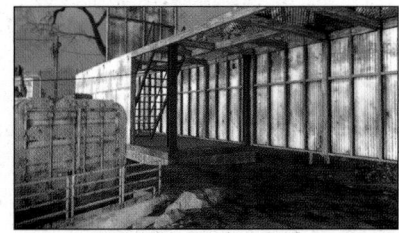

still fire on infiltrating foes. Add a second interior wall so foes breaking through the first wall have an inner wall to get through—if your budget allows. Then take a blueprint of this and construct a second, third, fourth, and fifth version of varying lengths, depending on the workshop's size.

Wall Defenses (Type B: Defenses Menu): The tall defensive wall of concrete and steel (with the climbing hooks on it) is a great barricade: It's tall enough so foes can't fire or climb over it. It erects quickly, can be sunk into the ground easily, doesn't need to "snap" into other objects, and can be used to seal gaps if your workshop already has a perimeter fence or defenses around

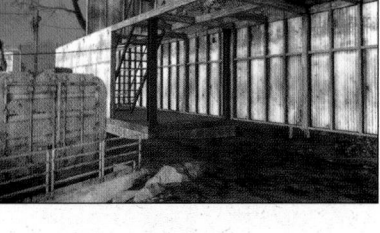

a resource collector. Position both types of defenses so you're forcing an enemy into a choke point.

Choke Points: A narrow gap between wall defenses Types A and B should be just wide enough so the enemy thinks this is the quickest and best way into a workshop. Naturally, you and your team should have clustered turrets aimed directly at this "choke point of death," along with traps, dead-end wall sections, turrets, and anything else you feel like throwing down to waylay enemies. If they get through this, give them a final hurdle:

Wall Defenses (Type C: Interior): Either paste in a blueprint of wall defense Type A (or a section of it), or create a final inner wall, perhaps attached to the structure that houses your most important collector or workshop workbench. It helps to look at the footprint of a fortified medieval castle, with an inner "bailey." Force foes up and down stairs through narrow areas. If you and your

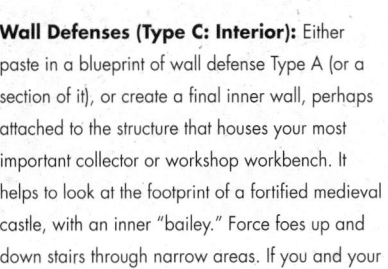

team have planned this, you can erect an inner wall first, building outward until you hit a perimeter.

Turret Towers and Defensive Towers: At the corners of your workshop, think about erecting a three- or four-floor tower, offering good lookout potential and advantageous sniping (due to your height). Make the tower high and narrow (the ready-made stairs with the mesh floor is a quick way to complete this). Populate the tower with turrets. Then copy the tower into a blueprint and

paste a second, third, and possibly fourth tower so your workshop is bristling with defenses!

TRAINING

CRAFTING AND C.A.M.P.ING

INVENTORY

QUESTS

ATLAS

BESTIARY

APPENDICES

Stations and Workbenches: Place any stations and workbenches you're likely to need during a protracted battle in an easy-to-reach location, but one that doesn't expose you to enemy fire when you're hammering away, crafting more ammo, or repairing your weapons: Place these inside a structure, against a defensive wall, and close to your workshop workbench and resource collectors.

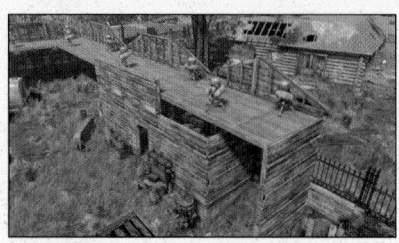

Switched Defenses: Check the list of object types at the end of this chapter, and figure out whether the more complex defenses can serve your purposes. Link your turrets to a switch so you have more control over them. Think about adding an alarm (triggered by trespassers). But be mindful that these accoutrements eat into your budget!

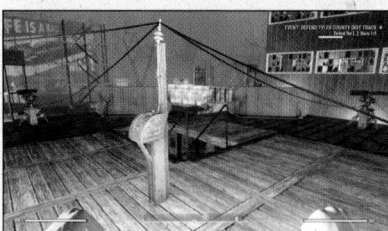

Camps and Other Building Types: While you can place a mess hall type of structure (which could even be a ready-made camp you've blueprinted), with beds, vending machines (which can be checked periodically for rare items to purchase), and paintings on the walls, this eats into your workshop budget. So think about moving your camp and including non-defensive objects (like a bed) to the edge of the workshop perimeter. Or have all your team craft four additional camps in the shape of a turret tower to really impact those defenses and act as early warning locations!

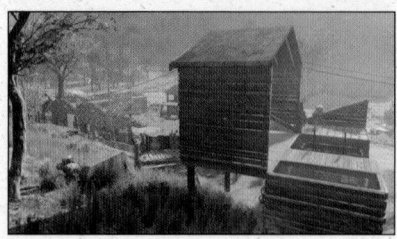

Distractions: Got a bit of budget left? Why not slap a Scorchbeast head on a wall, place a blinking arrow pointing in the direction of a choke point, spell out a neon-lit threat, or otherwise add some finishing touches to your workshop. Instead of making them aesthetically pleasing (as you might during camp construction), place these to cause your human foes to pause for a second, either to figure out what the distractions mean or to laugh at them. By which time, you're able to massacre them.

Helpful Hint from Vault-Boy!

BLUEPRINTS: THE KEY TO RAPID FORTIFICATION

Your first workshop is likely to take a while, so construct it in sections, and blueprint each one: That way, you can erect your next workshop in seconds, rather than hours!

RULE 4: CONTROLLING YOUR BUDGET

A good rule of thumb is to expect a workshop to have between three to five times the budget of a camp, depending on its size and location. This means you must stringently follow budgeting rules, knowing that turrets are going to be the costliest item by far. Unlike camps, you'll probably want all your budget to go into defenses, with objects such as floors, walls, roofs, turrets, traps, collectors, generators, and some lighting taking precedence. Make your workshop defensible first and aesthetically pleasing second.

RULE 5: TEAMWORK MAKES THE WORKSHOP WORK

Effective workshop claiming and defending depends on competence and working well with your teammates. As all four of you can essentially build your own Camp around a workshop perimeter, this can add a large amount of "free" defense to the workshop area. Divide your teammates into different responsibilities and ensure you're all part of the same team—if you aren't teamed up, turrets—which normally will not fire on teammates unless they are Wanted—may start firing on humans it thinks are intruders! Ensure your team leader is the "claimant"; he or she is responsible for the way your structures link to each other. Although anyone can build defenses, only the Vault Dweller who claimed the Workshop Workbench can remove defenses he or she doesn't like, even those built by teammates! Or, you can do it all yourself and invite teammates in afterward. Or, you can do it all yourself, ignore any other players, and try to defend it all by yourself, without a team: Which is far more difficult.

RULE 6: BATTLES, EXPLOITATION, AND ABANDONMENT

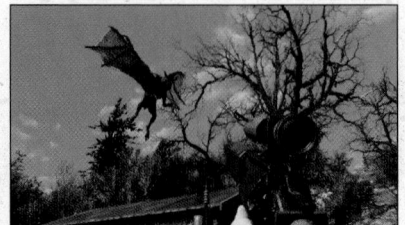

"A Scorchbeast is attacking! Prepare defenses and drive it back to keep the Workshop operational!"

With effective defenses, you must now prepare to repel any invaders. Spread out to vantage points; ensure you have enough provisions, ammunition, and quality gear and weapons to last a while; and hunker down! After you successfully purge waves of enemies, expect some quest reward loot, including plans and mods! Keep this up until enemies overrun the workshop, you run out of items to repair damaged turrets or defenses with, or you've exploited all the resources you want.

Even the finest defenses will fail one day: This is particularly true of workshops, which are ephemeral; that is, you can only keep a workshop until you log out, and it resets in the game world after one week: If you're on a team, the leader becomes the owner if you disconect. Don't expect to be here for months; instead, gather the resources you need, learn from your defensive structure building, take blueprints (especially your teammates' construction ideas that might be better than your own), and then move on. There's plenty more workshops out there to discover!

PART 3: THE CONSTRUCTION COLLECTION

THIS SECTION LISTS THE DIFFERENT BUILDING STRUCTURES AVAILABLE WHEN YOU ACCESS THE (ALMOST IDENTICAL) C.A.M.P. AND WORKSHOP BUILD MENUS, AS WELL AS LISTING THE RELEVANT PERKS AND BONUSES TO USE WHEN BUILDING.

Helpful Hint from Vault-Boy!

AN OVERVIEW, NOT A STATISTICS COURSE

The following information gives a thorough overview of every type of object you can build at a camp or workshop, but due to the ever-changing values of items (including what components they need and how many), a precise list of how many resources it costs to build everything just isn't possible. However, the type of components needed (listed approximately from most to least), a full list of items for each category (listed as they appear in the menu), and some specific information is provided, so you know what to expect when you gradually unlock all the plans necessary to use this massive amount of objects.

RECENT MENU

This offers access to objects you've previously utilized recently and is helpful if you've left your building to forage before returning and want to add some of the previously built objects (e.g., continuing a floor, wall, or roof). What were you doing when you last left your structure? Find out here!

STORED MENU

This is where you'll find objects you've previously built but haven't placed in the landscape, including the blueprints stored when you move your camp. This might be because you're rebuilding and you can't place the item yet (like a piece of roof when you're working on the foundations), it's something you're waiting to place, or it contains your previously built camp. Is your workshop budget almost full, with not much on the ground? Then you could have a lot of objects stored here. Storing is better than scrapping, as you get to keep and reuse the object, but don't get into the habit of hoarding stored items at the expense of your budget; sometimes you're going to make mistakes, scrap everything (for half the components of the original object), and start over!

BLUEPRINTS MENU

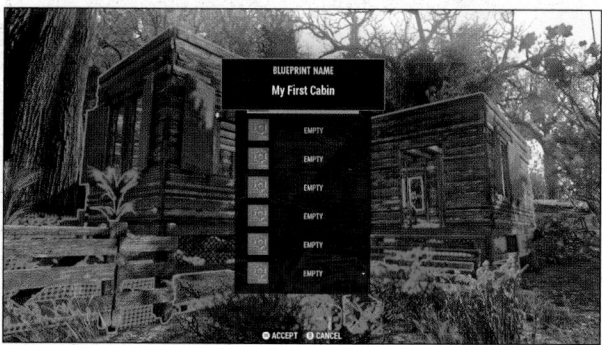

A list of blueprints, enabling fast rebuilding of past structures.

These are previously saved sections of a camp or workshop that you built and copied into a blueprint and named for later use. Ideally, these should be sections of a camp, a defensive tower, a wall, or another feature you want to instantly erect. This way you can make an impressive structure and place it down instantly when you reach a new location (or the same location that you want to rebuild in the same way). Blueprints save a considerable amount of time, so use them! You can select someone else's work and save it as a blueprint if you've unlocked all pieces in the blueprint; otherwise, you can take a photo of the structure (even if a rival Vault Dweller built it and you're attacking the camp or workshop!), study it, and rebuild it from the pictures before selecting and saving it as a blueprint yourself.

FLOORS

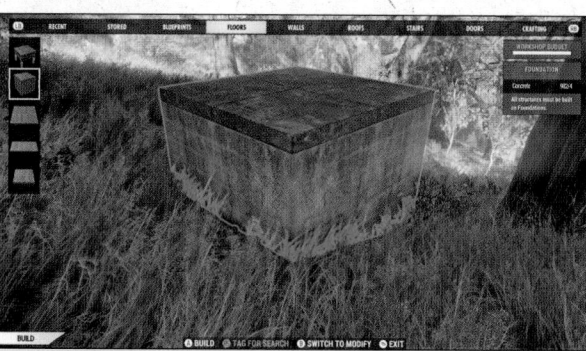

- **TYPES OF OBJECTS:** WOOD FOUNDATION, CONCRETE FOUNDATION, UPPER FLOOR
- **COMPONENTS NEEDED:** WOOD, CONCRETE

A wood or concrete foundation? That depends on the aesthetics and available materials. Foundations must be placed first, and a camp or workshop structure must have an "anchor" into the ground using this type of floor. However, the upper floor sections are of particular interest, as they are indestructible—the only piece of your camp that is. Create a "stilt" camp with a floor the enemy can't shoot through and with all your best stuff hidden in the air! Bear in mind that mesh flooring may be indestructible, but unlike the wood variant, it can be fired through; use your tactical forethought to determine if you want to fire down (or up) at foes during an attack, and place the right type of floors for this. On sloping ground, use the ramp foundation.

WALLS

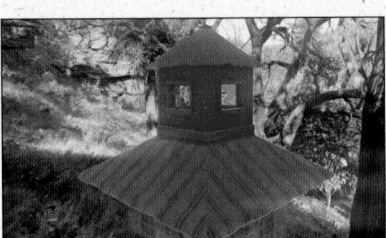

- **TYPES OF OBJECT:** WALLS (WOOD, RED BARN, SHACK METAL, BRICK, PANEL METAL); WALL SHAPES (HALF, SHAPES); ROLLING METAL DOOR; POWERED DOORS
- **COMPONENTS NEEDED:** WOOD, STEEL

There is a huge selection of styles and shapes in this menu, though many are locked, requiring plans to obtain them. There are doorways and shutter variants, as well as full wall sections. Leave the construction menu, and you can open any shutters, if you want to see outside! Play around with the styles and, most importantly, the shapes of the walls. Certain angled wall sections are used as battlement protection (as shown) or to create a dormer window or more complex roof. Use the rolling metal door to create your own garage, and use the powered doors (power link required) with a switch if you want a door opened with a timer. More expensive wall types, like brick and metal, have higher defensive values.

ROOFS

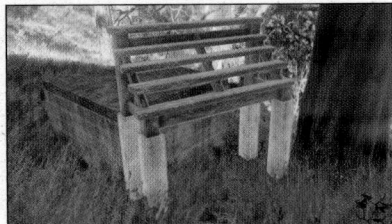

- **TYPES OF OBJECT:** ROOF (SHAPES)
- **COMPONENTS NEEDED:** STEEL, WOOD

Roof sections are designed to slot together in a variety of ways. To begin, just use the flat roof. Later on, add triangular wall sections and sloping roof lines for aesthetics and so grenades roll back down when thrown by an intruder. Create dormer windows (as shown), add a cupola to your barn, and note there are some roof sections with holes at the end for attaching to subsequent sections or for lobbing grenades through if you're inside and defending your home.

STAIRS

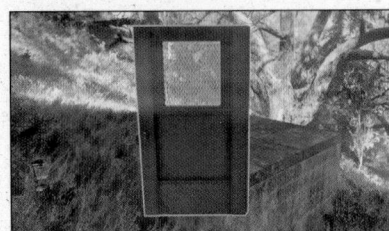

- **TYPES OF OBJECT:** STAIRS, STAIRS WITH FOUNDATION, POSTS
- **COMPONENTS NEEDED:** WOOD, STEEL

This is the method of reaching a second or subsequent floor, and allow you to build vertically with speed. The stairs with foundation offers an immediate two-floor structure you can quickly add walls to (when creating a defensive tower). Use the posts with wall sections of different shapes, or as stilts to lift up a building or for aesthetics if a building is "floating" and defying gravity. Connect them to the upper floor sections and ground.

DOORS

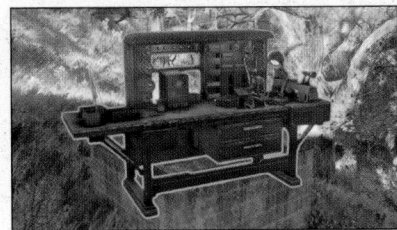

- **TYPE OF OBJECT:** DOOR
- **COMPONENTS NEEDED:** SCREW, STEEL, WOOD

These can be opened once you exit the Build menu. Close doors when you leave (so you can see if it was opened in your absence). Lay traps nearby to dissuade trespassing. Close doors to add protection. Doors can only be connected to the doorway wall sections. You can lock doors to keep other players out; you or your teammates can freely open locked doors.

CRAFTING

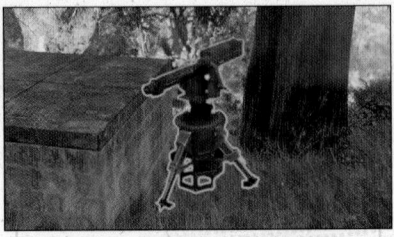

- **TYPES OF OBJECT:** COOKING STATION, CHEMISTRY STATION, POWER ARMOR STATION, ARMOR WORKBENCH, TINKER'S WORKBENCH, WEAPONS WORKBENCH
- **COMPONENTS NEEDED:** STEEL, WOOD, ALUMINUM, GEAR, OIL, SCREW, SPRING, COPPER, GLASS, RUBBER, CIRCUITRY, FIBERGLASS, PLASTIC, SCREW

This is relatively straightforward. When you receive the plans, choose any of the crafting benches you wish to place, and add some excellent functionality to your abode. If space is a consideration, and you have the plans, pick the smaller variant when picking a Cooking Station, Chemistry Station, Weapons Workbench, or Power Armor Station.

TURRETS AND TRAPS

- **TYPES OF OBJECT:** MACHINE GUN TURRET, HEAVY MACHINE GUN TURRET, LASER TURRET, HEAVY LASER TURRET, SHOTGUN TURRET, MISSILE TURRET, SPOTLIGHT, PUNJI BOARD, BONE CHIME, SPIKE BOARD TRAP, SPRING TRAP, SAWBLADE TRAP, TESLA ARC, FLAMETHROWER TRAP, RADIATION EMITTER
- **COMPONENTS NEEDED (TURRETS):** CIRCUITRY, GEAR, OIL, STEEL, ALUMINUM, FIBER OPTICS, GLASS, NUCLEAR MATERIAL, SCREW, CRYSTAL
- **PERKS NEEDED (TURRETS):** AGILITY: HOME DEFENSE, INTELLIGENCE: SCIENCE
- **COMPONENTS NEEDED (TRAPS):** STEEL, WOOD, BONE, CIRCUITRY, COPPER, ALUMINUM, OIL, RUBBER, SCREW, LEAD, NUCLEAR MATERIAL
- **PERKS NEEDED (TRAPS):** AGILITY: HOME DEFENSE, INTELLIGENCE: SCIENCE, ENDURANCE: FIREPROOF

Turrets: Be sure you have a selection of fast-firing turrets, especially at optimal locations around a workshop base, like higher ground, with ability to fire through mesh floors at foes or over wooden defenses (use the triangular wall sections with gaps where the gun points out). Link turrets to a terminal or switch so you can turn them off if a Wanted teammate saunters into camp (otherwise, the turrets are team-friendly). Use your perks to construct turrets with a higher defensive value, though machine-gun turrets are still very effective. Turrets are likely to suffer damage the most, so check on the components they need to be repaired with, and gather enough of them. And remember that nothing uses up your budget like placing turrets!

Traps: These range from jingling bone chimes announcing the arrival of someone to high-tech radiation and electrical emitters requiring perks and careful placement. Put traps close to high-value locations, like resource extractors (collectors) and your workshop workbench to dissuade even the most keen invader.

DEFENSES

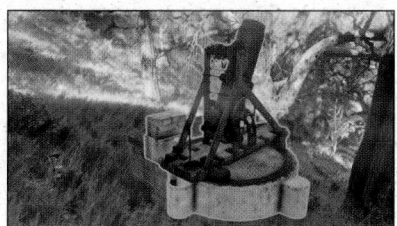

- **TYPES OF OBJECTS:** GUARD POST (WOOD), GUARD POST (CONCRETE), BARRICADE, DEFENSIVE WALL, PERIMETER WALL FRAME, PERIMETER WALL RAILING, FENCE, GATE, SIREN, ARTILLERY PIECE
- **COMPONENTS NEEDED:** STEEL, WOOD, CONCRETE, CERAMIC, COPPER, RUBBER, GEAR

Place these to discourage enemies from wandering into your camp or workshop; give your structures and high-value objects (like resource collectors) a bit of protection, as well as yourself and your team. Place barricades, especially the defensive wall (due to its height) along gaps in a workshop boundary. Create choke points where you can herd enemies. Hook up the siren to a different switch (from the Power Connectors menu) if you need to turn it on remotely. Use the perimeter wall frames just as their name suggests. Don't forget to hook up the artillery piece to power; it provides 6 Defense, launching mortars on foes marked by your smoke grenade!

GENERATORS

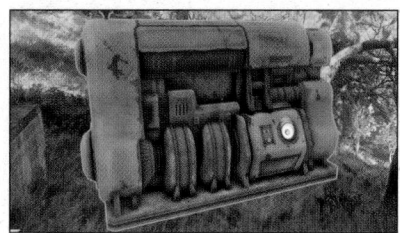

- **TYPES OF OBJECTS:** GENERATOR (SMALL, MEDIUM, LARGE, FUSION, WINDMILL)
- **COMPONENTS NEEDED:** CERAMIC, COPPER, GEAR, RUBBER, STEEL, SCREW, ALUMINUM, CRYSTAL, NUCLEAR MATERIAL.

There are five different types of generators. The usual ones are noisy, give off smoke, and allow you to connect powered devices that need up to 3/5/10 units of power (small/medium/large). The Fusion Generator is silent and requires some rare materials to make, but it gives you all the power you'll ever need (100 units); however, if an enemy destroys it, all power is lost, so keep it even more well defended than with normal generators). There's also a large but earth-friendly wind generator which is big but quiet (3 units an hour).

POWER CONNECTORS

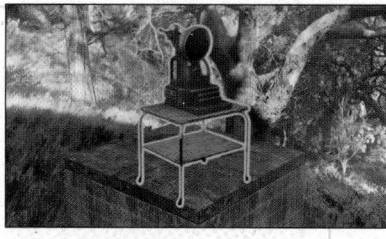

- **TYPES OF OBJECTS:** POWER PYLON, POWER CONDUIT, SWITCHED POWER PYLON, SWITCH, PRESSURE PLATE, CONDUIT JUNCTION, CONDUIT JUNCTION PASS-THROUGH, CONDUIT LIGHT, CONDUIT POWER RADIATOR, CONDUIT SWITCH, CONDUIT, TERMINAL, RANDOM SWITCH, SWITCHED POWER PYLON—KEYPAD ACCESS, LASER TRIPWIRE, POWERED SPEAKER (NORMAL, BLIP, EXPLOSIONS, PERCUSSION, PULSE VIBRATO, SINE, SQUARE, TRIANGLE), POWER COUNTER
- **COMPONENTS NEEDED:** CERAMIC, COPPER, STEEL, WOOD, RUBBER, SPRING, CRYSTAL, FIBER OPTICS, FUSION CELL, CIRCUITRY
- **PERK NEEDED:** DEMOLITION EXPERT (LASER TRIPWIRE)

This is perhaps the most involved menu, due to the large number of switchable and programmable objects, designed to automate, give you control, and neaten up the way power runs through your camp or workshop. The power pylons and power conduits are basically all you need to run wiring from a generator (or power plant box) to your object requiring power. But there are various additional features to think about:

- **SWITCHED POWER PYLONS AND SWITCHES:** ALLOWING YOU TO SWITCH THE POWERED DEVICE ON AND OFF, IN CASE YOU DON'T WANT LIGHTS OR A RESOURCE COLLECTOR ON WHILE YOU EXPLORE.
- **PRESSURE PLATE:** STAND ON THIS TO SWITCH A DEVICE ON, STEP OFF TO TURN IT OFF. USE THIS TO ADD A MEASURE OF SECURITY TO YOUR BASE, OPENING OTHERWISE-SEALED DOORS FOR TEAMMATES, FOR EXAMPLE.
- **CONDUITS:** THESE COPPER TUBES FEED POWER, AND SOME VARIANTS CAN BE PUSHED THROUGH WALLS, CONNECTED BY NEAT AND SNAKING PIPEWORK TO ALL YOUR INTERIOR SOURCES THAT NEED POWER, OR LIGHTING IF YOU WANT A SPECIFIC, TIDY LOOK. THERE'S A WIDE VARIETY OF JUNCTIONS, LIGHTS ATTACHED TO CONDUIT JUNCTIONS, AND CURVED SECTIONS TO CLAMP TO YOUR WALLS AND CEILINGS. AND EVEN FLOORS!
- **TERMINAL:** CONNECT A TERMINAL TO A CIRCUIT, AND YOU GAIN CONTROL OF SOME SWITCHES AND ALL SPOTLIGHTS, POWERED SPEAKERS, AND LIGHT BOXES THAT ARE RUNNING OFF THAT CIRCUIT. FROM HERE, YOU CAN TURN ANYTHING OFF AND ON. FOR TURRETS, THIS IS HELPFUL IF A FRIEND IS HEADING INTO YOUR BASE BUT THEY ARE WANTED (SO SWITCH OFF THE CONNECTED TURRETS TO AVOID THEM FIRING ON YOUR TEAMMATE). SPOTLIGHTS CAN BE USED TO TRAIN THEIR LIGHTS ON ENEMIES OR HUMANS. POWERED SPEAKERS ALLOW YOU TO SWITCH THEM OF AND ON IF YOU SUDDENLY WANT SILENCE. LIGHT BOXES CAN BE PROGRAMMED TO CHANGE COLOR; THIS IS A GREAT IDEA AS A FORM OF SIGNALING TO OTHER NEARBY TEAMMATES: PLACE LIGHT BOXES WHERE THEY CAN BE SEEN, AND CHANGE THE COLOR TO INDICATE THE TYPE OF ENEMY ATTACKING OR IF YOU'RE LOW ON A CERTAIN ITEM.
- **POWERED SPEAKERS:** PLACE THESE AROUND A WORKSHOP TO BEWILDER AND DISTRACT.

LIGHTS

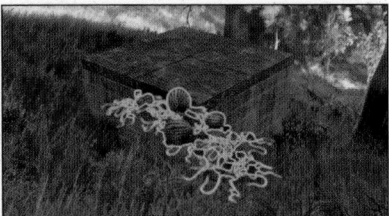

- **TYPES OF OBJECTS:** OIL LAMP, CANDLES, WALL SCONCE, LIGHTBULB, CEILING LIGHT, TRACK LIGHT, STRING OF LIGHTS, FLUORESCENT LIGHT, LAMP, CYCLING LIGHT, STROBE LIGHT CAGE WALL LIGHT, WALL LIGHT, INDUSTRIAL WALL LIGHT, SUBWAY LIGHT, TRAFFIC LIGHT, FANCY WALL LIGHT, YELLOW TABLE LAMP, BLUE TABLE LAMP, OVERSIZED NIXIE TUBE, LIGHTBOX, NEON LETTER, NEON SIGN—OPEN, MARQUEE ARROW, CAMP FIRE, MIRROR BALL, FIRE BARREL, CONSTRUCTION LIGHT, OIL LAMP POST, STREET LIGHT
- **COMPONENTS NEEDED:** CLOTH, GLASS, OIL, COPPER, STEEL, CERAMIC, WOOD

Need illumination? Then there's a whole host of lighting options, mainly split into two groups: those requiring power (usually just a power connector on the same wall or roof as the light is fixed to) and those requiring no power (candles and oil-based lighting). Naturally, you can hook up some of the cooler lights and signs (like the lightbox) to a terminal and program it to change color. Or you can create a message using neon letters, beckoning in strangers with a promise of high-value loot. Whether you keep that promise is entirely up to you!

FOOD

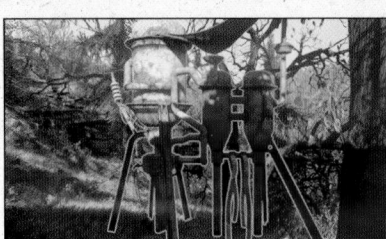

- **TYPES OF OBJECTS:** BLACKBERRY, CARROT, CORN, GOURD, MELON, MUTFRUIT PLANT, RAZORGRAIN, TATO PLANT
- **COMPONENTS NEEDED:** WILD BLACKBERRY, CARROT, CORN, GOURD, MELON, MUTFRUIT, RAZORGRAIN, TATO

While you have wilderness plants (like Soot Flowers and Glowing Fungus) that offer particular bonuses when made into a meal or drink at a cooking station, you also have a selection of crops, offering stable, free, and delicious consumables, with less chance of disease if cooked. Place them in dirt. For each point of food production in a location (always 1 at camps), one plant per cycle (17 cycles per hour) becomes harvestable. More plants allow more food storage, but not more production capacity. If you planted 17 plants at your camp, all of them would be harvestable in one hour. Remember these quickly spoil, but can be an easy meal when you return to your camp or workshop—if they haven't been harvested by someone else!

WATER

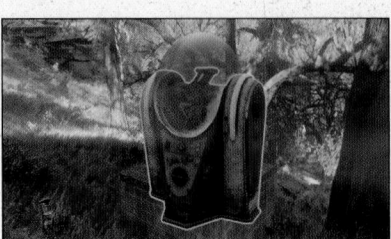

- **TYPES OF OBJECTS:** WATER PUMP, WATER PURIFIER
- **COMPONENTS NEEDED:** CONCRETE, GEAR, STEEL, CERAMIC, COPPER, OIL, RUBBER, SCREW, CLOTH

Need water quickly? Install a water pump, which allows you to obtain Dirty Water. To obtain water with no Rads, it needs to be purified. Instead of using a Chemistry Station and recipe, you could install one of three types of purifiers—small, large, or industrial—depending on how many units of water you want them to produce every hour (providing they are connected to power). This stops you from needing to forage for water once one is placed in water. Gather water frequently so they continue producing without reaching storage capacity, and keep them locked to protect from theft.

RESOURCES

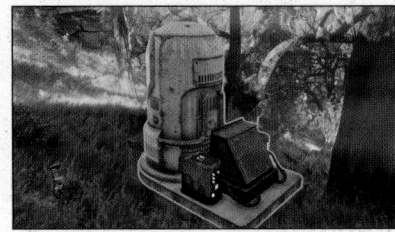

- **TYPES OF OBJECTS:** RESOURCE EXTRACTOR (COLLECTOR), SCAVENGING STATION, FERTILIZER PRODUCER
- **COMPONENTS NEEDED:** CIRCUITRY, COPPER, GEAR, STEEL, RAZORGRAIN

Are you tired of forging for items by yourself when you could have a couple of friendly Protectron types doing the work for you? Then place down one of these resource-generating machines; the Scavenging Station produces 13 junk units every hour. The fertilizer produces 25 units every hour. And if your camp or workshop is near a deposit, this menu automatically updates with a Resource Extractor (aka "Collector"), which, when powered up, will churn out a specific amount of valuable ore, mineral, or other material. Use the Locksmith perk to add locks to these devices, stopping thieves from stealing your resources.

APPLIANCES

- **TYPES OF OBJECTS:** RADIO, JUKEBOX, GRILL, ICE COOLER, CIGARETTE MACHINE, TELEVISION, STOVE, NUKA-COLA MACHINE, MILK VENDING MACHINE, EAT-O-TRONIC, TOILET, BATHTUB, ASHTRAY
- **COMPONENTS NEEDED:** CIRCUITRY, COPPER, PLASTIC, RUBBER, STEEL, ALUMINUM, WOOD, ASBESTOS, GLASS, CERAMIC

Stand-out objects in the appliance range definitely include both types of radios; switch them on and they'll either play Appalachia or Peacetime Radio, two of the stations your Pip-Boy picks up. The rest are more for decorative purposes, so if you've got a section of wall or yard that needs a large object to spruce it up a bit, drop in a toilet, ashtray, or non-working stove.

BEDS

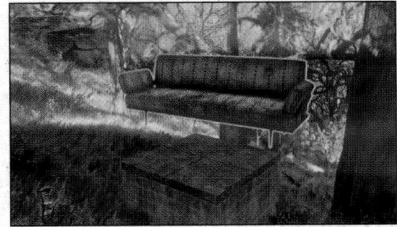

- **TYPES OF OBJECTS:** SLEEPING BAG, MATTRESS, BED, HOSPITAL BED, LARGE BED
- **COMPONENTS NEEDED:** CLOTH, WOOD, STEEL

Need a place to rest that's off the ground (so you're not susceptible to a disease) and that has the option for a Well Rested bonus? Then place some kind of sleeping quarters in your dwelling. It doesn't have to be fancy; though you can go functional or all out with a large carved bed, if space allows.

CHAIRS

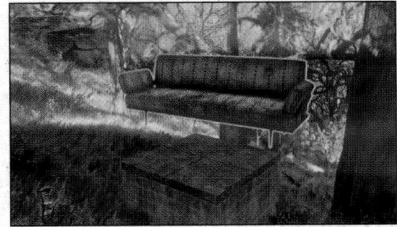

- **TYPES OF OBJECTS:** CHAIR, COUCH, LONG BENCH, STEEL BENCH, CONCRETE BENCH, STOOL, TUBA, GUITAR, DRUMS, PIANO
- **COMPONENTS NEEDED:** CLOTH, STEEL, WOOD, CONCRETE

Including airplane seats, an electric chair, rocking chairs, patio chairs, benches, pews, and couches, if you can sit on it, you can build it and add a rest spot in your abode. Don't stop there; if your plans allow, there's a number of different musical instruments you can place near a chair, and play to acquire the Well Tuned bonus. Expect a tuba, acoustic and steel guitars, a banjo, a bass, a snare drum, and an upright and a grand piano.

STASH BOXES

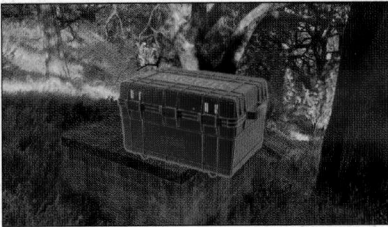

- **TYPES OF OBJECTS:** MY STASH BOX, FOOTLOCKER, COOLER, SUITCASE, TOOLBOX, SAFE, TOOL CHEST, WOODEN CRATE, LOCKER, NEWSSTAND, TRASH CAN, DESK, DRESSER, TABLE, VANITY, METAL BOX, SAFE (FLOOR), DUMPSTER, BEAR-PROOF TRASHCAN, FILE CABINET, DRESSER, CABINET, BUREAU, DESK
- **COMPONENTS NEEDED:** STEEL, WOOD, FIBERGLASS, CLOTH, GEAR, SPRING, RUBBER

Top of the list of "most important containers" is your My Stash Box, which is the key to placing and retrieving items. These all function in the same way; they are linked, no matter if they are in your camp or another location (meaning you can grab anything wherever you find one, and components in your Stash Box are used when crafting or building). Otherwise, these containers all look familiar, can be left unlocked (they can't be stolen from), and dress up your dingy hovel quite nicely.

FLOOR DECOR

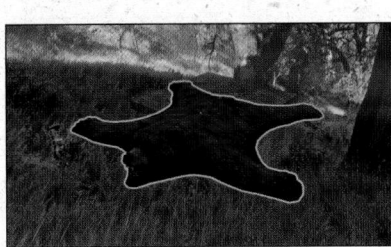

- **TYPES OF OBJECTS:** RUG, MAT, POTTED PLANT, VASE, VAULT-BOY STATUE, SPINNING WHEEL, LAWN FLAMINGO, SIGN, SCARECROW, CARDBOARD DISPLAY, BUST, VAULT-BOY LAWN GNOME, STONE PEDESTAL, STATUE (ROBED VAULT-BOY), STATUE (FEMALE), STATUE (BASEBALL PLAYER), FOUNTAIN (LARGE), LION (LARGE)
- **COMPONENTS NEEDED:** CLOTH, RUBBER, STEEL, WOOD, CERAMIC, CONCRETE, STEEL, PLASTIC, STEEL, COPPER

Designed to be placed on the ground or a table, there's a wide variety of carved object d'art. Use this for both interior and exterior placement to finish off a bare area or a field, or to act as a grand entrance, assuming you can spare the copper for those two lions and a fountain! Honor the classic Vault Boy in a variety of styles.

SHELVES

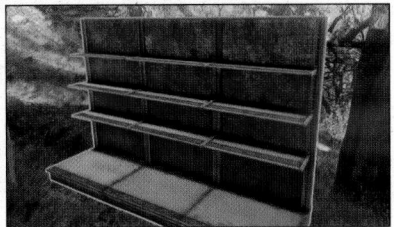

- **TYPES OF OBJECTS:** SHELF, BOOKCASE, SHELF (LARGE), MAGAZINE RACK
- **COMPONENTS NEEDED:** STEEL, WOOD, GLASS, SCREW

You can place your smaller containers on these shelving units of various styles and types. The display cases actually require power (after which, it can be opened or closed with a switch).

TABLES

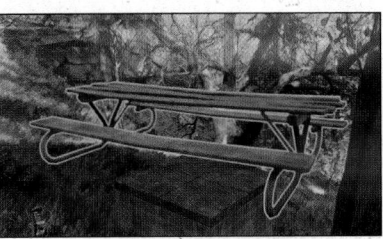

- **TYPES OF OBJECTS:** TABLE, COFFEE TABLE, END TABLE, KITCHEN TABLE, DRESSER, ORNATE TABLE, SQUARE TABLE, CONCRETE TABLE, BLACK AND WHITE ORNATE TABLE, BLACK ORNATE TABLE, RED TABLE, STEEL TABLE, DESK, ARCHITECT'S DESK, PATIO TABLE, POOL TABLE, PICNIC TABLE, STEEL PICNIC TABLE
- **COMPONENTS NEEDED:** STEEL, WOOD, PLASTIC, CONCRETE, CLOTH, RUBBER

Need something to put your lamps, radios, bric-a-brac, and containers on? Then there's a wide selection of every size, style, and (component) budget. Most are created using wood. If you want cohesiveness to your dwelling, try adding multiple types of tables of the same style. Or, vary your tables (and chairs) for that eclectic look.

TRAINING

CRAFTING AND C.A.M.P.ING

INVENTORY

QUESTS

ATLAS

BESTIARY

APPENDICES

WALL DECOR

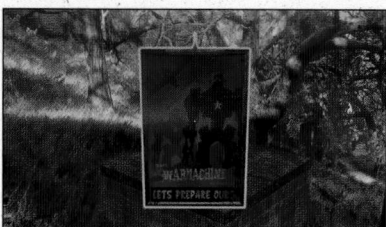

- **TYPES OF OBJECTS:** PAINTING, POSTER, POSTER (WITH LIGHT), SIGN (SMALL, METAL), U.S. FLAG, MIRROR CLOCK, SMALL LETTER/NUMBER, SMALL LETTER, SIGN, VAULT 76 POSTER, VAULT POSTER
- **COMPONENTS NEEDED:** WOOD, CLOTH, COPPER, GLASS, STEEL, SPRING, (CREATURE PARTS)

Wall decor is designed to fit on your interior and exterior walls. Add a touch of realism (and whimsy!) to your structures with some light posters (hook one of the types up to a wire). Get patriotic with the U.S. flag, or place a variety of clocks on your wall or a large selection of Vault posters.

MISC. STRUCTURES

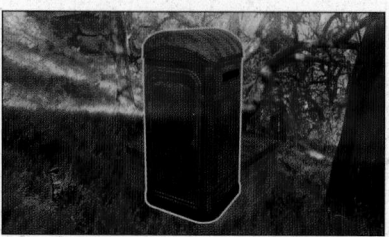

- **TYPES OF OBJECTS:** PORTABLE TOILET, BASKETBALL HOOP, TENT, FAST TRAVEL TARGET, DECONTAMINATION SHOWER
- **COMPONENTS NEEDED:** CLOTH, PLASTIC, STEEL, RUBBER, ALUMINUM, CIRCUITRY, COPPER, FIBER OPTICS

These are relatively large and functional objects, and ones that could be used to hide behind (the toilet and tent). The Fast-Travel Target is a floor mat that moves your Fast-Travel appearance spot to the mat. Use this if you want to appear at a specific location in your camp, like your Stash Box or a workbench. The decontamination shower requires power, but once activated, it will remove Rads—the perfect entrance to a camp in Toxic Valley!

PERKS AND MAGAZINES

Finally, the following table lists the available perks, along with their associated attribute and level, as well as two Magazines that are explicitly related to both camping and workshop-based activities. Be sure to have them active to get the very best bonuses to your construction.

ATTRIBUTE	PERK NAME	LEVEL	DESCRIPTION
Endurance	Homebody	19	Gain gradual health regeneration/improved health and limb regeneration while in your camp or workshop.
Endurance	Fireproof	27	Required to construct Flamethrower Trap.
Charisma	Happy Camper	3	Hunger and thirst grow 40/80% more slowly when in camp or in a team workshop.
Intelligence	Contractor	18	Crafting workshop items now cost 25/50% fewer materials.
Intelligence	Demolition Expert	10	Required to construct Laser Tripwire.
Intelligence	Grease Monkey	33	Workshop items are 30/60% cheaper to repair.
Intelligence	Locksmith	11	You can now craft Level 1/2/3 locks for your containers (plans required).
Intelligence	Science	20	Required to construct Laser Turret, Tesla Arc, Radiation Emitter
Intelligence	Wrecking Ball	29	You deal +40/80/120% damage to workshop objects.
Agility	Home Defense	22	Required to construct Heavy Machine-Gun Turret, Laser Turret, Missile Turret, Spotlight, Spring Board, Spike Trap, Tesla Arc, Flamethrower Trap, Radiation Emitter

MAGAZINE	DESCRIPTION
Backwoodsman 9	Repairs to your camp or workshop cost 50% fewer materials.
Backwoodsman 10	Turrets in your camp or workshop do 50% more damage.

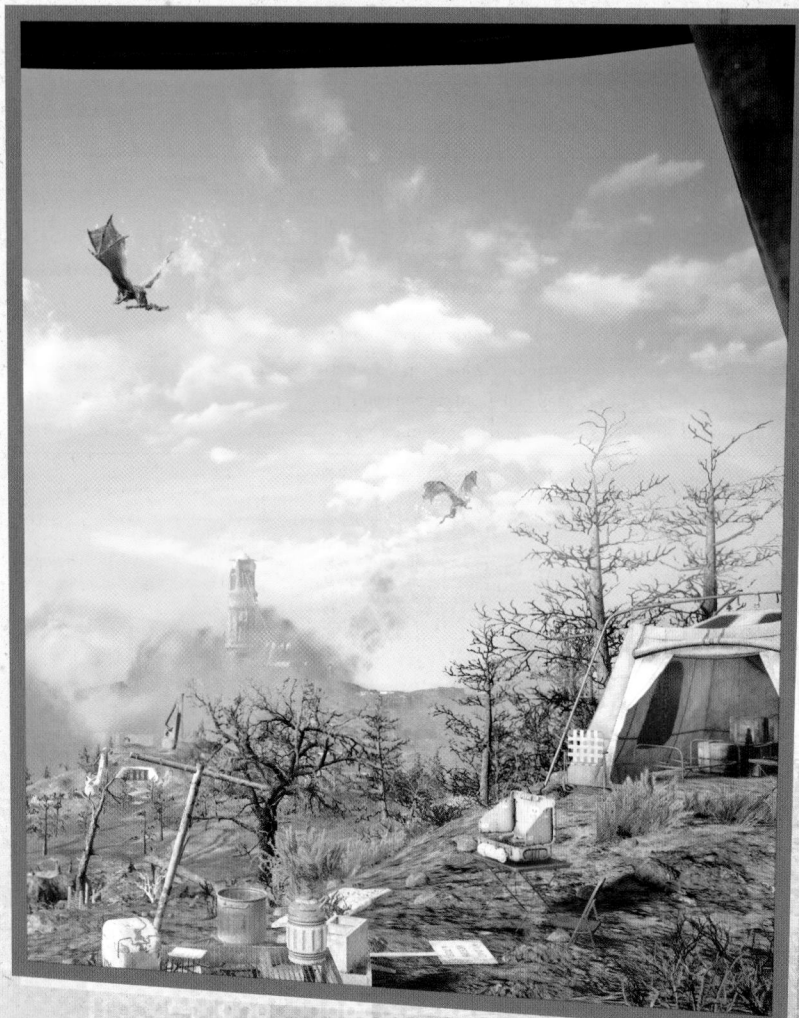

Inventory

WEAPONS

IT GOES WITHOUT SAYING THAT YOU WON'T SURVIVE THE POST-APOCALYPSE LONG WITHOUT A TRUSTY WEAPON OR TWO AT YOUR SIDE. BUT SIMPLY PICKING UP THE NEAREST POT LID AND BUTTER KNIFE ISN'T GOING TO KEEP YOU ALIVE FOR VERY LONG. THAT'S WHY KNOWLEDGE TRULY IS POWER, AND THIS CHAPTER HAS ALL THE KNOWLEDGE YOU NEED.

CRAFTING A WEAPON

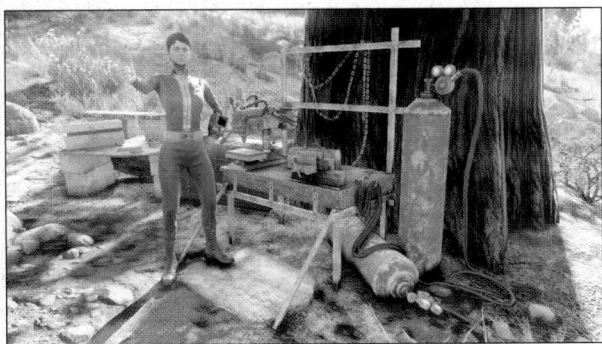

While there was plenty of crafting to go around in *Fallout 4*, crafting is an essential part of surviving in *Fallout 76*. Aside from being able to craft most of the weapons in the game, just about every weapon can be modded to suit your needs (and you definitely should mod whenever possible). However, your ability to craft anything is based on obtaining Plans, which are typically random rewards for completing Events and Daily Quests.

Plans, unfortunately, aren't the only limiters to crafting. You'll have to contend with individual level requirements, not only for using the weapon, but also for crafting it. You'll also have to keep Perk Card requirements in mind if you're working toward crafting a specific weapon or weapon type.

As you level up, you'll unlock the ability to craft weapons of higher levels. Every five levels unlocks a new level of weapon to craft, so you can craft the same weapon multiple times.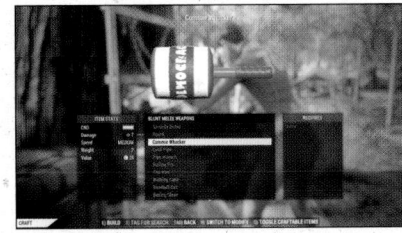

Another significant change from *Fallout 4* is how mods work. Whenever you craft a mod for a weapon, instead of the old mod automatically being placed in your inventory, it will simply disappear. Do your homework before picking mods. You may have the available parts for one mod, but how many more parts do you need for a mod that's the next step up? Is the mod you're looking at building going to give you the advantages you're hoping for? If you build it and then realize you want something else, you'll have to burn precious resources to craft a new one.

DAMAGE TYPES

You know how to craft and you have the information for how much damage a weapon can deal, but what about damage types? In addition to a weapon's damage value, you also must consider the type of damage that weapon deals. Thankfully, this is a simple system.

There are several types of damage: Radiation, Energy, Explosive, Poison, and Ballistic:

- **BALLISTIC:** THIS IS YOUR BREAD AND BUTTER DAMAGE. IT'S ON MOST WEAPONS AND IT'S EFFECTIVE AGAINST MOST ENEMIES. THINK OF THIS TYPE AS "PHYSICAL" DAMAGE. SOME ENEMIES ARE RESISTANT TO THIS TYPE; IN THIS CASE, SWAP OVER TO EITHER ENERGY OR RADIATION. BUT ASIDE FROM THOSE RARE INSTANCES, A WEAPON WITH BALLISTIC DAMAGE SHOULD ALWAYS BE IN YOUR HAND.
- **ENERGY DAMAGE:** THIS IS MORE OF A BLANKET TERM ENCOMPASSING ANY WEAPON THAT USES LASERS OR ELEMENTAL ATTACKS AS PRIMARY DAMAGE. WEAPONS WITH ICE AND FIRE ALSO FALL UNDER THE ENERGY DAMAGE UMBRELLA, THOUGH HOW EACH OF THESE SUBTYPES DEAL DAMAGE AND AFFECT ENEMIES IS DISTINCT FROM ONE ANOTHER.
- **RADIATION:** THIS IS MOST EFFECTIVE AGAINST PLAYERS, AS IT LOWERS THEIR MAXIMUM HP UNTIL THEY USE A RADAWAY. EVEN IF THEY HAVE A HEALTH ADVANTAGE ON YOU, CONTINUOUSLY USING WEAPONS WITH RADIATION WILL SLOWLY LOWER THEIR HEALTH UNTIL THEY'VE BARELY GOT A LEG TO STAND ON (SO TO SPEAK).
- **POISON:** THIS DAMAGE AFFECTS ENEMIES WELL BEYOND THE INITIAL ATTACK. ONCE STRUCK WITH A POISON WEAPON, THE ENEMY WILL CONTINUALLY TAKE DAMAGE FOR SEVERAL SECONDS, WHETHER YOU'RE HITTING THEM OR NOT. VERY FEW WEAPONS DEAL POISON DAMAGE, WHICH MIGHT BE FOR THE BEST, SINCE YOU'LL NEVER WANT TO USE IT AS A PRIMARY SOURCE OF DAMAGE ANYWAYS. IT WORKS BEST AS A WAY TO WEAKEN AN ENEMY WHILE YOU DUCK BEHIND COVER TO RELOAD OR HEAL UP.
- **EXPLOSIVE:** THIS IS THE MOST DEVASTATING DAMAGE TYPE IN TERMS OF RAW POWER. EXPLOSIVE WEAPONS DEAL SOME OF THE HIGHEST DAMAGE IN THE GAME; ANYTHING THAT UNWITTINGLY STEPS ON A MINE OR IS UNLUCKY ENOUGH TO HAVE A GRENADE ROLL BETWEEN ITS FEET WILL SUFFER MASSIVE HEALTH LOSS AND LIMB DAMAGE, IF NOT DIE OUTRIGHT. THE ONLY WAY TO SURVIVE EXPLOSIVE DAMAGE IS HAVING THE BEST ARMOR AVAILABLE TO YOU AT ALL TIMES. GET HIT WITH A WEAPON DEALING THIS DAMAGE TYPE WHILE WEARING LITTLE MORE THAN A SMILE AND YOU CAN CONSIDER YOUR EXPLORING DAYS OVER.

TRAINING

CRAFTING AND C.A.M.P.ING

INVENTORY

QUESTS

ATLAS

BESTIARY

APPENDICES

WEAPON TYPES

On top of damage types, weapons are also sorted into their own categories. While these don't provide immediate changes to combat, it's important to know your weapon's types to understand which Perk Cards to select or when to use Magazines and Bobbleheads to get the most out of your weapons.

There are 16 weapon types in all, most of which have more than one subtype. We'll list what Perk Cards work for each type, so if you're looking for information on how to get the most out of your weapon, find its type in this chapter.

GUNS AND PROJECTILE WEAPONS – OVERVIEW

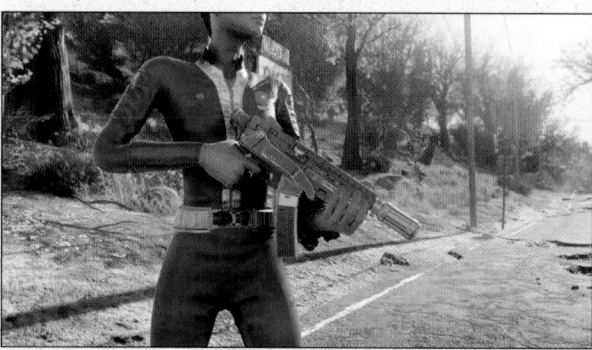

ENERGY GUNS

- CRYOLATOR
- FLAMER
- FLARE GUN
- GAMMA GUN
- GATLING LASER
- GATLING PLASMA
- GAUSS RIFLE
- LASER PISTOL
- PLASMA PISTOL
- PYROLYZER
- SALVAGED ASSAULTRON HEAD
- TESLA RIFLE
- ULTRACITE GATLING LASER
- ULTRACITE LASER PISTOL

Energy weapons fire lasers, ice, or fire. It's hard to pin down exactly what they are used for, since they come in all flavors, shapes, and sizes, but their variety is their strength. Lasers work well in penetrating enemy armor, while fire ignites enemies and ice freezes them.

If you're planning to use Energy Guns as your primary weapons, be prepared to work your way into multiple weapon categories. Every one of these weapons crosses over to another category, meaning each one will benefit from the Perk Cards of other weapon categories on top of the ones relating specifically to Energy Guns.

PERK CARDS
The perks to look out for are: ➡
- **SCIENCE (INT) SERIES OF PERK CARDS:** ALLOW YOU TO CRAFT ENERGY GUNS AND THEIR MODS WHILE REDUCING THE COST OF CRAFTING THEM.
- **BATTERIES INCLUDED (STR):** REDUCES THE TOTAL WEIGHT OF ALL ENERGY GUN AMMO.

EXPLOSIVE

- AUTO GRENADE LAUNCHER
- BROADSIDER
- BUNKER BUSTER
- DAISY CUTTER
- ENCLAVE PLASMA GUN
- FAT MAN
- FLARE GUN
- M79 GRENADE LAUNCHER
- MISSILE LAUNCHER

Explosive weapons could almost be considered a subcategory of Heavy Guns. A lot of what applies to those weapons applies to these as well. The Perk Cards that work here typically encompass all explosive weapons, including mines and grenades, so you're getting a little extra bang for your buck (it had to be done).

PERK CARDS
The perks of the trade are: ➡
- **DEMOLITION EXPERT (INT):** INCREASES ALL DAMAGE DEALT BY YOUR EXPLOSIVES
- **GRENADIER (PER):** INCREASES THE EXPLOSION RADIUS OF ANY EXPLOSIVE YOU USE.

EXOTIC WEAPONS

- BLACK POWDER BLUNDERBUSS
- BLACK POWDER PISTOL
- BLACK POWDER RIFLE
- BROADSIDER
- CROSSBOW
- GAUSS RIFLE
- HARPOON GUN
- PADDLE BALL
- RADIUM RIFLE
- RAILWAY RIFLE
- ROSE'S SYRINGER
- SALVAGED ASSAULTRON HEAD
- SYRINGER
- THE DRAGON
- VOX SYRINGER

Exotic Weapons cover the strange, different, and special. A good rule of thumb is if it can't be properly categorized, it's probably an Exotic Weapon.

Most Exotic Weapons fall under other umbrellas, so you won't find a lot of perks relating to weapons in this category. The only ones you'll find are the Exotic Weapons (INT) series of Perk Cards, which allow you to craft Exotic Weapons and progressively reduce their crafting costs as you get better cards.

HEAVY GUNS

- 50 CAL MACHINE GUN
- AUTO GRENADE LAUNCHER
- BUNKER BUSTER
- CRYOLATOR
- DAISY CUTTER
- FAT MAN
- FLAMER
- GATLING GUN
- GATLING LASER
- GATLING PLASMA
- HARPOON GUN
- LIGHT MACHINE GUN
- MINIGUN
- MISSILE LAUNCHER
- PYROLYZER
- TESLA RIFLE
- ULTRACITE GATLING LASER

These are the big bads of the weapons world. Where other weapon categories will allow for a certain level of flexibility, using Heavy Guns is a commitment of SPECIAL points, Perk Cards, and carrying capacity. What you get in exchange is a series of weapons that will decimate most things on the field. You won't be fast, you won't be accurate, but dang it you'll hit like a wrecking ball!

There is a lot of crossover between Heavy Guns, Explosive Weapons, and Energy Guns, so look at those sections if you're trying to maximize your Heavy Gunning potential.

PERK CARDS | The Perk Cards of the trade are: ⬇

- **LOCK AND LOAD (STR):** INCREASE RELOAD SPEED ON HEAVY GUNS.
- **ONE GUN ARMY (LCK):** GIVES YOU A CHANCE TO STAGGER ENEMIES AND CRIPPLE THEIR LIMBS WITH YOUR BULLETS.
- **STABILIZED (INT):** INCREASES YOUR ACCURACY AND ALLOWS YOUR HEAVY GUNS TO IGNORE A CERTAIN PERCENTAGE OF ENEMY ARMOR WHILE YOU'RE IN POWER ARMOR.
- **BEAR ARMS (STR):** REDUCES THE TOTAL WEIGHT OF YOUR HEAVY GUNS BY A SUBSTANTIAL AMOUNT.
- **BULLET SHIELD (STR):** INCREASES YOUR DAMAGE RESISTANCE WHILE YOU FIRE A HEAVY GUN.
- **HEAVY GUNNER (STR) SERIES OF PERK CARDS:** INCREASE THE DAMAGE OF YOUR NON-EXPLOSIVE HEAVY GUNS. THERE ARE PERK CARDS THAT SPECIFICALLY RAISE EXPLOSIVE DAMAGE THAT AFFECTS YOUR EXPLOSIVE HEAVY GUNS.

STR is going to be your primary SPECIAL stat, but Heavy Guns encompass a wide variety of weapons, so you might also consider looking at the Explosive and Energy Gun sections to see if there are any Perk Cards relating to your preferred weapons.

Also look to Perk Cards relating to Power Armor and resistances. Heavy Guns leave you exposed either while firing, reloading, or both. Being able to soak up damage is a must if you hope to stay alive.

PIPE GUNS

- **PIPE BOLT-ACTION PISTOL**
- **PIPE PISTOL**
- **PIPE REVOLVER**
- **ROSE'S SYRINGER**
- **SYRINGER**
- **VOX SYRINGER**

"Pipe Guns" functions more as a secondary label than its own unique weapon category. All of the Pipe Guns listed here fall under the Pistol category, meaning they benefit from the same perks. If you're looking to use Pipe Guns as your main mode of attack, look to the Pistols section to learn about what Perk Cards work for them.

There is one specific Perk Card that relates to Pipe Guns: Licensed Plumber (INT). This decreases the speed at which Pipe Guns degrade and decreases the costs of repairing them.

PISTOLS

Pistols are some of the most moddable and versatile weapons in the game. They can change into Automatic Rifles, Sniper Rifles, Non-Automatic Rifles, Automatic Pistols, and back again.

PERK CARDS | The Perk Cards of choice for all Pistol-wielding explorers are: ⬇

- **CRACKSHOT (PER):** INCREASES YOUR FIRING RANGING AND ACCURACY WHEN AIMING DOWN THE SIGHTS OF A PISTOL.
- **MODERN RENEGADE (AGI):** INCREASES HIP-FIRE ACCURACY AND GIVES YOU A CHANCE TO CRIPPLE ENEMY LIMBS WITH A SINGLE SHOT.
- **PACKIN' LIGHT (STR):** REDUCES THE WEIGHT OF YOUR PISTOLS, GIVING YOU THE OPPORTUNITY TO CARRY MORE PISTOLS WITH YOU FOR VERSATILITY OR FOR ADDED LOOT SPACE.

Those looking to use Pistols primarily will want to put their SPECIAL points into AGI primarily, with a handful of points into STR and PER for the Packin' Light and Crackshot Perk Cards.

AUTOMATIC PISTOLS

- **10 MM SUBMACHINE GUN**
- **PERFECT STORM**
- **SUBMACHINE GUN**
- **ANTI-SCORCHED TRAINING PISTOL**

Automatic Pistols are known for their high rate of fire and large ammo capacity. You're won't be sniping enemies with one, but if you're doing a lot of up-close-and-personal play, you'll find a lot to love here.

Any Pistol that can have an Automatic Receiver Mod applied to it can become an Automatic Pistol. If these are your preferred weapons, consider using the Guerrilla (AGI) series of Perk Cards. They increase your total damage done using Automatic Pistols and are stackable.

NON-AUTOMATIC PISTOLS

- **.44 PISTOL**
- **10 MM PISTOL**
- **BLACK POWDER PISTOL**
- **ENCLAVE PLASMA GUN**
- **GAMMA GUN**
- **LASER PISTOL**
- **PIPE BOLT-ACTION PISTOL**
- **PIPE PISTOL**
- **PIPE REVOLVER**
- **PLASMA PISTOL**
- **SINGLE ACTION REVOLVER**
- **SOMERSET SPECIAL**
- **ULTRACITE LASER PISTOL**
- **VOICE OF SET**
- **WESTERN REVOLVER**

These are excellent backup weapons, but anyone trying to create a character exclusively around Non-Automatic Pistols is in for a real challenge. That being said, if you are serious about using these weapons, you'll want to invest in the Gunslinger (AGI) series of Perk Cards, which increase your damage dealt with Non-Automatic Pistols.

RIFLES

Any weapon that can have a Stock mod applied to it is actually considered a Rifle, which means they also receive benefits from Rifle-based Perk Cards. You'll find that Pistols convert to Rifles more frequently than weapons of other types, so if you're looking for new Rifles to work with, start there first.

PERK CARDS | All Rifles benefit from several nonspecific Rifle Perk Cards: ⬇

- **LONG SHOT (PER):** INCREASES YOUR RANGE AND ACCURACY WHEN AIMING DOWN THE SIGHTS.
- **TANK KILLER (PER):** GIVES YOUR RIFLES INCREASED ARMOR PENETRATION AND HAS A HIGHER CHANCE TO STAGGER ENEMIES. BEST OF ALL, IT WORKS FOR ALL RIFLES!
- **TORMENTOR (LCK):** GIVES A CHANCE TO CRIPPLE LIMBS WITH A SINGLE SHOT FROM A RIFLE.

There are other Perk Cards that only work with Automatic or Non-Automatic rifles, but you'll find more information about those ahead.

Those looking to build a Rifle-focused character will want to focus more on PER as their main SPECIAL stat, with a few LCK points for Tormentor.

AUTOMATIC RIFLES

Looking at this list, you'll undoubtedly notice how empty it is. That's not because there are no Automatic Rifles that can be obtained in the game. It's because Non-Automatic Rifles, after being modified with an Automatic Receiver, become Automatic Rifles. Once you've slapped on that mod, all of the Perk Cards involving Automatic Rifles will apply.

PERK CARDS ➜ | For those looking to make the Automatic Rifles their main method of offensive, the Commando (PER) series of Perk Cards (which increase damage dealt with Automatic Rifles) will be your main point of focus.

As we mentioned before, any Pistol or Pipe Gun that has had a Rifle Stock mod applied to it is now considered a part of the Rifle family. Slap an Automatic Receiver and it's now an Automatic Rifle. Aren't mods grand?

NON-AUTOMATIC RIFLES

- **ASSAULT RIFLE**
- **BLACK POWDER RIFLE**
- **BROTHERHOOD RECON RIFLE**
- **COMBAT RIFLE**
- **GAUSS RIFLE**
- **HANDMADE RIFLE**
- **HUNTING RIFLE**
- **LEVER ACTION RIFLE**
- **RADIUM RIFLE**
- **THE DRAGON**

Most Rifles available in the game start out as Non-Automatic Rifles. They can be modded to become Automatic Rifles, but you can rest assured that if you find a Rifle in the wild, it's almost certainly going to fall under the Non-Automatic category.

As far as Non-Automatic Rifle Perk Cards are concerned, focus on the Rifleman (PER) series of Perk Cards, which increase your damage with Non-Automatic Rifles and are stackable. For additional benefits, you'll need to rely on general Rifle Perk Cards, like Tormentor, Long Shot (PER) and Tank Killer (PER).

TRAINING

CRAFTING AND C.A.M.P.ING

INVENTORY

QUESTS

ATLAS

BESTIARY

APPENDICES

SHOTGUNS

- BLACK POWDER BLUNDERBUSS
- CIVIL UNREST
- COMBAT SHOTGUN
- DOUBLE-BARREL SHOTGUN
- PUMP ACTION SHOTGUN

Shotguns are close-quarters weapons that pack a huge punch, but often have lengthy reload times, slow firing speeds, and limited ammo capacity. The damage they deal more than makes up for these cons, but you'll need to take those cons into account if you hope to use them effectively and avoid putting yourself in a bad position.

PERK CARDS
Perk Cards of note are: ➡

- ENFORCER (AGI): INCREASES YOUR CHANCE TO STAGGER ENEMIES AND CRIPPLE LIMBS.
- SCATTERSHOT (STR): LOWERS THE TOTAL WEIGHT OF YOUR SHOTGUNS AND INCREASES THEIR RELOAD SPEED.
- SHOTGUNNER (STR) SERIES: BOOSTS DAMAGE DEALT WITH SHOTGUNS.
- SKEET SHOOTER (PER): INCREASES YOUR ACCURACY AND REDUCES BULLET SPREAD.

Those looking to mainly Shotguns will want to focus their SPECIAL points into STR and AGI, while also adding a few points into PER for the Skeet Shooter Perk Card.

GUNS AND PROJECTILE WEAPONS

.44 PISTOL

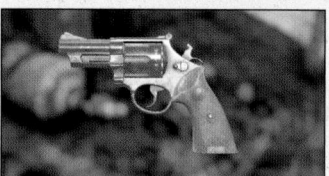

- STANDARD MODEL: SNUBNOSED .44 PISTOL
- TYPE 1: NON-AUTOMATIC PISTOL
- TYPE 2: —
- MINIMUM LEVEL: 5
- CRAFTING LEVEL: 5
- DAMAGE: 49 (BALLISTIC)
- AMMO: .44
- FIRE RATE: 6
- RANGE: 84 OR 156
- ACCURACY: 62 OR 63
- WEIGHT: 4.3
- VALUE: 36

This standard six-shooter won't turn any heads, but if you manage to get your hands on one of these early in the game, you'll have a pretty hefty damage dealer (as far as Pistols are concerned).

ATTACHABLE MOD TYPES ➡
- RECEIVER
- GRIP
- PAINT
- BARREL
- SIGHTS

10 MM PISTOL

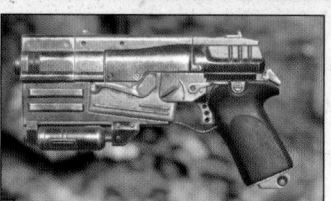

- STANDARD MODEL: 10 MM PISTOL
- TYPE 1: NON-AUTOMATIC PISTOL
- TYPE 2: —
- MINIMUM LEVEL: 5
- CRAFTING LEVEL: 15
- DAMAGE: 16 (BALLISTIC)
- AMMO: 10 MM
- FIRE RATE: 43
- RANGE: 120 OR 228
- ACCURACY: 61 OR 62
- WEIGHT: 4.3
- VALUE: 39

Unmodded, the 10 mm Pistol has modest damage but a solid rate of fire. You'll reload the 12-round magazine quickly and get back to firing without a hitch. This handgun really shines in its wealth of modding possibilities. You can specialize this weapon in just about any way you can hope for, from silenced and stealthy to full-auto. While it doesn't stack up to the guns you'll find later in your journey, it's a faithful friend for the earlier parts.

ATTACHABLE MOD TYPES ➡
- RECEIVER
- BARREL
- GRIP
- MAGAZINE
- SIGHTS
- MUZZLE
- PAINT

10 MM SUBMACHINE GUN

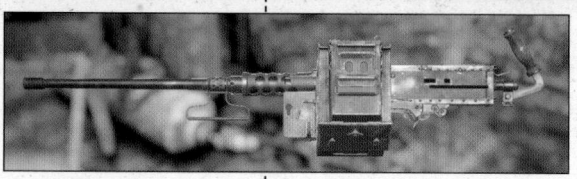

- STANDARD MODEL: SHORT 10 MM SUBMACHINE GUN
- TYPE 1: AUTOMATIC PISTOL
- TYPE 2: —
- MINIMUM LEVEL: 10
- CRAFTING LEVEL: 30
- CRAFTING RESTRICTIONS: GUERRILLA 1 (AGI)
- DAMAGE: 12 (BALLISTIC)
- AMMO: 10 MM ROUND
- FIRE RATE: 91
- RANGE: 84 OR 156
- ACCURACY: 47
- WEIGHT: 6.2
- VALUE: 97

It may lack in accuracy, but the 10 mm Submachine Gun fires bullets faster than you can count them. If you can get up close, you can watch enemy health simply melt away. Great for clearing interiors and for those looking for a more up-close-and-personal approach.

ATTACHABLE MOD TYPES ➡
- RECEIVER
- BARREL
- STOCK
- MAGAZINE

50 CAL MACHINE GUN

- STANDARD MODEL: 50 CAL MACHINE GUN
- TYPE 1: HEAVY GUN
- TYPE 2: —
- MINIMUM LEVEL: 25
- CRAFTING LEVEL: 30
- CRAFTING RESTRICTIONS: HEAVY GUNNER 1 (STR), COMMANDO 1 (PER)
- DAMAGE: 18 (BALLISTIC)
- AMMO: .50 CALIBER
- FIRE RATE: 91
- RANGE: 204 OR 395
- ACCURACY: 36 OR 37
- WEIGHT: 28.8
- VALUE: 183

The middle ground between an Automatic Rifle and a Gatling Gun, the 50 Cal is more than capable of standing tall when paired next to its distant cousins. You won't have to worry about spinning up the barrel to get this weapon screaming, but you will have to consider a low accuracy value and its overall size in your inventory. While its firing spread isn't as bad as other Heavy Guns, it's not a weapon to use for situations demanding carefully placed shots.

ATTACHABLE MOD TYPES ➡
- BARREL
- MUZZLE

ANTI-SCORCHED TRAINING PISTOL

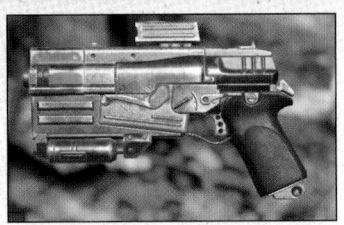

- **STANDARD MODEL:** ANTI-SCORCHED TRAINING PISTOL
- **TYPE 1:** AUTOMATIC PISTOL
- **TYPE 2:** –
- **MINIMUM LEVEL:** 1
- **CRAFTING LEVEL:** –
- **DAMAGE:** 12 (BALLISTIC)
- **AMMO:** 10 MM
- **FIRE RATE:** 75
- **RANGE:** 108
- **ACCURACY:** 64
- **WEIGHT:** 4.4
- **VALUE:** 196

This is a standard 10 mm Pistol with a Scorched-busting twist. Obtained during Main Quest: Into the Fire, this pistol deals an extra 25% damage to any Scorched you use it against, but all other enemy types will take 20% *less* damage with it. It's good for the earlier parts of the game if you encounter an abundance of Scorched (and you will).

ATTACHABLE MOD TYPES ➡ — **NONE**

ASSAULT RIFLE

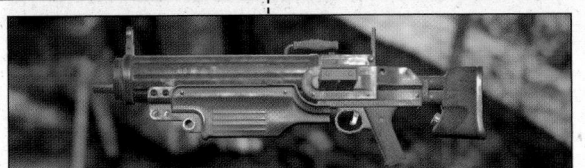

- **STANDARD MODEL:** SHORT ASSAULT RIFLE
- **TYPE 1:** NON-AUTOMATIC RIFLE
- **TYPE 2:** –
- **MINIMUM LEVEL:** 30
- **CRAFTING LEVEL:** 30
- **CRAFTING RESTRICTIONS:** RIFLEMAN 1 (PER)
- **DAMAGE:** 17 (BALLISTIC)
- **AMMO:** 5.56 AMMO
- **FIRE RATE:** 40
- **RANGE:** 120 OR 228
- **ACCURACY:** 65
- **WEIGHT:** 13.2
- **VALUE:** 199

Heavy, but very reliable, the Assault Rifle has a quick fire rate and decent accuracy. Mod it out and you can really make this weapon shine. Without an Automatic Receiver, this weapon is best served as a mid- to long-range weapon. Start experimenting with the mods, however, and you'll have a truly flexible weapon at your disposal.

ATTACHABLE MOD TYPES ➡ — **RECEIVER**   — **MAGAZINE**
— **BARREL**   — **SIGHTS**
— **STOCK**   — **MUZZLE**

AUTO GRENADE LAUNCHER

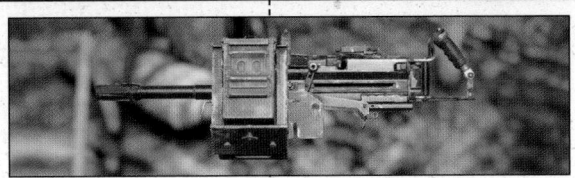

- **STANDARD MODEL:** AUTO GRENADE LAUNCHER
- **TYPE 1:** EXPLOSIVE
- **TYPE 2:** HEAVY GUN
- **CRAFTING RESTRICTIONS:** DEMOLITION EXPERT 1 (PER)
- **MINIMUM LEVEL:** 40
- **CRAFTING LEVEL:** 40
- **DAMAGE:** 118 (BALLISTIC)
- **AMMO:** 40MM AMMO
- **FIRE RATE:** 91
- **RANGE:** 395
- **ACCURACY:** 49
- **WEIGHT:** 18
- **VALUE:** 228

While it may fire slower than you might expect, the Auto Grenade Launcher is a powerhouse of violence and destruction. The ability to fire off a grenade round without having to wait for a lengthy reload makes this thing a nasty beast on the battlefield. Your greatest concern will almost certainly be trying to avoid blowing yourself straight to hell and back.

ATTACHABLE MOD TYPES ➡ — **BARREL**   — **GRIP**   — **MUZZLE**

BLACK POWDER BLUNDERBUSS

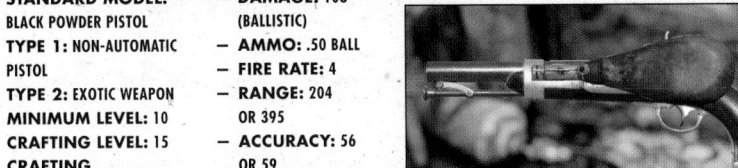

- **STANDARD MODEL:** BLACK POWDER BLUNDERBUSS
- **TYPE 1:** SHOTGUN
- **TYPE 2:** EXOTIC WEAPON
- **MINIMUM LEVEL:** 10
- **CRAFTING LEVEL:** –
- **CRAFTING RESTRICTIONS:** EXOTIC WEAPONS 1 (INT)
- **DAMAGE:** 108 (BALLISTIC)
- **AMMO:** .50 BALL
- **FIRE RATE:** 4
- **RANGE:** 12
- **ACCURACY:** 67
- **WEIGHT:** 3
- **VALUE:** 36

This packs a punch but comes at the cost of ammo capacity and reload speed. Luckily aiming isn't much of a factor in using a Blunderbuss, but if you don't take down your enemy in one shot, you might find yourself fleeing for your life. Take this weapon along with an immediate backup at the ready.

ATTACHABLE MOD TYPES ➡ — **NONE**

BLACK POWDER PISTOL

- **STANDARD MODEL:** BLACK POWDER PISTOL
- **TYPE 1:** NON-AUTOMATIC PISTOL
- **TYPE 2:** EXOTIC WEAPON
- **MINIMUM LEVEL:** 10
- **CRAFTING LEVEL:** 15
- **CRAFTING RESTRICTIONS:** EXOTIC WEAPONS 1 (INT)
- **DAMAGE:** 108 (BALLISTIC)
- **AMMO:** .50 BALL
- **FIRE RATE:** 4
- **RANGE:** 204 OR 395
- **ACCURACY:** 56 OR 59
- **WEIGHT:** 3
- **VALUE:** 53

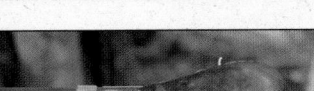

This is a powerful but incredibly slow Pistol. You'll have one shot in the chamber before having to reload—one shot to take your enemies out. Fail to land that shot and you'll be a sitting duck. Take this if you like the thrill and pressure of never being able to miss a shot. For everyone else, there are safe, more practical guns to keep at your hip.

ATTACHABLE MOD TYPES ➡ — **NONE**

TRAINING

CRAFTING AND C.A.M.P.ing

INVENTORY

QUESTS

ATLAS

BESTIARY

APPENDICES

BLACK POWDER RIFLE

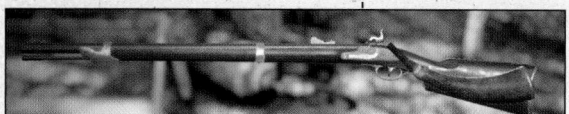

- **STANDARD MODEL:** BLACK POWDER RIFLE
- **TYPE 1:** EXOTIC WEAPON
- **TYPE 2:** NON-AUTOMATIC RIFLE
- **MINIMUM LEVEL:** 15
- **CRAFTING LEVEL:** 20
- **CRAFTING RESTRICTIONS:** EXOTIC WEAPONS 1 (INT)
- **DAMAGE:** 132 (BALLISTIC)
- **AMMO:** .50 BALL
- **FIRE RATE:** 4
- **RANGE:** 204 OR 395
- **ACCURACY:** 64 OR 67
- **WEIGHT:** 6
- **VALUE:** 98

Terribly powerful for a rifle but painfully slow on the reload, the Black Powder Rifle is more of a specialist's weapon than something sure and steady. If you've ever wanted the thrill of living or dying by the skill of your shots, look no further.

ATTACHABLE MOD TYPES ➡ — LARGE BAYONET

COMBAT SHOTGUN

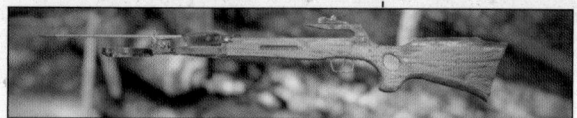

- **STANDARD MODEL:** COMBAT SHOTGUN
- **TYPE 1:** SHOTGUN
- **TYPE 2:** —
- **MINIMUM LEVEL:** 20
- **CRAFTING LEVEL:** 20
- **CRAFTING RESTRICTIONS:** SHOTGUNNER 1 (STR)
- **DAMAGE:** 61 (BALLISTIC)
- **AMMO:** SHELL
- **FIRE RATE:** 20
- **RANGE:** 72 OR 180
- **ACCURACY:** 10 OR 12 OR 22
- **WEIGHT:** 11.9
- **VALUE:** 148

The more practical and deadly of the shotgun family, the Combat Shotgun lacks most of the shortcomings of its brothers and sisters while adding a slew of benefits of its own. If you're looking for the unquestionable king of close-quarters, you've come to the right place.

ATTACHABLE MOD TYPES ➡
- RECEIVER
- SHORT BARREL
- STOCK
- MAGAZINE
- SIGHTS
- MUZZLE

BROADSIDER

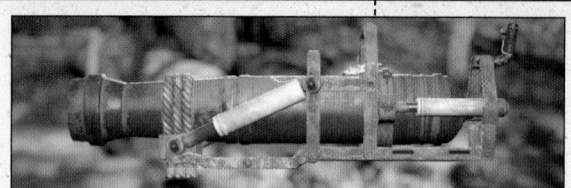

- **STANDARD MODEL:** BROADSIDER
- **TYPE 1:** EXPLOSIVE
- **TYPE 2:** EXOTIC WEAPON
- **MINIMUM LEVEL:** 25
- **CRAFTING LEVEL:** 40
- **CRAFTING RESTRICTIONS:** EXOTIC WEAPONS 1 (INT)
- **DAMAGE:** 104 (BALLISTIC)
- **AMMO:** CANNONBALL
- **FIRE RATE:** 3
- **RANGE:** 204 OR 395
- **ACCURACY:** 60 OR 62
- **WEIGHT:** 24.4
- **VALUE:** 139

This portable ship's cannon has a low fire rate, high reload time, and minimal explosive potential. It's not a bad weapon, but if you really want to get the most out of it, we've got two simple words for you: don't miss.

ATTACHABLE MOD TYPES ➡
- BARREL
- GRIP
- SHOT CANISTER

CROSSBOW

- **STANDARD MODEL:** CROSSBOW
- **TYPE 1:** EXOTIC WEAPON
- **TYPE 2:** —
- **MINIMUM LEVEL:** 15
- **CRAFTING LEVEL:** 15
- **CRAFTING RESTRICTIONS:** EXOTIC WEAPONS 1 (INT)
- **DAMAGE:** 100 (BALLISTIC)
- **AMMO:** BOLT
- **FIRE RATE:** 4
- **RANGE:** 168 OR 359
- **ACCURACY:** 67
- **WEIGHT:** 7.2
- **VALUE:** 70

This weapon is quiet and powerful but slow to fire. A great weapon for sneaky players, but hard to justify once you've been spotted. On the plus side, you can recollect any bolts you fire, which will keep you firing that much longer.

ATTACHABLE MOD TYPES ➡ — NONE

COMBAT RIFLE

- **STANDARD MODEL:** SHORT COMBAT RIFLE
- **TYPE 1:** NON-AUTOMATIC RIFLE
- **TYPE 2:** —
- **MINIMUM LEVEL:** 20
- **CRAFTING LEVEL:** 20
- **CRAFTING RESTRICTIONS:** COMMANDO 1 (PER)
- **DAMAGE:** 27 (BALLISTIC)
- **AMMO:** .45 AMMO
- **FIRE RATE:** 33
- **RANGE:** 120 OR 228
- **ACCURACY:** 61
- **WEIGHT:** 11.2
- **VALUE:** 168

Slower out of the box than an Assault Rifle but with higher damage potential, the Combat Rifle is just as flexible as its predecessor. You might get more out of it as a long-range weapon, but it will suit all of your needs with a few mod tweaks.

ATTACHABLE MOD TYPES ⬇
- RECEIVER
- BARREL
- STOCK
- MAGAZINE
- SIGHTS
- MUZZLE

CRYOLATOR

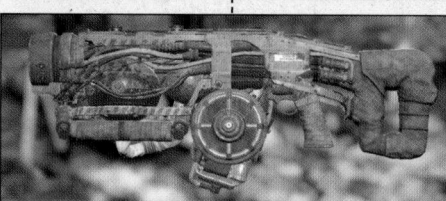

- **STANDARD MODEL:** CRYOLATOR
- **TYPE 1:** HEAVY GUN
- **TYPE 2:** ENERGY GUN
- **MINIMUM LEVEL:** 25
- **CRAFTING LEVEL:** 25
- **DAMAGE:** 14 (ENERGY)
- **AMMO:** CRYO
- **FIRE RATE:** 286
- **RANGE:** 120 OR 228
- **ACCURACY:** 56 OR 58
- **WEIGHT:** 13.3
- **VALUE:** 157

The ice to the Flamer's fire, the Cryolator fires a concentrated blast of liquid hydrogen to chill enemies to the bone (or to their processor, as the case may be). You'll have to be careful of the limited range to avoid getting caught out by attackers; in close-range, however, the Cryolator definitely keeps it cool.

ATTACHABLE MOD TYPES ➡ — BARREL — STOCK — SIGHTS

DOUBLE-BARREL SHOTGUN

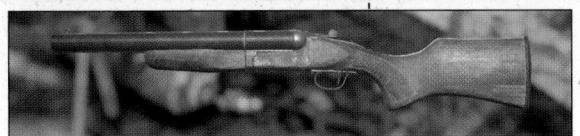

- **STANDARD MODEL:** SHORT DOUBLE-BARREL SHOTGUN
- **TYPE 1:** SHOTGUN
- **TYPE 2:** –
- **MINIMUM LEVEL:** 15
- **CRAFTING LEVEL:** 15
- **CRAFTING RESTRICTIONS:** SHOTGUNNER 1 (STR)
- **DAMAGE:** 87 (BALLISTIC)
- **AMMO:** SHELL
- **FIRE RATE:** 36
- **RANGE:** 180
- **ACCURACY:** 0
- **WEIGHT:** 9.6
- **VALUE:** 34

Quick to fire but slow to reload, the Double-Barrel Shotgun is a powerhouse as close range, especially when dealing with melee enemies. If a Super Mutant Berserk comes barreling down on you, draw this elephant's trunk out and drop them like the Sunday paper. Just make sure not to miss.

ATTACHABLE MOD TYPES ⬇
- RECEIVER
- BARREL
- STOCK
- SIGHTS
- MUZZLE

THE DRAGON

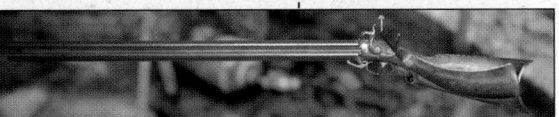

- **STANDARD MODEL:** THE DRAGON
- **TYPE 1:** EXOTIC WEAPON
- **TYPE 2:** NON-AUTOMATIC RIFLE
- **MINIMUM LEVEL:** 35
- **CRAFTING LEVEL:** 35
- **CRAFTING RESTRICTIONS:** EXOTIC WEAPONS 1 (INT)
- **DAMAGE:** 170
- **AMMO:** .50 BALL AMMO
- **FIRE RATE:** 4
- **RANGE:** 419
- **ACCURACY:** 65
- **WEIGHT:** 6
- **VALUE:** 36

The Dragon is practically a cannon in terms of both damage and the time it takes to reload. It will take huge chunks out of just about anything you hit with it, but the reload is maybe the longest out of any weapon in the game. Like the other Black Powder weapons, we suggest you use this weapon only if you've got something to prove.

ATTACHABLE MOD TYPES ➡ – LARGE BAYONET

ENCLAVE PLASMA GUN

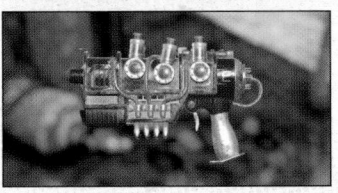

- **STANDARD MODEL:** SHORT ENCLAVE PLASMA GUN
- **TYPE 1:** NON-AUTOMATIC PISTOL
- **TYPE 2:** ENERGY GUN
- **MINIMUM LEVEL:** 25
- **CRAFTING LEVEL:** –
- **DAMAGE:** 18 (BALLISTIC), 18 (ENERGY)
- **AMMO:** PLASMA
- **FIRE RATE:** 33
- **RANGE:** 120 OR 228
- **ACCURACY:** 146
- **WEIGHT:** 4
- **VALUE:** 102

The Enclave Plasma Gun deals both Ballistic and Energy damage, making it a real powerhouse that's suited for most combat situations. Going up against a heavily armored enemy? The Energy damage will cut through them like butter while the Ballistic damage can handle enemies that eat energy damage for breakfast. Don't ignore this weapon if it lands in your lap. Its potential for damage is higher than it might seem at first blush.

ATTACHABLE MOD TYPES ➡
- CAPACITOR
- BARREL
- GRIP
- SIGHTS

FAT MAN

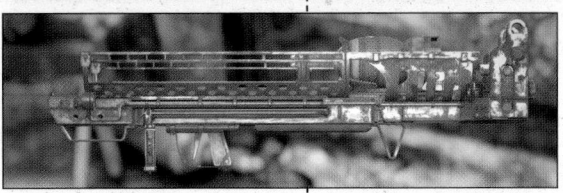

- **STANDARD MODEL:** FAT MAN
- **TYPE 1:** HEAVY GUN
- **TYPE 2:** EXPLOSIVE
- **MINIMUM LEVEL:** 25
- **CRAFTING LEVEL:** 25
- **CRAFTING RESTRICTIONS:** SCIENCE 1 (INT), DEMOLITION EXPERT 1 (INT)
- **DAMAGE:** 473 (BALLISTIC)
- **AMMO:** MININUKE
- **FIRE RATE:** 4
- **RANGE:** 117
- **ACCURACY:** 61
- **WEIGHT:** 20.5
- **VALUE:** 249

A mininuke-launching device of pure devastation. While its reload times are lengthy and its ammo both scarce and expensive, if you do decide to take the "nuclear option," you can be sure that nothing will be around to tell the tale.

ATTACHABLE MOD TYPES ⬇
- BOWLING BALL LAUNCHER
- MIRV LAUNCHER

FLAMER

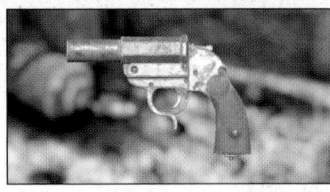

- **STANDARD MODEL:** SHORT FLAMER
- **TYPE 1:** ENERGY GUN
- **TYPE 2:** HEAVY GUN
- **MINIMUM LEVEL:** 30
- **CRAFTING LEVEL:** 30
- **DAMAGE:** 26 (ENERGY)
- **AMMO:** FUEL
- **FIRE RATE:** 91
- **RANGE:** 72
- **ACCURACY:** 53
- **WEIGHT:** 16.1
- **VALUE:** 131

Quick to burn but slow to fire, the Flamer relies as much on burning damage as much as direct damage. Your best bet is to start an enemy on fire, then take cover while the flames do their job. Shoot a few more burst rounds to keep the baddie cooking and you'll see exactly what this blowtorch can do.

ATTACHABLE MOD TYPES ➡
- TANK
- BARREL
- PROPELLANT TANK
- NOZZLE

FLARE GUN

- **STANDARD MODEL:** FLARE GUN
- **TYPE 1:** NON-AUTOMATIC PISTOL
- **TYPE 2:** EXPLOSIVE
- **MINIMUM LEVEL:** 1
- **CRAFTING LEVEL:** 1
- **DAMAGE:** 5 (BALLISTIC)
- **AMMO:** FLARE
- **FIRE RATE:** 6
- **RANGE:** 147
- **ACCURACY:** 74
- **WEIGHT:** 2
- **VALUE:** 41

More of a means to light darkened areas than to fend of enemies, the Flare Gun does exactly what you'd expect it to. You'll find its single-round chamber and sluggish reload time make it difficult to keep in your pocket at all times, but its ability to light enemies on fire definitely compensates for its lack of a damage value.

ATTACHABLE MOD TYPES ➡ – NONE

GAMMA GUN

- **STANDARD MODEL:** SHORT GAMMA GUN
- **TYPE 1:** NON-AUTOMATIC PISTOL
- **TYPE 2:** ENERGY GUN
- **MINIMUM LEVEL:** 15
- **CRAFTING LEVEL:** 25
- **CRAFTING RESTRICTIONS:** SCIENCE 1 (INT)
- **DAMAGE:** 33 (BALLISTIC), 50 (RADIATION)
- **AMMO:** GAMMA AMMO
- **FIRE RATE:** 67
- **RANGE:** 228
- **ACCURACY:** 69
- **WEIGHT:** 3.1
- **VALUE:** 79

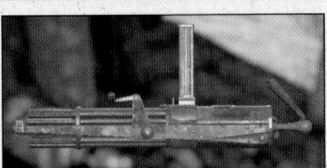

Gamma Guns deal radiation damage directly to enemies. While it's effective against normal enemies, you'll find it particularly useful against other players. Radiation damage temporarily lowers an enemy's max health, which means even the tankiest of enemies can be cut down to size if zapped with enough radiation.

ATTACHABLE MOD TYPES ➡ — DISH — GRIP — MUZZLE

GATLING GUN

- **STANDARD MODEL:** SHORT GATLING GUN
- **TYPE 1:** HEAVY GUN
- **TYPE 2:** —
- **MINIMUM LEVEL:** 20
- **CRAFTING LEVEL:** 25
- **CRAFTING RESTRICTIONS:** HEAVY GUNNER 1 (STR)
- **DAMAGE:** 27 (BALLISTIC)
- **AMMO:** 5MM AMMO
- **FIRE RATE:** 105
- **RANGE:** 120 OR 228
- **ACCURACY:** 49
- **WEIGHT:** 28.4
- **VALUE:** 222

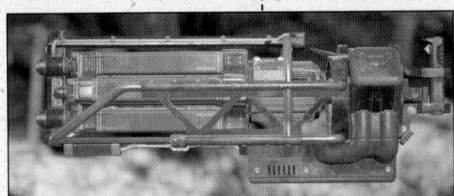

A more powerful, more manageable Gatling weapon that boasts a more modest fire rate than its contemporaries. With its high damage (for a Gatling weapon) and its solid accuracy, you could use this weapon in just about any close- to mid-range encounter and come out in good standing. Just be ready to spin up the barrel before walking headfirst into battle.

ATTACHABLE MOD TYPES ➡
- RECEIVER
- BARREL
- GRIP
- MAGAZINE
- SIGHTS
- MUZZLE

GATLING LASER

- **STANDARD MODEL:** GATLING LASER
- **TYPE 1:** HEAVY GUN
- **TYPE 2:** ENERGY GUN
- **MINIMUM LEVEL:** 25
- **CRAFTING LEVEL:** 25
- **CRAFTING RESTRICTIONS:** HEAVY GUNNER 1 (STR)
- **DAMAGE:** 9 (ENERGY)
- **AMMO:** CORE
- **FIRE RATE:** 273
- **RANGE:** 204 OR 395
- **ACCURACY:** 48
- **WEIGHT:** 19.4
- **VALUE:** 174

This is a weaker but more focused counterpart to the Gatling Plasma. Like any Gatling-style weapon, you'll get more out of this gun when using it for suppression or for tackling large groups of enemies in open areas, rather than for trying to carefully pick enemies off at a distance.

ATTACHABLE MOD TYPES ➡
- RECEIVER
- BARREL
- SIGHTS
- MUZZLE

GATLING PLASMA

- **STANDARD MODEL:** GATLING PLASMA
- **TYPE 1:** HEAVY GUN
- **TYPE 2:** ENERGY GUN
- **MINIMUM LEVEL:** 30
- **CRAFTING LEVEL:** 30
- **CRAFTING RESTRICTIONS:** HEAVY GUNNER 1 (STR)
- **DAMAGE:** 16 (ENERGY)
- **AMMO:** CORE
- **FIRE RATE:** 91
- **RANGE:** 204 OR 395
- **ACCURACY:** 23 OR 30
- **WEIGHT:** 30.6
- **VALUE:** 273

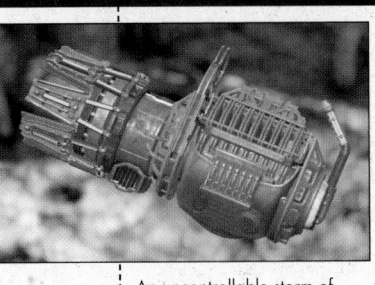

An uncontrollable storm of plasma rays, the Gatling Plasma has a firing spread that is hard to tame. If you can rein it in, you'll have a weapon perfect for keeping enemies locked down or for devastating large groups. Just keep an eye on your ammo count.

ATTACHABLE MOD TYPES ➡
- RECEIVER
- BARREL
- MAGAZINE
- SCOPE
- NOZZLE

GAUSS RIFLE

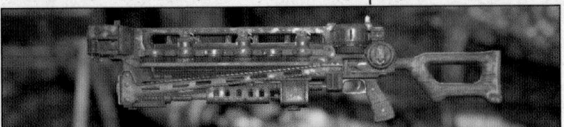

- **STANDARD MODEL:** GAUSS RIFLE
- **TYPE 1:** ENERGY GUN
- **TYPE 2:** NON-AUTOMATIC RIFLE
- **MINIMUM LEVEL:** 35
- **CRAFTING LEVEL:** 35
- **CRAFTING RESTRICTIONS:** SCIENCE 1 (INT)
- **DAMAGE:** 235 (BALLISTIC)
- **AMMO:** 2 MM ELECTROMAGNETIC CARTRIDGE
- **FIRE RATE:** 67
- **RANGE:** 204 OR 39
- **ACCURACY:** 56
- **WEIGHT:** 15.8
- **VALUE:** 247

Charge this weapon up for a powerful single shot, or mash the Fire button to unload a storm of semi-automatic shots. Incredibly powerful in the hands of a sharpshooter.

ATTACHABLE MOD TYPES ➡
- BARREL
- STOCK
- CAPACITOR
- SIGHTS
- MUZZLE

HANDMADE RIFLE

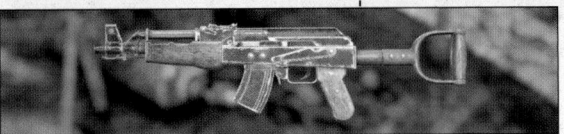

- **STANDARD MODEL:** SHORT HANDMADE
- **TYPE 1:** NON-AUTOMATIC RIFLE
- **TYPE 2:** —
- **MINIMUM LEVEL:** 15
- **CRAFTING LEVEL:** 25
- **DAMAGE:** 20 (BALLISTIC)
- **AMMO:** 5.56 AMMO
- **FIRE RATE:** 40
- **RANGE:** 120 OR 228
- **ACCURACY:** 65
- **WEIGHT:** 13.6
- **VALUE:** 107

This is a fairly standard Non-Automatic Rifle that shines with mods. Its stats are balanced across the board, which makes it more flexible than most weapons on offer.

ATTACHABLE MOD TYPES ➡
- RECEIVER
- BARREL
- STOCK
- MAGAZINE
- SIGHTS
- MUZZLE

HARPOON GUN

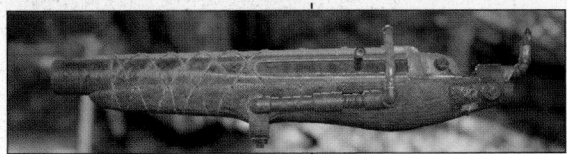

- **STANDARD MODEL:** HARPOON
- **TYPE 1:** EXOTIC WEAPON
- **TYPE 2:** HEAVY GUN
- **MINIMUM LEVEL:** 30
- **CRAFTING LEVEL:** 30
- **CRAFTING RESTRICTIONS:** EXOTIC WEAPONS 1 (INT)
- **DAMAGE:** 141 (BALLISTIC)
- **AMMO:** HARPOON
- **FIRE RATE:** 2
- **RANGE:** 120
- **ACCURACY:** 63
- **WEIGHT:** 16.4
- **VALUE:** 100

The Harpoon Gun is definitely in the lower bracket of weapons when it comes to shot speed, but when a shot lands, your enemies feel the pain. As an added bonus, any harpoons that you fire can be recollected, provided you can find them.

ATTACHABLE MOD TYPES ⬇

- **HARPOON**
- **SIGHTS**

LASER PISTOL

- **STANDARD MODEL:** SHORT LASER PISTOL
- **TYPE 1:** NON-AUTOMATIC PISTOL
- **TYPE 2:** ENERGY GUN
- **MINIMUM LEVEL:** 5
- **CRAFTING LEVEL:** 5
- **CRAFTING RESTRICTIONS:** SCIENCE 1 (INT)
- **DAMAGE:** 10 (ENERGY)
- **AMMO:** CELL
- **FIRE RATE:** 50
- **RANGE:** 120
- **ACCURACY:** 71
- **WEIGHT:** 4
- **VALUE:** 53

The Laser Pistol features a fast rate of fire and a ton of modding options. This gun is as easily converted to an Automatic Pistol as it is an Automatic Rifle. There are plenty of Energy Guns that deal heftier damage than the Laser Pistol, but few of them offer the same flexibility.

ATTACHABLE MOD TYPES ➡

- **CAPACITOR**
- **BARREL**
- **GRIP**
- **SIGHTS**
- **MUZZLE**
- **PAINT**

HUNTING RIFLE

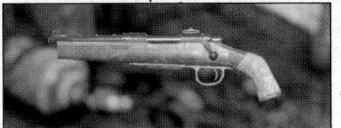

- **STANDARD MODEL:** SHORT HUNTING RIFLE
- **TYPE 1:** NON-AUTOMATIC RIFLE
- **TYPE 2:** —
- **MINIMUM LEVEL:** 1
- **CRAFTING LEVEL:** 5
- **CRAFTING RESTRICTIONS:** RIFLEMAN 1 (PER)
- **DAMAGE:** 45 (BALLISTIC)
- **AMMO:** .308 AMMO
- **FIRE RATE:** 3
- **RANGE:** 132 OR 240
- **ACCURACY:** 63 OR 62
- **WEIGHT:** 9.6
- **VALUE:** 45

The Hunting Rifle is slow but accurate. It's easily converted into a sniper rifle with a few tweaks at your local Weapon Workbench. Avoid close-quarters with this thing in hand and you'll have a rifle you can trust.

ATTACHABLE MOD TYPES ⬇

- **RECEIVER**
- **BARREL**
- **STOCK**
- **MAGAZINE**
- **SIGHTS**
- **MUZZLE**

LEVER ACTION RIFLE

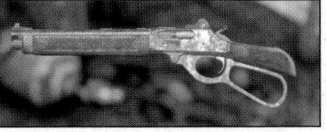

- **STANDARD MODEL:** SHORT LEVER ACTION RIFLE
- **TYPE 1:** NON-AUTOMATIC RIFLE
- **TYPE 2:** —
- **MINIMUM LEVEL:** 25
- **CRAFTING LEVEL:** 25
- **DAMAGE:** 82 (BALLISTIC)
- **AMMO:** .45 AMMO
- **FIRE RATE:** 5
- **RANGE:** 123 OR 231
- **ACCURACY:** 65
- **WEIGHT:** 9
- **VALUE:** 163

Slow to fire, but one of the most accurate semi-automatic rifles one can find in the whole of Appalachia. Slap a scope on top of this one, compensate for distance, and you've got a reliable mid- to long-range weapon that can give you control over a fight you've only dreamed of.

ATTACHABLE MOD TYPES ➡

- **RECEIVER**
- **BARREL**
- **STOCK**
- **SIGHTS**
- **MUZZLE**

LIGHT MACHINE GUN

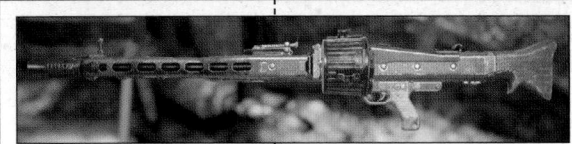

- **STANDARD MODEL:** LIGHT MACHINE GUN
- **TYPE 1:** HEAVY GUN
- **TYPE 2:** —
- **MINIMUM LEVEL:** 30
- **CRAFTING LEVEL:** 30
- **CRAFTING RESTRICTIONS:** COMMANDO 1 (PER)
- **DAMAGE:** 16 (BALLISTIC)
- **AMMO:** .308 AMMO
- **FIRE RATE:** 929
- **RANGE:** 156 OR 347
- **ACCURACY:** 66 OR 67
- **WEIGHT:** 21.6
- **VALUE:** 388

This Heavy Gun has a surprisingly tight bullet-spray pattern. Most other weapons of its kind (e.g., the Gatling series of weapons) have incredibly wide fire patterns, making it almost impossible to tell exactly where your bullet will go once you pull the trigger. That's not the case with the Light Machine Gun, though you will have to wrestle with a pretty violent recoil if you have a hope of utilizing it effectively.

ATTACHABLE MOD TYPES ➡

- **RECEIVER**
- **BARREL**
- **STOCK**
- **MAGAZINE**
- **MUZZLE BRAKE**

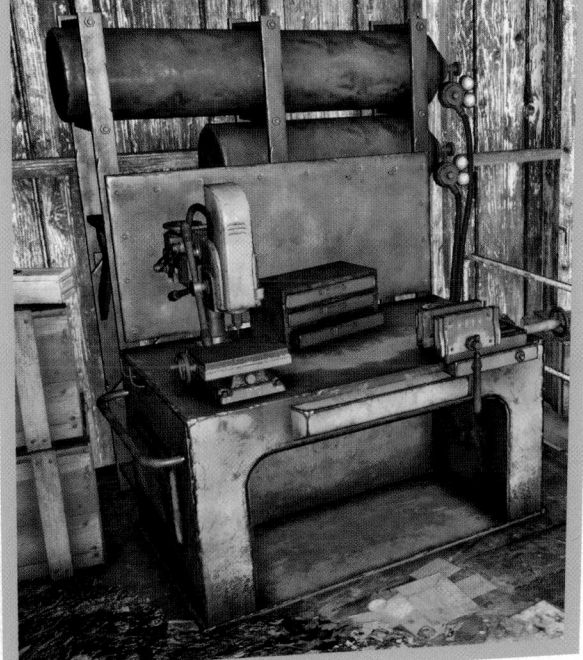

TRAINING

CRAFTING AND C.A.M.P.ING

INVENTORY

QUESTS

ATLAS

BESTIARY

APPENDICES

139

M79 GRENADE LAUNCHER

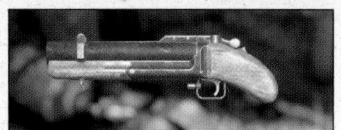

- STANDARD MODEL: M79 GRENADE LAUNCHER
- TYPE 1: EXPLOSIVE
- TYPE 2: —
- MINIMUM LEVEL: 15
- CRAFTING LEVEL: 40
- DAMAGE: 92 (BALLISTIC)
- AMMO: 40 MM AMMO
- FIRE RATE: 4
- RANGE: 120 OR 228
- ACCURACY: 18 OR 19
- WEIGHT: 8.9
- VALUE: 32

A sturdy Explosive weapon with a decent reload speed and ammo that's not hard to chase down. The arc on the M79's shots allow you to get behind enemy cover better than your standard Missile Launcher, but it definitely requires a bit of practice. If you're looking for a quality weapon to use as a master of Explosives, look no further.

ATTACHABLE MOD TYPES ➡
- RECEIVER
- BARREL
- STOCK
- MUZZLE

MINIGUN

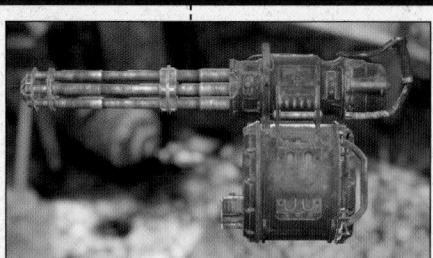

- STANDARD MODEL: MINIGUN
- TYPE 1: HEAVY GUN
- TYPE 2: —
- DAMAGE: 11 (BALLISTIC)
- MINIMUM LEVEL: 35
- CRAFTING LEVEL: 35
- REQUIRED: HEAVY GUNNER 1 (STR)
- DAMAGE: 25 (BALLISTIC)
- AMMO: 5 MM AMMO
- FIRE RATE: 273
- RANGE: 395
- ACCURACY: 36
- WEIGHT: 27.5
- VALUE: 207

A Heavy Gun user's bread and butter, the Minigun boasts a fast fire rate and a high ammo capacity. The damage may look small stats-wise, but don't be fooled. This weapon will tear through enemies like a kid tearing through presents on their birthday. Slap on some mods to further increase the fire rate and damage to really bring the Minigun to its fullest potential.

ATTACHABLE MOD TYPES ⬇
- BARREL
- SIGHTS
- MUZZLE
- PAINT

MISSILE LAUNCHER

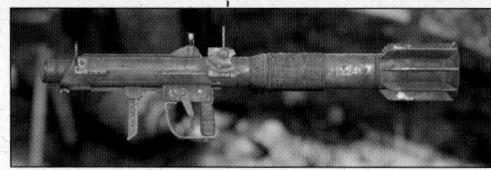

- STANDARD MODEL: MISSILE LAUNCHER
- TYPE 1: EXPLOSIVE
- TYPE 2: HEAVY GUN
- MINIMUM LEVEL: 20
- CRAFTING LEVEL: 20
- CRAFTING RESTRICTIONS: DEMOLITION EXPERT 1 (INT)
- DAMAGE: 124 (BALLISTIC)
- AMMO: MISSILES
- FIRE RATE: 4
- RANGE: 395
- ACCURACY: 65
- WEIGHT: 21
- VALUE: 254

Few Explosive weapons are as reliable as the Missile Launcher. The damage per shot is devastating on its own and the ammunition isn't hard to come by. Add in an excellent selection of mods that add a good bit of customization and you've got a Heavy Gun/ Explosive player's best friend.

ATTACHABLE MOD TYPES ⬇
- BARREL
- SIGHTS
- MUZZLE

PADDLE BALL

- STANDARD MODEL: PADDLE BALL
- TYPE 1: EXOTIC WEAPON
- TYPE 2: —
- MINIMUM LEVEL: 5
- CRAFTING LEVEL: 25
- DAMAGE: 1 (BALLISTIC)
- AMMO: BALL
- FIRE RATE: 25
- RANGE: 12
- ACCURACY: 152
- WEIGHT: 2
- VALUE: 41

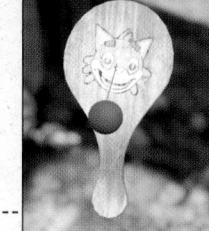

Obtained by turning in Mr. Fuzzy Tokens at Camden Park, the Paddle Ball may be goofy, but it's incredibly fun to use. It escaped being a melee weapon by the skin of its teeth, so expect to be up close and personal if you're hoping to use this in any serious capacity. The real meat of this weapon comes from its absolutely insane variety of mods (like creating micro-nuclear explosions with the Weaponized Nuka-Cola Quantum Ball mod). It's unlikely you'll take this weapon into endgame, but you'll definitely have some fun and some laughs if you're willing to commit your time to modding it.

ATTACHABLE MOD TYPES ⬇
- BLADED BALL
- ELECTRIFIED BALL
- FIRE BALL
- RUBBER BALL
- SPIKED BALL
- WEAPONIZED NUKA-COLA BALL
- WEAPONIZED NUKA-CHERRY BALL
- WEAPONIZED NUKA-COLA QUANTUM BALL

PIPE BOLT-ACTION PISTOL

- STANDARD MODEL: PIPE BOLT-ACTION PISTOL
- TYPE 1: PIPE WEAPON
- TYPE 2: NON-AUTOMATIC PISTOL
- MINIMUM LEVEL: 1
- CRAFTING LEVEL: 1
- DAMAGE: 40 (BALLISTIC)
- AMMO: .308 AMMO
- FIRE RATE: 3
- RANGE: 92 OR 168
- ACCURACY: 61 OR 62
- WEIGHT: 3.2
- VALUE: 28

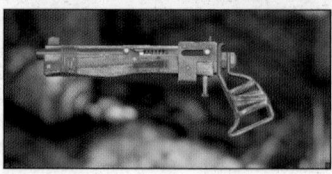

In its base form, the Pipe Bolt-Action Pistol is sluggish and used mostly at the start of your Appalachian journey (before other, better weapons become available). Hit the Weapon Workbench, however, and you'll find this gun has more than enough modding options to allow you to craft it into a weapon that will suit your needs as you take on greater and deadlier foes.

ATTACHABLE MOD TYPES ➡
- RECEIVER
- STUB BARREL
- GRIP
- SIGHTS
- MUZZLE

PIPE PISTOL

- STANDARD MODEL: PIPE PISTOL
- TYPE 1: PIPE WEAPON
- TYPE 2: NON-AUTOMATIC PISTOL
- MINIMUM LEVEL: 1
- CRAFTING LEVEL: 1
- DAMAGE: 14 (BALLISTIC)
- AMMO: .38 AMMO
- FIRE RATE: 60
- RANGE: 84 OR 156
- ACCURACY: 51 OR 53
- WEIGHT: 4.7
- VALUE: 20

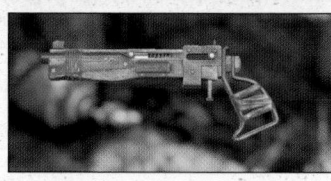

While it doesn't pack a punch like the Pipe Revolver, the Pipe Pistol is a quality handgun with near-limitless customization options. While most weapons will be left behind for something bolder and brighter, you'll find that the Pipe Pistol's modability makes it a gun you'll carry with you for a long, long time.

ATTACHABLE MOD TYPES ➡
- RECEIVER
- BARREL
- GRIP
- MAGAZINE
- SIGHTS
- MUZZLE

PIPE REVOLVER STANDARD MODEL: PIPE REVOLVER

- **TYPE 1:** PIPE WEAPON
- **TYPE 2:** NON-AUTOMATIC PISTOL
- **MINIMUM LEVEL:** 1
- **CRAFTING LEVEL:** 1
- **DAMAGE:** 40 (BALLISTIC)
- **AMMO:** .45 AMMO
- **FIRE RATE:** 6
- **RANGE:** 84 OR 156
- **ACCURACY:** 58 OR 60
- **WEIGHT:** 3.2
- **VALUE:** 24

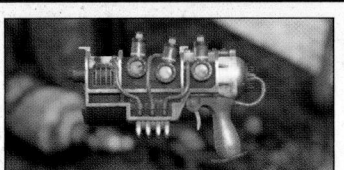

As far as handguns go, you'd be hard pressed to find a weapon more trustworthy than the Pipe Revolver. Excellent damage, a decent fire rate, reliable reloading speeds, and a range that allows for close to mid combat: the Pipe Revolver is dang near the perfect starting weapon.

ATTACHABLE MOD TYPES ▶
- RECEIVER – GRIP – MUZZLE
- BARREL – SIGHTS

PLASMA PISTOL

- **STANDARD MODEL:** SHORT PLASMA PISTOL
- **TYPE 1:** NON-AUTOMATIC PISTOL
- **TYPE 2:** ENERGY GUN
- **MINIMUM LEVEL:** 15
- **CRAFTING LEVEL:** 15
- **DAMAGE:** 20 (BALLISTIC), 20 (ENERGY)
- **AMMO:** PLASMA CARTRIDGE
- **FIRE RATE:** 33
- **RANGE:** 120 OR 228
- **ACCURACY:** 143
- **WEIGHT:** 4
- **VALUE:** 77

Powerful but uncommon. The Plasma Pistol's true strength lies in its dual damage output. Firing projectiles that deal both ballistic and energy damage will make most combat scenarios play in your favor (at least in the first half of the game), but the struggle to find more ammunition will make it nearly impossible to use this weapon exclusively. Use it for emergencies only, unless you have a surplus of Plasma Cartridges available.

ATTACHABLE MOD TYPES ▶
- CAPACITOR – GRIP
- BARREL – SIGHTS

PUMP ACTION SHOTGUN

- **STANDARD MODEL:** SHORT PUMP ACTION SHOTGUN
- **TYPE 1:** SHOTGUN
- **TYPE 2:** –
- **MINIMUM LEVEL:** 5
- **CRAFTING LEVEL:** 30
- **CRAFTING RESTRICTIONS:** SHOTGUNNER 1 (STR)
- **DAMAGE:** 67 (BALLISTIC)
- **AMMO:** SHELL
- **FIRE RATE:** 5
- **RANGE:** 72 OR 180
- **ACCURACY:** 11 OR 13
- **WEIGHT:** 11.2
- **VALUE:** 58

Not the fastest shotgun in Appalachia, but it will still serve anyone building a close-range character well. Make sure to account for the time it takes to pump the Shotgun between shots and you'll be just fine.

ATTACHABLE MOD TYPES ▶
- RECEIVER – GRIP – MUZZLE
- BARREL – SIGHTS –

RADIUM RIFLE

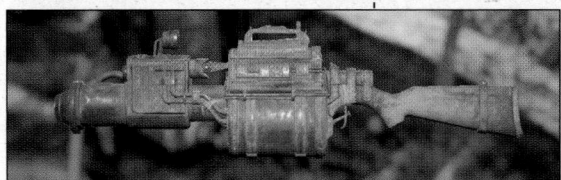

- **STANDARD MODEL:** SHORT RADIUM RIFLE
- **TYPE 1:** NON-AUTOMATIC RIFLE
- **TYPE 2:** EXOTIC WEAPON
- **MINIMUM LEVEL:** 40
- **CRAFTING LEVEL:** 40
- **CRAFTING RESTRICTIONS:** EXOTIC WEAPONS 1 (INT)
- **DAMAGE:** 30 (BALLISTIC), 13 (RADIATION)
- **AMMO:** .45 AMMO
- **FIRE RATE:** 40
- **RANGE:** 120 OR 228
- **ACCURACY:** 57 OR 58
- **WEIGHT:** 11.9
- **VALUE:** 89

The combination of Ballistic and Radiation damage makes this weapon a lean, mean fighting machine by itself, but slap an Automatic Receiver on it and it becomes something else entirely. You can't go wrong with a Radium Rifle slung across your shoulder.

ATTACHABLE MOD TYPES ▼
- RECEIVER – MAGAZINE
- BARREL – SIGHTS
- STOCK – MUZZLE

RAILWAY RIFLE

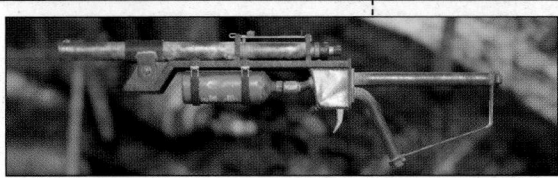

- **STANDARD MODEL:** RAILWAY RIFLE
- **TYPE 1:** NON-AUTOMATIC RIFLE
- **TYPE 2:** EXOTIC WEAPON
- **MINIMUM LEVEL:** 30
- **CRAFTING LEVEL:** 30
- **CRAFTING RESTRICTIONS:** EXOTIC WEAPONS 1 (INT)
- **DAMAGE:** 99 (BALLISTIC)
- **AMMO:** SPIKE
- **FIRE RATE:** 10
- **RANGE:** 120 OR 228
- **ACCURACY:** 56 OR 57
- **WEIGHT:** 14.4
- **VALUE:** 188

Powerful, reasonably accurate, decent range, but slow without an Automatic Receiver. If you can keep your Spike supply up, you'll find a lot to love with the Railway Rifle.

ATTACHABLE MOD TYPES ▶
- RECEIVER – STOCK – MUZZLE
- BARREL – SIGHTS

ROSE'S SYRINGER

- **STANDARD MODEL:** ROSE'S SYRINGER
- **TYPE 1:** PIPE GUN
- **TYPE 2:** EXOTIC WEAPON
- **MINIMUM LEVEL:** –
- **CRAFTING LEVEL:** –
- **DAMAGE:** 1 (BALLISTIC)
- **AMMO:** SYRINGER AMMO
- **FIRE RATE:** 4
- **RANGE:** 156
- **ACCURACY:** 72
- **WEIGHT:** 1.3
- **VALUE:** 100

Obtained as part of Main Quest: Flavors of Mayhem, Rose's Syringer is your typical Syringer in almost every way. You're granted it simply because Rose's request demands it of you.

ATTACHABLE MOD TYPES ▶ – BARREL

SALVAGED ASSAULTRON HEAD

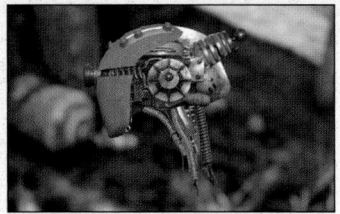

- STANDARD MODEL: SALVAGED ASSAULTRON HEAD
- TYPE 1: ENERGY GUN
- TYPE 2: EXOTIC WEAPON
- MINIMUM LEVEL: 25
- CRAFTING LEVEL: 25
- DAMAGE: 72 (ENERGY)
- AMMO: CELL
- FIRE RATE: 4
- RANGE: 94
- ACCURACY: 67
- WEIGHT: 8
- VALUE: 32

A semiautomatic severed head of an Assaultron, this weapon is charged by reloading repeatedly. The faster you press the Reload button, the more it charges. The more charged it is, the higher the damage. It also deals radiation damage to other players.

ATTACHABLE MOD TYPES ➡ — NONE

SINGLE ACTION REVOLVER

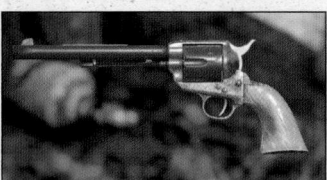

- STANDARD MODEL: SINGLE ACTION REVOLVER
- TYPE 1: NON-AUTOMATIC PISTOL
- TYPE 2: —
- MINIMUM LEVEL: 10
- CRAFTING LEVEL: 10
- DAMAGE: 45 (BALLISTIC)
- AMMO: .44 AMMO
- FIRE RATE: 6
- RANGE: 204 OR 395
- ACCURACY: 58 OR 62
- WEIGHT: 6.2
- VALUE: 215

This powerful Non-Automatic Pistol has some serious upgrade potential. You won't get a lot of flexibility out of the mods, and the fire rate leaves something to be desired, but the low crafting level requirements and high damage output will allow you to keep upgrading this weapon as you level up to make it a weapon to keep around for a long time.

ATTACHABLE MOD TYPES ➡ — RECEIVER — BARREL — GRIP

SUBMACHINE GUN

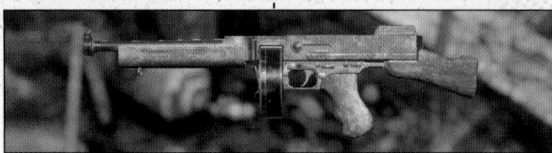

- STANDARD MODEL: SUBMACHINE GUN
- TYPE 1: AUTOMATIC PISTOL
- TYPE 2: —
- MINIMUM LEVEL: 10
- CRAFTING LEVEL: 15
- CRAFTING RESTRICTIONS: GUERRILLA 1 (AGI)
- DAMAGE: 12 (BALLISTIC)
- AMMO: 10 MM
- FIRE RATE: 91
- RANGE: 84
- ACCURACY: 48
- WEIGHT: 6.15
- VALUE: 147

A much slower-firing Submachine Gun than the 10 mm Submachine Gun, this is more of an entry-level weapon than the main event. Even with the lowered rate of fire, this gun still has monstrous recoil. You'll need to use Stock mods to get it under control.

ATTACHABLE MOD TYPES ⬇
- RECEIVER — MAGAZINE
- BARREL — SIGHTS
- STOCK — MUZZLE

SYRINGER

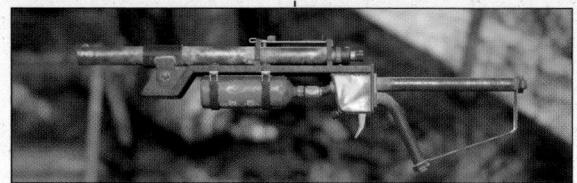

- STANDARD MODEL: SYRINGER
- TYPE 1: PIPE GUN
- TYPE 2: EXOTIC WEAPON
- MINIMUM LEVEL: —
- CRAFTING LEVEL: 1
- CRAFTING RESTRICTIONS: EXOTIC WEAPONS 1 (INT)
- DAMAGE: 1 (BALLISTIC)
- AMMO: SYRINGER AMMO
- FIRE RATE: 4
- RANGE: 156
- ACCURACY: 72
- WEIGHT: 5.3
- VALUE: 75

This is meant for putting status effects on enemies rather than for direct combat. This weapon is built for modding. If you want to get the best this weapon has to offer, you need to experiment with Barrel mods. Frenzy enemies, inject them with poison, and cause them to take bleeding damage and a slew of other status effects when you slap on a new Barrel.

ATTACHABLE MOD TYPES ➡ — BARREL — STOCK — SIGHTS

TESLA RIFLE

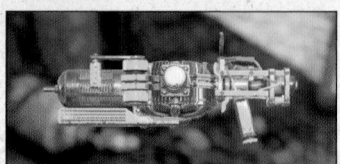

- STANDARD MODEL: TESLA RIFLE
- TYPE 1: HEAVY GUN
- TYPE 2: ENERGY GUN
- MINIMUM LEVEL: 40
- CRAFTING LEVEL: 40
- CRAFTING RESTRICTIONS: SCIENCE 1 (INT)
- DAMAGE: 48 (ENERGY)
- AMMO: CELL
- FIRE RATE: 40
- RANGE: 120 OR 228
- ACCURACY: 71
- WEIGHT: 8.2
- VALUE: 409

The Tesla Rifle is very powerful when used correctly. Any shots you fire will shoot off additional bolts to all enemies in close proximity. This fires an electrical discharge that arcs between targets.

ATTACHABLE MOD TYPES ⬇
- BARREL — SIGHTS

ULTRACITE GATLING LASER

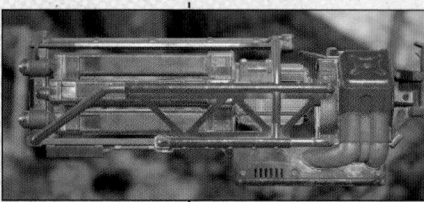

- STANDARD MODEL: ULTRACITE GATLING LASER
- TYPE 1: HEAVY GUN
- TYPE 2: ENERGY GUN
- MINIMUM LEVEL: 35
- CRAFTING LEVEL: 35
- DAMAGE: 16 (ENERGY)
- AMMO: CORE
- FIRE RATE: 273
- RANGE: 204 OR 395
- ACCURACY: 48
- WEIGHT: 19.4
- VALUE: 260

An unbelievably stable Gatling gun–type weapon that has a reasonably narrow bullet spread and very limited recoil pattern. It has a slew of mods that completely change the way the weapon is used, putting its versatility through the roof.

ATTACHABLE MOD TYPES ⬇
- RECEIVER — SIGHTS
- BARREL — MUZZLE

ULTRACITE LASER PISTOL

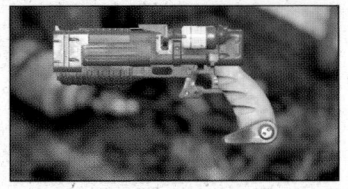

- **STANDARD MODEL:** SHORT ULTRACITE LASER PISTOL
- **TYPE 1:** NON-AUTOMATIC PISTOL
- **TYPE 2:** ENERGY WEAPON
- **MINIMUM LEVEL:** 30
- **CRAFTING LEVEL:** 35
- **DAMAGE:** 24 (ENERGY)
- **AMMO:** CELL
- **FIRE RATE:** 50
- **RANGE:** 120 OR 228
- **ACCURACY:** 70 OR 71
- **WEIGHT:** 4
- **VALUE:** 134

This is a significantly more powerful Laser Pistol but with some pretty beefy crafting requirements. You'll need to dig up a fair bit of Ultracite, which typically only shows up near fissure sites or in nuked areas. If you can manage to get the crafting components together, this is an Energy Gun worth having.

ATTACHABLE MOD TYPES ➡ — CAPACITOR — GRIP — MUZZLE — BARREL — SIGHTS

VOX SYRINGER

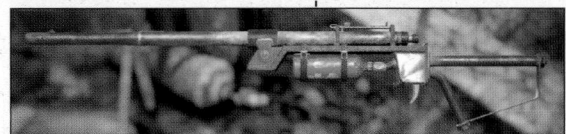

- **STANDARD MODEL:** VOX SYRINGER
- **TYPE 1:** PIPE GUN
- **TYPE 2:** EXOTIC WEAPON
- **MINIMUM LEVEL:** —
- **CRAFTING LEVEL:** —
- **DAMAGE:** 1 (BALLISTIC)
- **AMMO:** SYRINGER AMMO
- **FIRE RATE:** 4 OR 7
- **RANGE:** 204 OR 395
- **ACCURACY:** 75
- **WEIGHT:** 2.3
- **VALUE:** 86

While this weapon is technically an Exceptional Weapon, its only function is to allow you to complete Daily Quest: Someone to Talk To. It functions exactly as you would expect a Syringer to behave, but with the added bonus of making animals talk.

ATTACHABLE MOD TYPES ➡ — NONE

VOICE OF SET

- **STANDARD MODEL:** VOICE OF SET
- **TYPE 1:** NON-AUTOMATIC PISTOL
- **TYPE 2:** —
- **MINIMUM LEVEL:** 25
- **CRAFTING LEVEL:** 25
- **DAMAGE:** 56 (BALLISTIC)
- **AMMO:** .44
- **FIRE RATE:** 6
- **RANGE:** 84
- **ACCURACY:** 67
- **WEIGHT:** 4.6
- **VALUE:** 134

This modified .44 Pistol deals decent damage, but it excels at putting robotic enemies out of commission. Obtain this from the Mistress of Mystery quest line.

ATTACHABLE MOD TYPES ➡ — NONE

WESTERN REVOLVER

- **STANDARD MODEL:** SHORT WESTERN REVOLVER
- **TYPE 1:** NON-AUTOMATIC PISTOL
- **TYPE 2:** —
- **MINIMUM LEVEL:** 20
- **CRAFTING LEVEL:** 25
- **DAMAGE:** 67 (BALLISTIC)
- **AMMO:** .44
- **FIRE RATE:** 6
- **RANGE:** 120 OR 228
- **ACCURACY:** 65 OR 66
- **WEIGHT:** 5.3
- **VALUE:** 80

Very powerful, but with a painfully slow fire rate. We'd consider this one another trick weapon to challenge yourself, though modding it can certainly help with its negative traits.

ATTACHABLE MOD TYPES ➡ — RECEIVER — GRIP — BARREL — SIGHTS

MELEE WEAPONS – OVERVIEW

"Melee weapons in the gun-filled post-apocalypse? Preposterous!" We know how you feel, and yet you'll likely be as surprised as we were to learn that with the right Perk Cards, armor, and build, these weapons are not only viable, but also outright deadly. Ammunition and resources are scarce, and carrying capacity is at an all-time low—things melee weapons tend to ignore entirely. A single well-built melee weapon can make up for a dozen lackluster guns and without the need to carry bullets or a lot of your precious backpack space.

Now, that doesn't mean you can just grab a butter knife off the counter and take on Appalachia's most fearsome. Using melee weapons is a commitment to keeping your armor in tiptop shape, using the best melee-focused Perk Cards available, and ensuring your weapons are always upgraded and modified. If you're going to bring a bat to the wilderness, you better aim for the fences.

ALL MANNER OF MELEE

You'll have to choose between one-handed, two-handed, and punching weapons; even if you max out your STR, you won't have enough for all of the STR-related Perk Cards available. Gladiator (STR), Iron Fist (STR), and Slugger (STR) each offer damage increases to one-handed, punching, and two-handed melee weapons, respectively. We suggest you select one and stick with it. Which of the three types of melee weapons should you choose, though? Well, that also depends on your play style.

PERK CARDS ⬇

Just about every melee Perk Card is worth getting. The Perk Cards you avoid are based entirely on your play style. For example, Ninja (AGI), which increases stealth damage with melee weapons to up to three times normal, isn't going to work well if you like playing aggressively.

The Perk Cards to consider are:

- **INCISOR (STR):** INCREASES THE AMOUNT OF YOUR MELEE WEAPONS' ARMOR PENETRATION BY UP TO 75%.
- **MAKESHIFT WARRIOR (INT):** DECREASES THE RATE AT WHICH YOUR MELEE WEAPONS DEGRADE AND DECREASES THE COST TO REPAIR THEM
- **MARTIAL ARTIST (STR):** LOWERS THE TOTAL WEIGHT OF YOUR MELEE WEAPONS AND ALLOWS YOU TO SWING THEM UP TO 30% FASTER.
- **OVERLY GENEROUS (CHR):** BEING AFFLICTED WITH RADS GIVES YOU A CHANCE TO INFLICT 25 OR 50 RADIOACTIVE DAMAGE WITH YOUR MELEE ATTACKS.

TRAINING

CRAFTING AND C.A.M.PING

INVENTORY

QUESTS

ATLAS

BESTIARY

APPENDICES

ONE-HANDED MELEE

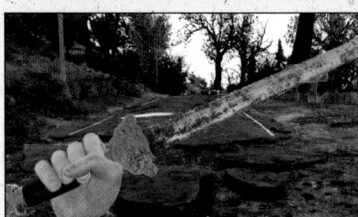

- ANCIENT BLADE
- ASSAULTRON BLADE
- BLACK DIAMOND
- BLADE OF BASTET
- BOWIE KNIFE
- CAMDEN WHACKER
- CHINESE OFFICER SWORD
- COMBAT KNIFE
- COMMIE WHACKER
- CULTIST BLADE
- CULTIST DAGGER
- DRILL
- GRANT'S SABER
- GUITAR AXE
- HATCHET
- LEAD PIPE
- MACHETE
- METEORIC SWORD
- NAILER
- REVOLUTIONARY SWORD
- RIPPER
- ROLLING PIN
- SECURITY BATON
- SHISHKEBAB
- SICKLE
- SKI SWORD
- SWITCHBLADE
- TIRE IRON
- WALKING CANE

One-handed melee weapons feature silent and swift knives, wide-slashing swords, and small bludgeoning clubs. They are typically quick and suit fast, agile play. Sneaking up and stabbing an enemy in the back with knives or moving in quickly, slashing, then putting distance between you and your enemy before striking again are the order of the day.

PUNCHING WEAPONS

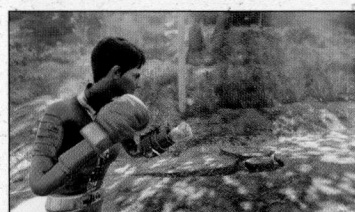

- BOXING GLOVE
- DEATH TAMBO
- DEATHCLAW GAUNTLET
- KNUCKLES
- MEAT HOOK
- MOLE MINER GAUNTLET
- POWER FIST

Punching weapons are similarly quiet and quick as a lot of one-handed melee weapons, but they tend to require a direct approach. One-handed melee weapons excel with players who move fast and don't stand still, while punching weapons require the player using them to commit and stay in close until the enemy is on the ground.

TWO-HANDED MELEE

- ALL RISE
- BASEBALL BAT
- BOARD
- CHAINSAW
- FIRE AXE
- GOLF CLUB
- GROGNAK'S AXE
- MR. HANDY BUZZ BLADE
- MULTI-PURPOSE AXE
- PICKAX
- PIPE WRENCH
- PITCHFORK
- POLE HOOK
- POOL CUE
- PROTEST SIGN
- SHOVEL
- SLEDGEHAMMER
- SPEAR
- SUPER SLEDGE
- WAR DRUM

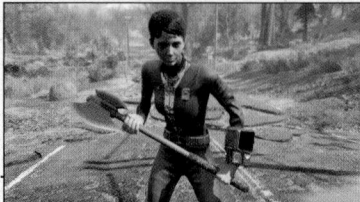

Two-handed melee weapons are typically powerful, sluggish, and loud. You should expect to be standing in the open whenever attacking enemies, which is why a good set of armor will come in handy. If you can grab a set of Power Armor and track down Perk Cards that add benefits to wearing it, you can really maximize the potential of these weapons.

MELEE WEAPONS

ANCIENT BLADE

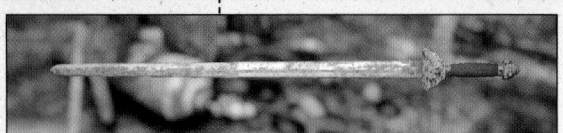

- **TYPE:** ONE-HANDED MELEE
- **DAMAGE:** 24 (BALLISTIC)
- **SPEED:** MEDIUM
- **WEIGHT:** 3
- **VALUE:** 61

This is a quick one-handed melee weapon with decent and balanced speed and damage. There are faster weapons and there are stronger ones, but few offer a bit of everything like this weapon does—at least not without a level requirement.

ATTACHABLE MOD TYPES ➡
- SERRATED BLADE
- ELECTRIFIED BLADE
- ELECTRIFIED SERRATED BLADE

ASSAULTRON BLADE

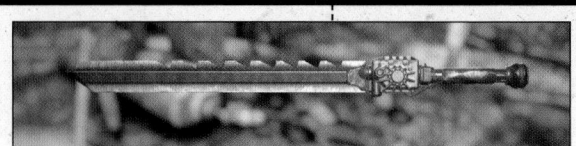

- **STANDARD MODEL:** ASSAULTRON BLADE
- **TYPE:** ONE-HANDED MELEE
- **MINIMUM LEVEL:** 25
- **CRAFTING LEVEL:** 25
- **DAMAGE:** 32 (BALLISTIC)
- **SPEED:** MEDIUM
- **WEIGHT:** 3
- **VALUE:** 57

Consider the Assaultron Blade a stronger version of the Ancient Blade with less modding possibilities and you'll know what to expect. If you don't have access to the Ancient Blade or the Blade of Bastet, this will fill in just fine.

ATTACHABLE MOD TYPES ➡
- ELECTRIFIED

BASEBALL BAT

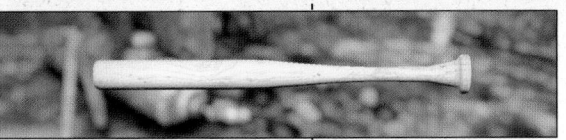

- **STANDARD MODEL:** BASEBALL BAT
- **TYPE:** TWO-HANDED MELEE
- **MINIMUM LEVEL:** 1
- **CRAFTING LEVEL:** 1
- **CRAFTING RESTRICTIONS:** SLUGGER 2 (STR)
- **DAMAGE:** 35 (BALLISTIC)
- **SPEED:** SLOW
- **WEIGHT:** 3
- **VALUE:** 20

Slow to swing and not the most powerful two-handed melee weapon in your arsenal, but a weapon that boasts some of the biggest (if not *the* biggest) mod support out of any melee weapon available. If you can't find a way to put this weapon to use, dig a little deeper.

ATTACHABLE MOD TYPES ⬇

- BARBED
- SHARP
- SPIKED
- CHAIN-WRAPPED
- BLADED
- HEATED COIL
- ROCKET
- SPIKED ROCKET
- PUNCTURING ROCKET
- BLADED ROCKET
- HEATED ROCKET
- SEARING PUNCTURING ROCKET

BINOCULARS

- **STANDARD MODEL:** BINOCULARS
- **TYPE:** NONE
- **MINIMUM LEVEL:** 1
- **CRAFTING LEVEL:** —
- **DAMAGE:** 7 (BALLISTIC)
- **FIRE RATE:** 1
- **RANGE:** 117
- **ACCURACY:** 88
- **WEIGHT:** 2
- **VALUE:** 5

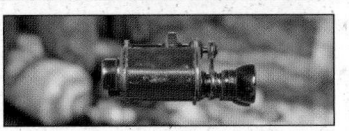

Not really meant as a weapon, Binoculars serve exactly the function you'd expect them to. The thing that gives them their weapon status is your ability to use a bash attack with them.

ATTACHABLE MOD TYPES ➡ — NONE

BLADE OF BASTET

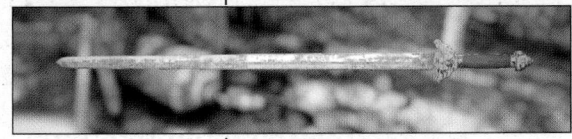

- **STANDARD MODEL:** BLADE OF BASTET
- **TYPE:** ONE-HANDED MELEE
- **MINIMUM LEVEL:** 25
- **CRAFTING LEVEL:** 25
- **DAMAGE:** 53 (BALLISTIC)
- **SPEED:** MEDIUM
- **WEIGHT:** 3
- **VALUE:** 65

Earned by playing through the Mistress of Mystery quest line, this is one of the best one-handed melee weapons you'll have access to from day 1. Quick, powerful, and with increased armor penetration, you can find a lot of use with this weapon if you're building a melee, Agility character—or perhaps you want to emulate the Mistress of Mystery herself. Whatever your reason, you can't go wrong with this sword in-hand.

ATTACHABLE MOD TYPES ➡ — NONE

BOARD

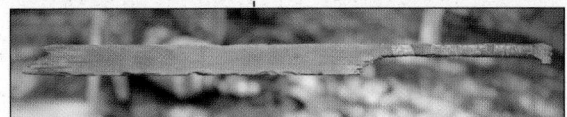

- **STANDARD MODEL:** BOARD
- **TYPE:** TWO-HANDED MELEE
- **MINIMUM LEVEL:** 1
- **CRAFTING LEVEL:** 5
- **DAMAGE:** 31 (BALLISTIC)
- **SPEED:** SLOW
- **WEIGHT:** 3
- **VALUE:** 8

Slow to swing and not the biggest damage dealer in the Two-Handed Melee family, but its mods offer a decent bit of flexibility in its use.

ATTACHABLE MOD TYPES ⬇

- BLADED
- PUNCTURING
- SPIKED

BOWIE KNIFE

- **STANDARD MODEL:** BOWIE KNIFE
- **TYPE:** ONE-HANDED MELEE
- **MINIMUM LEVEL:** 5
- **CRAFTING LEVEL:** 25
- **DAMAGE:** 17 (BALLISTIC)
- **SPEED:** FAST
- **WEIGHT:** 1
- **VALUE:** 28

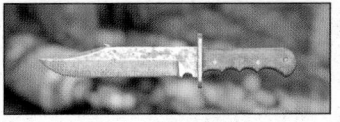

Quick and very portable. A nice melee weapon to have on hand for when ammo is low or you're attempting to take a stealth approach.

ATTACHABLE MOD TYPES ➡ — SERRATED BLADE — STEALTH BLADE

BOXING GLOVE

- **STANDARD MODEL:** BOXING GLOVE
- **TYPE:** PUNCHING WEAPON
- **MINIMUM LEVEL:** 5
- **CRAFTING LEVEL:** 5
- **CRAFTING RESTRICTIONS:** IRON FIST 2 (STR)
- **DAMAGE:** 23 (BALLISTIC)
- **SPEED:** MEDIUM
- **WEIGHT:** 1
- **VALUE:** 17

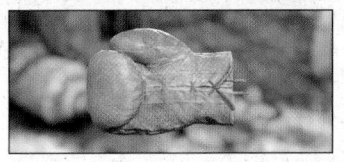

Super featherweights need not apply: These gloves are for heavy hitters only! If you've ever wanted to test an opponent's footwork, now is your chance. With solid speed and damage output (especially if you're using the Iron Fist Perk Card), this isn't bad for a melee user.

ATTACHABLE MOD TYPES ➡

- LEAD LINING
- PUNCTURING
- SPIKED

CAMDEN WHACKER

- **STANDARD MODEL:** CAMDEN WHACKER
- **TYPE:** ONE-HANDED MELEE
- **MINIMUM LEVEL:** —
- **CRAFTING LEVEL:** —
- **DAMAGE:** 6 (BALLISTIC)
- **SPEED:** MEDIUM
- **WEIGHT:** 2
- **VALUE:** 20

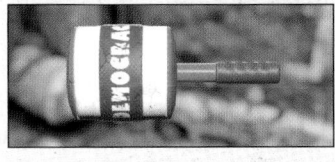

More a gag weapon than something you'd want to take out into the field, the Camden Whacker is obtained by trading Mr. Fuzzy Tokens at Camden Park in the Ash Heap.

ATTACHABLE MOD TYPES ➡ — BLADED

TRAINING

CRAFTING AND C.A.M.P.ING

INVENTORY

QUESTS

ATLAS

BESTIARY

APPENDICES

CHAINSAW

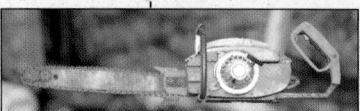

- **STANDARD MODEL:** CHAINSAW
- **TYPE:** TWO-HANDED MELEE
- **MINIMUM LEVEL:** 20
- **CRAFTING LEVEL:** —
- **DAMAGE:** 1 (BALLISTIC)
- **SPEED:** 45
- **RANGE:** 12
- **WEIGHT:** 12
- **VALUE:** 101

The perfect implement for those of us who need to rip and tear.

ATTACHABLE MOD TYPES ➡ — BAR — SCOPE

CHINESE OFFICER SWORD

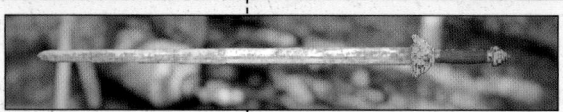

- **STANDARD MODEL:** CHINESE OFFICER SWORD
- **TYPE:** ONE-HANDED MELEE
- **MINIMUM LEVEL:** 5
- **CRAFTING LEVEL:** 5
- **DAMAGE:** 25 (BALLISTIC)
- **SPEED:** MEDIUM
- **WEIGHT:** 3
- **VALUE:** 41

This is an entry-level One-Handed Melee sword. Swords have a wide swinging arc that allows you to slash and move without slowing down. Swords are great weapons for AGI characters who prefer quickness and movement over standing still and taking aim.

ATTACHABLE MOD TYPES ➡ — SERRATED BLADE — ELECTRIFIED BLADE — ELECTRIFIED SERRATED BLADE

COMBAT KNIFE

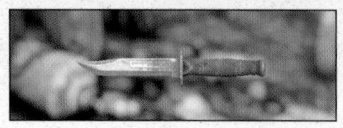

- **STANDARD MODEL:** COMBAT KNIFE
- **TYPE:** ONE-HANDED MELEE
- **MINIMUM LEVEL:** 1
- **CRAFTING LEVEL:** 5
- **DAMAGE:** 15 (BALLISTIC)
- **SPEED:** FAST
- **WEIGHT:** 1
- **VALUE:** 20

This quick stabbing blade is perfect for those in a sneaky mood or for anyone who needs a quick weapon in a pinch.

ATTACHABLE MOD TYPES ➡ — SERRATED BLADE — STEALTH BLADE

COMMIE WHACKER

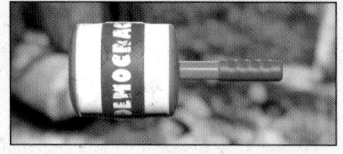

- **STANDARD MODEL:** COMMIE WHACKER
- **TYPE:** ONE-HANDED MELEE
- **MINIMUM LEVEL:** —
- **CRAFTING LEVEL:** —
- **DAMAGE:** 6 (BALLISTIC)
- **SPEED:** MEDIUM
- **WEIGHT:** 2
- **VALUE:** 20

All the power of a Whac-A-Mole mallet with the same amount of humor. You're not going to charge down enemy hordes with this thing, but if you really want to set another player on full tilt, bop them to death with it.

ATTACHABLE MOD TYPES ➡ — BLADED

CULTIST BLADE

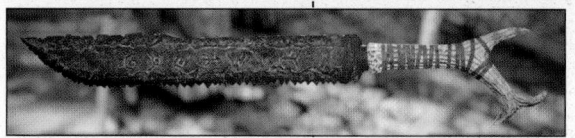

- **STANDARD MODEL:** CULTIST BLADE
- **TYPE:** ONE-HANDED MELEE
- **MINIMUM LEVEL:** 10
- **CRAFTING LEVEL:** 10
- **DAMAGE:** 29 (BALLISTIC)
- **SPEED:** MEDIUM
- **WEIGHT:** 3
- **VALUE:** 12

A decent One-Handed Melee weapon, but its lack of mods will keep it from staying with you for long.

ATTACHABLE MOD TYPES ⬇ — NONE

CULTIST DAGGER

- **STANDARD MODEL:** CULTIST DAGGER
- **TYPE:** ONE-HANDED MELEE
- **MINIMUM LEVEL:** 15
- **CRAFTING LEVEL:** 15
- **DAMAGE:** 20 (BALLISTIC)
- **SPEED:** FAST
- **WEIGHT:** 1
- **VALUE:** 20

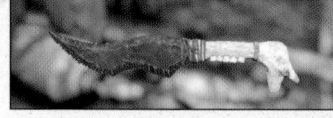

Quick and silent like any knife weapon, but the lack of mod support means you won't be using it for long.

ATTACHABLE MOD TYPES ➡ — NONE

DEATH TAMBO

- **STANDARD MODEL:** DEATH TAMBO
- **TYPE:** PUNCHING WEAPON
- **MINIMUM LEVEL:** 15
- **CRAFTING LEVEL:** 15
- **DAMAGE:** 28 (BALLISTIC)
- **SPEED:** MEDIUM
- **WEIGHT:** 0.5
- **VALUE:** 49

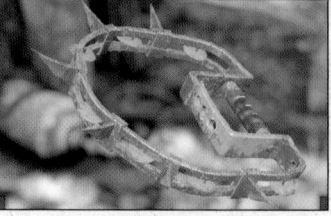

A Punching Weapon lacking in mod support. If you have it on hand and don't have access to any other Punching Weapons, it will get the job done. But there are other weapons that are more deserving of your time.

ATTACHABLE MOD TYPES ➡ — NONE

DEATHCLAW GAUNTLET

- **STANDARD MODEL:** DEATHCLAW GAUNTLET
- **TYPE:** PUNCHING WEAPON
- **MINIMUM LEVEL:** 30
- **CRAFTING LEVEL:** 30
- **DAMAGE:** 48 (BALLISTIC)
- **SPEED:** MEDIUM
- **WEIGHT:** 10
- **VALUE:** 69

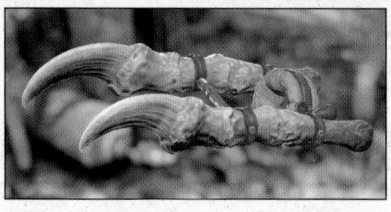

The upper echelon of Punching Weapons, the Deathclaw Gauntlet cuts through foes like the creature it was stolen from. Tack on the Extra Claw mod to really raise some hell!

ATTACHABLE MOD TYPES ➡ — EXTRA CLAW

DRILL

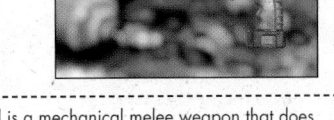

- **STANDARD MODEL:** DRILL
- **TYPE:** ONE-HANDED MELEE
- **MINIMUM LEVEL:** 20
- **CRAFTING LEVEL:** 30
- **DAMAGE:** 22 (BALLISTIC)
- **SPEED:** VERY FAST
- **WEIGHT:** 2.4
- **VALUE:** 84

Similar to the Chainsaw, the Drill is a mechanical melee weapon that does damage over time, instead of per strike. So long as you're next to an enemy and pointing the Drill in their direction.

ATTACHABLE MOD TYPES ➡ – PIERCING DRILL BIT

FIRE AXE

- **STANDARD MODEL:** FIRE AXE
- **TYPE:** TWO-HANDED MELEE
- **MINIMUM LEVEL:** 5
- **CRAFTING LEVEL:** 5
- **DAMAGE:** 42 (BALLISTIC)
- **SPEED:** SLOW
- **WEIGHT:** 3
- **VALUE:** 12

While it may be lacking in mods, the Fire Axe is still a hard-hitting weapon with low-level requirements. You'll be hard-pressed to find something that beats it, at least in the earlier stages of the game.

ATTACHABLE MOD TYPES ⬇
– NONE

GOLF CLUB

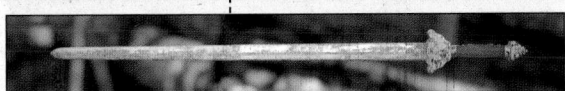

- **STANDARD MODEL:** GOLF CLUB
- **TYPE:** TWO-HANDED MELEE
- **MINIMUM LEVEL:** 1
- **CRAFTING LEVEL:** 1
- **CRAFTING RESTRICTIONS:** SLUGGER 2 (STR)
- **DAMAGE:** 31 (BALLISTIC)
- **SPEED:** SLOW
- **WEIGHT:** 3
- **VALUE:** 20

While not as powerful as a Fire Axe, the mod options give this weapon an edge in terms of versatility.

ATTACHABLE MOD TYPES ➡
- BLADED GOLF CLUB
- HEAVY CLUB
- SPIKED GOLF CLUB

GRANT'S SABER

- **STANDARD MODEL:** GRANT'S SABER
- **TYPE:** ONE-HANDED MELEE
- **MINIMUM LEVEL:** 1
- **CRAFTING LEVEL:** —
- **DAMAGE:** 26 (BALLISTIC)
- **SPEED:** MEDIUM
- **WEIGHT:** 3
- **VALUE:** 49

Obtained during Mistress of Mystery: Forging a Legend, this sword won't stay with you for long. While it's a decent melee weapon, its purpose is to be transformed into the Blade of Bastet—a significantly more powerful blade with excellent armor penetration.

ATTACHABLE MOD TYPES ➡ – NONE

GROGNAK'S AXE

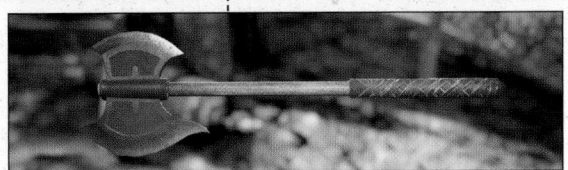

- **STANDARD MODEL:** GROGNAK'S AXE
- **TYPE:** TWO-HANDED MELEE
- **MINIMUM LEVEL:** 1
- **CRAFTING LEVEL:** 15
- **DAMAGE:** 40 (BALLISTIC)
- **SPEED:** MEDIUM
- **WEIGHT:** 10
- **VALUE:** 81

Grognak's Axe is both powerful and quick, which is a combination not often seen in Two-Handed Melee weapons. Its low level requirements also make it an excellent addition for anyone in the early stages of the melee-focused character build.

ATTACHABLE MOD TYPES ➡ – NONE

GUITAR SWORD

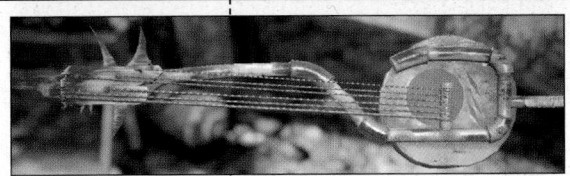

- **STANDARD MODEL:** GUITAR SWORD
- **TYPE:** ONE-HANDED MELEE
- **MINIMUM LEVEL:** 15
- **CRAFTING LEVEL:** 15
- **DAMAGE:** 40 (BALLISTIC)
- **SPEED:** MEDIUM
- **WEIGHT:** 3
- **VALUE:** 45

You'll get the expected speed from a One-Handed Melee weapon here but with the added bonus of a decent damage value. Per usual, the lack of mod support makes it less appealing long-term, but it's still a very solid One-Handed Melee weapon to have on hand.

ATTACHABLE MOD TYPES ➡ – NONE

HATCHET

- **STANDARD MODEL:** HATCHET
- **TYPE:** ONE-HANDED MELEE
- **MINIMUM LEVEL:** 1
- **CRAFTING LEVEL:** 1
- **DAMAGE:** 22 (BALLISTIC)
- **SPEED:** MEDIUM
- **WEIGHT:** 3
- **VALUE:** 12

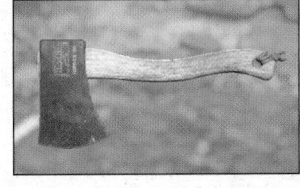

A standard One-Handed Melee weapon across the board. It does have a couple of modding options (one of which is cosmetic) that give it a bit of longevity. It's nothing to write home about, but for a weapon you can use from the start, it serves its purpose just fine.

ATTACHABLE MOD TYPES ➡ – ELECTRO FUSION – PAINT

KNUCKLES

- **STANDARD MODEL:** KNUCKLES
- **TYPE:** PUNCHING WEAPON
- **MINIMUM LEVEL:** 1
- **CRAFTING LEVEL:** 1
- **CRAFTING RESTRICTIONS:** IRON FIST 2 (STR)
- **DAMAGE:** 17 (BALLISTIC)
- **SPEED:** MEDIUM
- **WEIGHT:** 0.5
- **VALUE:** 8

Now, it's not the strongest Punching Weapon available, but it does feature a decent bit of customization due to its modding options. You'll find a replacement for it eventually, but until then this is a decent Punching Weapon to start with.

ATTACHABLE MOD TYPES ➡
- BLADED
- PUNCTURING
- SHARP
- SPIKED

TRAINING

CRAFTING AND C.A.M.P.ING

INVENTORY

QUESTS

ATLAS

BESTIARY

APPENDICES

LEAD PIPE

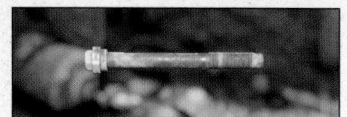

- **STANDARD MODEL:** LEAD PIPE
- **TYPE:** ONE-HANDED MELEE
- **MINIMUM LEVEL:** 1
- **CRAFTING LEVEL:** 1
- **DAMAGE:** 17 (BALLISTIC)
- **SPEED:** MEDIUM
- **WEIGHT:** 3
- **VALUE:** 12

A fairly standard One-Handed Melee weapon with a few bells and whistles in the form of mods. There are better weapons available, but if this is what you have, it will work just fine.

ATTACHABLE MOD TYPES ➡ — HEAVY — SPIKED

MACHETE

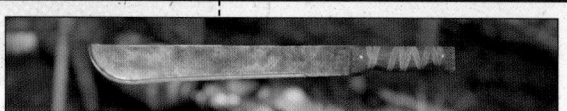

- **STANDARD MODEL:** MACHETE
- **TYPE:** ONE-HANDED MELEE
- **MINIMUM LEVEL:** 1
- **CRAFTING LEVEL:** 5
- **DAMAGE:** 22 (BALLISTIC)
- **SPEED:** MEDIUM
- **WEIGHT:** 2
- **VALUE:** 20

Likely one of the first melee weapons you'll find when you first exit Vault 76, the Machete is by no means a bad melee weapon. When accounting for your level and for modding potential, one might even feel inclined to say it's a pretty darn good melee weapon. At the very least, it will serve you until you can find an upgrade.

ATTACHABLE MOD TYPES ➡ — SACRIFICIAL BLADE — SERRATED BLADE

MEAT HOOK

- **STANDARD MODEL:** MEAT HOOK
- **TYPE:** PUNCHING WEAPON
- **MINIMUM LEVEL:** 5
- **CRAFTING LEVEL:** 15
- **DAMAGE:** 25 (BALLISTIC)
- **SPEED:** MEDIUM
- **WEIGHT:** 2
- **VALUE:** 16

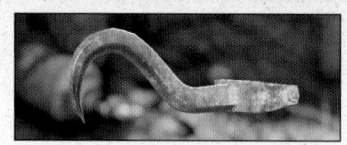

If you use the Meat Hook, you're going to need the Extra Hooks mod. If not for the damage increase, do it because it becomes a horror movie nightmare weapon.

ATTACHABLE MOD TYPES ➡ — EXTRA HOOKS

METEORIC SWORD

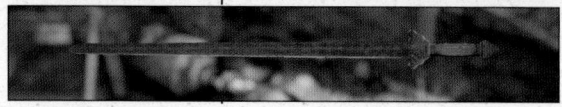

- **STANDARD MODEL:** METEORIC SWORD
- **TYPE:** ONE-HANDED MELEE
- **MINIMUM LEVEL:** 20
- **CRAFTING LEVEL:** —
- **DAMAGE:** 36 (BALLISTIC)
- **SPEED:** MEDIUM
- **WEIGHT:** 0.3
- **VALUE:** 122

A potential reward for completing Event: Lode Baring, the Meteoric Sword is lightweight, deals an additional 10% damage to human foes (other players, Scorched, and Feral Ghouls), and has 50% more durability than your stock standard sword weapon. You will likely have to work hard to obtain it, but it's worth the effort.

ATTACHABLE MOD TYPES ➡ — NONE

MOLE MINER GAUNTLET

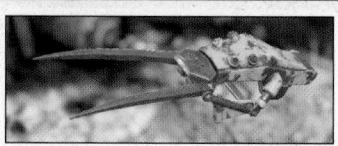

- **STANDARD MODEL:** MOLE MINER GAUNTLET
- **TYPE:** PUNCHING WEAPON
- **MINIMUM LEVEL:** 20
- **CRAFTING LEVEL:** 20
- **CRAFTING RESTRICTIONS:** IRON FIST 2 (STR)
- **DAMAGE:** 33 (BALLISTIC)
- **SPEED:** MEDIUM
- **WEIGHT:** 15
- **VALUE:** 91

The spiked knuckles of one of Appalachia's stranger enemies: the Mole Miner. It's a decent Punching Weapon made even better when the Extra Blade mod is attached.

ATTACHABLE MOD TYPES ➡ — EXTRA BLADE

MR. HANDY BUZZ BLADE

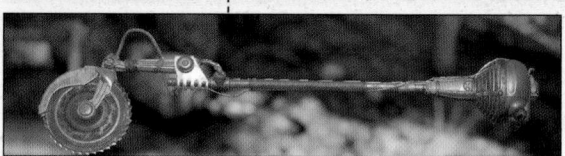

- **STANDARD MODEL:** MR. HANDY BUZZ BLADE
- **TYPE:** TWO-HANDED MELEE
- **MINIMUM LEVEL:** 15
- **CRAFTING LEVEL:** 15
- **DAMAGE:** 51 (BALLISTIC)
- **SPEED:** VERY FAST
- **WEIGHT:** 10
- **VALUE:** 41

A weapon that falls under the same camp as the Chainsaw and the Drill. Holding down the Attack button will hold the weapon out and begin spinning it violently. This one is particularly strong, especially when combined with the Electrified mod.

ATTACHABLE MOD TYPES ➡ — ELECTRIFIED

MULTI-PURPOSE AXE

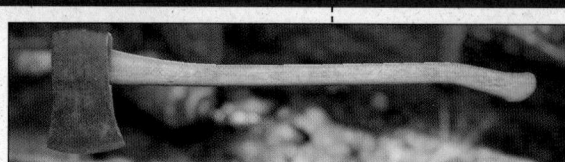

- **STANDARD MODEL:** MULTI-PURPOSE AXE
- **TYPE:** TWO-HANDED AXE
- **MINIMUM LEVEL:** 1
- **CRAFTING LEVEL:** 5
- **CRAFTING RESTRICTIONS:** SLUGGER 2 (STR)
- **DAMAGE:** 31 (BALLISTIC)
- **SPEED:** SLOW
- **WEIGHT:** 4
- **VALUE:** 32

This axe is listed as having a slow attack speed, but you won't really feel it. It's mostly an early game weapon that can be recrafted as you level up to keep its utility. There are few bells and whistles; just an axe for splitting heads. What more could you ask for?

ATTACHABLE MOD TYPES ➡ — NONE

NAILER

- **STANDARD MODEL:** NAILER
- **TYPE:** ONE-HANDED MELEE
- **MINIMUM LEVEL:** 15
- **CRAFTING LEVEL:** —
- **DAMAGE:** 32 (BALLISTIC)
- **SPEED:** MEDIUM
- **WEIGHT:** 3
- **VALUE:** 24

A One-Handed Melee weapon that gets stronger the lower your health. It's obtained as a reward for completing Event: One Violent Night.

ATTACHABLE MOD TYPES ➡ — NONE

PICKAXE

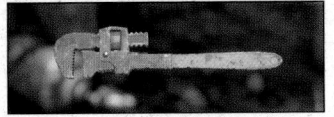

- **STANDARD MODEL:** PICKAXE
- **TYPE:** TWO-HANDED MELEE
- **MINIMUM LEVEL:** 5
- **CRAFTING LEVEL:** 5
- **CRAFTING RESTRICTIONS:** SLUGGER 2 (STR)
- **DAMAGE:** 37 (BALLISTIC)
- **SPEED:** SLOW
- **WEIGHT:** 3.5
- **VALUE:** 117

This is a decent melee weapon that performs as you'd expect. Like most melee weapons of its type, it will serve you well enough, but look to other melee weapons to truly get the most bang for your buck.

ATTACHABLE MOD TYPES ➡ — NONE

PIPE WRENCH

- **STANDARD MODEL:** PIPE WRENCH
- **TYPE:** ONE-HANDED MELEE
- **MINIMUM LEVEL:** 1
- **CRAFTING LEVEL:** 1
- **DAMAGE:** 24 (BALLISTIC)
- **SPEED:** MEDIUM
- **WEIGHT:** 2
- **VALUE:** 24

Bring out your inner mechanic with this One-Handed Melee weapon. Mod options will keep this weapon in your inventory longer than most.

ATTACHABLE MOD TYPES ➡ — EXTRA HEAVY — HOOKED — HEAVY — PUNCTURING

PITCHFORK

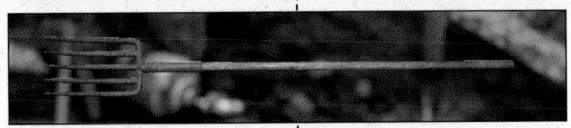

- **STANDARD MODEL:** PITCHFORK
- **TYPE:** TWO-HANDED MELEE
- **MINIMUM LEVEL:** 1
- **CRAFTING LEVEL:** 5
- **CRAFTING RESTRICTIONS:** SLUGGER 2 (STR)
- **DAMAGE:** 24 (BALLISTIC)
- **SPEED:** MEDIUM
- **WEIGHT:** 2
- **VALUE:** 12

A spear-type melee weapon that attacks more with lunges than strikes. If you're going to use the Pitchfork, be sure to take a look at its Flamer mods.

ATTACHABLE MOD TYPES ⬇
- BARBED FLAMING PITCHFORK
- BARBED PITCHFORK
- PITCHFORK FLAMER

POLE HOOK

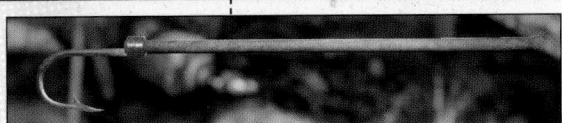

- **STANDARD MODEL:** POLE HOOK
- **TYPE:** TWO-HANDED MELEE
- **MINIMUM LEVEL:** 10
- **CRAFTING LEVEL:** 40
- **DAMAGE:** 46 (BALLISTIC)
- **SPEED:** SLOW
- **WEIGHT:** 7
- **VALUE:** 36

Not a particularly fast melee weapon, but it packs a punch. The level requirements for crafting will keep you from upgrading it beyond mods, ultimately limiting its usage, but if you manage to find it around Level 10, it's a decent melee weapon to have on hand.

ATTACHABLE MOD TYPES ➡ — PUNCTURING

POOL CUE

- **STANDARD MODEL:** POOL CUE
- **TYPE:** TWO-HANDED MELEE
- **MINIMUM LEVEL:** 1
- **CRAFTING LEVEL:** 30
- **CRAFTING RESTRICTIONS:** SLUGGER 2 (STR)
- **DAMAGE:** 31 (BALLISTIC)
- **SPEED:** SLOW
- **WEIGHT:** 1
- **VALUE:** 8

You'll run into the same problems with a Pool Cue as you would the Pole Hook. It's a decent weapon when taking into account its level requirements for usage, but the level and Perk Cards requirements for crafting it will keep you from upgrading it for far too long. If you find it early, it will serve you well, but any later and you'll likely have something in your arsenal that trumps it.

ATTACHABLE MOD TYPES ➡ — BLADED — SHARP

POWER FIST

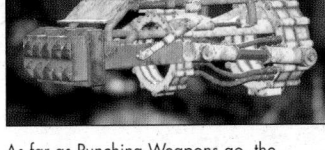

- **STANDARD MODEL:** POWER FIST
- **TYPE:** PUNCHING WEAPON
- **MINIMUM LEVEL:** 30
- **CRAFTING LEVEL:** 30
- **CRAFTING RESTRICTIONS:** IRON FIST 2 (STR)
- **DAMAGE:** 48 (BALLISTIC)
- **SPEED:** MEDIUM
- **WEIGHT:** 4
- **VALUE:** 81

As far as Punching Weapons go, the only rival the Power Fist knows is the Deathclaw Gauntlet. The Power Fist has one additional mod over its contemporary, but it also has crafting restrictions that the Deathclaw Gauntlet doesn't have. Really the choice is yours; you can't go wrong with either weapon.

ATTACHABLE MOD TYPES ➡ — PUNCTURING — HEATED COIL

TRAINING

CRAFTING AND C.A.M.P.ING

INVENTORY

QUESTS

ATLAS

BESTIARY

APPENDICES

PROTEST SIGN

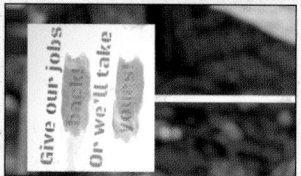

- STANDARD MODEL: PROTEST SIGN
- TYPE: TWO-HANDED MELEE
- DAMAGE: 11 (BALLISTIC)
- SPEED: SLOW
- WEIGHT: 3
- VALUE: 1

The Protest Sign is more a gag weapon than something to actually use in battle. There are two different signs in total. Can you find them both?

ATTACHABLE MOD TYPES → – NONE

REVOLUTIONARY SWORD

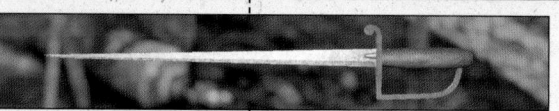

- STANDARD MODEL: REVOLUTIONARY SWORD
- TYPE: ONE-HANDED MELEE
- MINIMUM LEVEL: 10
- CRAFTING LEVEL: 20
- CRAFTING RESTRICTIONS: GLADIATOR 1 (STR)
- DAMAGE: 25 (BALLISTIC)
- SPEED: MEDIUM
- WEIGHT: 3
- VALUE: 41

This is a decent sword weapon when taking its level requirements into consideration. By the time you're able to craft newer, stronger versions of it, you'll be within spitting distance of using the Blade of Bastet, which you obtain from Mistress of Mystery: Forging a Legend. Use it while you have it; then make your way to that new, stronger sword.

ATTACHABLE MOD TYPES →
– SERRATED BLADE
– ELECTRIFIED

RIPPER

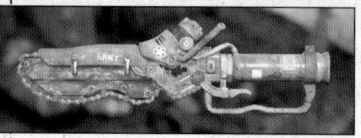

- STANDARD MODEL: RIPPER
- TYPE: ONE-HANDED MELEE
- MINIMUM LEVEL: 40
- CRAFTING LEVEL: 40
- DAMAGE: 4 (BALLISTIC)
- SPEED: VERY FAST
- WEIGHT: 6
- VALUE: 41

This portable Chainsaw-type melee weapon strikes as fast as its big brother but deals a good bit more damage. Add mods to further increase its power.

ATTACHABLE MOD TYPES →
– CURVED BLADE
– EXTENDED BLADE

ROLLING PIN

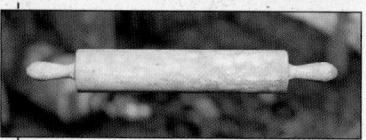

- STANDARD MODEL: ROLLING PIN
- TYPE: ONE-HANDED MELEE
- MINIMUM LEVEL: 1
- CRAFTING LEVEL: 1
- DAMAGE: 15 (BALLISTIC)
- SPEED: MEDIUM
- WEIGHT: 1
- VALUE: 8

This is one of the few weapons in the game that receives a damage boost from a Paint mod. Cover this cooking implement in an aluminum coating and it will hit harder. At an additional mod on top of that and you'll really be cooking.

ATTACHABLE MOD TYPES → – SHARP – SPIKED – PAINT

SECURITY BATON

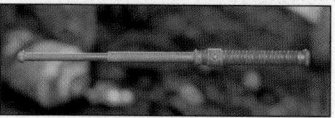

- STANDARD MODEL: SECURITY BATON
- TYPE: ONE-HANDED MELEE
- MINIMUM LEVEL: 5
- CRAFTING LEVEL: 5
- DAMAGE: 23 (BALLISTIC)
- SPEED: MEDIUM
- WEIGHT: 2
- VALUE: 12

Bring law and order to the lawless hordes of Appalachia with this weapon in hand. Equip a Responders Police Outfit and a .44 Pistol to really nail the police aesthetic.

ATTACHABLE MOD TYPES → – ELECTRIFIED

SHISHKEBAB

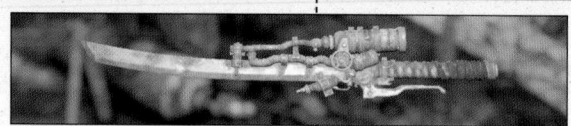

- STANDARD MODEL: SHISHKEBAB
- TYPE: ONE-HANDED MELEE
- MINIMUM LEVEL: 35
- CRAFTING LEVEL: 35
- DAMAGE: 41 (BALLISTIC), 37 (ENERGY)
- SPEED: MEDIUM
- WEIGHT: 3
- VALUE: 97

One of the best sword-type weapons in the game, the Shishkebab can deal damage that beats out just about everything else Appalachia has to offer. If you like slicing, dicing, and burning enemies to a fine crisp, look no further.

ATTACHABLE MOD TYPES → – EXTRA FLAME JETS

SHOVEL

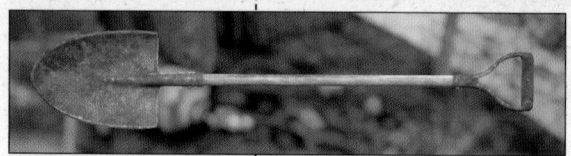

- STANDARD MODEL: SHOVEL
- TYPE: TWO-HANDED MELEE
- MINIMUM LEVEL: 1
- CRAFTING LEVEL: 1
- DAMAGE: 17 (BALLISTIC)
- SPEED: SLOW
- WEIGHT: 6
- VALUE: 32

The Shovel is more of a tool than an actual weapon. It's needed for digging up loot from dirt mounds, though it works fine as a melee weapon in a pinch. It's good to have one of these in your inventory at all times, but you're better off using just about any other melee weapon for combat.

ATTACHABLE MOD TYPES → – NONE

SICKLE

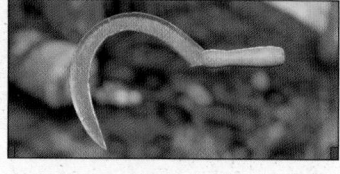

- STANDARD MODEL: SICKLE
- TYPE: ONE-HANDED MELEE
- MINIMUM LEVEL: 1
- CRAFTING LEVEL: 15
- DAMAGE: 22 (BALLISTIC)
- SPEED: MEDIUM
- WEIGHT: 3
- VALUE: 12

The Sickle is your basic One-Handed Melee weapon. It doesn't particularly excel in any way and its crafting restrictions, on top of its lack of mods, make it hard to recommend.

ATTACHABLE MOD TYPES → – NONE

SKI SWORD

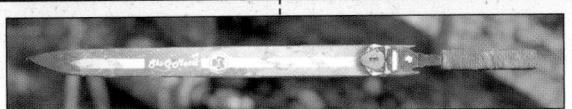

- **STANDARD MODEL:** SKI SWORD
- **TYPE:** ONE-HANDED MELEE
- **MINIMUM LEVEL:** 15
- **CRAFTING LEVEL:** 15
- **DAMAGE:** 35 (BALLISTIC)
- **SPEED:** MEDIUM
- **WEIGHT:** 3
- **VALUE:** 12

A sword quite literally made out of a ski. It has decent damage, which is further amplified by the Metal Shards or Skate Blade mods. If you're tired of hitting the slopes and crave to hit something else, this weapon might just be for you.

ATTACHABLE MOD TYPES ➡
- METAL SHARDS
- SKATE BLADE

SLEDGEHAMMER

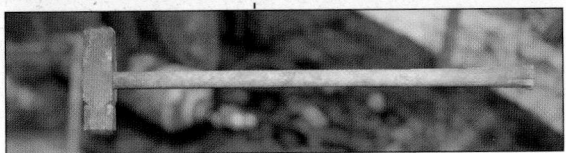

- **STANDARD MODEL:** SLEDGEHAMMER
- **TYPE:** TWO-HANDED MELEE
- **MINIMUM LEVEL:** 10
- **CRAFTING LEVEL:** 30
- **CRAFTING RESTRICTIONS:** SLUGGER 2 (STR)
- **DAMAGE:** 46 (BALLISTIC)
- **SPEED:** SLOW
- **WEIGHT:** 12
- **VALUE:** 32

Slow to swing but hard hitting and incredibly flexible. There are few melee weapons out there with as much modding potential as the Sledgehammer. The crafting requirements are a bit strict, but what you'll have available to you from the time you pick it up is still an impressive weapon that melee players will get a lot out of.

ATTACHABLE MOD TYPES ⬇
- HEAVY
- HEAVY ROCKET
- HEAVY SPIKED
- PUNCTURING
- SHARP
- HEAVY SHARP ROCKET
- HEAVY SPIKED ROCKET
- HEAVY SEARING SHARP ROCKET

SPEAR

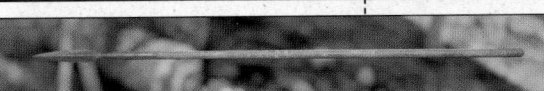

- **STANDARD MODEL:** SPEAR
- **TYPE:** TWO-HANDED MELEE
- **MINIMUM LEVEL:** 15
- **CRAFTING LEVEL:** 15
- **DAMAGE:** 25 (BALLISTIC)
- **SPEED:** MEDIUM
- **WEIGHT:** 2
- **VALUE:** 32

A melee weapon for those who want a more careful approach to combat. Instead of wide swings, you can pierce enemies with thrusting attacks.

ATTACHABLE MOD TYPES ➡ NONE

SUPER SLEDGE

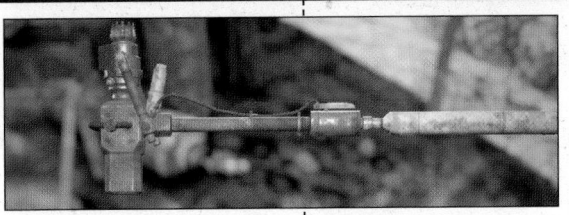

- **STANDARD MODEL:** SUPER SLEDGE
- **TYPE:** TWO-HANDED MELEE
- **MINIMUM LEVEL:** 30
- **CRAFTING LEVEL:** 30
- **CRAFTING RESTRICTIONS:** SLUGGER 2 (STR)
- **DAMAGE:** 77 (BALLISTIC)
- **SPEED:** SLOW
- **WEIGHT:** 20
- **VALUE:** 89

A truly devastating melee weapon. The Super Sledge doesn't have nearly as many options as the standard Sledgehammer, but it's hard to beat its raw damage output.

ATTACHABLE MOD TYPES ⬇
- HEATING COIL

SWITCHBLADE

- **STANDARD MODEL:** SWITCHBLADE
- **TYPE:** ONE-HANDED MELEE
- **MINIMUM LEVEL:** 10
- **CRAFTING LEVEL:** 10
- **DAMAGE:** 28 (BALLISTIC)
- **SPEED:** FAST
- **WEIGHT:** 1
- **VALUE:** 16

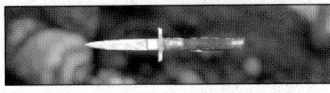

A surprisingly damaging knife-type weapon that has a quick strike speed. The mod options aren't the best, but there's still more than enough here to satisfy all the needs a knife user might have when out in the field.

ATTACHABLE MOD TYPES ➡ SERRATED BLADE

TIRE IRON

- **STANDARD MODEL:** TIRE IRON
- **TYPE:** ONE-HANDED MELEE
- **MINIMUM LEVEL:** 1
- **CRAFTING LEVEL:** 1
- **DAMAGE:** 22 (BALLISTIC)
- **SPEED:** MEDIUM
- **WEIGHT:** 2
- **VALUE:** 20

A decent melee weapon that you can upgrade as you level up. It's not going to change the melee-wielding game, but it's perfectly serviceable all the same. Be sure to tack on the Bladed mod for additional damage and the ability to cause enemies to bleed when hit.

ATTACHABLE MOD TYPES ➡ BLADED

WALKING CANE

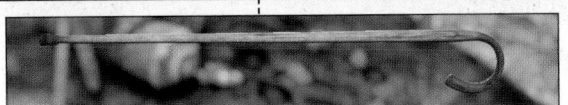

- **STANDARD MODEL:** WALKING CANE
- **TYPE:** ONE-HANDED MELEE
- **MINIMUM LEVEL:** 1
- **CRAFTING LEVEL:** 1
- **DAMAGE:** 22 (BALLISTIC)
- **SPEED:** MEDIUM
- **WEIGHT:** 2
- **VALUE:** 8

For the distinguished lady or gentleman in us all, the Walking Cane is well rounded, moddable, and has low crafting requirements, meaning you can upgrade it as you level to keep it doling damage to hooligans and ne'er-do-wells the world over. Pip, pip!

ATTACHABLE MOD TYPES ➡
- BARBED
- SPIKED

WAR DRUM

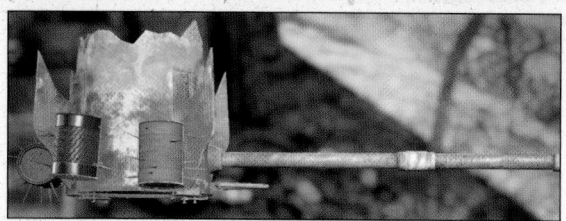

- **STANDARD MODEL:** WAR DRUM
- **TYPE:** TWO-HANDED MELEE
- **MINIMUM LEVEL:** 15
- **CRAFTING LEVEL:** 30
- **CRAFTING RESTRICTIONS:** SLUGGER 2 (STR)

- **DAMAGE:** 45 (BALLISTIC)
- **SPEED:** SLOW
- **WEIGHT:** 20
- **VALUE:** 93

The War Drum is a bit slow, but it hits hard. The crafting requirements make it hard to upgrade and the lack of mods limits its potential, but it will still satisfy the need to thump enemies over the head with a blunt object. Now that's music to our ears.

ATTACHABLE MOD TYPES ➡ - **NONE**

GRENADES AND THROWN WEAPONS

Grenades are perfect for taking out an enemy who is safely behind cover or dealing with a large group of enemies at once, while thrown weapons suit stealth play nicely. Grenades are single use, while thrown weapons can be recovered and easily crafted. You don't need to settle for just one, so why not bring plenty of both?

There aren't any Perk Cards specific to thrown weapons, but grenades will benefit greatly from most Perk Cards relating to explosive weapons and they also have a couple cards of their own. Fire in the Hole (PER) allows you to see an arc of where the grenade will travel and increases your throwing distance, while Ordnance Express (STR) decreases the overall weight of grenades in your inventory.

GRENADES

- BASEBALL GRENADE
- CRYOGENIC GRENADE
- FRAGMENTATION GRENADE
- FRAGMENTATION GRENADE MIRV

- HALLUCIGEN GAS GRENADE
- MOLOTOV COCKTAIL
- NUKA-GRENADE
- NUKA QUANTUM GRENADE
- ORBITAL MISSILE STRIKE BEACON
- ORBITAL SCAN BEACON

- ORBITAL STRIKE BEACON
- PLASMA GRENADE
- PULSE GRENADE
- PUMPKIN GRENADE
- SOUND GRENADE

THROWN WEAPONS

- DROSS
- THROWING KNIVES
- TOMAHAWK

BASEBALL GRENADE

- **TYPE:** GRENADE
- **CRAFTING RESTRICTIONS:** DEMOLITION EXPERT 1 (INT)
- **DAMAGE:** 125 (BALLISTIC)
- **FIRE RATE:** 0
- **RANGE:** 94

- **ACCURACY:** 0
- **WEIGHT:** 1
- **VALUE:** 20

An easy-to-make explosive that does a fair bit of damage. It won't reach the same levels as a Fragmentation Grenade, but the ease at which you can produce them more than makes up for it.

DROSS

- **TYPE:** THROWN WEAPON
- **DAMAGE:** 5 (BALLISTIC)
- **FIRE RATE:** 0
- **RANGE:** 94

- **ACCURACY:** 0
- **WEIGHT:** 0.5
- **VALUE:** 50

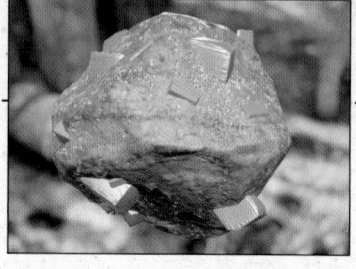

Exclusive to Daily Quest: Mistaken Identity, Dross is exactly as its name implies: total dross. It's used during the Dross Toss portion of that particular quest, wherein your goal is to throw these balls of trash into old tires. It may not be effective as a weapon, but it's a good time for those looking to let off some steam at Appalachia's one and only carnival.

CRYOGENIC GRENADE

- **TYPE:** GRENADE
- **CRAFTING RESTRICTIONS:** DEMOLITION EXPERT 3 (INT), SCIENCE 1 (INT)
- **DAMAGE:** 100 (BALLISTIC)
- **FIRE RATE:** 0
- **RANGE:** 94

- **ACCURACY:** 0
- **WEIGHT:** 0.5
- **VALUE:** 25

Instead of being bathed in a ball of fire, enemies will find themselves chilled to the bone and slowed to a near halt. Great for dealing with charging hordes of melee enemies or for giving you some vital time to reposition in a heated firefight.

FRAGMENTATION GRENADE

- **TYPE:** GRENADE
- **CRAFTING RESTRICTIONS:** DEMOLITION EXPERT 1 (INT)
- **DAMAGE:** 150 (BALLISTIC)
- **FIRE RATE:** 0
- **RANGE:** 94

- **ACCURACY:** 0
- **WEIGHT:** 0.5
- **VALUE:** 15

Your standard military-grade hand grenade. No bells or whistles, just pull the pin, throw the egg, and watch it explode. Simple as pie.

FRAGMENTATION GRENADE MIRV

- **TYPE:** GRENADE
- **CRAFTING RESTRICTIONS:** DEMOLITION EXPERT 3 (INT)
- **DAMAGE:** 100 (BALLISTIC)
- **FIRE RATE:** 0
- **RANGE:** 94

- **ACCURACY:** 0
- **WEIGHT:** 1
- **VALUE:** 50

A grenade that splinters off into a cluster of explosions, creating a blanket around the area it lands. It's not as powerful as a standard Fragmentation Grenade, but its coverage means enemies will have a harder time escaping once one of these things lands nearby.

HALLUCIGEN GAS GRENADE

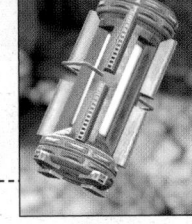

- **TYPE:** GRENADE
- **DAMAGE:** 1 (BALLISTIC)
- **FIRE RATE:** 0
- **RANGE:** 94
- **ACCURACY:** 0
- **WEIGHT:** 1
- **VALUE:** 25

Once thrown, a HalluciGen Gas Grenade will dispense gas that will cause all nearby enemies to frenzy and attack each other instead of you.

MOLOTOV COCKTAIL

- **TYPE:** GRENADE
- **DAMAGE:** 50 (BALLISTIC), 8 (ENERGY)
- **FIRE RATE:** 0
- **RANGE:** 94
- **ACCURACY:** 0
- **WEIGHT:** 0.5
- **VALUE:** 20

A Molotov Cocktail as you've always known it. Throw it at an enemy or on the ground to bathe your target in fire. The pool isn't the biggest, so either use it in a narrow choke point, or make sure it hits the enemy for max effect.

NUKA GRENADE

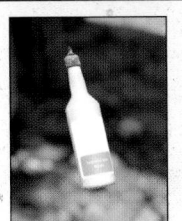

- **TYPE:** GRENADE
- **CRAFTING RESTRICTIONS:** DEMOLITION EXPERT 2 (INT)
- **DAMAGE:** 250 (BALLISTIC), 125 (RADIATION)
- **FIRE RATE:** 0
- **RANGE:** 94
- **ACCURACY:** 0
- **WEIGHT:** 0.5
- **VALUE:** 35

A pocket nuke ready to be thrown at a moment's notice. Don't expect to have these in your inventory often; the requirements for crafting them are demanding enough that you won't usually have more than a few in your inventory at any given time.

NUKA QUANTUM GRENADE

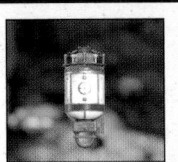

- **TYPE:** GRENADE
- **CRAFTING RESTRICTIONS:** DEMOLITION EXPERT 4 (INT)
- **DAMAGE:** 300 (BALLISTIC), 125 (RADIATION)
- **FIRE RATE:** 0
- **RANGE:** 94
- **ACCURACY:** 0
- **WEIGHT:** 0.5
- **VALUE:** 50

The Nuka Quantum Grenade is everything the Nuka Grenade is and more. If you have any hope of crafting these, you'll need to put your focus into building a character specialized in the INT stat. Few things will be able to stand up to an explosion created by one of these, which makes the price of admission worth the effort.

ORBITAL SCAN BEACON

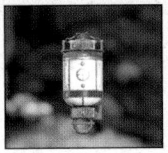

- **TYPE:** GRENADE
- **DAMAGE:** 1 (ENERGY)
- **FIRE RATE:** 0
- **RANGE:** 94
- **ACCURACY:** 0
- **WEIGHT:** 0.5
- **VALUE:** 50

If you've got a bad feeling in your gut, throw one of these out and a large scanning dome will appear around the immediate area. Any living thing caught in this dome will be marked with an icon that can even be seen behind objects and obstacles.

ORBITAL STRIKE BEACON

- **TYPE:** GRENADE
- **DAMAGE:** 1 (BALLISTIC)
- **FIRE RATE:** 0
- **RANGE:** 94
- **ACCURACY:** 0
- **WEIGHT:** 1
- **VALUE:** 50

Why go through the trouble of killing enemies when you can have an orbital missile platform do it for you? Throw one of these out and a targeting laser will appear on top of it. After a few seconds...BOOM! Nothing left but rubble and ash.

PLASMA GRENADE

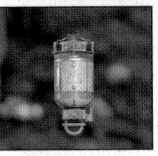

- **TYPE:** GRENADE
- **CRAFTING RESTRICTIONS:** DEMOLITION EXPERT 4 (INT), SCIENCE 1 (INT)
- **DAMAGE:** 200 (BALLISTIC), 200 (ENERGY)
- **FIRE RATE:** 0
- **RANGE:** 94
- **ACCURACY:** 0
- **WEIGHT:** 0.5
- **VALUE:** 30

This is a powerful grenade with hefty crafting restrictions. It has a relatively short delay before exploding. The explosion radius isn't particularly big, but you won't find a Grenade in Appalachia that deals more Energy damage than this one.

PULSE GRENADE

- **TYPE:** GRENADE
- **CRAFTING RESTRICTIONS:** DEMOLITION EXPERT 3 (INT), SCIENCE 1 (INT)
- **DAMAGE:** 175 (BALLISTIC), 175 (ENERGY)
- **FIRE RATE:** 0
- **RANGE:** 94
- **ACCURACY:** 0
- **WEIGHT:** 0.5
- **VALUE:** 20

Pulse Grenades are tailor-made to combat mechanical enemies. You wont get great results using them on the fleshy side of the bad-guy spectrum, but against robots? Let's just say that even a Genius Squad repair guy won't be able to put them back together again.

PUMPKIN GRENADE

- **TYPE:** GRENADE
- **DAMAGE:** 80 (BALLISTIC), 40 (RADIATION)
- **FIRE RATE:** 0
- **RANGE:** 94
- **ACCURACY:** 0
- **WEIGHT:** 0.5
- **VALUE:** 20

Obtained exclusively by completing Daily Quest: Trick or Treat?, Pumpkin Grenades deal both Ballistic and Energy damage, and anyone caught in its cloud will also take radiation damage for 5 seconds. A true triple threat.

THROWING KNIVES

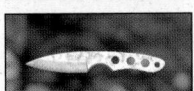

- **TYPE:** THROWN WEAPON
- **DAMAGE:** 75 (TYPE)
- **FIRE RATE:** 0
- **RANGE:** 12
- **ACCURACY:** 0
- **WEIGHT:** 0.25
- **VALUE:** 15

Sneaky, fast, deadly: Throwing Knives are the throwable weapon stealth players will always want at their side. As an added bonus, you'll also be able to pick up thrown knives, provided you can find where they landed.

TOMAHAWK

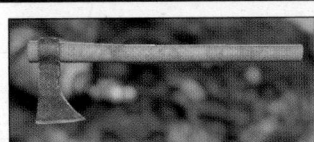

- **TYPE:** THROWN WEAPON
- **DAMAGE:** 100 (BALLISTIC)
- **FIRE RATE:** 0
- **RANGE:** 12
- **ACCURACY:** 0
- **WEIGHT:** 0.7
- **VALUE:** 15

Tomahawks are both quiet and deadly. Better yet, if you find where one landed, you can collect it and throw it again. Just make sure to practice a bit before using them in real combat; they are prone to losing altitude before reaching distant targets.

TRAINING

CRAFTING AND CAMPING

INVENTORY

QUESTS

ATLAS

BESTIARY

APPENDICES

MINES AND TRAPS

Mines and traps are tools for protecting your C.A.M.P. and for setting up a position on the battlefield that suits you much better than your opponent. Being chased by a group of foes? Get a little distance, throw a mine on the ground, and watch the sparks fly. Defending a Workshop? Drop some mines and traps in choke points and your enemies might think twice before pushing in. The more clever your placement, the more effective these tools of destruction are.

As far as Perk Cards are concerned, just about anything from the Explosive weapons section at the front of this chapter will work for mines as well. If you're looking to improve your traps, use Home Defense (AGI), which allows you to craft and disarm better traps.

MINES
— CRYO MINE
— EXPLOSIVE BAIT
— FRAGMENTATION MINE
— NUKE MINE
— PLASMA MINE
— PULSE MINE

CRYO MINE

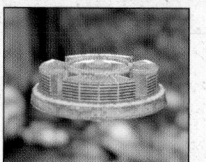

- TYPE: MINE
- CRAFTING RESTRICTIONS: DEMOLITION EXPERT 3 (INT), SCIENCE 1 (INT)
- DAMAGE: 175 (BALLISTIC)
- FIRE RATE: 0
- RANGE: 94
- ACCURACY: 0
- WEIGHT: 0.5
- VALUE: 30

This mine freezes enemies while doing a good bit of damage. They won't be frozen stiff, but they'll slow down enough for you to either take off running or finish them before they thaw out.

FRAGMENTATION MINE

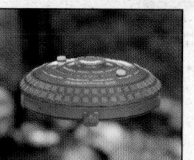

- TYPE: MINE
- CRAFTING RESTRICTIONS: DEMOLITION EXPERT 1 (INT)
- DAMAGE: 150 (BALLISTIC)
- FIRE RATE: 0
- RANGE: 94
- ACCURACY: 0
- WEIGHT: 0.5
- VALUE: 20

This is a standard explosive mine—no muss, no fuss. Throw it on the ground and wait for some poor sap to approach it. After a few quick beeps, they'll be little more than a folktale.

PLASMA MINE

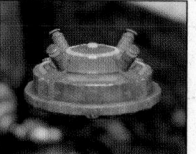

- TYPE: MINE
- CRAFTING RESTRICTIONS: DEMOLITION EXPERT 4 (INT), SCIENCE 1 (INT)
- DAMAGE: 200 (BALLISTIC), 200 (ENERGY)
- FIRE RATE: 0
- RANGE: 94
- ACCURACY: 0
- WEIGHT: 0.5
- VALUE: 35

The big brother of the Pulse Mine, the Plasma Mine is the perfect implement for dealing with pesky robotic enemies. It deals twice as much energy damage as the Pulse Mine but with increased Crafting Restrictions and components requirements.

EXPLOSIVE BAIT

- TYPE: MINE
- DAMAGE: 200 (BALLISTIC)
- FIRE RATE: 0
- RANGE: 94
- ACCURACY: 0
- WEIGHT: 0.5
- VALUE: 40

This mine draws in feral enemies and wild animals (Scorched and robotic enemies aren't particularly enchanted by it). Once the creatures gather around it, the mine detonates and sends them all to the forest in the sky.

NUKE MINE

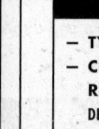

- TYPE: MINE
- CRAFTING RESTRICTIONS: DEMOLITION EXPERT 5 (INT)
- DAMAGE: 250 (BALLISTIC), 125 (RADIATION)
- FIRE RATE: 0
- RANGE: 94
- ACCURACY: 0
- WEIGHT: 0.5
- VALUE: 40

The most devastating mine in your arsenal, the Nuke Mine will sort just about any enemy that foolishly steps on it. You'll need to commit many of your SPECIAL points to INT to have even the slightest hope of seeing more than one of these during your journey, but those who make the effort will be rewarded with a truly devastating explosive.

PULSE MINE

- TYPE: MINE
- CRAFTING RESTRICTIONS: DEMOLITION EXPERT 3 (INT), SCIENCE 1 (INT)
- DAMAGE: 175 (BALLISTIC), 175 (ENERGY)
- FIRE RATE: 0
- RANGE: 94
- ACCURACY: 0
- WEIGHT: 0.5
- VALUE: 25

This is effective against robotic enemies, so you won't find much use for it against flesh-based enemies; a standard Fragmentation Mine will fit that purpose much better than this one.

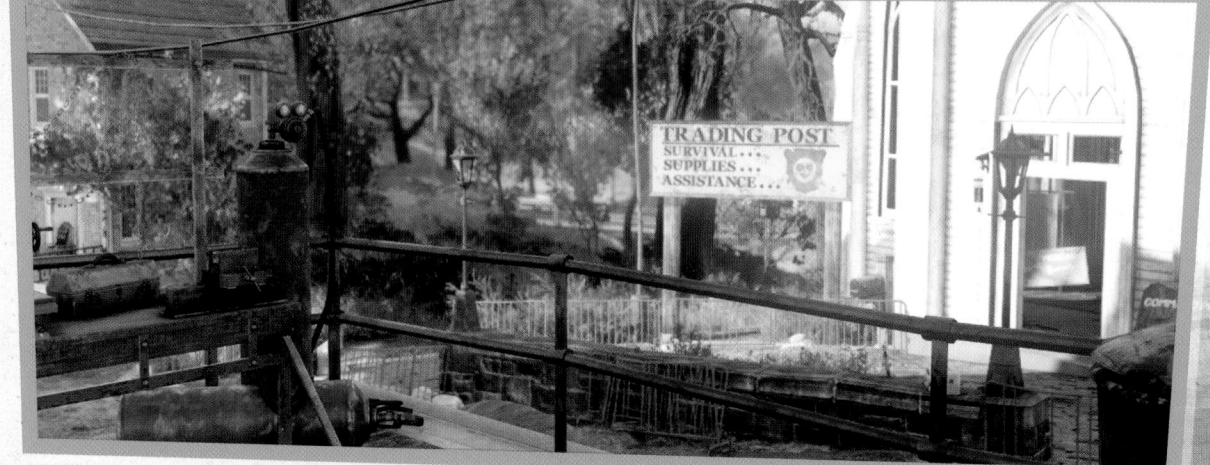

LEGENDARY EFFECTS

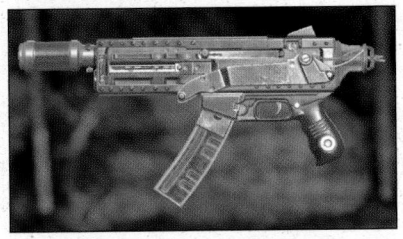

If you defeat a particularly strong enemy (i.e., one with stars next to its name), you will have a solid chance of receiving a Legendary piece of equipment (specifically a weapon or armor piece). Legendary equipment isn't new equipment, but equipment with a modifier that offers you bonuses and benefits while wearing or using it. You can identify a Legendary item by the modifier text in its title. For example: a Legendary 10 mm Pistol might appear as an Anti-Armor 10 mm Pistol or an Assassin's 10 mm Pistol.

Use the following list to learn about each modifier and how they benefit the weapons they are attached to.

LEGENDARY WEAPON EFFECTS

MODIFIER NAME	DESCRIPTION
Anti-Scorched	25% more damage against Scorched, 20% less against everything else.
Anti-Armor	Ignores 50% of your target's armor.
Assassin's	+10% damage to players.
Berserker's	Deal more damage the lower your Damage Resistance.
Bloodied	Does more damage the lower your health.
Concussive	+33% VATS hit chance
Executioner's	+50% more damage when your target is below 40% health.
Explosive	Bullets explode for 15 area damage.

MODIFIER NAME	DESCRIPTION
Exterminator's	Does 50% more damage against Mirelurks and bugs.
Furious	Damage increased after each consecutive hit on the same target.
Ghoul Slayer's	Does 50% more damage against Ghouls.
Hunter's	Does 50% more damage against animals.
Instigating	Does double damage if the target is at full health.
Junkie's	Deal more damage the more chem withdrawal effects you currently have.
Medic's	V.A.T.S. crits will heal you and your group.

MODIFIER NAME	DESCRIPTION
Mutant's	Damage increased by 10% if you are mutated.
Mutant Slayer's	+30% damage to Super Mutants.
Never Ending	Unlimited ammo capacity.
Nocturnal	Does increasing amounts of damage as the night grows longer, but less damage during the day.
Stalker's	If not in combat, +100% V.A.T.S. accuracy at +50% AP cost.
Suppressor's	Reduce your target's damage output by 20% for 3 seconds.
Troubleshooter's	+30% damage to robots
Two Shot	Shoots an additional projectile.
Zealot's	+30% damage to Ghouls.

EXCEPTIONAL WEAPONS

Exceptional Weapons are obtained as quest rewards for specific quests and only come in one flavor. Each one is a modification of a preexisting weapon, but with added bonuses that make them separate and distinct.

EXCEPTIONAL WEAPONS

NAME	WEAPON TYPE	BONUS	NOTES
All Rise	Two-Handed Melee	—	Obtained as a reward for completing Side Quest: Mayor for a Day.
Ancient Blade	One-Handed Melee	—	Obtained as part of Event: Breach and Clear.
Anti-Scorched Training Pistol	10 mm Automatic Pistol	+25% to Scorched, –20% to everything else	Given before entering the Belching Betty mine during Main Quest: Into the Fire.
Black Diamond	One-Handed Melee	—	Obtained as a reward for completing Main Quest: Flavors of Mayhem.
Blade of Bastet	One-Handed Melee	Increased armor penetration	Obtained as a reward for completing Mistress of Mystery Quest: Forging a Legend. Armor penetration increased when wearing the Eye of Ra.
Bunker Buster	Heavy Gun, Explosive	—	Obtained as a reward for completing Main Quest: One of Us.
Camden Whacker	One-Handed Melee	—	Purchased with Fuzzy Tokens at the Camden Park prize shop in the Ash Heap
Daisy Cutter	Explosive, Heavy Gun	—	Rewarded for completing Side Quest: An Organic Panic.
The Dragon	Exotic Weapon, Non-Automatic Rifle	Chance to cripple. Extra limb damage.	—
Dross	Thrown Weapon	None	Only usable during Daily Quest: Mistaken Identity as part of the Dross Toss minigame.
Grant's Saber	One-Handed Melee	—	Obtained as part of Mistress of Mystery: Forging a Legend.
Meteoric Sword	One-Handed Melee	+10% damage vs. Humans, 90% reduced weight, 50% more durability	Obtained as potential award from Event: Lode Baring

NAME	WEAPON TYPE	BONUS	NOTES
Nailer	One-Handed Melee	Does more damage the lower your health is.	Obtained as a reward for completing Event: One Violent Night.
Paddle Ball	Exotic Weapon	None	Obtained by trading in Mr. Fuzzy Tokens in Camden Park.
Pumpkin Grenades	Grenade	Target takes additional damage and radiation for 5s.	Obtained by completing Daily Quest: Trick or Treat.
Pyrolyzer	Heavy Gun, Energy Gun	Reduce your target's damage output by 20% for 3s	Obtained by completing Side Quest: Tracking Unknowns.
Rose's Syringer	Pipe Gun, Exotic Weapon	—	Obtained as part of Main Quest: Flavors of Mayhem.
Somerset Special	Non-Automatic Pistol	—	Obtained as a reward for completing Event: Back on the Beat.
Voice of Set	Non-Automatic Pistol	Additional electric damage vs. robots	Obtained as a reward for completing Mistress of Mystery Quest: Prototypical Problems. Does additional damage and has a chance to stun robots when wearing the Eye of Ra.
Vox Syringer	Pipe Gun, Exotic Weapon	Can make the target "speak"	Found in Monongah as the start of Daily Quest: Someone To Talk To.

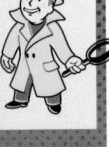

Helpful Hint from Vault Boy!
Several Mistress of Mystery items (the Voice of Set, Blade of Bastet, and Garb of Mysteries) can be upgraded to higher-level, higher-damage versions at weapon or armor workbenches as your level increases.

APPAREL

CLOTHING

These items provide little more than snappy fashion. You're not going to charge headlong into battle wearing little more than a bathrobe without losing an appendage in the process—but you'll definitely give your enemies something to think about if you do.

OUTFITS AND DRESSES

NAME	WEIGHT	VALUE	NOTES
Amusement Park Worker Outfit	1	10	—
Army Fatigues	1	12	—
Asylum Work Uniform	1	50	Also comes in blue, brown, forest, green, pink, red, weathered, white, dirtied white and yellow.
Baseball Uniform	1	10	—
Bathrobe	1	100	—
Black Fisherman's Overalls	1	115	Also comes in Brown
Black Vest and Slacks	1	10	—
Bomber Jacket	1	20	—
Brotherhood Lab Coat	1	19	—
BoS Jumpsuit	1	6	—
Bottle and Cappy Jacket & Jeans	1	5	This outfit comes in red or orange.
Brotherhood Fatigues	0.5	25	—
Camden Park Uniform	1	10	—
Cappy Jacket & Jeans	1	5	—
Casual Outfit	1	16	—
Civil War–Era Dress	1	10	—
Civil War Era–Suit	1	10	—
Clean Steel Worker Uniform	0.3	150	—
Clown Outfit	1	10	—
Confederate Uniform	1	10	—
Cop Uniform	1	10	—
Dirty Army Fatigues	1	12	—
Dirty Black Suit	1	14	—
Dirty Postman Uniform	1	10	—
Dirty Tan Suit	1	14	—
Drifter Outfit	1	14	—
Enclave Officer Uniform	0.3	15	—
Engineer's Uniform	1	15	—
Explorer Outfit	1	13	—
Farmhand Clothes	1	10	—
Field Scribe's Uniform	1	20	—
Fire Breather Uniform	1	10	—
Fireman Uniform	1	10	—
Fisherman's Outfit	1	10	—
Fisherman's Overalls	1	12	—
Forest Camo Jumpsuit	1	6	—
Golf Outfit	1	14	—
Golf Skirt	1	14	—
Grafton Monsters Jacket and Jeans	1	20	—

NAME	WEIGHT	VALUE	NOTES
Greaser Jacket and Jeans	1	20	—
Green Fisherman's Overalls	1	15	—
Green Shirt and Combat Boots	1	11	—
Grey Fisherman's Overalls	1	12	—
Halloween Costume Skeleton	1	10	—
Halloween Costume Skull	0.3	15	—
Halloween Costume Witch	1	10	—
Hunter's Long Coat	0.5	400	—
Lab Coat	1	10	—
Laundered Blue Dress	1	19	Also comes in cream or pink.
Leather Coat	1	13	—
Letterman's Jacket and Jeans	1	20	—
Longshoreman Outfit	1	10	—
Marine Tactical Armor	0.5	63	—
Mechanic Jumpsuit	1	6	—
Military Fatigues	0.5	10	—
Military Intel Officer Uniform	0.3	15	—
Military Officer Uniform	0.3	15	—
Miner Uniform	0.3	15	—
Mr. Fuzzy Mascot Suit	1	10	—
Nuka World Geyser Jacket & Jeans	1	5	—
Nuka World Jacket & Jeans	1	5	—
Nurse Uniform	1	10	—
Orange Shirt Western Outfit	1	13	—
Padded Blue Jacket	1	10	—
Pastor's Vestments	1	10	—
Patched Suit	1	10	—
Patched Three-Piece Suit	1	10	—
Prisoner Miner Uniform	0.3	15	—
Pristine Moe Outfit	1	10	—
Radstag Hide Outfit	1	13	—
Ranger Outfit	1	10	—
Ranger Outfit Clean	1	10	—
Ratty Skirt	1	11	—
Red and Khaki Shirt and Slacks	1	55	—
Red Dress	1	15	—

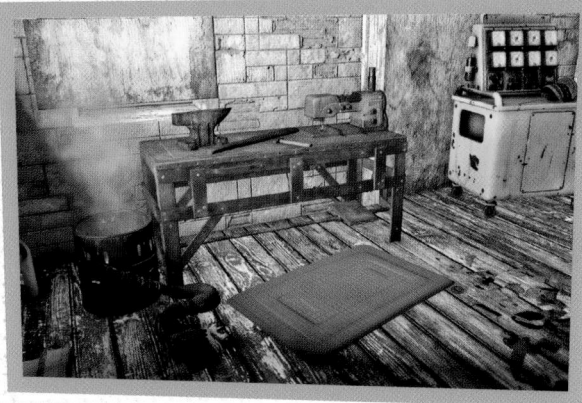

NAME	WEIGHT	VALUE	NOTES
Responder Cop Uniform	1	10	—
Responder Fireman Uniform	1	10	—
Responders Paramedic Jumpsuit	1	6	—
Ritual Bindings	1	10	—
Scavenger Outfit	1	13	—
Science Scribe's Uniform	1	15	—
Sequin Dress	1	31	—
Skiing Navy and Orange Outfit	1	10	Also comes in purple and white or red and green.
Skiing Outfit	1	10	—
Skiing Outfit Clean	1	10	—
Skiing Purple and White Outfit	1	25	—
Soiled Mr. Fuzzy Mascot Suit	1	10	—
Spacesuit	1	10	—
Spacesuit Clean	1	10	—
Spacesuit Jumpsuit	1	10	—
Steel Worker Uniform	0.3	15	—
Straight Jacket	1	10	—
Straight Jacket Clean	1	10	—
Summer Shorts	1	16	—
Surveyor Outfit	1	10	—
Suspenders and Slacks	1	10	—
Sweater Vest and Slacks	1	17	—
Swimsuit	1	10	—
Tattered Field Jacket	1	13	—
Tattered Moe Outfit	1	10	—
Tattered Rags	1	1	—
Traveling Leather Coat	1	13	—
T-Shirt and Slacks	1	14	—
Union Outfit	1	25	—
Union Uniform	1	10	—
Union Uniform	1	25	—
Vault-Tec Jumpsuit	1	6	—
VTU Jacket and Jeans	1	20	—
Western Outfit	1	13	—
Western Outfit & Chaps	1	13	—
White and Grey Shirt and Slacks	1	55	—
White Powder Jumpsuit	1	6	—
Whitespring Jumpsuit	1	6	—
Winter Jacket and Jeans	1	20	—

HELMETS AND HEADWEAR

NAME	WEIGHT	VALUE	NOTES
Asylum Worker Hat	1	15	Comes in blue, brown, forest, green, pink, red, weathered, white, dirtied white and yellow.
Baseball Cap	0.3	15	—
Battered Fedora	0.5	6	—
Beer Hat	0.3	15	—
Black Cowboy Hat	0.3	15	—
Black Prospector's Hat	0.3	15	—
Black-Rim Glasses	0.1	8	—
Blue Bandanna	0.1	1	—
Blue Batting Helmet	0.5	5	—
BoS Hood	0.5	25	—
Bottlecap Sunglasses	0.2	27	—
Bowler Hat	0.3	15	—
Camo Bandanna	0.1	1	—
Campaign Hat	0.3	15	—
Chef Hat	0.5	15	—
Civil War–Era Top Hat	0.5	10	—
Clown Hat	0.3	15	—
Combat Armor Helmet	0.5	25	—
Confederate Hat	0.5	10	—
Cop Cap	0.5	15	Comes in a Dirty or Clean form.
Crumpled Fedora	0.5	15	—
Dirty Army Helmet	1	20	—
Dirty Enclave Officer Hat	0.3	15	—
Dirty Fedora	0.5	8	—
Dirty Postman Hat	0.4	15	—
Enclave Officer Hat	0.4	15	—
Eyebot Helmet	0.5	20	—
Eyeglasses	0.1	7	—
Faded Visor	0.1	10	—
Faschnacht Death Skull Mask	0.5	10	—
Faschnacht Devil Mask	0.5	10	—
Faschnacht Harlequin Mask	0.5	10	—
Faschnacht Man Mask	0.5	10	—
Faschnacht Merman Mask	0.5	10	—
Faschnacht Napoleon Mask	0.5	10	—
Faschnacht Owl Mask	0.5	10	—
Faschnacht Second Man Mask	0.5	10	—
Faschnacht Witch Mask	0.5	10	—
Fashion Glasses	0.2	27	—
Field Scribe's Hat	0.5	8	—
Fireman Helmet	0.3	15	—
Fisherman's Hat	0.5	5	—
Flight Helmet	0.5	25	—
Gray Knit Cap	0.5	15	—
Green Bandanna	0.1	1	—
Green Hood	0.5	5	—
Halloween Costume Witch Hat	0.3	15	—
Hard Hat	0.5	15	—
Hooded Rags	1	7	—
Hunter's Hood	0.5	38	—
Leopard Print Bandanna	0.1	1	—
Marine Armor Helmet	0.5	250	—
Metal Helmet	0.5	38	—

NAME	WEIGHT	VALUE	NOTES
Military Cap	0.2	15	—
Military Intel Officer Dress Hat	0.3	15	—
Military Intel Officer Hat	0.3	15	—
Military Officer Dress Hat	0.3	15	—
Miner Hat	0.3	16	—
Miner Hat Clean	0.3	16	—
Mining Helmet	0.5	51	—
Monster Mask	0	0	—
Mr. Fuzzy Mascot Head	1	10	—
Mr. Fuzzy Mining Helmet	0.5	51	—
Newsboy Cap	0.5	5	—
Old Fisherman's Hat	0.5	5	—
Party Hat	0.3	15	—
Pompadour Wig	0.2	15	—
Prospector's Hat	0.3	15	—
Ranger Hat	0.3	10	—
Ranger Hat Clean	0.3	10	—
Red Bandanna	0.1	1	—
Responder Fireman Helmet	0.3	15	—
Ritual Headpiece	0.5	10	—
Ritual Hood	0.5	10	—
Ritual Mask	0.5	10	—
Sack Hood	0.5	5	—
Sea Captain's Hat	0.5	25	—
Sentry Bot Helmet	0.5	50	—
Skiing Outfit Hat	0.3	15	—
Skiing Outfit Hat Clean	0.3	15	—
Skull Bandanna	0.1	1	—
Soiled Mr. Fuzzy Mascot Head	1	10	—
Steel Worker Hat	0.3	15	—
Steel Worker Hat Clean	0.3	15	—
Striped Bandanna	0.1	1	—
Tin Foil Hat	0.3	15	—
Triggerman Bowler	0.3	15	—
Trilby Hat	0.5	5	—
Union Hat	0.5	10	—
Ushanka Hat	0.3	15	—
Vault-Tec Security Helmet	0.5	20	—
VTU Baseball Cap	0.5	15	—
Welding Helmet	0.5	20	—
Wood Helmet	3.5	15	—
Wool Fisherman's Cap	0.5	5	—
Wrapped Cap	0.5	5	—
Yellow Slicker Hat	0.3	15	—

ACCESSORIES

NAME	WEIGHT	VALUE
Medical Goggles	0.5	12
Old Ring	0.1	100
Patrolman Sunglasses	0.1	8
Prisoner Collar	0.5	15
Sunglasses	0.1	7
Surgical Mask	0.2	5
Wedding Ring	0.1	100
Welding Goggles	0.2	0
Wraparound Goggles	0.1	4

ARMOR

If clothing is all form and no function, armor is the other side of the coin. A few things to keep in mind with armor:

- UNDERARMOR DOESN'T REPLACE ANY OTHER ARMOR YOU PUT ON, SO BE SURE TO FIND A SUIT OF IT AND ALWAYS KEEP IT ON. YOU'LL GET RESISTANCE INCREASES AND WILL OFTEN GET S.P.E.C.I.A.L. STAT BOOSTS.
- MOST ARMOR IS PIECEMEAL, SO DON'T BE AFRAID TO MIX AND MATCH.
- PAY CLOSE ATTENTION TO A PIECE OF ARMOR'S WEIGHT. ALONE, MOST PIECES WON'T HURT YOUR STORAGE CAPACITY, BUT TOGETHER SOME SETS WILL LEAVE YOU HOBBLING ALONG APPALACHIA JUST BEGGING FOR A PLACE TO STORE SOME OF YOUR GEAR.
- MOST ARMOR CAN BE CRAFTED AT AN ARMOR WORKBENCH WITH THE PROPER PLANS, SO CHECK A BENCH REGULARLY TO UPGRADE YOUR GEAR.

UNDERARMOR

NAME	DAMAGE RESISTANCE	ENERGY RESISTANCE	RADIATION RESISTANCE	WEIGHT	VALUE	NOTE
Brotherhood Knight Suit	4	2	1	1.4	36	—
Brotherhood Officer Suit	4	2	1	1.4	36	—
Brotherhood Soldier Suit	4	2	1	1.4	36	—
Fireman Uniform	1	1	1	1.4	24	+1 CHR
Fireman Uniform	2	4	1	1.4	36	+1 PER
Flannel Shirt and Jeans	1	1	1	1.4	60	—
Forest Operative Underarmor	2	4	1	1.4	90	+1 PER
Harness	1	—	—	1.1	22	—
Long Johns	2	1	—	1.4	60	+1 AGI
Marine Wetsuit	2	2	2	2.8	105	+1 END
Raider Leathers	2	1	—	1.4	60	+1 AGI
Road Leathers	2	1	—	1.4	60	+1 AGI
Undershirt & Jeans	1	1	1	1.4	60	+1 CHR
Urban Operative Underarmor	2	4	1	1.4	90	+1 PER
Vault 76 Jumpsuit	1	1	1	1.4	60	+1 LCK
Vault-Tec University Jumpsuit	1	1	1	1.4	60	+1 LCK

STURDY ARMOR

NAME	LEVEL	DAMAGE RESISTANCE	ENERGY RESISTANCE	RADIATION RESISTANCE	WEIGHT	VALUE
Marine Armor Chest Piece	45	46	18	18	8	101
Marine Armor Left Arm	45	19	17	—	3.5	61
Marine Armor Left Leg	45	18	18	—	4	97
Marine Armor Right Arm	45	19	17	—	3.5	61
Marine Armor Right Leg	45	19	18	—	4	97
Sturdy Combat Armor Chest Piece	20	24	24	—	9.8	284
Sturdy Combat Armor Left Arm	20	9	8	—	3.85	243
Sturdy Combat Armor Left Leg	20	9	8	—	4.2	213
Sturdy Combat Armor Right Arm	20	9	8	—	3.85	243
Sturdy Combat Armor Right Leg	20	9	8	—	4.2	213
Sturdy Leather Chest Piece	—	7	8	—	5.6	132
Sturdy Leather Left Arm	—	2	3	—	2.8	69
Sturdy Leather Left Leg	—	2	3	—	3.15	73
Sturdy Leather Right Arm	—	2	3	—	2.8	69
Sturdy Leather Right Leg	—	2	3	—	3.15	73
Sturdy Metal Chest Piece	10	21	5	—	7.7	233

NAME	LEVEL	DAMAGE RESISTANCE	ENERGY RESISTANCE	RADIATION RESISTANCE	WEIGHT	VALUE
Sturdy Metal Left Arm	10	11	2	—	3.5	192
Sturdy Metal Left Leg	10	11	2	—	3.5	132
Study Metal Right Arm	10	11	2	—	3.5	192
Sturdy Metal Right Leg	10	11	2	—	3.5	132
Sturdy Raider Chest Piece	5	14	4	—	6.3	132
Sturdy Raider Left Arm	5	7	2	—	3.15	213
Sturdy Raider Left Leg	5	7	2	—	3.5	26
Sturdy Raider Right Arm	5	7	2	—	3.15	213
Sturdy Raider Right Leg	5	7	2	—	3.5	79
Sturdy Robot Chest Piece	10	11	10	6	8.4	203

NAME	LEVEL	DAMAGE RESISTANCE	ENERGY RESISTANCE	RADIATION RESISTANCE	WEIGHT	VALUE
Sturdy Robot Left Arm	10	4	3	4	3.5	182
Sturdy Robot Left Leg	10	4	3	4	3.85	134
Sturdy Robot Right Arm	10	4	3	4	3.5	182
Sturdy Robot Right Leg	10	4	3	4	3.5	122
Trapper Chest Piece	15	4	6	13	5	53
Trapper Left Arm	15	6	4	5	3	41
Trapper Left Leg	15	6	4	5	3.5	32
Trapper Right Arm	15	6	4	5	3	41
Trapper Right Leg	15	6	4	5	3.5	32

LIGHT ARMOR

NAME	LEVEL	DAMAGE RESISTANCE	ENERGY RESISTANCE	RADIATION RESISTANCE	WEIGHT	VALUE	NOTE
Combat Armor Chest Piece	20	17	16	—	7	49	—
Combat Armor Left Arm	20	7	6	—	2.8	49	—
Combat Armor Left Leg	20	7	6	—	3	20	—
Combat Armor Right Arm	20	7	6	—	2.8	49	—
Combat Armor Right Leg	20	7	6	—	3	20	—
Leather Chest Piece	1	5	6	—	4	32	—
Leather Left Arm	1	2	2	—	2	19	—
Leather Left Leg	1	2	2	—	2.3	21	—
Leather Right Arm	1	2	2	—	2	19	—
Leather Right Leg	1	2	2	—	2.3	21	—
Metal Chest Piece	10	15	3	—	5.5	32	—
Metal Left Arm	10	8	1	—	2.5	36	—
Metal Left Leg	10	8	1	—	2.5	12	—
Metal Right Arm	10	8	1	—	2.5	36	—
Metal Right Leg	10	8	1	—	2.5	12	—
Raider Chest Piece	5	10	3	—	4.5	41	—

NAME	LEVEL	DAMAGE RESISTANCE	ENERGY RESISTANCE	RADIATION RESISTANCE	WEIGHT	VALUE	NOTE
Raider Left Arm	5	5	1	—	2.5	28	—
Raider Left Leg	5	5	1	—	2.5	28	—
Raider Right Arm	5	5	1	—	2.5	28	—
Raider Right Leg	5	5	1	—	2.5	28	—
Robot Chest Piece	10	8	7	4	6	20	—
Robot Left Arm	10	3	2	1	2.5	32	—
Robot Left Leg	10	3	2	1	2.8	13	—
Robot Right Arm	10	3	2	1	2.5	32	—
Robot Right Leg	10	3	2	1	2.8	8	—
Spike Armor	11	10	12	—	7	41	—
Stand Fast	—	2	6	1	2.8	8	Modded Combat Armor; obtained after completing Main Quest: Early Warnings.
Wood Chest Piece	1	8	3	—	3.5	20	—
Wood Left Arm	1	3	1	—	1.8	12	—
Wood Left Leg	1	3	1	—	1.8	8	—
Wood Right Arm	1	3	1	—	1.8	12	—
Wood Right Leg	1	3	1	—	1.8	8	—

HEAVY ARMOR

NAME	LEVEL	DAMAGE RESISTANCE	ENERGY RESISTANCE	RADIATION RESISTANCE	WEIGHT	VALUE	NOTE
Cage Armor	—	25	27	—	10	73	—
Forest Scout Armor Chest Piece	45	56	36	—	7	49	—
Forest Scout Armor Left Arm	45	23	18	—	2.8	49	—
Forest Scout Armor Left Leg	45	23	18	—	3	20	—
Forest Scout Armor Right Arm	45	23	18	—	2.8	49	—
Forest Scout Armor Right Leg	45	23	18	—	3	20	—
Heavy Combat Armor Chest Piece	20	27	26	—	12.6	446	—
Heavy Combat Armor Left Arm	20	10	9	—	4.95	375	—
Heavy Combat Armor Left Leg	20	10	9	—	5.4	365	—

NAME	LEVEL	DAMAGE RESISTANCE	ENERGY RESISTANCE	RADIATION RESISTANCE	WEIGHT	VALUE	NOTE
Heavy Combat Armor Right Arm	20	10	9	—	4.95	375	—
Heavy Combat Armor Right Leg	20	10	9	—	5.4	365	—
Heavy Leather Chest Piece	—	7	10	—	7.2	182	—
Heavy Leather Left Arm	—	3	3	—	3.6	19	—
Heavy Leather Left Leg	—	3	3	—	4.05	93	—
Heavy Leather Right Arm	—	3	3	—	3.6	89	—
Heavy Leather Right Leg	—	3	3	—	4.05	93	—
Heavy Metal Chest Piece	10	25	5	—	9.9	385	—

TRAINING

CRAFTING AND C.A.M.P.ING

INVENTORY

QUESTS

ATLAS

BESTIARY

APPENDICES

NAME	LEVEL	DAMAGE RESISTANCE	ENERGY RESISTANCE	RADIATION RESISTANCE	WEIGHT	VALUE	NOTE
Heavy Metal Left Arm	10	13	3	—	4.5	294	—
Heavy Metal Left Leg	10	13	3	—	4.5	233	—
Heavy Metal Right Arm	10	13	3	—	4.5	233	—
Heavy Metal Right Leg	10	13	3	—	4.5	294	—
Heavy Raider Chest Piece	5	17	5	—	8.1	162	—
Heavy Raider Left Arm	5	8	3	—	4.05	365	—
Heavy Raider Left Leg	5	8	3	—	4.5	365	—
Heavy Raider Right Arm	5	8	3	—	4.05	365	—
Heavy Raider Right Leg	5	8	3	—	4.5	89	—
Heavy Robot Chest Piece	10	13	12	7	10.8	354	—
Heavy Robot Left Arm	10	5	4	5	4.5	284	—
Heavy Robot Left Leg	10	5	4	5	4.95	235	—
Heavy Robot Right Arm	10	5	4	5	4.5	284	—
Heavy Robot Right Leg	10	5	4	5	4.95	223	—
Helmeted Cage Armor	—	29	35	—	11	89	-2 PER, Prevents damage from airborne hazards.
Helmeted Spike Armor	—	13	15	—	17	53	Prevents damage from airborne hazards.
Hunter's Pelt Outfit	—	16	15	—	15	69	—
Urban Scout Armor Chest Piece	40	51	33	—	7	49	—
Urban Scout Armor Left Arm	45	12	18	—	2.75	49	—
Urban Scout Armor Left Leg	45	23	18	—	2.5	20	—
Urban Scout Armor Right Arm	45	12	18	—	2.75	49	—
Urban Scout Armor Right Leg	45	23	18	—	2.5	20	—

HAZMAT SUITS

Hazmat Suits aren't intended for combat, but they will offer you the best radiation protection available. Make sure to pick one up before heading into a blast zone.

HAZMAT SUITS

NAME	LEVEL	DAMAGE RESISTANCE	ENERGY RESISTANCE	RADIATION RESISTANCE	WEIGHT	VALUE
Damaged Hazmat Suit	—	1	0	500	4	45
Hazmat Suit	—	—	—	1,000	5	69
Prototype Hazmat Suit	—	1	—	1,000	5	69

REBREATHERS AND FACE MASKS

Gas masks and similar specialty headgear prevent damage and negative effects from airborne hazards, but they tend to reduce your Perception.

REBREATHERS AND FACE MASKS

NAME	WEIGHT	VALUE
Fire Breather Helmet	0.3	15
Forest Scout Armor Mask	0.5	25
Flight Helmet	0.5	25
Gas Mask	0.5	10
Gas Mask with Goggles	0.5	10
Marine Tactical Helmet	0.5	25
Red Flight Helmet	0.5	25
Sack Hood with Hoses	0.5	5
Sack Hood with Straps	0.5	5
Spacesuit Helmet	0.3	15
Spacesuit Helmet Clean	0.3	15
Spacesuit Jumpsuit Helmet	0.3	15
Urban Scout Armor Mask	7	49

LEGENDARY EFFECTS

Sometimes, after completing certain quests and after defeating enemies with stars next to their names, you'll earn a piece of Legendary equipment for your troubles. The most obvious indicator that a piece of equipment is Legendary is that it sports a Modifier Name next to its actual name. For example: "Mutant's Metal Torso," "Assassin's Leather Right Arm," and so on. Use this table to figure out precisely what each modifier does and what you should aim for if you're trying to make a specific build.

LEGENDARY ARMOR EFFECTS

NAME	DESCRIPTION
Acrobat's	Reduces falling damage by 50%.
Assassin's	Reduces damage from humans by 15%.
Bolstering	Grants increased Energy and Damage Resistance the lower your health.
Cavalier's	Reduces damage while blocking or sprinting by 15%.
Chameleon's	Enemies have a harder time detecting you while you're sneaking and not moving.
Duelist's	10% change to disarm melee attacker on hit.
Exterminator's	Reduces damage from Mirelurks and bugs by 15%.
Ghoul Slayer's	Recuces damage from Ghouls by 15%.
Hunter's	Reduces damage from animals by 15%.
Junkie's	Take less damage the more chem withdrawal effects you currently have.
Mutant Slayer's	Reduces damage to Super Mutants by 15%.
Sprinter's	Increases movement speed by 10%.
Troubleshooter's	Reduces damage from Robots by 15%.

UNIQUE APPAREL

UNIQUE APPAREL ITEMS

NAME	ITEM TYPE	BONUS	NOTES
Diver Suit	Hazmat Suit	Offers some protection from radiation.	—
Eye of Ra	Accessory	Enhances the Mistress of Mystery's regalia	Obtained as part of Mistress of Mystery Quest: The Mistress of Mystery. Must be worn with the Garb of Mysteries
Garb of Mysteries	Light Armor	Ballistic and Energy Resistance; Improves Perception and Sneak. Effects increased if wearing the Eye of Ra.	Obtained from the Fabricator after completing the Mistress of Mystery Quest: Initiate of Mysteries.
Last Bastion	Urban Enclave Torso	—	Obtained as a reward for completing "Officer on Deck."
Prototype Hazmat Suit	Hazmat Suit	—	Obtained as part of Side Quest: Tracking Unknowns.
Stand Fast	Combat Armor	—	Obtained as a reward for completing "Early Warnings."
Silver Lining	Leather Torso	—	Obtained as a reward for completing "Tentative Plans."
Trail Warden	Metal Torso	—	Obtained as a reward for completing "Bureau of Tourism."
Veil of Secrets	Headwear	Prevents damage and disease from airborne hazards	Obtained from the Fabricator after completing the Mistress of Mystery Quest: Into the Mystery.
Worn Veil	Headwear	—	Obtained as part of the Mistress of Mystery Quest: Into the Mystery.

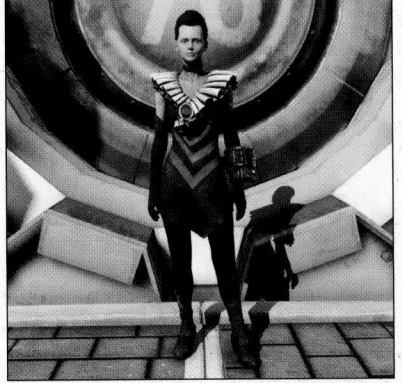

Eye of Ra, and Garb of Mysteries

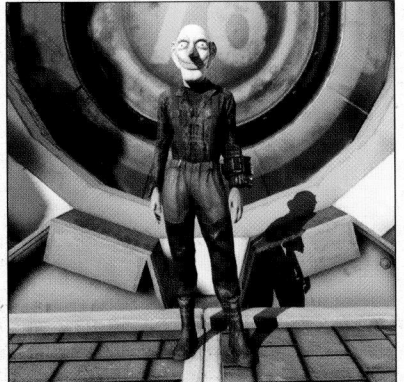

Faschnacht Man Mask and Fisherman's Outfit

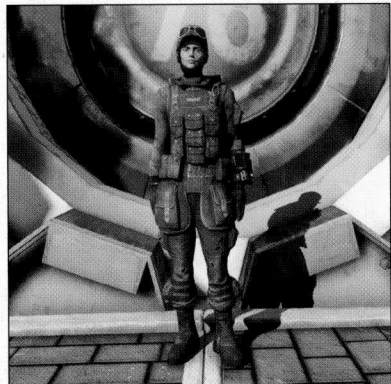

Field Scribe's Hat and Outfit

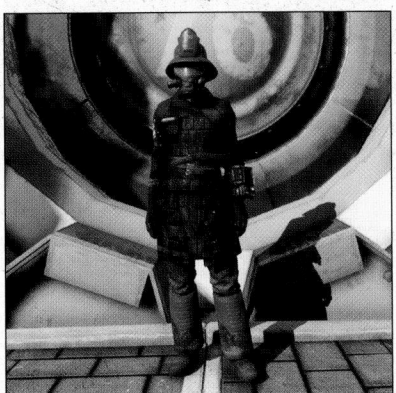

Fireman's Hat and Firebreather's Outfit

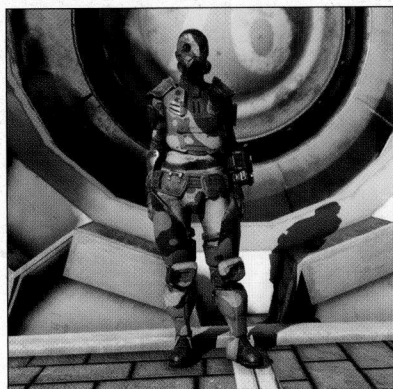

Forest Scout Armor

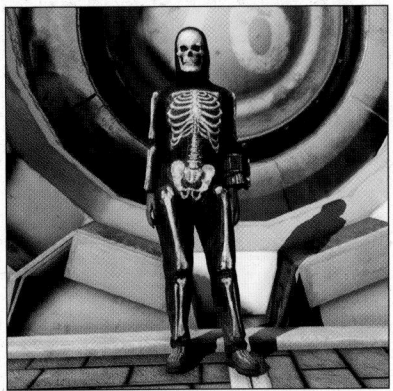

Halloween Skeleton Outfit

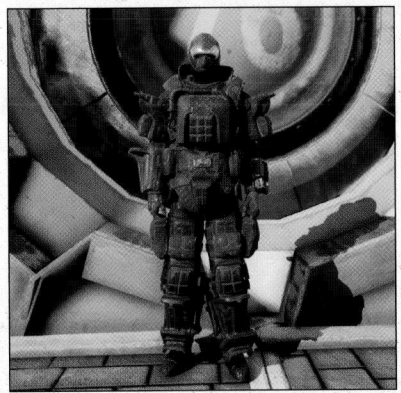

Marine Armor

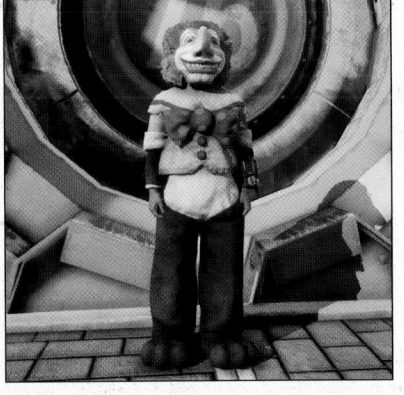

Monster Mask and Mr. Fuzzy Mascot Suit

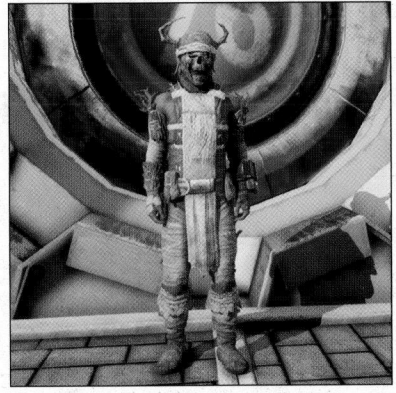

Ritual Mask and Bindings

TRAINING

CRAFTING AND C.A.M.P.ING

INVENTORY

QUESTS

ATLAS

BESTIARY

APPENDICES

POWER ARMOR

When it comes to saving your hide, Power Armor is second to none, and with storage restrictions at an all-time high, having a mechanized suit with loads of storage space simply can't be beat. You'll constantly have to be on the lookout for Fusion Cores, however—these suits require energy and they drink it down like a cold Nuka-Cola on a hot Appalachian summer day.

Most sets of Power Armor are found by scavenging loot off dead enemies and as random quest rewards (the Excavator set being the only exception). You can expect to complete a lot of Daily Quests and events to obtain all of the parts to most of these sets, so if you're struggling to put a complete suit together, don't take it personally; everyone traversing Appalachia is in the same boat.

If you're looking for more details on all of the suits of Power Armor available to you from day one, read on.

RAIDER POWER ARMOR

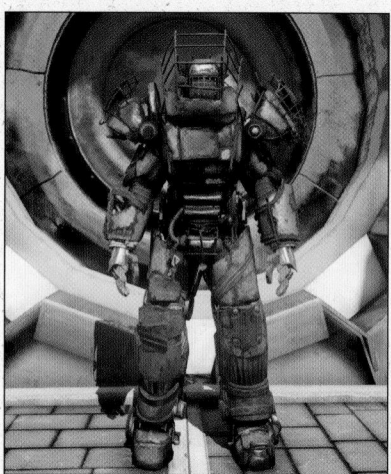

Your very first set of Power Armor isn't going to turn any heads, but it will get the job done (at least until your next set). While its resistances aren't particularly high, it will serve you well for the time you have it.

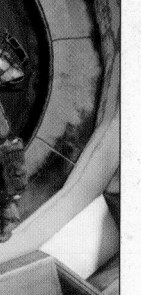

RAIDER POWER HELMET

- **LEVEL:** 15
- **DAMAGE RESISTANCE:** 24
- **ENERGY RESISTANCE:** 23
- **RADIATION RESISTANCE:** 23
- **WEIGHT:** 10
- **VALUE:** 41
- **NOTE: PREVENTS DAMAGE AND DISEASE FROM AIRBORNE AND WATERBORNE HAZARDS.**

RAIDER POWER RIGHT ARM

- **LEVEL:** 15
- **DAMAGE RESISTANCE:** 24
- **ENERGY RESISTANCE:** 23
- **RADIATION RESISTANCE:** 23
- **WEIGHT:** 10
- **VALUE:** 61

RAIDER POWER LEFT ARM

- **LEVEL:** 15
- **DAMAGE RESISTANCE:** 24
- **ENERGY RESISTANCE:** 23
- **RADIATION RESISTANCE:** 23
- **WEIGHT:** 10
- **VALUE:** 61

RAIDER POWER RIGHT LEG

- **LEVEL:** 15
- **DAMAGE RESISTANCE:** 24
- **ENERGY RESISTANCE:** 23
- **RADIATION RESISTANCE:** 23
- **WEIGHT:** 12
- **VALUE:** 61

RAIDER POWER LEFT LEG

- **LEVEL:** 15
- **DAMAGE RESISTANCE:** 24
- **ENERGY RESISTANCE:** 23
- **RADIATION RESISTANCE:** 23
- **WEIGHT:** 12
- **VALUE:** 61

RAIDER POWER TORSO

- **LEVEL:** 15
- **DAMAGE RESISTANCE:** 41
- **ENERGY RESISTANCE:** 40
- **RADIATION RESISTANCE:** 40
- **WEIGHT:** 14
- **VALUE:** 81

EXCAVATOR POWER ARMOR

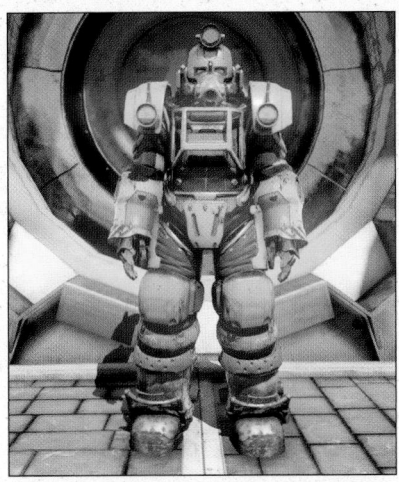

Obtained by completing Side Quest: Miner Miracles, the Excavator Power Armor is a powerhouse when it comes to survivability, especialy when in terms of Radiation Resistance. While it's not the best of the best when it comes to Damage and Energy Resistance, if you're heading into an uninhabitable environment, this suit will keep you safe and sound.

EXCAVATOR HELMET

- **LEVEL:** 25
- **DAMAGE RESISTANCE:** 25
- **ENERGY RESISTANCE:** 24
- **RADIATION RESISTANCE:** 35
- **WEIGHT:** 10
- **VALUE:** 49
- **NOTE:** PREVENTS DAMAGE AND DISEASE FROM AIRBORNE AND WATERBORNE HAZARDS.

EXCAVATOR RIGHT ARM

- **LEVEL:** 25
- **DAMAGE RESISTANCE:** 25
- **ENERGY RESISTANCE:** 24
- **RADIATION RESISTANCE:** 35
- **WEIGHT:** 11
- **VALUE:** 61
- **NOTE:** INCREASED YIELD WHEN MINING.

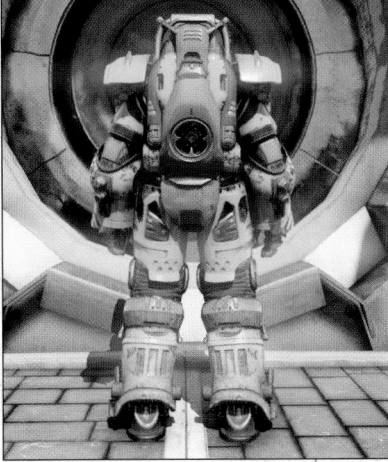

EXCAVATOR LEFT ARM

- **LEVEL:** 25
- **DAMAGE RESISTANCE:** 25
- **ENERGY RESISTANCE:** 24
- **RADIATION RESISTANCE:** 35
- **WEIGHT:** 11
- **VALUE:** 61
- **NOTE:** INCREASED YIELD WHEN MINING.

EXCAVATOR RIGHT LEG

- **LEVEL:** 25
- **DAMAGE RESISTANCE:** 25
- **ENERGY RESISTANCE:** 24
- **RADIATION RESISTANCE:** 35
- **WEIGHT:** 12
- **VALUE:** 81

EXCAVATOR LEFT LEG

- **LEVEL:** 25
- **DAMAGE RESISTANCE:** 25
- **ENERGY RESISTANCE:** 24
- **RADIATION RESISTANCE:** 35
- **WEIGHT:** 12
- **VALUE:** 81

EXCAVATOR TORSO

- **LEVEL:** 25
- **DAMAGE RESISTANCE:** 42
- **ENERGY RESISTANCE:** 41
- **RADIATION RESISTANCE:** 58
- **WEIGHT:** 12
- **VALUE:** 81

T-45 POWER ARMOR

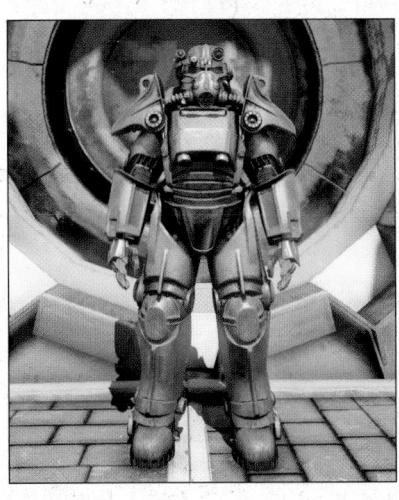

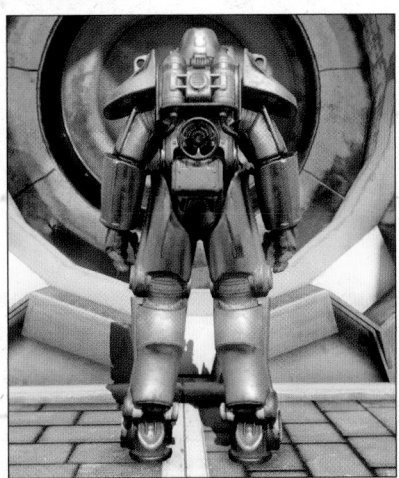

While the T-45 suit might not boast the same level of Radiation Resistance as the Excavator set, its balanced stats allow for a less nuanced approach to combat situations. You'll want to rethink entering a Rad storm for any serious amount of time while wearing it, but you won't find better armor for combat at this level.

TRAINING

CRAFTING AND C.A.M.P.ING

INVENTORY

QUESTS

ATLAS

BESTIARY

APPENDICES

T-45 HELMET

- **LEVEL:** 25
- **DAMAGE RESISTANCE:** 35
- **ENERGY RESISTANCE:** 34
- **RADIATION RESISTANCE:** 34
- **WEIGHT:** 11
- **VALUE:** 49
- **NOTE:** PREVENTS DAMAGE AND DISEASE FROM AIRBORNE AND WATERBORNE HAZARDS.

T-45 LEFT ARM

- **LEVEL:** 25
- **DAMAGE RESISTANCE:** 35
- **ENERGY RESISTANCE:** 34
- **RADIATION RESISTANCE:** 34
- **WEIGHT:** 12
- **VALUE:** 81

T-45 LEFT LEG

- **LEVEL:** 25
- **DAMAGE RESISTANCE:** 35
- **ENERGY RESISTANCE:** 34
- **RADIATION RESISTANCE:** 34
- **WEIGHT:** 14
- **VALUE:** 81

T-45 RIGHT ARM

- **LEVEL:** 25
- **DAMAGE RESISTANCE:** 35
- **ENERGY RESISTANCE:** 34
- **RADIATION RESISTANCE:** 34
- **WEIGHT:** 12
- **VALUE:** 81

T-45 RIGHT LEG

- **LEVEL:** 25
- **DAMAGE RESISTANCE:** 35
- **ENERGY RESISTANCE:** 34
- **RADIATION RESISTANCE:** 34
- **WEIGHT:** 14
- **VALUE:** 81

T-45 TORSO

- **LEVEL:** 25
- **DAMAGE RESISTANCE:** 58
- **ENERGY RESISTANCE:** 57
- **RADIATION RESISTANCE:** 57
- **WEIGHT:** 16
- **VALUE:** 113

T-51B POWER ARMOR

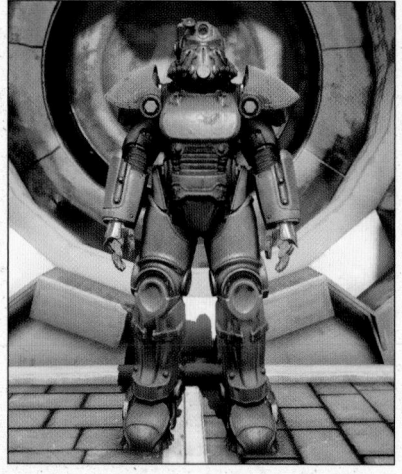 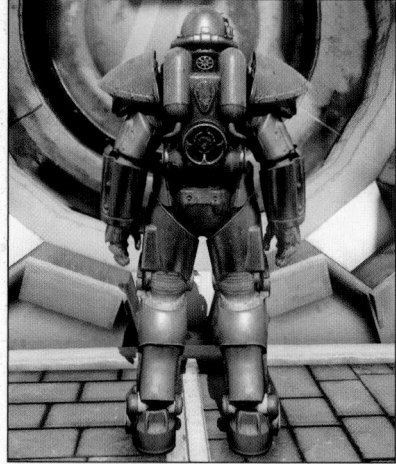

Jumping from the Excavator and T-45 suit to the T-51b might require a bit of consideration. If you're thinking of visiting a highly irradiated area, you would be better off hopping back into one of the two earlier mentioned suits. But if you're heading into a highly contested area and are expecting some fierce fighting, this walking brick wall will keep you safe and sound.

T-51B HELMET

- **LEVEL:** 30
- **DAMAGE RESISTANCE:** 45
- **ENERGY RESISTANCE:** 44
- **RADIATION RESISTANCE:** 27
- **WEIGHT:** 11
- **VALUE:** 65
- **NOTE:** PREVENTS DAMAGE AND DISEASE FROM AIRBORNE AND WATERBORNE HAZARDS.

T-51B LEFT ARM

- **LEVEL:** 30
- **DAMAGE RESISTANCE:** 45
- **ENERGY RESISTANCE:** 44
- **RADIATION RESISTANCE:** 27
- **WEIGHT:** 12
- **VALUE:** 105

T-51B LEFT LEG

- **LEVEL:** 30
- **DAMAGE RESISTANCE:** 45
- **ENERGY RESISTANCE:** 44
- **RADIATION RESISTANCE:** 27
- **WEIGHT:** 14
- **VALUE:** 105

T-51B RIGHT ARM

- **LEVEL:** 30
- **DAMAGE RESISTANCE:** 45
- **ENERGY RESISTANCE:** 44
- **RADIATION RESISTANCE:** 27
- **WEIGHT:** 12
- **VALUE:** 105

T-51B RIGHT LEG

- **LEVEL:** 30
- **DAMAGE RESISTANCE:** 45
- **ENERGY RESISTANCE:** 44
- **RADIATION RESISTANCE:** 27
- **WEIGHT:** 14
- **VALUE:** 105

T-51B TORSO

- **LEVEL:** 30
- **DAMAGE RESISTANCE:** 76
- **ENERGY RESISTANCE:** 75
- **RADIATION RESISTANCE:** 46
- **WEIGHT:** 17
- **VALUE:** 146

T-60 POWER ARMOR

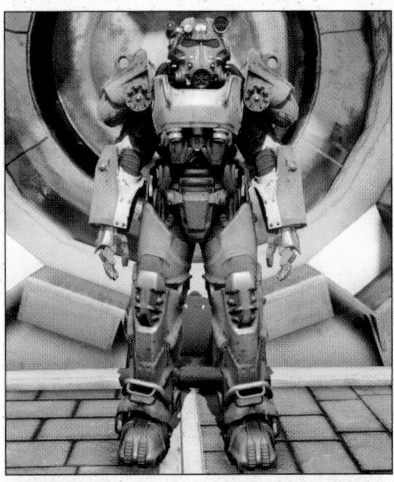

When it comes to Damage, Energy, and Radiation Resistances, there's no debate: the T-60 suit surpasses the stats of every other set before it. If you can get your hands on it, then you'll have a sturdy, well-rounded set of Power Armor that will serve you until you reach the level requirements for the next set.

T-60 HELMET

- **LEVEL:** 40
- **DAMAGE RESISTANCE:** 51
- **ENERGY RESISTANCE:** 49
- **RADIATION RESISTANCE:** 56
- **WEIGHT:** 11
- **VALUE:** 97
- **NOTE:** PREVENTS DAMAGE AND DISEASE FROM AIRBORNE AND WATERBORNE HAZARDS.

T-60 RIGHT ARM

- **LEVEL:** 40
- **DAMAGE RESISTANCE:** 51
- **ENERGY RESISTANCE:** 49
- **RADIATION RESISTANCE:** 56
- **WEIGHT:** 12
- **VALUE:** 130

T-60 LEFT ARM

- **LEVEL:** 40
- **DAMAGE RESISTANCE:** 51
- **ENERGY RESISTANCE:** 49
- **RADIATION RESISTANCE:** 56
- **WEIGHT:** 12
- **VALUE:** 130

T-60 RIGHT LEG

- **LEVEL:** 40
- **DAMAGE RESISTANCE:** 51
- **ENERGY RESISTANCE:** 49
- **RADIATION RESISTANCE:** 56
- **WEIGHT:** 14
- **VALUE:** 130

T-60 LEFT LEG

- **LEVEL:** 40
- **DAMAGE RESISTANCE:** 51
- **ENERGY RESISTANCE:** 49
- **RADIATION RESISTANCE:** 56
- **WEIGHT:** 14
- **VALUE:** 130

T-60 TORSO

- **LEVEL:** 40
- **DAMAGE RESISTANCE:** 84
- **ENERGY RESISTANCE:** 81
- **RADIATION RESISTANCE:** 94
- **WEIGHT:** 18
- **VALUE:** 162

X-01 POWER ARMOR

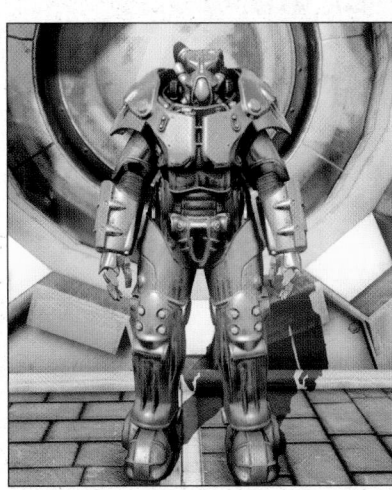
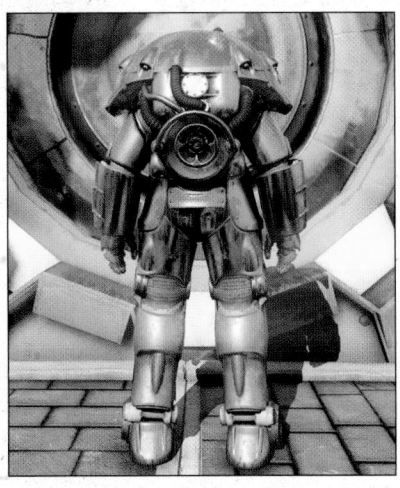

X-01 HELMET

- **LEVEL:** 45
- **DAMAGE RESISTANCE:** 55
- **ENERGY RESISTANCE:** 62
- **RADIATION RESISTANCE:** 62
- **WEIGHT:** 12
- **VALUE:** 113
- **NOTE:** PREVENTS DAMAGE AND DISEASE FROM AIRBORNE AND WATERBORNE HAZARDS.

X-01 LEFT ARM

- **LEVEL:** 45
- **DAMAGE RESISTANCE:** 55
- **ENERGY RESISTANCE:** 62
- **RADIATION RESISTANCE:** 62
- **WEIGHT:** 13
- **VALUE:** 162

The top of the mountain as far as Energy Resistance is concerned, the X-01 Power Armor is definitely in the upper echelon for reasons beyond its level requirements. While other sets handle physical damage a good deal better, the X-01 set can tank Energy attacks like, well...a tank! If combating Scorchbeasts and radioactive anomalies is in your near future, it might be in your best interest to take this mobile panic room for a spin.

TRAINING

CRAFTING AND C.A.M.P.ING

INVENTORY

QUESTS

ATLAS

BESTIARY

APPENDICES

X-01 LEFT LEG

- LEVEL: 45
- DAMAGE RESISTANCE: 55
- ENERGY RESISTANCE: 62
- RADIATION RESISTANCE: 62
- WEIGHT: 15
- VALUE: 162

X-01 RIGHT ARM

- LEVEL: 45
- DAMAGE RESISTANCE: 55
- ENERGY RESISTANCE: 62
- RADIATION RESISTANCE: 62
- WEIGHT: 13
- VALUE: 162

X-01 RIGHT LEG

- LEVEL: 45
- DAMAGE RESISTANCE: 55
- ENERGY RESISTANCE: 62
- RADIATION RESISTANCE: 62
- WEIGHT: 15
- VALUE: 162

X-01 TORSO

- LEVEL: 45
- DAMAGE RESISTANCE: 90
- ENERGY RESISTANCE: 103
- RADIATION RESISTANCE: 104
- WEIGHT: 19
- VALUE: 227

ULTRACITE POWER ARMOR

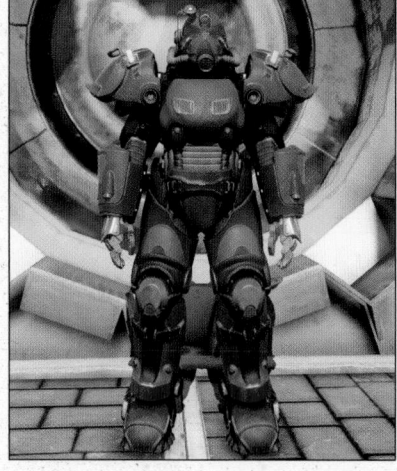 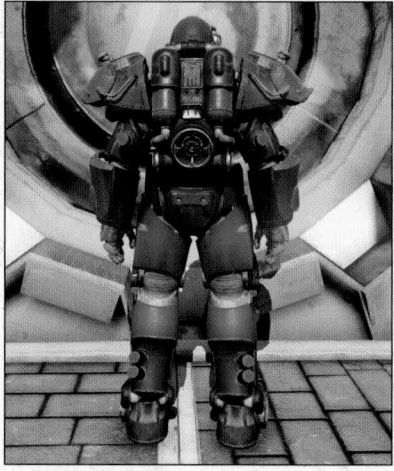

While the Ultracite set of Power Armor may be the last available on the list, that doesn't mean you can abandon every other set. The X-01 suit handles Energy-based damage much better than this one, but you can expect better physical Damage Resistance from this suit than any other.

The question on your mind might be, "Which one do I bring to a Fissure Site? Ultracite or X-01?" The truth is, it depends on what's giving you the hardest time. Scorchbeasts use Energy attacks almost exclusively, while the Scorched that surround it will attack you with physical damage attacks. If you find that Scorchbeasts are roughing you up the most, then consider the X-01, but Ultracite will work just fine in all other situations.

ULTRACITE HELMET

- LEVEL: 50
- DAMAGE RESISTANCE: 69
- ENERGY RESISTANCE: 59
- RADIATION RESISTANCE: 59
- WEIGHT: 12
- VALUE: 49
- NOTE: PREVENTS DAMAGE AND DISEASE FROM AIRBORNE AND WATERBORNE HAZARDS.

ULTRACITE LEFT ARM

- LEVEL: 50
- DAMAGE RESISTANCE: 68
- ENERGY RESISTANCE: 45
- RADIATION RESISTANCE: 45
- WEIGHT: 13
- VALUE: 81

ULTRACITE LEFT LEG

- LEVEL: 50
- DAMAGE RESISTANCE: 68
- ENERGY RESISTANCE: 45
- RADIATION RESISTANCE: 45
- WEIGHT: 15
- VALUE: 81

ULTRACITE RIGHT ARM

- LEVEL: 50
- DAMAGE RESISTANCE: 68
- ENERGY RESISTANCE: 45
- RADIATION RESISTANCE: 45
- WEIGHT: 13
- VALUE: 81

ULTRACITE RIGHT LEG

- LEVEL: 50
- DAMAGE RESISTANCE: 68
- ENERGY RESISTANCE: 45
- RADIATION RESISTANCE: 45
- WEIGHT: 15
- VALUE: 81

ULTRACITE TORSO

- LEVEL: 50
- DAMAGE RESISTANCE: 114
- ENERGY RESISTANCE: 98
- RADIATION RESISTANCE: 98
- WEIGHT: 20
- VALUE: 259

AID

The emphasis on survival has been amped up in a big way in *Fallout 76*, which is why knowing how to get food, water, and other Aid items is of the utmost importance.

You can find Aid items under the Aid menu on your Pip Boy. These items include cooked and raw food, drinks, chems, healing items, and many other items involved in the process of keeping healthy and well.

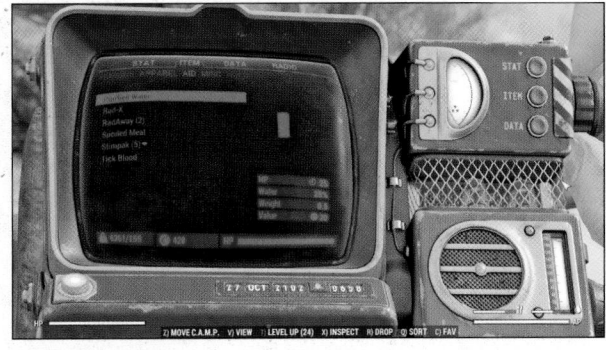

TRAINING

CRAFTING AND C.A.M.P.ING

INVENTORY

QUESTS

ATLAS

BESTIARY

APPENDICES

FOOD AND DRINK

You'll find plenty of meat off of fallen enemies, and while you can eat it raw, it's not only safer to cook it up first, it's also much more beneficial. Diseases are now a big part of the game too, so you'll constantly have to worry about catching them from both diseased enemies and raw or tainted food. Cooking your food and purifying your water help dramatically reduce the likelihood of catching anything from food in your inventory, and the way to cook it is by visiting a cooking station.

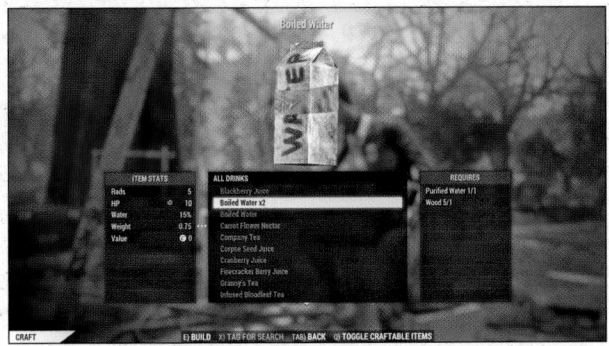

Like Armor and Weapon Workbenches, cooking stations are very common (the Overseer's C.A.M.P. has one, as does Flatwoods—both within spitting distance of Vault 76). If you have the proper food and spices, you can craft all sorts of delicious meals that not only fill up your hunger meter, but also occasionally offer buffs or other beneficial bonuses.

WORD OF WARNING FROM VAULT BOY

FOOD SAFETY IS SOMETHING WE TAKE VERY SERIOUSLY, SO WE'D FEEL A POWERFUL GUILT IF WE DIDN'T TELL YOU ABOUT FOOD SPOILAGE. IT IS NO LONGER OKAY TO LOAD UP YOUR BACKPACK WITH FOOD ITEMS AND EXPECT THEM TO ALWAYS BE FRESH AS A SPRING BREEZE. YOU'LL NEED TO PREPARE AND EAT THEM SHORTLY AFTER OBTAINING THEM IF YOU WANT TO AVOID LOSING YOUR FOOD TO SPOILAGE. YOU CAN STILL EAT SPOILED FOOD, BUT IT COMES WITH A HIGH RISK OF DISEASE.

Be sure to pick plants, loot fridges, and hunt non-hostile animals for opportunities to make delicious meals.

CHEMS

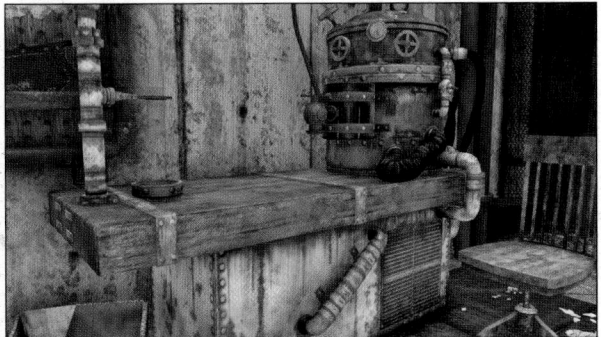

Made at a chemistry station, or found in the seedier corners of Appalachia, chems provide powerful boosts at the risk of a powerful addiction. Once used, chems only last for a short period, but they can turn the tide of battle by upping your attack damage, or even temporarily increase your carrying capacity, giving you the chance to get back to a My Stash Box to deposit a big haul of loot.

If you use too many chems, you'll suffer from withdrawals, which lowers your stats for a long period of time. You'll either need to wait until these symptoms clear on their own, or ingest food or medicine to remove the withdrawal effects altogether (Radscorpion Egg Omelettes usually do the trick). You'll find Perk Cards that help increase the length of chems, so if you find yourself not wanting to part with these deadly drugs, be sure to chase down those cards.

Helpful Hint from Vault Boy

Withdrawal effects can make your journey much more difficult, but there are pieces of Legendary equipment that boost your stats when you're going through withdrawals. If you're trying to live like a burned-out rockstar, look for equipment with the "Junkie's" Legendary Modifier on them.

FOOD

NAME	RADS	SATIATION	HP	EFFECTS	WEIGHT	VALUE	CRAFTABLE
Aged Mirelurk Queen Steak	5	25% Food	90	+3 END	1	44	Yes
Angler Meat	15	10% Food	—	7% Disease Chance	0.5	14	No
Ant Meat	15	10% Food	—	7% Disease Chance	0.25	3	No
Appalachili	5	15% Water, 10% Food	30	+2 LCK	1	6	Yes
Ash Rose	5	1% Food	—	2% Disease Chance	0.25	8	No
Aster	5	1% Food	—	2% Disease Chance	0.25	5	No
Awesome Opossum Bacon	5	15% Food	45	+2 LCK	0.3	12	Yes
Baked Bloatfly	2	10% Food	25	+10 Rad Resist	0.5	15	Yes
Black Bloodleaf	5	1% Food	—	2% Disease Chance	0.25	5	No
Blackberry Honey Crisp	2	20% Food	90	+300 AP, +5 AP Regen	0.25	23	Yes
Blamco Brand Mac and Cheese	0 or 1	10% Food	15	—	0.25	12	No
Blight	5	5% Food	—	4% Disease Chance	0.25	5	No
Blight Soup	5	10% Food, 15% Water	12	+20% Crit Dmg	0.5	5	Yes
Bloatfly Loaf	2	20% Food	60	+30 Rad Resist	0.5	15	Yes
Bloatfly Meat	15	10% Food	—	7% Disease Chance	0.5	8	No
Bloodbug Meat	10	10% Food	—	13% Disease Chance	0.5	18	No
Bloodbug Pepper Steak	2	20% Food	60	+0.25 Health Regen	0.5	24	Yes
Bloodbug Steak	5	15% Food	45	+30 Max HP	0.5	19	Yes
Bloodleaf	5	1% Food	—	2% Disease Chance	0.25	5	No
Brahmin Meat	15	15% Food	—	7% Disease Chance	1	12	No
Brain Bombs	5	25% Food	90	+3 INT, +300 AP	0.5	31	No
Brain Fungus	5	5% Food	—	4% Disease Chance	0.25	6	No
Brain Fungus Soup	5	10% Food, 15% Water	12	+2 INT	0.5	6	Yes
Broiled Scorchbeast Brain	10	25% Food	200	+3 INT	1.5	40	Yes
Bubblegum	1	—	8	50% slower hunger & thirst for 10 minutes	0.25	5	No
Cajun Rice & Beans	2	20% Food	25	—	0.5	14	No
Canned Dog Food	1	10% Food	25	—	0.5	6	No
Canned Meat Stew	2	20% Food, 15% Water	60	+5 Bonus XP, +2% XP gain for 1 hour	1	22	No
Carrot	5	5% Food	—	4% Disease Chance	0.25	3	No
Carrot Flower	5	1% Food	—	2% Disease Chance	0.25	6	No
Carrot Soup	5	10% Food, 15% Water	12	+2 PER	1	5	Yes
Cat Meat	15	10% Food	—	7% Disease Chance	0.5	8	No
Cat Meat Steak	5	15% Food	45	+2 AGI	0.5	8	Yes
Cave Cricket Gland	15	10% Food	—	7% Disease Chance	0.5	3	No
Cave Cricket Meat	15	10% Food	—	7% Disease Chance	0.5	13	No
Cave Fungus	5	5% Food	—	4% Disease Chance	0.25	8	No
Cave Fungus Soup	5	10% Food, 15% Water	12	+10 Poison Resist	0.5	8	Yes
Charred Scorchbeast Liver	10	25% Food	200	+3 LCK	1.5	40	Yes
Chew Stick	2	10% Food	25	+1 LCK	0.25	5	Yes
Chicken Noodle Soup	5	10% Food, 15% Water	30	+10 Disease Resist	0.5	19	Yes
Chicken Thigh	15	10% Food	—	7% Disease Resist	0.5	8	No
Chitlins Con Carne	5	15% Food	45	+2 END	1	6	Yes
Cola Perk Bubblegum	5	—	—	5% Slower hunger & thirst for two minutes	0.1	5	No
Cooked Softshell Meat	5	15% Food	45	+20 Max AP	0.5	28	Yes
Corn	5	5% Food	—	4% Disease Chance	0.5	6	No
Corn Pone	5	15% Food	45	+2 CHR	1	6	Yes
Corn Soup	5	10% Food, 15% Water	12	+3 AP Regen	0.5	6	Yes
Corpse Flower Stamen	5	5% Food	—	4% Disease Chance	0.25	8	No
Corpse Seeds	5	3% Food	—	4% Disease Chance	0.25	8	No
Cotton Candy Bites	1	6% Food	4	+60 AP	0.5	7	No
Cram	2	15% Food	20	—	0.5	15	No
Cramburger	10	20% Food	60	+20 Carry Weight	1	6	Yes
Cranberries	5	5% Food	—	4% Disease Chance	0.25	3	No
Cranberry Cobbler	5	10% Food	25	+5 Bonus XP	0.5	5	Yes
Cranberry Jam	1	15% Food	45	+10 DMG Resist	1	12	Yes
Cranberry Meatball Grinder	2	25% Food	250	+40 Max HP	1	47	Yes
Cranberry Relish	2	20% Food	60	+10 Bonus XP, +200 AP	1	12	Yes

NAME	RADS	SATIATION	HP	EFFECTS	WEIGHT	VALUE	CRAFTABLE
Crispy Cave Cricket	5	10% Food	25	+10 Energy Resist	0.5	25	Yes
Crispy Flying Ant Bits	2	10% Food	25	+120 AP	0.5	8	Yes
Crispy Squirrel Bits	2	10% Food	25	+2 AGI	0.25	6	Yes
Dandy Boy Apples	1	6% Food	10	—	0.5	7	No
Deathclaw Egg	15	10% Food	—	5% Disease Chance	0.25	15	No
Deathclaw Egg Omelette	5	15% Food	45	+0.13 Health Regen	0.25	38	Yes
Deathclaw Meat	15	20% Food	—	13% Disease Chance	2	17	No
Deathclaw Steak	10	20% Food	60	+2 STR	1.5	39	Yes
Deathclaw Wellington	5	25% Food	90	+3 STR	1	58	Yes
Disease Cranberries	5	5% Food	—	7% Disease Chance	0.25	3	No
Dog Meat Steak	2	20% Food	60	+3 END	1	12	Yes
Fancy Lads Snack Cakes	0 or 1	10% Food	15	—	0.25	12	No
Fever Blossom	5	1% Food	—	2% Disease Chance	0.25	4	No
Firecap	5	5% Food	—	4% Disease Chance	0.5	6	No
Firecap Soup	5	10% Food, 15% Water	10	+25 Energy Resist	0.5	5	Yes
Firecap Tasty Souffle	2	20% Food	60	+35 Energy Resist	1	22	Yes
Firecracker Berry	5	5% Food	—	4% Disease Chance	0.25	8	No
Flying Ant Meat	15	10% Food	—	7% Disease Chance	0.5	8	No
Fox Jerky	5	15% Food	45	+2 AGI	1	12	Yes
Fox Meat	15	10% Food	—	7% Disease Chance	0.25	2	No
Fried Deerskins	1	15% Food	45	+3 AP Regen	1	11	Yes
Fried Fog Crawler	5	15% Food	45	Damage Resistance increases in Foggy and Rainy weather conditions for 30 minutes	1	39	Yes
Fried Radtoad Legs	2	20% Food	60	+20 Carry Weight	1	12	Yes
Frog Egg	10	3% Food	—	7% Disease Chance	0.25	6	No
Frog Leg	10	5% Food	—	7% Disease Chance	0.25	0	No
Funnel Cake	2	15% Food	20	—	0.25	12	No
Ginseng Root	5	5% Food	—	4% Disease Chance	0.25	0	No
Glowing Fungus	5	5% Food	—	4% Disease Chance	0.25	6	No
Glowing Fungus Puree	2	20% Food, 15% Water	60	+35 Energy Resist	0.5	22	Yes
Glowing Fungus Soup	5	10% Food, 15% Water	12	+20 Rad Resist	0.5	6	Yes
Glowing Mass	30	20% Food	—	5% Disease Chance	2	65	No
Glowing Meat	30	20% Food	—	13% Disease Chance	2	25	No
Glowing Meat Steak	5	15% Food	45	+10% Melee Damage	1.5	42	Yes
Glowing Resin	5	5% Food	—	4% Disease Chance	0.5	12	No
Gourd	5	5% Food	—	4% Disease Chance	2	6	No
Gourd Blossom	5	1% Food	—	2% Disease Chance	0.25	6	Yes
Gourd Soup	5	10% Food, 15% Water	12	+2 PER	0.5	6	Yes
Grape Perk Bubblegum	—	—	—	+5 Damage Resist, 5% slower hunger & thirst for two minutes	0.1	5	No
Grilled Hermit Crab	5	10% Food	30	+1 END	1	39	Yes
Grilled Radroach	5	10% Food	25	+1 END	0.25	7	Yes
Grilled Radstag	10	20% Food	60	+20 Carry Weight	1.5	25	Yes
Grilled Radtoad	2	10% Food	25	+10 Carry Weight	0.25	32	Yes
Ground Mole Rat	2	20% Food	60	+3 AGI	0.5	11	Yes
Gulper Innards	15	10% Food	—	7% Disease Chance	1	12	No
Gulper Slurry	5	15% Food	45	Invisible for 10 seconds while in water	1	28	Yes
Gum Drops	1	6% Food	4	+60 AP	0.25	5	No
Halloween Candy	1	1% Food	—	+5 AP	0.01	0	No
Hermit Crab Meat	15	10% Food	—	7% Disease Chance	1	9	No
Honey	5	3% Food	—	+60 AP, 2% Disease Chance	0.25	5	No
Honeycomb	5	10% Food	—	+60 AP, 2% Disease Chance	0.25	5	No
Hotdog	5	15% Food	30	+30 Max HP	1	12	No
Iguana Bits	15	10% Food	—	7% Disease Chance	0.25	8	No
Iguana On A Stick	2	10% Food	25	+1 LCK	0.25	25	Yes
Iguana Soup	2	20% Food, 15% Water	60	+3 LCK	0.5	22	Yes
Imitation Seafood	2	15% Food	20	—	0.5	14	No
InstaMash	2	15% Food	20	—	0.5	9	No
Ionized Meat	30	20% Food	—	5% Disease Chance	0.5	30	No

TRAINING · CRAFTING AND C.A.M.P.ING · INVENTORY · QUESTS · ATLAS · BESTIARY · APPENDICES

NAME	RADS	SATIATION	HP	EFFECTS	WEIGHT	VALUE	CRAFTABLE
Lure Weed	5	5% Food	—	4% Disease Chance	0.25	5	No
Megasloth Meat	15	20% Food	—	7% Disease Chance	2	17	No
Megasloth Mushroom	5	5% Food	—	4% Disease Chance	0.25	6	No
Megasloth Mushroom Soup	5	10% Food, 15% Water	30	+20% Crit Dmg	0.5	6	Yes
Megasloth Tenderloin	5	25% Food	90	+35 Energy Resist	1	61	No
Melon	5	10% Food, 15% Water	—	4% Disease Chance	2	6	No
Melon Bloom	5	1% Food	—	2% Disease Chance	0.25	6	No
Melon Blossom	5	1% Food	—	2% Disease Chance	0.25	6	No
Mirelurk Cake	2	20% Food	60	Breathe underwater for 1 hour	1	22	Yes
Mirelurk Cake With Bloodleaf Aioli	2	25% Food	250	+30 Rad Resist	1	47	Yes
Mirelurk Egg	15	10% Food	—	7% Disease Chance	1	7	No
Mirelurk Egg Omelette	5	10% Food	25	+2 AP Regen	0.25	22	Yes
Mirelurk Jerky	2	20% Food	60	+15 DMG Resist	1	42	Yes
Mirelurk Meat	15	15% Food	—	13% Disease Chance	1	10	No
Mirelurk Queen Steak	5	15% Food	45	+2 END	1.5	39	Yes
Mirelurk Softshell Cake	2	20% Food	60	+3 AGI	0.5	33	Yes
Moldy Food	10	5% Food	—	11% Disease Chance	0.5	1	No
Mole Rat Chunks	5	10% Food	25	+1 STR	0.5	8	Yes
Mole Rat Meat	15	10% Food	—	7% Disease Chance	0.5	5	No
Mongrel Dog Meat	15	10% Food	—	7% Disease Chance	1	8	No
Mothman Egg	15	5% Food	—	7% Disease Chance	0.25	15	No
Mothman Egg Omelette	5	15% Food	45	+2 CHR	0.25	38	Yes
Mountain Hocks	5	10% Food	25	+10 Disease Resist	1	6	Yes
Mud Cookie	2	17% Food	25	+180 AP	1	6	Yes
Mutant Hound Chops	5	15% Food	45	+10% Melee Damage	1	12	Yes
Mutant Hound Meat	15	10% Food	—	7% Disease Chance	1	8	No
Mutant Hound Stew	2	20% Food, 15% Water	60	+15% Melee Damage	1	28	Yes
Mutated Fern Flower	5	1% Food	—	2% Disease Chance	0.25	4	No
Mutfruit	5	5% Food	—	4% Disease Chance	0.25	8	No
Mutt Chops	5	15% Food	45	+2 END	1	12	Yes
Noodle Cup	2	15% Food, 15% Water	20	—	1	10	No
Opossum Meat	15	10% Food	—	7% Disease Chance	0.25	2	No
Owlet Meat	15	10% Food	—	7% Disease Chance	0.25	2	No
Owlet Nuggets	2	10% Food	25	+1 INT	1	12	Yes
Pepper	5	1% Food	—	—	0.25	6	No
Perfectly Preserved Pie	1	15% Food	20	—	0.5	9	No
Perk Bubblegum	—	—	8	5% slower hunger & thirst for two minutes	0.1	5	No
Poached Angler	5	15% Food	45	+20 Max AP	0.5	28	Yes
Pork n' Beans	2	15% Food	20	—	0.5	8	No
Potato Crisps	1	6% Food	10	—	0.25	7	No
Pothole Potpie	15	10% Food, 15% Water	30	+10 DMG Resist	1	6	No
Preserved InstaMash	—	15% Food	20	—	0.5	13	No
Pumpkin	5	10% Food	—	4% Disease Chance	2	6	No
Pumpkin Pie	5	20% Food	45	+40 Max HP	1	11	Yes
Pumpkin Soup	5	10% Food, 15% Water	30	+2 PER	0.5	6	Yes
Queen Mirelurk Meat	15	20% Food	—	13% Disease Chance	1.5	19	No
Rabbit Leg	10	5% Food	—	7% Disease Chance	0.25	7	No
Rad-Rat Meat	15	10% Food	—	7% Disease Chance	0.5	5	No
Rad-Rat Steak	5	15% Food	45	+2 PER	0.5	8	Yes
Radroach Meat	15	10% Food	—	7% Disease Chance	0.25	3	No
Radscorpion Egg	15	5% Food	—	7% Disease Chance	0.25	13	No
Radscorpion Egg Omelette	2	10% Food	25	Cures a random addiction	0.25	25	Yes
Radscorpion Fillet	5	25% Food	90	+35 Energy Resist	1	20	Yes
Radscorpion Meat	15	20% Food	—	13% Disease Chance	2	15	No
Radscorpion Steak	10	20% Food	60	+25 Energy Resist	1.5	19	Yes
Radstag Meat	15	20% Food	—	7% Disease Chance	2	11	No
Radstag Stew	2	20% Food, 15% Water	60	+25 Energy Resist	1	44	Yes

NAME	RADS	SATIATION	HP	EFFECTS	WEIGHT	VALUE	CRAFTABLE
Radtoad Egg	15	5% Food	—	7% Disease Chance	0.25	9	No
Radtoad Leg	15	10% Food	—	7% Disease Chance	0.25	60	No
Radtoad Omelette	5	10% Food	25	+1 END	0.25	27	Yes
Raw Fog Crawler Meat	15	15% Food	—	7% Disease Chance	1	14	No
Raw Wolf Meat	15	15% Food	—	7% Disease Chance	1	8	No
Razorgrain	5	3% Food	—	4% Disease Chance	0.25	5	No
Razorgrain Soup	5	10% Food, 15% Water	30	+10 Disease Resist	0.5	5	Yes
Rhododendron Flower	5	1% Food	—	2% Disease Chance	0.25	0	No
Ribeye Steak	5	15% Food	45	+20 Carry Weight	1	29	Yes
Roast Megasloth	5	15% Food	60	+25 Energy Resist	1.5	39	Yes
Roasted Ant	2	10% Food	25	+10 Carry Weight	0.25	7	Yes
Roasted Mirelurk Meat	2	10% Food	25	+10 Max AP	1	28	Yes
Roasted Scorchbeast Heart	10	25% Food	200	+3 END	1.5	40	Yes
Royal Jelly Taffy	5	15% Food	30	+120 AP	0.5	39	Yes
Salisbury Steak	0 or 2	20% Food	25	—	0.5	13	No
Salt	5	1% Food	—	—	0.25	6	No
Scorchbeast Brain	15	20% Food	—	13% Disease Chance	2	27	No
Scorchbeast Heart	15	20% Food	—	13% Disease Chance	2	28	No
Scorchbeast Liver	15	20% Food	—	13% Disease Chance	2	23	No
Scorchbeast Lung	15	20% Food	—	13% Disease Chance	2	25	No
Scorchbeast Meat	15	20% Food	—	13% Disease Chance	2	22	No
Scorchbeast Mixed Meat Stew	2	34% Food, 41% Water	250	+1 LCK, +2 END, +1 INT, +1 AGI	1	66	Yes
Scorchbeast Steak	10	25% Food	200	+15 DMG Resist	1.5	40	Yes
Seared Venison With Berries	2	25% Food	250	+3 LCK	1	31	Yes
Seasoned Rabbit Skewers	2	10% Food	25	+1 LCK	0.25	15	Yes
Silt Bean	5	5% Food	—	4% Disease Chance	0.25	6	No
Silt Bean Puree	2	20% Food, 15% Water	60	+15 DMG Resist	0.5	22	Yes
Silt Bean Soup	5	10% Food, 15% Water	30	+2 END	0.5	6	Yes
Smoked Mirelurk Fillets	2	25% Food	250	+30 Carry Weight, Breathe underwater	1	47	Yes
Smoked Scorchbeast Lung	10	25% Food	200	+3 AGI	1.5	40	Yes
Snaptail Reed	5	5% Food	—	4% Disease Chance	0.25	5	No
Softshell Mirelurk Meat	15	10% Food	—	7% Disease Chance	0.5	16	No
Soot Flower	5	1% Food	—	2% Disease Chance	0.25	5	No
Spices	5	1% Food	—	—	0.25	6	No
Spoiled Fruit	5	10% Food	—	7% Disease Chance	0.1	0	No
Spoiled Meat	15	10% Food	—	13% Disease Chance	0.25	0	No
Spoiled Vegetables	5	10% Food	—	7% Disease Chance	0.1	0	No
Squirrel Bits	10	5% Food	—	7% Disease Chance	0.25	4	No
Squirrel On A Stick	2	15% Food	45	+3 AGI	0.25	15	Yes
Squirrel Stew	2	20% Food, 15% Water	60	+10 Bonus XP	1	16	Yes
Starlight Berries	5	5% Food	—	4% Disease Chance	0.25	8	No
Starlight Berry Cobbler	2	10% Food	25	+1 END	0.5	8	Yes
Stingwing Filet	5	15% Food	45	+2 STR	0.5	25	Yes
Stingwing Meat	15	10% Food	—	7% Disease Chance	0.5	12	No
Stingwing Stew	2	20% Food, 15% Water	60	+3 PER	1	20	Yes
Strangler Bloom	5	1% Food	—	2% Disease Chance	0.25	4	No
Strangler Pod	5	1% Food	—	2% Disease Chance	0.25	4	No
Strawberry Perk Bubblegum	—	—	—	+1 DMG Resist, 5% slower hunger & thirst for two minutes	0.1	5	No
Sugar	5	1% Food	—	+60 AP	0.25	6	Yes
Sugar Bombs	0 or 1	6% Food	10	+60 AP	0.5	9	No
Swamp Plant	5	5% Food	—	4% Disease Chance	0.5	12	No
Swamp Tofu	2	10% Food	25	+0.08 Health Regen	0.5	12	Yes
Swamp Tofu Soup	2	20% Food, 15% Water	60	+0.25 Health Regen	0.5	22	Yes
Sweet Roll	0.8	35% Food	90	+3 CHR	0.25	23	No
Sweet Tato Stew	2	20% Food, 15% Water	60	+0.25 Health Regen	1	22	Yes
Syrup	2	10% Food	25	+1 AGI	0.5	12	Yes
Tarberry	5	5% Food	—	4% Disease Chance	0.25	5	No

TRAINING

CRAFTING AND C.A.M.P.ING

INVENTORY

QUESTS

ATLAS

BESTIARY

APPENDICES

NAME	RADS	SATIATION	HP	EFFECTS	WEIGHT	VALUE	CRAFTABLE
Tasty Radscorpion Egg Omelette	1	15% Food	45	Cures all addictions	0.25	40	Yes
Tato	5	5% Food	—	4% Disease Chance	0.5	7	No
Tato Flower	5	1% Food	—	2% Disease Chance	0.25	7	No
Tato Salad Surprise	5	15% Food	45	+5 AP Regen	1	6	Yes
Tato Soup	5	10% Food, 15% Water	30	+10 Poison Resist	0.5	7	Yes
Thistle	5	1% Food	—	2% Disease Chance	0.25	5	No
Toxic Soot Flower	15	1% Food	—	2% Disease Chance	0.25	5	No
Vegetable Medley Soup	2	20% Food, 15% Water	60	+20 Disease Resist	0.5	22	Yes
Vegetable Starch	—	—	—	—	0.5	8	Yes
Vegetarian Ham	2	20% Food	25	—	0.5	14	Yes
Watermelon Perk Bubblegum	—	—	—	+42 AP, 5% slower hunger & thirst for two minutes	0.1	5	No
Wild Blackberry	5	5% Food	—	4% Disease Chance	0.25	8	No
Wolf Ribs	5	15% Food	45	+2 PER	1	16	Yes
Yao Guai Meat	15	20% Food	—	7% Disease Chance	2	17	No
Yao Guai Ribs	5	15% Food	45	+10% Melee Damage	1.5	29	Yes
Yao Guai Roast	5	25% Food	90	+15% Melee Damage	1	38	Yes
Yum Yum Deviled Eggs	2	15% Food	20	—	0.5	13	No

DRINKS

NAME	RADS	SATIATION	HP	EFFECTS	WEIGHT	VALUE	CRAFTABLE
Bioluminescent Fluid	1	8% Water	—	—	1	0	No
Blackberry Juice	2	15% Water	10	+2 AP Regen	0.5	8	Yes
Boiled Water	5	15% Water	10	—	0.75	0	Yes
Canned Coffee	2	25% Water	—	+300 AP	0.5	14	No
Carrot Flower Nectar	5	15% Water	10	+1 PER	1	5	Yes
Company Tea	2	41% Water	—	+10 AP Regen, +20 Disease Resist	0.5	10	Yes
Corpse Seed Juice	2	15% Water	10	+10 Max AP	0.5	8	Yes
Cranberry Juice	2	15% Water	10	+2 Bonus XP	0.5	5	Yes
Cream	—	15% Water	20	9% Disease Chance	0.5	5	Yes
Dirty Water	15	15% Water	—	5% Disease Chance	0.75	0	No
Firecracker Berry Juice	2	15% Water	10	—	0.5	8	Yes
Granny's Tea	2	25% Water	40	+0.13 Health Regen	0.5	6	Yes
Infused Bloodleaf Tea	1	25% Water	25	+20 Disease Resist	0.5	12	Yes
Infused Soot Flower Tea	1	25% Water	25	+20 Max AP	0.5	12	Yes
Melon Juice	2	15% Water	10	+0.08 Health Regen	0.5	6	Yes
Mutfruit Juice	2	15% Water	10	+1 AGI	0.5	8	Yes
Nuclear Wastewater	50	15% Water	—	11% Disease Chance	0.75	0	No
Nuka-Cherry	5	15% Water	50	+25 AP	1	40	No
Nuka-Cola	2	15% Water	40	+10 AP	1	10	No
Nuka-Cola Wild	5	15% Water	40	+25 AP	1	15	No
Purified Water	—	25% Water	25	—	0.5	20	Yes
Simple Ash Rose Tea	2	15% Water	10	+1 CHR	0.5	5	Yes
Simple Aster Tea	2	15% Water	10	+1 INT	0.5	5	Yes
Simple Bloodleaf Tea	5	15% Water	10	+5 Disease Resist	0.5	5	Yes
Simple Fern Flower Tea	5	15% Water	10	+1 STR	0.5	5	Yes
Simple Soot Flower Tea	2	15% Water	10	+10 Max AP	0.5	5	Yes
Soot Flower Herb Paste	5	15% Food, 8% Water	12	+20 Rad Resist	0.5	6	Yes
Spoiled Bio Fluid	10	8% Water	—	—	1	0	No
Steeped Ash Rose Tea	1	25% Water	25	+2 CHR	0.5	14	Yes
Steeped Aster Tea	1	25% Water	25	+2 INT	0.5	12	Yes
Steeped Black Bloodleaf Tea	1	25% Water	25	+10 Poison Resist	0.5	12	Yes
Steeped Carrot Flower Tea	1	25% Water	25	+2 PER	0.5	12	Yes
Steeped Fern Flower Tea	1	25% Water	25	+2 STR	0.5	11	Yes
Steeped Fever Blossom Tea	1	25% Water	25	+5 AP Regen	0.5	11	Yes
Steeped Gourd Blossom Tea	1	25% Water	25	+2 END	0.5	12	Yes
Steeped Melon Bloom Tea	1	25% Water	25	+20 Max AP	0.5	12	Yes
Steeped Melon Blossom Chai	1	25% Water	25	+2 AGI	0.5	12	Yes

NAME	RADS	SATIATION	HP	EFFECTS	WEIGHT	VALUE	CRAFTABLE
Steeped Strangler Bloom Tea	5	25% Water	25	+20 Rad Resist	0.5	11	Yes
Steeped Strangler Pod Tea	5	25% Water	25	+20 Rad Resist	0.5	11	Yes
Steeped Tato Flower Tea	1	25% Water	25	+2 INT	0.5	13	Yes
Steeped Thistle Tea	1	25% Water	25	+20% Crit Dmg	0.5	12	Yes
Sweet Blackberry Tea	1	25% Water	25	+200 AP	0.5	14	Yes
Sweet Labrador Tea	1	25% Water	40	+5 AP Regen	0.5	6	Yes
Sweet Mutfruit Tea	1	25% Water	25	+20% Crit Dmg	0.5	14	Yes
Sweetwater Special Blend	0.4	25% Water	—	+2 PER	0.5	15	Yes
Tarberry Juice	2	15% Water	10	+120 AP	0.5	5	Yes
Tato Juice	2	15% Water	10	+10 Max AP	0.5	7	Yes
Tick Blood	15	15% Water	20	13% Disease Chance	0.75	7	No
Toxic Water	30	15% Water	—	13% Disease Chance	0.75	0	No

HEALING AND CHEMS

NAME	RADS	SATIATION	HP	EFFECTS	WEIGHT	VALUE	CRAFTABLE
Antibiotics	—	-3% Food, -5% Water	—	+50 Disease Resist	0.25	40	Yes
Berry Mentats	—	-3% Water	—	+5 INT	0.18	35	Yes
Blood Pack	—	35% Water	125	—	0.25	20	Yes
Buffout	—	-3% Water, -5% Food	—	+25 Max HP, +2 END, +2 STR	0.1	45	No
Bufftats	—	-3% Water, -1% Food	—	+40 Max HP, +3 END, +3 STR, +3 PER	0.18	40	Yes
Day Tripper	—	-3% Water	—	+3 CHR, +3 LCK, -2 STR	0.18	30	No
Detoxing Salve	—	—	—	Removes 75 Rads	0.25	15	Yes
Disease Cure	—	-1% Food, -3% Water	—	Cures one disease	0.25	0	Yes
Fury	—	-3% Food, -3% Water	—	-5 PER, +25 DMG Resist	0.18	40	Yes
Glowing Blood Pack	—	35% Water	40	+75 Rad Resist	0.25	30	No
Grape Mentats	—	-3% Water	—	+5 CHR	0.18	35	Yes
Healing Salve	—	—	20%	—	0.5	20	Yes
Med-X	—	-1% Food, -3% Water	—	+25 DMG Resist	0.18	40	No
Mentats	—	-3% Water	—	+2 INT, +2 PER	0.18	30	Yes
Orange Mentats	—	-3% Water	—	+5 PER	0.18	35	Yes
Overdrive	—	-3% Food, -3% Water	—	+15% Damage, +25% Critical Chance	0.18	40	Yes
Phantom Device	—	—	—	Frenzies nearby creatures and renders you almost completely invisible. Duration increased if wearing the Eye of Ra.	1	100	Yes
Psycho	—	-1% Food, -3% Water	—	+25 DMG Resist	0.18	30	Yes
Psychobuff	—	-3% Food, -3% Water	—	+3 STR, +3 END, +65 Max HP	0.18	40	Yes
Rad-X	—	-3% Water	—	+100 Rad Resist	0.18	25	No
Rad-X: Diluted	—	-3% Water	—	+50 Rad Resist	0.18	15	Yes
RadAway	-300	-1% Food, -3% Water	—	-50 Disease Resist	0.25	25	Yes
RadAway: Diluted	-150	-1% Food, -3% Water	—	-50 Disease Resist	0.25	15	Yes
RadShield	—	—	—	+100 Rad Resist	0.25	80	Yes
Refreshing Beverage	-1,000	-3% Food	—	Removes all Rads and cures addictions	0.35	80	Yes
Scorched Fever Inoculation	—	-3% Food, -5% Water	—	—	0.1	0	No
Skeeto Spit	—	-3% Water	—	+25 Max HP	0.18	35	Yes
Soot Flower Herb Paste	5	15% Food, 8% Water	12	+20 Rad Resist	0.5	6	Yes
Stealth Boy	—	—	—	Invisible for 30 seconds	1	100	No
Stimpak	—	—	40%, 20%	Restores HP with an initial burst followed by a slower rate of healing.	0.7	40	Yes
Stimpak: Diluted	—	—	20%, 10%	Restores HP with an initial burst followed by a slower rate of healing.	0.35	15	Yes
Stimpak: Super	—	—	80% HP, 40% HP	Restores health with an initial burst followed by a slower rate of healing	1.5	60	Yes
Sunshine Oil	2	—	—	+15 DMG Resist, +400 AP	1	6	Yes
Toxic Goo	125	—	—	—	0.75	0	No

TRAINING

CRAFTING AND C.A.M.P.ING

INVENTORY

QUESTS

ATLAS

BESTIARY

APPENDICES

SERUMS

NAME	WEIGHT	VALUE	CRAFTABLE
Adrenal Reaction Serum	0.25	500	Yes
Bird Bones Serum	0.25	500	Yes
Carnivore Serum	0.25	500	Yes
Chameleon Serum	0.25	500	Yes
Eagle Eyes Serum	0.25	500	Yes
Egg Head Serum	0.25	500	Yes
Electricity Charged Serum	0.25	500	Yes
Empath Serum	0.25	500	Yes
Grounded Serum	0.25	500	Yes
Healing Factor Serum	0.25	500	Yes
Herbivore Serum	0.25	500	Yes
Herd Mentality Serum	0.25	500	Yes
Marsupial Serum	0.25	500	Yes
Plague Walker Serum	0.25	500	Yes
Scaly Skin Serum	0.25	500	Yes
Speed Demon Serum	0.25	500	Yes
Talons Serum	0.25	500	Yes
Twisted Muscles Serum	0.25	500	Yes
Unstable Isotope Serum	0.25	500	Yes

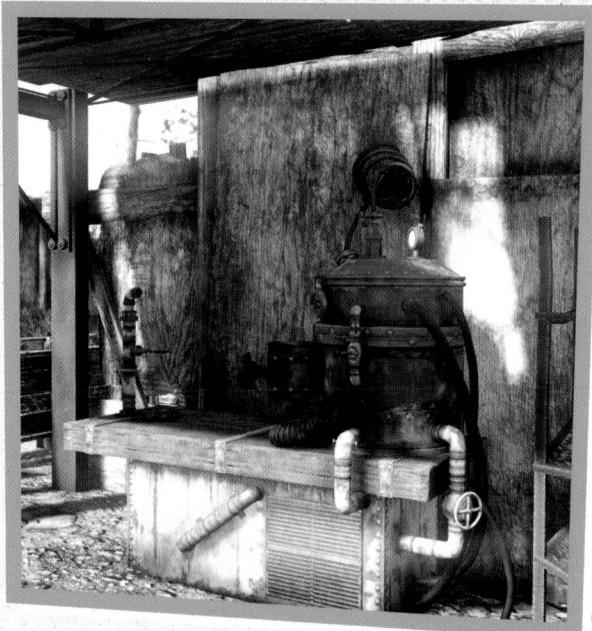

NUKED FLORA

NAME	RADS	SATIATION	HP	EFFECTS	WEIGHT	VALUE	CRAFTABLE
Inert Flux	5	25% Water	—	+5 Disease Resist	1	10	No
Raw Cobalt Flux	5	25% Water	—	+5 Disease Resist	0.2	50	No
Raw Crimson Flux	5	25% Water	—	+5 Disease Resist	0.2	50	No
Raw Fluorescent Flux	5	25% Water	—	+5 Disease Resist	0.2	50	No
Raw Violet Flux	5	25% Water	—	+5 Disease Resist	0.2	50	No
Raw Yellowcake Flux	5	25% Water	—	+5 Disease Resist	0.2	50	No
Stable Cobalt Flux	—	—	—	—	1	30	Yes
Stable Crimson Flux	—	—	—	—	1	30	Yes
Stable Fluorescent Flux	—	—	—	—	1	30	Yes
Stable Violet Flux	—	—	—	—	1	30	Yes
Stable Yellowcake Flux	—	—	—	—	1	30	Yes

ALCOHOL

NAME	RADS	SATIATION	HP	EFFECTS	WEIGHT	VALUE	CRAFTABLE
Beer	—	15% Water	—	+1 CHR, +1 STR, -1 INT	1	5	No
Blackwater Brew	—	15% Water	—	+1 CHR, +1 STR, -1 INT	1	5	No
Bourbon	—	15% Water	—	+1 END, +1 STR, -1 INT	1	7	No
Cranberry Moonshine	—	15% Water	—	+25 Max HP, +1 CHR, +1 STR, -1 INT	1.2	20	No
Mountain Honey	—	15% Water	25	+1 CHR, +1 STR, -1 INT	1.2	20	No
Muttberry Shine	—	15% Water	—	+25 Max HP, +1 CHR, +1 STR, -1 INT	1.2	10	No
New River Red Ale	—	15% Water	—	+1 STR, +1 CHR, -1 INT	1	5	No
Nuka-Cola Quantum	5	15% Water	400	+100 AP	1	50	No
Oak Holler Lager	—	15% Water	—	+1 STR, +1 CHR, -1 INT	1	5	No
Old Possum	—	15% Water	—	+1 STR, +1 CHR, -1 INT	1	5	No
Pickaxe Pilsner	—	15% Water	—	+1 STR, +1 CHR, -1 INT	1	5	No
Rodgers' Reserve Beer	—	15% Water	—	+1 CHR, +1 STR, -1 INT	1	5	No
Rum	—	15% Water	—	+1 STR, +1 AGI, -1 INT	1	8	No
Sunday Shine	—	15% Water	—	+25 Max HP, +1 CHR, +1 STR, -1 INT	1.2	10	No
Tater Shine	—	15% Water	—	+25 Max HP, +1 CHR, +1 STR, -1 INT	1.2	10	No
Vodka	—	15% Water	—	+25 Max HP, +1 STR, -1 INT	1	5	No
Whiskey	—	15% Water	—	+2 STR, -1 INT	1	5	No
Wine	—	15% Water	—	+1 STR. -1 INT	1	6	No

UTILITY

NAME	WEIGHT	VALUE	CRAFTABLE
Cutting Fluid	1	13	Yes (At Chemistry Station)
Solvent Attractant	1.5	0	Yes (At Chemistry Station)
Solvent Deterrent	1.5	0	Yes (At Chemistry Station)
Solvent Enhancer	1.5	0	Yes (At Chemistry Station)
Solvent Suppressor	1.5	0	Yes (At Chemistry Station)
Vegetable Starch	0.5	8	Yes (At Cooking Station)
Water Filter	0.5	0	Yes (At Chemistry Station)

PERK AND BONUS ITEMS

BOBBLEHEADS

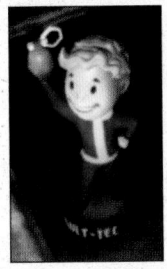

Each Bobblehead you collect grants a temporary perk-like benefit, once you decide to utilize it. You're free to sell these valuable figurines, swap them, or hoard them. Note that the location of every Bobblehead across Appalachia (detailed in this guide's Appendices) is definite, but the item's appearance is random: The Bobblehead will appear at the location eventually, but it might not have spawned, or it might have been taken by another player.

MAGAZINES

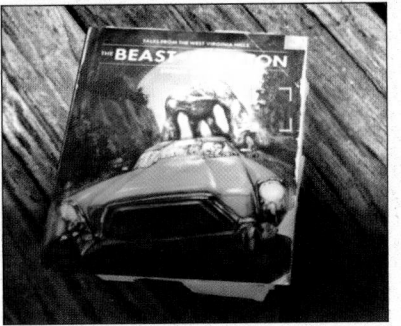

You'll find informative magazines scattered across Appalachia. Each time you collect one of these items, you're rewarded with a temporary bonus. You're free to sell them, swap them, or hoard them. Note that the location of every Magazine across Appalachia (detailed in this guide's Appendices) is definite, but the item's appearance is random: The Magazine will appear at the location eventually, but it might not have spawned, or it might have been taken by another player.

Statistical information for Bobbleheads and Magazines is provided in the Training: Being a Better You! chapter. Location information is provided in the guide's Appendices chapter. Expect Bobbleheads/Magazines to have a Weight of 0/0 and a Value of 300/100.

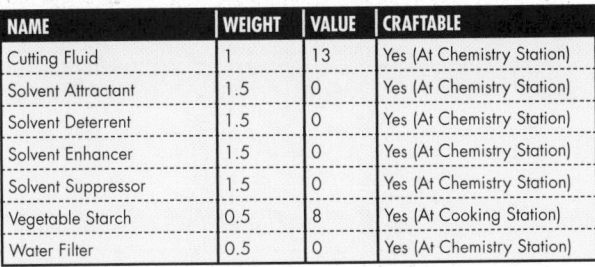

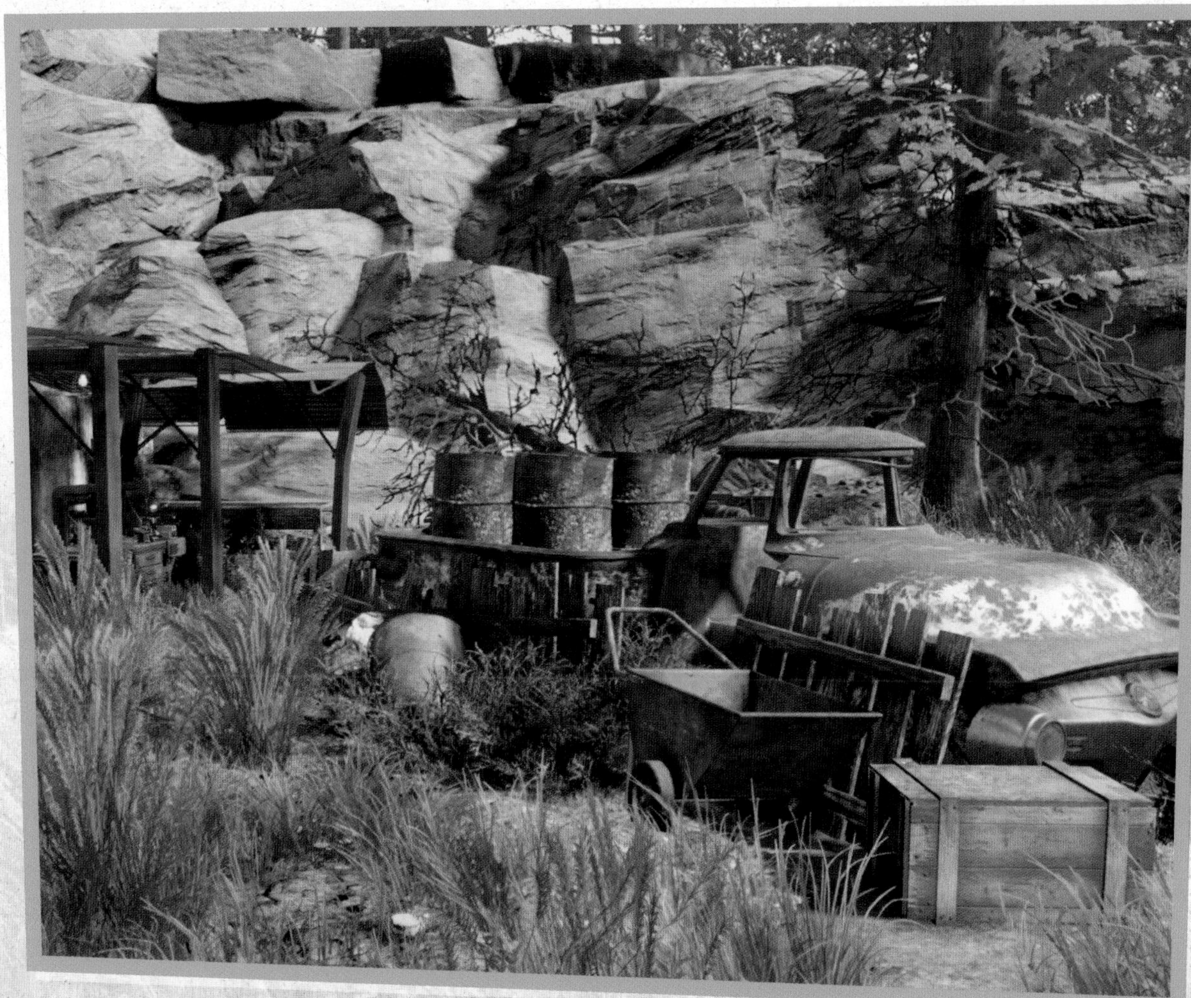

TRAINING

CRAFTING AND C.A.M.P.ING

INVENTORY

QUESTS

ATLAS

BESTIARY

APPENDICES

JUNK

You'll find junk on defeated enemies, stashed in containers, and scattered around virtually every location you explore. You can, of course, sell these bits and bobs for extra Caps, but a junk item's true value lies in the components it yields. Battered clipboards are made from springs and wood; desk fans contain gears, screws, and steel; an old fuse can be salvaged for copper and glass. With the right junk items, you can build everything from extra ammunition, to C.A.M.P. objects, to advanced Power Armor Mods.

Whenever you build an item, the required components are automatically salvaged from the junk items, or the components that you scrapped from any junk items, that are currently in your inventory or stored within your My Stash Box. This makes managing your collected junk items incredibly easy—when you attempt to craft an object, you'll instantly see which components can be salvaged from the available junk or parts.

When a lack of materials is holding up construction, use the "Tag for Search" function. From that point on, your Pip-Boy automatically indicates if a targeted junk item contains the tagged component. Repeat the process at any time to add or remove tracked components from your list.

BASE COMPONENTS

COMPONENT	RARITY	DESCRIPTION
Acid	Rare	Acid is primarily used in the Chemistry Station for crafting chems and explosives. Found both in junk and rare environmental deposits.
Adhesive	Uncommon	Fashioned from glue and Vegetable Starch, this essential component is used in a range of mods and explosives, and is useful when upgrading your gear.
Aluminum	Uncommon	Used in almost all types of crafting, this is an essential component, especially for more complex Power Armor and Weapon Mods, as well as turrets, generators, and appliances.
Antiseptic	Uncommon	Usually used when Medicinal Mods and chems are required, grab an Abraxo Cleaner for a quick addition to your Antiseptic stockpile.
Asbestos	Rare	If you need to boost an item's Energy Resistance, or create a few mods and chems or appliances, then search out this base material.
Ballistic Fiber	Very Rare	Found in only two junk items (Military Ammo Bag (2), Military Grade Duct Tape (2)), this is used in high-level mods, especially light-weight armor and apparel items.
Black Titanium	Very Rare	Found in deposits and veins as Black Titanium Ingot or Raw Black Titanium, this rare metal is mainly used in extremely high-level Power Armor Mods.
Bone	Common	Found in bone fragments in sections throughout Appalachia, use it if you need Cutting Fluid or some Raider Armor Mods, as well as a Bone Chime for your camp.
Ceramic	Common	While this is useful for occasional modding work, it is a critical component to most of your camp's power-related objects, such as Defenses, Generators, Power Connectors (switches), Lights, Water, and more.
Circuits	Rare	A large number of more advanced mods and a few chems and explosives, as well as electronic devices and turrets, require circuitry. Your camp's crafting, defenses, power connectors, and some appliances also need this.
Cloth	Common	Use this when making furniture for your camp (as well as lights, water sources, beds, and more), as well as armor and related modifications.

COMPONENT	RARITY	DESCRIPTION
Concrete	Common	Need a camp foundation or a Water Pump? Then seek out gravel pits and concrete bags.
Copper	Uncommon	Found in veins and deposits as well as in junk devices, copper is important in most electronic objects, like generators, defenses, turrets, switches, lights, and advanced mods.
Cork	Uncommon	Need to reduce your armor weight using a mod? Then cork is going to help with this. Grab a Baseball or Antique Globe to help you with this.
Crystal	Rare	Also found in veins and deposits, and an integral part of devices requiring lasers (like tripwires, turrets, and laser weaponry). Scopes and high-tech items (like fancier generators and traps) need this too.
Fertilizer	Uncommon	Until you start churning out your own fertilizer at your camp with a Resource Extractor, look for phosphate nodes and take the fertilizer to a workbench to make chems and explosives with it.
Fiber Optics	Rare	Fiber optics are required to craft a variety of high-tech mods and devices. These components are particularly important to laser-based weapons and switches, but fiber optics are used in the creation and modification of several items (including turrets and traps, and power connectors).
Fiberglass	Uncommon	Both lightweight and durable, fiberglass is used in a variety of weapons, armor, and Power Armor. Energy Weapon Mods, in particular, tend to require a good amount of fiberglass. This versatile component is also required to craft a small selection of explosives and workshop items (crafting and containers).
Flux	Very Rare	Gathered only after a nuclear strike, when the blast zone has been razed, this rare and irradiated plant (with variants known as Cobalt Flux, Fluorescent Flux, Violet Flux, Crimson Flux, and Yellowcake Flux) is a key component for some extremely rare items like the Fusion Core.
Gears	Uncommon	Gears are required for a variety of applications. From simple ceiling fans to massive generators and other camp resources, nearly any device that involves moving parts includes some amount of gears. These low-tech components are particularly important in turret production and gun modification, so restock your supply as often as possible.
Glass	Uncommon	Glass is used in several recipes, but is crucial when crafting lights, scopes, syringes, and laser-based Weapon Mods.

COMPONENT	RARITY	DESCRIPTION
Gold	Rare	Also found in veins and deposits, gold is needed for a variety of high-tech mods and devices. It's particularly important for laser weapon enthusiasts.
Lead	Uncommon	Also found in deposits, most lead applications involve boosting the Radiation Resistance offered by a piece of apparel, but any item meant to reflect or contain radiation is likely to require some amount of lead (including a camp trap).
Leather	Common	Leather has a few different uses, but the component you primarily claim from animal hides is most often used at an Armor Workbench.
Nuclear Material	Rare	Also found in rare deposits (as raw Uranium), nuclear material is required to craft a variety of mods, explosives, and workshop items. Most of the rare devices that use nuclear materials are fairly advanced (like the camp's fusion generator), but this rare component is also needed to craft simple weapon sights and camp traps. Need some quick? Find the Blast Radius Board Game.
Oil	Common	Oil is essential to most mechanical devices like Gun Mods, turrets, and water purifiers, but it's also used in a variety of Armor Mods and explosives. It has a low-tech use too: to power lights that don't require a generator.
Plastic	Common	Plastic is involved in almost every type of crafting, but it's most commonly needed for building furniture or modifying armor and energy weapons.
Rubber	Common	The unique properties of rubber make it an essential part of many items. It serves as insulation for mechanical devices like generators and pylons, it adds flexibility to weapons and armor, and it's an important component of various furniture pieces and decorative items.

COMPONENT	RARITY	DESCRIPTION
Screw	Uncommon	Whether you're constructing mechanical devices or reinforcing armor, you'll find a lot of uses for this component. Screws aren't as rare as some materials, but if you plan on modifying your gear, building turrets, or crafting doors and shelves for your camp, you'll want to salvage as many screws as possible.
Silver	Rare	Silver is primarily used for modifying weapons. It's required for a wide variety of Energy Weapon Mods, but it's also a featured component of most sights and scopes.
	Uncommon	Small coiled wiring used to create turrets and some weapon mods. Found in items with springs in their component parts, like Alarm Clocks, Typewriters, Giddyup Buttercups, Lighters, Cameras, and Toasters.
Steel	Common	Steel is an essential building material, as well as used in a variety of mods. Fortunately, it is relatively common, and can also be mined at deposits or veins of iron, and then smelted (at the Chemistry Station).
Ultracite	Very Rare	Found occasionally in deposits, this extremely rare and dangerous substance is a key component when crafting the most devastating laser and gatling weaponry and mods, and the infamous Ultracite armor.
Wood	Common	Wood is used most often in basic construction. Camp and workshop structures, furniture, and decorative items all tend to require large amounts of wood. Find the majority of the wood you need from harvesting logs or log piles.

JUNK ITEMS

Over time, you'll develop an eye for junk you find particularly useful, but Appalachia is absolutely packed with discarded treasures. Every junk item has its uses, but some are far more valuable than you might expect. Note the "#" (number) value gives a very approximate value of how many of each junk item is available loose in the world (i.e., not randomly found in a container), so you can determine how rare it is. Then check the Atlas and see the examples of the type of junk you can expect to find in each location.

#	NAME	VALUE	WEIGHT	COMPONENTS
1	.308 Casing	0	0.1	1 Steel, 1 Lead
4	.44 Casing	0	0.1	1 Steel, 1 Lead
4	.50 Casing	0	0.1	1 Steel, 1 Lead
13	10lb Weight	14	10	7 Lead
25	10mm Casing	0	0.1	1 Steel, 1 Lead
7	160lb Barbell	40	160	20 Lead
35	20lb Dumbbell	14	20	7 Lead
37	25lb Weight	20	25	7 Lead
11	40lb Barbell	14	40	7 Lead
27	5lb Weight	4	5	2 Lead
18	5mm Casing	0	0.1	1 Steel, 1 Lead
4	80lb Barbell	20	80	10 Lead
6	80lb Curlbar	20	80	10 Lead
275	Abraxo Cleaner	5	0.8	1 Acid, 2 Antiseptic, 1 Fiberglass

#	NAME	VALUE	WEIGHT	COMPONENTS
121	Abraxo Cleaner Industrial Grade	28	0.8	2 Acid, 3 Antiseptic, 2 Fiberglass
4	Accordion	0	0.2	2 Plastic, 1 Steel, 1 Wood
98	Acetone Canister	5	0.8	1 Steel, 1 Copper
5	Acoustic Guitar	0	4	2 Wood
299	Adjustable Wrench	5	1	1 Gears, 2 Steel
119	Alarm Clock	12	1	2 Aluminum, 1 Glass, 1 Springs
8	All-Star Basketball	6	1	3 Rubber
724	Aluminum Can	5	0.5	1 Aluminum, 1 Lead
244	Aluminum Canister	12	1.5	1 Aluminum, 1 Fiberglass, 1 Oil

#	NAME	VALUE	WEIGHT	COMPONENTS
4	Aluminum Oil Can	9	0.5	2 Oil, 1 Steel
2	Aluminum Ore	0	0.25	None
7	Aluminum Scrap	3	0.1	1 Aluminum
2	Aluminum Tray	1	0.5	2 Steel
2	Amontillado Bottle	9	1	3 Glass
158	Anti Freeze Bottle	4	2	2 Acid, 2 Plastic
75	Antique Globe	7	2	2 Cork, 2 Plastic, 1 Screws
4	Antique Table Knife	3	0.2	2 Steel
2	Army Training Graduation Papers	0	0	None
1	Arthur Wood's Lighter	17	0.5	1 Gold, 1 Oil, 1 Steel
2	Artifica Benzate Sample	0	0	None
251	Ashtray	2	0.5	1 Ceramic
2	Assaultron Circuit Board	22	2	2 Circuitry, 2 Silver

#	NAME	VALUE	WEIGHT	COMPONENTS
38	Atomic Roller Ball	0	0	None
22	Autopsy Board Game	8	1	2 Wood, 1 Antiseptic, 1 Plastic, 1 Bone
58	Baby Rattle	3	0.2	1 Plastic, 1 Lead
396	Bag of Cement	5	8	5 Concrete
42	Bag of Chlorine	11	4	2 Cloth, 3 Acid
258	Bag of Fertilizer	11	3.5	1 Acid, 4 Fertilizer
251	Ball-Peen Hammer	4	1.5	1 Wood, 2 Steel
32	Bandage Scissors	1	0.2	1 Steel
14	Banjo	0	2	2 Plastic
98	Baseball	6	0.5	2 Cork, 2 Leather
9	Baseball Base	4	3	2 Plastic, 2 Cloth
48	Baseball Glove	6	1	3 Leather
124	Basketball	6	1	3 Rubber
822	Battered Clipboard	4	0.2	1 Springs, 1 Wood
11	Beaker	1	0.5	2 Glass
64	Beaker Stand	4	0.5	2 Copper
3,298	Beer Bottle	3	0.5	1 Glass
2	Bioluminescent Fluid	0	5	None
10	Biometric Scanner	28	3	1 Fiber Optics, 1 Asbestos, 1 Nuclear Material
48	Bird Decoration	5	0.6	1 Copper, 1 Steel
32	Black Bowl	2	0.5	1 Ceramic
1	Black Box	0	0	None
56	Black Drinking Glass	3	0.5	1 Glass
48	Black Napkin	2	0.1	1 Cloth
3	Black Titanium Ingot	21	1	3 Black Titanium
1	Black Transmitter	0	3	None
28	Blacksmith Hammer	4	3	2 Wood, 2 Steel
48	Blackwater Brew Bottle	3	0.5	2 Glass
62	Blast Radius Board Game	17	1	2 Wood, 1 Nuclear Material
54	Blasting Caps Box	6	0.5	2 Aluminum
159	Blowtorch	15	2.5	2 Steel, 1 Oil
109	Blue Garden Gnome	4	1.5	2 Ceramic
70	Blue Paint	10	3	2 Oil, 2 Steel, 7 Lead
104	Blue Table Lamp	10	2	1 Copper, 2 Glass
1	Blue Transmitter	0	3	None
116	Bobby Pin	5	0.1	None
29	Bobby Pin Box	15	0.25	None

#	NAME	VALUE	WEIGHT	COMPONENTS
2	Bolton Greens Place Setting	7	1	None
42	Bone Cutter	8	3	2 Plastic, 2 Gears, 1 Copper
54	Bonesaw	5	1.5	1 Rubber, 2 Steel
1	Bourbon	4	1	2 Glass
42	Bourbon Bottle	9	0.8	3 Glass
115	Bowl	2	0.5	1 Ceramic
15	Bowling Ball	5	8	5 Plastic
51	Bowling Pin	4	3	2 Plastic, 2 Wood
6	Box of San Francisco Sunlights	40	0.5	2 Wood, 3 Cloth
6	Box of Shooting Targets	0	0	None
32	Brahmin Hide	8	1.2	4 Leather
31	Brahmin Skull	5	3	5 Bone
39	Brass Miner's Lamp	14	2	2 Glass, 2 Copper
33	Bread Box	3	1	3 Plastic
1	Broken Doll	2	0.4	1 Cloth, 1 Plastic
4	Broken Doll	7	1	2 Leather, 2 Cloth
5	Broken Doll	2	1	1 Plastic, 1 Cloth
11	Broken Femur	2	0.5	2 Bone
32	Broken Garden Gnome	3	1.5	2 Ceramic
148	Broken Lamp	7	2	1 Copper, 1 Glass
12	Broken Light Bulb	4	0.5	1 Copper
19	Broken Tibia	2	0.5	2 Bone
1	Broken Uplink	0	0	None
208	Broom	3	1	1 Wood, 1 Plastic
76	Brown Bottle	6	0.5	2 Glass
55	Bubblegum Bear	5	1	2 Leather, 1 Cloth
28	Bumblebear	7	1	2 Leather, 1 Cloth
54	Bunsen Burner	6	0.8	2 Steel, 1 Copper
53	Burger Tray	1	1	1 Cloth
91	Burgundy Bottle	6	0.5	2 Glass
595	Burnt Book	1	1	None
52	Burnt Fashion Magazine	1	0.1	None
43	Burnt Grognak Comic	1	0.1	None
80	Burnt Lifestyle Magazine	1	0.1	None
58	Burnt Manta-Man Comic	1	0.1	None
22	Burnt Mistress of Mystery Comic	1	0.1	None
468	Burnt Textbook	1	1	None
97	Burnt Trade Magazine	1	0.1	None
39	Burnt Unstoppables Comic	1	0.1	None
10	Butterchurn Stick	0	0.2	1 Wood

#	NAME	VALUE	WEIGHT	COMPONENTS
9	Butterchurn Top	0	0.2	1 Wood
195	Cafeteria Tray	2	1	2 Plastic
33	Cake Pan	9	0.5	3 Aluminum
66	Camera	11	3	1 Gears, 1 Springs, 1 Crystal
454	Can	4	0.2	2 Steel, 1 Lead
13	Candy Fan Mr. Fuzzy	7	0.6	2 Leather, 2 Cloth
2	Capacitor	0	0	None
23	Capless Skull	1	0.2	1 Bone
25	Carlisle Typewriter	24	5	5 Gears, 4 Screws, 5 Springs, 2 Aluminum
2	Cartridge	0	0	None
80	Cat Bowl	2	0.5	2 Plastic
22	Catch the Commie Board Game	8	1	2 Wood, 1 Asbestos, 1 Steel
19	Ceramic Bowl	2	1	1 Ceramic
5	Ceramic Scrap	1	0.05	1 Ceramic
78	Chalk	6	0.2	1 Asbestos
14	Charleston Herald	2	0.1	1 Cloth
1	Chattingham's Passcode	0	0.3	None
2	Checker Tie Mr. Fuzzy	7	0.6	2 Leather, 2 Cloth
32	Chemistry Jar	1	0.5	2 Glass
114	Chessboard	2	0.6	2 Wood
2	Chez Vivi Typewriter	20	5	2 Aluminum, 5 Springs, 4 Screws, 5 Gears
14	Chinese Ornamental Vase	25	10	2 Copper, 3 Ceramic
63	Cigar	1	0.2	1 Cloth
146	Cigar Box	15	0.5	2 Wood, 2 Fiberglass, 3 Cloth
257	Cigarette	1	0.1	1 Cloth
208	Cigarette Carton	15	1	2 Plastic, 1 Cloth, 2 Asbestos
19	Circuits	6	0.15	1 Circuitry
25	Clarksburg Brew Bottle	3	0.5	1 Glass
27	Claw Hammer	4	3	2 Wood, 2 Steel
5	Clean Bowl	4	0.5	2 Ceramic
13	Clean Broom	3	0.8	2 Wood, 1 Plastic
3	Clean Cake Pan	6	0.5	2 Aluminum
15	Clean Coffee Cup	2	0.5	1 Ceramic
14	Clean Coffee Tin	6	1	2 Aluminum
1	Clean Dog Bowl	2	0.5	2 Plastic
28	Clean Drinking Glass	3	0.5	1 Glass

#	NAME	VALUE	WEIGHT	COMPONENTS
3	Clean Globe	7	3	2 Cork, 2 Plastic, 1 Screws
11	Clean Pepper Mill	4	0.5	2 Screws, 2 Plastic
7	Clean Red Plate	1	0.6	2 Ceramic
6	Clean Salt Shaker	1	0.5	2 Plastic
44	Clean Umbrella	8	1.5	2 Springs, 2 Plastic
45	Clean Umbrella Stand	4	2	2 Ceramic
6	Clean White Plate	1	0.6	2 Ceramic
9	Clipboard	7	0.2	2 Springs, 1 Wood
268	Clothes Hanger	1	0.5	1 Steel
27	Clothing Iron	3	3	1 Plastic, 2 Steel
47	Clown	7	1	2 Leather, 1 Cloth
13	Coal	10	0.1	1 Coal
1415	Coffee Cup	4	0.5	2 Ceramic
343	Coffee Pot	16	1	2 Plastic, 2 Steel, 2 Asbestos
48	Coffee Tin	3	1	2 Aluminum
29	Colander	1	0.5	1 Steel
3	Collectible Baseball	6	0.5	2 Cork, 2 Leather
290	Combination Wrench	5	1.2	1 Steel, 2 Lead
36	Comfy Pillow	3	1	3 Cloth
2	Commendation	0	0	None
3	Completed FEV Virus Canister	0	0	None
64	Composite Ski	10	3	2 Fiberglass
30	Comrade Chubs	7	1	2 Leather, 1 Cloth
3	Concrete Scrap	3	0.05	1 Concrete
89	Connecting Rod	2	5	2 Steel
109	Cooking Oil	9	0.5	2 Oil, 1 Plastic
152	Cooking Pan	2	0.5	2 Steel
142	Cooking Pot	6	0.8	1 Copper, 2 Steel
112	Coolant	7	1.2	2 Acid, 1 Plastic
44	Coolant Cap	6	1	2 Aluminum
2	Copper Ore	0	0.25	None
1	Cork Scrap	3	0.03	1 Cork
48	Cotton Yarn	1	0.5	1 Cloth
21	Covered Metal Tub	2	2	2 Steel
24	Covered Sauce Pan	2	0.8	2 Steel
6	Cracked Bowl	1	1	1 Ceramic
11	Cracked Deathclaw Egg	4	0.2	1 Bone, 1 Acid
41	Cracked Glass Bowl	6	1	2 Glass
1	Creature Attractant Recipe	0	0.1	None

#	NAME	VALUE	WEIGHT	COMPONENTS
1	Creature Deterrent Recipe	0	0.1	None
110	Crushed Acetone Canister	1	0.5	1 Steel
136	Crushed Orange Canister	1	0.5	1 Steel
131	Crushed Rusty Canister	1	0.5	1 Steel
148	Crushed Yellow Canister	1	0.5	1 Steel
64	Crystal Liquor Decanter	16	3	1 Cork, 3 Crystal
1	Crystal Shards	5	0.1	1 Crystal
29	Cue Ball	1	0.4	1 Plastic
31	Cutting Board	3	8	3 Wood
78	Cutting Board	2	0.5	2 Wood
4	Cutting Fluid	13	1	3 Oil, 1 Steel
2	Crystalline Scorched Head	2	1	1 Glass, 2 Bone
2	Deflated Kickball	6	0.5	3 Rubber
9	Dehydrated Beef Stock	5	1	1 Copper, 1 Steel
209	Desk Fan	14	3	2 Gears, 2 Screws, 2 Steel
20	Detective Case File	1	0.25	1 Cloth
8	Diced Vegetable Mix	5	1	1 Copper, 1 Steel
135	Dinner Fork	1	0.2	1 Steel
227	Dinner Plate	1	0.6	1 Steel
3	Diode	0	0	None
550	Dirty Ashtray	2	0.6	1 Ceramic
171	Dirty Desktop Frame	2	1	2 Wood
1	Dirty Old Teddy Bear	7	1	2 Leather, 3 Cloth
2	Dirty Pillow	4	0.8	2 Cloth
11	Dirty Pillow	4	0.8	2 Cloth
463	Dishrag	3	0.2	1 Cloth
1	Distress Beacon	0	0	None
104	Dog Bowl	1	0.5	2 Plastic
27	Dog Tags	1	0.2	1 Steel
32	Doll	7	1.5	3 Leather, 2 Cloth
6	Doll Head	7	0.4	2 Leather, 3 Cloth
3	Doll Left Arm	1	0.4	1 Plastic
5	Doll Right Arm	7	1	2 Leather, 3 Cloth
68	Drinking Glass	3	0.5	1 Glass
11	Drumstick	3	0.2	1 Wood
313	Duct Tape	7	0.2	1 Adhesive, 1 Cloth
130	Economy Wonderglue	30	0.75	5 Adhesive
19	Eight Ball	2	0.4	1 Plastic
2	Electroaquiam Sample	0	0	None
17	Eleven Ball	2	0.4	2 Plastic

#	NAME	VALUE	WEIGHT	COMPONENTS
7	Emerald Tie Mr. Fuzzy	7	0.6	2 Leather, 2 Cloth
32	Empty Blood Pack	1	0.5	1 Plastic
1	Empty Can	1	0.5	2 Steel
6	Empty Can	1	0.5	2 Steel
56	Empty Coolant	1	0.5	1 Plastic
17	Empty Floral Barrel Vase	2	2	1 Ceramic
22	Empty Floral Bud Vase	2	2	1 Ceramic
18	Empty Floral Flared Vase	2	2	1 Ceramic
26	Empty Floral Rounded Vase	2	2	1 Ceramic
50	Empty Floral Vaulted Vase	2	2	1 Ceramic
220	Empty Milk Bottle	6	0.8	2 Glass
265	Empty Paint Can	2	0.5	2 Steel
11	Empty Teal Barrel Vase	2	2	1 Ceramic
17	Empty Teal Bud Vase	2	2	1 Ceramic
13	Empty Teal Flared Vase	2	2	1 Ceramic
14	Empty Teal Rounded Vase	2	2	1 Ceramic
17	Empty Teal Vaulted Vase	2	2	1 Ceramic
39	Empty Willow Barrel Vase	2	2	1 Ceramic
18	Empty Willow Bud Vase	2	2	1 Ceramic
29	Empty Willow Flared Vase	2	2	1 Ceramic
22	Empty Willow Rounded Vase	2	2	1 Ceramic
32	Empty Willow Vaulted Vase	2	2	1 Ceramic
563	Enamel Bucket	2	1.5	1 Steel, 1 Plastic
1	Energy Cell	0	0.15	1 Plastic, 1 Lead
47	Enhanced Targeting Card	17	0.2	1 Plastic, 1 Silver, 2 Circuitry
5	Excess Adhesive	6	0.05	1 Adhesive
303	Extinguisher	13	6	2 Rubber, 1 Steel, 1 Asbestos
3	Eyebot Model	6	0.2	2 Aluminum
1	Fan Motor	0	0	None
8	Fancy Framed Lighthouse	2	0.8	2 Wood
51	Fancy Hairbrush	7	0.5	1 Plastic, 1 Silver
16	Feather Duster	1	1	2 Plastic, 1 Cloth
38	Femur	2	1	2 Bone
6	Fiber Optics Bundle	6	0.05	1 Fiber Optics
12	Fiberglass Spool	6	0.05	1 Fiberglass
19	Fifteen Ball	2	0.4	2 Plastic
111	Fishing Rod	10	2.5	2 Gears, 1 Springs, 1 Wood

TRAINING

CRAFTING AND C.A.M.P.ING

INVENTORY

QUESTS

ATLAS

BESTIARY

APPENDICES

#	NAME	VALUE	WEIGHT	COMPONENTS
10	Five Ball	2	0.4	2 Plastic
51	Flask	3	0.5	1 Glass
1	Flight Data Recorder	23	3	1 Circuitry, 2 Fiber Optics, 1 Copper
124	Flip Lighter	8	0.5	1 Oil, 1 Springs, 1 Steel
14	Floral Barrel Vase	2	2	1 Ceramic
20	Floral Bud Vase	2	2	1 Ceramic
15	Floral Flared Vase	2	2	1 Ceramic
10	Floral Rounded Vase	2	2	1 Ceramic
16	Floral Vaulted Vase	2	2	1 Ceramic
429	Flower Pot	3	1	2 Ceramic
2	Flute	0	0.6	2 Steel, 1 Silver
307	Folder	1	0.25	1 Cloth
12	Food Dehydrator	0	5	2 Steel, 1 Plastic, 1 Glass
8	Fork	1	0.2	1 Steel
14	Four Ball	2	0.4	2 Plastic
19	Fourteen Ball	2	0.4	2 Plastic
47	Fox Hide	4	0.5	2 Leather
6	Framed Lighthouse Photo	2	0.8	2 Wood
49	Frying Pan	2	1	2 Steel
75	Fuel Tank	0	5	2 Oil, 2 Steel
51	Fumigus Blowtorch	25	3	3 Steel, 3 Oil
181	Fuse	7	0.2	1 Copper, 1 Glass
659	Gas Canister	7	3	3 Steel, 1 Oil
80	Gear	1	1	1 Steel
45	Giddyup Buttercup	35	8	3 Gears, 5 Steel, 3 Springs, 4 Screws
5	Giddyup Buttercup Back Leg	13	1.5	2 Springs, 1 Steel, 2 Gears
3	Giddyup Buttercup Body	14	3	2 Steel, 2 Springs, 2 Screws
6	Giddyup Buttercup Front Leg	13	1.5	2 Gears, 1 Steel, 2 Springs
11	Giddyup Buttercup Head	8	2.5	2 Steel, 2 Springs
40	Glass Bowl	6	1	2 Glass
1	Glass Bud Red Vase	6	3	2 Glass
249	Glass Pitcher	6	1	2 Glass
1	Glass Rounded Vase	6	3	2 Glass
4	Glass Shards	3	0.05	1 Glass
31	Globe	9	3	2 Screws, 2 Cork, 1 Plastic
3	Gold Fork	12	0.2	1 Gold
15	Gold Ore	0	0.25	None
56	Gold Plated Flip Lighter	17	0.4	1 Gold, 1 Oil, 1 Steel
28	Gold Pocket Watch	30	0.5	1 Gears, 2 Gold, 1 Springs
31	Gold Scrap	9	0.05	1 Gold
2	Gold Table Knife	12	0.2	1 Gold
4	Gold Table Spoon	6	0.2	1 Silver
2	Gold Tie Mr. Fuzzy	7	0.6	2 Leather, 2 Cloth
5	Gold-Plated Glass	15	0.5	1 Glass, 1 Gold
424	Golf Ball	2	0.1	1 Cork, 1 Plastic
18	Golf Tee	1	0.1	1 Wood
27	Graduated Cylinder	1	0.5	2 Glass
2	Green Transmitter	0	3	None
1	Grey & Gould Pocket Watch	25	0.5	2 Gears, 2 Silver, 2 Springs
1	Growth Enhancer Recipe	0	0.1	None
1	Growth Suppressor Recipe	0	0.1	None
2	Gunpowder	3	0.1	None
49	Hack Saw	3	2	2 Steel, 1 Wood
63	Hairbrush	2	0.5	2 Plastic
1	HalluciGen Gas Canister	17	3	2 Steel, 5 Acid
3	Hammer	3	1.5	1 Wood, 2 Steel
68	Handcuffs	8	0.5	1 Screws, 1 Springs, 2 Steel
55	Handmade Glue	3	0.6	1 Glass, 1 Adhesive
1	Hardened Mass	20	0.6	1 Ultracite
10	Harmonica	0	0.2	1 Wood, 1 Steel, 1 Plastic
2	Heating Coil	0	0	None
3	HH-3A Capacitor	7	1	1 Aluminum, 1 Ceramic
31	Hide Bundle	35	0.5	3 Leather
29	High-Powered Magnet	29	5	3 Copper, 1 Ceramic, 1 Nuclear Material
30	Hoe	6	2	3 Steel, 3 Wood
10	Home Plate	4	2	2 Plastic, 2 Cloth
44	Honey Jar	3	0.5	1 Glass
118	Hot Dog Tray	1	1	1 Cloth
214	Hot Plate	12	3	1 Circuitry, 1 Copper, 1 Screws
20	House Teapot	15	0.6	2 Ceramic
9	Hubcap	5	3	2 Screws, 2 Aluminum
3	Huffwarbler Teapot	2	1	2 Ceramic
16	Human Jaw	2	0.2	2 Bone
1	Hunting Rifle Long Scope	25	1	2 Steel
14	Ice Tongs	0	2	1 Steel
6	Ignition Core	38	1	3 Nuclear Material, 7 Lead, 2 Steel
33	Imported Chinese Panda	7	1	2 Leather, 3 Cloth
3	Incomplete FEV Virus Canister	0	0	None
1	Indus-tro Coffee Pot	5	1	2 Steel
11	Industrial Cleaner	10	8	2 Plastic, 2 Acid, 2 Fiberglass
95	Industrial Oil Canister	14	2	2 Aluminum, 2 Oil
52	Industrial Size Shortening	16	4	4 Oil
61	Industrial Solvent	15	1	3 Steel, 3 Antiseptic
2	Inert Bomb	0	0	None
19	Iron Ore	0	0.25	None
72	IV Bag	1	0.2	1 Plastic
55	Jangles the Moon Monkey	9	2	3 Cloth, 1 Plastic, 1 Fiberglass
4	Jarred Scorched Foot	2	1	1 Glass, 1 Bone
3	Jarred Scorched Hand	2	1	1 Bone, 1 Glass
3	Jarred Scorched Head	2	1	2 Bone, 1 Glass
65	Jawless Brahmin Skull	1	3	5 Bone
42	Kickball	6	0.5	3 Rubber
2	KidSecure ID	0	0	None
47	Kitchen Scale	12	2	3 Steel, 3 Springs
42	Lab Bottle	3	0.5	1 Glass
63	Ladle	1	0.5	1 Steel
12	Lantern	0	3	2 Glass, 2 Steel
290	Lantern	17	2.5	2 Glass, 2 Oil, 3 Steel
30	Large Baby Bottle	8	1	2 Glass, 1 Rubber
47	Large Beaker	3	1	2 Glass
35	Large Glass Jar	2	0.8	1 Glass
36	Large Glass Jar Lid	5	0.8	1 Aluminum
2	Large Glass Jar Ring	5	0.8	1 Aluminum
2	Large Glass Jar Top	3	0.2	1 Aluminum
74	Large Left Antler	2	1	3 Bone
90	Large Right Antler	2	1	3 Bone
98	Large Sealed Glass Jar	2	0.8	1 Glass
15	Late Edition Newspaper	2	0.25	1 Cloth

#	NAME	VALUE	WEIGHT	COMPONENTS
2	Lead Ore	0	0.5	None
5	Lead Scrap	3	0.1	1 Lead
17	League Bowling Pin	4	3	2 Plastic, 2 Wood
42	Left Arm Bones	3	1.25	3 Bone
44	Left Foot Bones	2	1.2	2 Bone
52	Left Hand Bones	2	0.8	1 Bone
41	Left Leg Bones	3	1.25	3 Bone
99	Life Preserver	6	3	3 Plastic, 1 Springs
102	Light Bulb	7	0.5	1 Glass, 1 Copper
4	Lighthouse Souvenir	8	0.2	2 Copper
27	Lil' Ginger Snuggles	7	1	2 Leather, 1 Cloth
2	Liquid Noctmate Sample	0	0	None
189	Liquor Bottle	6	0.5	2 Glass
10	Lit Cigar	1	0.2	1 Cloth
5	Lit Cigarette	1	0.1	1 Cloth
2	Lit Stogie	1	0.2	1 Cloth
17	Loose Gears	3	0.1	1 Gears
41	Loose Screws	3	0.03	1 Screws
5	Loose Spring	3	0.1	1 Springs
8	Lumberjack Saw	4	2	3 Steel, 1 Wood
67	Luxobrew Coffee Pot	16	1	2 Plastic, 2 Steel, 2 Asbestos
50	Magnifying Glass	15	0.5	2 Glass, 1 Copper, 1 Crystal
142	Makeshift Battery	12	6	2 Lead, 2 Wood, 2 Acid
176	Mason Jar	2	0.5	2 Glass
15	Masonry Hammer	3	3	1 Wood, 2 Steel
8	Meat-flavored Soy Chunks	5	1	1 Copper, 1 Steel
40	Medical Liquid Nitrogen Dispenser	12	5	2 Steel
4	Megasloth Claw	10	0.2	2 Bone
1	Megasloth Pelt	25	5	5 Leather
2	Memor-Eaze Coffee Cup	1	0.5	2 Ceramic
2	Metabolizer	0	5	None
14	Metal Beer Stein	9	2	1 Steel, 1 Silver, 2 Wood
734	Metal Bucket	2	0.6	1 Steel
69	Metal Tub	2	2	1 Steel
18	Metal Tub Lid	2	1	1 Steel
97	Microscope	18	3.5	1 Gears, 1 Glass, 1 Crystal, 1 Fiber Optics
81	Military Ammo Bag	4	3	2 Antiballistic Fiber
63	Military Grade Duct Tape	22	0.2	2 Antiballistic Fiber, 4 Adhesive
60	Military-Grade Circuit Board	25	1.5	5 Circuitry
48	Miner's Lamp	5	2.5	2 Steel, 1 Glass
1	Mining Headlamp	100	1	1 Steel
29	Mining Light	0	2	2 Glass, 2 Steel
7	MiniNuke Beryllium Cap	17	3	2 Steel, 1 Nuclear Material
10	MiniNuke Detonator Shell	33	5	2 Nuclear Material, 3 Steel
3	MiniNuke Stabilizer Fins	9	1.5	3 Steel, 2 Screws
2	Mirelurk Deterrent	0	0.5	None
1	Moist Radkelp	0	0	None
3	Molded Plastic	1	0.05	1 Plastic
13	Mole Rat Hide	4	0.5	2 Leather
3	Mole Rat Teeth	2	0.2	2 Bone
129	Moonshine Jug	0	1	2 Glass
166	Mop	4	2	2 Wood, 2 Cloth
1	Mouth Harp	0	0.25	1 Plastic, 1 Steel, 1 Wood
1	Mr. Gutsy Model	6	0.2	2 Aluminum
1	Mr. Handy Fuel	19	5	4 Oil, 3 Steel
71	Mr. Handy Fuel	11	5	2 Oil, 3 Steel
5	Mr. Handy Model	6	0.2	2 Aluminum
2	Mutated Scorched Head	2	1	2 Bone, 1 Glass
29	Napkin	1	0.1	1 Cloth
1	New Floral Barrel Vase	2	2	1 Ceramic
3	New Floral Barrel Vase	2	2	1 Ceramic
73	New Floral Bud Vase	2	2	1 Ceramic
6	New Floral Flared Vase	2	2	1 Circuitry
1	New Floral Rounded Vase	2	2	1 Ceramic
2	New Floral Rounded Vase	2	2	1 Ceramic
1	New Floral Vaulted Vase	2	2	1 Ceramic
13	New Floral Vaulted Vase	2	2	1 Ceramic
16	New River Red Ale Bottle	3	0.5	2 Glass
1	New Teal Barrel Vase	2	2	1 Ceramic
5	New Teal Bud Vase	2	2	1 Ceramic
1	New Teal Flared Vase	2	2	1 Ceramic
9	New Teal Flared Vase	2	2	1 Ceramic
2	New Teal Vaulted Vase	2	2	1 Ceramic
5	New Teal Vaulted Vase	2	2	1 Ceramic
8	New Toy Car	7	0.8	1 Screws, 2 Wood, 1 Lead
3	New Toy Truck	13	1.5	2 Steel, 3 Screws, 1 Lead
1	New Willow Barrel Vase	2	2	1 Ceramic
9	New Willow Barrel Vase	2	2	1 Ceramic
1	New Willow Bud Vase	2	2	1 Ceramic
35	New Willow Bud Vase	2	2	1 Ceramic
7	New Willow Flared Vase	2	2	1 Ceramic
5	New Willow Rounded Vase	2	2	1 Ceramic
1	New Willow Vaulted Vase	2	2	1 Ceramic
40	New Willow Vaulted Vase	2	2	1 Ceramic
18	Nine Ball	2	0.4	2 Plastic
2	Nitrous Extrematis Sample	0	0	None
19	Nuclear Waste	10	0.1	1 Nuclear Material
485	Nuka-Cola Bottle	6	0.5	2 Glass
464	Nuka-Cola Cup	1	1	1 Cloth
125	Nuka-Cola Cup and Straw	2	1	1 Cloth, 1 Plastic
47	Nuka-Cola Cup Pack	2	1	1 Cloth, 1 Plastic
17	Oak Holler Lager Bottle	3	0.5	2 Glass
265	Office Desk Fan	11	2.5	2 Gears, 1 Screws, 2 Steel
43	Oil Can	19	0.5	4 Oil, 1 Aluminum
223	Oil Canister	10	1.5	2 Steel, 2 Oil
34	Old Possum Bottle	3	0.5	2 Glass
15	One Ball	2	0.4	2 Plastic
40	Orange Bowl	2	0.5	1 Ceramic
114	Orange Canister	5	1	1 Copper, 1 Steel
50	Orange Drinking Glass	3	0.5	1 Glass
52	Orange Napkin	2	0.1	1 Cloth
3	Orange Tie Mr. Fuzzy	7	0.6	2 Leather, 2 Cloth
1	Orbital Strike Beacon Schematics	5	0	None
16	Ornamental Vase	10	10	1 Ceramic, 2 Copper
86	Oven Mitt	8	1	1 Asbestos, 2 Cloth
357	Pack of Cigarettes	8	0.25	1 Plastic, 1 Cloth, 1 Asbestos

TRAINING

CRAFTING AND C.A.M.P.ING

INVENTORY

QUESTS

ATLAS

BESTIARY

APPENDICES

#	NAME	VALUE	WEIGHT	COMPONENTS
66	Pack of Duct Tape	26	0.2	4 Adhesive, 2 Cloth
148	Paint Can	24	3	2 Oil, 2 Steel, 7 Lead
102	Paintbrush	2	0.5	1 Wood, 1 Cloth
12	Paper Cutter	0	0	2 Steel
24	Paper Cutter	0	0	2 Steel
39	Pelvis Bones	3	1	3 Bone
175	Pen	1	0.2	1 Plastic
367	Pencil	3	0.2	1 Lead, 1 Wood
32	Pepper Mill	2	0.5	2 Screws, 2 Plastic
1	Phosphate	0	0.25	None
19	Pickaxe Pilsner Bottle	3	0.5	2 Glass
145	Pillow	2	0.8	2 Cloth
293	Pillow	2	0.8	2 Cloth
71	Pizza Tray	1	1	1 Cloth
49	Plastic Bowl	2	0.5	2 Plastic
20	Plastic Fork	1	0.2	1 Plastic
22	Plastic Fork	1	0.2	1 Plastic
41	Plastic Fork	1	0.2	1 Plastic
1	Plastic Gas Canister	10	3	2 Oil, 2 Plastic
14	Plastic Knife	1	0.2	2 Plastic
19	Plastic Knife	1	0.2	2 Plastic
21	Plastic Knife	1	0.2	2 Plastic
9	Plastic Plate	1	0.2	1 Plastic
23	Plastic Plate	1	0.2	1 Plastic
34	Plastic Plate	1	0.2	1 Plastic
46	Plastic Plate	1	0.2	1 Plastic
104	Plastic Plate	1	0.2	1 Plastic
105	Plastic Pumpkin	2	1	2 Plastic
17	Plastic Spoon	1	0.2	1 Plastic
22	Plastic Spoon	1	0.2	1 Plastic
66	Plastic Spoon	1	0.2	1 Plastic
9	Plate	1	0.6	1 Steel
4	Pleasant Valley Claim Ticket	0	0	None
227	Plunger	5	1	2 Rubber, 1 Wood
133	Portable Fuel Tank	10	5	2 Oil, 2 Steel
7	Power Relay Coil	10	0.5	2 Copper, 2 Steel
15	Pre-War Lamp	18	2.5	3 Copper, 2 Glass
406	Pre-War Money	0	0.2	1 Cloth
3	Preserved Cigarette Pack	15	0.25	1 Plastic, 2 Cloth, 2 Asbestos
13	Pristine Teddy Bear	7	1	2 Leather, 1 Cloth
3	Propaganda Flyer	1	0.5	1 Cloth
26	ProSnap Camera	33	4	3 Gears, 3 Springs, 3 Crystal
5	Protectron Model	6	0.2	2 Aluminum

#	NAME	VALUE	WEIGHT	COMPONENTS
5	Purple Tie Mr. Fuzzy	7	0.6	2 Leather, 2 Cloth
49	Quantum Bear	7	1	2 Leather, 1 Cloth
50	Rabbit Hide	4	0.5	2 Leather
32	Rack	2	0.5	2 Wood
25	Rad Poker Board Game	18	1	2 Wood, 1 Nuclear Material, 1 Plastic
33	Radbear	7	1	2 Leather, 1 Cloth
16	Radio Jammer	16	3	2 Circuitry, 2 Steel, 1 Copper
9	Radioactive Pumpkin Seeds	10	0.1	4 Fertilizer
17	Radstag Hide	8	1.2	4 Leather
191	Rat Poison	17	0.5	1 Asbestos, 1 Fiberglass, 7 Lead
2	Raw Black Titanium	0	0.25	None
2	Raw Black Titanium	6	0.1	1 Black Titanium
9	Raw Cloth	1	0.05	1 Cloth
1	Raw Crystal	0	0.25	None
3	Raw Fertilizer	1	0.1	1 Fertilizer
5	Raw Leather	3	0.05	1 Leather
44	Red Garden Gnome	4	1.5	2 Ceramic
20	Red Paint	24	3	2 Oil, 2 Steel, 7 Lead
97	Red Plate	4	0.6	2 Ceramic
3	Red Tie Mr. Fuzzy	7	0.6	2 Leather, 2 Cloth
1	Red Transmitter	0	3	None
2	Relay	0	0	None
2	Repair Beacon	0	0	None
4	Requisition Note	8	1	None
8	Research Test Tube	3	0.2	1 Glass
3	Resistor	0	0	None
1	Responder ID	5	1	None
3	Responder Manual	0	0	None
6	Restored Desk Fan	14	3	2 Steel, 2 Screws, 2 Gears
59	Rib Cage	5	1	5 Bone
46	Rib Cage and Pelvis	3	2	3 Bone
43	Rib Cage and Spine	3	1.25	3 Bone
70	Right Arm Bones	3	1.25	3 Bone
40	Right Foot Bones	2	1.2	2 Bone
33	Right Hand Bones	2	0.8	1 Bone
32	Right Leg Bones	3	1.25	3 Bone
5	Ring Stand	4	3	1 Steel, 1 Aluminum
1	Robot Parts Model	0	0.1	2 Aluminum
1	Robot Parts Model	0	0.1	2 Aluminum

#	NAME	VALUE	WEIGHT	COMPONENTS
2	Robot Parts Model	0	0.1	2 Aluminum
80	Rolled Charleston Herald	1	0.25	1 Cloth
2	Royal Jelly	15	0.6	1 Glass, 3 Antiseptic
5	Ruby Tie Mr. Fuzzy	7	0.6	2 Leather, 2 Cloth
62	Rum Bottle	9	1	3 Glass
41	Ruptured HalluciGen Gas Canister	10	3	1 Steel
106	Rusty Canister	5	0.8	1 Copper, 1 Steel
32	Salt Shaker	1	0.5	1 Plastic
31	Sauce Pan	2	1	2 Steel
7	Sauce Pan Lid	1	0.5	1 Steel
116	Saucer	1	0.4	2 Ceramic
85	Saw	5	3	3 Steel, 1 Rubber
19	Scalpel	1	0.2	1 Steel
72	Scissors	2	0.2	1 Plastic, 1 Steel
4	Scorched Ashes	1	0.5	None
349	Screwdriver	3	0.4	2 Steel, 1 Wood
87	Sealed Charleston Herald	1	0.5	1 Cloth
69	Sealed Mason Jar	2	0.6	1 Glass
83	Sealed Specimen Jar	2	0.6	1 Glass
49	Sealed Wonderglue	24	0.2	4 Adhesive
15	Sensor Module	23	1.2	1 Steel, 5 Circuitry, 2 Copper
1	Sentry Bot Model	6	0.2	2 Aluminum
10	Seven Ball	2	0.4	2 Plastic
22	Shadeless Lamp	10	3	1 Copper, 2 Glass
72	Shadeless Table Lamp	10	3	1 Copper, 2 Glass
11	Shaped Charge	1	1	None
232	Shopping Basket	4	0.8	1 Plastic, 3 Steel
155	Shot Glass	3	0.2	1 Glass
19	Shotgun Shell Casing	0	0.15	1 Steel, 1 Plastic
1	Signal Booster	0	0	None
28	Silver Bowl	12	1	2 Silver
10	Silver Fork	12	0.2	1 Silver
30	Silver Locket	12	0.2	2 Silver
3	Silver Ore	0	0.25	None
47	Silver Plate	6	1	1 Silver
29	Silver Pocket Watch	24	0.5	2 Gears, 2 Silver, 2 Springs
5	Silver Scrap	6	0.05	1 Silver
23	Silver Table Knife	6	0.2	1 Silver
23	Silver Table Spoon	6	0.2	1 Silver

#	NAME	VALUE	WEIGHT	COMPONENTS
9	Silver Tie Mr. Fuzzy	7	0.6	2 Leather, 2 Cloth
12	Six Ball	2	0.4	2 Plastic
176	Ski Pole	20	1	3 Aluminum
200	Skull	3	2.5	3 Bone
11	Skull Cap Bone	2	0.2	2 Bone
13	Skull Eye Socket	2	0.2	2 Bone
6	Skull Faceplate	2	1	2 Bone
6	Skull Fragment	2	0.2	2 Bone
34	Small Baby Bottle	8	1	2 Glass, 1 Rubber
2	Small Covered Sauce Pan	1	0.8	1 Steel
60	Small Drinking Glass	1	0.5	2 Glass
137	Small Glass Jar	2	0.5	1 Glass
16	Small Glass Jar Lid	5	0.2	1 Aluminum
1	Small Glass Jar Ring	5	0.2	1 Aluminum
2	Small Glass Jar Top	5	0.2	1 Aluminum
81	Small Left Antler	2	1	2 Bone
12	Small Picture Frame	2	0.8	2 Wood
52	Small Picture Frame	2	1	2 Wood
95	Small Right Antler	2	1	2 Bone
15	Small Sauce Pan	1	1	1 Steel
4	Small Sauce Pan Lid	1	0.2	1 Steel
114	Small Sealed Glass Jar	2	0.6	1 Glass
2	Snare Drum	0	2.5	2 Plastic, 2 Wood
1	Soap	4	0.5	1 Oil
231	Soap	4	0.4	1 Oil
2	Soldier's Remains	5	0	None
1	Souvenir Coffee Cup	1	0.5	2 Ceramic
6	Souvenir Sloth Toy	9	1	3 Cloth, 2 Leather, 1 Lead
4	Souvenir Teddy Bear	3	1	2 Cloth, 3 Leather
5	Souvenir Teddy Bear	3	1	2 Cloth, 3 Leather
3	Souvenir Toy Car	7	1	1 Screws, 2 Wood, 1 Lead
61	Spatula	3	0.5	1 Rubber, 1 Steel
48	Specimen Jar	2	0.5	1 Glass
34	Spine	5	1	5 Bone
1	Spooky Mr. Fuzzy Pencil	3	0.2	1 Lead, 1 Wood
6	Spooky Time Mr. Fuzzy	7	0.6	2 Leather, 2 Cloth
4	Steel Guitar	0	4	1 Aluminum, 2 Steel
24	Steel Scrap	1	0.1	1 Steel
95	Stew Pot	6	3	2 Steel, 1 Copper

#	NAME	VALUE	WEIGHT	COMPONENTS
1	Sticky Tar	11	0.6	2 Oil, 1 Glass
2	Stogie	1	0.2	1 Cloth
163	Straw Pillow	1	1	1 Cloth
2	Strontium 90	0	0	None
42	Stuffed Grizzly	7	1	2 Leather, 1 Cloth
23	Stuffed Polar Bear	7	1	2 Leather, 1 Cloth
4	Super Mutant Head	0	1	None
4	Super Mutant Left Lower Arm	0	1	None
2	Super Mutant Left Lower Leg	0	1	None
4	Super Mutant Left Upper Arm	0	1	None
5	Super Mutant Right Hand	0	1	None
5	Super Mutant Right Lower Arm	0	1	None
1	Super Mutant Right Lower Leg	0	1	None
6	Super Mutant Right Thigh	0	1	None
80	Suprathaw Antifreeze	8	2	2 Acid, 2 Plastic
36	Surgical Scalpel	5	0.2	1 Steel
272	Surgical Tray	6	0.5	2 Aluminum
85	Table Knife	1	0.2	1 Steel
83	Table Spoon	1	0.2	1 Steel
41	Tabletop Picture Frame	2	1	2 Wood
21	Tack Hammer	3	1.5	2 Wood, 1 Steel
727	Tall Drinking Glass	3	0.5	1 Glass
84	Tall Flask	3	0.5	1 Glass
23	Tea Kettle	2	1.5	2 Steel
148	Teacup	2	0.2	1 Ceramic
7	Teal Barrel Vase	2	2	1 Ceramic
27	Teal Bud Vase	2	2	1 Ceramic
15	Teal Flared Vase	2	2	1 Ceramic
15	Teal Rounded Vase	2	2	1 Ceramic
17	Teal Vaulted Vase	2	2	1 Ceramic
57	Teapot	10	1	2 Ceramic, 1 Asbestos
1	Technical Schematics	1	0	None
197	Teddy Bear	7	0.8	2 Leather, 1 Cloth
45	Teddy Fear	7	1	2 Leather, 1 Cloth
287	Telephone	14	2	1 Circuitry, 1 Copper, 1 Fiberglass
15	Ten Ball	2	0.4	2 Plastic
1	Test Misc Item	0	0	None
112	Test Tube	3	0.5	1 Glass
63	Test Tube Rack	2	0.8	2 Wood
1	TestSmoke Bonesaw	5	1.5	1 Rubber, 2 Steel

#	NAME	VALUE	WEIGHT	COMPONENTS
1	TestSmoke Fuse	7	0.25	1 Copper, 1 Glass
1	TestSmoke Lamp	14	2	2 Glass, 2 Copper
1	TestSmoke Tall Flask	3	0.5	1 Glass
2	Tetratoxus-6 Sample	0	0	None
25	Thin Beaker	3	0.5	1 Glass
15	Thirteen Ball	2	0.4	2 Plastic
11	Three Ball	2	0.4	2 Plastic
91	Tibia	2	1	2 Bone
8	Tick Blood Sac	8	0.2	2 Antiseptic
787	Tin Can	4	0.5	2 Steel, 1 Lead
64	Tin Pitcher	6	1	2 Aluminum
3	Toaster	8	3	2 Springs, 2 Steel
70	Toaster	8	2.5	2 Springs, 2 Steel
296	Toilet Paper	1	0.25	1 Cloth
53	Token	0	0.1	None
35	Tongs	5	3	2 Steel, 1 Screws
60	Toothbrush	1	0.2	1 Plastic
44	Toothpaste	5	0.25	1 Plastic, 1 Antiseptic
104	Torque Rod End	1	3	2 Steel
3	Toxic Barrel	0	15	None
2	Toy Alien	5	0.6	2 Plastic, 2 Rubber
52	Toy Alien	5	0.5	2 Plastic, 2 Rubber, 1 Lead
1	Toy Car	5	1	1 Screws, 2 Wood
90	Toy Car	7	1	1 Screws, 2 Wood, 1 Lead
1	Toy Rocketship	5	0.6	1 Aluminum, 2 Plastic
68	Toy Rocketship	7	0.5	1 Aluminum, 2 Plastic, 1 Lead
79	Toy Truck	7	1.5	2 Steel, 1 Screws, 1 Lead
1	Triangle	0	0.1	1 Steel
31	Trifold American Flag	3	3	2 Wood, 2 Cloth
2	Triphosphal Irradium Sample	0	0	None
4	Trumpet	0	2	3 Copper
165	Tube Flange	2	5	2 Steel
2	Tungsten Dominium Sample	0	0	None
155	Turpentine	10	1	2 Steel, 2 Antiseptic
202	TV Dinner Tray	9	0.5	3 Aluminum
14	Twelve Ball	2	0.4	2 Plastic
14	Two Ball	2	0.4	1 Plastic

#	NAME	VALUE	WEIGHT	COMPONENTS
145	Typewriter	12	4	2 Gears, 1 Screws, 1 Springs
2	Ultracite Ore	0	0.25	None
24	Ultracite Scrap	10	0.1	1 Ultracite
38	Umbrella	8	1.5	2 Springs, 2 Plastic
40	Umbrella Stand	4	0.8	2 Ceramic
24	Undamaged Abraxo Cleaner	16	0.8	1 Acid, 2 Antiseptic, 1 Fiberglass
5	Undamaged American Flag	6	3	2 Wood, 4 Cloth
1	Undamaged Baseball Glove	6	0.8	3 Leather
5	Undamaged Camera	17	3	2 Gears, 2 Springs, 1 Crystal
1	Undamaged Cigarettes	20	0.8	2 Plastic, 3 Cloth, 2 Asbestos
16	Unfilled Kickball	1	0.5	3 Rubber
1	Unrefined Coal	0	0.25	None
43	Unrusted Tin Can	4	0.5	1 Steel, 1 Aluminum
2	Unscorched Oven Mitt	8	1	1 Asbestos, 2 Cloth
24	Unstoppables! Board Game	16	1	2 Wood, 1 Leather, 1 Gold
4	Untarnished Coffee Pot	9	1	1 Plastic, 2 Steel, 1 Asbestos
11	Untarnished Metal Bucket	2	3	2 Steel
60	Unused Ashtray	4	0.5	2 Ceramic
19	Unused Enamel Bucket	2	3	2 Steel
4	Unused Flip Lighter	21	0.5	1 Oil, 1 Springs, 1 Steel
2	Upgraded Motor	0	0	None
95	Upper Skull	1	0.2	1 Bone

#	NAME	VALUE	WEIGHT	COMPONENTS
2	Uranium Ore	0	0.5	None
308	Used Oil Can	5	0.8	1 Steel, 1 Oil
49	Vacuum Tube	10	0.2	1 Copper, 2 Glass
369	Valid Ballot	0	0	None
51	Vase	2	2	1 Ceramic
2	Vault-Tec Alarm Clock	15	1	1 Nuclear Material, 2 Springs, 2 Glass, 1 Aluminum
14	Vegetable Starch	8	0.5	4 Adhesive
7	Violin	0	2	2 Wood
4	Violin Bow	0	0.2	1 Wood
2	Vodka	6	1	2 Glass
40	Vodka Bottle	9	0.8	3 Glass
37	Volatile Materials Box	15	0.1	1 Nuclear Material
13	VTU Coffee Cup	4	0.5	2 Ceramic
31	Wakemaster Alarm Clock	15	1	1 Aluminum, 2 Glass, 2 Springs, 1 Nuclear Material
8	Waste Acid	3	0.05	1 Acid
6	Waste Antiseptic	3	0.1	1 Antiseptic
5	Waste Oil	4	0.1	1 Oil
2	Water Filter	0	0.5	None
1	Water Testing Kit	0	0	None
4	Whiskey	2	1	2 Glass
68	Whiskey Bottle	2	0.8	2 Glass
111	White Bottle	2	0.5	2 Glass
31	White Ornamental Vase	6	8	3 Ceramic
177	White Plate	4	0.6	2 Ceramic

#	NAME	VALUE	WEIGHT	COMPONENTS
29	Willow Barrel Vase	2	2	1 Ceramic
23	Willow Bud Vase	2	2	1 Ceramic
30	Willow Flared Vase	2	2	1 Ceramic
75	Willow Rounded Vase	2	2	1 Ceramic
57	Willow Vaulted Vase	2	2	1 Ceramic
139	Wine Bottle	6	0.8	3 Glass
94	Wonderglue	12	0.2	2 Adhesive
19	Wood Bucket	2	3	2 Wood
17	Wood Scraps	1	0.1	1 Wood
21	Wooden Beer Stein	25	1	2 Wood, 2 Steel
102	Wooden Block - B & Y	3	0.2	1 Wood, 1 Lead
83	Wooden Block - I & D	3	0.2	1 Wood, 1 Lead
68	Wooden Block - N & S	3	0.2	2 Wood, 1 Lead
64	Wooden Block - V & F	3	0.2	1 Wood, 1 Lead
237	Wooden Ski	2	2	2 Wood
70	Wooden Spoon	1	0.2	2 Wood
132	Wrench	2	0.8	1 Steel
2	Xenxoate Sample	0	0	None
4	Yao Guai Hide	8	2.5	4 Leather
77	Yardstick	2	0.75	2 Wood
99	Yellow Canister	5	0.8	1 Steel, 1 Copper
62	Yellow Paint	24	3	2 Steel, 2 Oil, 7 Lead
138	Yellow Plate	2	0.6	1 Ceramic
92	Yellow Table Lamp	10	2	1 Copper, 2 Glass
2	Yellow-Trimmed Plate	4	0.6	2 Ceramic

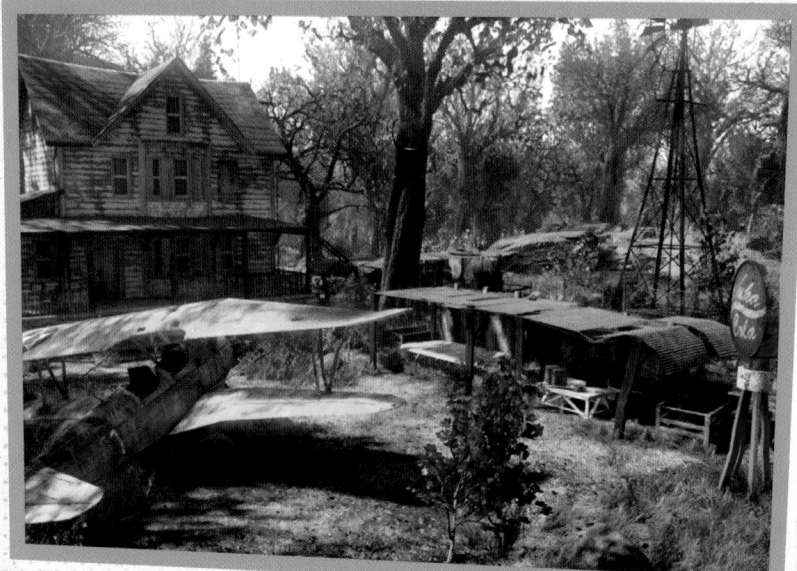

Helpful Hint from Vault Boy

COMPONENT BREAK DOWN

Need to see a chart showing all the junk items listed by the base component (and amount) they break down into? You'll want the online version of this guide, free with this tome!

WEAPON AND ARMOR MODS

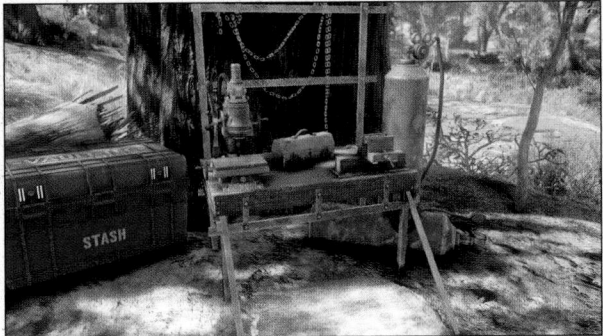

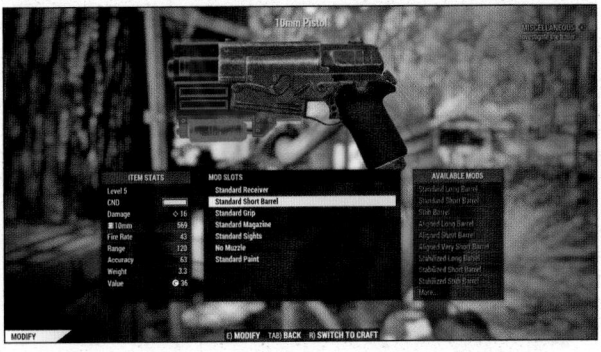

Mods are attachments for your weapons and armor that boost stats and allow for a wide range of customization.

You craft mods by looking at the armor or weapon you're trying to modify while on a workbench. While on the Workbench menu, look at the bottom of the screen and press the button marked "Modify" to get to the Mod Crafting menu.

Mods are broken down into categories, most of which have a slew of mods within them. If you want to know more about each of these categories, read further into this chapter to get a breakdown of each one. You can select a category, then look through each of the mods, read their descriptions, and see how each mod will change your current weapon or piece of armor.

Finding the proper menu isn't enough to craft a mod, however; you also need to have the proper components, which are shown on the right side of the screen (for more information about components check out the "Crafting" chapter). Once you have the parts necessary you can create your mod of choice with the touch of a button.

A weapon can only have one mod from each mod category equipped at once. If you decide to equip a new mod in a category you already have a mod equipped from, the previous mod will be unequipped and destroyed as the new one takes its place. Be sure to consider your options when looking through your mod options so you don't waste precious components.

More mods can be unlocked by obtaining Plans from Events, Daily Quests, and Workshop Defenses. You may also find them while scavenging bodies and containers across Appalachia.

WEAPONS MODS

Early on in the game you'll find that just about any weapon in your inventory will suit your needs, but if you're hoping to survive some of the challenges you'll face in the game's later stages you're going to need mods. Mods offer you the ability to change and rework just about everything about a weapon (depending on the weapon), allowing you to turn basic melee weapons into tactical damage dealers, and most guns into wildly varied damage dealers.

GUN MODS

Guns in their base forms typically lack the punch and utility of a fully modded gun. From automatic Barrels to long-range sniper Sights, mods have the potential to completely rework the way you think about a weapon and how you use it.

RECEIVERS

Receivers are the damage-enhancing part of any weapon (called a Capacitor on most Energy Guns and a Tank on a Flamer). There is a wide variety of Receiver Mods that offer small tweaks and benefits on top of a damage increase—though, some forego a damage increase for other benefits, like an increased critical hit chance. If you want your weapon to hit harder, this is where you should look first.

BARRELS

Barrels (called a Rubber Ball on the Paddle Ball, a Canister on a Broadsider, and a Launcher on a Fat Man) offer some of the most dramatic changes a gun can have. You won't have access to many automatic weapons without first attaching an Automatic Barrel; likewise, you won't find a lot of sniper rifles without a Sniper Barrel. Barrels should be considered the foundation of your weapon and should be first on your list when you're thinking about making a change to any gun in your inventory.

It should be noted that a Gamma Gun comes with Dishes instead of Barrels, but the basic usage is still the same.

GRIPS AND STOCKS

Grips and Stocks stabilize a weapon and help further determine if it's a close-range or long-range weapon. Grips make for more accurate hipfiring, which is perfect for SMGs and Shotguns, while Stocks convert any weapon they're on into a Rifle, perfect for mid- to long-range combat.

TRAINING

CRAFTING AND C.A.M.P.ING

INVENTORY

QUESTS

ATLAS

BESTIARY

APPENDICES

MAGAZINES

Magazines affect everything related to reloading, from reload speed to the amount of bullets you can fire before having to switch mags. If you've got a powerhouse of a weapon with a small magazine and brutal reload time, try putting on a Magazine with more rounds. If you've got a weapon with plenty of rounds, but you could watch yourself age while waiting to reload, try adding a Magazine mod with a faster reload speed.

SIGHTS

While Sights need very little in the way of explanation, they are the mods that offer some of the most flexibility in the way you build your weapons. From standard, snappy Reflex Sights for close- to mid-range engagements to vision-enhancing Holographic Sights, the way you tackle an encounter is largely going to be influenced by what Sight you have equipped. If you're looking to turn a mid-range weapon into a sniper rifle, slap on a 4x or 8x Scope.

MUZZLES

Bayonets, Suppressors, Compensators: if it goes on the end of a gun, it can rightly be called a Muzzle. Aside from that, you'll find little in common with each Muzzle mod you find. Bayonets increase melee damage with the weapon it's attached to, while Compensators, Muzzle Breaks, and Suppressors reduce recoil at the cost of firing range. Suppressors do, however, have the added benefit of quieting your shots, making it harder for enemies to detect you.

PAINT MODS

These mods aren't going to modify or improve your weapon stats in any way, but they offer a personal touch that can really make a weapon feel like yours and yours alone.

MELEE MODS

While not categorized in the same fashion as Gun Mods, Melee Mods do offer dramatic changes to the weapons they are attached to. Want an extra claw on your Deathclaw Gauntlet? An electrified Security Baton? What about a Pitchfork with fire jets? While you won't find the level of customization here that you'll find in Gun Mods, you'll still get more options for radically reworking your melee weapons in ways that Gun Mods can't hope to achieve.

MATERIAL MODS

Found as a Paint Mod, these mods will change the material a melee weapon is made up of to increase its damage. Unfortunately, the only melee weapons that allow for this kind of modification are the Rolling Pin and the Baseball Bat, both of which can be changed to an aluminum material. If you're planning on using either of those weapons, be sure not to leave without coating them in an aluminum Material Mod first.

UPGRADE MODS

As we mentioned earlier, you're not going to get the same level of customization with a melee weapon as you would a gun, but you also won't find singular mods that dramatically change a weapon's appearance and damage output like you will with Upgrade Mods. Some Upgrade Mods merely boost a melee weapon's damage output, but others change the damage type entirely. It's not uncommon to add Energy damage, a bleeding debuff, or armor penetration to a melee weapon with certain mods, though the amount of options you have varies from weapon to weapon.

ARMOR MODS

Armor Mods don't necessarily offer the same level of customization as Weapon Mods, but they are perfect complements to any play style. You can up your resistances to different types of damage, increase your encumbrance capacity, or even increase your sneaking ability. While Weapon Mods affect how you take on each encounter, Armor Mods reinforce those tactics in beneficial ways that simply can't be ignored.

Individual pieces of armor tend to have far fewer modding options than full sets (Leather or Metal Armor, for example). You'll want to keep that in mind before sinking precious components into pieces of armor that don't have a set. That's not to say that modding non-set armor is a mistake, but it's something you should do after first considering your options.

MATERIAL MODS

The vast majority of Material Mods improve your resistances to different types of damage, though some offer other buffs, like the improved stealth buff found in Shadowed Mods.

BALLISTIC WEAVE MODS

Lightweight armor doesn't have the same defense potential as most other sets you'll find, which is why Ballistic Weave Mods should always be considered. They are your main method of improving defense on otherwise low-defense armor. That's not to say every piece of thin armor should have a Ballistic Weave Mod on it. But if you're not planning on doing a lot of evading, you should make a point to bulk up your defenses a little bit—you'll be glad you did.

MISCELLANEOUS MODS

For everything that isn't a Material Mod or Ballistic Weave Mod, Miscellaneous Mods offer a wide array buffs and bonuses not found in their contemporaries. Increased carrying capacity, faster sprinting, longer chem durations: if you're looking to make a truly specialized set of armor, Miscellaneous Mods are going to be your number one go-to.

HEADLAMPS

Mining helmets can have a Headlamp attached to them as a replacement for the normal Pip-Boy flashlight. These lights have a more focused beam, which is brighter than the Pip-Boy, but lights up less of the environment.

POWER ARMOR MODS

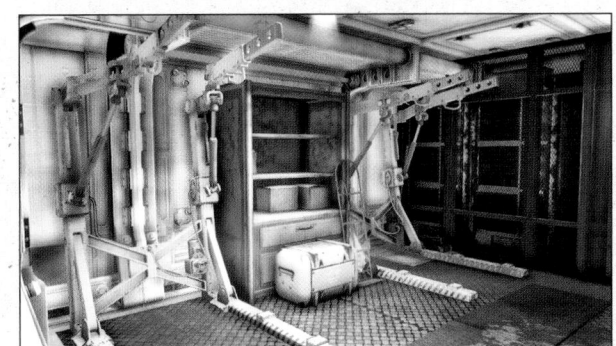

Power Armor Mods aren't dramatically different from Armor Mods, but where you create them is. While Armor Workbenches can be found with relative ease, if you don't have the Plans necessary to build a Power Armor Station in your C.A.M.P., you can go a long time without ever finding one.

Be sure to use the Atlas section of this guide to find Power Armor Stations around West Virginia with ease.

BASE MODS

Base Mods provide the bulk of the defensive improvements you'll find in Power Armor Mods. If you're hoping to take on the hardest challenges the game has to offer, you're going to need to wear Power Armor. Even with a full set of the best armor available to you, you'll still find plenty of challenges that require more defense than your Power Armor's base stats can provide. Base Mods will allow you to up that defense beyond base values to give you armor that can handle whatever Appalachia throws at you.

MISCELLANEOUS MODS

In a similar fashion to Armor Mods, Miscellaneous Mods provide a slew of benefits beyond improvements to defense. Adding a Miscellaneous Mod to your arms, for instance, can potentially provide increased melee damage, while adding a mod to your Power Armor's legs can increase sprint speed or carrying capacity.

HEADLAMPS

Like mining helmets, you can strap a Headlamp onto any Power Armor helmet in the game. Like Headlamps on a mining helmet, the light shines brighter but is much more focused, which causes it to brighten less of the room than your Pip-Boy would.

AMMO

With limited backpack space, you'll have to be more selective than ever with what ammo you carry. Below is a list of all ammo types and their weight and Cap value, so you make the hard choice of what to take with you, what to leave behind, and what to sell for valuable Caps.

STANDARD AMMUNITION

NAME	WEIGHT	VALUE
.308 Round	0.006	2
.38 Round	0.003	1
.44 Round	0.004	3
.45 Round	0.003	2
.50 Caliber Ball	0.1	5
.50 Round	0.005	5
10-mm Round	0.005	1
5.56 Round	0.005	2
5-mm Round	0.001	1
Cannonball	1	8
Crossbow Bolt	0.06	8
Harpoon	0.2	1
Modified Bowling Ball	1	10
Paddle Ball String	0.01	1
Railway Spike	0.2	1
Shotgun Shell	0.06	2
Syringer Ammo	0	1

ENERGY AMMUNITION

NAME	WEIGHT	VALUE
2-mm Electromagnetic Cartridge	0.1	10
Cryo Cell	0.03	10
Flare	0.1	1
Fuel	0.1	1
Fusion Cell	0.005	3
Fusion Core	3	162
Gamma Round	0.01	10
Plasma Cartridge	0.03	5
Plasma Core	1	162

EXPLOSIVE AMMUNITION

NAME	WEIGHT	VALUE
40-mm Grenade Rounds	0.2	25
Mini Nuke	12	100
Missile	2	25

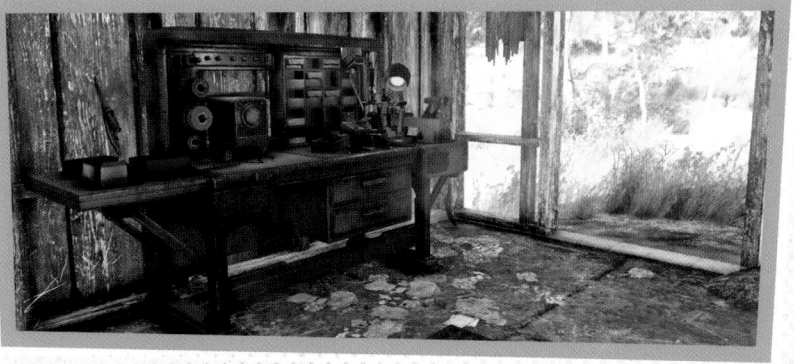

Quests

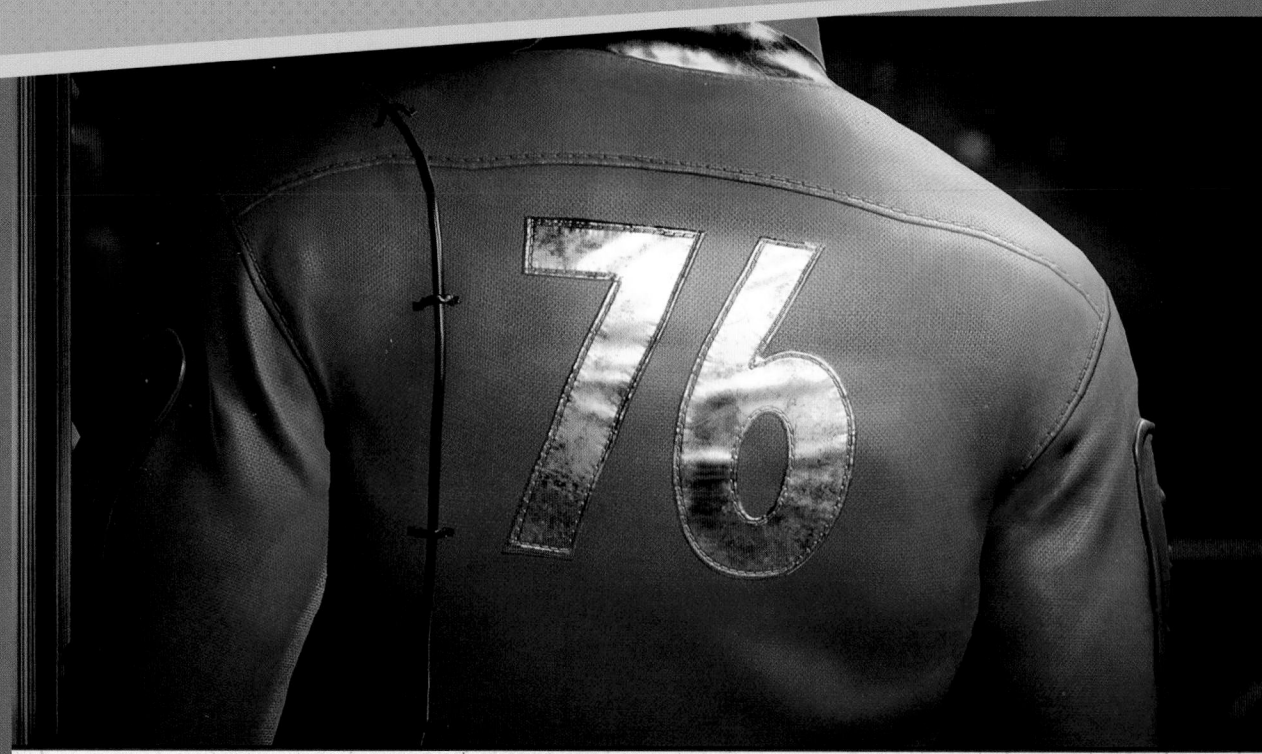

THE QUESTS IN THIS CHAPTER MAKE UP THE GAME'S MAIN NARRATIVE. IT'S WELL WORTH DOING, AS IT WILL UNLOCK A SLEW OF GOODIES, TAKE YOU ON A TOUR OF APPALACHIA, AND UNLOCK THE ABILITY TO FIRE NUKES (MORE ON THAT LATER).

FASCINATING FACTS FROM VAULT BOY!

FALLOUT 76 HAS A SIMILAR SCALING DIFFICULTY STRUCTURE TO *FALLOUT 4*, BUT THE SCALING IS A BIT MORE AGGRESSIVE THIS TIME AROUND. HERE IS A BREAKDOWN OF THE LEVEL RANGES YOU CAN EXPECT ENEMIES TO BE IN FOR EACH AREA. THESE ARE GOING TO BE SIGNIFICANTLY HIGHER OR LOWER THAN YOUR OWN LEVEL AS FREQUENTLY AS THEY ACTUALLY MATCH IT. DON'T ASSUME THAT ENTERING SAVAGE DIVIDE AT LEVEL 21 IS GOING TO GIVE YOU ENEMIES IN THE 20 RANGE; YOU MIGHT END UP BUMPING IN TO A 45 OR A 50. WITHOUT WARNING. BE READY FOR ANYTHING!

- THE FOREST: LEVELS 1-9
- TOXIC VALLEY: LEVELS 10-14
- SAVAGE DIVIDE: LEVELS 15-24
- ASH HEAP: LEVELS 25-29
- THE MIRE: LEVELS 30-34
- CRANBERRY BOG: LEVELS 35+

TO HAMMER THE POINT HOME, THERE ARE ALSO FISSURE SITES AROUND APPALACHIA (ALMOST EXCLUSIVELY IN SAVAGE DIVIDE, THE MIRE, AND CRANBERRY BOG) THAT ARE GUARDED BY POWERFUL SCORCHED AND THE MONSTROUS BAT-LIKE SCORCHBEASTS. THESE WILL ALWAYS PRODUCE POWERFUL ENEMIES, AND SCORCHBEASTS ARE ALWAYS BETWEEN LEVELS 50 AND 65. STAY THE HECK AWAY FROM THOSE UNTIL YOU REACH A MAIN QUEST THAT REQUIRES IT.

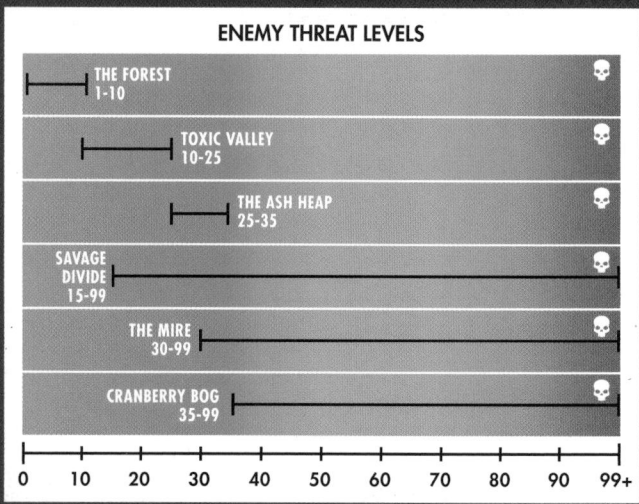

ENEMY THREAT LEVELS

THE FOREST 1-10		💀
TOXIC VALLEY 10-25		💀
THE ASH HEAP 25-35		💀
SAVAGE DIVIDE 15-99		💀
THE MIRE 30-99		💀
CRANBERRY BOG 35-99		💀

0   10   20   30   40   50   60   70   80   90   99+

NOTES BEFORE YOU GO

Now, before you set off, there are a some things to keep in mind while questing. Most of these quests are meant to be played with more than one person. That doesn't mean you can't play them solo, but it means you'll need to be more prepared for each quest. There are plenty of places in Appalachia that will constantly throw enemies at you. If you don't have the means to take a beating and still press onward, go off, explore, loot, craft and level, and then try the quest again.

PACE YOURSELF

Which leads us to another important thing to note: patience. This looks like *Fallout*, sounds like *Fallout*, and plays like *Fallout*, but unlike any other *Fallout* entry, rushing through the main quest is ill-advised. The jump in difficulty from region to region is significant; even if you crush quests in one region, a quest in a different region will likely have devastatingly powerful enemies in it. For this reason, take your time. Focus more on exploring individual regions rather than completing the main quest. There are plenty of Daily, Event, and side quests to keep you busy in a single region for hours. Take those on, get plenty of gear, and level up before moving on.

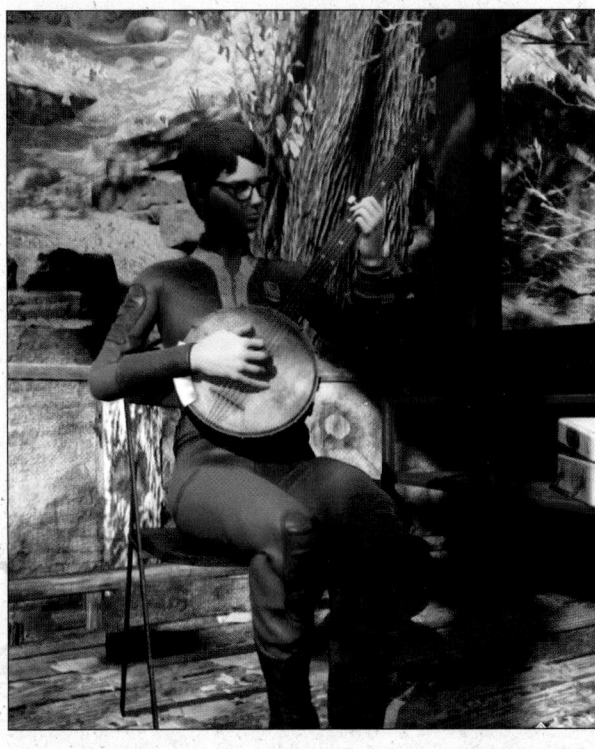

On top of dealing with high-level enemies, you'll also encounter quests that have you hop all over Appalachia, or quests that require very specific crafting materials without telling you specifically where to find them. These are more reasons to pace yourself. Instead of pulling your hair out looking for those crafting materials, or having to constantly head into unknown territory for a single quest objective, explore and loot and adventure. If you end up in the general vicinity of your quest objective, great! Go knock it out and get the next one going. If you stumble onto the crafting materials required for an objective, excellent! Go use those ASAP so you don't accidentally burn them on crafting something else (a situation we are all too familiar with here).

Think of questing in *Fallout 76* as a tour, rather than a train ride. There are plenty of fun things to see, but you can also explore without feeling like the quest is your de facto destination.

READ AHEAD

Our last tip before we set you loose: Don't be afraid to read ahead a bit. We've largely kept story bits out of this walkthrough, so it's unlikely that you'll turn the page and see a real SHOCKER of a plot twist right in your face. Some quests will have you coming and going from a central location. If you know this ahead of time, you can plant your C.A.M.P. somewhere near the main quest location to save yourself some caps on fast traveling.

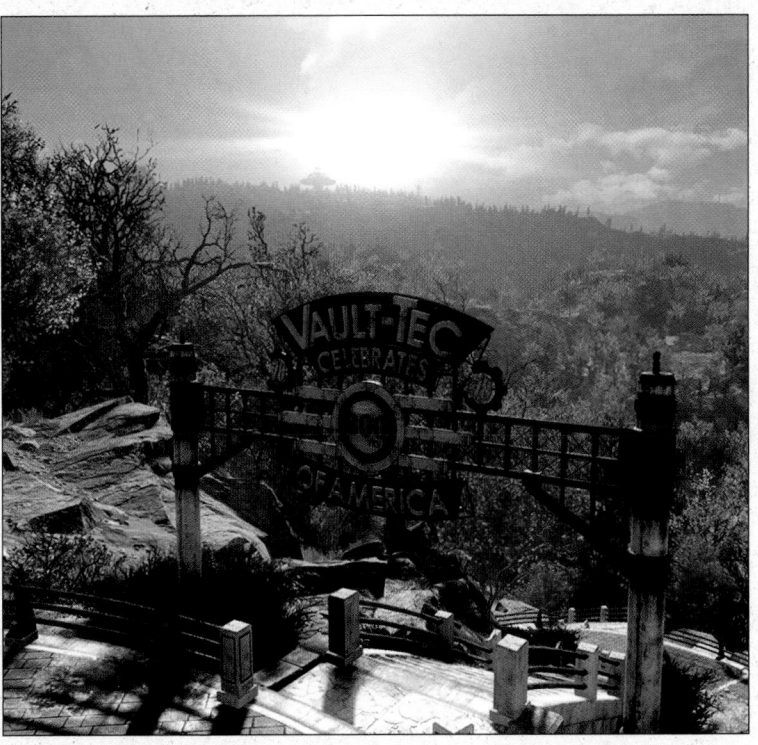

We also suggest using the Atlas chapter for each area you explore. For these quest chapters, we've focused almost exclusively on getting you through each objective as smoothly as possible and have left the deep diving of each location to the Atlas. Using the Atlas at each new location will give you the information you need to find all the best loot each area has to offer.

With that, go forth! We had a great time playing through these quests and we found the story fascinating and surprising every time we played through it. Whether you're playing by yourself or with friends, we're sure you're going to fall in love with Appalachia just like we did. Good luck and have fun, Vault Dweller!

TRAINING

CRAFTING AND C.A.M.P.ING

INVENTORY

QUESTS

ATLAS

BESTIARY

APPENDICES

QUEST INDEX

MAIN QUEST

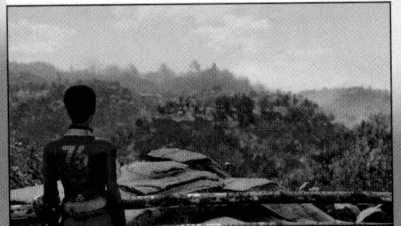

SIDE QUESTS

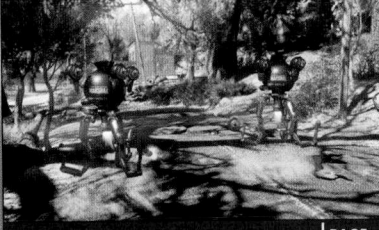

MISTRESS OF MYSTERY

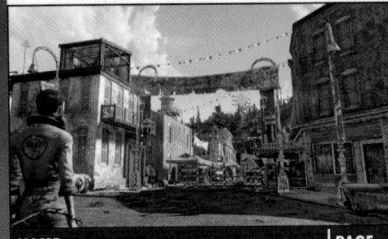

DAILY, REPEATABLE, AND DROP QUESTS

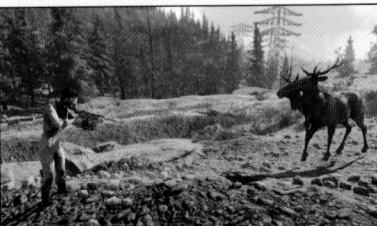

EVENTS

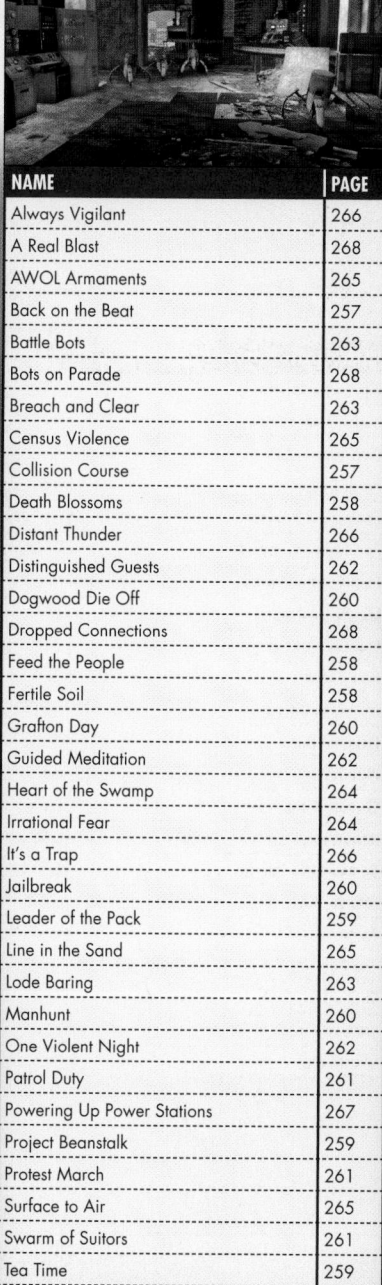

PVP

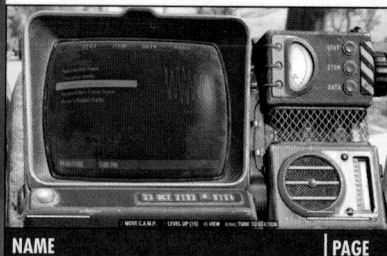

TRAINING

CRAFTING AND C.A.M.P.ING

INVENTORY

QUESTS

ATLAS

BESTIARY

APPENDICES

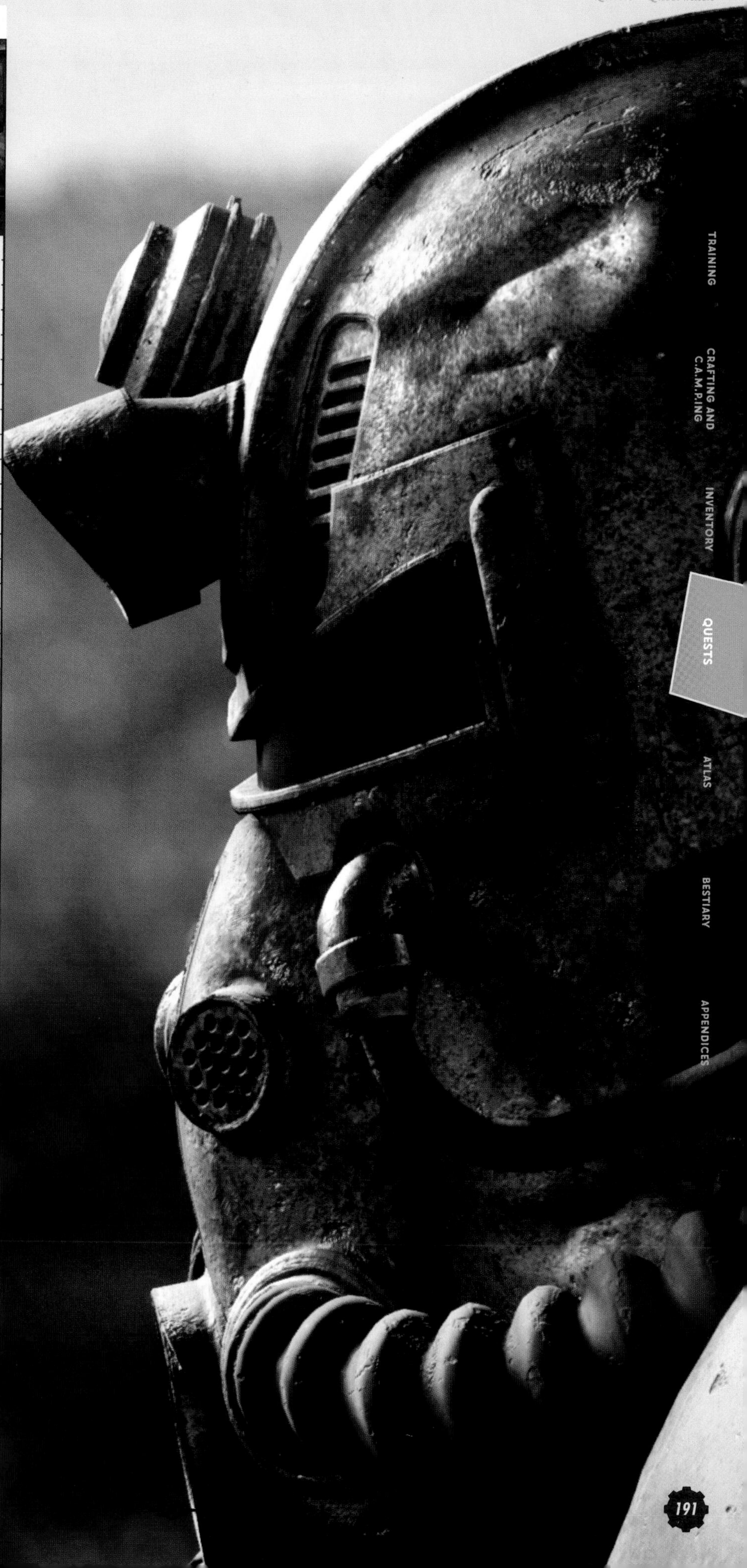

Quest RECLAMATION DAY

OBJECTIVES	REWARDS
– LEAVE VAULT 76.	– RANDOM AMMO
– DISCOVER THE OVERSEER'S MISSION.	– RANDOM AID ITEM
LOCATIONS TO EXPLORE	PREREQUISITES
– VAULT 76	– NONE

I JUST WANT TO START...

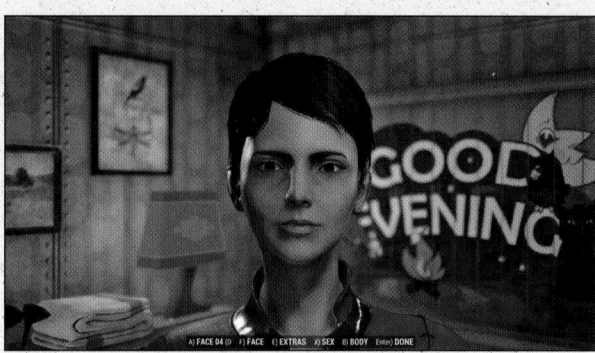

Rise and shine! After adjusting your appearance after last night's festivities, eject the Nuka Tapper game from the terminal, inspect your room, and clamp the Pip-Boy to your wrist. Then head out into the mezzanine forecourt. Mr. Handy robots are here to grant you verbal encouragement as you pass the other vault rooms (all inaccessible), and head down the stairs from the cafeteria.

ITEMS ➡ ❭ HOLOTAPE GAME: NUKA TAPPER
❭ PIP-BOY 2000 CONSOLE

FASCINATING FACTS FROM VAULT BOY!
OUR BEST TAPOLOGISTS WERE ABLE TO GET A SOLID 55,425 POINTS AND MANAGED TO CLIMB TO LEVEL 10 IN NUKA TAPPER. SEE IF YOU CAN DETHRONE THE NUKA TAPPER CHAMPS!

Pass by Crutchley, and follow the cardboard Vault-Boy's pointed finger up the stairs to the first Vault-Tec standee, designed to grant some friendly reminders before you go. They are numbered so you don't miss any. Check each one as you continue on your way:

1: Stay Hydrated: Learn about the importance of water and gather Purified water as well as Rad-X.

ITEMS ➡ ❭ PURIFIED WATER   ❭ RAD-X

2: Health & Medication: Learn about Stimpaks and gather five as well as some RadAway.

ITEMS ➡ ❭ STIMPAK (5)   ❭ RADAWAY

3: Power Is Key: Learn about the infrastructure (there isn't any) and grab a bag of building supplies.

ITEM ➡ ❭ BUILDING SUPPLIES: EXCESS ADHESIVE (3), RAW CLOTH (5), STEEL SCRAP (5), WOOD SCRAPS (5)

4: Join a Team: Learn about other vault dwellers who have already left Vault 76. Grab a party hat.

ITEM ➡ ❭ PARTY HAT

FASCINATING FACTS FROM VAULT-BOY!
RUMMAGE AROUND IN YOUR PIP-BOY AND INSPECT THE ITEMS YOU'VE JUST GATHERED, INCLUDING THOSE INSIDE THE BAG OF BUILDING SUPPLIES (REMEMBER YOU CAN USE ITEMS WITH COMPONENTS FOR CRAFTING). BE SURE TO LEARN HOW TO ACCESS THE EMOTES MENU AND THE SOCIAL MENU; YOU DON'T WANT TO BE AN ANTISOCIAL HERMIT, DO YOU? EVEN IF YOU DO, IF YOU FIND FRIENDS, YOUR CHANCES OF SURVIVAL ARE EXPONENTIALLY INCREASED!

...A FLAME IN YOUR HEART

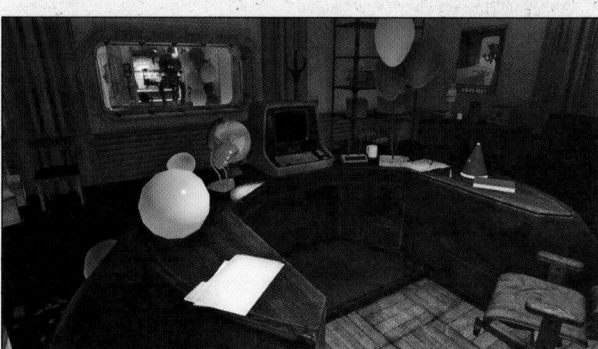

Just after the fourth Vault Tec informational standee, veer off into the adjacent Overseer's room and access her terminal. Check her reports and learn about her mission by ejecting the holotape in the terminal and playing it on your Pip-Boy (from the ITEMS > HOLO menu).

ITEM ➡ ❭ HOLOTAPE: OVERSEER'S LOG—VAULT 76

Continue to check out the Vault-Tec standees as you head toward the exit:

5: Camping Made Easy: Learn about the rudiments of C.A.M.P.ing, and grab a portable unit to use yourself.

ITEM ➡ ❭ C.A.M.P.

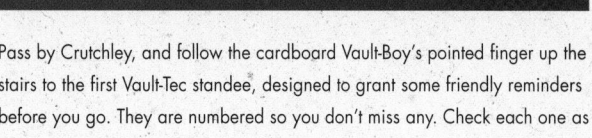

6: Get a Job: Gather your Perk Cards, and assign the first of them. Nab the pencil and black-rimmed glasses while you're at it; there's no reason to leave loot behind, especially when the loot contains a slick pair of spectacles.

ITEMS ➡	› BLACK-RIMMED GLASSES	› PERK CARDS
	› PENCIL	

After this, it's simply a matter of waving goodbye to your robot chums and stepping out into the world.

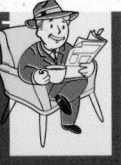

FASCINATING FACTS FROM VAULT-BOY!

AH, THE THRILL OF C.A.M.P.ING! ONCE YOU'RE IN THE WILDERNESS, BUILD A SMALL (BUT PERFECTLY FORMED) BASE OF OPERATIONS. DON'T WORRY; WE'LL TELL YOU WHEN! ALSO DON'T WORRY TOO MUCH ABOUT PERK CARDS; THERE'S A SPLENDID SECTION IN THIS GUIDE ON WHICH ONES TO PICK AND HOW THEY CAN AID YOU WHEN YOU WISH TO SPECIALIZE IN A CHOSEN PROFESSION.

Quest FIRST CONTACT

FASCINATING FACTS FROM VAULT BOY!

LOOKING AT THE TEXT AT THE START OF A QUEST WALKTHROUGH IN THIS BOOK MIGHT SEEM OVERWHELMING TO START, BUT WE'LL BREAK IT DOWN FOR YOU:

OBJECTIVES: THIS SECTION PROVIDES A BRIEF SUMMARY OF THE TASKS YOU'LL DO THROUGHOUT THE QUEST.

LOCATIONS TO EXPLORE: ALL THE LOCATIONS YOU MUST EXPLORE DURING THE QUEST. IF IT'S NOT MANDATORY, IT WON'T SHOW UP HERE.

REWARDS: ALL THE ITEMS YOU'LL EARN AS REWARDS FOR COMPLETING THE QUEST. SOME SAY "RANDOM," WHICH MEANS YOU'LL GET THAT TYPE OF ITEM, BUT WHICH ONE YOU GET IS COMPLETELY RANDOM.

- PHOTO FRAMES ARE USED IN PHOTO MODE, SO IF YOU UNLOCK ONE OF THESE AND CONSIDER YOURSELF A SHUTTER BUG, GO TAKE A LOOK AT THE NEW FRAMES!

- IF ONE OF THE REWARDS SAYS "RANDOM LEGENDARY WEAPON OR ARMOR," THAT MEANS YOU'LL GET A WEAPON OR PIECE OF ARMOR THAT HAS A LEGENDARY EFFECT ON IT (YOU CAN SEE ALL OF THE LEGENDARY EFFECTS AND WHAT THEY DO AT THE END OF THE WEAPONS CHAPTER).

- IF A REWARD SAYS "CHANCE FOR A LEGENDARY WEAPON OR ARMOR," IT MEANS JUST THAT: YOU HAVE A CHANCE TO GET SOMETHING GOOD, BUT NO GUARANTEES. YOU'RE MOSTLY GOING TO SEE THIS IN THE REGIONAL QUESTS AND EVENT QUESTS SECTIONS OF THE BOOK, WHERE THE QUESTS ARE REPEATABLE. QUESTS WITH THESE AS A REWARD ARE GREAT TO DO AGAIN AND AGAIN TO GET BETTER GEAR.

OBJECTIVES

- FIND THE OVERSEER'S C.A.M.P.
- (MISC) CRAFT A PIECE OF ARMOR.
- (MISC) CRAFT A WEAPON.
- LISTEN TO THE OVERSEER'S LOG—C.A.M.P.
- FIND THE OVERSEER IN FLATWOODS.
- LISTEN TO THE OVERSEER'S LOG—FLATWOODS.
- REGISTER AS A VOLUNTEER.

LOCATIONS TO EXPLORE

- OVERSEER'S C.A.M.P.
- FLATWOODS

REWARDS

- HATCHET (WEAPON)
- PARAMEDIC JUMPSUIT (APPAREL)
- HEALING SALVE RECIPE
- RANDOM AMMO
- PHOTO FRAME

PREREQUISITES

- COMPLETE "RECLAMATION DAY."

COUNTRY ROAD

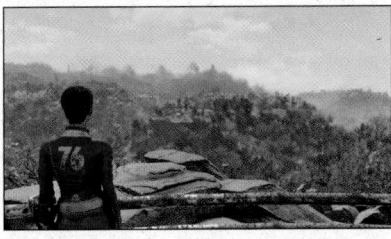

Survey the hills and forests stretching out to the horizon, as well as the larger landmarks you can use to orientate yourself. Then head down the Vault-Tec entrance steps and speak to a Mr. Handy robot about the Overseer's whereabouts. Head down to the road and walk roughly south. Before your exploration goes any further, it's worth scavenging for a few weapon-based items.

Helpful Hint from Vault-Boy!

Normally, Vault-Tec provides simple and unequivocal facts pertinent only to the quest at hand. However, due to the imminent dangers present in every direction, it is worth spending a few moments surveying the area:

- Inspect a Responder corpse atop the steps on the same level as the Vault entrance, by a lamppost and the steps leading down to the parking lot. Search the corpse for chems and your first ranged weapon (a gun).
- Inspect a Responder corpse along the entrance steps (lower level) for a hand weapon and a note.
- Remain on the upper Vault-Tec walkways and vehicle ramp and scavenge the area for additional goods.
- Be aware of Liberator Mk.0 robot threats and neutralize them with hand weapons before you locate a gun.
- Bring up your map and look for a waypoint roughly south-southeast of Vault 76. This is where you need to head. Bringing up your map (or Pip-Boy) does not pause the action, so learn how to use your "Quick-Boy"!
- Be ready to investigate a variety of Locations to Explore at the base of the rocky promontory that Vault 76 sits on. The Wixon Homestead and Gilman Lumber Mill have their own threats—and rewards—for you to find.

TRAINING

CRAFTING AND C.A.M.P.ING

INVENTORY

QUESTS

ATLAS

BESTIARY

APPENDICES

C.A.M.P.ING TRIP

Head along Route 88 East, across a covered bridge, and find the Overseer's C.A.M.P. just above the road junction. Though it may lack the most basic of defenses, it does have some key crafting stations and is empty of occupants (unless another Vault Dweller is active in the area). Start by inspecting the indicated Locations to Explore within the camp.

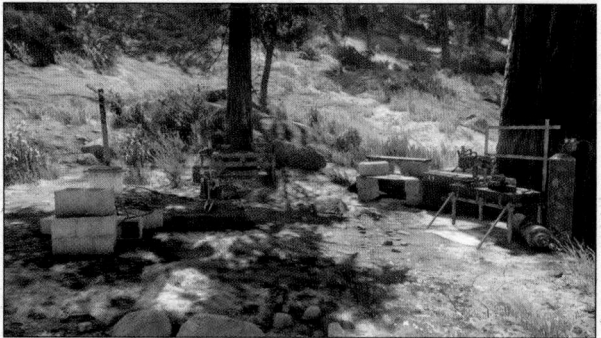

ITEM ➡	› HOLOTAPE: OVERSEER'S LOG—C.A.M.P.

SURVIVAL BASICS

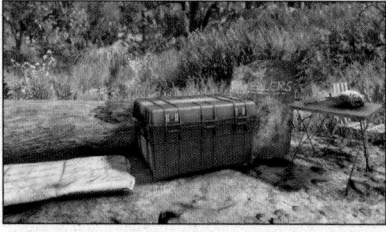

You now have two Miscellaneous Quest objectives to fulfill: crafting a piece of armor and a weapon. Continue your inspection of the C.A.M.P., and discover some pertinent objects to interact with (all of which were built using the C.A.M.P., so you can too!):

- **THE OVERSEER'S CACHE:** CONTAINS HELPFUL ITEMS AND A HOLOTAPE TO PLAY TO FURTHER THIS QUEST LINE.
- **MY STASH BOX:** ALLOWS YOU TO REMOVE AND CLAIM ITEMS, THEN GATHER THEM AGAIN AT SUBSEQUENT MY STASH BOXES DOTTED THROUGHOUT THE WORLD.
- **TOOLBOX:** CONTAINERS LIKE THE RED TOOLBOX TO THE LEFT OF THE WEAPONS WORKBENCH CONTAIN A SLEW OF JUNK ITEMS THAT CAN BE USED AS COMPONENTS FOR CRAFTING. ALSO LOOK FOR CHESTS, BOXES, AND OTHER CONTAINERS LIKE THIS ONE TO FIND THE GOODS YOU NEED TO SURVIVE IN APPALACHIA.
- **ARMOR WORKBENCH:** CRAFT, SCRAP, REPAIR, OR MODIFY WEARABLE ARMOR AT THESE BENCHES.
- **WEAPONS WORKBENCH:** CRAFT, SCRAP, REPAIR, OR MODIFY WEAPONS AT THESE BENCHES.
- **COOKING STATION:** USE THESE TO CRAFT RECIPES MAINLY RELATED TO FOOD AND DRINK.

Complete both the Miscellaneous Quests by scavenging all the components on the table just left of the My Stash Box; this should give you enough components to craft some armor and a weapon at the respective workbenches.

FLATWOODS OR BUST

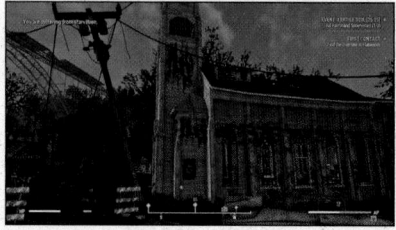

When the Overseer's Log finishes playing, you realize she headed to the town of Flatwoods. Head there by journeying southwest along the road, passing the Green Country Lodge and eventually reaching the town, which was once a hub of activity for a group known as the Responders. Various structures in the town have been repurposed, and many of the buildings have signs or are adorned with a heart sign—the logo of the Responders.

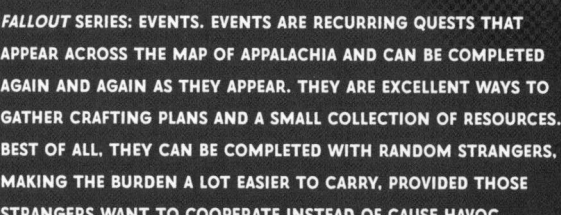

Enter the church at Flatwoods, which has a "Command Post" sign outside its entrance. Though the Overseer isn't here, another one of her caches is: Open it and claim the contents. Among the items is another holotape to listen to. The Overseer stresses the importance of working with the Responders (if any are still alive).

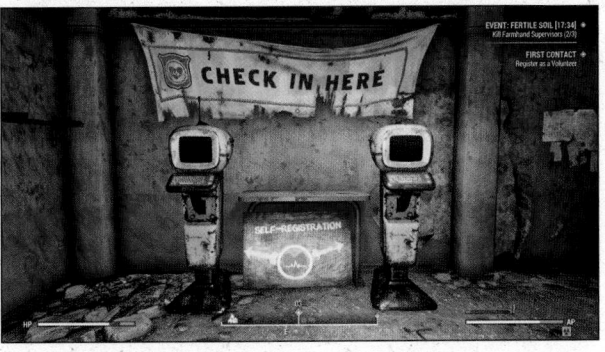

Having found the Responder's Outposts at Flatwoods and listened to the Overseer's remarks, head inside the Flatwoods Tavern (with the "Volunteers Needed!" sign outside). Access either of the Self-Serve Registration Kiosks.

Register as a volunteer, after which you're instructed to find one of the responders, Kesha McDermott. Optionally look her up in the Responder database at the kiosk.

> **ITEM ➡** > HOLOTAPE: OVERSEER'S LOG—FLATWOODS

FASCINATING FACTS FROM VAULT BOY!

AS YOU ENTERED FLATWOODS, YOU MAY HAVE STUMBLED INTO A NEW TYPE OF QUEST, KNOWN AS AN EVENT. THESE ARE WORTH ATTEMPTING, AND THEY ARE REPLAYABLE, FEATURE EXCELLENT REWARDS, AND ALLOW YOU TO EXPLORE MORE OF THE IMMEDIATE AREA. FOR EXAMPLE, THE VAULT-TEC AGRICULTURAL RESEARCH CENTER (A NEW LOCATION ON THE SOUTH SIDE OF FLATWOODS, WHERE EVENT: FERTILE SOIL CONCLUDES) HAS AN ADDITIONAL HOLOTAPE CLUE FROM THE OVERSEER HERSELF. FIND IT ON THE GROUND FLOOR COUNTER IN THE ENTRANCE FOYER OF THE MAIN BUILDING AND LISTEN TO OVERSEER'S JOURNAL: ENTRY 1 TO FURTHER THE STORY OF THE OVERSEER'S PAST.

Quest THIRST THINGS FIRST

OBJECTIVES
- **LOCATE KESHA MCDERMOTT.**
- **(OPTIONAL) SEARCH FOR HER LOCATION IN THE SYSTEM.**
- **SEARCH FOR KESHA ALONG THE NEARBY RIVER.**
- **RETRIEVE THE WATER TESTING KIT FROM KESHA MCDERMOTT.**
- **TEST A SAMPLE OF WATER FROM THE RIVER.**
- **TEST A SAMPLE OF WATER FROM FLATWOOD'S WATER PUMPS.**
- **ANALYZE THE WATER TESTING KIT'S RESULTS IN KESHA'S LAB.**
- **BOIL WATER USING DIRTY WATER AND WOOD FUEL.**
- **(OPTIONAL) COLLECT DIRTY WATER.**
- **(OPTIONAL) HARVEST WOOD.**
- **CHECK IN WITH THE SELF-SERVE KIOSK.**

LOCATIONS TO EXPLORE
- **FLATWOODS**

REWARDS
- **BOILED WATER**
- **CHEMISTRY WORKBENCH PLAN**
- **RANDOM ARMOR**
- **RANDOM AMMO**
- **A RANDOM AID ITEM**

PREREQUISITES
- **COMPLETE "FIRST CONTACT."**

WATER, WATER EVERYWHERE

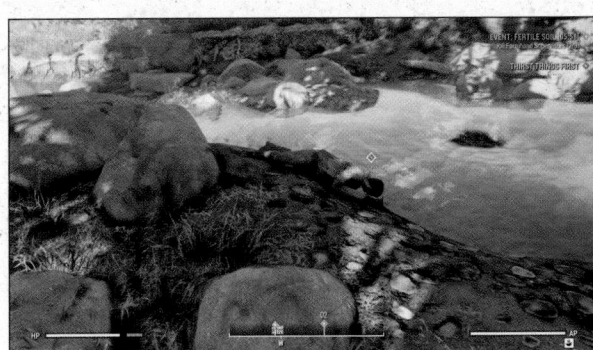

Head west to the river within the town's boundaries, where you find Kesha's remains. Search her for a holotape and Water Testing Kit. Then crouch at the water's edge and collect some Dirty Water. Stay on the bank rather than wading into the river to avoid radiation. Then wander roughly south to the Community Garden, collecting water from either of the water pumps near the shed.

> **ITEMS ➡** > WATER TESTING KIT

Helpful Hint from Vault-Boy!
Collecting water is both easy and necessary! Walk up to a river, well, or water pump and complete the instructions. But don't drink it yet; you don't want to poison yourself, do you?

CREATING A DROP TO DRINK

Journey back to the church and enter. Head to the back where the makeshift lab is located. Access the diagnostic terminal. Choose "Analyze Water Sample": As expected, the results aren't good; the water needs to be purified before being fit for human consumption:

- **PLAN A:** IF YOU HAVEN'T COLLECTED ANY WATER OR WOOD YET, DO SO NOW. FIND SOME LOGS AT THE WOOD PILE AND A LOG IN THE GRAVEYARD NEAR THE CHURCH'S NORTH SIDE. THEN FIND ANY COOKING STATION (LIKE THE TWO LOCATED IN THE PARKING LOT ON THE TAVERN'S SOUTH SIDE) AND BOIL THE DIRTY WATER. THE REQUIREMENTS FOR BOILED WATER ARE DIRTY WATER (2) AND WOOD (1).

- EVEN IF YOU ALREADY HAVE BOILED WATER IN YOUR INVENTORY, YOU CAN'T SKIP THIS PART.

| ITEMS ➡ | > DIRTY WATER (2) | > WOOD (1) | > BOILED WATER |

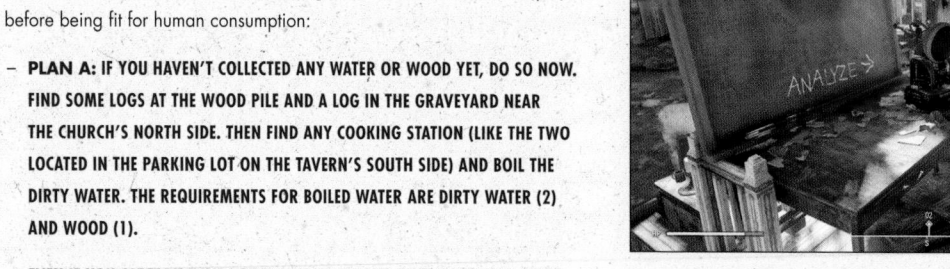

Once you have crafted the Boiled Water, check back at the self-serve kiosk, check your Volunteer status, and conclude this quest. Responder Quest: Second Helpings now begins.

Quest SECOND HELPINGS

OBJECTIVES

- FIND DELBERT WINTERS IN FLATWOODS.
- (OPTIONAL) SEARCH FOR DELBERT WINTERS IN THE PEOPLE DIRECTORY.
- LOOK FOR DELBERT WINTERS AT HIS HOME.
- SEARCH FOR TRAINING INSTRUCTIONS AROUND DELBERT'S HOUSE.
- COOK A RIBEYE STEAK.
- (OPTIONAL) GET A PIECE OF BRAHMIN MEAT.
- (OPTIONAL) GET SOME WOOD FOR FUEL.
- CHECK IN WITH THE SELF-SERVE KIOSK.
- CONTACT THE RESPONDERS USING THE DATABASE.

LOCATIONS TO EXPLORE

- FLATWOODS

REWARDS

- WOOD
- TINKER'S WORKBENCH PLAN
- A RANDOM PLAN
- RANDOM AMMO
- A RANDOM AID

PREREQUISITES

- COMPLETE "THIRST THINGS FIRST."

MAN OF GOD

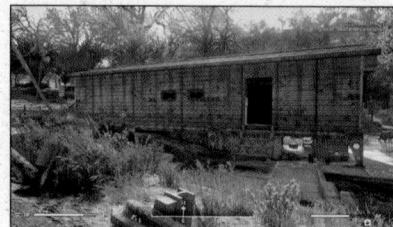

Look up Delbert Winters in the People Directory, then head to his trailer on the south side of town. Enter, and inspect his dwelling until you uncover Reverend Delbert. Access Delbert's terminal. Now you know the password, you can access all of his entries. It seems Delbert had a hankering for some juicy ribeye steak!

MAKING A MEAL

Cooking a ribeye steak is a simple process:

- **PLAN A:** STEP OUT OF DELBERT'S TRAILER, SEARCH ONE OF THE NEARBY BRAHMIN CORPSES, OR KILL AND LOOT ANY LIVING BRAHMIN IN THE VICINITY. GATHER BRAHMIN MEAT FROM THE CORPSE, AND THEN VISIT ANY COOKING STATION (SUCH AS ONE OF THE TWO ADJACENT TO THE TAVERN IN THE PARKING LOT). CRAFT A RIBEYE STEAK BY COMBINING BRAHMIN MEAT (1) AND WOOD (1).

- EVEN IF YOU ALREADY HAVE A RIBEYE STEAK IN YOUR INVENTORY, YOU WILL HAVE TO GO THROUGH THE PROCESS OF COOKING ONE FOR THIS OBJECTIVE.

| ITEM ➡ | > RIBEYE STEAK |

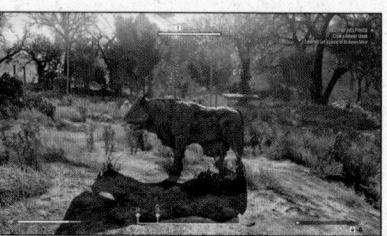

Head back to the Flatwoods tavern, enter the pantry, access the nearby kiosk, and become a full volunteer. Next, head inside to the back of the church and access the Responders Database Terminal. You can now log on as a volunteer (not just a guest), which enables you to contact the main Responders Headquarters. Once you've read the emergency message, the quest concludes.

Quest FINAL DEPARTURE

OBJECTIVES
- INVESTIGATE MORGANTOWN AIRPORT.
- LEARN THE FATE OF THE RESPONDERS.
- LISTEN TO OVERSEER'S LOG—MORGANTOWN.
- LEARN ABOUT THE INOCULATION PROJECT.

LOCATIONS TO EXPLORE
- MORGANTOWN AIRPORT
- MORGANTOWN AIRPORT TERMINAL

REWARDS
- PATROLMAN'S SUNGLASSES (APPAREL)
- RANDOM AMMO
- A RANDOM AID ITEM
- SOMERSET SPECIAL (MODDED .44 PISTOL)

PREREQUISITES
- COMPLETE "SECOND HELPINGS."

WORD OF WARNING FROM VAULT-BOY!
MORGANTOWN IS OVERRUN BY THE MOST UNFRIENDLY OF FOLK, KNOWN LOCALLY AS THE SCORCHED. THEY CAN'T BE TRADED WITH, OR EVEN TALKED TO, WITHOUT THE SITUATION BECOMING TRICKY. IT'S BEST TO REASON WITH THEM USING WEAPONRY, SO BE SURE YOU'RE PACKED ACCORDINGLY!

CATCHING A FLIGHT

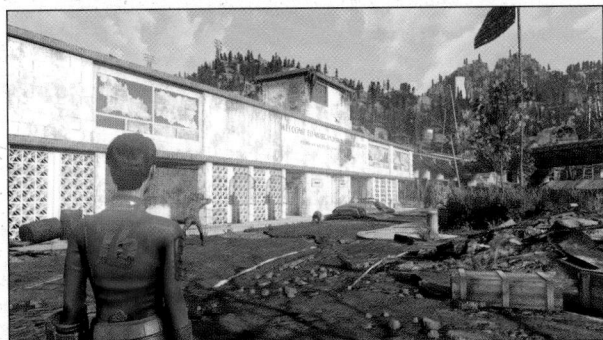

Trek northeast from Flatwoods, along Interstate 59, to eventually reach the remains of Morgantown Airport. On the way, feel free to tune your radio to the Responders Emergency Signal. Enter the grounds, and go interior the Morgantown Airport Terminal. Find the marked room on the upper floor and inspect the Overseer's Cache inside. Among other items, grab and listen to the Overseer's Log.

ITEM ➡ ❯ OVERSEER'S LOG—MORGANTOWN

INOCULATION INVESTIGATIONS

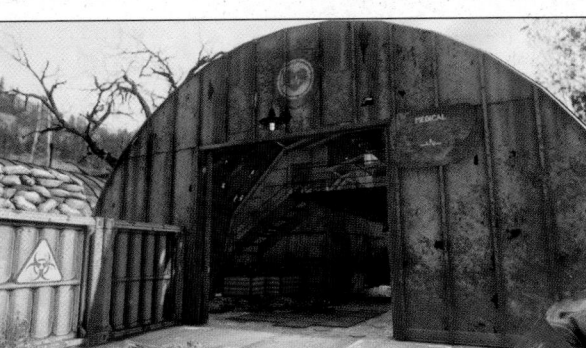

The report mentions an "Inoculation Project"; further your search outside, passing the old field-ops tower. Head east along the runway camp to an area marked "Quarantine." Expect heavy resistance from Scorched forces. Fight your way into the curved-roofed hangars labeled "Medical," and use the terminal on the second floor. Select "Inoculation Project Announcement" to complete the quest.

Quest AN OUNCE OF PREVENTION

OBJECTIVES
- STUDY DOCTOR HUDSON'S RESEARCH.
- COLLECT A TYPE-T FUSE.
- COLLECT A BLOOD SAMPLE FROM A MOLE RAT.
- COLLECT A BLOOD SAMPLE FROM A FERAL GHOUL.
- COLLECT A BLOOD SAMPLE FROM A WOLF.
- ANALYZE THE BLOOD SAMPLES.
- USE THE SYMPTO-MATIC TO ADMINISTER THE VACCINE.

LOCATIONS TO EXPLORE
- AVR MEDICAL CENTER
- GREG'S MINE SUPPLY

REWARDS
- DILUTED RAD-X
- DILUTED RAD-X RECIPE
- RADAWAY
- RADAWAY RECIPE
- A PHOTO FRAME
- A RANDOM LEGENDARY WEAPON OR ARMOR

PREREQUISITES
- COMPLETE "FINAL DEPARTURES."

FASCINATING FACTS FROM VAULT BOY!
THERE'S A BODY TUCKED AWAY NEAR THE CENTER OF THE BUILDING'S EXTERIOR. LOOT THE WORN VEIL AND DAMAGED HOLOTAPE OFF THE BODY TO START THE "INTO THE MYSTERY" QUEST. YOU CAN READ MORE ABOUT THIS QUEST AND ALL OTHER QUESTS IN ITS LINE IN THE "SIDE QUESTS" CHAPTER.

DOCTOR'S VISIT

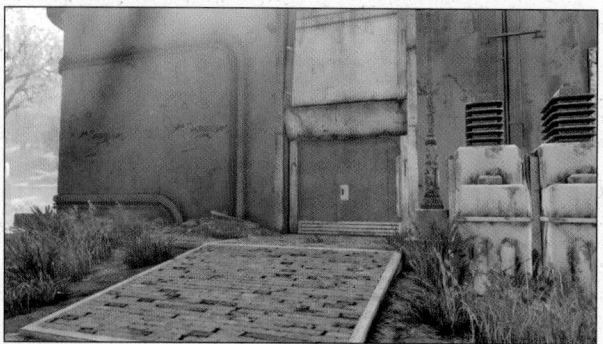

Helpful Hints from Vault Boy!

The objective is downstairs, so you might be tempted to drop down the hole in the center of the entry room if you entered through the building's north entrance. While there is a locked door with a handful of items down there, this path will not lead you to the next objective (not directly anyway) and there's a good chance you'll take damage from the fall. Use the stairs to the right after entering from the building's north entrance to save yourself a headache.

Head to the basement of the Scorched-filled AVR Medical Center. The easiest way to do that is to use the stairs to the right of the building's north entrance. Be careful and take things slow. If you are impatient, you can easily become surrounded by the hordes of Scorched occupying this space. Once down below, use the AVR Medical Laboratory Terminal and read the "Inoculation Project Overview" entry.

SCIENCE EXPERIMENT

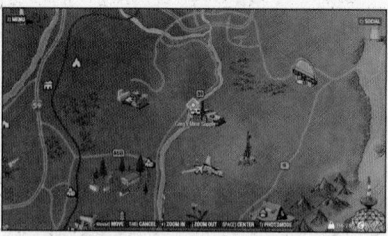

You will need to collect a handful of items to complete this next series of objectives. We'll start with the Type-T Fuse, which is located in Greg's Mine Supply northeast of the AVR Medical Center and south of the Morgantown Airport.

FASCINATING FACTS FROM VAULT BOY!

IF YOU HEAD STRAIGHT FROM THE AVR MEDICAL CENTER WITHOUT FAST-TRAVELING, YOU'LL LIKELY PASS THROUGH WADE AIRPORT (A SHORT TRIP NORTHEAST OF AVR MEDICAL CENTER), WHICH WILL START THE "CLAIM WORKSHOP AT WADE AIRPORT" QUEST, AND CAMP MCCLINTOCK (MARKED BY THE CIRCLE ICON WITH A STAR IN IT ON YOUR RADAR, ON THE EAST SIDE OF THE TRAIN TRACKS), WHERE YOU CAN FIND THE "BACK TO BASIC" QUEST BY SPEAKING WITH MASTER SERGEANT GUTSY ON THE SECOND FLOOR OF THE CENTRAL BUILDING.

YOU CAN READ ABOUT CLAIMING WORKSHOPS IN THE "OTHER QUESTS" SECTION OF THIS BOOK, WHILE YOU CAN FIND INFORMATION ON THE "BACK TO BASIC" QUEST LATER IN THIS CHAPTER.

YOU'LL HAVE TO COMPLETE "BACK TO BASIC" LATER ON AS PART OF THE MAIN QUEST, SO YOU CAN COMPLETE IT NOW TO SAVE SOME TIME OR JUST IGNORE IT FOR LATER.

After reaching Greg's Mine Supply, head to the house across the street and use the basement at the rear of the house. Follow the path through the basement and you'll eventually end up inside Greg's Mine Supply. Find the Type-T Fuse inside the yellow wooden crate just up the stairs out of the basement.

ITEM ➡ 〉 TYPE-T FUSE

SAMPLING THE WILD LIFE

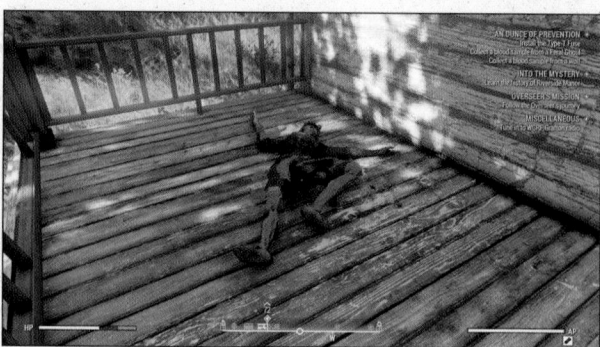

Once you have the fuse in your possession, head back to the AVR Medical Center. Hold off from installing the fuse. Your next task is to get blood samples from a Feral Ghoul, a Wolf, and a Mole Rat, all of which are located at the objective markers east and west of the medical center.

To collect blood samples, kill one of the three enemies listed, then approach them as if you were looting their bodies. Look in the bottom-right corner of the loot window for the button to press for collecting a sample. You only need to do this once for each enemy type, so after you get a sample, move on to the remaining enemies.

WORD OF WARNING FROM VAULT BOY!

WHILE COLLECTING THE THREE BLOOD SAMPLES, YOU'LL COME DANGEROUSLY CLOSE TO ENTERING THE ASH HEAP. IF YOU DO CROSS INTO THE REGION, YOU'LL RECEIVE A WARNING IN THE SCREEN'S TOP-LEFT CORNER INFORMING YOU THAT THE AIR IS TOXIC. IF YOU DON'T HAVE A GAS MASK OR A MOUTH-COVERING PIECE OF CLOTHING THAT'S NOTED AS PROTECTING YOU FROM AIRBORNE DISEASES, BACK OUT. THE AIR IN THE ASH HEAP IS DEADLY AND WILL QUICKLY FILL YOU WITH AILMENTS AND POISONS. WE GET A GAS MASK IN THE NEXT QUEST, SO DON'T WORRY—A LITTLE PATIENCE GOES A LONG WAY HERE.

After collecting all three samples, head back to the AVR Medical Center, insert the Type-T Fuse into the fuse box to the terminal's right, insert the blood samples into the centrifuge, and use the terminal to analyze them. Once done, use the Sympto-Matic (one of the gigantic tubes to the terminal's left) to administer the newly created vaccine. You'll immediately start the next quest, "Into the Fire," after completing this one.

Quest INTO THE FIRE

OBJECTIVES
- JOIN THE "FIRE BREATHERS."
- PASS THE KNOWLEDGE EXAM.
- COMPLETE THE PHYSICAL EXAM.
- HEAD TO THE FINAL EXAM SITE.
- ACTIVATE THE EMERGENCY BEACON.
- RETURN TO BERNIE.
- REGISTER WITH THE FIRE BREATHER'S COMPUTER SYSTEM.
- LISTEN TO THE PRIORITY MESSAGE.

LOCATIONS TO EXPLORE
- CHARLESTON FIRE DEPARTMENT
- CHARLESTON
- CHARLESTON HERALD
- BELCHING BETTY

REWARDS
- FIRE BREATHERS UNIFORM (APPAREL)
- FIRE BREATHERS HELMET (APPAREL)
- ANTI-SCORCHED TRAINING PISTOL
- ANTI-SCORCHED WEAPON MOD RECIPES
- RANDOM AMMO
- A RANDOM AID ITEM

PREREQUISITES
- COMPLETE "AN OUNCE OF PREVENTION."

KNOWLEDGE IS POWER

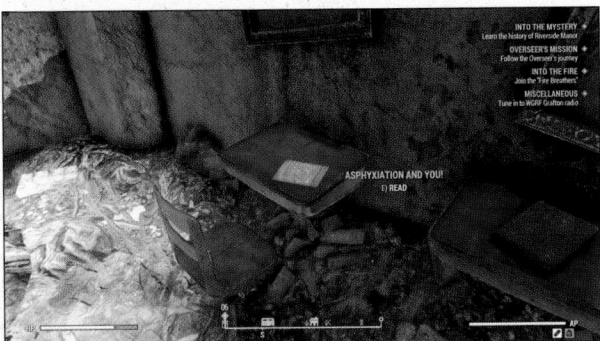

Head to the Charleston Fire Department, which is located southeast of AVR Medical Center. You'll need to take the Fire Breather Knowledge Exam to be granted entry in the ranks of the prestigious Fire Breathers. The questions mostly require common sense (danger bad, safety good), but if you're an overachiever, you can collect the answer key from the main office upstairs, or search the room the terminal is in and read marked notes scattered around the station. You can find two of the marked notes on the desks in the same room as the terminal; another one is in the locker room next door in an open locker. The final note is in the fire truck garage inside another open locker.

When you're ready to take the test, use the Fire Breather Training System terminal and select the Knowledge Exam entry.

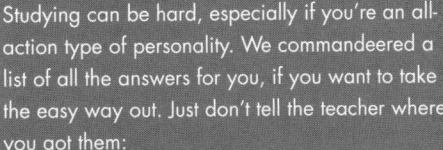

Helpful Hint from Vault Boy!
Studying can be hard, especially if you're an all-action type of personality. We commandeered a list of all the answers for you, if you want to take the easy way out. Just don't tell the teacher where you got them:

- Question 1: Evacuate as quickly as possible
- Question 2: A water-soaked rag
- Question 3: Gently bind the burn with clean bandages
- Question 4: Retreat immediately
- Question 5: 1 pt. Purified Water, 2 Ash Rose, 2 Blight, 2 Soot Flower
- Question 6: Fall back and engage from a distance with firearms
- Question 7: End his life as mercifully as possible

Once you've completed the Knowledge Exam, leave the department and head north toward your next destination.

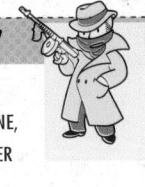

WORD OF WARNING FROM VAULT BOY!
THE PATH TO THE NEXT OBJECTIVE WILL TAKE YOU DIRECTLY THROUGH THE HEART OF CHARLESTON, WHICH IS A WAR ZONE, COMPLETE WITH SCORCHED, SUPER MUTANTS, AND ALL OTHER MANNER OF TERRIBLE BEASTIES. TREAD CAREFULLY.

BUT MIGHT MAKES RIGHT

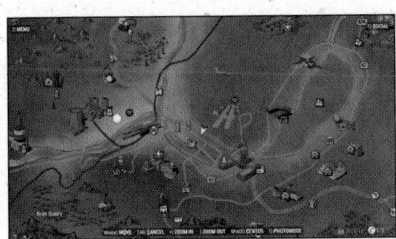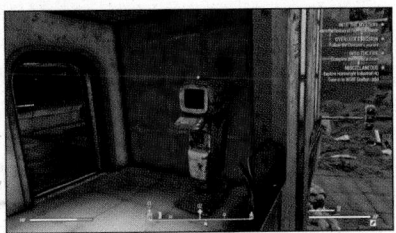

You'll need to reach a terminal inside the Charleston Herald building in order to start the physical exam. While this isn't Charleston proper, it is still Charleston, and Charleston spells danger. The easiest and safest route up to the terminal is to stay on the outskirts of the town and head to its east side. You'll see a set of stairs attached to the outside of a tall apartment building not far from the objective. Climb to the top of the stairs, enter the building, then head down a floor and head west toward the objective. You'll cross a bridge of scrap onto the next building. Once there, drop down another floor and follow the red, painted arrows lining the floor and walls, but do so backward. They'll lead you to the next building, where you'll reach the terminal.

A NEED TO SPEED

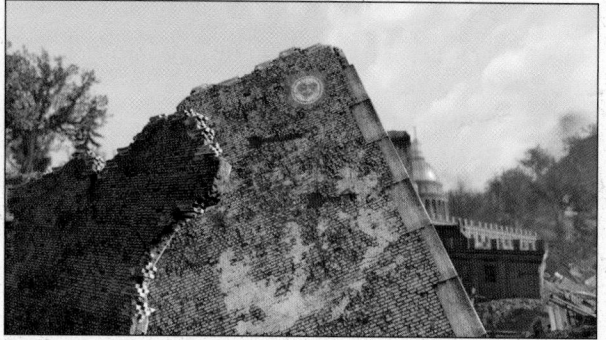

Once you initiate the physical exam, hit Button A—which is right in front of the terminal—then race to the south side of Charleston Herald and hit Button B. Return and hit Button A again. Oh! And you'll need to do it while avoiding Scorched and also within a three-minute time limit.

We're making it sound more intimidating than it actually is. You really just need to focus on getting off and out of the buildings into Charleston Herald proper as quickly as you can. From there, head toward the objective marker while following the arrows marking the walls. Once you hit Button B, head around the outside of the city, making your way to the east set of stairs we took up to the terminal the first time. Once you reach the stairs, just follow the path you took to the terminal and you're home free.

A REAL FIRE BREATHER

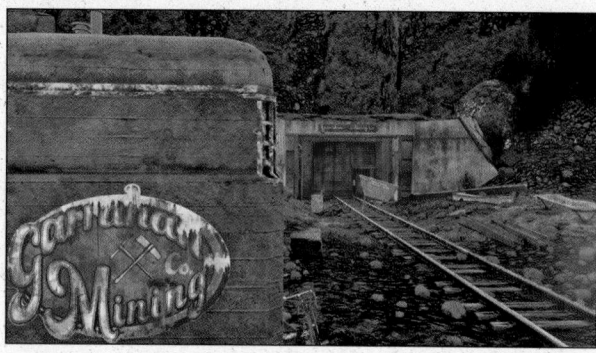

Initiate the final exam on the terminal, then head southwest of Charleston Herald to Belching Betty to reach your next objective. Once you arrive, pick up your gear and get ready for your final test.

ITEMS ➡	> FIRE BREATHER HELMET
	> FIRE BREATHER UNIFORM
	> FIRE BREATHERS FINAL EXAM BRIEFING HOLOTAPE
	> ANTI-SCORCHED TRAINING PISTOL

WORD OF WARNING FROM VAULT BOY!

BE SURE TO EQUIP YOUR FIRE BREATHER HELMET AS SOON AS YOU GET IT. THE AIR INSIDE THE BELCHING BETTY MINE (AND THE SMOKE PLUMES THROUGHOUT THE THE ASH HEAP) IS HIGHLY TOXIC. PUTTING ON THE FIRE BREATHER HELMET WILL PROTECT YOU IN THESE ENVIRONMENTS.

Listen to the Fire Breathers Final Exam Briefing Holotape in your inventory. Once you've listened to your final exam instructions, suit up and enter the mine.

FASCINATING FACTS FROM VAULT BOY!

THE ANTI-SCORCHED TRAINING PISTOL DEALS AN ADDITIONAL 25% DAMAGE TO SCORCHED, BUT 20% LESS TO ALL NON-SCORCHED ENEMIES. IF YOU DON'T HAVE ANYTHING STRONGER AND YOU'VE GOT PLENTY OF 10 MM ROUNDS, EQUIP IT BEFORE TACKLING THE NEXT PART OF THE QUEST.

ONLY YOU CAN PREVENT...

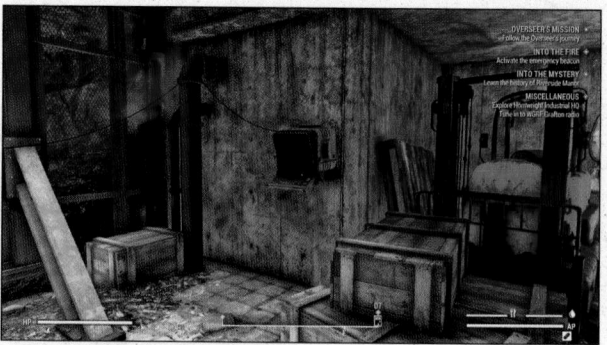

Once inside, use the terminal to the right of the locked door to unlock it. Follow the path and eventually you'll reach a fork in the road. You can pick either path: both have plenty of resistance and both lead you to your destination.

After you push the emergency beacon, more Scorched enter the room. Get behind cover and fight your way out carefully. Once you've back on the surface, speak with Bernie, then head back to the Charleston Fire Department and register yourself in the Fire Breather's computer system.

| ITEM ➡ | > WELCOME TO THE FIRE BREATHERS HOLOTAPE |

Head to the room next to the second-floor terminal and hit the button to play the priority message to complete the quest. You'll be launched into the "The Missing Link" quest immediately following this one.

Quest THE MISSING LINK

OBJECTIVES
- FOLLOW MADIGAN'S TRAIL.
- COMPLETE ROSE'S QUESTS TO GAIN HER TRUST.
- RETRIEVE THE UPLINK.
- GO TO THE FREE STATES BUNKER.

LOCATIONS TO EXPLORE
- TOP OF THE WORLD
- PLEASANT VALLEY SKI RESORT
- ABBIE'S BUNKER

REWARDS
- RANDOM AMMO, ARMOR, PLANS OR WEAPON
- A PHOTO FRAME

PREREQUISITES
- COMPLETE "INTO THE FIRE."

ON TOP OF THE TOP OF THE WORLD

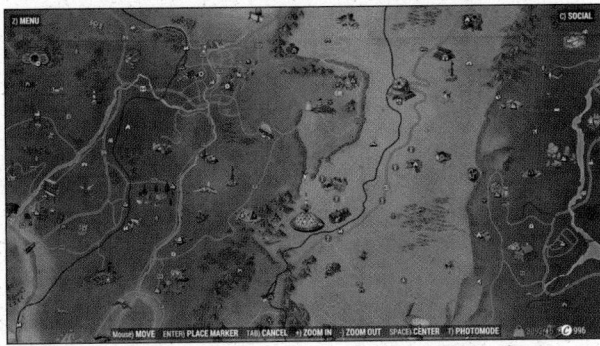

You need to reach Top of the World in the center of the map. It's a long journey, but a relatively quiet one, provided you take the proper route. If you take the southern route, you'll run straight through 98 NAR Regional, a checkpoint that is filled with deadly robots—most of whom explode shortly after getting destroyed by gunfire. It's a deadly place, so proceed with caution. Instead, Fast-Travel to Morgantown (or Morgantown Airport) northwest of Top of the World and approach from the northern path. There are Mole Men, Super Mutants, and plenty of combat hot zones, but you'll be encountering enemies that are roughly around Levels 5 to 10, which is a far cry from Levels 25 to 30.

FASCINATING FACTS FROM VAULT BOY!

AS YOU APPROACH TOP OF THE WORLD, YOU'LL RECEIVE A SIGNAL FOR A TOP OF THE WORLD RADIO STATION AND A MISCELLANEOUS QUEST. LISTEN TO THE RADIO STATION FOR A BIT, THEN HEAD TO TOP OF THE WORLD TO INITIATE THE "SIGNAL STRENGTH" QUEST. SIGNAL STRENGTH IS DIRECTLY TIED TO YOUR CURRENT QUEST. YOU'LL NEED TO COMPLETE IT, FLAVORS OF MAYHEM, AND KEY TO THE PAST IN ORDER TO PROGRESS WITH THIS QUEST.

After you build Rose's Signal Repeater, she'll let you take the elevator up to the third floor of Top of the World. Once there, you'll find where Madigan's trail ended. Rose knows what Madigan was looking for, but she's not willing to share that info unless you help her out with something else.

At this point, you need to complete all of Rose's other quests to progress beyond this objective.

BACK ON TRACK

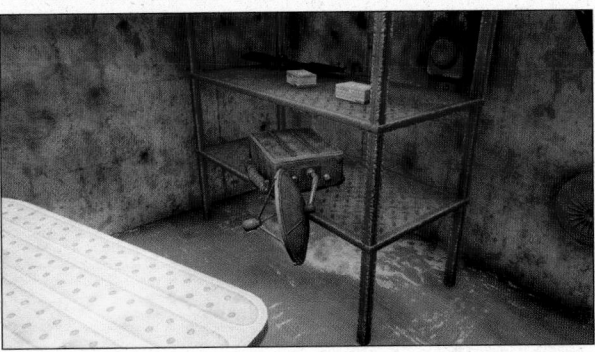

After you finish Rose's quest, grab the Broken Uplink from inside the Raider's Cache. We're taking a long trip to the Mire in the northeast corner of Appalachia. Fast-Travel to Sunnytop Ski Lanes or the Palace of the Winding Path, and start making your way east.

Once at the door to Abbie's Bunker, hack the terminal next to the door and head on in. When you do, the quest will be complete (finally!).

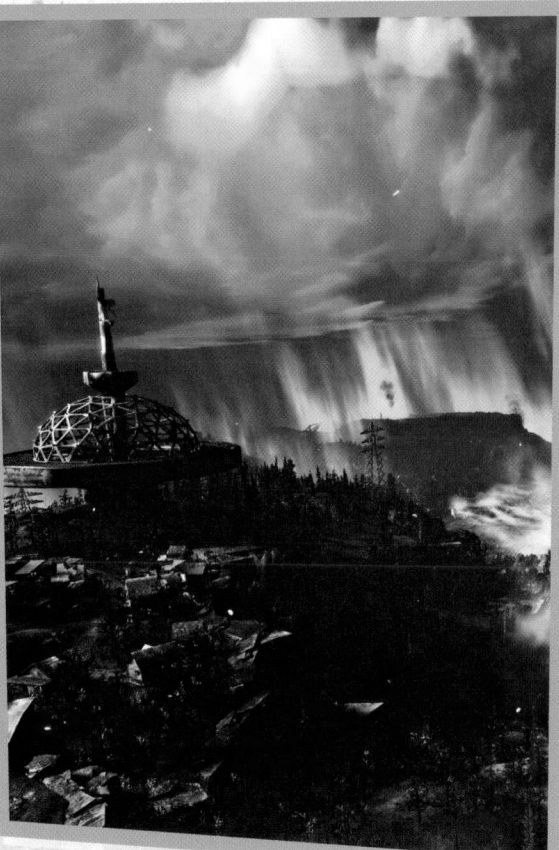

TRAINING

CRAFTING AND C.A.M.P.ING

INVENTORY

QUESTS

ATLAS

BESTIARY

APPENDICES

SIGNAL STRENGTH

OBJECTIVES

- FIND THE SIGNAL REPEATER SCHEMATIC.
- READ SIGNAL REPEATER NOTES.
- SEARCH FOR AN RCX01-A39 DUPLEXER.
- SEARCH FOR AN SMU-97 TRANSPONDER.
- CONSTRUCT THE SIGNAL REPEATER AT ANY TINKER'S WORKBENCH.
- GO TO THE NATIONAL ISOLATED RADIO ARRAY.
- INSTALL THE SIGNAL REPEATER.
- DIVERT POWER TO THE REPEATER.
- RETURN TO SPEAK WITH ROSE.

LOCATIONS TO EXPLORE

- TOP OF THE WORLD
- SENECA ROCKS VISITOR CENTER
- HORIZON'S REST
- 98 NAR REGIONAL
- NATIONAL ISOLATED RADIO ARRAY

REWARDS

- A CHANCE FOR A DEATH TAMBO OR GUITAR SWORD
- RANDOM AMMO
- A RANDOM AID ITEM
- A RANDOM PLAN
- A PHOTO FRAME

PREREQUISITES

- YOU'LL RECEIVE A MISCELLANEOUS QUEST TO LISTEN TO THE TOP OF THE WORLD RADIO STATION WHEN YOU GET ANYWHERE NEAR TOP OF THE WORLD. LISTEN TO IT, THEN REACH TOP OF THE WORLD TO START THIS QUEST.

RUNNING ERRANDS

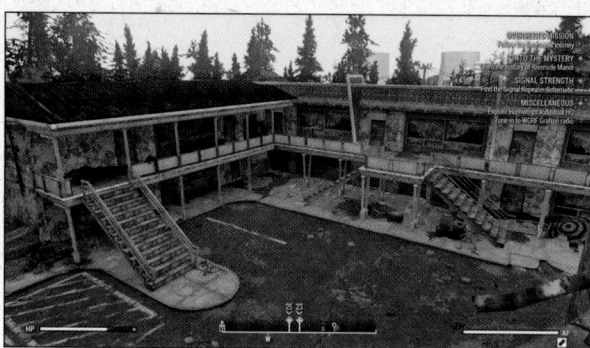

Rose wants you to find a Signal Repeater Schematic and she won't help you until you do. Head north of Top of the World until you reach the Seneca Rocks Visitor Center. Head slightly northwest of that to find a small motel. You need to loot the Signal Repeater Notes and Signal Repeater Schematics off of Major Darion Jones's body on the second floor.

ITEM ➡ 〉 SIGNAL REPEATER SCHEMATICS

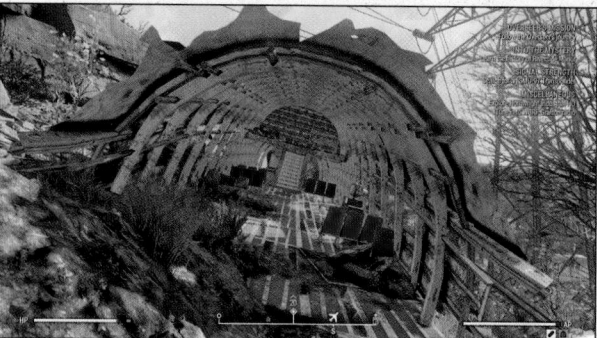

Read the Signal Repeater Notes and you'll be tasked with tracking down two parts necessary for constructing the Repeater: one west and slightly south of your position and one south of Top of the World. The western part is just south of Greg's Mine Supply, so you can Fast-Travel there to shorten the trip. You'll need to scale up Horizon's Rest and enter the plane wreckage therein. The SMU-97 Transponder is in the plane's cockpit.

ITEM ➡ 〉 SMU-97 TRANSPONDER

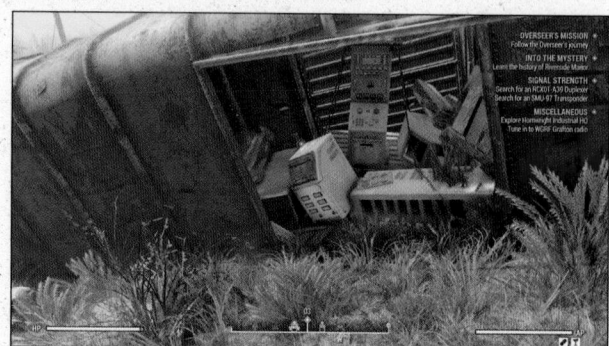

Fast-Travel back to Top of the World and make your way south while following the train tracks on your map. You'll eventually reach 98 NAR Regional: an apparent train graveyard. You'll find the RCX01-A39 Duplexer in a circuitry panel sitting in a busted train car on the north side of 98 NAR Regional.

ITEM ➡ 〉 RCX01-A39 DUPLEXER

With both parts in hand, find your nearest Tinker's Workbench and construct the Signal Repeater under the "Quest Items" option.

ITEM ➡ 〉 SIGNAL REPEATER

Helpful Hint from Vault Boy!

You can find a Tinker's Workbench in the trailer at Tygart Water Treatment, which is a location on your map south and slightly west of Horizon's Rest (the busted plane we visited earlier).

REACHING THE MASSES

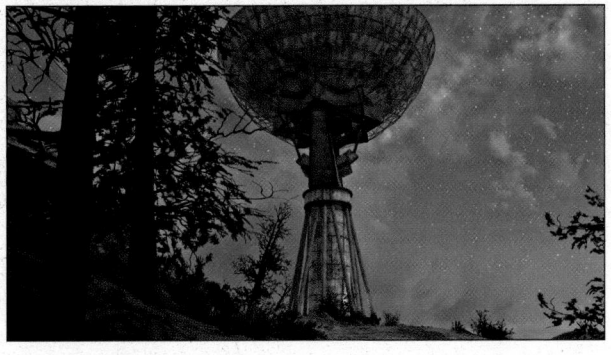

Your next task is to install the Repeater at the National Isolated Radio Array, located southeast of Top of the World. After you install it, you must divert power to it from a terminal in a small station just southwest of the Repeater's position. Select "Auxiliary Component Control," then "Divert Power to Auxiliary Component" to get the Repeater the energy it needs to function.

Head back to Top of the World. Now that Rose has what she wants, she's willing to let you up to the third floor. Speak with her to complete the quest.

Quest FLAVORS OF MAYHEM

OBJECTIVES
- ADD A KARMA SYRINGE BARREL MOD TO ROSE'S SYRINGER.
- SHOOT A YAO GUAI WITH A KARMA SYRINGE.
- KILL YOUR TARGET WHILE IT IS AFFECTED BY KARMA.
- CRAFT EXPLOSIVE BAIT AT ANY TINKER'S WORKBENCH.
- (OPTIONAL) FIND MATERIALS TO CRAFT EXPLOSIVE BAIT.
- USE EXPLOSIVE BAIT ON A CREATURE.
- APPROACH A DEATHCLAW AND "MAKE FRIENDS."
- (CHOOSE ONE) KILL OR ESCAPE THE DEATHCLAW.
- STEAL FROM A SUPER MUTANT CAMP.
- KILL A FERAL GHOUL.
- (OPTIONAL) EQUIP THE CANNIBAL PERK AND CANNIBALIZE A FERAL GHOUL.
- SPEAK WITH ROSE.

LOCATIONS TO EXPLORE
- BECKWITH FARM
- MONONGAH POWER PLANT
- WEST TEK RESEARCH CENTER
- R & G PROCESSING SERVICES

REWARDS
- ROSE'S SYRINGER
- BLACK DIAMOND (MODDED SKI SWORD)
- EXPLOSIVE BAIT RECIPE
- RAIDER HEADGEAR
- A RANDOM AID ITEM
- A PHOTO FRAME

PREREQUISITES
- COMPLETE "SIGNAL STRENGTH."

JUST A LITTLE PRICK

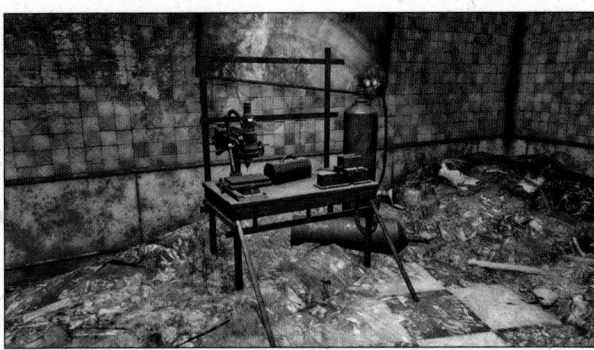

Helpful Hint from Vault Boy!

Rose's quests have you running all over Appalachia to collect specific items and kill elusive enemies. Our suggestion is don't try to marathon these quests. Figure out what Rose wants from you for an objective, then go off on some other adventure. As you stumble onto the items and Locations to Explore you need to visit, complete another objective, then go off and complete different quests, rinse, repeat.

To start, head to the second floor of Top of the World (the mezzanine level), and use the marked Weapons Workbench. Switch to the Modify menu and select Rose's Syringer. Rose provides everything you need to make the necessary modifications: two Firecracker Berries, one Glowing Resin, one Psycho, and one Steel. Some of these are perishable, so don't delay.

ITEM ➡	❯ ROSE'S SYRINGER

TRAINING

CRAFTING AND C.A.M.P.ING

INVENTORY

QUESTS

ATLAS

BESTIARY

APPENDICES

FASCINATING FACTS FROM VAULT BOY!

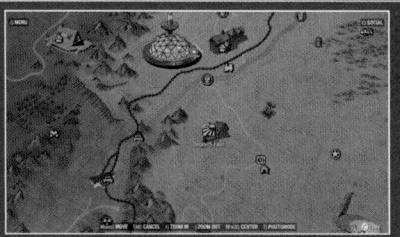

YOU CAN FIND GLOWING RESIN AND FIRECRACKER BERRIES IN THE AREA SURROUNDING BECKWITH FARM, WHICH IS THE BUILDING SOUTHEAST OF TOP OF THE WORLD ON YOUR MAP. IT WILL TAKE A BIT OF SEARCHING, BUT THERE ARE PLENTY OF PLANTS THERE TO MEET YOUR NEEDS. JUST GRAB THE FIRECRACKER BERRIES QUICKLY AND AVOID WALKING THROUGH THEIR BUSHES—THEY ARE EXTREMELY VOLATILE AND WILL DETONATE WHEN TOUCHED.

GLOWING RESIN CAN BE A BEAR TO FIND. YOUR BEST BET IS TO SEARCH AT NIGHT, WHEN THE RESIN IS SHINING BRIGHTEST. GLOWING RESIN ONLY GROWS ON THE SIDES OF TREES, SO SEARCH THE TREES YOU PASS AS YOU LOOK FOR FIRECRACKER BERRIES.

PSYCHO CAN ALSO BE A TOUGH FIND. YOU'LL NEED TO EITHER LUCK INTO FINDING ONE FROM LOOTING A CONTAINER OR AN ENEMY, OR YOU NEED TO STUMBLE ONTO THE PLANS FOR IT AND CRAFT AT A CHEMISTRY STATION (THERE'S ONE IN THE BACK OF THE FLATWOODS CHURCH INTERIOR).

STEEL IS FOUND BY BREAKING DOWN STEEL-BASED COMPONENTS AT A WORKBENCH. WRENCHES, DESK FANS, AND SO ON . . . IF IT SEEMS LIKE IT'S MADE OF METAL, YOU CAN PROBABLY GET STEEL OUT OF IT.

NO ONE BEAR SHOULD HAVE ALL THAT POWER

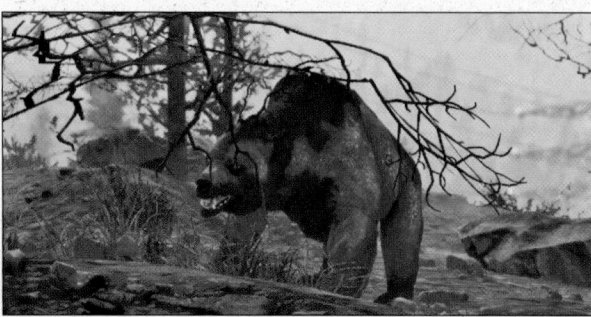

Your next task is to shoot a Yao Guai with Rose's Syringer equipped with the Karma Syringe Barrel, survive its terrible 60-second rampage, and then kill it when the effects of the drugs wear off. You can find a Yao Guai north of Top of the World. Fast-Travel to Seneca Rocks Visitor Center and head north from there to reach the marked destination faster. Now, you could just shoot any organic enemy and kill them while they're jacked up on Karma, but Rose wouldn't like that and we wouldn't want to upset Rose . . . would we?

Helpful Hint from Vault Boy!

You'll receive Miscellaneous Quest: Investigate the House if you pass through Monongah to reach the Yao Guai. Completing this will start the Daily quest "Someone to Talk To."

BUT WAIT!

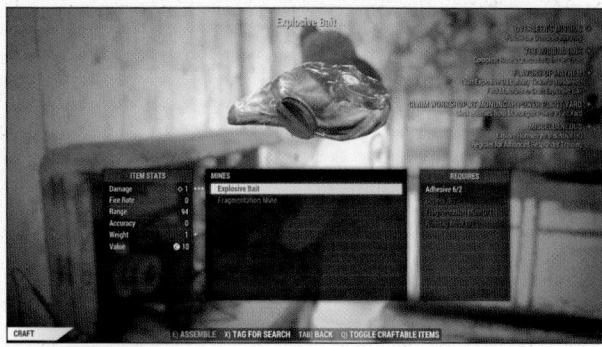

Your next task is to locate a Tinker's Workbench and craft Explosive Bait. The objective marker will lead you to both a Tinker's Workbench and a nearby container holding all of the components you need to craft Explosive Bait. Once at the Workbench, craft the Explosive Bait from the "Mines" crafting category, then head back outside and use it on some poor, unsuspecting, irradiated monstrosity.

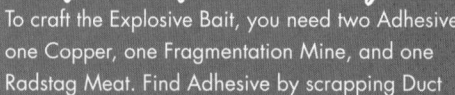

ITEM ➡ | > EXPLOSIVE BAIT

Helpful Hint from Vault Boy!

To craft the Explosive Bait, you need two Adhesive, one Copper, one Fragmentation Mine, and one Radstag Meat. Find Adhesive by scrapping Duct Tape, and obtain Copper by scrapping Fuses or Power Relay Coils. For the Fragmentation Mine, you can either try to disarm one around the base of Top of the World, craft one yourself, or find a local merchant who sells them.

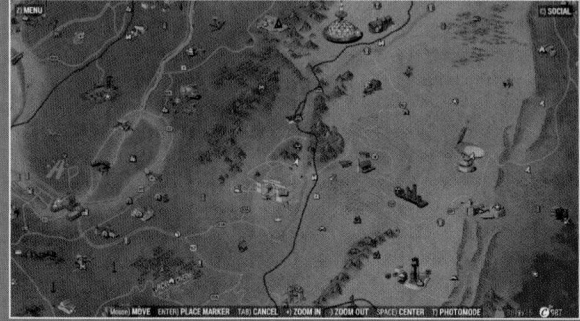

Radstags are tricky to find, as they are quite rare. The best place to locate one is on the northern tip of The Whitespring Resort, which is south and slightly west of Top of the World. Two of them are drinking from a small pond behind a house. They're higher level, so hit them with something heavy if you want to get them before they flee. You can find more on the southern end of the resort, so be sure to explore if things go south the first time.

IT GETS EVEN BETTER!

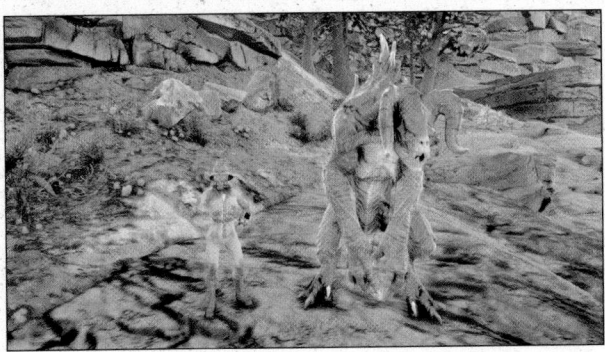

Because Rose has a few screws loose (no pun intended), your next task is to . . . "make friends" with a Deathclaw. You have to approach it and hit the Activate button to complete the objective. After that, you'll be given the choice to either flee from the Deathclaw or kill it. If you've approached it and it saw you, fleeing probably isn't going to help. Use obstacles and drops to keep the Deathclaw at a distance. If it gets close, you're toast, but dropping off of ridges and keeping trees between you and it can help you keep it at a distance while you unload your strongest weapon on it.

ROSE IS TRYING TO KILL US ...

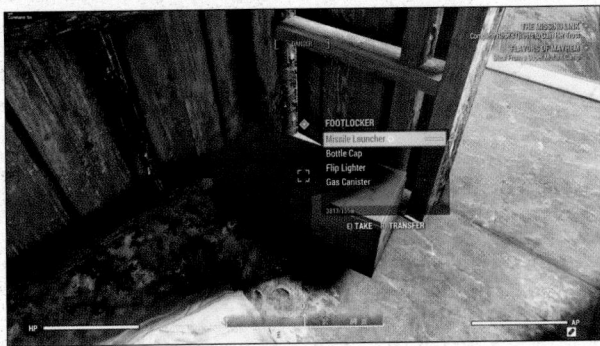

Now, because what we've done isn't absurd enough, your next objective is to steal from a Super Mutant Camp. Your objective marker will lead you to a container holding the item you need to steal (a Missile Launcher) to complete this objective.

ITEM ➡ ❯ MISSILE LAUNCHER

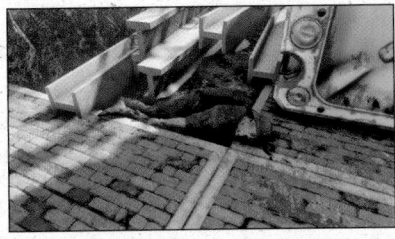

Rose's next little field trip leads us to the south side of the Savage Divide. If you visited The Whitespring Resort to get the Radstag meat, Fast-Travel there and head south. If you didn't, you've got a longer trip ahead of you.

When you arrive, you need only dispatch a Feral Ghoul or two while in the circle to complete the objective. You can equip the Cannibalize perk (if you have it and meet the level requirement) to snack on the dead Ghoul for Rose's amusement. Once you're done, head back to Rose in Top of the World.

Quest KEY TO THE PAST

OBJECTIVES
- CHECK THE TERMINAL AT BLACKWATER MINE.
- FIND THE BLACKWATER BANDITS' KEY FRAGMENT.
- FIND THE TRAPPER'S KEY FRAGMENT.
- CHECK MARGIE'S LAST KNOWN LOCATION FOR CLUES.
- DUPLICATE THE DIEHARD'S KEY FRAGMENT.
- FIND THE GOURMANDS' KEY FRAGMENT.
- KILL DAVID AND GET THE CUTTHROAT'S KEY FRAGMENT.
- BRING THE KEY FRAGMENTS TO ROSE.
- GO TO THE RAIDER CACHE.

LOCATIONS TO EXPLORE
- BLACKWATER MINE
- DEVIL'S BACKBONE
- SUNNYTOP SKI LANES
- PALACE OF THE WINDING PATH
- BOLTON GREENS
- WENDIGO CAVE
- BIG FRED'S BBQ SHACK
- CHARLESTON CAPITOL BUILDING
- PLEASANT VALLEY SKI RESORT

REWARDS
- RAIDER POWER ARMOR (FULL SET)
- A RANDOM WEAPON PLAN
- RANDOM AMMO
- A RANDOM AID ITEM
- A PHOTO FRAME

PREREQUISITES
- COMPLETE "FLAVORS OF MAYHEM."

PASSWORD PLEASE!

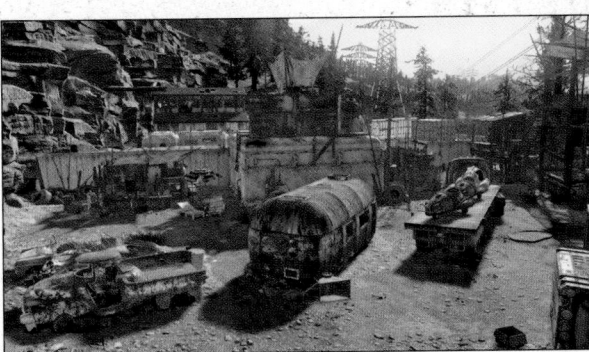

The quest to please Rose continues. This time, we're collecting five fragments of a password to open a Raid cache filled with treasure. Head south from Top of the World, or use The Whitespring Resort, which is slightly west of your destination; then head for the objective marker.

Enter Blackwater Mine and use the terminal just inside. Select any entry (except that last one of the main three options) to complete the objective; then head deeper into the mine. You'll have to kill an irradiated woman by the name of Freddie Lang to find the mine's Key Fragment. Grab the fragment; then leave the mine.

ITEM ➡ ❯ BLACKWATER BANDITS KEY FRAGMENT

LATE TO THE PARTY

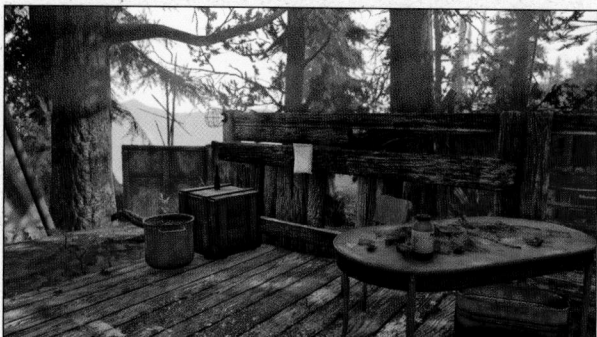

Your next Key Fragment is east of the Blackwater Mine at a local Trappers' Camp on the Devil's Backbone. You can Fast-Travel from the National Isolated Radio Array north of the objective, but the West Tek Research Center below it is a dangerous place; you might end up spending more time there than if you had just walked from Blackwater Mine.

The camp was hit by a local Super Mutant group, and they took the one guy carrying our next Key Fragment. Follow the road west to Huntersville. You'll find the Trappers' Key Fragment on the body of Walter Griswold in the center of the town.

WORD OF WARNING FROM VAULT BOY!

IF YOU HAVE YOUR PERCEPTION AT 2 OR HIGHER, YOU'LL RECEIVE A MESSAGE NOTING THAT THE CORPSE MIGHT BE BOOBY TRAPPED. ACT FAST! YOU CAN EITHER DISARM THE TRAP OR OPT TO RUN FOR IT AS SOON AS YOU GRAB THE KEY! AFTER ABOUT 30 SECONDS, A MININUKE WILL DETONATE, BLOWING UP EVERYTHING SURROUNDING THE BODY.

ITEM ➡ **❭ TRAPPERS' KEY FRAGMENT**

SKI TRIP

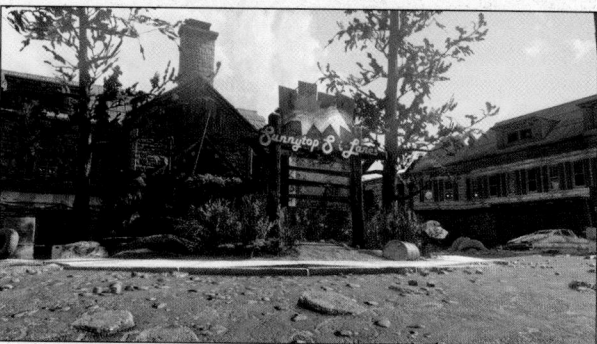

Your next stop is Sunnytop Ski Lanes on the north side of the Savage Divide. You can Fast-Travel to Monongah Power Plant or Seneca Rocks Visitor Center (both of which are north of Top of the World); then head northeast to reach the marked location.

WORD OF WARNING FROM VAULT BOY!

AS YOU PASS MONONGAH MINES WHILE IT'S WEST OF THE ROAD, TRY AND STAY ON THE OUTSIDE OF THIS COLLECTION OF CARS. FRAGMENTATION MINES ARE SCATTERED THROUGHOUT THIS AREA. JUST ONE OF THESE WILL SET OFF EVERY CAR AND MINE IN A GLORIOUS FLASH OF RED-HOT DEATH; YOU'LL BE DEAD BEFORE YOU REALIZED WHERE THINGS WENT WRONG. GIVE IT A WIDE BERTH AND YOU'LL MAKE IT OUT WITH ALL YOUR BITS IN THEIR RIGHTFUL PLACE.

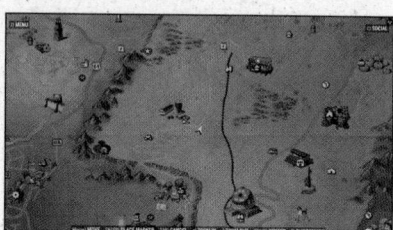

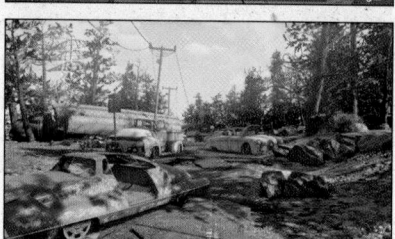

HITTING THE SLOPES

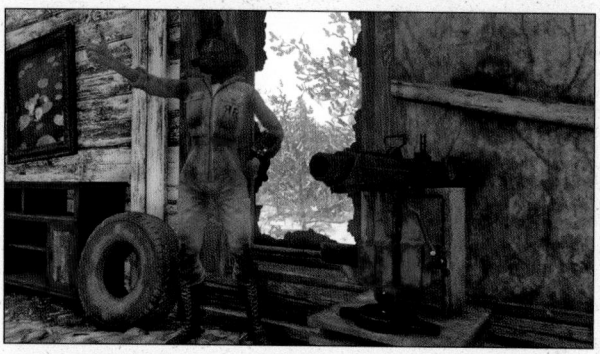

Sunnytop is packed with enemies and mountains of traps. Move through this place carefully if you want to avoid getting blown up by a hanging grenade trap or a missile launcher trip wire. Thankfully, you don't have to do a lot of exploring to find what you're looking for. Just enter through the front entrance (watch out for the Punji Board in front of the front door), then hang a left. You can't access the room the objective is in from outside, but getting there once inside is just a matter of clearing the rooms of Super Mutants, then walking on over.

ITEM ➡ **❭ MARGIE MCCLINTOCK'S HOLOTAPE**

Helpful Hints from Vault Boy!

Some of the rooms in Sunnytop Ski Lanes are locked, but one in particular holds a bit of loot that is worth diverting for. Look on the wall behind the front desk of the ski lodge. You'll find the Sunnytop Ski Lanes Room 6 Key hanging from a hook. Grab it, then head to the southeast side of the building (the right side if you're standing at the entrance to the building). Head up the flight of stairs at the end of the building and use the key to the door at the top of the stairs. Enter carefully: there's a missile launcher trap on the door's other side that will launch when you enter the room. You'll find an ammo box and a steamer trunk in here, along with the missiles and missile launcher from the trap.

After listening to the holotape, go to the opposite end of the lodge and head downstairs the first chance you get. You'll find a terminal at the far end of the lower floor. Use it, select "Inbox," then read the "Admin Password" entry.

DOUBLE DIGITS

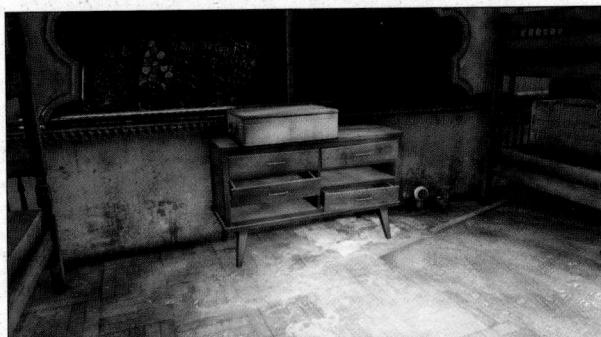

Margie's group's Key Fragment has been destroyed, but a way to replicate it has been preserved. Head northwest from the lodge to reach the Palace of the Winding Path. You'll find the Palace Admin Password in a dresser just a short trip into the palace.

ITEM ➡	❯ PALACE ADMIN PASSWORD

Once you have the password, head downstairs and use the Holotape Duplication Terminal to create the Diehards Key Fragment by selecting "DUPLICATE FROM ARCHIVES," then "Diehards Key Fragments."

ITEM ➡	❯ DIEHARDS KEY FRAGMENT

A ROUND OF GOLF

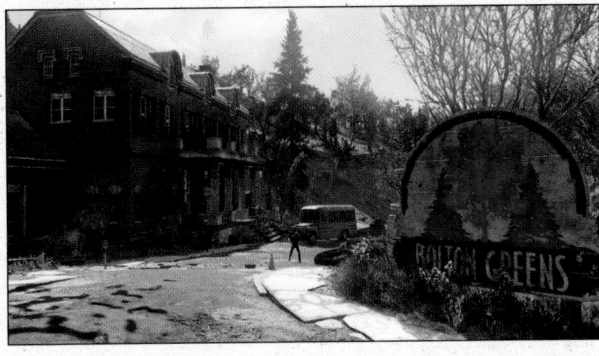

Your next task is to search around Bolton Greens for notes on the next Key Fragment. Reach it quickly by Fast-Traveling to Monongah Power Plant, then heading west. Once you reach Bolton Greens, go inside and head to the top floor to find the Gourmands Note.

ITEM ➡	❯ GOURMANDS NOTE

The note leads us back to Savage Divide to find the Gourmands' Key Fragment in a place known ominously as the Wendigo Cave. Fast-Travel back to Top of the World and go northeast from there to reach the Wendigo Cave.

THERE'S A WENDIGO IN THE WENDIGO CAVE

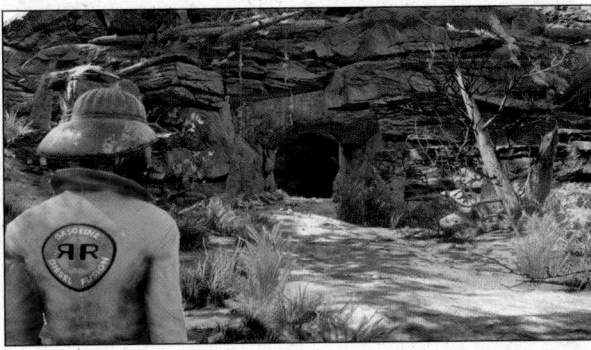

The Wendigo Cave is a winding, twisting, Mirelurk-filled death maze. You'll have a lot of fighting ahead of you, and the enemies are powerful. It's a tough place, but if you use the map we've provided in the Atlas, you can keep this trip as short and sweet as a cave full of murdering, hate-beasts will allow.

Reach the objective, grab the Gourmands Key Fragment, and get the hell out of Dodge.

ITEM ➡	❯ GOURMANDS KEY FRAGMENT

TRAINING

CRAFTING AND C.A.M.P.ING

INVENTORY

QUESTS

ATLAS

BESTIARY

APPENDICES

DAVID MUST DIE

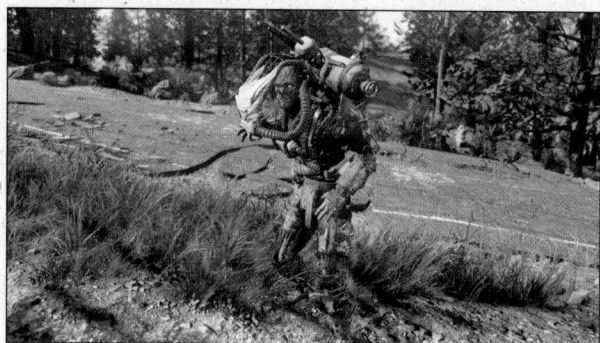

Fast-Travel back to Top of the World and head southeast. Your next destination, Big Fred's BBQ Shack, is a short trip from there. When you arrive at your destination, Feral Ghouls almost immediately swarm you. Find the nearest cover and take them down. David Thorpe, now a Scorched, will be attacking the Feral Ghouls along with you. Use this distraction to target David, as he is significantly more powerful than the other enemies here.

Once he's dead and gone, loot his body to find the Cutthroats Key Fragment.

ITEM ➡	> CUTTHROATS KEY FRAGMENT

DIGGING UP THE PAST

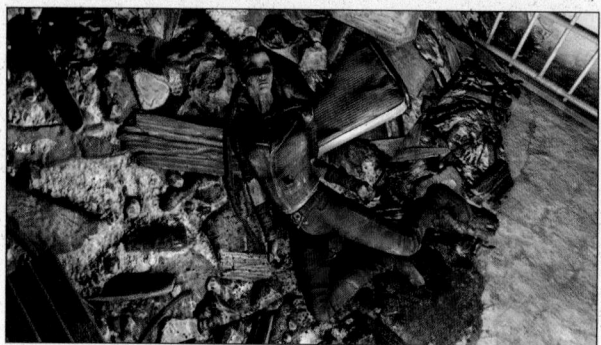

With all the Key Fragments in hand, head back to Rose at Top of the World and slide them her way. Rose will task you with heading into Charleston to find the body of a woman named Rosalynn at the Charleston Capitol Building. It's not a place we'd suggest you go if it wasn't a necessity; it's a dangerous, unfriendly place with plenty of dangers around, above and below you.

You can hop to Charleston Fire Department just southwest of the Capitol Building. It's a short trip and a much safer journey than coming in from Charleston proper. Head into the Charleston Capitol Courthouse and head down to the basement. Use the marked terminal and select the entry on "Doe, J." Head into the room behind the terminal.

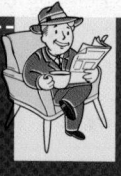

FASCINATING FACTS FROM VAULT BOY!
IF YOU'RE KEEN ON LEARNING A BIT ABOUT ROSE'S FATE BEFORE SHE BECAME A MISS NANNY. LISTEN TO THE HOLOTAPE ON THE TABLE IN THE CENTER OF THE CELL ROOM.

JUST LIKE OLD TIMES

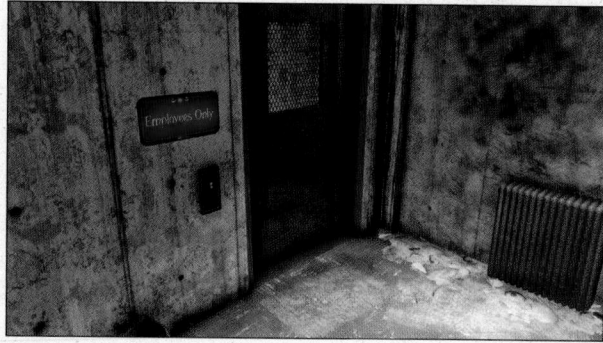

Head back to Top of the World and head east to the Pleasant Valley Ski Resort. Enter the resort and head down into the basement. The door to the cache is locked; check under the welcome mat for the key. Use the keycard you find on the keycard reader to the left of the door. Enter the cache to complete the quest.

ITEM ➡	> RAIDER CACHE KEYCARD

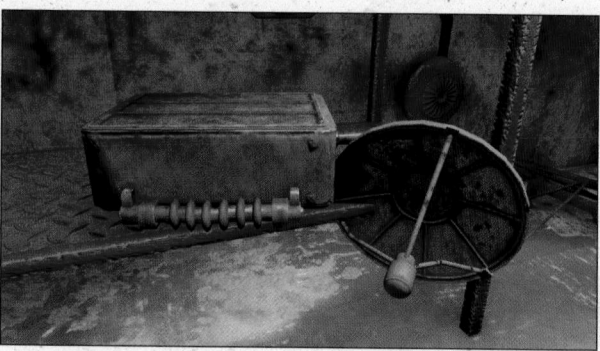

Although the quest is technically over, head to the back left corner of the room and grab the Broken Uplink before leaving.

ITEM ➡	> BROKEN UPLINK

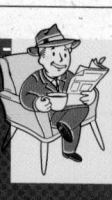

FASCINATING FACTS FROM VAULT BOY!
WITH THIS QUEST COMPLETE, YOU'VE FINALLY WRAPPED UP ROSE'S QUEST. JUMP BACK TO "THE MISSING LINK" SECTION OF THIS CHAPTER TO FIND OUT WHAT TO DO NEXT.

BUNKER BLUNDERS

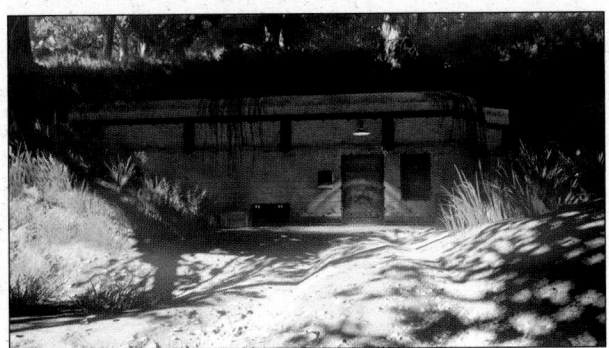

Head to Abbie's Bunker on the north side of the Mire. Enter the back room and use the marked Tinker's Workbench. Head down to the Quest Items tab and select "Uplink." Create the Uplink to "repair" it. Head back to the entry room and use the Scorched Detection System Terminal at the objective marker. Select the "Communications Uplink Repaired" entry to check in; then back out and listen to what Abbie has to say via the intercom.

ITEM ➡ ❯ **RALEIGH'S PASSWORD**

NUMBER ONE FANS

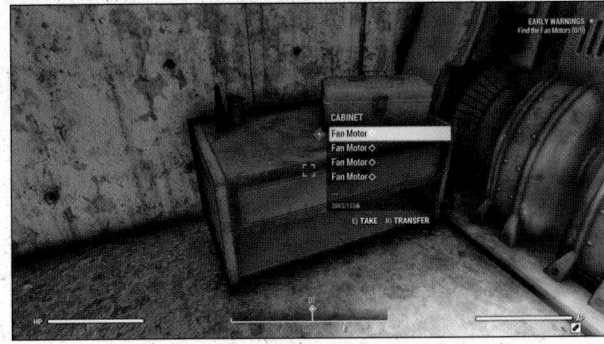

EARLY WARNINGS
Find the Fan Motors (0/5)

CABINET
Fan Motor
Fan Motor ◇
Fan Motor ◇
Fan Motor ◇

Exit the bunker and follow the road south to reach Raleigh Clay's Bunker. Use the terminal to unlock the front door; then head inside. Listen to Abbie and you'll receive your next objective: Find the Fan Motors.

Enter the hall on the bunker's southeastern side and you'll receive an optional quest to find Raleigh's Schematics. Find them by entering the first door on the right of the southeastern hall. The Schematics are on the cabinet on the room's north side.

ITEM ➡ ❯ **PLAN: SHROUDED WOOD ARMOR MOD**

Now head to the room on the hall's opposite side and investigate the marked cabinet to find all five of the Fan Motors.

Next, you must locate a series of Heating Coils from several locations to explore across the Mire (and one in Savage Divide). To find the first coil, head to the room at the hall's end and open the toolbox at the objective marker.

ITEM ➡ ❯ **HEATING COIL**

OBJECTIVES
- FIND THE MISSING UPLINK.
- REPAIR THE BROKEN UPLINK.
- CHECK IN AT SDS TERMINAL.
- ENTER RALEIGH'S BUNKER.
- FIND FIVE FAN MOTORS.
- FIND HEATING COILS ACROSS THE MIRE.
- CRAFT FIVE UPGRADED MOTORS.
- CHECK IN AT THE SDS TERMINAL.

PREREQUISITES
- COMPLETE "THE MISSING LINK."

LOCATIONS TO EXPLORE
- ABBIE'S BUNKER
- RALEIGH CLAY'S BUNKER
- ELLA AMES' BUNKER
- RELAY TOWER LW-B1-22

REWARDS
- SHADOWED COMBAT ARMOR MODS
- STAND FAST (MODDED COMBAT ARMOR TORSO)
- RANDOM AMMO
- A RANDOM AID ITEM
- A PHOTO FRAME

BEAT THE HEAT

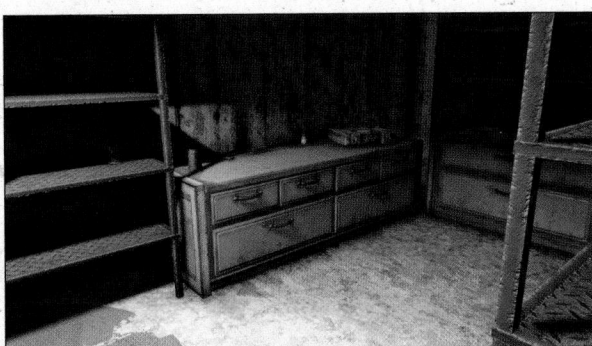

Leave the bunker and follow the road north; then head off-road a bit west to reach Ella Ames' Bunker. Once inside the main room, use the door on the south side and then take the door on the left to track down the second Heating Coil.

ITEM ➡ ❯ **HEATING COIL**

FASCINATING FACTS FROM VAULT BOY

YOU'LL RECEIVE A MISCELLANEOUS TASK TO "INVESTIGATE ELLA'S BUNKER." THIS JUST INVOLVES LOOKING AT HER COMPUTER TERMINAL, WHICH IS AT THE END OF THE SAME HALL THE HEATING COIL ROOM IS ATTACHED TO. READ THE "RADSHIELD" ENTRY UNDER "RESEARCH STUDIES" TO COMPLETE THE OBJECTIVE AND START "AN ORGANIC SOLUTION."

Exit the bunker and head west to Relay Tower LW-B1-22; wrap around the mountains between the tower and Ella Ames' Bunker. Enter the Relay Tower and grab the Heating Coil from the toolbox on the room's southeast side.

ITEM ➡ ❯ **HEATING COIL**

TRAINING

CRAFTING AND C.A.M.P.ING

INVENTORY

QUESTS

ATLAS

BESTIARY

APPENDICES

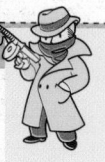
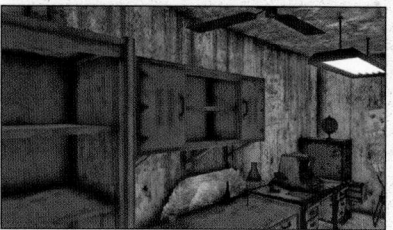

Fast-Travel back up to Abbie's Bunker on the north side of the Mire. Head to the back room on the building's north side (where the Tinker's Workbench is located). Look in the cupboards on the room's left side to find your last two Heating Coils; then go to the Tinker's Workbench and craft five Upgraded Motors under the Quest Items tab. Once you have all five, head back to the SDS Terminal in the main room and select "Motors Upgraded" to complete the quest. You'll roll right into "Reassembly Required" from here.

ITEMS ➡	❯ HEATING COILS X2
	❯ UPGRADED MOTORS X5

Helpful Hint from Vault Boy

Loot all of the junk items around the bunker if you're missing anything to craft the Upgraded Motors. You can find plenty of items containing Copper, as well as Steel. If you're still short, check the Crafting chapter and the Atlas for mining Locations to Explore.

Quest REASSEMBLY REQUIRED

OBJECTIVES

- TAKE THE HOLOTAPE FOR ROSE.
- UPGRADE FIVE SCORCHED DETECTORS.
- TAKE THE HOLOTAPE TO ROSE.
- RETURN TO ABBIE'S BUNKER.

LOCATIONS TO EXPLORE

- ABBIE'S BUNKER
- TOP OF THE WORLD

REWARDS

- NUKE MINES
- NUKE MINE RECIPE
- FRAGMENTATION GRENADE MIRVS
- FRAGMENTATION GRENADE MIRV RECIPE
- A RANDOM AID ITEM

PREREQUISITES

- COMPLETE "EARLY WARNINGS."

UPDATING SECURITY

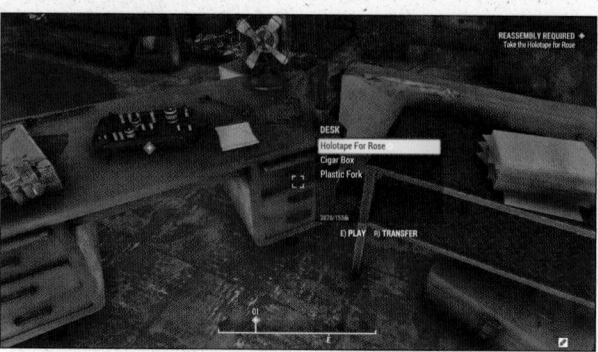

Grab the holotape For Rose from in the desk in front of the SDS Terminal; then exit the bunker.

ITEM ➡	❯ HOLOTAPE FOR ROSE

Next, you must walk along Route 65 and install the Upgraded Motors into the Scorched Detectors lining the road. The first is on the road a short trip northeast of the bunker. Head there, then follow the road south, upgrading the Scorched Detectors as you go.

OLD FRIENDS

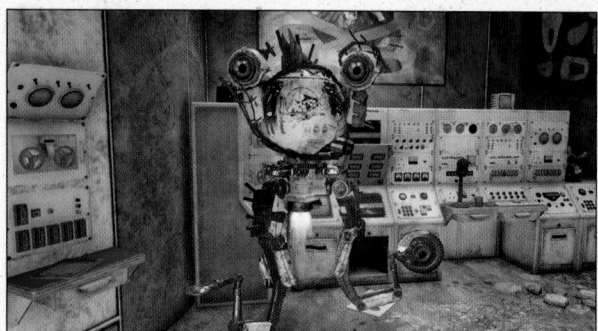

After you finish upgrading all the Scorched Detectors, Fast-Travel to Top of the World and hand Rose the holotape you picked up in Abbie's Bunker.

When you're finished with Rose, Fast-Travel back to Abbie's Bunker and enter it to complete the quest. You'll immediately start the next quest, "Coming to Fruition," after wrapping up this one.

COMING TO FRUITION

OBJECTIVES
- TAKE AND LOAD THE MASTER HOLOTAPE IN THE ARMORY TERMINAL.
- LOAD THE MASTER HOLOTAPE IN RALEIGH'S TERMINAL.
- LOAD THE MASTER HOLOTAPE IN SAM'S TERMINAL.
- LOAD THE MASTER HOLOTAPE IN A RELAY TOWER TERMINAL.
- UPLOAD THE DATA.
- REBOOT THE SYSTEM.

LOCATIONS TO EXPLORE
- ABBIE'S BUNKER
- HARPERS FERRY
- CHARLESTON CAPITOL BUILDING
- ANY RELAY TOWER

PREREQUISITES
- COMPLETE "REASSEMBLY REQUIRED."

REWARDS
- ELECTRICAL ARC PLANS
- FLAMETHROWER TRAP PLANS
- RANDOM LEGENDARY WEAPON OR ARMOR
- RANDOM AID
- A RANDOM AID ITEM
- A PHOTO FRAME

ON THE ROAD AGAIN

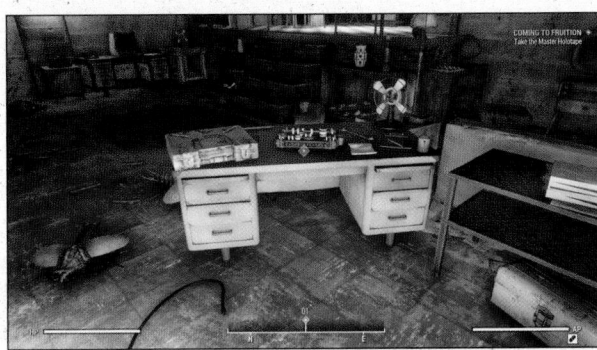

Head to the bunker's main room and grab the Master Holotape out of the desk in front of the Scorched Detection System Terminal. Exit the bunker and head south down Route 65 to reach the Harpers Ferry. Go to the Armory Access Terminal on the south side of Harpers Ferry and insert the Master Holotape. Select "Play Holotape" to hack the terminal; then unlock the door to the armory.

ITEM ➡	> MASTER HOLOTAPE

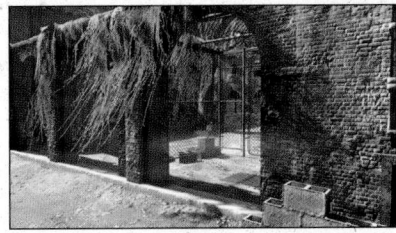

After entering the armory compound, take a right through the first opening available to enter the armory proper. Use the door terminal ahead to open the sealed door and pass through the large gray fence. Head upstairs, turn around, and use the planks to cross into the building ahead.

SMASH THE STATE

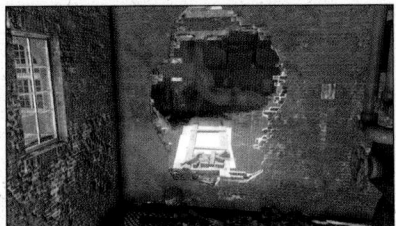

Drop downstairs and use the next terminal up ahead to open a second door. Exit the building from the door ahead and enter the neighboring building. Go upstairs and hack the terminal to gain access to Raleigh's terminal. Insert the Master Holotape, then listen to what Abbie has to say.

A CAPITOL IDEA!

Fast-Travel to the Charleston Capitol Building on the southwest side of Appalachia. Head to the third floor, where you find Sam's terminal. No dice! The terminal is locked tight. Head down to the basement and use the marked security terminal. Select "Accounts/Account Lockdowns/Samuel Blackwell" to unlock Sam's computer. Now head back up to the third floor and try loading the Master Holotape again.

Helpful Hint from Vault Boy!
When you exit Sam Blackwell's office, you can drop down the hole in the floor, then drop down the larger hole on the next floor to reach the basement quicker.

RELAY RACE

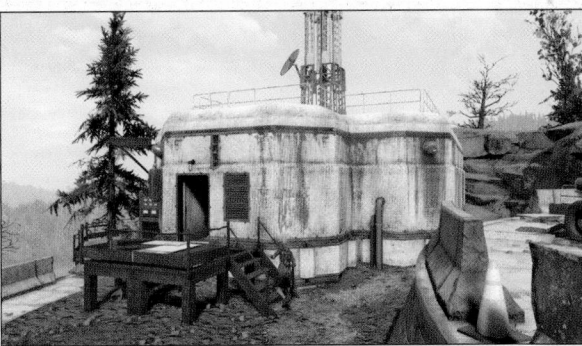

Your next task is to put the Master Holotape into a Relay Tower computer. You can head to the Relay Tower southwest of you in the Ash Heap, or you can Fast-Travel to the one you already visited during "Early Warnings"—Relay Tower LW-B1-22, in the map's northeastern corner. Whatever you choose, head to a Relay Tower and use the Master Holotape on the terminal there.

After you insert the Master Holotape and download the data, head back to Abbie's Bunker and restart the system from the Scorched Detection System Terminal in the main room to complete the quest.

You'll roll right into "Defiance Has Fallen" from here.

Quest DEFIANCE HAS FALLEN

OBJECTIVES

- FIND THE LOCATION OF FORT DEFIANCE.
- DISCOVER THE BROTHERHOOD'S FATE.
- POWER UP THE ASYLUM.

LOCATIONS TO EXPLORE

- TOP OF THE WORLD
- CAMP VENTURE
- FORT DEFIANCE

REWARDS

- BOS SOLDIER'S UNIFORM
- GATLING GUN
- 5 MM AMMO
- BOS UNDERARMOR MOD
- A RANDOM AID ITEM
- A PHOTO FRAME

PREREQUISITES

- READ THE "FORT DEFIANCE" POST ON THE TERMINAL IN ABBIE'S BUNKER.

HUNTING FORT DEFIANCE

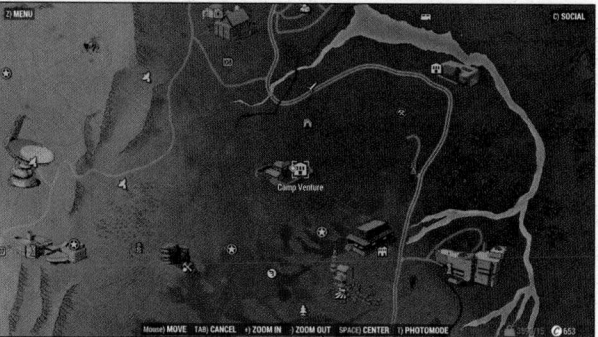

In order to find Fort Defiance, you'll need to find clues. The best place to look is Camp Venture. If you follow Route 65 south and keep going south after it turns east, you'll be on track to reach the camp.

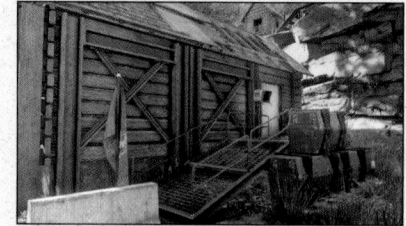

When you arrive, head to the camp's upper level to find the Command Center. The room is locked and you'll need to locate the password to the terminal next to the door to get inside. Check the terminal to get an optional objective to locate the password to the terminal. You didn't need the objective, but the marker will help you locate the password with greater ease.

BREAKING AND ENTERING

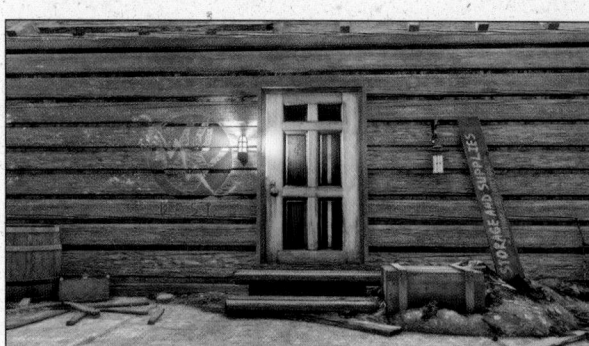

From here, head back to the Command Center terminal, input the password, and then enter. There are two tables in the center of the room; read the note on the back of the table on the right to find Fort Defiance's location.

ITEM ➡ ❯ LETTER TO TOMMY

Now head to the camp's lower level and enter the Storage and Supplies building (its sign is sitting sideways next to the front entrance of the building). Enter and head left; then go downstairs. Use your lockpick abilities to unlock the door ahead; then approach the locked door at the end of the basement. Read the note to the door's right to receive an optional quest to locate the room's key.

To find the key, head back to the camp's upper level and enter the building south of the Command Center terminal. Loot the marked locker to find the key to the storage closet. Head back to the Storage and Supplies building and open the door. Read the note on the table to get the password to the Command Center terminal.

ITEM ➡ ❯ COMMAND CENTER PASSWORD

Helpful Hints from Vault Boy!

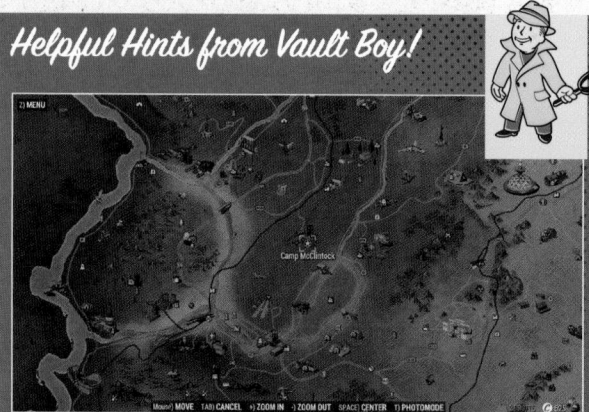

If you haven't completed the Camp McClintock quest "Back to Basic" yet, this is a good time. It will make the next portion of this quest go much smoother. Camp McClintock is located just south of the center of the Forest. You'll get a Miscellaneous Quest as soon as you approach it.

For more info on "Back to Basic," see its section next in this chapter.

THE ACTS OF DEFIANCE

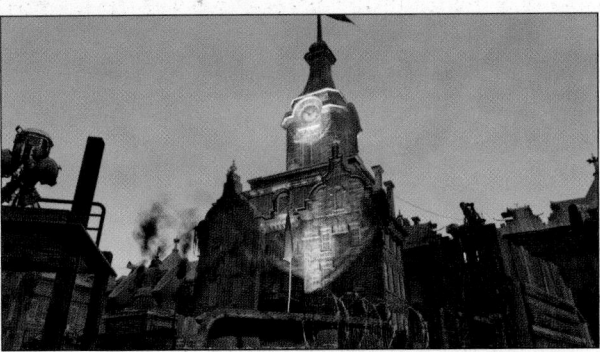

Fort Defiance is located southwest of Camp Venture, right on the border between Savage Divide and Cranberry Bog. Fort Defiance was built out of an old asylum and has not seen a lot of activity in some time. We're here to discover what happened to the Brotherhood of Steel, but to do that we need to repower the building by flipping the circuit breaker on the top floor.

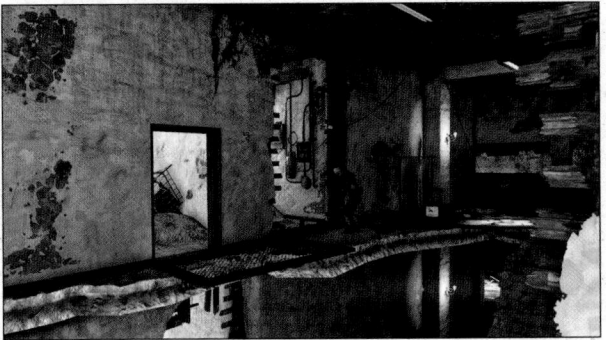

The path to the circuit breaker is very straightforward. Head down the hall and up each floor and you'll arrive at the top floor quickly. Once there, you find that most of it has broken apart and fallen to the floor below. With the gap in front of you, head through the door on your left. From here, progress through the rooms ahead, then cross over the makeshift bridge to the room's right side. Continue this pattern of room hopping and bridge crossing to arrive at the circuit breaker. Activate it, then head back downstairs via the ramp just outside the circuit breaker's room.

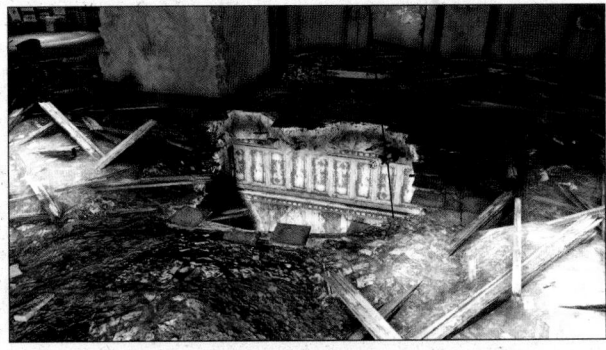

If you keep moving toward the objective marker, you'll find a hole in the ground that will drop you right back in front of the locked room near the building's entrance. Read the note to complete the quest.

ITEM ➡	> FINAL STAND

Quest BACK TO BASIC

OBJECTIVES
- **COLLECT YOUR UNIFORM.**
- **PRESENT YOURSELF TO THE MASTER SERGEANT.**
- **COMPLETE THE MARKSMANSHIP TRAINING COURSE.**
- **COMPLETE THE AGILITY TRAINING COURSE.**
- **COMPLETE THE PATRIOTISM TRAINING COURSE.**
- **COMPLETE THE LIVE FIRE EXERCISE.**

LOCATIONS TO EXPLORE
- **CAMP MCCLINTOCK.**

REWARDS
- **RANDOM AMMO AND AID ITEM**

PREREQUISITES
- **INITIALLY APPEARS AS A MISCELLANEOUS QUEST TO "START YOUR TRAINING AT CAMP MCCLINTOCK."**

YOU'RE IN THE ARMY NOW!

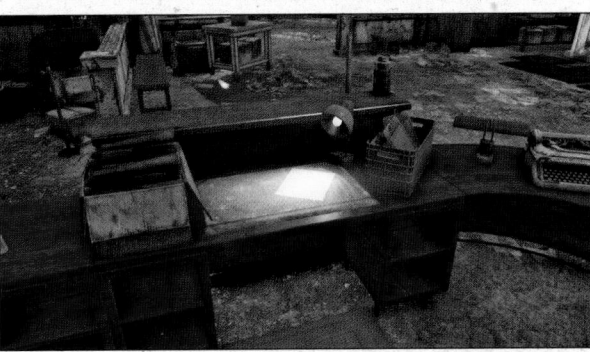

After speaking with Master Sergeant Gutsy, leave the room and drop to the first-floor foyer. You find a Uniform Disbursement Log on the desk in the center of the room. Take it to discover the location of a Uniform Voucher.

ITEM ➡	> UNIFORM DISBURSEMENT LOG

Exit the building and head to the barracks on the base's south side. Enter the first set of barracks. The Uniform Voucher is in a container somewhere in this building. It changes every time you do this quest, so we can only tell you it's in this building.

ITEM ➡	> UNIFORM VOUCHER

Take the voucher back into the first-floor foyer of the main building and use the Uniform Dispenser to get your fatigues and helmet. Go into your inventory and equip the Dirty Army Fatigues and Dirty Army Helmet, both of which are under the Apparel tab in the Item menu. Once you're geared up, head back up to Master Sergeant Gutsy to continue your training.

ITEMS ➡	> DIRTY ARMY FATIGUES > DIRTY ARMY HELMET

Your next task is to complete each of the camp's three basic training courses: Marksmanship, Agility, and Patriotism. You can do these in any order, but we're going to start with the Agility course.

AGILITY COURSE

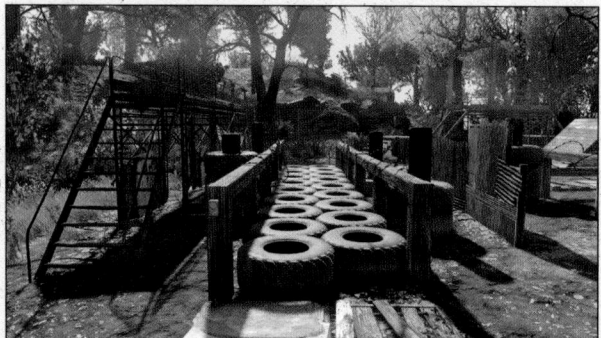

Use the training terminal and select "Begin Course" when you're ready to go. You'll have two minutes to run through the obstacle course and hit every button along the way. Follow the objective markers and make sure to walk or crawl through any marked obstacle; it's not enough to simply hit the buttons. If you miss an objective marker, the next set won't appear, so be thorough. You need to keep moving, but don't rush.

PATRIOTISM COURSE

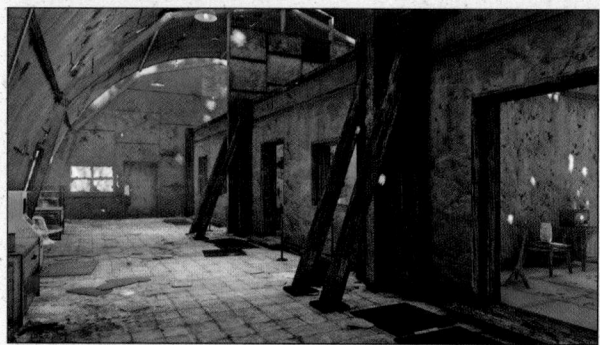

This is a test of your ability to root out Commie threats to the good and decent people of the U.S. of A. You'll need to investigate Jimmy's, Topher's, and Jianjun's rooms, and speak with each of them to figure out who bleeds red and who bleeds red, white, and blue. Once you feel you have enough evidence to support your argument, head back to the Patriotism Training Terminal to make your accusation.

A Helpful Hint from Vault Boy

We could tell you who the culprit is, but the answer is so obvious that only a Commie wouldn't be able to see it from the word "go."

MARKSMAN COURSE

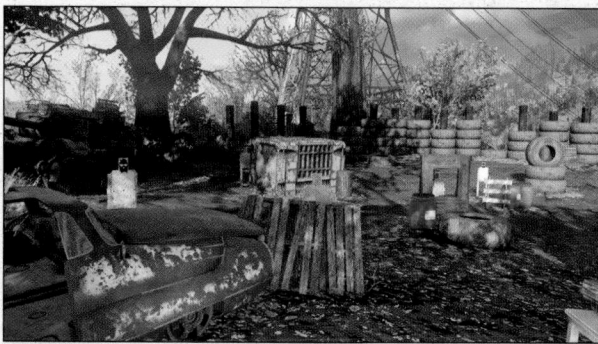

You'll have 30 seconds to hit all the targets as quickly as possible. Before starting, equip a weapon with decent range and a fast fire rate—something explosive is totally acceptable as well. Once you hit "Begin Course," you'll have a short countdown before all of the targets pop up in front of you. Shoot them all within the time to complete the course.

LIVE FIRE

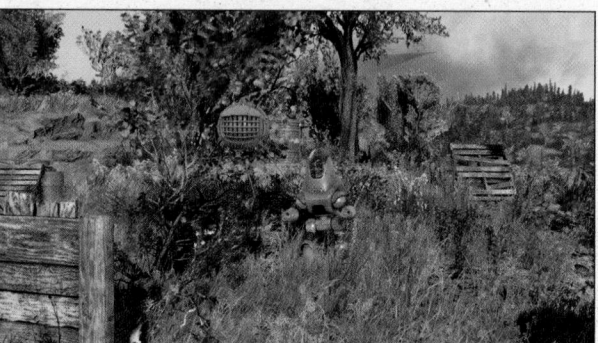

Now that you've got the speed of a cheetah, the aim of a trickshooter, and the wits of fiction's finest detective, it's time to put your life on the line with a live fire exercise. Head southwest out of the base to reach the live fire test grounds.

You must defeat and destroy three waves of "Communist" robots to complete this leg of the quest. There are no tricks to this objective. Simply use your natural ability to shoot and dodge your way to victory. Be warned that the last will drop tougher enemies on you, so be sure to reload and heal up between waves.

After you finish the Live Fire Training Exercise, head back to the Master Sergeant and report your results to complete the quest.

FASCINATING FACTS FROM VAULT BOY

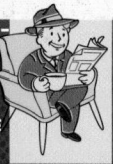

IF YOU WERE COMPLETING THIS QUEST AS PART OF "RECRUITMENT BLUES," HOP BACK TO THAT TEXT TO SEE WHAT TO DO NEXT.

Quest RECRUITMENT BLUES

OBJECTIVES	LOCATIONS TO EXPLORE	REWARDS
– TAKE THE ELEVATOR TO THE TOP FLOOR.	– FORT DEFIANCE	– BOS FIELD SCRIBE OUTFIT
– REGISTER FOR ELEVATOR SECURITY.	– CAMP MCCLINTOCK	– ULTRACITE LASER PISTOL
– SEARCH FOR CLUES TO BYPASS SECURITY.	– CHARLESTON	– FUSION CELL AMMO
– COMPLETE "BACK TO BASIC."	– CHARLESTON CAPITOL DMV	– A RANDOM AID ITEM
– SURVIVE THE DMV.	– CHARLESTON CAPITOL COURTHOUSE	**PREREQUISITES**
– REGISTER FOR THE BROTHERHOOD OF STEEL.		– COMPLETE "DEFIANCE HAS
– INVESTIGATE THE BROTHERHOOD AND SCORCHBEASTS.		FALLEN."

CRACKING THE CODE

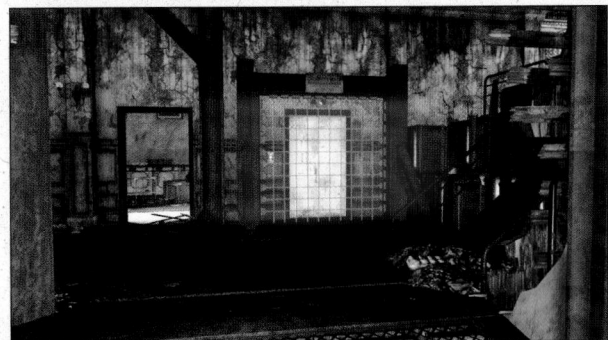

Starting from the bulletin board where you finished "Defiance Has Fallen," look to the right and head into the opening ahead. Take another right to find an elevator with a laser grid blocking your path.

You must register yourself on the fort's security system. To do that, head back to the bulletin board. Now follow the hall and up the first ramp you see. Follow the hall on the second floor and climb the metal stairs at the end. Take the hall on the third floor and eventually you'll come to another laser-grid-blocked elevator. Use the terminal in front of the laser grid and select "Register new personnel." Access will be denied, which means we have to find clues on how to bypass security.

Head to the room at the hall's other end and read the note on the set of shelves near the middle of the room labeled "Squire Evelyn's Journal—Page 16."

ITEM ➡	ᐳ SQUIRE EVELYN'S JOURNAL—PAGE 16

You need a military-issue ID, which you can obtain by completing basic training at Camp McClintock. If you've done that already, you must have your ID printed. Buckle up, because you're going to the DMV.

FASCINATING FACTS FROM VAULT BOY

IN ORDER TO PROGRESS WITH "RECRUITMENT BLUES," YOU MUST FIRST COMPLETE "BACK TO BASIC." THEY ARE INSEPARABLY LINKED, SO DOING ONE WILL ALLOW YOU TO PROGRESS IN THE OTHER. IF YOU'VE ALREADY COMPLETED "BACK TO BASIC." SKIP TO THE NEXT STEP.

THREE LETTERS, ENDLESS DREAD

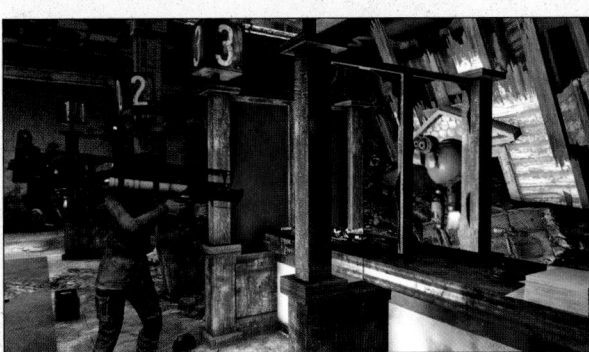

Your next stop is the Charleston Capitol Building southwest of your location. Enter the Charleston Capitol DMV building. Use the terminal on the room's left side and select "Government ID Application." Fill out the information, then approach DMV Bot B2. Print a number from the printer to the robot's right, then head to the computer terminal in the center of the room. Select "Boot up Department B." The DMV Bots now start working their way through the numbers. Fight off waves of Feral Ghouls as you wait for your number to be called.

Once your number is called, speak with DMV Bot B2; then leave the building. Head west from the DMV and follow the objective marker to an old mailbox on the ground. Pull the Junk Mail out of it, and then reenter the DMV.

ITEM ➡	ᐳ JUNK MAIL

Hand the Junk Mail over to DMV Bot B2 and he tells you that you need to get YET ANOTHER form.

EVEN IN THE APOCALYPSE THE DMV IS THE WORST

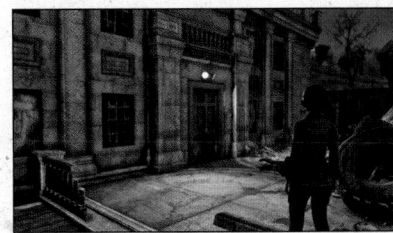

Exit the DMV again and head west a short distance to reach the Charleston Capitol Courthouse. Drop to the bottom floor and grab the DMV form.

ITEM ➡	ᐳ BLANK DMV-AT-21C-V FORM

With form in hand, head back to the DMV yet again. Hand the form to DMV Bot B2, and then openly weep when he tells you you're in the wrong department. Speak with DMV Bot C1; then use the number printer next to him. Use the terminal in the center of the room, select "Boot up Department C," and fight over Feral Ghouls while waiting for your number to be called. Once your number is called, talk to DMV Bot C1. Wait for him to finish his awful, awful coffee break, and then have an emotional breakdown when he asks you to obtain a birth certificate.

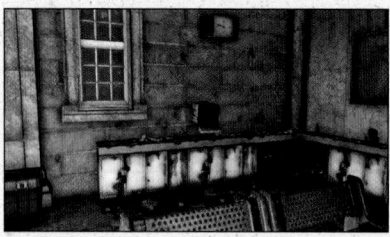

Use the terminal on the room's west side to learn about Error 34B/1. As DMV Bot C1 mentioned earlier, the error occurred because you don't have a valid birth certificate. You must use a stamp from the governor's office in order to validate your application. Head through the doors on the room's south side and continue south; then go west to find the Governor's Seal. Use it to stamp your document, and return to the DMV to turn it in. Get your picture taken and you'll earn your ID. Now let's get back to Fort Defiance.

ITEMS ➡
> **BLANK DMV-AT-21C FORM (STAMPED)**
> **MILITARY ID CARD**

BECOMING THE BROTHERHOOD

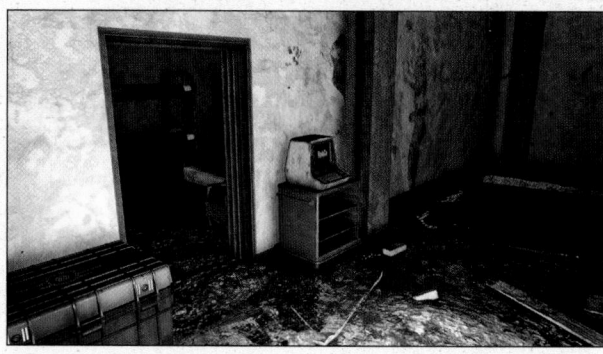

Once inside Fort Defiance, head through the left door and go to the top of the building. Once you reach the terminal, select "Register new personnel" and then "Scan military ID card." You are now a full-fledged member of the Brotherhood of Steel.

With your name registered in the Brotherhood of Steel database, you are now free to use the elevator. Head to the fourth floor and enter the room at the end of the hall on the left. At the computer terminal here, select "URGENT: Touchdown Recovery" to complete the quest.

The next quest, "Belly of the Beast," begins immediately after concluding this one.

Quest BELLY OF THE BEAST

OBJECTIVES
- USE THE BROTHERHOOD EMERGENCY TRANSPONDER RADIO TO FIND TAGGERDY.
- SEARCH TAGGERDY'S REMAINS.
- LEARN MORE ABOUT THE SCORCHED AT TAGGERDY'S QUARTERS.

PREREQUISITES
- COMPLETE "RECRUITMENT BLUES."

LOCATIONS TO EXPLORE
- SURVEY CAMP ALPHA
- DROP SITE V9
- GLASSED CAVERN
- FORT DEFIANCE

REWARDS
- ULTRACITE POWER ARMOR (FULL SET)
- RANDOM LEGENDARY WEAPON OR ARMOR
- RANDOM WEAPON PLAN
- RANDOM AID ITEM
- PHOTO FRAME

TRANSPONDER HUNTING

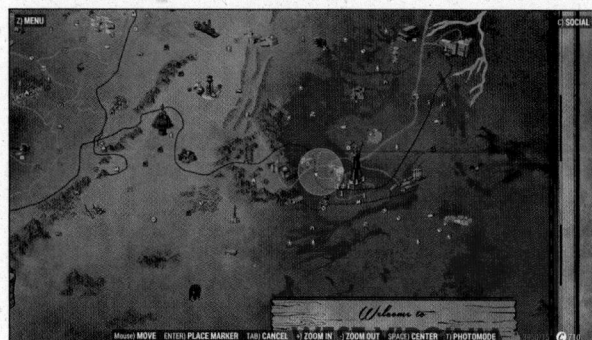

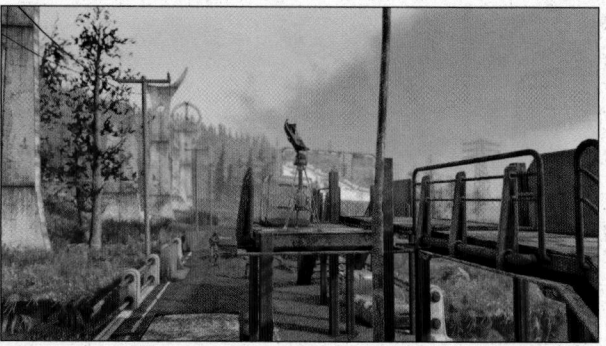

If you're still in Fort Defiance after completing the last quest, exit the building and head northeast. When you enter the boundary of the quest objective, turn on the Brotherhood Emergency Transponder radio station. You need to use periodically use the signal strength indicator that appears in the screen's top-left corner to locate a transponder. You'll find the first transponder atop a bridge near the center of the circle. Sync with the transponder; then head east to search for a second one.

THE SECOND TRANSPONDER

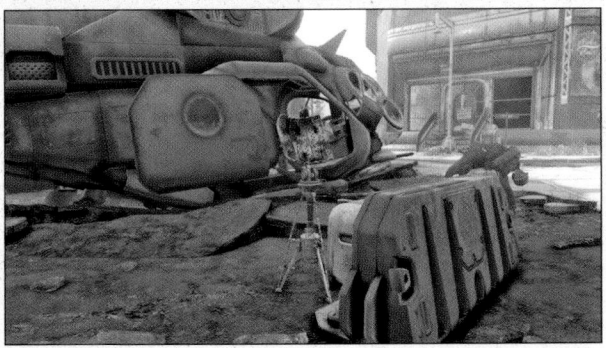

The next transponder is in the center of the circle. It's sitting next to a crashed aircraft. When you find it, sync with the transponder and continue east.

THE THIRD TRANSPONDER

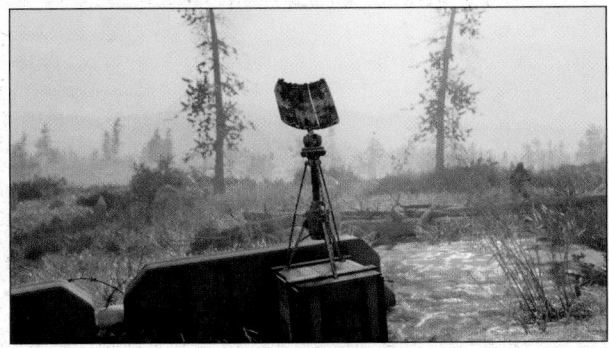

The third transponder is in Survey Camp Alpha slightly to the left of the circle's center. When you've synced with the transponder, continue east.

WORD OF WARNING FROM VAULT BOY!

TAKE CARE WHILE HEADING TO THE NEXT TRANSPONDER. IF YOU'RE HEADING DIRECTLY EAST FROM SURVEY CAMP ALPHA, YOU'LL WALK RIGHT PAST A FISSURE SITE. THIS AREA CONTAINS HIVES FOR THE SCORCHED AND SCORCHBEASTS AND IS NOT GENERALLY MEANT FOR INDIVIDUAL PLAYERS TO CHALLENGE, AT LEAST NOT AT THIS STAGE IN THE GAME.

THE FOURTH TRANSPONDER

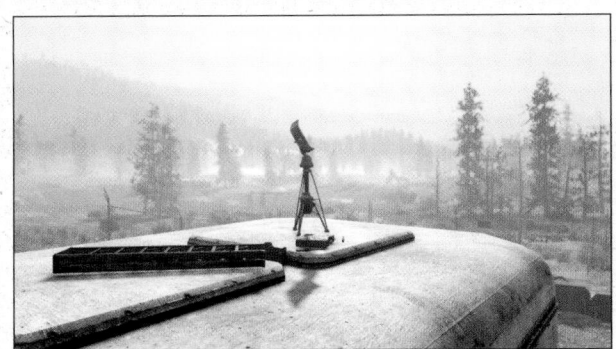

The fourth transponder is atop Drop Site V9 just left of the circle's center. Sync with it, and then head east until you reach the Glassed Cavern.

DANGER AROUND EVERY TURN

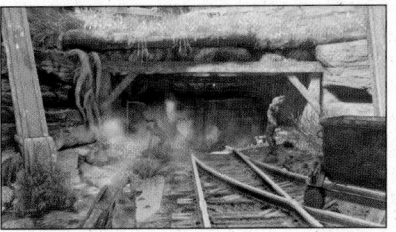

Things start out quiet in the Glassed Cavern, but they definitely don't end that way. Use the Brotherhood Emergency Transponder and the objective marker to find your way through the cave (the Atlas section also has a handy detailed map that makes navigating this area a breeze).

The cavern containing the transponder is also home to a living Scorchbeast. You must fight it and its Scorched minions in order to reach the transponder. It's not an easy fight, so make sure you're prepared when your transponder starts receiving 50 percent signal.

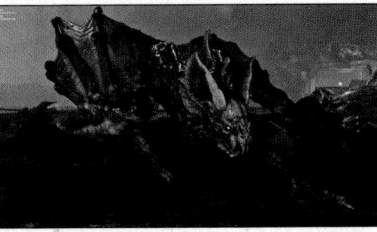

The cave's restricted space definitely favors you and not the Scorchbeast in this fight. It won't take flight, limiting its mobility tremendously, but that doesn't mean it's not still a complete killer. It shoots out energy waves from its mouth repeatedly, which is the attack you'll spend the most time avoiding. Spring to the left or right of the Scorchbeast while it's shooting these waves and you'll have a good chance of avoiding them completely.

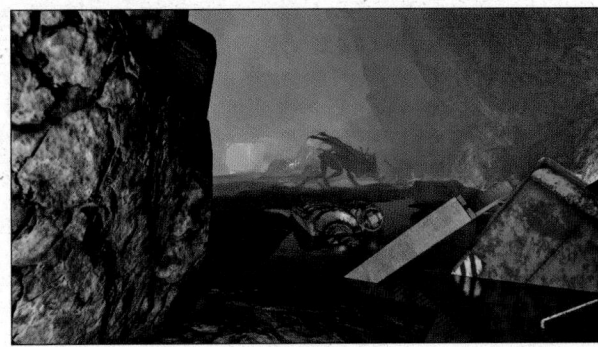

Keep your distance and use the rocky terrain to your advantage. Getting in close will push the Scorchbeast to swat at you with its claws and release a burst of toxic gas into the air around it. Use the giant rock near the room's center to keep the Scorchbeast away from you, and take potshots at it while it tries to catch up. If you have any mines, place them while you run—the Scorchbeast sets them off when it follows you.

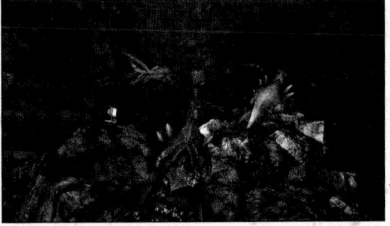

After defeating the Scorchbeast and its lackies, investigate the transponder and Taggerdy's body next to it. Loot Taggerdy's ID, then return to Fort Defiance.

ITEM ➡ **> LIEUTENANT ELIZABETH TAGGERDY'S ID**

TRAINING

CRAFTING AND C.A.M.P.ING

INVENTORY

QUESTS

ATLAS

BESTIARY

APPENDICES

WHAT ARE THE SCORCHED?

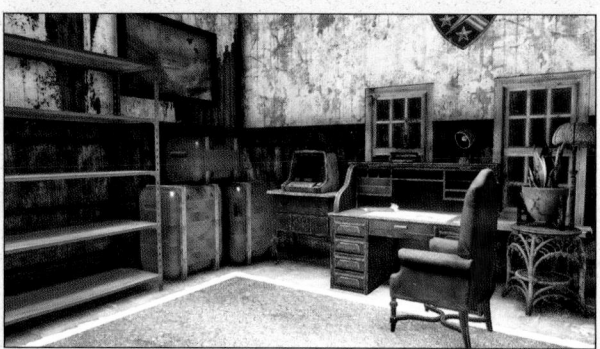

Once back in Fort Defiance, head through the door on the left; then make an immediate right to reach the elevator. Take the elevator to the fourth floor. Use Taggerdy's terminal and select "Ultimate Solution" to finish the quest.

You'll start the next quest, "Uncle Sam," immediately after this one.

Quest UNCLE SAM

OBJECTIVES
- SEARCH THE CHARLESTON HERALD FOR INFO ON SAM BLACKWELL.
- FIND SAM BLACKWELL'S BUNKER.

LOCATIONS TO EXPLORE
- CHARLESTON HERALD
- ABANDONED WASTE DUMP

REWARDS
- RANDOM AMMO AND AID ITEM

PREREQUISITES
- COMPLETE "BELLY OF THE BEAST."

A STUDY OF SAM

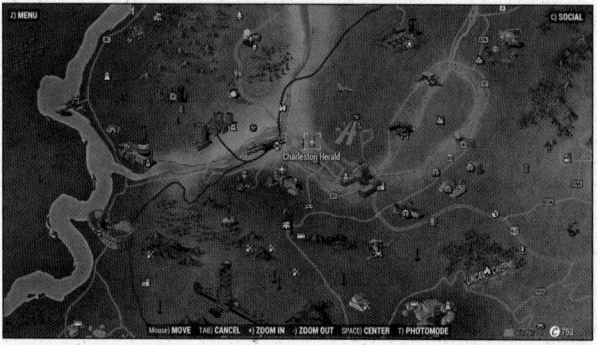

Fast-Travel to Charleston Herald. If you don't have it as a Fast-Travel location, visit any Charleston location (all of which are in the southwest corner of the map, right on the border of the Ash Heap). Follow the objective marker into the nearby building and read the note hidden inside a box of papers on the upper floor of the Herald.

ITEM ➡	❯ SAM BLACKWELL INTERVIEW NOTES

WHAT A DUMP!

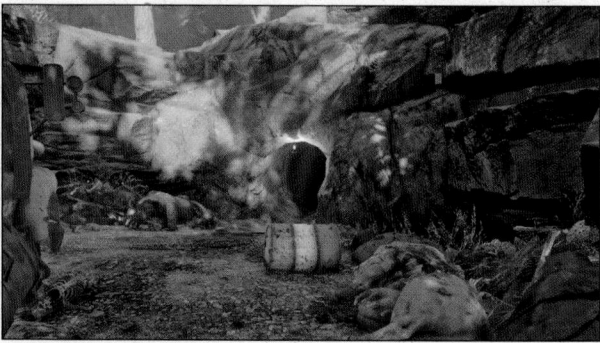

Sam Blackwell's Bunker is on the map's east side, hidden deep in the Deathclaw-filled Abandoned Waste Dump. Find the dump east of Route 65 in the Mire.

Finding the bunker's entrance can be a bit of a challenge. As we mentioned before, the dump is no stranger to Deathclaws and you'll find a couple of them every time you enter these caves.

Once you reach the elevator, use the control panel. You're denied access and the quest concludes, but you start "Bunker Buster" immediately afterward.

Quest BUNKER BUSTER

OBJECTIVES

- SEARCH THE AREA FOR A WAY INSIDE THE BUNKER.
- SEARCH THE CAVERN FOR THE "BYPASS HOLOTAPE."
- USE THE "BYPASS HOLOTAPE" TO GRANT YOURSELF ACCESS TO THE BUNKER.
- ENTER THE BUNKER.
- EXPLORE THE BUNKER.
- FIND A WAY TO BYPASS THE BUNKER'S LASER GRID.
- REGISTER YOUR HANDPRINT WITH THE SECURITY SYSTEM.
- EXPLORE THE BUNKER'S SECURE ROOM.
- INVESTIGATE THE SOUND COMING FROM THE PAINTING.
- LISTEN TO THE HOLOTAPE "WELCOME TO THE WHITESPRING."

LOCATIONS TO EXPLORE

- ABANDONED WASTE DUMP

REWARDS

- DEATHCLAW GAUNTLET
- RANDOM AMMO
- RANDOM AID ITEM
- RANDOM ARMOR MOD

PREREQUISITES

- COMPLETE "UNCLE SAM."

HUNTING FOR HOLOTAPES

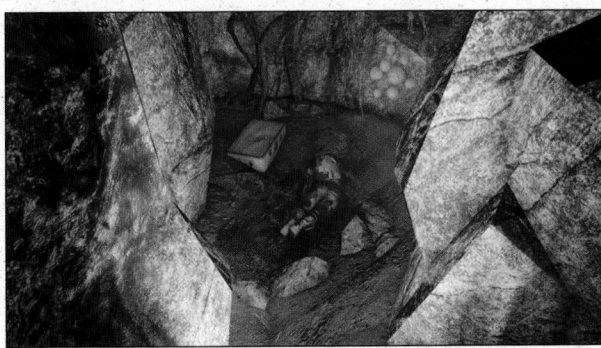

Head to the cave's northern corner to find an agent's body. Loot the Operation Summary—Blackwell Holotape off of it.

ITEM ➡	> OPERATION SUMMARY—BLACKWELL HOLOTAPE

Listening to the tape will reveal the existence of a Bypass Holotape, which you can use to crack through Blackwall's bunker security. You must search through the Deathclaw Nests (the pile of refuse on the ground) around the cave to find the holotape. When you find it, take it back to the elevator.

ITEM ➡	> BYPASS HOLOTAPE

While in the elevator, pull up your Pip-Boy and use the Bypass Holotape under the Holo tab in your Items menu. This unlocks the panel to the elevator, giving you full access to its functions. You can now use the elevator to enter Sam Blackwell's bunker.

MISSION: IMPREGNABLE

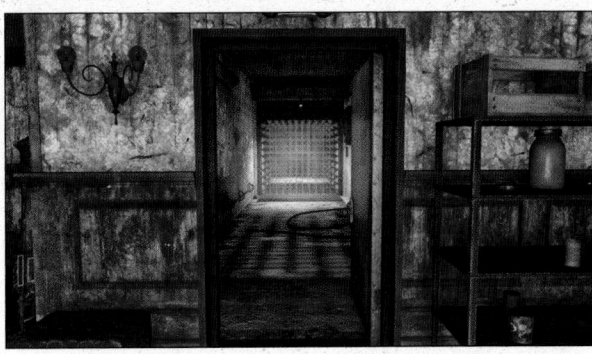

Once in the bunker, head down the stairs and through the blue door ahead of you. Take the northern door to reach a laser grid; you must find a way to pass this laser grid if you want to have any hope of exploring deeper into the bunker.

Turn around, head back up the stairs, and exit the bunker's main room. Hang a right and head through the door. Follow the path until it dead ends at a room with a large set of blue machinery. One of those machines is a computer terminal that you can hack to shut off the laser grid below. If you don't have the Hacking skill level to break through, you can force a system restart by following these three steps:

1. FROM THE BLUE TERMINAL ROOM, BACKTRACK UNTIL YOU'RE ON THE CATWALK IN THE CENTER OF THE PREVIOUS ROOM. WALK ONTO THE AIR 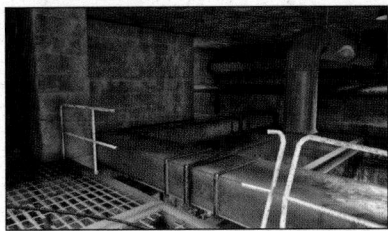 DUCTS AHEAD AND HEAD LEFT. NOW PRESS THE SWITCH ON THE WALL TO ACTIVATE THE CIRCUIT CONDUIT.

2. RETURN TO THE BUNKER'S MAIN ROOM AND HEAD THROUGH THE DOOR ON THE LEFT. OPEN THE CIRCUIT BREAKER LID TO THE LEFT OF THE 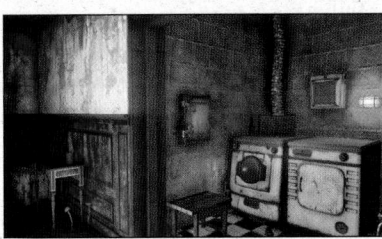 WASHING MACHINE, AND ACTIVATE THE CIRCUIT BREAKER.

3. HEAD TO THE DOOR ON THE OTHER SIDE OF THE BUNKER'S MAIN ROOM. TAKE THE FIRST LEFT, AND ACTIVATE THE AIR FLUE VALVE STATIONED ON THE 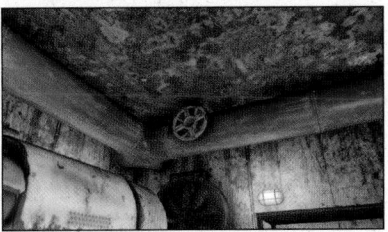 PIPES IN THE ROOM'S TOP-LEFT CORNER (ABOVE THE TWO RED LIGHTS).

After you perform a system reboot or hack the terminal, return to the laser grid room and use the hand scanner to register yourself and gain control over the grid.

021584

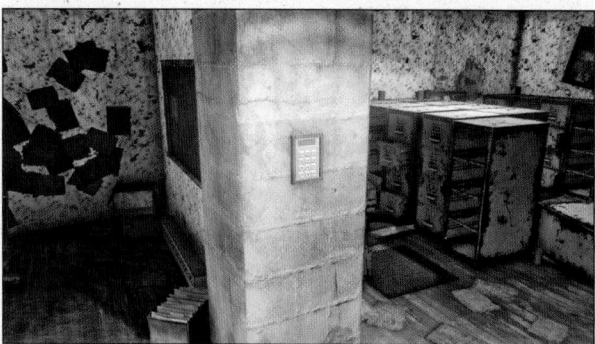

There's a keypad on the dividing wall in the center of the room. Sam Blackwell has some well-guarded secrets in here, but to reach them you must crack that code.

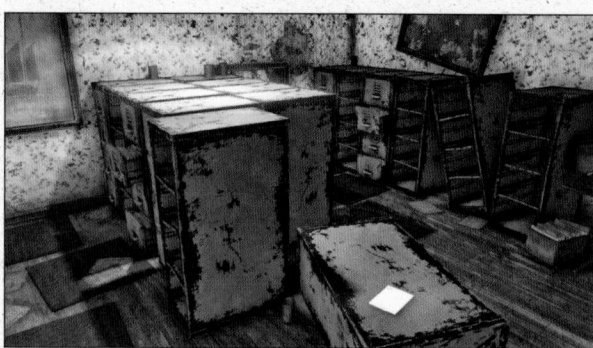

Return to the room and search through the filing cabinets. One of them contains the "Senate Orientation Letter," another holds "Record of Divorce: The Blackwells," and a third has "Intelligence Memo—8/16/77." Find and read all three, and then read the "Judy's Gone" entry on Sam's terminal. One of these holds Sam Blackwell's access code.

ITEMS ➡	> SENATE ORIENTATION LETTER
	> RECORD OF DIVORCE: THE BLACKWELLS
	> INTELLIGENCE MEMO—8/16/77

Approach the keypad mounted on the wall separating the first half of the room from the second, and input the codes until one of them works.

SAM I AM

After inputting the proper code, return to the other half of the room and investigate the indicated painting. You'll get the Welcome to The Whitespring Holotape and the Congressional Access Card from the back of the painting.

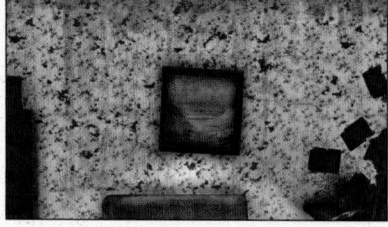

| ITEMS ➡ | > WELCOME TO THE WHITESPRING HOLOTAPE |
| | > CONGRESSIONAL ACCESS CARD |

Listen to the Welcome to The Whitespring Holotape to complete the quest and start "One of Us."

Quest ONE OF US

OBJECTIVES
- EXPLORE THE WHITESPRING BUNKER.
- MEET THE BUNKER'S RESIDENT.
- LOAD THE SYSTEM ACCESS TAPE INTO A SIGINT SYSTEM TERMINAL.
- COLLECT MODUS' LOST DATA.
- DEPLOY THE UPLINK MODULE AT THE CONNECTION SITE.

LOCATIONS TO EXPLORE
- THE WHITESPRING BUNKER
- SUGAR GROVE
- RADIO ASTRONOMY RESEARCH CENTER

REWARDS
- BUNKER BUSTER (MODDED MISSILE LAUNCHER)
- ORBITAL STRIKE BEACON (WEAPON)
- ORBITAL STRIKE BEACON SCHEMATIC
- ORBITAL SCAN BEACON (WEAPON)
- ORBITAL SCAN BEACON SCHEMATICS
- RANDOM AMMO
- RANDOM AID
- RANDOM PLAN
- PHOTO FRAME

PREREQUISITES
- COMPLETE "BUNKER BUSTERS."

MODUS OPERANDI

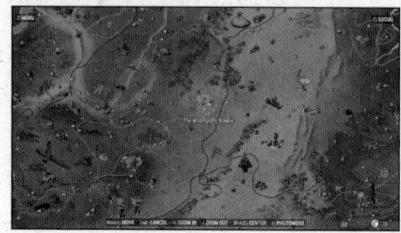

The Whitespring Resort, if you recall, is located almost directly south of Top of the World. We mentioned visiting it when you were tasked with making Explosive Bait for Rose; if you took that advice, you can simply Fast-Travel there now. If not, you can Fast-Travel to either Top of the World or 98 NAR Regional and head south to the The Whitespring Bunker.

The bunker entrance is blocked by a vault door, but a mysterious figure inside the bunker will open it and let you in. Accept his invitation and enter.

WORD OF WARNING FROM VAULT BOY!

YOU MIGHT BE TEMPTED TO CAUSE A LITTLE HAVOC ONCE INSIDE THE BUNKER BY SHOOTING SOME OF THE ROBOTS PATROLLING ABOUT, BUT RESTRAIN YOURSELF! THIS PLACE IS A FORTRESS AND CAN QUICKLY DISPATCH ANY INTERLOPERS WITHIN, AS WELL AS WITHOUT. HOLSTER YOUR WEAPON, OR FACE THE CONSEQUENCES OF AN ITCHY TRIGGER FINGER.

IN OTHER WORDS: SHOOT A GUN AND YOU'RE DONE.

Make your way down the right corridor. Approach the marked button and press it to have your picture taken. Head over to the dispenser slightly to your left and activate it to obtain some Operative Underarmor, courtesy of the house. Now head through the "Orientation" door and go downstairs.

| ITEM ➡ | > OPERATIVE UNDERARMOR |

EXAM WEEK

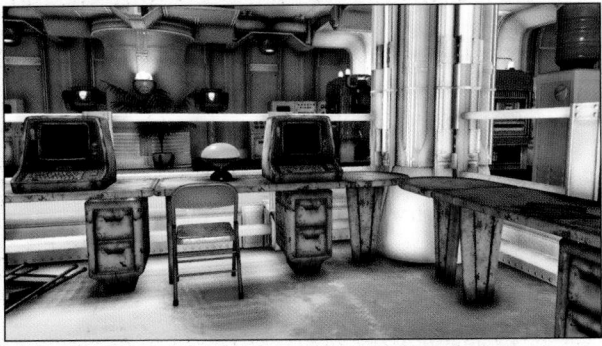

After speaking with our benevolent host, head farther downstairs by following the passage to the left. MODUS will request that you take an exam to prove your intelligence. If you're not in the mood, or find tests anxiety provoking, you can use the MODUS terminal behind the testing computer to skip the exam altogether. Scoring well on the test is recommended; MODUS will immediately reward you for any score higher than four points, and send backup to aid you later if you score well enough.

Helpful Hints from Vault Boy

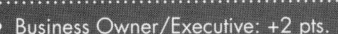

The first two questions tell MODUS about your personality. Here's how points are awarded:

- Business Owner/Executive: +2 pts.
- Lawyer: +1 pt.
- Military/Law Enforcement: +0 pts.
- Doctor/Scientist: +2 pts.
- Agriculture/Food Service: +0 pts.
- Other: +0 pts.
- St. Thomas Aquinas: +1 pt.
- Adam Smith: +3 pts.
- John Stuart Mill: +2 pts.
- Karl Marx: +0 pts.
- Elvis: +1 pt.

The last three questions have factual answers:

- Ulysses S. Grant was the 18th president of the United States.
- An oyster fork is the only one that goes on the right side of the plate.
- General Constantine Chase led the reclamation of Anchorage, Alaska.

MODUS will grant you an item based off the result of the examination and a System Access Tape, which you'll need to help him hack into a SigInt System terminal in Sugar Grove, near Route 65.

ITEM ➤	❯ SYSTEM ACCESS TAPE

CORPORATE ESPIONAGE

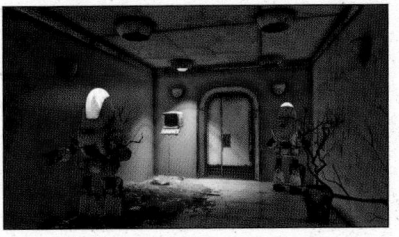

Fast-Travel to Camp Venture on the east side of the Appalachia (on the border between Cranberry Bog and the Ash Heap); then head toward the objective marker to reach Sugar Grove. The southern door requires a key to open, but the northern door is available with the touch of a button on a nearby computer terminal.

Go downstairs to the SigInt System terminal and insert the System Access Tape; then follow the terminal prompts. Head up a floor and use the Archival Dispenser to get MODUS's lost data. Fast-Travel back to The Whitespring Bunker.

THIS IS DEFINITELY A GOOD IDEA

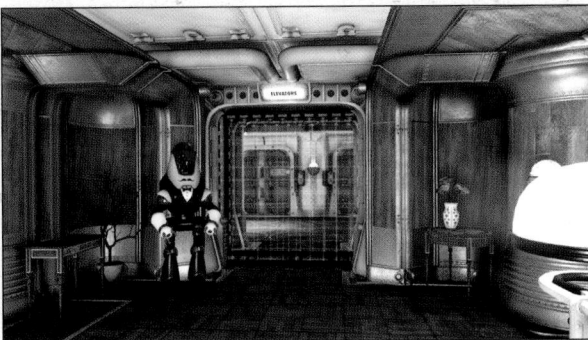

Once back in The Whitespring Bunker, use the control panel to open the vault door back into the bunker. This time, instead of heading to the right to enter the room where you got your picture taken, take a left through the laser grid. Use the elevator to reach the exam room. Follow MODUS's directions and he'll pass you an Uplink Module with instructions to install it.

ITEMS ➤	❯ MODULE INSTRUCTIONS
	❯ UPLINK MODULE

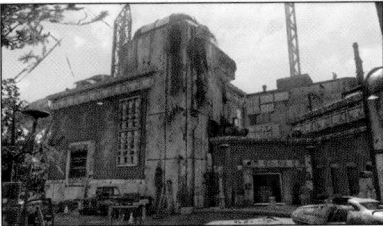

Just south of Sugar Grove (or between the National Isolated Radio Array and Camp Venture) is the Radio Astronomy Research Center, which is your next destination. Enter the building and head to the top floor to reach the roof. Insert the Uplink Module on the Connection Platform machine on the research center roof.

Leave the research center and head east along the road a short distance to find a care package containing both an Orbital Scan Beacon and an Orbital Strike Beacon. Grab the care package's contents, and head back to The Whitespring Bunker. Take the elevator back down to the exam room and speak with MODUS to complete the quest.

ITEMS ➤	❯ ORBITAL SCAN BEACON
	❯ ORBITAL STRIKE BEACON

OFFICER ON DECK

OBJECTIVES	REWARDS
– SPEAK WITH MODUS IN THE BUNKER MILITARY WING.	– LAST BASTION (MODDED URBAN ENCLAVE ARMOR TORSO)
– REGISTER WITH THE PROMOTION SYSTEM.	– ENCLAVE OFFICER'S UNIFORM
– EARN PROMOTION COMMENDATION.	– ENCLAVE OFFICER'S HAT
LOCATION	– RANDOM AID ITEM
– THE WHITESPRING BUNKER	– PHOTO FRAME
	PREREQUISITE
	– COMPLETE "ONE OF US."

COMMENDABLE

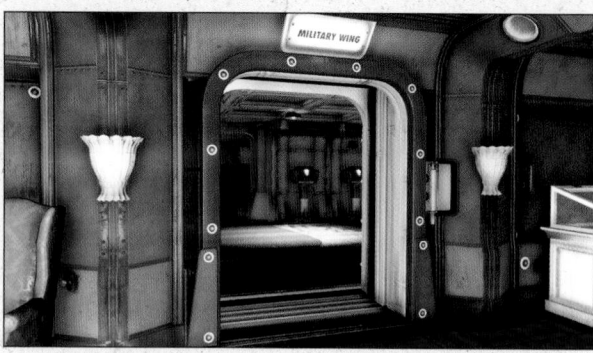

Make your way to the Military Wing. Go through the laser grid in the exam room, head downstairs, and go to the end of the restaurant. Take the door on the left, then head down the stairs. The Military Wing is through the first door on your left.

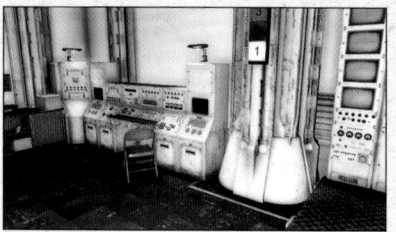

As soon as you enter the Military Wing, MODUS begins explaining the American military's nuclear system (more on that later). Once he's finished, use the terminal in the room's back corner to activate the Automated Promotion System.

From here, you must rise up the ranks of The Whitespring Automated Promotion System, which requires you to complete a myriad of tasks and objectives to earn Promotion Commendations. Earn enough and you'll gain a promotion; get promoted enough and you'll gain power and influence in The Whitespring Bunker, which unlocks some fascinating new opportunities.

Let's break down how Promotion Commendations work:

- Basic Combat Commendations: earned by killing Epic Creatures with three or fewer stars next to their names. Each time you accomplish this, you'll earn a single Commendation.

- High-Risk Combat Commendations: earned by killing Scorchbeasts or Epic Creatures with four or five stars next to their names. Every time you kill a creature that falls into one of these categories, you'll earn a single Commendation.

- You'll also earn Commendations for completing Enclave Events. Completing "Dropped Connection" and "Bots on Parade" earn one Commendation each; "A Real Blast" earns two Commendations.

Once you have enough Commendations, you'll be promoted automatically and the quest will conclude. The next quest, "I Am Become Death," begins immediately after.

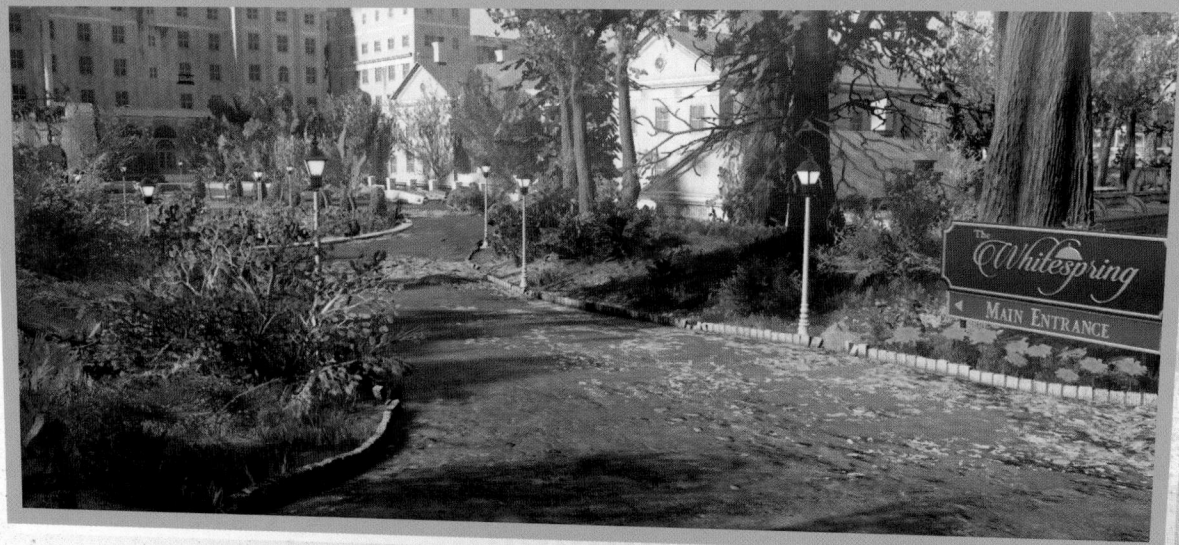

Quest I AM BECOME DEATH

TRAINING

CRAFTING AND C.A.M.P.ING

INVENTORY

QUESTS

ATLAS

BESTIARY

APPENDICES

OBJECTIVES	LOCATIONS
– EXPLORE THE WHITESPRING COMMAND CENTER.	– THE WHITESPRING BUNKER
– COMPLETE ALL THE NUCLEAR TRAINING TUTORIALS.	– MAMA DOLCE'S FOOD PROCESSING
– SPEAK TO MODUS.	– FUJINIYA INTELLIGENCE BASE
– ACQUIRE A NUCLEAR CODE PIECE.	**REWARDS**
– SEARCH THE ARCHIVES FOR INFO ON THE LAUNCH CODE ENCRYPTION.	– RANDOM LEGENDARY WEAPON OR ARMOR
– TRACK DOWN INFORMATION ABOUT THE CODE ENCRYPTION.	– ENCLAVE SCOUT UNIFORM
– LAUNCH A NUCLEAR MISSILE.	– GATLING PLASMA
– (OPTIONAL) NUKE FISSURE SITE PRIME [8+ PLAYERS RECOMMENDED].	– FUSION CORE
PREREQUISITES	– RANDOM AID ITEM
– COMPLETE "OFFICER ON DECK."	– PHOTO FRAME

WAR NEVER CHANGES

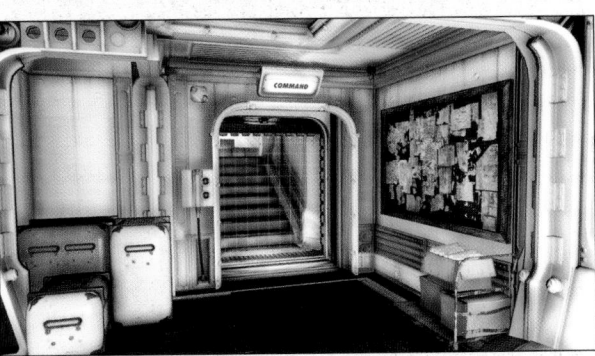

Head back into The Whitespring Bunker and reenter the Military Wing. Take a right and head through the laser grid that has the "Command" label above its door. Go upstairs and you'll receive the task of using each of four terminals; all are meant to teach you the fine art of firing a nuke.

Helpful Hint from Vault-Boy!

Attention! Launching a nuke is not a one-person activity. To accomplish anything, you need to work together with friends and strangers, which means you'll want to talk to others online and see if they've made any strides toward cracking the Launch Codes.

Now let's break the steps down:

- **Step 1:** Obtain a Nuclear Keycard. There are several security measures that have been implemented so that some sociopath with a loathing for humanity can't launch a nuke. You have to locate a Vertibot, which is being escorted somewhere around Appalachia. Shoot it down, then take the Nuclear Keycard out of its supply box. These are single-use keycards, so once you fire a nuke (or if you enter the wrong Launch Code), you'll have to get back out there and track down another Vertibot to find a new card.

- **Step 2:** Obtain the Launch Codes: While exploring Appalachia, you'll occasionally see a Ghoul or Scorched Officer carrying a beacon on its back that beeps loud enough to be heard over vast distances. There are three nuclear missile silos— Alpha, Bravo,

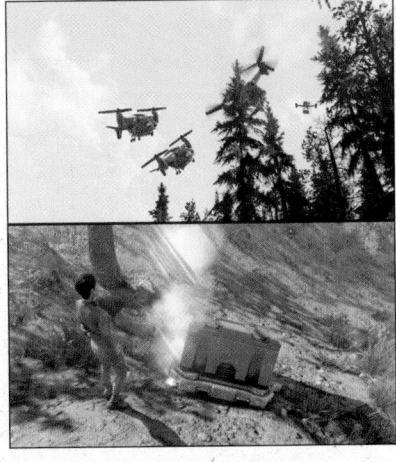

and Charlie. To fire a nuke from any of them, you must gather eight Silo Codes for a specific silo, put the numbers together, then use a cypher key to decode the Launch Code. If that wasn't enough of a challenge, your codes last for only one week before dissolving into nothing.

- We can't tell you the exact method for deciphering the Silo Codes or government assassins will promptly escort us to the afterlife. We'd tell you everything, we swear! But, sadly, our hands are tied and our lips are sealed.

- Wait...were those letters on the wall in the command center always there? It seems like they spell something. It almost looks like

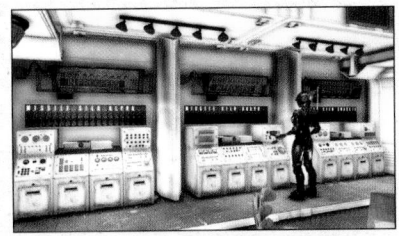

an actual **word**. Whoever created it **is** either a genius or a maniac. We've never been good at de**ciph**ering word scrambles...They take a **kee**n eye that we simple don't possess.

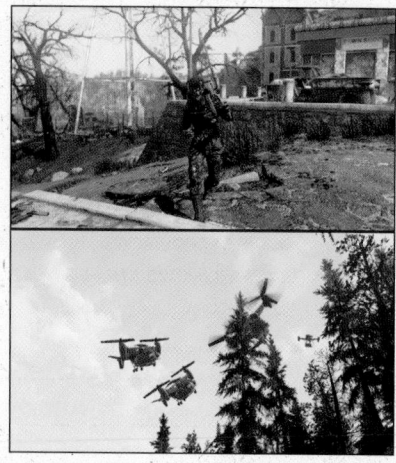

Step 3: Once you have the Nuclear Keycard and the Launch Codes, you must overcome the automated silos. These are some of the toughest areas in the game; if you want to survive them, you must work with a group of people. You'll receive a quest at the start of a silo; completing its objectives is the only way to reach the launch console.

• If you activate each of the pins on the maps inside the command center, the locations of each site will be permanently revealed on your map.

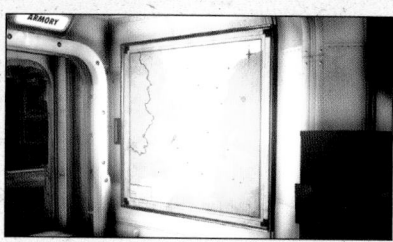

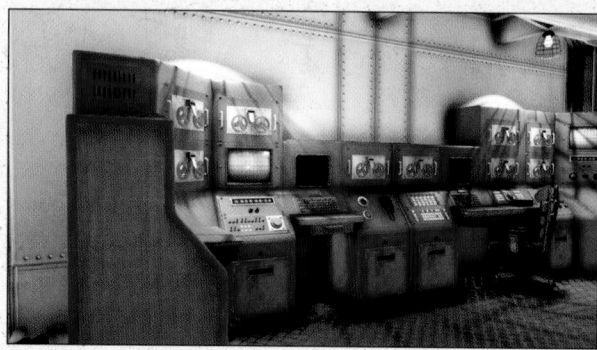

• We can tell you that the solution for the code is global, but it changes from week to week. If someone has figured it out and puts the code online, it will work for you just as well as it worked for them. Once your codes dissolve, you need a fresh code and a new code hunt.

Step 4: Nuclear fallout. After you complete a silo and reach the launch console, you'll be asked to select your target. While the Forest from Vault 76 down to Flatwoods is off-limits, the rest of Appalachia is your plaything. Select a spot, then fire and the area will become irradiated for a time—you'll also kill all players caught in the blast for good measure. While the area is irradiated, the creatures, flora, and mining locations will be transformed. Enemies will be stronger and drop better gear and the obtainable resources will become irradiated versions of themselves, which can only be obtained in a fallout zone.

CRACKING THE CODE

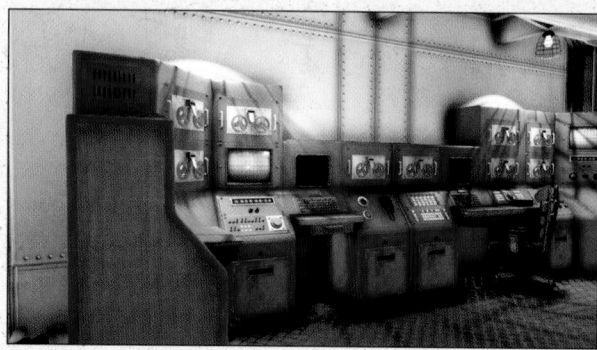

Now it's time to put the pieces together and launch a nuke (undoubtedly with the help of others). First things first, head into the back room and use the terminal. Select Ellen Santiago's archive, then choose "The Code Pieces" entry. You'll receive the Fujiniya Facility Password. You can also use the Surveillance System terminal on the southeast side of the command room to track the location of the Nuclear Keycard and Nuclear Code Pieces. Using it to track either the Keycard or the Code Pieces will initiate the "Hide and Seek and Destroy" quest. Use this quest to locate both until you have everything you need.

ITEM ➡ ❯ FUJINIYA FACILITY PASSWORD

Once you have all eight Code Pieces for a single silo and a Launch Keycard, head to Mama Dolce's Food Processing, right next to Morgantown in the Forest. We're going to learn about how to crack this code.

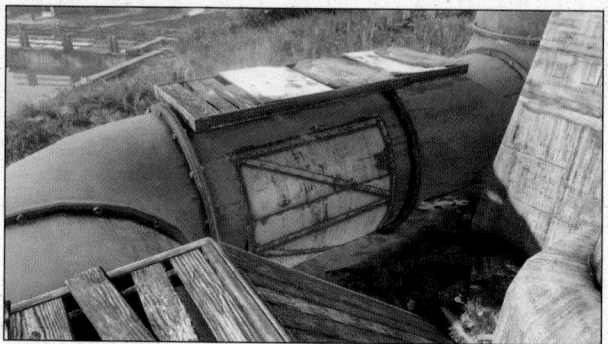

Go to the southeastern corner of Mama Dolce's and drop behind the giant blue pipe. There's a hatch on the pipe's side; head inside it. You'll eventually reach a card-locked door. Use the card reader and enter to reach the Fujiniya Intelligence Base.

PARTY TIME

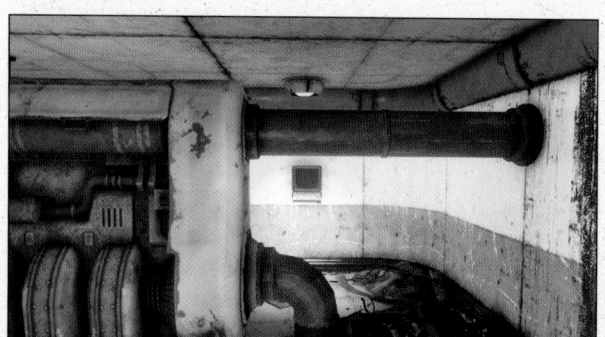

Once you reach the end of the road, open the hatch on your left to enter the base. Head to the lowest floor and follow the objective marker until you reach the open room with the set of tables sitting in front a large piece of blue machinery. Head northwest and use the terminal behind this machinery. Put in the password you acquired in The Whitespring Bunker.

Quest MISSION: COUNTDOWN

LOCATIONS TO EXPLORE
- SITE ALPHA
- SITE BRAVO
- SITE CHARLIE

REWARDS
- MISSILE AMMO
- RANDOM AID ITEM
- RANDOM PLAN, ARMOR, MOD, OR WEAPON
- CHANCE FOR A RANDOM LEGENDARY WEAPON OR LEGENDARY ARMOR

PREREQUISITES
- COMPLETE "OFFICER ON DECK" TO GAIN ACCESS TO THE SILOS.
- COMPLETE "I AM BECOME DEATH" TO ACQUIRE A NUCLEAR KEYCARD AND THE LAUNCH CODE.

DOWN FOR THE COUNT

Mission: Countdown is a gauntlet of enemies and obstacles that will test even the most seasoned band of survivors. If you don't feel up to the challenge just yet, spend more time on other quests and exploration first. Set out for new adventures and return once you've gained the levels, items, perks, and techniques you need to take on this penultimate challenge.

Here's what you're up against:

- EACH SILO HAS FIVE MAJOR EVENTS. IN EACH, YOU'LL HAVE TO TAKE DOWN THE INITIAL DEFENDERS, THEN COMPLETE A SERIES OF OBJECTIVES WHILE HOLDING THE LINE AGAINST AN ENDLESS STREAM OF POWERFUL ROBOTS, INCLUDING ASSAULTRONS, ROBOBRAINS, PROTECTRONS, AND MR. GUTSYS.
- THIS IS A WAR OF ATTRITION. YOUR FOES REALLY ARE ENDLESS, AND AWARD LITTLE EXPERIENCE OR USEFUL LOOT, SO YOU NEED TO PRESS FORWARD AS QUICKLY AS YOU CAN WITHOUT BEING OVERWHELMED. TAKE TOO LONG, AND THEY'LL WEAR YOU DOWN TO THE POINT THAT YOU CAN'T CONTINUE.
- REGARDLESS OF THE SILO YOU SELECT, STUDY THE MAPS, LEARN THE ROUTE, AND KNOW WHERE YOU'RE GOING. EVERY SECOND COUNTS.
- ONLY AFTER YOU COMPLETE ALL FIVE EVENTS CAN YOU ACCESS THE LAUNCH CONTROL SYSTEM. IF YOU'RE HERE TO LAUNCH A NUKE, BE ABSOLUTELY SURE YOU HAVE A NUCLEAR KEYCARD AND THE CORRECT LAUNCH CODE BEFORE YOU GET STARTED. YOU ONLY GET ONE SHOT AT THIS—IF YOU MISTYPE THE CODE (AND DIDN'T BRING AN EXTRA KEYCARD), YOU'LL HAVE TO DO IT ALL OVER AGAIN.
- GLUTTON FOR PUNISHMENT? YOU CAN CHALLENGE MISSION: COUNTDOWN AS OFTEN AS YOU WANT. YOU'LL ONLY EARN THE QUEST'S REWARDS ONCE PER SILO PER DAY.

I DO WANT TO SET THE WORLD ON FIRE

If you're determined to press on, here are some tips to help you prepare:

1. GATHER YOUR TEAM. WHILE IT IS POSSIBLE TO SOLO MISSION: COUNTDOWN, IT'S DRAMATICALLY EASIER TO COMPLETE WITH A TEAM. TALK THINGS OVER WITH YOUR GROUP IN ADVANCE, DISCUSS YOUR BUILDS, AND MAKE SURE EVERYONE KNOWS THEIR ROLE. ARE YOU GOING TO FOCUS ON THE OBJECTIVES FOR EACH EVENT? RUN INTERFERENCE AND TANK THE ENEMY ROBOTS? WHO'S HANDLING SUPPORT SKILLS? IF YOU HAVE A LARGE ENOUGH GROUP, IT MAY BE WORTH HAVING ONE PLAYER SET UP CAMP OUTSIDE THE SILO AND RUN SUPPLIES TO THE REST OF THE GROUP AS THEY PUSH FORWARD.

2. REBUILD YOUR BUILD. THIS IS A GOOD TIME TO REVIEW AND HONE YOUR BUILD. IF THERE ARE PERK CARDS YOU AREN'T TAKING FULL ADVANTAGE OF, DUPLICATE THE ABILITIES OF SOMEONE ELSE ON YOUR TEAM, OR JUST AREN'T USEFUL IN A COMBAT-INTENSIVE ENVIRONMENT (LIKE AQUAGIRL OR WOODCHUCKER), SWAP THEM OUT FOR SOMETHING YOU CAN USE. YOU CAN ALWAYS SWITCH BACK LATER.

3. CONSIDER HACKING AND PICKLOCK. IF YOU'RE ON A TEAM, IT PAYS TO BRING TOP-TIER HACKER AND PICKLOCK SKILLS—BOTH ARE USEFUL THROUGHOUT THE SILO, AND TOGETHER, THEY ALLOW YOU TO SKIP ONE OF THE FIVE EVENTS ENTIRELY.

4. OPTIMIZE YOUR INVENTORY. AT A MINIMUM, YOU'RE GOING TO WANT:

- 2-3 OF YOUR PREFERRED WEAPONS AND HUNDREDS OF ROUNDS OF AMMO. IF THERE'S ANY CHANCE YOU MIGHT RUN OUT, BRING A FALL-BACK WEAPON THAT USES A DIFFERENT TYPE OF AMMO.
- FULLY MODDED AND REPAIRED WEAPONS AND ARMOR. AS YOU REPAIR YOUR GEAR, KEEP TRACK OF THE COMPONENTS YOU USE TO REPAIR IT. YOUR GEAR WILL BREAK DOWN (PROBABLY MULTIPLE TIMES) DURING THIS MISSION, AND THERE'S NO GUARANTEE YOU'LL FIND THE COMPONENTS YOU NEED TO REPAIR IT ALONG THE WAY. MAKE SURE TO BRING THEM WITH YOU.
- THE BEST FOOD AND DRINK YOU CAN FIND. STOCK UP ON STEAKS AND PURIFIED WATER, OR FOCUS ON MEALS THAT FORTIFY YOUR COMBAT ATTRIBUTES.
- ALL THE STIMPAKS YOU CAN CARRY.
- SEVERAL RADAWAYS.
- MEDX, RADX, AND ANY OTHER CHEMS OR ITEMS THAT SUPPORT YOUR BUILD OR PLAYSTYLE.
- A HAZMAT SUIT (FROM "TRACKING UNKNOWNS," OR FOUND RANDOMLY IN THE WORLD), OR THE BEST RADIATION PROTECTION YOU CAN FIND, PLUS EVEN MORE RADX AND RADAWAY.
- EXPLOSIVES. BASIC FRAGMENTATION GRENADES ARE FINE, ALTHOUGH BETTER GRENADES OR A MISSILE LAUNCHER WORK, TOO. GIVEN THE CLOSE QUARTERS, MINI NUKES ARE NOT RECOMMENDED.
- FOR THE STORAGE AREA, ONE PERSON ON YOUR TEAM SHOULD BRING 45 SCRAP STEEL AND 30 CIRCUITS TO QUICKLY REBUILD THE MAINFRAME CORES IN THAT EVENT.

Helpful Hint From Vault Boy

Intent on going it alone? While it is possible for a very well-equipped high-level character (50+) to fight their way through the silo, characters with a focused stealth build will have a much easier time. Your secret agent should focus on:

- Very high Agility
- Sneak Perks
- The Chameleon Mutation
- Armor or Mods that enhance stealth, like the Garb of Mysteries.
- The Covert Operative, Rifleman, and Sandman Perks for one-shot sneak kills.
- High-end Hunting, Lever-Action, or Gauss Rifles.
- Stealth Boys or Umbra Devices, for those times when you have to break cover to use a terminal.

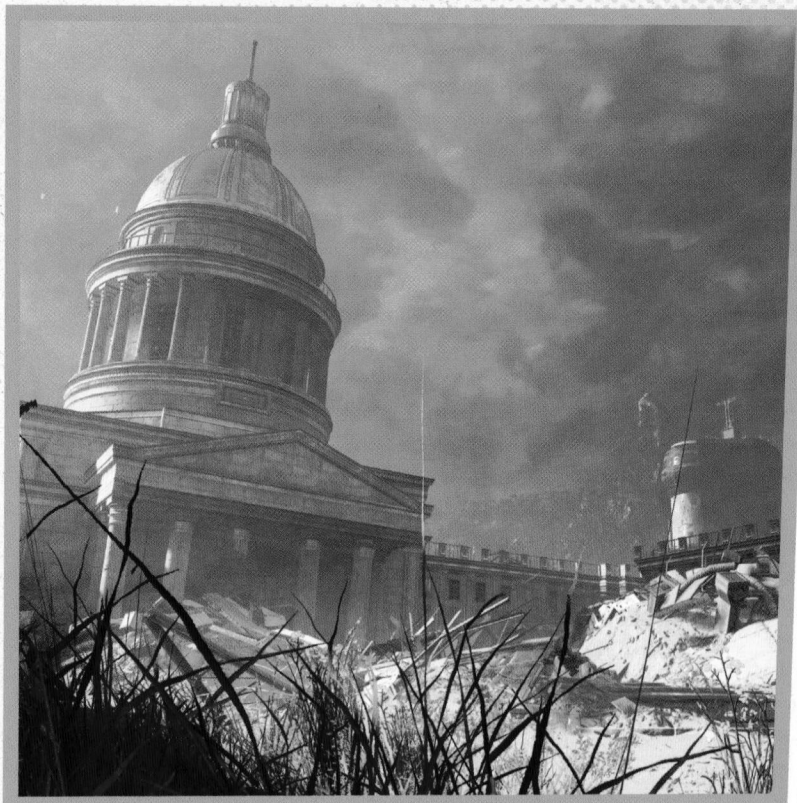

INTO THE FIRE

There are a variety of ways to approach each event, depending on the size of your group and your particular assortment of skills, but a good general strategy is:

- **TAKE A DEEP BREATH.** BEFORE HEADING INTO EACH EVENT SPACE, MAKE SURE YOU'VE HEALED UP, RELOADED YOUR WEAPONS, REPAIRED YOUR GEAR, AND DEALT WITH ANY HUNGER OR THIRST YOU'VE BUILT UP.

- **HACK IN.** EACH EVENT AREA INCLUDES MULTIPLE TERMINALS TO HACK. THE MOST VALUABLE IS USUALLY THE ONE NEAREST THE ENTRANCE, WHICH OFTEN ALLOWS YOU TO FRENZY OR DISABLE THE TURRETS IN THE NEXT FEW ROOMS, AND DEACTIVATE THE ROBOBRAIN SUPERVISOR FOR THAT SECTOR. MANY TERMINALS ALSO PROVIDE SPECIFIC BONUSES THAT ARE WELL WORTH YOUR TIME, SUCH AS ENABLING ALLIED ROBOTS, OR ACTIVATING THE DECONTAMINATION ARCHES IN THE RADIATION-FILLED REACTOR AREA.

- **CLEAR THE ROOM.** IN TWO OF THE FIVE AREAS (REACTOR AND CONTROL), THE SECURITY SYSTEM ISN'T TRIGGERED UNTIL YOU ACTUALLY BEGIN WORKING ON THE TASK FOR THAT AREA. TAKE A MOMENT TO CLEAR OUT THE INITIAL ROBOTS AND TURRETS, ORIENT YOURSELF, AND HEAL UP BEFORE YOU GET TO WORK.

- **YOUR FOES ARE ENDLESS.** ONCE THE SECURITY SYSTEM IS TRIPPED, THE ONLY WAY TO STEM THE TIDE OF SECURITY ROBOTS IS TO FINISH THE EVENT. FOCUS ON COMPLETING THOSE OBJECTIVES!

- **DON'T GET SWARMED.** KEEP AN EYE ON THE ROBOTS, AND DON'T LET YOURSELF GET OVERWHELMED OR BOXED INTO A CORNER. WHILE IT MAY BE TEMPTING TO CONCENTRATE YOUR FIRE ON WEAKER ROBOTS, IT PAYS TO TAKE DOWN THE ASSAULTRONS FIRST— WAIT TOO LONG, AND YOU MAY FIND YOURSELF FACING TWO OR MORE OF THEM SIMULTANEOUSLY. IF THINGS DO GET ROUGH, RETREAT, RECOVER, AND RETRY.

- **FOCUS ON MANDATORY OBJECTIVES.** OUR AGENTS HAVE IDENTIFIED A NUMBER OF OBJECTIVES (MARKED WITH AN * IN THE DESCRIPTIONS BELOW) THAT AREN'T STRICTLY NECESSARY. IF YOU DON'T COMPLETE THEM, YOU MAY MISS OUT ON GUIDANCE ABOUT WHAT TO DO NEXT, BUT YOU CAN BUY YOURSELF TIME.

A few other key notes, before you get started:

- **DON'T GIVE UP.** IF YOU LEAVE A SILO FOR MORE THAN A FEW MINUTES, ALL OF YOUR PERSONAL PROGRESS WILL BE LOST, AND YOU'LL HAVE TO COMPLETE THE RESIDENTIAL AREA AGAIN BEFORE REJOINING YOUR GROUP. IF YOUR ENTIRE GROUP LEAVES THE SILO FOR A FEW MINUTES, THE ENTIRE SPACE WILL RESET. DON'T DALLY!

- **FIND THE REPAIR STATIONS.** THERE ARE A NUMBER OF WORKBENCHES LOCATED THROUGHOUT THE SILO. TAKE A MOMENT TO STOP AND REPAIR YOUR GEAR BEFORE PRESSING FORWARD.

- **OPEN THE SHORTCUT.** ONCE YOU REACH THE STORAGE AREA, YOU CAN USE A TERMINAL TO UNLOCK A DOOR THAT CONNECTS BACK TO THE FIRST PART OF THE SILO. IF YOU RESPAWN (OR WIPE), THIS ALLOWS YOU TO GET BACK TO THE ACTION MUCH MORE QUICKLY.

Quest THE RUNDOWN

MAP LEGEND

MY STASH BOX
OVERSEER'S CACHE
TRUNK
TRADER

COLLECTIBLES
BOBBLEHEAD
MAGAZINE
POWER ARMOR

IMPORTANT
DOOR/GATE
LOCKED DOOR/GATE
SAFE
SCANNER
TERMINAL

CRAFTING
ARMOR WORKBENCH
CHEMISTRY WORKBENCH
COOKING STATION
POWER ARMOR STATION
TINKER'S WORKBENCH
WEAPONS WORKBENCH
WORKSHOP WORKBENCH

Missile Silo (Interior)

LEGEND

1. FOYER
2. RESIDENTIAL ROOM (BIOMETRICS)
3. BUNKS
4. GYM
5. SHOWERS
6. CAFETERIA
7. STORAGE (PANTRY)
8. LIVING ROOMS AND GAME ROOM
9. SECURITY CONTROL ROOM
10. MEDICAL AND BIOMETRIC SCANNER ROOM
11. LASER GRID
12. MAIN STORAGE CORRIDOR
13. POWER HOUSE: MONITORING ROOM
14. POWER HOUSE: FUMIGATION CORRIDOR
15. POWER HOUSE: REACTOR ROOM
16. POWER HOUSE: REACTOR CONTROL ROOM
17. POWER HOUSE: SECURITY COMMAND ROOM AND EXIT
18. MAINFRAME: ACCESS CONTROL ROOM
19. MAINFRAME: ACCESS CONTROL CORRIDOR
20. MAINFRAME: CENTRAL CHAMBER
21. MAINFRAME: EXIT
22. STORAGE AND FACILITIES: ENTRANCE
23. STORAGE AND FACILITIES: MECHANICAL ROOM
24. STORAGE AND FACILITIES: MAINFRAME COMPUTERS AND EXIT
25. LAUNCH SILO: ENTRANCE
26. LAUNCH SILO: MAIN CHAMBER
27. LAUNCH SILO (UPPER): LAUNCH CONTROL BALCONY
28. LAUNCH SILO (LOWER): LAUNCH KEYCARD, CODE, AND TARGETING COMPUTER
29. EXIT TUNNEL
30. ELEVATOR TO SURFACE

EVENT 1: THE RESIDENTIAL AREA

OBJECTIVES

- FIND A WAY PAST THE LASER GRIDS.*
- FIND A WAY TO MAKE A BIOMETRIC ID CARD.*
- FIND AN OLD BIOMETRIC ID CARD.
- ERASE THE OLD BIOMETRIC ID CARD.
- ACQUIRE YOUR BIOMETRIC DATA.
- CREATE YOUR BIOMETRIC ID CARD.
- REGISTER YOUR BIOMETRIC ID CARD.

Hack the terminal in the entryway, and use it to disable the Supervisor and turrets. Then head in and clear out the rest of the area. If you're careful (don't kill the Supervisor!), you can avoid triggering the security system here and buy yourself some time to look around.

Each member of your team must complete this event individually. A good strategy is to have half your team run through the objectives while the other half fends off the robots, and then alternate. Once everyone has acquired and registered their own Biometric ID, the security system shuts down, and you can make your way forward.

TRAINING

CRAFTING AND C.A.M.P.ING

INVENTORY

QUESTS

ATLAS

BESTIARY

APPENDICES

EVENT 2: THE REACTOR AREA

> **OBJECTIVES**
> - **FIND A WAY TO END THE REACTOR SECURITY LOCKDOWN.***
> - **SHUT DOWN THE REACTOR FOR REPAIRS.**
> - **REPAIR THE REACTOR PIPES.**
> - **(OPTIONAL) RESTART THE REACTOR.**

The Reactor Area is flooded with lethal levels of radiation. If you brought a Hazmat Suit, equip it before getting anywhere near the door to this area. Otherwise, equip your best radiation protection gear, take a RadX, and have your RadAway favorited. A couple of Hazmat Suits can be found in the first room of this area, although you'll be taking significant radiation damage already by that point.

In the first room, hack the terminal and use it to disable the Supervisor and turrets. You can also use it to turn on the Decontamination Arches, which is highly recommended—it's much faster and cheaper than burning through your own supply of RadAway. Terminals elsewhere in the Reactor Area will allow you to activate robot allies to help in the fight that follows.

If your entire team has Hazmat Suits, it's worth clearing the room, and then taking a minute to locate all of the broken pipes. You can't repair them until you shut down the reactor (which also sets off the security system here), but you can map them out and make sure your team is spread out and ready to hit them as soon as the system shuts down.

Once you do shut down the reactors, repair the pipes as quickly as possible, and then restart the reactor to end the security alarm. If you have a small team, it may be worth ignoring the enemies entirely and just rushing the repairs—you don't have a lot of time, and you're likely to run out if you keep stopping to fight.

Helpful Hints from Vault-Boy!

There is an alternate approach. If you have top-tier Picklock skills, you can pick the lock on the door in the middle of the Reactor Area. Inside, use your top-tier Hacker skills to hack the Security Command Terminal and override the lockdown. The doors will open, and you can skip the entire event.

You can find Weapon, Armor, and Power Armor Workbenches in one of the side rooms on the far side of the Reactor chamber.

EVENT 3: THE OPERATIONS CENTER

> **OBJECTIVES**
> - **DESTROY THE MAINFRAME CORES.**

There's no time to waste here—the security alarm sounds as soon as you set foot in the Operations Center. A terminal in the first room will allow you to disable the Supervisor and turrets, though.

The key to completing the Operations Center efficiently is explosives—a single well-placed grenade can take out an entire bank of console panels and their Mainframe Cores (as well as any nearby robots). Be careful to coordinate your actions with your team, though—grenade accidents can be messy.

EVENT 4: THE STORAGE AREA

> **OBJECTIVES**
> - **FIND A WAY TO OPEN THE SECURITY DOORS.***
> - **REPLACE 15 MAINFRAME CORES.**
> - **(OPTIONAL) FIND SPARE MAINFRAME CORES.**
> - **(OPTIONAL) REPAIR DAMAGED MAINFRAME CORES.**
> - **OPEN THE SECURITY DOOR.**

In the first room of the Storage Area, pick the lock on the side office door to get to the terminal, where you can disable the Supervisor and turrets. Then head into the main room and deal with the Sentry Bot and the other robots.

Once you've cleared the room, find the terminal on the side wall and use it to open the terminal-locked door leading back to the entrance—if you have to respawn, this shortcut makes rejoining your group a whole lot quicker.

The security system in this area will trip as soon as you interact with the Facilities Mainframe terminal or any of the Mainframe Cores. If you want, you can take a moment to locate (but don't pick up) the Mainframe Cores you're going to need.

An even better solution is to repair the damaged cores. Have one member of your team quickly remove all 15 Damaged Mainframe Cores from the Facilities Mainframe, then head in to the Tinker's Workbench in the next room. If you brought the Scrap Steel and Circuits we recommended, you can quickly repair all 15 cores, return to the mainframe, and slot them in, no scrounging required.

Helpful Hint from Vault-Boy!

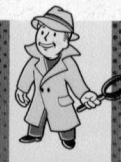

Need a pit stop? After finishing this event, take advantage of the Weapon, Armor, Power Armor, and Tinker's Workbenches in the side rooms off the main Storage Area.

EVENT 5: THE CONTROL ROOM

> **OBJECTIVES**
> - **INITIATE LAUNCH PREP.**
> - **COMPLETE LAUNCH PREP.**
> - **DEFEND THE SECTION CHIEFS.**
> - **REPLACE THE SECTION CHIEFS.**

At the top of the stairs, find the terminal in the first room and use it to deal with the Supervisor and Turrets. Then head in and clear the Control Room.

In this event, your team needs to defend the Section Chiefs as they make their way to their posts and complete the launch prep process. There are no shortcuts here and no avoiding combat. But you have all the time you need to orient yourself, find good defensive spots, and (ideally) lay down some mines. The security alarm won't sound until you initiate launch prep.

Ideally, keep one (or two) members of your team on the upper level, near the Launch Control Chief's post—he's the easiest to defend, and as long as he's active, launch prep will finish eventually. Larger groups can take a more aggressive approach, holding the entrances to the main room.

If a Section Chief is destroyed, you can use the terminal near its fabrication pod to construct a new one. But don't do this unless you feel you have the fight well under control—there's nothing worse than rebuilding one Chief, only to return to the room and find you've lost another.

As soon as launch prep is completed, Mission: Countdown comes to an end.

IT'S BEEN A BLAST

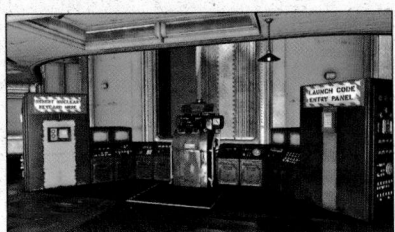

With launch prep completed, the launch control console is now active. Insert your Nuclear Keycard into the keycard receptacle. Once you do this, there's no turning back. If you enter the wrong Launch Code, you'll have to track down another Nuclear Keycard and repeat the entire silo—so enter the code carefully.

Once your code is accepted, approach the targeting computer and choose the location you want to nuke. A suggested target is available, but you're free to select any point in Appalachia except portions of the Forest region. Confirm your choice, and you'll exit the targeting system.

Quest DEATH FROM ABOVE

If you like, you can watch the launch from inside the silo. Shortly after the launch, you'll be notified of an automated lockdown. Collect your belongings and exit the silo. The silo will be locked down until a new missile is ready for launch (in about three hours).

If you hurry outside (don't forget to loot the chest on your way out), you can also watch the launch from there. And, depending on the target you selected, you may be able to see the blast, too. It's always spectacular, and all three silos provide excellent vantage points.

Any players in the blast zone will receive an automated warning of the incoming nuke, and have a short time to run to safety. Anyone who doesn't make it out will be killed, and any workshops or camps caught in the blast will be utterly destroyed.

IN THE AFTERMATH

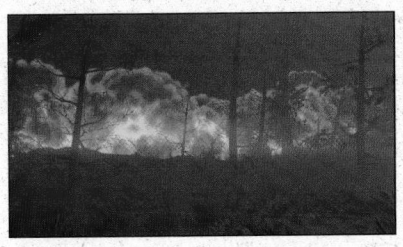

Steel yourself for the most difficult (and rewarding) challenge yet. Put on your Hazmat Suit and head into the blast zone, where all of the flora and fauna are now heavily irradiated. Expect far more difficult encounters, and rare resources that can be obtained nowhere else.

Helpful Hint from Vault-Boy!

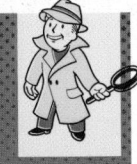

For a little extra firepower, set up a C.A.M.P. in the blast zone and build some turrets to help you tear through the enemy population.

RINSE, REPEAT

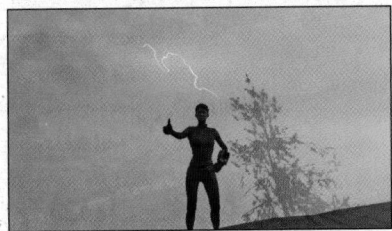

Launching a nuke is hardly the end of the game. You can repeat the process anytime you're willing to track down a Nuclear Keycard and decipher the Launch Codes.

There's no better way to get high-end gear and resources, and you definitely won't get everything you need on the first go.

Good luck! And watch out for the Scorchbeasts...

Quest SCORCHED EARTH

EVENT LOCATION
- **CRANBERRY BOG AT A RANDOM LOCATION**

REWARDS
- **ULTRACITE ORE**
- **RANDOM AMMO**
- **RANDOM AID ITEM**
- **RANDOM PLAN, ARMOR, MOD, OR WEAPON**
- **CHANCE FOR A RANDOM LEGENDARY WEAPON OR ARMOR**

DETAILS

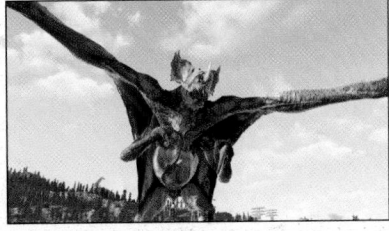

The Prime Fissure has opened, disgorging an enormous Scorchbeast Queen. Defeat her before she leaves to make a new nest elsewhere!

SIDE QUESTS

Side Quests are typically as long as a Main Quest, but they aren't directly tied to one. You will often have to complete a specific Main Quest in order to participate in a Side Quest, but they are stand-alone, one-off adventures that don't tie into other quests.

Quest AN ORGANIC SOLUTION

ORGANIC PANIC

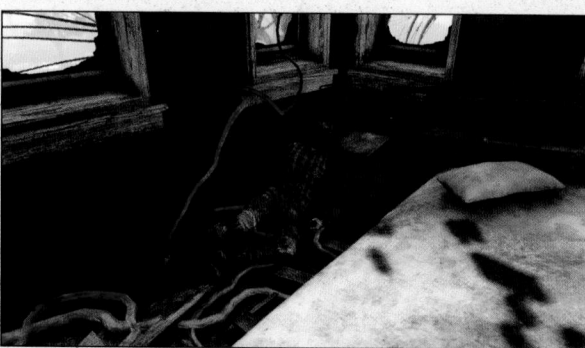

Exit the bunker and head into the forest to the north to reach Southhampton Estate. Find Ella's Research on Ella Ames' body on the estate's second floor.

ITEM ➡	❯ ELLA'S RESEARCH HOLOTAPE

Access Ella's Research Holotape under the Holo tab in the Items menu. It will bring up a terminal screen. Read through the entries, then select "Install Radio Tracking" under "Tracking Bone Meal." Now set your radio to "Radiation Signal Tracker" and start your hunt for bone meal.

Pay attention to the signal strength percentage in the screen's top-left corner. If it goes up while you're moving in a direction, keep moving in that direction. If it goes down, switch gears and start moving toward a new location.

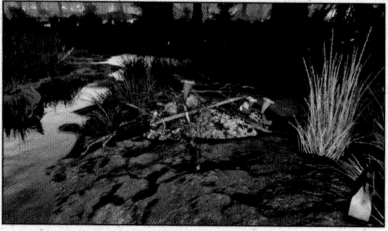

Head southeast of Southhampton Estate toward the Crevasse Dam to reach the objective circle. Once inside, follow your Radiation Signal Tracker to locate a Deathclaw nest on the western bank of the Mire lake. Be warned: Where there are Deathclaw nests, there are inevitably Deathclaws.

Once you've grabbed the bone meal, head south on Route 65 to Dyer Chemical, where you'll need to find nitrogen, phosphorous, and potassium.

ITEM ➡	❯ BONE MEAL

NITROGEN

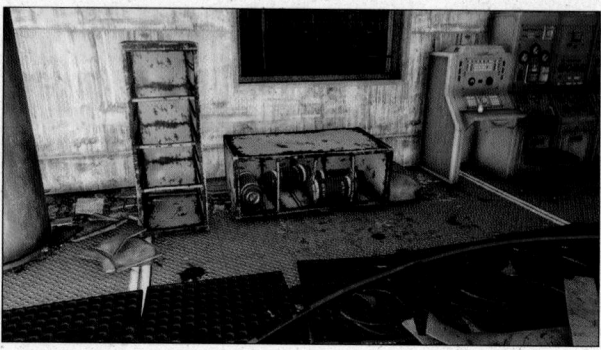

The nitrogen is in the office on the second floor of the building on Dyer Chemical's north side.

ITEM ➡	❯ NITROGEN

POTASSIUM

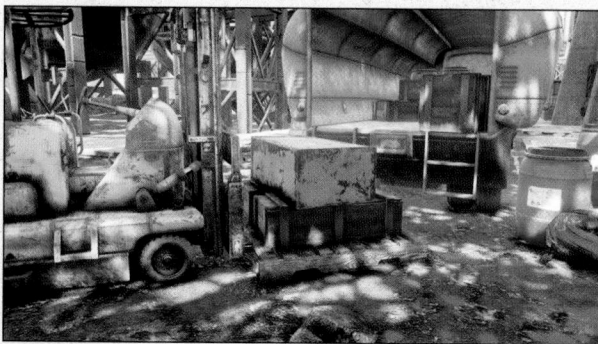

The potassium is in the back of a large blue truck on the south side of Dyer Chemical.

ITEM ➡	❯ POTASSIUM

PHOSPHOROUS

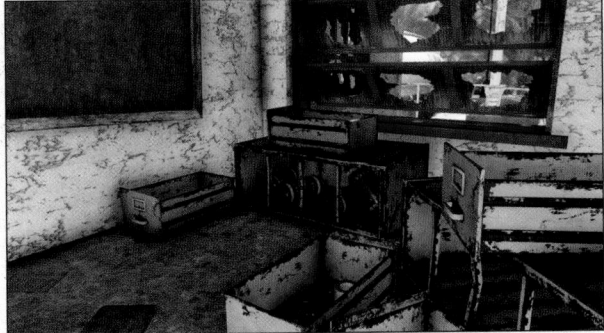

Phosphorous is inside the small building attached to the southwestern corner of Dyer Chemical.

ITEM ➡	❯ PHOSPHOROUS

CONSTRUCTING RADSHIELD

Once you have all three chemicals, take them and the bone meal up to the facility's third floor and insert them into the marked terminal. Select "Confirm." Once complete, select "Flush" to dump the fertilizer into the river.

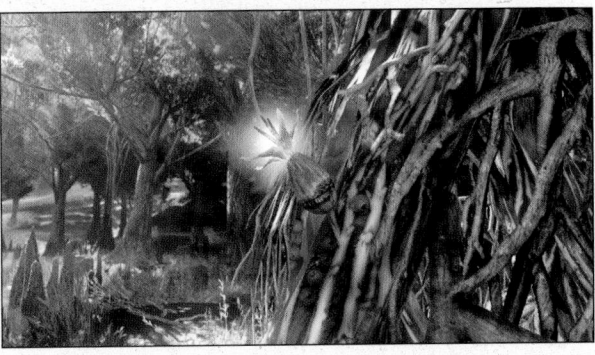

Jump into the western river and pull one of the glowing Strangler Blooms off a tree lining the riverbank. Head to the marked Chemistry Station and craft RadShield, which is under the "Healing" category. Once you craft the RadShield, the quest completes.

ITEMS ➡	❯ STRANGLER BLOOM	❯ RADSHIELD

Quest BUREAU OF TOURISM

OBJECTIVES
- TALK TO GRAFTON MAYOR
- OPEN THE WATER VALVE AT WAVY WILLARD'S WATERPACK
- PICK UP 10 BEER BOTTLES AT THE SHOOTING RANGE
- REPAIR PRICKETT'S FORT TOKEN DISPENSER
- REPAIR BLACK BEAR LODGE CHECK-IN TERMINAL

LOCATIONS
- GRAFTON
- CLARKSBURG SHOOTING CLUB
- PRICKETT'S FORT
- WAVY WILLARD'S WATER PARK

REWARDS
- TRAIL WARDEN (MODDED METAL TORSO ARMOR)
- COMPONENTS
- RANDOM AMMO
- RANDOM AID ITEM

PREREQUISITES
- AS YOU APPROACH GRAFTON, YOU'LL RECEIVE A MISCELLANEOUS QUEST TO LISTEN TO THE WGRF GRAFTON RADIO STATION. COMPLETE THAT TO INITIATE THE QUEST.

HANDY MAN

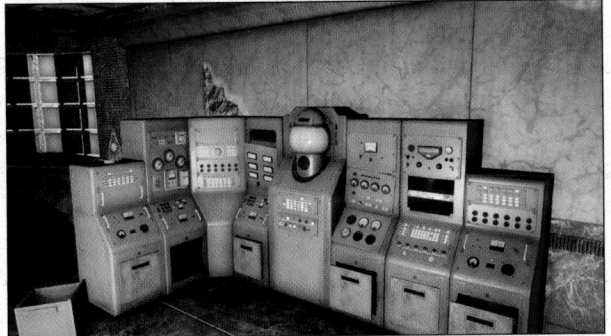

Head into Grafton and use the terminal at the objective marker. Grafton Mayor will send you off to repair tourist attractions around Toxic Valley. Most of these are as simple as walking to an objective and activating something, but there are some things to note.

TOURIST TRAPS

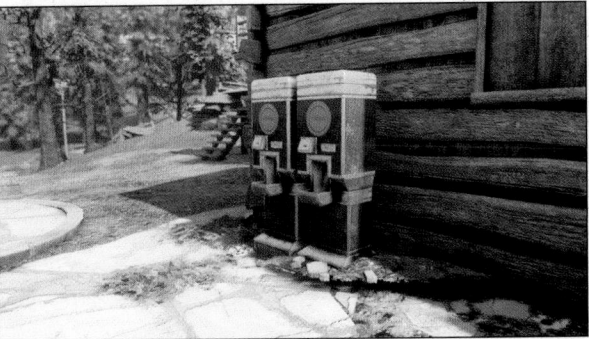

Start by repairing the token dispenser. It takes a few base components, which are common and easy enough to find.

TRAINING
CRAFTING AND C.A.M.P.ING
INVENTORY
QUESTS
ATLAS
BESTIARY
APPENDICES

Repairing the Black Bear Lodge Check-in Terminal requires a Screw and one Circuitry. If you have those items in your inventory, you only need to interact with the terminal to fix it—finding it is a breeze.

When you're off to repair the water valve at Wavy Willard's Water Park, head under the facility. There's a set of stairs in the park's northeastern side that lead to the park's lower levels. You can also use a hole in the bottom of one of the cobra pools slightly north of the objective marker.

Once you finish all four tasks, the quest concludes.

Helpful Hint from Vault Boy!

Consult the "Junk" chapter for information on what to break down for components if you're lacking the means to repair anything during this quest.

Quest COLD CASE

OBJECTIVES
- **ACCESS THE SECURITY SYSTEM**
- **PLAY THE HOLOTAPE CLUES**
- **SEARCH FOR FREDDY'S ID**
- **SEARCH THE MAILBOX**
- **GO TO CLARKSBURG POST OFFICE**
- **(OPTIONAL) REPAIR THE KIDSECURE USING A TINKER'S BENCH**
- **SEARCH OTIS PIKE'S HOUSE**
- **ENTER THE GRAFTON DAM AND SEARCH FOR CLUES**
- **SEARCH THE WOODS ESTATE**

LOCATIONS
- **WAVY WILLARD'S WATER PARK**
- **CLARKSBURG**
- **GRAFTON DAM**
- **WOODS ESTATE**

PREREQUISITES
- **SPEAK WITH MISS ANNIE, WHO IS SITTING BELOW THE GIANT CROCODILE'S MOUTH IN WAVY WILLARD'S WATER PARK TO INITIATE THIS QUEST.**

REWARDS
- **PERFECT STORM (MODDED 10-MM SMG)**
- **MULTIPLE RANDOM AMMO TYPES**
- **RANDOM AID ITEM**

A COLD, WET MYSTERY

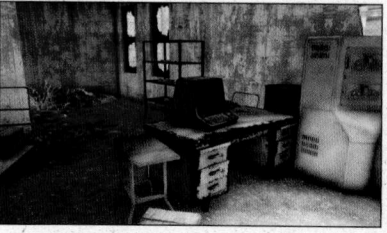

Access the security terminal in the building near the center of Wavy Willard's Water Park. The front door is locked with a Level 2 lock, but you can access the building from a hole in the building's northeastern corner.

Read through all the "Holotape Review" entries; then unlock the safe behind the terminal and listen to the holotape within. Head down the stairs beneath the Slither Slide Terminal to find the second holotape.

 ITEMS ➡
> **WWP LOG RIDE ENTRY 10172077 DAILY HOLOTAPE**
> **WWP SLITHER SLIDE 10172077 DAILY HOLOTAPE**

Head back upstairs and grab the notes out of the mailbox; then head to the top of Slither Slide in the park's northeast corner to find the KidSecure ID.

 ITEMS ➡
> **LETTER TO THE MEDIA**
> **CLARKSBURG P.O. BOX 12**
> **KIDSECURE ID**

You can repair the KidSecure ID at a Tinker's Workbench in the southeast building in Willard Corporate Housing (east of Wavy Willard's Water Park), but it will require a Nuclear Material, three Adhesive, and one Circuitry. If you don't have the time or patience to wrangle the components for the SecureKid ID, head to Clarksburg Post Office to continue the quest.

MAIL CALL

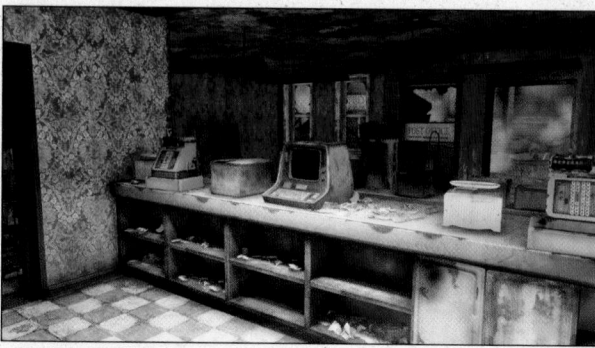

Once in the Clarksburg Post Office, select "Search by BOX NUMBER," then "Box 012." Your next task is to search Otis Pike's house, which is on the south end of Grafton. Use the terminal in Pike's basement and select "Correspondence," then "Dam Safety Inquiry."

You will need a Lockpicking skill of 3 in order to enter the dam directly. Otherwise, there's a hidden way in; follow your objective marker along the walkway around the building and drop down into a broken spill tube. You'll find keys to the dam inside.

ITEMS ➡
> **DIARY OF OTIS PIKE**
> **FREDDY'S ADVENTURE #1**
> **FREDDY'S ADVENTURE #2**
> **FREDDY'S ADVENTURE #3**
> **ARTHUR'S WOOD LIGHTER**

Head northwest to the Woods Estate and head upstairs. Check the desk beneath the terminal and grab "Freddy's Hasty Note"; then head back to Miss Annie at Wavy Willard's Water Park to conclude the quest.

ITEM ➡
> **FREDDY'S HASTY NOTE**

Quest FALSELY ACCUSED

OBJECTIVES
- TALK TO THE WARDEN ABOUT THE MARSHALS
- CLEAR YOUR GOOD NAME

LOCATIONS
- EASTERN REGIONAL PENITENTIARY (TOXIC VALLEY)

REWARDS
- CIVIL UNREST (MODDED PUMP-ACTION SHOTGUN)
- ROBOT TORSO ARMOR
- RANDOM AMMO
- RANDOM AID ITEM

PREREQUISITES
- APPEARS RANDOMLY WHILE IN TOXIC VALLEY, BUT ONLY AFTER COMPLETING THE "BUREAU OF TOURISM" SIDE QUEST.

FUGITIVE FROM JUSTICE

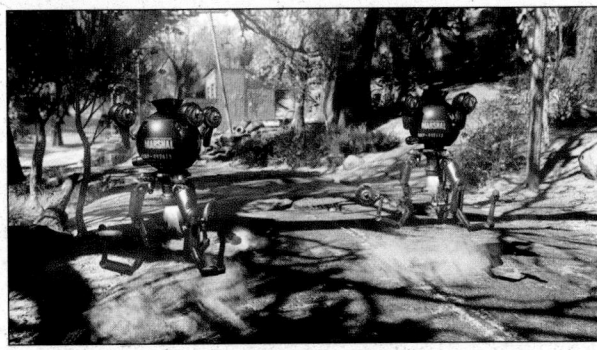

While trekking about Toxic Valley, you'll find yourself suddenly and unceremoniously attacked by Protectron Marshals. It turns out that you've been mistaken for a notorious criminal and the law will stop at nothing to see you dead or put behind bars.

Kill the Marshals and loot the warrant off their bodies. Head to the Eastern Regional Penitentiary and speak with the warden. You'll need to visit each of the security stations marked on your map and authorize turret activation. Once you've done that, return to the warden to complete the quest.

Quest MAYOR FOR A DAY

OBJECTIVES
- LEARN MORE ABOUT THE SABOTEUR
- FIND THE SABOTEUR'S HIDEOUT
- SEARCH THE HIDEOUT FOR CLUES
- INVESTIGATE THE SABOTEUR'S WORK TERMINAL
- TAKE THE VIRUS HOLOTAPE TO MAIA
- START UPLOAD PROCESS
- PREVENT SECURITY FROM STOPPING THE UPLOAD

LOCATIONS
- WATOGA MUNICIPAL CENTER
- ABANDONED BOG TOWN
- ROBCO RESEARCH CENTER

REWARDS
- ALL RISE (MODDED SUPER SLEDGE)
- MAYOR'S HAT
- MAYOR'S CLOTHES
- WATOGA MAYOR SAFE COMBINATION
- RANDOM AMMO
- RANDOM AID ITEM

PREREQUISITES
- WHILE APPROACHING WATOGA IN CRANBERRY BOG, YOU'LL RECEIVE A TRANSMISSION FROM THE MAYOR OF WATOGA. THIS WILL GIVE YOU A MISCELLANEOUS QUEST TO GO TO THE MAYOR'S OFFICE. COMPLETE THAT QUEST TO START THIS ONE.

STALKING THE SABOTEUR

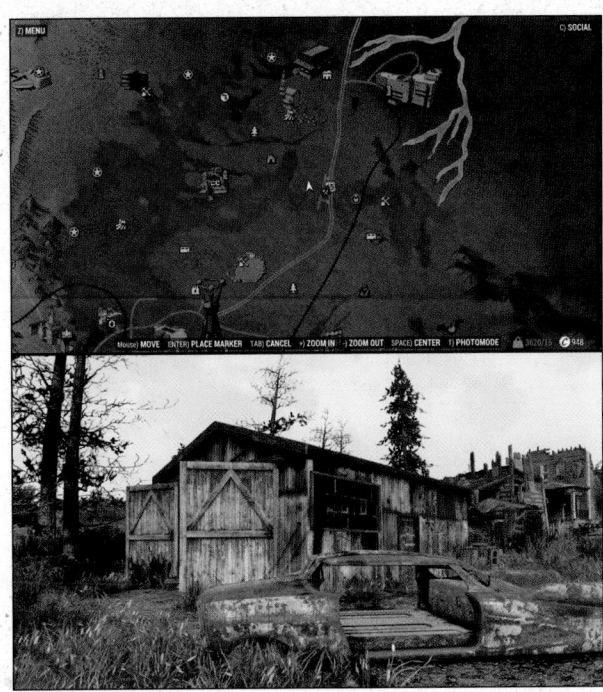

Use the terminal on the mayor's desk and select "Read this! [HIGH PRIORITY]"; then select "Mayor for a Day." Exit the municipal building and head north up Route 65. The Saboteur's house is inside a small warehouse with the words "Private Property No Trespassing Keep Out" written on the door.

TRAINING

CRAFTING AND C.A.M.P.ING

INVENTORY

QUESTS

ATLAS

BESTIARY

APPENDICES

You'll need to hunt down five clues inside the hideout, so search all the likely places. Start with the body of Scott Turner, crack into the terminal on the desk and read the entries. Select "Safe Control" and unlock the safe on the ground under the cabinet on the desk's left side. Continue thoroughly investigating until you have all five necessary pieces of evidence.

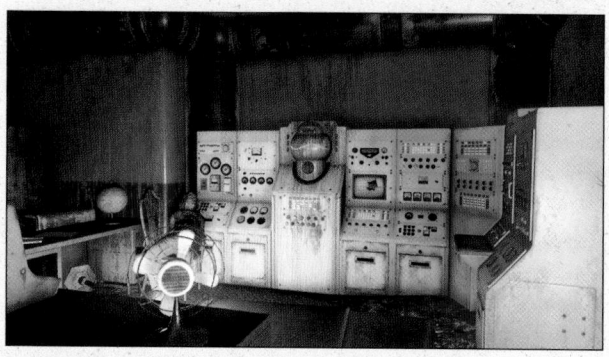

| ITEMS ➡ | ❯ ROBCO RESEARCH FACILITY KEYCARD |
| | ❯ SABOTEUR'S WORK PASSWORD |

HUMBLE BEGINNINGS

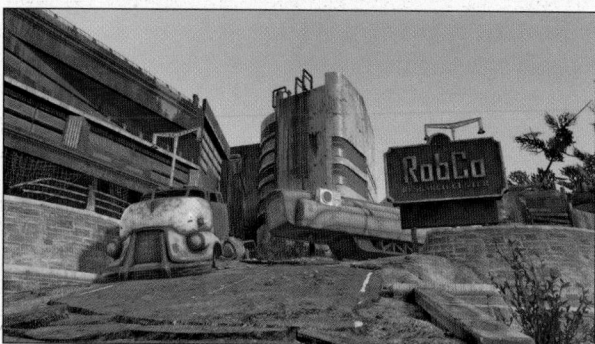

Head north from the Saboteur's house to find the RobCo where the Saboteur once worked. Enter the building and head to the Saboteur's office on the building's east side. Use his terminal and select "Scan Likeness" to obtain the Robot Virus Holotape. Now exit the building and go to the Watoga Municipal Center.

| ITEM ➡ | ❯ ROBOT VIRUS HOLOTAPE |

Return to the mayor's office and interact with MAIA on the office's west wall. She'll instruct you to go up to the building's roof and upload the virus from a relay tower. Exit the office, go down the hall, and use the elevator on the left to reach the roof. Use the marked terminal to start the upload. You'll have to guard the terminal for a full 5 minutes while fending off waves of robotic enemies and a Scorchbeast. Once you do, the quest will be complete.

You'll earn the Watoga Mayor Safe Combination for your troubles, and the robots in Watoga will no long be hostile. Not too bad! You can use the safe combination on the safe in the mayor's office (on the desk's left side).

FASCINATING FACTS FROM VAULT BOY!

COMPLETING THIS QUEST WILL MAKE MOST OF THE ROBOTS IN WATOGA STOP ATTACKING YOU (SO LONG AS YOU DON'T ATTACK THEM). THIS ONLY APPLIES TO THOSE WHO HAVE COMPLETED THIS QUEST, SO IF YOU HAVE TEAMMATES WHO HAVEN'T UPLOADED THE VIRUS, THEY'LL STILL GET ATTACKED BY THE ROBOTS IN WATOGA.

Quest MINER MIRACLES

OBJECTIVES
- **INVESTIGATE GARRAHAN MINING'S HEADQUARTERS**
- **CONSULT THE PROJECT MANAGER'S TERMINAL**
- **BUILDING EXCAVATOR POWER ARMOR**

LOCATIONS
- **GARRAHAN MINING HEADQUARTERS**

REWARDS
- **EXCAVATOR POWER ARMOR PLANS**
- **POWER ARMOR WORKBENCH PLAN**
- **RANDOM AMMO**
- **RANDOM AID ITEM**

PREREQUISITES
- **THIS QUEST STARTS AFTER YOU COMPLETE A MISCELLANEOUS QUEST WITH THE OBJECTIVE "DISCOVER GARRAHAN MINING'S INNOVATION."**

DIG DEEP

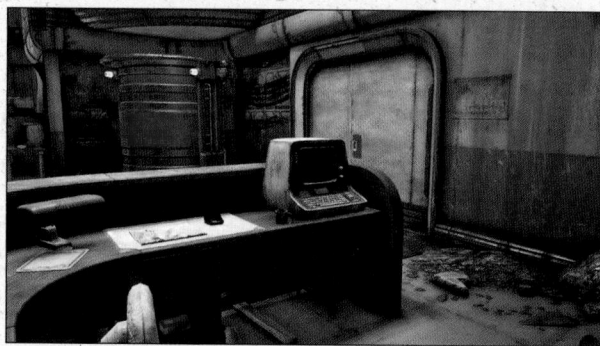

Head into the Garrahan Mining Headquarters, but do so slowly. The path leading into the building is loaded with fragmentation mines. Once inside, find the terminal near the back of the building and select "Memo: Excavator Queries."

Now go to the project manager's terminal on the building's east side. Select "Excavator Module Blueprints" to download plans for all of the Excavator Power Armor parts.

ORE TOUR

At this point you'll need to take a suit of Power Armor to a Power Armor Station and craft all the parts for the Excavator Power Armor. The greatest challenge you'll have to face from here on is that it requires some difficult-to-find materials, such as Nuclear Material and Black Titanium.

Helpful Hints from Vault Boy

If you're looking for Nuclear Material, you can flip to the "Junk" chapter of this book to figure out the best items to scrap to get it.

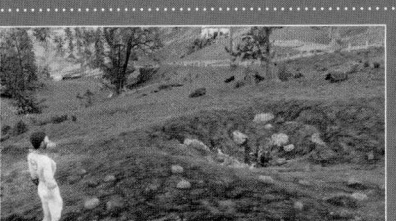

If you're trying to quickly locate Black Titanium, leave Garrahan Mining Headquarters and head directly north until you reach the northwest corner of Lewisburg. The Black Titanium is just slightly off the road around that area. Use the screenshot we've included above to find the exact location.

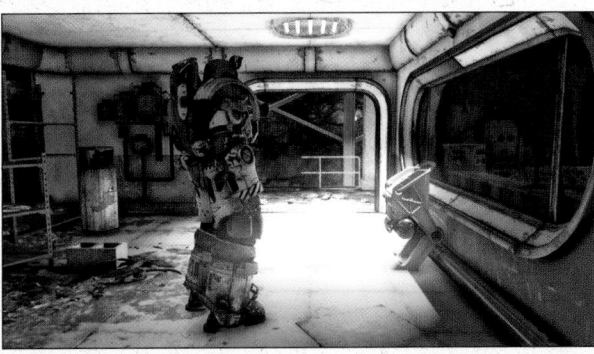

Once you've built the Excavator Power Armor parts, head back to Garrahan Mining Headquarters and register it by using the marked button on the building's east side.

Quest OVERSEER'S MISSION

OBJECTIVES

- FOLLOW THE OVERSEER'S JOURNEY

LOCATION	REWARDS	PREREQUISITES
– CAMP MCCLINTOCK	– NONE	– NONE

HOT ON THE TRAIL

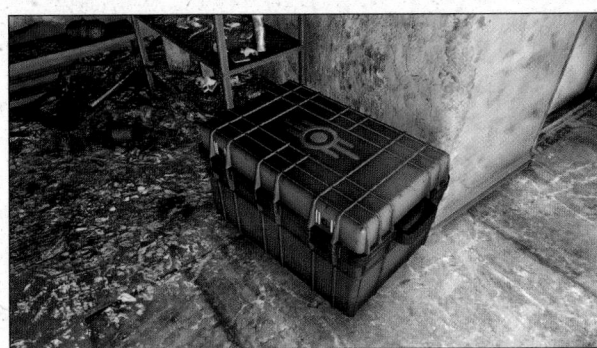

The Overseer has been a busy lady, as evidenced by the number of Overseer's Caches and holotapes around Appalachia. Finding each one is key to this quest, which is only as difficult as putting one foot in front of the other. Whenever you're in close proximity to an Overseer's Cache, you'll receive an objective marker for it.

Find the Overseer's Caches in the following locations:

- **C.A.M.P. SOUTHEAST OF VAULT 76**
- **FLATWOODS INSIDE THE WHITE CHURCH**
- **MORGANTOWN AIRPORT TERMINAL**
- **CHARLESTON FIRE DEPARTMENT**
- **NEXT TO THE FIRST-FLOOR ELEVATOR AT TOP OF THE WORLD**
- **CHARLESTON CAPITOL DMV**
- **NEXT TO ABBIE'S BUNKER ENTRANCE**
- **CAMP VENTURE (ON THE SOUTHERN BORDER OF THE MIRE AND CRANBERRY BOG)**
- **FORT DEFIANCE NEAR THE ELEVATOR ON THE THIRD FLOOR**
- **FORT DEFIANCE NEAR THE ELEVATOR ON THE FOURTH FLOOR**
- **GRAFTON**
- **CAMP MCCLINTOCK**
- **NEAR THE ELEVATOR DOWN TO SITE ALPHA**
- **NEAR THE ELEVATOR DOWN TO SITE BRAVO**
- **R&G PROCESSING SERVICES NEAR THE ELEVATOR TO SITE CHARLIE**
- **R&G PROCESSING SERVICES NEAR THE ELEVATOR TO SITE CHARLIE— THIS ONE APPEARS IN THE OVERSEER'S CACHE AFTER RECEIVING THE FIRST HOLOTAPE AND AFTER SOMEONE HAS LAUNCHED A NUKE AT A NON-FISSURE SITE TARGET ON THE SERVER YOU'RE IN.**

None of these Overseer's Caches are hidden, and they all have the same appearance and shape. As we mentioned earlier, when you're near one, you'll receive an objective marker, so jump to this book's Atlas to find each location listed and the Overseer's Caches. Each one contains loot on top of a holotape chronicling the Overseer's journey through Appalachia. There's an additional holotape to be found (without a cache) at the Mountainside B&B.

TRAINING
CRAFTING AND C.A.M.P.ING
INVENTORY
QUESTS
ATLAS
BESTIARY
APPENDICES

Quest PERSONAL MATTERS

OBJECTIVES
- FIND THE OVERSEER'S JOURNALS

REWARDS
- RANDOM AMMO AND AID ITEM

LOCATIONS
- VAULT-TEC AGRICULTURAL CENTER
- SUTTON
- MORGANTOWN HIGH SCHOOL
- VAULT-TEC UNIVERSITY
- WELCH
- MOUNT BLAIR

PREREQUISITES
- FIND AND LISTEN TO THE OVERSEER'S JOURNAL, ENTRY 1 HOLOTAPE TO START THIS QUEST

INVASION OF PRIVACY

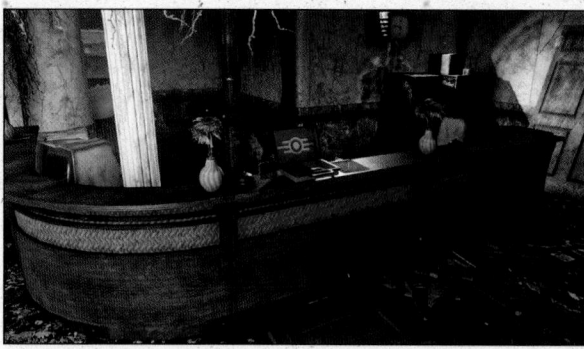

Aside from the Overseer's Cache Holotapes, there are a small handful of personal journals from the Overseer.

You can find the journals in any order (except for Entry 1 in the Vault-Tec Agricultural Center, which initiates the quest). Upon reaching the location, you'll receive an objective marker that will point you to the location of the next journal.

The journals can be found in the following locations:

- **VAULT-TEC AGRICULTURAL CENTER, WHICH INITIATES THE QUEST**
- **SUTTON**
- **MORGANTOWN HIGH SCHOOL**
- **VAULT-TEC UNIVERSITY**
- **WELCH**
- **MOUNT BLAIR**

Find and listen to each one; then find Evan to complete the quest.

Quest SAFE FOR WORK

OBJECTIVES
- LISTEN TO THE PATROL: TRAINING EXERCISE HOLOTAPE
- CHECK THE SUPPLIES IN THE TRIAGE CENTER
- USE THE SECURITY TERMINAL TO UNLOCK THE SAFE
- LISTEN TO THE PATROL: TRIAGE CENTER HOLOTAPE
- PATROL THE PROCESSING CENTER
- GET THE SUPPLY CACHE KEY FROM RESPONDER ROCKY
- CHECK THE SUPPLIES IN THE SAFE
- LISTEN TO THE PATROL: PROCESSING CENTER HOLOTAPE
- REPORT TO THE MEDICAL CENTER
- CHECK THE SUPPLIES IN THE STORAGE CHEST
- LISTEN TO THE PATROL: MEDICAL CLINIC HOLOTAPE
- REPORT TO THE TRAFFIC CONTROL TOWER
- GET THE LAST HOLOTAPE FROM THE CONTROL TOWER TERMINAL
- LISTEN TO THE PATROL: CONTROL TOWER HOLOTAPE
- CHECK IN AT THE RESPONDERS TERMINAL

LOCATIONS
- MORGANTOWN AIRPORT

REWARDS
- BOBBY PINS
- RANDOM AMMO
- RANDOM AID ITEM
- RANDOM LEGENDARY WEAPON OR ARMOR

PREREQUISITES
- COMPLETE THE "TENTATIVE PLANS" QUEST TO UNLOCK A MISCELLANEOUS OBJECTIVE REQUIRING YOU TO "REGISTER FOR MORE ADVANCED RESPONDER TRAINING." USE THE TERMINAL ON THE SECOND FLOOR OF MORGANTOWN AIRPORT AND SELECT "VOLUNTEERS: ADVANCED TRAINING" TO START THIS QUEST.

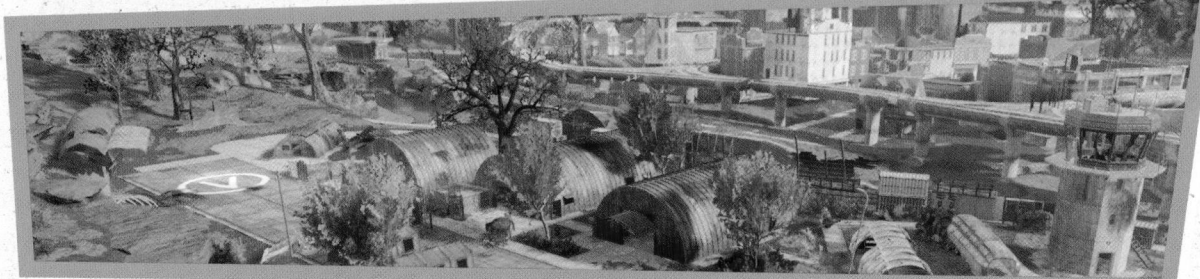

FIRST DAY ON THE JOB

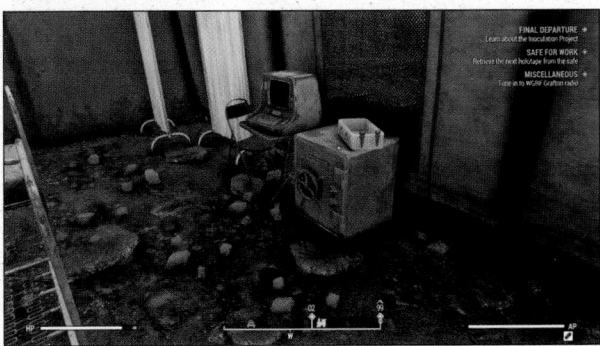

To start, open your Pip-Boy and listen to the Patrol: Training Exercise Holotape. Now head to the triage center terminal in the tent in front of Morgantown Airport. Select "Safe Control," then disengage the lock to the safe to the terminal's right. Loot and listen to the Patrol: Triage Center Holotape.

ITEM ➡ 〉 **PATROL: TRIAGE CENTER HOLOTAPE**

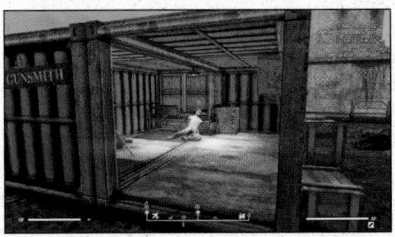

Head to the airport's north side and take the Responders Bravo Station Key off of Responder Rocky, who is lying on the bed in the large blue storage container. Use the key to open the safe next to Rocky's bed, grab the Patrol: Processing Center Holotape, and head to the airport's east side to reach the medical center. It may be a bit confusing, but the building with the "Laboratory" sign on it is the one you're gunning for (the beginning of the post-apocalypse was a chaotic time).

ITEMS ➡ 〉 **RESPONDERS BRAVO STATION KEY**
〉 **PATROL: PROCESSING CENTER**

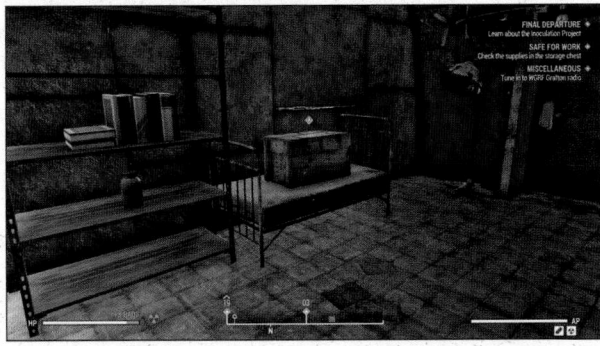

Open the wooden crate inside the medical center, then grab and listen to the Patrol: Medical Clinic Holotape. Now head to the traffic control tower near the center of the airport. Climb to the tower's top and use the terminal. Select "Resource Requests," then "Requests" to obtain a copy of the Patrol: Control Tower Holotape. Listen to the holotape to complete the quest.

ITEMS ➡ 〉 **PATROL: MEDICAL CLINIC HOLOTAPE**
〉 **PATROL: CONTROL TOWER HOLOTAPE**

Quest TENTATIVE PLANS

OBJECTIVES

– **LISTEN TO "VOLUNTEER TRAINING: CAMPING 101"**
– **INVESTIGATE RESPONDER MIGUEL'S CAMPSITE**
– **SEARCH THE CAMPSITE**
– **INVESTIGATE THE PROTECTRON**
– **SEARCH MIGUEL'S TERMINAL FOR C.A.M.P. PLANS**
– **FIND THE "CAMP GUIDE PROGRAM" FOR THE PROTECTRON**
– **GIVE HOLOTAPE TO MIGUEL'S PROTECTRON**
– **DEPLOY YOUR C.A.M.P.**
– **(OPTIONAL) DEPLOY YOUR C.A.M.P. NEAR MIGUEL'S CAMPSITE**
– **BUILD A BASIC COOKING FIRE**
– **BUILD A SIMPLE STASH BOX**
– **BUILD A GENERATOR AT YOUR C.A.M.P.**

LOCATIONS

– **MORGANTOWN AIRPORT TERMINAL**
– **MIGUEL'S CAMPSITE**

REWARDS

– **SILVER LINING (MODDED LEATHER TORSO ARMOR)**
– **SCREWS**
– **RANDOM AMMO**
– **RANDOM AID ITEM**

PREREQUISITES

– **COMPLETE THE "THIRST THINGS FIRST" AND "SECOND HELPINGS" QUESTS. USE THE RESPONDERS HQ TERMINAL ON THE SECOND FLOOR OF THE MORGANTOWN AIRPORT TERMINAL AND SELECT "VOLUNTEERS: ADVANCED TRAINING" TO BEGIN THIS MISCELLANEOUS QUEST.**

C.A.M.P. GROUNDS

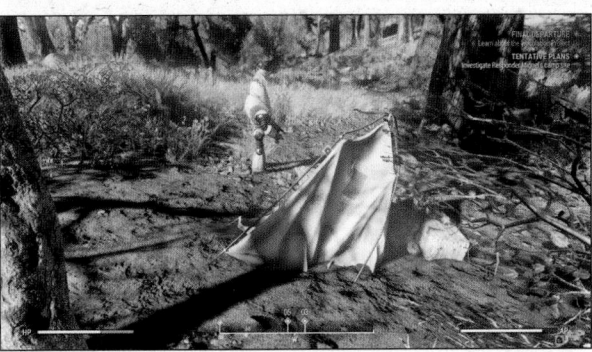

Bring up your Pip-Boy and play the Volunteer Training: Camping 101 Holotape. Head north from Morgantown Airport to reach Responder Miguel's campsite. Search his tent, read through the Camping Syllabus hidden within, then speak with the nearby Protectron.

Head back down to the Morgantown Airport and search the area near Miguel's terminal for the Camp Guide Program 3.4 Holotape. Head back to Miguel's camp and hand the holotape over to his Protectron. If you've already deployed a C.A.M.P. before delivering the holotape, you'll be instructed to complete the quest by building a generator. Otherwise, you'll be tasked with building a cooking fire and stash box.

ITEM ➡ 〉 **CAMP GUIDE PROGRAM 3.4**

BUILDER'S BASICS

Pull up your Pip-Boy and press the Move C.A.M.P. button, as shown on the bottom of the screen. Place the C.A.M.P. next to Miguel's camp; then approach the C.A.M.P. device and press the Build button to enter build mode. Move to the Stash Boxes tab and build a My Stash Box. Place the My Stash Box on the ground, then move to the Crafting tab and create a cooking station. Place this on the ground to complete the quest.

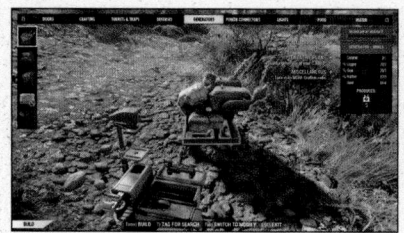

FASCINATING FACTS FROM VAULT BOY!
COMPLETING THIS QUEST WILL UNLOCK ANOTHER MISCELLANEOUS OBJECTIVE: REGISTER FOR MORE ADVANCED RESPONDER TRAINING. HEAD BACK TO THE MORGANTOWN AIRPORT TERMINAL AND USE THE COMPUTER TERMINAL ON THE SECOND FLOOR.

Quest THE MOTHERLODE

OBJECTIVES

- **SEARCH PENNY'S OFFICE FOR INFO ABOUT THE "MOTHERLODE"**
- **FIND AN ID CARD PRINTER**
- **OBTAIN A SENIOR EXECUTIVE ID**
- **EXPLORE THE BUILDING'S UPPER FLOOR**
- **SEARCH THE AREA FOR A REPAIR BEACON**
- **DEPLOY THE REPAIR BEACON**
- **COLLECT MOTHERLODE'S GIFT**

LOCATIONS

- **HORNWRIGHT INDUSTRIAL HEADQUARTERS**

REWARDS

- **ULTRACITE ORE**
- **RANDOM WEAPON**
- **RANDOM ORE**
- **RANDOM COMPONENTS**

PREREQUISITES

- **TIED TO A MISCELLANEOUS QUEST THAT APPEARS UPON APPROACHING THE HORNWRIGHT INDUSTRIAL HEADQUARTERS. ENTER, USE THE TERMINAL IN THE FOYER, AND READ THE ARCHIVED MESSAGES TO BEGIN THIS QUEST AND COMPLETE THE MISCELLANEOUS QUEST.**

CORPORATE ESPIONAGE

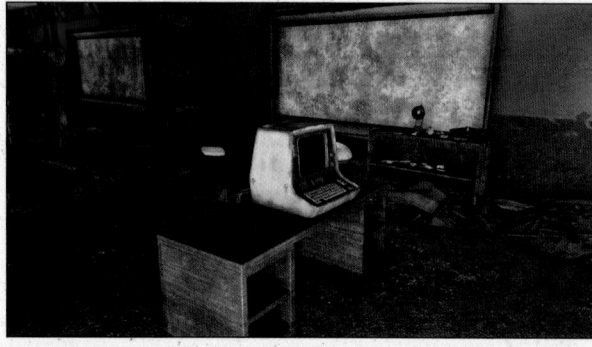

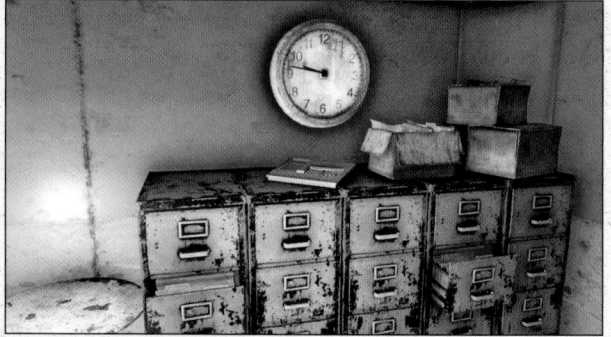

Head to the second to top floor and use the Penelope Hornwright's Terminal. Select "Archived Message—9.30.77" after accessing the archived messages to receive the Hornwright HR Password.

Head to the third floor and enter the Human Resources Department. Immediately look atop the filing cabinets to your right to find an ID Card Printer. Use this to create an Executive Key Card. To do that, you'll need to find a way to prove you're an executive.

ITEM ➡ **❭ HORNWRIGHT HR PASSWORD**

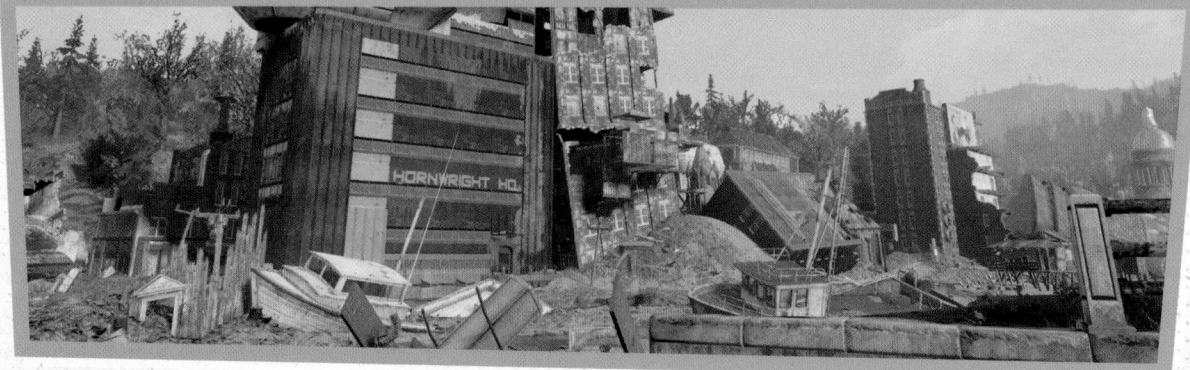

CLIMBING THE LADDER

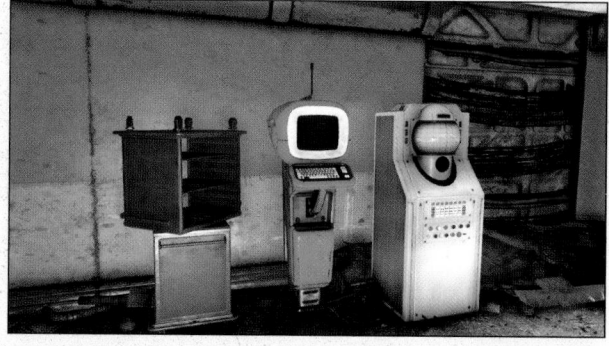

Head to the office next door and use one of the Hiring System Terminals. You must take an exam to prove you've got what it takes to be a Hornwright Industrial top-shelf exec. If you're keen on figuring out the answers to this quiz on your own, head down a floor and search the Technology Support Department to find something to help you out. If you're the impatient sort, read the Helpful Hints from Vault Boy! box for the answers.

Helpful Hints from Vault Boy!

Whoever said "cheaters never prosper" has never had the answers to the Hornwright Industrial Mining executive exam placed in their laps, which is what we happen to have here for you.

Q1: 2	Q3: 1	Q5: 1
Q2: 2 or 3	Q4: 2	

After you complete the exam, reenter the Human Resources Department next door and use the ID Card Printer to collect your Senior Executive ID.

HITTING THE MOTHERLODE

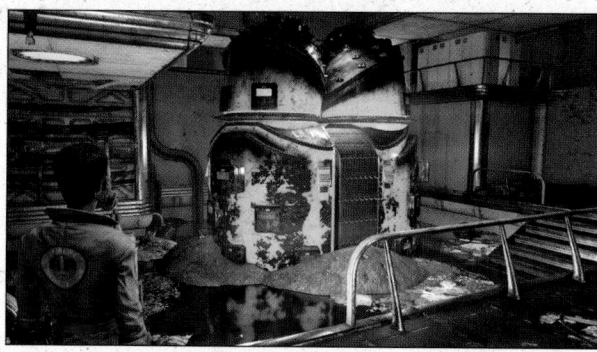

ITEM ➡ ❭ HORNWRIGHT SENIOR EXECUTIVE ID

Head back down to the bottom floor and use the elevator on the room's northeastern side. Slide your card through the ID Reader to head to the executive floor.

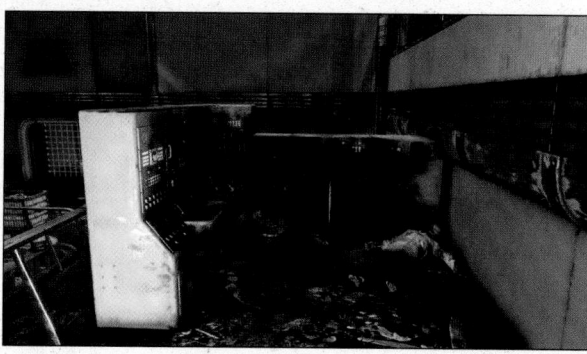

Once on the executive floor, enter the room on the left and inspect one of the External Connection Systems. You'll be tasked with searching the area for a repair beacon. Head up the small flight of stairs and go to the northeast wall.

There's a red computer terminal there. Use it, then select "Power Struggles" to learn the repair beacon acquisition code. Head back down the stairs and use one of the keypads on the opposite side of the red computer terminal. Punch in the requisition code (it's part of your current mission objective); then collect the Repair Beacon from the dispenser on your left.

ITEM ➡ ❭ REPAIR BEACON

Exit the room and head to the room on the floor's opposite end. Use the elevator behind the laser grid, then enter the center of the next room and put the Repair Beacon into the yellow Beacon Launcher. A giant, seemingly sentient machine called "Motherlode" will appear from the ground near the center of the room, then dig its way back down into the earth. Once the dust settles, head up the small flight of stairs and use the marked Docking Station Dispenser to collect Motherlode's gift: some Ultracite Ore, a random assortment of other Ores and components, and a random weapon.

FASCINATING FACTS FROM VAULT BOY!

HAVING COMPLETED THIS QUEST, MOTHERLODE WILL SHOW UP IN APPALACHIA FROM TIME TO TIME TO OFFER YOU AN EVENT QUEST CALLED "THE MOTHERLODE," WHICH SHOWS UP EXCLUSIVELY IN ASH HEAP.

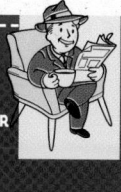

TRAINING

CRAFTING AND C.A.M.P.ING

INVENTORY

QUESTS

ATLAS

BESTIARY

APPENDICES

TRACKING UNKNOWNS

OBJECTIVES

- INVESTIGATE THE AREA NORTH OF VALLEY GALLERIA
- FIND A SIGNAL BOOSTER
- SUMMON A CARGOBOT
- ATTACH THE SIGNAL BOOSTER
- TRACK THE DISTRESS BEACON TO ITS SOURCE
- ENTER THE DYER CHEMICAL SEWERS
- DISCOVER THE FATE OF THE TRACKING PARTY

LOCATIONS

- HARPERS FERRY
- VALLEY GALLERIA
- CAMP VENTURE
- DYER CHEMICAL

REWARDS

- PYROLYZER (MODDED FLAMER)
- RADAWAY
- RANDOM AMMO
- RANDOM AID ITEM

PREREQUISITES

- STARTS AS A MISCELLANEOUS QUEST TO "INVESTIGATE HARPERS FERRY" UPON VISITING HARPERS FERRY IN THE MIRE. USE ANY OF THE THREE MARKED TERMINALS, SELECT "MISSING PERSONS," THEN "MISSING HUNTING PARTY" TO START THIS QUEST.

A GRIM FATE

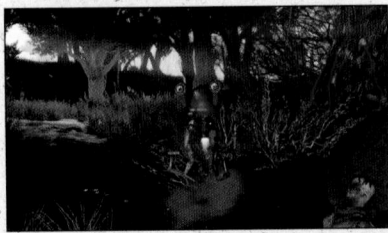

Search the bottom of the marked circle to find a Mr. Gutsy named "Hardball." Speak with Hardball to learn about what happened to the hunting party he was accompanying. He'll task you with tracking down a Signal Booster in either Harpers Ferry or Valley Galleria. We suggest going to the Valley Galleria. Harpers Ferry is a veritable fortress that can be difficult to traverse, while the Signal Booster in Valley Galleria is a short walk once inside the building.

ITEM ➡	> SIGNAL BOOSTER

SPECIAL DELIVERY

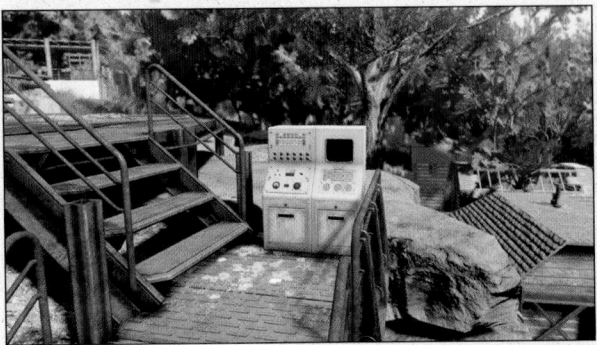

After obtaining the Signal Booster, head to Camp Venture in the south; then go to the helipad at the top of the camp. Use the control terminal to summon a Cargobot, and wait for it to arrive. Once it has lowered to the helipad, approach it and attach the Signal Booster by pressing the Activate button. Once the Cargobot lifts off, bring up your Pip-Boy and listen to the Distress Beacon radio station.

HOT AND COLD

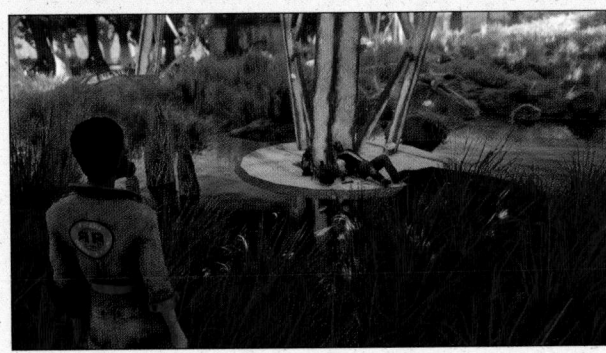

You'll need to track a Distress Beacon by following the signal strength indicator in the screen's top-left corner. The Distress Beacon is on the southern leg of the large white and red electrical tower, almost dead center of the triangle created by Southern Belle Motel, the Abandoned Waste Dump, and Haven Church. The Southern Belle Motel and Haven Church are both along Route 65, while the Abandoned Waste Dump is east of the Southern Belle Motel.

After grabbing the Distress Beacon, loot Randy's Holotape off his body (right next to the beacon) and listen to it.

ITEMS ➡	> RANDY'S HOLOTAPE > DISTRESS BEACON

Head to the rusted car on the northwestern leg of the electrical tower to find Nari Samir's body resting on the car's left side. Collect the Dyer Chemical ID Card and Nari's Holotape off of her body; then grab the Prototype Hazmat Suit from the backpack next to her.

ITEMS ➡	> DYER CHEMICAL ID CARD > NARI'S HOLOTAPE > PROTOTYPE HAZMAT SUIT

PARTY'S OVER

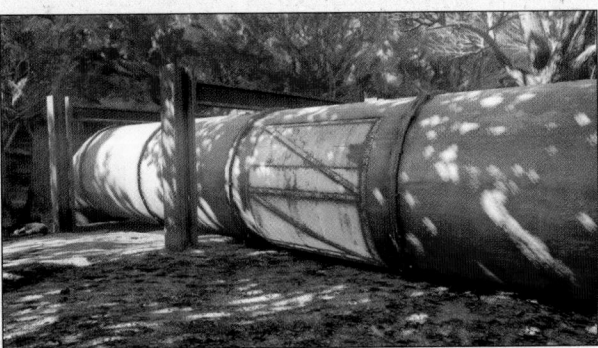

Head to Dyer Chemical, which is north of the electrical tower. Use the hatch to enter the pipes on the plant's west side. Use the ID Reader to the door's right to enter the Dyer Chemical Sewer. Go into the control room and grab Lucy's Holotape off her body to complete the quest.

ITEM ➡	> LUCY'S HOLOTAPE

MISTRESS OF MYSTERY QUEST LINE

The Mistress of Mystery quest line follows the rise and fall of the Order of Mysteries: a group of young women led by an ex-actress to bring justice to a world gone mad.

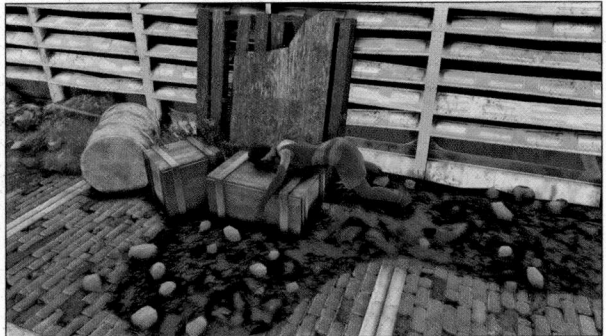

The line starts after you investigate the body of one of its fallen members. You'll find these bodies occasionally, but we've focused on the one you are guaranteed to encounter if you complete some of the earliest Main Quests. You'll find her lying next to a trash can in the center of the AVR Medical Center's exterior. Loot the Worn Veil and Damaged Holotape off of her to begin the first quest.

INTO THE MYSTERY

OBJECTIVES
- LISTEN TO THE DAMAGED HOLOTAPE
- LEARN THE HISTORY OF RIVERSIDE MANOR
- SEARCH THE FRONT PARLOR WHILE WEARING A VEIL
- DISCOVER THE SECRET OF RIVERSIDE MANOR

PREREQUISITES
- FIND A BODY WITH A WORN VEIL AND DAMAGED HOLOTAPE.

LOCATIONS
- RIVERSIDE MANOR

REWARDS
- VEIL OF SECRETS
- RANDOM AMMO
- RANDOM AID ITEM

FASCINATING FACTS FROM VAULT BOY

ALMOST 20 FORMER MEMBERS OF THE ORDER OF MYSTERIES CAN BE FOUND THROUGHOUT THE FOREST, THE ASH HEAP, AND SAVAGE DIVIDE. YOU CAN ACQUIRE THE WORN VEIL AND DAMAGED HOLOTAPE FROM MOST OF THEIR BODIES, BUT ONLY THE FIRST CORPSE YOU FIND WILL HAVE THEM.

UNRAVELING THE MYSTERY

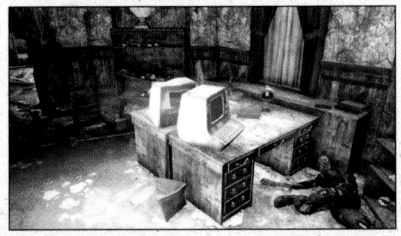

The holotape mentions Riverside Manor. Head to the manor's second floor study and read the journal entry for 7/29/77. Head back downstairs and equip the Worn Veil from the Apparel tab in your Items menu and begin searching the marked room. Inspect the folding screen in eastern corner and it will fold back automatically, revealing a hidden door.

INITIATE OF MYSTERIES

OBJECTIVES
- REGISTER AS AN INITIATE
- LISTEN TO THE INITIATE HOLOTAPE
- REQUEST A MENTOR ASSIGNMENT
- MEET YOUR MENTOR IN LEWISBURG
- (OPTIONAL) SEARCH FOR RAIDERS IN LEWISBURG
- REPORT TO CRYPTOS
- FIND A WAY TO AUTHORIZE YOUR OWN PROMOTION
- LOG IN TO CLAIM YOUR PROMOTION

PREREQUISITES
- COMPLETE "INTO THE MYSTERY."

LOCATIONS
- RIVERSIDE MANOR
- LEWISBURG

REWARDS
- GARB OF MYSTERIES
- RANDOM AMMO
- RANDOM AID ITEM

INITIATE INITIATION

Use one of the terminals in the center and register yourself as an Initiate. Open your Pip-Boy and listen to the "Order of Mysteries—Rank: Initiate" Holotape, which was added when you registered on the terminal. When you're done, use the terminal again and log in; then select "Database Queries," followed by "Initiate | Mentor Assignment."

ITEM ➡	> ORDER OF MYSTERIES—RANK: INITIATE

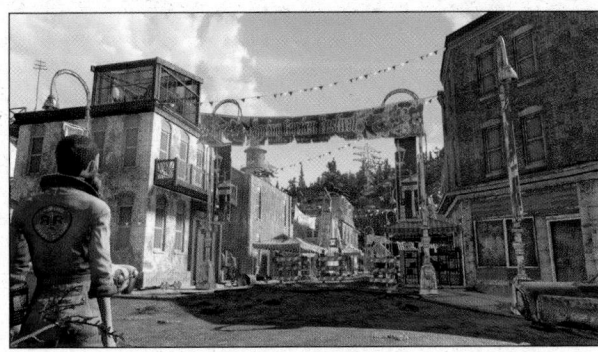

Once you have your mentor assignment, head out of the Riverside Manor and go to Lewisburg, which is southeast of the manor.

Helpful Hints from Vault Boy

Before you head out to track down your mentor, you can use the Fabricator down the stairs on the room's south side to repair the Worn Veil you acquired when you started this quest. Repairing it will grant you the Veil of Secrets, which prevents damage and diseases from toxic air—a very helpful tool since you'll be entering the Ash Heap, which is rife with toxic air.

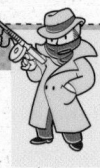

THE AIR IN LEWISBURG IS POISONOUS. DON'T ENTER UNLESS YOU'VE PROCURED SOME SORT OF MOUTH COVERING. FOR A QUICK SOLUTION, READ THE NEARBY "HELPFUL HINTS FROM VAULT BOY" TIP.

Once in Lewisburg, clear out the local Ghoul population; then look next to the Nuka-Cola machine to the right of the Ice Cream sign on the corner of W. Foster St. to find Natasha Hunt's body. Take the login password and holotape from her corpse, and listen to the holotape.

| ITEMS ➡ | ➤ MISTRESS NATASHA HUNT'S LOGIN |
| | ➤ ORDER OF MYSTERIES—LEWISBURG |

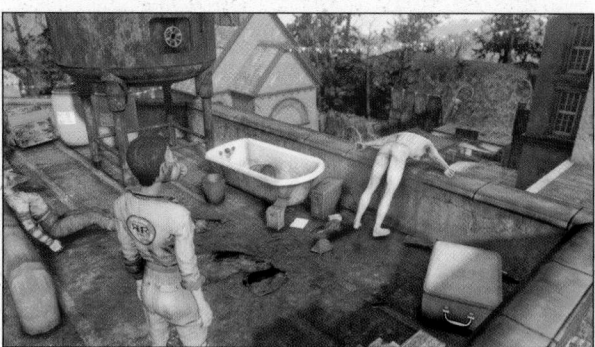

Head to the building across the street from Natasha, make your way to the back alley, and climb the stairs. Follow the path to the roof. Loot Kerry's body and pick up Note—Kerry's Orders.

| ITEM ➡ | ➤ NOTE—KERRY'S ORDERS |

With note in hand, return to Riverside Manor and use the terminal again. You'll quickly discover that only your mentor is allowed to authorize your promotion. So back out, log in with Natasha Hunt's ID, select "Administrative Actions," then "Authorize Promotion," and allow yourself the right to be promoted. Backtrack to the login screen and log in again, but this time as yourself.

Helpful Hints from Vault Boy

With Natasha Hunt's login details, you can access the terminal in the infirmary, which is up the northern stairs. Select "Safe Control" to open a safe to the terminal's right. You can also use it to access the terminal in the Council Chamber, on the opposite side of the room, to learn more about the Order's deliberations

You will complete the quest and also be given the ability to fabricate the Garb of Mysteries from the Fabricator in this basement.

NOVICE OF MYSTERIES

OBJECTIVES
- LISTEN TO THE NOVICE HOLOTAPE
- MASTER THE TOOLS OF THE MISTRESS OF MYSTERY
- EARN THE PHANTOM DEVICE
- EARN THE BLADE OF BASTET
- EARN THE VOICE OF SET
- LOG IN TO CLAIM YOUR PROMOTION

LOCATIONS
- RIVERSIDE MANOR

PREREQUISITES
- COMPLETE "INITIATE OF MYSTERIES."

REWARDS
- STEALTH BOY
- RANDOM AMMO
- RANDOM AID ITEM

LOOKING THE PART

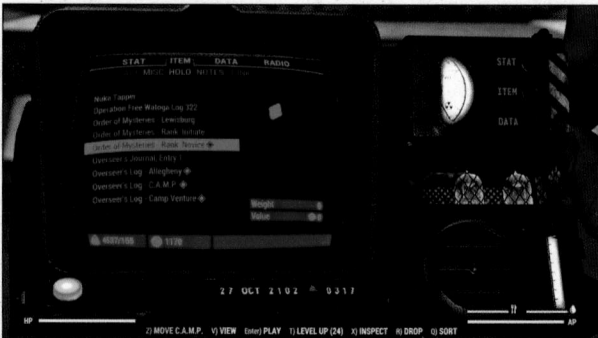

To get things rolling, open your Pip-Boy and listen to the Order of Mysteries—Rank: Novice Holotape. You will be tasked with earning several items to become a full-fledged member of the Order of Mysteries. You can find each of the three listed items in whatever order you choose. For simplicity's sake, we cover them in the order they appear in your objectives, but feel free to branch out in whatever way you choose.

Use the terminal, log in, and select "Mission Board" to see all three items. Select any of the items to start new quests, which will point you in the direction of the items. Once you've completed those three quests, return to this section and continue.

BACK ON TRACK

After you craft the Phantom Device, the Blade of Bastet, and the Voice of Set, return to Cryptos in the Riverside Manor basement and log in to claim your promotion to complete the quest.

FASCINATING FACTS FROM VAULT BOY!

MANY OF THE ITEMS YOU EARN FROM THE ORDER OF MYSTERIES CAN BE UPGRADED AS YOUR LEVEL INCREASES. YOU CAN UPGRADE THE GARB OF MYSTERIES AT ANY ARMOR WORKBENCH, AND THE BLADE OF BASTET AND VOICE OF SET AT ANY WEAPONS WORKBENCH.

CHASING SHADOWS

CRAFTING THE PHANTOM DEVICE

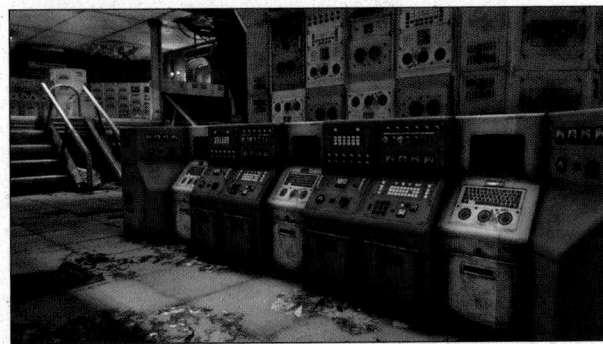

Listen to the Order of Mysteries—the Phantom Device Holotape to complete the first objective. Afterward, use Cryptos, the terminal in the basement, to select "Database Queries," then "Novice | Phantom Device Components" to locate the components necessary for building the device. You'll need to track down a Stealth Boy in North Cutthroat Camp and Hallucigen Gas in Garrahan Mining HQ.

Helpful Hints from Vault Boy

If you already have Hallucigen Gas or a Stealth Boy, you can use them and skip a step.

STEALING A STEALTH BOY

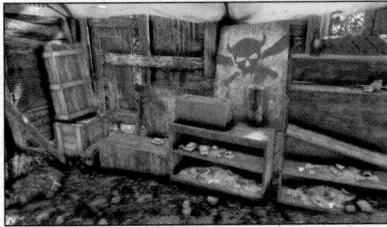

North Cutthroat Camp is located almost dead center of Savage Divide. The trek there is quite dangerous, so if you run into trouble, feel free to back off and do some other questing. You'll eventually end up back in the Savage Divide while doing other quests, so there's no shame in delaying this quest.

ITEM ➡ › STEALTH BOY

GRABBING HALLUCIGEN GAS

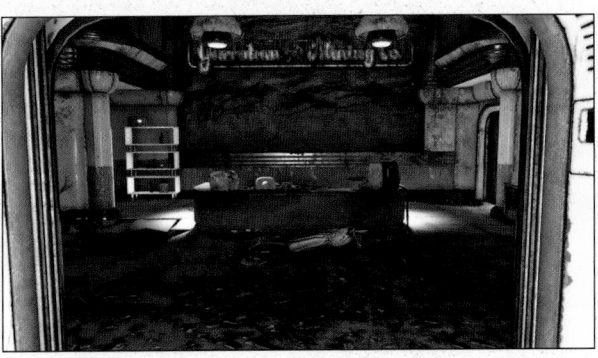

To reach the Hallucigen Gas, head south from Riverside Manor to reach Garrahan Mining Headquarters. Approach the objective marker and locate the safe in that back room. You'll need to either pick the lock on the safe or hack the nearby terminal to open the safe remotely.

ITEM ➡ › HALLUCIGEN GAS

When you have both components, return to Riverside Manor and use the Fabricator to craft the Phantom Device. You'll find it under the Aid tab in your Items menu. Take note, however, that it is single-use (and has a rather low time limit too). You can craft more from the Tinker's Workbench, but you'll need another Stealth Boy and canister of Hallucigen Gas.

ITEM ➡ › PHANTOM DEVICE

With the Phantom Device in hand, the quest concludes. Complete the other quests; then head back and read the rest of the "Novice of Mysteries" walkthrough to wrap up this overarching quest.

FORGING A LEGEND

TRAINING • CRAFTING AND C.A.M.P.ING • INVENTORY • QUESTS • ATLAS • BESTIARY • APPENDICES

HISTORIC HEIST

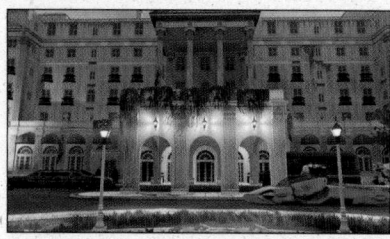

Finding the Historic Sword isn't too challenging. Simply head to The Whitespring Resort area east of Riverside Manor. The sword is locked in a case in the Presidential Cottage. To unlock the case, search the Protectron in the next room, and take the Presidential Cottage Password from its remains. Then locate the terminal next to the display case.

ITEM ➡	> PRESIDENTIAL COTTAGE PASSWORD HOLOTAPE

Use the terminal and select "STAFF ACCESS," followed by "Display Case Access" to open the case. You'll find Grant's Saber inside, which is our Historic Sword. Grab it, then return to Riverside Manor. Use the Fabricator on the basement's south end to craft a Swing Analyzer; then use the Weapon Workbench in the Fabricator room and add the Swing Analyzer to Grant's Saber.

ITEMS ➡	> GRANT'S SABER
	> SWING ANALYZER

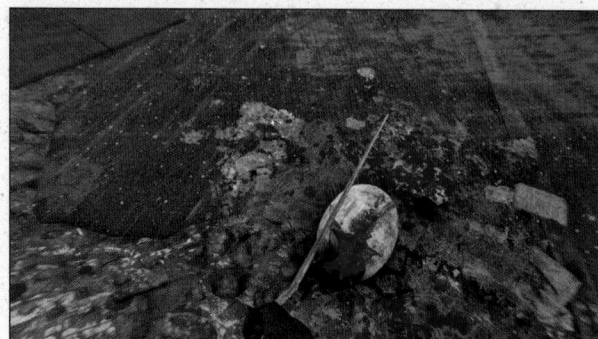

Your next step is to test Grant's Saber by killing six different types of enemies. This isn't terribly difficult, but it does require a good deal of patience and a willingness to do a bit of wandering. The Savage Divide has a very diverse ecology, and simply exploring new locations will allow you to find most of the targets you need. Or proceed with the other quests, Chasing Shadows and Prototypical Problems, and use the saber to confront the enemies you encounter while exploring their locations.

Once you kill six different enemy types, return to the Riverside Manor and use the Fabricator to create the Blade of Bastet and complete this quest.

ITEM ➡	> BLADE OF BASTET

PROTOTYPICAL PROBLEMS

> **OBJECTIVES**
> - **LISTEN TO THE VOICE OF SET HOLOTAPE**
> - **SEARCH CRYPTOS FOR EXPERIMENTAL WEAPONS RESEARCH**
> - **LOCATE THE EMP RESEARCH PROGRAM**
> - **FIND A WAY TO COPY THE EMP RESEARCH PROGRAM DATA**
> - **GET A PROJECT SIPHON HOLOTAPE**
> - **USE THE PROJECT SIPHON HOLOTAPE TO EXTRACT THE DATA**
> - **UPLOAD THE DATA INTO THE FABRICATOR**
> - **USE THE FABRICATOR TO MAKE THE VOICE OF SET**
>
> **LOCATIONS**   **REWARDS**
> - **SUGAR GROVE**   – **VOICE OF SET**
> - **RIVERSIDE MANOR**   – **RANDOM AMMO**
>   – **RANDOM AID ITEM**
>
> **PREREQUISITES**
> - **USE THE TERMINAL DURING "NOVICE OF MYSTERIES" AND SELECT "THE VOICE OF SET" TO BEGIN THIS QUEST.**

A VOICE TO DIE FOR

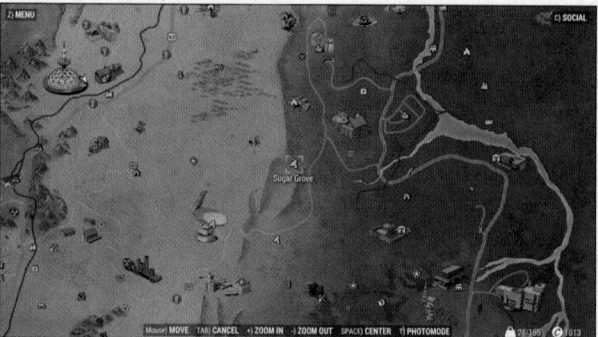

Sugar Grove is located on the east side of Savage Divide, due east of Top of the World. It's also the location for the EMP item we need to develop the Voice of Set. Once inside, head to the rear of the facility to find an advanced research terminal. The Blank Holotapes scattered around the terminal are a red herring, but they hint at your next problem. Read through the terminal's project reports and mail messages to learn more.

ITEM ➡	> BLANK HOLOTAPE

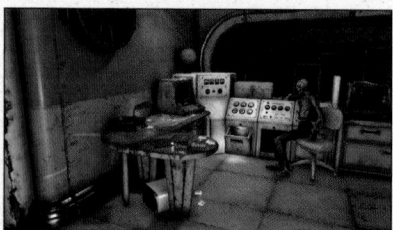

Your goal is the EMP research data, but you won't be able to download it without the proper tools. Fortunately, those tools can be found here in Sugar Grove. Follow your new quest target to the analyst's terminal in the nearby office, and dispense the last Project SIPHON holotape. Then return to the advanced research terminal, insert the Project SIPHON holotape, and download the data.

ITEM ➡	> PROJECT SIPHON HOLOTAPE

Once back at the manor, head to the Fabricator and insert the Project Siphon Holotape. Select "Play Holotape," then upload the data. Now select "Fabrication Services" and fabricate the Voice of Set to complete this quest.

ITEM ➜	❯ VOICE OF SET

SEEKER OF MYSTERIES

OBJECTIVES
- LISTEN TO THE SEEKER HOLOTAPE
- ACCEPT A MISTRESS-RANK MISSION
- LISTEN TO THE PLEASANT VALLEY HOLOTAPE
- INFILTRATE PLEASANT VALLEY SKI RESORT
- SEARCH FOR INFORMATION ABOUT THE ORDER OF MYSTERIES
- LOCATE BRODY'S ROOM
- BREAK INTO BRODY'S ROOM
- (OPTIONAL) FIND A KEY TO BRODY'S ROOM
- FIND BRODY'S HOLOTAPE
- (OPTIONAL) FIND A PASSWORD FOR BRODY'S TERMINAL

LOCATIONS
- RIVERSIDE MANOR
- PLEASANT VALLEY SKI RESORT

REWARDS
- RANDOM RAIDER TORSO ARMOR MOD
- RANDOM AMMO
- RANDOM AID ITEM

PREREQUISITES
- COMPLETE "NOVICE OF MYSTERIES."

HIDE AND SEEKER

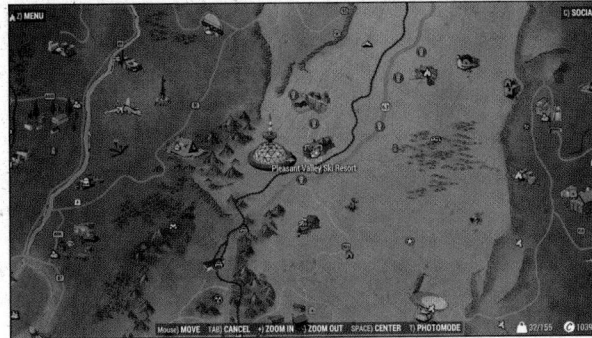

To kick things off, listen to the Order of Mysteries—Rank: Seeker Holotape; then use Cryptos to pick up a Mistress-rank mission from the "Mission Board" entry. The Order of Mysteries—Pleasant Valley Holotape will be added to your inventory. Listen to it, then put on your snow gear, because we're heading to Pleasant Valley Ski Resort (conveniently located east of Top of the World in Savage Divide).

ITEM ➜	❯ ORDER OF MYSTERIES—PLEASANT VALLEY HOLOTAPE

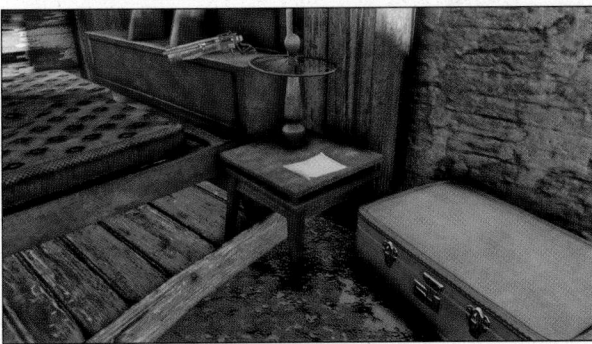

At the resort, visit each of the notes at the objective markers. Read them to get a broader perspective on the Raiders and their interactions with the Order of Mysteries. It sounds like one of the Raiders, Brody, had some valuable intel about the order.

If your lockpicking skill is up to Level 3, you can pick your way straight into Brody's room. If it's not, read the "Yo Brody" entry on the nearby terminal; this will give you the location of his room key—specifically by placing an objective marker on the map for you to follow.

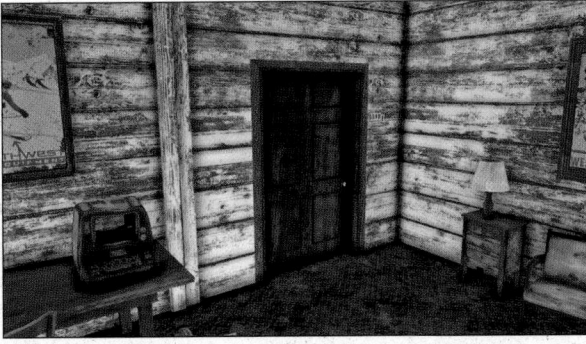

After you enter Brody's room, your next goal is to access his terminal. However, it requires a Level 3 Hacking skill to crack it. If you happen to have a Bobby Pin handy, you can crack open the footlocker at the base of the bed, pull out the note, and give it a read to learn the location of the password to the terminal. Either hack the computer or return to the main lodge of the ski resort. Head upstairs, and use the terminal to reset the user password for "Torrance, Brody."

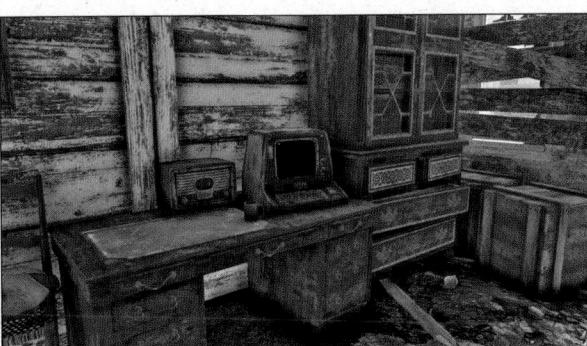

Whatever your method, once you're on the terminal, select the second prompt. Follow it through and take the holotape to complete the quest.

TRAINING

CRAFTING AND C.A.M.P.ING

INVENTORY

QUESTS

ATLAS

BESTIARY

APPENDICES

OBJECTIVES
- GAIN ACCESS TO THE HEADMISTRESS' OFFICE
- SEARCH THE HEADMISTRESS' OFFICE
- LOCATE THE MEETING PLACE
- (OPTIONAL) LOOK FOR CLUES TO THE MEETING PLACE
- SEARCH THE BODIES
- BECOME A MISTRESS OF MYSTERY

LOCATIONS
- RIVERSIDE MANOR

REWARDS
- EYE OF RA
- RANDOM AMMO
- RANDOM AID ITEM

PREREQUISITES
- COMPLETE "SEEKER OF MYSTERIES."

THE FALL OF THE ORDER OF MYSTERIES

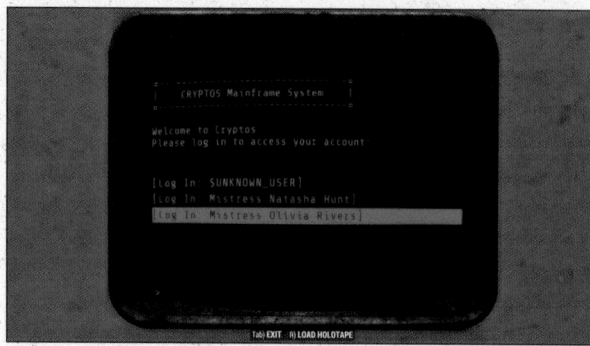

Use the Cryptos terminal in the Riverside Manor basement and log in with your new login account. Select "Administrative Actions," "Authorize Access," then "Authorize Access—Headmistress' Office." Make your way down the personnel list and select yourself to have authorized access. Now head up the west steps and use the hand scanner to enter the Headmistress's office.

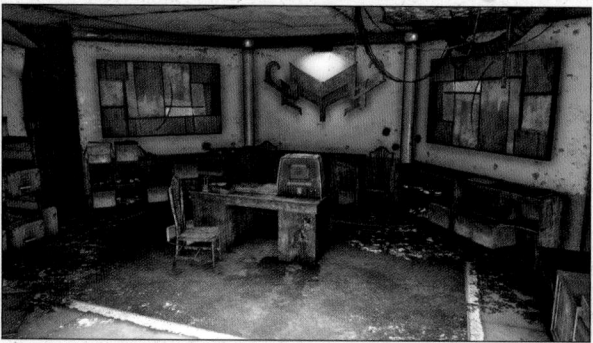

Use the Headmistress's terminal and select the first entry. You can also read through her personal journal to learn about the rise and tragic fall of the Order of Mysteries. Once finished, go to the manor's second floor and use the study terminal.

Read the first entry of the "Personal Journal"; then make your way to the terminal on the other side of the house. Read the first entry of the "Personal Journal" on this terminal to get the location: just northeast of Top of the World.

When you arrive, grab the items from the bodies, and return to Riverside Manor.

ITEMS ➡	> HEADMISTRESS SHANNON RIVERS' LOGIN
	> SHANNON RIVERS' RECORDING
	> EYE OF RA

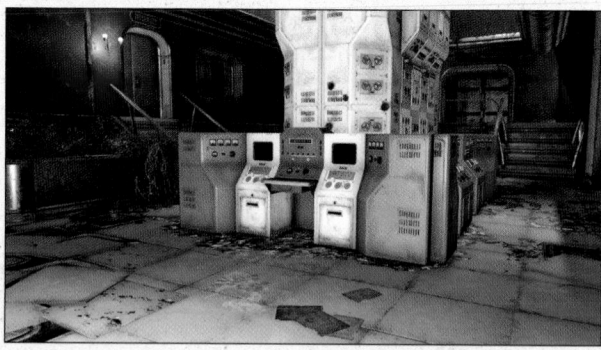

Once back in the manor basement, log in to Cryptos with Headmistress Shannon Rivers's account. Select "Administrative Actions," "Authorize Promotion," then "Authorize Promotion—Mistress of Mystery." Move down the personnel list and select yourself for the promotion, then back out and log in on your own account to become a full-fledged Mistress of Mystery and complete the quest.

You'll pick up the Order of Mysteries—Rank: Mistress Holotape upon signing in and you'll have the Eye of Ra as your prize for completing the quest line.

FASCINATING FACTS FROM VAULT BOY!
THE EYE OF RA EMPOWERS THE MISTRESS OF MYSTERY'S ITEMS, OFTEN DOUBLING THEIR POWERS OR EFFECTIVENESS. IT REQUIRES SOME COMMITMENT, THOUGH: IN ORDER TO EQUIP IT, YOU MUST BE WEARING THE GARB OF MYSTERIES.

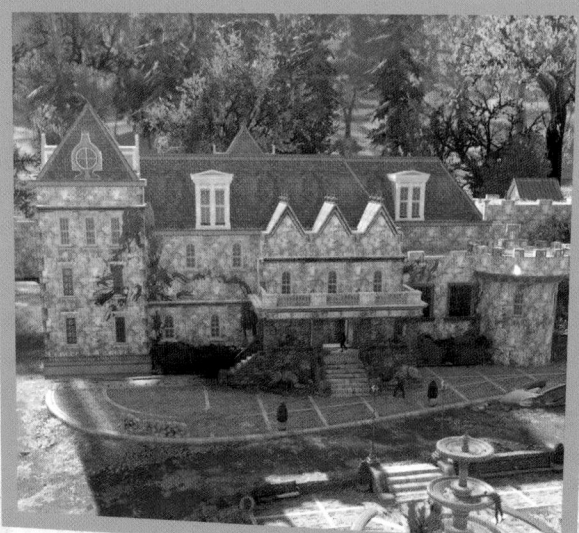

DAILY, REPEATABLE, AND DROP QUESTS

Aside from events, Main Quests, and Side Quests, you'll find smaller adventures that follow a very different set of rules.

DAILY QUESTS

As the name implies, Daily Quests can be played once a day. Though replayable like events, Daily Quests are always in the same fixed location. The first location you find one in is the place it will be 24 hours later.

REPEATABLE QUESTS

Repeatable Quests are the only quests in the game that you can play as frequently as you want. There aren't many of them, but you can play them again and again for loot and a chance to obtain a Legendary weapon or piece of armor.

DROP QUESTS

Truly, Drop Quests might have more in common with Side Quests than Daily and Repeatable Quests, but their odd starting method puts them in a league of their own. In order to start a Drop Quest, you must find a specific item dropped by a random enemy or in a random container. These items will be indicated with an objective marker, so they are a bit hard to miss. Once you loot them, the quest begins.

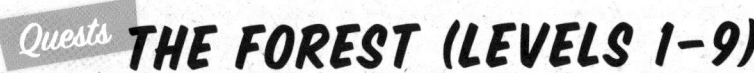

Quests THE FOREST (LEVELS 1–9)

ECOLOGICAL BALANCE

OBJECTIVES
- **INVESTIGATE THE TRAILER**
- **LISTEN TO THE "MESSAGE FOR JEFF" HOLOTAPE**
- **LEARN AMY KERRY'S LOCATION**
- **RETRIEVE AMY'S TERMINAL PASSWORD**
- **ACCESS THE ENVIRONMENTAL MONITORING PROGRAM**
- **ESTABLISH A DEVICE LINK WITH THE TERMINAL**
- **COLLECT AND UPLOAD THE WATER, SOIL, AND AIR HOLOTAPES**
- **PROCESS THE SENSOR DATA**

LOCATIONS
- **TYGART WATER TREATMENT**
- **COW SPOTS CREAMERY**

REWARDS
- **ANTISEPTIC**
- **RANDOM AMMO**
- **RANDOM AID ITEM**
- **RANDOM PLAN, ARMOR, MOD, OR WEAPON**
- **CHANCE FOR A RANDOM LEGENDARY WEAPON OR ARMOR**

PREREQUISITES
- **FIND AND LISTEN TO THE HOLOTAPE IN THE TRAILER ON THE NORTH SIDE TYGART WATER TREATMENT.**

ENVIRONMENTAL INVESTIGATIONS

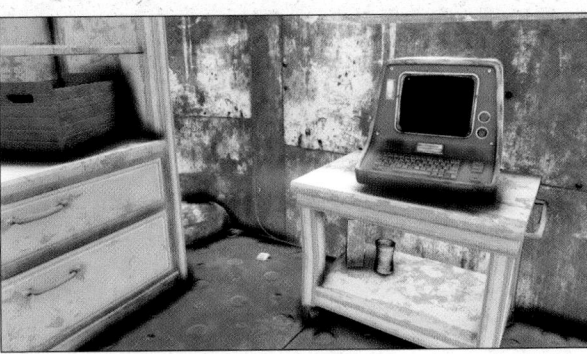

As you approach the trailer, an objective marker and the "Investigate the Trailer" Miscellaneous Quest will appear. Grab and listen to the holotape at the objective marker; then use the terminal. Select "Messages," then "Date Night?"

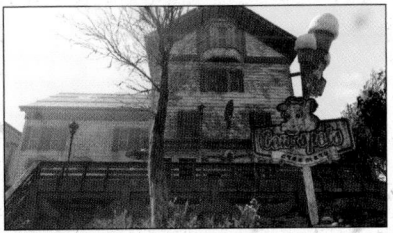

Head to Cow Spots Creamery at the marked location and loot Amy Kerry's corpse. Read "Amy's Note"; then return to Tygart Water Treatment. Use the terminal and select "Environmental Monitoring Program." Select "Establish Portable Device Link." Your job now is to collect data on the local water, soil, and air quality, then upload via this terminal.

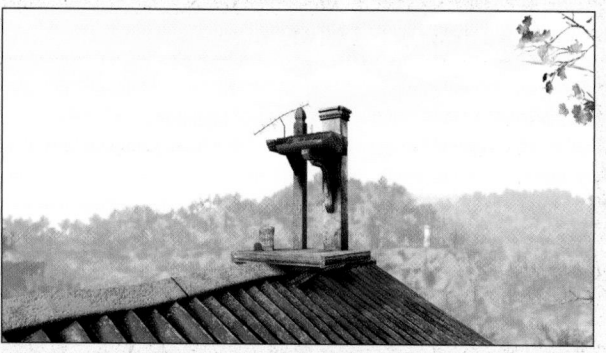

The Air Data Holotape is on the roof of the building at the marked location. Climb up the stairs, then jump onto the roof to reach it. The data's locations change every time you play through this quest, but they are never hard to reach. You can find all three Data Holotapes marked on your map.

ITEMS ➜	> AIR DATA HOLOTAPE > WATER DATA HOLOTAPE > SOIL DATA HOLOTAPE

After collecting all three holotapes, return to the Tygart Water Treatment Terminal and upload each one. Afterward, either step off the terminal and use it again, or select another entry and back out. When you return, a new entry labeled "Begin Data Processing" will appear. Select it to complete the quest.

HEART OF THE ENEMY

OBJECTIVES	REWARDS
– FIND THE AUTOMATED RESEARCH TERMINAL	– RANDOM WEAPON
– POWER UP THE AUTOMATED RESEARCH TERMINAL	– RANDOM AMMO
– RETRIEVE VIABLE SCORCHBEAST DNA	– RANDOM AID ITEM
LOCATIONS	– RANDOM PLAN, ARMOR, MOD, OR WEAPON
– VAULT-TEC UNIVERSITY	– CHANCE FOR A GATLING LASER
	– CHANCE FOR A RANDOM LEGENDARY WEAPON OR ARMOR

PREREQUISITES

– PICK UP THE "MISSION 099-01 ORDERS" NOTE FROM INSIDE THE DESK UNDER SENIOR KNIGHT WILSON'S TERMINAL ON THE FOURTH FLOOR OF FORT DEFIANCE TO START THIS QUEST (YOU MUST COMPLETE "RECRUITMENT BLUES" TO ACCESS THE FOURTH FLOOR).

BACK TO SCHOOL

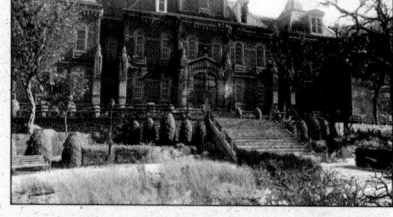

Head to Vault-Tec University on the east side of the Forest (right next to Morgantown). Enter the building and use the Automated Research Terminal. Select the top entry, then "Execute automated test."

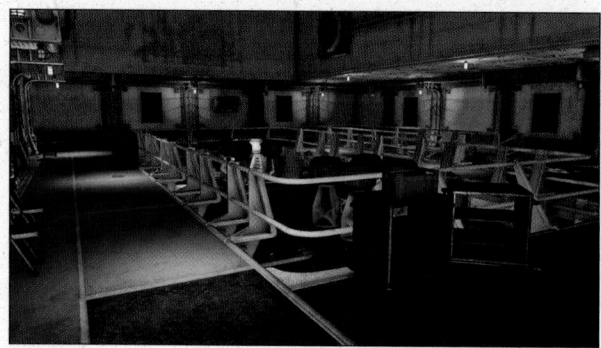

You can't perform an automated test until you give more power to the terminal. To do this, head north, then drop down a floor when you reach the room with the large power generators. Hack into the Power Terminal and select "Allocate power to Automated Research Lab." Now return to the Automated Research Terminal, select the first entry again, and click "Execute automated test" once more.

BIOLOGY CLASS

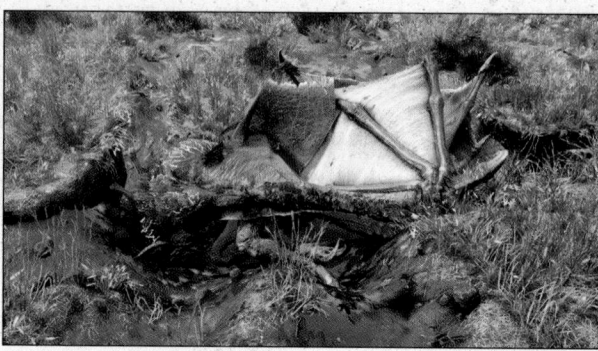

You must obtain some Scorchbeast DNA, which means heading to Scorchbeast country: Cranberry Bog. You'll need to harvest DNA off a dead Scorchbeast (by pressing the button displayed in the bottom-right corner of the loot window), but thankfully it doesn't have to be one you killed yourself. Unfortunately, you still must face off with one if you can't find a fresh kill.

ITEM ➜	> VIABLE SCORCHBEAST DNA

Head back to Vault-Tec University and insert the Scorchbeast DNA into the Automated Centrifuge; then use the terminal. Select the top entry, then "Execute automated test" to complete this quest.

STRANGE BREW

OBJECTIVES	LOCATIONS
– COLLECT 10 HONEY	– GIANT TEAPOT
– DELIVER HONEY TO SWEETWATER	

REWARDS
- SPECIAL BLEND DRINK RECIPE
- HONEY
- RANDOM AMMO
- RANDOM AID ITEM
- RANDOM PLAN, ARMOR, MOD, OR WEAPON
- CHANCE FOR A RANDOM LEGENDARY WEAPON OR ARMOR

PREREQUISITES
- APPROACH THE GIANT TEAPOT, THEN SPEAK WITH SWEETWATER (SOMEWHERE NEARBY) TO BEGIN THIS QUEST.

A SMACKERAL OF HONEY

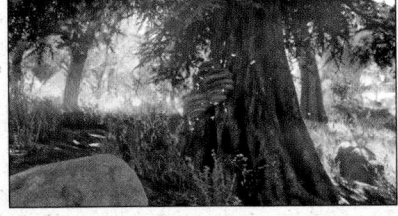

Head to one of the objective markers and search the area for beehives. You'll find honey within them, but you'll also be attacked by angry Bee Swarms. Defeat them with melee attacks, then harvest the hives.

Once you have 10 Honey in hand, return to Sweetwater and deliver the goods to complete the quest.

THE BELL TOLLS (REPEATABLE)

EVENT LOCATION
- CHARLESTON (NEAR THE CHARLESTON HERALD—THE FOREST)

REWARDS
- RANDOM AMMO AND AID ITEM

DETAILS

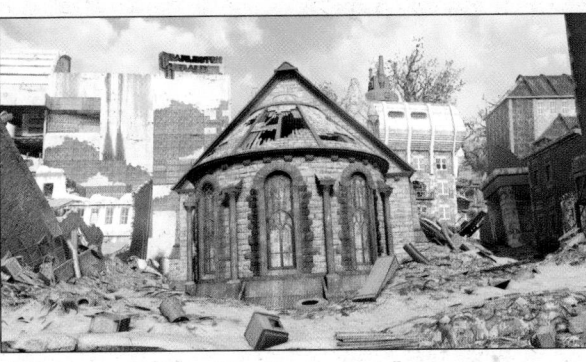

Collect loot being dug up from in and around a Charleston church—just watch out for the agitated Mole Rats that are being drawn up by the digging.

Quests TOXIC VALLEY (LEVELS 10-14)

BIG GAME HUNT

OBJECTIVES	REWARDS
– KILL ONE RADSTAG	– HUNTER PERK
– KILL ONE STINGWING	– RANDOM AMMO
– KILL ONE SNALLYGASTER	– RANDOM AID ITEM
LOCATIONS	– RANDOM PLAN, ARMOR, MOD, OR WEAPON
– BLACK BEAR LODGE	– CHANCE FOR A RANDOM LEGENDARY WEAPON OR ARMOR

PREREQUISITES
- YOU'LL RECEIVE A MISCELLANEOUS QUEST TO SPEAK WITH THE HUNTMASTER IN THE BASEMENT OF BLACK BEAR LODGE. SPEAK WITH HIM TO START THE QUEST.

HUNTING SEASON

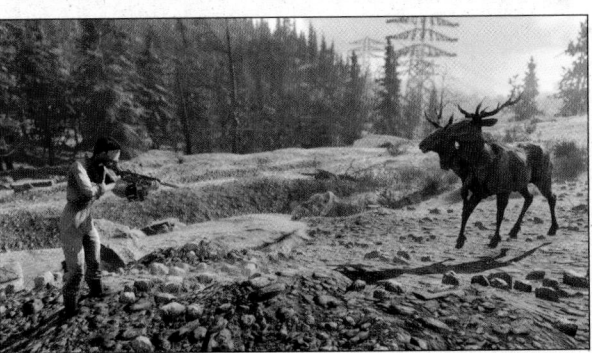

Head to each of the three marked locations and search in their general vicinity to track down your targets. If they are not there, head to the next location and come back. You shouldn't have too much trouble finding the Stingwing or the Snallygaster, since both of them are hostile and will likely chase you harder than you chase them. The Radstag, on the other hand, can be really skittish and hard to locate. Search its area first, then leave and come back as needed.

TRAINING

CRAFTING AND C.A.M.P.ING

INVENTORY

QUESTS

ATLAS

BESTIARY

APPENDICES

BURIED WITH HONOR

OBJECTIVES
- TALK TO THE CURATOR
- GET THE REMAINS
- PUT THE REMAINS IN AN OPEN GRAVE
- BURY THE REMAINS

LOCATIONS
- PHILIPPI
- BATTLEFIELD
- CEMETERY
- PRICKETT'S FORT

REWARDS
- BLACK POWDER AMMO
- RANDOM AMMO
- RANDOM AID ITEM
- RANDOM PLAN, ARMOR, MOD, OR WEAPON
- CHANCE FOR A RANDOM LEGENDARY WEAPON OR ARMOR

PREREQUISITES
- NONE

RESPECT FOR THE DEAD

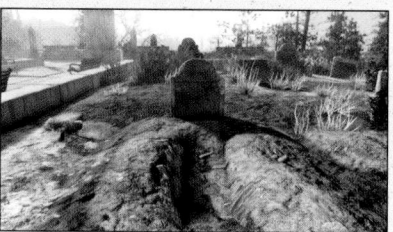

In order to truly start the quest, you must speak with the Curator at Prickett's Fort, up the road north. Enter the fort and grab the remains; then head back, place them in the open grave, pick up the shovel in front of the dirt pile next to the grave, and bury the remains.

ITEM ➡ > SOLDIER'S REMAINS

PASS THE BUCK

OBJECTIVES
- PICK UP THREE BARRELS
- (OPTIONAL) SINK THE BARRELS
- DUMP THE BARRELS

LOCATIONS
- PIONEER SCOUT CAMP
- HEMLOCK HOLES

REWARDS
- NUCLEAR MATERIAL
- RANDOM AMMO
- RANDOM AID ITEM
- RANDOM PLAN, ARMOR, MOD, OR WEAPON
- CHANCE FOR A RANDOM LEGENDARY WEAPON OR ARMOR

PREREQUISITES
- NONE

TARGET RICH ENVIRONMENT

OBJECTIVES
- GET NEW PAPER TARGETS

LOCATIONS
- CLARKSBURG SHOOTING CLUB
- WAVY WILLARD'S WATER PARK

REWARDS
- RANDOM WEAPON
- RANDOM AMMO
- RANDOM AID ITEM
- RANDOM PLAN, ARMOR, MOD, OR WEAPON
- CHANCE FOR A RANDOM LEGENDARY WEAPON OR ARMOR

PREREQUISITES
- YOU'LL RECEIVE A MISCELLANEOUS QUEST WHEN YOU REACH THE CLARKSBURG SHOOTING CLUB. APPROACH THE SHOOTING RANGE ATTENDANT AND THE QUEST WILL BE AUTOMATICALLY ADDED.

DON'T FORGET YOUR RADAWAY

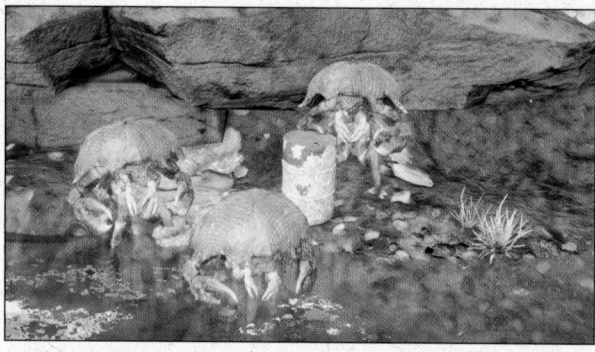

You'll have to go in and around the irradiated lake to find and dispose of the three Toxic Barrels. If you have three AGI, you can dispose of them on the spot. Otherwise, you have to carry them northwest to Hemlock Holes to dump them in the Dumpster there. Once you dump the barrels, however, the quest completes.

ITEM ➡ > TOXIC BARREL X 3

MENIAL LABOR

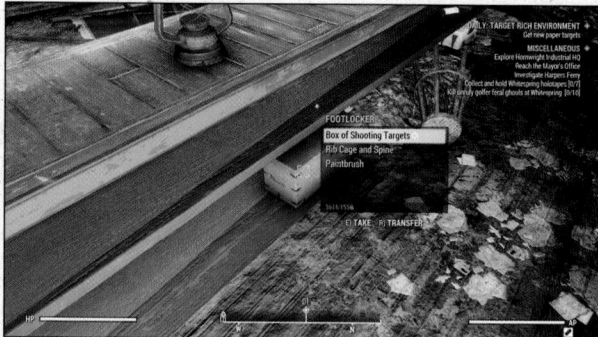

Head to Wavy Willard's Water Park northwest of Clarksburg Shooting Club. Grab the Box of Shooting Targets from the level below the park. You can access the lower level through the hole in the empty cobra pool, from underneath the highest point of the crocodile slide, or from a set of stairs on the right side of the Crocolossus Mountain entrance building.

Once you have the targets, head back and put them on the shooting range to complete the quest.

THRILL OF THE GRILL

OBJECTIVES
- GATHER FOOD FOR THE CHEF

LOCATIONS
- HEMLOCK HOLES (TOXIC VALLEY)

REWARDS
- COOKING RECIPE
- RANDOM AMMO
- RANDOM AID ITEM
- RANDOM PLAN, ARMOR, MOD, OR WEAPON
- CHANCE FOR A RANDOM LEGENDARY WEAPON OR ARMOR

PREREQUISITES
- NONE

WET HOT VIRGINIAN SUMMER

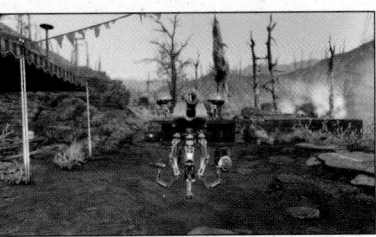

The robot cook at Hemlock Holes Country Club is having a cookout, but he's fresh out of meat and vegetables. Track down some good eats for the chef to make this a post-apocalyptic barbecue to remember.

Quests SAVAGE DIVIDE (LEVELS 15-24)

SOMEONE TO TALK TO

OBJECTIVES
- LOAD THE VOX INTERPRETER HOLOTAPE INTO YOUR PIP-BOY
- SHOOT THE THREE MARKED ANIMALS WITH A VOX DART

LOCATIONS
- MONONGAH

REWARDS
- SYRINGER AMMO
- RANDOM AMMO
- RANDOM AID ITEM
- RANDOM PLAN, ARMOR, MOD, OR WEAPON
- CHANCE FOR A RANDOM LEGENDARY WEAPON OR ARMOR

PREREQUISITES
- THIS QUEST STARTS VIA A MISCELLANEOUS QUEST IN MONONGAH (NORTH OF TOP OF THE WORLD). YOU MUST USE THE COMPUTER TERMINAL IN THE BASEMENT OF THE MARKED HOUSE, SELECT "BEGIN VOX INTERPRETER DATA COLLECTION EXERCISE," AND TAKE THE VOX SYRINGER OUT OF THE BOX TO THE LEFT OF THE TERMINAL TO BEGIN THIS QUEST.

IF I COULD TALK WITH THE ANIMALS

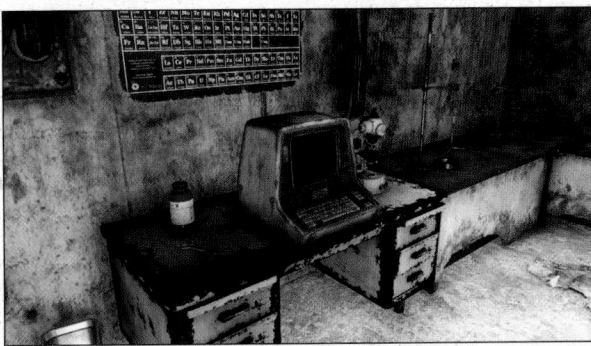

Open your Pip-Boy and insert the Vox Interpreter Holotape. You'll be tasked with hunting down and shooting three randomly-selected animals with your Vox Syringer. Afterward, you must wait for a timer to tick down while your Pip-Boy analyzes their speech patterns.

After shooting all three animals, head back to the basement in Monongah and return the Vox Syringer to the container you took it from. Also return the Vox Interpreter Holotape to the terminal by selecting the bottom option to complete the quest.

TRICK OR TREAT?

OBJECTIVES
- COLLECT 10 PUMPKINS
- DELIVER PUMPKINS TO JACK

LOCATIONS
- PUMPKIN HOUSE

REWARDS
- PUMPKIN GRENADES
- PUMPKIN GRENADE RECIPE
- RADIOACTIVE PUMPKIN SEEDS

PREREQUISITES
- APPEARS AS A MISCELLANEOUS QUEST FIRST; LISTEN TO JACK AT THE PUMPKIN HOUSE AND IT WILL START THIS QUEST.

THE PUMPKIN KING

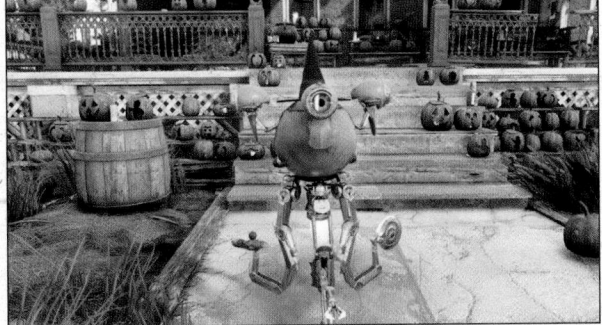

Follow the marker to a kids' hay ride with plenty of pumpkins to go around. Beware of Scorchbeasts from the nearby fissure! Deliver the pumpkins to complete the quest and earn some Pumpkin Grenades as a reward.

EARTH MOVER (REPEATABLE)

LOCATIONS	REWARDS
– MOUNT BLAIR	– RANDOM ORE
PREREQUISITES	– RANDOM AMMO
– CLAIM THE	– RANDOM AID ITEM
MOUNT BLAIR	– RANDOM PLAN, ARMOR, MOD, OR
WORKSHOP	WEAPON
	– CHANCE FOR A RANDOM LEGENDARY
	WEAPON OR ARMOR

CAN YOU DIG IT?

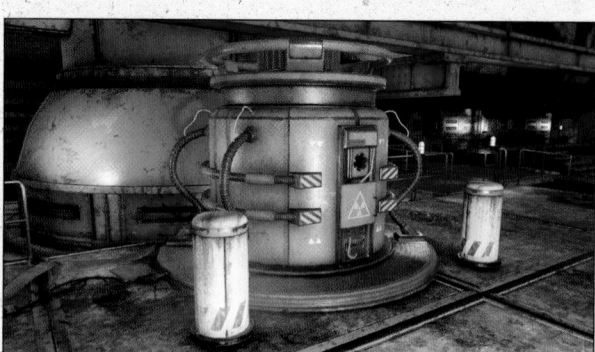

Perched atop Mount Blair, the "Rockhound" Bucket-Wheel Excavator has defiantly stood the test of time. Armed with the proper blueprints and a bit of determination, it's time to bring this sleeping beast back to life.

Follow your objective marker to the terminal in the Control Room and access it to learn how to power up the Rockhound. Find or craft four Ignition Cores and insert each one into a reactor and the Rockhound noisily comes on.

Defend the Rockhound from the waves of enemies attracted to all the noise! Enemies will focus their attacks on the reactors, and you'll have to repair them to keep the Rockhound running. The Rockhound will deposit metal in a collector for thirty minutes until its Ignition Cores are spent, so fend off foes and keep the reactors in good repair to maximize your metal production.

LOST AND FOUND (DROP)

OBJECTIVES
– USE THE MOLE MINER KEY TO OPEN A RANDOM CHEST
LOCATIONS
– RANDOM
REWARDS
– RANDOM JUNK ITEMS
– RANDOM AMMO
– RANDOM AID ITEM
PREREQUISITES
– LOOT A RANDOM KEY OFF OF A MOLE MINER'S CORPSE.

WHERE DID I PLACE MY KEYS?

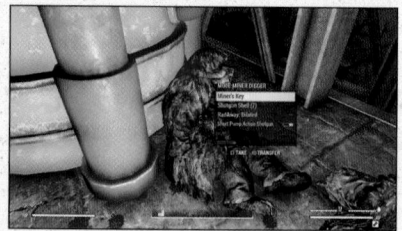

Sometimes when you kill a Mole Miner, they'll drop a key. This key will unlock one of several supply lockers around Appalachia. Which one it unlocks is completely random, but once you have the key, you'll know exactly which locker to visit.

Mole Miners are most common to the mines of the Ash Heap. You'll find them in pretty much any location listed as a "Mine" on the map, but if you're specifically trying to track down one of their keys, hunting them in the Ash Heap will prove the most fruitful.

After you loot the designated chest, the quest completes. This quest is repeatable, however. Find another key on another dead Mole Miner and the hunt begins anew.

LUCKY STRIKE

LOCATIONS
– RANDOM MINING LOCATION
REWARDS
– THE LOCATION OF AN ORE DIG SITE
– RANDOM AMMO
– RANDOM AID ITEM
PREREQUISITES
– PURCHASE A MAP FROM THE U-MINE-IT! MACHINE.

TREASURE HUNTING

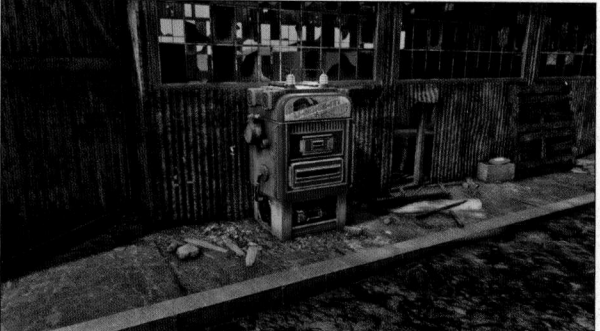

Purchase a map from the "U-Mine-It!" machine to start the quest. The location it points you to is random, but the objective once you arrive is simple: excavate the ore.

These quests aren't complicated: simply complete the tasks as they appear and you'll have them wrapped up in no time. Just be prepared for resistance along the way—and a good bit of on-foot traveling.

MISTAKEN IDENTITY

OBJECTIVES

- GO TO THE CAMDEN PARK MAIN ENTRANCE
- REPORT FOR YOUR SHIFT
- PUT ON YOUR UNIFORM
- CLOCK IN FOR YOUR SHIFT

- CALIBRATE MR. FUZZY'S GAMES
- GO TO THE CHOW LINE
- GO TO THE DROSS TOSS
- GO TO THE LUCKY MUCKER
- VISIT THE COMPANY STORE

PREREQUISITES

- THIS QUEST WILL BE ADDED AUTOMATICALLY UPON APPROACHING CAMDEN PARK.

LOCATIONS

- CAMDEN PARK (NORTHWEST SIDE OF THE ASH HEAP)

REWARDS

- MR. FUZZY TOKEN
- RANDOM AMMO
- RANDOM AID ITEM
- RANDOM PLAN, ARMOR, MOD, OR WEAPON
- CHANCE FOR A RANDOM LEGENDARY WEAPON OR ARMOR

MR. FUZZY'S WILD RIDE

Head to the objective marker and pull the Camden Park Uniform out of the locker. Put on your new uniform; then use the time clock next to the door to clock in for your shift.

ITEM ➡ 〉 CAMDEN PARK UNIFORM

At this point, three new Daily Quests will be added, but they are all a part of your current quest. We will cover them as if they were objectives in this quest, rather than quests on their own, since you can't activate them without starting "Mistaken Identity"—at least not on your first go-round.

THE CHOW LINE

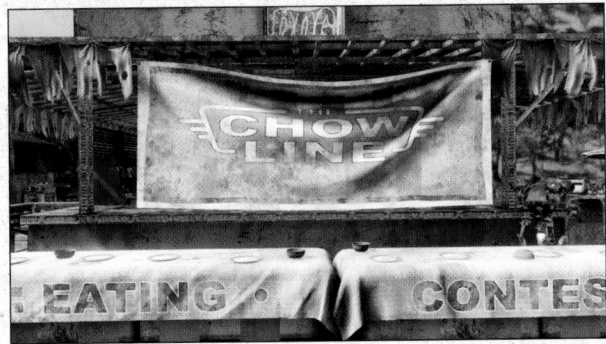

Go speak with Zoe and she'll explain the rules of the Chow Line. In case you need a reminder, as soon as you grab the paper towel, you'll need to eat six moldy hot dogs within 60 seconds as Zoe brings them out. Eat them fast enough and you'll earn a few Mr. Fuzzy Tokens. Fail and...well, if it means not eating six moldy hot dogs, maybe failing is the only real way to win.

DROSS TOSS

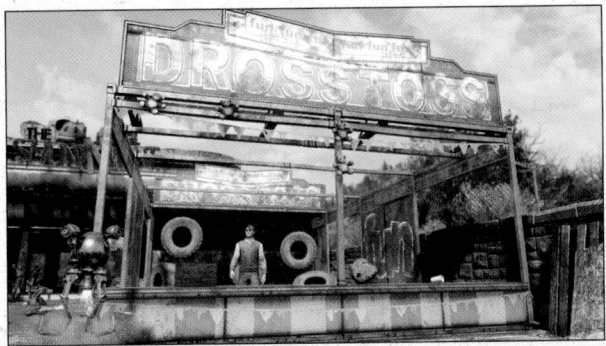

In order to calibrate this game, you need to throw dross into the used tires within the time limit. Once you start, hold and release the Grenade button to throw the dross. To start, pick up the dross off the counter.

LUCKY MUCKER

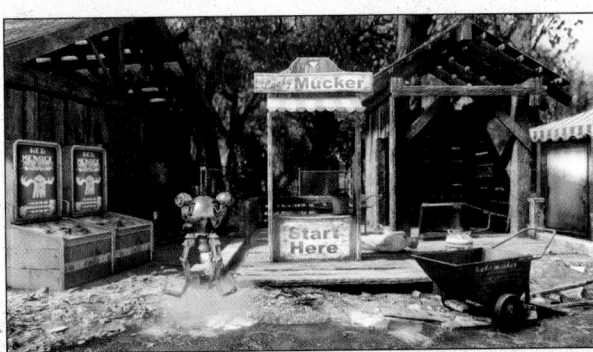

To complete this game, you must run to wheelbarrows scattered around the park and deposit coal into them within the time limit. It can be a bit tricky to spot them when you're around the objective marker, but don't panic! You have plenty of time to scan the area; the circles created by the objective markers will help narrow your search. When you're ready to start, grab the coal bucket. Once you locate all the wheelbarrows around the park, return to Zeke to complete this game.

BIG TOKENS! BIG PRIZES! I LOVE IT!

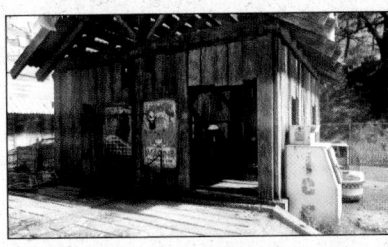

After you complete all three games, head to the Boss to complete the quest. If you want to redeem your Mr. Fuzzy Tokens, you must remove your Camden Park Uniform, then use the terminals next to the Boss. Save up enough and you can get a Paddle Ball, a Camden Whacker, or even a fabulous Mr. Fuzzy Costume!

FASCINATING FACTS FROM VAULT BOY

IF YOU'RE STRUGGLING TO REMEMBER WHAT THE PRIZE SHOP AT CAMDEN PARK HAS, ALWAYS REMEMBER THIS PAGE:

NAME	COST	NAME	COST
Mr. Fuzzy Pencil	5 tokens	Paddle Ball	50 tokens
10 Paddle Ball Ammo	5 tokens	Camden Whacker	50 tokens
Cotton Candy Bites	5 tokens	Super Comic Book	100
Gumdrops	5 tokens	Mr. Fuzzy Costume	150
Jumbo Mr. Fuzzy Plush	20 tokens	Mr. Fuzzy Costume Head	300
Mr. Fuzzy Mining Helmet	20 tokens		

TRAINING

CRAFTING AND C.A.M.P.ING

INVENTORY

QUESTS

ATLAS

BESTIARY

APPENDICES

IDLE EXPLOSIVES

OBJECTIVES
- **TALK TO BOOMER**
- **LOCATE INERT BOMBS**

LOCATIONS
- **SOUTHERN BELLE MOTEL**

REWARDS
- **ALUMINUM**
- **ADHESIVE**
- **BLAST MINE PLANS**
- **RANDOM AMMO**
- **RANDOM AID ITEM**
- **CHANCE FOR A RANDOM LEGENDARY WEAPON OR ARMOR**

PREREQUISITES
- **APPROACH BOOMER NEAR THE CENTER OF THE SOUTHERN BELLE MOTEL MAP MARKER TO START THIS QUEST.**

PLAY TIME

OBJECTIVES
- **COMPLETE A TASK GIVEN BY CHLOE**

LOCATIONS
- **BERKELEY SPRINGS**

REWARDS
- **PYROLYZER (MODDED FLAMER)**
- **RADAWAY**
- **RANDOM AMMO**
- **RANDOM AID ITEM**
- **RANDOM PLAN, ARMOR, MOD, OR WEAPON**
- **CHANCE FOR A RANDOM LEGENDARY WEAPON OR ARMOR**

PREREQUISITES
- **SPEAK WITH CHLOE IN BERKELEY SPRINGS TO START THIS QUEST.**

TICK, TICK, BOOM!

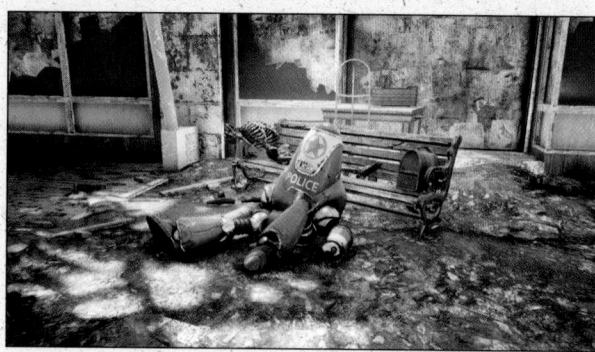

Speak with Boomer and he'll task you with recovering bombs from somewhere in Appalachia. Head to the objective markers and locate each of the Inert Bombs scattered around the area to complete the quest.

TASKS FOR CHLOE

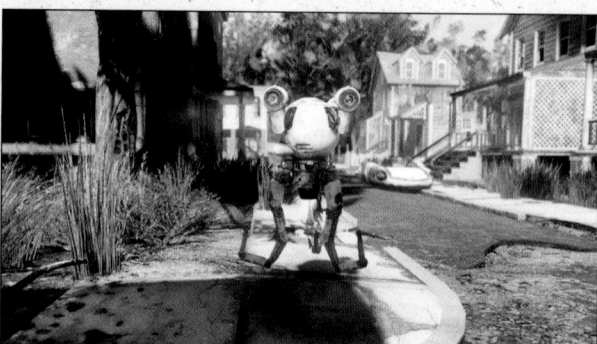

Chloe will ask you to complete one of the following tasks: Collect science project samples, collect flowers, attend a playdate, or retrieve toys. Return with the task accomplished to complete the quest.

QUEEN OF THE HUNT

OBJECTIVES
- **INVESTIGATE THREE SITES**
- **KILL THE CRYPTID**
- **EXTRACT THE SAMPLE**
- **DEPOSIT THE TISSUE SAMPLE**

LOCATIONS
- **HUNTER'S SHACK**

REWARDS
- **CRYPTID PERK**
- **RANDOM AMMO**
- **RANDOM AID ITEM**
- **RANDOM PLAN, ARMOR, MOD, OR WEAPON**
- **CHANCE FOR A CASUAL UNDERARMOR MOD**
- **CHANCE FOR A RANDOM LEGENDARY WEAPON OR ARMOR**

PREREQUISITES
- **CHECK THE COMPUTER TERMINAL IN THE HUNTER'S SHACK IN THE MIRE AND SELECT "UPLOAD DATA" TO START THIS QUEST.**

HUNTER KILLER

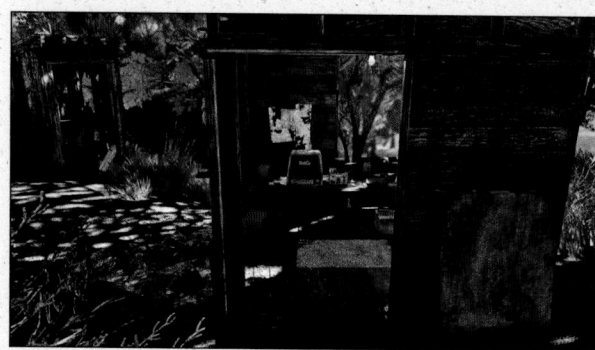

After checking the terminal in the Hunter's Shack, you must visit three locations around the Mire. These locations are random every time you do the quest, but they are usually in the top half of the Mire, so you don't have to go too far to reach your destination.

Investigate the sites until you discover the Cryptid. After you take it out, press the button prompt while looting the creature to take a tissue sample from it. Once you have extracted the Cryptid's tissue sample, take it back to the Hunter's Shack to complete the quest.

WASTE NOT

OBJECTIVES

- EXAMINE THE MAINTENANCE TERMINAL
- RECOVER THREE RED ROCKET CORES

LOCATIONS

- RED ROCKET MEGA STOP (ON THE NORTHEASTERN BORDER BETWEEN SAVAGE DIVIDE AND THE MIRE)

REWARDS

- COPPER
- RUBBER
- RANDOM AMMO
- RANDOM AID ITEM
- RANDOM PLAN, ARMOR, MOD, OR WEAPON
- CHANCE FOR A RANDOM LEGENDARY WEAPON OR ARMOR

PREREQUISITES

- THIS QUEST WILL BEGIN AUTOMATICALLY UPON VISITING THIS RED ROCKET MEGA STOP.

CORE CONUNDRUM

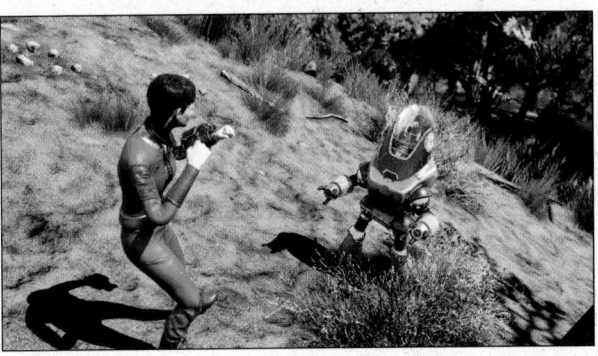

Use the marked terminal in the Red Rocket Mega Stop garage and select "ALERTS." Head to the marked location to track down the Red Rocket Protectrons. Destroy them, loot their Red Rocket Cores, and head back to the Mega Stop and deposit them to complete the quest.

Quests CRANBERRY BOG (LEVEL 35+)

COP A SQUATTER

OBJECTIVES

- REMOVE SQUATTERS FROM LOCATION

REWARDS

- RANDOM WEAPON MOD
- RANDOM AMMO
- RANDOM AID ITEM
- RANDOM PLAN, ARMOR, MOD, OR WEAPON
- CHANCE FOR A RANDOM LEGENDARY WEAPON OR ARMOR

PREREQUISITES

- NONE

LOCATIONS

- WATOGA EMERGENCY SERVICES

CLEANING UP THE STREETS

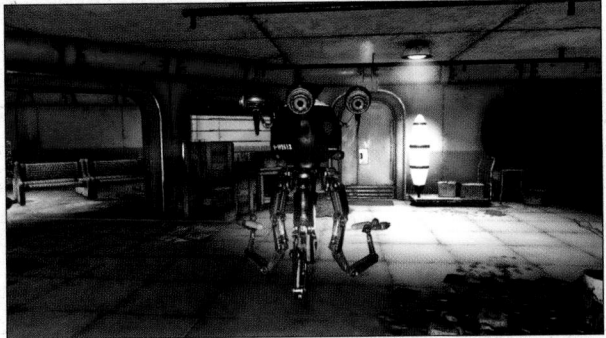

The Watoga Police Chief asks you to "deal with some squatters" (Read: Kill things). Head to the specified location and "politely" ask them to move.

FORBIDDEN KNOWLEDGE

OBJECTIVES

- FIND A PLACE TO SECURE THE TECHNICAL SCHEMATIC

LOCATIONS

- FORT DEFIANCE
- CAMP VENTURE

REWARDS

- BOS UNDERARMOR MOD
- RANDOM AMMO
- RANDOM AID
- CHANCE FOR BOS CLOTHES

PREREQUISITES

- YOU MUST COMPLETE "DEFIANCE HAS FALLEN" TO GAIN ACCESS TO THIS QUEST.

TRAINING

CRAFTING AND C.A.M.P.ING

INVENTORY

QUESTS

ATLAS

BESTIARY

APPENDICES

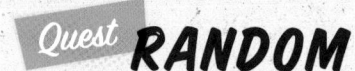

REQUEST GOVERNMENT AIR DROP (DROP)

OBJECTIVES	LOCATIONS	REWARDS
– UPLOAD THE US GOVERNMENT SUPPLY REQUISITION HOLOTAPE AT THE MARKED RELAY LOCATION	– RANDOM	– RANDOM AMMO AND AID ITEM

PREREQUISITES

– FIND THE US GOVERNMENT SUPPLY REQUISITION HOLOTAPE RANDOMLY IN A CONTAINER OR BY LOOTING AN ENEMY.

AIR SUPPORT

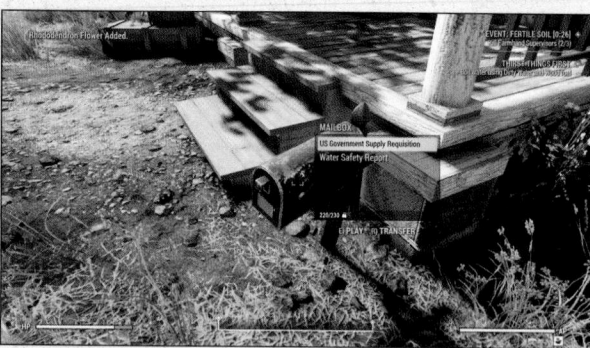

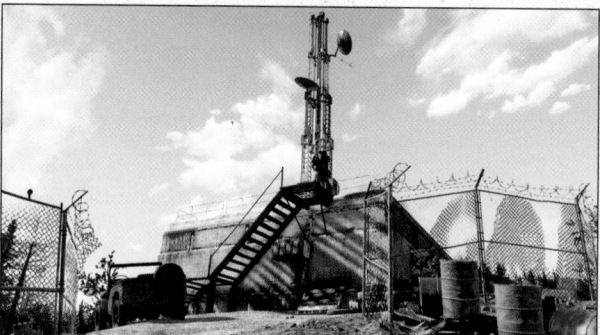

Occasionally, while looting through containers, you'll find a US Government Supply Requisition Holotape, which will launch the "Request Government Air Drop" quest. Your task is to go to the relay station marked on your map and use the terminal among the large computers lining the center interior of the building. Load the US Government Supply Requisition Holotape into the terminal and select "Request Emergency Air Drop."

The quest will technically be complete after you use the terminal, but you still need to collect your reward. Look around the map of Appalachia to find Miscellaneous Quest: Find the Supply Drop. Head to that location and look for the pillar of smoke that marks a Supply Drop. Collect its contents and consider the quest complete.

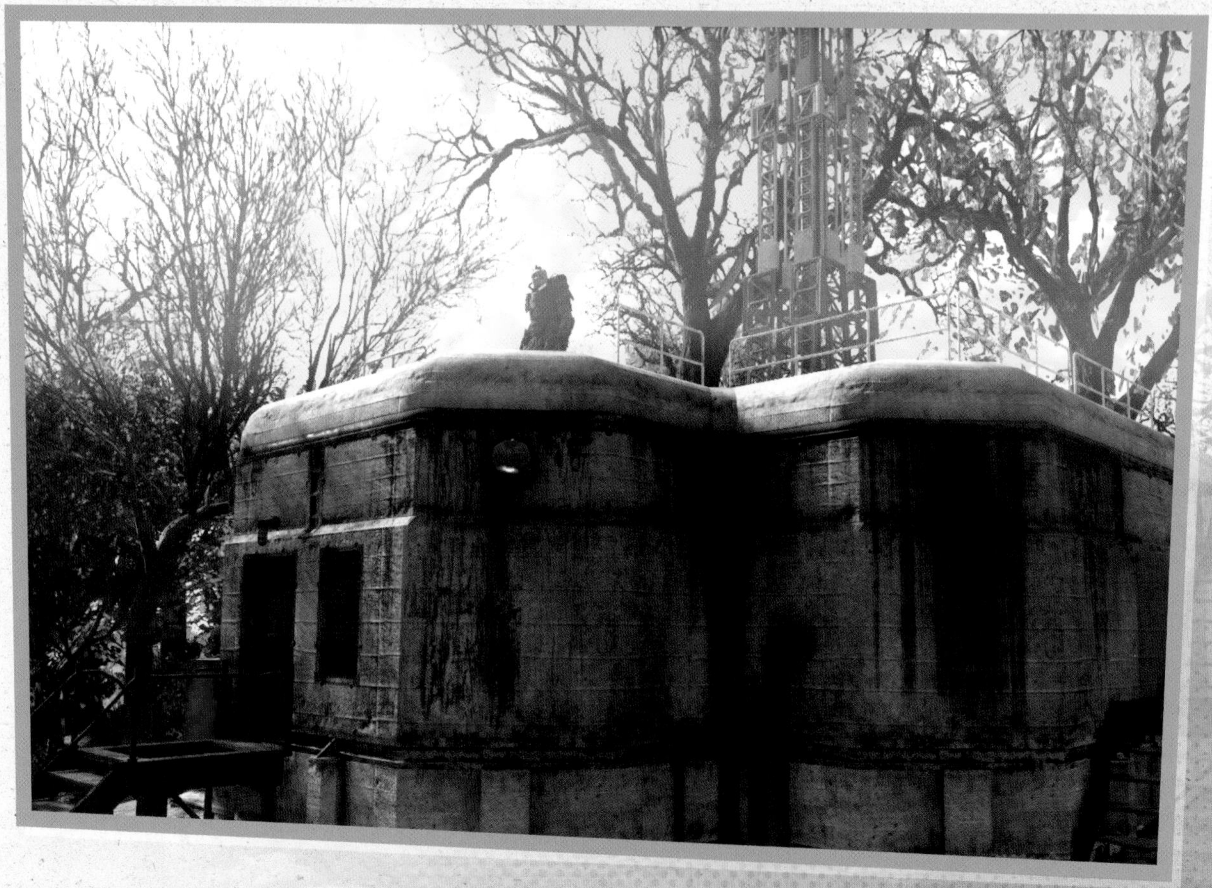

EVENT QUESTS

Events are quests that randomly appear on the map and can be played by anyone in the area. Completing an event gives you a chance at earning a Legendary weapon or piece of armor. Events are also endlessly repeatable, meaning you can play it again anytime it appears on the map.

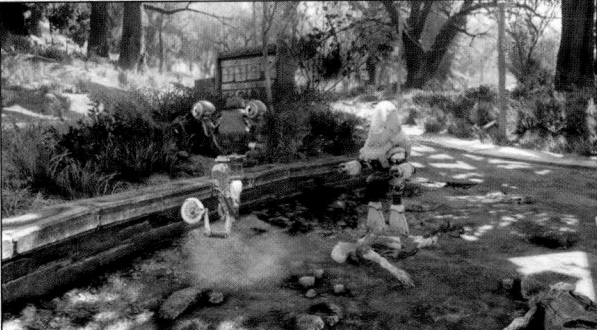

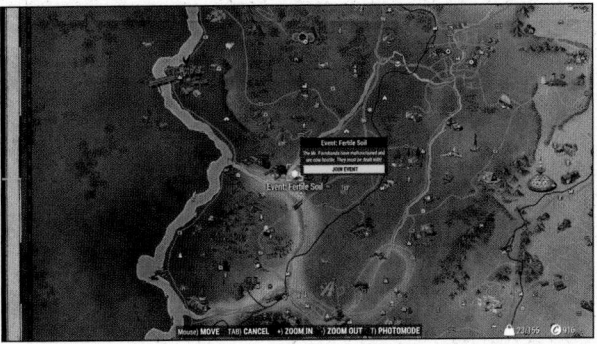

Avoid events early in the game, as some of them can be truly challenging and most will soak up more of your tiny backpack of supplies than you'll want to share at that point in the game. Once you've got a decent gun, a sturdy set of armor, and a backpack full of ammo and supplies, visit events whenever you can. On top of getting a chance to earn a Legendary, you'll also earn crafting plans just about every time you complete one.

For convenience's sake, you can Fast-Travel to any event so long as it's visible to you on the map—even if you haven't yet visited the area it takes place in!

One thing you need to be aware of is that most Event Quests have timers that are actively ticking down whether you're participating in the event or not. If you're fishing for Legendaries and Plans, don't sleep when you see an event marker appear. Some of these require all the time you're allowed if you're hoping to complete them.

Quests THE FOREST (LEVELS 1-9)

BACK ON THE BEAT

> *EVENT LOCATION*
> - **WEST SIDE OF MORGANTOWN (THE FOREST)**
>
> *REWARDS*
> - **RESPONDER COP UNIFORM**
> - **RANDOM AMMO**
> - **RANDOM AID ITEM**
> - **RANDOM PLAN, ARMOR, MOD, OR WEAPON**

DETAILS

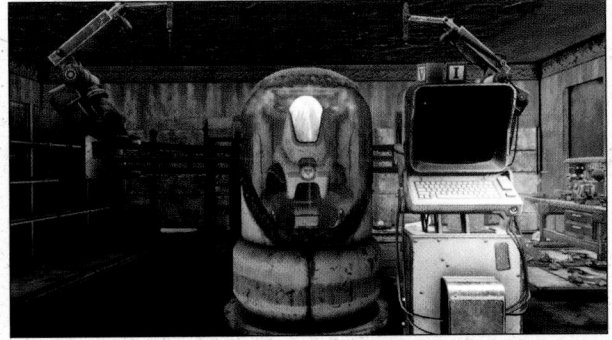

Among the Responders' various projects to protect the people of Appalachia was Steelheart, a stout and loyal Protectron. Power Steelheart up and join him on his patrol through the streets of Morgantown to unlock Responder stash rooms.

COLLISION COURSE

> *EVENT LOCATION*
> - **MORGANTOWN AIRPORT (THE FOREST)**
>
> *REWARDS*
> - **CONCRETE**
> - **RANDOM AMMO**
> - **RANDOM AID ITEM**
> - **RANDOM PLAN, ARMOR, MOD, OR WEAPON**
> - **CHANCE FOR A RANDOM LEGENDARY WEAPON OR ARMOR**

DETAILS

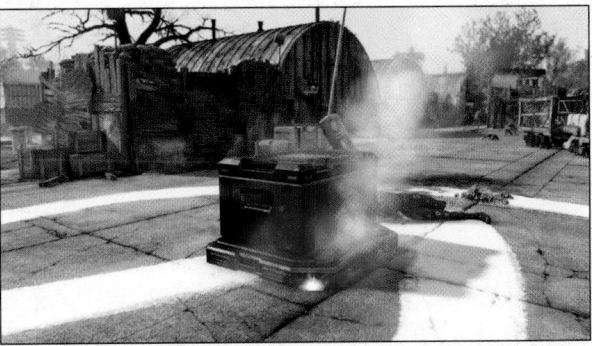

Defeat waves of Scorched to give a Vertibot a safe spot to land and make a supply drop. Be sure to wait for the Vertibot to drop off the Government Aid Drop and loot it for additional rewards.

DEATH BLOSSOMS

EVENT LOCATION

- **RANDOM LOCATIONS IN THE FOREST**

REWARDS

- **CORPSE FLOWER SEEDS**
- **RANDOM AMMO**
- **RANDOM AID ITEM**
- **RANDOM PLAN, ARMOR, MOD, OR WEAPON**
- **CHANCE FOR A RANDOM LEGENDARY WEAPON OR ARMOR**

DETAILS

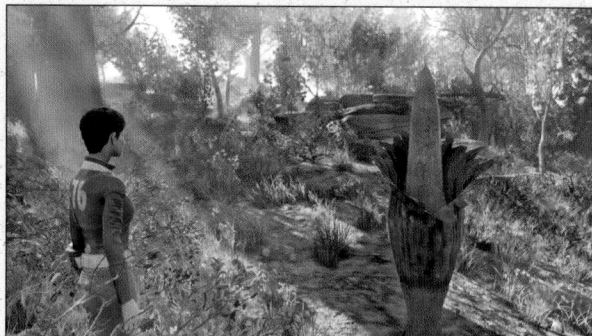

Five Corpse Flowers around the event area are about to bloom, which is driving the local wildlife population absolutely mad. Guard all five Corpse Flowers from waves of enemies until the timer runs out.

FEED THE PEOPLE

EVENT LOCATION

- **MAMA DOLCE'S FOOD PROCESSING (THE FOREST)**

REWARDS

- **PROCESSED FOOD**
- **RANDOM AMMO**
- **RANDOM AID ITEM**
- **RANDOM PLAN, ARMOR, MOD, OR WEAPON**
- **CHANCE FOR A RANDOM LEGENDARY WEAPON OR ARMOR**

DETAILS

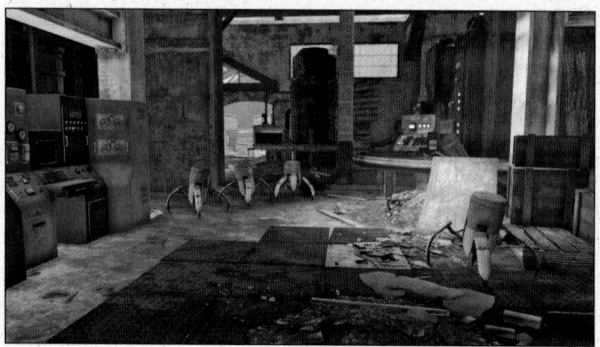

Hunt down and deposit canisters of food into food-processing machines in Mama Dolce's Food Processing while fending off enemies and repairing the machines as they break.

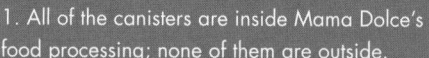
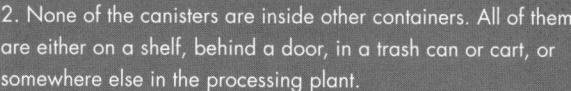

Helpful Hints from Vault Boy!

There are a few things to note to make this event go as smooth as possible:

1. All of the canisters are inside Mama Dolce's food processing; none of them are outside.

2. None of the canisters are inside other containers. All of them are either on a shelf, behind a door, in a trash can or cart, or somewhere else in the processing plant.

3. All of the canisters have the same appearance, except for the label in the center—if you find one canister, you'll know exactly what all the others look like.

FERTILE SOIL

EVENT LOCATION

- **FLATWOODS (SOUTH OF THE OVERSEER'S C.A.M.P.—THE FOREST)**

REWARDS

- **FERTILIZER**
- **RANDOM AMMO**
- **RANDOM AID ITEM**
- **RANDOM PLAN, ARMOR, MOD, OR WEAPON**
- **CHANCE FOR A RANDOM LEGENDARY WEAPON OR ARMOR**

DETAILS

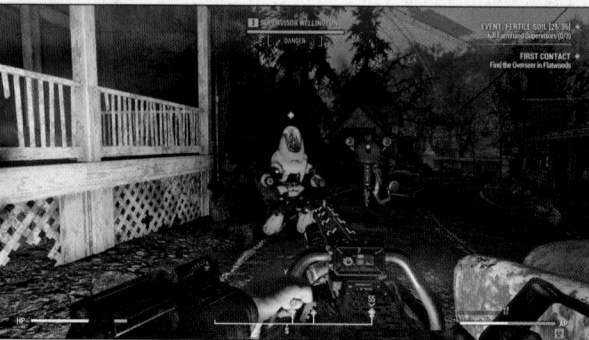

Robotic farmhands from the nearby Vault-Tec Agricultural Research Center (and Its surrounding farms) have begun to run amok around the Flatwoods area. Destroy them, then enter the Vault-Tec Agricultural Research Center and reprogram them.

LEADER OF THE PACK

EVENT LOCATION
- TYLER COUNTY FAIRGROUNDS (NORTHWEST CORNER OF THE FOREST)

REWARDS
- RANDOM AMMO AND AID ITEM

DETAILS

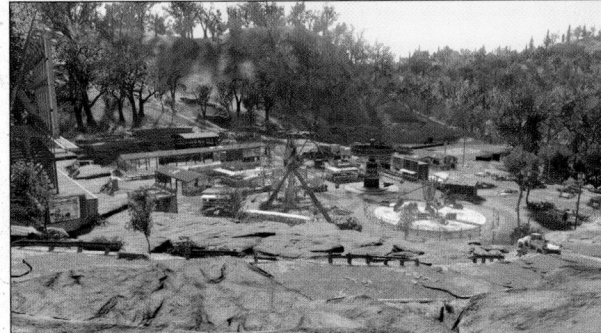

Head to each of the marked locations north and south of Tyler County Fairgrounds, and hunt down the Wolf Pack Leaders. They'll be accompanied by a pack of Wolves, so expect a fight.

PROJECT BEANSTALK

EVENT LOCATIONS
- WEST SIDE OF THE FOREST
- SILVA HOMESTEAD (THE FOREST)

REWARDS
- BUFFOUT
- RANDOM AMMO
- RANDOM AID ITEM
- RANDOM PLAN, ARMOR, MOD, OR WEAPON
- CHANCE FOR A RANDOM LEGENDARY WEAPON OR ARMOR

DETAILS

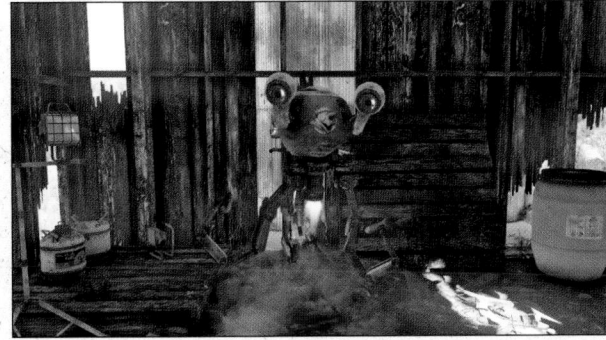

Follow a Pharmabot and protect it while it takes care of (and destroys) crops around a local farm.

THE PATH TO ENLIGHTENMENT

EVENT LOCATION
- THE FOREST AT A RANDOM LOCATION

REWARDS
- NUCLEAR MATERIAL
- RANDOM AMMO
- RANDOM AID ITEM
- RANDOM PLAN, ARMOR, MOD, OR WEAPON
- CHANCE FOR A RANDOM LEGENDARY WEAPON OR ARMOR

DETAILS

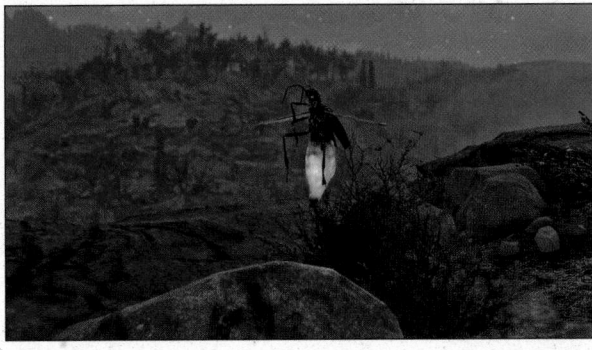

Some call the Cult of the Mothman a bunch of lunatics, but Brother Moncrief knew otherwise. To prove his devotion, he was determined to light the lamp at the Landview Lighthouse in hopes of summoning the Mothman for a holy communion. Now you must follow in his footsteps.

TEA TIME

EVENT LOCATION
- GIANT TEAPOT

REWARDS
- SWEETWATER TEA
- SWEETWATER TEA RECIPE
- RANDOM AMMO
- RANDOM AID ITEM
- RANDOM PLAN, ARMOR, MOD, OR WEAPON
- CHANCE FOR A RANDOM LEGENDARY WEAPON OR ARMOR

DETAILS

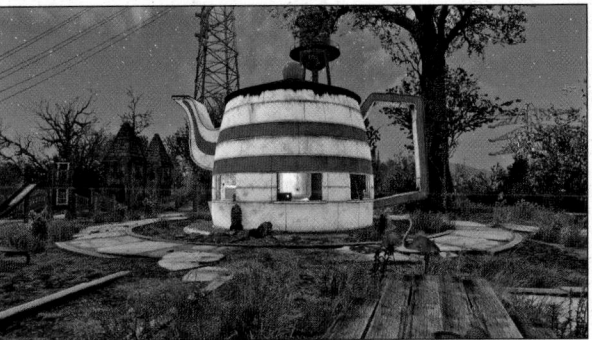

There's nothing like a fresh cuppa to lift your spirits—something the proprietors of the Giant Teapot know all too well. Unfortunately, enemy attacks are keeping the Giant Teapot from brewing up its famous Sweetwater Tea. Protect the water pipes leading into the Giant Teapot while it finishes its tasty brew.

DOGWOOD DIE OFF

EVENT LOCATION
- BECKER FARM (SOUTHWEST TOXIC VALLEY)

REWARDS
- BLEACH DOGWOOD
- RANDOM AMMO
- RANDOM AID ITEM
- RANDOM PLAN, ARMOR, MOD, OR WEAPON
- CHANCE FOR A RANDOM LEGENDARY WEAPON OR ARMOR

DETAILS

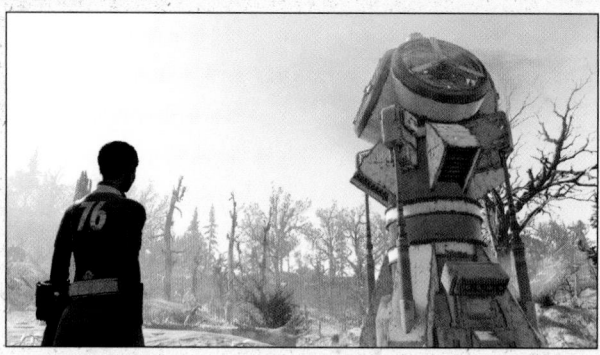

Find and repair three aerosolizers around Toxic Valley.

GRAFTON DAY

EVENT LOCATION
- TOXIC VALLEY AT A RANDOM LOCATION

REWARDS
- FRAG MINES
- RANDOM AMMO
- RANDOM AID ITEM
- RANDOM PLAN, ARMOR, MOD, OR WEAPON
- CHANCE FOR A RANDOM LEGENDARY WEAPON OR ARMOR

DETAILS

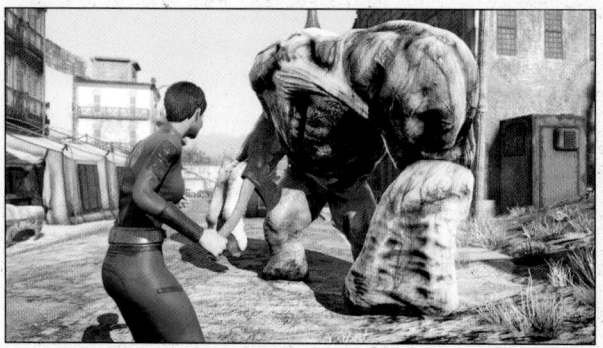

It's Grafton Day in Grafton. Again! And the Grafton Monster is on parade... well, rampage actually.

JAILBREAK

EVENT LOCATION
- EASTERN REGIONAL PENITENTIARY (TOXIC VALLEY)

REWARDS
- RANDOM ARMOR MOD
- RANDOM AMMO
- RANDOM AID ITEM
- RANDOM PLAN, ARMOR, MOD, OR WEAPON
- CHANCE FOR A RANDOM LEGENDARY WEAPON OR ARMOR

DETAILS

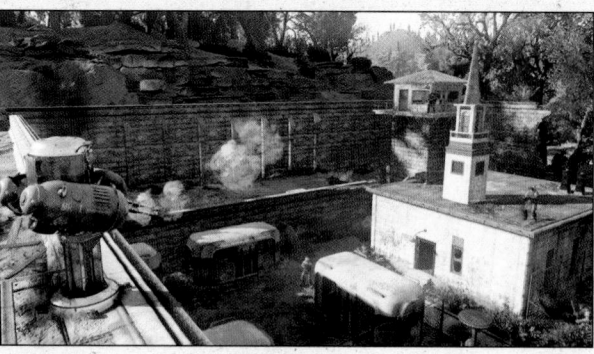

An onslaught of Super Mutants is pouring into the Eastern Regional Penitentiary in an attempt to break Mad Dog Malone out of prison. Run along the prison's rooftops and repair turrets to keep them from freeing this notorious prisoner.

MANHUNT

EVENT LOCATION
- GRAFTON DAM (TOXIC VALLEY)

REWARDS
- RADAWAY
- RANDOM ARMOR MOD
- RANDOM AMMO
- RANDOM AID ITEM
- RANDOM PLAN, ARMOR, MOD, OR WEAPON
- CHANCE FOR A RANDOM LEGENDARY WEAPON OR ARMOR

DETAILS

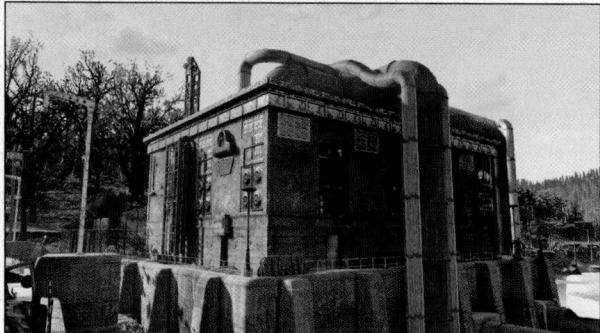

Find a way into Grafton Dam and take out the Super Mutant criminal known as "Mad Dog Malone."

PROTEST MARCH

EVENT LOCATION
- GRAFTON (TOXIC VALLEY)

REWARDS
- RANDOM WEAPON MOD
- RANDOM AMMO
- RANDOM AID ITEM
- RANDOM PLAN, ARMOR, MOD, OR WEAPON
- CHANCE FOR A RANDOM LEGENDARY WEAPON OR ARMOR

DETAILS

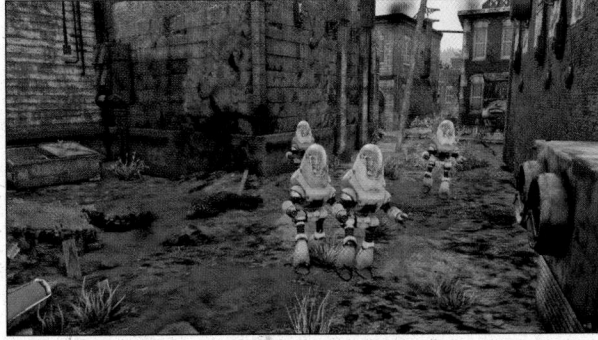

Grafton's mayor has caught wind of a protest and wants you to break it up. Head to the protesters' location and get ready for a fight.

PATROL DUTY

EVENT LOCATION
- EASTERN REGIONAL PENITENTIARY (TOXIC VALLEY)

REWARDS
- RANDOM RANGED WEAPON RECIPE
- RANDOM ARMOR MOD
- RANDOM AMMO
- RANDOM AID ITEM
- RANDOM PLAN, ARMOR, MOD, OR WEAPON
- CHANCE FOR A RANDOM LEGENDARY WEAPON OR ARMOR

DETAILS

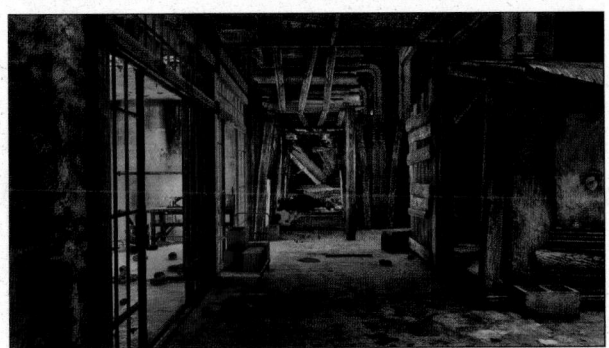

Escort a penitentiary guard through the prison on its daily rounds.

SWARM OF SUITORS

EVENT LOCATION
- TOXIC VALLEY AT A RANDOM LOCATION

REWARDS
- MIRELURK EGGS
- RANDOM AMMO
- RANDOM AID ITEM
- RANDOM PLAN, ARMOR, MOD, OR WEAPON
- CHANCE FOR A RANDOM LEGENDARY WEAPON OR ARMOR

DETAILS

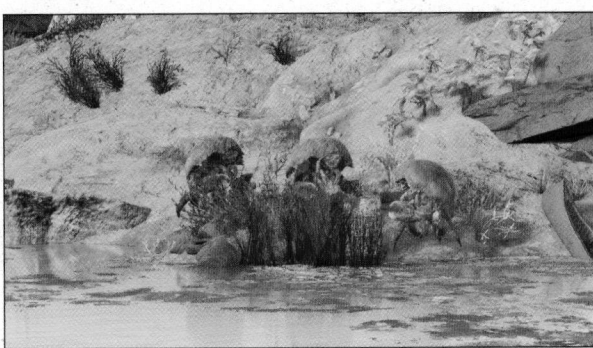

A horde of Mirelurks has been spotted heading toward their breeding ground in Grafton Lake. Stop them before they call the Mirelurk Queen.

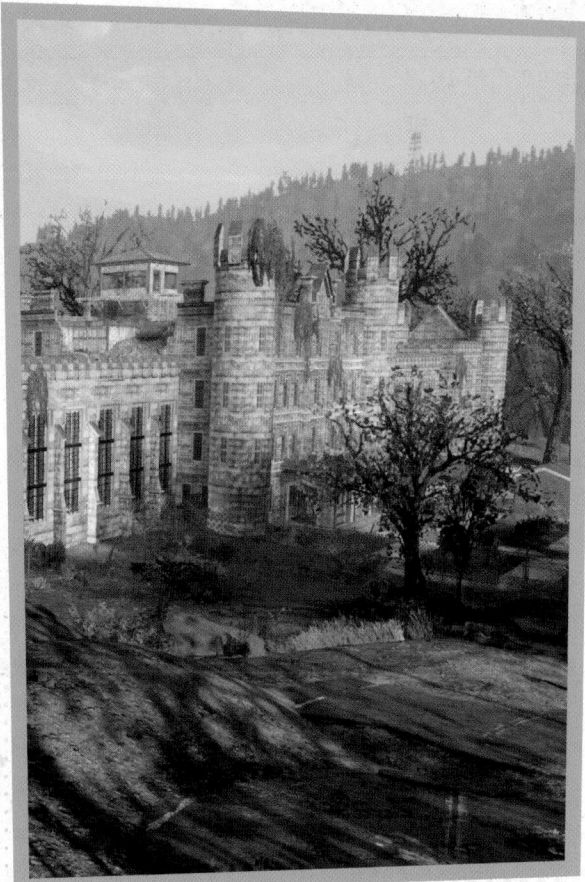

TRAINING

CRAFTING AND C.A.M.P.ING

INVENTORY

QUESTS

ATLAS

BESTIARY

APPENDICES

SAVAGE DIVIDE (LEVELS 15–24)

DISTINGUISHED GUESTS

EVENT LOCATION
- SAVAGE DIVIDE AT A RANDOM LOCATION

REWARDS
- RANDOM COOKING RECIPE
- RANDOM AMMO
- RANDOM AID ITEM
- RANDOM PLAN, ARMOR, MOD, OR WEAPON
- CHANCE FOR A RANDOM LEGENDARY WEAPON OR ARMOR

DETAILS

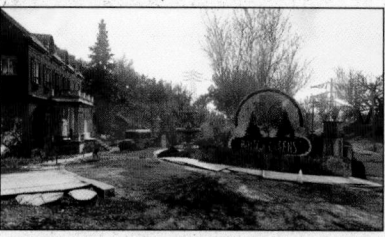

The Maître d' at Bolton Greens, Billingsley, is in distress. He is convinced that distinguished guests will be arriving at any moment for the Halloween Gala, but the club is in such disarray! In addition to getting the robot waitstaff back to work and setting the tables, uninvited guests must be turned away and kept out of the function room so as not to disturb the guests' delicate sensibilities.

GUIDED MEDITATION

EVENT LOCATION
- PALACE OF THE WINDING PATH (NORTHERN SAVAGE DIVIDE)

REWARDS
- ADDICTOL
- RANDOM AMMO
- RANDOM AID ITEM
- RANDOM PLAN, ARMOR, MOD, OR WEAPON
- CHANCE FOR A GAMMA GUN
- CHANCE FOR A RANDOM LEGENDARY WEAPON OR ARMOR

DETAILS

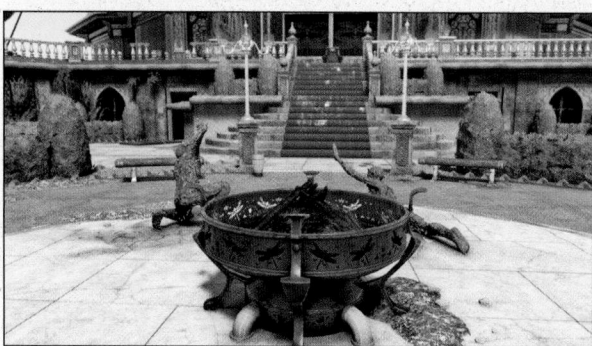

Light the Brazier of Transcendence in the courtyard of the Palace of the Winding Path; then get ready for guided meditation. Breathe in, exhale. Take in positivity, eject negativity. Protect the four speakers around the palace from enemy attacks to synchronize your chakras.

ONE VIOLENT NIGHT

EVENT LOCATION
- SAVAGE DIVIDE AT A RANDOM LOCATION

REWARDS
- BEER OR A BEER HAT
- RANDOM AMMO
- RANDOM AID ITEM
- RANDOM PLAN, ARMOR, MOD, OR WEAPON
- CHANCE FOR A NAILER SWORD
- CHANCE FOR A RANDOM LEGENDARY WEAPON OR ARMOR

DETAILS

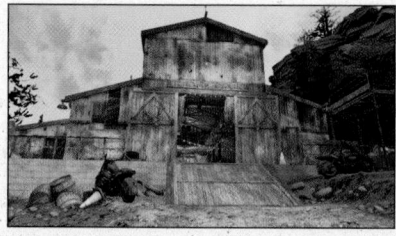

The Nightstalker, a murderous abomination with a taste for human flesh, attacked residents of the Sons of Dane Compound every night while they partied at the Buck's Den Beer House. Making noise and playing raucous music is the key to luring in one of the region's deadliest threats and finally killing this monster of legend.

URANIUM FEVER

EVENT LOCATION
- BLACKWATER MINE (SOUTH OF TOP OF THE WORLD—SAVAGE DIVIDE)

REWARDS
- NUCLEAR MATERIAL
- RANDOM AMMO
- RANDOM AID ITEM
- RANDOM PLAN, ARMOR, MOD, OR WEAPON
- CHANCE FOR A RANDOM LEGENDARY WEAPON OR ARMOR

DETAILS

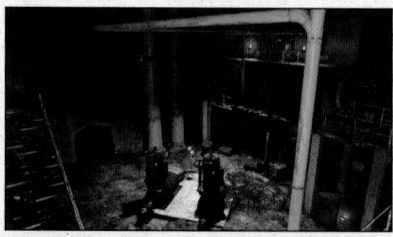

Enter the Blackwater Mine and protect uranium extractors from waves of Mole Miners.

WORD OF WARNING FROM VAULT BOY

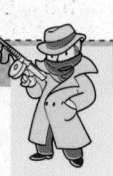

THIS MINE IS A HOTBED FOR RADIATION. THE EVENT IS ALMOST IMPOSSIBLE TO COMPLETE WITHOUT A HAZMAT SUIT. MAKE SURE YOU'RE WEARING ONE BEFORE PROGRESSING PAST THE MINE'S OPENING.

THE ASH HEAP (LEVELS 25–29)

BATTLE BOTS

EVENT LOCATION
- MOUNT BLAIR TRAINYARD (SOUTHERN ASH HEAP)

REWARDS
- SCREWS
- RANDOM AMMO
- RANDOM AID ITEM, RANDOM PLAN, ARMOR, MOD, OR WEAPON
- CHANCE FOR AN ASSAULTRON HEAD
- CHANCE FOR A RANDOM LEGENDARY WEAPON OR ARMOR

DETAILS

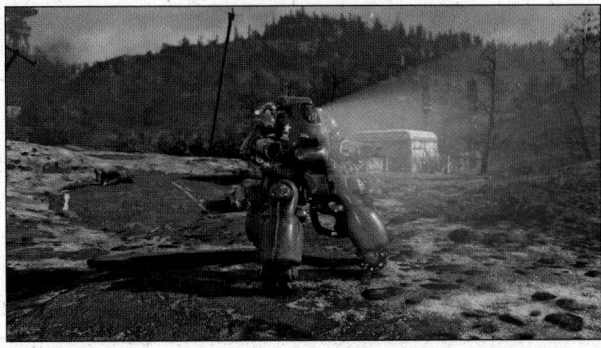

Destroy a roaming Sentry Bot and shut down the security system in the nearby bunker it was protecting.

BREACH AND CLEAR

EVENT LOCATION
- THE ASH HEAP AT A RANDOM LOCATION

REWARDS
- RANDOM ORE
- RANDOM AMMO
- RANDOM AID ITEM
- RANDOM PLAN, ARMOR, MOD, OR WEAPON
- CHANCE FOR A METEORIC CHINESE SWORD
- CHANCE FOR A RANDOM LEGENDARY WEAPON OR ARMOR

DETAILS

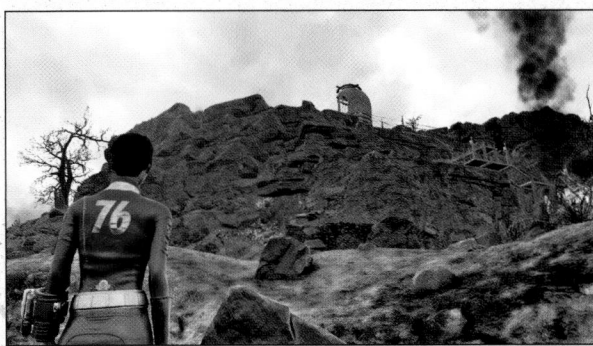

Clear the work site of trouble; then grab as many goodies as you can from the mining apparatus.

LODE BARING

EVENT LOCATION
- ABANDONED MINE SITE KITTERY (NORTHEAST OF MOUNT BLAIR—ASH HEAP)

REWARDS
- CLAIM TOKENS
- RANDOM AMMO
- RANDOM AID ITEM
- RANDOM PLAN, ARMOR, MOD, OR WEAPON
- CHANCE FOR A RANDOM LEGENDARY WEAPON OR ARMOR

DETAILS

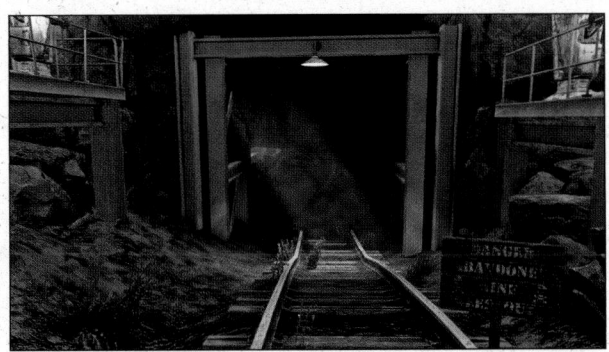

Enter Mine Site Kittery and repair a trio of Auto-Miner robots to get them digging again. Keep them safe from enemy attacks and they'll kick you back some of their findings—just make sure to escape the mine before the 60-second timer runs out at the end of the dig.

TRAINING

CRAFTING AND C.A.M.P.ing

INVENTORY

QUESTS

ATLAS

BESTIARY

APPENDICES

THE MIRE (LEVELS 30-34)

HEART OF THE SWAMP

EVENT LOCATIONS
- THE MIRE AT A RANDOM LOCATION

REWARDS
- RAD-X
- RANDOM AMMO
- RANDOM AID ITEM
- RANDOM PLAN, ARMOR, MOD, OR WEAPON
- CHANCE FOR A RANDOM LEGENDARY WEAPON OR ARMOR

IRRATIONAL FEAR

EVENT LOCATION
- THE MIRE AT A RANDOM LOCATION

REWARDS
- SCREWS
- RANDOM AMMO
- RANDOM AID ITEM
- RANDOM PLAN, ARMOR, MOD, OR WEAPON
- CHANCE FOR A RANDOM LEGENDARY WEAPON OR ARMOR

DETAILS

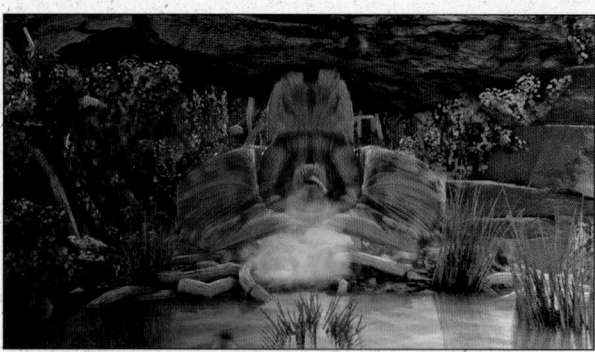

Fight and destroy a Strangler Heart and its Mirelurk and Feral Ghoul reinforcements in the Mire. Avoid the Heart's poison gas and take down the boss (usually a Strangler Queen, with a 50% chance to be a Mirelurk Queen or Grafton Monster) that appears when the Strangler Heart is at 25% health.

DETAILS

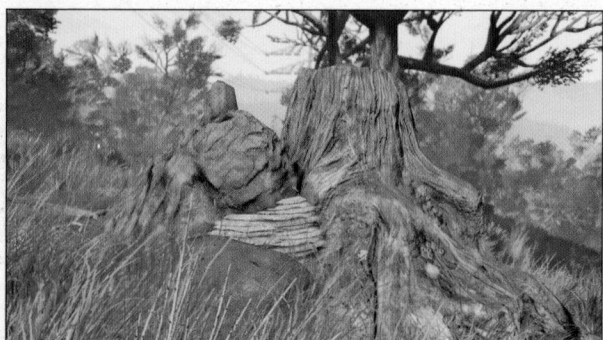

Protect the apiphobic Beckham from waves of Raging Honey Beasts and Yao Guai while he visits beehives to harvest honey.

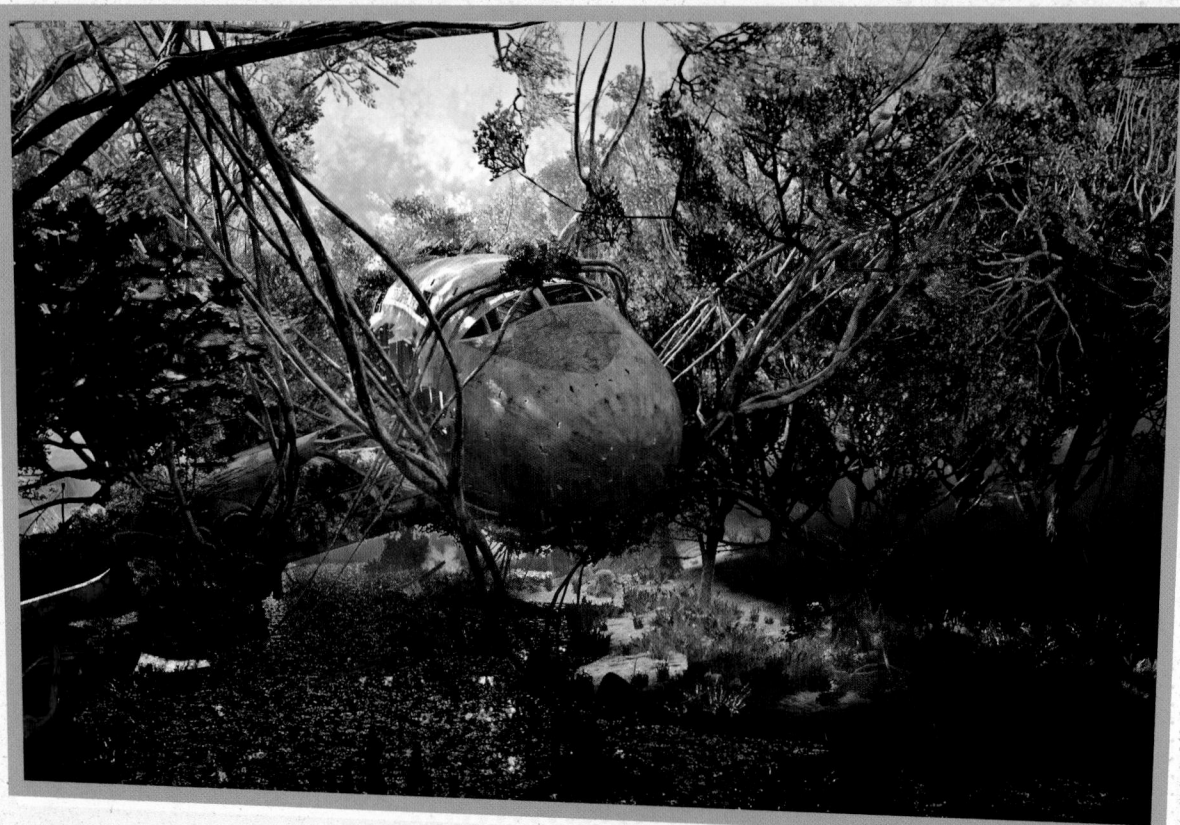

CRANBERRY BOG (LEVEL 35+)

AWOL ARMAMENTS

> **EVENT LOCATION**
> – CRANBERRY BOG AT A RANDOM LOCATION
>
> **REWARDS**
> – ARMOR MOD
> – RANDOM AMMO
> – RANDOM AID ITEM
> – RANDOM PLAN, ARMOR, MOD, OR WEAPON
> – CHANCE FOR A RANDOM LEGENDARY WEAPON OR ARMOR

DETAILS

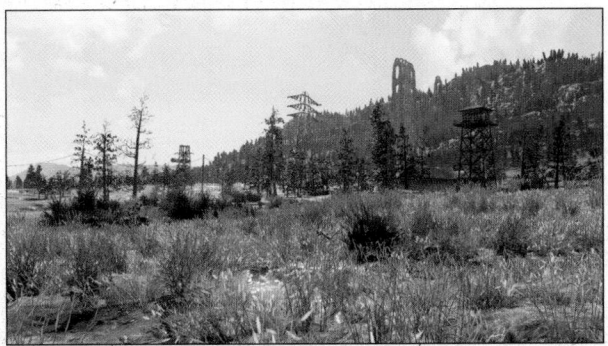

Fight off waves of misbehaving military-grade robots.

CENSUS VIOLENCE

> **EVENT LOCATION**
> – CRANBERRY BOG AT A RANDOM LOCATION
>
> **REWARDS**
> – RANDOM PLAN
> – RANDOM AMMO
> – RANDOM AID ITEM
> – RANDOM PLAN, ARMOR, MOD, OR WEAPON
> – CHANCE FOR MARINE ARMOR MODS
> – CHANCE FOR MARINE UNDERARMOR MODS
> – CHANCE FOR A RANDOM LEGENDARY WEAPON OR ARMOR

DETAILS

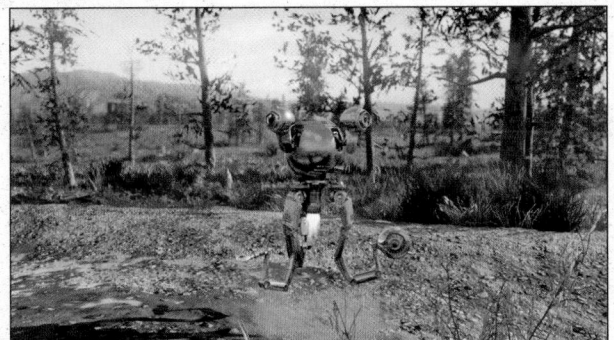

Defend a robotic census taker as he "fixes" his count (through killing incorrectly tallied creatures, naturally.)

LINE IN THE SAND

> **EVENT LOCATION**
> – FORT DEFIANCE (WESTERN CRANBERRY BOG)
>
> **REWARDS**
> – FUSION CORE
> – RANDOM AMMO
> – RANDOM AID ITEM
> – RANDOM PLAN, ARMOR, MOD, OR WEAPON
> – CHANCE FOR A RANDOM LEGENDARY WEAPON OR ARMOR

DETAILS

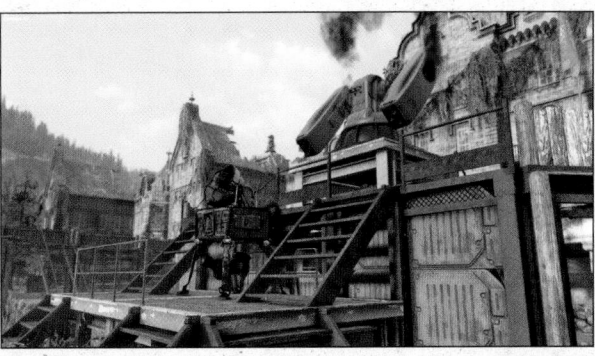

Build up your defenses, repair the walls, enable the turrets, and arm the ASAM: A Scorchbeast is in the area and it's looking to tear your Sonic Generator to pieces. Fell the beast and protect the generator to claim victory in another event.

SURFACE TO AIR

> **EVENT LOCATION**
> – CRANBERRY BOG AT A RANDOM LOCATION
>
> **REWARDS**
> – T-51 POWER ARMOR PIECE
> – RANDOM AMMO
> – RANDOM AID ITEM
> – RANDOM PLAN, ARMOR, MOD, OR WEAPON
> – CHANCE FOR A RANDOM LEGENDARY WEAPON OR ARMOR

DETAILS

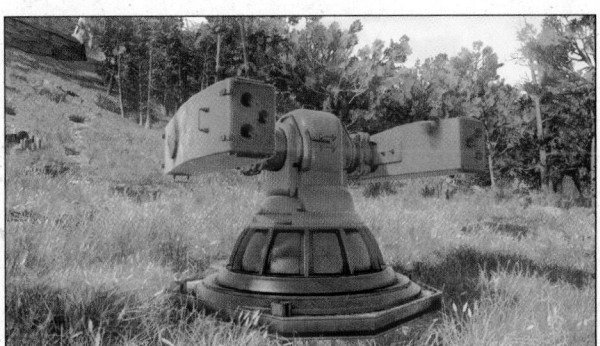

Defend and repair an automated surface-to-air missile launcher while Scorchbeasts do everything in their power to destroy it.

TRAINING

CRAFTING AND C.A.M.PING

INVENTORY

QUESTS

ATLAS

BESTIARY

APPENDICES

ALWAYS VIGILANT

EVENT LOCATION
- ANY RELAY TOWER

REWARDS
- SPRINGS
- ACID
- RANDOM AMMO
- RANDOM AID ITEM
- RANDOM PLAN, ARMOR, MOD, OR WEAPON
- CHANCE FOR A RANDOM LEGENDARY WEAPON OR ARMOR

DETAILS

Repair Rover the Eyebot and protect him from waves of enemies for 5 minutes while he repairs a relay tower. Rover's timer will pause whenever he's damaged, so keep him repaired to keep the timer running!

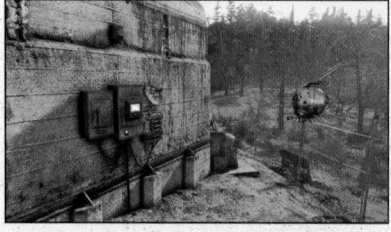

DISTANT THUNDER

EVENT LOCATION
- RANDOM

REWARDS
- RANDOM WEAPON
- RANDOM AMMO
- RANDOM AID ITEM
- RANDOM PLAN, ARMOR, MOD, OR WEAPON
- CHANCE FOR A RANDOM POWER ARMOR PIECE
- CHANCE FOR A RANDOM LEGENDARY WEAPON OR ARMOR

DETAILS

Use a Recon Scope to mark enemies as targets for a destructive air strike. Mop up the leftovers and you'll be home free.

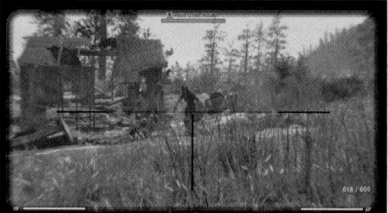

Helpful Hints from Vault Boy

To mark an enemy with a Recon Scope, just zoom in on them with the scope—the rest is automatic. This can help you keep track of enemies during the chaos of a heated firefight or let you approach a situation more tactically and stealthily.

IT'S A TRAP

EVENT LOCATION
- THE MIRE, THE ASH HEAP, OR CRANBERRY BOG AT A RANDOM LOCATION

REWARDS
- SCORCHBEAST PARTS
- RANDOM AMMO
- RANDOM AID ITEM
- RANDOM PLAN, ARMOR, MOD, OR WEAPON
- CHANCE FOR A RANDOM LEGENDARY WEAPON OR ARMOR

DETAILS

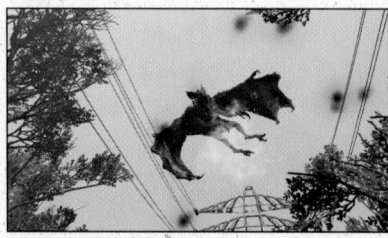

You will have the opportunity to defeat one of the most feared creatures in Appalachia: the Scorchbeast. The work done to restore the Free States detector system pays off with the opportunity to isolate and lure the powerful creature and its allies into a trap. This fight is difficult and dangerous!

THE MESSENGER

EVENT LOCATION
- RANDOM

REWARDS
- STIMPAKS
- RANDOM AMMO
- RANDOM AID ITEM
- RANDOM PLAN, ARMOR, MOD, OR WEAPON
- CHANCE FOR A RANDOM LEGENDARY WEAPON OR ARMOR

DETAILS

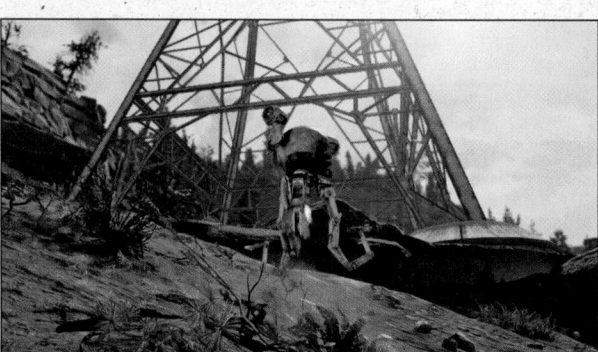

Repair and then safely escort Mr. Messenger to his destination. Expect a long, quiet countryside walk, as Mr. Messenger doesn't have the sharpest memory on the market.

POWERING UP POWER STATIONS

EVENT LOCATIONS

- POSEIDON ENERGY PLANT WV-06
- MONONGAH POWER PLANT
- THUNDER MOUNTAIN POWER PLANT

REWARDS

- POWER BOX POWER (SEE BELOW)
- POWER GENERATOR PLAN
- NUCLEAR MATERIAL
- COPPER
- FUSION CELL AMMO
- RANDOM AID ITEM
- RANDOM PLAN, ARMOR, MOD OR WEAPON
- CHANCE FOR A RANDOM LEGENDARY WEAPON OR ARMOR

DETAILS

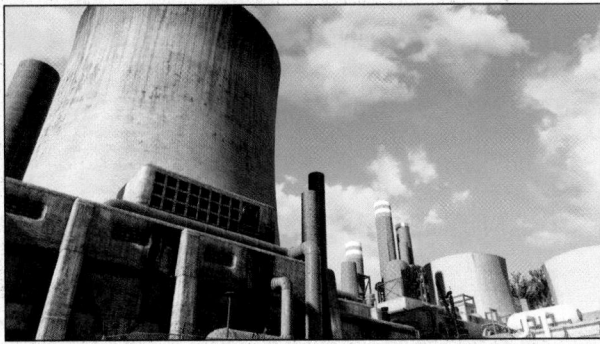

Power Boxes can be found throughout Appalachia. If the local Power Plant has broken down, these still have a bit of residual power you can draw on (only 10 power). But once the local Power Plant has been repaired, Power Boxes provide substantially more (100 power in most locations, or 400 power for Power Boxes at the plant itself).

If you have big plans for a Workshop, or just want to build the C.A.M.P. of your dreams, Power Boxes can save you a fortune in generators. But that means you'll need to get those plants back online.

POWERING UP A POWER PLANT

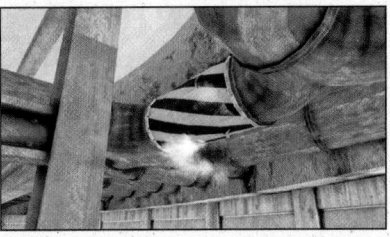

Once at the Power Plant of your choosing, you'll need to locate the plant's Cooling Towers, Turbine Hall, and Reactor Room. In each area, you'll find a number of broken black-and-yellow-striped pipes spewing steam, and several sparking control consoles. You need only activate them to repair them—no materials required.

There are a lot of objects to find. Initially, you're on your own, with no quest targets to guide you, but once you've repaired about half of the objects in each area, quest targets will point you to the remaining broken objects. It may be helpful to turn off any other quests you're tracking to focus in on the targets all around you.

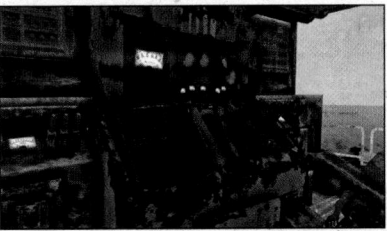

Once you've finished basic repairs to each system, you can restart the Power Plant by using the terminal in the plant's control room; that completes the event and restores the power. But if you have a few more minutes, take the time to finish fully repairing all three systems: you'll get a better much reward for your efforts.

Helpful Hints From Vault Boy

Once a Power Plant has been repaired, you won't have to worry about it breaking down for several hours. Take advantage of this by harvesting resources from as many of the Workshops on its power grid as you can.

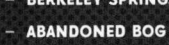

FASCINATING FACTS FROM VAULT BOY

THE POSEIDON ENERGY PLANT WV-06 CONTROLS THE GRID IN THE WESTERN THIRD OF THE MAP. ITS POWER BOXES CAN BE FOUND AT:

- POSEIDON ENERGY PLANT YARD
- POSEIDON POWER SUBSTATION PX-01
- POSEIDON POWER SUBSTATION PX-02
- POSEIDON POWER SUBSTATION PX-03
- WADE AIRPORT
- LAKESIDE CABINS
- SUTTON
- GRAFTON STEEL
- BILLINGS HOMESTEAD
- SUNSHINE MEADOWS INDUSTRIAL FARM

THE MONONGAH POWER PLANT CONTROLS THE GRID IN THE CENTRAL THIRD OF THE MAP. ITS POWER BOXES CAN BE FOUND AT:

- MONONGAH POWER PLANT YARD
- MONONGAH POWER SUBSTATION MZ-01
- MONONGAH POWER SUBSTATION MZ-02
- MONONGAH POWER SUBSTATION MZ-03
- CONVERTED MUNITIONS FACTORY
- RED ROCKET HIGHWAY MEGA STOP
- FEDERAL DISPOSAL FIELD HZ-21

THE THUNDER MOUNTAIN POWER PLANT CONTROLS THE GRID IN THE EASTERN THIRD OF THE MAP. ITS POWER BOXES CAN BE FOUND AT:

- THUNDER MT. POWER PLANT YARD
- THUNDER MOUNTAIN SUBSTATION TM-01
- THUNDER MOUNTAIN SUBSTATION TM-02
- BERKELEY SPRINGS
- ABANDONED BOG TOWN

TRAINING

CRAFTING AND C.A.M.P.ING

INVENTORY

QUESTS

ATLAS

BESTIARY

APPENDICES

A REAL BLAST

EVENT LOCATION	REWARDS
– RANDOM	– ENCLAVE UNDERARMOR
	– RANDOM AMMO
	– RANDOM AID ITEM
	– RANDOM PLAN, ARMOR, MOD, OR WEAPON
	– CHANCE FOR A RANDOM LEGENDARY WEAPON OR ARMOR

DETAILS

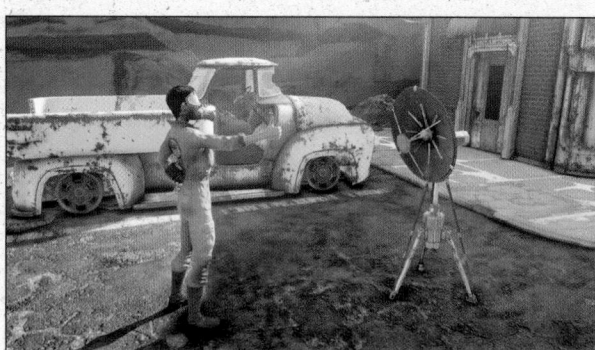

Initialize arrays in the marked area to start an orbital bombardment strike. Continuously repair the arrays as they break until the orbital bombardment is ready to fire; then hightail it out of there! You have only 15 seconds to clear the area before getting blown back into the Stone Age.

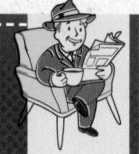

FASCINATING FACTS FROM VAULT BOY!
THIS EVENT WILL UNLOCK AFTER REACHING "OFFICER ON DECK" IN THE MAIN QUEST LINE.

BOTS ON PARADE

EVENT LOCATION		
– RANDOM		
REWARDS		
– ROBOT ARMOR	– RANDOM PLAN, ARMOR, MOD, OR WEAPON	
– RANDOM AMMO		
– RANDOM AID ITEM	– CHANCE FOR A RANDOM LEGENDARY WEAPON OR ARMOR	

DETAILS

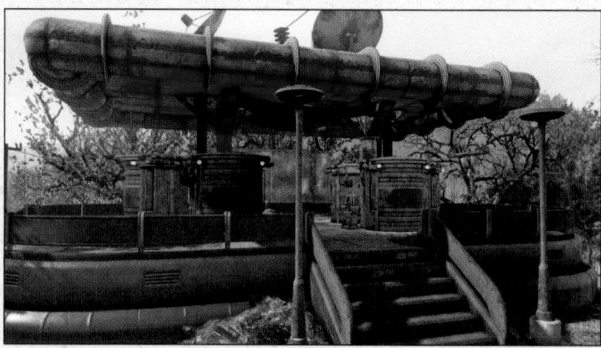

Protect a small squad of bots from enemies while MODUS reprograms them. Guard them until the timer runs out; then kill off any remaining enemies to wrap things up.

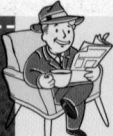

FASCINATING FACTS FROM VAULT BOY!
THIS EVENT WILL UNLOCK AFTER REACHING "OFFICER ON DECK" IN THE MAIN QUEST LINE.

DROPPED CONNECTIONS

EVENT LOCATION
– RANDOM
REWARDS
– ENCLAVE STRONGBOX
– RANDOM AMMO
– RANDOM AID ITEM
– RANDOM PLAN, ARMOR, MOD, OR WEAPON
– CHANCE FOR A RANDOM LEGENDARY WEAPON OR ARMOR

FASCINATING FACTS FROM VAULT BOY!
THIS EVENT WILL UNLOCK AFTER REACHING "OFFICER ON DECK" IN THE MAIN QUEST LINE.

DETAILS

Move around the enemy-filled event location while activating marked arrays. Once you finish activating each of them, an orbital supply drop will plunge to the earth. Kill or destroy all of the enemies drawn to the supply drop, and claim its inventory as your own to complete the event.

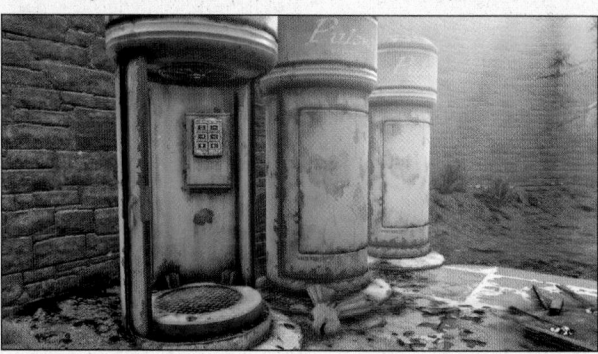

OTHER QUESTS

There are other quests besides the ones listed in the previous chapters, but they are less structured and inconsistent than those quests. Read on to learn about all the other wild and weird events that you can expect to encounter a time or two in Appalachia.

RANDOM ENCOUNTERS

While exploring Appalachia, you'll encounter strange characters and happenings entirely at random. Most of these encounters are either good for a laugh or a small stash of items, but some of them warn of dangers ahead. Keep your eyes peeled for odd events (especially the traveling Super Mutant merchant Grahm and his "Moo Moo" Chally), and listen to any strange NPCs you happen upon.

ENEMY HORDES

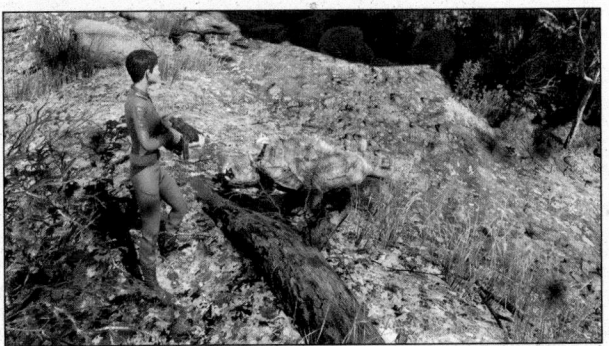

Every now and then, a horde of a particular enemy type will appear somewhere on the map. You can avoid them, but if you're sporting for a fight and decide to dive in and challenge their numbers, there are some things you need to know. Namely, hordes always have a leader, which will be marked on the map after encountering the horde. So long as that leader lives, the horde will continue to restore its members regardless of how many of them you kill.

WORKSHOP DEFENSE

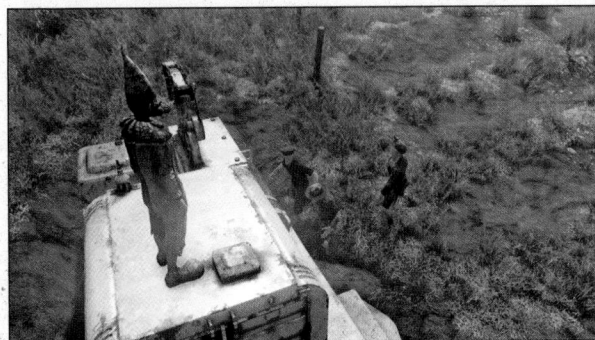

Capturing a workshop is relatively effortless, but hanging on to it is a different story. Aside from having to deal with hostile players trying to steal workshops from you, you'll occasionally have to fend off waves of attacks by the local wildlife.

Attacks like these will come at regular intervals, so if you're willing to hunker down and protect your workshop, they are a great way to gather loot and Plans. Set up some turrets in high, safe places and carefully place traps around the area and you'll hardly have to lift a finger.

SUPPLY DROPS

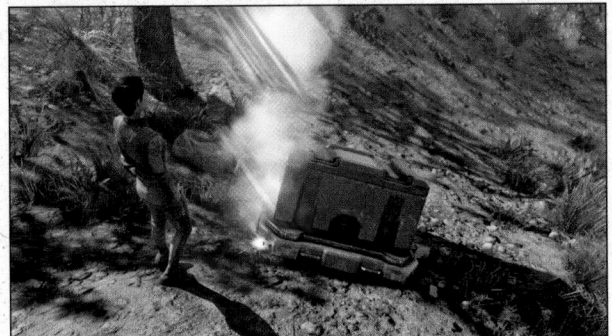

Vertibots will occasional swoop in and drop off a box of supplies before taking to the sky again. Any players in the region will receive a Miscellaneous Quest pointing them in the direction of the box. The supplies inside are well worth the journey, so head for the drops when you want to stock up!

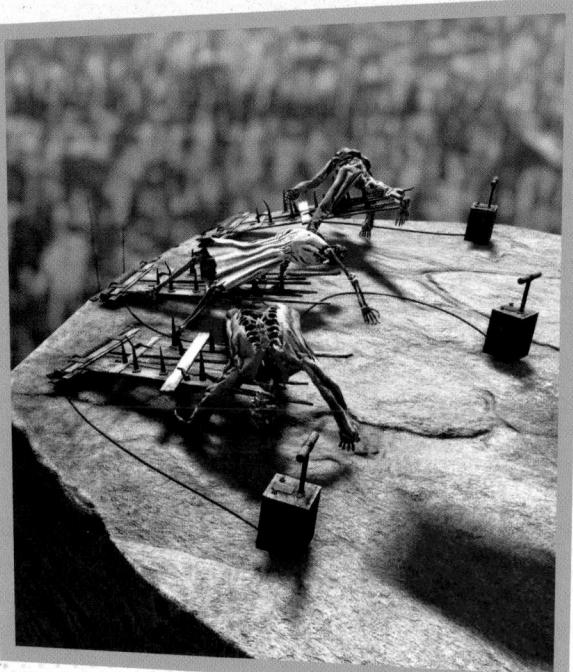

TRAINING

CRAFTING AND C.A.M.P.ING

INVENTORY

QUESTS

ATLAS

BESTIARY

APPENDICES

COMPETITIVE MULTIPLAYER

While most other Vault Dwellers you encounter in Appalachia will be civil (or evasive), things don't always have to be hunky dory. If you're looking to throw down the gauntlet and challenge other players to games of skill and speed, check out each of these quests.

HUNTER HUNTED

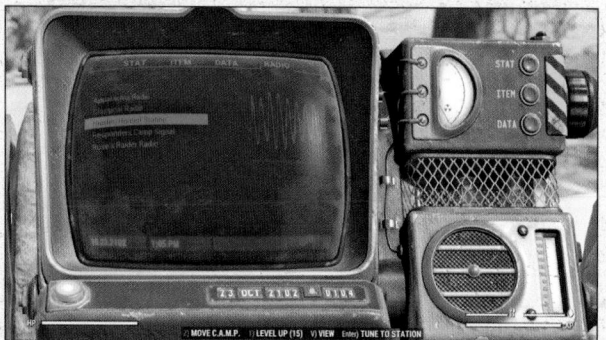

Bring up your Pip-Boy and turn to the Radio tab to find the Hunter Hunted radio station. If you and at least three other players are listening to that station, you'll initiate Hunter Hunted: a game where you are both hunter and prey. Kill your target and avoid getting killed by the other player targeting you to win.

MONSTER MASH

EVENT LOCATION
- WATOGA HIGH SCHOOL (CRANBERRY BOG)

REWARDS
- UNIQUE CANDY
- RANDOM AMMO
- RANDOM AID ITEM
- RANDOM PLAN,
- ARMOR, MOD, OR WEAPON
- CHANCE FOR A RANDOM LEGENDARY WEAPON OR ARMOR

DETAILS

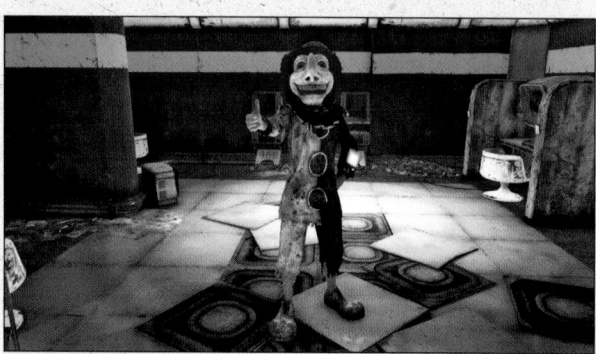

Battle with up to six other players to wrangle candy and complete a slew of objectives in Watoga High.

THE BATTLE THAT NEVER WAS

OBJECTIVE
- TALK TO THE CURATOR

EVENT LOCATION
- PRICKETT'S FORT (TOXIC VALLEY)

REWARDS
- AMMO FOR BLACK POWDER WEAPONS
- RANDOM AMMO
- RANDOM AID ITEM
- RANDOM PLAN, ARMOR, MOD, OR WEAPON
- CHANCE FOR A BLACK POWDER PISTOL
- CHANCE FOR A RANDOM LEGENDARY WEAPON OR ARMOR
- CIVIL WAR CLOTHING (IF YOUR TEAM WINS)
- RANDOM AMMO (IF YOUR TEAM LOSES)

DETAILS

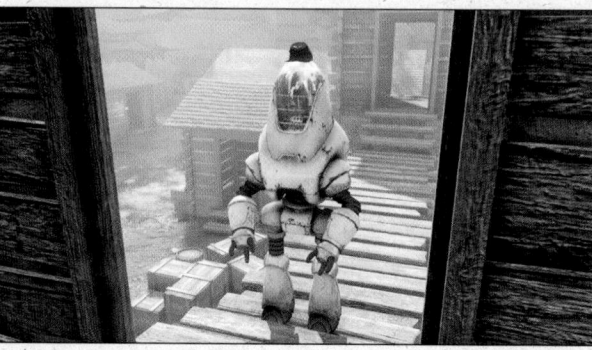

Partake in a faux historic battle between the Union and the Confederates at an old Civil War–era fort. The team with the most kills (including robot kills) is the winner.

MISCELLANEOUS QUESTS

While exploring Appalachia, you'll discover Miscellaneous Quests—nameless quests that are added to your quest log automatically. Most of these will simply lead to a small collection of loot, but others will lead into new, more expansive quests. There are dozens of Miscellaneous Quests scattered around Appalachia and more being added all the time. This isn't all of them, but it's enough to let you know what to expect when you bump into one. Explore every area extensively and you're bound to find even more!

OBJECTIVE	LOCATION	DESCRIPTION
Clear out New Gad	New Gad	Defeat the marked enemies in New Gad to complete this quest.
Clear out the Flooded Trainyard	Flood Trainyard	Kill enemies around the Flooded Trainyard until an elite enemy appears. Kill that enemy (who will be marked by an objective marker) to complete this Miscellaneous Quest.
Clear out the Watoga Emergency Services building	Watoga Emergency Services	Enter Watoga Emergency Services in central Cranberry Bog and kill any enemies you see. Eventually an elite enemy will appear. Kill and loot that enemy to complete the Miscellaneous Quest.
Clear out Watoga Civic Center	Watoga Civic Center	Enter Watoga Civic Center in central Cranberry Bog and kill any enemies you see. Eventually an elite enemy will appear. Kill and loot that enemy to complete the Miscellaneous Quest.
Collect and hold The Whitespring Holotapes	The Whitespring Resort	Explore The Whitespring Resort and its surrounding areas to locate holotapes. There are 10, and most of them are inside The Whitespring buildings.
Contact Miss Annie	Wavy Willard's Water Park	Speak with Miss Annie at Wavy Willard's Water Park in Toxic Valley to initiate "Cold Case."
Discover Garrahan Mining's innovation	Garrahan Mining Headquarters in southeast Ash Heap	This will appear as you approach Garrahan Mining Headquarters. Investigate the poster at the objective marker to start "Miner Miracles."
Explore Hornwright Industrial HQ	Hornwright Industrial HQ in Charleston	Enter Hornwright Industrial HQ and use the reception terminal in the foyer. Select "Archived Messages," then "Archived Message—9.29.77" to initiate the "The Motherlode" quest.
Find Grafton's Mayor's office	Morgantown Airport Terminal	Use the Responders HQ terminal on the second floor of the Morgantown Airport Terminal and select "Complaint 15-J." Reading that entry will initiate this Miscellaneous Quest. Head north to Grafton in Toxic Valley to find the office.
Find jukeboxes to bring music back to Summersville	Summersville	Head to the objective markers and activate the nearby jukeboxes. All three of them are inside buildings within the objective marker. They're not particularly hard to find, and once you locate them, you only need to activate them to complete the quest.
Find the church	Next to Hornwright Industrial HQ in Charleston	Related to "The Bell Tolls" event.
Get the Supply Drop	Random	Every now and then a Government Aid Drop will land in Appalachia. Race to reach one, as they have plenty of quality loot you won't want to miss getting your hands on.
Investigate Berkeley Springs	Berkeley Springs	Speak with Chloe the Ms. Nanny in Berkeley Springs to start "Play Time."
Investigate Ella's Bunker	Ella Ames' Bunker	Appears when you are near Ella Ames' Bunker. Use Ella's terminal in the room at the end of the hall on the right side of the main room. Select "Research Studies," then "RadShield" to complete the Miscellaneous objective and start "An Organic Solution."
Investigate Harpers Ferry	Harpers Ferry	Use any of the marked terminals around Harpers Ferry. Select "Missing Persons," then "Missing Hunting Party" to complete this quest and start "Tracking Unknowns."
Investigate the House	Monongah (in the basement of the marked house)	Pull the Vox Syringer out of the box to the left of the terminal; then use the terminal and select "Begin Vox Interpreter Data Collection Exercise" to start the quest "Someone to Talk To."
Investigate the shack	Hunter's Shack	Check the terminal inside the Hunter's Shack and select "Upload Data" to start the quest "Queen of the Hunt."
Investigate the Southern Belle Motel	Southern Belle Motel off of Route 65	Appears when you approach Southern Belle Motel. Speak with Boomer the broken Police Protectron in front of the hotel to start "Idle Explosives."
Investigate the trailer	Tygart Water Treatment	Pick up and listen to the Message for Jeff Holotape on the floor on the right side of the Tinker's Workbench. Starts the "Ecological Balance" quest.
Jangles got lost at the fair—find him!	Tyler County Fairgrounds	Jangles the Moon Monkey can be found next to the ice box in the Farm to Food booth.
Kill 10 unruly golfer Feral Ghouls at Whitespring	The Whitespring Resort	Kill Feral Ghouls roaming around The Whitespring Resort sporting golf attire.
Find Responder Supply Caches	Morgantown Trainyard	Search the trainyard to find the three supply caches needed to complete the quest and net some extra loot.
Find Duchess's Stash	Welch	Uncover the quest to loot the ill-gotten gains of the pre-war crime boss called Duchess.
Play music on the rooftops of Beckley	Beckley in the southwestern corner of the Ash Heap	Climb to the rooftops of the buildings in Beckley and head to each of the instruments at the marked locations. Play each instrument to complete this Miscellaneous Quest.
Reach the Mayor's Office	Watoga	While exploring Cranberry Bog near Watoga, you'll receive a transmission from the mayor of Watoga. Enter the Watoga Municipal Center and make your way to the mayor's office on the top floor. Completing this objective will start "Mayor for a Day."
Read Scribe Grant's terminal	Fort Defiance fourth floor	Appears when you reach the fourth floor of Fort Defiance.
Search General's Steakhouse for supplies	General's Steakhouse	Find and loot all of the containers at the objective markers to complete this quest.
Search Monongah Mine for supplies	Monongah Mine	Locate and unlock a safe in the Monongah Mine exterior. If you don't have the skill to pick the lock, just remember: "The gnome holds the key."
Search the body	Multiple locations in Appalachia (the easiest one is at AVR Medical Center near the center of the building's exterior)	Take the Worn Veil and Damaged Holotape off the body to begin the "Into the Mystery" quest.

OBJECTIVE	LOCATION	DESCRIPTION
Search the cabin for survivors	Sunday Brothers' Cabin	Recover each of the holotapes at the objective markers to complete this Miscellaneous Quest.
Sign up for Advanced Responder Training	Morgantown Airport Terminal	Use the terminal next to the Overseer's Cache in the Morgan Town Airport Terminal and select "Volunteers: Advanced Training" to start "Tentative Plans."
Speak to the Shooting Range Attendant	Grafton	Appears when you're near the shooting range. Complete this Miscellaneous Quest to start the "Target Rich Environment" Daily Quest.
Speak with Jack at the Pumpkin House	Pumpkin House	Appears when you're anywhere near the Pumpkin House in Savage Divide; initiates the "Trick Or Treat?" Daily Quest.
Start your training at Camp McClintock	Camp McClintock	Starts Main Quest: Back to Basic (you can read more about it in the Main Quests section of this book).
Talk to the Huntmaster of Black Bear Lodge	Black Bear Lodge	Head to the basement of Black Bear Lodge and speak with the Huntmaster computer terminal to begin "Big Game Hunt."
Tune in to WGRF Grafton radio	Eastern Regional Penitentiary	Turn your Pip-Boy radio station to WGRF Grafton Radio to start the "Bureau of Tourism" quest.
Visit the Giant Teapot	The Giant Teapot	Approach the Giant Teapot; then enter the red house next to it and speak with Sweetwater the Mr. Handy to initiate "Strange Brew."

SEARCH BIG BEND TUNNEL FOR SURVIVORS

This is a Miscellaneous Quest, but it's a bit more involved than most others. It will be added automatically upon visiting Big Bend Tunnel East or West.

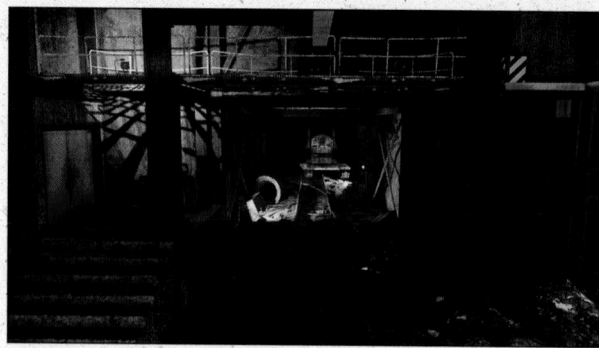

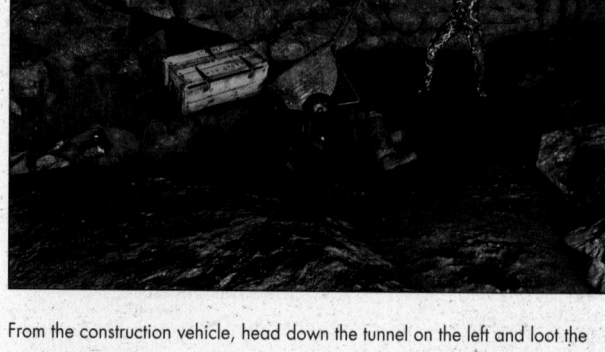

Loot the notes off of Sgt. Allemane's body (Sgt. Holstein if you're coming from the east side), and then enter the tunnel. When you reach the open corridor in the center of the tunnel, head through the south passage.

From the construction vehicle, head down the tunnel on the left and loot the notes off Sgt. Cominsky's body.

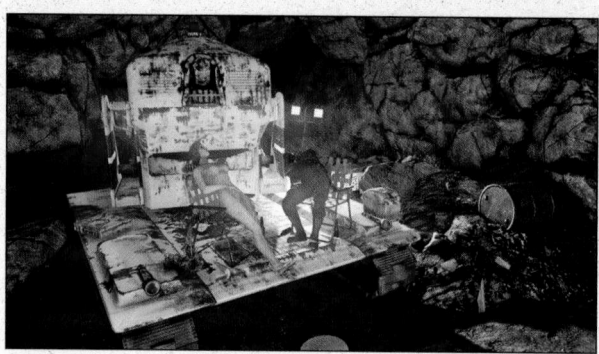

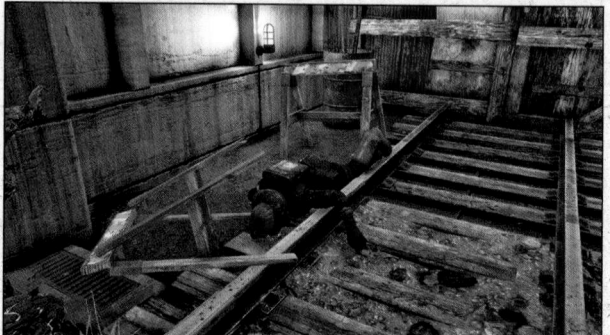

If you want access to the locked doors back in the central corridor, you can grab the Big Bend Tunnel Door Key off the body sitting in the chair on the large yellow construction vehicle.

Head to the opposite end of the tunnel and loot the Fire Breather's body (Sgt. Allemane on the west side, Sgt. Holstein on the east) to complete this Miscellaneous Quest.

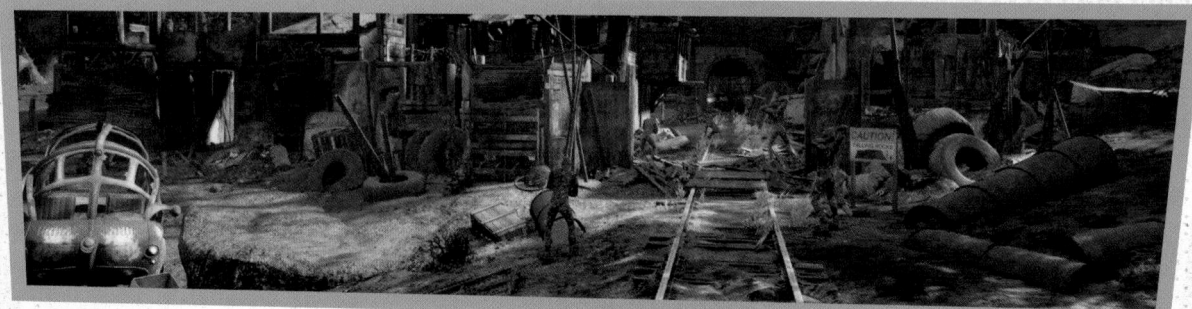

CHALLENGES

Challenges provide extra incentive to complete, see, craft and kill things that maybe you would have ignored before—the incentive being Atoms, which are the currency for the in-game online store.

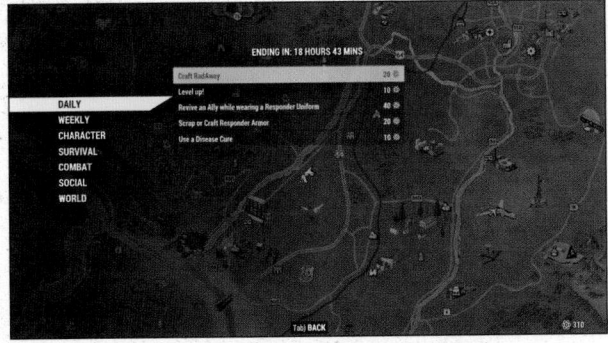

There are three different categories of Challenges: Daily, Weekly, and Lifetime. Daily and Weekly Challenges change regularly, while Lifetime Challenges are permanent and fixed to your account.

It likely goes without saying, but you will obtain greater rewards for completing more difficult Challenges. Most are tiered; you'll need to repeat the same things multiple times to complete the harder version of the same Challenge. For example: Collecting 25 Wood will net you the easiest Challenge, while collecting 50 will knock out the medium Challenge. Jump that up to 100 Wood and you'll have completed the hard version of that Challenge, earning you Atoms for each difficulty completed.

A SMALL SAMPLING

The following list isn't all of the Challenges in the game—not by a long shot—but it should give you a good idea of exactly how Challenges work. As a quick note: the numbers in parentheses represent the number of times you need to complete the specific task listed before the Challenge is complete ("Collect a Bobblehead (1)" means collect a single Bobblehead, while "Take a photo using Photo Mode (1)" means take a single photo, and so on...).

DAILY CHALLENGES

COLLECTING ITEMS

EASY	MEDIUM	HARD
Collect a Bobblehead (1)	Collect Bobbleheads (2)	Collect Bobbleheads (3)
Collect a Magazine (1)	Collect Magazines (2)	Collect Magazines (3)
Collect a Holotape (1)	Collect Holotapes (2)	Collect Holotapes (3)
—	Collect Burned Books (5)	Collect Burned Books (10)

WEEKLY CHALLENGES

COMBAT

EASY	MEDIUM	HARD
Deal Critical Hits to Enemies (10)	Deal Critical Hits to Enemies (25)	Deal Critical Hits to Enemies (50)
Destroy Assorted Robots (5)	Destroy Assorted Robots (5)	Destroy Assorted Robots (5)
Kill Cryptids while wielding a Laser, Plasma, or Energy Gun (5)	Kill Creatures that have become Scorched (3)	Kill Cryptids while wearing a Cultist Outfit or Tinfoil Hat (5)

LIFETIME CHALLENGES

Lifetime Challenges are attached to your account, so any Challenges you complete with one character don't need to be done again with another. Some Lifetime Challenges only appear after completing others. For instance: completing the "Reach level 4!" Challenge will unlock the "Reach level 6!" Challenge, while others unlock after you discover a new region or when you reach certain levels. These Level Up Lifetime Challenges are the only ones that can be re-earned on new characters.

CRAFTING

EASY	MEDIUM	HARD
Craft Grenades (76)	Craft Mines (76)	Craft or Scrap 1H Bladed (76)
Craft or Scrap a Melee Weapon (1)	Craft or Scrap 1H Melee (76)	Craft or Scrap 2H Blunt (76)
Craft or Scrap a Ranged Weapon (1)	Craft or Scrap 2H Melee (76)	—

TRAINING

CRAFTING AND C.A.M.P.ING

INVENTORY

QUESTS

ATLAS

BESTIARY

APPENDICES

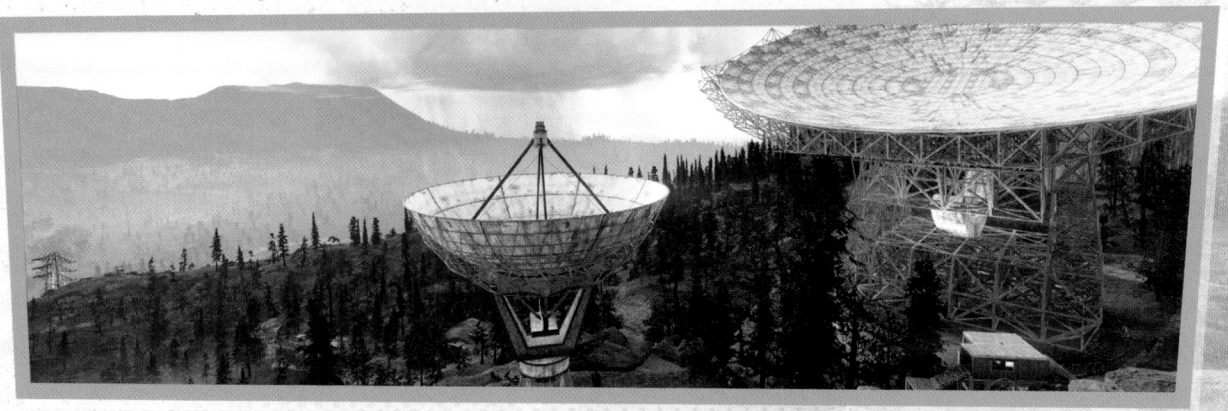

TREASURE MAPS

Occasionally, while looting containers and fallen foes, you'll find a treasure map. These maps have a simple sketch on them which will point you to a small cache of items: X marks the spot! The difficulty comes in trying to decode these visual riddles. If you pay close attention to the scenery presented in the image, you should be able to figure out where the treasure is located. Once you reach the X, you simply need to use the activate button on the ground where the treasure is hidden to dig it up and make it your own.

Here are a few tips that will make your treasure hunting experience a lot simpler:

- **TAKE IN THE SCENERY.** WE SAID IT BEFORE, BUT IT BEARS REPEATING. THERE WILL BE PLENTY OF TIMES WHERE YOU'LL OPEN UP A MAP AND SCRATCH YOUR HEAD AT ITS APPARENT VAGUENESS. DON'T LET THAT DISSUADE YOU! REALLY COMB THE IMAGE, PAY ATTENTION TO MOUNTAINS, LOOK AT POWER LINES, WATER TOWERS, ANYTHING! THERE'S ALWAYS A CLUE THAT WILL LEAD YOU TO WHERE YOU NEED TO GO.

- **ANGLE YOUR VIEW.** IF A MAP SHOWS A PARTICULAR LANDMARK (TOP OF THE WORLD, FOR INSTANCE) ON THE LEFT OF THE X, THEN MAKE SURE YOU TAKE THE SAME ANGLE. IF YOU'RE STRUGGLING TO LINE UP A LANDMARK IN THE SAME WAY THAT IS SHOWN IN THE MAP, YOU MIGHT BE IN A COMPLETELY DIFFERENT LOCATION THAN WHAT'S BEING SHOWN.

- **(N), (S), (E), (W).** WHENEVER YOU SEE A LETTER WITH A CIRCLE AROUND IT, YOU'RE LOOKING AT A COMPASS DIRECTION. IF THE IMAGE HAS AN E CIRCLED ON THE LEFT SIDE OF THE IMAGE, WHILE THE X IS ON THE RIGHT, YOU CAN BET THAT YOUR TREASURE IS SOMEWHERE ON THE WEST SIDE OF THE REGION.

THE FOREST

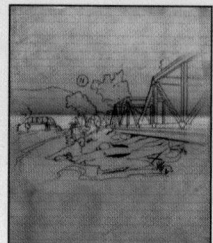

The Forest Treasure Map #01

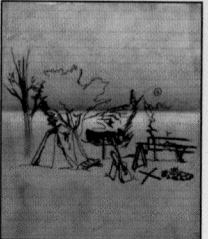

The Forest Treasure Map #02

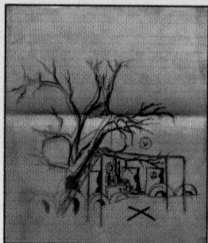

The Forest Treasure Map #03

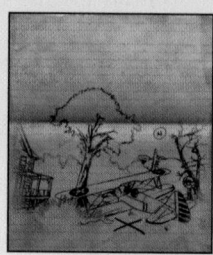

The Forest Treasure Map #04

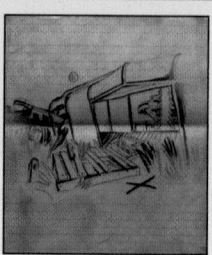

The Forest Treasure Map #05

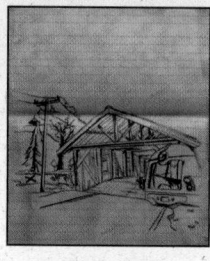

The Forest Treasure Map #06

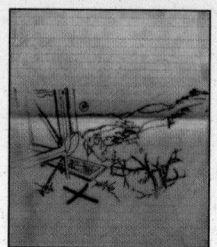

The Forest Treasure Map #07

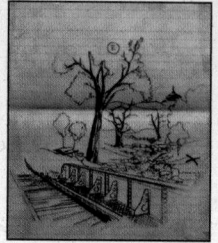

The Forest Treasure Map #08

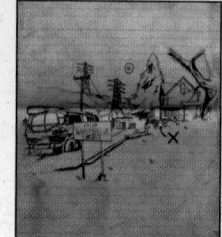

The Forest Treasure Map #09

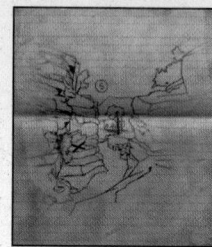

The Forest Treasure Map #10

TOXIC VALLEY

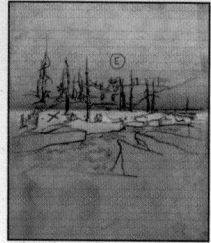

Toxic Valley Treasure Map #01

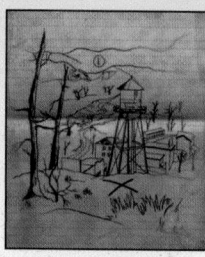

Toxic Valley Treasure Map #02

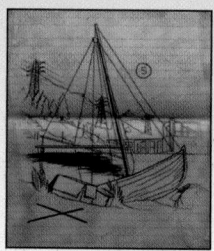

Toxic Valley Treasure Map #03

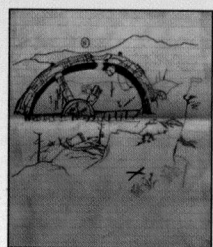

Toxic Valley Treasure Map #04

THE ASH HEAP

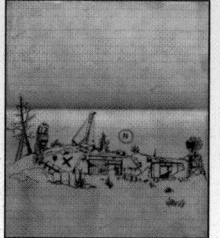

**The Ash Heap
Treasure Map #01**

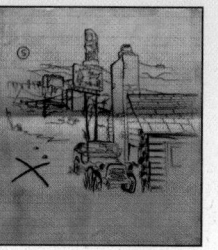

**The Ash Heap
Treasure Map #02**

SAVAGE DIVIDE

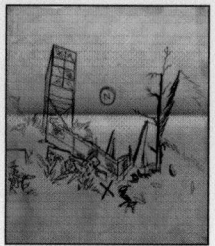

**Savage Divide
Treasure Map #01**

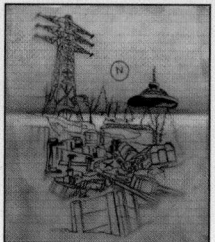

**Savage Divide
Treasure Map #02**

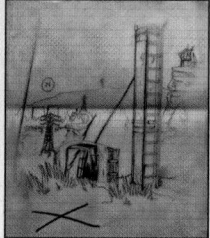

**Savage Divide
Treasure Map #03**

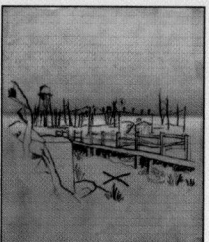

**Savage Divide
Treasure Map #04**

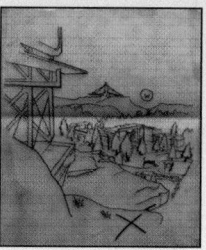

**Savage Divide
Treasure Map #05**

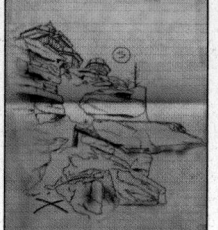

**Savage Divide
Treasure Map #06**

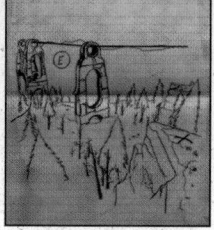

**Savage Divide
Treasure Map #07**

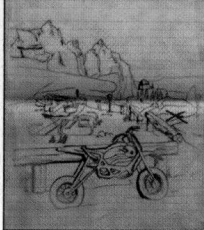

**Savage Divide
Treasure Map #08**

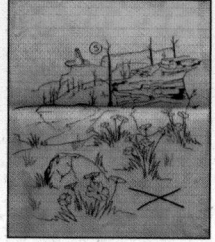

**Savage Divide
Treasure Map #09**

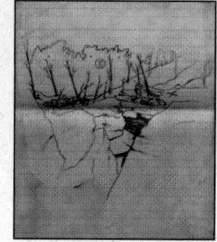

**Savage Divide
Treasure Map #10**

THE MIRE

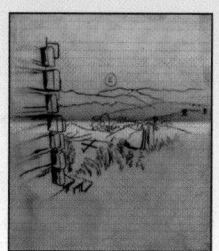

**The Mire
Treasure Map #01**

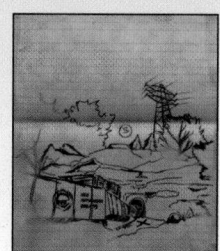

**The Mire
Treasure Map #02**

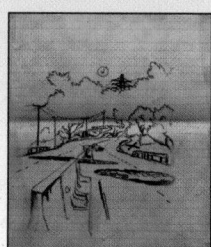

**The Mire
Treasure Map #03**

**The Mire
Treasure Map #04**

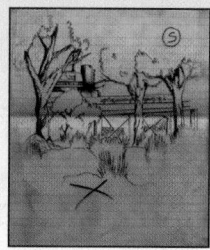

**The Mire
Treasure Map #05**

CRANBERRY BOG

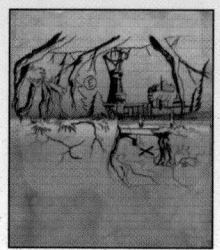

**Cranberry Bog
Treasure Map #01**

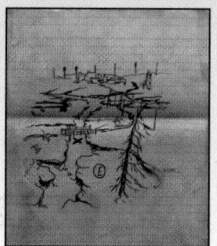

**Cranberry Bog
Treasure Map #02**

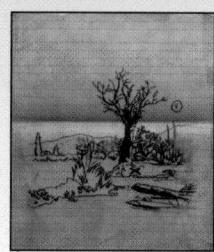

**Cranberry Bog
Treasure Map #03**

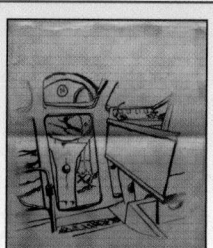

**Cranberry Bog
Treasure Map #04**

TRAINING

CRAFTING AND C.A.M.P.ING

INVENTORY

QUESTS

ATLAS

BESTIARY

APPENDICES

Atlas of Appalachia

INTRODUCTION

AN OVERVIEW OF APPALACHIA

WELCOME TO WEST VIRGINIA, VAULT DWELLER! IN THIS EXPANSIVE CHAPTER, YOU'RE ABLE TO FULLY EXPLORE THE MAJORITY OF LOCATIONS DOTTED THROUGHOUT THE VAST APPALACHIAN WILDERNESS. WE PROVIDE CAREFULLY CURATED INFORMATION ON EVERY POINT OF INTEREST, FROM THE GOLDEN DOME OF THE CHARLESTON CAPITOL BUILDING TO THE SMALLEST, MOST DILAPIDATED AND REMOTEST HUT. TO START WITH, HERE'S HOW ALL THIS INFORMATION BREAKS DOWN:

LOCATION TYPES

To avoid consternation, the land of Appalachia has been segmented into various regions and zones, from large to small.

REGIONS

All of Appalachia is divided into six major regions. Though your in-game world (parchment) map doesn't delineate exact borders, this guide does. These are massive areas of wilderness, townships, and cities, each with their particular flavor (even if that flavor is sometimes bitter radioactive ash). Expect to find a multitude of primary locations within each region, and even more secondary locations. The six regions are as follows:

REGION LOCATIONS

#	REGION NAME	ZONES	THREAT LEVEL	PRIMARY LOCATIONS	SECONDARY LOCATIONS
1	The Forest	5 (A, B, C, D, E)	1–10	95	121*
2	Toxic Valley	1	10–25	29	41*
3	The Ash Heap	2 (A, B)	25–35	50	38*
4	Savage Divide	3 (A, B, C)	15–99	92	155*
5	The Mire	2 (A, B)	30–99	43	66*
6	Cranberry Bog	2 (A, B)	35–99	49	73*
Total	Appalachia (852*)	14	1–99	358	494*

*There are likely to be even more secondary locations than this guide tracks. Can you find them all?

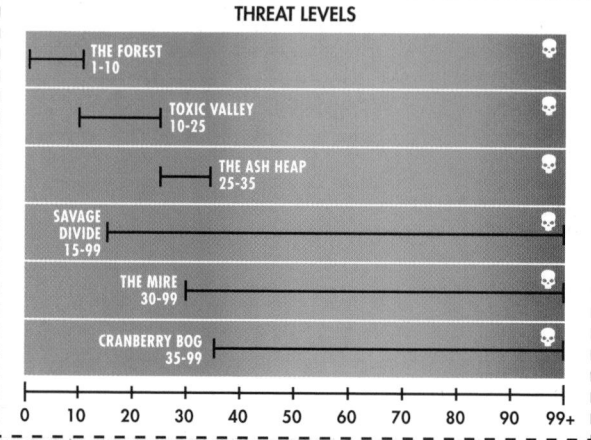

With some light reading of this chapter, you're therefore able to learn where more than 850 different locations are outside of Vault 76.

ZONES

If a region is simply too unwieldy for us to easily impart information, we subdivided it into smaller zones (which don't appear in the game). These are still very large-scale areas where upward of 20 to 30 primary locations are listed. Boundaries are drawn based on the topography of the area (usually divided at roads, railroads, rivers, or cliffs).

MAP LEGENDS: WORLD MAP

Before embarking from the Vault, learn what the different icons that appear on the world map mean:

WORLD MAP LEGEND
— REGION BOUNDARY ... 🏠 04 PRIMARY LOCATION
— ZONE BOUNDARY ... 22 SECONDARY LOCATION

This legend appears at the beginning of each region and zone and refers to the world map.

REGION AND ZONE BOUNDARIES

This is the perimeter of the region. This usually follows an easy-to-spot route, such as along a fence, road, or river, or at the base of a cliff.

PRIMARY LOCATIONS

🏠 **04** Also known as "marked locations," these are usually large locations that, once you discover them, appear and remain on your in-game world map. Fortunately, for those with this guide, every primary location has been spotted prior to discovery! These may require interior investigations; if necessary, we provide a local map in the guide with further detail. Each location has a Vault-Tec approved number designation; for example, Vault 76 has the number [01], indicating it is the first location listed in The Forest region.

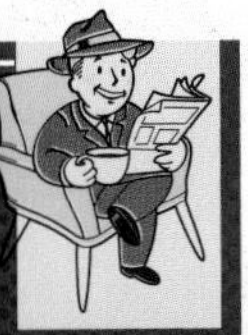

FASCINATING FACT FROM VAULT BOY!
WORLD AND LOCAL MAPS

WORLD MAP: THIS IS THE COLORFUL MAP OF APPALACHIA YOU CAN BRING UP WHILE IN GAME. IT HAS PRIMARY LOCATIONS ON IT, AND YOU CAN PINPOINT LOCATIONS, SEE OTHERS, AND BRING UP YOUR MAIN MENU.

LOCAL MAP: THIS IS THE LOCALIZED AREA MAP OF AN INDIVIDUAL PLACE. LOCAL MAPS ARE AVAILABLE ONLY IN THIS GUIDE AND SHOW BOTH DETAILED EXTERIORS AND INTERIORS OF PLACES LARGE ENOUGH TO WARRANT THIS EXTRA SCRUTINY.

SECONDARY LOCATIONS

22 Also known as "unmarked locations" or "points of interest" (POIs), these are usually much smaller locations that vary in size, from a large shack to a single corpse. These locations have excellent scavenging, photography, C.A.M.P. placement, or other potential. They do not feature an in-game World Map icon and don't ever appear on your in-game map. These are flagged so you can maximize your exploration!

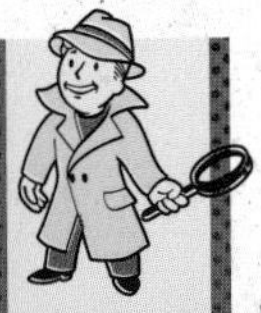

Helpful Hint from Vault-Boy!
LOOKING FOR LOCATIONS IN ALL THE RIGHT PLACES
Want to pinpoint a secondary location on your in-game map? Use the Map Marker function! Place it at the secondary location you want to visit, and head there without the hassle of stumbling upon it by chance!

MAP LEGENDS: LOCAL MAPS

The following legend appears whenever a location is big enough to require an interior map. Most of the icons are self-explanatory, as they indicate doors, collectibles, and workbenches. If there's a letter by some interactive elements (doors, safes, terminals), this indicates how you can access it.

LOCAL MAP LEGEND

MAP LEGEND
- MY STASH BOX
- OVERSEER'S CACHE
- TRUNK
- TRADER

COLLECTIBLES
- BOBBLEHEAD
- MAGAZINE
- POWER ARMOR

CRAFTING
- ARMOR WORKBENCH
- CHEMISTRY WORKBENCH
- COOKING STATION
- POWER ARMOR STATION
- TINKER'S WORKBENCH
- WEAPONS WORKBENCH
- WORKSHOP WORKBENCH

IMPORTANT
- DOOR/GATE
- LOCKED DOOR/GATE
- SAFE
- SCANNER
- TERMINAL

TRAINING
CRAFTING AND C.A.M.P.ING
INVENTORY
QUESTS
ATLAS
BESTIARY
APPENDICES

LOCATION STATISTICS

Every primary location in Appalachia has a list under its name and picture—a complete breakdown of pertinent information to better inform you of what to expect when you visit it. The following section explains what all of this is. If you require more information on better methods of scavenging particular items, consult the Junk, C.A.M.P., and Workshop sections of this guide.

Helpful Hint from Vault-Boy!

HASHTAG TRIPLE PLUS!

Many of the items or bits of information have one of two symbols after it. But what do they mean?

(#): This indicates the item is tracked precisely, and the exact number of items found at a location is shown. This is mainly confined to important collectibles (Bobbleheads, Caps Stashes, Magazines, and Power Armor), as well as each type of crafting workbench or station.

(+++): This indicates the item is tracked imprecisely: Due to the random nature of where everything is, estimates are made regarding exactly how many there are of each item:

(+): This indicates either a small scattering of the item or item type at the location. For Item Examples, between 1 and 2 of a particular item.

(++): This indicates a moderate amount of the item or item type. For Item Examples, around 3 to 6 of a particular item.

(+++): This indicates a copious amount of the item or type. For Item Examples, expect more than 6 of a particular item.

WORD OF WARNING FROM VAULT-BOY!

WHY ISN'T MY POWER ARMOR, BOBBLEHEAD, OR MAGAZINE HERE?

REMEMBER THAT THE LOCATIONS SHOWN ARE ONLY *POSSIBLE* PLACES WHERE A BOBBLEHEAD, CAPS STASH, MAGAZINE, OR POWER ARMOR FRAME *MIGHT* APPEAR. THERE IS A CHANCE THE COLLECTIBLE WON'T BE THERE, AND YOU SHOULD RETURN AFTER A DAY TO SEE IF IT'S APPEARED. OF COURSE, IF THE COLLECTIBLE IS MISSING, IT MIGHT BE BECAUSE ANOTHER VAULT DWELLER GOT THERE BEFORE YOU!

WORD OF WARNING FROM VAULT-BOY!

HEY! WHERE'S MY COPY OF TUMBLERS TODAY?

IT IS ALSO WORTH REMEMBERING THAT THE POSSIBLE LOCATIONS WHERE A BOBBLEHEAD OR MAGAZINE MIGHT APPEAR ALSO GRANT YOU A *RANDOM* TYPE OF BOBBLEHEAD OR MAGAZINE. THIS MEANS THAT THE SAME MAGAZINE LOCATION COULD GIVE YOU ISSUE #1 OF THE UNSTOPPABLES THE FIRST TIME YOU FIND IT, AND AFTER WAITING A DAY, THE LOCATION MAY GIVE YOU ISSUE #4 OF TUMBLERS TODAY (OR ANY OTHER MAGAZINE, OR NO MAGAZINE AT ALL). SO GRAB A BOBBLEHEAD OR MAGAZINE, EVEN IF YOU DON'T WANT TO USE IT RIGHT AWAY.

COLLECTIBLES

These are particularly helpful or impressive items that can aid your progress. Make finding them a priority (especially if others are in the area!):

BOBBLEHEAD (#)

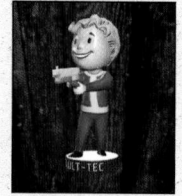

There is a possibility of one (or more) randomly determined limited-edition Vault-Tec Bobblehead (from a selection of 20) at this location, each with a particular statistical improvement. Note the Curator perk grants you longer benefits when you decide to use this item. Also note the Percepti-Bobble perk grants you directional audio to more easily find this item.

CAPS STASH (#)

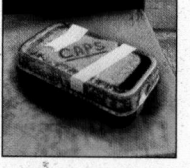

There is a possibility of one (or more) Caps Stashes; you can use tins of Caps to bolster your funds. Note the Cap Collector perk grants you more Caps per Stash, and the Fortune Finder perk grants you directional audio to more easily find this item.

HOLOTAPE (+++)

One or more holotapes are available at this location. These orange and white plastic tapes are played on your Pip-Boy or at any terminal. They offer information and sometimes give you quests. RobCo game holotapes are not included, as they randomly appear in the same location as Magazines.

HOLOTAPE: OVERSEER

This location has a holotape with remarks from the Vault 76 Overseer, which offers more insight into her life as you track her progress through Appalachia.

MAGAZINE (#)

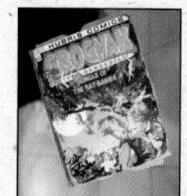

There is a possibility of one (or more) randomly determined Magazines at this location, each with a particular statistical improvement or holotape game. There are 12 different types of Magazines, and each type has a number of volumes or issues (meaning there's 104 different Magazines you can find). The Curator perk grants you longer benefits when you use this item. The Pannapictagraphist perk grants you directional audio to more easily find this item.

NUKA-COLA CHERRY (+++)

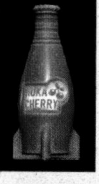

Sometimes, a normal Nuka-Cola at this location is replaced by a Nuka-Cherry, with an intense flavor and additional benefits. If a Nuka-Cherry has been spotted at this location, it is flagged there.

NUKA-COLA QUANTUM (+++)

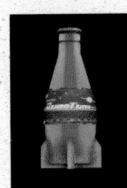

Sometimes, a normal Nuka-Cola at this location is replaced by a Nuka-Cola Quantum, with a robust flavor and additional benefits. If one has been spotted at this location, it is flagged here.

NUKA-COLA (OTHER) (+++)

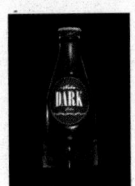

Occasionally, a location may have another, extremely rare Nuka-Cola flavor. Nuka-Grape, anyone?

POWER ARMOR (#)

 There is a possibility of a Power Armor Frame at this location, with pieces of armor attached to it. You can't 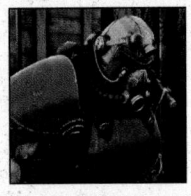 access some of the more impressive suits until you reach the appropriate level. If a corpse wearing Power Armor is at this location, it is also flagged.

CRAFTING

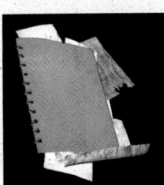

If a particular crafting station or workbench has been spotted, it is flagged at this location and (for the more important stations) placed on any pertinent local maps.

ARMOR (#)

Craft, repair, or modify armor and break down junk at the Armor Workbench, one or more of which are at this location.

CHEMISTRY (#)

Craft chems, smelt items, and break down junk at the Chemistry Workbench, one or more of which are at this location.

COOKING (#)

 Cook meals and prepare drinks at the Cooking Station, one or more of which are at this location.

POWER ARMOR (#)

Craft, repair, or modify Power Armor and break down junk at the Power Armor Station, one or more of which are at this location.

TINKER (#)

 Craft, repair, or modify ammunition and break down junk at the Tinker's Workbench, one or more of which are at this location.

WATER PUMP (#)

Find a supply of Dirty Water from the Water Pump, one or more of which are at this location.

WEAPONS (#)

 Craft, repair, or modify weapons and break down junk at the Weapons Workbench, one or more of which are at this location.

WORKSHOP

Build resource generators, buildings, and defenses at a Public Workshop, one of which is at this location.

DANGER!

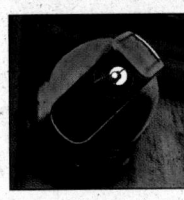

Many locations may feature one or more of the following dangers; check here before venturing in to see what troubles you might find.

CAN CHIME!

Disarm these hanging cans for junk or jingle them to attract attention.

BONE CHIME!

Disarm these hanging bones for junk or jingle them to attract attention.

EXPLOSIVE CANISTER!

This area has one or more red pressurized canisters or a large red plastic barrel; these are designed to explode when shot. Don't stand close by during an explosion.

FLAMETHROWER!

These flamethrower turrets are designed to burn you alive. One or more are at this location.

GRENADE!

Tension traps (such as those using bathroom scales or wires) usually release a "bouquet" of grenades when triggered. Look for these and add them to your projectiles before they drop.

HEAT!

This location features extreme temperatures, and specialized outfits are recommended (a firefighter's attire or Power Armor).

PUNJI BOARD

A spiked board you can easily stand on is at this location. Step over or around it.

LONG DROP!

This location is very tall, sits atop a long fall, or has narrow platforms over a long fall. Plummeting off a location is usually fine in Power Armor but can lead to a terrible and crushing death if you're just larking about and slip while in regular armor.

MINE!

That beeping sound indicates a mine is about to cripple you at this location. Disarm it before this happens, or flee the immediate area.

OIL!

A rainbow hue of leaking fluid can be ignited if flammable projectiles or explosions touch it. That's fine if enemies are standing on the oil, but isn't great if you're caught in the fire.

RADIATION!

This location is either mildly (+), moderately (++), or severely (+++) radioactive. It is important to wear additional protective gear (such as Hazmat Suits or Power Armor) for particularly bad areas to avoid radiation poisoning. Keep Rad-X and RadAway with you as a precaution when exploring this location.

RADTOAD MINE!

The cryptid Radtoad has been active in this area and may have laid explosive egg mines. Creep to avoid detonation, and retreat to avoid an explosion if the eggs are about to detonate.

TRAINING

CRAFTING AND C.A.M.P.ING

INVENTORY

QUESTS

ATLAS

BESTIARY

APPENDICES

SPIKE BOARD!

The location has a spike on a door with a spring; once triggered (usually via a tension trigger or tripwire), it swings around and pierces you. Jump back, take greater care, and avoid it when at all possible.

TENSION TRIGGER!

A spring has been set against an object that, when released, detonates an explosive of some kind. Disarm these so the explosion never occurs.

TESLA ARC!

An electrical device that's as impressive to look at as it is foolish to take damage from. Disarm these wall-mounted devices if you can, or face a surge of energy damage.

TRIPWIRE!

A length of wire (or a laser beam) is in this area. Hitting it releases a trap—sometimes a weapon on a stand fires at you or a previously mentioned trap is triggered. Disarm these to avoid the hurting.

TURRET!

The location features unmanned tripod or wall turrets, usually controlled by a nearby terminal you can hack, if you don't wish to sneak by or manually blow the turrets up. Sometimes a turret may be non-hostile or in need of repair, after which you or your team can use it.

ITEM: ITEMS INFORMATION

This entry explains what value the location has in terms of the items you can acquire.

ARMS AND AMMO (+++)

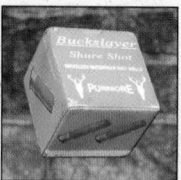

Expect ammunition here, and if the rating is increased, add weapons to that list. Expect a large settlement with an armory to necessitate a +++ rating.

HARVESTABLE

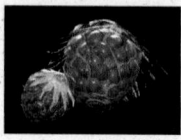

The preeminent types of crop to harvest or resources to mine are listed here. They include plant life, minerals, and rocks you need for object creation and item modifications. Note that the area immediately around a location has been checked for flora, though some harvestable items not listed may be at the location.

HEALTH AND CHEMS (+++)

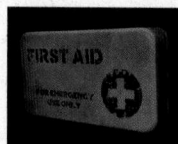

This location has Stimpaks and chems of some description. The higher the rating, the more you'll find.

MY STASH BOX

 A Vault blue chest is available at this location. It allows you to offload any items or gather those you have 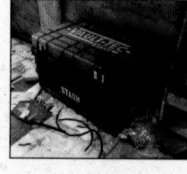 placed in any other My Stash Box. This is helpful if you are overburdened, need to free some room before exploring a location, or need to retrieve an item you already stored. Think about using these locations (or your camp) as a base from which you and your team can start and finish an exploration.

OVERSEER'S CACHE

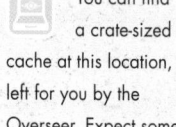 You can find a crate-sized cache at this location, left for you by the Overseer. Expect some items that can aid you, as well as a possible holotape with the Overseer's progress, as part of the "Overseer's Mission" Side Quest.

RECIPE/MOD/PLAN (+++)

This location has one or more recipes, weapons, or armor modification, or you can plan to build a particular object.

TRUNK

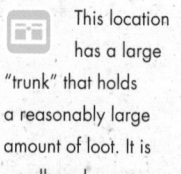 This location has a large "trunk" that holds a reasonably large amount of loot. It is usually red or green 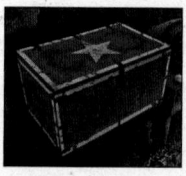 and has various names (e.g., Steamer Trunk or Industrial Trunk). It is usually a "reward" chest for clearing a location, so if you see one, you're likely to have explored most of the location. It holds random loot.

VENDING MACHINE

This location has a trash-can-sized receptacle that allows you to purchase (or gather) a particular type of item. Expect 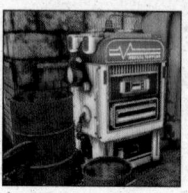 the following, with the vast majority of vending machines offering either ammunition or health and supplies, providing you have the Caps.

Type of Vending Machine: Ammunition, Archival Dispenser, Health and Supplies, Map Dispenser (U-Mine It!), Resume Receptacle, Token Dispenser, Uniform Dispenser.

INFO: INFORMATION

Every location has several different aspects to it. All the most pertinent (and trackable) information is listed in this entry.

AEROSOLIZER (TOXIC VALLEY)

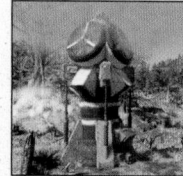

This location features an Air Purifier unit, which when running, produces more breathable air for a short time.

AIR PURIFIER (THE ASH HEAP)

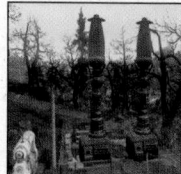

This location features an Air Purifier unit, which, when running, produces more breathable air for a short time.

C.A.M.P. POWER

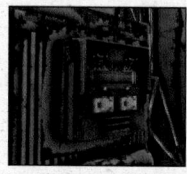

This location (usually a substation) has a power box attached to it, allowing you to hang wire from it to any camp item that requires power, in lieu of a generator. However, you may need to bring a nearby power plant online first.

EXPECTED ENEMY

When visiting a location, there is a chance that a random enemy type may appear, but this entry flags the type of enemy you should expect, based on previous experience.

INSTRUMENT

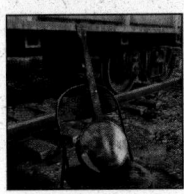

The location contains one or more musical instrument that you can play (or take with you and played) for the "Well Tuned" bonus.

LANDMARK

This location is particularly impressive, has historical significance, and can be seen from far away. Optionally use it to orient yourself when exploring the immediate vicinity or a region.

NOTE

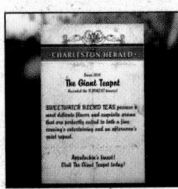

One or more notes (usually on paper) are at this location, usually adding flavor, but sometimes a quest, to your exploration.

QUEST

One or more quests begin at this location.

SCAVENGE RATING (0–5+)

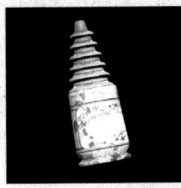

If you're here for the junk, ammo, and chems, then this rating is important:

- **0: THERE'S NOTHING OF WORTH HERE.**
- **1: EXPECT A FEW SCRAPS OF JUNK BUT NOTHING ELSE.**
- **2: A SMALL COLLECTION OF JUNK; NOT WORTH GOING OUT OF YOUR WAY TO FIND.**
- **3: A FEW REASONABLE PIECES OF JUNK; WORTH YOUR TIME TO SCAVENGE HERE.**
- **4: A LARGE AMOUNT OF JUNK, ONE OR TWO RARER BITS AND PIECES, PERHAPS REQUIRING A VISIT TO A MY STASH BOX. DEFINITELY RANSACK THIS PLACE!**
- **5: A MASSIVE QUANTITY OF JUNK, INCLUDING RARER ITEMS THAT GRANT GOOD RESOURCES. GET HERE BEFORE EVERYONE ELSE DOES!**
- **5+: USUALLY A CITY-SIZED LOCATION WITH MULTIPLE PLACES TO SCAVENGE, AND AT LEAST TWO TRIPS TO THE MY STASH BOX.**

SIZE (1–5+)

The location's size is listed. The number is based on the following:

- **1: A TINY LOCATION, USUALLY NO BIGGER THAN A SHACK.**
- **2: A LOCATION ABOUT THE SIZE OF A COUPLE HUTS, A MEDIUM-SIZED POND, OR A FARMHOUSE.**
- **3: A SMALL HAMLET, A LARGE SINGLE STRUCTURE WITH ONE OR TWO FLOORS, AND PERHAPS A SMALL INTERIOR AREA.**
- **4: A SMALL TOWN, OR VERY LARGE SINGLE STRUCTURE WITH MULTIPLE FLOORS AND INTERIORS.**
- **5: A LARGE TOWN, WITH MULTIPLE SEPARATE LOCATIONS TO INVESTIGATE.**
- **5+: A CITY-SIZED SETTLEMENT, WITH NUMEROUS REGULARLY SIZED LOCATIONS WITHIN ITS BOUNDARIES.**

SLEEPING

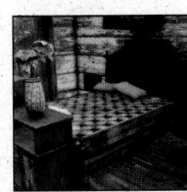

A sleeping bag, mattress, or bed is available at this location. Once you neutralize all hostiles, you can use it to obtain the Well Rested bonus.

SURVEY AREA

This location is usually a lookout tower that allows you to survey the immediate area from the top of the location, so additional primary locations appear on your in-game map.

THREAT LEVEL (1–99)

The threat level of this location is listed, which is usually the same as the region the location is in.

TRADER

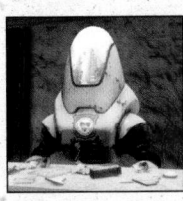

A stationary Vendor Bot is at this location, ready to trade with you. Note that Vendor Bots from different regions will have regular items, as well as those specific to the region in question. Remember to use the Hard Bargain perk to get better deals!

LOCK: LOCKED

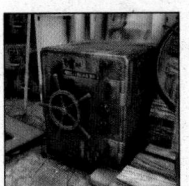

At this location, there are one or more doors, safes, or terminals that require some time to unlock them.

DOOR (TYPE)

A door—whether it be wooden or metal, a gate, a security gate, or other doorway-blocking device—is at this location. Most are unlocked, but some have a type of associated lock (see below). Those normally locked require Bobby Pins and a Lockpick minigame to unlock.

SAFE (TYPE)

A small safe, sitting on the ground, built into the wall, or sunk into the floor, is available and (unless unlocked) requires Bobby Pins and a Lockpick minigame to unlock.

SCANNER (TYPE)

This location has a Scanner, which is usually accessed via a handprint and circumvented during a particular quest.

TERMINAL (TYPE)

A desk or wall terminal, requiring a brief "word match" hacking minigame to unlock.

LOCK TYPES

- **B—BARRED: THE DOOR HAS A BAR ACROSS IT, ONLY ACCESSIBLE FROM ONE SIDE.**
- **C—CHAINED: THE DOOR HAS A CHAIN ACROSS IT, ONLY ACCESSIBLE FROM ONE SIDE.**
- **0—NOVICE LEVEL; 1—ADVANCED LEVEL; 2—EXPERT LEVEL; 3—MASTER LEVEL: THE DOOR, SAFE, OR TERMINAL REQUIRES A MINIGAME TO COMPLETE AND A PARTICULAR PERK RANK LEVEL FOR DOORS (PICKLOCK), SAFES (PICKLOCK), OR TERMINALS (HACKER), RESPECTIVELY.**
- **KEY—KEY: A KEY, ID CARD, OR OTHER DEVICE IS NEEDED TO OPEN THIS DOOR.**
- **T—UNLOCKED VIA TERMINAL: THIS DOOR (USUALLY A SECURITY GATE) IS USUALLY UNLOCKED AT AN ADJACENT TERMINAL).**
- **IN—INACCESSIBLE: THE DOOR IS INACCESSIBLE AND CANNOT BE OPENED.**

TRAINING

CRAFTING AND C.A.M.P.ING

INVENTORY

QUESTS

ATLAS

BESTIARY

APPENDICES

ITEM EXAMPLES (+++)

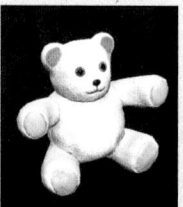

Each location also features a list of the type of (mainly junk) items you're likely to discover while searching the immediate vicinity. These are items that are visible, on the ground or surfaces, and do not include any that are inside containers. These are listed to give you a flavor of the item types available here; the list is by no means exhaustive.

Helpful Hint from Vault-Boy!

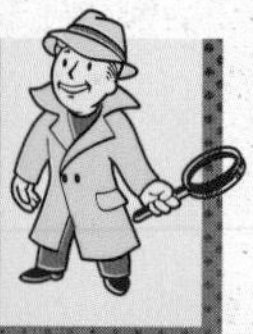

CONTAINING YOUR DELIGHT

Remember that each location has much more than the Item Examples shown in this guide. Search for tool boxes, lunch pails, wooden crates, furniture of every kind, ammo boxes, and other containers (whether locked or not), as you'll gather the vast majority of items from these. Remember that just because a location doesn't flag, for example, a recipe, that doesn't mean a container won't have one! As items in containers are random, they cannot be tracked.

FASCINATING FACTS FROM VAULT-BOY!

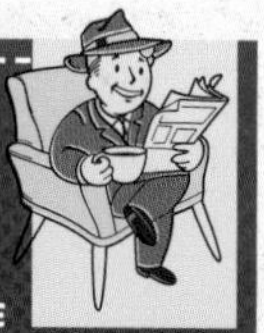

WHERE ARE MY MINI NUKES, FUSION CORES, AND UNIQUE WEAPONS, THEN?

ASIDE FROM FINDING THESE IN CONTAINERS, THE GUIDE DOES FLAG MINI NUKES AND FUSION CORES THAT ARE LOCATED IN THE LANDSCAPE. HOWEVER, YOU SHOULD THINK ABOUT CRAFTING MINI NUKES AND HARVESTING FUSION CORES FROM GENERATORS AT POWER PLANTS (FOR A NEVER-ENDING SUPPLY!). UNIQUE WEAPONS (AND OTHER FANCY ITEMS) ARE ALMOST NEVER FOUND LYING AROUND; THEY ARE ALMOST ALWAYS GIVEN AS A QUEST REWARD OR FOUND ON A PARTICULARLY TOUGH OR NAMED ENEMY.

WORK: PUBLIC WORKSHOP INFORMATION

If the location is a Public Workshop, information on the various resources you can extract, mine, and harvest are detailed here, once you or your team have claimed the workshop.

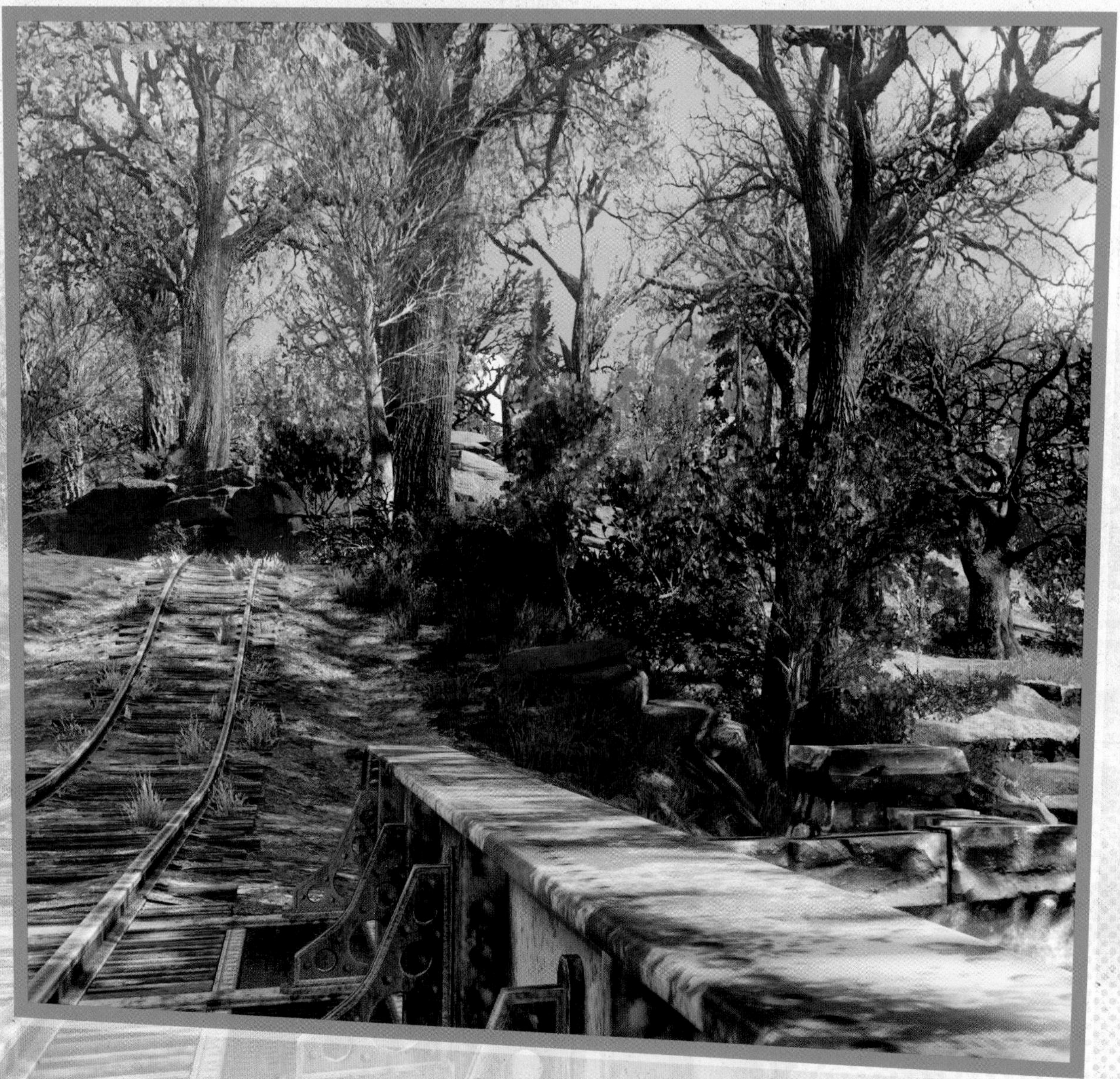

Appalachia: WORLD MAP

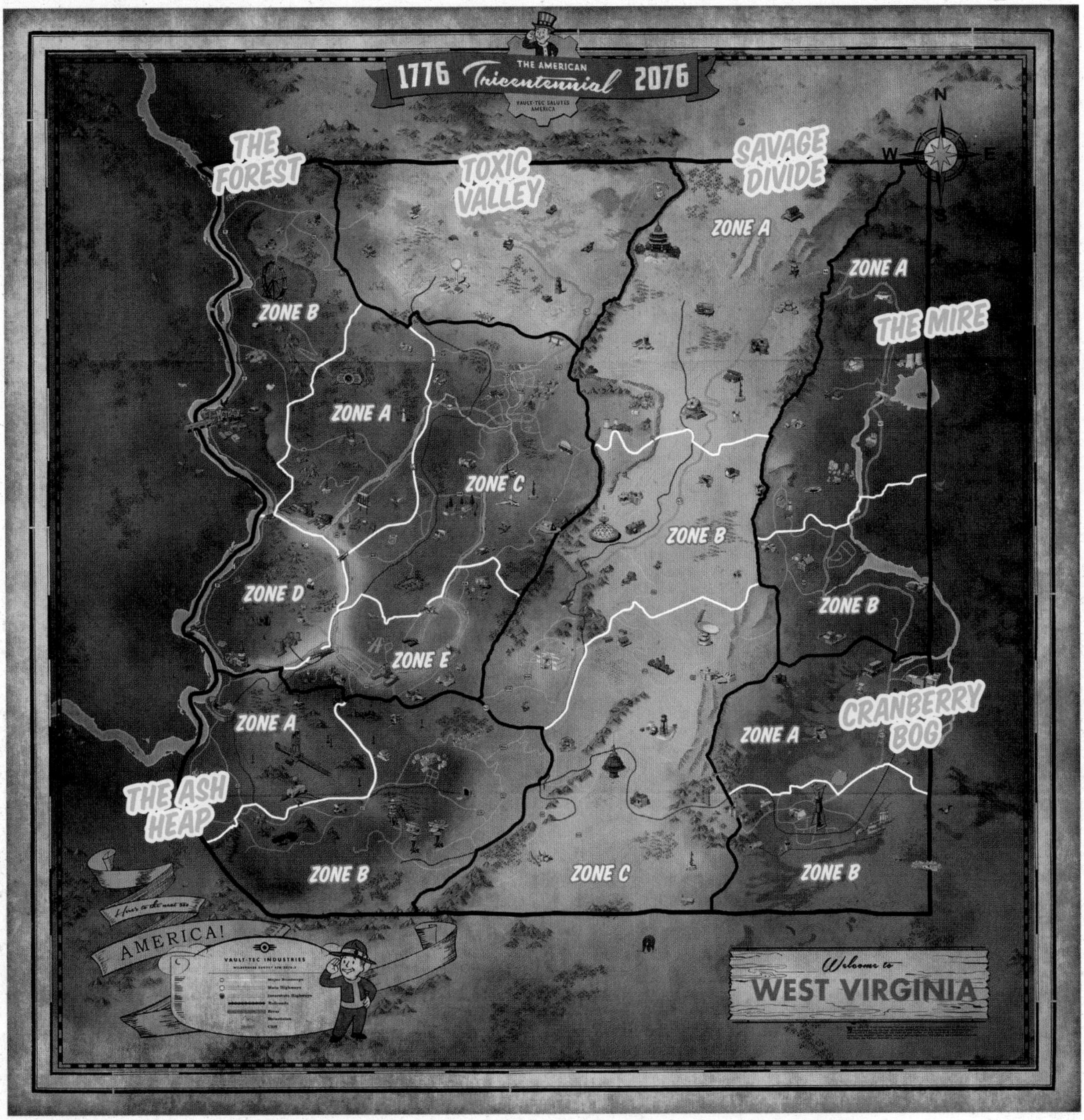

THE AMERICAN
1776 *Tricentennial* **2076**
VAULT-TEC SALUTES
AMERICA

THE FOREST

TOXIC VALLEY

SAVAGE DIVIDE

ZONE A

ZONE A

THE MIRE

ZONE B

ZONE A

ZONE C

ZONE B

ZONE D

ZONE B

ZONE E

ZONE A

ZONE A

CRANBERRY BOG

THE ASH HEAP

ZONE B

ZONE C

ZONE B

AMERICA!

VAULT-TEC INDUSTRIES

Welcome to **WEST VIRGINIA**

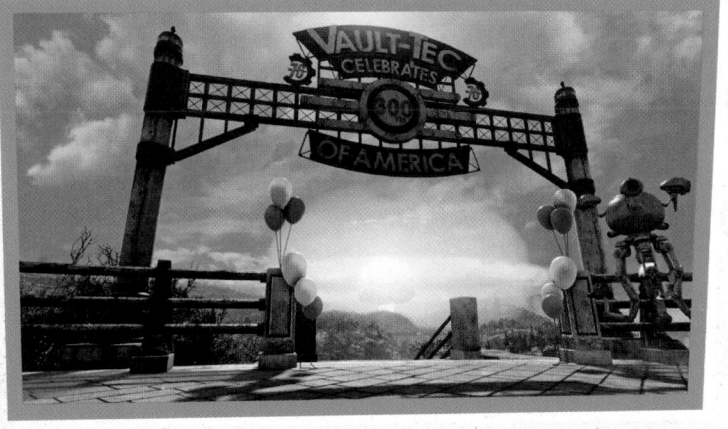

REGION 1: THE FOREST

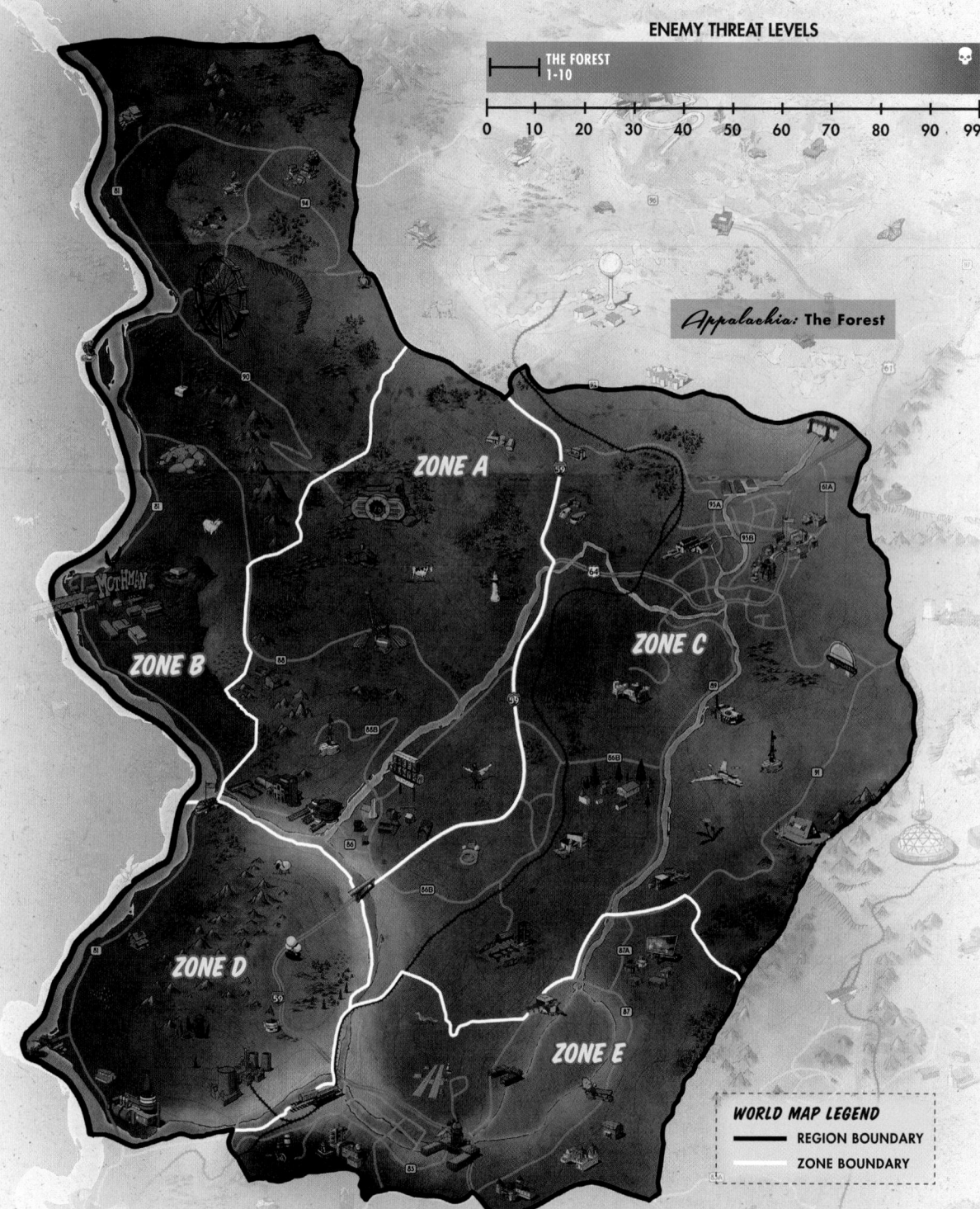

ENEMY THREAT LEVELS

| THE FOREST |
| 1-10 |

0 10 20 30 40 50 60 70 80 90 99+

Appalachia: The Forest

ZONE A

ZONE B

ZONE C

ZONE D

ZONE E

WORLD MAP LEGEND
— REGION BOUNDARY
— ZONE BOUNDARY

Mostly untouched by the ravages of nuclear fallout, the gigantic Appalachian forest area comprises the central, western, and northwestern parts of the map (mainly areas in and around Kanawha County). This area offers exceptional scavenging opportunities, remote places to hide out in or near, numerous strange settlements, and many towns, including Point Pleasant (to the west), Morgantown (northeast), Sutton and Helvetia (toward the center), Summersville (north of the large dry lake), and the capital itself, Charleston, which has almost been razed to the ground. Expect some lengthy explorations across the New Gorge Bridge and through the Kanawha Nuka-Cola Plant, battling Super Mutants at Wade Airport, losing your footing at Horizon's Rest...and that's just scratching the surface! Stay here if you want to scavenge more easily, in less inclement weather conditions, with enemies that are still a threat but usually won't cause you to flee in terror (especially if you have a friend or three along for the romp). Check the various Public Workshops for areas you can claim and mine the resources just a little more easily than elsewhere in Appalachia. And finally...did you see those glowing eyes staring at you from the woods? Beware the Mothman!

ZONE A—VAULT 76 AND FLATWOODS

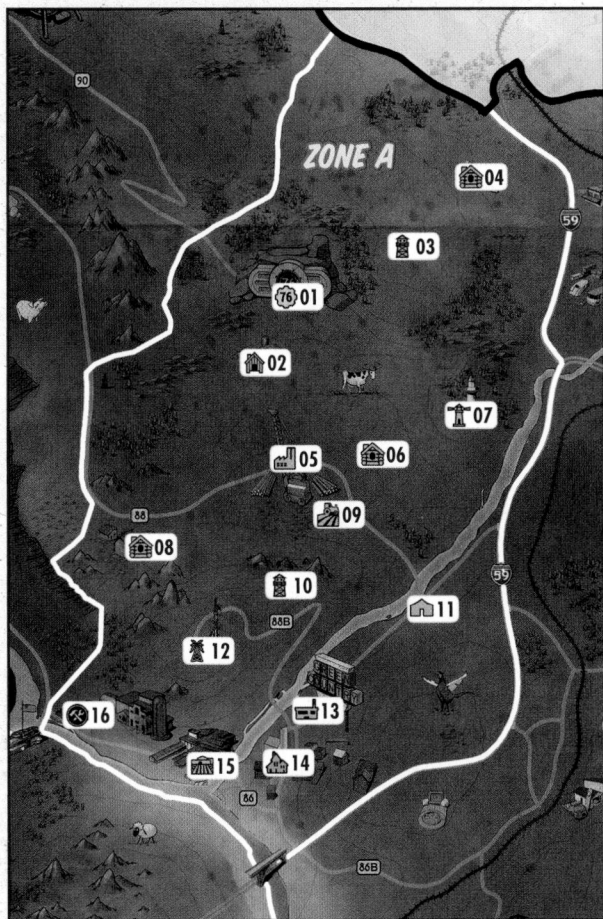

Appalachia: The Forest (Zone A) – Primary Locations

Vault 76 is located near the northern climbs of this undulating forest valley, which encompasses some rich farm and logging land, as well as the river that leads to the town of Flatwoods (make this your first settlement to explore). You are in relative safety if you remain in this zone. There's plenty to scavenge, and there are odd and interesting locations to visit (including a landlocked lighthouse and many Bobbleheads and Magazines), as well as some secondary location points of interest that don't show up on your map. Remember you can flee back to the Overseer's Camp or Vault 76 if you need workbenches or safety, respectively. Now get exploring; there's people to see, places to visit, and a Flatwoods Monster to hunt!

Helpful Hint from Vault-Boy!

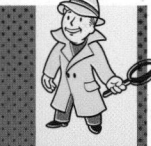

Though each location listed has its own crafting stations and workbenches called out, the closest workbenches to Vault 76 are as follows:

Armor Workbench: 09. Wixon Homestead

Chemistry Workbench: 02. Moonshiner's Shack

Cooking Station: 02. Moonshiner's Shack

Power Armor Station: 30. Wilson Brother's Auto Repair (Zone C)

Tinker's Workbench: 05. Gilman Lumber Mill

Water Pump: 03. North Kanawha Lookout

Weapons Workbench: 02. Moonshiner's Shack

Helpful Hint from Vault-Boy!

Make Zone A your initial playground! Once you emerge, you may be worried about attacks from the vicious and unknown beasts of West Virginia, but staying within the confines of this zone allows you to explore thoroughly and gather junk, recipes, mods, plans, weapons, armor, and other useful items without drifting too far away, so you aren't spending too many Caps on Fast-Travel.

WORLD MAP LEGEND

—— REGION BOUNDARY   —— ZONE BOUNDARY

PRIMARY LOCATIONS

				icon	NAME
	1			76 01	VAULT 76
				02	MOONSHINER'S SHACK
				03	NORTH KANAWHA LOOKOUT
	1			04	TWIN PINE CABINS
				05	GILMAN'S LUMBER MILL
				06	ISOLATED CABIN
2	2			07	LANDVIEW LIGHTHOUSE
2	2			08	ALPINE RIVER CABINS
1	1			09	WIXON HOMESTEAD
				10	FLATWOODS LOOKOUT
				11	OVERSEER'S CAMP
				12	RELAY TOWER EM-B1-27
				13	GREEN COUNTRY LODGE
				14	FLATWOODS
4	5	4		15	VAULT-TEC AGRICULTURAL RESEARCH CENTER
				16	SUNSHINE MEADOWS INDUSTRIAL FARM

● BOBBLEHEADS   ■ CAP STASHES   ● MAGAZINES   ■ POWER ARMOR

ZONE A: PRIMARY LOCATIONS

76 01. VAULT 76 (VAULT)

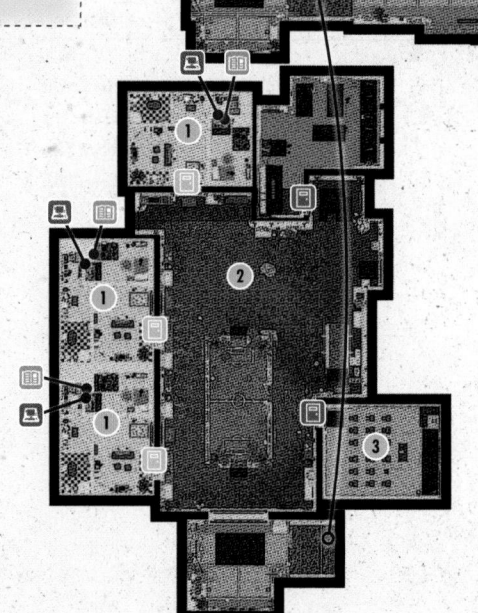

Vault 76 (Interior)

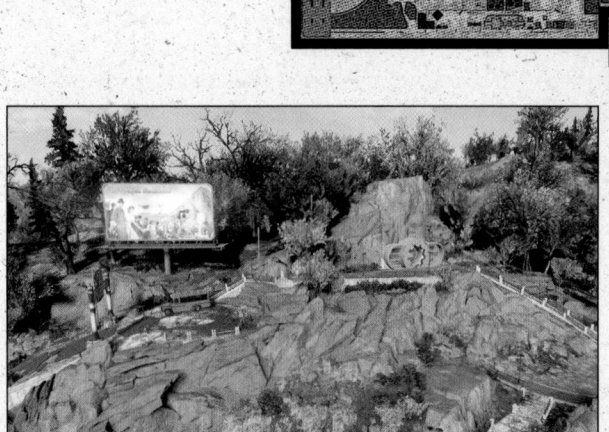

- **COLLECTIBLE: MAGAZINE**
- **ITEMS: HEALTH AND CHEMS**
- **INFO: INSTRUMENT; NOTE; QUEST: RECLAMATION DAY;
  SCAVENGE RATING: 3; SIZE: 3; THREAT LEVEL: 1–10.**
- **ITEM EXAMPLES: BLACK-RIMMED GLASSES, BUILDING
  SUPPLIES, C.A.M.P., PARTY HAT, PEN, PERK CARDS, PIP-
  BOY 2000, PURIFIED WATER, RAD-X, STIMPAK**

LEGEND

1. VAULT DWELLER ROOM
2. RECREATION AREA
3. CAFETERIA AND CLASSROOM
4. OVERSEER'S OFFICE
5. CLASSROOM
6. SCREENING
7. VAULT DOOR (EXIT)

Welcome to Vault 76! We hope you had a wonderful Reclamation Day shindig, but it's now time to leave. Follow the onscreen instructions, visiting each of the locations on the map, before heading out into the Appalachian wilderness. Remember you can return to the (relative) protection of the Vault entrance when using Fast-Travel without having to spend any Caps. Usually, though, you should gather all items you can before leaving.

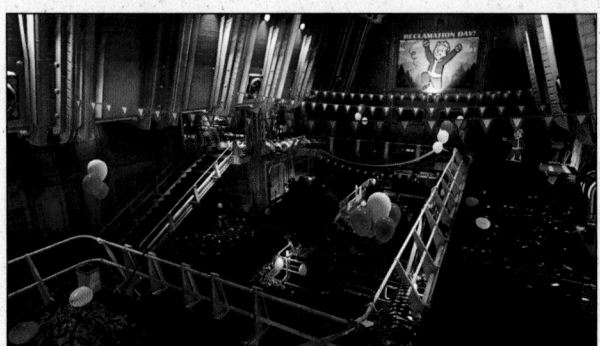

02. MOONSHINER'S SHACK

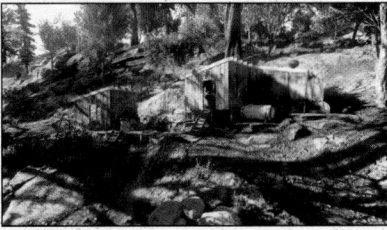

- **CRAFTING:** CHEMISTRY; COOKING; WEAPONS
- **DANGER:** RADIATION!+ (TICK)
- **ITEMS:** HARVESTABLE: TATO PLANT
- **INFO:** EXPECTED ENEMY: TICK; SCAVENGE RATING: 2; SIZE: 1; SLEEPING; THREAT LEVEL: 1-5
- **ITEM EXAMPLES:** ANTI-FREEZE BOTTLE, MOUNTAIN HONEY, INDUSTRIAL CLEANER

A small hut structure on the slope of steep wooded terrain, inhabited by some pesky bloodsuckers.

03. NORTH KANAWHA LOOKOUT

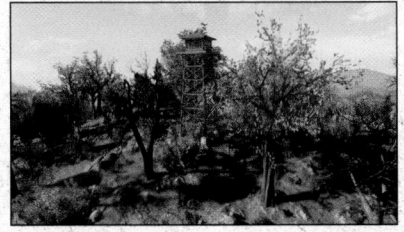

- **CRAFTING:** COOKING (2), WEAPONS, WATER PUMP
- **DANGER:** LONG DROP!
- **ITEMS:** ARMS AND AMMO; HARVESTABLE: RHODODENDRON, SOOT FLOWER; RECIPE/MOD/PLAN
- **INFO:** EXPECTED ENEMY: MOLE RAT, SCORCHED; SCAVENGE RATING: 2; SIZE: 3; SURVEY AREA; THREAT LEVEL: 1-5
- **LOCK:** SAFE (KEY)
- **ITEM EXAMPLES:** DANDY BOY APPLES, LOOSE GEARS, WASTE ANTISEPTIC, TOOTHPASTE

Beware of Sickleman! At least, that's what the graffiti in the crawl space of the cabin on the grounds of this lookout tower states. Crawl up through the hole here to explore the cabin interior. Then check the tower and nearby outhouse for a key (atop an outhouse roof) to the safe atop the tower.

04. TWIN PINE CABINS

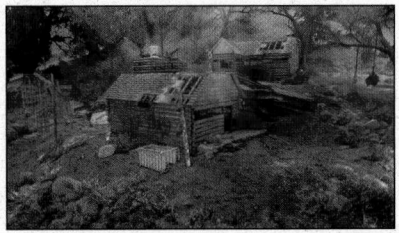

- **COLLECTIBLE:** MAGAZINE
- **CRAFTING:** WEAPONS
- **DANGER:** MINES!
- **ITEMS:** ARMS AND AMMO; HARVESTABLE: RHODODENDRON; HEALTH AND CHEMS; TRUNK
- **INFO:** EXPECTED ENEMY: SCORCHED; SCAVENGE RATING: 1; SIZE: 1; THREAT LEVEL: 1-5
- **ITEM EXAMPLES:** FRAGMENTATION MINE, MINI NUKE, WONDERGLUE

Intermittent battles for territory between the Scorched and Super Mutants have resulted in this once-idyllic pair of cabins being turned into a place of bloodshed. Come for the meat bags: Stay for the Truck scavenge.

05. GILMAN LUMBER MILL

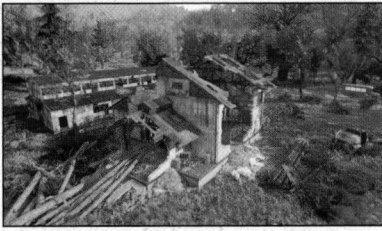

- **CRAFTING:** TINKER
- **DANGER:** RADIATION!+ (TICK)
- **ITEMS:** ARMS AND AMMO; HARVESTABLE: GLOWING FUNGUS, RHODODENDRON, SOOT FLOWER, WOOD; HEALTH AND CHEMS+
- **INFO:** EXPECTED ENEMY: TICK; SIZE: 2; THREAT LEVEL: 1-5
- **ITEM EXAMPLES:** ALUMINUM SCRAP, CONCRETE SCRAP, LOOSE GEARS

Two dilapidated warehouses still stand in this overgrown lumberyard, tended by a nearby (relatively friendly) robots. Come here for the initial scavenging opportunities.

06. ISOLATED CABIN

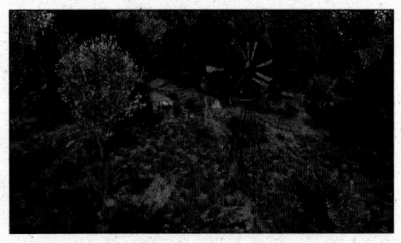

- **CRAFTING:** COOKING, WATER PUMP, WEAPONS
- **DANGER:** RADIATION!+ (TICK)
- **ITEMS:** ARMS AND AMMO; HARVESTABLE: RHODODENDRON, STARLIGHT CREEPER; HEALTH AND CHEMS
- **INFO:** EXPECTED ENEMY: TICK; NOTES; SCAVENGE RATING: 2; SIZE: 1; THREAT LEVEL: 1-5
- **LOCK:** SAFE (0)
- **ITEM EXAMPLES:** FOX HIDE, MEDICAL LIQUID NITROGEN DISPENSER, VOLATILE MATERIALS BOX

This modest shack is set in the woods; the inhabitant is long gone. Read the notes scattered about to get a glimpse of a past life. Check the tent and outhouse. Either the world's cleverest dog resided here, or a chemist was using the shack's kennel as a hiding place.

07. LANDVIEW LIGHTHOUSE

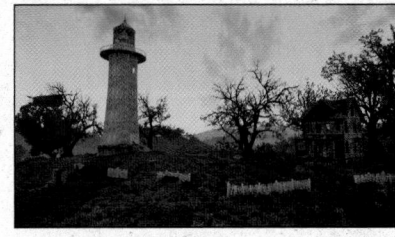

- **COLLECTIBLES:** BOBBLEHEAD (2), HOLOTAPE, MAGAZINE (2)
- **DANGER:** LONG DROP!
- **ITEMS:** HARVESTABLE: BLACKBERRY, RHODODENDRON, SOOT FLOWER; HEALTH AND CHEMS
- **INFO:** EXPECTED ENEMY: GHOUL, RADROACH; LANDMARK; NOTES; SCAVENGE RATING: 2; SIZE: 2; THREAT LEVEL: 1-10
- **LOCK:** SAFE (1)
- **ITEM EXAMPLES:** ALUMINUM CAN, LANTERN, LIGHTHOUSE SOUVENIR

This landmark oddity offers views of the surrounding countryside. To reach the lighthouse perched on the cliff, head south up the path that starts near the road to the north, near a covered picnic area. Check the upstairs and downstairs of the small white house for a couple collectibles. Explore a second covered picnic area for some light reading, a holotape, and some combat with the revolting deceased.

TRAINING

CRAFTING AND C.A.M.P.ING

INVENTORY

QUESTS

ATLAS

BESTIARY

APPENDICES

08. ALPINE RIVER CABINS

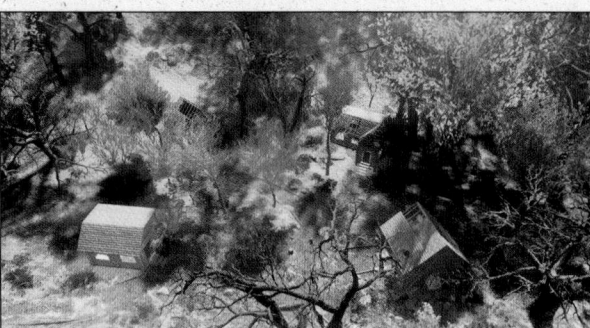

- COLLECTIBLES: BOBBLEHEAD (2), HOLOTAPE (2), MAGAZINE (2)
- CRAFTING: WATER PUMP
- DANGER: RADIATION!
- ITEMS: HARVESTABLE: BLOODLEAF, GLOWING FUNGUS; HEALTH AND CHEMS; RECIPE/MOD/PLAN
- INFO: EXPECTED ENEMY: GHOUL; NOTES; SCAVENGE RATING: 1; SIZE: 2; SLEEPING; THREAT LEVEL: 1–10.
- LOCK: SAFE (0)
- ITEM EXAMPLES: CARROT; HOT DOG, RABBIT HIDE

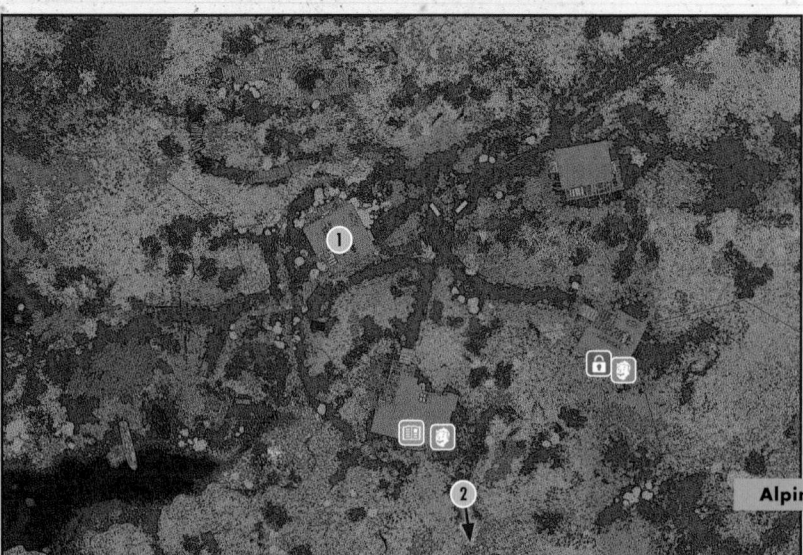

Hidden in the woods, just off Highway 88, is a quaint collection of cabins. However, the strange seismic disturbances and distant screaming make this a most unnerving place to visit, especially at night! Perhaps there's a way to "turn off" these unnerving occurrences? That treehouse up the hill to the south looks interesting...;

LEGEND
1. BEAR RUG CABIN
2. TO TREEHOUSE

Alpine River Cabins (Exterior)

09. WIXON HOMESTEAD

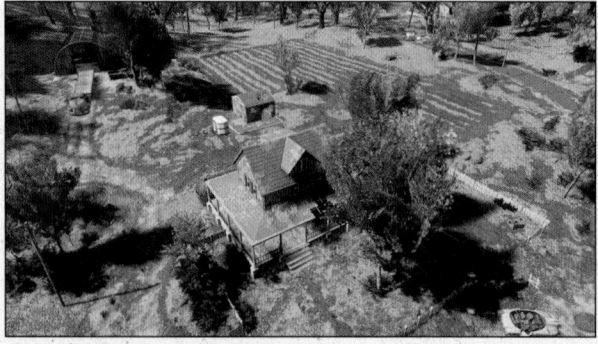

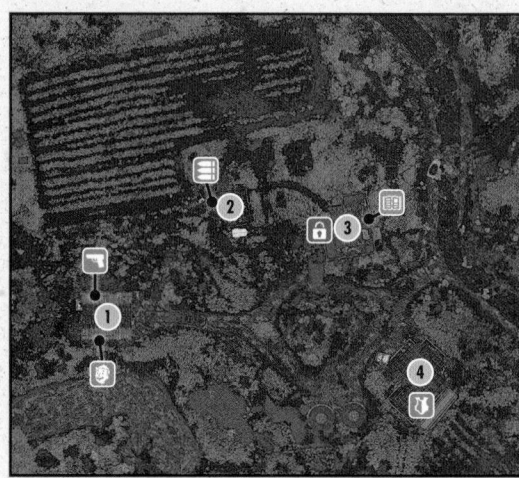

- COLLECTIBLES: BOBBLEHEAD, MAGAZINE
- CRAFTING: ARMOR, TINKER'S, WEAPONS
- ITEMS: HARVESTABLE: RHODODENDRON, SOOT FLOWER, WILD MUTFRUIT
- INFO: EXPECTED ENEMY: SCORCHED; SCAVENGE RATING: 2; SIZE: 2; SLEEPING; THREAT LEVEL: 1–5
- LOCK: SAFE (1)
- ITEM EXAMPLES: ALARM CLOCK, BAG OF FERTILIZER, OAK HOLLER LAGER, TYPEWRITER, USED OIL CAN

Wixon Homestead (Exterior)

LEGEND
1. EQUIPMENT BARN
2. SHED
3. FARMHOUSE
4. SILO BARN

At the foot of the valley below Vault 76 is a small farmstead, now the home to a clan of Scorched. Check under the porch for a safe, and remember to locate more items in the main farmhouse, the equipment barn, and the larger barn near the two silos. The field nearby is one of the flattest areas in all of Appalachia; try building a camp there if you want.

10. FLATWOODS LOOKOUT

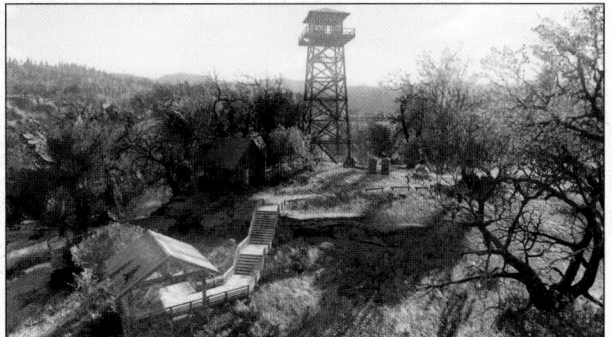

- **DANGER:** LONG DROP!
- **ITEMS:** HARVESTABLE: WILD MUTFRUIT, WOOD, RECIPE/MOD/PLAN
- **INFO:** EXPECTED ENEMY: GHOUL; INSTRUMENT; SCAVENGE RATING: 2; SIZE: 1; THREAT LEVEL: 1–10
- **ITEM EXAMPLES:** DIRTY ASHTRAY, LANTERN, PACK OF CIGARETTES, PIPE PISTOL, RANGER HAT, SHORT HUNTING RIFLE

This tower offers stunning views of the valley and woods as well as the town of Flatwoods. There's a small deck and cottage on the premise to ransack too.

11. OVERSEER'S CAMP

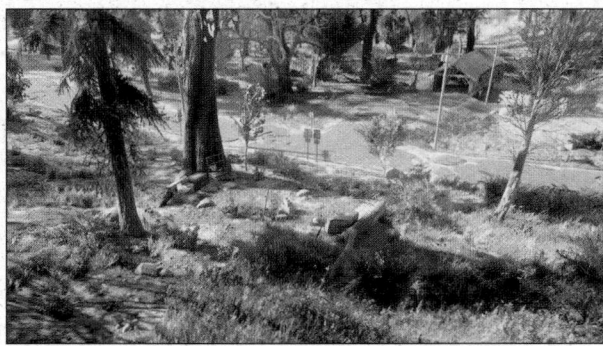

- **COLLECTIBLE:** HOLOTAPE
- **CRAFTING:** ARMOR, COOKING, WEAPONS
- **ITEMS:** HARVESTABLE: WOOD, MY STASH BOX, OVERSEER'S CACHE
- **INFO:** EXPECTED ENEMY: GHOUL; QUEST: FIRST CONTACT, MISC; SCAVENGE RATING: 3; SIZE: 1; SLEEPING; THREAT LEVEL: 1–5
- **ITEM EXAMPLES:** BALL-PEEN HAMMER, LOOSE GEARS, MOLE RAT MEAT, WASTE OIL.

The first clue in the journey of the Overseer is at her recently abandoned C.A.M.P. Learn the basics of crafting here, and remember the three crafting stations can help you during the creation of your own first C.A.M.P.

12. RELAY TOWER EM-B1-27

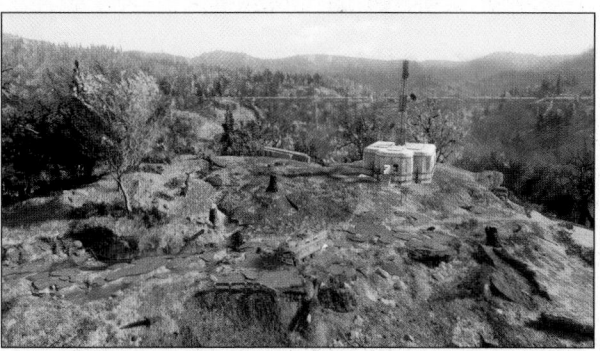

- **COLLECTIBLE:** BOBBLEHEAD, HOLOTAPE, MAGAZINE
- **DANGER:** EXPLOSIVE CANNISTER!
- **ITEMS:** ARMS AND AMMO; FUSION CORE; HARVESTABLE: BLOODLEAF, RHODODENDRON; HEALTH AND CHEMS; POWER ARMOR
- **INFO:** EXPECTED ENEMY: ROBOTS; SCAVENGE RATING: 2; SIZE: 1; QUEST: REQUEST GOVERNMENT AIR DROP; THREAT LEVEL: 1–10
- **ITEM EXAMPLES:** CIGARETTE CARTON, IV BAG

This small hilltop military relay tower has a parked APC and possible access to a Vertibot drop.

13. GREEN COUNTRY LODGE

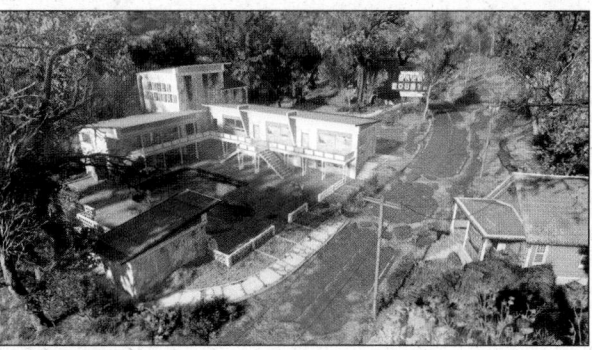

- **COLLECTIBLES:** HOLOTAPE+, NUKA-COLA QUANTUM
- **DANGER:** RADIATION!
- **ITEMS:** HARVESTABLE: RHODODENDRON; HEALTH AND CHEMS
- **INFO:** EXPECTED ENEMY: MOLE RAT, RADROACH; SCAVENGE RATING: 2; SIZE: 2; THREAT LEVEL: 1–5.
- **ITEM EXAMPLES:** 160 LB DUMBBELL, ALARM CLOCK, PACK OF CIGARETTES, LEATHER RIGHT ARM

At the north entrance into Flatwoods is a welcome sign to the town and the Faction known as the Responders. There are a few boarded-up houses and the Lodge. The ruined motel still features an accessible gym, if you wish to test the limits of your carry weight. The swimming pool is definitely closed, though; it's irradiated.

Flatwoods (Exterior)

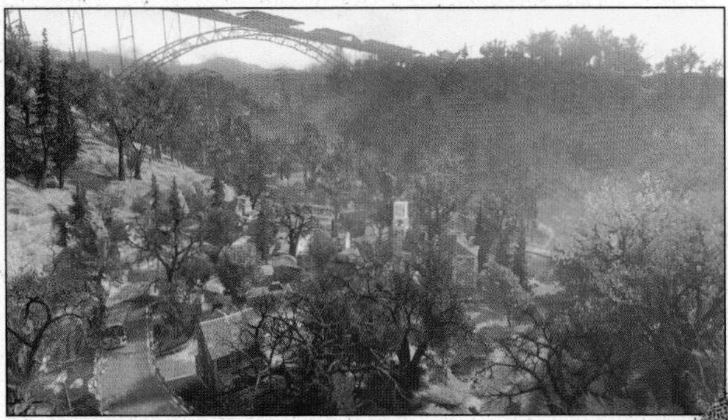

- **COLLECTIBLES:** HOLOTAPE++, NUKA-CHERRY
- **CRAFTING:** ARMOR, COOKING (2), TINKER'S, WATER PUMP, WEAPONS (2)
- **DANGER:** RADIATION!
- **ITEMS:** ARMS AND AMMO; HARVESTABLE: GLOWING FUNGUS, RHODODENDRON, SILT BEAN, SNAPTAIL, SOOT FLOWER, WILD MUTFRUIT; HEALTH AND CHEMS++; MY STASH BOX (2); RECIPE/MOD/PLAN+
- **INFO:** EXPECTED ENEMY: BRAHMIN, GHOUL, MOLE RAT, RADROACH, OPOSSUM; NOTES; OVERSEER'S CACHE; QUEST: FIRST CONTACT, THIRST THINGS FIRST, SECOND HELPINGS; EVENT: FERTILE SOIL; SCAVENGE RATING: 4; SIZE: 3; THREAT LEVEL: 1–5; TRADER: VENDOR BOT
- **LOCK:** SAFE (1), TERMINAL (0)
- **ITEM EXAMPLES:** BAG OF CHLORINE, BEER BOTTLE, FLORAL BARREL VASE, FLOWER POT, GARDEN GNOME, JAWLESS BRAHMIN SKULL, KITCHEN SCALES, MR. HANDY FUEL, SOUVENIR TEDDY BEAR, TUBE FLANGE, WASTE OIL

This rural town was home to a group of maverick holdouts with a willingness to help others, a ragtag bunch known as the Responders. Sadly, they are all departed, but their legacy lives on: As you pass under the bridge from Green Country Lodge, the main drag is Church Street, named after the Church ("Command Post") with a trading robot, Overseer's Cache. There are also Responder quest terminals inside, including the Responders Database and a lab terminal (as well as a couple of Chemistry Stations).

Check the Flatwoods Tavern ("Volunteers Needed") for two Self-Serve Registration Kiosks (to begin your work as a volunteer), as well as a holotape, a Kitchen Terminal (0), and an Automated Pantry you can donate to. Upstairs is another holotape.

Reverend Winters's trailer is also here; search inside for clues during the Responder Quest: Second Helpings. Along the western side of town runs a river. Seek out Kesha McDermott here; she was testing the water supply.

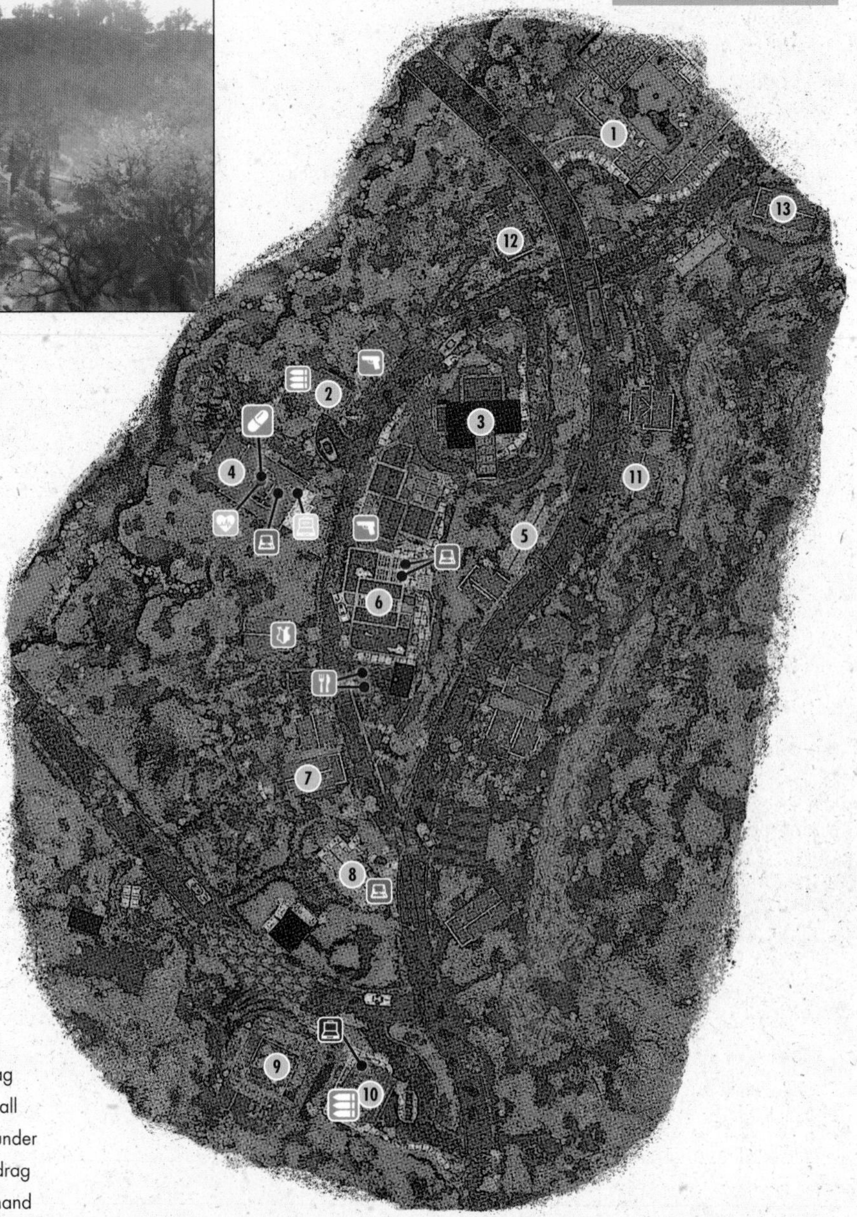

LEGEND

1	GREEN COUNTRY LODGE	8	DELBERT WINTERS' TRAILER
2	YELLOW HOUSE	9	COMMUNITY GARDEN
3	FUNERAL HOME ("MEETING HALL")	10	RED ROCKET GAS STATION ("SUPPLIES")
4	CHURCH ("COMMAND POST")	11	RESPONDER COLONEL'S HOME
5	JEREMIAH WARD'S HOME	12	SOFIE'S HOME
6	FLATWOODS TAVERN ("VOLUNTEERS NEEDED")	13	WILLIE MAE'S HOME
7	NURSE SCOTT'S HOME		

On the far south side of town, across the road, are military tents, the Community Garden (with Water Pump), and the Red Rocket Gas Station ("Supplies"), where you find a Stash Box.

Perhaps your questing might reveal the secrets of the Flatwoods Green Monster? Start with Nurse Scott's Holotape.

There are 10 Survivor Story holotapes in Flatwoods, most of which are on the corpses of the deceased Responders and refugees. There are a couple in coolers, chests, and on tables as well.

15. VAULT-TEC AGRICULTURAL RESEARCH CENTER

- **COLLECTIBLES:** BOBBLEHEAD (4), CAPS STASH (5), HOLOTAPE, HOLOTAPE (OVERSEER), MAGAZINE (4)
- **CRAFTING:** CHEMISTRY (2)
- **DANGER:** RADIATION!
- **ITEMS:** ARMS AND AMMO, CAPS; HARVESTABLE: FIRECAP, SNAPTAIL, SOOT FLOWER; HEALTH AND CHEMS+
- **INFO:** EXPECTED ENEMY: GHOUL, ROBOT; NOTES; QUEST: EVENT: FERTILE SOIL; SCAVENGE RATING: 4; SIZE: 3; SLEEPING; THREAT LEVEL: 1–10
- **LOCK:** DOOR (0), FERTILIZER STORAGE (0, TERMINAL)
- **ITEM EXAMPLES:** ABRAXO CLEANER INDUSTRIAL GRADE, BAG OF CEMENT, FLOWER POT, GARDEN GNOME, HOT PLATE, KITCHEN SCALES, PENCIL, RAW FERTILIZER, STARLIGHT BERRIES, SUPRATHAW ANTIFREEZE, WASTE ACID

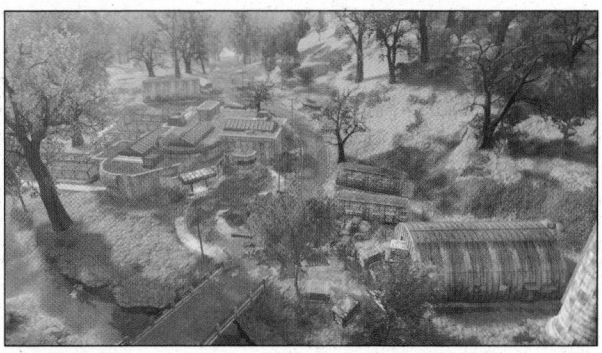

Vault-Tec Agricultural Research Center (Exterior)

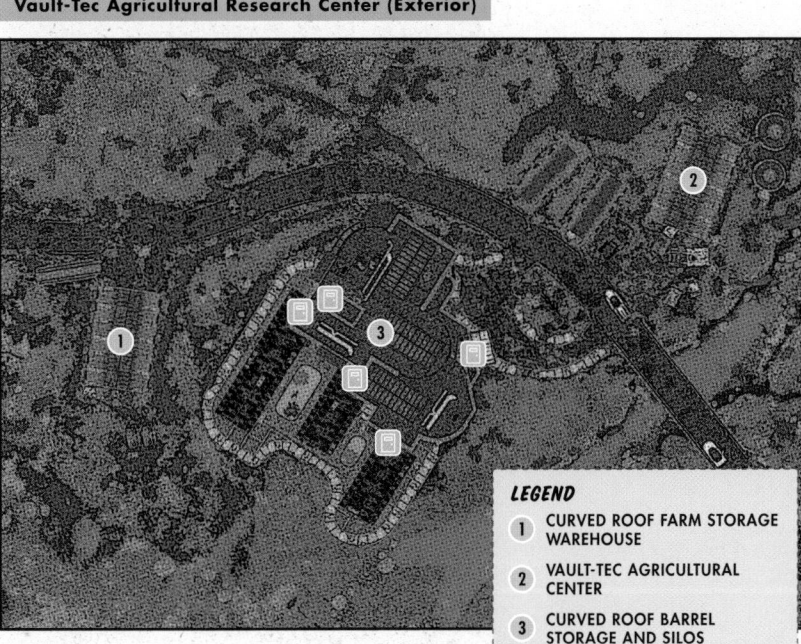

Vault-Tec Agricultural Research Center (Interior)

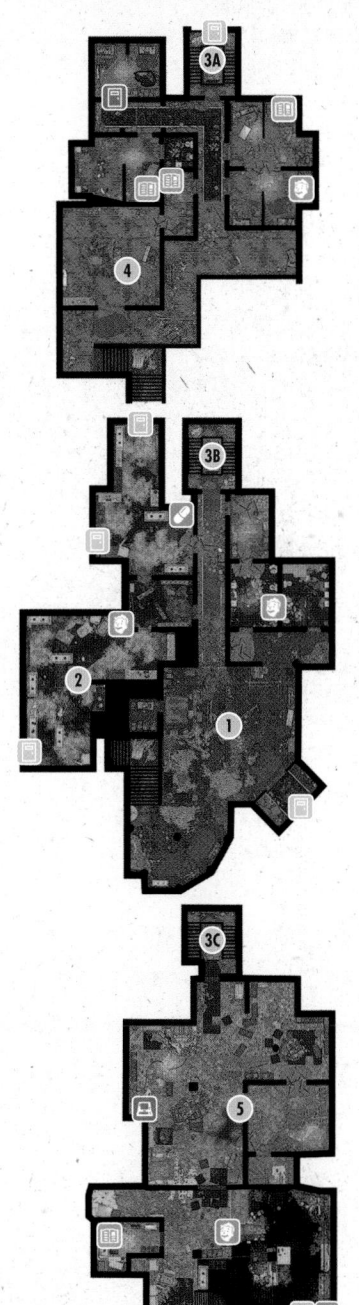

LEGEND

1. CURVED ROOF FARM STORAGE WAREHOUSE
2. VAULT-TEC AGRICULTURAL CENTER
3. CURVED ROOF BARREL STORAGE AND SILOS
1. LOBBY (GROUND)
2. HYDROPONICS ROOM (GROUND)
3A. STAIRWELL (UPPER)
3B. STAIRWELL (GROUND)
3C. STAIRWELL (LOWER)
4. OFFICES (UPPER)
5. BASEMENT (LOWER)

On the southern outskirts of Flatwoods is a cluster of low-rise rusting structures: a curved storage building with two others on the road's north side and the main center with two connected exterior greenhouses. Check under the road bridge for additional items.

Reach the Center's interior via the main foyer doors, the roadside doors, a side door, or the roof. Access the basement via the easily overlooked stairwell; here you find the Agricultural Center Mainframe, a computer you must access during the event.

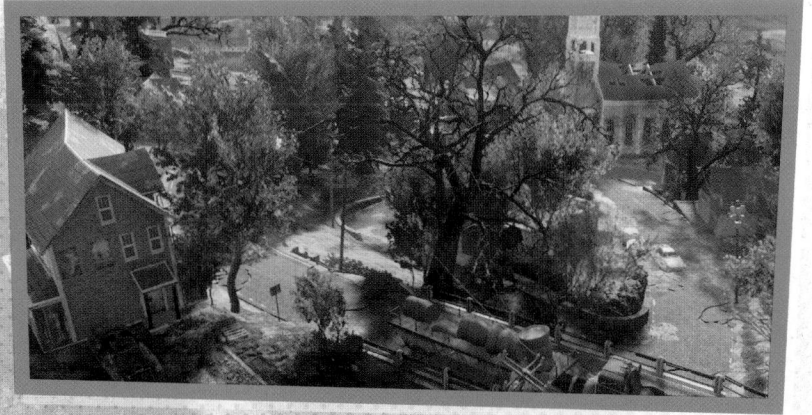

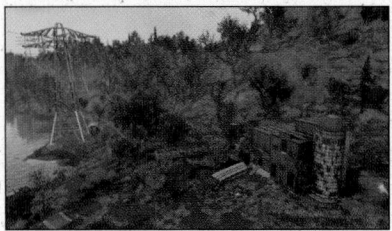

- **DANGER: LONG DROP!**
- **ITEMS: HARVESTABLE:** JUNK PILE, PHOSPHATE DEPOSIT
- **INFO: EXPECTED ENEMY:** VARIES; SCAVENGE RATING: 1(4); SIZE: 2; THREAT LEVEL: 1–10
- **ITEM EXAMPLES:** STEEL WORKER HAT, METAL BUCKET
- **WORK: FOOD [10], WATER [3], PACKAGED FOOD [1], FERTILIZER [3], JUNK [1], ALUMINUM [1], CONCRETE [1]**

This midsize factory and unloading dock has a trio of curve-roofed barracks at the back. Learn the choke points (gaps in the fencing and locations of enemy incursions) to ensure you can build and hold this resource-heavy farm. Be aware of the upper offices and storage area leading to the rear roof access atop the factory.

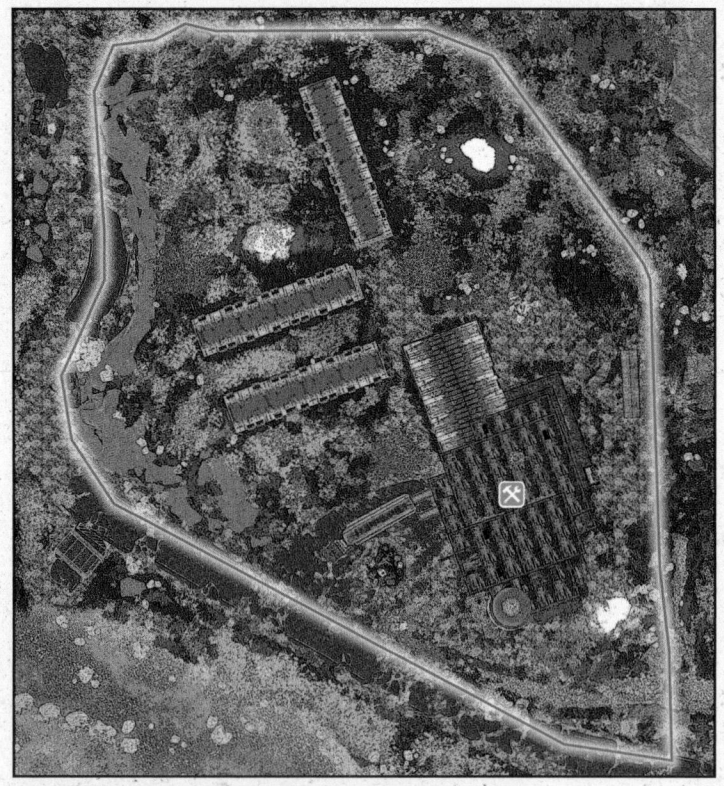

Sunshine Meadows Industrial Farm (Exterior)

ZONE A: SECONDARY LOCATIONS

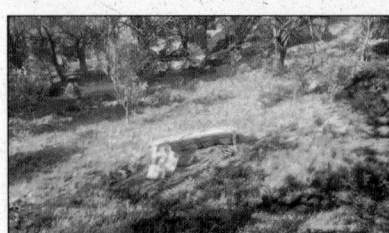

Long Way from a Lake

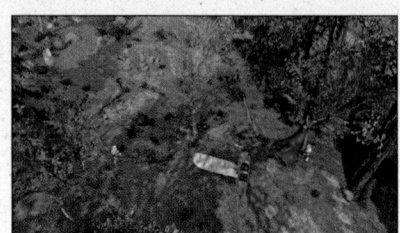

Biplane Crash ("HELP")

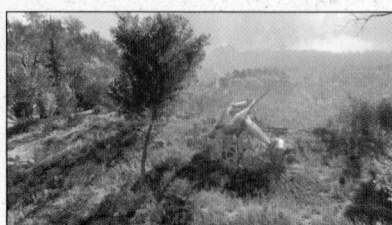

**Vertibird Crash Site
(west of Moonshiner's Shack)**

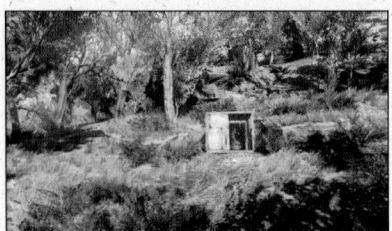

Rusty Hillside Shed

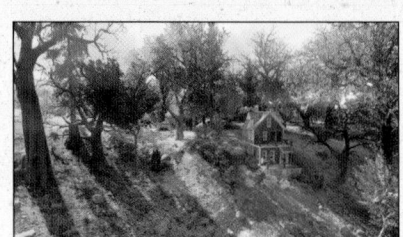

Old Gray Cottage

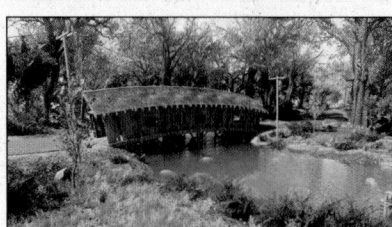

Covered Bridge (Route 88)

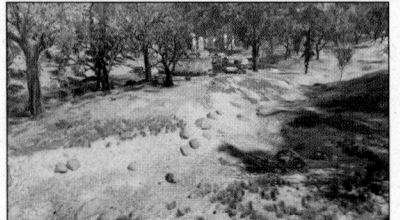

The Beached Boat

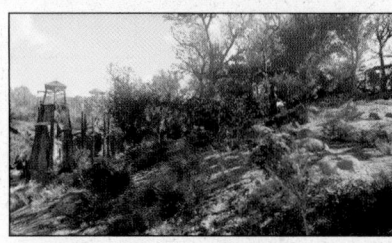

New River Gorge Resort Adventure Park

#	NAME	DESCRIPTION
1	Biplane Crash (northeast of Anchor Farm)	Gather any chems you can from the burned ground in the wooded area where a small plane has crashed.
2	Long Way from a Lake	A small upturned boat with a cooking station.
3	Boat Breakdown (Route 94)	A truck bringing a boat along the main road has broken, and so has the boat—split in two with some minor items to scavenge.
4	Earthen Hole: Tin-Roof Shack Lair	Half-hidden at the bottom of a dell is a patriotic camp with a tin roof.
5	Outcrop Altar of Burned Branches	A meeting place of chairs, candles, and burned branches on a flat rock altar. Are cultists active in these woods?
6	Beehive: North Kanawha	Gather honey and try not to get stung at this beehive, stuck to an old tree.
7	Settler's Cabin	A ruined cabin with crops, Nuka-Cola, a mattress, and a cooking station.
8	Cultist Totem (east of Vault 76)	A cultist totem seems to be claiming (and digesting) bones and corpses in this small, Silt Bean clearing.
9	Biplane Crash ("HELP")	An enterprising survivor of a plane crash fashioned a crude message in the hillside, near her crashed plane.
10	Marksman's Cave	A small rock cave with an archery target on top of it. There's a crack you can fall down, so watch out!
11	Cultist Totem (west of Vault 76)	A sacrificed skeleton and a cultist totem; worrying developments in the woods just west of Vault 76.
12	Grass Camp (northwest of Moonshiner's Shack)	A small tent and camp with a cooking station and sleeping bag, in the relative flat grass area close to the Vault.
13	Banjo Tower	A small lookout tower with a sleeping bag and instruments to play at the top platform.
14	Kanawha Cave Alcove	A small rock alcove with a skeleton and a chem box, as well as a weapon to brandish.
15	Weapon Worker's Hide	One of the nearest Weapons Workbenches is under the lookout at this cooking station tent and small camp.
16	Terminal Log Jam on Route 88	Two big-rigs have collided on this stretch of road, with their contents (logs and terminals) scattered throughout.
17	Vertibird Crash Site (west of Moonshiner's Shack)	A military craft made a rough landing on the grassy hilltop; there's a First Aid Kit still accessible on the craft.
18	Rusty Hillside Shed	A small, box-like shed with items inside and a cooking station. Perhaps you could build your camp around it?
19	Prehistoric Bones Camp	Evidence of old bones is present in the small hillside excavation and tent, with a cooking station.
20	Wixon Pond	A small pond with a dock with good plant life harvesting potential.
21	Beehive: Wixon's Pond	Gather honey and try not to get stung at this beehive, stuck on the bank of the pond.
22	Beehive: Alpine River	Gather honey and try not to get stung at this beehive, stuck to a pine tree and log.
23	Corpse Pile	A pile of corpses near a field of cut trees, west of Wixon Homestead.
24	The Doghouse	Three bears (and a prostrate corpse) appear to have made this dog kennel their home, in the flat woods east of old Wixon's place.

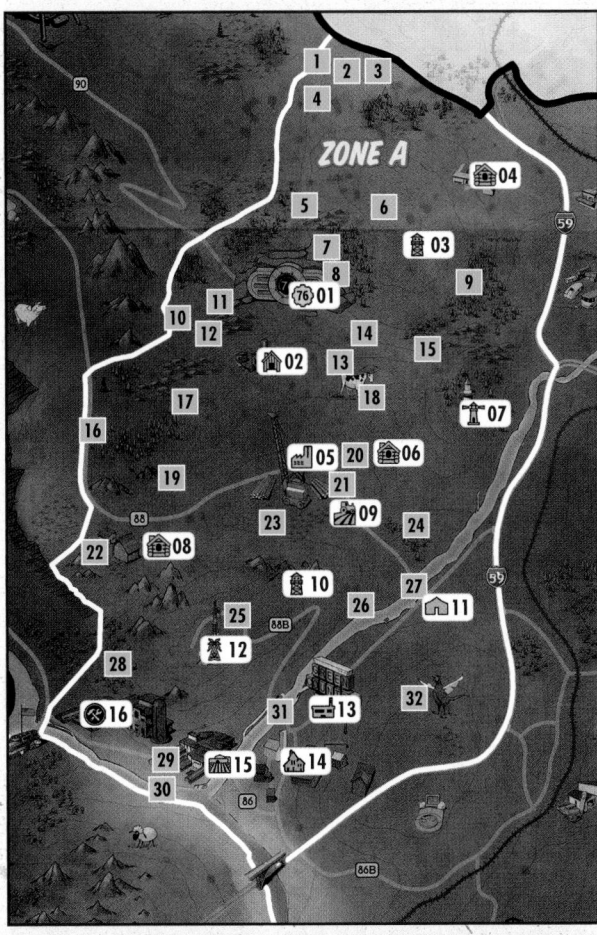

Appalachia: The Forest (Zone A) – Secondary Locations

#	NAME	DESCRIPTION
25	Old Gray Cottage	A small cottage on the road to the Relay Tower, with a pool table and Armor Workbench.
26	Flatwoods River Camp	A good alternate place to use a cooking station, by the river near two canoes, a cooler, and some bloodleaf.
27	Covered Bridge (Route 88)	A pickup has fallen through the covered bridge close to the Overseer's Camp. Don't ignore the goods inside the crate in the pickup.
28	Game of Thrones	Two skeletons face off on a leafy hillside, each sitting on a toilet. The duel doesn't end well for either party.
29	Delivery Van Crash (Vault-Tec Ag Research Center)	A half-buried van, with a wood crate still ripe for opening, on the low hillside by the main road south of Flatwoods.
30	The Beached Boat	A long rowboat dry-docked on the southern shore of what was once a river, close to the Vault-Tec Research Center.
31	Green Country Bridge	The bridge to Flatwoods has a camp under it and a vehicular altercation on the bridge itself.
32	New River Gorge Resort Adventure Park	A series of vista decks, stepping stones, and tree platforms to navigate to a small adventure tower with possible Bobblehead reward.

TRAINING

CRAFTING AND C.A.M.P.ING

INVENTORY

QUESTS

ATLAS

BESTIARY

APPENDICES

THE FOREST: ZONE B—
NORTHWEST FOREST AND POINT PLEASANT

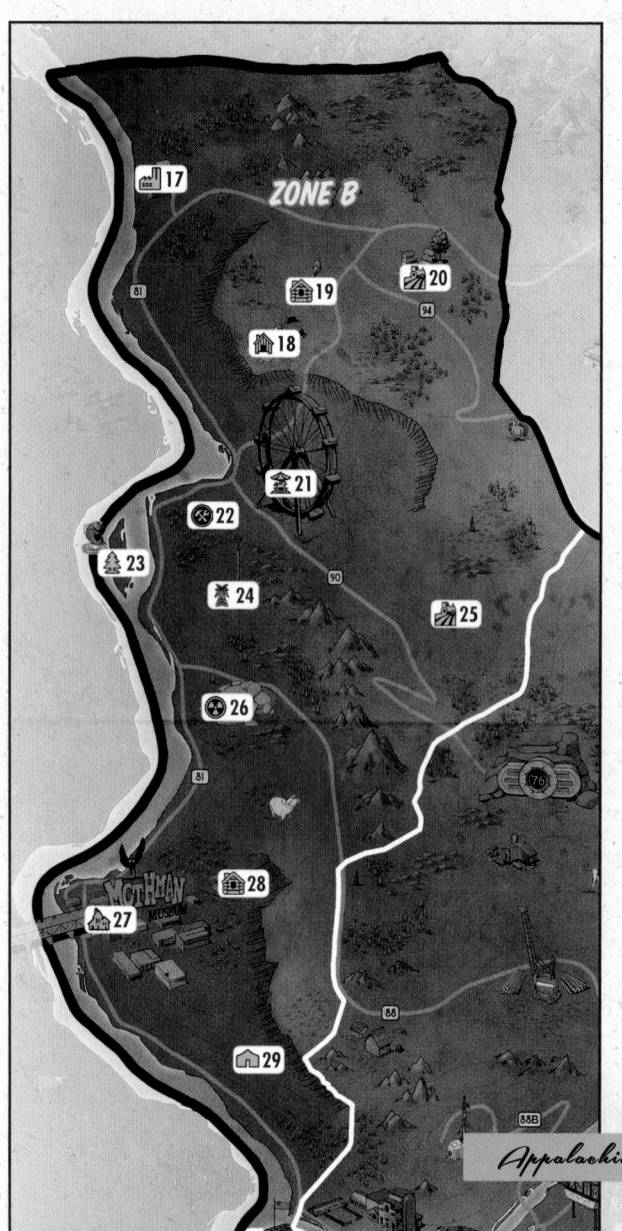

ZONE B

This sliver of the Forest follows the winding Ohio River, the western boundary of Appalachia, and is mainly comprised of wooded and mountainous terrain. It is more remote and has fewer large settlements, with the exception of Point Pleasant, where a strange band of cultists have started to worship a possibly apocryphal shadow creation known as the Mothman. Thoroughly explore this wilderness, and you may find evidence of cultist totems built to honor this cryptid. Journey farther north to reach a disused lumber mill and scattered dwellings well off the beaten path. Elsewhere, there are small farms, cabins to ransack, and a large fairground with an adjacent dirt track, where all the fun of both the fair and resource gathering come together. That fun might be short-lived if you venture too close to the aptly named Deathclaw Island and aren't prepared to repel savagery!

Appalachia: **The Forest (Zone B) – Primary Locations**

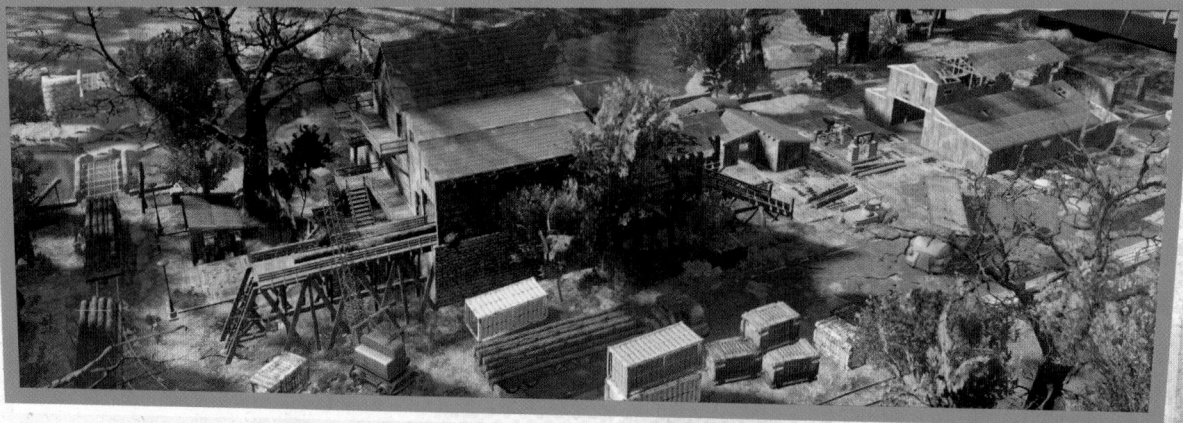

ZONE B: PRIMARY LOCATIONS

TRAINING

CRAFTING AND C.A.M.P.ING

INVENTORY

QUESTS

ATLAS

BESTIARY

APPENDICES

MAP LEGEND

- 🖥 MY STASH BOX
- 📋 OVERSEER'S CACHE
- 🧰 TRUNK
- 👤 TRADER

COLLECTIBLES

- 🎲 BOBBLEHEAD
- 📖 MAGAZINE
- 🦾 POWER ARMOR

CRAFTING

- 🛡 ARMOR WORKBENCH
- ⚗ CHEMISTRY WORKBENCH
- 🍴 COOKING STATION
- 🦾 POWER ARMOR STATION
- 📚 TINKER'S WORKBENCH
- 🔫 WEAPONS WORKBENCH
- 🔧 WORKSHOP WORKBENCH

IMPORTANT

- 🚪 DOOR/GATE
- 🚪 LOCKED DOOR/GATE
- 🔒 SAFE
- ✋ SCANNER
- 💻 TERMINAL

🏭 17. WV LUMBER CO.

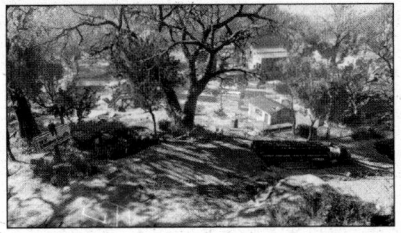

- **COLLECTIBLES:** BOBBLEHEAD (2), MAGAZINE (2), NUKA-CHERRY, POWER ARMOR
- **CRAFTING:** ARMOR, CHEMISTRY (2), COOKING, POWER ARMOR (2), TINKER
- **ITEMS:** ARMS AND AMMO; HARVESTABLE: BRAIN FUNGUS, FIRECAP, RHODODENDRON, SOOT FLOWER, WOOD PILE++; HEALTH AND CHEMS++; VENDING MACHINE: MEDICAL SUPPLIES
- **INFO:** EXPECTED ENEMY: SUPER MUTANT; INSTRUMENT SCAVENGE RATING: 3; SIZE: 3; SLEEPING; THREAT LEVEL: 1–10
- **ITEM EXAMPLES:** ABRAXO CLEANER, ALARM CLOCK, ANTIFREEZE BOTTLE, BOBBY PIN BOX, CAN+, CHESSBOARD, CLEAN RED PLATE, COFFEE CUP, COOLANT CAP, EMPTY PAINT CAN, ENAMEL BUCKET, FUEL TANK, FUSE, FUSION CORE, GEAR, HARD HAT, LEFT HAND BONES, LOOSE SCREWS, PIPE WRENCH, PLASTIC FORK, PORTABLE FUEL TANK+, RECOIL COMPENSATED PUMP ACTION SHOTGUN, RIGHT ARM BONES, SCREWDRIVER+, SKULL, SUPRATHAW ANTIFREEZE, TURPENTINE, VOLATILE MATERIALS BOX, WELDING GOGGLES.

In the remote northwestern corner of Appalachia is an abandoned lumber mill, close to the river and the blocked railroad tunnel to the north. There are telltale signs of Super Mutant activity, so enter with care and with enough room in your inventory to gather the copious scavengeable items. Check the main metal warehouse for a possible Power Armor frame.

LEGEND

1. RED WAREHOUSE
2. LUMBER GARAGE
3. LUMBER MILL
4. METAL WAREHOUSE
5. MECHANIC'S GARAGE
6. PLATFORM TOWER AND SILO

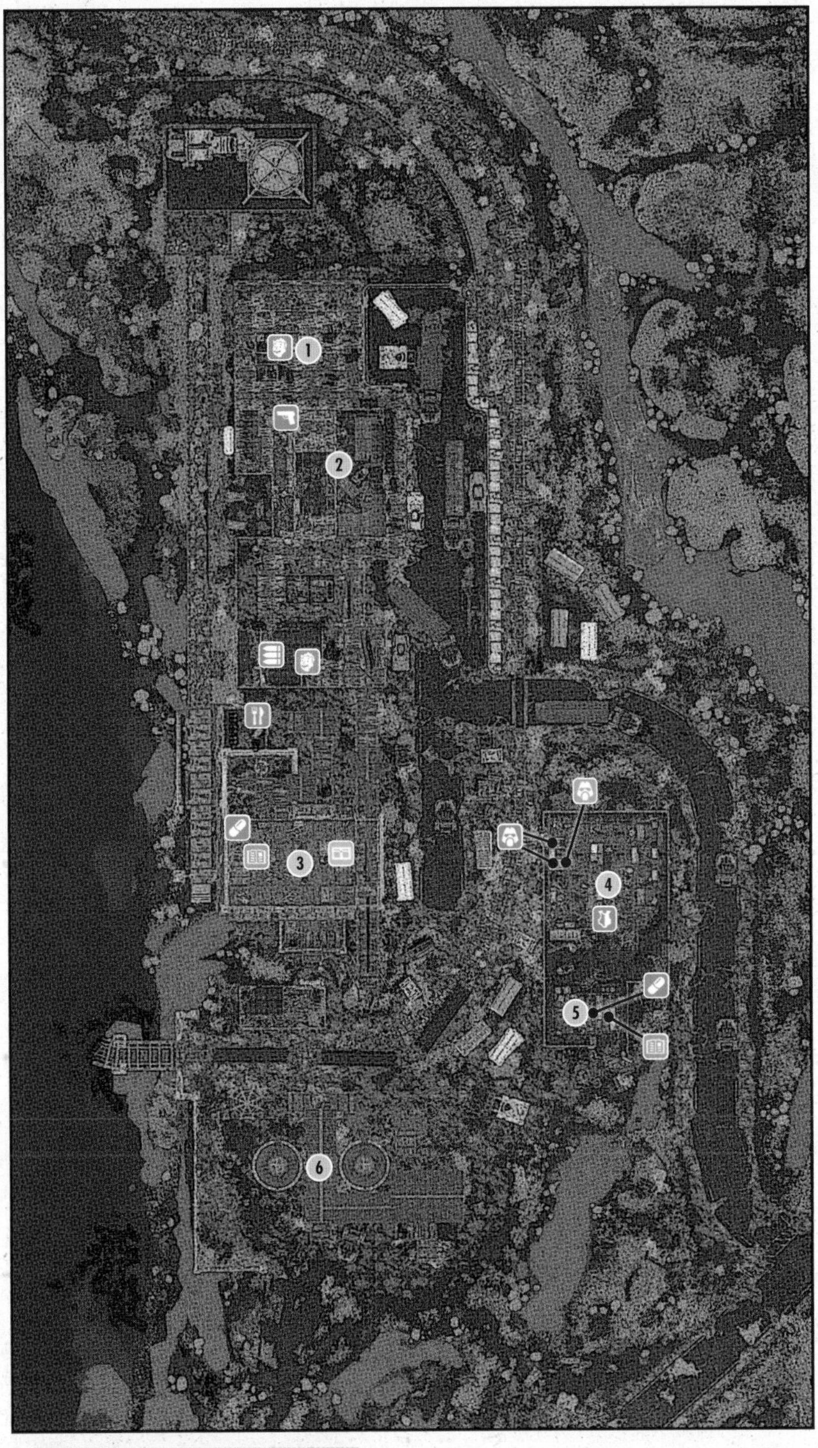

WV Lumber Company (Exterior)

18. DARLING SISTER'S LAB

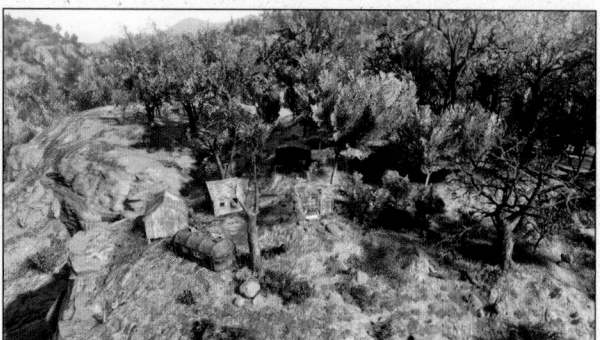

- **COLLECTIBLES:** BOBBLEHEAD, MAGAZINE, NUKA-COLA QUANTUM
- **CRAFTING:** CHEMISTRY, TINKER
- **ITEMS:** ARMS AND AMMO, HEALTH AND CHEMS
- **INFO:** EXPECTED ENEMY: IRRADIATED ANIMAL; SCAVENGE RATING: 3; SIZE: 1; SLEEPING; THREAT LEVEL: 1–10
- **LOCK:** SAFE (2)
- **ITEM EXAMPLES:** ABRAXO CLEANER, BOBBY PINS, BOWIE KNIFE, FUEL TANK, HALLUCIGEN GAS CANISTER, SMALL LEFT ANTLER, SMALL RIGHT ANTLER, SOAP+, TIN PITCHER

A collection of small, ramshackle structures atop the long rock ridge to the east of Route 81. The Darling Sisters seem to have been chem… connoisseurs.

19. GROVES FAMILY CABIN

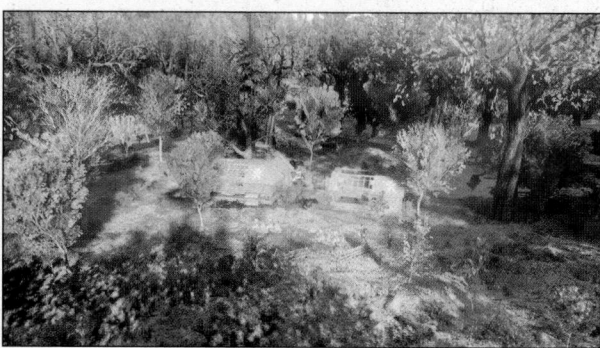

- **COLLECTIBLES:** BOBBLEHEAD, MAGAZINE
- **CRAFTING:** COOKING
- **ITEMS:** HARVESTABLE: CARROT, FIRECAP, GOURD, LOG, WILD MUTFRUIT; HEALTH AND CHEMS; TRUNK
- **INFO:** EXPECTED ENEMY: SCORCHED; NOTES; SCAVENGE RATING: 2; SIZE: 1; SLEEPING; RECIPE/MOD/PLANS; THREAT LEVEL: 1–10
- **ITEM EXAMPLES:** LANTERN, MACHETE, SUGAR

A pair of hunter's cabins and a small garden of harvestable items sits in once-idyllic woodland.

20. AARONHOLT HOMESTEAD

- **COLLECTIBLES:** BOBBLEHEAD (3), MAGAZINE (2), POWER ARMOR
- **CRAFTING:** ARMOR, COOKING (2), POWER ARMOR, WATER PUMP, WEAPONS
- **ITEMS:** ARMS AND AMMO; HARVESTABLE: FIRECAP, FIRECRACKER BERRY, JUNK, RHODODENDRON, SILT BEAN, SOOT FLOWER, TATO PLANT, WILD MELON BLOSSOM, WOOD PILE; RECIPE/MOD/PLAN
- **INFO:** EXPECTED ENEMY: BEE SWARM; IRRADIATED ANIMAL; IRRADIATED INSECT; QUEST: LEADER OF THE PACK; SCAVENGE RATING: 4; SIZE: 4; SLEEPING; THREAT LEVEL: 1–10
- **LOCK:** DOOR (0), SAFE (0)
- **ITEM EXAMPLES:** ALARM CLOCK, ALUMINUM CANISTER, BEER BOTTLE, BOBBY PIN BOX, BOURBON BOTTLE, CAMPAIGN HAT, CARLISLE TYPEWRITER, DANDY BOY APPLES, EMPTY MILK BOTTLE+, ENAMEL BUCKET, FISHING HAT, FOOD DEHYDRATOR, INDUSTRIAL SIZE SHORTENING, KITCHEN SCALE, LARGE RIGHT ANTLER, MACHETE, METAL BUCKET, METAL TUB, NUKA-COLA, PAPER CUTTER, PUMPKIN+, RABBIT HIDE, RADAWAY, SALT, SKULL, SUPRATHAW ANTIFREEZE, TEA POT, TOILET PAPER+, WALKING CANE, WELDING GOGGLES, WINE BOTTLE

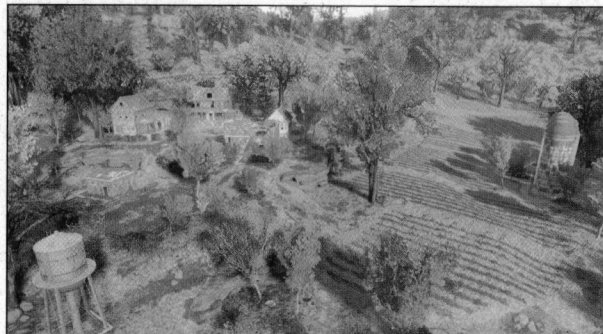

Close to a section of sagging road are a group of farm structures. The three main structures (and small hay barn) house a variety of junk and collectibles (and the corpse of farmer Aaronholt). The locked silo warehouse (0) to the south is also of considerable interest, possibly housing a Power Armor frame. Check the junk pile near a ruined shed on the eastern edge of the farmstead too.

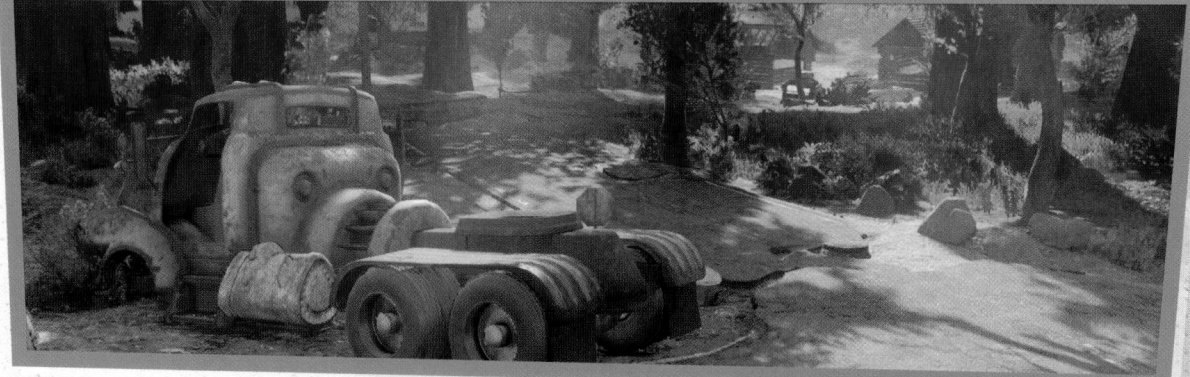

21. TYLER COUNTY FAIRGROUNDS

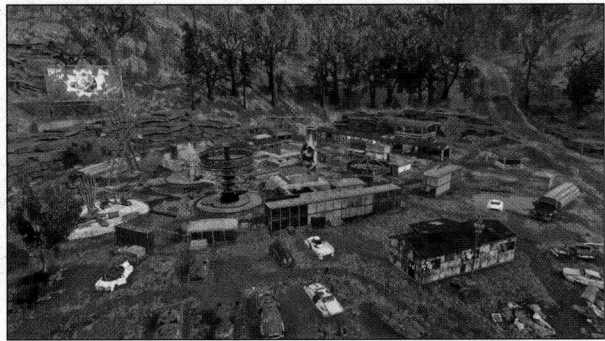

- **COLLECTIBLES:** BOBBLEHEAD (3), CAPS STASH, MAGAZINE (3), NUKA-CHERRY+
- **CRAFTING:** COOKING, TINKER
- **ITEMS:** ARMS AND AMMO+; HARVESTABLE: RHODODENDRON, SOOT FLOWER, STARLIGHT CREEPER; HEALTH AND CHEMS+; VENDING MACHINE: AMMUNITION; MEDICAL SUPPLIES; TRUNK
- **INFO:** EXPECTED ENEMY: RADROACH, SCORCHED, WOLF; QUEST: LEADER OF THE PACK; SCAVENGE RATING: 4; SIZE: 3; THREAT LEVEL: 1–10
- **LOCK:** CRATE OR BOX (0)
- **ITEM EXAMPLES:** BASKETBALL, CANNED DOG FOOD, CLOWN HAT, COMMIE WHACKER, GLASS JAR+++, SPOOKY TIME MR. FUZZY, SUGAR, TEDDY BEAR++, TOY ALIEN, TOY ROCKETSHIP+

"All the fun of the fair" has been replaced by "all the salivating horror of the Scorched." This large area of rusting fairgrounds is a great place to find uncommon items and search for health as you secure the nearby Tyler County Dirt Track (Public Workshop). Don't overlook the mechanic's warehouse either—a must-visit if you're a fan of pumpkin displays.

Tyler County Fairgrounds (Exterior)

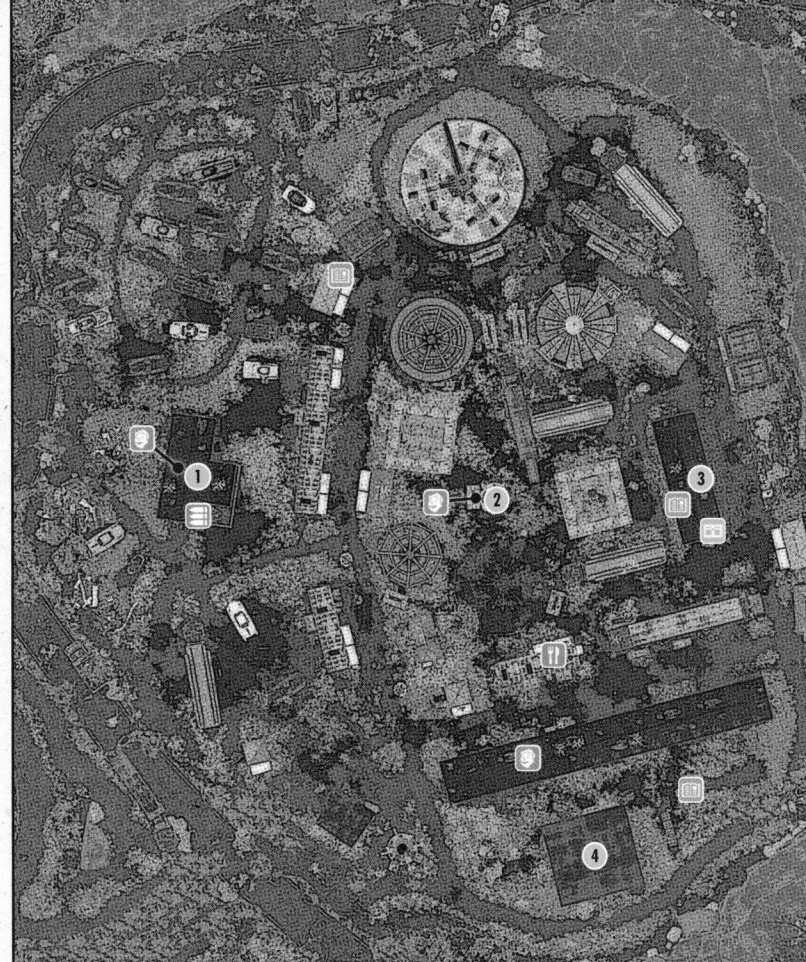

LEGEND

1. MECHANIC'S WAREHOUSE
2. GIANT NUKA-COLA BOTTLE
3. HAY BARN PETTING ZOO
4. APPLES AND HOT DOGS STAND

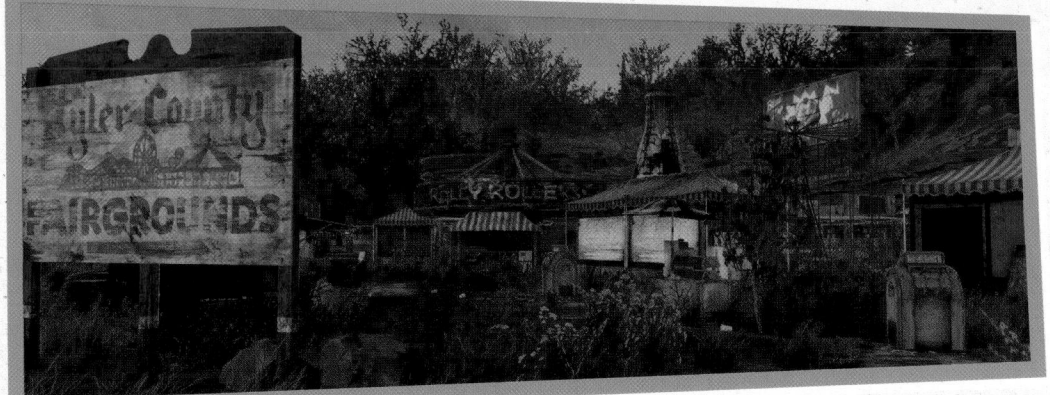

TRAINING

CRAFTING AND C.A.M.P.ING

INVENTORY

QUESTS

ATLAS

BESTIARY

APPENDICES

22. TYLER COUNTY DIRT TRACK (WORKSHOP)

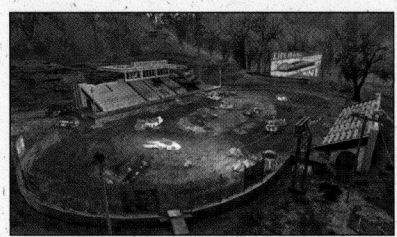

- **CRAFTING:** CHEMISTRY, WORKSHOP
- **ITEMS:** HARVESTABLE: ALUMINUM DEPOSIT, IRON DEPOSIT, SILVER DEPOSIT, SOOT FLOWER; HEALTH AND CHEMS
- **INFO:** EXPECTED ENEMY: VARIES; QUEST: CLAIM THE WORKSHOP AT TYLER COUNTY DIRT TRACK; SCAVENGE RATING: 1(5+); SIZE: 3; THREAT LEVEL: 1–10

- **ITEM EXAMPLES:** DANDY BOY APPLES, MR. HANDY MODEL, TYPEWRITER
- **WORK:** FOOD (1), WATER (3), FERTILIZER (1), JUNK (1), SILVER (3), ALUMINUM (1), STEEL (1)

Tyler County Dirt Track (Exterior)

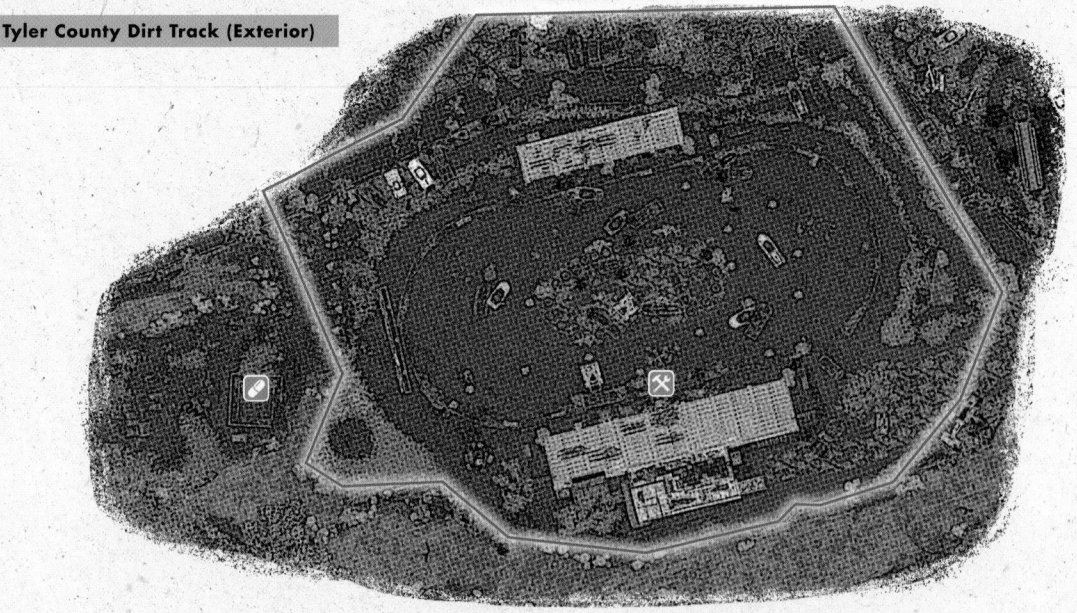

Here you battle a random assortment of foes and waves of enemies once you stake your claim to the workshop at this old demolition derby dirt track, adjacent to the fairgrounds. If your team can keep both locations, you can enjoy a plethora of scavenged resources.

23. DEATHCLAW ISLAND

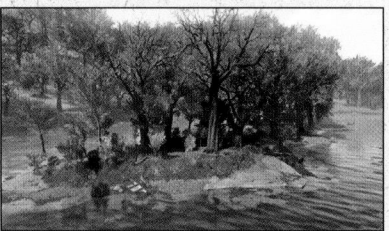

- **COLLECTIBLES:** BOBBLEHEAD, CAPS STASH, MAGAZINE
- **DANGER:** RADIATION!
- **ITEMS:** ARMS AND AMMO; HEALTH AND CHEMS; TRUNK
- **INFO:** EXPECTED ENEMY: DEATHCLAW; SCAVENGE RATING: 1; SIZE: 2; THREAT LEVEL: 1–10
- **LOCK:** SAFE (3)
- **ITEM EXAMPLES:** NEW RIVER RED ALE, PEPPER, RIB CAGE

This island is seemingly devoid of inhabitants, if you don't count the scattered and skeletal remains dotted around various fishing and picnic spots— and the Deathclaw nest, of course.

24. TRANSMISSION STATION 1AT-U03

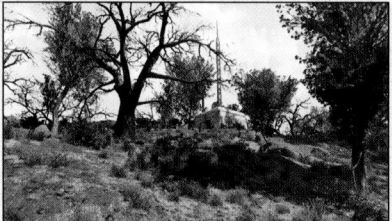

- **COLLECTIBLE:** MAGAZINE
- **CRAFTING:** TINKER
- **ITEMS:** ARMS AND AMMO, TRUNK
- **INFO:** EXPECTED ENEMY: MOLE RAT; NOTES; SCAVENGE RATING: 1; SIZE: 1; THREAT LEVEL: 1–10
- **LOCK:** DOOR (0)
- **ITEM EXAMPLES:** BASEBALL UNIFORM, GREEN RAG HAT, INSTAMASH

Assuming you have the necessary bobby pins to unlock the door, this small transmission structure atop a wooded hill seems to have been a hideout for a family.

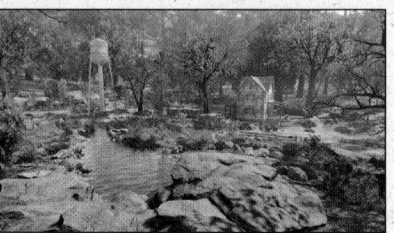
25. ANCHOR FARM

- **CRAFTING:** ARMOR
- **DANGER:** RADIATION!+
- **ITEMS:** ARMS AND AMMO; HARVESTABLE: GLOWING FUNGUS, RHODODENDRON, SOOT FLOWER, TATO PLANT; HEALTH AND CHEMS
- **INFO:** EXPECTED ENEMY: GHOUL; SCAVENGE RATING: 1; SIZE: 1; THREAT LEVEL: 1–10
- **ITEM EXAMPLES:** METAL CHEST PIECE, MENTATS, SHORT HUNTING RIFLE

This small farmstead has a large rusting anchor (the namesake of the abode) that is slowly rotting into the moist earth. A parked (and unusable) plane sits close to the (inaccessible) farmhouse. Check the road for a military APC for a better scavenging potential.

26. BLACK MOUNTAIN ORDNANCE WORKS

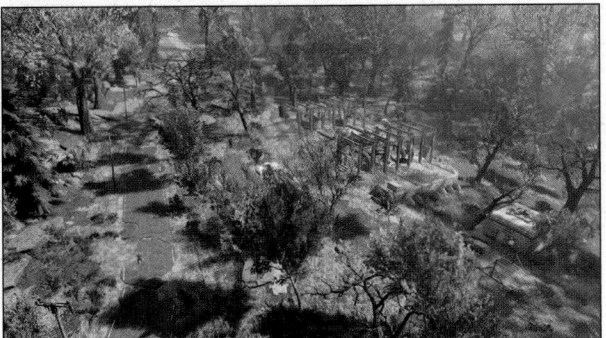

- **COLLECTIBLE: POWER ARMOR**
- **CRAFTING:** ARMOR, COOKING, POWER ARMOR, WEAPONS
- **DANGER:** EXPLOSIVE CANNISTERS! RADIATION!++
- **ITEMS:** ARMS AND AMMO+; HARVESTABLE: BLOODLEAF, BRAIN FUNGUS, GLOWING FUNGUS, RHODODENDRON, SOOT FLOWER, STARLIGHT CREEPER; HEALTH AND CHEMS++; POWER ARMOR (NUKA-COLA); RECIPE/MOD/PLAN
- **INFO:** EXPECTED ENEMY: GHOUL; SCAVENGE RATING: 1(5); SIZE: 3; THREAT LEVEL: 1–10
- **ITEM EXAMPLES:** BIOMETRIC SCANNER+, CANNED COFFEE+, COOKING OIL+, FANCY LAD SNACK CAKES+, HARD HAT, HAZMAT SUIT, MICROSCOPE, MILITARY-GRADE CIRCUIT BOARD, MR. HANDY FUEL, SHORT PUMP-ACTION SHOTGUN, SPINE, ULTRACITE SCRAP, UNRUSTED TIN CAN++
- **LOCK:** TERMINAL (U)

Black Mountain Ordnance Works (Exterior)

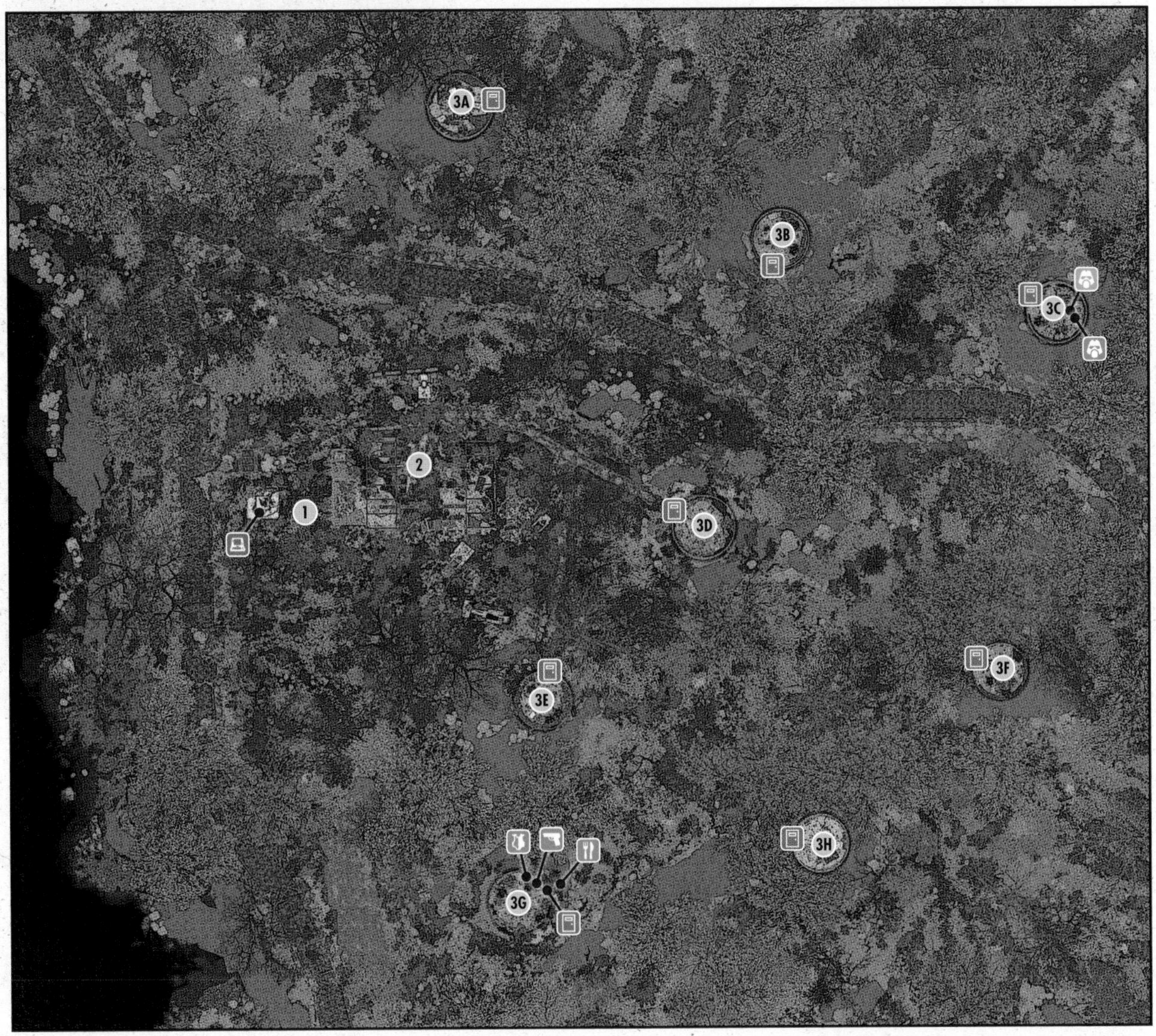

Improper disposal of irradiated waste ensures you may become sick if you spend too long at this ruined works area. The terminal in the security hut informs you of eight various domes built into the wooded hills to the south and north of this location. Accessing them yields various chambers, some with more junk items than others (some of the listed item examples come from sealed domes). One is even said to feature a variety of Nuka-Cola products from a private collector!

LEGEND
1. ORDNANCE WORKS SECURITY ENTRANCE
2. ORDNANCE WORKS GROUNDS
3A [3A-3H] DOMES (8)

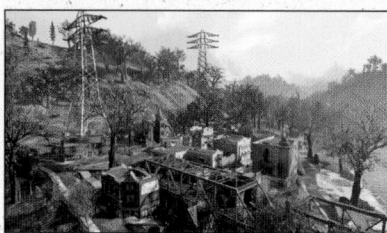

- **COLLECTIBLES:** CAPS STASH, HOLOTAPE+, POWER ARMOR
- **CRAFTING:** CHEMISTRY, COOKING, POWER ARMOR, TINKER'S (2), WEAPONS (2)
- **DANGER:** GRENADES! LONG DROP!
- **ITEMS:** ARMS AND AMMO+++; CAPS; HARVESTABLE: FEVER BLOSSOM, JUNK PILE, MOTHMAN EGG; HEALTH AND CHEMS+++; POWER ARMOR; RECIPE/MOD/PLAN++; VENDING MACHINE: AMMO

- **INFO:** EXPECTED ENEMY: BLOODBUG, RADROACH, SCORCHER; NOTES; SCAVENGE RATING: 4; SIZE: 4; THREAT LEVEL: 1–10
- **LOCK:** DOOR (0, 0, 1, 1, 2), SAFE (1, 1, 3)
- **ITEM EXAMPLES:** BUBBLE GUM, COMBAT ARMOR HELMET, CULT OUTFIT, FUEL TANK, GREASER JACKET AND JEANS, PEPPER, RAIDER STRENGTHENED LIMB MOD, SUGAR, TEDDY BEAR, WHISKEY

Point Pleasant (Exterior)

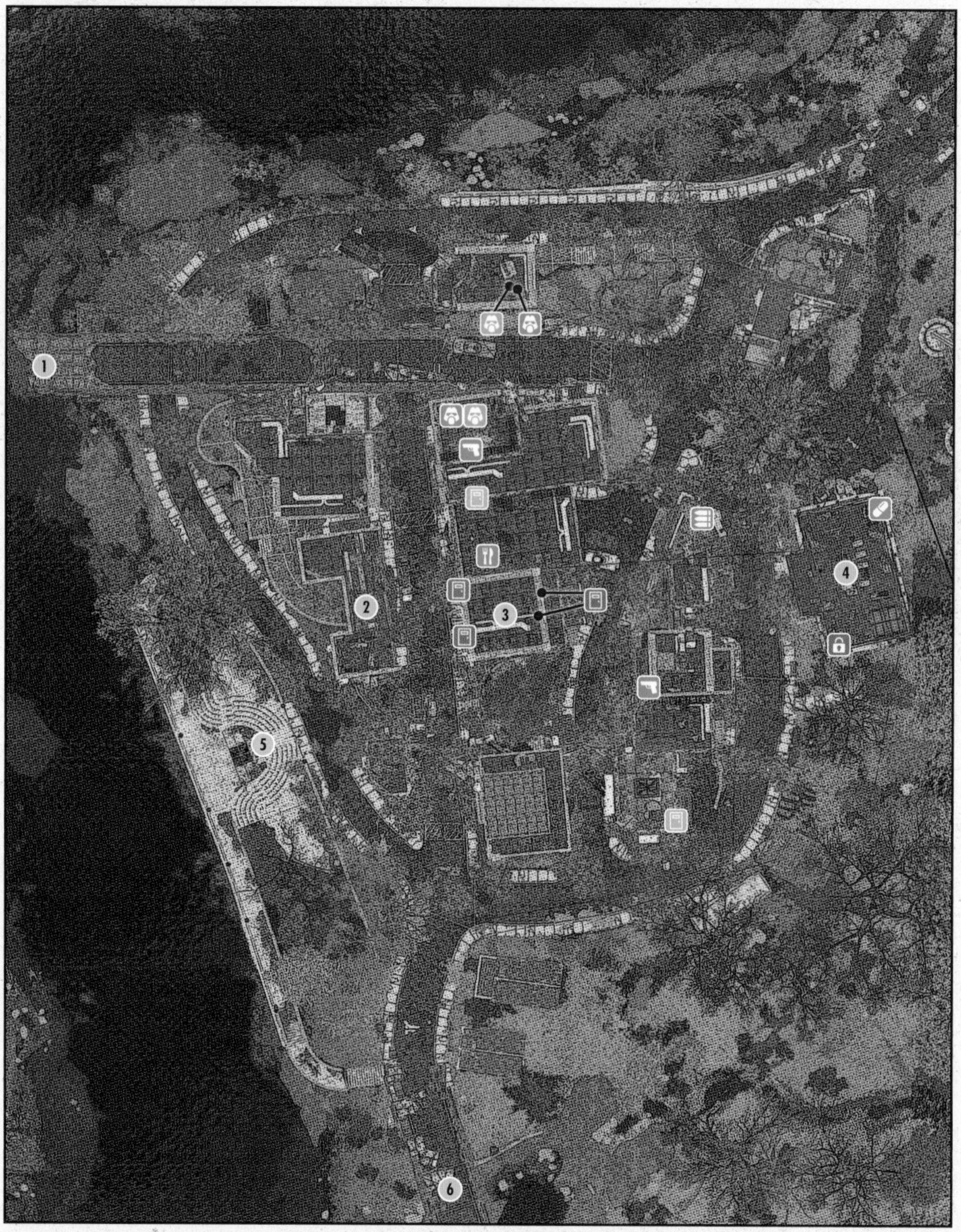

LEGEND

1. NORTH ROAD BRIDGE (DESTROYED)
2. STORE AND APARTMENTS (EXTERIOR AND INTERIOR)
3. MOTHMAN MUSEUM (EXTERIOR AND INTERIOR)
4. POINT PLEASANT CHURCH
5. SACRIFICIAL GATHERING SPOT
6. SOUTH ROAD BRIDGE

Point Pleasant: Mothman Museum (Interior)

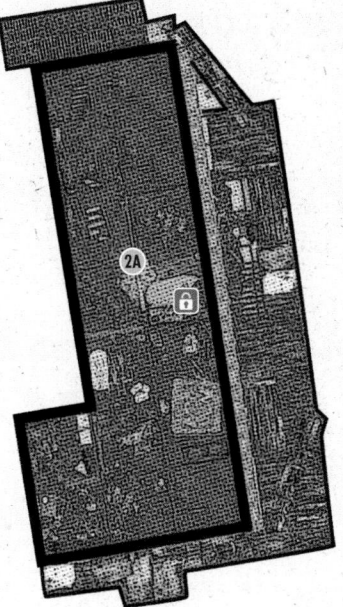

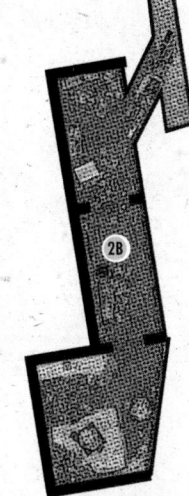

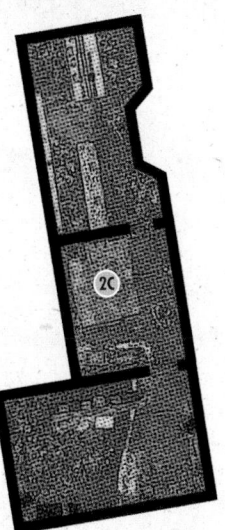

TRAINING

CRAFTING AND C.A.M.P.ING

INVENTORY

QUESTS

ATLAS

BESTIARY

APPENDICES

LEGEND

2A POINT PLEASANT: STORE AND APARTMENTS (ROOF INTERIOR)

2B POINT PLEASANT: STORE AND APARTMENTS (UPPER INTERIOR)

LEGEND

3A MOTHMAN MUSEUM (UPPER INTERIOR)

3B MOTHMAN MUSEUM (STORE: GROUND INTERIOR)

3C MOTHMAN MUSEUM (LOWER INTERIOR: CELLAR SHRINE)

Point Pleasant is home to the Mothman Museum and the adjacent statue. Its recent past has seen it change hands from a Raider to a Responder camp, though the current inhabitants are Scorchers and some mutated and unpleasant wildlife. Expect a number of inaccessible dwellings, upper rooftops with ramps, and bridges connecting them to narrow interiors, allowing for you to dodge violence as well as explore. Clear the rooftops of Scorchers first, before venturing into structures and finally securing the town.

Don't forget to search for "The Mothman Cometh" holotapes (parts 1 and 2), and observe the worrying sacrificial display by the river. Check the church for the remains of a Responders triage center. Attempt to enter the Mothman Museum via either the locked front door (1) or the rear upper back door (0); then unlock the toilet door (2), which leads to a secret staircase into the basement, where true cultist horrors await!

28. MARIGOLD PAVILION

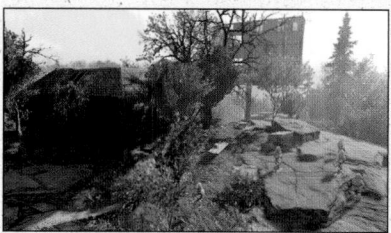

- **COLLECTIBLES:** BOBBLEHEAD, MAGAZINE
- **CRAFTING:** COOKING, WEAPONS
- **DANGER:** RADIATION!
- **ITEMS:** HARVESTABLE: SNAPTAIL; HEALTH AND CHEMS; TRUNK
- **INFO:** EXPECTED ENEMY: IRRADIATED ANIMALS; SCAVENGE RATING: 1; SIZE: 1; SLEEPING; THREAT LEVEL: 1–10
- **ITEM EXAMPLES:** BANJO, FISHING ROD, TOY TRUCK

To the east of Point Pleasant, atop a rugged hillside, is an old wooden structure, along with an irradiated lake, which once beckoned tourists and hikers. Check the lake for a sunken safe to open.

29. HUNTER'S RIDGE

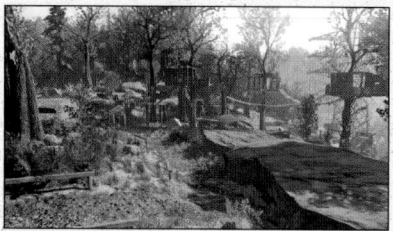

- **COLLECTIBLES:** BOBBLEHEAD, MAGAZINE
- **CRAFTING:** ARMOR, COOKING
- **DANGER:** CAN CHIMES!+, GRENADES!
- **ITEMS:** ARMS AND AMMO; HEALTH AND CHEMS
- **INFO:** EXPECTED ENEMY: SCORCHER; NOTES; SCAVENGE RATING: 2; SIZE: 2; SLEEPING; THREAT LEVEL: 1–10
- **LOCK:** BOX (0)
- **ITEM EXAMPLES:** BEER BOTTLE, BLACK BOWL, GARDEN GNOME, PORTABLE FUEL TANK, USED OIL CAN

A hilltop camp, set with traps for the unwary, is now home to a cluster of shambling Scorchers. Ascend the suspended bridges for a spot of scavenging after clearing the threats (both living and trap-based).

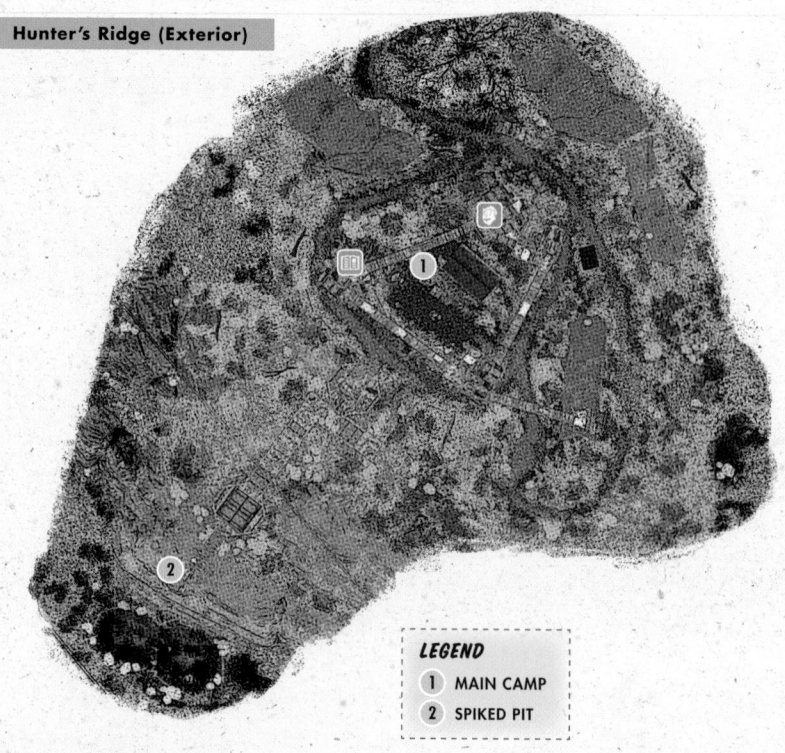

Hunter's Ridge (Exterior)

LEGEND
1 MAIN CAMP
2 SPIKED PIT

ZONE B: SECONDARY LOCATIONS

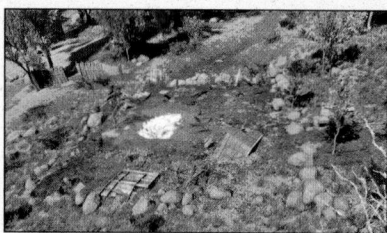

Wrecked Warehouse (WV Lumber)

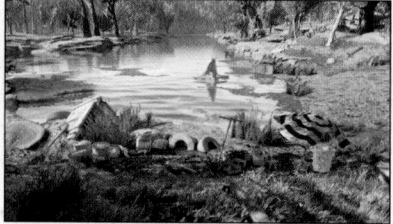

River Raft (north of Tyler County Dirt Track)

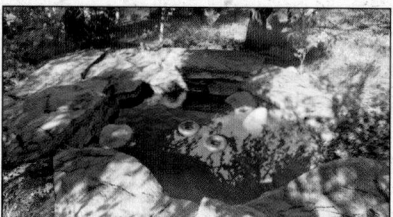

Rubber Tire Pond

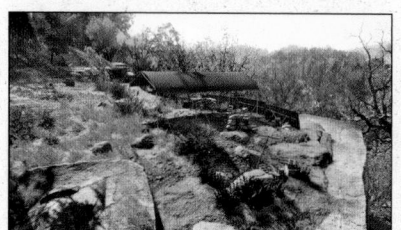

The Competent Campsite

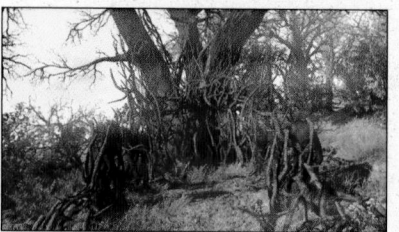

Cultist Totems (Point Pleasant Tangle Tree)

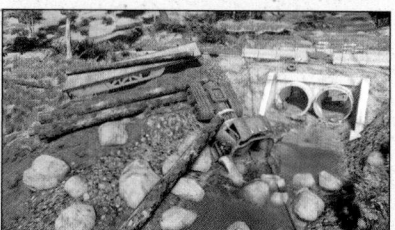

Tank Landslide (south of Hunter's Ridge)

#	NAME	DESCRIPTION
33	Wrecked Warehouse (WV Lumber)	A phosphate deposit and some flattened structures might make a good camping spot.
34	Abandoned Hill Farm	A small barn and farm structure at the base of the rock outcrop with a variety of crops to gather.
35	The Golfer's Camp	A green tent atop the rock outcrop with Firecaps and a golf club on the ledge edge.
36	Rocky Outcrop Camp	A small camp with a pitiful lean-to structure and a skeleton in a water ring.
37	Birdwatcher's Roost	A small deck of birdhouses and empty nectar bottles.
38	Crash on R81 (east of WV Lumber Co.)	A rusty car and nearby pickup were involved in an ancient altercation. Now you can grab the goods still on both vehicles.
39	The Safecrackers' Lament	A small pond with an open safe and the remains of a heist gone wrong.
40	Beehive: Aaronholt Homestead	Gather honey and try not to get stung at this beehive, stuck to the remains of a small barn near the corpse of Farmer Aaronholt.
41	Nuka-Cola Carnage	A crashed Nuka-Cola truck on the highway.
42	Ridgetop Lake	A small lake with sleeping bags and floating platforms.
43	Two Barn Farm	A small farm with Tato crops and two small sheds.
44	River Raft (north of Tyler County Dirt Track)	A rusting big-rig, a river raft with a blue tarp, and a small camp with a cooking station are all located by the river.
45	Tinker's Shed (Tyler County Dirt Track)	A small barn with a Tinker's Workbench, corn and tato crops, and a tall windmill, at the edge of the dirt track.
46	Party Time Diners	A dining room table stocked with food, board games, and balloons, out by the rocky promontory.
47	The Scarecrow and the Pickup	A rusty vehicle, cooking station, and open safe at the base of a scarecrow.
48	The Safecracker's Shack	A refuse-strewn trailer with multiple safes to crack.
49	Jackknifed on Route 90	A flipped truck and trailer on the road, near some Firecracker berries.
50	Decommissioned Transmission Station	An old transmission antenna and outhouse, slowly succumbing to the elements atop a rock bluff.
51	Rubber Tire Pond	It's worth taking a quick dip into this small pond with a beehive and two rubber tires; there's a safe (0) at the bottom.
52	Irradiated Dock	A small concrete dock with strewn radioactive barrels.
53	Ohio River Antics	A small white fishing boat, half-buried radioactive barrels, a table and parasol, and a junk pile.
54	Billboard Junk Camp (Route 88)	A Nuka-Cola sign and rusting billboard along the roadside is worth your time; there's plants, wood, and junk to harvest from this ruined shack camp.
55	The Competent Campsite	A tarp-tent and cooking station set atop a rocky outcrop, on the forested hillside.
56	Cultist Totems (Point Pleasant Tangle Tree)	A grand altar; a place where multiple totems and the tangled roots of an old tree beckon you to worship the Mothman!
57	Beehive: Point Pleasant	Gather honey and try not to get stung at this beehive, stuck to both sides of a three-trunked tree.
58	Teddy Bears' Picnic	If you go down the footpath junction north of Hunter's Ridge, you're sure for a small surprise.
59	The Rickety Dock	A series of hastily constructed wood dock sections, a small shack, and a toilet.
60	Tank Landslide (south of Hunter's Ridge)	A tank has run over its operator; there's road sinkage and piles of junk to mine at the water's edge. It's a real mess around here!
61	Road Pipes and Pylon	An electrical pylon is close to a crashed truck, item boxes, and pipes spewing water into the river.

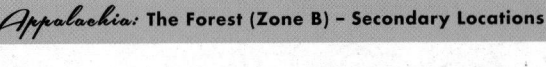

Appalachia: **The Forest (Zone B) – Secondary Locations**

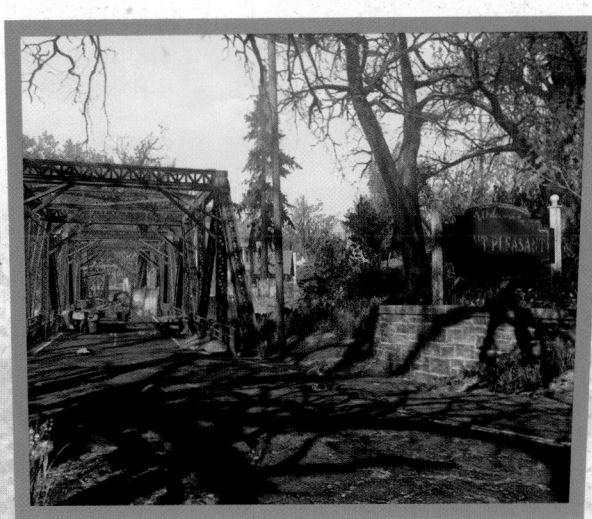

THE FOREST: ZONE C—
MORGANTOWN AND EASTERN FOREST

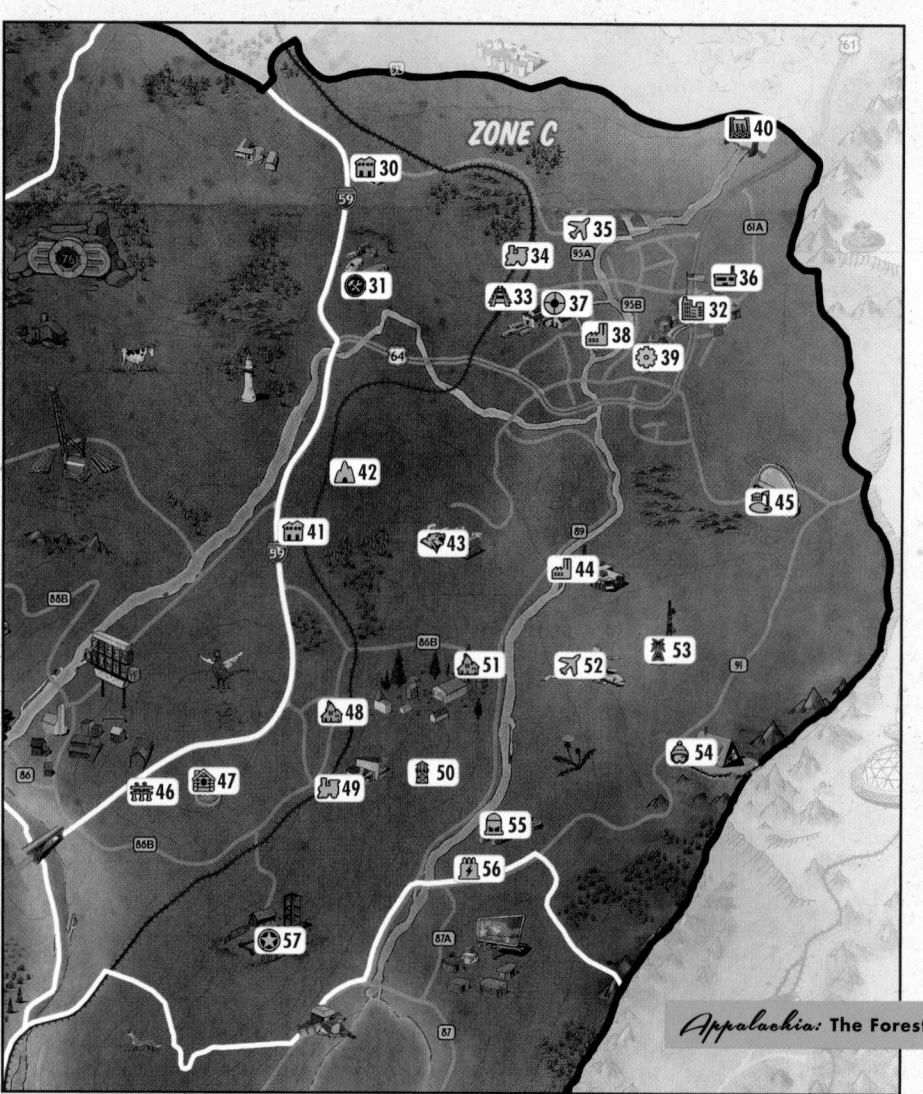

ZONE C

Appalachia: **The Forest (Zone C) – Primary Locations**

The northeastern part of The Forest comprises the lower, more manageable terrain stretching from the poisonous wastes of the Toxic Valley to the north (the boundary is Route 92), as well as all the waste to the outer reaches of Charleston. This zone is dominated by the large settlement of Morgantown, with its airport, school, warehouses, and even a Vault-Tec University, which seems to admit anybody these days. Trek farther south to discover a multitude of interesting places, from the hilltop chem complex of Arktos Pharma, to the gigantic green New River Gorge Bridge (a trek so long, you end up in another zone!). Don't miss visiting the town of Sutton, the hifalutin mansion at Bolton Greens, and the clifftop crash site of a passenger plane. Head east, and you can start the treacherous ascent to the mountains demarcating the Savage Divide— though you're wise to level up a few times (and travel via road for an easier ascent) first.

WORLD MAP LEGEND

—— REGION BOUNDARY   —— ZONE BOUNDARY

■ BOBBLEHEADS   ■ CAP STASHES   ■ MAGAZINES   ■ POWER ARMOR

PRIMARY LOCATIONS

				icon	NAME
				🏚30	WILSON BROTHER'S AUTO REPAIR
			1	🌀31	GORGE JUNKYARD
	9			🏢32	MORGANTOWN
1	6	2	1	🅰33	MORGANTOWN TRAINYARD
				🚉34	MORGANTOWN STATION
1		2		✈35	MORGANTOWN AIRPORT
3	1	3		🏫36	MORGANTOWN HIGH SCHOOL
1		1		✦37	PORTSIDE PUB
4	1	4	2	🏭38	MAMA DOLCE'S FOOD PROCESSING
3	2	3		⚙39	VAULT-TEC UNIVERSITY
1		1	1	🏙40	GRAFTON DAM
1		1		🏚41	SLOCUM'S JOE
3		2		🔺42	GAULEY MINE
1		2	1	◈43	ARKTOS PHARMA

		icon	NAME
1	1	🏭44	GREG'S MINE SUPPLY
5	3	🏰45	BOLTON GREENS
1		🏛46	NEW RIVER GORGE BRIDGE—EAST
1	1	🏠47	NEW RIVER GORGE RESORT
2	2	🏘48	SUTTON
		🚉49	SUTTON STATION
1		🗼50	EAST KANAWHA LOOKOUT
1		🏔51	HELVETIA
1	1	✈52	HORIZON'S REST
1	1	☗53	RELAY TOWER HN-B1-12
		⛷54	WHITE POWDER WINTER SPORTS
1	1	🚰55	TYGART WATER TREATMENT
		⚡56	POSEIDON POWER SUBSTATION PX-02
	1	★57	CAMP MCCLINTOCK

ZONE C: PRIMARY LOCATIONS

MAP LEGEND

- MY STASH BOX
- OVERSEER'S CACHE
- TRUNK
- TRADER

COLLECTIBLES
- BOBBLEHEAD
- MAGAZINE
- POWER ARMOR

CRAFTING
- ARMOR WORKBENCH
- CHEMISTRY WORKBENCH
- COOKING STATION
- POWER ARMOR STATION
- TINKER'S WORKBENCH
- WEAPONS WORKBENCH
- WORKSHOP WORKBENCH

IMPORTANT
- DOOR/GATE
- LOCKED DOOR/GATE
- SAFE
- SCANNER
- TERMINAL

30. WILSON BROTHER'S AUTO REPAIR

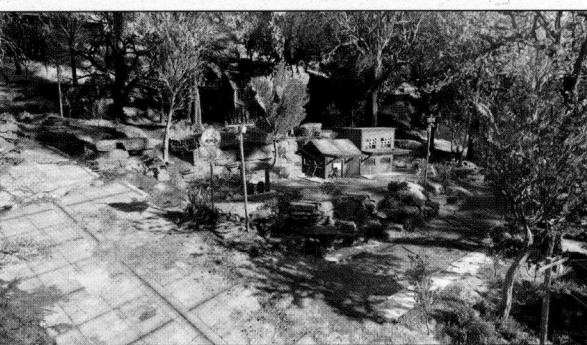

- **CRAFTING:** ARMOR, POWER ARMOR
- **ITEMS:** ARMS AND AMMO; HARVESTABLE: SOOT FLOWER; HEALTH AND CHEMS
- **INFO:** EXPECTED ENEMY: SCORCHED; SCAVENGE RATING: 2; SIZE: 2; THREAT LEVEL: 1–10
- **LOCK:** SAFE (2)
- **ITEM EXAMPLES:** COOKING POT, TELEPHONE, TORQUE ROD END, TURPENTINE

This small repair shop consists of three separate structures: a white house with a yellow door (and a basement safe), a garage and workshop area with workbenches, and a red house on the upper rocky ground. This house's cellar shows evidence of Mothman Cultist activity!

31. GORGE JUNKYARD (WORKSHOP)

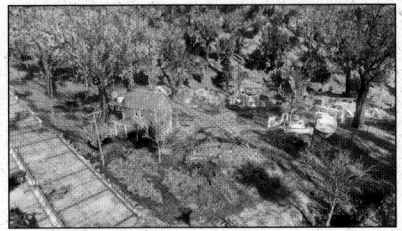

- **COLLECTIBLE:** POWER ARMOR
- **CRAFTING:** CHEMISTRY, POWER ARMOR
- **ITEMS:** ARMS AND AMMO; HARVESTABLE: CONCRETE, JUNK, TITANIUM, WOOD; HEALTH AND CHEMS
- **INFO:** EXPECTED ENEMY: IRRADIATED ANIMALS, ROBOTS; QUEST: CLAIM WORKSHOP AT GORGE JUNKYARD; SCAVENGE RATING: 4; SIZE: 2; THREAT LEVEL: 1–10
- **LOCK:** INACCESSIBLE AREA (KEY), TRAILER DOOR (3)
- **ITEM EXAMPLES:** CAMERA, COMBAT KNIFE, DESK FAN, GREEN BANDANNA, FUSION CORE, MINI NUKE, PORK N' BEANS, TYPEWRITER, USED OIL CAN
- **WORK:** FOOD (5), WATER (3), JUNK (1), TITANIUM (1), CONCRETE (1), WOOD (1)

Gorge Junkyard (Exterior)

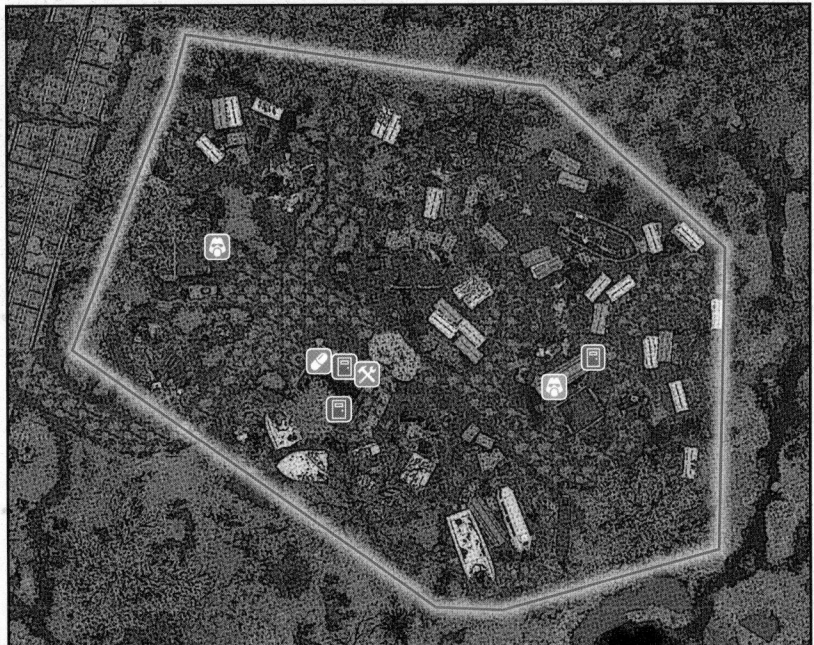

With a Black Titanium and Concrete Deposits, as well as a plentiful supply of junk and other helpful items, this is bound to be a hard-fought location to claim and keep. Check the locked shed by the workshop for a Chem bench and some choice items. Unlock the military (green) trailer (3) to secure some possible Power Armor as well.

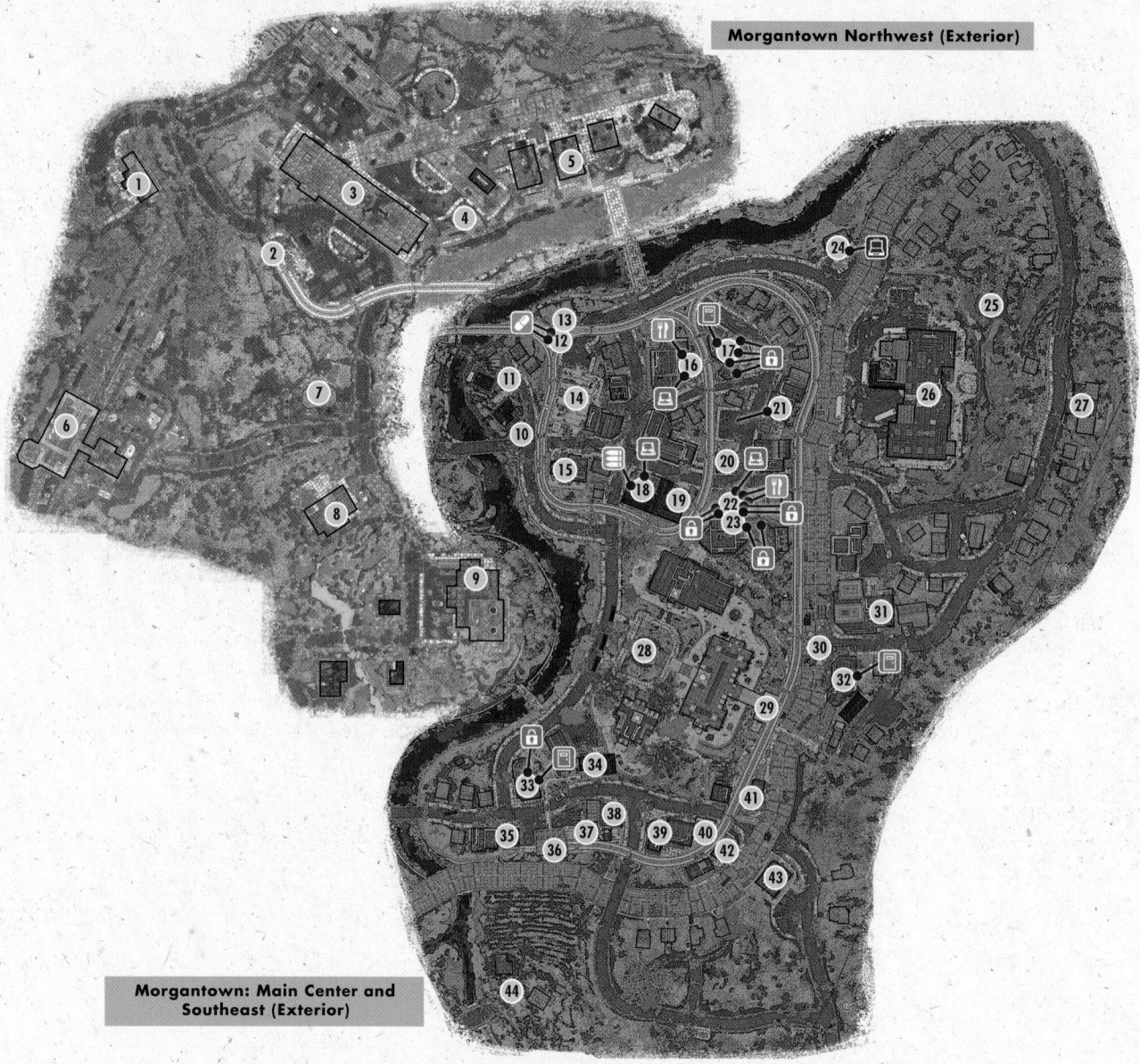

Morgantown Northwest (Exterior)

Morgantown: Main Center and Southeast (Exterior)

LEGEND

1. PRIMARY LOCATION: MORGANTOWN STATION
2. MORGANTOWN MONORAIL STATION: AIRPORT
3. PRIMARY LOCATION: MORGANTOWN AIRPORT (TERMINAL)
4. PRIMARY LOCATION: MORGANTOWN AIRPORT (CONTROL TOWER)
5. PRIMARY LOCATION: MORGANTOWN AIRPORT (RESPONDER HANGARS)
6. PRIMARY LOCATION: MORGANTOWN TRAINYARD
7. ROBCO BOT SHOP
8. PRIMARY LOCATION: PORTSIDE PUB
9. PRIMARY LOCATION: MAMA DOLCE'S FOOD PROCESSING
10. WELCOME TO MORGANTOWN SIGN
11. PIPE PILE METAL GARAGE AND WAREHOUSES
12. STUDENT SURVIVORS' CHEM LAB (MONORAIL TRACKS)
13. PULOWSKI PRESERVATION SHELTER (NORTH)
14. MORGANTOWN MONORAIL STATION: NORTH (AND PARKING LOT)
15. MONORAIL ACCESS PLANKS

16. DELICATESSEN (RESPONDER STASH ROOM), AND APARTMENTS (INTERIOR AND ROOF ACCESS)
17. SHADOWBREEZE APARTMENTS (SCAFFOLD APARTMENTS, AND MOORMAN'S) (INTERIOR AND ROOF ACCESS)
18. LIQUOR STORE: RESPONDER HEADQUARTERS
19. ROOF SHACK (ACCESS FROM MONORAIL TRACKS)
20. BAR AND WINE CELLAR
21. ATTORNEY (RESPONDER STASH ROOM)
22. BANK (RESPONDER STASH ROOM)
23. NUKA-COLA BILLBOARD APARTMENTS (INTERIOR AND ROOF ACCESS)
24. RED ROCKET GAS STATION
25. WATER TOWER AND NORTHWEST HILLSIDE HOMES
26. PRIMARY LOCATION: MORGANTOWN HIGH SCHOOL
27. APARTMENTS (INACCESSIBLE INTERIOR)
28. PRIMARY LOCATION: VAULT-TEC UNIVERSITY
29. MORGANTOWN MONORAIL STATION: UNIVERSITY
30. TENT CITY AND DEFENSIVE WALL

31. PARKING LOT
32. DRUGSTORE TENEMENT BLOCK (ROOF CAMP)
33. [33] BOOK & STATIONERY SHOP, AND BARBERS
34. BANK OF MORGANTOWN (UNIVERSITY BRANCH)
35. YELLOW APARTMENT BLOCK (ROOF ACCESS)
36. MORGANTOWN MONORAIL STATION: SOUTH
37. PULOWSKI PRESERVATION SHELTER (SOUTH)
38. PAWN SHOP AND POST OFFICE (INACCESSIBLE INTERIOR)
39. MORGANTOWN TAVERN
40. APARTMENT TOWER (INTERIOR, ROOF, AND MONORAIL ACCESS)
41. LIMESTONE TENEMENT (ROOF AND MONORAIL ACCESS)
42. GRAVIANO'S ITALIAN EATERY
43. SUPER DUPER MART (INACCESSIBLE INTERIOR)
44. SOUTH MORGANTOWN FARMSTEAD

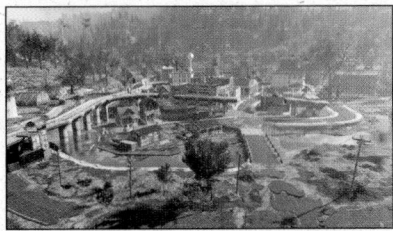

- COLLECTIBLES: CAPS STASH (9), HOLOTAPE, NUKA-CHERRY
- CRAFTING: CHEMISTRY, COOKING (2), TINKER'S, WATER PUMP
- DANGER: GRENADE! LONG DROP! MINE! TURRET!
- ITEMS: ARMS AND AMMO+++; HARVESTABLE: BRAIN FUNGUS, GLOWING FUNGUS, MUTATED FERN, RHODODENDRON, SOOT FLOWER, WILD MUTFRUIT; HEALTH AND CHEMS+++; MY STASH BOX
- INFO: EXPECTED ENEMY: GHOUL, SCORCHED; INSTRUMENT; LANDMARK; NOTE; EVENT: BACK ON THE BEAT; SCAVENGE RATING: 5+++; SIZE: 5+++; SLEEPING; THREAT LEVEL: 1–10
- LOCK: DOOR (1, 1), SAFE (0, 0, 1, 1, 1, 2, 2, 2, 2), TERMINAL (0)
- ITEM EXAMPLES: ABRAXO CLEANER, ABRAXO CLEANER INDUSTRIAL GRADE, BAG OF FERTILIZER, BALL-PEEN HAMMER, BASEBALL BAT, BEER BOTTLE+, BLAST RADIUS BOARD GAME, BLUE PAINT+, BOILED WATER, BOWLER HAT, BROKEN LAMP, BUBBLEGUM, CAP++, CHEF HAT, CIGAR BOX, CIGARETTE CARTON, CLEAN BROOM, COFFEE CUP++, CRAM, DANDY BOY APPLES+, DESK LAMP+, DOG BOWL, DOLL, DIRTY ASHTRAY, DUCT TAPE, ECONOMY WONDERGLUE, ENAMEL BUCKET+, EYEGLASSES, GARDEN GNOME+, GAS CANISTER+, GLOWING FUNGUS PUREE, HARD HAT, HOT PLATE, INSTAMASH+, KITCHEN SCALE, LANTERN+, MAKESHIFT BATTERY, OFFICE DESK FAN, ORANGE DRINKING GLASS, OVEN MITT, PACK OF CIGARETTES, PARTY HAT, PENCIL, POOL BALL++, POOL CUE, PRE-WAR MONEY++, PURIFIED WATER, ROLLED CHARLESTON HERALD, RUBY TIE MR. FUZZY, SAW, SCREWDRIVER, SENSOR MODULE, SHADELESS TABLE LAMP, SHOT GLASS, SOAP+, SOUVENIR COFFEE CUP, SUGAR BOMBS, TALL DRINKING GLASS+, TEAL BUD CASE, TEAL VAULTED VASE, TEDDY BEAR, TIN CAN+, TOILET PAPER, TOY ALIEN, TURPENTINE+, VAULT-TEC LUNCHBOX, VODKA BOTTLE+, WASTE ACID, WINE, WHISKEY, WOOD BLOCK+, WONDERGLUE, YARDSTICK, YELLOW PAINT, YELLOW PLATE, YELLOW TABLE LAMP.

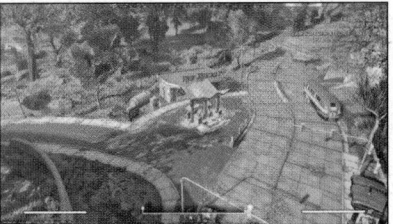

Red Rocket Gas Station

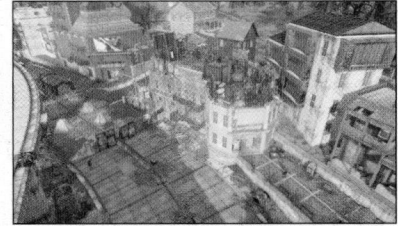

Drugstore Tenement Block (Roof Camp)

The town of Morgantown encompasses this and the subsequent seven Primary Locations, all within a relatively easy-to-distinguish border (once you hit railroad, grass, or forest, you're out of town). Therefore, all information regarding Crafting, Dangers, Items, Information, Locked areas, and Item Examples are also specified for those individual locations. This entry simply gives you a short overview of the entirety of the settlement and areas of interest outside these locations.

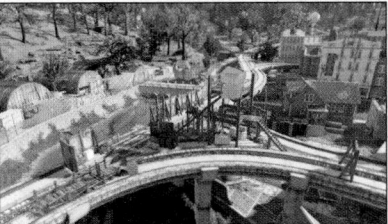

Student Survivors' Chem Lab (Monorail Tracks)

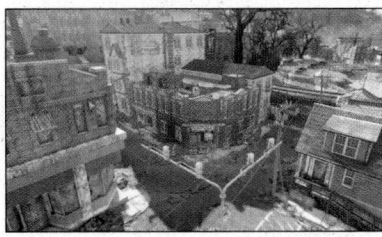

Liquor Store (Responder Headquarters)

Navigating Morgantown can be tricky due to the complex maze of structures, the ruined city streets, and dilapidated apartment blocks and other buildings, some of which feature interior and rooftop access. Your first step is figuring out a base of operations; this could be at the Responders Headquarters (in a liquor store close to the center of town), but a better bet is to stay to the north, at the Red Rocket Gas Station, which has a My Stash Box you can utilize. There is a camp with a few chemistry stations and traps built on the elevated rail line itself.

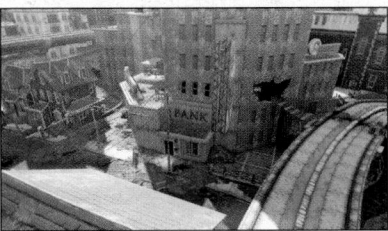

Bank (Responder Stash Room)

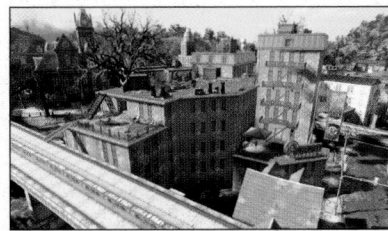

Nuka-Cola Billboard Apartments

There are numerous apartment structures (and to a lesser extent, stores) with interiors you can explore. It's worth checking the multiple exits—at street level, onto the monorail, or onto the rooftops. Expect at least two city blocks to have this type of access. Over on the eastern side, where the buildings aren't as tall, there's still some interiors and rooftops to check. Of particular note are three Responder Stashes; access the monitor at a bank, attorneys, and deli (all relatively close to the headquarters) for a wealth of additional junk (mainly foodstuffs). These are accessible once the Event: Back on the Beat has been completed.

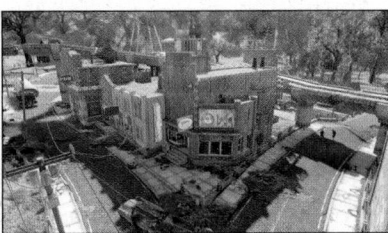

Morgantown Tavern

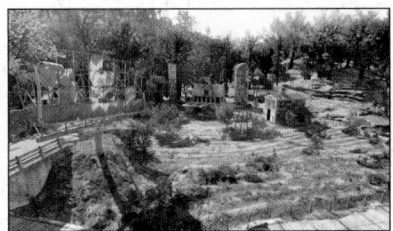

South Morgantown Farmstead

The taller structures in town are surrounded by a monorail loop and several stations (North, South, University, and Airport) you can reach by wandering on or below the rails. When you reach the southern edge of Morgantown's sprawling settlement, there's a small farmstead with a cottage (and flooded basement), a silo, and a red barn.

TRAINING

CRAFTING AND CAMPING

INVENTORY

QUESTS

ATLAS

BESTIARY

APPENDICES

33. MORGANTOWN TRAINYARD

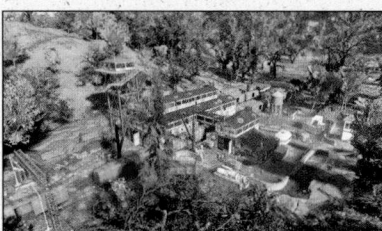

- **COLLECTIBLES:** BOBBLEHEAD, CAPS STASH (6), MAGAZINE (2), POWER ARMOR
- **CRAFTING:** ARMOR, CHEMISTRY, COOKING (X2), WEAPONS

- **DANGER:** LONG DROP! RADIATION!++
- **ITEMS:** ARMS AND AMMO; HEALTH AND CHEMS; RECIPE/MOD/PLAN; TRUNK
- **INFO:** EXPECTED ENEMY: SCORCHED; INSTRUMENT; NOTES; SCAVENGE RATING: 4; SIZE: 3; SLEEPING; THREAT LEVEL: 1–10
- **LOCK:** SAFE (X2), (U, 1)
- **ITEM EXAMPLES:** ASHTRAY, BOBBY PIN BOX, BUFFOUT, COFFEE CUP+, COFFEE POT, DESK FAN+, DESK LAMP, DUCT TAPE, GAS CANISTER, MAKESHIFT BATTERY, OIL CANISTER, OVEN MITT, RADIO JAMMER+, SUGAR, TIN CANISTER+, VACUUM TUBE.

34. MORGANTOWN STATION

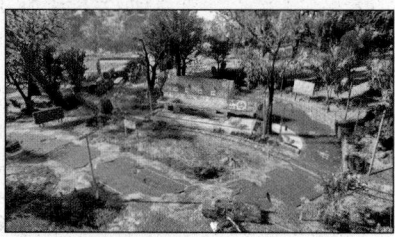

- **CRAFTING:** CHEMISTRY
- **ITEMS:** ARMS AND AMMO; HEALTH AND CHEMS; MY STASH BOX; VENDING MACHINE: AMMUNITION, MEDICINAL SUPPLIES
- **INFO:** SCAVENGE RATING: 2; SIZE: 1; THREAT LEVEL: 1–10. TRADER: VENDOR BOT
- **ITEM EXAMPLES:** ALARM CLOCK, MENTATS, TOILET PAPER+

Serving Morgantown, the railway station is on the town's northwestern edge and offers a great regrouping area to offload items and to trade and heal.

Morgantown Station (Exterior and Interior)

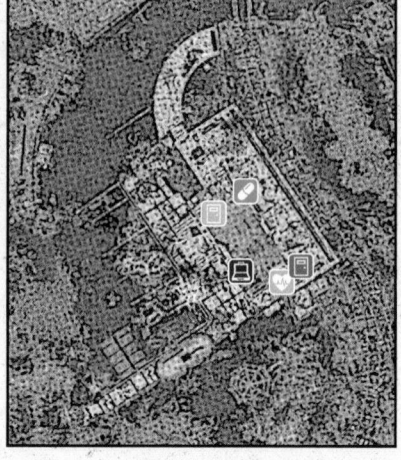

Morgantown Trainyard (Exterior and Interior)

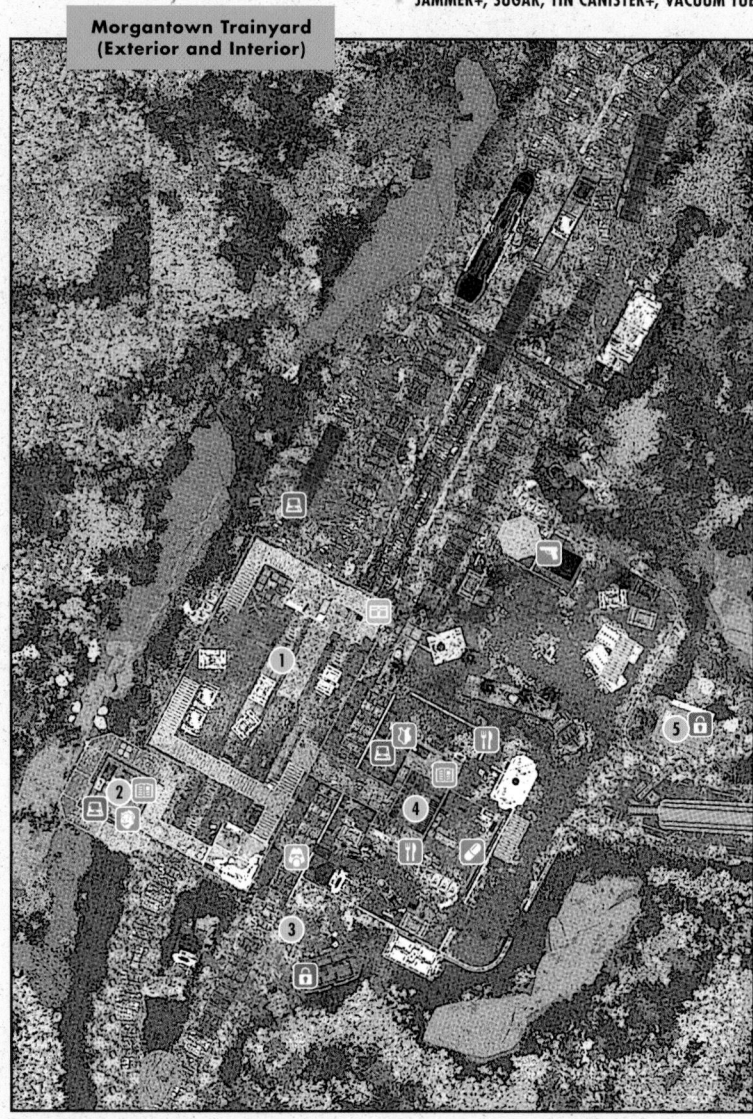

LEGEND
1. MAIN TRAINYARD TERMINUS WAREHOUSE
2. SUPERVISOR'S TOWER
3. METAL CARAVAN AND BANJO
4. MAIN WAREHOUSE
5. SIGNAL TOWER

The southwestern edge of Morgantown is comprised of this large trainyard, full of rusting cargo carriages and lurking foes. Follow the derailed containers up to the Station, checking any open ones for possible scavenging opportunities. The large corrugated metal warehouses have a gantry leading to control huts and a tall tower. Outside on the east side is a large mechanic's warehouse (with workbenches), an unloading area marked with two flag poles with open containers, a signal tower, a small mechanic's hut, and an open carriage with possible Power Armor.

✈ 35. MORGANTOWN AIRPORT

- **COLLECTIBLES:** BOBBLEHEAD, HOLOTAPE, MAGAZINE (2)
- **CRAFTING:** ARMOR (2), CHEMISTRY, COOKING (4), POWER ARMOR (2), TINKER (2), WEAPONS (3)
- **DANGER:** EXPLOSIVE CANNISTER! TURRET!
- **ITEMS:** ARMS AND AMMO+; HARVESTABLE: PUMPKIN, TATO PLANT, WILD CORN; HEALTH AND CHEMS++; RECIPE/MOD/PLAN; OVERSEER'S CACHE; TRUNK
- **INFO:** EXPECTED ENEMY: SCORCHED; INSTRUMENT; QUEST: AN OUNCE OF PREVENTION; NOTE; SCAVENGE RATING: 5; SIZE: 5; SLEEPING; THREAT LEVEL: 1–10

- **LOCK:** GATE (1), SAFE (T, 0, 1)
- **ITEM EXAMPLES:** ASHTRAY, BALL-PEEN HAMMER, BLAMCO BRAND MAC AND CHEESE, BLAST RADIUS BOARD GAME, BOARD, BROOM, CAKE TRAY, COFFEE CUP+, COFFEE POT+, CREAM, DOG BOWL, ENAMEL BUCKET, FUSION CORE, GAS CANISTER, IV BAG, LAB COAT, MEDICAL LIQUID NITROGEN DISPENSER+, MICROSCOPE, PACK OF CIGARETTES, PATCHED THREE-PIECE SUIT, PILLOW, PORTABLE FUEL TANK, RAD POKER BOARD GAME, RADAWAY, SALT, SCORCHED SPECIMEN JAR+, SHORT LASER PISTOL, SHORT PIPE RIFLE, SURGICAL MASK, SURGICAL TRAY, TIN CAN, TOILET PAPER+, USED OIL CAN

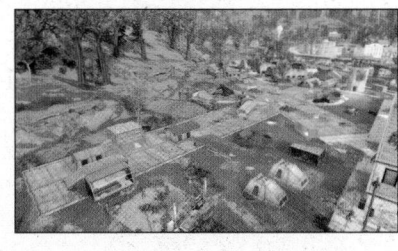

Morgantown Airport (Exterior)

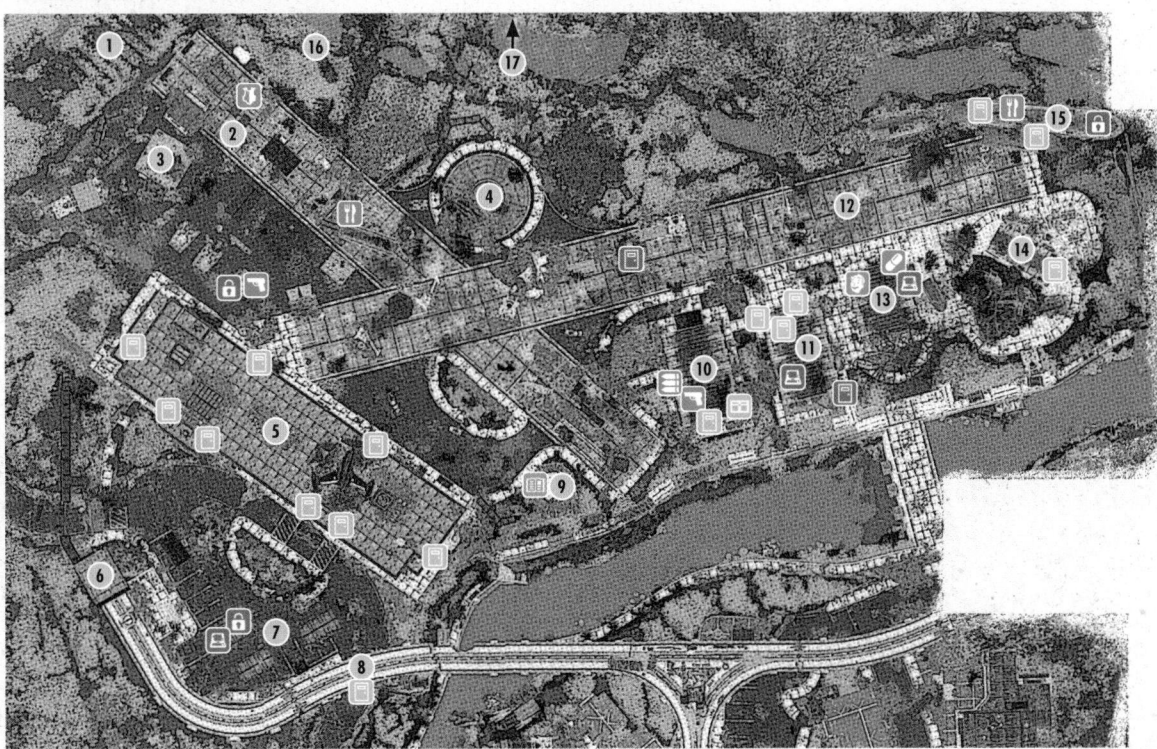

LEGEND

1	COMMUNITY GARDEN	9	CONTROL TOWER (FIELD OPS)
2	CONTAINER TOWN	10	BOT SHOP HANGAR
3	MUSIC STAGE	11	MEDICAL HANGAR
4	CRASHED VERTIBIRD	12	INNER RUNWAY
5	TERMINAL BUILDING (TRADING POST)	13	LABORATORY HANGAR
6	MONORAIL STATION	14	QUARANTINE HANGAR
7	MILITARY TENTS	15	QUARANTINE GUARD BARRACKS
8	MAIN GATE	16	RESPONDERS CEMETERY
		17	TO MIGUEL'S CAMPSITE

Morgantown Airport: Terminal (Interior)

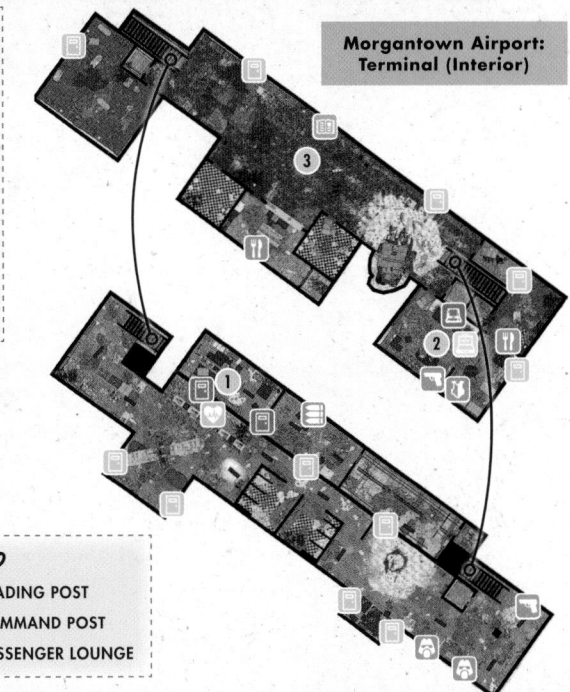

LEGEND

1	TRADING POST
2	COMMAND POST
3	PASSENGER LOUNGE

Spanning most of the northern part of Morgantown is the expansive airport, recently turned into a large-scale Responders base, before a horde of Scorched descended upon the area. Behind the main terminal building (which houses a trading post as well as Power Armor Stations and an Overseer's Cache) is the main airport runway, turned into a shantytown with a modicum of turret defenses at the control tower. Head east to reach the hangars and quarantine area, where you find additional information on the Responders' experiments. Pick up Responder Volunteers: Advanced Training quests at the Responders HQ Terminal in the Command Post.

TRAINING · CRAFTING AND C.A.M.P.ING · INVENTORY · QUESTS · ATLAS · BESTIARY · APPENDICES

- **COLLECTIBLES:** BOBBLEHEAD (3), CAPS STASH, HOLOTAPE, MAGAZINE (3), NUKA-CHERRY
- **CRAFTING:** CHEMISTRY
- **DANGER:** EXPLOSIVE CANNISTER! GRENADE!
- **ITEMS:** ARMS AND AMMO; HARVESTABLE: PUMPKIN+; HEALTH AND CHEMS++; TRUNK
- **INFO:** EXPECTED ENEMY: IRRADIATED INSECT, SCORCHED; SCAVENGE RATING: 5; SIZE: 4; SLEEPING; THREAT LEVEL: 1–10
- **LOCK:** DOOR (0, 0, 1, 2, 2, C), TERMINAL (1), SAFE (2, 2)
- **ITEM EXAMPLES:** ABRAXO CLEANER, AUTOPSY BOARD GAME, BASEBALL BAT, BASEBALL GLOVE, BEAKER STAND, BEER BOTTLE+, BLACK DRINKING GLASS+, BLUE PAINT, BOWLING PIN+, BURNT BOOK+, CAKE PAN, CANDY FAN MR. FUZZY, CAP, CIGARETTE CARTON, DUCT TAPE, ENAMEL BUCKET, GLOBE, GOLF BALL+, HOT PLATE+, MICROSCOPE+, MOP, NAPKIN+, NUKA-COLA CUP, ORANGE BOWL, ORANGE DRINKING GLASS, OVEN MITTS, PLASTIC PUMPKIN+++, POTATO CRISPS, PRE-WAR MONEY+, PRINCIPAL'S SAFE KEY, PURIFIED WATER, RAT POISON, SALISBURY STEAK, SOAP, SOUVENIR TOY CAR, TALL FLASK, TV DINNER TRAY+, WHISKEY

Morgantown High School (Interior)

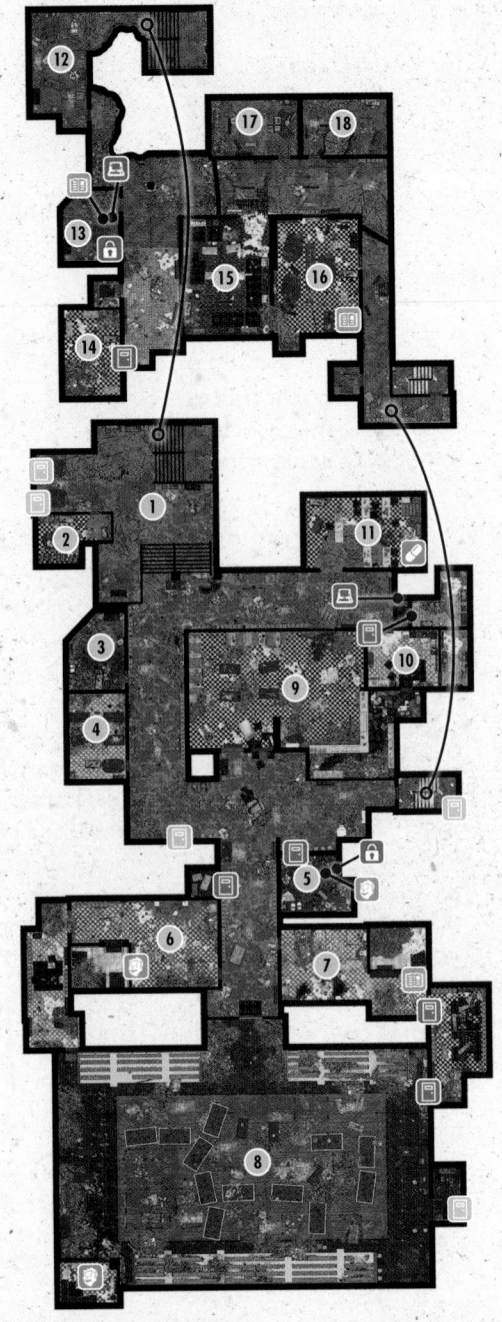

Morgantown High School (Exterior)

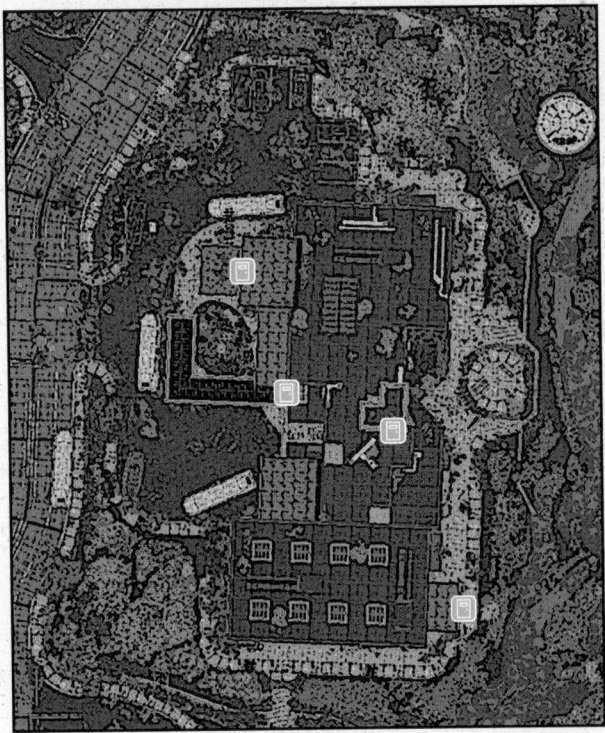

The exterior of this high school is mostly overgrown (especially at the rear of the premises), while the front road and parking area is strewn with vehicles— mostly school buses with the odd piece of junk to grab. Find fire escape stairs on the north side to reach the roof. There are two white double doors to access the main entrance foyer and a blue side door to the right of these doors, or you can use the rear green door (into the gym) or the door on the roof. There are two main interior levels to explore. The place is in relatively good shape, with only a few damaged rooms.

LEGEND

1 ENTRANCE FOYER AND STAIRS	**10** KITCHENS AND STORAGE
2 FILING OFFICE	**11** BIOLOGY CLASSROOM
3 SMALL LOUNGE	**12** TEACHERS' LOUNGE
4 CLASSROOM	**13** MEZZANINE OFFICE
5 COMMON ROOM	**14** SMALL CLASSROOM
6 BOYS' RESTROOM AND LOCKERS	**15** COOKING CLASSROOM
7 GIRLS' RESTROOMS AND LOCKERS	**16** LIBRARY
8 GYMNASIUM	**17** BLUE DESK CLASSROOM
9 CAFETERIA	**18** RUINED CLASSROOM

⊕ 37. PORTSIDE PUB

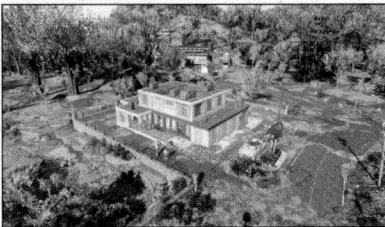

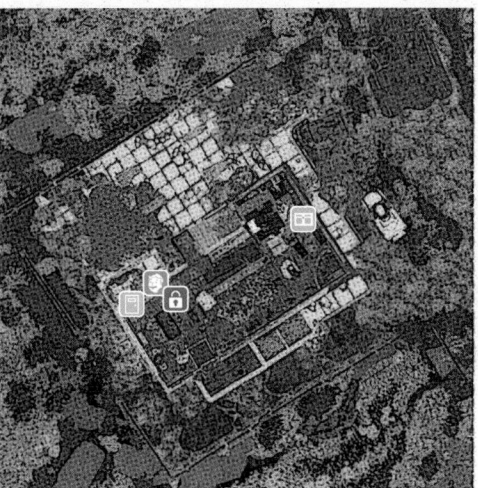

- **COLLECTIBLES:** BOBBLEHEAD, MAGAZINE
- **ITEMS:** HARVESTABLE: WILD CARROT, HEALTH AND CHEMS, TRUNK
- **INFO:** EXPECTED ENEMY: ROBOT; INSTRUMENT; SCAVENGE RATING: 3; SIZE: 2; THREAT LEVEL: 1–10
- **LOCK:** SAFE (1)
- **ITEM EXAMPLES:** BLACKWATER BREW, CATCH THE COMMIE BOARD GAME, CHESSBOARD, GLASS JAR+, FUEL TANK, LANTERN, NUKA-COLA CUP, PEPPER, SALT

**Portside Pub
(Exterior and Interior)**

Look for the sailboat on a pole outside this two-story, run-down tavern. There is ample room for parking and a low stone wall around the perimeter. Use a propped ladder to reach the upper roof with the skylights and safe.

🏭 38. MAMA DOLCE'S FOOD PROCESSING

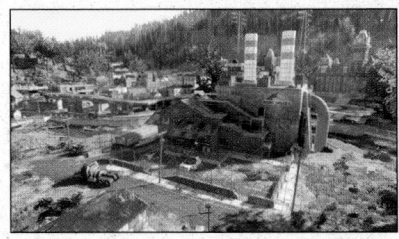

- **COLLECTIBLES:** BOBBLEHEAD (4), CAPS STASH, MAGAZINE (4), POWER ARMOR (2)
- **CRAFTING:** POWER ARMOR, WEAPONS
- **DANGER:** EXPLOSIVE CANNISTER! GRENADES! MINES! TENSION TRIGGER!
- **ITEMS:** ARMS AND AMMO++; HARVESTABLE: RHODODENDRON, SOOT FLOWER, SNAP TAIL, WILD MUTFRUIT; HEALTH AND CHEMS+; RECIPE/MOD/ PLAN
- **INFO:** EXPECTED ENEMY: IRRADIATED ANIMAL, ROBOT; NOTE; EVENT: FEED THE PEOPLE; SCAVENGE RATING: 3; SIZE: 4; THREAT LEVEL: 1–10

- **LOCK:** DOOR (0, 1, B), SAFE (2)
- **ITEM EXAMPLES:** ALARM CLOCK, BASEBALL GRENADE, BEER BOTTLE+, BLAMCO BRAND MAC AND CHEESE, BLUE PAINT, BOBBY PIN BOX, CAP, COFFEE CUP, COFFEE POT, COOLANT CAP, DOG BOWL, FANCY LAD SNACK CAKES, FUSION CORE, HALLUCIGEN GAS CANISTER, MAKESHIFT BATTERY, MAMA DOLCE'S MANAGER ID CARD, NUKA-COLA BOTTLE+, OIL CANISTER, RAT POISON, SALISBURY STEAK, TELEPHONE, TOILET PAPER, TORQUE ROD END, TYPEWRITER, YELLOW PAINT, YUM YUM DEVILED EGGS

**Mama Dolce's Food Processing
(Exterior and Interior)**

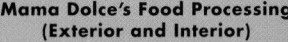

LEGEND

1. MECHANIC'S GARAGE
2. SCAFFOLD WAREHOUSE
3. MECHANIC SHED AND OFFICE
4. SECURITY BARRIER
5. PROCESSING PLANT
6. MANAGER'S OFFICE
7. EXECUTIVE OFFICE

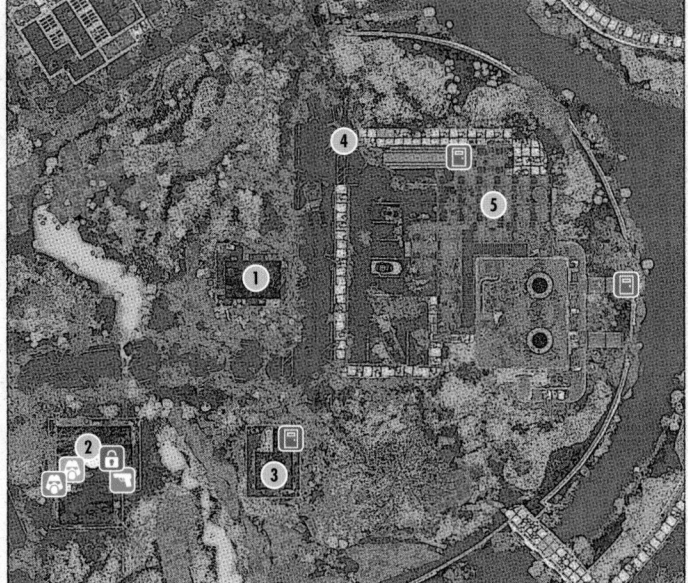

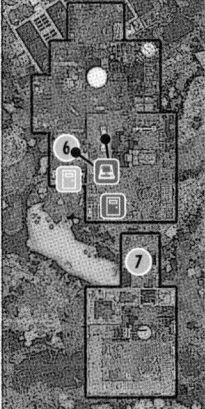

For all your reconstituted canned goods, Mama Dolce is the place to go! Currently, the company's processing facility is in need of a makeover. Check the three metal structures outside the main building for a variety of junk and some explosive traps (at the scaffold warehouse). Inside the plant is an unloading dock (unlock the trailer [1] for some extra ammo). Also inside the facility is a security gate (0) with items to scavenge behind it. Check upstairs for the Mama Dolce's Manager ID Card, in the executive office area. The upstairs gantry also allows access to the roof; use this for defensive positioning or to check views of Morgantown to the north.

⊖

TRAINING

CRAFTING AND C.A.M.P.ING

INVENTORY

QUESTS

ATLAS

BESTIARY

APPENDICES

FUJINIYA INTELLIGENCE BASE

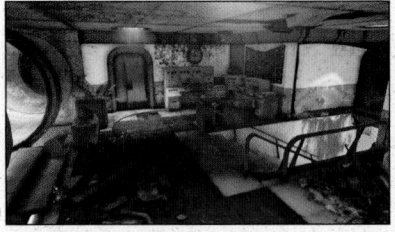

- **CRAFTING:** CHEMISTRY (4)
- **ITEMS:** ARMS AND AMMO++, HEALTH AND CHEMS++, RECIPE/MOD/PLAN, TRUNK
- **INFO:** EXPECTED ENEMY: IRRADIATED INSECT, ROBOT; QUEST: I AM BECOME DEATH; SCAVENGE RATING: 3; SIZE: 3; THREAT LEVEL: 1–10
- **LOCK:** DOOR (1), SAFE, TERMINAL (1)
- **ITEM EXAMPLES:** ALUMINUM CANISTER, BASEBALL GRENADE, BEAKER STAND, COFFEE CUP, COFFEE POT, BOILED WATER+, CANNED DOG FOOD, CRAM, CHINESE OFFICER SWORD, FUSION CORE, MICROSCOPE, PILLOW+, PIPE PISTOL, PORK N' BEANS, SALISBURY STEAK, STEALTH BOY, TALL DRINKING GLASS+, TALL FLASK, TOILET PAPER+, WINE

With the appropriate Quest and ID Reader card active, you can explore the secret Chinese base underneath this processing facility! Access it from the hatch on one of the large drainage pipes outside the plant, close to the river. Inside the Intelligence Base is a three-level, subterranean hideaway stocked with ammunition, chems, and collectibles!

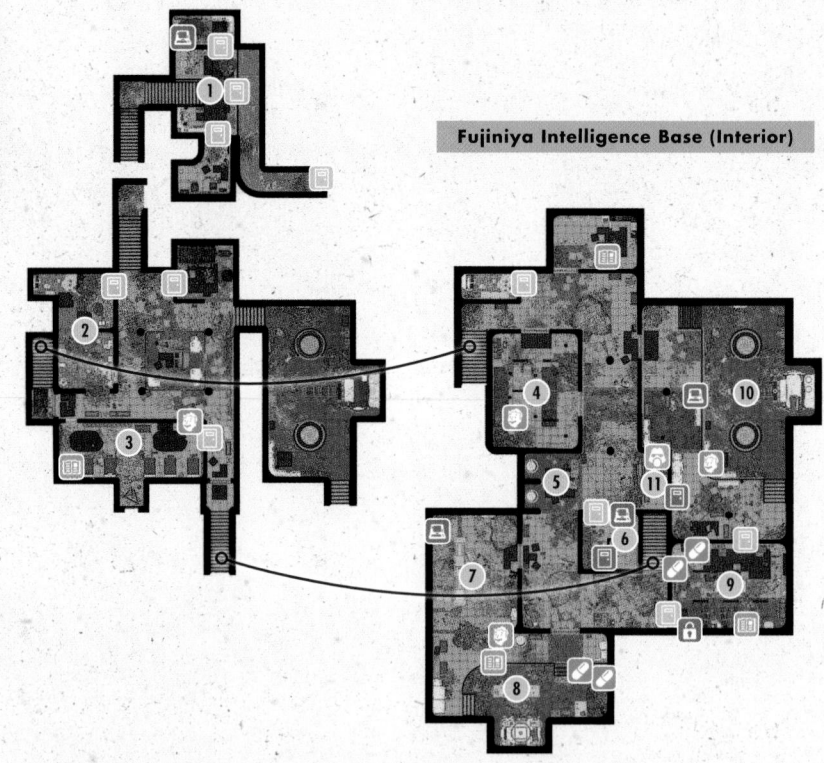

Fujiniya Intelligence Base (Interior)

LEGEND

1	ENTRANCE AND SECURITY	5	PROTECTRON PODS	9	OPERATING ROOM
2	RESTROOMS	6	SECURITY ROOM	10	MAIN PROCESSING
3	DORMITORY	7	GENERATOR ROOM	11	ARMORY CLOSET
4	COMPUTER ROOM	8	LABORATORY		

 ## 39. VAULT-TEC UNIVERSITY

- **COLLECTIBLES:** BOBBLEHEAD (3), CAPS STASH (2), HOLOTAPE, MAGAZINE (3)
- **CRAFTING:** ARMOR, WEAPONS
- **ITEMS:** HARVESTABLE: RHODODENDRON; HEALTH AND CHEMS+++; RECIPE/MOD/PLAN; TRUNK
- **INFO:** EXPECTED ENEMY: GHOUL; SCAVENGE RATING: 5; SIZE: 5; SLEEPING; THREAT LEVEL: 1–10
- **LOCK:** SAFE (3, 3), TERMINAL (0)
- **ITEM EXAMPLES:** 20 LB WEIGHT, BUBBLEGUM, BREAD BOX, BURNT BOOK++, CAFETERIA TRAY+, CANNED DOG FOOD, CHESSBOARD, DISHRAG, DRINKING GLASS+, ENAMEL BUCKET, FANCY LAD SNACK CAKES, GIDDYUP BUTTERCUP, GLASS BEAKER, GLASS PITCHER, INSTAMASH, MAGNIFYING GLASS, MED-X, METAL BUCKET, MICROSCOPE, NEW RIVER RED ALE, NUKA-COLA, OFFICE DESK FAN, PAPER CUTTER, PAPER CUTTER, PLUNGER, POOL BALL, POOL CUE, POTATO CRISPS, PURIFIED WATER++, SOAP, SILVER POCKET WATCH, TEAL VAULTED VASE, TOOTHBRUSH, TOOTHPASTE, VAULT JUMPSUIT, VTU COFFEE CUP+, WHISKEY, WOOD BLOCK+, YELLOW TABLE LAMP, YUM YUM DEVILED EGGS

Vault-Tec University (Exterior)

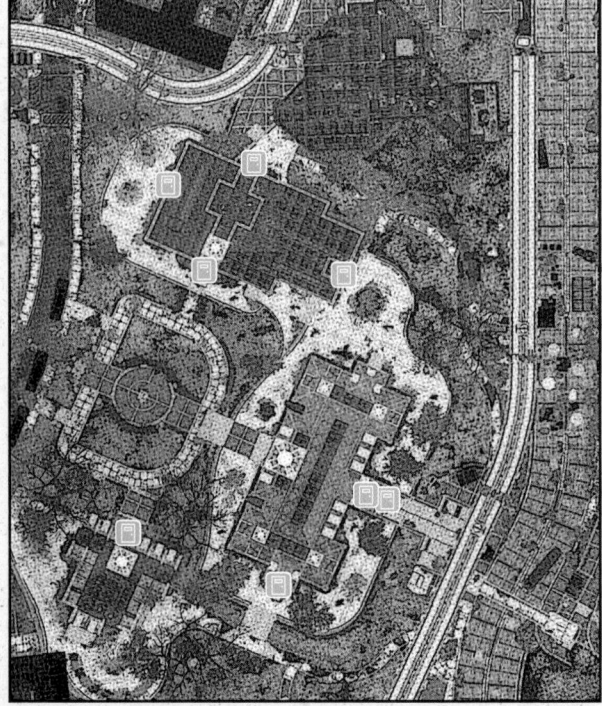

Exterior: The university is comprised of three campus structures made of old imposing brick edifices, all with red doors that are easily entered. The interiors of the structure link underground to each other, while a skybridge links one of the campus buildings to the Monorail station. Check the area under the monorail station for a small tent city, which has a few additional items to scavenge.

Vault-Tec University (Interior)

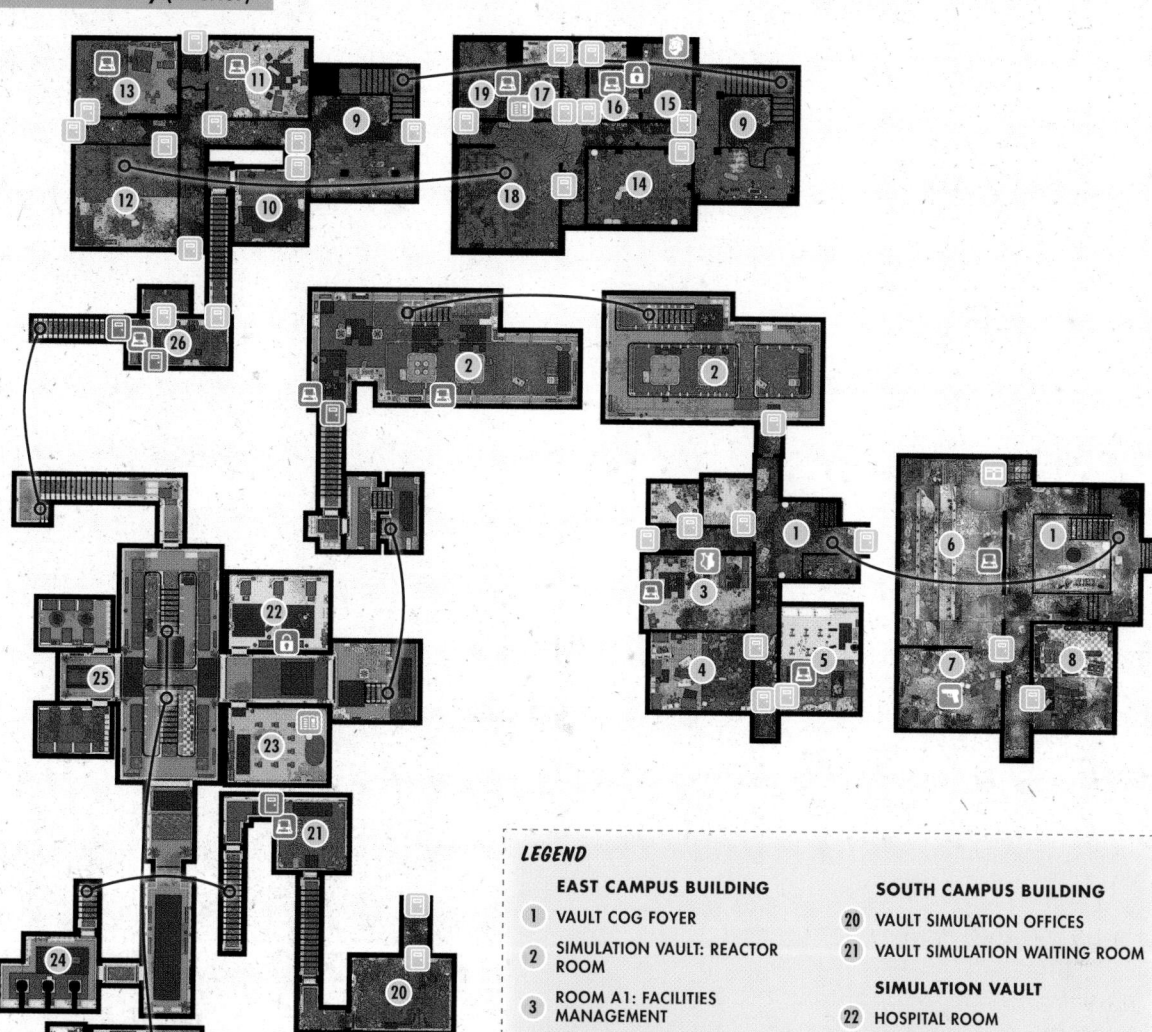

TRAINING

CRAFTING AND C.A.M.P.ING

INVENTORY

QUESTS

ATLAS

BESTIARY

APPENDICES

LEGEND

EAST CAMPUS BUILDING

1. VAULT COG FOYER
2. SIMULATION VAULT: REACTOR ROOM
3. ROOM A1: FACILITIES MANAGEMENT
4. ROOM A2: SLEEP AND HOUSING LAB
5. ROOM A3: PHYSICAL ACTIVITY LAB
6. EUGENE DAVIDSON LECTURE HALL
7. ROOM B2: STORAGE
8. ROOM B3: FOOD PREPARATION LAB

NORTH CAMPUS BUILDING

9. RECEPTION AND STAIRWELL
10. ROOM 101: TRAINING VAULT ENTRANCE
11. ROOM 102: MEDICAL EMERGENCY CARE
12. ROOM 103: FACILITIES TRAINING
13. ROOM 104: YOUNG DWELLER DEVELOPMENT
14. ROOM 201: COMPUTER LAB
15. ROOM 202: OFFICE OF THE DEAN OF ADMISSION
16. ROOM 203: OFFICE OF THE DEAN, OVERSEER TRAINING
17. ROOM 204: LOUNGE
18. ROOM 207. PROF. G. ESPINO, PROF. J. HOLLAR
19. ROOM 208: PROF. M. BLAKE

SOUTH CAMPUS BUILDING

20. VAULT SIMULATION OFFICES
21. VAULT SIMULATION WAITING ROOM

SIMULATION VAULT

22. HOSPITAL ROOM
23. CLASSROOM
24. LOCKER ROOM AND SHOWERS
25. POOL ROOM AND BUNK DORMS
26. OVERSEER'S ROOM
27. GYM AND SHOWERS
28. CAFETERIA
29. MAINTENANCE ROOM
30. RECORDS CHAMBER

EAST CAMPUS BUILDING

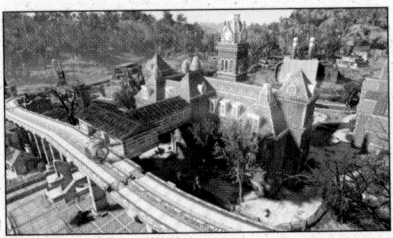

The largest of the three campus buildings is east of the Vault Boy garden statue and links the gardens (west) with the monorail (east). Inside is a central foyer with a "cog" display and access to four main corridors and stairs, including an entrance to the Simulation Vault via a terminal. Three classrooms are on the ground floor. Up the stairs is the Overseer's Holotape, access to the monorail bridge, a large lecture hall, and the "B" wing of rooms.

NORTH CAMPUS BUILDING

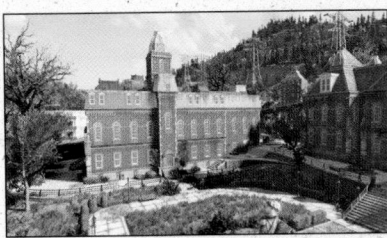

Evidence of violence is present in the north campus structure. A barricade prevents access from the north red entrance door (use the hole in the wall of Room 102 to access this instead). There's gloomy corridors and academic chambers to pick through, including the "official" entrance to the vault, which allows access into the Overseer's room. Some of the rooms (such as 103) are in particularly bad condition, with fallen ceilings allowing access to an upper floor of rooms, including a large (and ruined) archival office.

SOUTH CAMPUS BUILDING

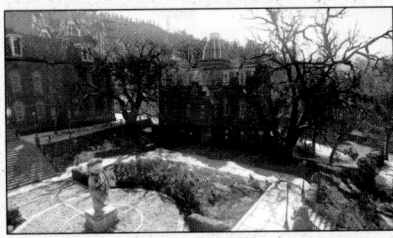

Enter via the only accessible exterior doors into a large office room, picked clean of most junk. Stairs lead down to a waiting room with benches and a terminal that allows access to the locker room and showers within the Simulation Vault.

SIMULATION VAULT

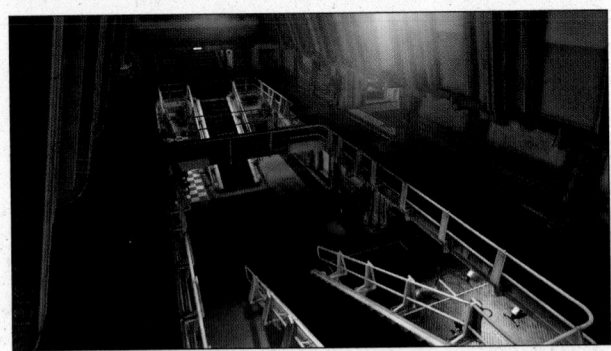

Aside from the entrance chambers, this simulation of a vault is in spectacular condition! It is centered around a main mezzanine level, which has all the usual and recognizable elements of a vault. There is also a hidden Records Chamber on the lowest level.

---

40. GRAFTON DAM

- **COLLECTIBLES:** BOBBLEHEAD, HOLOTAPE, MAGAZINE, POWER ARMOR
- **CRAFTING:** COOKING, POWER ARMOR, TINKER, WEAPONS
- **DANGER:** LONG DROP! RADIATION! TENSION TRIGGER!
- **ITEMS:** ARMS AND AMMO; HARVESTABLE: MIRELURK EGG, MUTATED FERN; HEALTH AND CHEMS; RECIPE/MOD/PLAN; TRUNK
- **INFO:** EXPECTED ENEMY: IRRADIATED INSECT, MIRELURK, SUPER MUTANT; NOTE; QUEST: PASS THE BUCK; SCAVENGE RATING: 3; SIZE: 3; SLEEPING; THREAT LEVEL: 1–10
- **LOCK:** DOOR (3, 3, 3)
- **ITEM EXAMPLES:** ABRAXO CLEANER, BURGUNDY BOTTLE, CAMERA, CAN, CONNECTING ROD, COOLANT, ENAMEL BUCKET, GAS CANISTER, FUSION CORE, HALLUCIGEN GAS CANISTER, GLASS JAR, MINI NUKE, ORANGE CANISTER, PACK OF CIGARETTES, SALT, SPICES, STEEL WORKER HAT, TORQUE ROD END, TOY ROCKETSHIP, VOLATILE MATERIALS BOX, WASTE ACID.

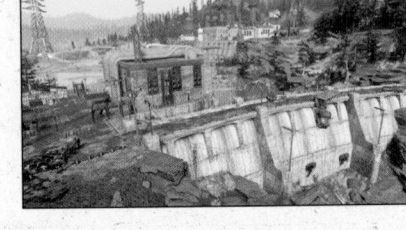

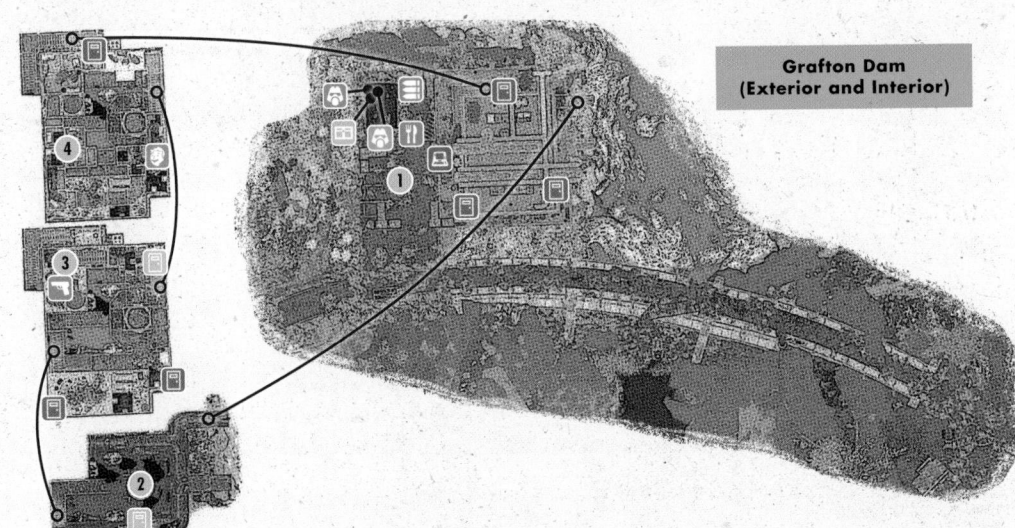

Grafton Dam (Exterior and Interior)

LEGEND

1. PARKING LOT AND STORAGE WAREHOUSE
2. LOWER GENERATOR ROOM
3. WORKBENCH STAIRWELL (TRAP)
4. UPPER MAINTENANCE HUTS

Route 92 to the north of Morgantown crosses the remains of Grafton Dam, on the border between The Forest and Toxic Valley. The irradiated waters of Grafton Lake are being held back by the intact dam wall. The actual dam structure is much more dilapidated and usually overrun by Super Mutants, though this was once a Brotherhood of Steel compound.

Getting into the dam building may be tricky, as the three exterior doors are all locked tight (3). Drop off the northeast exterior balcony onto the large outflow pipe with the skeletal corpse hanging from it. Sneak inside this way. Once inside, head to the ground-level gantry and up two more floors (watching for traps and foes); head to a series of blue metal maintenance huts on the gantry.

41. SLOCUM'S JOE

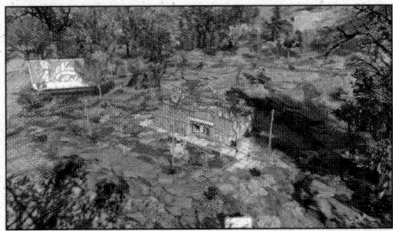

- **CRAFTING:** WATER PUMP, TINKER
- **ITEMS:** ARMS AND ARMOR; HARVESTABLE: RHODODENDRON
- **INFO:** EXPECTED ENEMY: GHOULS, SCORCHED; SCAVENGE RATING: 2; SIZE: 1; THREAT LEVEL: 1–10
- **ITEM EXAMPLES:** COFFEE POT, ENAMEL BUCKET, GAS CANISTER

Though this coffee shop is closed for business, there's a small alcove in the back with a Tinker's bench. Expect Scorched to fire on you from the roof. Use the rusty fire escape to reach this area, where you can leap to the rocks above.

42. GAULEY MINE

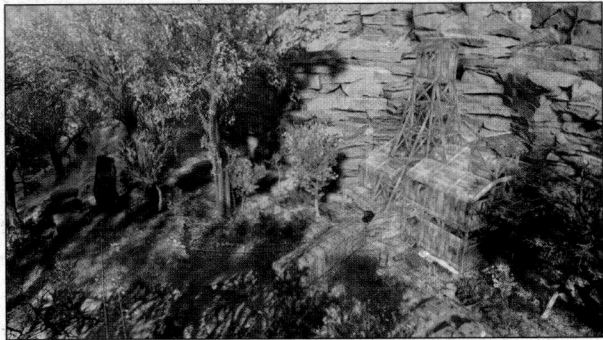

- **COLLECTIBLES:** BOBBLEHEAD (3), HOLOTAPE, MAGAZINE (2)
- **CRAFTING:** WEAPONS
- **DANGER:** EXPLOSIVE CANNISTER! RADIATION!
- **ITEMS:** ARMS AND AMMO; HARVESTABLE: BRAIN FUNGUS, GLOWING FUNGUS; HEALTH AND CHEMS; TRUNK
- **INFO:** EXPECTED ENEMY: IRRADIATED ANIMAL, ROBOT, SCORCHED; SCAVENGE RATING: 3; SIZE: 3; THREAT LEVEL: 1–10
- **LOCK:** SAFE (2)
- **ITEM EXAMPLES:** BAG OF FERTILIZER, BALL PEEN HAMMER, BEER BOTTLE+, COOLANT, CONNECTING ROD, DUCT TAPE+, GAS CANISTER+, GLASS BOWL, ENAMEL BUCKET, LANTERN+, MAKESHIFT BATTERY, PICKAX, PRE-WAR MONEY, TIN CANISTER, USED OIL CAN

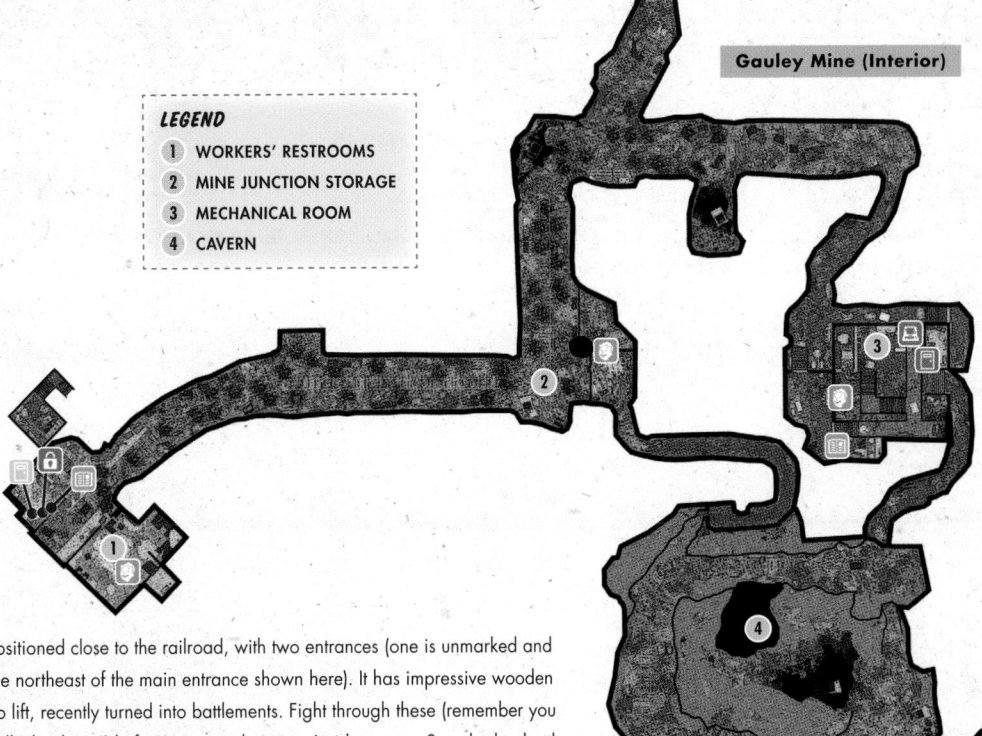

LEGEND
1 WORKERS' RESTROOMS
2 MINE JUNCTION STORAGE
3 MECHANICAL ROOM
4 CAVERN

Gauley Mine (Interior)

This mining facility is positioned close to the railroad, with two entrances (one is unmarked and set into the hillside to the northeast of the main entrance shown here). It has impressive wooden scaffolding and a cargo lift, recently turned into battlements. Fight through these (remember you can descend from the hillside above!) before entering the mine. Inside, expect Scorched to battle you as you work your way through the chambers, finding narrow tunnels to the cavern and the secondary entrance/exit.

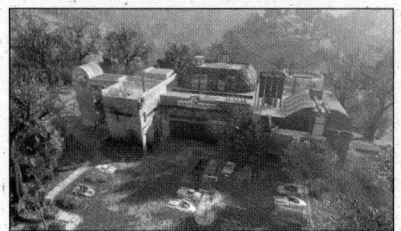

Arktos Pharma (Interior)

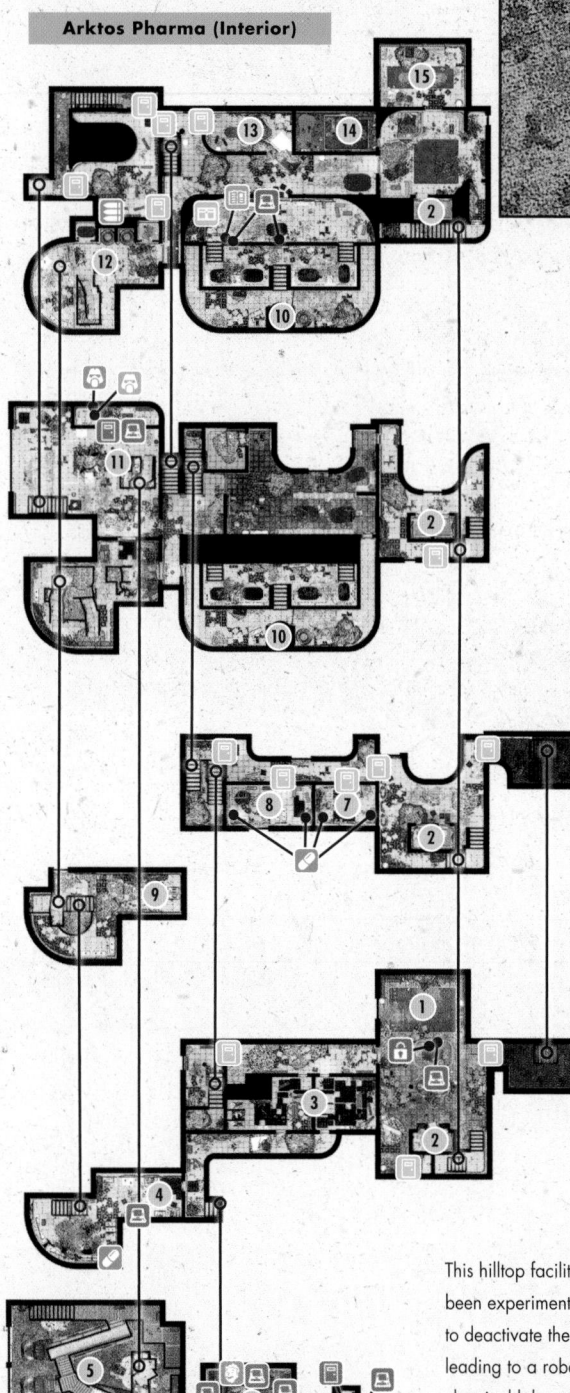

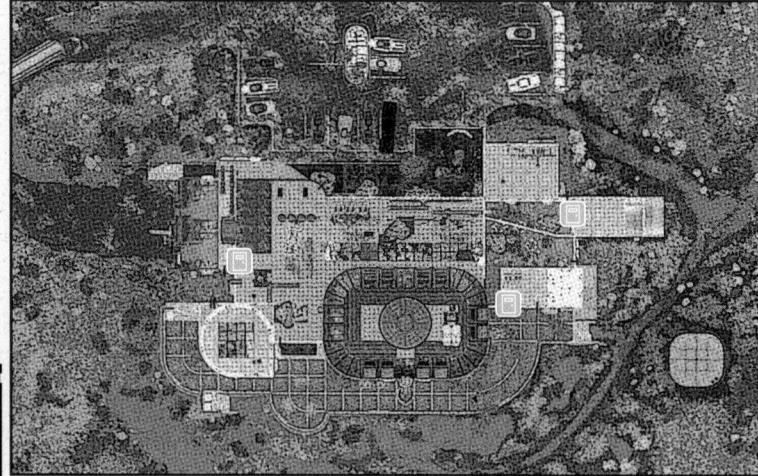

Arktos Pharma (Exterior)

- **COLLECTIBLE:** BOBBLEHEAD, HOLOTAPE, MAGAZINE (2), NUKA-CHERRY, POWER ARMOR
- **CRAFTING:** ARMOR, CHEMISTRY (5), POWER ARMOR, TINKER, WEAPONS
- **DANGER:** EXPLOSIVE CANNISTER! TURRETS!
- **ITEMS:** ARMS AND AMMO; HEALTH AND CHEMS; RECIPE/MOD/PLAN, TRUNK (2); VENDING MACHINE: MEDICINAL SUPPLIES
- **INFO:** EXPECTED ENEMY: SCORCHED, ROBOT, VERTIBOT; SCAVENGE RATING: 3; SIZE: 4; THREAT LEVEL: 1–10.
- **LOCK:** DOOR (0), SAFE (2), TERMINAL X3 (0, 1, 1)
- **ITEM EXAMPLES:** COOLANT, FLASK, FUSION CORE+, HOT PLATE

LEGEND

1. LOBBY
2. ELEVATORS
3. RESTROOMS AND LOCKERS
4. FLORA RESEARCH
5. LOADING DOCK
6. PROTEIN SEQUENCING CHAMBER
7. LABORATORY (EAST)
8. LABORATORY (WEST)
9. OFFICE CUBICLES
10. CARGOBOT CONTROL CHAMBER
11. VERTIBOT DOCK
12. ANIMAL LABORATORY
13. EXECUTIVE CONFERENCE ROOM
14. CEO'S OFFICE
15. EXECUTIVE MEETING ROOM

This hilltop facility is the headquarters of the Arktos Company, an organization that appears to have been experimenting with new strains of plant life. Enter the lobby to hack the terminal (1) if you wish to deactivate the turrets in this facility. Check the unloading area for a security door and terminal (1) leading to a robotron maintenance area. Check the Protein Sequencer Terminal before investigating chemical labs and a large command room with Cargobot Controls. The upper floors can be reached via stairs or planks atop a trailer from the unloading area. Another security terminal (0) allows access to a Power Armor Station (and possible armor). The ruined upper level includes a test chamber and executive offices. Expect your intrusion to summon Vertibots on the roof, which is also accessible via exterior or interior stairs.

44. GREG'S MINE SUPPLY

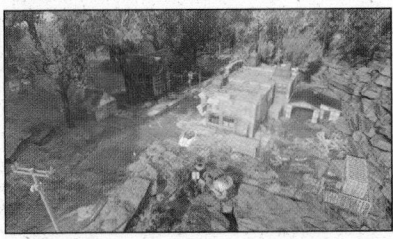

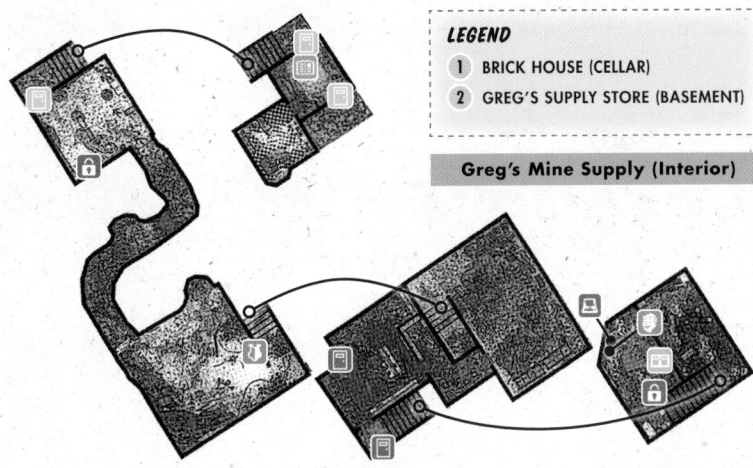

Greg's Mine Supply (Interior)

- **COLLECTIBLES:** BOBBLEHEAD, MAGAZINE, NUKA-CHERRY
- **CRAFTING:** ARMOR, WEAPONS
- **DANGER:** MINES! RADIATION!
- **ITEMS:** HEALTH AND CHEMS, RECIPE/MOD/PLANS, TRUNK
- **INFO:** EXPECTED ENEMY: SCORCHED; SCAVENGE RATING: 3; SIZE: 3; SLEEPING; THREAT LEVEL: 1–10
- **LOCK:** SAFE X2 (0, 1)

- **ITEM EXAMPLES:** ABRAXO CLEANER, ASHTRAY, BEER BOTTLE, BLAMCO BRAND MAC AND CHEESE, COMBINATION WRENCH, COOKING POT, CUTTING BOARD, GARDEN GNOME, GLASS JAR+, GOLD SCRAP, OIL CANISTER, PICKAX, TALL DRINKING GLASS

This hamlet is dominated by Greg's construction store, for all your mining needs! The store is locked up tight, but some enterprising individuals have burrowed under and across the road from the brick house, allowing access through a short tunnel. The supply shop has an upstairs area where you can secure Greg's Mine Supply Keys. Use them to open the door to the side yard.

45. BOLTON GREENS

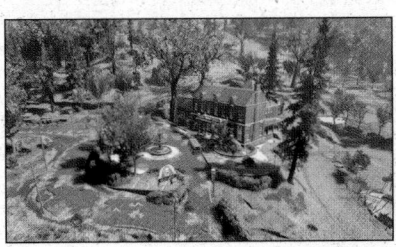

- **COLLECTIBLES:** BOBBLEHEAD (5), HOLOTAPE, MAGAZINE (3)
- **DANGER:** PUNJI BOARD!
- **ITEMS:** ARMS AND AMMO+; HARVESTABLE: SNAPTAIL; HEALTH AND CHEMS; RECIPE/MOD/PLAN+; TRUNK
- **INFO:** EXPECTED ENEMY: SCORCHED; NOTES; SCAVENGE RATING: 3; SIZE: 3; SLEEPING; THREAT LEVEL: 1–10

- **LOCK:** DOOR (X2) (0, 2); SAFE (X2) (1, 2)
- **ITEM EXAMPLES:** BEER, BOILED WATER+, COFFEE CUP, DOLL, ENAMEL BUCKET, GIDDYUP BUTTERCUP, GOLF BALL+, PEPPER+, PLASTIC PUMPKIN, POOL BALL+, SALT+, SUGAR, TELEPHONE, TOY CAR, TRIGGERMAN BOWLER, WINE, WOOD BLOCK+

Bolton Greens (Exterior)

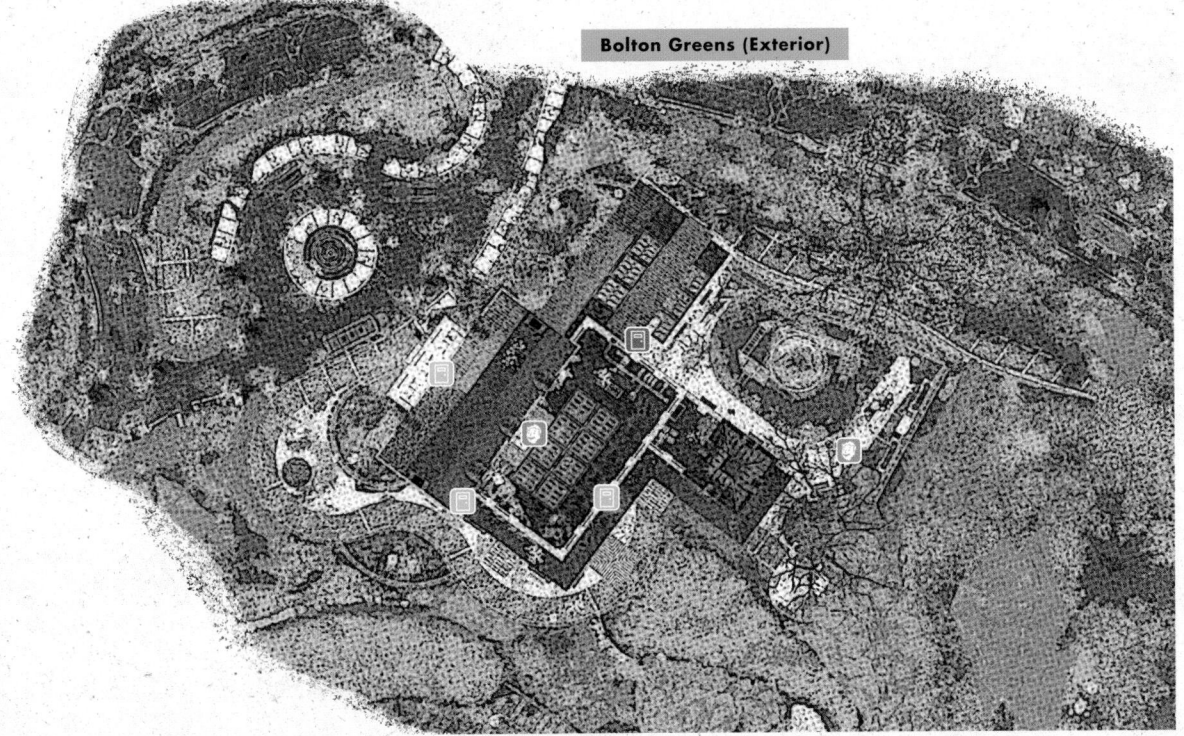

TRAINING

CRAFTING AND C.A.M.P.ING

INVENTORY

QUESTS

ATLAS

BESTIARY

APPENDICES

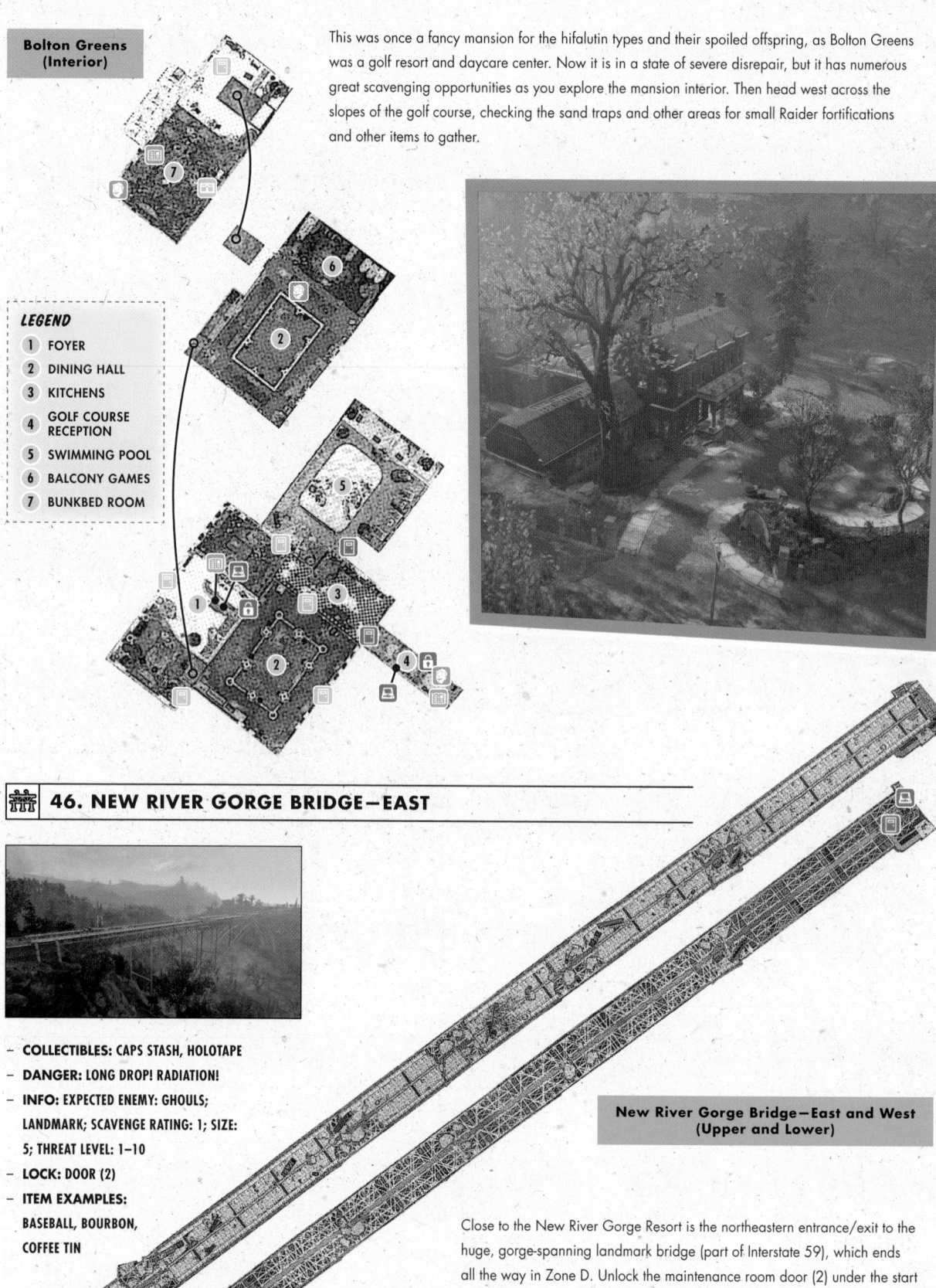

Bolton Greens (Interior)

This was once a fancy mansion for the hifalutin types and their spoiled offspring, as Bolton Greens was a golf resort and daycare center. Now it is in a state of severe disrepair, but it has numerous great scavenging opportunities as you explore the mansion interior. Then head west across the slopes of the golf course, checking the sand traps and other areas for small Raider fortifications and other items to gather.

LEGEND
1. FOYER
2. DINING HALL
3. KITCHENS
4. GOLF COURSE RECEPTION
5. SWIMMING POOL
6. BALCONY GAMES
7. BUNKBED ROOM

46. NEW RIVER GORGE BRIDGE—EAST

- **COLLECTIBLES:** CAPS STASH, HOLOTAPE
- **DANGER:** LONG DROP! RADIATION!
- **INFO:** EXPECTED ENEMY: GHOULS; LANDMARK; SCAVENGE RATING: 1; SIZE: 5; THREAT LEVEL: 1–10
- **LOCK:** DOOR (2)
- **ITEM EXAMPLES:** BASEBALL, BOURBON, COFFEE TIN

New River Gorge Bridge—East and West (Upper and Lower)

Close to the New River Gorge Resort is the northeastern entrance/exit to the huge, gorge-spanning landmark bridge (part of Interstate 59), which ends all the way in Zone D. Unlock the maintenance room door (2) under the start of the eastern span to check a small office. The lengthy bridge span features ruined gantries under a tarmac highway road, with derelict sections to carefully maneuver through. Consult "New River Gorge Bridge—West" for information on the maintenance room on the gorge's opposite (southwest) side.

47. NEW RIVER GORGE RESORT

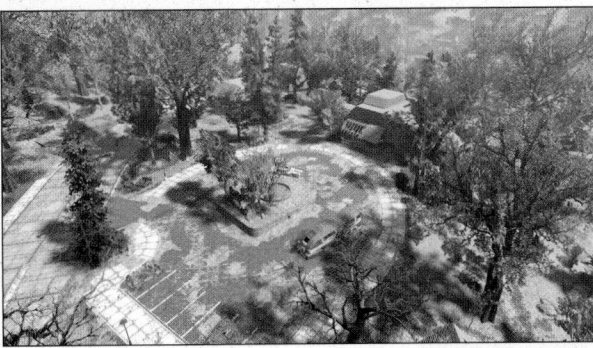

- COLLECTIBLES: BOBBLEHEAD, CAPS STASH, HOLOTAPE
- CRAFTING: COOKING
- ITEMS: ARMS AND AMMO+; HARVESTABLE: GLOWING FUNGUS, RHODODENDRON, SOOT FLOWER; HEALTH AND CHEMS++; RECIPES/MODS/PLANS
- INFO: EXPECTED ENEMY: GHOULS, IRRADIATED INSECTS, MIRELURKS; SCAVENGE RATING: 3; SIZE: 3; THREAT LEVEL: 1–10
- LOCK: SAFE (1)
- ITEM EXAMPLES: ABRAXO CLEANER, ANTISEPTIC, AUTOPSY BOARD GAME, BLAST RADIUS BOARD GAME, CAMERA, EMPTY MILK BOTTLE, FLIP LIGHTER, LANTERN, OVEN MITT, SCREWDRIVER, WAKEMASTER ALARM CLOCK, WOODEN BLOCK.

The majority of this dilapidated resort is located on the south side of Interstate 59. It consists of a main lodge, a swimming pool, and a few cabins dotted around. All are accessible in some way (one you enter via the floor). This is a good choice for a scavenging mission after you visit Flatwoods.

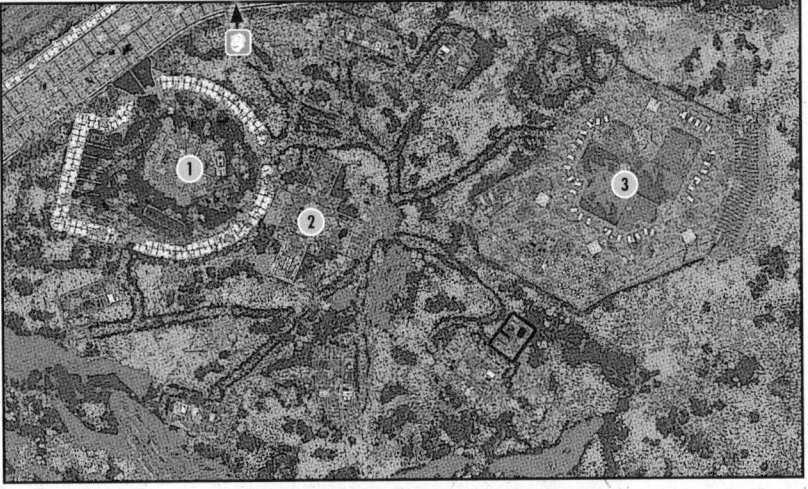

LEGEND
1. PARKING LOT
2. MAIN LODGE
3. SWIMMING POOL

New River Gorge Resort (Exterior)

NEW RIVER GORGE NATURE TRAIL AND ADVENTURE PARK

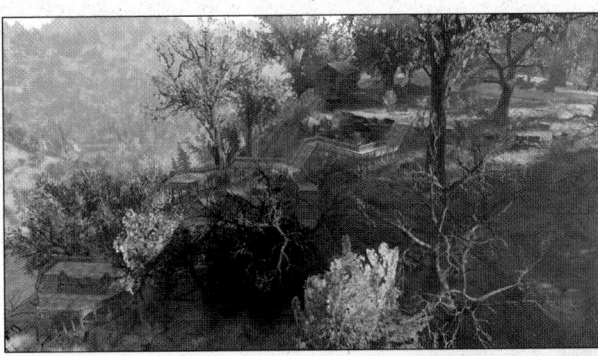

Technically located in Zone A but part of the resort, this wooded area has a nature trail, numerous wooden deck platforms, a covered picnic area with great views of the gorge bridge, and an adventure path: Test your jumping dexterity with a series of increasingly narrower platforms, ending with some precision jumping across log poles to a small tower with a possible Bobblehead prize.

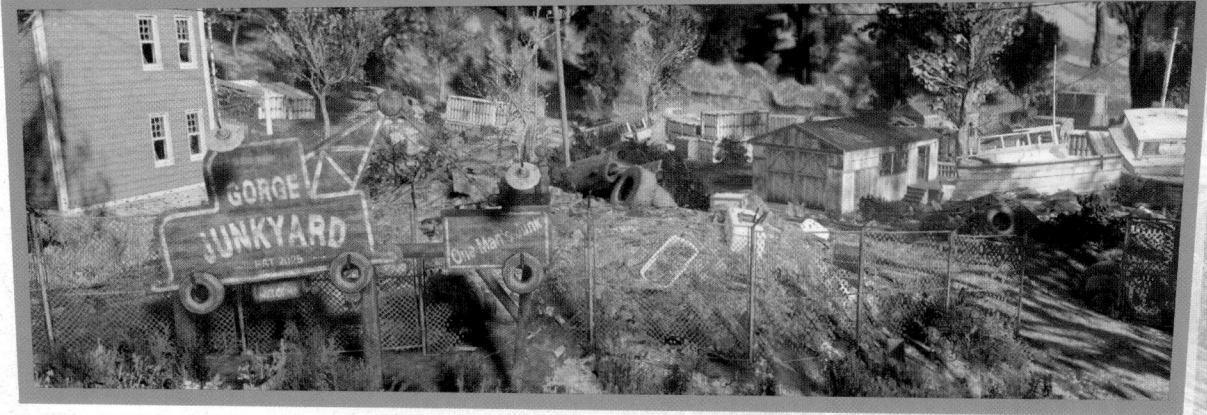

TRAINING

CRAFTING AND C.A.M.P.ING

INVENTORY

QUESTS

ATLAS

BESTIARY

APPENDICES

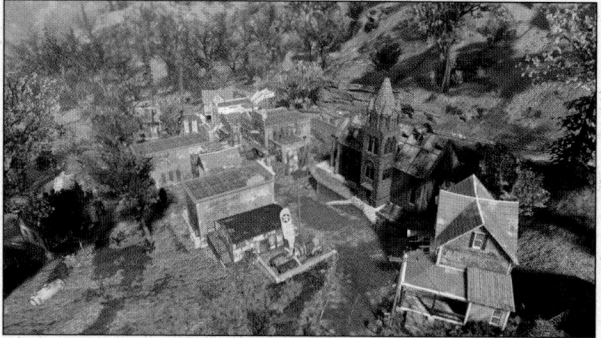

- **COLLECTIBLES:** BOBBLEHEAD (2), HOLOTAPE (OVERSEER), MAGAZINE (2)
- **CRAFTING:** ARMOR, CHEMISTRY, TINKER, WEAPONS
- **ITEMS:** ARMS AND AMMO+, HEALTH AND CHEMS, MY STASH BOX, TRUNK
- **INFO:** EXPECTED ENEMY: IRRADIATED ANIMALS, SCORCHED; NOTES; SCAVENGE RATING: 4; SIZE: 4; SLEEPING; THREAT LEVEL: 1–10
- **LOCK:** SAFE X3 (0, 2, 2)
- **ITEM EXAMPLES:** 2 MM ELECTROMAGNETIC CARTRIDGE, ABRAXO CLEANER INDUSTRIAL GRADE, ADJUSTABLE WRENCH, ALARM CLOCK, ALUMINUM CANISTER, BEER BOTTLE+, BLAST RADIUS BOARD GAME, COFFEE CUP+, CIRCUITS, ENAMEL BUCKET, PILLOW, PLUNGER, SOAP, TALL DRINKING GLASS+, TIN PITCHER+, WONDERGLUE.

The town of Sutton was once a major hub for the timber industry, with an excellent transportation network (the I-59 and railroad) and nearby train station (also shown on the map). Now the place shows the signs of recent Raider activity. A ramshackle wall prevents progress down Main Street. Use the roof planks and building interiors to navigate through and around. Scavenge at the indicated places of interest; grab whatever you need, as there's a My Stash Box at the Red Rocket Gas Station. Pay particular attention to the blue house at the north (lower) end of Main Street; it has a packed cellar and an Overseer Holotape upstairs: This is the Overseer's childhood home.

LEGEND

1. METAL TRAILER
2. THE BLUE HOUSE
3. RED ROCKET GAS STATION
4. METAL SHED
5. LIQUOR STORE
6. CLOTHING SHOP
7. RAIDER WALL
8. CHURCH
9. MECHANIC'S SHED
10. SUTTON STATION

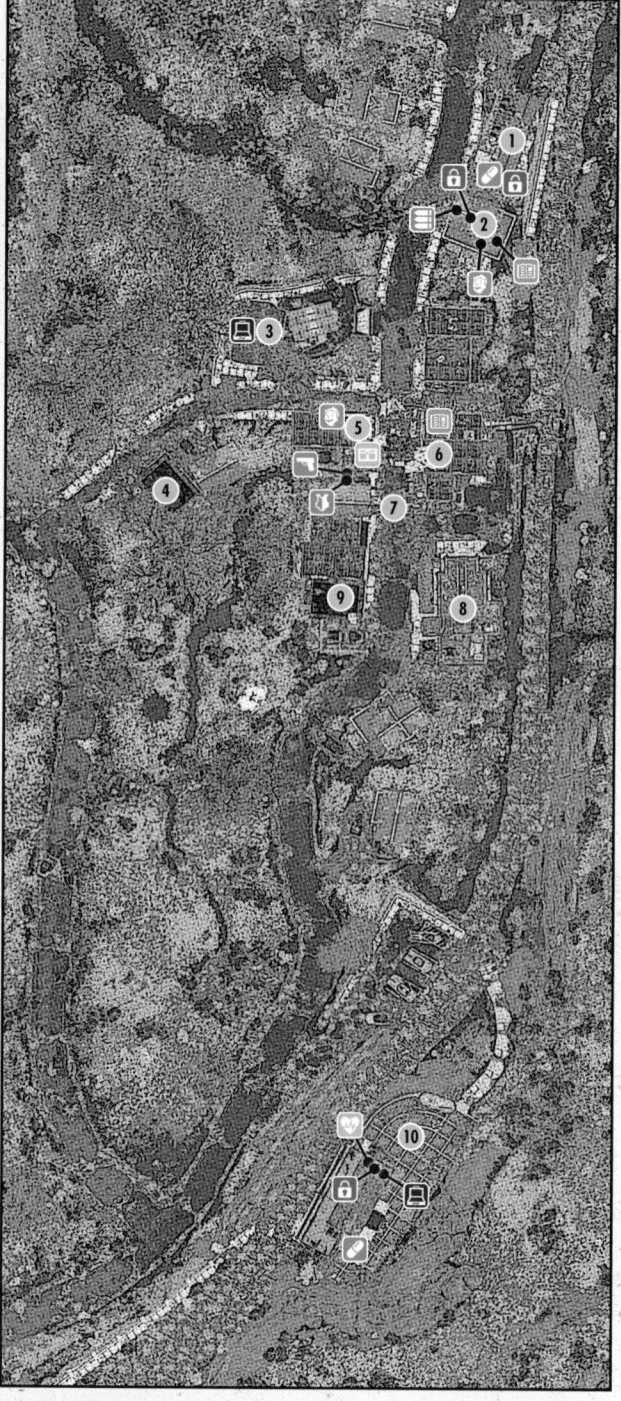

Sutton (Exterior)

🧩 **49. SUTTON STATION**

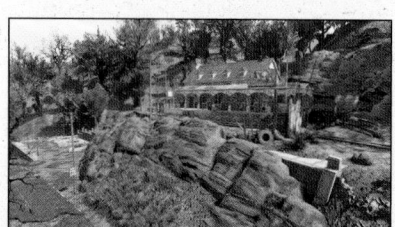

- **COLLECTIBLES:** CAPS STASH, NUKA-CHERRY
- **CRAFTING:** CHEMISTRY
- **ITEMS:** HEALTH AND CHEMS; MY STASH BOX; VENDING MACHINE: AMMO, MEDICAL SUPPLIES
- **INFO:** INSTRUMENT; NOTES; SCAVENGE RATING: 3; SIZE: 1; THREAT LEVEL: 1–10; TRADER: VENDOR BOT

- **ITEM EXAMPLES:** BEER BOTTLE, BOBBY PIN BOX, DIRTY POSTMAN HAT, GARDEN GNOME, TOILET PAPER+

To the south of Sutton, along the road and on higher ground, is the town's train station. The main station structure is in relatively good shape, offering a place to stash your belongings and purchase more from the Vendor Bot.

50. EAST KANAWHA LOOKOUT

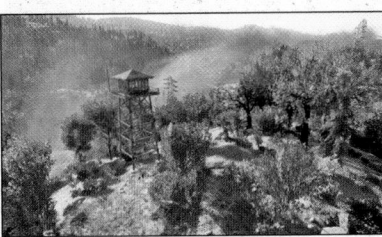

- COLLECTIBLE: CAPS STASH
- DANGER: LONG DROP!
- ITEMS: HARVESTABLE: RHODODENDRON, SILT BEAN, SOOT FLOWER
- INFO: EXPECTED ENEMY: GHOULS; LANDMARK; SCAVENGE RATING: 2; SIZE: 1; SLEEPING; SURVEY AREA; THREAT LEVEL: 1–10.

- ITEM EXAMPLES: COMBINATION WRENCH, MAKESHIFT BATTERY, RANGER HAT, RANGER OUTFIT, TOY CAR, WOODEN BLOCK.

This relatively sturdy lookout tower offers excellent views of Sutton, and the countryside north and east. Climb to the top to find new locations and access a HELP terminal.

51. HELVETIA

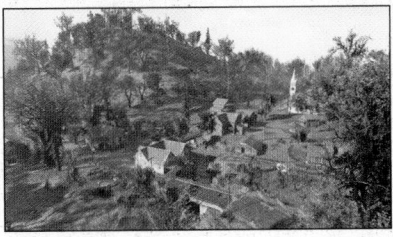

- CRAFTING: CHEMISTRY, COOKING, WATER PUMP, WEAPONS (2)
- DANGER: RADIATION!
- ITEMS: ARMS AND AMMO; HARVESTABLE: WOOD; HEALTH AND CHEMS++
- INFO: EXPECTED ENEMY: IRRADIATED ANIMALS, SCORCHED; INSTRUMENTS; NOTES; RECIPE/MOD/PLANS; SCAVENGE RATING: 5; SIZE: 3; THREAT LEVEL: 1–10

- COLLECTIBLES: CAPS STASH, HOLOTAPE

- LOCK: DOOR (1), SAFE X2 (1, 3)
- ITEM EXAMPLES: ASHTRAY, BLAST RADIUS BOARD GAME, BOILED WATER+, CANNED DOG FOOD, COFFEE CUP, DESK FAN, DUCT TAPE, HONEY, PEPPER, POOL BALLS, PORTABLE FUEL TANK, POTATO CRISPS, SALT, SUGAR BOMBS, TALL DRINKING GLASS, TEAPOT, TEDDY BEAR, TYPEWRITER, WHISKEY

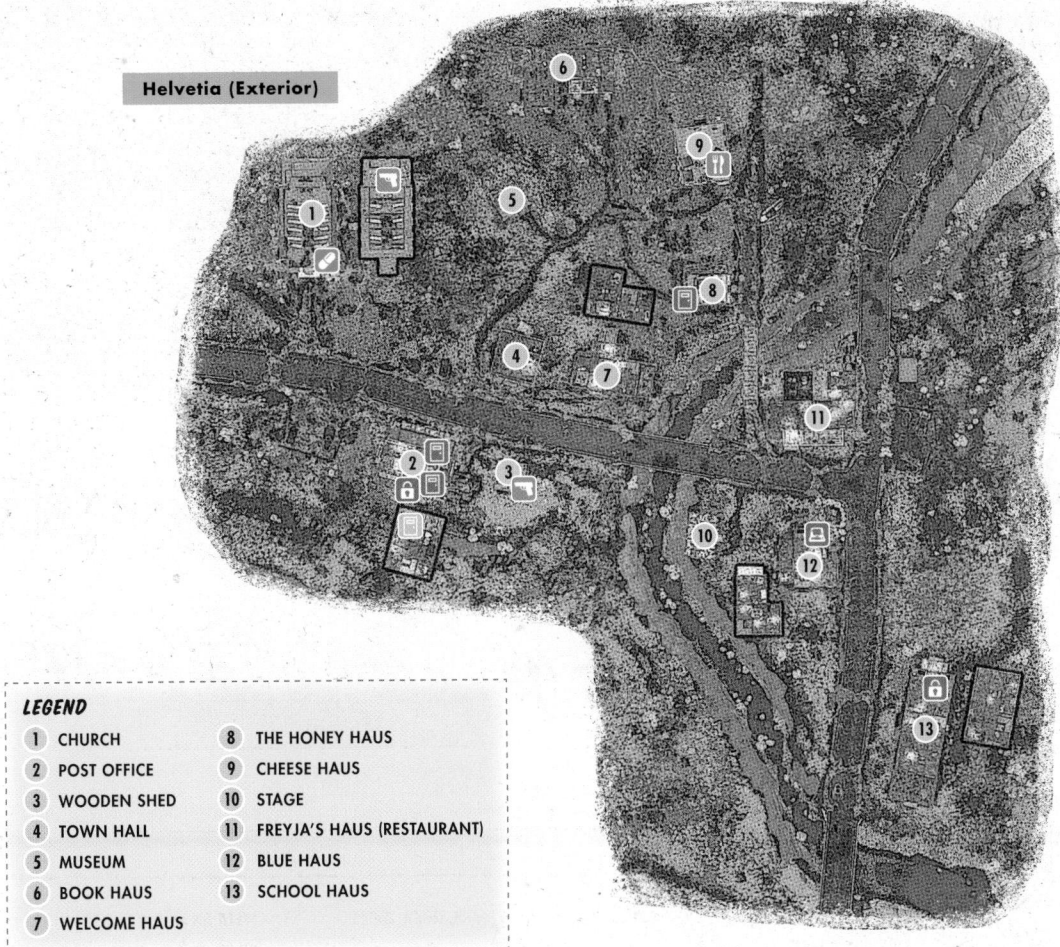

Helvetia (Exterior)

LEGEND

1	CHURCH	8	THE HONEY HAUS
2	POST OFFICE	9	CHEESE HAUS
3	WOODEN SHED	10	STAGE
4	TOWN HALL	11	FREYJA'S HAUS (RESTAURANT)
5	MUSEUM	12	BLUE HAUS
6	BOOK HAUS	13	SCHOOL HAUS
7	WELCOME HAUS		

Settled by Swiss and German immigrants after the Civil War, Helvetia was known for its Fasnacht festival, where grotesque masks were worn by revelers. Perhaps this headgear can be found when an Event of the same name is active? Check the settlement along Pickens Road for scavengable items. The church shows signs of cultist (and chem addict) activity. The post office front door is locked (1), but you can climb up the metal lean-to and through the upper balcony door. The other structures have a variety of odd and helpful junk items to gather.

✈ 52. HORIZON'S REST

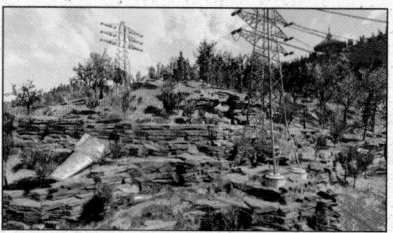

Horizon's Rest (Exterior)

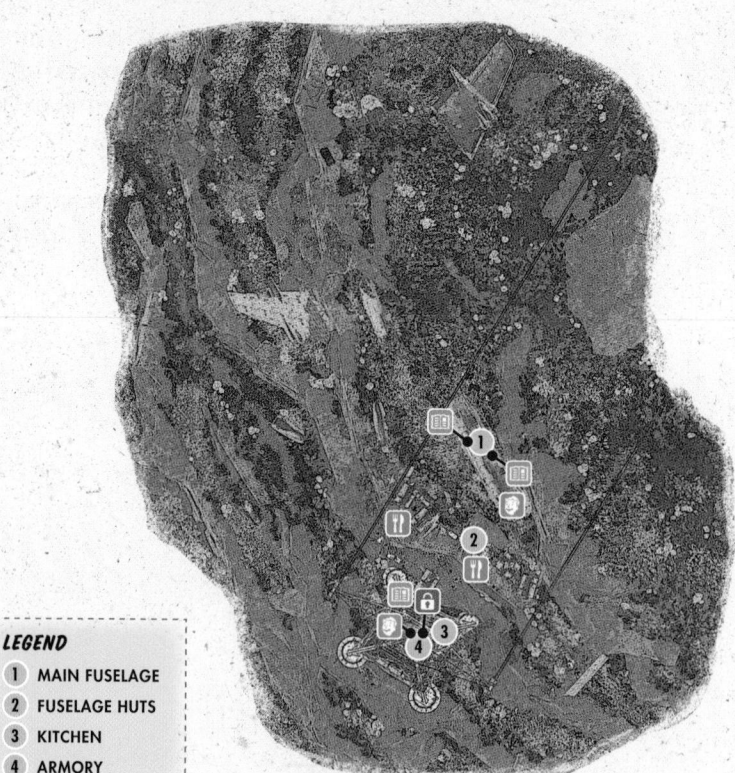

- **COLLECTIBLES:** BOBBLEHEAD (2), MAGAZINE (3)
- **CRAFTING:** COOKING (2)
- **DANGER:** LONG DROP!
- **ITEM:** ARMS AND ARMOR++; HARVESTABLE: RHODODENDRON, SOOT FLOWER; HEALTH AND CHEMS; RECIPE/MOD/PLAN
- **INFO:** EXPECTED ENEMY: SCORCHED, SUPER MUTANT; SCAVENGE RATING: 4; SIZE: 3; SLEEPING; THREAT LEVEL: 1–10
- **LOCK:** SAFE (1)
- **ITEM EXAMPLES:** ADJUSTABLE WRENCH, BEER BOTTLE++, COMBAT ARMOR HELMET, COOKING PAN, COOKING POT+, DESK FAN, HACK SAW, HOT PLATE, OVEN MITT, PAINT CAN+, RED PLATE+, SALT+ TALL DRINKING GLASS, TIN CAN+, WOODEN SPOON, YELLOW TABLE LIGHT

LEGEND
1 MAIN FUSELAGE
2 FUSELAGE HUTS
3 KITCHEN
4 ARMORY

The remains of a Horizon flight that struck the hillside and a nearby electrical pylon have been fashioned into a rudimentary camp, which is now under the control of more base creatures. The upper camp consists of the fuselage and sections of plane constructed into small huts. Descend the precarious cliff to cross to the pylon platforms, where a kitchen and numerous shanty huts are located, including a small armory (with a key to find back at the Fuselage Huts, under a flower pot).

🌴 53. RELAY TOWER HN-B1-12

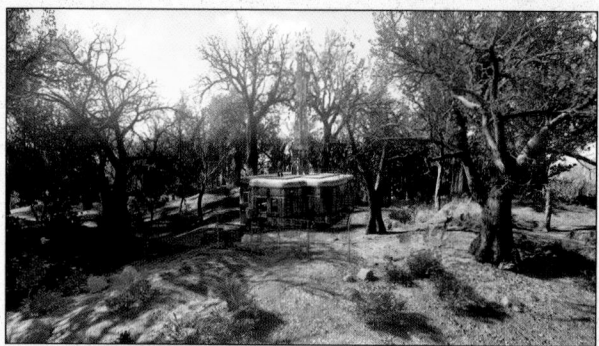

- **COLLECTIBLES:** BOBBLEHEAD, HOLOTAPE, MAGAZINE
- **DANGER:** EXPLOSIVE CANNISTER! TURRETS!
- **ITEMS:** HARVESTABLE: BLACKBERRY; HEALTH AND CHEMS
- **INFO:** EXPECTED ENEMY: SUPER MUTANT; EVENT: ALWAYS VIGILANT; SCAVENGE RATING: 2; SIZE: 1; THREAT LEVEL: 1–10
- **ITEM EXAMPLES:** ADJUSTABLE WRENCH, BOILED WATER+, DUCT TAPE, OFFICE DESK FAN, PACK OF CIGARETTES, SUGAR BOMBS

A small relay tower is located in the upper woodland area, close to the crashed plane. Watch for turrets on the exterior corner of the structure's roof. Feel free to access and repair the Emergency Management System Relay Terminal inside the building.

🧢 54. WHITE POWDER WINTER SPORTS

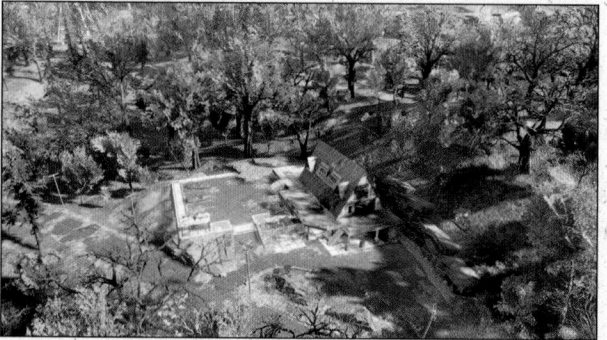

- **COLLECTIBLES:** CAPS STASH, NUKA-CHERRY
- **CRAFTING:** COOKING, WEAPONS
- **ITEMS:** ARMS AND AMMO; HARVESTABLE: SOOT FLOWER; RECIPE/MOD/PLAN
- **INFO:** EXPECTED ENEMY: IRRADIATED ANIMALS, GHOULS; SCAVENGE RATING: 2; SIZE: 1; THREAT LEVEL: 1–10
- **LOCK:** SAFE (0)
- **ITEM EXAMPLES:** BOILED WATER, BURGER TRAY, HOT DOG, NUKA-COLA CUP+, SKIING OUTFIT HAT, TALL DRINKING GLASS, TEDDY BEAR

A chalet-sized store and outside eating area is now slowly decomposing at the foot of the mountains near the western side of the Savage Divide. Check the lower diner for more scavenging potential and a safe.

55. TYGART WATER TREATMENT

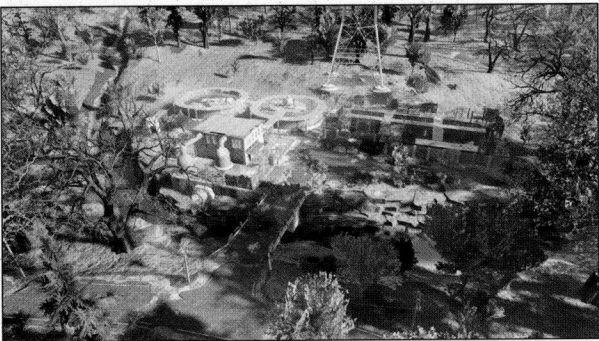

- **COLLECTIBLES:** BOBBLEHEAD, CAPS STASH, MAGAZINE
- **CRAFTING:** ARMOR, COOKING (X2)
- **DANGER:** RADIATION!
- **ITEMS:** ARMS AND AMMO; HEALTH AND CHEMS; RECIPE/MOD/PLAN; TRUNK
- **INFO:** EXPECTED ENEMY: ROBOT; SCAVENGE RATING: 2; SIZE: 2; SLEEPING; THREAT LEVEL: 1–10
- **LOCK:** DOOR (X2) (I, I)
- **ITEM EXAMPLES:** BEER BOTTLE, DIRTY ASHTRAY, LANTERN, PEPPER, RADAWAY (DILUTED), TEDDY BEAR, TIN CAN

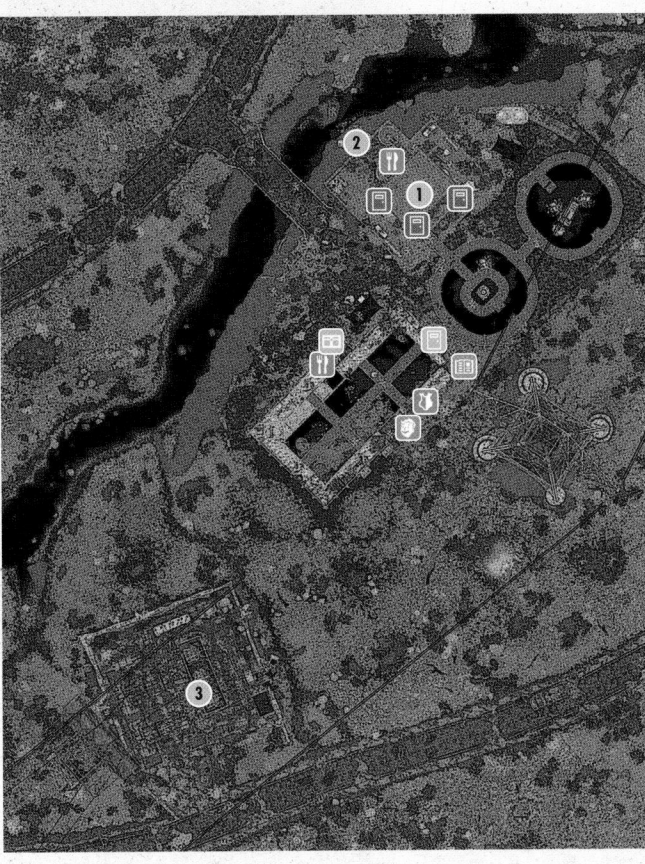

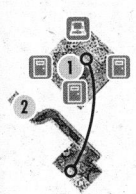

Tygart Water Treatment (Exterior)

LEGEND

1. DRAINAGE PIPE
2. CONTROL HUT
3. PRIMARY LOCATION: POSEIDON POWER SUBSTATION PX-02

This compact and excellent defensive location features a river to the west and a high barbed-wire fence surrounding the facility. Most of the fencing is still intact, and getting into the plant's vat walkways can be tough, as the control hut's doors are locked from the inside. Either jump from the Raider-built platform, across the top of the barbed-wire fence near the blown-out wall terminal and sandbags, or head in via the lower drainage pipe by the river. Once inside the control hut, use the interior wall terminal to open all doors.

56. POSEIDON POWER SUBSTATION PX-02

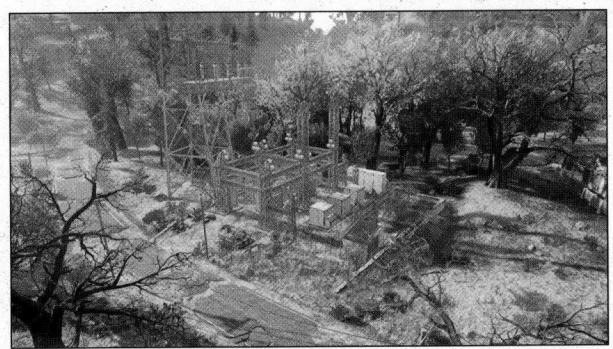

- **ITEMS:** ARMS AND AMMO; **HARVESTABLE:** LOGS, SOOT FLOWER
- **INFO:** C.A.M.P. POWER; EXPECTED ENEMY: MOLE RAT; SCAVENGE RATING: 1; SIZE: 1; THREAT LEVEL: 1–10
- **ITEM EXAMPLES:** BALL-PEEN HAMMER, LOOSE SCREWS, SCREWDRIVER, WASTE ACID

Just northeast of a blockade over the river, with a tractor and some scavengable items, is a small power substation between two electrical pylons. Check the power box near the green portable toilets if you need to quickly power up your C.A.M.P.

TRAINING

CRAFTING AND C.A.M.P.ING

INVENTORY

QUESTS

ATLAS

BESTIARY

APPENDICES

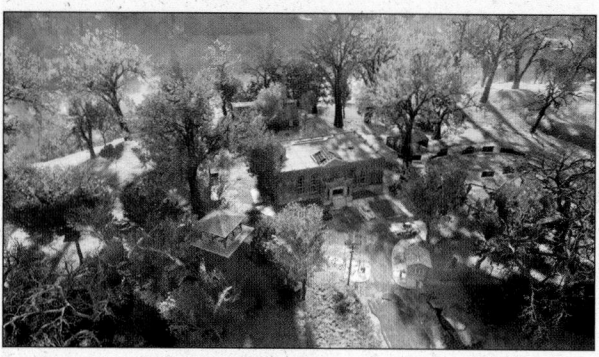

- **COLLECTIBLES:** HOLOTAPE, MAGAZINE
- **CRAFTING:** ARMOR, WEAPONS
- **ITEMS:** ARMS AND AMMO+; HARVESTABLE: RHODODENDRON, SOOT FLOWER; HEALTH AND CHEMS+; OVERSEER'S CACHE; VENDING MACHINE: AMMUNITION; UNIFORM DISPENSER
- **INFO:** EXPECTED ENEMY: ROBOT; NOTES; QUEST: BACK TO BASIC; SCAVENGE RATING: 4; SIZE: 4; SLEEPING; THREAT LEVEL: 1–10
- **LOCK:** DOOR (0), SAFE (1)
- **ITEM EXAMPLES:** ALARM CLOCK, BASEBALL GLOVE, BLOOD PACK, BOILED WATER+, BOWIE KNIFE, COMBAT ARMOR HELMET, COMFY PILLOW, CRAM, DESK FAN, DUCT TAPE, EMPTY WILLOW BUD VASE, ENAMEL BUCKET, EXTINGUISHER, FANCY HAIRBRUSH, HALLUCIGEN GAS CANISTER, INSTAMASH, MILITARY AMMO BAG, SALT, SILVER POCKET WATCH, SMALL LEFT ANTLER, TABLE KNIFE, TALL DRINKING GLASS, TIN PITCHER, TOASTER, TOILET PAPER, TRIFOLD AMERICAN FLAG+, TV DINNER TRAY, WHISKEY, YELLOW FLIGHT HELMET, YELLOW PLATE

Camp McClintock: Main Building (Interior)

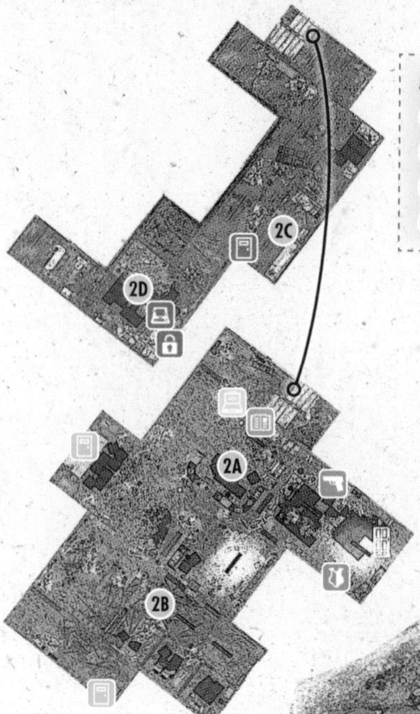

LEGEND

2A RECEPTION
2B OFFICES
2C EQUIPMENT CLOSET
2D ADMINISTRATION OFFICE

Camp McClintock (Exterior)

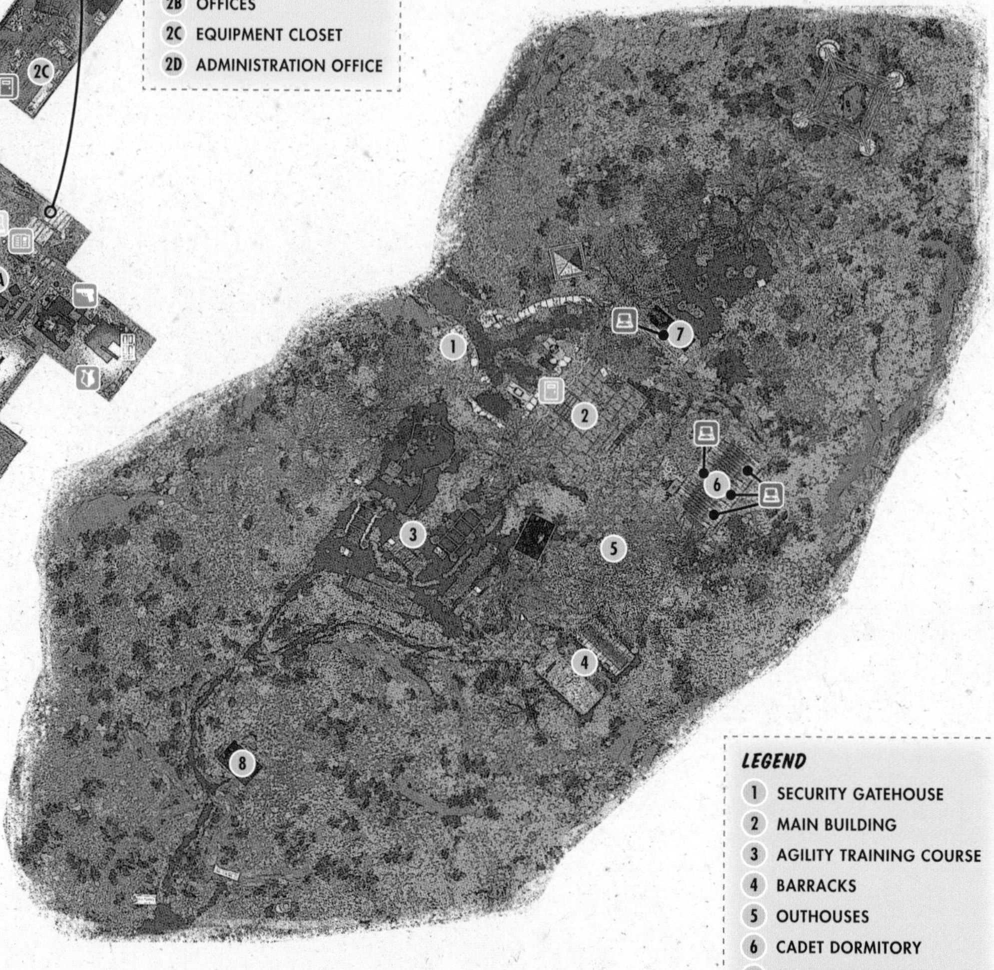

LEGEND

1 SECURITY GATEHOUSE
2 MAIN BUILDING
3 AGILITY TRAINING COURSE
4 BARRACKS
5 OUTHOUSES
6 CADET DORMITORY
7 SHOOTING RANGE
8 LIVE FIRE EXERCISE RANGE

A military academy, where robotic Master Sergeants hone and chisel raw recruits into the fighting force of the future! The Mr. Gutsys here are still programmed to train, so expect them to holler but remain non-hostile. The base itself consists of a large area of hilltop woodlands that extends farther southwest than you'd think and is dotted with various barracks, ranges, and other structures.

ZONE C: SECONDARY LOCATIONS

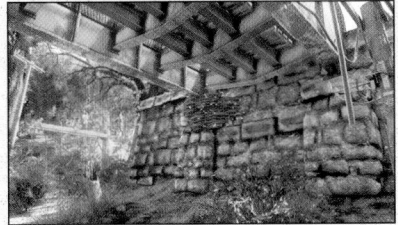

Beehive: Under Grafton Rail Bridge

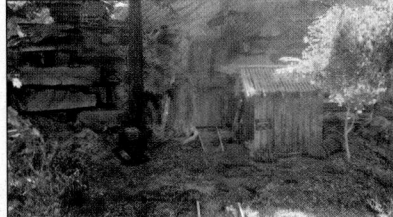

Gauley Mine Exit

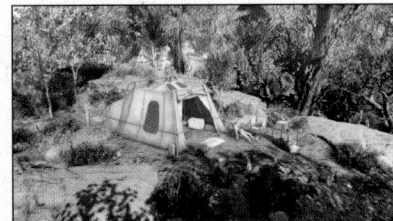

Forest and Rock Camp

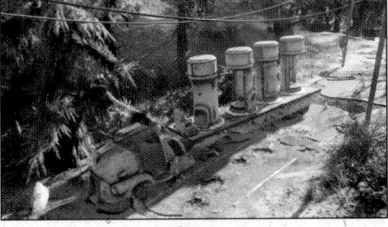

Pulowski Preservation Shelter Transport (Route 91)

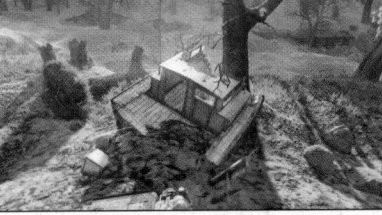

Broken Boat and River Debris

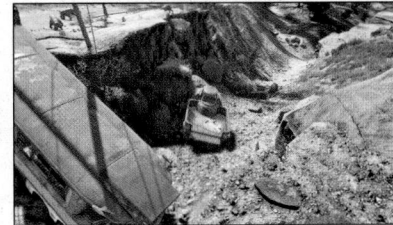

Road Subsidence (Route 91)

Appalachia: **The Forest (Zone C) – Secondary Locations**

ZONE C

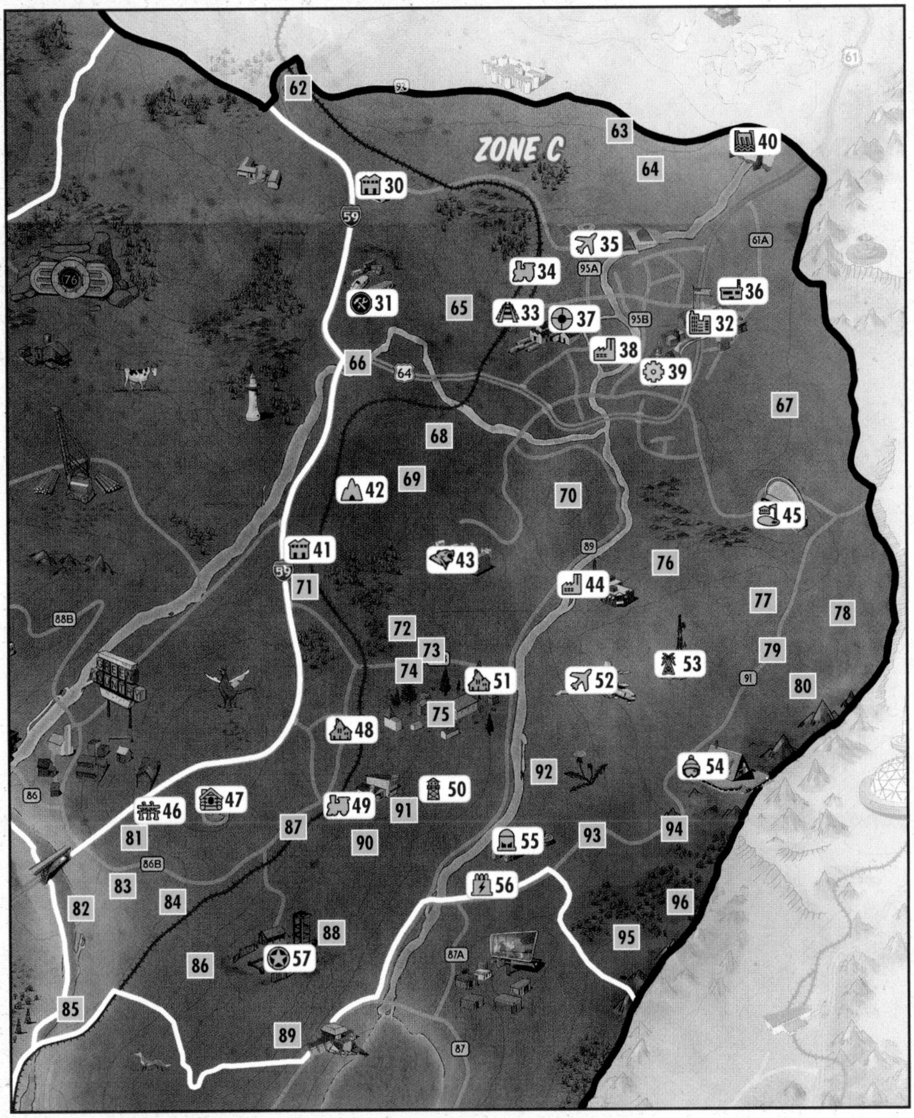

TRAINING

CRAFTING AND C.A.M.P.ING

INVENTORY

QUESTS

ATLAS

BESTIARY

APPENDICES

#	NAME	DESCRIPTION
62	Beehive: Under Grafton Rail Bridge	Gather honey and try not to get stung at this beehive, stuck on the underside of the rail bridge.
63	Crash on Route 92	If you inspect this vehicle crash closely, you'll see just how horrific the accident was.
64	Responder Tent	Learn the basics of C.A.M.P. management from the Protectron in the woods north of Morgantown.
65	Beehive: Woods West of Morgantown	Gather honey and try not to get stung at this beehive, stuck on a tree on a rocky hillside.
66	Gravel Pit Bus	A school bus, used as a camp (watch for traps!), close to a good source of concrete scraps.
67	The Ailurophile's Farm	A small farm with crops, cats, and some interesting trophy heads adorning the home's interior.
68	Gauley Mine Exit	The exit from inside Gauley Mine, offering quick access to the railroad tracks and Morgantown.
69	Green Tent Camp	A green tent in the woods, with basic camping equipment, just east of Gauley Mine.
70	Forest and Rock Camp	A tent in a relatively small and flat area of rocks, in the forest north of Greg's Mine Supply.
71	The Sutton Salmon House	A salmon-colored house with garage and kennel and an interior (with a safe) to explore.
72	The Emergency Outhouse	An outhouse with a First Aid Box on the side of it, in the woods north of Helvetia.
73	Picnic Area and Trail (Helvetia)	A flat-topped hill offers some great picnicking opportunities, providing you aren't being mauled by the denizens of Helvetia.
74	Cargo Box Pickup (Route 86B)	A rusty pickup with items to scavenge from the back of it, stranded on the road from Helvetia.
75	Helvetia Hill Tent	A small tent above the town on a rocky bluff, with views north toward the hilltop Pharma facility.
76	Military Comms Tower Bolton	A small, quest-related comms dish sitting on an electrical pylon platform with a cooking station and a mounted machine-gun golf cart.
77	Bolton Greens Lookout	A lookout tower on the hill south of Bolton Greens.
78	The Radstag Hunter's Pylon Camp	Platforms and hanging meat from one of the large electrical pylons.
79	Pulowski Preservation Shelter Transport (Route 91)	A truck bringing a quartet of tube shelters has stopped for a fallen branch. Ransack all four shelters; one has duffel bags in it.

#	NAME	DESCRIPTION
80	Yao Guai Cave Alcove	A shallow rock alcove and cliff where mutated bears like to prowl.
81	Beehive: Under New River Gorge Bridge—East	Gather honey and try not to get stung at this beehive, stuck on a tree below the bridge.
82	Broken Boat and River Debris	Silt Bean grows where the river left its boat and vehicle-related debris deposits, in the gorge beneath the bridge.
83	Rotten Tent	A copper deposit and a drab camp next to the road.
84	Soapy Skeleton	A skeletal wallowing in a bathtub full of soap, under an electrical pylon. This will keep you in oil for a bit!
85	Scuppered Boat and Bathtub	A white boat, broken in half, sits where a river used to be, close to a duffel bag in a bathtub.
86	Beehive: Camp McClintock	Gather honey and try not to get stung at this beehive, stuck all around a tree trunk.
87	Road and Rail Truck Camp	A small concrete breeze block defense near a rusting vehicle and a skeleton guarded by his red Garden Gnome friend.
88	Teddy's RV Room Under the Pylon	A strange locked door (0) with no walls leading to a TV-watching bear pair, under the electrical pylon.
89	Chem and Hoop Shack	David seems to be the better hoop player at this hillside shack with a Chemistry Workbench and a small wood bridge with basketballs.
90	The Red Shed	A small shed with a birdhouse nailed to the tree next to it, as well as some items to scavenge.
91	Truck Trailer Camp	A red big-rig trailer; now a small camp in the ravine southeast of Sutton.
92	River Bend Canoe Camp	Two canoes, a submerged corpse, and a quaint little turn in the river where you can use the cooking station. Just watch for undesirables.
93	Tygart Scrap Truck (191)	A flatbed truck has spilled its scrap on the steep hill east of Tygart Water Treatment.
94	Road Subsidence (Route 91)	A coach has hit a dip in the road, along with a rusty pickup you can check for bottles.
95	The Violinist's Picnic	The radio may still be playing as you reach a skeletal violinist slumped against a tree; he stopped serenading a while ago.
96	One Man and His Dog	By a rusting pickup: The final resting place of a man and his best friend, both now worm meat.

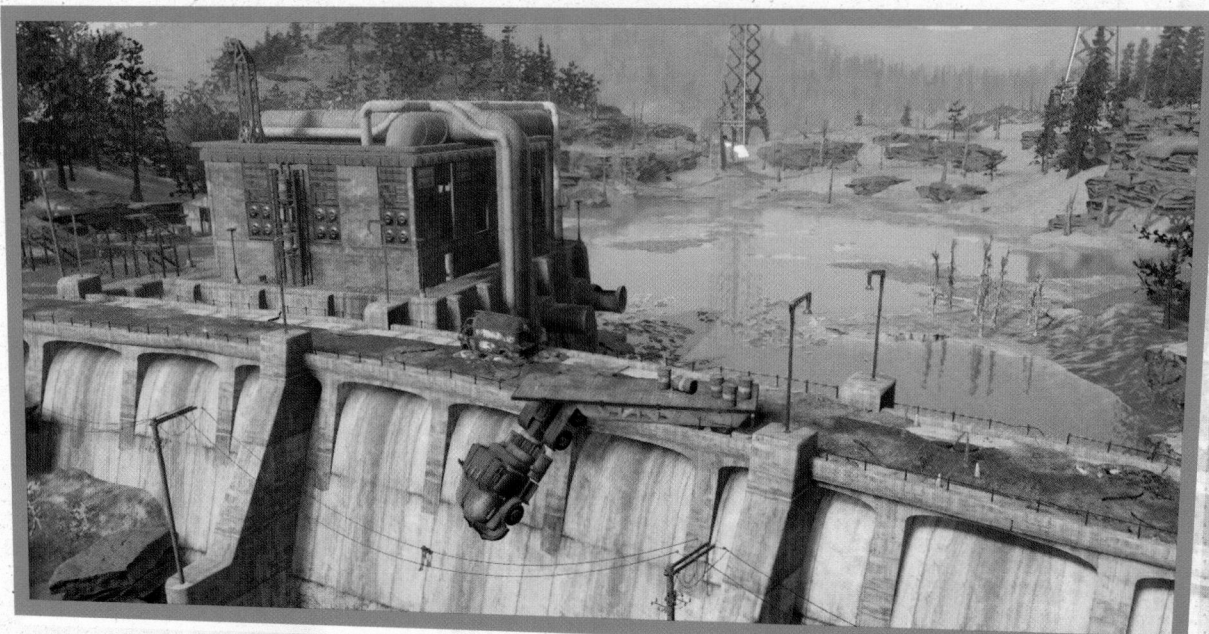

THE FOREST: ZONE D—SOUTHWEST FOREST

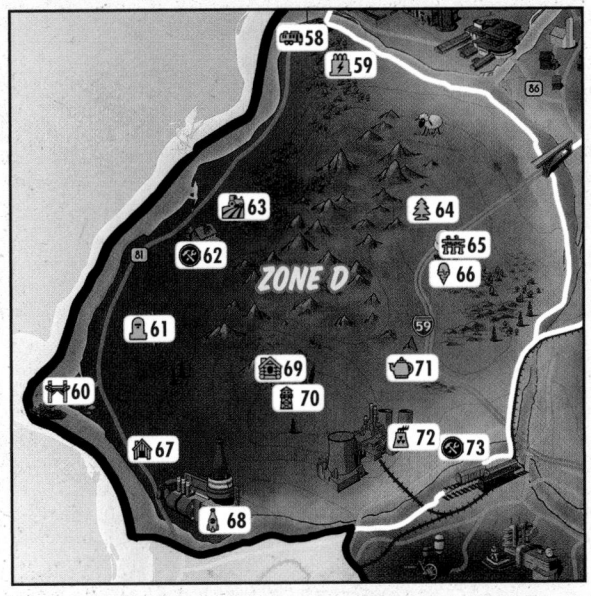

WORLD MAP LEGEND

— REGION BOUNDARY   — ZONE BOUNDARY

PRIMARY LOCATIONS

				icon	NAME
				🚌 58	HILLFOLK HOTDOGS
				🏚 59	POSEIDON POWER SUBSTATION PX-01
1		1		⛩ 60	OHIO RIVER ADVENTURES
		1		⚰ 61	KANAWHA COUNTY CEMETERY
				⊗ 62	BILLINGS HOMESTEAD
2		2	1	🏚 63	SILVA HOMESTEAD
				🌲 64	ORWELL ORCHARDS
			1	🌉 65	NEW RIVER GORGE BRIDGE—WEST
				🍦 66	COW SPOTS CREAMERY
3		3	1	🏛 67	LEWIS & SONS FARMING SUPPLY
3	3	3	1	🏭 68	KANAWHA NUKA-COLA PLANT
			1	🏠 69	CAMP ADAMS
				🗼 70	CAMP ADAMS LOOKOUT
2		2		🫖 71	THE GIANT TEAPOT
5	21	8	1	🏭 72	POSEIDON ENERGY PLANT WV-06
				⊗ 73	POSEIDON ENERGY PLANT YARD

■ BOBBLEHEADS   ■ CAP STASHES   ■ MAGAZINES   ■ POWER ARMOR

Though The Forest is technically a gigantic island, its southwestern area features hilly wooded terrain across the central spine, with slopes toward the rivers on every side. It is in this zone that you'll explore the wonders of the large Nuka-Cola Plant and will learn the hard work it takes to keep an arable farm Public Workshop going. You will also discover the terrors of wandering around a Giant Teapot and a Creamery at night when Ghouls (or worse!) are prowling about. Take time to pay your respects at the local church on the western side of this zone (though the church and cemetery have seen an uptick in cultist activity before humans disappeared from the region). If you have a considerable amount of time to kill, investigate the colossal Poseidon Energy Plant, which dominates the southeastern part of this region. If you need an endless supply of Fusion Cores, want to stake a claim to a workshop in the biggest location in Appalachia, and want to restore power to part of the region, it's well worth the trip.

ZONE D: PRIMARY LOCATIONS

MAP LEGEND

📱 MY STASH BOX
📖 OVERSEER'S CACHE
🗄 TRUNK
♥ TRADER

COLLECTIBLES
🧠 BOBBLEHEAD
📖 MAGAZINE
🦾 POWER ARMOR

IMPORTANT
🚪 DOOR/GATE
🔒 LOCKED DOOR/GATE
🔓 SAFE
✋ SCANNER
💻 TERMINAL

CRAFTING
🛡 ARMOR WORKBENCH
⚗ CHEMISTRY WORKBENCH
🍴 COOKING STATION
🔋 POWER ARMOR STATION

🔧 TINKER'S WORKBENCH
🔫 WEAPONS WORKBENCH
⚙ WORKSHOP WORKBENCH

🚌 58. HILLFOLK HOTDOGS

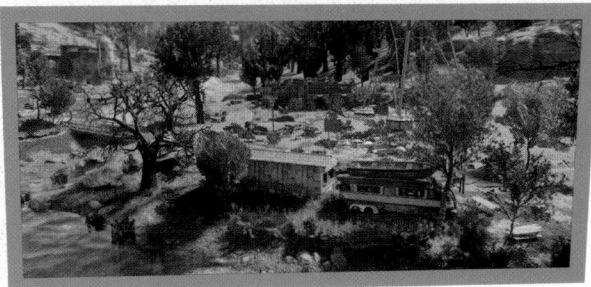

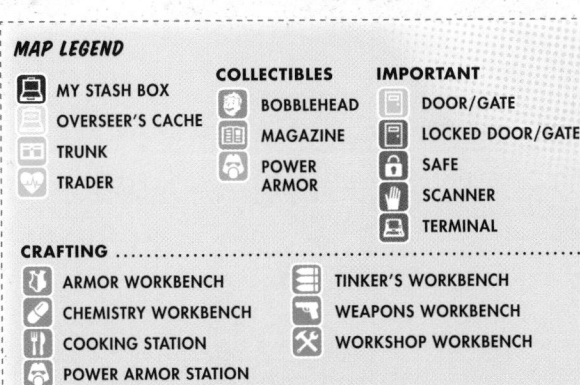

- **CRAFTING:** COOKING
- **DANGER:** CAN CHIMES!
- **ITEMS:** HARVESTABLE: BLOODLEAF, GLOWING FUNGUS, SNAPTAIL; RECIPE/MOD/PLAN
- **INFO:** EXPECTED ENEMY: MOLE RAT; NOTE; SCAVENGE RATING: 2; SIZE: 1; THREAT LEVEL: 1–10
- **LOCK:** (1)
- **ITEM EXAMPLES:** DIRTY ASHTRAY, FLIP LIGHTER, INDUSTRIAL SIZE SHORTENING, OVEN MITT, PEPPER, PILLOW, RAT POISON, SALT, SPATULA, TEDDY BEAR, TOASTER, TOY CAR, YELLOW PLATE

A small roadside (and riverside) hot-dog stand, rusting coach, and trailer are across the road from a slightly less bucolic pile of tires.

59. POSEIDON POWER SUBSTATION PX-01

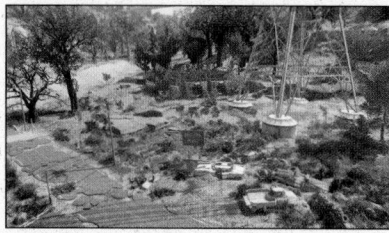

- **DANGER:** EXPLOSIVE CANNISTER!
- **ITEMS:** HARVESTABLE: LOG, RHODODENDRON, SOOT FLOWER
- **INFO:** C.A.M.P. POWER; EXPECTED ENEMY: SCORCHED; SCAVENGE RATING: 1; SIZE: 1; THREAT LEVEL: 1–10
- **ITEM EXAMPLES:** BALL-PEEN HAMMER, GAS CANISTER, OFFICE DESK LAMP

Close to an electrical pylon, and requiring Poseidon Power Plant to be activated is a substation that allows you to draw power to your C.A.M.P. if it's positioned nearby.

60. OHIO RIVER ADVENTURES

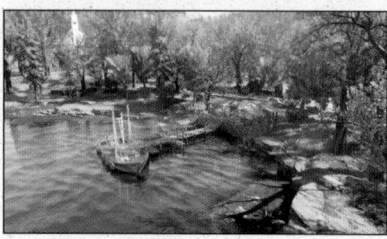

- **COLLECTIBLE:** BOBBLEHEAD, MAGAZINE
- **CRAFTING:** WEAPONS
- **DANGER:** RADIATION!
- **ITEMS:** ARMS AND AMMO; HARVESTABLE: BLOODLEAF, RHODODENDRON, SNAPTAIL, WILD MUTFRUIT
- **INFO:** EXPECTED ENEMY: GHOUL; SCAVENGE RATING: 3; SIZE: 2; THREAT LEVEL: 1–10
- **ITEM EXAMPLES:** BOBBY PIN BOX, FIBER OPTICS BUNDLE, FISHERMAN'S HAT, FISHING ROD, GOLF BALL+, GOLF CLUB, JANGLES AND MOON MONKEY, LIFE PRESERVER++, LIGHTBULB, MENTATS, METAL BUCKET+, METAL HELMET, SCREWDRIVER.

This small boat dock, with the remains of a once-flourishing river boat cruise business, now slowly sags and rots into the lightly radioactive water.

61. KANAWHA COUNTY CEMETERY

- **COLLECTIBLE:** MAGAZINE
- **CRAFTING:** COOKING
- **ITEM:** ARMS AND AMMO; HARVESTABLE: FIRECAP, LOG, RHODODENDRON, SOOT FLOWER, TATO PLANT
- **INFO:** EXPECTED ENEMY: GHOUL, ROBOT, SUPER MUTANT; INSTRUMENT; SCAVENGE RATING: 1; SIZE: 3; SLEEPING; THREAT LEVEL: 1–10
- **LOCK:** SAFE (1)
- **ITEM EXAMPLES:** ALUMINUM CAN, BOBBY PIN BOX, CLEAN DRINKING GLASS+, DESK FAN, GLASS PITCHER, MED-X, MENTATS, PAINT CAN+, PASTOR'S VESTMENTS, PORTED TUNED SNIPER RIFLE, RAT POISON+, SPICES, STIMPAK, SUGAR, TIN CAN, TYPEWRITER.

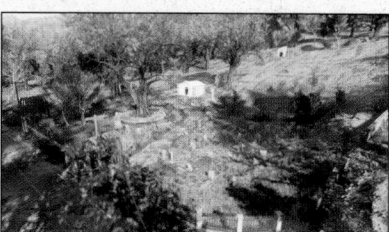

From a distance, this county church and adjacent cemetery appears peaceful, but closer inspection reveals the possible cause of death for the skeletal parishioners and evidence of cultist totems inside both the church and cemetery shed.

62. BILLINGS HOMESTEAD (WORKSHOP)

- **CRAFTING:** ARMOR, WORKSHOP
- **DANGER:** EXPLOSIVE CANNISTER!
- **ITEMS:** ARMS AND AMMO; HARVESTABLE: CRYSTAL, COPPER, GOLD, PHOSPHATE, SOOT FLOWER, WILD MUTFRUIT; HEALTH AND CHEMS
- **INFO:** EXPECTED ENEMY: VARIES; QUEST: CLAIM WORKSHOP AT BILLINGS HOMESTEAD; SCAVENGE RATING: 3 (5); SIZE: 3; THREAT LEVEL: 1–10
- **LOCK:** SAFE (2)
- **ITEM EXAMPLES:** ANTIFREEZE BOTTLE, BLOWTORCH, BREAD BOX, COTTON YARN, CRYSTAL LIQUOR DECANTER, DINNER FORK, DIRTY ASHTRAY, DUCT TAPE, ENAMEL BUCKET, FLOWER POT, FUSE, PUMPKIN+, SHORT HUNTING RIFLE, SILVER PLATE, TURPENTINE, UNSTOPPABLE SHINDIG BOARD GAME, WAKEMASTER ALARM CLOCK, YELLOW CANISTER
- **WORK:** FOOD (5), WATER (3), FERTILIZER (1), CRYSTAL (1), GOLD (1), COPPER (1)

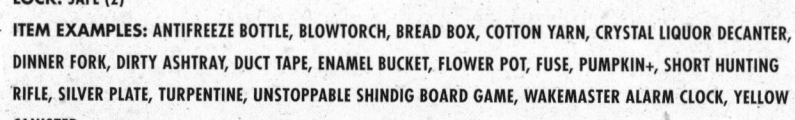

Billings Homestead (Exterior)

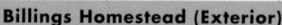

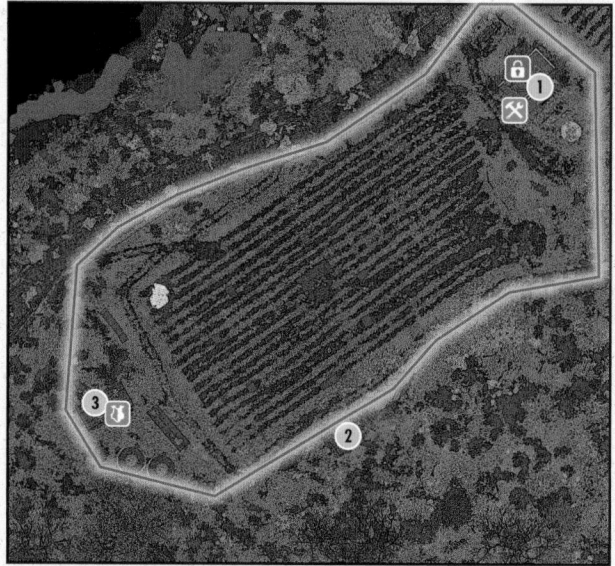

LEGEND
1 BILLINGS FARMHOUSE
2 HAY SHED
3 TRACTOR BARN

Adjacent and slightly southwest of Silva Homestead is a small farm dwelling, large field, tractor shed and silo, and a number of resource deposits along with a workshop outside the farmhouse. Claim this area for yourself or your team, and start that resource acquisition!

63. SILVA HOMESTEAD

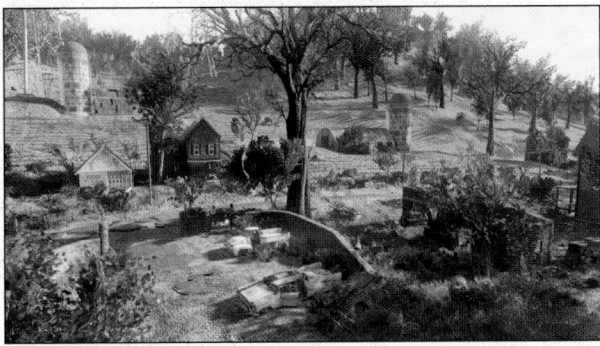

- COLLECTIBLES: BOBBLEHEAD (2), MAGAZINE (2), POWER ARMOR
- CRAFTING: POWER ARMOR, TINKER, WEAPONS (3)
- ITEMS: ARMS AND AMMO; HARVESTABLE: ASH ROSE, BLACKBERRY, CARROT, LOG, TATO PLANT, WILD CORN; HEALTH AND CHEMS
- INFO: EXPECTED ENEMY: IRRADIATED INSECT, ROBOT, SCORCHED, SUPER MUTANT; SCAVENGE RATING: 5; SIZE: 4; THREAT LEVEL: 1–10
- LOCK: SAFE (1)
- ITEM EXAMPLES: ALARM CLOCK, ANTIFREEZE BOTTLE, AUTOPSY BOARD GAME, BLAST RADIUS BOARD GAME, CANDY FAN MR. FUZZY, COOLANT+, COTTON YARD, CRUSHED ACETONE CANISTER, CRUSHED RUSTY CANISTER+, CRUSHED YELLOW CANISTER, DUCT TAPE+ EXPLORER OUTFIT, FLARE, FLOWER POT+, FOOD DEHYDRATOR, GIDDY UP BUTTERCUP, GLASS JAR+, HUFFWARBLER TEAPOT, JANGLES THE MOON MONKEY, METAL TUB, MICROSCOPE, MR. HANDY FUEL+, PLASTIC PUMPKIN, SENSOR MODULE, SILVER PLATE, TALL DRINKING GLASS+, TORQUE ROD END, UNFILLED KICKBALL, USED OIL CAN, WILLOW ROUNDED VASE, WOOD BLOCK+

Silva Homestead (Exterior)

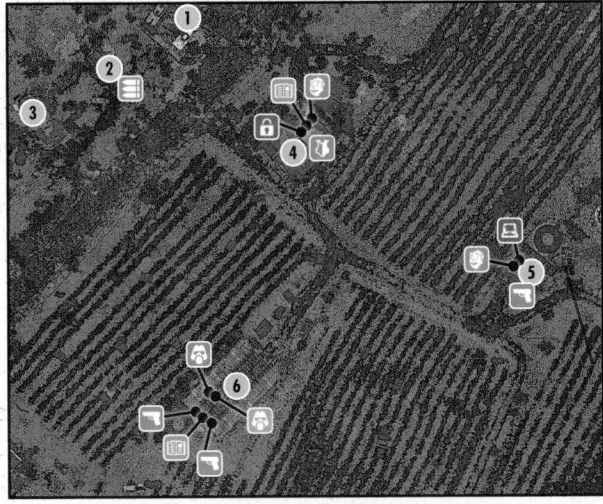

LEGEND

1	PARKING LOT	4	SILVA FARMHOUSE
2	DERELICT CRATE SHED	5	SILO BARN
3	TALL COTTAGE	6	TRACTOR BARN

This area contains a small farm, a farrow field, a rusting tractor, and a cottage across the road along with its own dilapidated shed. Of considerable interest is an Arktos Pharma Terminal inside the silo up the sloping corn field, as well as the tractor barn (for its workbenches) and the farmhouse; all have masses of junk to accrue.

64. ORWELL ORCHARDS

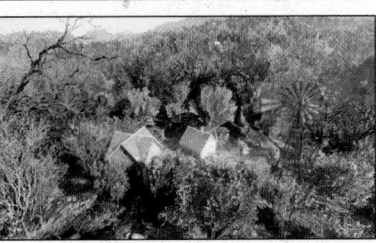

- COLLECTIBLE: HOLOTAPE
- CRAFTING: ARMOR, WEAPONS
- DANGER: RADIATION!+
- ITEMS: ARMS AND AMMO; HARVESTABLE: LOG, RHODODENDRON, SOOT FLOWER, WILD MUTFRUIT
- INFO: EXPECTED ENEMY: ROBOT; NOTE; SCAVENGE RATING: 2; SIZE: 3; THREAT LEVEL: 1–10
- LOCK: SAFE (0, 0)
- ITEM EXAMPLES: CRUSHED YELLOW CANISTER, DIRTY ASHTRAY, GAS CANISTER, MOP, TIN CAN, TOY TRUCK

This hilltop orchard, now devoid of fruit, has a cluster of buildings in various stages of dereliction. Watch for the dumped radioactive barrels in one of the red sheds.

65. NEW RIVER GORGE BRIDGE—WEST

- COLLECTIBLE: POWER ARMOR
- CRAFTING: POWER ARMOR, TINKER
- DANGER: LONG DROP! RADIATION!
- INFO: EXPECTED ENEMY: GHOULS; SCAVENGE RATING: 3; SIZE: 5; THREAT LEVEL: 1–10
- LOCK: DOOR (KEY)
- ITEM EXAMPLES: GUM DROPS, FUSION CORE, PAINT CAN, POTATO CHIPS, RAT POISON, STEEL WORKER HAT

Just below and north of the Cow Spots Creamery, the start of the massive New River Gorge Bridge (part of Interstate 59) leads you across to the northeastern side (in Zone C). Once you have the necessary key, you can open the maintenance room under the road at the start of the bridge's span; there is possibly a suit of Power Armor to obtain. The long bridge span features rusting gantries, alarming gaps, and a tarmac road with derelict areas to move across without falling. Consult "New River Gorge Bridge—East" for the map and information on the maintenance room on the gorge's opposite (northeast) side.

66. COW SPOTS CREAMERY

- CRAFTING: TINKER
- ITEMS: HARVESTABLE: RHODODENDRON, SILT BEAN, SOOT FLOWER, WILD MUTFRUIT
- INFO: EXPECTED ENEMY: GHOUL, IRRADIATED INSECT; SCAVENGE RATING: 2; SIZE: 2; THREAT LEVEL: 1–10
- LOCK: SAFE (0)
- ITEM EXAMPLES: CREAM++, EMPTY MILK BOTTLE+, PRE-WAR MONEY, SUGAR+, TALL DRINKING GLASS

This small roadside ice cream shop, complete with children's playground and impressive views of the bridge, features a tiny factory where cream was made and can now be scavenged.

67. LEWIS & SONS FARMING SUPPLY

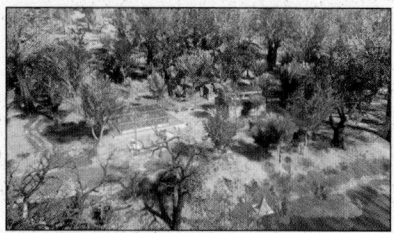

- **COLLECTIBLE:** BOBBLEHEAD (3), MAGAZINE (3), POWER ARMOR
- **CRAFTING:** CHEMISTRY, POWER ARMOR
- **ITEMS: HARVESTABLE:** BLACKBERRY, COPPER, CORN PLANTER, LOG, MELON PLANTER, SOOT FLOWER; HEALTH AND CHEMS+; RECIPE/MOD/PLAN
- **INFO: EXPECTED ENEMY:** IRRADIATED INSECT; SCAVENGE RATING: 4; SIZE: 3; SLEEPING; THREAT LEVEL: 1–10
- **ITEM EXAMPLES:** BOILED WATER+, BROOM, CAT BOWL, COOLANT+, CONNECTING ROD+, CRUSHED ACETONE CANISTER, CRUSHED RUSTY CANISTER, CRUSHED YELLOW CANISTER, DUCT TAPE, GLASS JAR+, FLOWER POT++, INSTAMASH, KITCHEN SCALES, MULTI-PURPOSE AXE, OIL CANISTER, PIPE WRENCH, MAKESHIFT BATTERY, RAT POISON, RED PAINT+ SHOVEL, TURPENTINE

Lewis & Sons Farming Supply (Exterior)

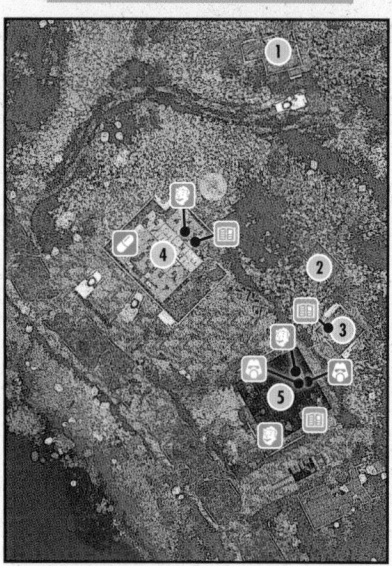

LEGEND
1. FARM COTTAGE
2. HAY SHED
3. WORK SHED
4. GREENHOUSE
5. WAREHOUSE

An excellent source of both junk and collectible items, this supply store consists of a smattering of small structures across from the road and river. This is a must-stop location you can return to time and again.

68. KANAWHA NUKA-COLA PLANT

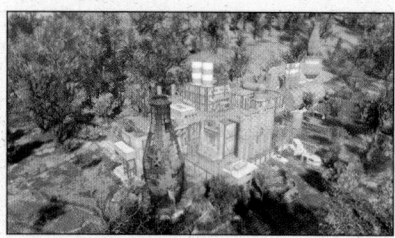

- **LOCK:** DOOR (0, 1, 1, 2), SAFE (2, 3)
- **ITEM EXAMPLES:** ALUMINUM CAN+, ALUMINUM CANISTER+, BALL-PEEN HAMMER, BEER BOTTLE+, BLOWTORCH, BLUE PAINT, BOILED WATER+, BONE CUTTER, BUFFOUT, COFFEE CUP+, COFFEE POT, DIRTY ASHTRAY, EMPTY PAINT CAN, ENAMEL BUCKET, FUEL TANK, FUSION CORE++, GAS CANISTER, HACKSAW, HOT PLATE, INDUSTRIAL OIL CANISTER, MASONRY HAMMER, MICROSCOPE, MOP, NUKA-COLA+++, NUKA-COLA BOTTLE+++, NUKA-COLA CUP, NUKA-COLA CUP AND STRAW, NUCLEAR WASTE+, PACK OF DUCT TAPE, PAINT CAN+, PAPER CUTTER, RADAWAY, RESTORED DESK FAN, RUSTY CANISTER+, SALISBURY STEAK, SAW, SCREWDRIVER, SUGAR, TIN CAN+, TONGS, USED OIL CAN+, VODKA BOTTLE, WILLOW BUD VASE, WINE, WONDERGLUE, YELLOW PAINT.

- **COLLECTIBLE:** BOBBLEHEAD (3), CAPS STASH (5), HOLOTAPE, MAGAZINE (3), NUKA-CHERRY+++, NUKA-COLA QUANTUM+++, POWER ARMOR
- **CRAFTING:** ARMOR, CHEMISTRY, POWER ARMOR, TINKER, WEAPONS
- **DANGER:** RADIATION!
- **ITEMS:** ARMS AND AMMO; HARVESTABLE: BRAIN FUNGUS, GLOWING FUNGUS, LOG; HEALTH AND CHEMS; TRUNK; VENDING MACHINE: U-MINE-IT!
- **INFO: EXPECTED ENEMY:** GHOUL, IRRADIATED ANIMAL; NOTE; SCAVENGE RATING: 5; SIZE: 4; SLEEPING; THREAT LEVEL: 1–10

Kanawha Nuka-Cola Plant (Interior)

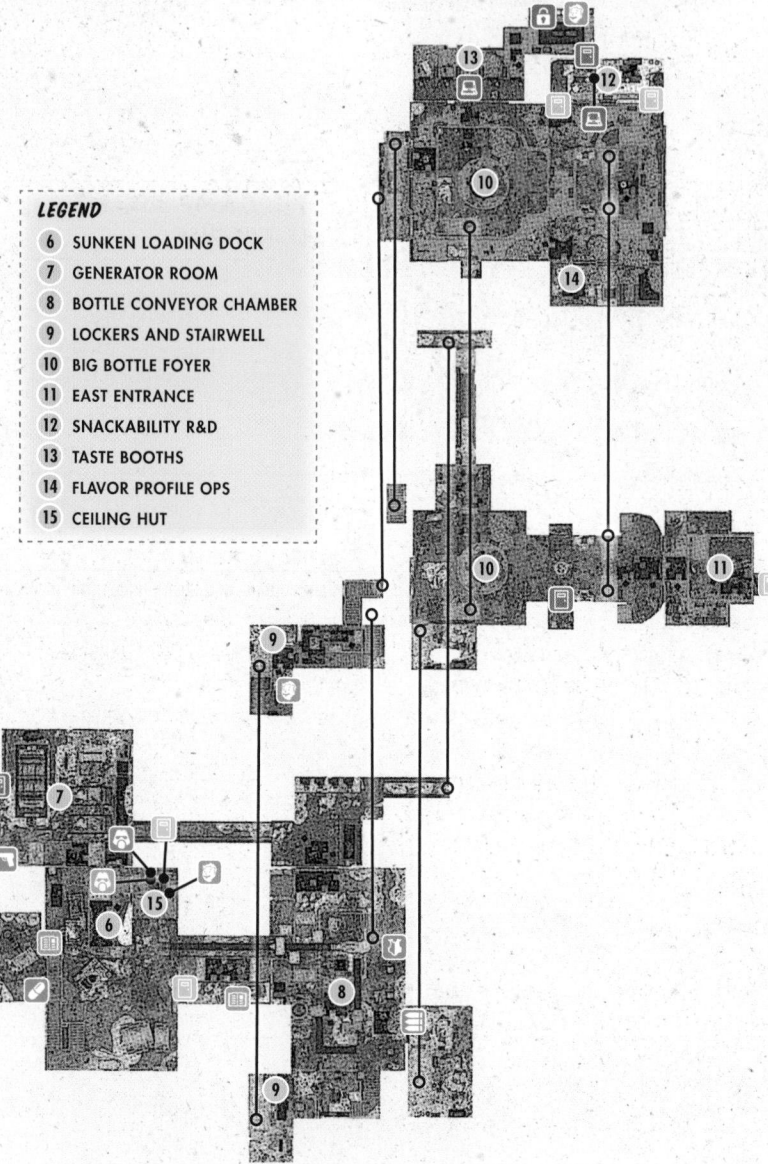

LEGEND
6. SUNKEN LOADING DOCK
7. GENERATOR ROOM
8. BOTTLE CONVEYOR CHAMBER
9. LOCKERS AND STAIRWELL
10. BIG BOTTLE FOYER
11. EAST ENTRANCE
12. SNACKABILITY R&D
13. TASTE BOOTHS
14. FLAVOR PROFILE OPS
15. CEILING HUT

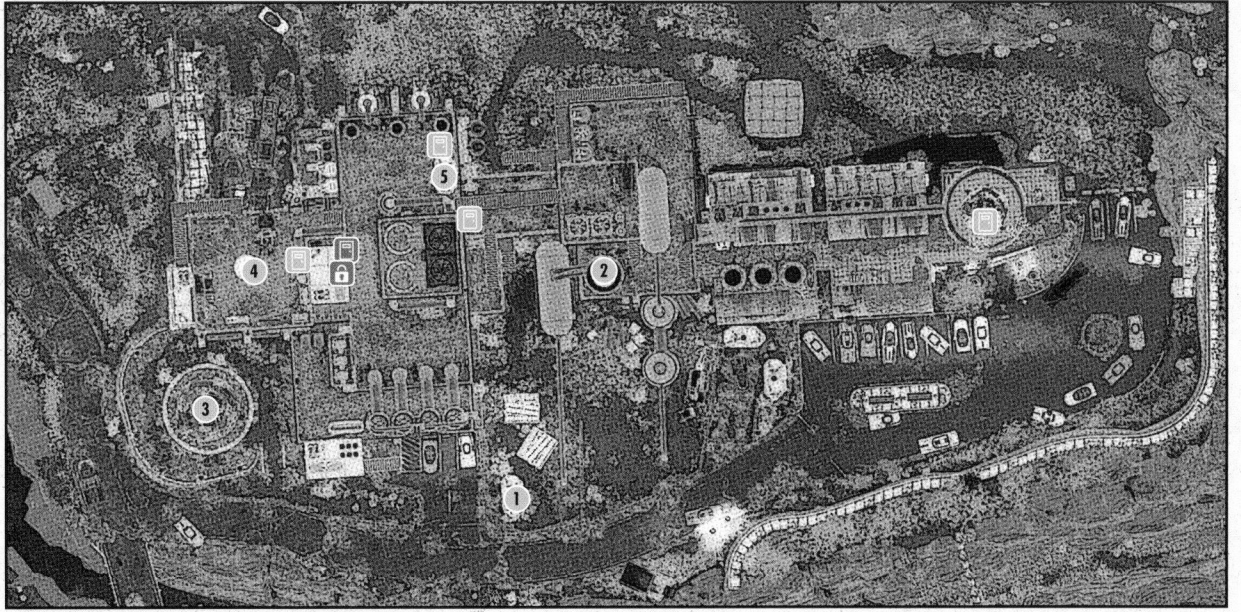

Kanawha Nuka-Cola Plant (Exterior)

LEGEND

1. MAIN SECURITY GATE AND TRAILER (ENTRANCE)
2. MAIN PLANT BUILDING
3. GIANT NUKA-COLA BOTTLE
4. LOADING DOCK
5. ROOF MAINTENANCE TRAILER (ROOF HATCH ENTRANCE)

If you've a hankering for some nice ice-cold soda and won't be too appalled when you read just what ingredients go into Nuka-Cola, then why not visit the large bottling plant, where more than your thirst will be quenched—assuming you're also here to gather junk and collectibles. The facility is divided into two massive chambers, with numerous side rooms and connecting areas, all of which have excellent scavenging (and photographic) potential! Don't leave without accessing the roof hatch, which is the only way to reach a blue maintenance hut clamped to the ceiling, with its gantry fallen away; inside are some choice beverages!

69. CAMP ADAMS

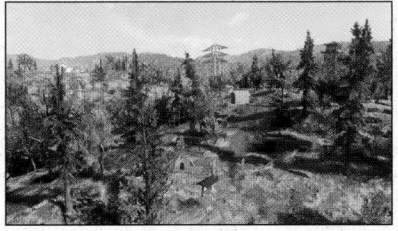

- **COLLECTIBLE:** MAGAZINE
- **CRAFTING:** COOKING
- **ITEMS:** ARMS AND AMMO; HARVESTABLE: BLACKBERRY, LOG, RHODODENDRON, SOOT FLOWER; HEALTH AND CHEMS; TRUNK
- **INFO:** EXPECTED ENEMY: IRRADIATED ANIMAL; SUPER MUTANT; NOTE; SCAVENGE RATING: 2; SIZE: 3; SLEEPING; THREAT LEVEL: 1–10
- **ITEM EXAMPLES:** BOURBON BOTTLE, COFFEE CUP, DIRTY ASHTRAY, EMPTY CAN, GLASS JAR, RANGER HAT, SEALED CHARLESTON HERALD, SPICES

Expect long grass, cabins dotted throughout a hilltop wilderness, and two towers; one is the lookout to come and the other is a smaller adventure tower with a rickety platform you must use to reach the top. Pick the area clean of junk.

70. CAMP ADAMS LOOKOUT

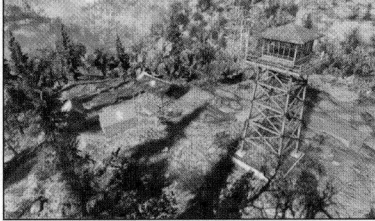

- **DANGER:** LONG DROP!
- **ITEMS:** ARMS AND AMMO; HEALTH AND CHEMS
- **INFO:** EXPECTED ENEMY: IRRADIATED ANIMAL; SCAVENGE RATING: 1; SIZE: 1; SURVEY AREA; THREAT LEVEL: 1–10
- **ITEM EXAMPLES:** ASHTRAY, DESK LAMP

Atop the hill is a fenced tower. Below are small cabins of Camp Adams. Climb to the top. The platform has been picked clean, but you can survey other locations.

71. THE GIANT TEAPOT

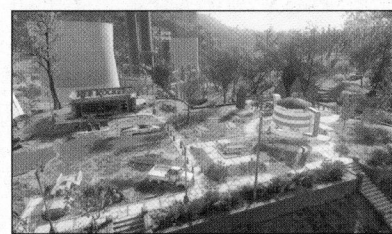

- **COLLECTIBLES:** BOBBLEHEAD (2), MAGAZINE (2)
- **ITEMS:** HEALTH AND CHEMS; MY STASH BOX
- **INFO:** EXPECTED ENEMY: GHOUL, IRRADIATED ANIMAL, IRRADIATED INSECT; NOTE; QUEST: STRANGE BREW, TEA TIME; SCAVENGE RATING: 3; SIZE: 2; THREAT LEVEL: 1–10
- **ITEM EXAMPLES:** BEER BOTTLE, BLASTING CAPS BOX, BOBBY PIN BOX, BOURBON, CIGAR BOX, COTTON YARN, HOUSE TEAPOT+, INSTAMASH, MECHANIC JUMPSUIT, OLD POSSUM, RABBIT HIDE, RADAWAY, SAUCER, SHADELESS LAMP, SHORT PUMP ACTION SHOTGUN, SUGAR, SUGAR BOMBS, TABLETOP PICTURE FRAME, TOY TRUCK, TRILBY HAT, WOOD BLOCK+, WRENCH

There are three separate structures at this roadside tourist spot: a red house, which is a gift shop containing the most junk; the teapot; and a Red Rocket Gas Station with a My Stash Box; the latter is especially helpful when returning to this location while exploring the general area.

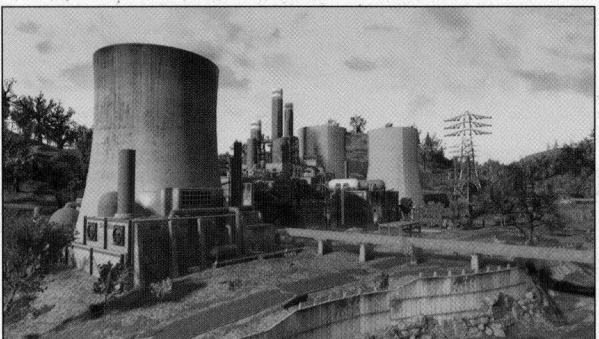

- **COLLECTIBLES:** BOBBLEHEAD (5), CAPS STASH (21), HOLOTAPE, MAGAZINE (8), POWER ARMOR
- **CRAFTING:** ARMOR, COOKING (2), POWER ARMOR (2), TINKER (2), WEAPONS
- **DANGER:** CAN CHIMES! FLAMETHROWER! GRENADE! MINE! OIL! RADIATION!+++ TESLA ARC! TURRET!

- **ITEMS:** ARMS AND AMMO; HARVESTABLE: GLOWING FUNGUS; HEALTH AND CHEMS; TRUNK
- **INFO:** EXPECTED ENEMY: GHOUL, SCORCHED; LANDMARK; SCAVENGE RATING: 4; SIZE: 5; SLEEPING; THREAT LEVEL: 15–99
- **LOCK:** DOOR (0, 1, 2, 2, 2, 2, 3), SAFE (1, 2, 3), TERMINAL (1, 3, 3, 3, 3)
- **ITEM EXAMPLES:** 10-MM AUTO PISTOL, ALARM CLOCK, ANTIFREEZE BOTTLE, BAG OF CEMENT+, BALL-PEEN HAMMER, BATTERED CLIPBOARD, BEER BOTTLE+, BOBBY PIN BOX, BROKEN LAMP, COFFEE CUP+, COFFEE POT+, COMBAT KNIFE, DAMAGED HAZMAT SUIT+, DIRTY ASHTRAY+, ECONOMY WONDERGLUE, ENAMEL BUCKET+, EXTINGUISHER, FARMHAND CLOTHES, FUSION CORE+++, GAS MASK, HALLUCIGEN GAS CANISTER, HALLUCIGEN GAS CANISTER, HARD HAT, HAZMAT SUIT, HOT PLATE, INSTAMASH, MENTATS, METAL BUCKET, NUKA-COLA BOTTLE+, OLD POSSUM, PACK OF CIGARETTES+, PAPER CUTTER, PLASTIC PLATE, PLASTIC PUMPKIN, POSEIDON HAZMAT STORAGE KEY, POSEIDON PLANT MANAGER'S PASSWORD, PROTEST SIGN+, RAD-X, SALT, SCREWDRIVER, SECURITY BATON, STEEL WORKER HAT, SUPRATHAW ANTIFREEZE, TACK HAMMER, TELEPHONE, USED OIL CAN, WILLOW VAULTED VASE, YELLOW TABLE LAMP.

Poseidon Energy Plant WV-06 (Exterior)

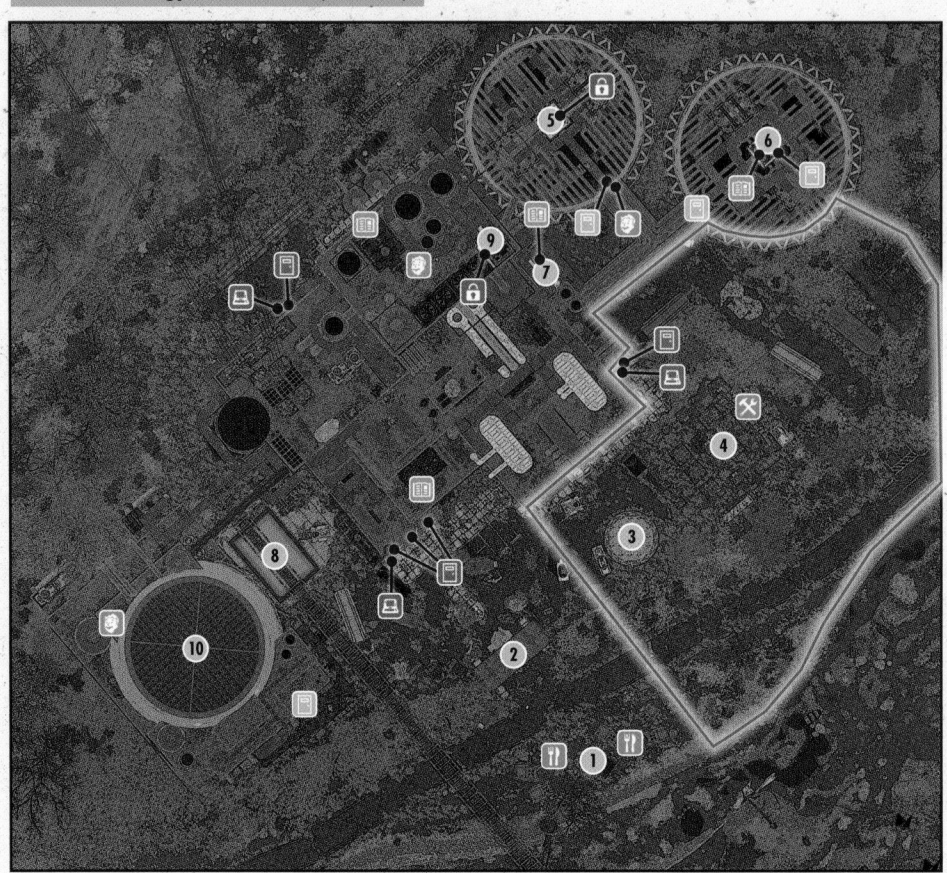

LEGEND

1. MINERS' PROTEST CAMP
2. MAIN PLANT ENTRANCE
3. VERTIBOT LANDING PAD
4. PRIMARY LOCATION: POSEIDON POWER PLANT YARD
5. COOLING TOWER #1

6. COOLING TOWER #2
7. GANTRY HUT (NORTHEAST)
8. TOXIC POOL AND ROOF GANTRIES
9. GANTRY HUT (ROOF)
10. SOUTH EXPANSION COOLING TOWER

Poseidon Energy Plant WV-06 (Interior)

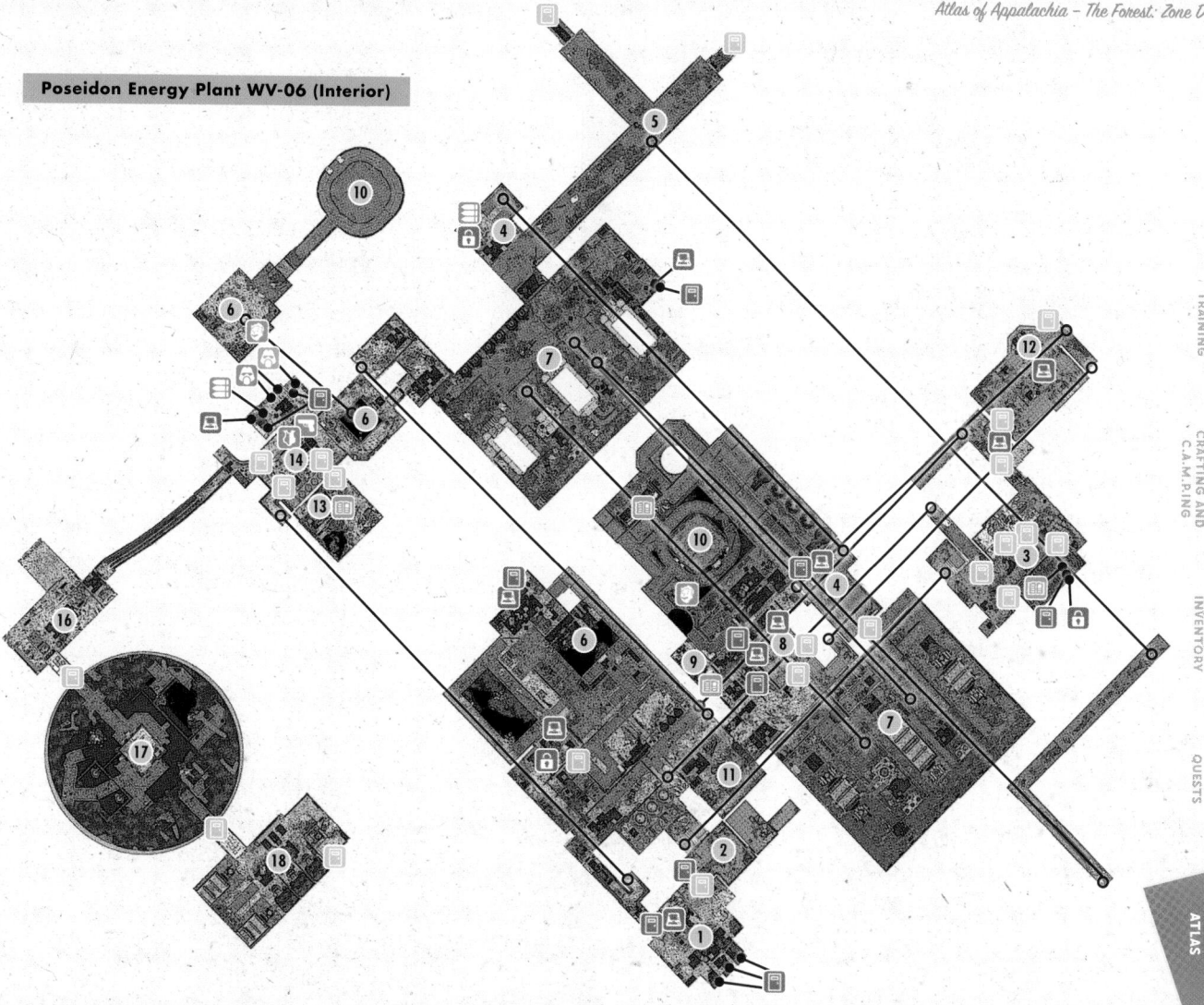

TRAINING

CRAFTING AND C.A.M.P.ING

INVENTORY

QUESTS

ATLAS

BESTIARY

APPENDICES

LEGEND

1. MAIN ENTRANCE
2. LOBBY
3. PLANT OFFICE
4. PIPE INTERCHANGE (AND GANTRY STAIRS)
5. COOLING TOWER #1 AND #2 CORRIDOR
6. FUEL STORAGE
7. TURBINE HALL
8. SECURITY (AND DECONTAMINATION)
9. SECURITY: LOCKER ROOM
10. REACTOR ROOM
11. LOADING DOCK
12. CONTROL ROOM
13. BASEMENT: LOCKER ROOM
14. BASEMENT: WORKROOM
16. EXPANSION PLANT: STORAGE (BASEMENT)
17. EXPANSION PLANT: COOLING TOWER #3
18. EXPANSION PLANT: BOILERS

Note this location also encompasses the Poseidon Energy Plant Yard (workshop), so check that location for more information on additional resources and items. This gargantuan power plant is so big, many reckon it's the largest structure in all of Appalachia! Bigger than other power plants, before Poseidon Power decided to add a third cooling tower, this used to power all of Charleston and the surrounding region. The exterior is dominated by the three towers (a pair to the northeast and one to the southwest). The roadside entrance is close to a strike camp, and the place is mined; there are other threats as well. Check the toxic pool between the main and south structures (avoiding a swim), and use the gantry platforms to reach both rooftops; from here you can reach other roof areas, and there are hidden collectibles to gather. Enter the plant via the locked terminals (3) at the main entrance (three double doors), the South Expansion, the Fuel Storage (north side), the Turbine Hall (east, by the workshop substation), or the unlocked doors at Cooling Tower #1 (Pipe Interchange) or Cooling Tower #2 (Pipe Interchange).

Once inside, check the guide maps to ensure you don't get lost. Remove any foes, and beware of chambers with multiple gantry platforms and increased radiation (like the Reactor Room, Fuel Storage, and Cooling Tower #3). Set about restoring power and collect the loot. If you're lost, look for the red signposts leading you to each named chamber. Don't forget the south expansion plant is mainly the interior of Cooling Tower #3, which you can access from the outside or via a basement workroom area where the majority of the workbenches and possible Power Armor is located.

73. POSEIDON ENERGY PLANT YARD (WORKSHOP)

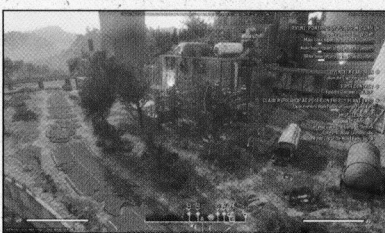

- **CRAFTING:** WORKSHOP
- **DANGER:** EXPLOSIVE CANNISTER! TURRET! RADIATION!
- **ITEMS:** ARMS AND AMMO; HARVESTABLE: GRAVEL PIT, LEAD, LOG, URANIUM
- **INFO:** EXPECTED ENEMY: VARIES; QUEST: CLAIM WORKSHOP AT POSEIDON ENERGY PLANT YARD; SCAVENGE RATING: 2 (5+); SIZE: 3; THREAT LEVEL: 1–10
- **ITEM EXAMPLES:** BOBBY PIN BOX, BROOM, EMPTY PAINT POT, GEAR, PACK OF CIGARETTES, PENCIL, PITCHFORK, MR. HANDY FUEL, SYRINGER AMMO, TUBE FLANGE
- **WORK:** FOOD [9], WATER [8], FUSION CORE [3], LEAD [1], ALUMINUM [1], NUCLEAR [1], CONCRETE [1]

The map for this location is within the perimeter of the Poseidon Energy Plant WV-06 (previous location). Find the workshop at the substation in the eastern part of the exterior perimeter. Scour the area for resources, and build your defenses around the ones you wish to keep for the longest time. Note the Fusion Core Processors, as well as the gun emplacements, vertibot landing pad, and power box, which you can use (after some repair work on the power plant) to further bolster your base.

ZONE D: SECONDARY LOCATIONS

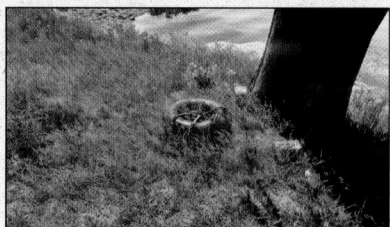

Riverbank Canoe

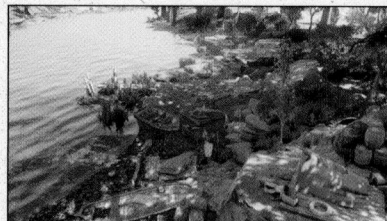

Billings River Dock

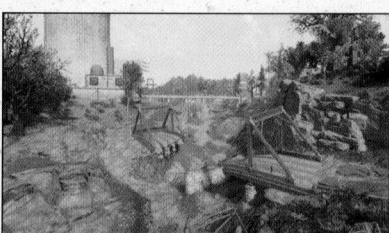

West Charleston Bridge

Appalachia: **The Forest (Zone D) – Secondary Locations**

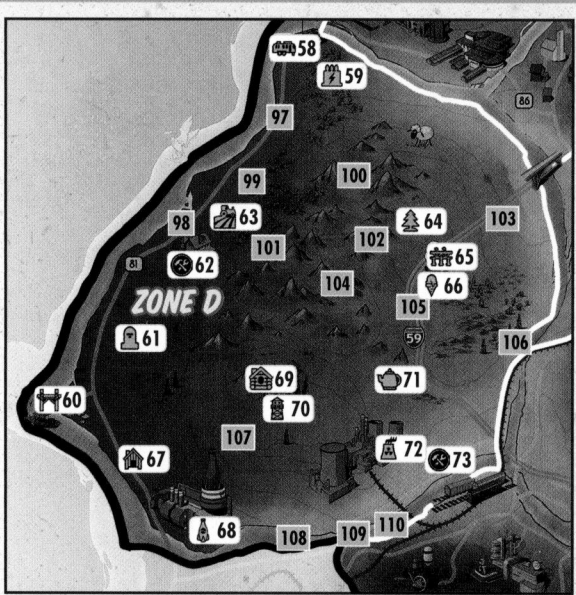

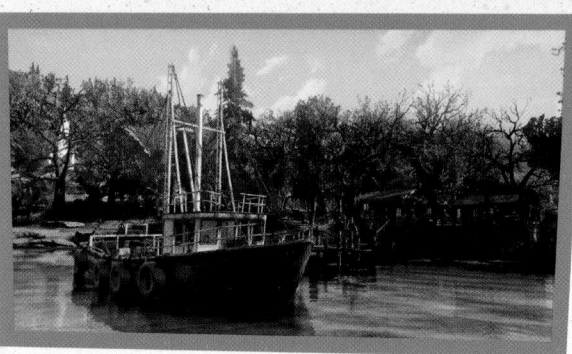

#	NAME	DESCRIPTION
97	Riverbank Canoe	A rubber tire, a skeletal canoeist, and his cooler and Rads are all that's left on this part of the Ohio River.
98	Billings River Dock	A Tinker's Workbench, moored boats, a sleeping bag, and junk to gather on a riverside camp.
99	Beheaded at the Drainage Gully	A machete and a headless corpse sit at the drainage pipe, near boards over what's left of the main road.
100	Orchard Woods Hilltop Camp	A duffel bag, bones, and an axe; a hilltop white tent offers good views but little to scavenge.
101	Tractor and Bones	A yellow tractor seems to have dug up more than just carrots in the upper fields of Silva Farmstead.
102	Outhouse and Platform Path	Part of the trail takes you past a pond, shopping cart (ammo box), and a rickety outhouse. Look for oil to gather at the top of the trail.
103	Jangles' Sofa Safe	The Moon Monkey and his best friend the Tedster are keeping that locked safe (3) secure, under the New Gorge Bridge.
104	Beehive: Camp Adams Hills	Gather honey and try not to get stung at this beehive, stuck to a large old tree.
105	Underpass Camp and Truck Trailer Crash (Highway 59)	A fallen big-rig and large-scale freeway subsidence, along with a small camp under the upper edge of the underpass destruction.
106	Gunsmith's Overlook Shack	Perched on rocks above the river and rail line, expect excellent bridge views, a Weapons Workbench, and a place to sleep.
107	Camp Adams Cookout	A spit roast, tent, and picnic table on the hillside south of Camp Adams.
108	River Rope Bridge	The dry ravine where a river used to be has a footbridge leading to an abandoned stall.
109	West Charleston Bridge	How do you get from the power plant to the landfill? Not via this bridge; it's out. Check for a rusty van with items inside.
110	Fisherman's Lament	A skeletal fisherman in what's left of his rowboat, in the concrete river channel.

THE FOREST: ZONE E—
CHARLESTON AND SURROUNDINGS

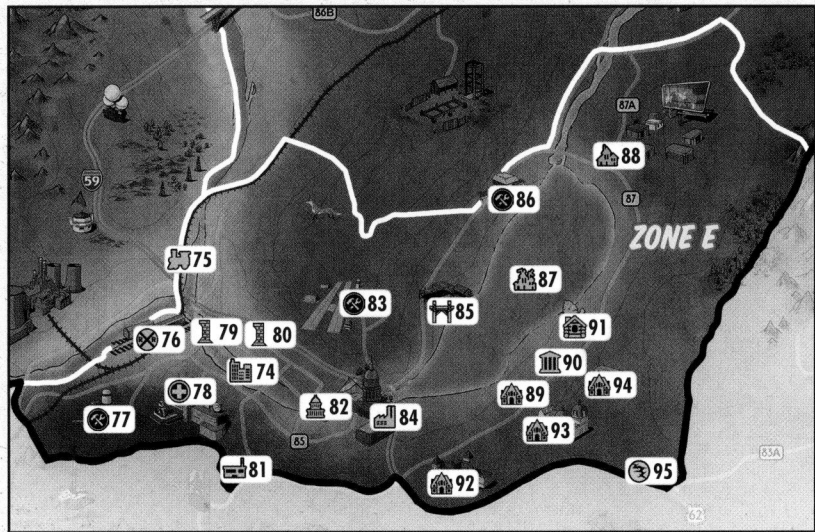

Appalachia: **The Forest (Zone E) – Primary Locations**

Though you should make time to explore the north lakeside community of Summersville, and the shanty dwellings scattered across the deceptively dry Summersville Lake, you'll probably spend most of your time surveying the damage the city of Charleston suffered after the dam broke, sending the contents of the Kanawha River rushing through town (and that's not counting the bomb damage). The unscathed gleaming gold dome of the Capitol may fill you with hope, but the debris, collapsed tenement buildings, fallen skyscrapers, and ruined city blocks may put a damper on your thoughts of rebuilding: Better to sift through the debris for good quality junk (especially at the Landfill workshop), then trade it at the Fire Department, before finally investigating the cluster of imposing mansions on the lake's southeast shores. What secrets are contained within these once-opulent dwellings? Don't get lost in that hedge maze!

WORLD MAP LEGEND

— REGION BOUNDARY   — ZONE BOUNDARY

■ BOBBLEHEADS   ■ CAP STASHES   ■ MAGAZINES   ■ POWER ARMOR

PRIMARY LOCATIONS

				icon	NAME						icon	NAME
				74	CHARLESTON	3		3		85	SUMMERSVILLE DOCKS
				75	CHARLESTON STATION					86	LAKESIDE CABINS
1		1		76	CHARLESTON RAILYARD					87	NEW GAD
				77	CHARLESTON LANDFILL					88	SUMMERSVILLE
4	1	3		78	AVR MEDICAL CENTER	2	1	2		89	BURDETTE MANOR
3	1	3	1	79	HORNWRIGHT INDUSTRIAL HEADQUARTERS		1			90	SUGARMAPLE
				80	CHARLESTON HERALD	2	3	2		91	OVERLOOK CABIN
				81	CHARLESTON FIRE DEPARTMENT	2	7	4		92	RIVERSIDE MANOR
1		1		82	CHARLESTON CAPITOL BUILDING	2		2		93	TORRANCE HOUSE
	1		2	83	WADE AIRPORT	1	1	2		94	HORNWRIGHT SUMMER VILLA
				84	SUMMERSVILLE DAM					95	FISSURE SITE

ZONE E: PRIMARY LOCATIONS

MAP LEGEND

- MY STASH BOX
- OVERSEER'S CACHE
- TRUNK
- TRADER

COLLECTIBLES

- BOBBLEHEAD
- MAGAZINE
- POWER ARMOR

CRAFTING

- ARMOR WORKBENCH
- CHEMISTRY WORKBENCH
- COOKING STATION
- POWER ARMOR STATION
- TINKER'S WORKBENCH
- WEAPONS WORKBENCH
- WORKSHOP WORKBENCH

IMPORTANT

- DOOR/GATE
- LOCKED DOOR/GATE
- SAFE
- SCANNER
- TERMINAL

TRAINING

CRAFTING AND C.A.M.P.ING

INVENTORY

QUESTS

ATLAS

BESTIARY

APPENDICES

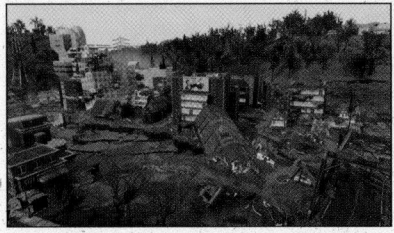

- **INFO:** EXPECTED ENEMY: GHOUL, IRRADIATED ANIMAL, IRRADIATED INSECT, SCORCHED, SUPER MUTANT; LANDMARK; NOTE; EVENT: THE BELL TOLLS; SCAVENGE RATING: 5+++; SIZE: 5+++; SLEEPING; THREAT LEVEL: 1–10
- **LOCK:** DOOR (0, 1), SAFE (U, 1, 1)
- **ITEM EXAMPLES:** ABRAXO CLEANER, ABRAXO CLEANER INDUSTRIAL GRADE, BASEBALL GLOVE, BLUE TABLE LAMP, CAT BOWL, CHARLESTON HERALD—BELL ARTICLE, CHEF HAT, CLOWN, COFFEE CUP+++, COFFEE POT+, COOKING PAN, COOKING POT, COOLANT, COP CAP, COVERED SAUCEPAN, CRAM, CRANBERRY MOONSHINE, CUTTING BOARD, EMPTY FLORAL BUD VASE, EMPTY MILK BOTTLE, EYEGLASSES, FADED VISOR, FANCY LADS SNACK CAKES, FRYING PAN, GLASS PITCHER, GLOBE, HAIRBRUSH, HOT PLATE, MEDICAL LIQUID NITROGEN DISPENSER, MOUNTAIN HONEY, NOODLE CUP, NURSE UNIFORM, OVEN MITT, PACK OF CIGARETTES, PORK N' BEANS, SAUCE PAN, SHORT LASER PISTOL, SWEATER VEST AND SLACKS, SWIMSUIT, TABLETOP PICTURE FRAME, TALL DRINKING GLASS, TELEPHONE, TEST TUBE RACK, TIN PITCHER, TOY CAR, TOY ROCKETSHIP, WAKEMASTER ALARM CLOCK, WILLOW BUD VASE, YELLOW TABLE LAMP+

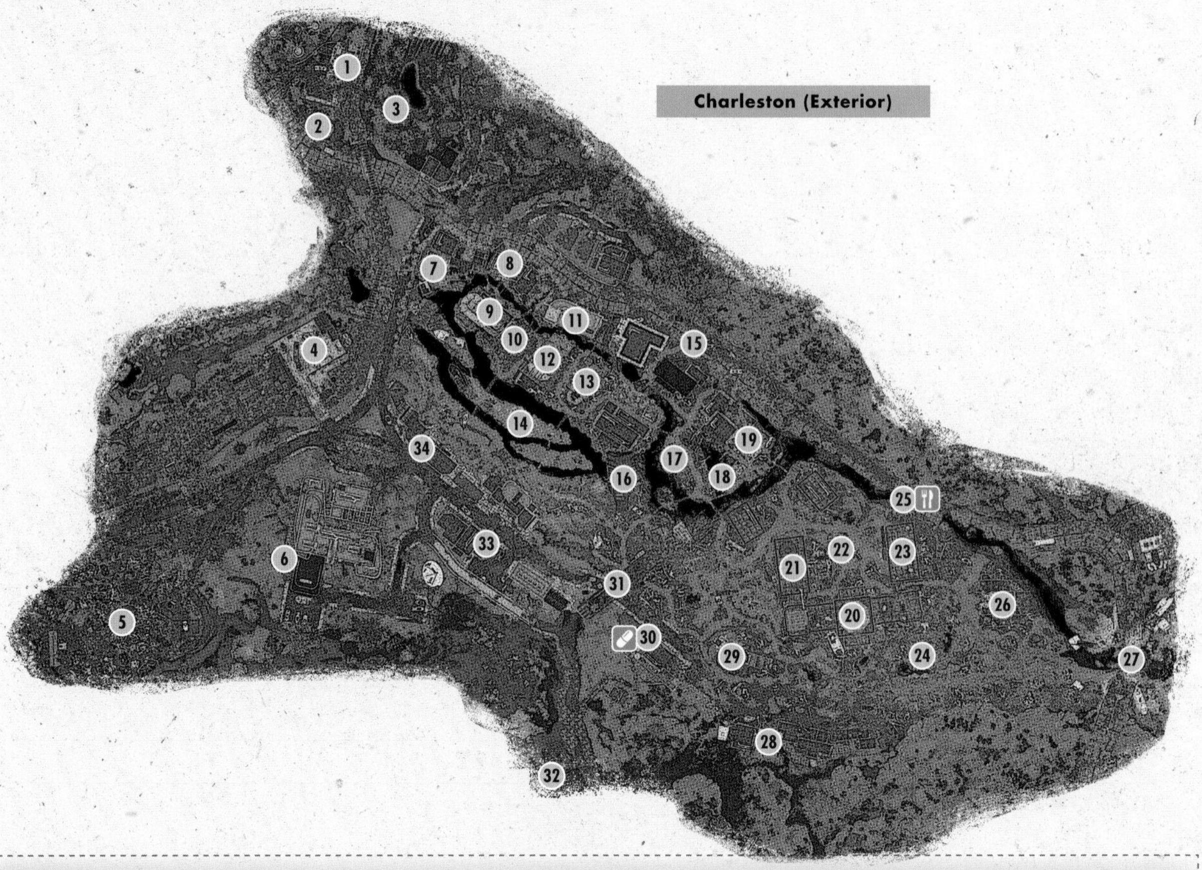

- **CRAFTING:** CHEMISTRY, COOKING
- **DANGER:** LONG DROP! RADIATION! TURRET!
- **ITEMS:** ARMS AND AMMO, HARVESTABLE: BLOODLEAF, RHODODENDRON, SOOT FLOWER, WILD MUTFRUIT; HEALTH AND CHEMS; RECIPE/MOD/ PLAN; TRUNK

Charleston (Exterior)

LEGEND

1. PRIMARY LOCATION: CHARLESTON STATION
2. CHARLESTON BOT-STOP
3. RED BARN
4. PRIMARY LOCATION: CHARLESTON RAILYARD
5. PRIMARY LOCATION: LANDFILL
6. PRIMARY LOCATION: AVR MEDICAL CENTER
7. DESTROYED APARTMENTS
8. COFFEE SHOP
9. PRIMARY LOCATION: HORNWRIGHT INDUSTRIAL HEADQUARTERS
10. LEANING RESPONDER TENEMENT BLOCK (LIMESTONE BRICK)
11. PRIMARY LOCATION: CHARLESTON HERALD

12. SPLIT TENEMENT BLOCK (RED BRICK)
13. CHARLESTON CHURCH
14. KANAWHA RIVER STILT SHACK
15. INTERSTATE 59 OVERPASS SIGN
16. TOPPLED TOWER OF RUST (INACCESSIBLE INTERIOR)
17. RUINED RED HOUSE
18. OPEN PLAN OFFICE
19. MELODY'S CAMP (RESPONDER)
20. PRIMARY LOCATION: CHARLESTON CAPITOL BUILDING
21. CHARLESTON CAPITOL COURTHOUSE
22. RESPONDER BELL
23. DEPARTMENT OF MOTOR VEHICLES (CAPITOL DMV)

24. OLD GLORY
25. UNDERPASS CAMP
26. APARTMENTS TOWER (INTERIOR)
27. PRIMARY LOCATION: SUMMERSVILLE DAM
28. SOUTHEAST APARTMENTS
29. BLUE METAL TOWER (INACCESSIBLE)
30. PHARMACY AND APARTMENT (SHOPPING PROMENADE)
31. ROAD BRIDGE: SUPER MUTANT CAMP
32. PRIMARY LOCATION: CHARLESTON FIRE DEPARTMENT
33. SLOCUM'S JOE (SOUTH CHARLESTON)
34. BOOK STORE, BARBER'S AND CLOTHING SHOP (SOUTH CHARLESTON)

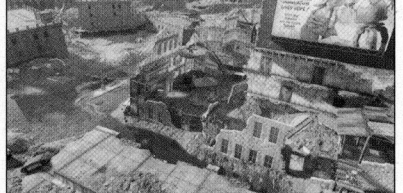

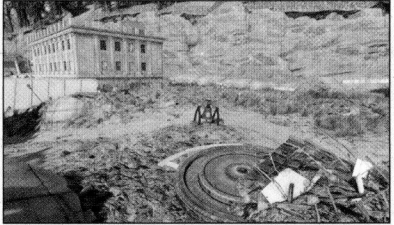
Kanawha River Stilt Shack

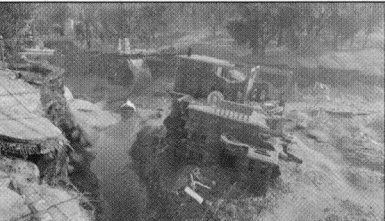
Melody's Camp

The city of Charleston encompasses this and the next eight Primary Locations, all within a relatively delineated border (basically the ruins on either side of the empty Kanawha River). Therefore, all information regarding Crafting, Dangers, Items, Information, Locked areas, and Item Examples are specified for those individual locations: This entry simply flags areas of interest outside these locations.

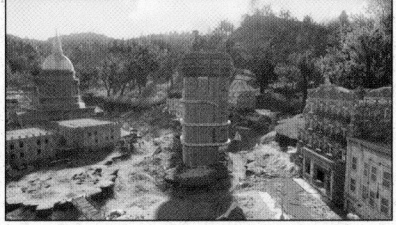
Responder Bell

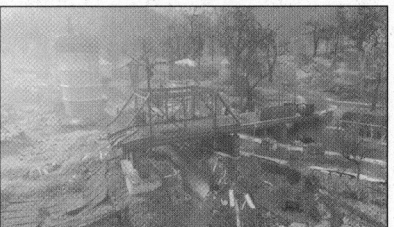
Apartments Tower

Working northwest to south, there's plenty to see and do outside of the major locations to investigate. Far west, look for the bridge across Route 83, close to the railyard, with I-59 running east to west, just north of the Hornwright Industrial Headquarters. The major tenement towers (where the Responders have set up a maneuverability test and turret camp) are just east of the Hornwright skyscraper. All are in terrible disrepair. There are plank paths across the (relatively) dry riverbed and a small camp beneath the road underpass when it breaks apart to the northeast. Move toward the remains of Summersville Dam, and there's a tall apartment building that's fully explorable (watch your step; it's a long drop!).

Blue Metal Tower

Road Bridge: Super Mutant Camp

To the south is a grassy cliff, set of shops, apartments, and the remains of a road bridge that Super Mutants have recently used in their incessant gore-collecting plan. Closer to the AVR Medical Center is a Slocum's Joe coffee shop, and a barber's, book store, and clothing emporium; all have scraps of loot to pillage. Before you leave Charleston, be sure to visit the Fire Department to the south, where the Responders have set up a trading post.

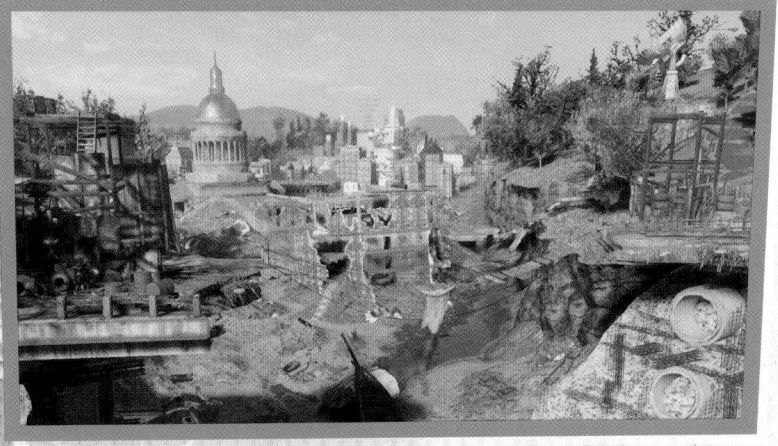

75. CHARLESTON STATION

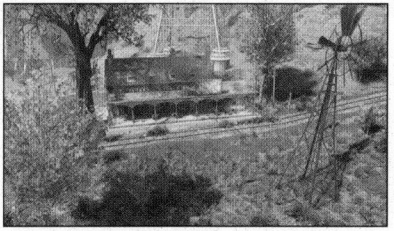

- **COLLECTIBLE: NUKA-CHERRY**
- **CRAFTING: WEAPONS**
- **ITEMS: MY STASH BOX; VENDING MACHINE: AMMUNITION, MEDICAL SUPPLIES**
- **INFO: SCAVENGE RATING: 2; SIZE: 2; THREAT LEVEL: 1–10; TRADER: VENDOR BOT**
- **ITEM EXAMPLES: BEER BOTTLE++, BOILED WATER, BOURBON, COP UNIFORM, TOILET PAPER+**

North of the main ruins of Charleston is the almost-untouched train station, which has a Vendor Bot and a My Stash Box to aid in your item management. Return here from your exploration of the capital to offload and retool.

76. CHARLESTON RAILYARD

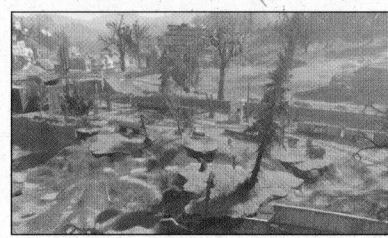

- **COLLECTIBLES: BOBBLEHEAD, MAGAZINE**
- **CRAFTING: ARMOR, COOKING, WEAPONS**
- **ITEMS: ARMS AND AMMO+; HEALTH AND CHEMS; TRUNK**
- **INFO: EXPECTED ENEMY: ROBOT; NOTE; SCAVENGE RATING: 3; SIZE: 3; THREAT LEVEL: 1–10**
- **LOCK: SAFE (1)**
- **ITEM EXAMPLES: 10-MM AUTO PISTOL, ALARM CLOCK, BOURBON BOTTLE, COFFEE CUP, DINNER PLATE, HUNTING RIFLE, LIGHTBULB, LUXOBREW COFFEE POT, RAD-X, SHADELESS LAMP, STEALTH BOY, STEEL WORKER HAT+, TIN PITCHER, WALKING CANE**

TRAINING

CRAFTING AND C.A.M.P.ING

INVENTORY

QUESTS

ATLAS

BESTIARY

APPENDICES

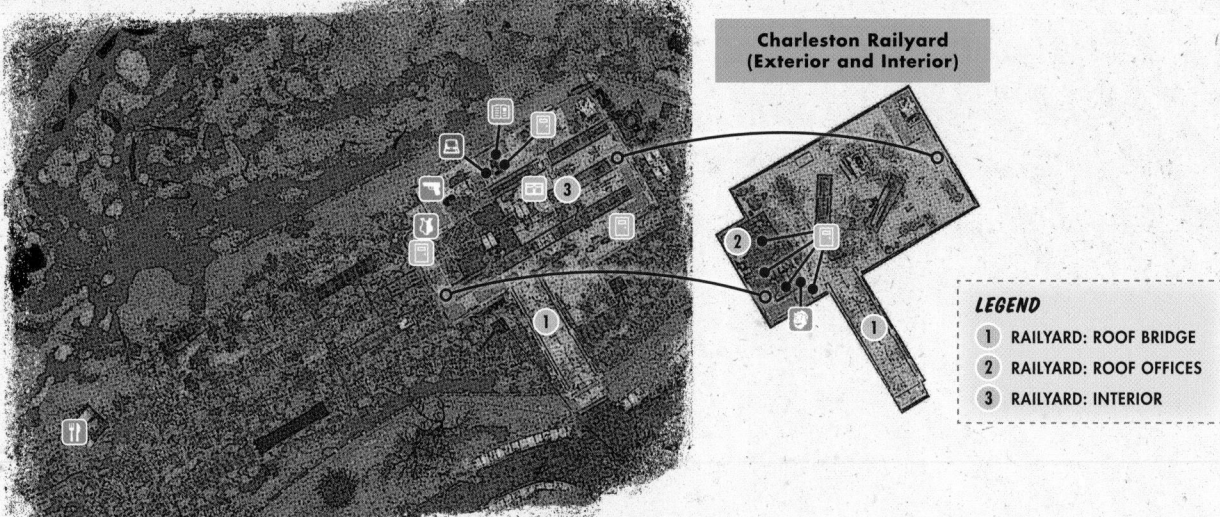

Charleston Railyard (Exterior and Interior)

LEGEND

1. RAILYARD: ROOF BRIDGE
2. RAILYARD: ROOF OFFICES
3. RAILYARD: INTERIOR

Between the power plant and river to the north and the rest of Charleston to the southeast is an abandoned railyard, with rusting railroad carriages and a large brick yard warehouse to explore. Use the gantry to reach the roof (and unloading area), as well as the three offices and an "open air" lounge. A bridge connects the roof to the road. Inside are two ground-floor offices (diagonally opposite) with rail tracks running through the structure and metal gantry huts above.

77. CHARLESTON LANDFILL (WORKSHOP)

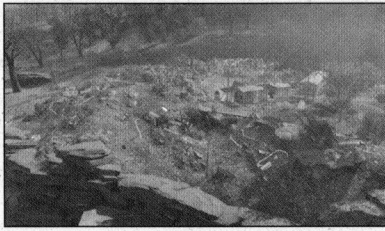

Charleston Landfill (Exterior)

LEGEND

1. RUSTY TRAILER
2. RUINED TRAILER

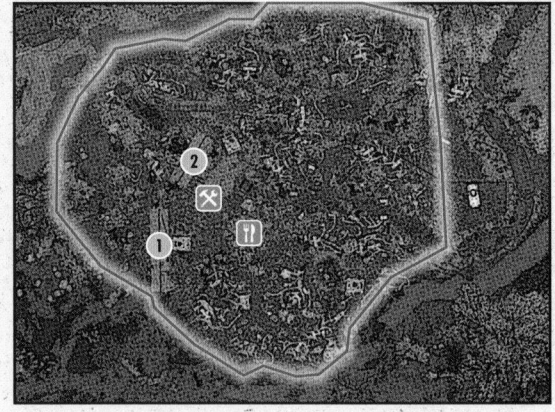

- **CRAFTING:** COOKING, WORKSHOP
- **ITEMS:** ARMS AND AMMO; HARVESTABLE: ALUMINUM, ASH, COPPER, JUNK, STEEL
- **INFO:** EXPECTED ENEMY: VARIES; QUEST: CLAIM WORKSHOP AT CHARLESTON LANDFILL; SCAVENGE RATING: 5 (5); SIZE: 3; SLEEPING; THREAT LEVEL: 1–10
- **ITEM EXAMPLES:** BABY RATTLE, BEER BOTTLE, BLAMCO BRAND MAC AND CHEESE, BOBBY PIN BOX, BROKEN LAMP, CLOTHING IRON, COFFEE POT, GARDEN GNOME, PIPE BOLT-ACTION PISTOL, PLUNGER, OVEN MITT, PEPPER MILL, SCAVENGER OUTFIT, SOAP, SMALL BABY BOTTLE, SUGAR BOMBS, TEDDY BEAR, WOOD BLOCK+
- **WORK:** FOOD (6), WATER (8), JUNK (3), ASH (1), ALUMINUM (1), COPPER (1), STEEL (1)

On the western edge of town, up a short tarmac road, is what used to be an eyesore—the landfill dump for the city. Now it's a source of scavenging and is fought over, so ensure you find the workshop (sitting between the two junk-filled trailers), clear the area of foes, and build up defenses to quickly gather those resources! Watch for attacks from the higher ground to the southwest.

78. AVR MEDICAL CENTER

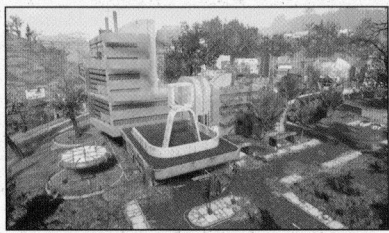

- **ITEMS:** HARVESTABLE: GLOWING FUNGUS; HEALTH AND CHEMS++; RECIPE/MOD/PLAN; TRUNK; VENDING MACHINE: MEDICAL SUPPLIES
- **INFO:** EXPECTED ENEMY: SCORCHED; SCAVENGE RATING: 5; SIZE: 4; SLEEPING; THREAT LEVEL: 1–10
- **LOCK:** DOOR (1), SAFE (1, 2), TERMINAL (0, 1, 1, 2)
- **ITEM EXAMPLES:** ABRAXO CLEANER+, ALARM CLOCK, BAG OF CEMENT, BLAST RADIUS BOARD GAME, BLOWTORCH, BLUE TABLE LAMP, BOILED WATER, BROKEN LAMP+, BROOM, CAFETERIA TRAY++, COFFEE CUP, COMBINATION WRENCH, COOKING PAN, COOKING POT+, COTTON CANDY BITES, EMPTY TEAL BARREL VASE, ENAMEL BUCKET, EYEGLASSES, HOT PLATE, JANGLES THE MOON MONKEY, LOOSE SCREWS, LUXOBREW COFFEE POT, MEDICAL LIQUID NITROGEN DISPENSER, MICROSCOPE+, NUKA-COLA, OFFICE DESK FAN, OIL CANISTER, OVEN MITT, PACK OF DUCT TAPE, PAINTBRUSH, PEPPER, PIPE WRENCH, PLUNGER, SALISBURY STEAK, SALT, SCISSORS, SCREWDRIVER, SHOPPING BASKET, SLEDGEHAMMER, STEEPED TATO FLOWER TEA, SURGICAL TRAY+, TALL DRINKING GLASS+, TELEPHONE, TEST TUBE RACK, TOILET PAPER+, TOY TRUCK, TURPENTINE, VAULT-TEC LUNCH BOX, WHITE PLATE+

- **COLLECTIBLES:** BOBBLEHEAD (4), CAPS STASH, MAGAZINE (3), NUKA-CHERRY
- **CRAFTING:** CHEMISTRY
- **DANGER:** EXPLOSIVE CANNISTER! LONG DROP! OIL!

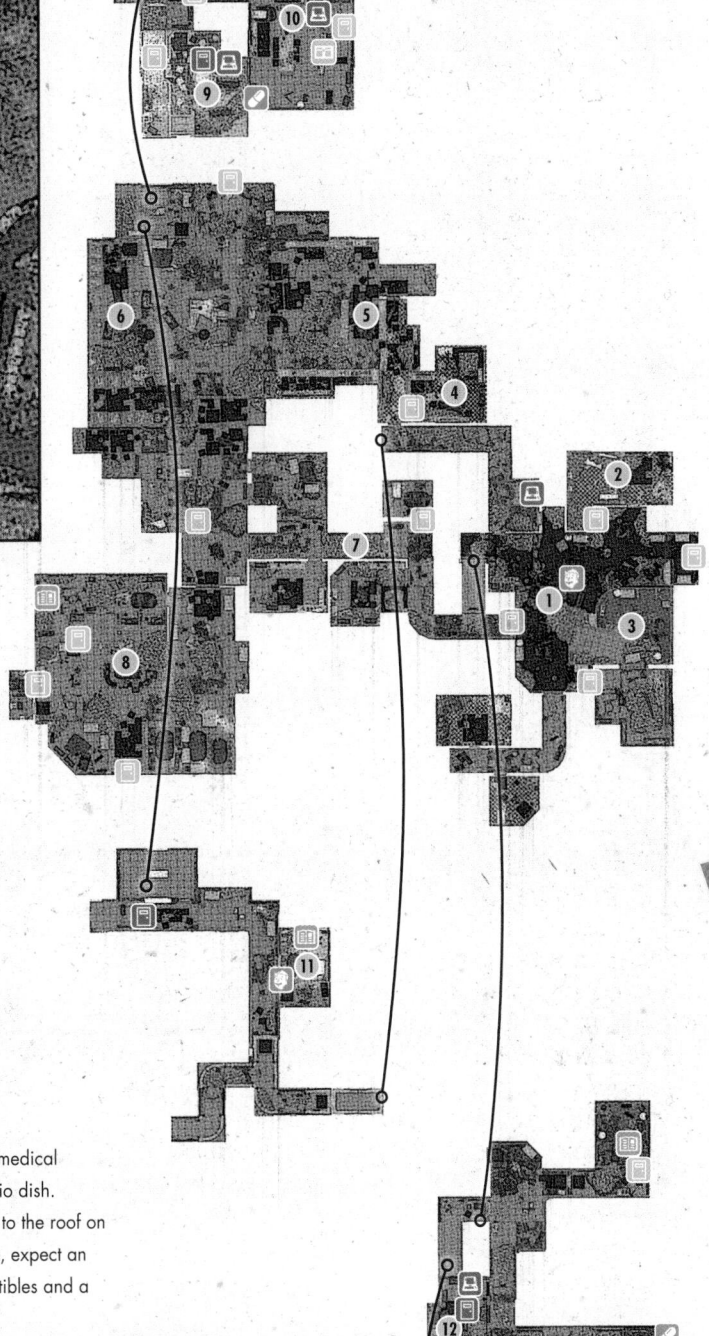

AVR Medical Center (Interior)

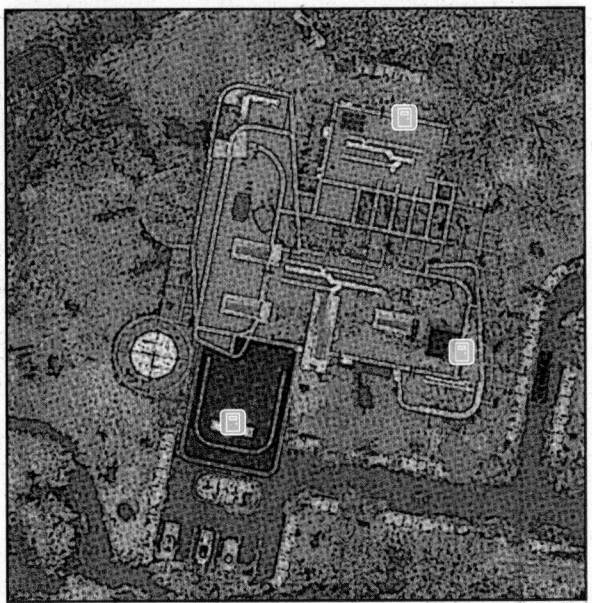

AVR Medical Center (Exterior)

LEGEND

1. EAST FOYER
2. RESTROOMS
3. PHARMACY
4. KITCHENS
5. CAFETERIA
6. BOOTH SEATING
7. LAB ROOMS
8. SOUTHWEST FOYER
9. BASEMENT GENERATOR ROOM
10. BASEMENT LABORATORY
11. ADMINISTRATOR'S ROOM
12. SECURITY CHEM CLOSET
13. UPPER LAB ROOM
14. MARVIN WEXIM'S OFFICE

Over on the upper grassy banks of Southwest Charleston is a rusting medical facility. The main entrance in on the eastern side, close to a large radio dish. There's a secondary entrance on the north wall and fire escape stairs to the roof on the south side (leading to a small computer bank under a tarp). Inside, expect an impressive (if derelict) four-floor hospital to explore, with ample collectibles and a huge amount of medical junk to gather.

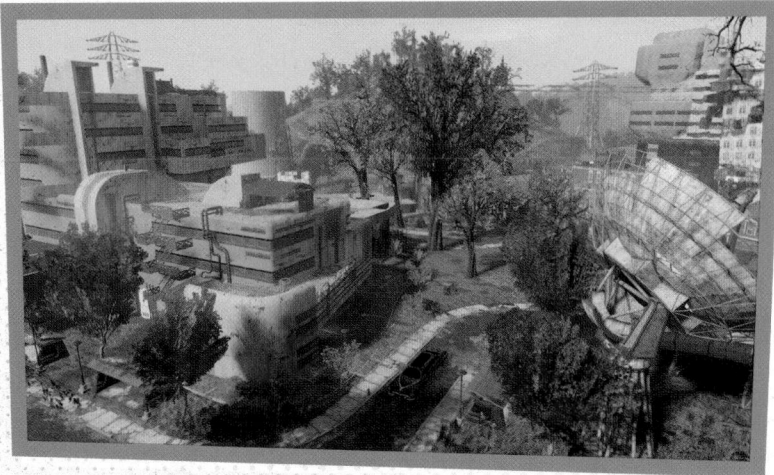

TRAINING

CRAFTING AND C.A.M.P.ING

INVENTORY

QUESTS

ATLAS

BESTIARY

APPENDICES

- **COLLECTIBLES:** BOBBLEHEAD (3), CAPS STASH, MAGAZINE (3), POWER ARMOR
- **CRAFTING:** CHEMISTRY, COOKING (2), TINKER, WEAPONS
- **DANGER:** LONG DROP!+++
- **ITEMS:** ARMS AND AMMO+; HARVESTABLE: GLOWING FUNGUS; HEALTH AND CHEMS; RECIPE/MOD/PLAN; TRUNK; VENDING MACHINE: DOCKING STATION, RESUME RECEPTACLE
- **INFO:** EXPECTED ENEMY: GHOUL, SCORCHED; LANDMARK; NOTE; QUEST: THE MOTHERLODE; SCAVENGE RATING: 4; SIZE: 4; SLEEPING; THREAT LEVEL: 1–10
- **LOCK:** SAFE (0, 1, KEY), TERMINAL (1)
- **ITEM EXAMPLES:** BEAKER STAND, BEER BOTTLE+, BOBBY PIN BOX, CLAW HAMMER, COFFEE CUP+, COFFEE POT, DESK FAN+, FUSION CORE, GLASS JAR, GOLD SCRAP, GOLF CLUB, HOT PLATE, IRON ORE+, MACHETE, MOUNTAIN HONEY, NUKA-COLA, OLD POSSUM, OVEN MITT, PACK OF CIGARETTES, PEPPER, SALISBURY STEAK, SALT, SPICES, STEALTH BOY, STIMPAK, SUGAR, SUGAR BOMBS, TALL FLASK, TATO SOUP, TELEPHONE, URANIUM ORE, VACUUM TUBE, WILLOW ROUNDED VASE, WONDERGLUE, YELLOW TABLE LAMP+

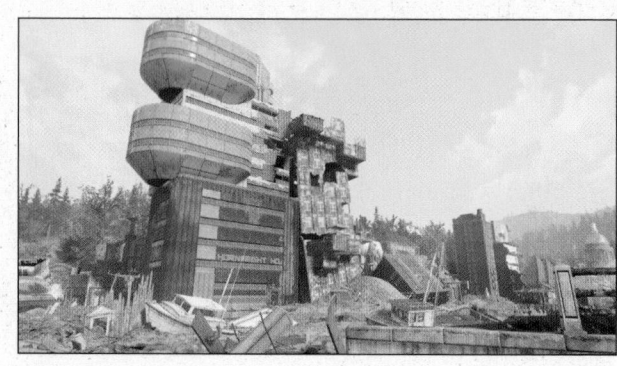

Though not lurching at an alarming angle like the brick tenement block adjacent to this location, the Hornwright tower is still in a frightful state of disrepair. Though you can enter the place via some treacherous tenement block maneuvering (from the Charleston Herald structure), and you can enter the structure from the fifth level, it's easier to work your way up from the ground floor, via the south-facing entrance.

Hornwright Industrial Headquarters (Interior)

Inside, the Hornwrights have thoughtfully labeled each level with a number so you know where you are. Enter the passageway between the walls on Level 03 or 04 to reach the otherwise-inaccessible office on Level 05. Or, with the appropriate ID card, you can use the lobby elevator to reach the executive level. Once you shut down the laser grids, you can reach the sublevel basement.

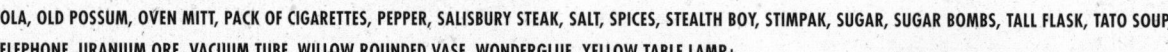

LEGEND

1. LOBBY
2. ARCHIVAL OFFICE
3. LEVEL 02: TECHNOLOGY SUPPORT DEPARTMENT
4. LEVEL 03: HUMAN RESOURCES (FILING ROOM)
5. LEVEL 03: HUMAN RESOURCES (CANDIDATE TESTING)
6. LEVEL 03: LABORATORY
7. LEVEL 04: CONFERENCE ROOM
8. LEVEL 04: PENELOPE HORNWRIGHT'S OFFICE
9. LEVEL 05: R. VARGAS'S OFFICE
10. EXECUTIVE LEVEL: CEO'S OFFICE
11. EXECUTIVE LEVEL: EXTERNAL CONNECTION SYSTEM CHAMBER
12. SUBLEVEL BASEMENT

80. CHARLESTON HERALD

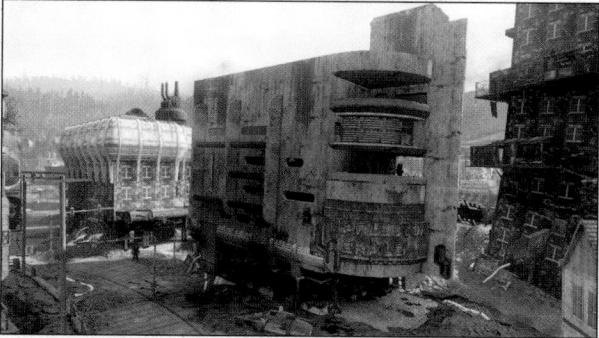

- **COLLECTIBLE:** HOLOTAPE++
- **DANGER:** LONG DROP! TRIPWIRE!
- **ITEM:** RECIPE/MOD/PLAN
- **INFO:** EXPECTED ENEMY: SCORCHED; LANDMARK; NOTE; QUEST: INTO THE FIRE; SCAVENGE RATING: 2; SIZE: 3; THREAT LEVEL: 1–10
- **LOCK:** DOOR (0), SAFE (2)
- **ITEM EXAMPLES:** BOURBON BOTTLE, BROKEN LAMP, COFFEE POT, COFFEE CUP, CRYSTAL LIQUOR DECANTER, GAS CANISTER, LANTERN, OFFICE DESK FAN, TELEPHONE+, TYPEWRITER+, WHISKEY BOTTLE

LEGEND
1 FOYER
2 RESPONDER TEST START
3 C. QUINN'S OFFICE
4 B. BREYER'S OFFICE
5 EDITOR'S OFFICE

The newspaper of note for all of Appalachia is close to the Hornwright building, but this rusting office structure is in even worse condition. Enter the lobby from the street outside to check out an old printing press. Climb through the ceiling to reach an upper level with two doors; one leads to a small balcony, and the other leads to an apartment building that has fallen away in a most spectacular fashion. If you don't head out to the terminal to begin the Responders' physical fitness test, continue up to the purple-walled level of the Herald offices and check out the reporters' offices. One floor up is the editor's office, an outside balcony, and a rickety bridge to the limpet shacks that are adjacent to the Hornwright building.

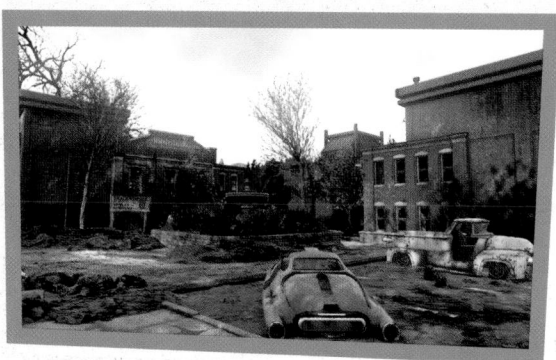

Charleston Herald (Interior)

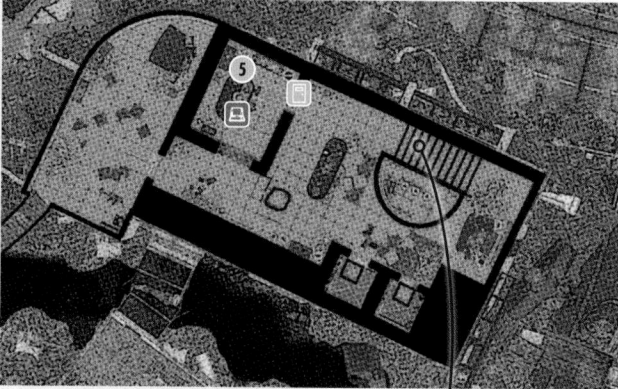
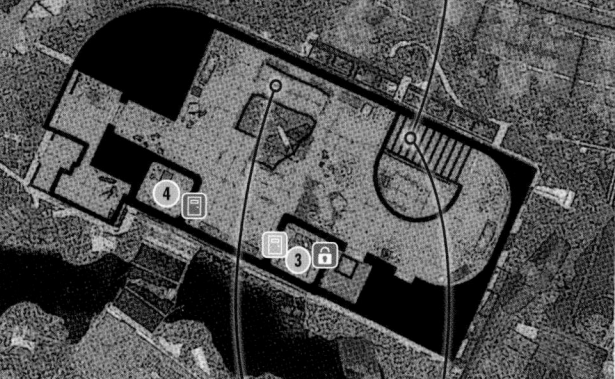
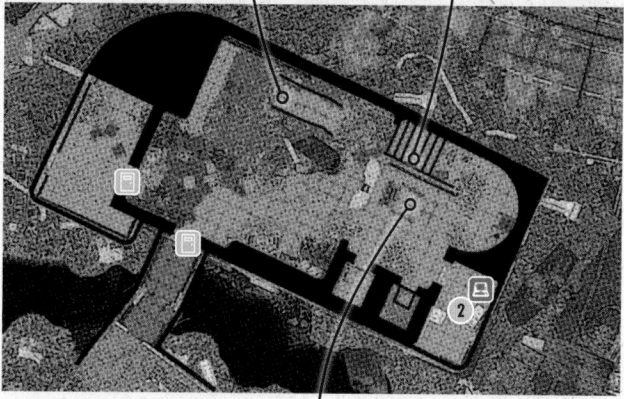
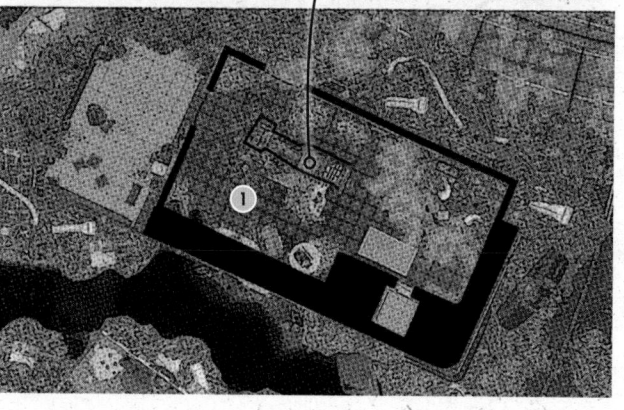

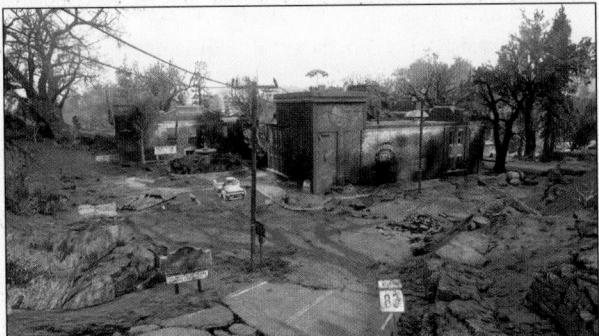

- **COLLECTIBLE:** HOLOTAPE
- **CRAFTING:** ARMOR, WEAPONS
- **DANGER:** EXPLOSIVE CANNISTER!
- **ITEMS:** ARMS AND AMMO; HEALTH AND CHEMS+; OVERSEER'S CACHE
- **INFO:** EXPECTED ENEMY: ROBOTS; SCAVENGE RATING: 4; SIZE: 3; SLEEPING; THREAT LEVEL: 1–10; TRADER: VENDOR BOT
- **LOCK:** DOOR (1), SAFE (0)
- **ITEM EXAMPLES:** 10-MM AUTO PISTOL, 20-LB DUMBBELL, ASHTRAY, BINOCULARS, BONE SAW, BROKEN LAMP, CANNED DOG FOOD, CHEF HAT, COFFEE CUP+, COFFEE POT, COMBINATION WRENCH, DUCT TAPE, ECONOMY WONDERGLUE, EMPTY MILK BOTTLE+, EXTINGUISHER, GAS CANISTER, GREEN RAG HAT, HOT PLATE, LIT CIGAR, LOOSE GEARS, PADDED BLUE JACKET, PAINT CAN, PIPE PISTOL, PORK N' BEANS, SCREWDRIVER, SHORT HUNTING RIFLE, SOAP, STEEL WORKER HAT, SWEET ROLL, TEDDY BEAR+, TELEPHONE+, TOY ALIEN, VODKA, WHISKEY, WINE

This is a good option for a base camp, from which you can explore Charleston. The Fire Department was recently a Responder Trading Post and is far enough away from the dangers down the hill. Feel free to ransack the place for loot, including the roof, which is also reasonably defensible.

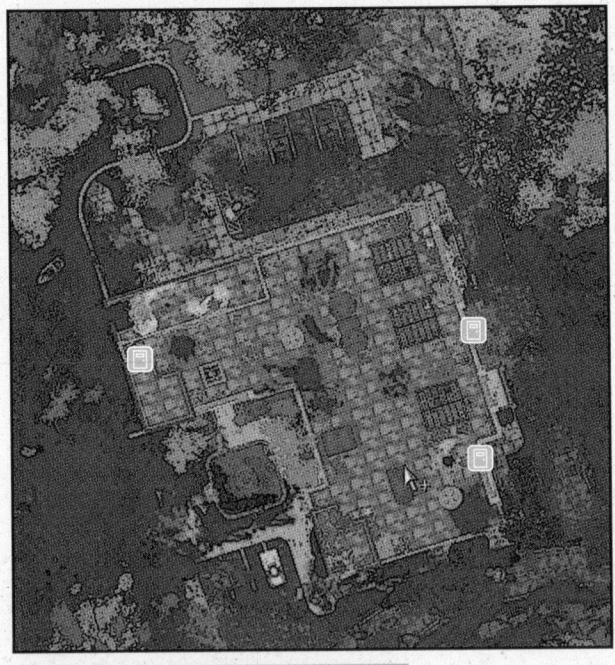

Charleston Fire Department (Exterior)

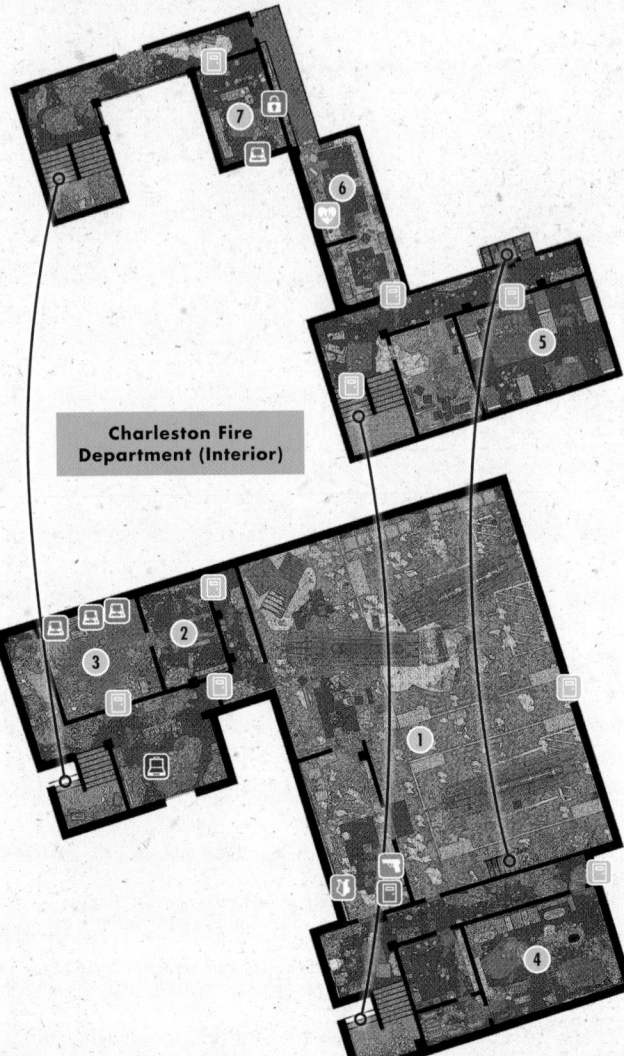

Charleston Fire Department (Interior)

LEGEND
1. FIRE TRUCK GARAGE
2. GYM
3. KNOWLEDGE EXAM & REGISTRATION ROOM
4. BREAK ROOM
5. DORMITORY
6. TRADING POST
7. FIRE BREATHERS OFFICE

82. CHARLESTON CAPITOL BUILDING

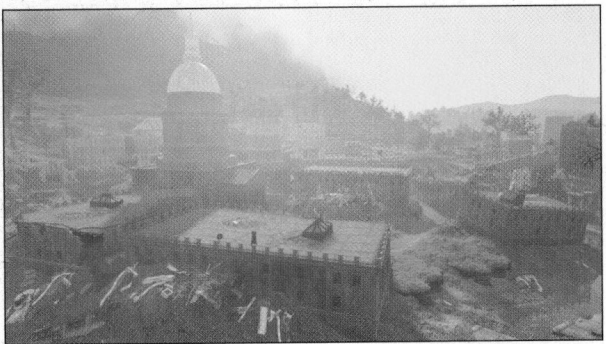

- **COLLECTIBLES:** BOBBLEHEAD, HOLOTAPE, MAGAZINE, NUKA-CHERRY
- **CRAFTING:** ARMOR, CHEMISTRY, COOKING, WEAPONS
- **DANGER:** RADIATION!
- **ITEMS:** ARMS AND AMMO+; HEALTH AND CHEMS; OVERSEER'S CACHE; RECIPE/MOD/PLAN; TRUNK

- **INFO:** EXPECTED ENEMY: GHOUL, IRRADIATED ANIMAL; LANDMARK; NOTE; SCAVENGE RATING: 4; SIZE: 4; SLEEPING; THREAT LEVEL: 1–10
- **LOCK:** DOOR (0, 0, 0, 0, 2), SAFE (2, 3), TERMINAL (1)
- **ITEM EXAMPLES:** ALARM CLOCK, BANDAGE SCISSORS, BLAMCO BRAND MAC AND CHEESE, BLAST RADIUS BOARD GAME, BLUE PAINT, BOILED WATER+, BONE CUTTER, CAFETERIA TRAY, CAMERA, COFFEE CUP+, COFFEE POT, COFFEE TIN, COMBAT ARMOR HELMET, DANDY BOY APPLES, DINNER PLATE, DIRTY BLACK SUIT, ENAMEL BUCKET+, EYEGLASSES, FUSION CORE, HOT DOG, HOT PLATE, INSTAMASH, GLASS JAR+, GLASS PITCHER, GLOBE, LOOSE SCREWS, LUXOBREW COFFEE POT, KEY TO HOLBROOKE'S STASH, MEDICAL LIQUID NITROGEN DISPENSER, MOUNTAIN HONEY, NUKA-COLA, NUKA-COLA BOTTLE+, PACK OF CIGARETTES, PAINTBRUSH, PEPPER, PILLOW+, POTATO CRISPS, PURIFIED WATER, SALISBURY STEAK, SALT, SCREWDRIVER, SHADELESS LAMP, SHORT LASER PISTOL, SLEDGEHAMMER, SUGAR BOMBS, SURGICAL TRAY, SWEET ROLL, TALL DRINKING GLASS, TELEPHONE, TOILET PAPER, TV DINNER TRAY, TYPEWRITER+, VODKA BOTTLE, TVU COFFEE CUP, WALKING CANE, WHISKEY BOTTLE, WILLOW VAULTED VASE

Charleston Capitol Building (Interior)

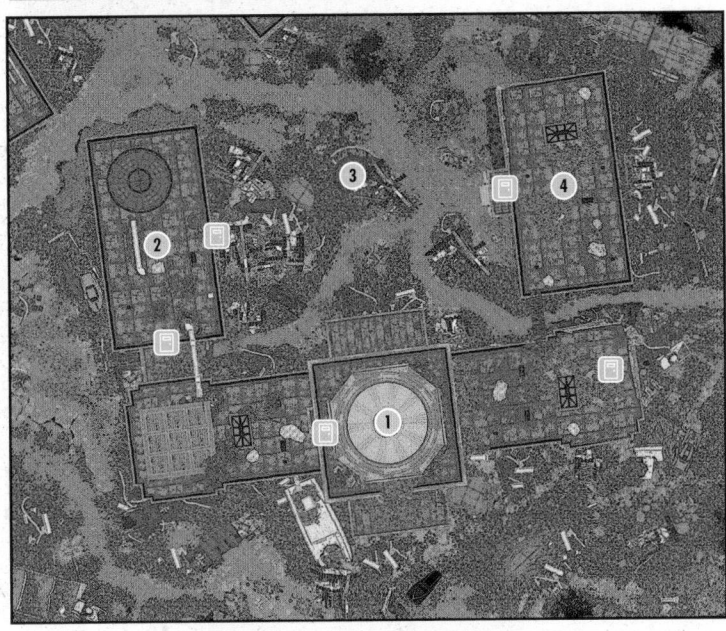

LEGEND
1. CHARLESTON CAPITOL BUILDING
2. CHARLESTON CAPITOL COURTHOUSE
3. RESPONDERS' BELL
4. CHARLESTON CAPITOL DMV

The pride of Appalachia was this temple to legislation, an edifice of limestone with a gold-topped dome that's more robust than many survivors expected. The dome is still intact, though the interior of the three main Capitol structures have been ransacked almost beyond recognition, and there is a sizable amount of rubble (thanks to the bursting of the dam) to trek across. There are three separate structures (a fourth is inaccessible) with entrances to the interior, which provides access to all three buildings beneath the rubble. There's an entrance via an office exposed by a large hole in the exterior of the main building (northeast corner). There are also entrances on the domed roof, two in the central courtyard near the bell (one to the DMV, the other to the Capitol Courthouse via a tunnel of trash), and another into the courthouse at the narrow (south) end where the trash is piled the highest (near a quest-related Responders button).

Starting inside the Capitol DMV, perhaps the most important object in this chamber is the Overseer's Cache, which gives you information and an immediate influx of items. Then methodically check all other rooms for junk, paying special attention to stairwells, fallen ceiling ramps, and other methods of getting to every nook and cranny within these structures. Expect three floors and a basement to explore.

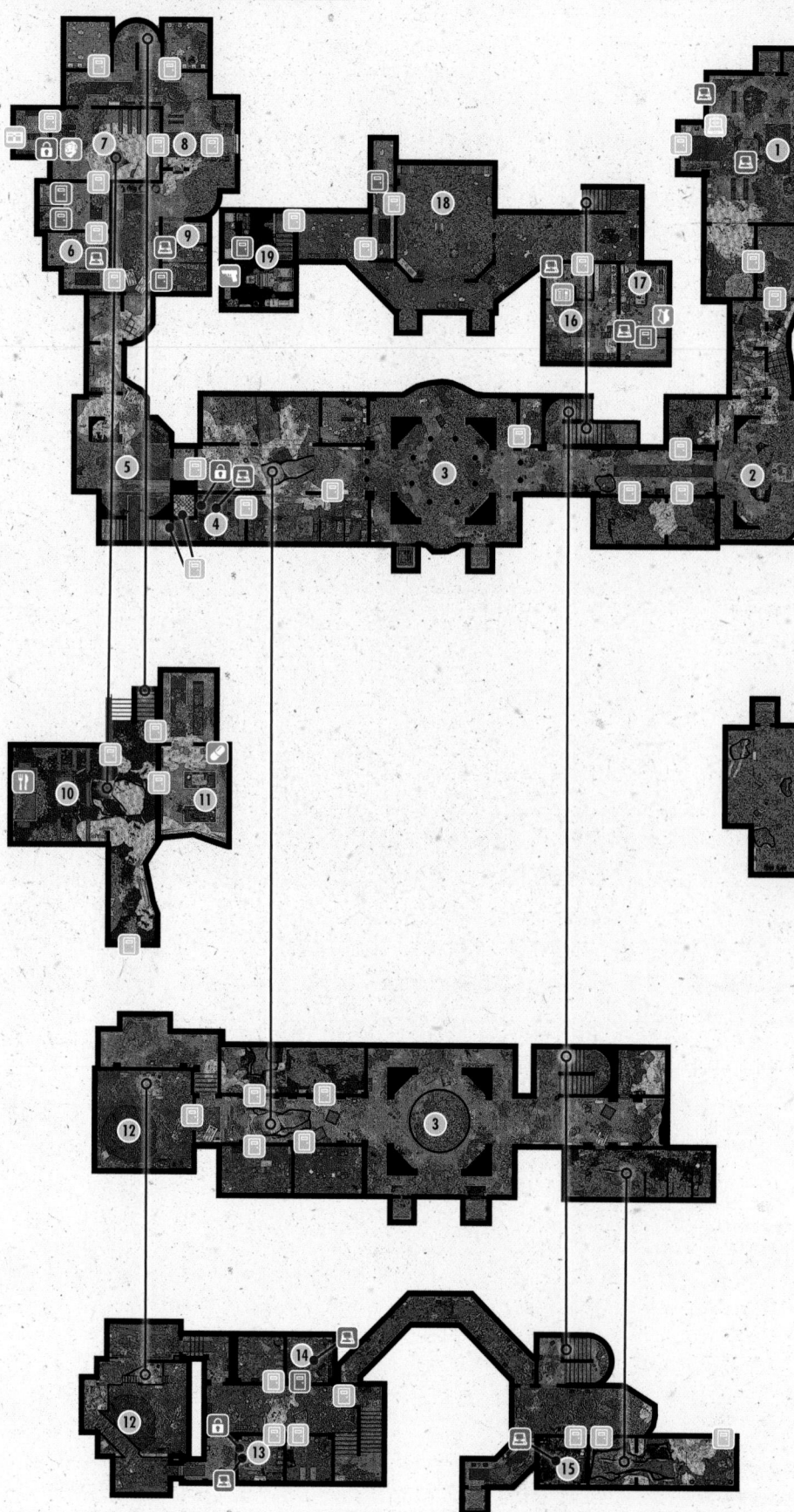

LEGEND

1 DMV WAITING ROOM
2 STATUE JUNCTION ROOM
3 GOLDEN DOME ROTUNDA
4 GOVERNOR'S OFFICE
5 PODIUM ROOM (TV)
6 CAPITOL POLICE OFFICE
7 STATE COURTHOUSE
8 COURTHOUSE ENTRANCE
9 OFFICE OF THE REGISTRAR
10 PODIUM ROOM (PRESS)
11 CONFERENCE ROOM (TRIAGE)
12 RAIDER ROTUNDA
13 SPEAKER POOLE'S OFFICE
14 SENATOR BLACKWELL'S OFFICE
15 TANNER HOLBROOKE'S OFFICE
16 BASEMENT: FILING AND ARCHIVES
17 BASEMENT: MACHINE ROOM
18 BASEMENT: CAPITOL FOOD COURT
19 BASEMENT: FLOODED GENERATOR ROOM

83. WADE AIRPORT (WORKSHOP)

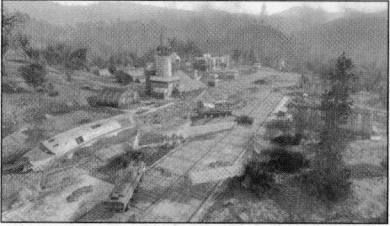

Wade Airport (Exterior)

- **COLLECTIBLES:** CAPS STASH, POWER ARMOR (2)
- **CRAFTING:** WORKSHOP
- **DANGER:** EXPLOSIVE CANNISTER! TURRET! MINE!
- **ITEMS:** HARVESTABLE: COPPER, OIL, SILVER; HEALTH AND CHEMS; TRUNK
- **INFO:** EXPECTED ENEMY: SUPER MUTANT; NOTE; QUEST: CLAIM WORKSHOP AT WADE AIRPORT; SCAVENGE RATING: 3; SIZE: 5; THREAT LEVEL: 1–10
- **LOCK:** DOOR (2)
- **ITEM EXAMPLES:** ABRAXO CLEANER, ANTIFREEZE BOTTLE, BAG OF FERTILIZER, BOBBY PIN BOX, BLUE PAINT, BONE CUTTER, CLEAN COFFEE TIN, COFFEE CUP, COFFEE POT, ECONOMY WONDERGLUE, EMPTY PAINT CAN+, ENAMEL BUCKET, GAS CANISTER+, HOT PLATE, MENTATS, MICROSCOPE, PAINT CAN, PACK OF DUCT TAPE, PICKAX PILSNER, PIPE PISTOL, PLUNGER, RAD-X, SURGICAL TRAY, TEST TUBE RACK, TUBE FLANGE, USED OIL CAN, YELLOW CANISTER, YELLOW PAINT.
- **WORK:** FOOD (5), WATER (5), SILVER (1), COPPER (1), OIL (3)

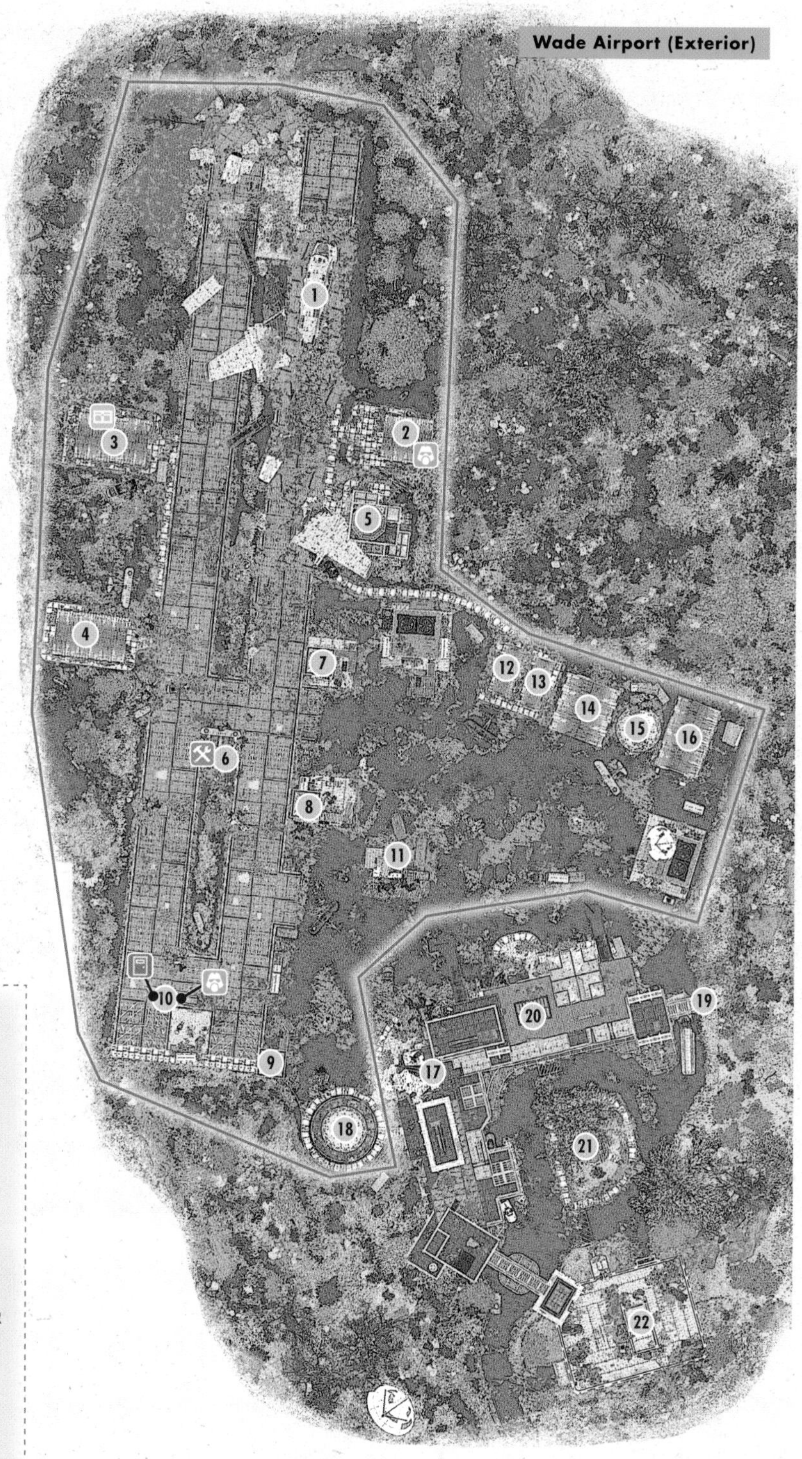

LEGEND

1. CRASHED PLANE FUSELAGE
2. HANGAR: STORAGE AND POWER ARMOR
3. HANGAR: TANK (AND TRUNK)
4. HANGAR: TRUCK
5. CONTROL TOWER (AND PLANE WING)
6. RUNWAY PLATFORM (WORKSHOP)
7. RUNWAY TOWER A
8. RUNWAY TOWER B
9. RUNWAY TOWER C
10. LOCKED AND BOOBY-TRAPPED BLUE TRAILER
11. RADIO MAST AND CONTAINER DEFENSES
12. GARAGE: STORAGE
13. GARAGE: MECHANIC'S
14. HANGAR: BIPLANES
15. VERTIPOD LANDING PAD
16. HANGAR: FIELD HOSPITAL
17. CRASHED VERTIBIRD
18. VERTIPOD LANDING PAD
19. SECURITY HUT
20. ARRIVALS AND DEPARTURES (BUILDING)
21. ARRIVALS AND DEPARTURES (ROUNDABOUT)
22. PARKING STRUCTURE

Wade Airport was in considerable disrepair before Super Mutants arrived, destroyed anything not contained in crates, and started hanging their revolting meat bags everywhere. The terminal structure is mostly devoid of items; concern yourself with the runway area (and the hangars if you're scavenging): The workshop is away from the main terminal building, on a rickety defensive structure by the runway. This workshop also allows you to repair gun emplacements and summon Vertipods to aid in your efforts. Check the landing pads to summon the robotic craft.

TRAINING

CRAFTING AND C.A.M.P.ING

INVENTORY

QUESTS

ATLAS

BESTIARY

APPENDICES

84. SUMMERSVILLE DAM

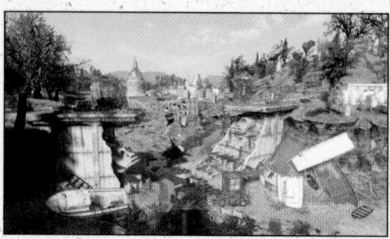

- **DANGER:** EXPLOSIVE CANNISTER! GRENADE! LONG DROP! OIL! RADIATION! TENSION TRIGGER! TRIPWIRE!
- **ITEMS:** ARMS AND AMMO; RECIPE/MOD/PLAN
- **INFO:** EXPECTED ENEMY: SCORCHED; NOTE; SCAVENGE RATING: 2; SIZE: 3; SLEEPING; THREAT LEVEL: 1–10
- **ITEM EXAMPLES:** COFFEE CUP, DESK FAN, FRAGMENTATION GRENADE, GUM DROPS, INSTAMASH, PILLOW, POTATO CRISPS, PROTECTRON MODEL, SHORT DOUBLE-BARREL SHOTGUN, SUGAR, TELEPHONE, TYPEWRITER, YELLOW PLATE

At the eastern end of the Charleston ruins are the remains of the main dam. Those with a penchant for understatement could describe this structure as "compromised." This was recently a Raider camp, and these deceased thugs have left some traps for the unwary. Head up from the lake bed (check the green boat cabin for a trunk) via the ladders and wreckage on the north side of the dam ruins. There's a small pump house and a rope bridge across the gap where the dam was. Watch for those traps!

85. SUMMERSVILLE DOCKS

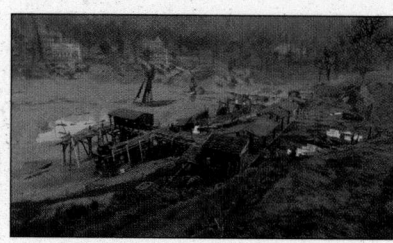

- **COLLECTIBLES:** BOBBLEHEAD (3), MAGAZINE (3)
- **CRAFTING:** COOKING (3)
- **DANGER:** EXPLOSIVE CANNISTER!
- **ITEMS:** ARMS AND AMMO+; HARVESTABLE: SOOT FLOWER; HEALTH AND CHEMS; RECIPE/MOD/PLAN; TRUNK
- **INFO:** EXPECTED ENEMY: IRRADIATED ANIMAL, IRRADIATED INSECT, SCORCHED; SCAVENGE RATING: 4; SIZE: 3; THREAT LEVEL: 1–10
- **LOCK:** DOOR (1)
- **ITEM EXAMPLES:** BAG OF CEMENT, BALL-PEEN HAMMER, BATTERED FEDORA, BEER BOTTLE+, BLOWTORCH, BOBBY PIN BOX, BOURBON, BUBBLEGUM, BUFFOUT, CANNED DOG FOOD, COOLANT, CUTTING BOARD, DUCT TAPE, EXTINGUISHER, FANCY LAD SNACK CAKES, FARMHAND CLOTHES, FISHING ROD+, FRYING PAN, GAS MASK, INSTAMASH, LIFE PRESERVER+, LUXOBREW COFFEE POT, METAL TUB, RADSTAG HIDE OUTFIT, RUM, SUGAR, SUGAR BOMBS

Summersville Docks (Exterior)

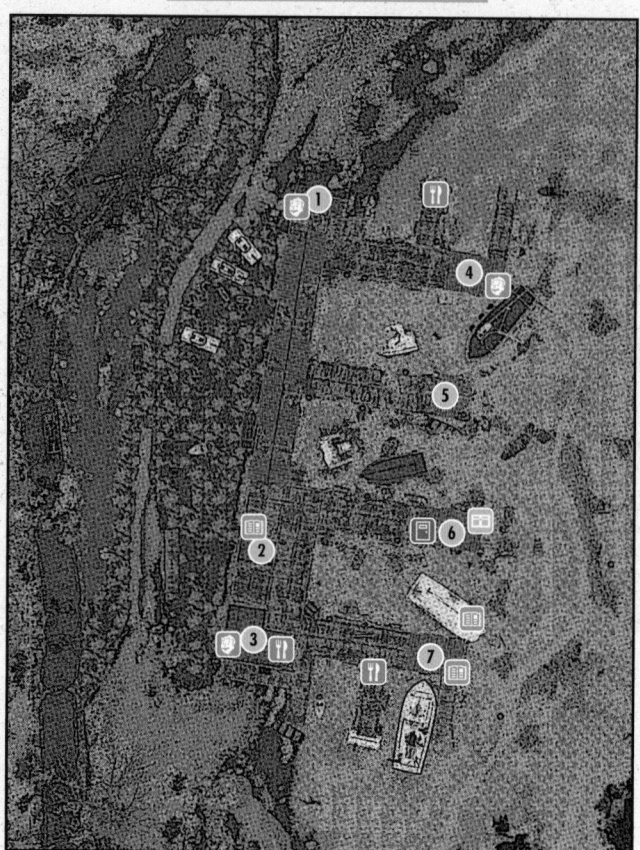

LEGEND

1. STORAGE SHED
2. DRYING SHED
3. FISH SHOP
4. NORTH BOATHOUSE
5. EAST BOATHOUSE
6. SOUTHEAST BOATHOUSE
7. SOUTH BOATHOUSE

Search this rotting series of covered docks, small wooden shops, and riverside boathouses, starting at the parking lot and working your way toward the dry lake. Check for additional sleeping and enemy locations under each boathouse.

86. LAKESIDE CABINS (WORKSHOP)

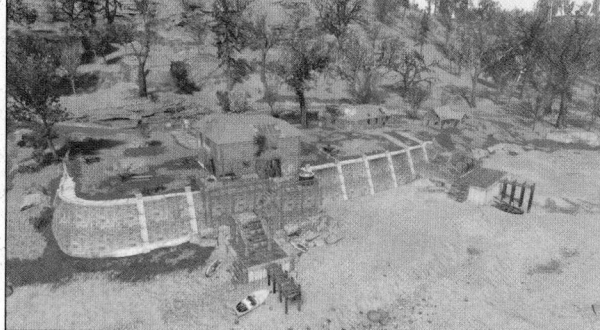

Lakeside Cabins (Exterior)

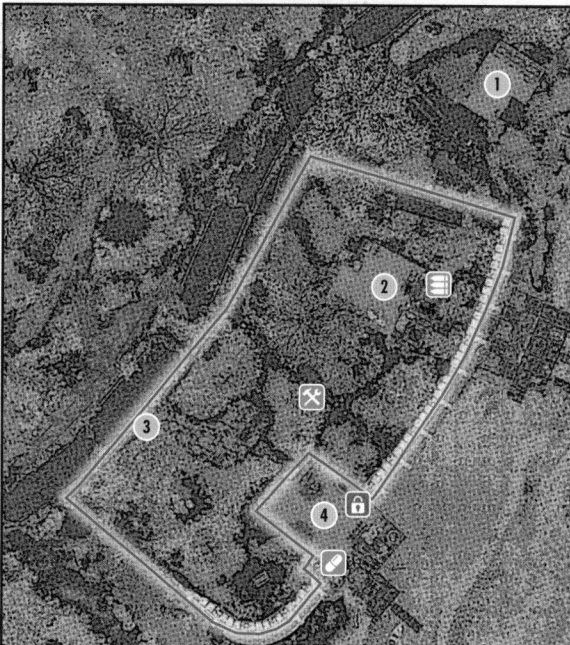

- **CRAFTING:** CHEMISTRY, TINKER, WORKSHOP
- **ITEMS:** ARMS AND AMMO; HARVESTABLE: CRYSTAL, LEAD, SILVER, RHODODENDRON, SOOT FLOWER, WOOD PILE; RECIPE/MOD/PLAN
- **INFO:** EXPECTED ENEMY: VARIES; QUEST: CLAIM WORKSHOP AT LAKESIDE CABINS; SCAVENGE RATING: 4(5+); SIZE: 3; THREAT LEVEL: 1–10
- **LOCK:** SAFE (2)
- **ITEM EXAMPLES:** BOILED WATER, CANNED DOG FOOD, CLOWN OUTFIT, COOKING POT, COFFEE CUP, FISHING ROD, GAS CANISTER, GLOWING FUNGUS PUREE, FRYING PAN, HOT PLATE, INDUSTRIAL SIZE SHORTENING, KITCHEN SCALE, LIFE PRESERVER+, OFFICE DESK FAN, OVEN MITT, PLASTIC FORK+, PUMPKIN PIE, RIB CAGE, SKULL, WILLOW BARREL VASE, YELLOW PLATE+, YUM YUM DEVILED EGGS.
- **WORK:** FOOD (6), WATER (6), SILVER (1), CRYSTAL (1), LEAD (1), WOOD (1)

LEGEND

1. NORTH CABIN
2. NORTHEAST CABIN
3. POSEIDON POWER BOX
4. MAIN CABIN

Running along the lake's northwestern edge are four cabins, two of which are well within the boundary of this public workshop. There is extra power available from a box if you started up the Poseidon Power Plant. The workshop is outside the large main cabin. Command this location, check to see if the resources are needed, and start resource gathering at your earliest convenience.

87. NEW GAD

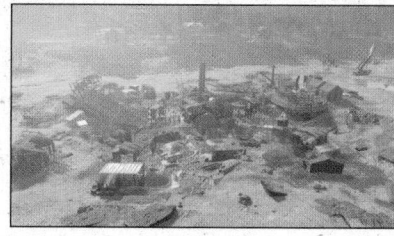

New Gad (Exterior)

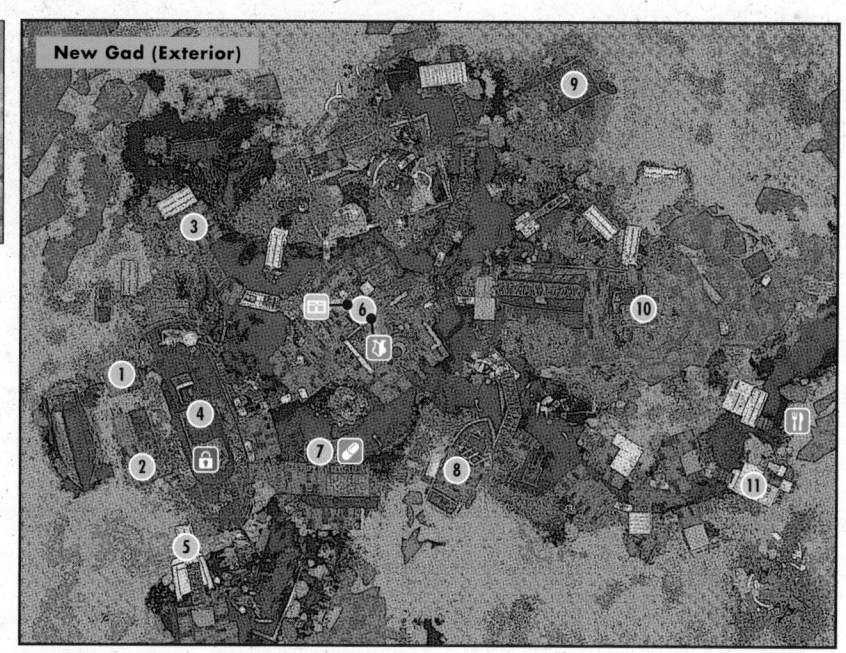

- **COLLECTIBLE:** NUKA-CHERRY
- **CRAFTING:** ARMOR, CHEMISTRY, COOKING
- **DANGER:** RADIATION!
- **ITEMS:** ARMS AND AMMO+; HARVESTABLE: GLOWING FUNGUS; HEALTH AND CHEMS; TRUNK
- **INFO:** EXPECTED ENEMY: SUPER MUTANT; SCAVENGE RATING: 3; SIZE: 3; SLEEPING; THREAT LEVEL: 1–10
- **LOCK:** SAFE (1)
- **ITEM EXAMPLES:** 10-MM AUTO PISTOL, BLACKWATER BREW, BOILED WATER+, BROWN BOTTLE, CANNED DOG FOOD, CHESSBOARD, COFFEE CUP, DANDY BOY APPLES, DOG BOWL, ENAMEL BUCKET+, GLASS PITCHER, HUNTING RIFLE, INSTAMASH, MENTATS, NEW RIVER RED ALE, OAK HOLLER LAGER, POTATO CRISPS, SALISBURY STEAK, SHOT GLASS+, SHOVEL, TATTERED RAGS, TEST TUBE RACK, TOY ALIEN

LEGEND

1. CAT SHED
2. POOL TABLE SHACK
3. BUNK BED SHACK
4. GREEN TUG-BOAT SHACK
5. ORANGE CONTAINER ARMORY
6. THE BIG SHACK
7. CHEMISTRY CARAVAN
8. RED BOAT SHACK
9. RED SHED (AND GREEN DINGHY)
10. SHACK ON THE ROCK
11. HOSPITAL SHACK

TRAINING · CRAFTING AND C.A.M.P.ING · INVENTORY · QUESTS · ATLAS · BESTIARY · APPENDICES

Before Summersville Lake was created, an old farming community set up a village named Gad. With the lake now "drained," a shanty town has appeared over the original town's foundations. It is a maze of tiny, interconnecting shacks. Learn to situate yourself by remembering the central "Big Shack" has four levels and is in the center of town, with rickety planks out to other sections.

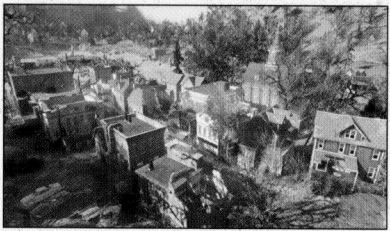

- **CRAFTING:** COOKING (2)
- **DANGER:** EXPLOSIVE CANNISTER! GRENADE! LONG DROP! OIL! TENSION TRIGGER!
- **ITEMS:** ARMS AND AMMO; HARVESTABLE: RHODODENDRON, SILT BEAN, SOOT FLOWER, WILD MUTFRUIT; HEALTH AND CHEMS; TRUNK
- **INFO:** EXPECTED ENEMY: SUPER MUTANT; SCAVENGE RATING: 4; SIZE: 4; SLEEPING; THREAT LEVEL: 1–10
- **ITEM EXAMPLES:** ABRAXO CLEANER, BATTERED CLIPBOARD+, BEER BOTTLE++, BLAMCO BRAND MAC AND CHEESE, BOURBON, BROKEN LAMP+, CAMPAIGN HAT, CIGARETTE CARTON, CLOTHES HANGER+, COFFEE CUP, COFFEE POT, COOKING POT, CRACKED DEATHCLAW EGG, CRAM, CUTTING BOARD, DANDY BOY APPLES, DISHRAG, DOG BOWL, FRYING PAN, HOT PLATE, INDUSTRIAL SIZE SHORTENING, KITCHEN SCALES, LADLE, METAL BUCKET, MULTIPURPOSE AXE, OFFICE DESK FAN, PILLOW, PUMPKIN PIE, RED PLATE, RIGHT HAND BONES, SOAP, SPATULA, TEDDY BEAR+, TOASTER, TOY TRUCK, TELEPHONE, WHISKEY

The once-bucolic town on the north end of the lake that shares its name is now a trap-filled hunting ground for wayward Vault Dwellers and mutated undesirables. The fire escapes at the playground or the eastern edge of the settlement provide quick access to the rooftop areas, where it's easiest to hide and attack; remove the traps and many explosive cannisters first.

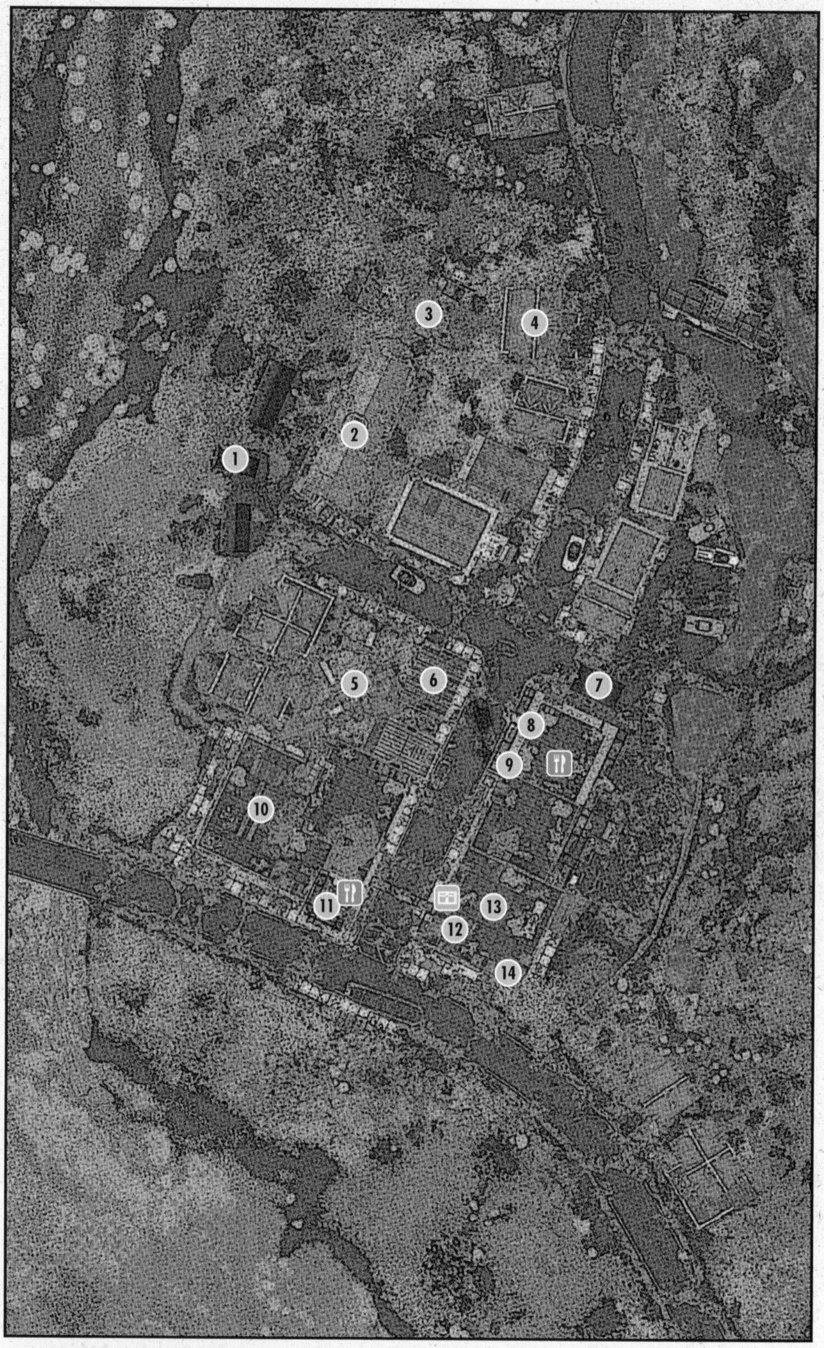

Summersville (Exterior)

LEGEND

1 VOTER SERVICES TENTS	8 DRY CLEANING STORE (INTERIOR)
2 SUMMERSVILLE CHURCH	9 DELICATESSEN (INTERIOR)
3 GRAVEYARD PICNIC	10 ICE CREAM PARLOR (INTERIOR)
4 OVERGROWN ABODE	11 DRUNKEN SNIPER'S NEST
5 OVERGROWN PLAYGROUND	12 JEWELRY AND CLOTHING STORE (INTERIOR)
6 LAUNDRETTE (INTERIOR)	13 ACCESSIBLE APARTMENT (ROOF AND INTERIOR)
7 VOTING TENT	14 ALMOST INACCESSIBLE APARTMENT (INTERIOR)

🏠 89. BURDETTE MANOR

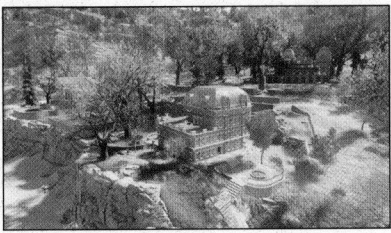

- **COLLECTIBLES:** BOBBLEHEAD (2), CAPS STASH, MAGAZINE (2)
- **ITEMS:** HARVESTABLE: BRAIN FUNGUS, SOOT FLOWER; HEALTH AND CHEMS; RECIPE/MOD/PLAN; TRUNK;
- **INFO:** EXPECTED ENEMY: IRRADIATED ANIMAL; INSTRUMENT; SCAVENGE RATING: 3; SIZE: 3; THREAT LEVEL: 1–10
- **LOCK:** SAFE (2)
- **ITEM EXAMPLES:** ALARM CLOCK, CIGAR BOX, EMPTY FLORAL VAULTED VASE+, ENAMEL BUCKET, FLOWER POT, MILK BOTTLE+, MOP, PEPPER MILL, PITCHFORK, POTATO CRISPS, RED PLATE, SUGAR BOMBS, TALL DRINKING GLASS, TEDDY BEAR, TOILET PAPER, TYPEWRITER, YELLOW TABLE LAMP+

This imposing yellow-bricked mansion has elements of the Italianate style, with a fire pit and the remains of some steps down to where the water's edge once was. One corner of the mansion has crumbled away, close to an exterior door; both allow access into much of the ground floor. You can go up a spiral staircase to a bar area, a bedroom, and an attic area. Both upper floor chambers have sections of wall missing, allowing access to an upper balcony. They connect to each other.

🏛 90. SUGARMAPLE

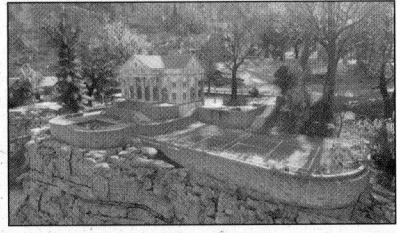

- **COLLECTIBLE:** CAPS STASH
- **ITEMS:** HARVESTABLE: RHODODENDRON, SNAPTAIL, SOOT FLOWER
- **INFO:** EXPECTED ENEMY: IRRADIATED ANIMAL; SCAVENGE RATING: 1; SIZE: 2; THREAT LEVEL: 1–10
- **ITEM EXAMPLES:** NOT MUCH!

An immense Greek Revival mansion on the shores of the dry lake, complete with a lion fountain and stone-walled patio and tennis court. The house itself is inaccessible.

🏠 91. OVERLOOK CABIN

- **COLLECTIBLE:** BOBBLEHEAD (2), CAPS STASH (3), HOLOTAPE, MAGAZINE (2)
- **CRAFTING:** COOKING, ARMOR
- **ITEMS:** HARVESTABLE: BRAIN FUNGUS, GLOWING FUNGUS, RHODODENDRON, SOOT FLOWER; HEALTH AND CHEMS; RECIPE/MOD/PLAN; TRUNK
- **INFO:** EXPECTED ENEMY: SCORCHED; SCAVENGE RATING: 3; SIZE: 3; THREAT LEVEL: 1–10
- **LOCK:** SAFE (2)
- **ITEM EXAMPLES:** ABRAXO CLEANER INDUSTRIAL GRADE, ACETONE CANISTER, BLAST RADIUS BOARD GAME, BLASTING CAPS BOX, BOWLER HAT, COFFEE CUP+, COTTON YARN, CRUSHED RUSTY CONTAINER, DESK FAN, DUCT TAPE, FLORAL VAULTED VASE+, FUSE, GARDEN GNOME, GIDDYUP BUTTERCUP, HOUSE TEAPOT, INDUSTRIAL SIZE SHORTENING, INDUSTRIAL SOLVENT, POOL BALL+, PUMPKIN PIE, SOAP, TALL DRINKING GLASS+, TEAPOT, TIN CAN, TIRE IRON, TOILET PAPER, USED OIL CAN, WOOD BLOCK++, YELLOW TABLE LAMP

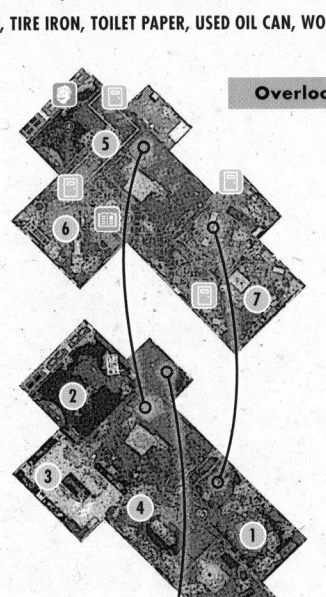

Overlook Cabin (Interior)

LEGEND
1. RECEPTION
2. GAME ROOM
3. KITCHEN
4. DINING ROOM
5. UPSTAIRS LANDING
6. CHILD'S BEDROOM
7. MASTER BEDROOM
8. CELLAR

Built to mimic the much smaller mountain cabins, this large lodge is in relatively good shape, with only part of the interior's upper floor falling into the reception area. There are three floors' worth of junk-collecting you can attempt here.

🏠 92. RIVERSIDE MANOR

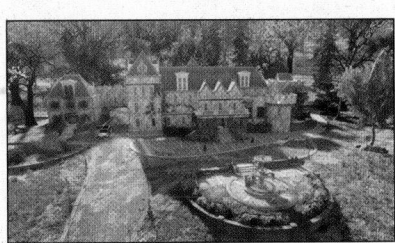

- **COLLECTIBLES:** BOBBLEHEAD (2), CAPS STASH (7), HOLOTAPE, MAGAZINE (4)
- **CRAFTING:** ARMOR (2), CHEMISTRY, TINKER'S, WEAPONS
- **ITEMS:** ARMS AND AMMO+; HARVESTABLE: RHODODENDRON, SOOT FLOWER; HEALTH AND CHEMS; TRUNK
- **INFO:** EXPECTED ENEMY: IRRADIATED ANIMAL, SCORCHED; INSTRUMENT; QUESTS: MISTRESS OF MYSTERY; SCAVENGE RATING: 4; SIZE: 4; THREAT LEVEL: 1–10
- **LOCK:** DOOR (3, S), SAFE (2, 3, 3)

ABRAXO CLEANER, ALARM CLOCK, BASEBALL BAT, BASEBALL CAP, BLUE TABLE LAMP, BOBBY PIN BOX, BONE CUTTER, BOURBON, BROKEN LAMP, BURNT BOOK+, CHESSBOARD, CLOTHES HANGER+, DIRTY BLACK SUIT, DIRTY DESKTOP FRAME+, EMPTY FLORAL VAULTED VASE+, ENAMEL BUCKET+, EXTINGUISHER, FANCY LADS SNACK CAKES, FRAGMENTATION MINE, GEAR, HAIRBRUSH, HOUSE TEAPOT, MICROSCOPE, MOLOTOV COCKTAIL, NUKA-COLA BOTTLE+, OIL CANISTER, ORANGE CANISTER, OVEN MITT, PEPPER, POOL BALL+, POOL CUE, PLUNGER, RACK, SALT, SHOVEL, SPICES, SUGAR BOMBS, T-SHIRT AND SLACKS, TALL DRINKING GLASS+, TATO, TOILET PAPER, TOY ALIEN, TOY TRUCK, TURPENTINE, UNSTOPPABLE SHINDIG BOARD GAME, VASE, WHISKEY, WINE BOTTLE, WOOD BLOCK+, WRENCH, YELLOW PLATE+, YELLOW TABLE LAMP+

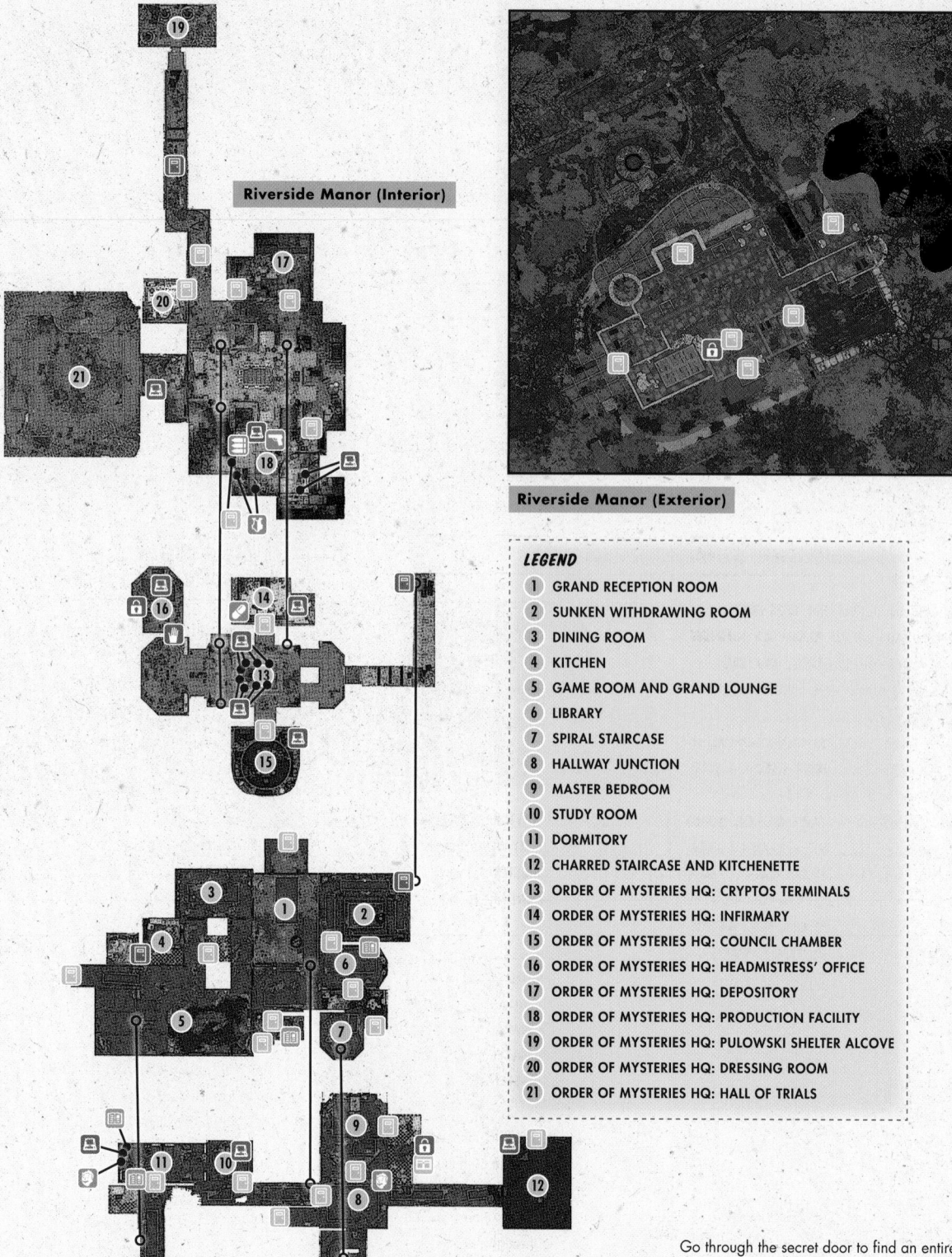

Riverside Manor (Interior)

Riverside Manor (Exterior)

LEGEND

1. GRAND RECEPTION ROOM
2. SUNKEN WITHDRAWING ROOM
3. DINING ROOM
4. KITCHEN
5. GAME ROOM AND GRAND LOUNGE
6. LIBRARY
7. SPIRAL STAIRCASE
8. HALLWAY JUNCTION
9. MASTER BEDROOM
10. STUDY ROOM
11. DORMITORY
12. CHARRED STAIRCASE AND KITCHENETTE
13. ORDER OF MYSTERIES HQ: CRYPTOS TERMINALS
14. ORDER OF MYSTERIES HQ: INFIRMARY
15. ORDER OF MYSTERIES HQ: COUNCIL CHAMBER
16. ORDER OF MYSTERIES HQ: HEADMISTRESS' OFFICE
17. ORDER OF MYSTERIES HQ: DEPOSITORY
18. ORDER OF MYSTERIES HQ: PRODUCTION FACILITY
19. ORDER OF MYSTERIES HQ: PULOWSKI SHELTER ALCOVE
20. ORDER OF MYSTERIES HQ: DRESSING ROOM
21. ORDER OF MYSTERIES HQ: HALL OF TRIALS

Perhaps the most imposing homes on Mansions Row is the Riverside abode, with its large footprint, cannons on a low roof turret, and faded grandeur both inside and out. There are multiple entrances, but roof access is only available from the interior. Methodically check each room for items and collectibles. If you have the quest active, try to find the cunningly hidden secret door (hint: check the sunken withdrawing room thoroughly)!

Go through the secret door to find an entire level underneath the mansion, which is sealed unless a specific Mistress of Mystery Quest is active. It features various chambers that help illuminate your ongoing antics with this group. Consult the Side Quests section of this guide for more information.

93. TORRANCE HOUSE

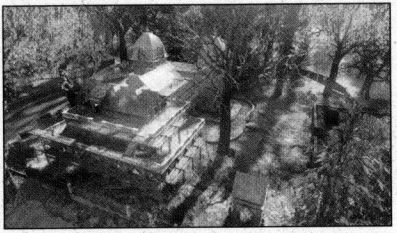

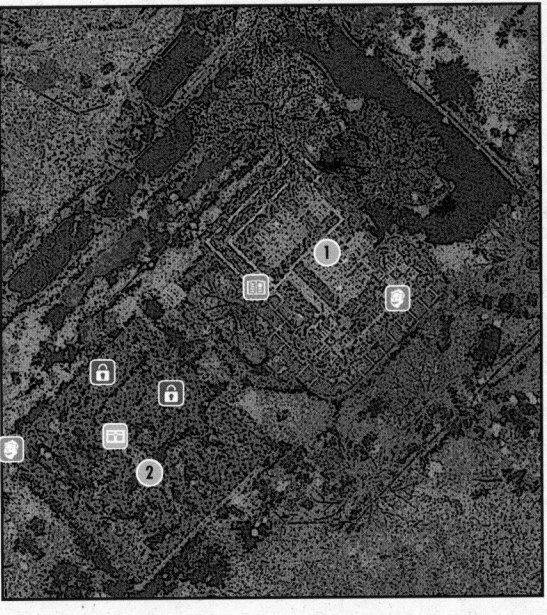

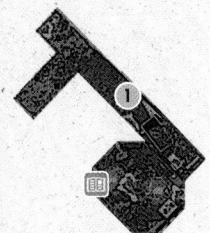

Torrance House (Exterior and Interior)

- **COLLECTIBLES:** BOBBLEHEAD (2), MAGAZINE (2)
- **DANGER:** LONG DROP!
- **ITEMS:** HARVESTABLE: RHODODENDRON, SOOT FLOWER; TRUNK
- **INFO:** EXPECTED ENEMY: IRRADIATED ANIMAL, ROBOT; SCAVENGE RATING: 2; SIZE: 3; THREAT LEVEL: 1–10
- **LOCK:** SAFE (2, 2)
- **ITEM EXAMPLES:** BOILED WATER, ENAMEL BUCKET+, NUKA-COLA BOTTLE, RAD-X, TEDDY BEAR, WOOD BLOCK ("REDRUM")++

LEGEND
1. TORRANCE HOUSE
2. HEDGE MAZE

Wonderful parties were once held in this imposing mansion; now, small sections of the ground floor have been broken into. Scaffolding allows access to the roof, where *midnight, the stars, and you* are all that's needed for a good time. The real treasures are located in the adjacent hedge maze, which is thoughtfully mapped here so you don't have to chase your wayward offspring around to "correct" him.

94. HORNWRIGHT SUMMER VILLA

- **COLLECTIBLES:** BOBBLEHEAD, CAPS STASH, HOLOTAPE, MAGAZINE (2), NUKA-COLA QUANTUM
- **CRAFTING:** ARMOR (2), TINKER, WEAPONS
- **ITEMS:** HARVESTABLE: CORN, GOURD; RECIPE/ MOD/PLAN; TRUNK
- **INFO:** EXPECTED ENEMY: IRRADIATED ANIMAL, ROBOT; INSTRUMENT; SCAVENGE RATING: 4; SIZE: 3; SLEEPING; THREAT LEVEL: 1–10
- **ITEM EXAMPLES:** ADJUSTABLE WRENCH, ALUMINUM CAN, BINOCULARS, BLOWTORCH, CIGARETTE CARTON, COMBINATION WRENCH, COTTON YARN, CRUSHED ACETONE CANISTER, ECONOMY WONDERGLUE, EMPTY TEAL ROUNDED VASE, ENAMEL BUCKET, FANCY LAD SNACK CAKES, FIRE AXE, OIL CANISTER, FLOWER POT+, GARDEN GNOME, ORANGE CANISTER, NUKA-COLA CUP+, SUGAR BOMBS, SUPRATHAW ANTIFREEZE, TALL DRINKING GLASS, TOY TRUCK, USED OIL CAN, YELLOW PLATE

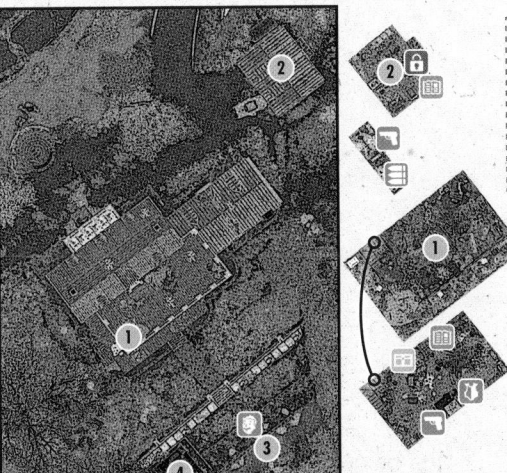

LEGEND
1. VILLA AND WINE CELLAR
2. GARAGE AND STORAGE
3. GAZEBO
4. GREENHOUSE

The hifalutin coal mining family used to own this summer villa, which is now mostly boarded up. However, you can rummage through the garage, then head around to the opening in the rear of the property, close to the greenhouse. Descend into a wine cellar for a trove of now-useful junk items.

Hornwright Summer Villa (Exterior)

95. FISSURE SITE (FISSURE)

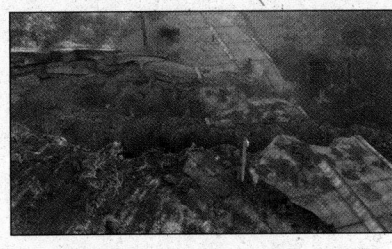

- **DANGER:** LONG DROP! RADIATION!++
- **ITEMS:** HARVESTABLE: RHODODENDRON, SCORCHBEAST GUANO PILE, SOOT FLOWER, ULTRACITE
- **INFO:** EXPECTED ENEMY: SCORCHBEAST, SCORCHED; SCAVENGE RATING: 1; SIZE: 1; THREAT LEVEL: 1–10
- **ITEM EXAMPLES:** NOT MUCH!

It isn't wise to head up or down the hill on I-62 at this particular point, as there's a fissure in the road; a terrifying Scorchbeast and her minions appear from this. Tackle these foes only when you're strong enough!

ZONE E: SECONDARY LOCATIONS

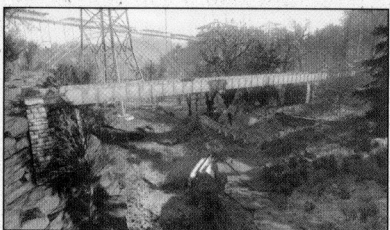

The Scuppered Tug

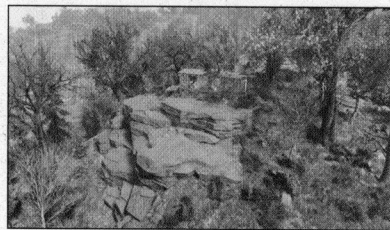

Trailer Overlook (north of Summersville)

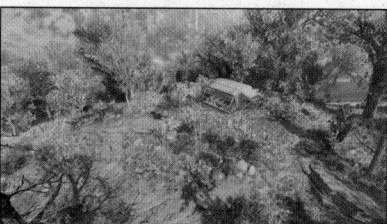

Summersville Glampers

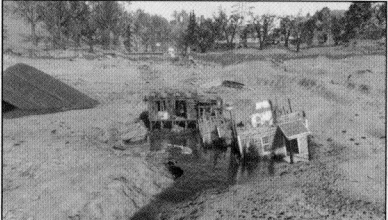

The Plastic People's Shack (Dry Lake)

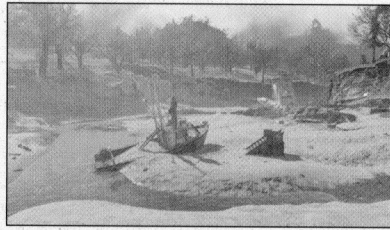

Military Comms Tower Summersville

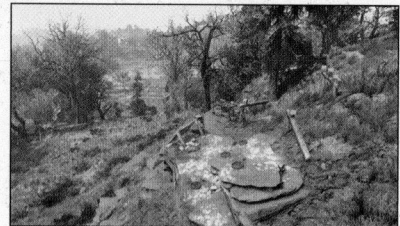

Birdhouse Maker

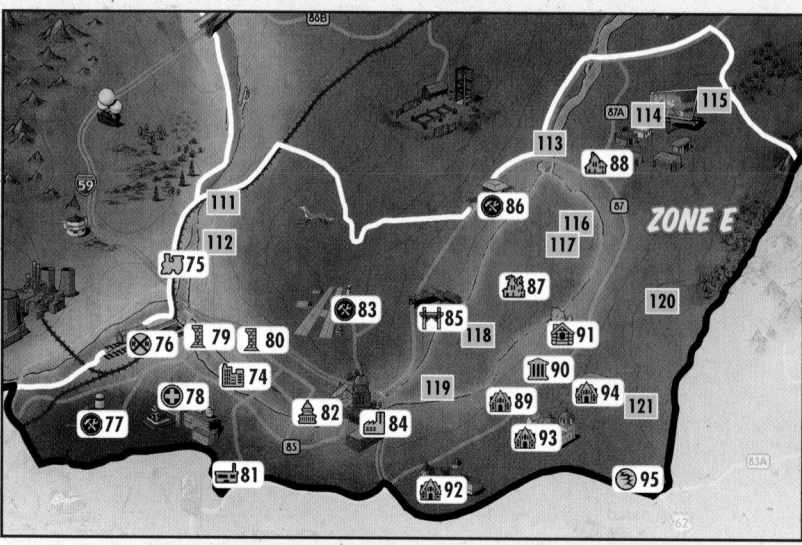

Appalachia: **The Forest (Zone E) – Secondary Locations**

#	NAME	DESCRIPTION
111	The Scuppered Tug	A rusty green tug boat with a safe (3) inside, below the railbridge north of Charleston.
112	Beached Tall Ship	An older shipping vessel is stuck in the dry river northeast of Charleston Station; there's beer and a cooking station under the mast.
113	Summersville Suburbs	A collection of homes by the road and river, including a garage and voting tent, west of town.
114	Trailer Overlook (north of Summersville)	A busted-up trailer home on the rocks above Summersville, with some weaponry and a Mod to scavenge.
115	Summersville Glampers	The latest in green caravan trailers, an acoustic guitar, and more junk than many primary locations; time to visit this glampground.
116	Cargo Container Flotsam (Dry Lake)	An open container close to a skeleton on a rowboat offers protection and minor items to scavenge.

#	NAME	DESCRIPTION
117	The Plastic People's Shack (Dry Lake)	There's a party going on inside this stilt shack, but the skeletal and the plastic outnumber the living. What's on the jukebox?
118	Tugboat and Rowboat (The Domestics)	Two plastic people argue on a rowboat while a large tug vessel slowly sinks into Lake Summersville.
119	Military Comms Tower Summersville	A small, quest-related comms dish sits atop a half-sunken boat with a 50-cal machine gun and turret, in the dry lake.
120	Raider Outcrop Camp	Offering weapons, armor, and cooking stations, this three-tier shack also has some of the best views of the dry lake.
121	Birdhouse Maker	Someone has been busy capturing birds and constructing birdhouses. If you're after Pumpkin Seeds, this wooded hillside is the place.

REGION 2: TOXIC VALLEY

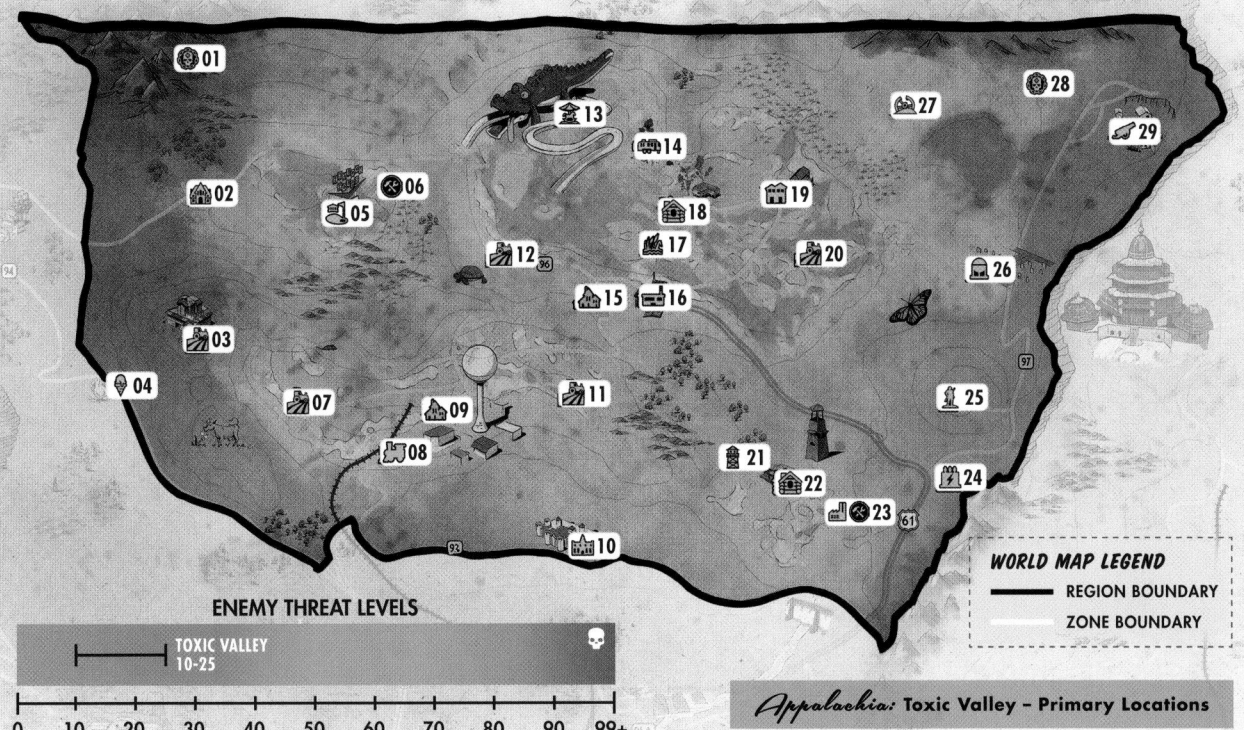

ENEMY THREAT LEVELS

TOXIC VALLEY
10-25

| 0 | 10 | 20 | 30 | 40 | 50 | 60 | 70 | 80 | 90 | 99+ |

Appalachia: **Toxic Valley – Primary Locations**

WORLD MAP LEGEND
— REGION BOUNDARY
ZONE BOUNDARY

The far northwestern Region of Appalachia is covered in a lightly irradiated blanket of white toxic materials. Much of the landscape (most noticeably the rivers and lakes) is now a choked mess of orange filth and noxious clouds; the environment is unpleasant, rough going, and the tree cover has been ripped away. Now the atmosphere is dead. That's not to say nothing has survived, but the non-robotic entities you'll meet as you visit this stark and unforgiving depression aren't going to be trading anything with you but diseases and savage wounding. As you discover more locations, prepare to visit dilapidated farmsteads, lakeside cabins, and a scout camp where poisonous effluent has replaced clear waters. The main town is Grafton, which is in a rough state, even before reports of its headless monster were confirmed. Seek small respite at the Wavy Willard's Water Park, where there's some frivolity to be had, and ignore the golf course at Hemlock Holes. Instead, spend time cultivating your drive to mine resources at the nearby workshop. There's also tough battles at close quarters with denizens inside the penitentiary along the southern border, a few scattered Raider camps to uncover, and a crashed satellite to the northeast. Finally, pay some respects at the historic sites along the eastern edge of this forsaken region.

WORLD MAP LEGEND
— REGION BOUNDARY   ZONE BOUNDARY

■ BOBBLEHEADS   ■ CAP STASHES   ■ MAGAZINES   ■ POWER ARMOR

PRIMARY LOCATIONS

				icon	NAME
1	1	1	1	01	THE CROSSHAIR
2		2		02	CLANCY MANOR
1		1		03	COBBLETON FARM
1		1		04	LADY JANET'S SOFT SERVE
				05	HEMLOCK HOLES
				06	HEMLOCK HOLES MAINTENANCE
2		1		07	BECKER FARM
				08	GRAFTON STATION
	2			09	GRAFTON
4	19	7	1	10	EASTERN REGIONAL PENITENTIARY
				11	SMITH FARM
				12	WOODS ESTATE
4		2		13	WAVY WILLARD'S WATER PARK
1		1		14	WILLARD CORPORATE HOUSING
	2		1	15	CLARKSBURG

			icon	NAME
			16	CLARKSBURG SHOOTING CLUB
			17	TOXIC DRIED LAKEBED
1	2		18	KIDDIE CORNER CABINS
1	1	1	19	BLACK BEAR LODGE
			20	GRANINGER FARM
			21	PIONEER SCOUT LOOKOUT
2	2		22	PIONEER SCOUT CAMP
			23	GRAFTON STEEL AND GRAFTON STEEL YARD
			24	POSEIDON POWER SUBSTATION PX-03
			25	COLONEL KELLY MONUMENT
1	1		26	PHILIPPI BATTLEFIELD CEMETERY
		1	27	CRASHED SPACE STATION
	1		28	KNIFE EDGE
			29	PRICKETT'S FORT

TRAINING
CRAFTING AND C.A.M.P.ING
INVENTORY
QUESTS
ATLAS
BESTIARY
APPENDICES

TOXIC VALLEY: PRIMARY LOCATIONS

MAP LEGEND
- MY STASH BOX
- OVERSEER'S CACHE
- TRUNK
- TRADER

COLLECTIBLES
- BOBBLEHEAD
- MAGAZINE
- POWER ARMOR

CRAFTING
- ARMOR WORKBENCH
- CHEMISTRY WORKBENCH
- COOKING STATION
- POWER ARMOR STATION
- TINKER'S WORKBENCH
- WEAPONS WORKBENCH
- WORKSHOP WORKBENCH

IMPORTANT
- DOOR/GATE
- LOCKED DOOR/GATE
- SAFE
- SCANNER
- TERMINAL

01. THE CROSSHAIR

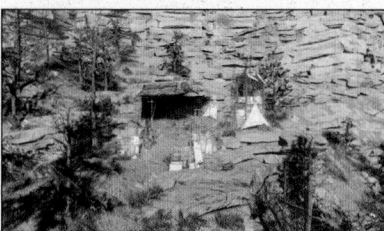

- **COLLECTIBLES:** BOBBLEHEAD (2), MAGAZINE, POWER ARMOR
- **CRAFTING:** ARMOR, COOKING, WEAPONS
- **ITEMS:** ARMS AND AMMO, HEALTH AND CHEMS
- **INFO:** EXPECTED ENEMY: SCORCHED; SCAVENGE RATING: 1; SIZE: 1; THREAT LEVEL: 10–25
- **ITEM EXAMPLES:** BINOCULARS, BOURBON, LANTERN, MOLOTOV COCKTAIL, SALISBURY STEAK

Up in the remote northwest mountains is a small Raider camp, usually overrun by Scorched. Come for the views and the possibility of some collectibles.

02. CLANCY MANOR

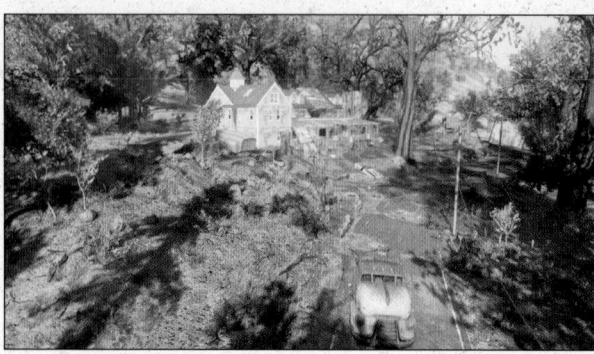

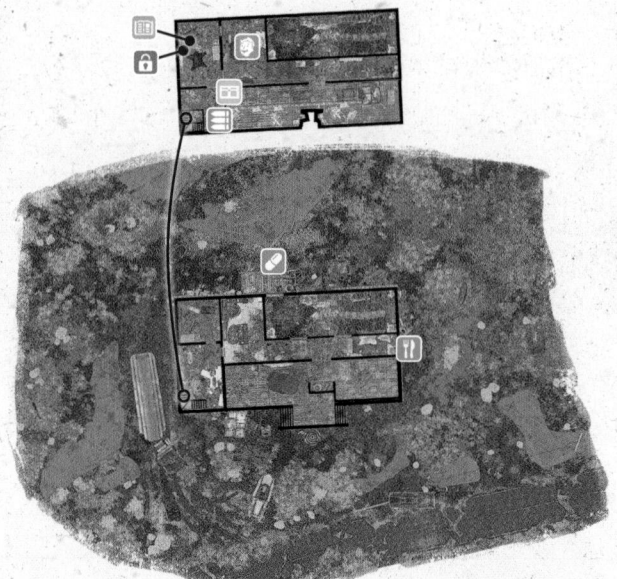

Clancy Manor (Exterior)

- **COLLECTIBLES:** BOBBLEHEAD, MAGAZINE
- **CRAFTING:** CHEMISTRY, COOKING, TINKER
- **DANGER:** RADIATION!
- **ITEMS:** ARMS AND AMMO; HARVESTABLE: FIRECAP; HEALTH AND CHEMS; TRUNK
- **INFO:** EXPECTED ENEMY: SCORCHED; SCAVENGE RATING: 4; SIZE: 2; SLEEPING; THREAT LEVEL: 10–25
- **LOCK:** SAFE (1)
- **ITEM EXAMPLES:** ANTIQUE GLOBE, BROKEN LAMP, DESK FAN, KITCHEN SCALE, MILITARY-GRADE CIRCUIT BOARD, MILITARY GRADE DUCT TAPE+, SMALL PICTURE FRAME, SOAP, TEDDY BEAR+, TOILET PAPER, TURPENTINE, WONDERGLUE, WINE

A historic home was once commandeered by Raiders and is now home to even less desirable residents. Aside from the Teddy cooking show in the kitchen, check the Tinker's Workbench upstairs for some excellent junk. Then inspect the roof.

03. COBBLETON FARM

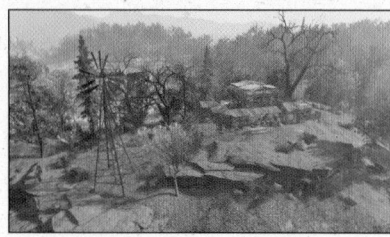

- **COLLECTIBLES:** BOBBLEHEAD, MAGAZINE
- **CRAFTING:** CHEMISTRY, TINKER, WATER PUMP
- **ITEMS:** ARMS AND AMMO; HARVESTABLE: BLACKBERRY, MUTFRUIT PLANT, RAZOR GRAIN, TATO PLANT, WILD CORN; TRUNK
- **INFO:** EXPECTED ENEMY: SUPER MUTANT; SCAVENGE RATING: 3; SIZE: 2; SLEEPING; THREAT LEVEL: 10–25
- **ITEM EXAMPLES:** ALUMINUM CAN, BEER BOTTLE+, CRAM, GAS CANISTER, RUM, TIN CAN+, USED OIL CAN

Nestled on a hilltop with little of the toxic debris that litters the majority of the valley, this small farmstead is still highly dangerous, thanks to the influx of foes. Aside from an outhouse and small vegetable garden, the majority of the scavenging (and fighting) takes place inside the main shack-like structure.

04. LADY JANET'S SOFT SERVE

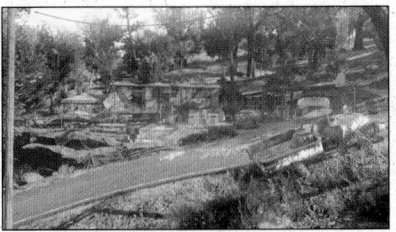

- **COLLECTIBLES:** BOBBLEHEAD, MAGAZINE
- **CRAFTING:** CHEMISTRY, WEAPONS
- **ITEMS:** HEALTH AND CHEMS, TRUNK
- **INFO:** EXPECTED ENEMY: GHOUL; SCAVENGE RATING: 1; SIZE: 1; THREAT LEVEL: 10–25
- **LOCK:** SAFE (0)
- **ITEM EXAMPLES:** BEER BOTTLE, GAS MASK WITH GOGGLES, HOT DOG, MOUNTAIN HONEY, TEDDY BEAR

A roadstop ice cream parlor. There's no rum and raisin, but there might be a well-hidden Magazine behind the locked safe.

05. HEMLOCK HOLES

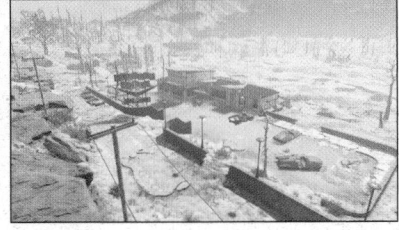

- **COLLECTIBLE:** NUKA-CHERRY
- **DANGER:** RADIATION!++
- **ITEM:** ARMS AND AMMO
- **INFO:** EXPECTED ENEMY: IRRADIATED INSECT, SCORCHED; QUEST: THRILL OF THE GRILL; SCAVENGE RATING: 3; SIZE: 2; THREAT LEVEL: 10–25
- **LOCK:** SAFE (1)
- **ITEM EXAMPLES:** BOBBY PIN BOX, COFFEE CUP, FADED VISOR, GLASS PITCHER, GOLF BALL++, GOLF CLUB, PEPPER, SALT, SILVER PLATE+, TALL DRINKING GLASS

Apparently this toxic mire used to be a golf course. Check in with the cook for a spot of meat hunting, then scavenge the cafe and gift shop. The course is a little more challenging now; check a small satellite dish and crashed Vertibird to the south. See the Hemlock Holes Maintenance map for a closer look at the entrance building.

06. HEMLOCK HOLES MAINTENANCE (WORKSHOP)

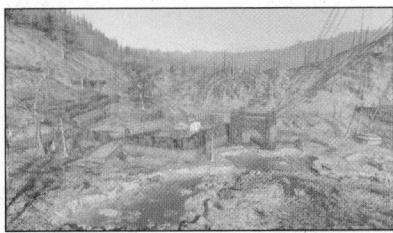

- **DANGER:** RADIATION!++
- **ITEMS:** HARVESTABLE: ACID, BLOODLEAF, CRYSTAL, GOLD
- **INFO:** EXPECTED ENEMY: VARIES; SCAVENGE RATING: 1(5); SIZE: 2; THREAT LEVEL: 10–25
- **ITEM EXAMPLES:** DUCT TAPE
- **WORK:** FOOD (3), WATER (3), CRYSTAL (1), GOLD (1), ACID (3)

Hemlock Holes Maintenance (Workshop)

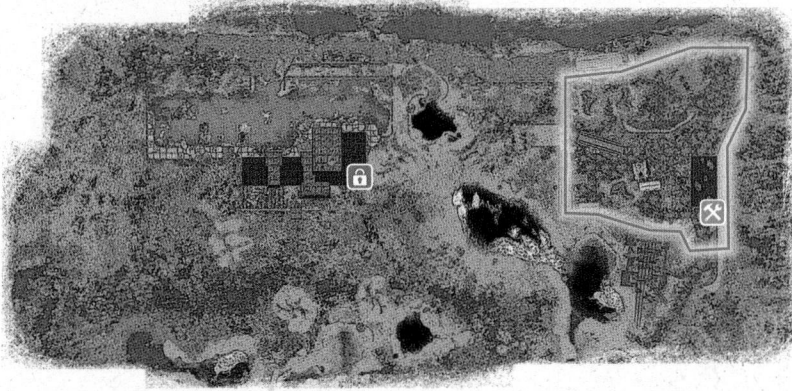

This small substation and maintenance yard doesn't have much to scavenge initially, except for the deposits of acid, crystal, and gold. Get your workshop up and running and defend this resource-heavy place; there should be power from the substation you can use instead of (or in addition to) generators.

07. BECKER FARM

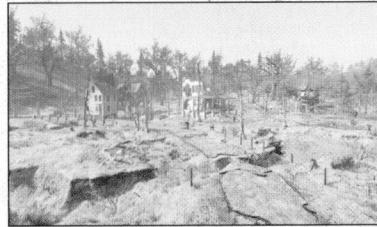

A small collection of ruined dwellings and barns to the west of Grafton, this was once a thriving farm belonging to the Becker family. Now the more intact structures house some good-quality junk and possible collectibles.

- **COLLECTIBLES:** BOBBLEHEAD (2), MAGAZINE
- **CRAFTING:** CHEMISTRY, COOKING
- **DANGER:** RADIATION!+
- **ITEMS:** HARVESTABLE: MUTATED FERN, TATO PLANT, WILD CARROT, WILD CORN; HEALTH AND CHEMS; RECIPE/MOD/PLAN; TRUNK
- **INFO:** AEROSOLIZER; EXPECTED ENEMY: GHOUL; SCAVENGE RATING: 4; SIZE: 3; SLEEPING; THREAT LEVEL: 10–25
- **ITEM EXAMPLES:** BASEBALL UNIFORM, BEER BOTTLE++, BOBBY PIN BOX, CARTON OF CIGARETTES, COFFEE POT, COOKING POT, COP CAP, DIRTY ASHTRAY, DIRTY BLACK SUIT, DISH RAG, GLASS JAR+, MOONSHINE JUG, PEN, SHOT GLASS, SUGAR+, TABLETOP PICTURE FRAME, TEDDY BEAR+, TIN CAN+, TOILET PAPER+, TYPEWRITER, WAKEMASTER ALARM CLOCK+, WILLOW BARREL VASE+

Becker Farm (Exterior)

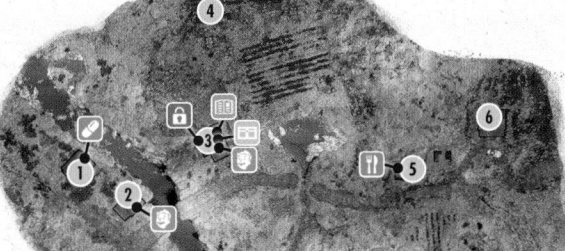

LEGEND

1. WHITE AND GREEN HOUSE
2. WHITE HOUSE
3. WHITE ROOFLESS HOUSE
4. DILAPIDATED SHED
5. WHITE BARN
6. WHITE FARMHOUSE

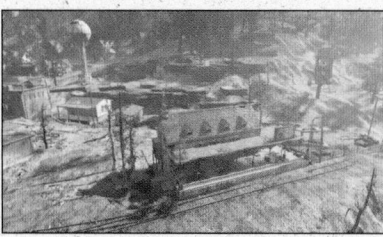

– **CRAFTING:** COOKING, TINKER'S
– **ITEMS:** ARMS AND AMMO; HEALTH AND CHEMS; MY STASH BOX; RECIPE/MOD/PLAN; VENDING MACHINE: AMMUNITION, MEDICAL SUPPLIES
– **INFO:** QUEST: GRAFTON DAY; SCAVENGE RATING: 2; SIZE: 1; THREAT LEVEL: 10–25; TRADER: VENDOR BOT
– **ITEM EXAMPLES:** BOILED WATER, BOURBON, TOILET PAPER+

On the southwest outskirts of town, this serves as the entrance to the town of Grafton for those heading here via the railroad tracks. The station should be a tactical gathering point before you explore Grafton. It is also a drop-off spot due to the Vendor Bot and Stash Box available here.

🏠 **09. GRAFTON**

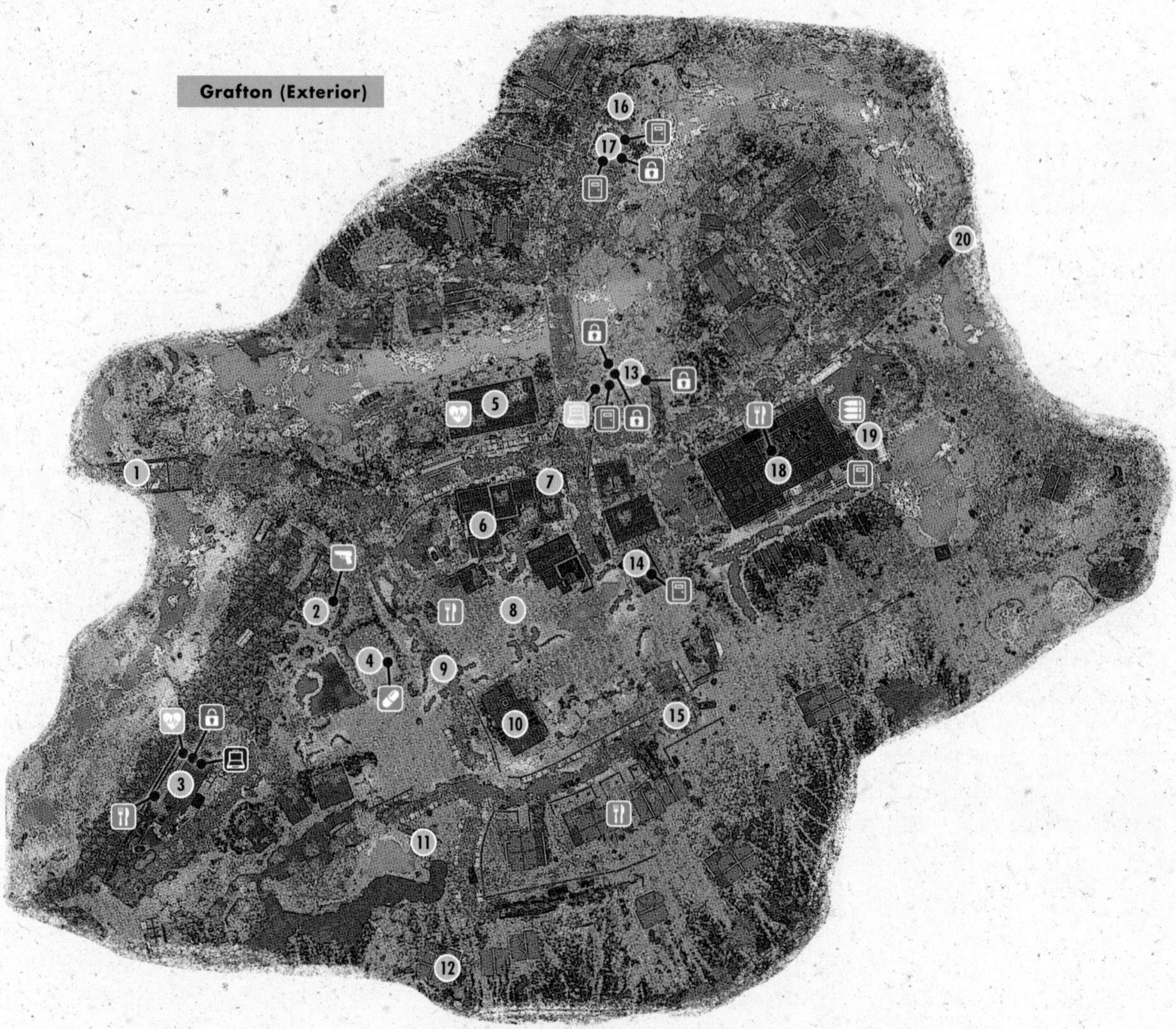

Grafton (Exterior)

LEGEND

1. GRAFTON BRIDGE (WEST)
2. RAILROAD WAREHOUSE (INTERIOR)
3. PRIMARY LOCATION: GRAFTON STATION (INTERIOR)
4. CONCRETE STORAGE (INTERIOR)
5. MUSEUM: TRADING POST (INTERIOR)
6. CIGARETTE SHOP (INTERIOR)
7. SCAFFOLD CORNER APARTMENTS (INTERIOR)
8. NARROW TENEMENT APARTMENTS (INTERIOR)
9. VOTING TENTS
10. GRAFTON CHURCH (INACCESSIBLE)
11. WATER TOWER
12. GRAFTON HOME (INTERIOR)
13. GRAFTON CITY HALL (INTERIOR)
14. GRAFTON POLICE STATION (INTERIOR)
15. VOTING TENT
16. VOTING TENT
17. BEECH STREET GAS STATION (INTERIOR)
18. GRAFTON HIGH SCHOOL (INTERIOR)
19. TINKER'S COACH
20. GRAFTON BRIDGE (NORTHEAST)

- **INFO:** AEROSOLIZER; EXPECTED ENEMY: IRRADIATED ANIMAL, RADTOAD, SUPER MUTANT; NOTE; QUEST: BUREAU OF TOURISM, GRAFTON DAY; SCAVENGE RATING: 5; SIZE: 5; SLEEPING; THREAT LEVEL: 10–25. TRADER: VENDOR BOT.
- **LOCK:** DOOR (0, 1, 1, 1, 2), SAFE (0, 1, 1, 1)
- **ITEM EXAMPLES:** ABRAXO CLEANER+, ASHTRAY, BASEBALL+, BASEBALL BASE, BASEBALL BAT, BASEBALL CAP, BASEBALL GLOVE, BASKETBALL+, BEER BOTTLE+, BLUE PAINT, BOILED WATER, BOTTLECAP SUNGLASSES, BREAD BOX, BROWN BOTTLE, CIGAR BOX, CIGARETTE CARTON, COFFEE POT, COOKING OIL, COOKING POT, COTTON CANDY BITES, CRAM, DESK FAN, DOG BOWL, DUCT TAPE, EMPTY MILK BOTTLE++, ENAMEL BUCKET+, EXTINGUISHER+, FANCY LADS SNACK CAKES, GAS CANISTER, GREEN RAG HAT, HUNTING RIFLE, INSTAMASH, LETTERMAN'S JACKET AND JEANS, MENTATS, METAL BUCKET, MOONSHINE JUG, NUKA-COLA BOTTLE, OVEN MITTS, PEPPER, PIPE WRENCH, PLASTIC PLATE+, POOL BALL+, POOL CUE, POTATO CRISPS, RACK, SALT, SKULL, SOAP, SOUVENIR SLOTH TOY, SUGAR BOMBS, TALL DRINKING GLASS, TEDDY BEAR, TELEPHONE, TIN CAN, TIN CANISTER, TYPEWRITER, WHITE PLATE, YUM YUM DEVILED EGGS

- **COLLECTIBLES:** CAPS STASH (2), HOLOTAPE, NUKA-CHERRY
- **CRAFTING:** CHEMISTRY, COOKING (3), TINKER, WEAPONS
- **DANGER:** GRENADE! MINE! RADIOACTIVE!++, RADTOAD MINE!
- **ITEMS:** ARMS AND AMMO++; HARVESTABLE: BLOODLEAF, MUTATED FERN, TATO PLANT; HEALTH AND CHEMS+; OVERSEER'S CACHE; VENDING MACHINE: MEDICAL SUPPLIES

The town of Grafton grew at the confluence of a creek, though the current river conditions can best be described as "toxic" and "sludge-like." When you're not fleeing from a roaming monster that shares its name with this town, you'll be dropping your junk at the Grafton Station stash box and thoroughly exploring the town, including the tenement apartments and rooftops that are accessible (the school, police station, city hall, and tenement block all have upper exteriors to explore). Also visit Robotic Grafton Mayor in city hall; the Overseer's Cache is here too. There is also the vendor at the museum farther along the main street. Otherwise, head here to gather copious junk to add to your collection.

10. EASTERN REGIONAL PENITENTIARY

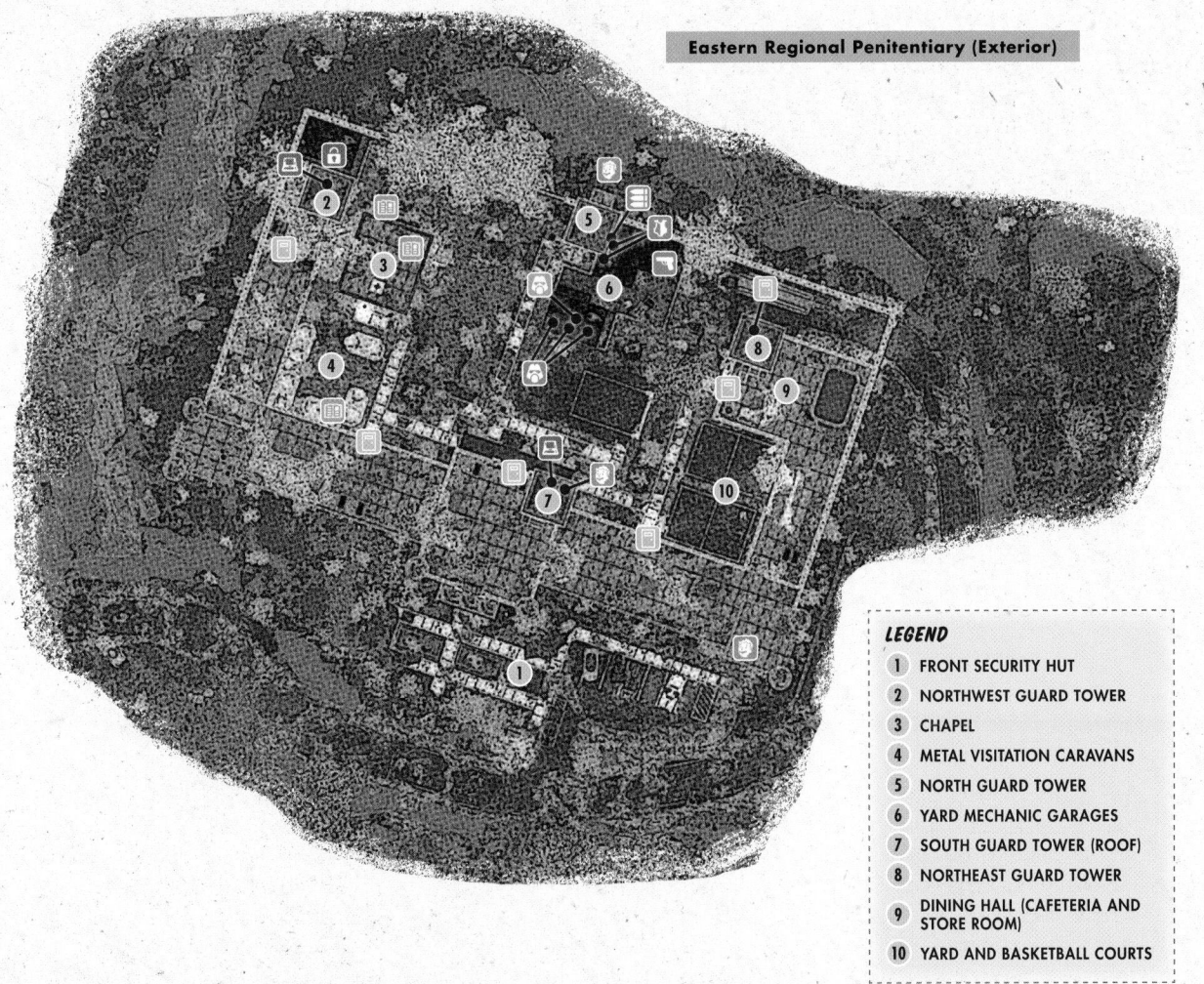

Eastern Regional Penitentiary (Exterior)

LEGEND

1. FRONT SECURITY HUT
2. NORTHWEST GUARD TOWER
3. CHAPEL
4. METAL VISITATION CARAVANS
5. NORTH GUARD TOWER
6. YARD MECHANIC GARAGES
7. SOUTH GUARD TOWER (ROOF)
8. NORTHEAST GUARD TOWER
9. DINING HALL (CAFETERIA AND STORE ROOM)
10. YARD AND BASKETBALL COURTS

TRAINING

CRAFTING AND C.A.M.P.ING

INVENTORY

QUESTS

ATLAS

BESTIARY

APPENDICES

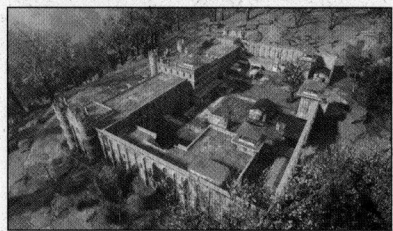

- **COLLECTIBLES:** BOBBLEHEAD (4), CAPS STASH (19), MAGAZINE (7), POWER ARMOR
- **CRAFTING:** ARMOR (3), CHEMISTRY, COOKING (2), POWER ARMOR (3), TINKER (2), WEAPONS (2)
- **DANGER:** CAN CHIMES! ESCAPING GAS! FLAMETHROWER! GRENADE! LONG DROP! MINE! OIL! TESLA ARC! TRIPWIRE! TURRET!
- **ITEMS:** ARMS AND AMMO+; HARVESTABLE: RHODODENDRON, SOOT FLOWER; HEALTH AND CHEMS++; RECIPE/MOD/PLAN; TRUNK
- **INFO:** EXPECTED ENEMY: SUPER MUTANT; SCAVENGE RATING: 5; SIZE: 4; SLEEPING; THREAT LEVEL: 10–25
- **LOCK:** DOOR (0, 0, 1, 2, 2), SAFE (1, 2, 2), TERMINAL (1, 2, 2)
- **ITEM EXAMPLES:** ABRAXO CLEANER, ADDICTOL, ADJUSTABLE WRENCH, ALARM CLOCK, BEER BOTTLE++, BLAST RADIUS BOARD GAME, BLOOD PACK+, BLUE PAINT, BOBBY PIN BOX, BONESAW, BROKEN LAMP, BUNSEN BURNER, BURNT FASHION MAGAZINE, CAFETERIA TRAY+, CHESSBOARD, CLOTHING IRON+, COFFEE CUP+, COFFEE POT, COOLANT, DESK FAN+, DIRTY ASHTRAY, ECONOMY WONDERGLUE+, EXPLORER OUTFIT, EXTINGUISHER, FUSION CORE, HANDCUFFS, HOODED RAGS, INSTAMASH, LAB BOTTLE, LEFT ARM BONES, MAKESHIFT BATTERY+, MICROSCOPE, MR. HANDY FUEL, NUKA-COLA+, NUKA-COLA BOTTLE+, PACK OF CIGARETTES+, PEN, PENITENTIARY KEY+, PLUNGER, PRISON COLLAR++, RAT POISON, SALT, SCAVENGER OUTFIT, SHORT 10-MM AUTO PISTOL, SPATULA, SPICES, STEW POT, STRAIGHT JACKET+, SURGICAL SCALPEL, SURGICAL TRAY, SURVEYOR OUTFIT, TABLETOP PICTURE FRAME, TEDDY BEAR, TELEPHONE+, TIN CAN, TIN CANISTER, TOASTER, TUBE FLANGE, WOOD BLOCK+, YARDSTICK, YELLOW PAINT

Holding infamous ne'er-do-wells like Mad Dog Malone, this large and ancient prison is brimming with foes and a variety of nasty traps; watch your step when exploring. The prison's walls are mostly intact along the front (south) side, but become increasingly derelict as you reach the rear of the premises, allowing easy access from multiple directions into the exterior yard and multitude of outbuildings, as well as access into the structure itself (which you can also enter via the front doors). The yard's two garages have almost every type of work station you need to access, though the surrounding towers have turrets that may cause havoc on top of the enemy threats.

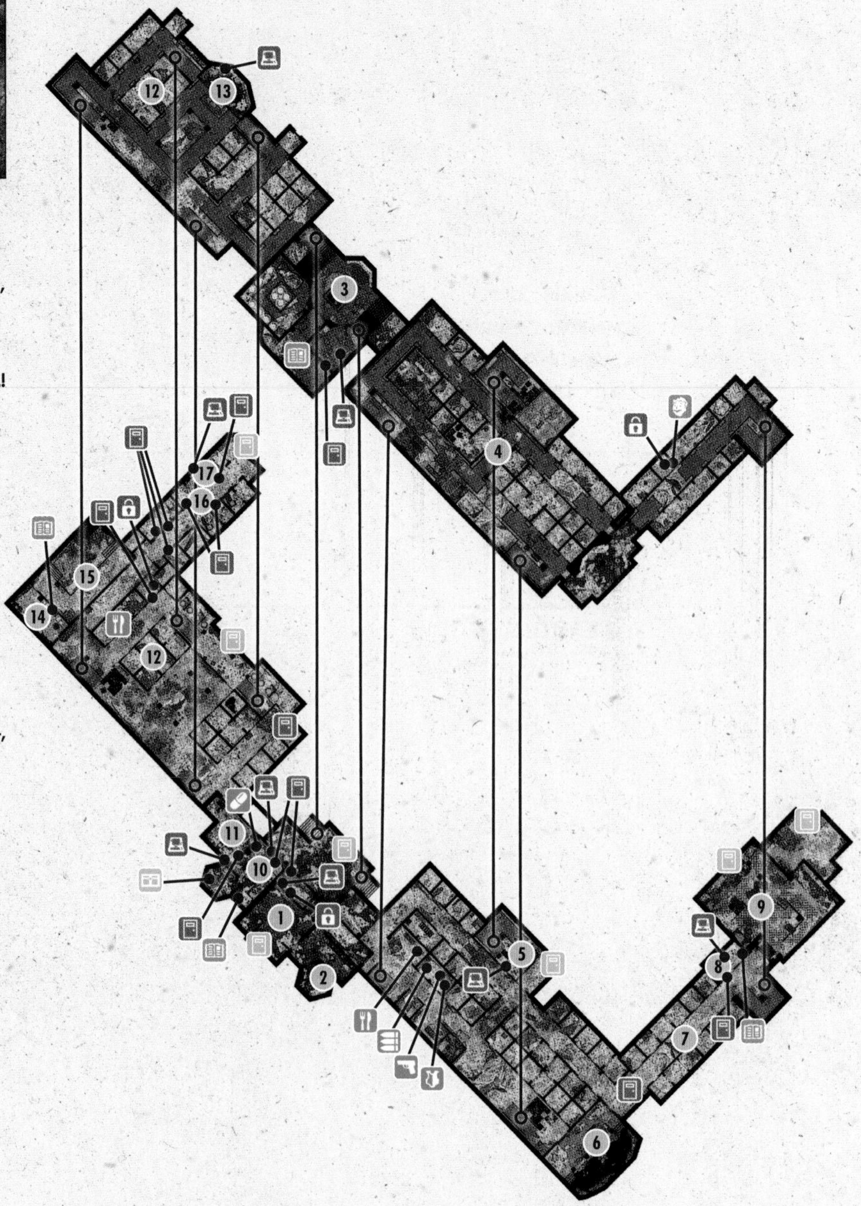

LEGEND

1	ENTRANCE	**10**	RECEPTION AND INTAKE (ELECTRIC CHAIRS)
2	VISITING ROOM	**11**	INFIRMARY
3	WARDEN BRENNAN'S OFFICES AND CONTROL ROOM	**12**	CELL BLOCK D
4	CELL BLOCK A	**13**	SECURITY (D)
5	SECURITY (A)	**14**	LAUNDRY
6	SHOWERS	**15**	GENERATOR ROOM
7	CELL BLOCK B	**16**	SOLITARY BLOCK (CELL BLOCK C)
8	SECURITY (B)	**17**	SECURITY (SOLITARY)
9	DINING AND STORE ROOM		

Inside, the prison is a confusing mess of tangled metal blocking your path, locked doors (find a penitentiary key in any security room), and a maze of prison cells. Study the adjacent map, and check the names of the areas you're visiting above each door until you memorize the layout. Expect two main levels to explore, and watch your step!

11. SMITH FARM

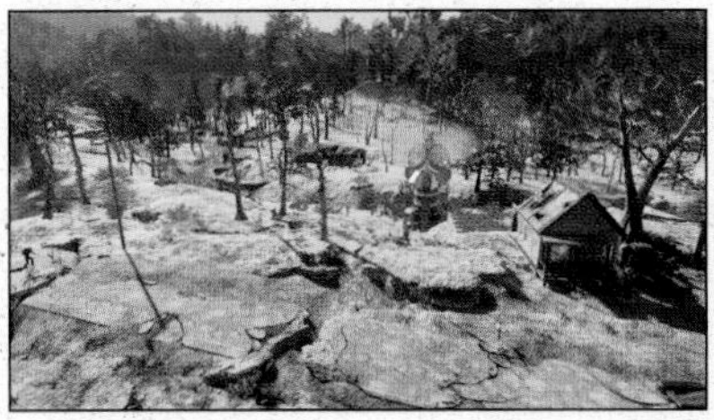

- **COLLECTIBLE:** NUKA-CHERRY
- **CRAFTING:** COOKING
- **DANGER:** RADIATION!
- **ITEMS: ARMS AND AMMO; HARVESTABLE:** TATO PLANT, WILD CARROT; HEALTH AND CHEMS
- **INFO:** AEROSOLIZER; EXPECTED ENEMY: IRRADIATED ANIMAL; SCAVENGE RATING: 1; SIZE: 1; SLEEPING; THREAT LEVEL: 10–25
- **ITEM EXAMPLES:** BOILED WATER, EMPTY WILLOW ROUNDED VASE, ENAMEL BUCKET, SHOT GLASS

On the outskirts of northeast Grafton is a small cluster of farm buildings close to what was once a freshwater stream. Leap the toxic water to reach the metal shed across from the farm cottage.

12. WOODS ESTATE

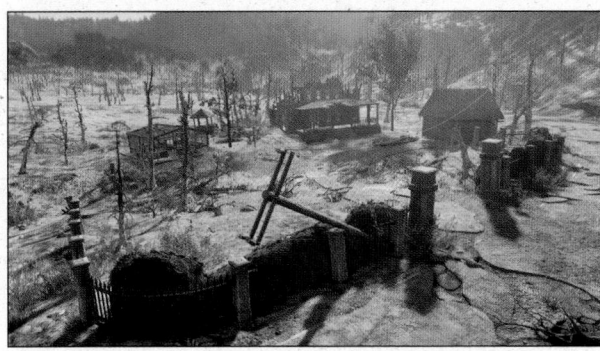

- **ITEMS: ARMS AND AMMO; HARVESTABLE:** BLEACHED DOGWOOD
- **INFO:** SCAVENGE RATING: 1; SIZE: 1; THREAT LEVEL: 10–25
- **ITEM EXAMPLES:** FLOWER POT+, GLASS JAR, PAINT POT, WINE BOTTLE

North of Grafton is the estate of the long-dead Arthur Wood, southeast of the water park sign. This is in a miserable state of repair. Check the greenhouse, then the main house, for a smattering of scavengables and ammo.

13. WAVY WILLARD'S WATER PARK

Wavy Willard's Water Park (Exterior)

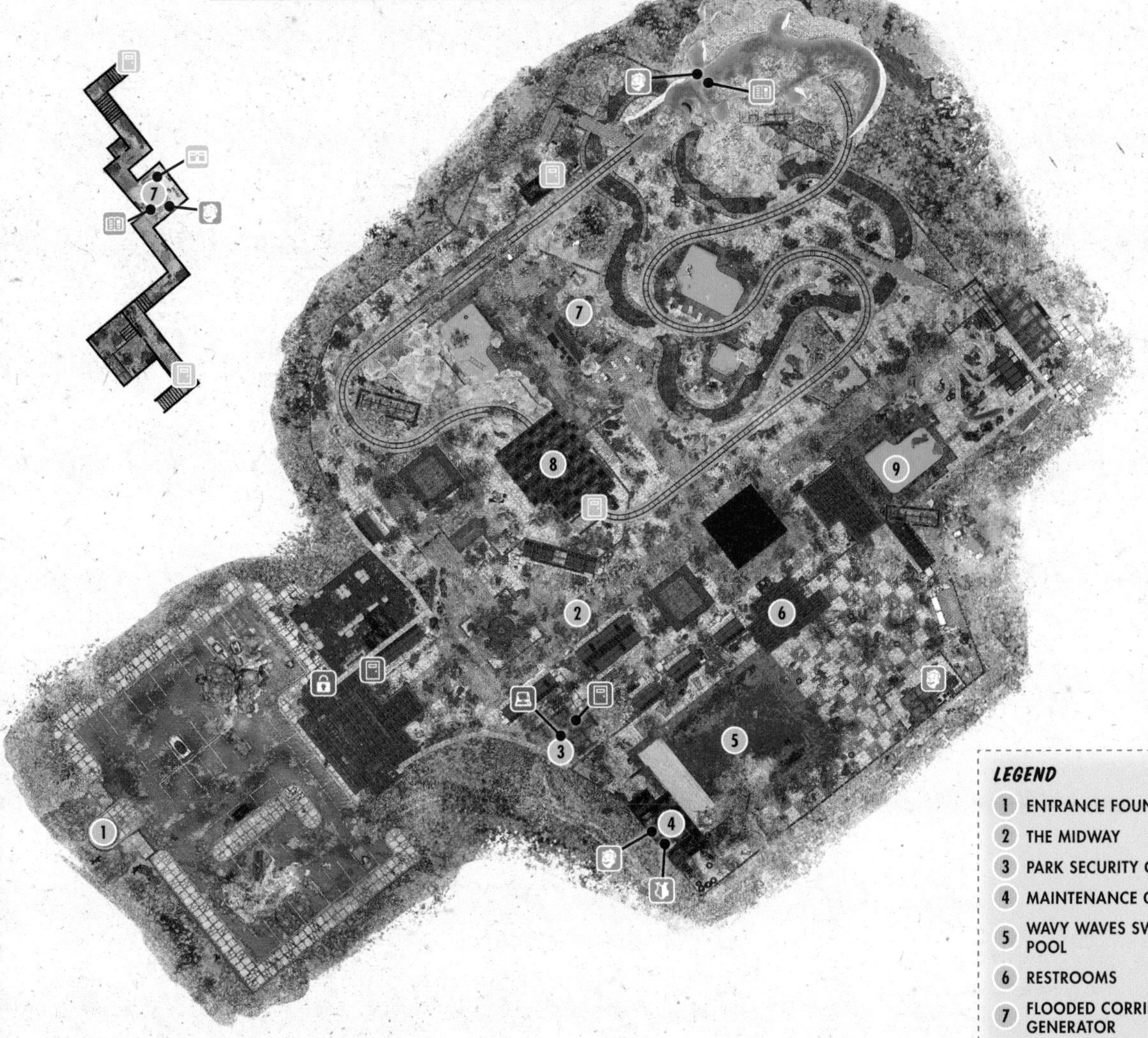

LEGEND

1. ENTRANCE FOUNTAIN
2. THE MIDWAY
3. PARK SECURITY OFFICE
4. MAINTENANCE GARAGE
5. WAVY WAVES SWIMMING POOL
6. RESTROOMS
7. FLOODED CORRIDOR AND GENERATOR
8. CROCOLOSSUS MOUNTAIN
9. SSSLITHER SLIDE

TRAINING

CRAFTING AND C.A.M.P.ING

INVENTORY

QUESTS

ATLAS

BESTIARY

APPENDICES

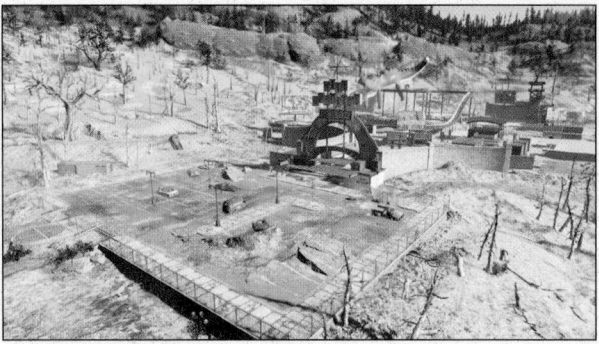

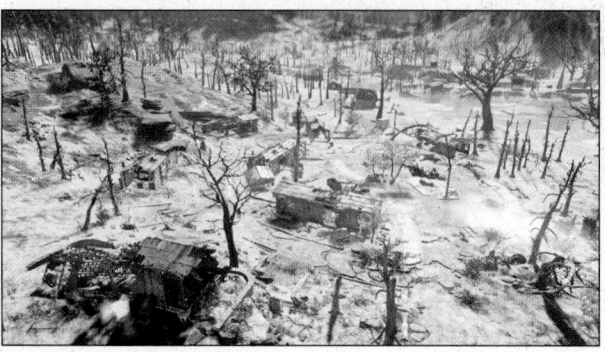

- **COLLECTIBLES:** BOBBLEHEAD (4), MAGAZINE (2)
- **CRAFTING:** ARMOR
- **DANGER:** PUNJI BOARD! RADIATION!
- **ITEMS:** ARMS AND AMMO; HEALTH AND CHEMS; TRUNK
- **INFO:** EXPECTED ENEMY: IRRADIATED ANIMAL, SCORCHED; SCAVENGE RATING: 4; SIZE: 4; SLEEPING; THREAT LEVEL: 10–25
- **LOCK:** DOOR (2, 2), SAFE (2)
- **ITEM EXAMPLES:** ABRAXO CLEANER+, ANTIFREEZE BOTTLE+, BALL-PEEN HAMMER, BASEBALL+, BEER BOTTLE+, BLOWTORCH, BURGER TRAY+, COFFEE POT, COOLANT+, DOG BOWL, ENAMEL BUCKET+, FUSE+, FUSION CORE, GAS CANISTER+, GLASS JAR+++, GOLF BALL+, HARD HAT, HOT PLATE, JANGLES THE MOON MONKEY, KICKBALL, LIFE PRESERVER, METAL BUCKET+, MOP, NUKA-COLA BOTTLE, NUKA-COLA CUP+, NUKA-COLA CUP AND STRAW, NUKA-COLA CUP PACK, OFFICE DESK FAN, OIL CAN, OIL CANISTER, PACK OF DUCT TAPE, PIZZA TRAY, PLASTIC PUMPKIN, PLUNGER, ROLLING PIN+, SCREWDRIVER, SHORT 10-MM PISTOL, TOY ALIEN+, TOY CAR, TOY TRUCK, TEDDY BEAR, TURPENTINE+, TV DINNER TRAY+, USED OIL CAN, VACUUM TUBE, WONDERGLUE, YELLOW PAINT

- **COLLECTIBLE:** BOBBLEHEAD
- **CRAFTING:** TINKER
- **ITEMS:** ARMS AND AMMO; HARVESTABLE: BLEACH DOGWOOD, SOOT FLOWER; HEALTH AND CHEMS; RECIPE/MOD/PLAN; TRUNK
- **INFO:** EXPECTED ENEMY: IRRADIATED ANIMALS, IRRADIATED INSECTS; SCAVENGE RATING: 1; SIZE: 1; THREAT LEVEL: 10–25
- **ITEM EXAMPLES:** COFFEE CUP, MENTALS, PEN, SALT

Just southeast of the water park are the remains of around six trailers, which used to house the park's workforce. Now these wrecked and tangled metal huts are rusting in the inclement weather.

Bring more than your swimming costume to the remains of this aquatic fun park; the place is run-down and the water is toxic. However, Wavy Willard's signature ride (the giant croc) is still here, slowly fading in the nuclear sun. The park's edge is surrounded by a stone wall, but there are several intrusion points allowing access, and you can enter via the main entrance and parking lot. Once inside, there's lots of (broken and dry) rides to explore, as well as a big croc to visit. Come for the views, and stay for the junk collecting!

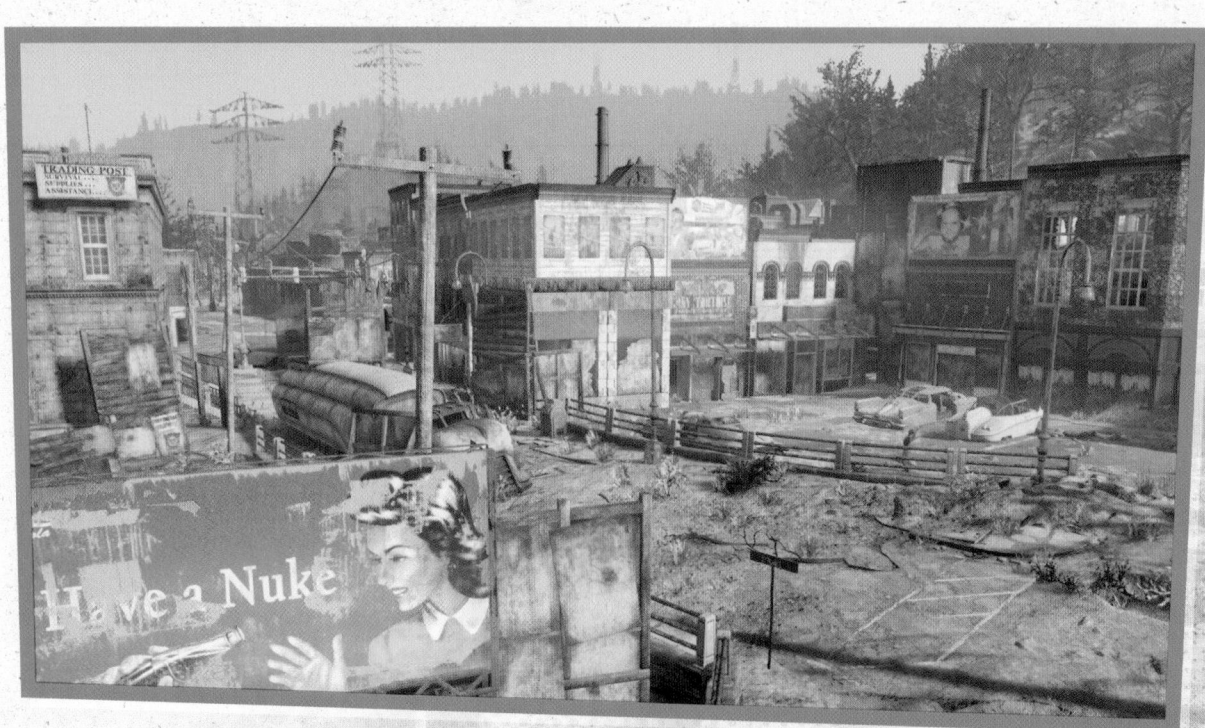

15. CLARKSBURG

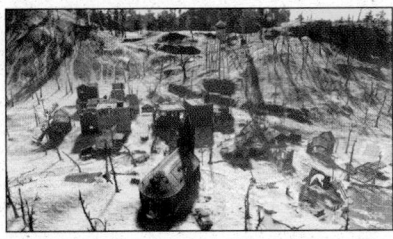

- **COLLECTIBLES:** CAPS STASH (2), POWER ARMOR
- **CRAFTING:** ARMOR, COOKING (3), WEAPONS

- **DANGER:** RADIATION! TENSION TRIGGER!
- **ITEMS:** ARMS AND AMMO++; HARVESTABLE: SOOT FLOWER, WOOD PILE; HEALTH AND CHEMS+; RECIPE/MOD/PLAN, TRUNK
- **INFO:** EXPECTED ENEMY: IRRADIATED ANIMAL; SCAVENGE RATING: 4; SIZE: 4; SLEEPING; THREAT LEVEL: 10–25
- **LOCK:** DOOR (0), SAFE (0, 1, 1, 2, 2), TERMINAL (0, 3)
- **ITEM EXAMPLES:** ALARM CLOCK, ASHTRAY, BLAMCO BRAND MAC AND CHEESE, BLUE TABLE LAMP, BIOMETRIC SCANNER, BOBBY PIN BOX, BOILED WATER, CANNED DOG FOOD, CAP, CIGAR BOX, COFFEE CUP, COFFEE POT, COLANDER, CUTTING BOARD, EMPTY PAINT CAN+, ENAMEL BUCKET, FUSION CORE, GLASS PITCHER, KITCHEN SCALES, METAL BUCKET, MISSILE LAUNCHER, MOP. NUKA-COLA, PIPE RIFLE, PLUNGER+, PORK N' BEANS, PRE-WAR MONEY, PROTEST SIGN+, RAW WOLF MEAT, SALISBURY STEAK, SOAP, SUGAR BOMBS, TELEPHONE, TIN CANISTER, TOILET PAPER, USED OIL CAN, YELLOW PLATE, YELLOW TABLE LAMP+

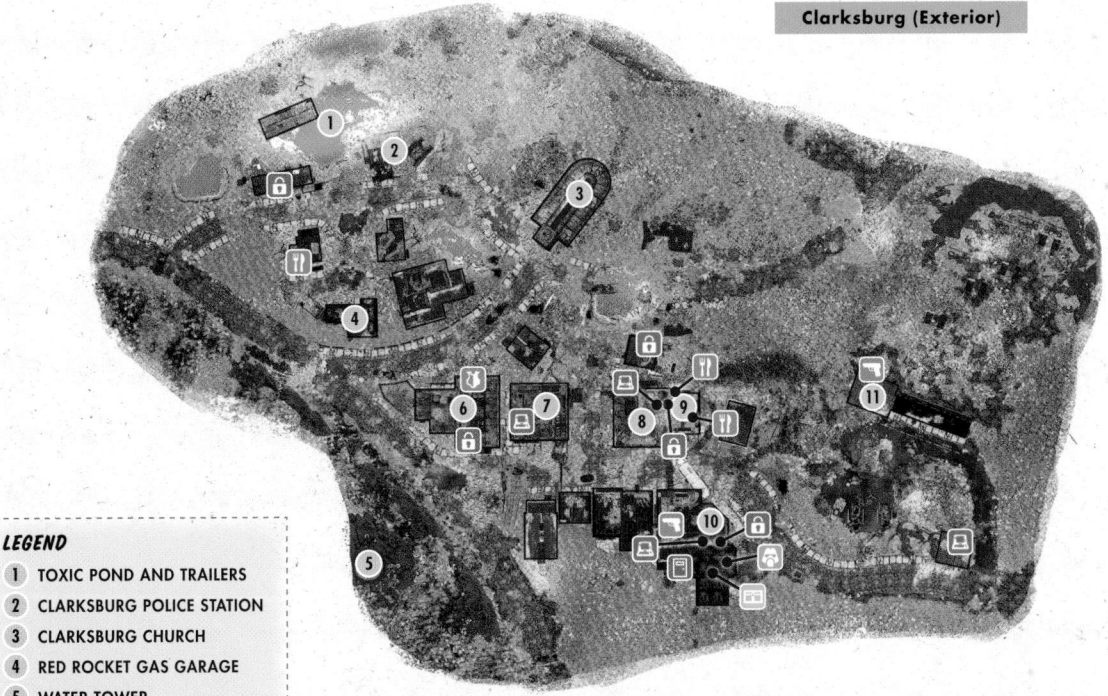

Clarksburg (Exterior)

LEGEND

1. TOXIC POND AND TRAILERS
2. CLARKSBURG POLICE STATION
3. CLARKSBURG CHURCH
4. RED ROCKET GAS GARAGE
5. WATER TOWER
6. HARDWARE STORE
7. POST OFFICE
8. PHARMACY (AND APARTMENT)
9. ICE CREAM STORE
10. GUN SHOP AND HARDWARE TOWER
11. PRIMARY LOCATION: CLARKSBURG SHOOTING CLUB

This area encompasses both the town of Clarksburg and the Clarksburg Shooting Club, at the town's east end. Clarksburg had seen better days even before the bombs dropped; miners were protesting due to an increasing reliance on robotic workers, and the economy was depressed. Naturally, it's a tad more unpleasant to live in Clarksburg now; most of the residential homes are almost completely destroyed, Raiders have erected rough defenses on the main street, and there are numerous rooftops to fire from (or expect fire yourself). Still, the place is worth a visit for the possible junk loot.

16. CLARKSBURG SHOOTING CLUB

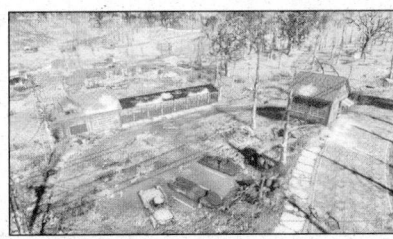

- **CRAFTING:** WEAPONS
- **ITEMS:** ARMS AND AMMO+; RECIPE/MOD/PLAN; VENDING MACHINE: AMMUNITION
- **INFO:** EXPECTED ENEMY: GHOUL, IRRADIATED INSECT; QUEST: TARGET RICH ENVIRONMENT; SCAVENGE RATING: 3; SIZE: 2; SLEEPING; THREAT LEVEL: 10–25
- **ITEM EXAMPLES:** BEER BOTTLE+, COFFEE CUP, COOKING PAN, COOKING POT, DISHRAG, GAS CANISTER, METAL BUCKET, RAT POISON, SPICES

The eastern side of Clarksburg is mostly taken up by a shooting club on the shore of the lakebed. Check the roadside hut for the attendant, and check the range structure for ammo, a weapon, and a station. The target range can be tested, too.

17. TOXIC DRIED LAKEBED

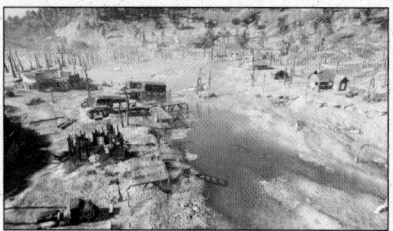

- **DANGER:** RADIATION!+
- **ITEMS:** ARMS AND AMMO; HARVESTABLE: BLOODLEAF; HEALTH AND CHEMS
- **INFO:** EXPECTED ENEMY: GHOUL, MIRELURK; SCAVENGE RATING: 3; SIZE: 3; THREAT LEVEL: 10–25
- **LOCK:** DOOR (2)
- **ITEM EXAMPLES:** COFFEE CUP+++, COFFEE POT, GAS CANISTER, HOT PLATE, PACK OF CIGARETTES, SALT, SPATULA, SUGAR, TEDDY BEAR, TYPEWRITER

Stretching north from Clarksburg is a marsh of dangerous, radioactive sludge, with a wrecked coffee shop and dock on the southeastern shore. Head west to the remains of the Lakeside Grill, a cafe with junk to gather inside. There's also a crab shack; only a rooftop picnic area is accessible around this structure. Then inspect the sagging docks and boat sheds, one of which is locked (2). The lake is radioactive, with a small sludge island and half-sunken boat to inspect, and the possibility of enemies both disgusting and glowing.

18. KIDDIE CORNER CABINS

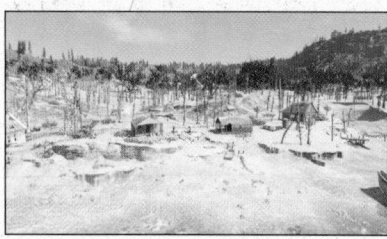

- **COLLECTIBLES:** BOBBLEHEAD, MAGAZINE (2)
- **CRAFTING:** ARMOR
- **ITEMS:** ARMS AND AMMO; HEALTH AND CHEMS; RECIPE/MOD/PLAN; TRUNK
- **INFO:** EXPECTED ENEMY: IRRADIATED INSECT; SCAVENGE RATING: 2; SIZE: 2; SLEEPING; THREAT LEVEL: 10–25
- **ITEM EXAMPLES:** ALARM CLOCK, ANTIQUE GLOBE, BLAMCO BRAND MAC AND CHEESE, CAN, COFFEE POT, CRAM, MILK BOTTLE, SHADELESS TABLE LAMP, TABLE SPOON, TOILET PAPER, TYPEWRITER

On the north side of the toxic lakebed are four cabins and cottages in various stages of disrepair. Search them all for a variety of junk and the possibility of some light reading materials.

19. BLACK BEAR LODGE

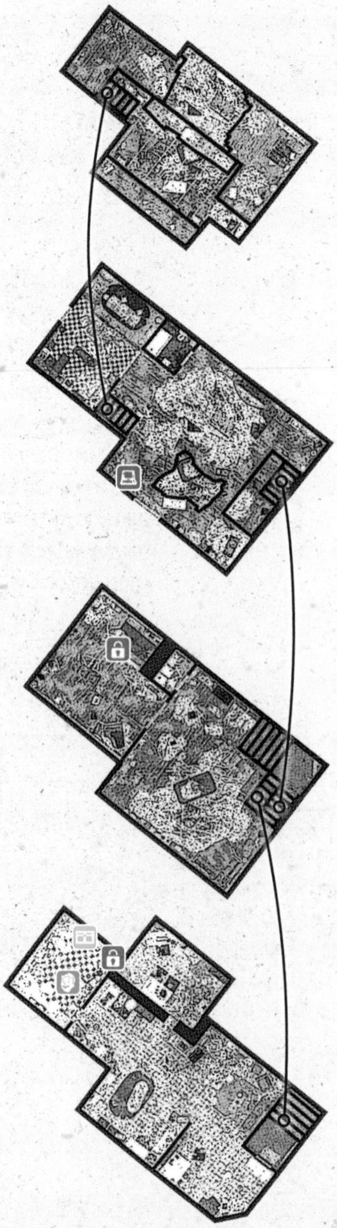

Black Bear Lodge (Exterior and Interior)

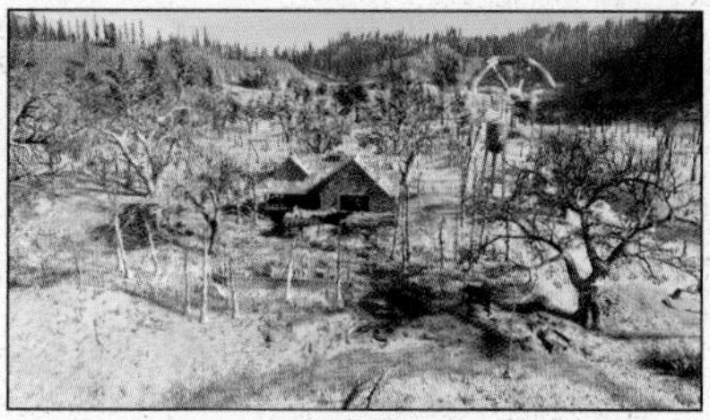

- **COLLECTIBLES:** BOBBLEHEAD, MAGAZINE, NUKA-CHERRY, POWER ARMOR
- **CRAFTING:** COOKING, WATER PUMP
- **DANGER:** EXPLOSIVE CANNISTER! RADIATION!++
- **ITEMS:** HEATH AND CHEMS; TRUNK; VENDING MACHINE: AMMUNITION
- **INFO:** EXPECTED ENEMY: IRRADIATED ANIMAL; QUEST: BIG GAME HUNT; SCAVENGE RATING: 4; SIZE: 3; SLEEPING; THREAT LEVEL: 10–25
- **LOCK:** SAFE (X2) (2, 2)
- **ITEM EXAMPLES:** ALUMINUM CAN, BEER BOTTLE++, BEER HAT, BLOWTORCH, BOBBY PIN BOX, FLORAL VASE+, FUSE, GAS CANISTER, GLASS JAR, GLOBE, INDUSTRIAL SIZE SHORTENING, MAKESHIFT BATTERY, METAL BUCKET, PAINT CAN, POOL BALL+, TURPENTINE, WAKEMASTER ALARM CLOCK+

This lodge was once a hunter's paradise. There's still some impressive game to be tagged and mounted, if the interior lounge walls of this lodge is anything to go by! Visit the Huntmaster in the basement to find out more, and don't forget your beer hat! Then check the irradiated outside red shed for a possible suit of Power Armor. The Magazine is in an upper attic that is only accessible from the outside north corner.

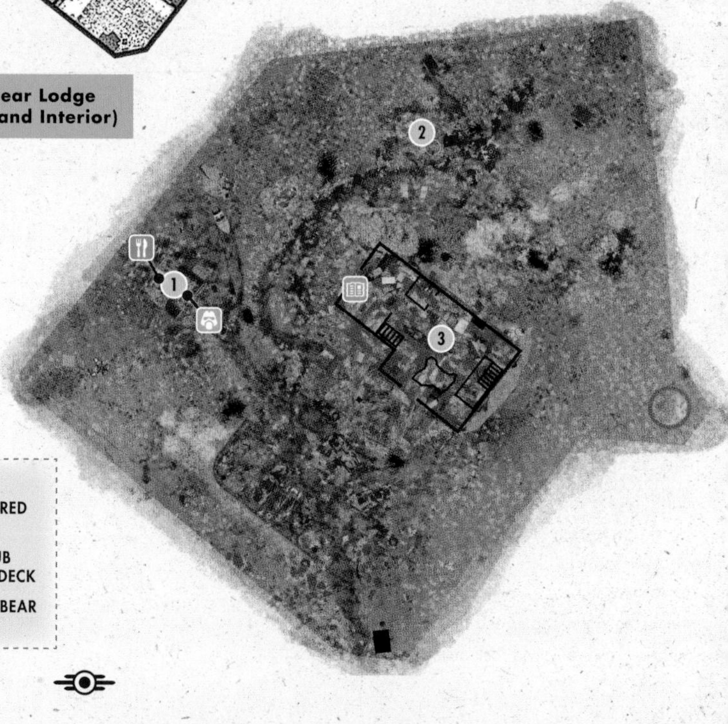

LEGEND

1. SMALL RED SHED
2. HOT TUB PARTY DECK
3. BLACK BEAR LODGE

20. GRANINGER FARM

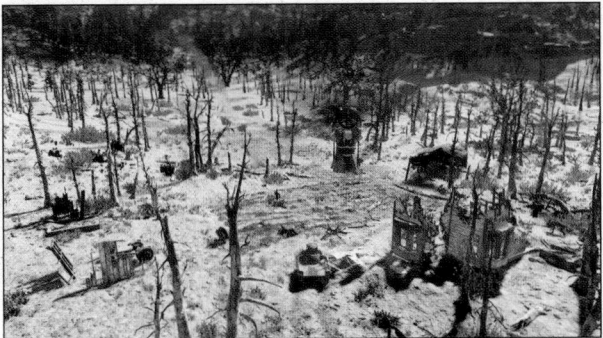

- **CRAFTING:** COOKING
- **ITEMS:** HARVESTABLE: TATO PLANT, WILD CORN; HEALTH AND CHEMS
- **INFO:** AEROSOLIZER; EXPECTED ENEMY: SUPER MUTANT; SCAVENGE RATING: 1; SIZE: 1; SLEEPING; THREAT LEVEL: 10–25
- **LOCK:** SAFE (1)
- **ITEM EXAMPLES:** BEER BOTTLE+, METAL BUCKET, PILLOW, TEDDY BEAR, TIN CAN.

Slowly sinking into the toxic marshland is a small farmstead, with a ruined home and equally disheveled mechanic's shed.

21. PIONEER SCOUT LOOKOUT

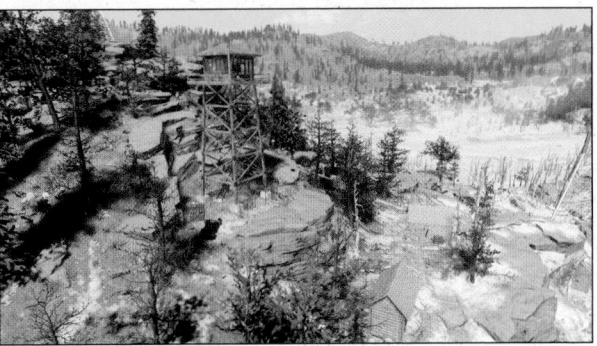

- **CRAFTING:** COOKING
- **DANGER:** LONG DROP!
- **ITEMS:** ARMS AND AMMO; HEALTH AND CHEMS
- **INFO:** EXPECTED ENEMY: GHOUL; LANDMARK; SCAVENGE RATING: 2; SIZE: 1; SURVEY AREA; THREAT LEVEL: 10–25
- **ITEM EXAMPLES:** CAMERA, ECONOMY WONDERGLUE, GAS CANISTER, HOT PLATE, METAL BUCKET, PAINT CAN, WILLOW BUD VASE

Standing tall on the western upper rock outcrop, surrounded by the main Scout Camp, is a tall lookout tower with surveying possibilities (and minor items) at the top.

22. PIONEER SCOUT CAMP

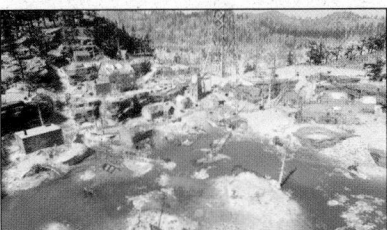

- **COLLECTIBLES:** BOBBLEHEAD (2), MAGAZINE (2), NUKA-CHERRY
- **CRAFTING:** COOKING (3)
- **DANGER:** RADIATION!++
- **ITEMS:** HARVESTABLE: MUTATED FERN; HEALTH AND CHEMS; RECIPE/MOD/PLAN

- **INFO:** EXPECTED ENEMY: GHOUL, IRRADIATED ANIMAL, MIRELURK; NOTES; SCAVENGE RATING: 3; SIZE: 3; SLEEPING; THREAT LEVEL: 10–25
- **LOCK:** SAFE (2)
- **ITEM EXAMPLES:** BLAST RADIUS BOARD GAME, CANNED DOG FOOD, CLEAN COFFEE TIN, CREAM, FISHING ROD+, LANTERN, PEPPER, PILLOW+, SALT, SUGAR, TIN CAN+, TOOTHPASTE

Pioneer Scout Camp and Lookout (Exterior)

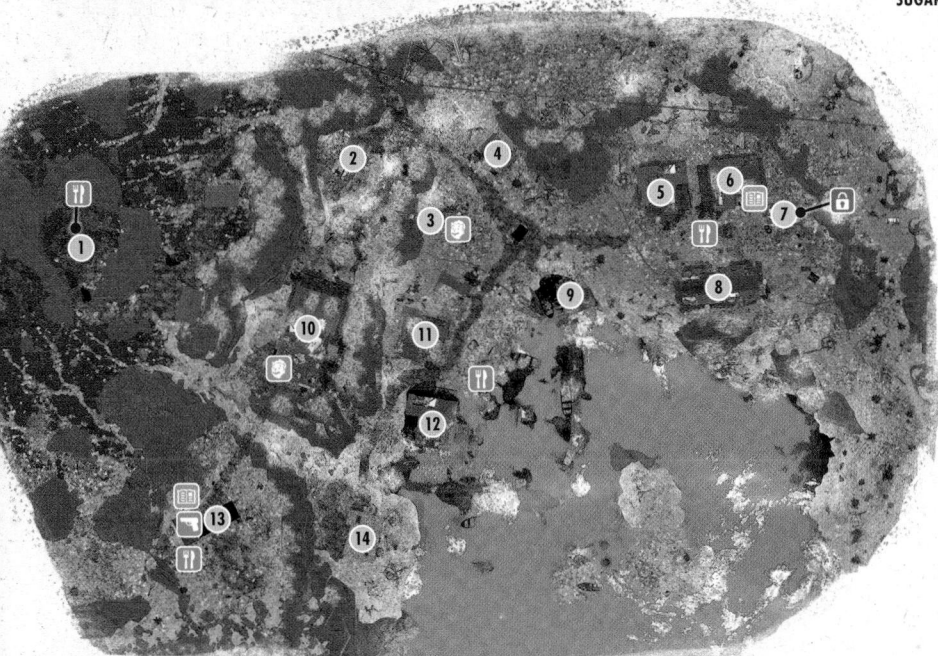

LEGEND

1. PRIMARY LOCATION: PIONEER SCOUT LOOKOUT
2. STORAGE CABIN
3. ADVENTURE TOWER
4. OFFICE CABIN
5. BUNK CABIN A01
6. BUNK CABIN A02
7. EXPEDITION CABIN
8. BUNK CABIN A03
9. BOATHOUSE
10. MESS HALL
11. BUNK CABIN B01
12. BUNK CABIN B02
13. SHOOTING RANGE
14. SHOWERS

The remains of Camp Lewis are below an electrical pylon, by a fetid lake, west of the Grafton Steel. The camp is comprised of scattered cabins, the lower ones being waterlogged and treacherous; a small tower (and a larger, marked one previously listed); and a mess hall that lives up to its name. To the camp's southwest, on the raised rock outcrop, is a small target range.

TRAINING

CRAFTING AND C.A.M.P.ING

INVENTORY

QUESTS

ATLAS

BESTIARY

APPENDICES

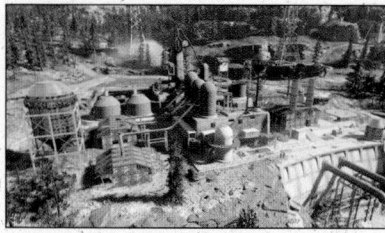

- **COLLECTIBLE:** HOLOTAPE
- **CRAFTING:** ARMOR (2), CHEMISTRY, POWER ARMOR, TINKER, WEAPONS, WORKSHOP
- **DANGER:** LONG DROP!
- **ITEMS:** ARMS AND AMMO; HARVESTABLE: COPPER, IRON, OIL, STEEL; HEALTH AND CHEMS; RECIPE/ MOD/PLAN
- **INFO:** EXPECTED ENEMY: VARIES; NOTE; QUEST: CLAIM THE WORKSHOP AT GRAFTON STEEL; SCAVENGE RATING: 3 (5+); SIZE: 5; THREAT LEVEL: 10–25.
- **ITEM EXAMPLES:** ALARM CLOCK, ALUMINUM CANISTER, COFFEE CUP, COTTON YARN, DIRTY ASHTRAY, ENAMEL BUCKET+, FUEL TANK+, FUSION CORE, HARD HAT, PIPE WRENCH, PROTEST SIGN, SUPRATHAW COOLANT, TEDDY BEAR, YELLOW CANISTER
- **WORK:** FOOD [2], WATER [2], LEAD [1], COPPER [1], STEEL [4], OIL [1]

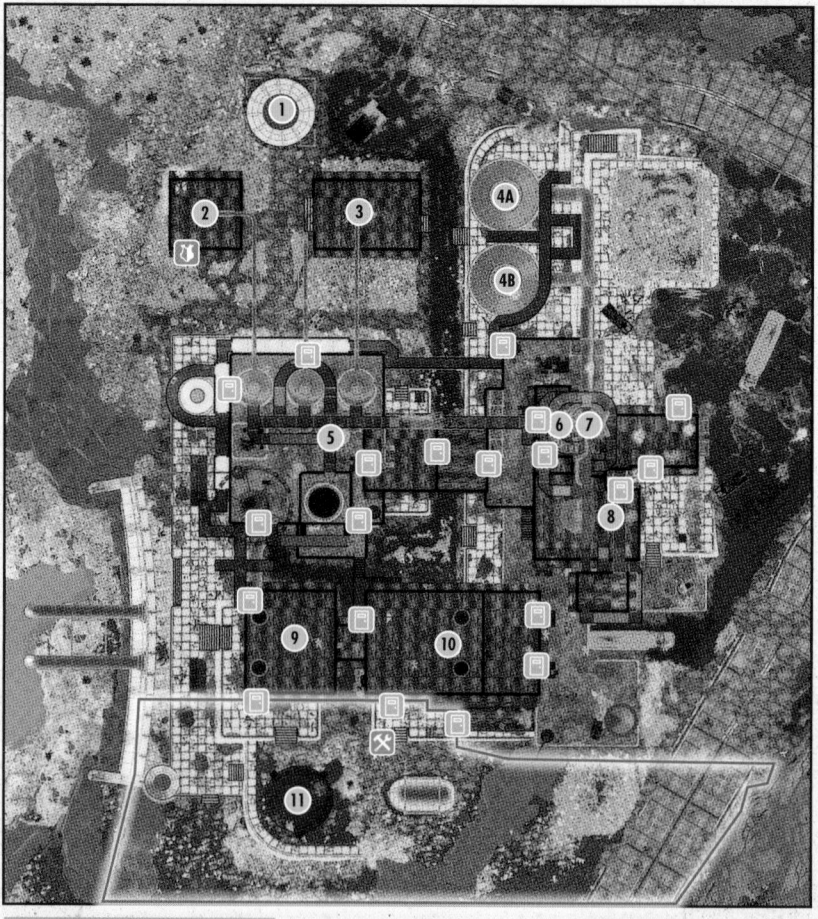

Grafton Steel (Exterior)

LEGEND

1. RAILYARD SILO
2. UNLOADING WAREHOUSE
3. LOADING WAREHOUSE
4A. [4A, 4B] COOLING STACKS
5. SMELTER
6. BLAST FURNACE
7. BLAST FURNACE CHIMNEY
8. WORKROOM
9. ROLLING MILL (LOWER)
10. ROLLING MILL (UPPER)
11. VERTIBOT PAD

Grafton Steel (Interior)

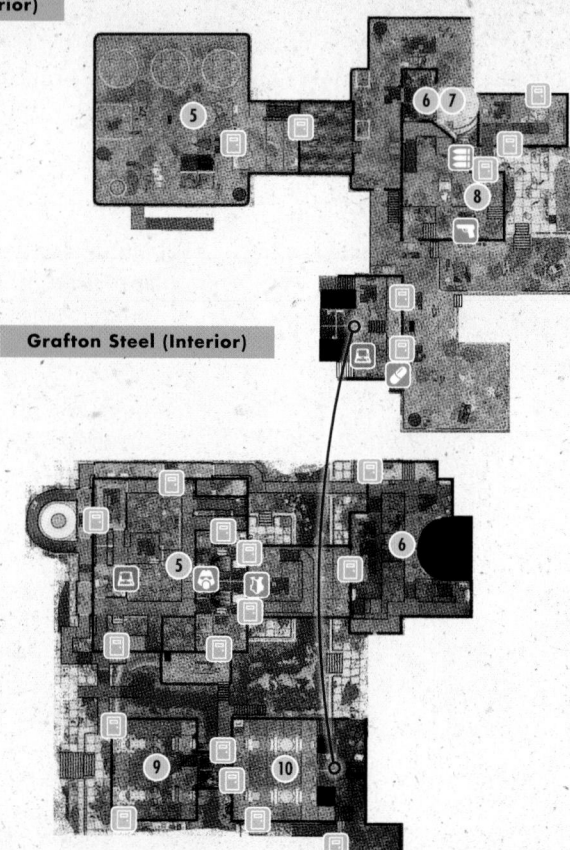

This pride of Appalachia is currently in disrepair but can be an excellent resource if you can claim and keep it. The place is large, but as long as you realize the blast furnace and smelter are linked chambers, and the workroom has gantry steps leading to the top of the cooling tower, you can easily remove all threats everywhere. Check the red signs near most entrances and exits to see which building you're in, and note the workshop base is mostly constructed on the facility's south side. Note there's a power coupling on the wall outside the blast furnace chamber.

24. POSEIDON POWER SUBSTATION PX-03

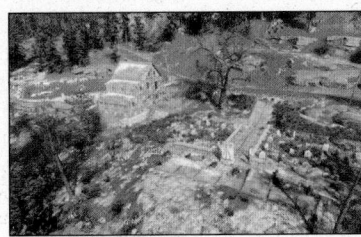

- **DANGER: EXPLOSIVE CANNISTER!**
- **ITEM: HARVESTABLE: BLACKBERRY**
- **INFO:** C.A.M.P. POWER; EXPECTED ENEMY: SCORCHED; SCAVENGE RATING: 0; SIZE: 1; THREAT LEVEL: 10–25
- **ITEM EXAMPLES: NOT MUCH!**

A small substation at the foot of the Savage Divide mountains, usually with a few Scorched foes roaming the electrical machinery. Hook up a C.A.M.P. power instead of a generator here, if you wish.

25. COLONEL KELLY MONUMENT

- **ITEM: HEALTH AND CHEMS**
- **INFO:** EXPECTED ENEMY: IRRADIATED INSECT; LANDMARK; SCAVENGE RATING: 1; SIZE: 1; THREAT LEVEL: 10–25
- **ITEM EXAMPLES:** FLIP LIGHTER, PACK OF CIGARETTES

Visit this monument to the Civil War general for a spot of introspection. The vista point close to the statue offers an audio tour, as well as good views to the west, across the Toxic Valley.

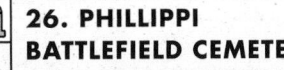

26. PHILLIPPI BATTLEFIELD CEMETERY

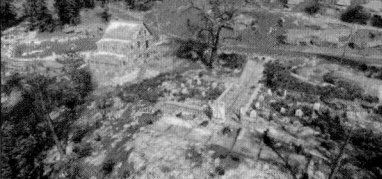

- **COLLECTIBLES: BOBBLEHEAD, MAGAZINE**
- **ITEM: ARMS AND AMMO**
- **INFO:** EXPECTED ENEMY: GHOUL, IRRADIATED INSECT, YAO GUAI; QUEST: BURIED WITH HONOR; SCAVENGE RATING: 3; SIZE: 2; THREAT LEVEL: 10–25
- **ITEM EXAMPLES:** ASHTRAY, BLAMCO BRAND MAC AND CHEESE, BLACK POWDER PISTOL, BLACK POWDER RIFLE, BOBBY PIN BOX, CIGAR, CIVIL WAR ERA SUIT, CIVIL WAR ERA TOP HAT, CONFEDERATE UNIFORM, SHOVEL, SPICES, UNION UNIFORM

Along a lonely stretch of Route 97 is a Civil War cemetery and museum on the Phillippi Battlefield grounds. Check inside the museum to flip the wall switches and unlock the display cases with guns and uniforms to purloin.

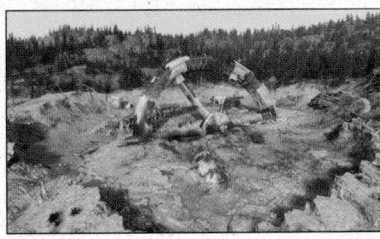

27. CRASHED SPACE STATION

- **COLLECTIBLE: POWER ARMOR**
- **ITEM: TRUNK (2)**
- **INFO:** EXPECTED ENEMY: MIRELURK; SUPER MUTANT; LANDMARK; SCAVENGE RATING: 2; SIZE: 3; THREAT LEVEL: 10–25
- **LOCK: DOOR (2)**
- **ITEM EXAMPLES:** JANGLES THE MOON MONKEY, SPACE SUIT, SPACESUIT HELMET, SPACESUIT JUMPSUIT

Protruding from a giant impact crater are the sections of a wrecked space station, now picked clean by Super Mutants and other scavengers. Though there's little to find that isn't in trunks or boxes, if you can open the locked door to a small section of sealed station corridor, there's three parts of a spacesuit to grab. That's not all; if you trek south to the rim of the crater, there's a small shack with a Jangles the Moon Monkey to keep you company and a possible Power Armor frame.

28. KNIFE EDGE

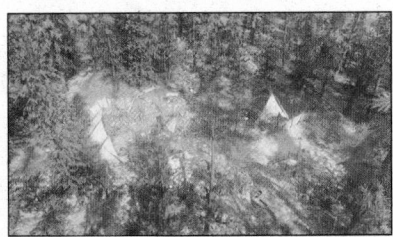

- **COLLECTIBLE: MAGAZINE**
- **CRAFTING: COOKING (2), TINKER**
- **ITEMS: ARMS AND AMMO; HARVESTABLE: MUTATED FERN; RECIPE/MOD/PLAN**
- **INFO:** EXPECTED ENEMY: IRRADIATED ANIMAL; NOTES; SCAVENGE RATING: 3; SIZE: 1; SLEEPING; THREAT LEVEL: 10–25
- **ITEM EXAMPLES:** BEER BOTTLE+, CLOWN, EMPTY FLORAL BARREL VASE, ENAMEL BUCKET, GAS MASK, HOT PLATE, METAL BUCKET, TURPENTINE

A small Raider camp, where violent scavengers have been heading to and from the crashed space station in search of junk.

29. PRICKETT'S FORT

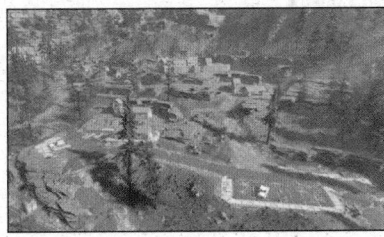

- **CRAFTING: COOKING (2)**
- **ITEMS: ARMS AND AMMO+; HARVESTABLE: BLACKBERRY, WOOD; HEALTH AND CHEMS**
- **INFO:** EXPECTED ENEMY: GHOUL, IRRADIATED INSECT; QUEST: BURIED WITH HONOR; SCAVENGE RATING: 4; SIZE: 3; SLEEPING; THREAT LEVEL: 10–25
- **ITEM EXAMPLES:** BEAR TRAP+, BLACK POWDER PISTOL, CAMERA, CIVIL WAR ERA TOP HAT, FANCY LADS SNACK CAKES, FOX HIDE, FUEL TANK, LANTERN, LUMBERJACK SAW, MULTI-PURPOSE AXE, RADIOACTIVE PUMPKIN SEEDS, SPICES, WHITE PLATE+, WOOD BUCKET, WOODEN BLOCK+

This Civil War–era fort, first erected in 1774, is a presentation of the Society for the Preservation of Historical Recreations and consists of a number of wooden ramparts, towers, and other fortifications set against the mountain slope. Speak to the curator, and visit each of the exhibit locations for the fullest experience.

TRAINING

CRAFTING AND C.A.M.P.ING

INVENTORY

QUESTS

ATLAS

BESTIARY

APPENDICES

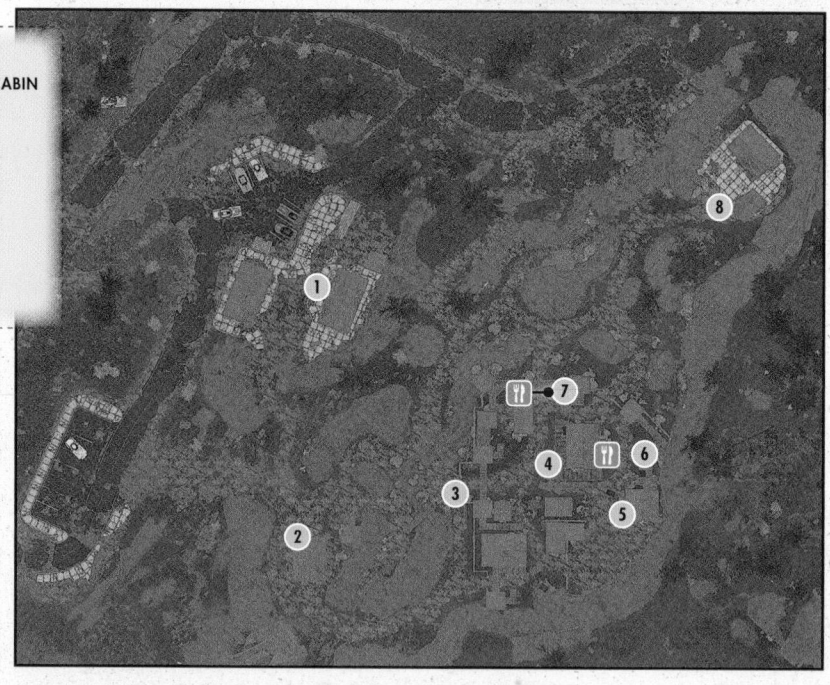

LEGEND

1 LOCATION 1: MUSEUM AND RECEPTION CABIN
2 LOCATION 2: BLACKSMITH SHOP
3 LOCATION 3: MAIN FORT ENTRANCE
4 LOCATION 4: MESS HALL
5 LOCATION 5: BARRACKS
6 LOCATION 6: NORTH WALL
7 LOCATION 7: NORTH ENTRANCE
8 LOCATION 8: MAIN GIFT SHOP

TOXIC VALLEY: SECONDARY LOCATIONS

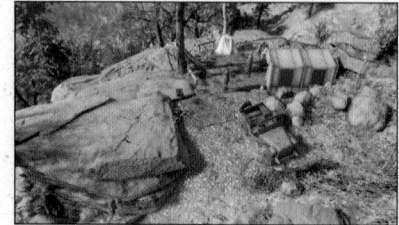

Campground (south of Crosshairs)

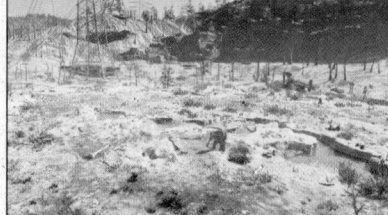

Vertibird Crash Site (Hemlock Holes)

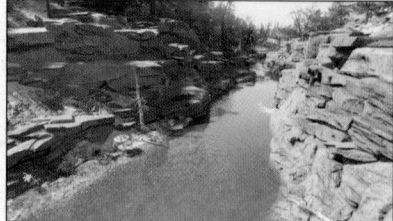

Grafton Lake Jetskiers
(West Grafton Lake)

Appalachia: Toxic Valley – Secondary Locations

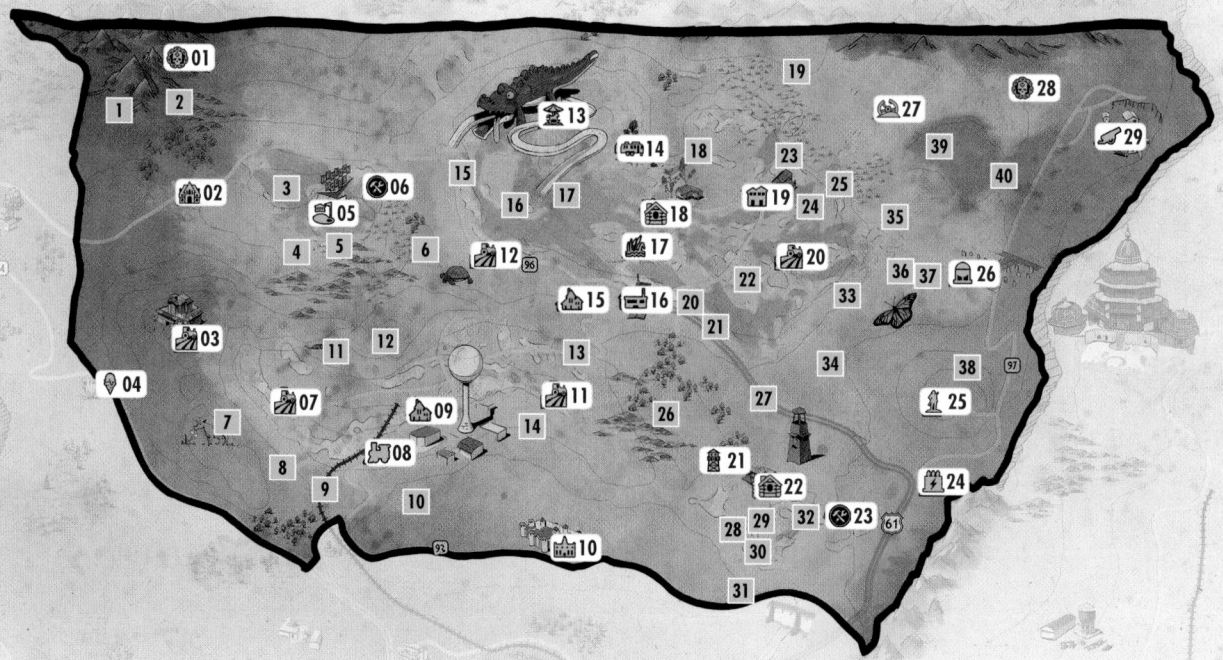

#	NAME	DESCRIPTION
1	Fancy Photo Studio (Rock Outcrop)	A wood chair, room dividers, and two side tables with flower vases; a great place to take a photo; a rock outcrop in the remote woods.
2	Campground (south of Crosshairs)	A foothills campsite with an orange tent, Tinker's Workbench and cooking station, and various debris, along with views to the south and east.
3	The Small Stage (Hemlock Holes)	A stage for amateur dramatists and a box full of hats; find a Tinker's Workbench around the back at this old hay bale karaoke place.
4	Oily Camp at Hemlock Holes	A leaky fuel tank and a cooking station, with a corpse at the edge of the golf course.
5	Vertibird Crash Site (Hemlock Holes)	This crash site yields items but no survivors, though a small military comms tower was erected before the crew died.
6	Spotter's Pylon (west of Woods Estate)	A toxic corpse may be cause for worry, but the views from this electrical pylon are worth it; there are binoculars you can use here, too.
7	Rusty Truck (edge of Toxic Valley)	A truck faced off against an old tree and lost; find it close to the edge where forest meets valley.
8	Grafton Hills Camp (southwest)	Though the campers are long dead, their tarp tent camp on the low rocky woodland hills still has a cooking station and mattress you can use.
9	The Missing Cyclist	A cyclist squashed by a boulder is by the railroad tracks at the edge of Toxic Valley, near a burned-out home with a bathtub.
10	Burned Graves (south of Grafton)	Someone really wanted these coffin corpses burned, but they left their flammable junk evidence ready for you to utilize.
11	Junk Tower Windmill	An impressive amateur engineering feat and landmark windmill with mechanical junk and an Armor Workbench.
12	Piano Bar Camp (north of Grafton)	A tarp tent, a bar, and an upright piano, along with dozens of beer bottles and other alcohol. Have a knees-up in no time!
13	Mr. Fuzzy's Boardgame Tent Pylon	A small camp with sleeping bags, a cooking station, and two soft toys overlooking Clarksburg.
14	Smith Pond Rowboat	Skeletal remains on a rotting boat, moored at a tiny toxic pond south of the Smith residence.
15	Wavy Willard's Sign	Knowing the exact spot where the Water Park entrance sign is helps you congregate here before exploration begins.
16	Marksmens' Campsite	Two green tents with sleeping bags inside, a rusty truck, a comfy sofa, and some sniping weaponry to gather.
17	Cyclists' Picnic	A couple of cyclists brought their board games to this picnic, near what used to be a river.
18	Patriot's Bone Camp	Bone chimes and a sledgehammer of justice await you here. Come for the bones and the weapon.
19	Rusting Car Camp	A cluster of cars around a small tent; the skeletal remains lie by their beer bottles.
20	Clarksburg Suburbs	Three ruined houses in various stages of disrepair can be found on the road east of town; check them for items.
21	Military Comms Tower Clarksburg	A small, quest-related comms dish standing near defensive spikes, sandbags, and a rusting van, close to the road.
22	Clarksburg Restrooms	There's usually something interesting in the parking lot above the restrooms, near a small public pool and pond with a tree island.

#	NAME	DESCRIPTION
23	Fetid Pond (Black Bear Lodge)	It's almost worth the radiation poisoning to gather the items from the ammo box on the half-sunken pickup in this pond.
24	Toxic Barrel and Tire Dump (east of Black Bear Lodge)	A couple of barrel-tippers succumbed to the elements in this lightly radioactive waterway.
25	Toxic Farmhouse (east of Black Bear Lodge)	A small, roofless farmhouse with adjacent red shed, caked in dust.
26	Hilltop Pylon Camp	Candy Fan Mr. Fuzzy and his pumpkin friends are sitting in a green tent camp, under a hilltop electrical pylon.
27	Camp Lewis North Entrance (161)	Though there are many ways to reach it, the Pioneer Scout Camp's main entrance is close to rusting traffic and half-buried bulldozers.
28	Grafton Lake Jetskiers (West Grafton Lake)	A couple of plastic people, kitted out in some natty toggle (and junk items to nab) are enjoying the orange waters on the west side of the lake.
29	Safe Cracker's Rowboat (Grafton Lake)	A half-sunken rowboat scuppered on the lake shore; one has a safe to crack.
30	Rifleman's Raft (West Lake)	Perhaps one of the least pleasant locations to take a nap; a raft with a blue tarp on the edge of the toxic lake.
31	Roadside Hilltop Lean-to	A small camp with a cooking station, tatos, and views of the edge of the Toxic Valley.
32	Mirelurk Shell Camp (Grafton Lake)	Some ingenious (and now dead) soul has fashioned a lakeside tent from Mirelurk carapaces. Also come here for the junk.
33	Toxic Pond and Wreckage	A ruined home slowly sinks into a toxic pond, creating an otherworldly atmosphere; possibly explains the toy alien in the bathtub.
34	The Domestics (Home)	Is a house without walls still a home? Come for the domestic bliss, witnessing the plastic faces (and the steel guitar).
35	Crashed Biplane (east of Graninger Farm)	Buried in mud, the pilot extricated herself from the plane but succumbed to her wounds. She left some chems for you, though.
36	Toxic Dust Dump	A favorite spot for Mirelurks, a truck trailer snowed under with toxic dust, is parked next to a half-buried hole of radioactive barrels.
37	Debris Camp	A rusty car, sharp metal, a duffel bag infuriatingly difficult to unlock (3), and soot flowers are here in what passes for a camp in these parts.
38	Road Vista and Rustbuckets	Two vehicles are parked at this dead-end vista point; take in the view, then take a look at the items in the vehicles.
39	Observation Shack (south of Crashed Space Station)	A Tinker's Workbench and cooking station, possible Power Armor, mattresses, and a moon monkey await at this clifftop shack filled with junk.
40	Biplane Pieces	This plane likely hit the sparse forest with great force, judging from where all the pieces (and tins of Mentats) landed.
41	Dilapidated Woodshed	Someone liked collecting tires, which are the only objects holding up the shed in the woods in northeast Toxic Valley.

TRAINING

CRAFTING AND C.A.M.P.ING

INVENTORY

QUESTS

ATLAS

BESTIARY

APPENDICES

REGION 3: THE ASH HEAP

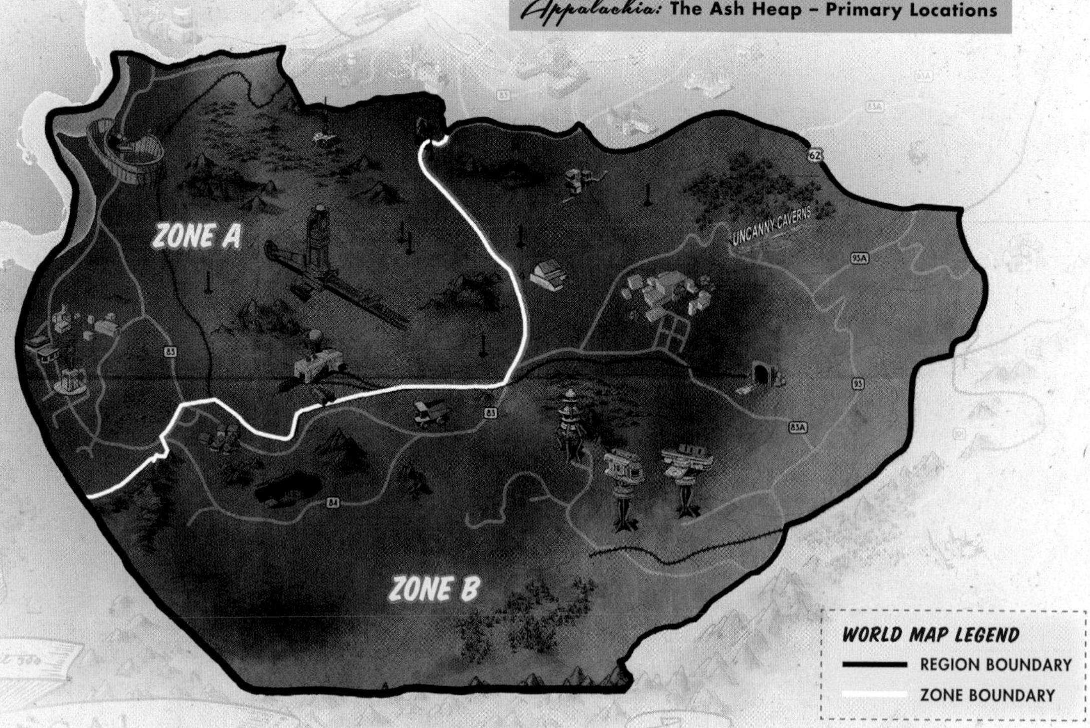

ZONE A

UNCANNY CAVERNS

ZONE B

WORLD MAP LEGEND
— REGION BOUNDARY
— ZONE BOUNDARY

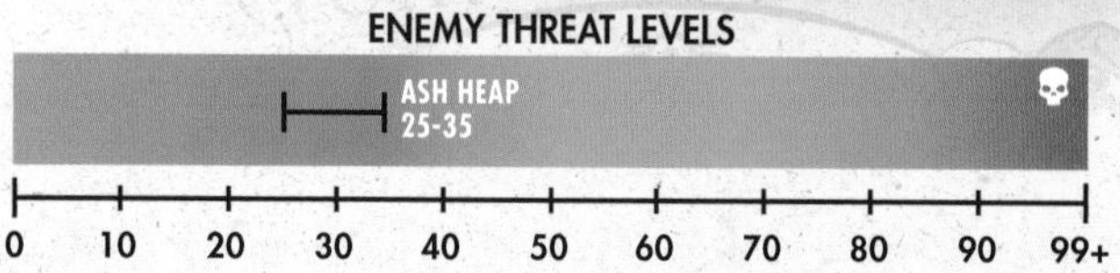

ENEMY THREAT LEVELS

ASH HEAP
25-35

0   10   20   30   40   50   60   70   80   90   99+

The Ash Heap is the center of mining in this part of Appalachia. The air wasn't the cleanest here before the bombs dropped, and now with mountains of ash mixing in with the nuclear fallout, you have a virulent and choking atmosphere where a gas mask (or other protective measures) is a must. While maintaining a backup breathing apparatus is a good idea, this region cannot be described as "oxygen-friendly." There are great gouts of smoke you should steer well clear of, especially as you head inevitably to the main landmark: the gigantic bucket-wheel excavator sitting on what's left of Mount Blair. You don't want to be gasping for breath on top of the local risk of attacks from the mysterious Mole Miners or the threat of an encroaching Rad Storm. There are some hard-scrapping old mining towns, like Beckley and Lewisburg, to visit and scavenge and a special suit of Power Armor to obtain, if your questing takes you to the headquarters of Garrahan Mining, owned by one of the prominent mining families in this region. The vertical tower mansions to the southeast still exist to this day.

Expect periodic bouts of seismic activity and instability, mainly brought about by decades of incautious mining by the AMS Corporation. AMS conducted some early Ultracite tests in the region, leading to seismic rumblings, while other shaking seems to be caused by Scorchbeasts burrowing and the infamous "Motherlode." Prior to the bombs dropping, an earthquake revealed a vein of Ultracite under some homes in the impoverished town of Welch. AMS attempted to evict the residents in order to reach the vein, and these tactics resulted in a riot, which swept the region about three weeks before the War. Rioters hit the Bucket Wheel Excavator on Mount Blair, blowing up one of the Mega Mansions and defacing the home of the Hornwrights. The Garrahan family's holdings were mainly left intact due to their tendency to work with, rather than against, the miners.

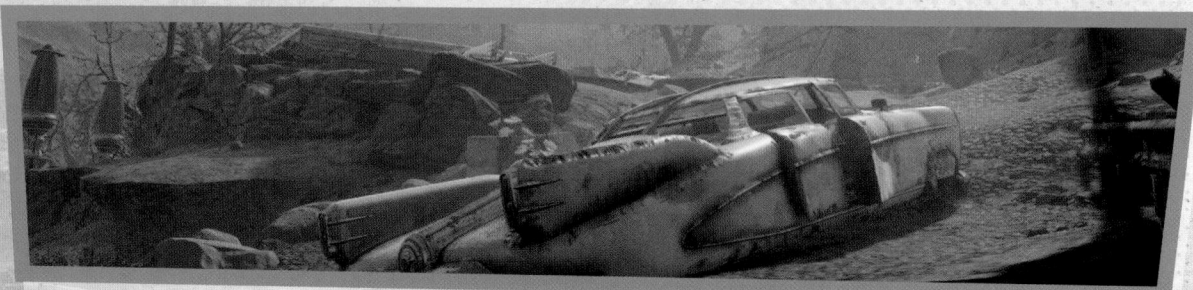

THE ASH HEAP: ZONE A—
BECKLEY AND MOUNT BLAIR

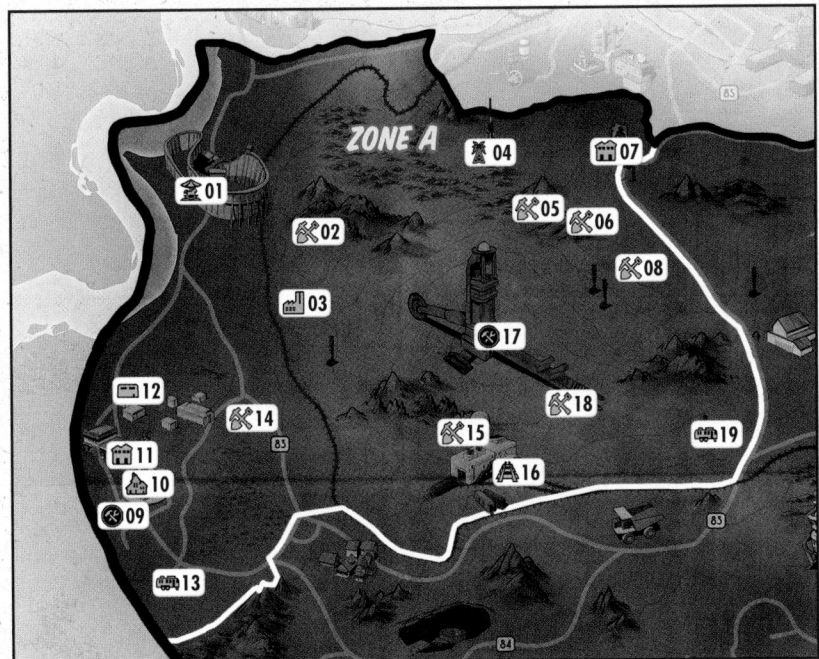

TRAINING

CRAFTING AND C.A.M.P.ING

INVENTORY

QUESTS

ATLAS

BESTIARY

APPENDICES

Appalachia: **The Ash Heap (Zone A) – Primary Locations**

WORLD MAP LEGEND

— REGION BOUNDARY　　— ZONE BOUNDARY

PRIMARY LOCATIONS

				icon	NAME
4	1	3	1	🏛 01	CAMDEN PARK
				⚒02	BRIM QUARRY
				🏭03	HORNWRIGHT TESTING SITE #04
1		1		📡 04	RELAY TOWER HG-B7-09
				⚒05	ABANDONED MINE SHAFT 5
4		4	1	⚒06	BELCHING BETTY
2		2	1	🏚07	THE RUSTY PICK
				⚒08	ABANDONED MINE SITE KITTERY
	1			🎡09	BECKLEY MINE EXHIBIT
2		2	1	🏘10	BECKLEY
2		1		🏚11	SAL'S GRINDERS
				📟12	HORNWRIGHT AIR CLEANSER SITE #04
	1			🚌13	NICHOLSON'S END
				⚒14	ABANDONED MINE SHAFT 4
	1			⚒15	ABANDONED MINE SHAFT ELAINE
4	2	3	1	🚂16	MOUNT BLAIR TRAINYARD
2		2	1	🎡17	MOUNT BLAIR
				⚒18	ABANDONED MINE SHAFT 6
1		1	1	🚌19	ROLLINS WORK CAMP

🟢 BOBBLEHEADS　⬛ CAP STASHES　🟪 MAGAZINES　⬜ POWER ARMOR

The western side of this region is dominated by the monumental bucket excavator, which is also an impressive workshop. It is located on the strip-mined Mount Blair, surrounded by several warehouses and mines (some on fire, some inaccessible, and all with good scavenging opportunities). When you're ready to try something other than clambering across massive metal structures, seek out the mining town of Beckley, with a small and relatively manageable workshop and a main street that's seen havoc of many kinds, from fallen buildings to Raider fortifications to battles against the military. There's also evidence of mining protests against the companies that own this land and their incessant march toward automation. But if all of this gets too grim, frolic through Camden Park, the kiddie funfair on the northern tip of this zone (though it's been recently marred by Raider activity too).

ZONE A: PRIMARY LOCATIONS

01. CAMDEN PARK

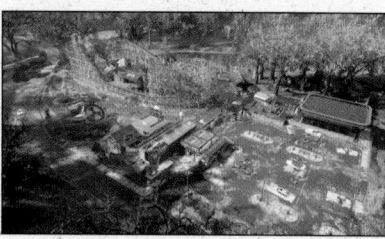

- **COLLECTIBLES:** BOBBLEHEAD (4), CAPS STASH, MAGAZINE (3), NUKA-COLA QUANTUM, POWER ARMOR
- **CRAFTING:** ARMOR, COOKING (3), POWER ARMOR

- **DANGER:** CAN CHIMES!+ EXPLOSIVE CANNISTER! OIL!
- **ITEMS:** ARMS AND AMMO+, HEALTH AND CHEMS+, RECIPE/MOD/PLAN, TRUNK, VENDING MACHINE: MEDICAL SUPPLIES
- **INFO:** EXPECTED ENEMY: IRRADIATED INSECT, SCORCHED; QUEST: MISTAKEN IDENTITY; SCAVENGE RATING: 4; SIZE: 4; SLEEPING; THREAT LEVEL: 25–35; TRADER: VENDOR BOT
- **LOCK:** DOOR (2), SAFE (1, 2, 2)
- **ITEM EXAMPLES:** ATOMIC ROLLER BALL++,

BASKETBALL++, BEER BOTTLE+, BEER HAT, BOBBY PIN BOX, BOILED WATER+, BUBBLEGUM, CAP, CLOWN HAT, COMMIE WHACKER, COTTON CANDY BITES, CRAM, CRUSHED ACETONE CANISTER, ENAMEL BUCKET, FUSION CELL, FUSION CORE, INSTAMASH, MR. HANDY FUEL, NUKA-COLA BOTTLE+, NUKA-COLA CUP+, NUKA-COLA CUP PACK, ORANGE TIE MR. FUZZY, PACK OF CIGARETTES, PORTABLE FUEL TANK+, RUBY TIE MR. FUZZY, SKULL, SMALL LEFT ANTLER, SPOOKY TIME MR. FUZZY, TEDDY BEAR++, TOILET PAPER+, UPPER SKULL, WAKEMASTER ALARM CLOCK, WOOD BLOCK++

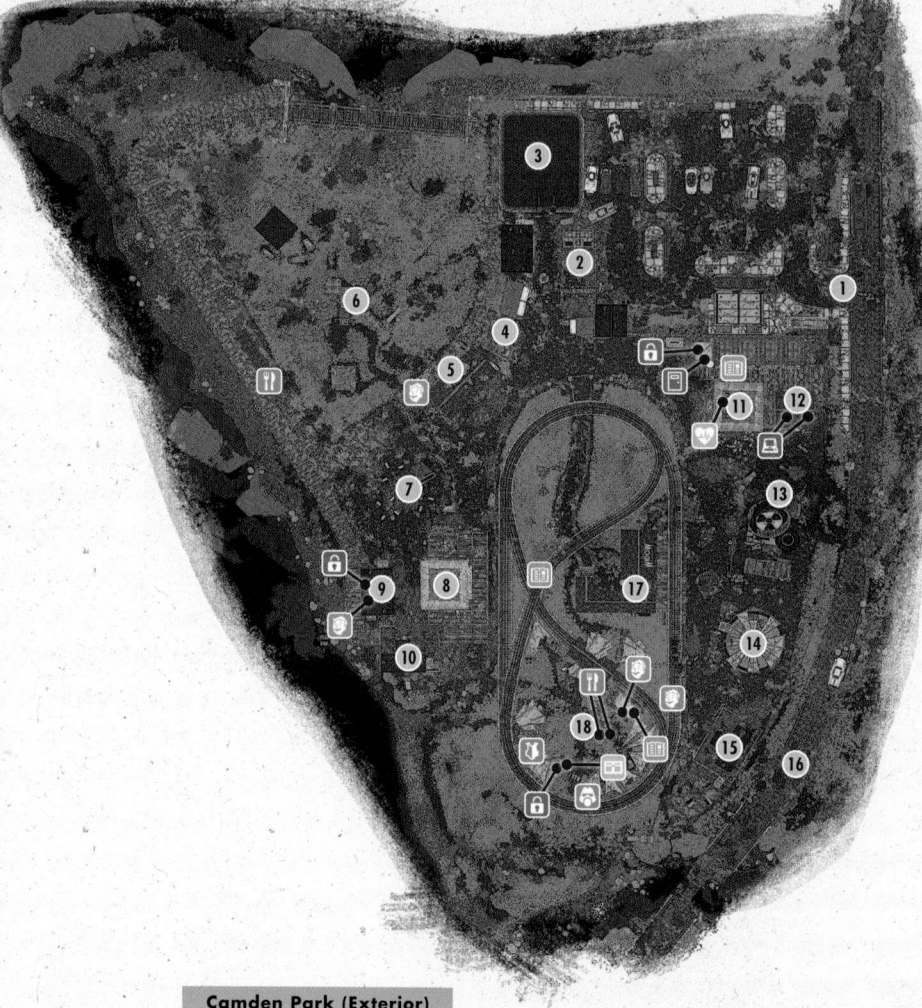

Camden Park (Exterior)

LEGEND

1. ENTRANCE
2. DROSS TOSS (QUOITS)
3. THE SHUNT N' BUNT (BUMPER CARS)
4. LUCKY MUCKER (GAME OF SKILL)
5. CAMDEN PARK EXPRESS (MINIATURE TRAIN)
6. MINOR MINER ZONE (WOODLAND PLAY PARK)
7. STRIP MINER (WURLITZER)
8. CHOW LINE (REFRESHMENT STAND)
9. EMPLOYEES ONLY METAL SHED
10. RESTROOMS
11. SUGAR HEAPS (TRADING POST)
12. THE COMPANY STORE (GIFT SHOP: TOKEN REDEMPTION)
13. RADIOACTIVE ROUNDUP (BROKEN SPINNER RIDE)
14. CAROUSEL
15. RESTROOMS
16. SHACK UNDER THE ROAD
17. THE WIDOW MAKER (ROLLER-COASTER)
18. OLD RAIDER CAMP

The Responders recently commandeered this funfair and turned it into a trading post, with supplies and medical facilities, before the place was abandoned and overrun. Now you can help the robots maintain order, as well as investigate the different attractions, including a small abandoned Raider camp in the grassy central area surrounded by the roller coaster.

02. BRIM QUARRY

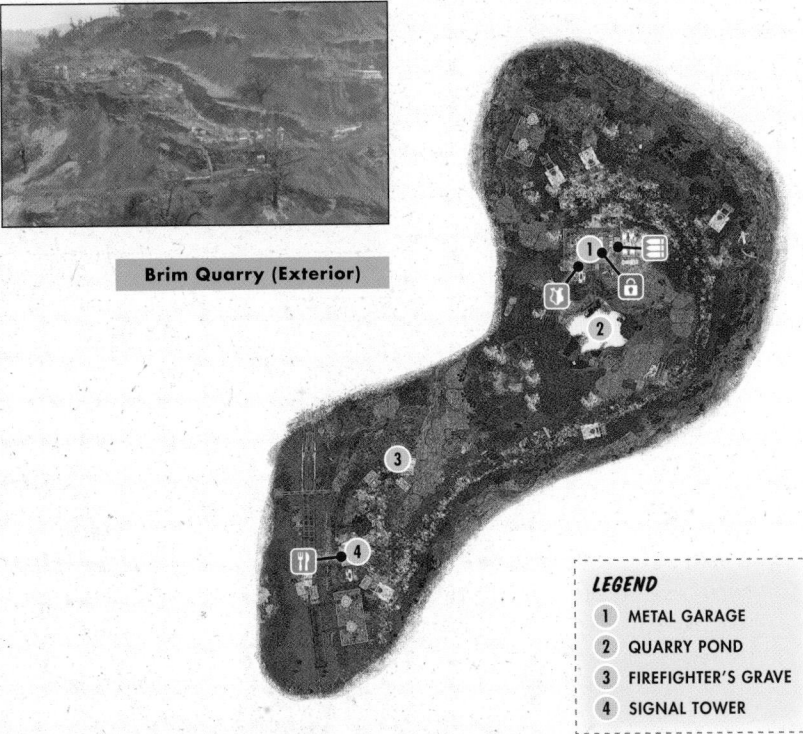

Brim Quarry (Exterior)

LEGEND
1. METAL GARAGE
2. QUARRY POND
3. FIREFIGHTER'S GRAVE
4. SIGNAL TOWER

- **CRAFTING:** ARMOR, COOKING, TINKER, WATER PUMP
- **DANGER:** RADIATION!
- **ITEMS:** ARMS AND AMMO, HEALTH AND CHEMS
- **INFO:** EXPECTED ENEMY: MOLE MINER; NOTE; SCAVENGE RATING: 3; SIZE: 3; SLEEPING; THREAT LEVEL: 25–35

- **LOCK:** WALL SAFE (1)
- **ITEM EXAMPLES:** ACETONE CANISTER, BLOWTORCH, BOX OF SAN FRANCISCO SUNLIGHTS, BUFFOUT, GAS CANISTER, FUSION CORE, HANDMADE GLUE, HIGH-POWERED MAGNET, MAKESHIFT BATTERY, METAL BUCKET, OFFICE DESK FAN, TYPEWRITER.

On the rough-hewed side of the mining slopes is a small quarry, now waterlogged with a metal garage structure and a variety of rusting machinery. Below and west is a railroad with an open carriage. Scavenge the entire area, including the wooden box submerged in the quarry pond.

03. HORNWRIGHT TESTING SITE #04

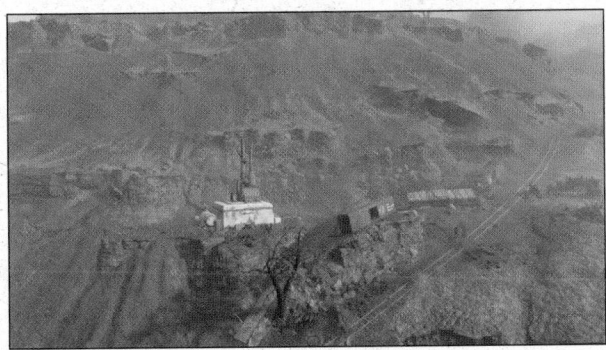

- **ITEMS:** HEALTH AND CHEMS
- **INFO:** SCAVENGE RATING: 1; SIZE: 1; THREAT LEVEL: 25–35
- **LOCK:** DOOR (B), TERMINAL (KEY)
- **ITEM EXAMPLES:** COFFEE CUP, COFFEE POT, EXTINGUISHER, FUSE, GAS CANISTER PAINT CAN, TIN CAN+

Close to a collection of derailed carriages is a small monitoring structure with a barred door. Inside is a meager collection of scraps and junk.

04. RELAY TOWER HG-B7-09

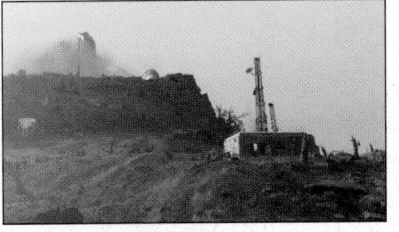

- **COLLECTIBLES:** BOBBLEHEAD, HOLOTAPE, MAGAZINE
- **DANGER:** TURRET!
- **ITEM:** HEALTH AND CHEMS
- **INFO:** EXPECTED ENEMY: SCORCHED; EVENT: ALWAYS VIGILANT; SCAVENGE RATING: 2; SIZE: 1; THREAT LEVEL: 25–35
- **ITEM EXAMPLES:** COMBINATION WRENCH, ENAMEL BUCKET, GAS CANISTER+, GLASS JAR, OFFICE DESK FAN, USED OIL CAN, WELDING GOGGLES

Aside from the roaming foes and automatic roof turrets, this transmission tower has a relay terminal that's worth repairing, if only to request a possible supply drop.

05. ABANDONED MINE SHAFT 5

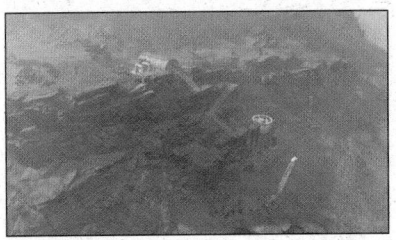

- **CRAFTING:** CHEMISTRY,
- **DANGER:** EXPLOSIVE CANNISTER!
- **ITEM:** HARVESTABLE: HIGH-YIELD MINING SITE
- **INFO:** EXPECTED ENEMY: GHOUL; SCAVENGE RATING: 3; SIZE: 2; THREAT LEVEL: 25–35
- **ITEM EXAMPLES:** BUNSEN BURNER, DESK FAN, DRILL, FUSION CORE, LUXOBREW COFFEE POT, PRISTINE MINER UNIFORM, RADIO JAMMER, SHAPED CHARGE, TALL FLASK

This shaft is one of the many abandoned shafts in this region, and is farther down the mountain. Access it from the curved-roof laboratory via a gantry.

TRAINING

CRAFTING AND C.A.M.P.ING

INVENTORY

QUESTS

ATLAS

BESTIARY

APPENDICES

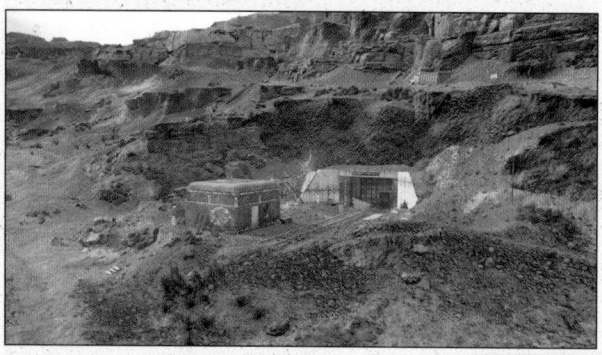

- **COLLECTIBLES:** BOBBLEHEAD (4), MAGAZINE (4), NUKA-CHERRY, POWER ARMOR
- **CRAFTING:** ARMOR, CHEMISTRY, COOKING, TINKER, WEAPONS
- **DANGER:** EXPLOSIVE CANNISTER! HEAT!
- **ITEMS:** ARMS AND AMMO; HARVESTABLE: BLACK TITANIUM; HEALTH AND CHEMS+; TRUNK; VENDING MACHINE: KIT DISPENSER
- **INFO:** EXPECTED ENEMY: SCORCHED; QUEST: INTO THE FIRE; SCAVENGE RATING: 4; SIZE: 4; THREAT LEVEL: 25–35
- **LOCK:** SAFE (0)
- **ITEM EXAMPLES:** BLAST RADIUS BOARD GAME, BOILED WATER, BOURBON, COFFEE CUP+, COFFEE POT, ENAMEL BUCKET, FUSION CORE, GAS CANISTER, HARD HAT, HOT PLATE, OFFICE DESK FAN, OIL CANISTER, ORANGE CANISTER, RADAWAY, SOAP, TACTICAL COMBAT SHOTGUN, TOXIC WATER, WHISKEY.

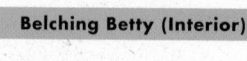

Belching Betty (Interior)

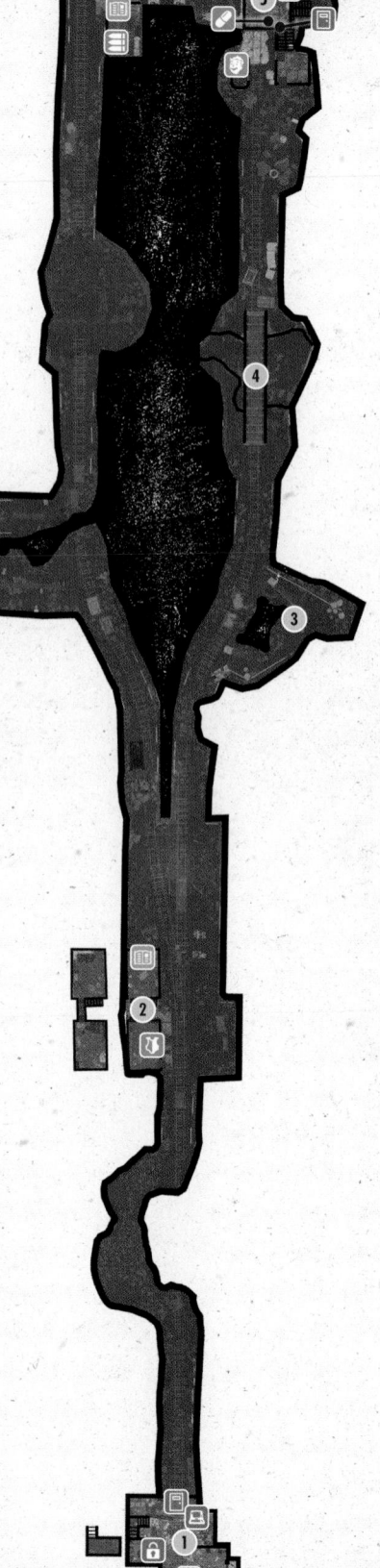

LEGEND

1. ENTRANCE AND SECURITY GATE
2. LOCKER ROOM AND CONTROL HUTS
3. SIDE TUNNEL (BLACK TITANIUM)
4. BRIDGE
5. SECURITY GATE AND GENERATOR
6. ELEVATOR SHAFT AND STAIRS
7. MAIN CAVERN: GENERATORS AND OFFICE
8. CONVEYOR TUNNEL A
9. CONVEYOR TUNNEL B

Check the maintenance hut on the surface first: Be sure you're properly protected with a fireproof kit (or Power Armor) before entering "Mine Shaft Beatrice," the official name of this fiery and hellish molten mine interior. Despite the extreme heat, there are some choice items to gather, as well as some rare Black Titanium to mine.

07. THE RUSTY PICK

- **COLLECTIBLES:** BOBBLEHEAD (2), MAGAZINE (2), POWER ARMOR
- **CRAFTING:** COOKING, WATER PUMP, WEAPONS
- **DANGER:** CAN CHIMES!
- **ITEMS:** ARMS AND AMMO; HARVESTABLE: BRAIN FUNGUS, GLOWING FUNGUS, RHODODENDRON, SOOT FLOWER; HEALTH AND CHEMS; RECIPE/MOD/PLAN; VENDING MACHINE: U-MINE IT!
- **INFO:** EXPECTED ENEMY: IRRADIATED ANIMAL, IRRADIATED INSECT, MOLE MINER, SUPER MUTANT; INSTRUMENT; NOTE; SCAVENGE RATING: 3; SIZE: 3; THREAT LEVEL: 25–35
- **LOCK:** SAFE (2)
- **ITEM EXAMPLES:** ASHTRAY, CLOWN HAT, COFFEE CUP, COFFEE POT, COOKING POT, BEER BOTTLE, FIRECAP TASTY SOUFFLÉ, GLASS PITCHER, LANTERN, MOONSHINE JUG, MOUNTAIN HONEY, PACK OF CIGARETTES, PEPPER, PORTABLE FUEL TANK, PLUNGER, RADAWAY, SALT, SOAP, TACTICAL AUTOMATIC COMBAT SHOTGUN, TEDDY BEAR, VOLATILE MATERIALS BOX, WRAPPED CAP

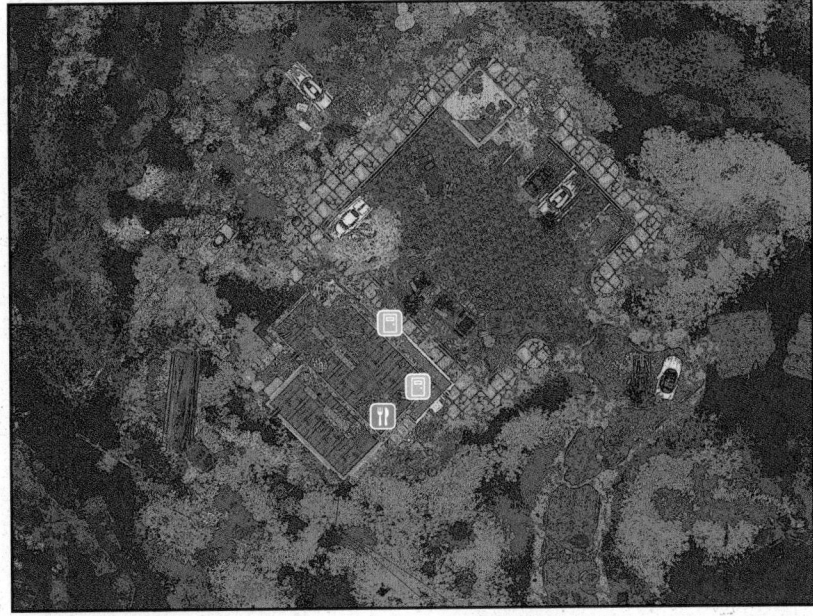

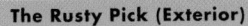
The Rusty Pick (Exterior)

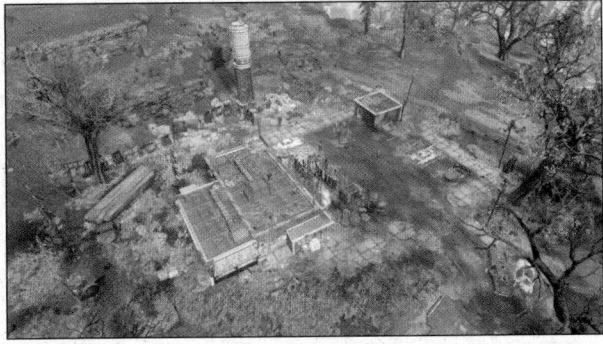

Micky Flanagan's miners' tavern was a popular watering hole in the region, but after the Raiders ransacked it and more mutated foes roam the exterior parking lot and interior of the place, it's definitely lost its customer base. Check the cellar for a possible suit of Power Armor and small mine tunnel addition.

LEGEND (INTERIOR)

1. BAR AND KITCHEN
2. MICK FLANAGAN'S CELLAR
3. MINE TUNNEL
4. DEAD-END CAVERN

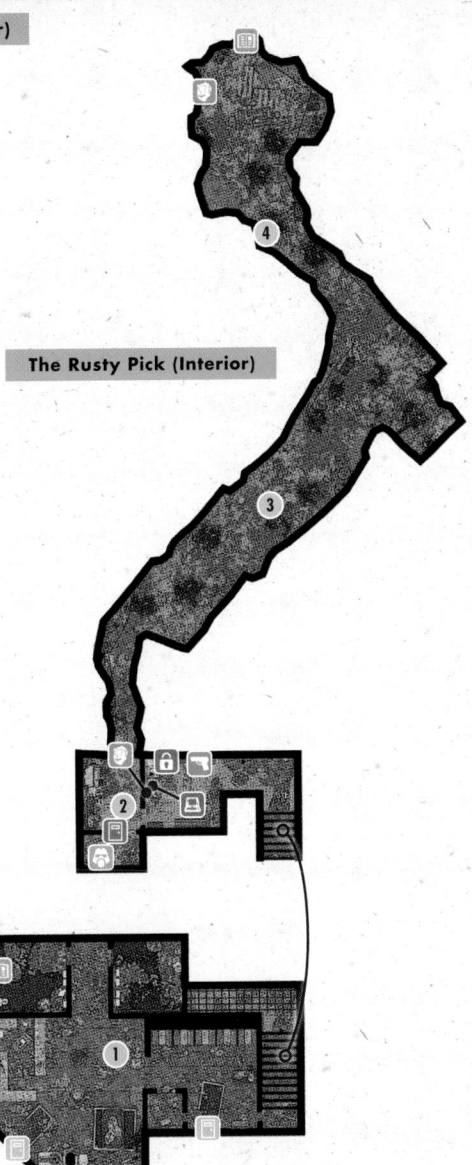

The Rusty Pick (Interior)

08. ABANDONED MINE SITE KITTERY

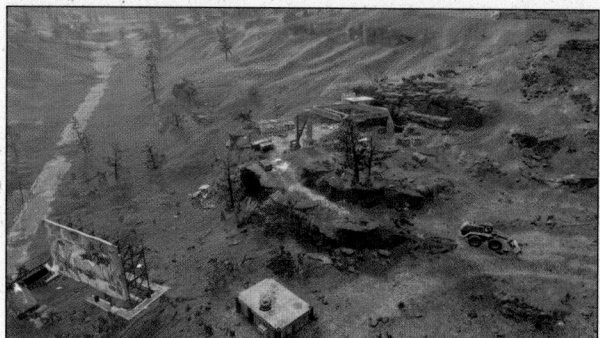

- **ITEMS:** ARMS AND AMMO; HEALTH AND CHEMS
- **INFO:** EXPECTED ENEMY: IRRADIATED ANIMAL; SCAVENGE RATING: 2; SIZE: 3; THREAT LEVEL: 25–35
- **ITEM EXAMPLES:** BEER BOTTLE+, BOILED WATER, LANTERN, PIPE REVOLVER, TEDDY BEAR

The mine entrance is atop a mountain of black dirt. Ascend the road with a miners' blockade and strewn and rusting vehicles. A curved-roof warehouse sits at the edge of the mine shaft, with miner lockers inside. Head to the blocked mine entrance, and check the Token Exchange terminal to swap tokens for gifts. There's a metal hut atop a gantry and another halfway down the hill; visit both to gather more important junk.

09. BECKLEY MINE EXHIBIT (WORKSHOP)

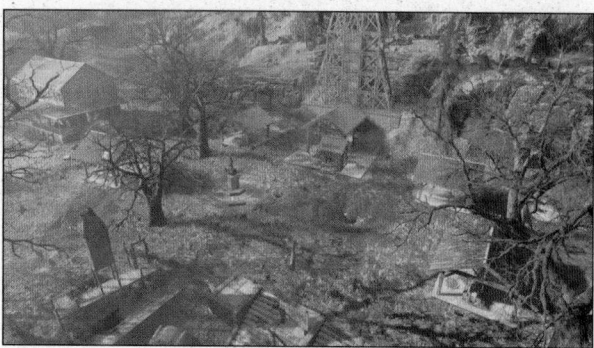

- **COLLECTIBLE:** CAPS STASH
- **CRAFTING:** WORKSHOP
- **ITEMS:** HARVESTABLE: ASH, CRYSTAL, GOLD, OIL
- **INFO:** EXPECTED ENEMY: VARIES; QUEST: CLAIM WORKSHOP AT BECKLEY MINE EXHIBIT; SCAVENGE RATING: 1(5); SIZE: 3; THREAT LEVEL: 25–35
- **ITEM EXAMPLES:** BOILED WATER, NUKA-COLA BOTTLE
- **WORK:** FOOD [6], WATER [8], CRYSTAL [1], GOLD [1], OIL [3]

Part of the town of Beckley, this area of park and cordoned-off mine was once an educational exhibit. Now the resources present here make this an even more popular destination!

10. BECKLEY

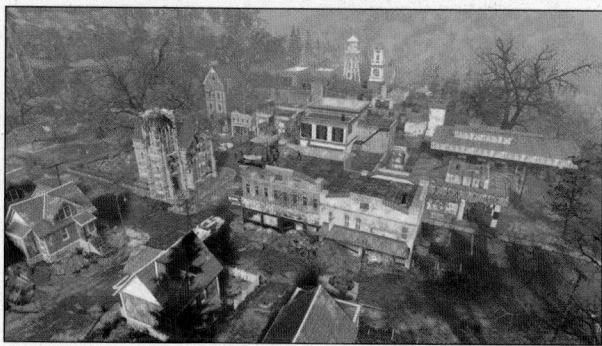

- **COLLECTIBLES:** BOBBLEHEAD (2), HOLOTAPE, MAGAZINE (2), POWER ARMOR
- **CRAFTING:** CHEMISTRY, COOKING (3), WEAPONS
- **DANGER:** LONG DROP!
- **ITEMS:** ARMS AND AMMO, HEALTH AND CHEMS
- **INFO:** EXPECTED ENEMY: GHOUL; INSTRUMENT; SCAVENGE RATING: 3; SIZE: 5; SLEEPING; THREAT LEVEL: 25–35
- **LOCK:** DOOR (0), SAFE (0, 2)
- **ITEM EXAMPLES:** ABRAXO CLEANER, BEER, BLUE PAINT, BOILED WATER, COFFEE CUP+, COOLANT, EMPTY PAINT CAN, HALLUCIGEN GAS CANISTER, MAKESHIFT BATTERY, MINING HELMET+, PAINT CAN, PAINTBRUSH, PORK N' BEANS, PROTEST SIGN+, PURIFIED WATER, SENSOR MODULE, SHORT HUNTING RIFLE

The town of Beckley has seen some of the most acrimonious rivalry between mine workers and operators bringing robot automation to Appalachia. Remnants of miner blockades can still be seen, especially on the north side of town, as you travel uphill to main street, where Raiders further augmented the pre-bombs defenses. Now the place is filled with other foes. Locate the rusty fire escape stairs on the outer sides of the buildings to most easily reach the rooftop shacks as you explore and scavenge this old mining town.

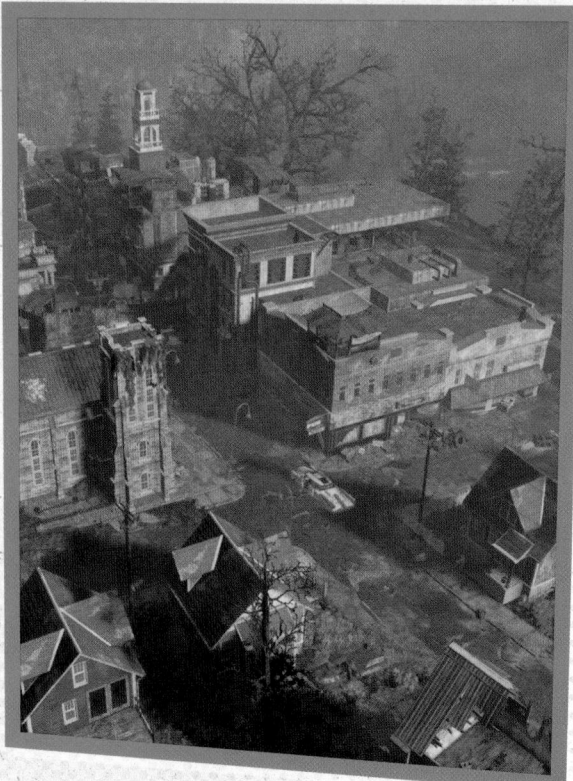

Beckley (Exterior)

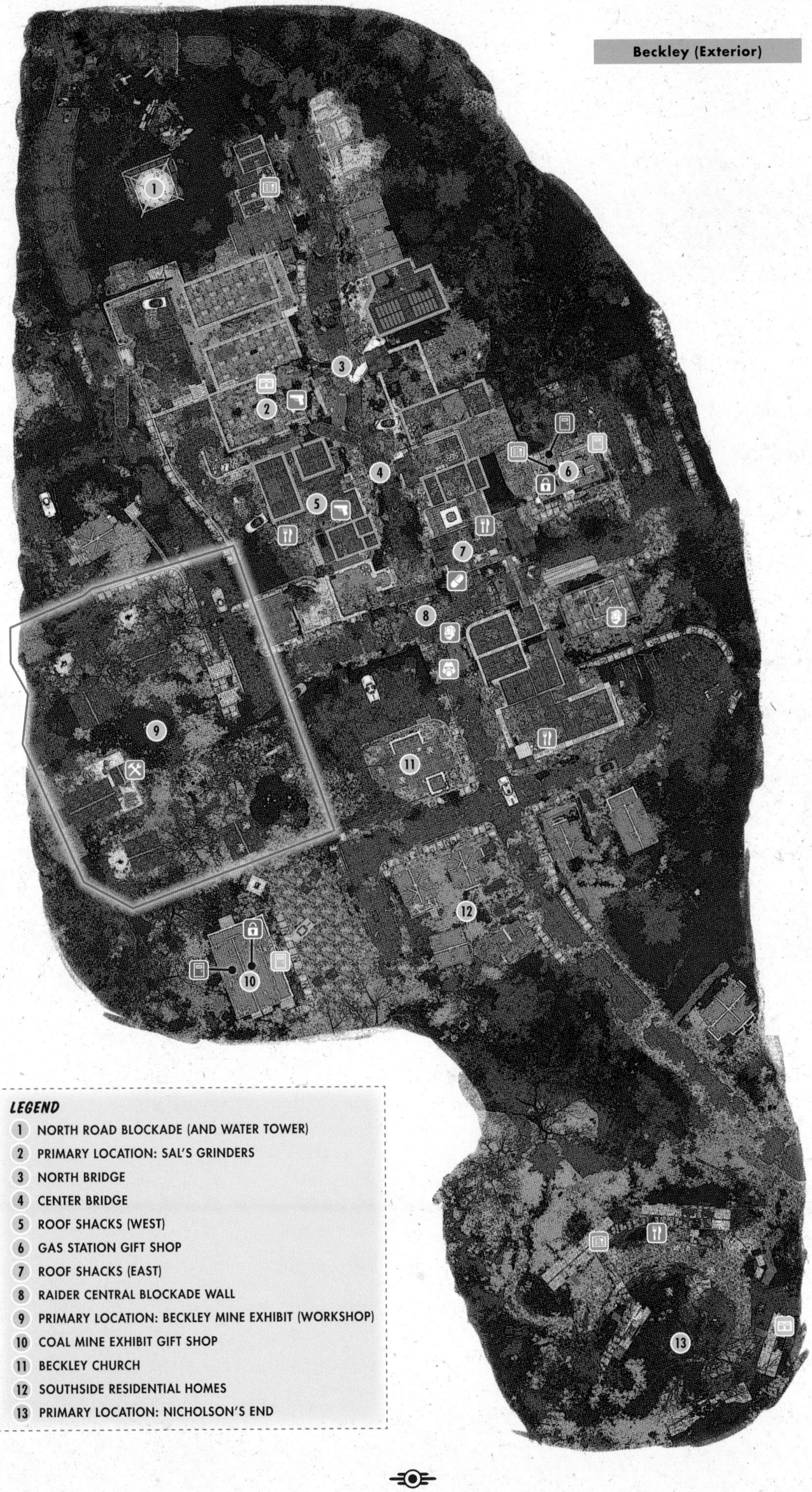

TRAINING

CRAFTING AND C.A.M.PING

INVENTORY

QUESTS

ATLAS

BESTIARY

APPENDICES

LEGEND

1 NORTH ROAD BLOCKADE (AND WATER TOWER)
2 PRIMARY LOCATION: SAL'S GRINDERS
3 NORTH BRIDGE
4 CENTER BRIDGE
5 ROOF SHACKS (WEST)
6 GAS STATION GIFT SHOP
7 ROOF SHACKS (EAST)
8 RAIDER CENTRAL BLOCKADE WALL
9 PRIMARY LOCATION: BECKLEY MINE EXHIBIT (WORKSHOP)
10 COAL MINE EXHIBIT GIFT SHOP
11 BECKLEY CHURCH
12 SOUTHSIDE RESIDENTIAL HOMES
13 PRIMARY LOCATION: NICHOLSON'S END

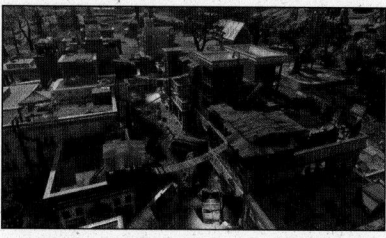

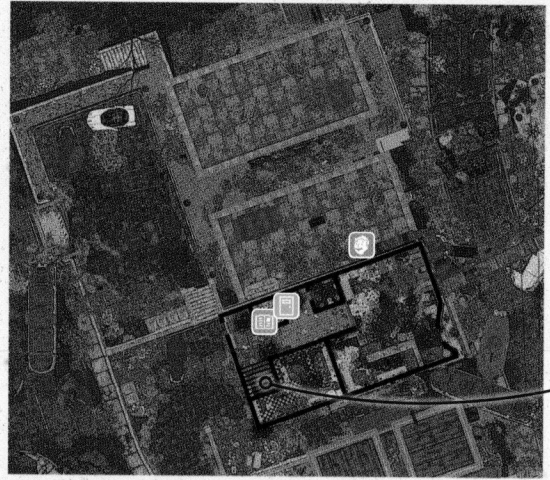

- **COLLECTIBLES:** BOBBLEHEAD (2), HOLOTAPE, MAGAZINE
- **CRAFTING:** WEAPONS
- **DANGER:** LONG DROP!
- **ITEMS:** ARMS AND AMMO; HARVESTABLE: GLOWING FUNGUS; HEALTH AND CHEMS; TRUNK (2); VENDING MACHINE: U-MINE-IT!
- **INFO:** EXPECTED ENEMY: GHOUL; SCAVENGE RATING: 4; SIZE: 3; SLEEPING; THREAT LEVEL: 25–35
- **LOCK:** DOOR (1), SAFE (1)
- **ITEM EXAMPLES:** ALARM CLOCK, BEER BOTTLE, BINOCULARS, BLUE TABLE LAMP, BOBBY PIN BOX, BOILED WATER, CAKE PAN, DINNER PLATE, FLOWER POT+, GLASS PITCHER, HOT PLATE, IGUANA ON A STICK, INDUSTRIAL SIZE SHORTENING, LATE EDITION NEWSPAPER, METAL BUCKET, MOP, PILLOW, PLUNGER, PROTEST SIGN, SOAP, TURPENTINE

Sal's Grinders (Exterior and Interior)

The best sandwiches in town? No. But this does feature some of the best loot in Beckley! Located near the center of town is a large coffee shop and diner, with apartments above and a shanty dwelling on the roof, along with two trunks and a good possibility of collectible scavenging. Otherwise, treat this as the most defensible part of Beckley, with good access to the rickety bridges and other rooftops.

🚐 **12. HORNWRIGHT AIR CLEANSER SITE #04**

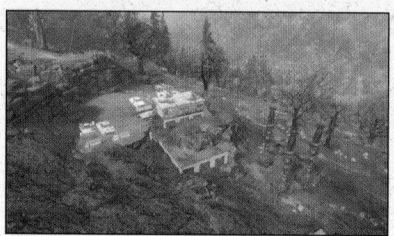

- **ITEM:** HEALTH AND CHEMS
- **INFO:** AIR PURIFIER; EXPECTED ENEMY: SCORCHED; SCAVENGE RATING: 2; SIZE: 2; THREAT LEVEL: 25–35
- **LOCK:** TERMINAL (KEY)
- **ITEM EXAMPLES:** BLASTING CAPS BOX, COFFEE CUP, COFFEE POT, COMBINATION WRENCH, HARD HAT, HERMIT CRAB MEAT, HIGH-POWERED MAGNET, HOT DOG, OIL CANISTER, SCREWDRIVER,

If you're hankering for some tinned crab meat, visit this cleanser site.

🚌 **13. NICHOLSON'S END**

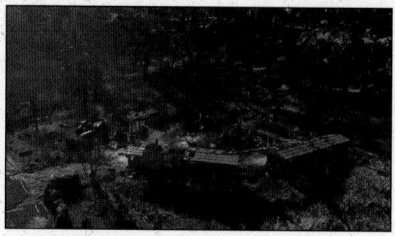

- **COLLECTIBLES:** MAGAZINE, NUKA-CHERRY
- **CRAFTING:** COOKING
- **ITEMS:** ARMS AND AMMO; HARVESTABLE: RHODODENDRON, SOOT FLOWER
- **INFO:** EXPECTED ENEMY: IRRADIATED ANIMAL, SUPER MUTANT; SCAVENGE RATING: 2; SIZE: 2; THREAT LEVEL: 25–35; TRUNK
- **ITEM EXAMPLES:** BOILED WATER, BROKEN LAMP, COFFEE CUP, COLANDER, DISHRAG, DOG BOWL, GLASS PITCHER, INDUSTRIAL SIZE SHORTENING, MINI NUKE, PEPPER, PLUNGER, TALL DRINKING GLASS, TELEPHONE, TOILET PAPER, TV DINNER TRAY

Part of the southern edge of Beckley township, this collection of trailer homes are in various states of disrepair. Some have been moved and metal sheets added to create ramps and rooftop battlements, possibly by Super Mutants as signs of their revolting activities are present here.

⛏️ **14. ABANDONED MINE SHAFT 4**

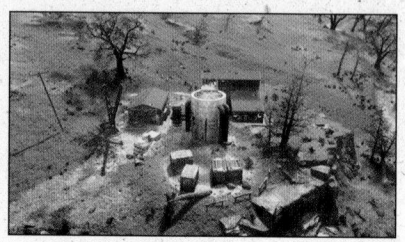

- **CRAFTING:** ARMOR, POWER ARMOR, TINKER, WEAPONS
- **ITEMS:** ARMS AND AMMO; HEALTH AND CHEMS
- **INFO:** EXPECTED ENEMY: SCORCHED; SCAVENGE RATING: 3; SIZE: 2; SLEEPING; THREAT LEVEL: 25–35
- **LOCK:** SAFE (3)
- **ITEM EXAMPLES:** BLOWTORCH, BUBBLEGUM, COFFEE CUP, COFFEE POT, LANTERN, MOLE RAT MEAT+, OIL CAN, PILLOW, RADAWAY, SUPRATHAW ANTIFREEZE, TIN CAN, TURPENTINE, WRENCH

This small cluster of structures is above a road with an abandoned truck and green caravan. Check both the warehouses for some junk, close to a vat-like structure (which is the inaccessible sealed mine mouth).

15. ABANDONED MINE SHAFT ELAINE

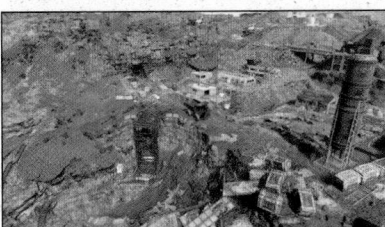

- COLLECTIBLE: POWER ARMOR
- CRAFTING: POWER ARMOR
- DANGER: RADIATION!
- ITEM: HEALTH AND CHEMS
- INFO: EXPECTED ENEMY: MOLE MINER; SCAVENGE RATING: 2; SIZE: 3; THREAT LEVEL: 25–35
- ITEM EXAMPLES: BASEBALL, BLASTING CAPS BOX, COFFEE CUP, MOP, MR. HANDY FUEL, OIL CANISTER, PROTEST SIGN+, RED PLATE, SCREWDRIVER, TALL DRINKING GLASS+, TUBE FLANGE, USED OIL CAN

This is part of Mount Blair Trainyard. Follow a rickety path of corrugated metal and rusting steps from Welch Station (Zone B), or wander west from the trainyard, to investigate this abandoned shaft. Rail carriages have slipped down the unsafe mountainside. At the top of the mountain is a small, rust-covered cargo elevator, two upper metal huts, and a curved-roof locker room, with a power armor station just outside.

16. MOUNT BLAIR TRAINYARD

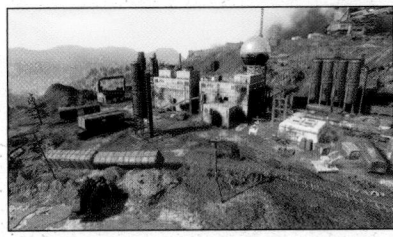

- INFO: EXPECTED ENEMY: MOLE MINER, ROBOT; NOTE; SCAVENGE RATING: 5; SIZE: 4; THREAT LEVEL: 1–10
- LOCK: DOOR (2, KEY, KEY), SAFE (1, 2)
- ITEM EXAMPLES: ABRAXO CLEANER INDUSTRIAL GRADE, BAG OF CEMENT, BEAKER STAND, BERRY MENTATS, BLASTING CAPS BOX+, BLOWTORCH, BOILED WATER, BOWLING PIN, CANNED DOG FOOD, COFFEE CUP+, COFFEE POT, COOLANT, COOLANT CAP, DANDY BOY APPLES, DISHRAG, DESK FAN, ECONOMY WONDERGLUE, ENAMEL BUCKET+, EXTINGUISHER, FUMIGUS BLOWTORCH+, FUSE+, FUSION CORE+, GAS CANISTER++, HANDMADE GLUE, HARD HAT++, HOT PLATE+, LIGHT BULB, MAGNIFYING GLASS, METAL BUCKET, MICROSCOPE, MILITARY GRADE CIRCUIT BOARD, MINING HELMET+, NUCLEAR WASTE, NUKA-COLA TRUCK, OFFICE DESK FAN, OIL CANISTER, PACK OF CIGARETTES, PACK OF DUCT TAPE, PORTABLE FUEL TANK, PROTEST SIGN, RADAWAY, SCREWDRIVER, SOAP, SURGICAL TRAY, TALL DRINKING GLASS+, TALL FLASK+, TEDDY BEAR, TIN CAN, TORQUE ROD END, TURPENTINE, WAKEMASTER ALARM CLOCK, WOOD BLOCK+

- COLLECTIBLES: BOBBLEHEAD (4), CAPS STASH (2), HOLOTAPE, MAGAZINE (3), NUKA-CHERRY, POWER ARMOR
- CRAFTING: CHEMISTRY, COOKING (2), POWER ARMOR, TINKER
- DANGER: EXPLOSIVE CANNISTER! LONG DROP!
- ITEMS: ARMS AND AMMO; HEALTH AND CHEMS; TRUNK

Mount Blair Trainyard (Exterior)

LEGEND

1. PRIMARY LOCATION: ABANDONED MINE SHAFT ELAINE
2. SMALL WAREHOUSE (NORTHWEST)
3. COAL CONVEYOR GENERATOR
4. OPEN CARGO CARRIAGES (WEST)
5. LARGE TRAIN WAREHOUSE (WEST)
6. SMALL TRAIN WAREHOUSE (SOUTHWEST)
7. PAYROLL HUT (INTERIOR)
8. SUPERVISOR HUT (INTERIOR)
9. MAIN OFFICE
10. METAL ROOF HUT (LOCKED)
11. KEYPAD STORAGE HUT
12. SMALL TRAIN WAREHOUSE (EAST)
13. OPEN CARGO CARRIAGE (EAST)
14. SIGNAL TOWER

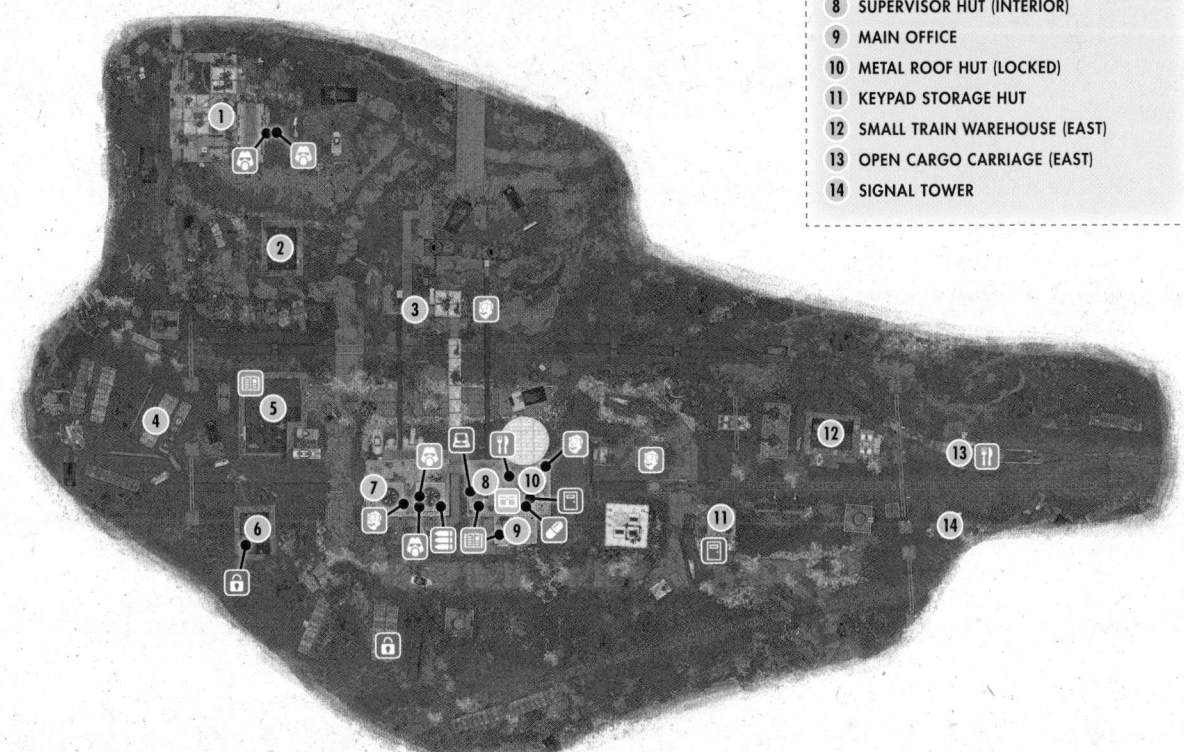

On the upper ridge overlooking the main trainyard (close to Abandoned Mine Shaft Elaine) are numerous containers, rusting carriages, wrecked structures, generators, and other machinery. Upon the hill sits a large coal conveyor, which brings coal to the trainyard below. At the base of the hill is the trainyard, with coal trucks still waiting inside the yard buildings. There are also several exterior warehouses and a storage room accessible only via a key. Feel free to chat to the robot Mount Blair Payroll Terminal in one of the two upper metal huts, and try some vertigo-inducing parkour to reach a Bobblehead or two on and near the roof.

17. MOUNT BLAIR (WORKSHOP)

Mount Blair (Exterior)

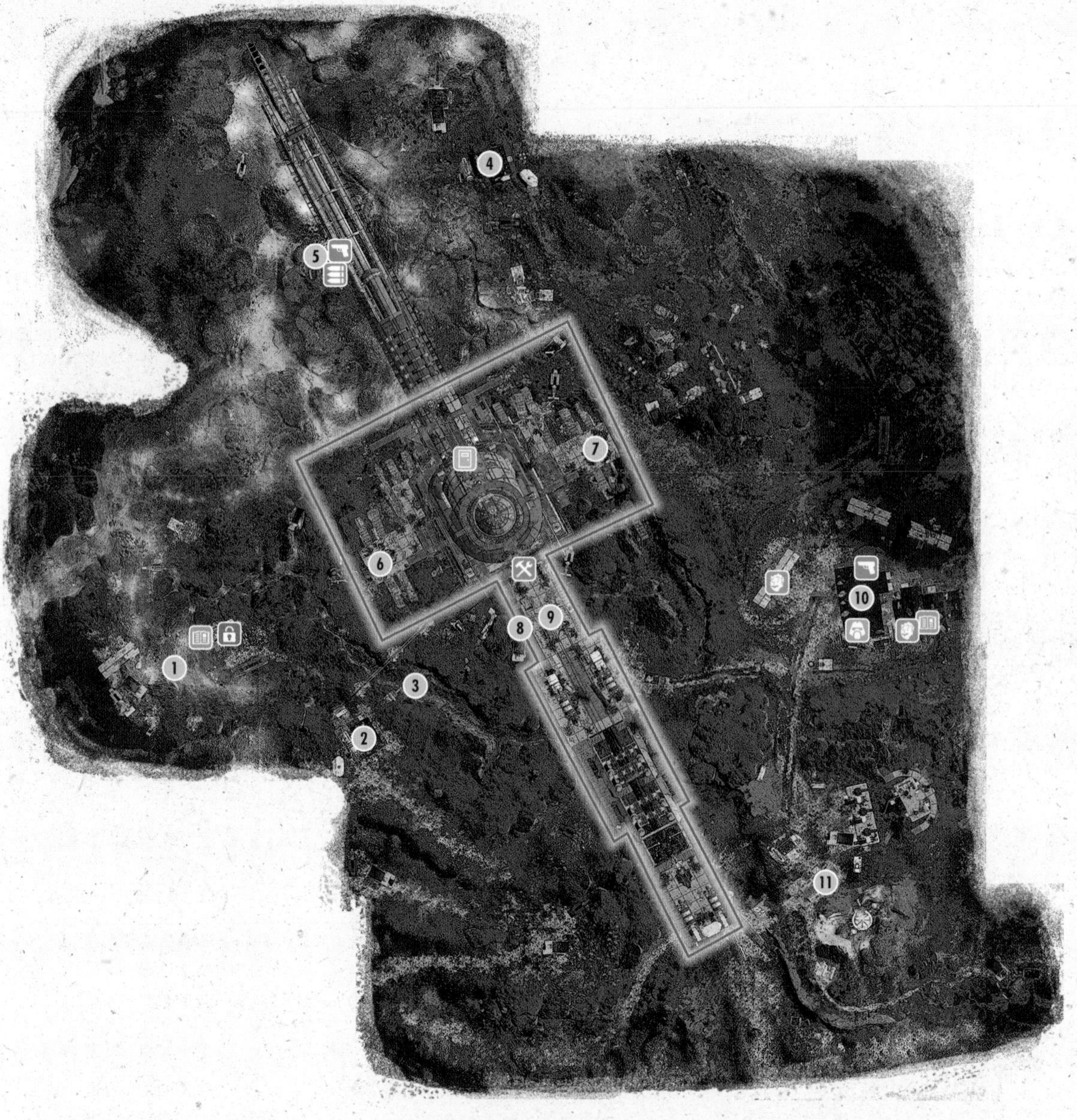

LEGEND

1. OUTER TRAILERS
2. GENERATOR WAREHOUSE
3. MINING CHANNELS
4. GENERATOR SHED AND FIELD HOSPITAL
5. NORTHWEST SCAFFOLD ACCESS
6. WEST GANTRY ACCESS AND OPERATOR HUT

7. EAST SCAFFOLD ACCESS
8. SOUTH SCAFFOLD ACCESS
9. SUPERSTRUCTURE ARM (WORKSHOP)
10. WEST BULLDOZER GARAGES AND TRAILER HOUSES
11. PRIMARY LOCATION: ABANDONED MINE SHAFT 6

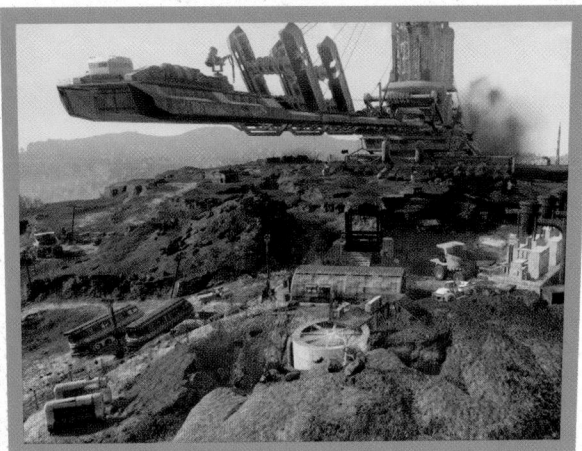

- COLLECTIBLES: BOBBLEHEAD (2), HOLOTAPE (2), MAGAZINE (2), POWER ARMOR
- CRAFTING: TINKER, WEAPONS (2), WORKSHOP
- DANGER: EXPLOSIVE CANNISTER! HEAT! LONG DROP!+++ RADIATION!
- ITEMS: ARMS AND AMMO; HARVESTABLE: ASH, IRON; HEALTH AND CHEMS+
- INFO: EXPECTED ENEMY: VARIES; LANDMARK; SCAVENGE RATING: 3 (5+); SIZE: 5+; SLEEPING; THREAT LEVEL: 25–35
- LOCK: DOOR (KEY, B), SAFE (2)
- ITEM EXAMPLES: ANTIFREEZE BOTTLE, ADJUSTABLE WRENCH, BALL-PEEN HAMMER, BLASTING CAPS BOX+, BLOOD PACK, BOBBY PIN BOX, BONE CUTTER, CANNED DOG FOOD, COFFEE CUP, COFFEE POT, COOKING PAN, COOKING POT, DUCT TAPE, ECONOMY WONDERGLUE, FUMIGUS BLOWTORCH, FUSE+, FUSION CORE, GUM DROPS, LANTERN, MISSILE LAUNCHER, OFFICE, PACK OF DUCT TAPE, PICKAX, PILLOW, PURIFIED WATER, SEALED CHARLESTON HERALD, TABLE SPOON, TURPENTINE, USED OIL CAN, WALKING CANE.
- WORK: FOOD [9], WATER [8], ORE [1]

Mount Blair has been strip-mined, with its original summit removed before the bombs dropped. The gigantic bucket wheel excavator is still in operation, and the huge surface area means only a small portion of the superstructure forms the workshop base. Note the steep mining channel that snakes from the scaffold entrance to the superstructure's south; these can trap you if you fall in, so locate the sloped exit (by a small red digging machine) to avoid being pinned down. Elsewhere, expect hotspots of fire and craggy, rough ground. The workshop is on the superstructure; access it via the excavator arm to the northwest or the conveyor arm to the southeast (via numerous gantry steps or scaffold step access points). Climb the main tower to reach an elevator leading to two upper levels; both are small but offer some incredible views of almost all of Appalachia! Also check to the southeast; there's two large bulldozer garages and two ruined metal trailer houses to check for additional junk. One of the bulldozer garages is of particular interest. If you have the ID card, you can head past an Overseer's holotape box, enter a basement, and gather some choice junk from the generator room under the garage.

18. ABANDONED MINE SHAFT 6

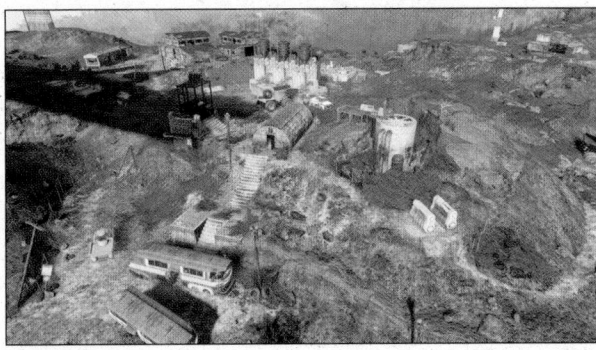

- CRAFTING: ARMOR
- DANGER: LONG DROP! RADIATION!
- ITEM: HEALTH AND CHEMS
- INFO: EXPECTED ENEMY: MOLE MINER, MOLE RAT; SCAVENGE RATING: 2; SIZE: 2; SLEEPING; THREAT LEVEL: 25–35
- ITEM EXAMPLES: BLOWTORCH, FUSION CORE, MINER UNIFORM, MOLE RAT MEAT, MOONSHINE JUG, SOAP, TURPENTINE, WRENCH

This is part of the Blair Mountain mining complex. Southeast of the main gargantuan-wheel excavator are a couple of parked coaches below a curved-roof locker room, some yellow metal conveyor belts and other machinery, a slag heap with a steep drop into lava, and the remains of shaft 6, which is inaccessible.

19. ROLLINS WORK CAMP

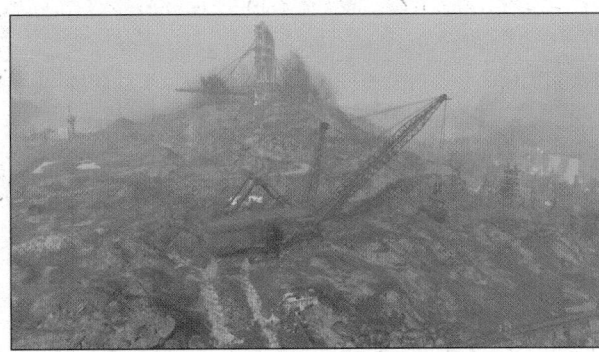

- COLLECTIBLES: BOBBLEHEAD, MAGAZINE, POWER ARMOR
- ITEMS: ARMS AND AMMO; HEALTH AND CHEMS; RECIPE/MOD/PLAN; TRUNK
- INFO: EXPECTED ENEMY: IRRADIATED INSECT; SCAVENGE RATING: 2; SIZE: 2; SLEEPING; THREAT LEVEL: 25–35
- LOCK: SAFE (2)
- ITEM EXAMPLES: ANTIFREEZE, BLOWTORCH, CRAM, ENHANCED TARGETING CARD, USED OIL CAN, PACK OF DUCT TAPE, SPICES, WONDERGLUE

Close to a large bucket excavator is a group of stacked containers, three metal caravans serving as dorms and junk storage, and some portable toilets close to a small parking area.

ZONE A: SECONDARY LOCATIONS

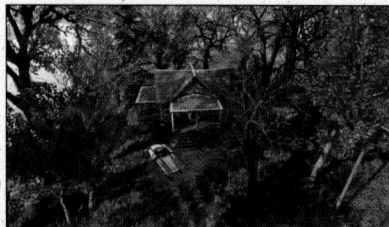
Riverside Cottage

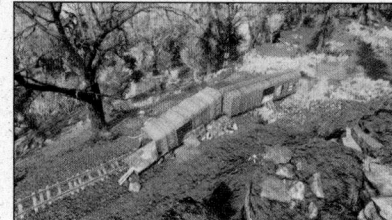
Camden Railroad Wreckage

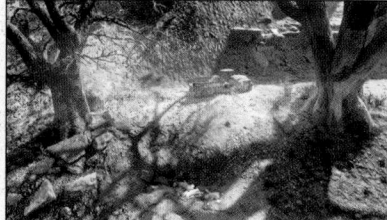
Rusty Pickup and Grave

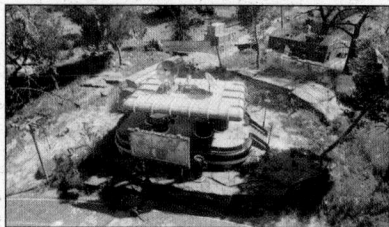
Bot Stop and Red Barn

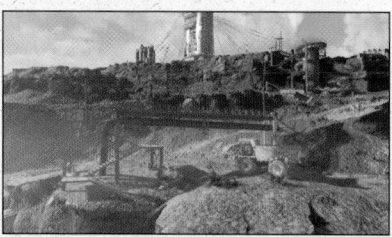
Mount Blair Truck Turn

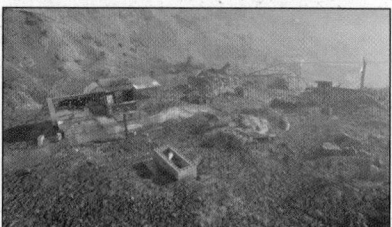
Mount Blair Coffee Shack

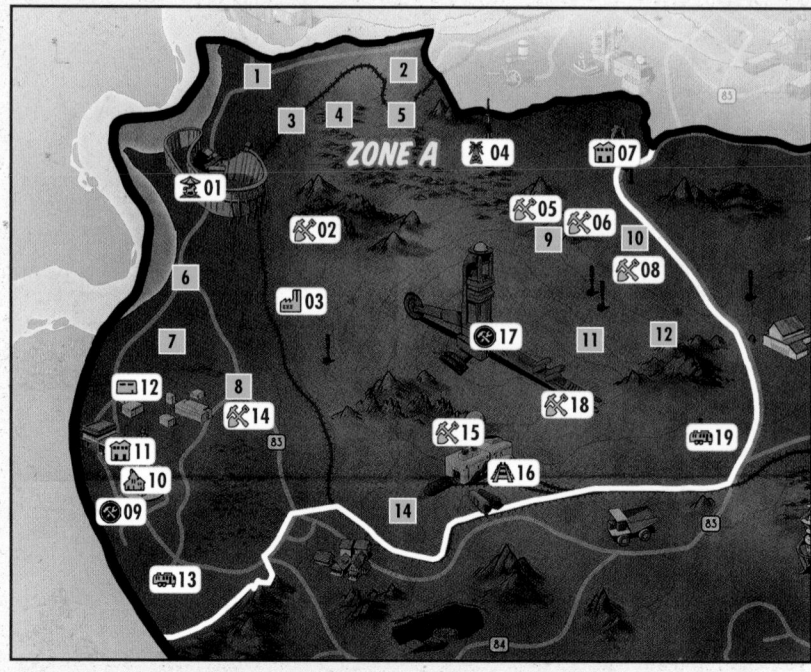

Appalachia: **The Ash Heap (Zone A) – Secondary Locations**

#	NAME	DESCRIPTION
1	Riverside Cottage	A small white cottage in the woods by the river, just south of the Nuka-Cola Plant.
2	Rusty Caravan Cabin	There's wild gourds to gather and a safe to crack at this trailer in the hills at the edge of The Ash Heap.
3	Camden Railroad Wreckage	A trio of open cargo carriages were turned into a makeshift camp, with sleeping bags and junk and some unwelcome foes.
4	Rusty Pickup and Grave	Alcohol, ammo, and a shovel are just some of the items to snag from a pickup and nearby grave.
5	Chemical Carriage Derailment	A rockfall seems to have derailed a collection of tanker trucks, now rusting in the fetid breeze.
6	Bot Stop and Red Barn	Aside from the robot terminals, seek out junk scattered in and around overturned trucks, inside containers, and in a rickety red barn off the road.
7	Toxic Pond Gulley	A muddy mess on the hillside marking the edge of the Ash Heap.

#	NAME	DESCRIPTION
8	Lost Truck and Trailer	A small "glamping" caravan being pulled by a rusty pickup, on the road.
9	Northeast Mount Blair Bridge	A footbridge and coal truck, offering access across what's left of the mining road north of Mount Blair.
10	Kittery Junk Storage Hut	A great maintenance hut to pillage from, including military-grade circuit boards, fuses, and duct tape.
11	Mount Blair Truck Turn	A small concrete lookout and green metal stairs, with a first aid kit and other minor items, and good views from the Mount.
12	Kittery Road Outhouse	A metal and concrete platform near a parked red truck; come here for the fuel tanks and other junk.
13	Workshack at Mount Blair	A large, two-level shack on the outskirts of Mount Blair, with a safe and a Tinker's Workbench inside.
14	Mount Blair Coffee Shack	On the corrugated trail from Welch Station to the trainyard, there's a metal shanty store that used to sell coffee. It now sells despair.

THE ASH HEAP: ZONE B—LEWISBURG, WELCH, AND GARRAHAN MINING

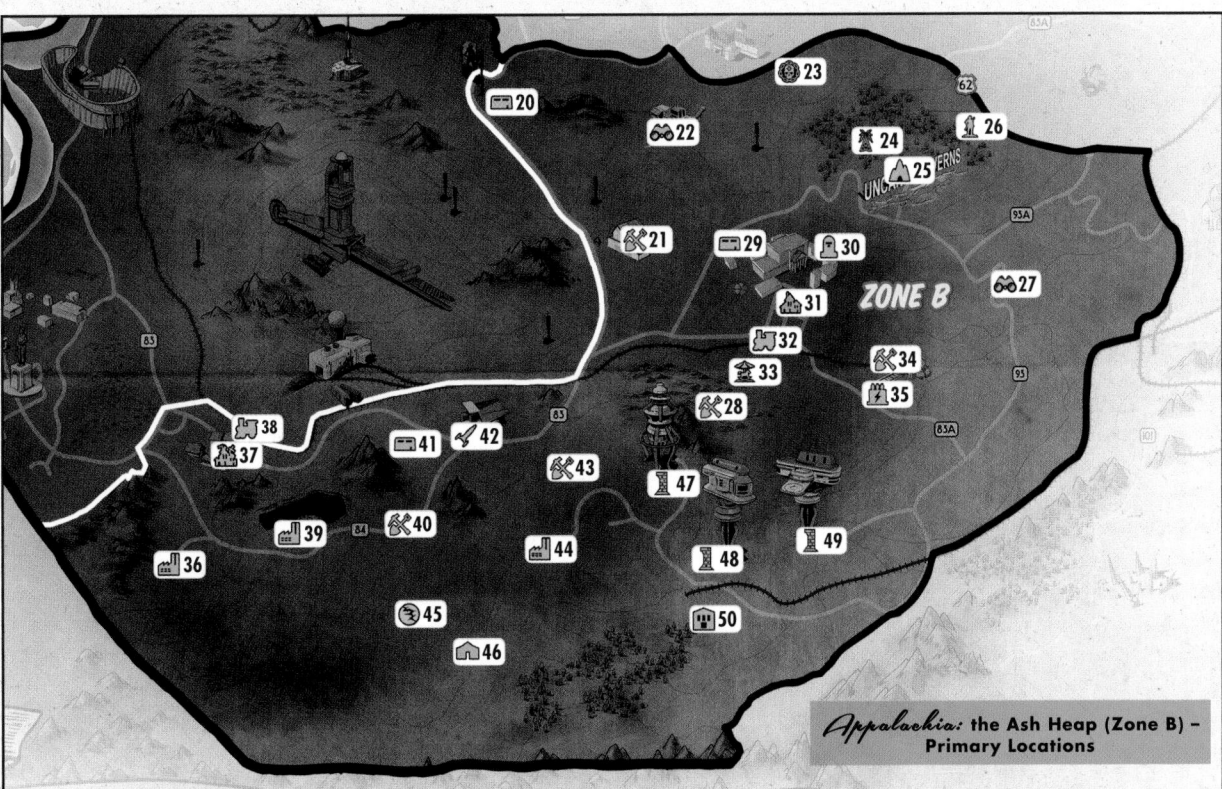

Appalachia: the Ash Heap (Zone B) – Primary Locations

TRAINING

CRAFTING AND C.A.M.P.ING

INVENTORY

QUESTS

ATLAS

BESTIARY

APPENDICES

WORLD MAP LEGEND

—— REGION BOUNDARY ······ ZONE BOUNDARY

● BOBBLEHEADS ■ CAP STASHES ■ MAGAZINES ■ POWER ARMOR

PRIMARY LOCATIONS

			icon	NAME
4	4	1	20	HORNWRIGHT AIR CLEANSER SITE #01
4	4	1	21	THE BURNING MINE
1	1		22	WIDOW'S PERCH
			23	BLEEDING KATE'S GRINDHOUSE
			24	RELAY TOWER DP-B5-21
4	4		25	UNCANNY CAVERNS
			26	MINERS MONUMENT
1	1		27	BASTION PARK
			28	ABANDONED MINE SHAFT 3
			29	HORNWRIGHT AIR CLEANSER SITE #02
	1	1	30	PLEASANT HILLS CEMETERY
2	2		31	LEWISBURG
1			32	LEWISBURG STATION
			33	LAKE REYNOLDS
1	1	1	2	34	BIG BEND TUNNEL WEST
			35	MONONGAH POWER SUBSTATION MZ-03

			icon	NAME
			36	HORNWRIGHT TESTING SITE #02
			37	WELCH
			38	WELCH STATION
			39	ABANDONED MINE SHAFT 1
1		1	1	40	AMS TESTING SITE
1	1	1	1	41	HORNWRIGHT AIR CLEANSER SITE #03
			42	RED ROCKET FILLING STATION
1			43	ABANDONED MINE SHAFT 2
			44	HORNWRIGHT TESTING SITE #03
2		2	1	45	FISSURE SITE
			46	STRIKER ROW
	1		47	UNFINISHED MANSION
			48	GARRAHAN ESTATE
			49	HORNWRIGHT ESTATE
1		1	5	50	GARRAHAN MINING HEADQUARTERS

If you're trudging through the Ash Heap and think, "I wish the environment was even more difficult to stay alive in," then visit the Burning Mine, where the terrible, choking air quality meets the heat of molten slag heaps. It's well worth the extra protection to gather the quality resources hidden within (Black Titanium anyone?). Elsewhere, you have the inaptly named Pleasant Hills Cemetery on the north side of Lewisburg, a place where grave-robbing, evidence of mining protests, election voting, and festivities collide in a dichotomy of the past. It's good to look up once in a while, so visit the rooftop gardens on top of Lewisburg and pick some of the fancier crops for your cooking pot. Don't forget the ruined hillside town of Welch (though everyone except the Mole Miners already have gone) and touring the Uncanny Caverns (where subterranean audio tours and irradiated monstrosities await). Finally, save some time to explore the three towers of the old mining families, vertical mansions in the sky, still standing and waiting for the correct ID card to be used.

ZONE B: PRIMARY LOCATIONS

MAP LEGEND

- ▣ MY STASH BOX
- ▤ OVERSEER'S CACHE
- ▦ TRUNK
- ♥ TRADER

COLLECTIBLES
- ▣ BOBBLEHEAD
- ▤ MAGAZINE
- ▣ POWER ARMOR

CRAFTING
- ▣ ARMOR WORKBENCH
- ▣ CHEMISTRY WORKBENCH
- ▣ COOKING STATION
- ▣ POWER ARMOR STATION
- ▣ TINKER'S WORKBENCH
- ▣ WEAPONS WORKBENCH
- ▣ WORKSHOP WORKBENCH

IMPORTANT
- ▣ DOOR/GATE
- ▣ LOCKED DOOR/GATE
- ▣ SAFE
- ▣ SCANNER
- ▣ TERMINAL

▦ 20. HORNWRIGHT AIR CLEANSER SITE #01

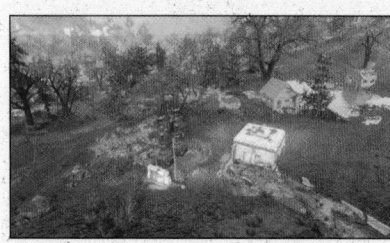

- CRAFTING: CHEMISTRY
- DANGER: RADIATION!
- ITEMS: ARMS AND AMMO; HARVESTABLE: WOOD PILE+; HEALTH AND CHEMS; RECIPE/MOD/PLAN
- INFO: AIR PURIFIER; EXPECTED ENEMY: GHOUL; INSTRUMENT; SCAVENGE RATING: 3; SIZE: 3; SLEEPING; THREAT LEVEL: 25–35
- LOCK: DOOR (1)

- ITEM EXAMPLES: BALL-PEEN HAMMER, BOBBY PIN BOX, CANNED DOG FOOD, COFFEE CUP, COFFEE POT, DIRTY ASHTRAY, DIRTY FEDORA, FLORAL BARREL VASE, FUEL TANK, FUSION CORE, MR. HANDY FUEL, PACK OF CIGARETTES, PORTABLE FUEL TANK, POTATO CRISPS, SALT, TIN CAN+

Across from The Rusty Pick on Route 83, on the edge of Charleston's city limits, is one of the Hornwright Air Purifier Systems. Unlock the concrete maintenance hut (1); then check the two ruined structures around the fetid pond for more junk.

⛏ 21. THE BURNING MINE

The Burning Mine (Interior)

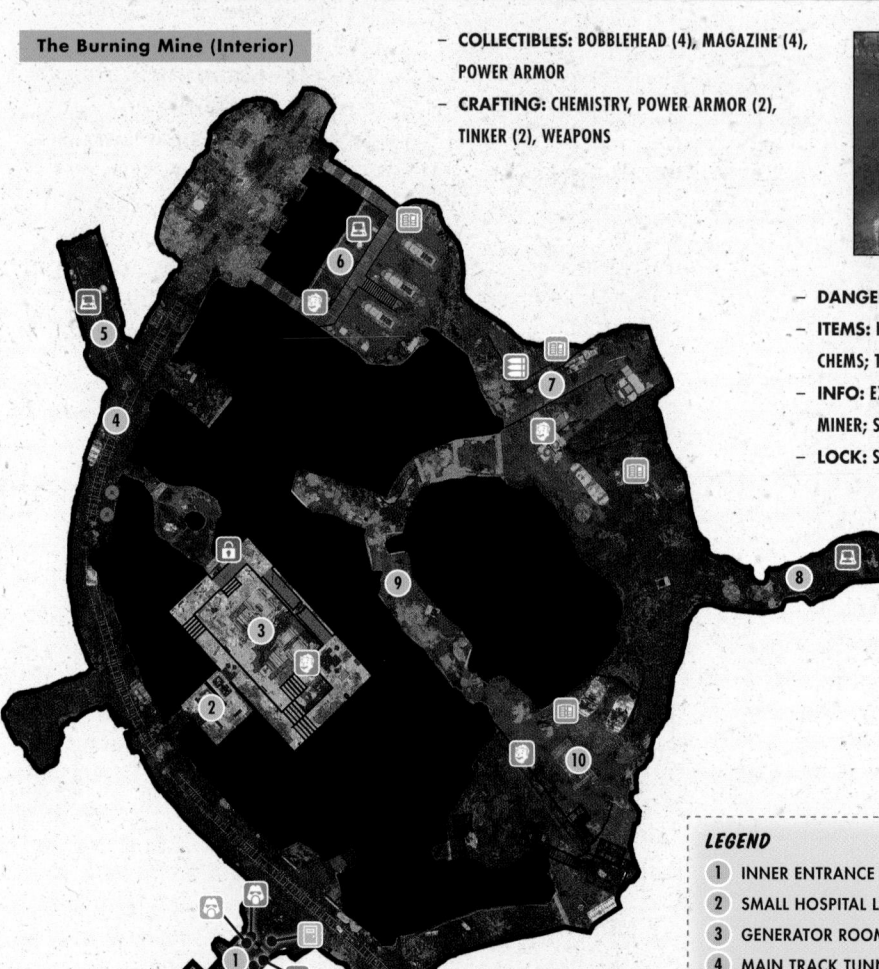

- COLLECTIBLES: BOBBLEHEAD (4), MAGAZINE (4), POWER ARMOR
- CRAFTING: CHEMISTRY, POWER ARMOR (2), TINKER (2), WEAPONS

- DANGER: EXPLOSIVE CANNISTER! HEAT! LONG DROP!
- ITEMS: HARVESTABLE: GLOWING FUNGUS; HEALTH AND CHEMS; TRUNK
- INFO: EXPECTED ENEMY: IRRADIATED ANIMAL, MOLE MINER; SCAVENGE RATING: 3; SIZE: 4; THREAT LEVEL: 25–35
- LOCK: SAFE (1, 2), TERMINAL (0, 2)
  - ITEM EXAMPLES: BEAKER STAND, BEER BOTTLE+, BLAST RADIUS BOARD GAME, BOILED WATER, CANNED DOG FOOD, CHESSBOARD, COFFEE CUP, CRUSHED ACETONE CANISTER, DOG BOWL, ENAMEL BUCKET+, FUSION CORE+, GAS CANISTER, HACKSAW, HARD HAT, MICROSCOPE, MUZZLED LASER RIFLE, OIL CANISTER, RADAWAY, RUSTY CANISTER, TALL DRINKING GLASS, TIN CAN, TONGS, TURPENTINE, VOLATILE MATERIALS BOX.

LEGEND
1. INNER ENTRANCE
2. SMALL HOSPITAL LAB
3. GENERATOR ROOM
4. MAIN TRACK TUNNEL
5. UPPER AUTO-MINER TUNNEL
6. BLUE CONVEYOR PISTONS AND GANTRY
7. TIERED COAL CONVEYOR CAVERN
8. LOWER AUTO-MINER TUNNEL
9. INFERNO TUNNEL
10. MINE SHAFT AND WHITE GENERATOR CAVERN

Dangerously soft ground has caused the lower mining structure at this location to break in half; this isn't anything compared to the searing heat and inhospitable conditions when you actually enter a mine that is mostly *on fire*. Before entering the main orange door, check the metal steps to an upper warehouse with workbenches and a possible weapon. Then enter with proper protective clothing. Once inside, remove threats and gather as much loot as you can, for as long as you're able to withstand the heat. The place is easy to get lost in, so look for landmarks, such as large pieces of machinery, noting their color so you can retrace your steps.

22. WIDOW'S PERCH

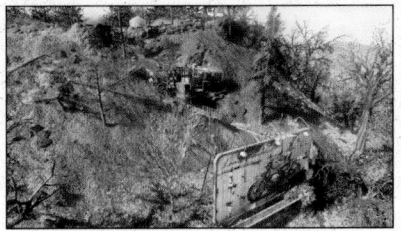

- **COLLECTIBLES:** BOBBLEHEAD, MAGAZINE
- **CRAFTING:** TINKER
- **DANGER:** LONG DROP!
- **ITEM: HARVESTABLE:** SOOT FLOWER
- **INFO:** EXPECTED ENEMY: IRRADIATED ANIMAL; SCAVENGE RATING: 2; SIZE: 2; SLEEPING; THREAT LEVEL: 25–35
- **ITEM EXAMPLES:** 10-MM PISTOL, ENAMEL BUCKET, FUSION CORE, WONDERGLUE

An apt name for a precarious shanty hut and rickety platforms that stretch out to an old billboard.

23. BLEEDING KATE'S GRINDHOUSE

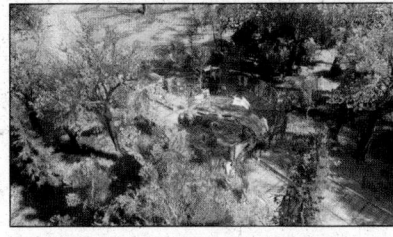

- **ITEMS:** ARMS AND AMMO; HARVESTABLE: WILD MUTFRUIT; HEALTH AND CHEMS; TRUNK
- **INFO:** EXPECTED ENEMY: IRRADIATED INSECT; SCAVENGE RATING: 2; SIZE: 2; THREAT LEVEL: 25–35
- **ITEM EXAMPLES:** FUSION CORE, HUNTING RIFLE, MOONSHINE JUG, PIPE AUTO PISTOL

When Raiders ruled the roads, they used this blockade as a defensive fort along I-62 and as an outdoor cinema.

24. RELAY TOWER DP-B5-21

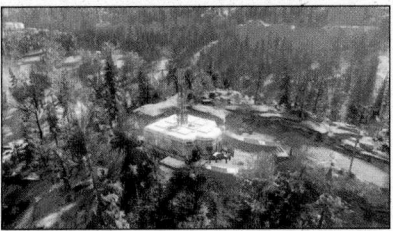

- **COLLECTIBLE:** HOLOTAPE
- **ITEMS:** ARMS AND AMMO; HEALTH AND CHEMS; RECIPE/MOD/PLAN
- **INFO:** EXPECTED ENEMY: SCORCHED; EVENT: ALWAYS VIGILANT; SCAVENGE RATING: 2; SIZE: 1; THREAT LEVEL: 25–35
- **ITEM EXAMPLES:** ADJUSTABLE WRENCH, BOILED WATER, DUCT TAPE, GAS CANISTER, MAKESHIFT BATTERY, MENTATS, OFFICE DESK FAN, RECOIL COMPENSATED AUTOMATIC PLASMA RIFLE, VODKA, WELDING GOGGLES

On the edge of the Ash Heap, on a hilltop road, is a small transmission tower, with an interior relay terminal in need of repair. Call on a possible supply drop from here, too.

25. UNCANNY CAVERNS

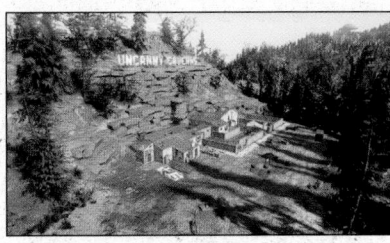

- **ITEMS:** ARMS AND AMMO; HARVESTABLE: BRAIN FUNGUS, CORN, GLOWING FUNGUS, WOOD PILE; HEALTH AND CHEMS; RECIPE/PLAN/MOD; TRUNK
- **INFO:** EXPECTED ENEMY: GHOULS, IRRADIATED ANIMAL, IRRADIATED INSECT, WENDIGO; SCAVENGE RATING: 4; SIZE: 4; SLEEPING; THREAT LEVEL: 25–35
- **LOCK:** DOOR (1), SAFE (1, 2)
- **ITEM EXAMPLES:** BLAST RADIUS BOARD GAME, BOURBON BOTTLE, BUBBLEGUM, CAMERA, CRAM, DANDY BOY APPLES, ENAMEL BUCKET, GAS CANISTER, GLASS JAR, HOUSE TEAPOT, LANTERN, MOONSHINE JUG, NUKA-COLA BOTTLE, NUKA-COLA CUP+, PORTABLE FUEL TANK, PROTEST SIGN+, RAD-X, RIB CAGE, RUM BOTTLE, SUGAR BOMBS, TEDDY BEAR, TELEPHONE, TOILET PAPER, TOY TRUCK, WINE, WINE BOTTLE
- **COLLECTIBLES:** BOBBLEHEAD (4), HOLOTAPE, MAGAZINE (4)
- **CRAFTING:** COOKING (2)
- **DANGER:** PUNJI BOARD! SPIKE BOARD! RADIATION!+

Uncanny Caverns (Exterior)

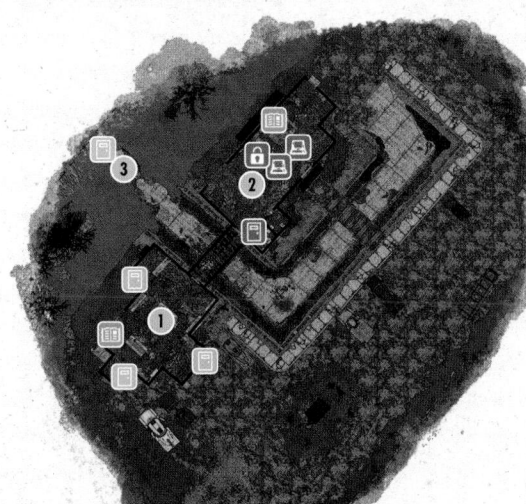

LEGEND
1. GIFT SHOP
2. RECEPTION
3. CAVE ENTRANCE

TRAINING

CRAFTING AND C.A.M.P.ING

INVENTORY

QUESTS

ATLAS

BESTIARY

APPENDICES

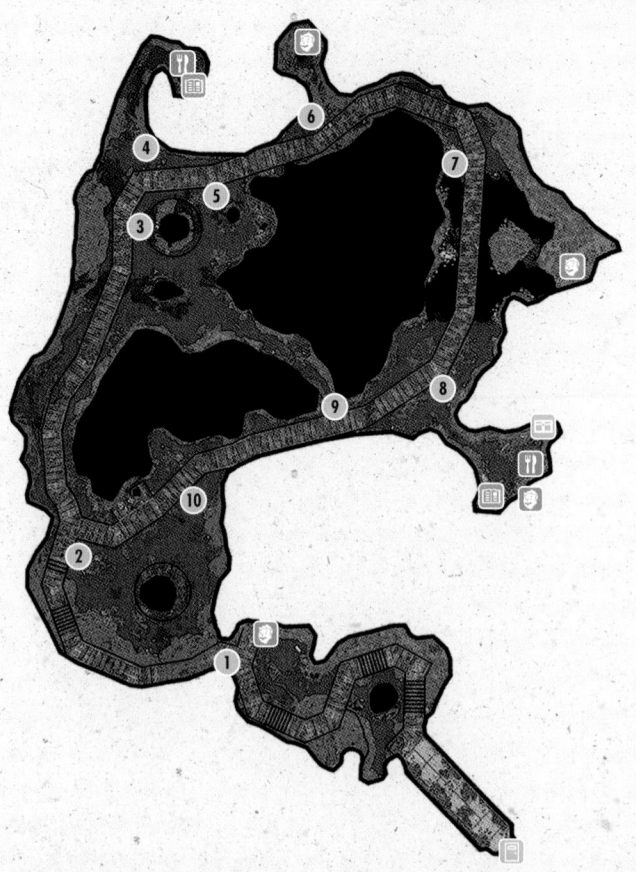

LEGEND

1	AUDIO TOUR STATION 1 AND PHOTO BACKDROP
2	AUDIO TOUR STATION 2
3	AUDIO TOUR STATION 3
4	AUDIO TOUR STATION 4
5	AUDIO TOUR STATION 5
6	AUDIO TOUR STATION 6
7	AUDIO TOUR STATION 7
8	AUDIO TOUR STATION 8
9	AUDIO TOUR STATION 9
10	AUDIO TOUR STATION 10

After stopping at the roadside stall and outside gift shop, descend into a lost world and witness spectacular rock formations, including stalagmites, naturally occurring pillars, and a host of junk, sprawled corpses, and deadly shambling foes. Check the 10 different audio tour locations for more information on what you're seeing, when you're not clearing out revolting creatures from your view.

26. MINERS MONUMENT

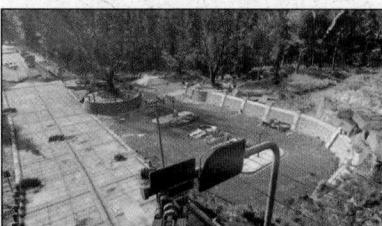

- **CRAFTING:** WEAPONS
- **ITEMS:** ARMS AND AMMO; HARVESTABLE: RHODODENDRON
- **INFO:** EXPECTED ENEMY: IRRADIATED ANIMAL; ROBOT; SCAVENGE RATING: 1; SIZE: 1; THREAT LEVEL: 25–35
- **ITEM EXAMPLES:** PICKAX, PICKAX PILSNER, PROTEST SIGN++, TUBE FLANGE

A monument to the hardworking, salt-of-the-earth folk of Appalachia. Now this monument has seen recent protests against robot automation.

27. BASTION PARK

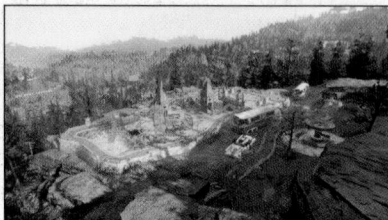

- **COLLECTIBLES:** BOBBLEHEAD (2), MAGAZINE (2)
- **ITEM:** HARVESTABLE: BLACKBERRY
- **INFO:** EXPECTED ENEMY: IRRADIATED ANIMAL, ROBOT; SCAVENGE RATING: 2; SIZE: 2; THREAT LEVEL: 25–35
- **ITEM EXAMPLES:** DINNER TRAY, DOLL, NUKA-COLA, NUKA-COLA BOTTLE+, PURIFIED WATER, SALT, SHOPPING BASKET, SOUVENIR TEDDY BEAR, TEDDY BEAR, TOY ALIEN, TOY TRUCK

Halfway up the winding Route 93, a picnic area and playground offers once-spectacular views to the north and west. Now there's junk scraps to gather and collectibles to hope for.

28. ABANDONED MINE SHAFT 3

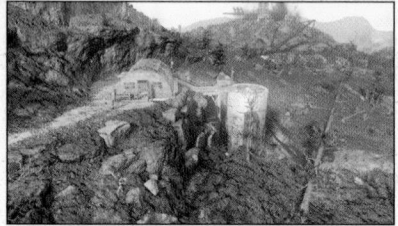

- **CRAFTING:** ARMOR, COOKING
- **DANGER:** LONG DROP! RADIATION!+
- **ITEMS:** ARMS AND AMMO, HEALTH AND CHEMS
- **INFO:** EXPECTED ENEMY: MOLE MINER; SCAVENGE RATING: 2; SIZE: 2' SLEEPING; THREAT LEVEL: 25–35
- **ITEM EXAMPLES:** ASHTRAY, BLOWTORCH, CATCH THE COMMIE BOARD GAME, COMBAT SNIPER RIFLE, HOT PLATE, HUNTING RIFLE, LEFT FOOT BONES, MENTATS, MINER UNIFORM, NUKA-COLA BOTTLE, RADAWAY (DILUTED), SCREWDRIVER

North of the mansion towers, on lower ash-filled slopes close to Lewisburg, is another sealed mine shaft. Access the platform to this huge vat-sized cylinder (with a precarious drop to avoid!) via a gantry from a curved-roof maintenance shed.

29. HORNWRIGHT AIR CLEANSER SITE #02

- **CRAFTING:** TINKER
- **ITEMS:** ARMS AND AMMO, HEALTH AND CHEMS
- **INFO:** AIR PURIFIER; SCAVENGE RATING: 2; SIZE: 1; THREAT LEVEL: 25–35

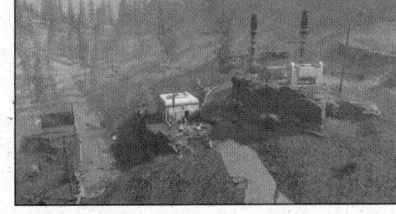

- **ITEM EXAMPLES:** BUFFOUT, COFFEE CUP, DIRTY ASHTRAY, ENHANCED TARGETING CARD, INDUSTRIAL SOLVENT, MR. HANDY FUEL, PACK OF CIGARETTES, RAD-X, TALL DRINKING GLASS, TIN CAN

The site is set into the hills northwest of Lewisburg and is technically part of the township.

30. PLEASANT HILLS CEMETERY

- **COLLECTIBLES:** CAPS STASH, MAGAZINE
- **ITEMS:** HARVESTABLE: RHODODENDRON, SOOT FLOWER, WILD CARROT FLOWER; RECIPE/MOD/PLAN
- **INFO:** EXPECTED ENEMY: IRRADIATED INSECT; SCAVENGE RATING: 2; SIZE: 2; THREAT LEVEL: 25–35

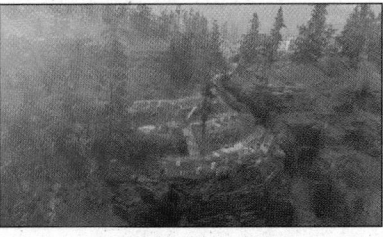

- **LOCK:** SAFE (3, 3, 3)
- **ITEM EXAMPLES:** MINING HELMET, MOUNTAIN HONEY, SHOVEL, VODKA BOTTLE

This is located on the hillside northeast of Lewisburg. Desecrated with scattered coffins, this is hardly a befitting resting place for the lucky ones. Still, someone has unearthed a few expertly sealed safes for you to crack!

31. LEWISBURG

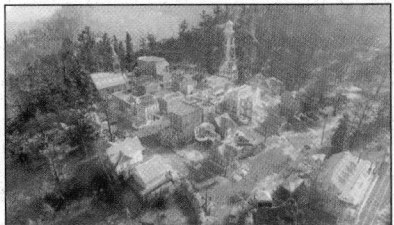

- **COLLECTIBLES:** BOBBLEHEAD (2), MAGAZINE (2)
- **CRAFTING:** CHEMISTRY, COOKING (2)
- **DANGER:** LONG DROP!
- **ITEMS:** ARMS AND AMMO+; HARVESTABLE: ASH ROSE, CARROT, RHODODENDRON, SOOT FLOWER, WILD CARROT FLOWER; HEALTH AND CHEMS; TRUNK
- **INFO:** EXPECTED ENEMY: SUPER MUTANT; INSTRUMENT; NOTE; SCAVENGE RATING: 4; SIZE: 4; SLEEPING; THREAT LEVEL: 25–35
- **LOCK:** SAFE (1, 2)
- **ITEM EXAMPLES:** BAG OF FERTILIZER+, BASEBALL BAT, BATTERED CLIPBOARD, BINOCULARS, BOBBY PIN BOX, BOWLING PIN, CAMERA, CIGAR BOX, COFFEE CUP, COFFEE POT, COOKING OIL, CRANBERRY MOONSHINE, CRUSHED ACETONE CANISTER, CRUSHED ORANGE CANISTER, CIVIL WAR ERA DRESS, CIVIL WAR ERA TOP HAT, EMPTY TEAL ROUNDED VASE+, ENAMEL BUCKET, EXTINGUISHER, FLOWER POT+, FUEL TANK, HOT DOG, HOT PLATE, MARKSMAN'S SNIPER RIFLE, METAL BUCKET+, MOP, NUKA-COLA+, NUKA-COLA CUP++, NUKA-COLA CUP AND STRAW, PEPPER, PLASTIC PLATE+, POTATO CRISPS, PURIFIED WATER, SHOVEL, STEALTH BOY, TOILET PAPER, TOY TRUCK, TV DINNER TRAY+, VAULT-TEC LUNCH BOX, VODKA BOTTLE, WHISKEY BOTTLE+, WILLOW ROUNDED VASE+, WOOD BLOCK+, YUM YUM DEVILED EGGS

Lewisburg (Exterior)

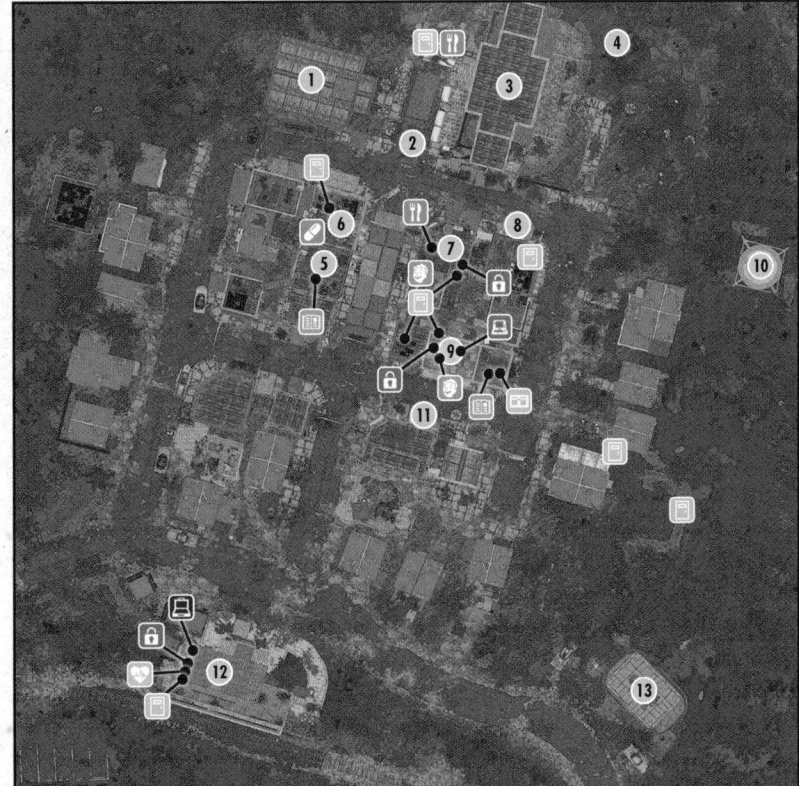

LEGEND

1. LEWISBURG CHURCH (INACCESSIBLE)
2. PICNIC TABLES AND FOOD STALLS
3. CITY HALL (INACCESSIBLE)
4. MUSICIANS' STAGE
5. DESTROYED DINER
6. ROOFTOP GREENHOUSE
7. SERENITY ROAD ART GALLERY
8. GUN STALL
9. LEWISBURG VISITOR CENTER AND ROOF ALLOTMENTS
10. WATER TOWER
11. ART STALL
12. PRIMARY LOCATION: LEWISBURG STATION
13. ROBCO BOT SHOP

TRAINING

CRAFTING AND C.A.M.P.ING

INVENTORY

QUESTS

ATLAS

BESTIARY

APPENDICES

Lewisburg's miners may have been striking along the southern perimeter of town, but the majority of the townsfolk still came out to vote and celebrate Halloween with a festival, complete with stalls and a live band. All that has been replaced with crumbling buildings, dilapidated and faded bunting, and ferocious enemies ready to cut you from gizzard to throat. The town is initially a little mazelike, but most of the fire escapes provide access onto one of the two rooftop garden areas in the center of town (this has an excellent selection of plants to harvest). You can also visit a few of the stores still standing.

32. LEWISBURG STATION

- **CRAFTING:** ARMOR
- **ITEMS:** ARMS AND AMMO; MY STASH BOX; VENDING MACHINE: AMMUNITION, MEDICAL SUPPLIES
- **INFO:** SCAVENGE RATING: 2; SIZE: 2; THREAT LEVEL: 25–35; TRADER: VENDOR BOT
- **ITEM EXAMPLES:** BEER BOTTLE++, BROKEN LIGHT BULB, OIL CANISTER, PACK OF CIGARETTES, PAINT CAN, PLUNGER, RADAWAY, TEDDY BEAR, WINE BOTTLE, YELLOW PAINT

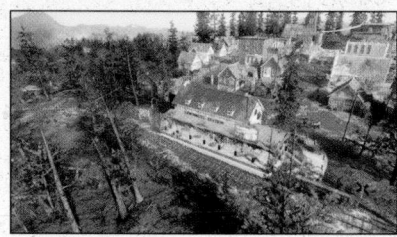

On the south side of town (by a couple of voting tents) is the railway station offering a brief respite, a place to stash your items, and a trader to barter with. Why not use this as a base camp when exploring this part of the Ash Heap?

33. LAKE REYNOLDS

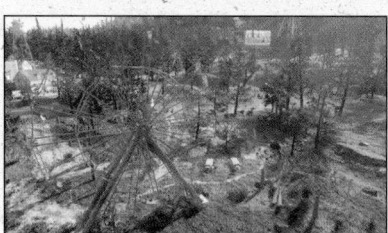

- **CRAFTING:** WEAPONS
- **DANGER:** RADIATION!
- **INFO:** EXPECTED ENEMY: MIRELURK; SCAVENGE RATING: 2; SIZE: 3; SLEEPING; THREAT LEVEL: 25–35
- **LOCK:** SAFE (2)
- **ITEM EXAMPLES:** COFFEE CUP+, CRUSHED ACETONE CANISTER+, CRUSHED ORANGE CANISTER+, FUSION CORE, GLASS JAR, HIDE BUNDLE, TOY ALIEN

This part of Lewisburg consists of a once-idyllic lake and children's fun park. Now the carousel and Ferris wheel are covered in detritus, and the place is a real dump (in fact, it was abandoned even before the War). Recently, Responders were active here. Check farther east for some odd signs and an open railroad carriage. Have you dived down for the fusion core inside the tiniest toy alien spacecraft of all?

34. BIG BEND TUNNEL WEST

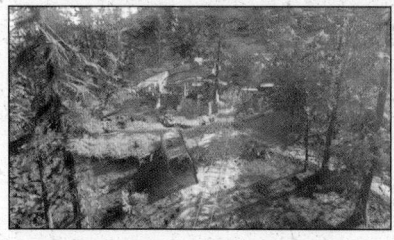

- **INFO:** EXPECTED ENEMY: IRRADIATED ANIMAL, IRRADIATED INSECT, SCORCHED; NOTE; QUEST: SEARCH BIG BEND TUNNEL FOR SURVIVORS; SCAVENGE RATING: 5; SIZE: 4; SLEEPING; THREAT LEVEL: 25–35.
- **LOCK:** DOOR (1, KEY), SAFE (1)
- **ITEM EXAMPLES:** ABRAXO CLEANER, ABRAXO CLEANER INDUSTRIAL GRADE, BAG OF CEMENT, BALL-PEEN HAMMER, BEER BOTTLE+, BLAMCO BRAND MAC AND CHEESE, BOILED WATER+, BOURBON, BROKEN LIGHTBULB, BUNSEN BURNER, CAN, CANNED DOG FOOD, COFFEE CUP, COOLANT+, DANDY BOY APPLES, DUCT TAPE+, ENAMEL BUCKET+, FUSION CORE, GAS CANISTER+, GEAR, GLASS JAR, HOT PLATE, LANTERN, LEAD PIPE, LIQUOR BOTTLE, MAKESHIFT BATTERY+, MENTATS, METAL BUCKET, NEW RIVER RED ALE, OIL CAN, OIL CANISTER, PLASTIC PUMPKIN, RAT POISON, RUSTY CANISTER, SENSOR MODULE, SHORT ASSAULT RIFLE, SHOT GLASS, SKULL, STEALTH BOY+, SURVEYOR OUTFIT, TIBIA, TOILET PAPER, TORQUE ROD END, VODKA BOTTLE, VOLATILE MATERIALS BOX, WHISKEY

- **COLLECTIBLES:** BOBBLEHEAD, CAPS STASH, HOLOTAPE, MAGAZINE, NUKA-CHERRY, POWER ARMOR (2)
- **CRAFTING:** ARMOR (2), CHEMISTRY, COOKING, POWER ARMOR; TINKER; WEAPONS
- **DANGER:** EXPLOSIVE CANNISTER! RADIATION!+
- **ITEMS:** ARMS AND AMMO+; HARVESTABLE: ALUMINUM, BRAIN FUNGUS, GLOWING FUNGUS; HEALTH AND CHEMS

LEGEND

1. WEST ENTRANCE
2. SHANTY BLOCKADE
3. MAIN MAINTENANCE JUNCTION
4. MAINTENANCE WAREHOUSE
5. ALUMINUM MINING TUNNEL
6. SHANTY BLOCKADE
7. EAST ENTRANCE

Big Bend Tunnel East and West (Interior)

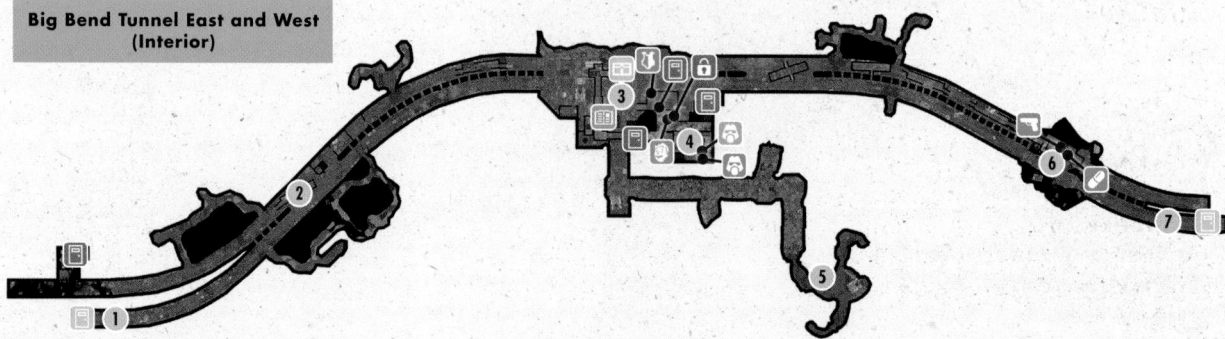

This vast underground tunnel system links Mount Blair to Big Bend Tunnel East (Watoga), over in Cranberry Bog Region. It is an alternate method to an overland crossing. Head east from Lewisburg along the railroad tracks to reach the entrance; Raider defenses and a (well-stocked) shanty are now overrun by even more deranged foes.

Inside, the tunnel has two main railroad tracks, so check both sides for foes and loot as you progress. Also investigate the various side passages—narrow mining tunnels filled with fungus and other loot. As you reach the main maintenance junction, dodge the containers and stilts, and investigate the large mining tunnel; here you can mine for aluminum. Eventually the tunnel ends at digging equipment and a corpse with the Big Bend Tunnel Door Key, allowing access into the maintenance junction building. When you're done exploring, head to either entrance/exit, passing another shanty blockage as you go.

35. MONONGAH POWER SUBSTATION MZ-03

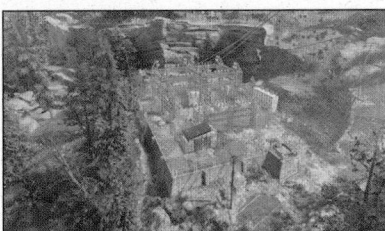

- **DANGER: EXPLOSIVE CANNISTER!**
- **INFO:** C.A.M.P. POWER; EXPECTED ENEMY: RADANT, ROBOT, SCORCHED; SCAVENGE RATING: 1; SIZE: 1; THREAT LEVEL: 25–35
- **ITEM EXAMPLES:** BAG OF CEMENT+

Close to the Big Bend Tunnel entrance, on a steep part of the ruined Route 83A, is a small substation with power access if you're intending on siphoning to your C.A.M.P..

36. HORNWRIGHT TESTING SITE #02

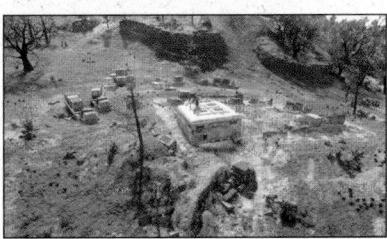

- **CRAFTING: WEAPONS**
- **ITEM: HARVESTABLE: BLIGHT**
- **INFO:** EXPECTED ENEMY: IRRADIATED ANIMAL; SCAVENGE RATING: 2; SIZE: 2; THREAT LEVEL: 25–35
- **LOCK:** DOOR (2)
- **ITEM EXAMPLES:** ASHTRAY, BROWN BOTTLE, CAMERA, COFFEE CUP, COFFEE POT, EXTINGUISHER, HOT PLATE, LIQUOR BOTTLES, OFFICE DESK FAN, ORANGE CANISTER, WONDERGLUE

Tucked away on the southwestern edge of the Ash Heap is an old testing location, with numerous parked (and rusting) trucks, containers, and a small concrete office structure with a locked (2) storage room.

37. WELCH

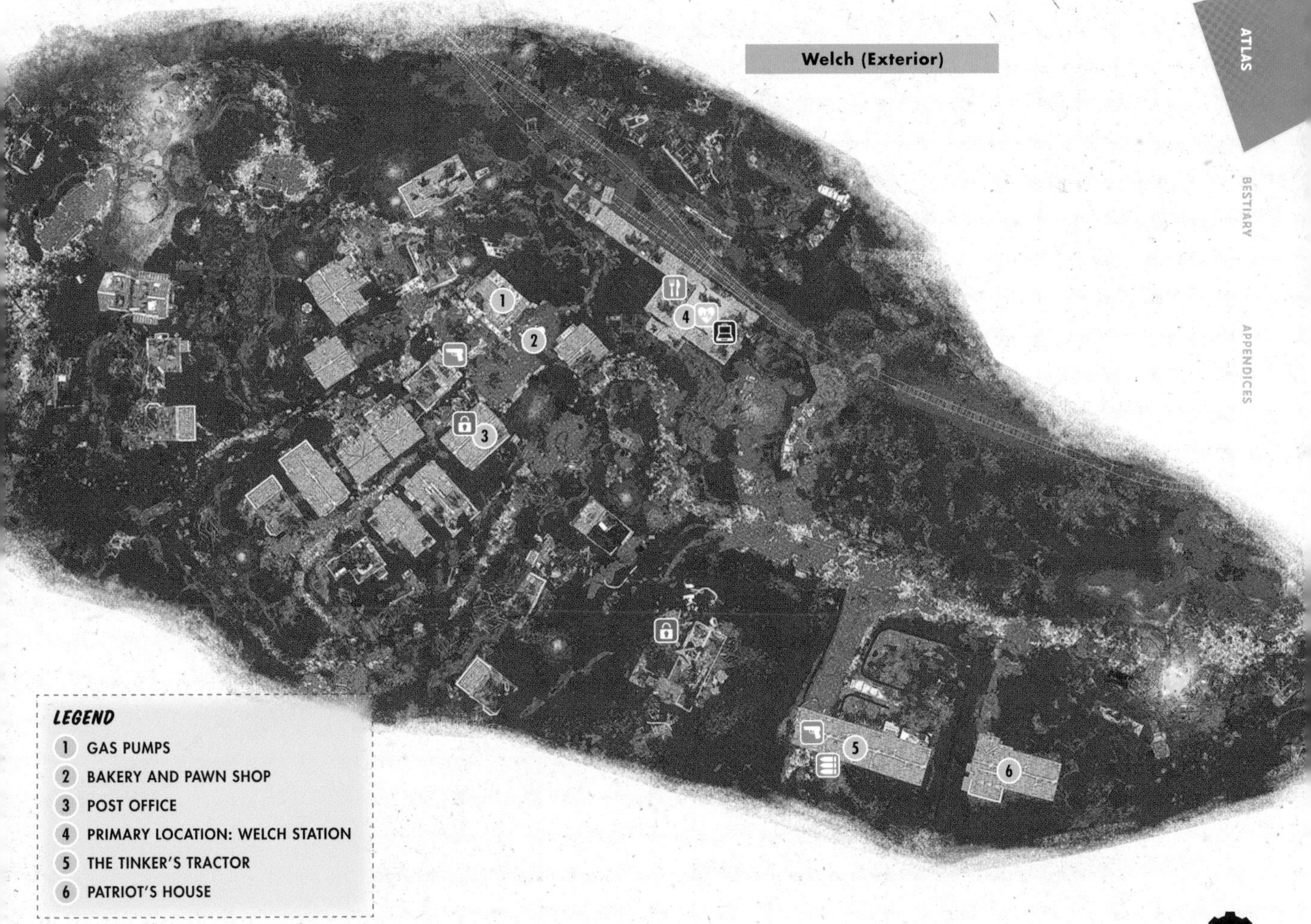

Welch (Exterior)

LEGEND
1 GAS PUMPS
2 BAKERY AND PAWN SHOP
3 POST OFFICE
4 PRIMARY LOCATION: WELCH STATION
5 THE TINKER'S TRACTOR
6 PATRIOT'S HOUSE

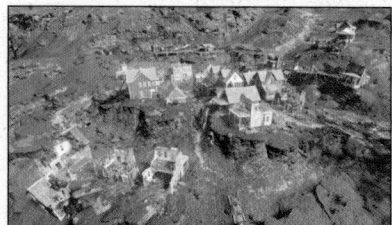

- **COLLECTIBLES:** HOLOTAPE, HOLOTAPE (OVERSEER), NUKA-CHERRY
- **CRAFTING:** TINKER, WEAPONS (2)
- **ITEMS:** ARMS AND AMMO; HEALTH AND CHEMS; RECIPE/MOD/PLAN; VENDING MACHINE: U-MINE-IT!
- **INFO:** EXPECTED ENEMY: MOLE MINER, ROBOT; NOTE; SCAVENGE RATING: 3; SIZE: 4; SLEEPING; THREAT LEVEL: 25–35
- **LOCK:** SAFE (U, 2)
- **ITEM EXAMPLES:** 10-MM AUTO PISTOL, ASHTRAY, BLAMCO BRAND MAC AND CHEESE, BOBBY PINS BOX, BOILED WATER+, BREAD BOX, CAFETERIA TRAY, CARTON OF CIGARETTES, COFFEE CUP+, COOKING POT, CRAM, DESK FAN, FLOWER POT, GAS CANISTER, GLASS PITCHER, INDUSTRIAL SIZE SHORTENING, INSTAMASH, LIT CIGAR, MED-X, MENTATS, MOP, OVEN MITT, PEPPER, PIPE BOLT-ACTION PISTOL, PLASTIC PLATE, PLUNGER, PORK N' BEANS, PROTEST SIGN+, PURIFIED WATER, RAT POISON, STRAW PILLOW, TEDDY BEAR+, TELEPHONE, TOILET PAPER, TYPEWRITER, YELLOW TABLE LAMP

A small town where striking miners had blocked the main road well before the entire hillside started to slip down into the valley. Now you must pick through the wreckage of the wooden homes and small central stores for possible loot and lament the loss of Welch.

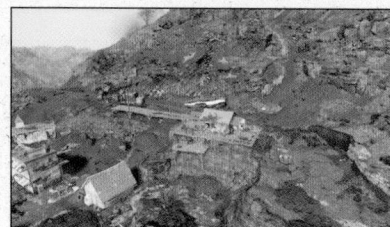

- **CRAFTING:** ARMOR, COOKING
- **ITEMS:** ARMS AND AMMO; HEALTH AND CHEMS; MY STASH BOX; VENDING MACHINE: AMMUNITION, MEDICAL SUPPLIES
- **INFO:** EXPECTED ENEMY: IRRADIATED ANIMAL; INSTRUMENT; SCAVENGE RATING: 2; SIZE: 2; SLEEPING; THREAT LEVEL: 25–35; TRADER: VENDOR BOT
- **ITEM EXAMPLES:** ABRAXO CLEANER, BEER BOTTLE+, BOURBON, CANDY FAN MR. FUZZY, CAT BOWL, COFFEE CUP+, MONGREL DOG MEAT, PILLOW, PIPE PISTOL, PROTEST SIGN+, PSYCHO, RADSTAG MEAT, STEW POT

Part of Welch township, the station is on the upper north side of the settlement. It is worth using as a base camp when exploring Welch and the surrounding locations. Also check out the rickety uphill path north of the tracks (technically in the previous zone). It leads to a small, abandoned trading post with a safe (1).

39. ABANDONED MINE SHAFT 1

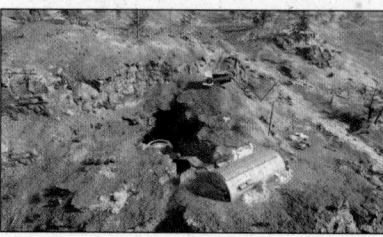

- **CRAFTING:** WEAPONS (2)
- **DANGER:** LONG DROP! RADIATION!++
- **ITEMS:** ARMS AND AMMO; HARVESTABLE: BLIGHT
- **INFO:** EXPECTED ENEMY: MOLE MINER; SCAVENGE RATING: 2; SIZE: 2; THREAT LEVEL: 25–35
- **ITEM EXAMPLES:** BEER BOTTLE, DESK FAN, FUSION CORE, MONGREL DOG MEAT, TUBE FLANGE, TURPENTINE

Perched on a promontory southeast of Welch is a curved-roof mechanical storage room, close to a short gantry and sealed mine shaft mouth. Watch the drop into highly irradiated waste!

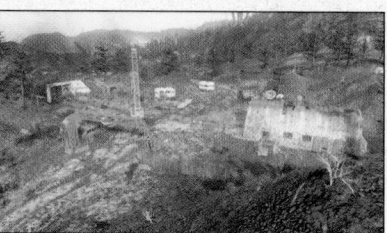

- **COLLECTIBLES:** BOBBLEHEAD, MAGAZINE, POWER ARMOR
- **CRAFTING:** CHEMISTRY, POWER ARMOR (2), TINKER, WEAPONS
- **DANGER:** RADIATION!+
- **ITEMS:** HARVESTABLE: BLIGHT, WILD CARROT FLOWER; TRUNK
- **INFO:** EXPECTED ENEMY: IRRADIATED ANIMAL, MOLE MINER, SUPER MUTANT; SCAVENGE RATING: 3; SIZE: 2; THREAT LEVEL: 25–35
- **LOCK:** SAFE (2)
- **ITEM EXAMPLES:** ALARM CLOCK, ANTIFREEZE, BLOOD PACK, BLUE PAINT, BOILED WATER, CAP, FUSE+, FUSION CORE, OIL CAN, OIL CANISTER, PACK OF DUCT TAPE, RAD POKER BOARD GAME, TURPENTINE, YELLOW PAINT

The Automated Mining Systems company constructed a site to test its non-human workforce, and this collection of outbuildings and caravans near a (sealed) mine entrance is the result.

41. HORNWRIGHT AIR CLEANSER SITE #03

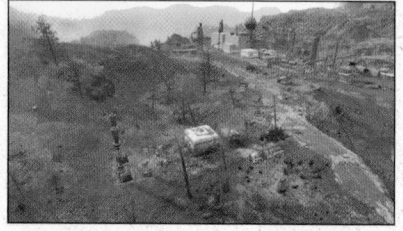

- **ITEMS:** ARMS AND AMMO; HEALTH AND CHEMS
- **INFO:** AIR PURIFIER; EXPECTED ENEMY: MOLE MINER, ROBOT; SCAVENGE RATING: 2; SIZE: 1; THREAT LEVEL: 25–35
- **LOCK:** DOOR (0)
- **ITEM EXAMPLES:** ABRAXO CLEANER, BLOWTORCH, CRAM, EXTINGUISHER, INDUSTRIAL SOLVENT, LANTERN, MR. HANDY FUEL, PACK OF CIGARETTES, PORTABLE FUEL TANK, TIN CAN, WAKEMASTER ALARM CLOCK, WONDERGLUE

Seek out this location for the light scavenging potential.

42. RED ROCKET FILLING STATION

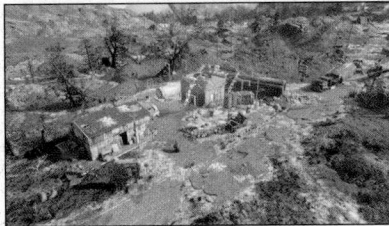

- **COLLECTIBLES:** BOBBLEHEAD, CAPS STASH, MAGAZINE, POWER ARMOR
- **CRAFTING:** CHEMISTRY, POWER ARMOR
- **DANGER:** OIL!
- **ITEMS:** HEALTH AND CHEMS; MY STASH BOX; VENDING MACHINE: U-MINE IT!
- **INFO:** EXPECTED ENEMY: MOLE MINER; SCAVENGE RATING: 2; SIZE: 2; THREAT LEVEL: 25–35
- **ITEM EXAMPLES:** FUMIGUS BLOWTORCH, MOP, PEPPER, PORTABLE FUEL TANK, RADAWAY, SALT, SOAP, SUPRATHAW ANTIFREEZE

A small gas station, with a miners' blockade to the east side of the property and a small metal garage housing a My Stash Box and the majority of the scavengable junk on the other.

43. ABANDONED MINE SHAFT 2

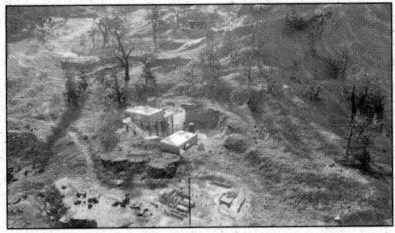

- **CRAFTING:** WEAPONS
- **DANGER:** LONG DROP! RADIATION!+
- **ITEMS:** ARMS AND AMMO+; HEALTH AND CHEMS
- **INFO:** EXPECTED ENEMY: GHOUL; SCAVENGE RATING: 2; SIZE: 1; THREAT LEVEL: 25–35
- **ITEM EXAMPLES:** ADJUSTABLE WRENCH, ASHTRAY, BLOOD PACK, BLOWTORCH, COFFEE CUP, COFFEE POT, FUSION CORE, RECOIL COMPENSATED PIPE BOLT-ACTION RIFLE, SHORT PUMP ACTION SHOTGUN, TACTICAL AUTOMATIC COMBAT SHOTGUN

Close to a particularly fetid pond (with some small, rudimentary structures), are two blue metal maintenance huts dug into the hillside. Expect more weaponry here than you usually scavenge. The upper hut leads to the sealed shaft and a drop to avoid.

44. HORNWRIGHT TESTING SITE #03

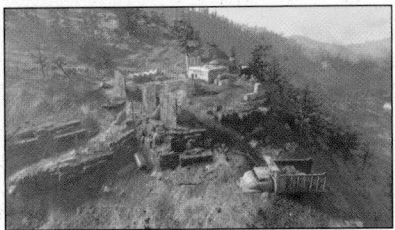

- **COLLECTIBLE:** BOBBLEHEAD
- **DANGER:** EXPLOSIVE CANNISTER!
- **ITEMS:** HARVESTABLE: SOOT FLOWER; HEALTH AND CHEMS
- **INFO:** EXPECTED ENEMY: IRRADIATED INSECT; SCAVENGE RATING: 2; SIZE: 1; SLEEPING; THREAT LEVEL: 25–35
- **ITEM EXAMPLES:** BAG OF CEMENT, BALL-PEEN HAMMER, BLASTING CAPS BOX, HIGH-POWERED MAGNET, OIL CANISTER, ORANGE CANISTER, SCREWDRIVER, USED OIL CAN

This small maintenance structure has meager pickings and a yard of strewn barrels; a small, half-destroyed shed; and a half-buried giant bucket with a sofa in it. Still, there's views of the Garrahan mansion towers.

45. FISSURE SITE (FISSURE)

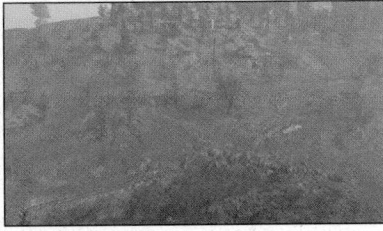

- **DANGER:** LONG DROP! RADIATION!++
- **ITEMS:** HARVESTABLE: ASH ROSE, BLIGHT, ULTRACITE
- **INFO:** EXPECTED ENEMY: SCORCHBEAST, SCORCHED; SCAVENGE RATING: 2; SIZE: 1; THREAT LEVEL: 25–35.
- **ITEM EXAMPLES:** NOT MUCH!

Perhaps it's best to avoid the low ash-covered hills close to Striker Row on this region's southern edge; a horde of Scorched and their queen are guarding this fissure. Avoid unless you're powerful enough!

46. STRIKER ROW

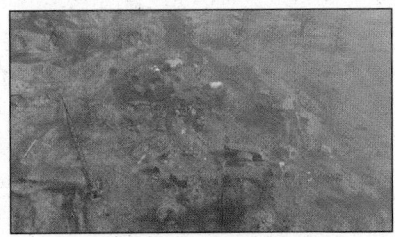

- **COLLECTIBLE:** BOBBLEHEAD (2), MAGAZINE (2), POWER ARMOR
- **CRAFTING:** COOKING
- **ITEMS:** ARMS AND AMMO; HARVESTABLE: SOOT FLOWER; HEALTH AND CHEMS; RECIPE/MOD/PLAN; TRUNK
- **INFO:** EXPECTED ENEMY: IRRADIATED INSECT; SCAVENGE RATING: 3; SIZE: 2; SLEEPING; THREAT LEVEL: 25–35
- **ITEM EXAMPLES:** BEER BOTTLE+, BOILED WATER, CAFETERIA TRAY, CANNED DOG FOOD, DESK FAN, FIRE AXE, FLIP LIGHTER, GLASS JAR, HOT PLATE, LANTERN+, PILLOW, PORTABLE FUEL TANK, PROTEST SIGN+, RUM, SALT, SHORT ASSAULT RIFLE

A small camp of striking miners seem to have had an altercation with the robots that helped replace them; though the Fissure site probably played a part in leaving this location mostly deserted of life. Check the lower tent camp, and the upper hut and tarp tent as well.

47. UNFINISHED MANSION

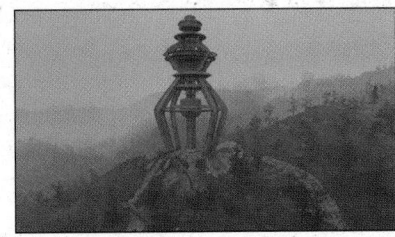

- **INFO:** LANDMARK; SCAVENGE RATING: 1; SIZE: 1; THREAT LEVEL: 25–35
- **ITEM EXAMPLES:** ALUMINUM CANISTER, PROTEST SIGN+, TIRE IRON

One of a trio of monolithic housing structures created by the Garrahan Mining company. However, this one wasn't completed, and the structure is little more than a giant (and inaccessible) shell. The views of Mount Blair to the northwest are impressive, but the Dumpster-diving potential is not.

TRAINING

CRAFTING AND C.A.M.P.ING

INVENTORY

QUESTS

ATLAS

BESTIARY

APPENDICES

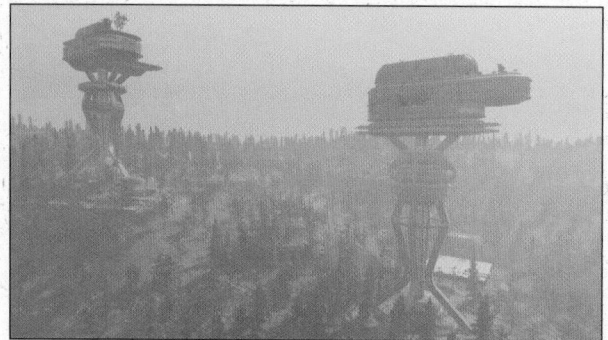

Garrahan Estate (Interior)

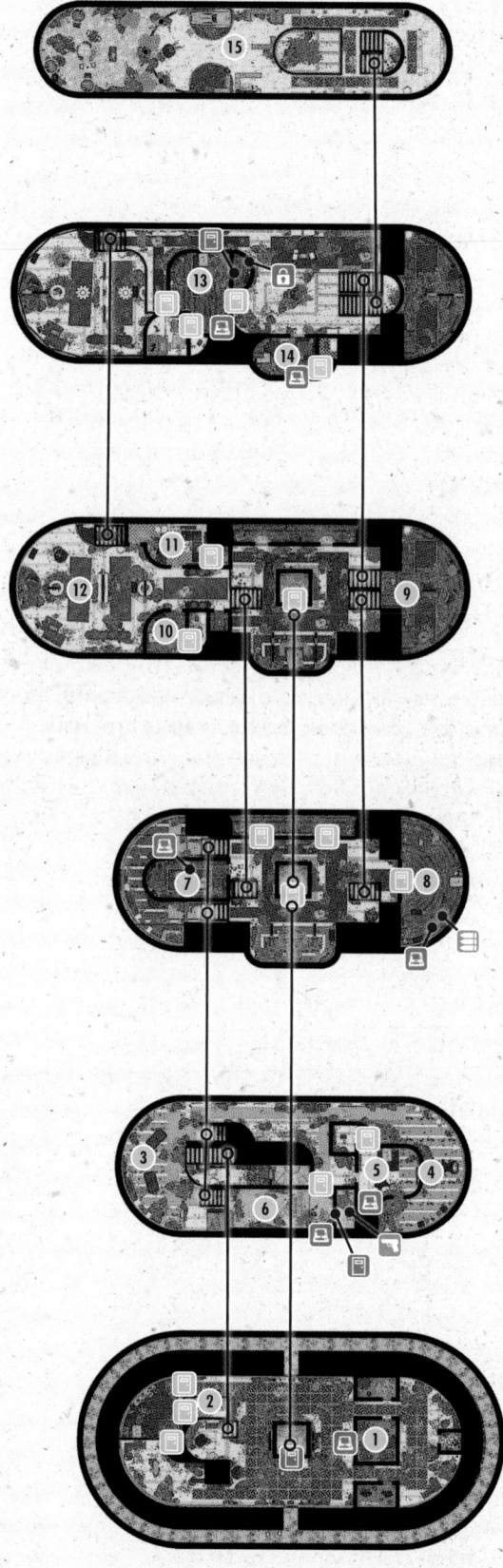

- **COLLECTIBLE:** NUKA-CHERRY, NUKA-COLA QUANTUM
- **CRAFTING:** CHEMISTRY, COOKING, TINKER, WEAPONS
- **DANGER:** LONG DROP! MINES! OIL!
- **ITEMS:** ARMS AND AMMO++; HARVESTABLE: MUTATED FERN; HEALTH AND CHEMS+; RECIPE/MOD/PLAN
- **INFO:** EXPECTED ENEMY: IRRADIATED INSECT, ROBOT; INSTRUMENT++; LANDMARK; NOTE; SCAVENGE RATING: 5; SIZE: 4; SLEEPING; THREAT LEVEL: 25–35
- **LOCK:** DOOR (0, 1, KEY), SAFE (1), TERMINAL (3)
- **ITEM EXAMPLES:** ABRAXO CLEANER+, ADJUSTABLE WRENCH, ALARM CLOCK, ANTIQUE GLOBE, BALL-PEEN HAMMER, BEER BOTTLE+++, BLACKWATER BREW, BLAMCO BRAND MAC AND CHEESE, BLAST RADIUS BOARD GAME, BLASTING CAPS BOX, BOBBY PIN BOX, BOILED WATER+, BOURBON BOTTLE, BROKEN LAMP, CATCH THE COMMIE BOARD GAME, CERAMIC BOWL+, CIGARETTE CARTON, CLOWN, CLOWN HAT, COFFEE CUP, COOKING OIL, COP CAP, CRUMPLED FEDORA, CRYSTAL LIQUOR DECANTER, DESK FAN+, DIRTY ASHTRAY+, DIRTY DESKTOP FRAME+, DOLL HEAD, DUCT TAPE, ECONOMY WONDERGLUE, FEATHER DUSTER, FOOD DEHYDRATOR, HANDCUFFS, HOT PLATE, INDUSTRIAL SOLVENT, INSTAMASH, KICKBALL, MINIGUN, MR. HANDY FUEL, NUKA-COLA, NUKA-COLA BOTTLE, NUKA-COLA CUP+, ORNAMENTAL VASE, PACK OF CIGARETTES+, PIPE REVOLVER, PLUNGER, POOL BALL+ POOL CUE, PORTABLE FUEL TANK, PROSNAP CAMERA, PURIFIED WATER, RAD POKER BOARD GAME, RACK, SEQUIN DRESS, SERRATED COMBAT KNIFE, SILVER TIE MR. FUZZY, SKULL, STEW POT, STRAIGHT JACKET, SURGICAL TRAY, SWEATER VEST AND SLACKS, TALL DRINKING GLASS+++, TELEPHONE, TIN CAN+, TIN PITCHER, TOASTER, TOILET PAPER, TV DINNER TRAY, USED OIL CAN, VASE, VEGETABLE STARCH, VODKA BOTTLE+, WALKING CANE, WASTE ACID, WHITE PLATE, WOODEN BEER STEIN

The Garrahan Tower is a self-contained vertical mansion with the latest in robotic servants. This impressive feat of engineering is still standing and has exceptional views (and dangerous drops from the top deck!). Head into the main tower and the sprawling, vertical living quarters by using the ID at the elevator door on the mine-trapped ground floor. Then explore the five or so levels, searching for a massive amount of useful junk.

LEGEND

1. CAGES
2. KITCHEN
3. GAME ROOM
4. LOUNGE AND BAR
5. BILL'S BEDROOM
6. FIRING RANGE
7. BRIGHTON'S OFFICE
8. BRYCE'S BEDROOM
9. BAR AND MUSIC ROOM
10. UPPER BEDROOM
11. UPPER KITCHEN
12. DINING AND MUSIC ROOM
13. VIVIAN'S BEDROOM (AND KINKY CLOSET)
14. ANGELICA'S BEDROOM
15. GRAND ROOF DECK

49. HORNWRIGHT ESTATE

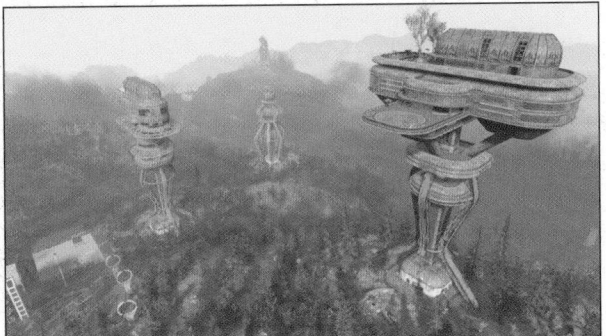

Hornwright Estate (Interior)

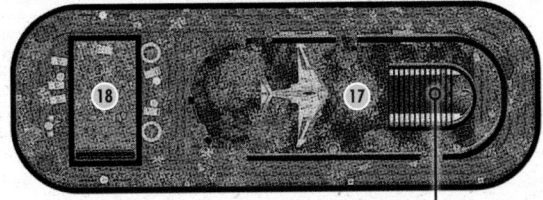

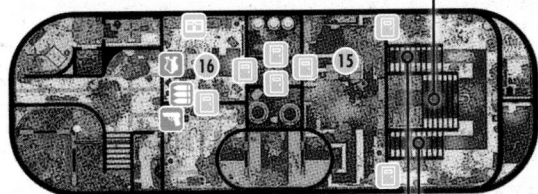

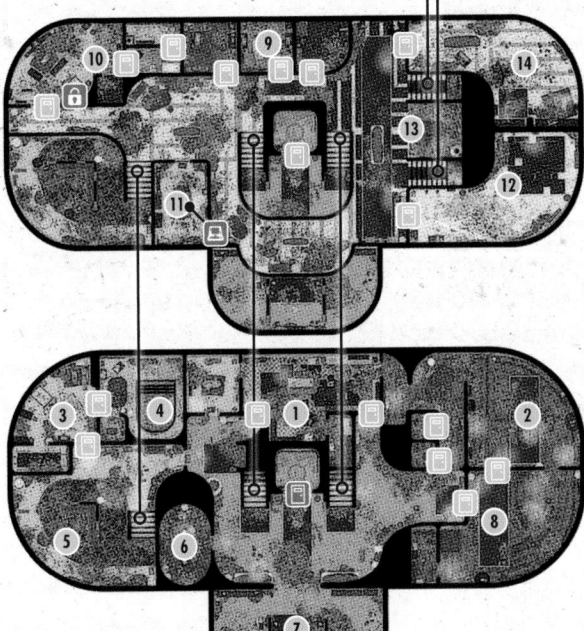

- **COLLECTIBLES:** CAPS STASH, NUKA-CHERRY
- **CRAFTING:** ARMOR, TINKER (2), WEAPONS
- **DANGER:** EXPLOSIVE CANNISTER! LONG DROP!
- **ITEMS:** ARMS AND AMMO; HEALTH AND CHEMS; RECIPE/MOD/PLAN; TRUNK
- **INFO:** EXPECTED ENEMY: GHOUL, IRRADIATED ANIMAL; LANDMARK; INSTRUMENT+; SCAVENGE RATING: 5; SIZE: 4; SLEEPING; THREAT LEVEL: 25–35
- **LOCK:** DOOR (KEY), SAFE (U)
- **ITEM EXAMPLES:** 40-LB BARBELL, ABRAXO CLEANER, ACETONE CANISTER, ALARM CLOCK, ASHTRAY, BEER BOTTLE+++, BOURBON, BROKEN LAMP+, BURGER TRAY, CAFETERIA TRAY, CAN+, CIGARETTE CARTON, CHESS BOARD, CLOTHES HANGER++, CLOWN, COFFEE CUP++, COFFEE POT, COOKING PAN, CRAM, DESK FAN+, DINNER PLATE+, DIRTY ASHTRAY, DIRTY DESKTOP FRAME, ECONOMY WONDERGLUE, EMPTY MILK BOTTLE, FUEL TANK, FUSION CORE, GAS CANISTER+, GLASS JAR+, GLOBE, HOT PLATE, LIGHTBULB, METAL TUB, MICROSCOPE, MOONSHINE JUG, NUKA-COLA, NUKA-COLA CUP, PENCIL, POOL BALL+, POOL CUE, PILLOW, PLASTIC SPOON, POTATO CRISPS, PUMPKIN PIE, RUM, SAUCE PAN, SAUCER, SHOT GLASS+, SOAP, SPATULA, STEW POT, TALL DRINKING GLASS+, TEDDY BEAR+, TIN CAN++, TIN PITCHER, TOASTER, TOOTHBRUSH, TOOTHPASTE, VASE, WHISKEY+, WILLOW FLARED VASE+, WINE, WOODEN SPOON, WONDERGLUE, YELLOW CANISTER, YELLOW TABLE LAMP+

This structure belongs to another of Appalachia's prominent mining families. It has a well-stocked bar on the ground floor, but the real riches become available once you use the ID card on the elevator and enter this vertical mansion tower. Search the upper floors for a variety of loot and important junk. The top floors get decidedly more oily.

LEGEND

1 KITCHENS	8 LOUNGE, MUSIC ROOM AND BAR	15 MECHANIC'S ROOM
2 DINING ROOM	9 GUEST BEDROOMS	16 ROBOT PARTS ROOM
3 MASTER BEDROOM	10 PENNY'S BEDROOM SUITE	17 ROOFTOP HANGAR
4 MASTER BATHROOM	11 PENNY'S OFFICE	18 EXTERIOR SWIMMING POOL
5 GREAT ROOM	12 GYM	
6 CONFERENCE ROOM	13 POOL TABLE ROOM	
7 TROPHY CABINET ROOM AND LANDING PAD	14 LOUNGE	

TRAINING

CRAFTING AND C.A.M.P.ING

INVENTORY

QUESTS

ATLAS

BESTIARY

APPENDICES

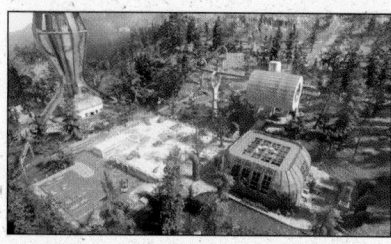

- **DANGER:** EXPLOSIVE CANNISTER! OIL! MINE!
- **ITEMS:** ARMS AND AMMO+; HARVESTABLE: IRON; HEALTH AND CHEMS+; RECIPE/MOD/PLAN; TRUNK
- **INFO:** EXPECTED ENEMY: ROBOT; NOTE; QUEST: MINER MIRACLES; SCAVENGE RATING: 5; SIZE: 4; THREAT LEVEL: 25–35
- **LOCK:** DOOR (0, 0), SAFE (1, 3), TERMINAL (0, 0, 1)
- **ITEM EXAMPLES:** BEAKER STAND, BLADED MOLE MINER GAUNTLET, BLOOD PACK, BUNSEN BURNER, CAFETERIA TRAY, CAN, CIGARETTE CARTON, CIVIC CENTER BOOTH KEY, COFFEE CUP+, COFFEE POT+, COFFEE TIN, COOKING PAN, COOKING POT, CRAM, CUTTING BOARD, DANDY BOY APPLES, DESK FAN+, DOLL, DUCT TAPE, EMPTY PAINT CAN, EXTINGUISHER, FANCY LADS SNACK CAKES, FIRE AXE, FLARE GUN, FRYING PAN, FUSION CORE, GARRAHAN ESTATE ACCESS KEYCARD, GUM DROPS, INSTAMASH, IRON ORE, LANTERN, MICROSCOPE, MINER'S LAMP, MOUNTAIN HONEY, NUKA-COLA BOTTLE, OLD POSSUM, PAINT CAN, PIPE WRENCH, POTATO CRISPS, PRISTINE MINER'S UNIFORM, PROTEST SIGN+, ROLLING PIN, SHOT GLASS, SMALL DRINKING GLASS, SOAP, TACTICAL COMBAT SHOTGUN, TALL DRINKING GLASS, TEACUP+, TOASTER, TOILET PAPER, WHISKEY BOTTLE, WINE, YUM YUM DEVILED EGGS

- **COLLECTIBLES:** BOBBLEHEAD, HOLOTAPE, MAGAZINE, POWER ARMOR (4), POWER ARMOR (EXCAVATOR)
- **CRAFTING:** CHEMISTRY, POWER ARMOR (2), TINKER, WEAPONS

Garrahan Mining Headquarters (Interior)

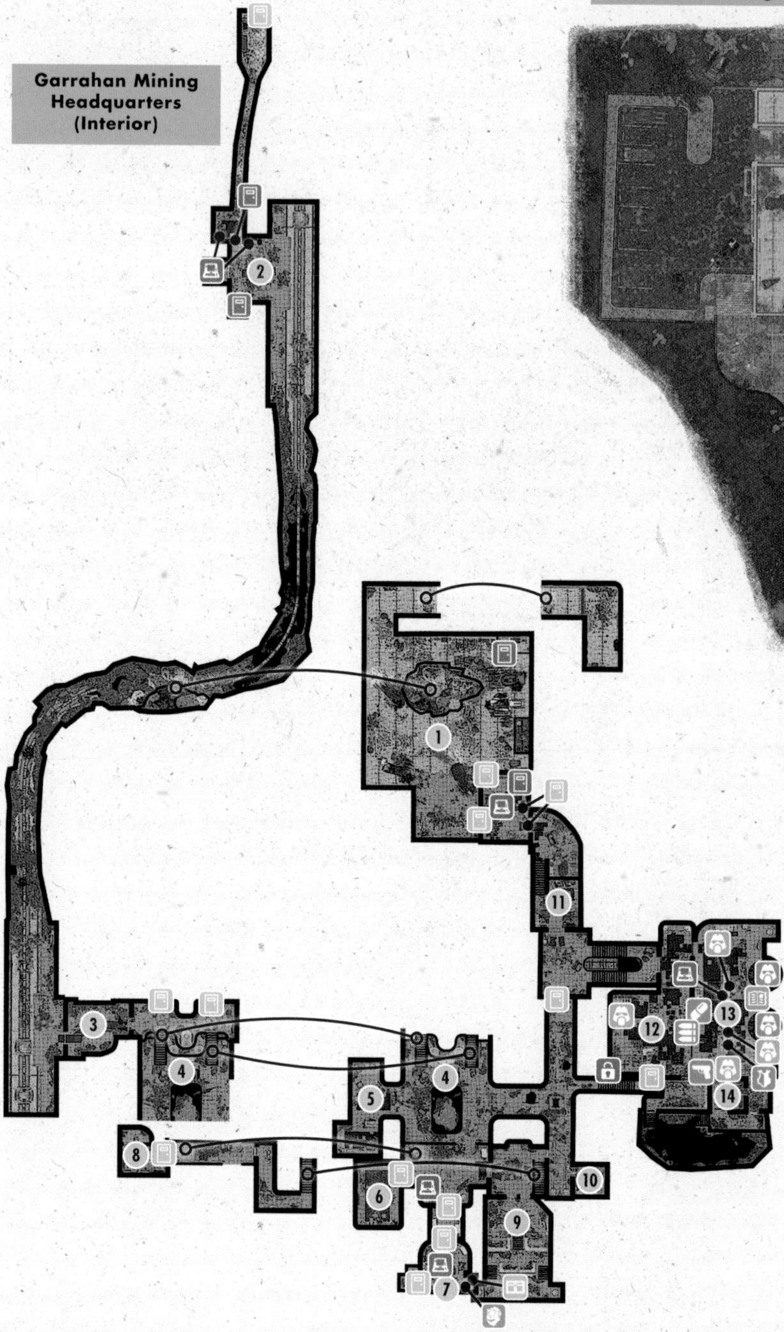

Garrahan Mining Headquarters (Exterior)

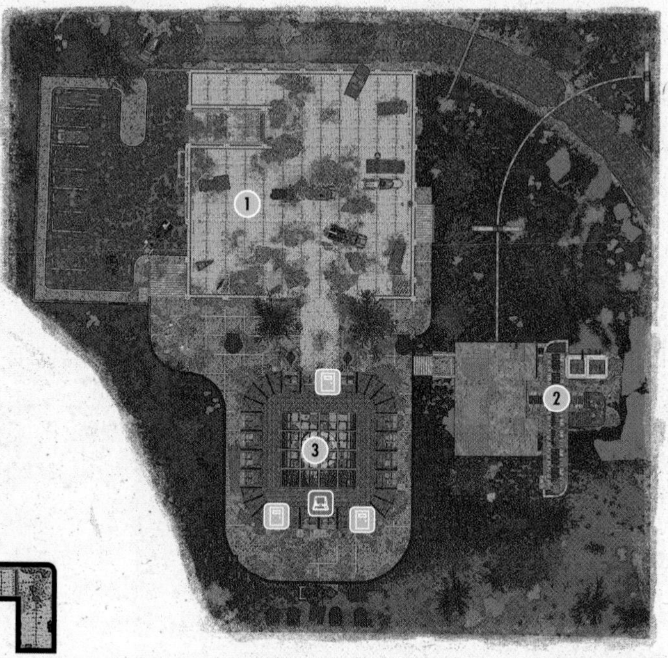

LEGEND

1. PARKING LOT
2. MONORAIL STATION
3. GARRAHAN MINING ENTRANCE AND LOBBY

LEGEND

1. PARKING LOT
2. GARRAHAN STATION A (TO BUNKER EXIT)
3. GARRAGAN STATION B (TO HEADQUARTERS)
4. GARRAHAN MINING LOBBY
5. KITCHEN
6. CONFERENCE ROOM
7. CEO'S OFFICE
8. ADMIN
9. CONTROL ROOM
10. RESTROOMS
11. MEZZANINE BREAK ROOM
12. R&D: TESTING, CONTROL AND ASSESSMENT
13. R&D: FABRICATION AND TESTING
14. R&D: POWER ARMOR REGISTRATION SCANNER

The headquarters of the infamous mining company has its fair share of secrets, including a maintenance hut with a secret exit, away from the main parking lot near the three towering mansion structures. There's a monorail station and two more stations underground. Access this via the lobby or from inside the parking lot. The headquarters is a treasure trove of junk, and if a certain quest is active, you will find a special suit of Power Armor (the Excavator Class) here as well. There's also a possible Power Armor frame and two pieces of Power Armor to pick up from the R&D department, as well as some keys from the CEO's office.

ZONE B: SECONDARY LOCATIONS

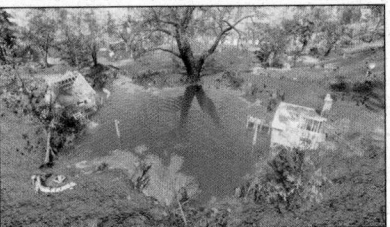

Military Comms Tower Kittery

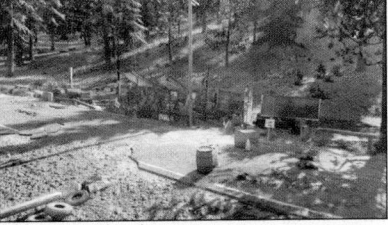

Roadside Stalls (Uncanny Caverns)

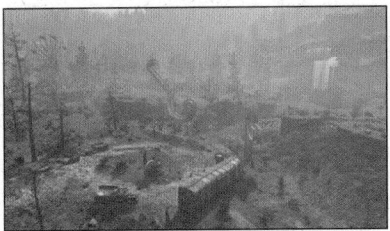

Lake Reynolds Dump

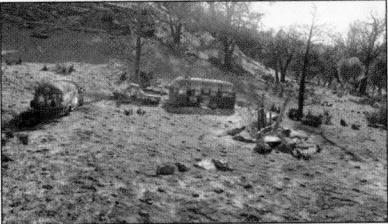

Gnome Sweet Gnome Camp

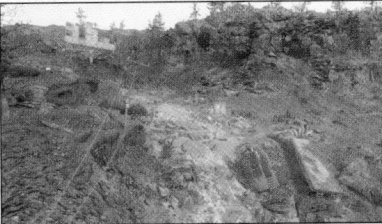

Welch Miner Blockade

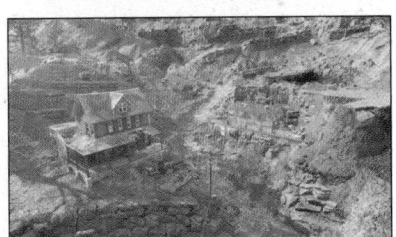

Vault 63 (Entrance)

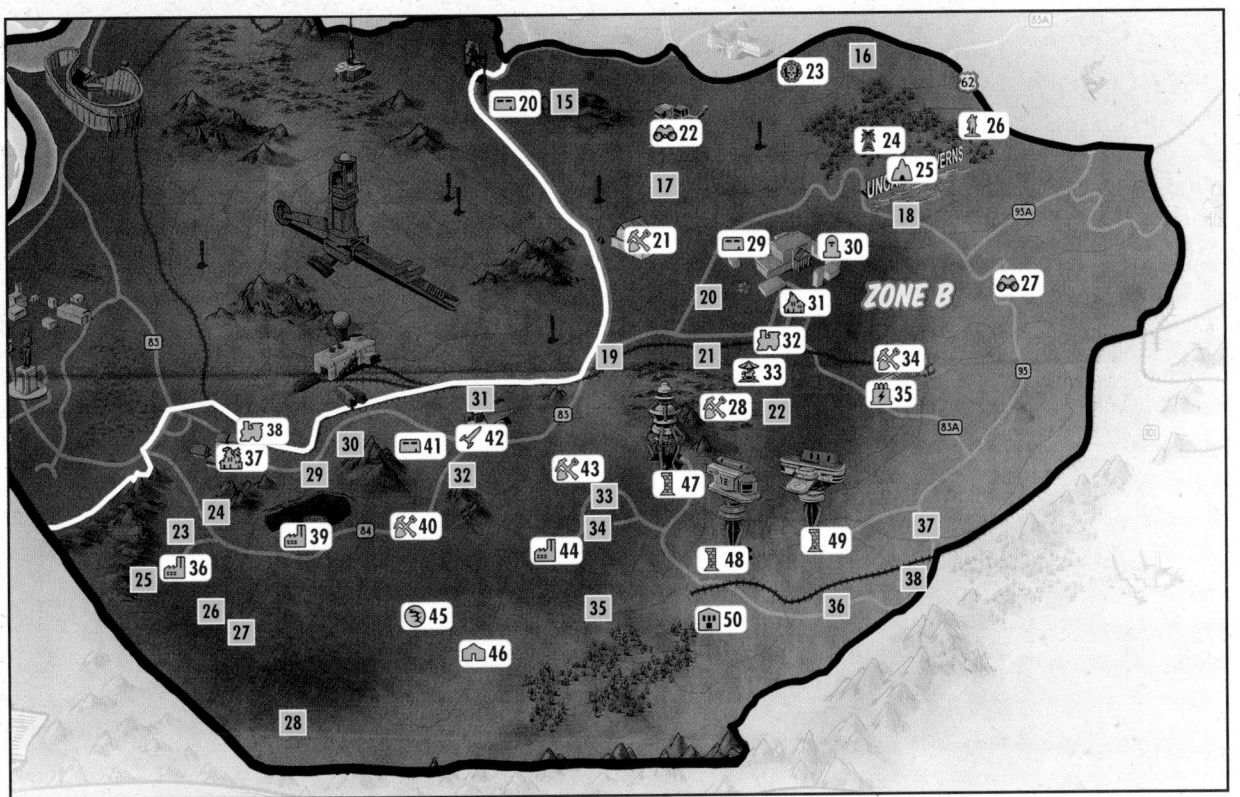

Appalachia: the Ash Heap (Zone B) – Secondary Locations

TRAINING

CRAFTING AND C.A.M.P.ING

INVENTORY

QUESTS

ATLAS

BESTIARY

APPENDICES

#	NAME	DESCRIPTION
15	Military Comms Tower Kittery	A small, quest-related comms dish standing near the Air Cleanser Site pond with two shacks.
16	Cultist Totem (east of Bleeding Kate's)	Those seeking clues to the Mothman cult (as well as Iron Deposits and a teddy bear) should seek this totem out.
17	Hilltop Sludge Hut	A locked safe (2) sinking into a shallow pond, along with a log cabin with a cooking station inside and no proper ventilation.
18	Roadside Stalls (Uncanny Caverns)	There's still some pickings to be had at this miners' stall, if you like corn, alcohol, and potato crisps.
19	Cement Pipe Excavation and Railroad Carriages	There are two safes (1, 2), one in the west signal tower and the other in an orange carriage to the east. Grab some weaponry and junk here, too.
20	Propeller Head's Shack	A small curved-roof shack and billboard, with a propeller generator atop the rock outcrop above.
21	Lake Reynolds Dump	Rusting fairground signs, a cargo carriage with an impromptu office in it, and a rusty pickup to pick over.
22	Small Raider Camp	White tarp sheets offer a modicum of protection at this pole and breeze block camp, with sleeping bags and a duffel bag.
23	Oak Tree Vista	An old oak tree, dead but still atop the hill with a pile of breeze blocks and views of Beckley to the north.
24	Route 84 Turnout	A cluster of rusty military vehicles and Old Glory on a flagpole indicate what used to be a road turnout.
25	Gnome Sweet Gnome Camp	A dirt field of earth, gnomes, a golf cart, gnomes, a rusty trailer, gnomes, a van, and yet more gnomes.
26	Cultist Altar (south of Hornwright Testing Site #02)	Scattered skeletal bodies, bones and skulls, the Ash Rose, and a tangled cult totem.

#	NAME	DESCRIPTION
27	Orange Tarp Scavenger's Stall	An old stall constructed from a tipped truck trailer, which still has a safe (3) inside and some weaponry to gather from a display case.
28	Top of the Heap	A single orange chair sits atop a frightening clifftop fall; head here for a selfie across most of the Ash Heap, if the weather cooperates.
29	Welch Miner Blockade	The upper western blockage of Welch yields more than just empty paint cans; there's aluminum veins here, too.
30	Golden Quarry Pond	A sunken pond with plants and gold veins to pillage from.
31	Sludge Trailer	A rusting metal trailer with junk to gather, a place to sleep, and an outdoor space best described as "gunky."
32	Military Comms Tower Mount Blair South	A small, quest-related comms dish standing on a low dirt hill near telephone poles and wires.
33	Red Star Roadside Home	Across from the small warehouse and Vault 63 entrance is a large home to check for items.
34	Vault 63	A small, unassuming metal warehouse has a door inside leading to a cave entrance, cog door, and Vault 63.
35	Vertibird Crash Site (South part of The Ash Heap)	Skeletal remains, a crate or two, and the rusting remains of an aircraft that crashed after the bombs dropped.
36	Wild Wolf Homestead	A farmhouse, garage, scarecrow, and mutfruit greenhouse await those exploring the southeastern edge of the Ash Heap.
37	Miners' Road Block	A blockade across the road to the east of the mine owners' vertical mansions.
38	Halloween Horror Hamlet	A Halloween-themed farmstead on both sides of the room, where pumpkins are plentiful.

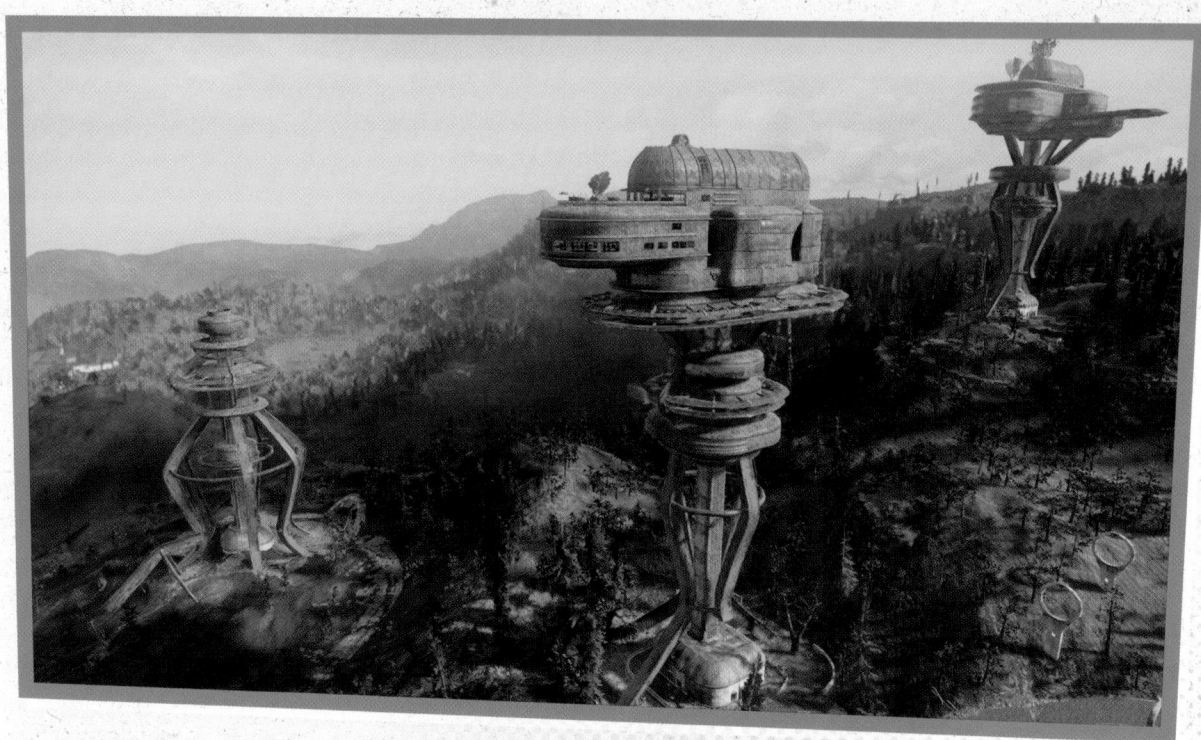

Atlas of Appalachia
REGION 4: SAVAGE DIVIDE

ENEMY THREAT LEVELS

SAVAGE
DIVIDE
15-99 💀

0 10 20 30 40 50 60 70 80 90 99+

When visiting Savage Divide, remember the ground is more unforgiving than in other regions, so stay on paths or roads to prevent stepping off a sheer drop! This region splits West Virginia between the west and east; the mountainous topography stretches north to south across the map and consists mainly of steep slopes, large craggy rock scree, forests, and some idyllic spots with incredible views. There are many interesting and unique dwellings to chance upon, ranging from a temple of enlightenment close to the northern border, to a house filled with pumpkins, to caves where the strangest of cryptids reside. Slap bang in the middle of the map is the "giant red thumbtack" known as Top of the World; as you'd expect, this observation tower and hifalutin shopping mall that once catered to the well-to-do skiers at Pleasant Valley is now a rusting landmark with which to orient yourself. Those seeking peace and quiet might do well to visit the array of large radio astronomy structures, including a massive dish in the mountains, once part of the United States National Radio Quiet Zone.

WORLD MAP LEGEND
—— REGION BOUNDARY
—— ZONE BOUNDARY

Appalachia: **Savage Divide**

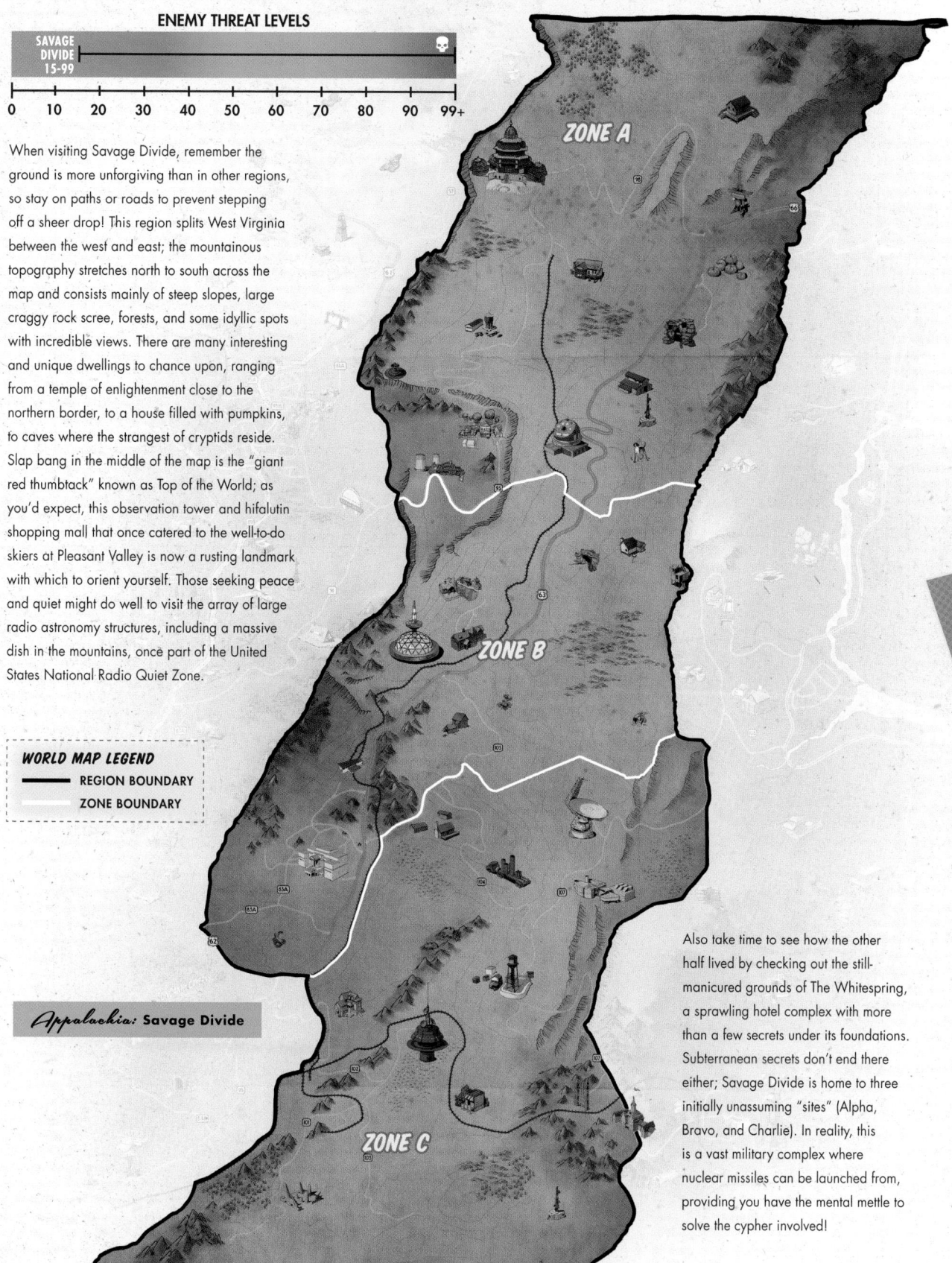

ZONE A

ZONE B

ZONE C

Also take time to see how the other half lived by checking out the still-manicured grounds of The Whitespring, a sprawling hotel complex with more than a few secrets under its foundations. Subterranean secrets don't end there either; Savage Divide is home to three initially unassuming "sites" (Alpha, Bravo, and Charlie). In reality, this is a vast military complex where nuclear missiles can be launched from, providing you have the mental mettle to solve the cypher involved!

TRAINING

CRAFTING AND C.A.M.P.ING

INVENTORY

QUESTS

ATLAS

BESTIARY

APPENDICES

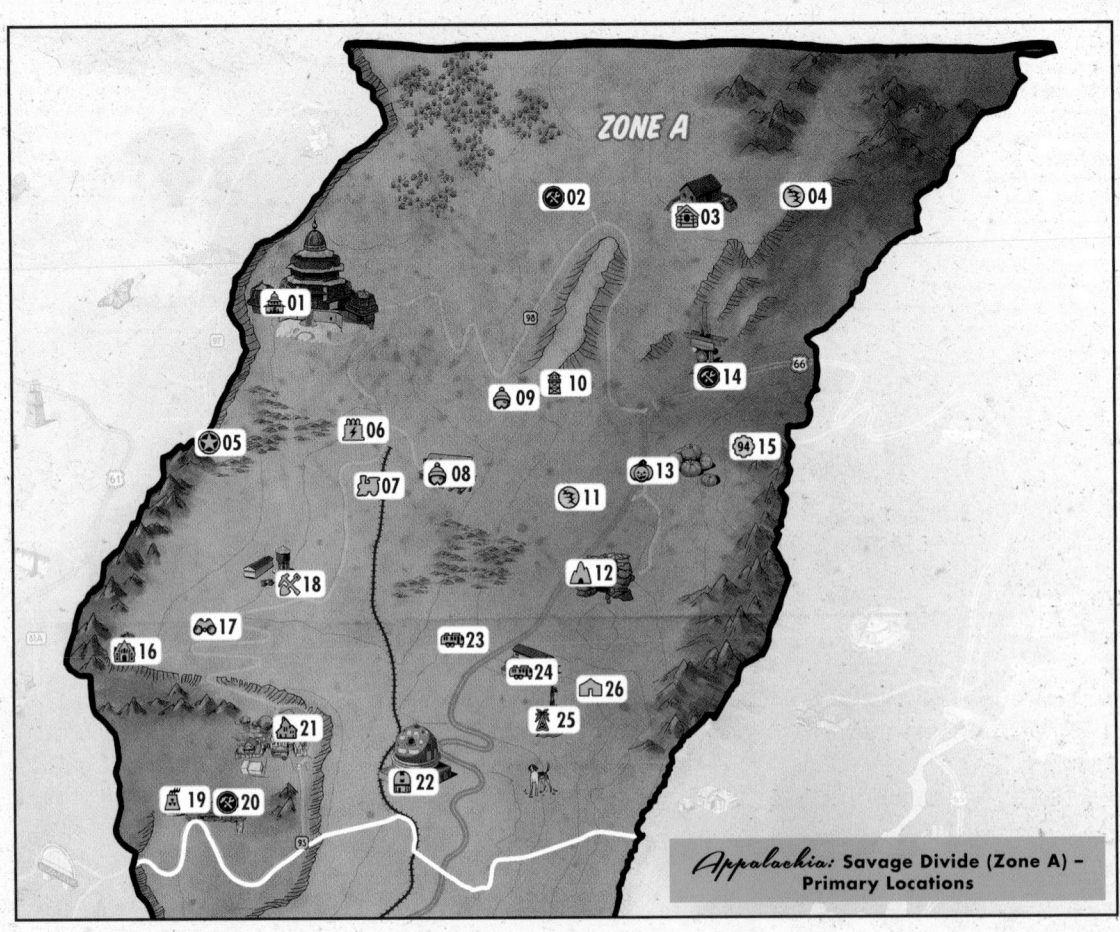

ZONE A

Appalachia: Savage Divide (Zone A) – Primary Locations

WORLD MAP LEGEND

— REGION BOUNDARY   — ZONE BOUNDARY

■ BOBBLEHEADS   ■ CAP STASHES   ■ MAGAZINES   ■ POWER ARMOR

PRIMARY LOCATIONS

				icon	NAME						icon	NAME
1		1	1	🏯 01	PALACE OF THE WINDING PATH				1		🎯 14	RED ROCKET MEGA STOP
1		1	1	🎯 02	CONVERTED MUNITIONS FACTORY	1	14	1			94 15	VAULT 94
1		1		🏚 03	BAILEY FAMILY CABIN	1		2			🏛 16	INGRAM MANSION
				⊗ 04	FISSURE SITE BETA						🔭 17	MONONGAH OVERLOOK
4		3	1	◉ 05	SITE BRAVO						⚒ 18	MONONGAH MINE
				⚡ 06	MONONGAH POWER SUBSTATION MZ-01				1		⛏ 19	MONONGAH POWER PLANT
				🚂 07	SUNNYTOP STATION						⊗ 20	MONONGAH POWER PLANT YARD
4		4	1	⛷ 08	SUNNYTOP SKI LANES						🏔 21	MONONGAH
2		2	1	⛷ 09	SUNNYTOP SKI LANES BASE LODGE	1		1			🏢 22	OBSERVATORY
				🗼 10	NORTH MOUNTAIN LOOKOUT				1		🚚 23	AMMO DUMP
				⊗ 11	FISSURE SITE SIGMA	3		3	1		🚚 24	SONS OF DANE COMPOUND
1		1	1	🏔 12	HOPEWELL CAVE	1		1			📡 25	RELAY TOWER LW-B1-22
				🎃 13	PUMPKIN HOUSE	2		2			🏠 26	SYLVIE & SONS LOGGING CAMP

The northern wilds of Savage Divide have mountainous forest you can get lost in for days, remote cabins, strange militia compounds, abandoned camps, and odd caves abound (if you can discover them). Stay on the main roads, though, to discover the largest Red Rocket Gas Station ever seen (a great workshop to defend), a pumpkin house with a suitably orange Mr. Handy, and a huge domed telescope observatory. The southwestern part of the zone encompasses the foothills of Monongah, with the ruined town and idle power plant of the same name. Lest you think mining is just confined to the Ash Heap, it's also worth exploring the mine workings too; here you'll find sealed shafts, old (and particularly spiky) Raider camps and checkpoints, and strange, hunched atrocities known as Mole Miners, who don't take kindly to trespassers.

ZONE A: PRIMARY LOCATIONS

MAP LEGEND

- MY STASH BOX
- OVERSEER'S CACHE
- TRUNK
- TRADER

COLLECTIBLES

- BOBBLEHEAD
- MAGAZINE
- POWER ARMOR

CRAFTING

- ARMOR WORKBENCH
- CHEMISTRY WORKBENCH
- COOKING STATION
- POWER ARMOR STATION
- TINKER'S WORKBENCH
- WEAPONS WORKBENCH
- WORKSHOP WORKBENCH

IMPORTANT

- DOOR/GATE
- LOCKED DOOR/GATE
- SAFE
- SCANNER
- TERMINAL

01. PALACE OF THE WINDING PATH

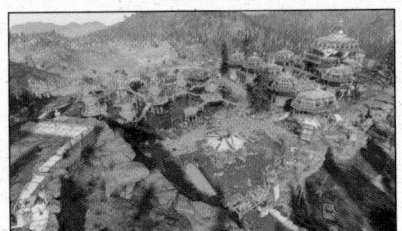

- **COLLECTIBLES:** BOBBLEHEAD, HOLOTAPE, MAGAZINE, NUKA-CHERRY, POWER ARMOR
- **CRAFTING:** ARMOR, CHEMISTRY (2), COOKING (3), TINKER (2), WEAPONS
- **DANGER:** RADIATION!
- **ITEMS:** ARMS AND AMMO; HARVESTABLE: BLOODLEAF, RHODODENDRON, SOOT FLOWER, WILD CARROT FLOWER, WOOD PILE; RECIPE/MOD/PLAN; TRUNK
- **INFO:** EXPECTED ENEMY: SCORCHED; INSTRUMENT; LANDMARK; NOTE; SCAVENGE RATING: 5; SIZE: 4; SLEEPING; THREAT LEVEL: 15–99
- **ITEM EXAMPLES:** ABRAXO CLEANER+, ABRAXO CLEANER INDUSTRIAL GRADE, ANTIFREEZE BOTTLE, BEER BOTTLE, BLUE TABLE LAMP+, BOWIE KNIFE, BREAD BOX, CAFETERIA TRAY+, CAKE PAN, CHALK+, CIGAR BOX, COOKING OIL, COOKING POT, DINNER PLATE, FLOWER POT+, FUSION CORE, HOT PLATE, GLASS PITCHER, LANTERN, MAKESHIFT BATTERY, MICROSCOPE, MUZZLED CROSSBOW, OLD POSSUM+, ORNAMENTAL VASE++, OVEN MITT, PILLOW++, POOL BALL++, POOL CUE, RAT POISON, SALT, SHOT GLASS+, SKULL, SOAP, SPICES, SURGICAL TRAY, TEA CUP++, TEAPOT+, TEAL FLARED VASE++, UPPER SKULL+, VODKA BOTTLE+, WHISKEY BOTTLE, WOOD BLOCK++

LEGEND

1. TARGET RANGE
2. CAVE ENTRANCE (TO BASEMENT)
3. TINKER'S PAVILION
4. PALACE COURTYARD

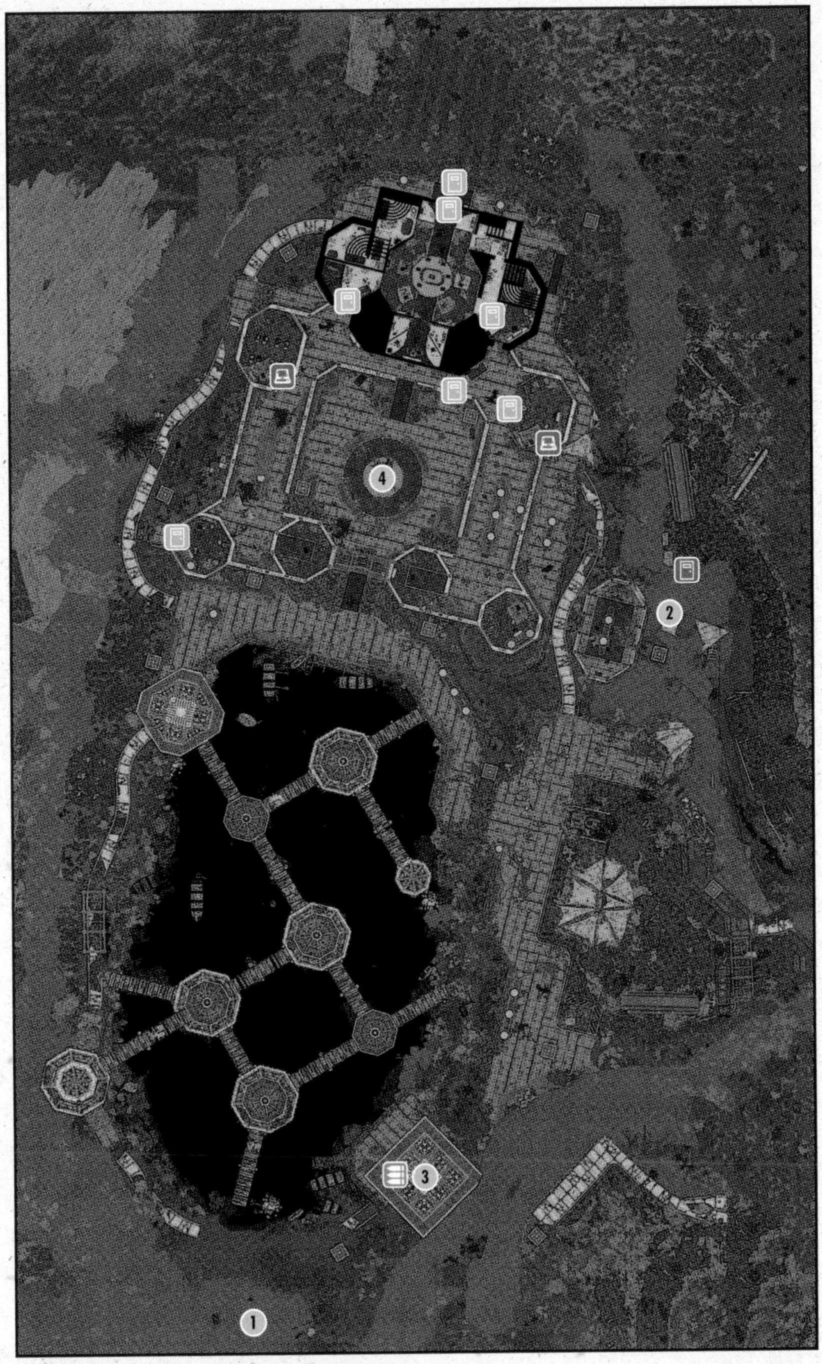

Palace of the Winding Path (Exterior)

TRAINING
CRAFTING AND C.A.M.P.ING
INVENTORY
QUESTS
ATLAS
BESTIARY
APPENDICES

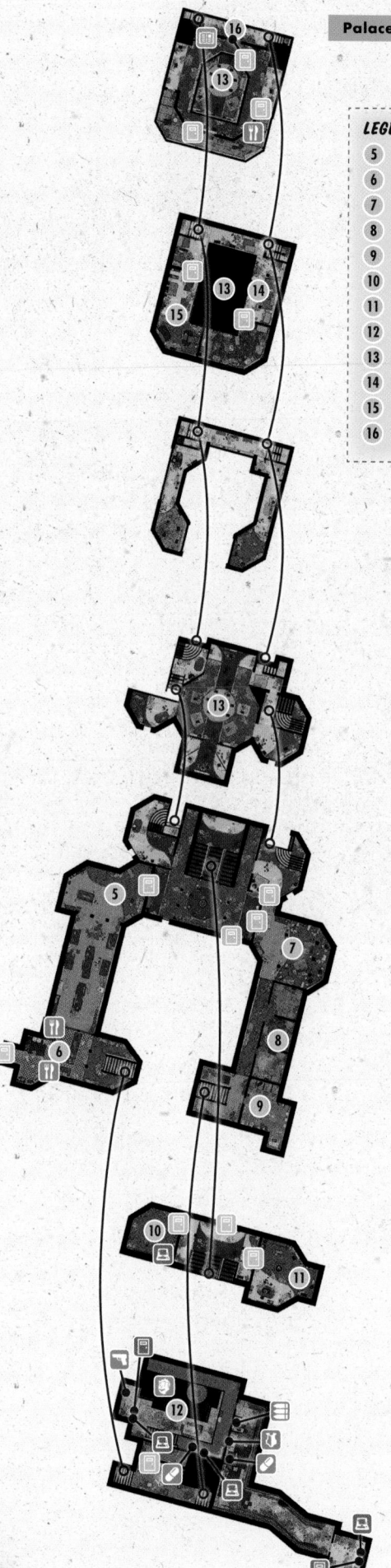

LEGEND

5 GREEN LOUNGE
6 KITCHENS
7 MEDITATION ROOMS
8 BUNK BEDS
9 SHOWERS
10 HOLOTAPE DUPLICATION ROOM
11 MAIN OFFICE
12 LOWER GENERATOR ROOM
13 GRAND CHAMBER OF ENLIGHTENMENT
14 RAIDERS' SLEEPING QUARTERS
15 BAR AND BEDROOM
16 UPPER BALCONY

Wholeness Through Transcendence! This oddity of architecture has been here before the war and still has a faded grandeur about it, even after it was turned into a Raider camp. View it from the vista turnout along the road, or better yet, explore the small water pavilions before venturing into the multilevel interior in search of loot and one of the best views over Toxic Valley. Also note the Holotape Duplication Terminal; if you have a spare holotape (e.g., from Sugar Grove), you may be able to record a tape (or even a game!) for your fellow explorers. Finally, check the two parked trailers in the wilderness north of here; there might be a Power Armor frame in it for you.

 02. CONVERTED MUNITIONS FACTORY (WORKSHOP)

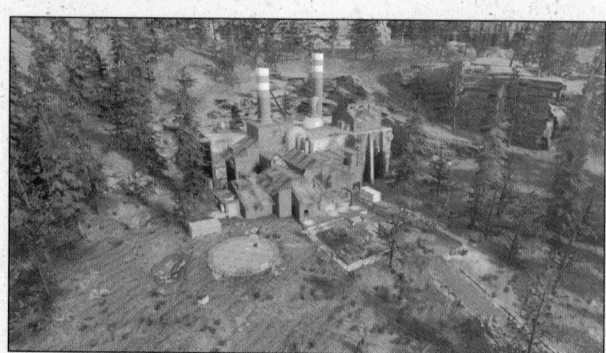

- **COLLECTIBLE:** POWER ARMOR
- **CRAFTING:** ARMOR, WEAPONS, WORKSHOP
- **DANGER:** EXPLOSIVE CANISTER!
- **ITEMS:** ARMS AND AMMO+++; HARVESTABLE: AMMUNITION, JUNK PILE, ALUMINUM; COPPER; LEAD; OIL; SILVER; HEALTH AND CHEMS
- **INFO:** EXPECTED ENEMY: VARIES; NOTES; SCAVENGE RATING: 3(5+); SIZE: 3; THREAT LEVEL: 15–99
- **LOCK:** DOOR (X2) (1, 2), SAFE (2)
- **ITEM EXAMPLES:** ABRAXO CLEANER, BLAST RADIUS BOARD GAME, BLOWTORCH, COFFEE CUP, EMPTY PAINT CAN, FUSION CORE, MENTATS, METAL BUCKET, MILITARY GRADE CIRCUIT BOARD, MILITARY GRADE DUCT TAPE, OFFICE DESK FAN, PLASTIC PUMPKIN+, PLUNGER, SHORT HUNTING RIFLE, SLEDGEHAMMER, TEDDY BEAR, TOY ROCKETSHIP
- **WORK:** FOOD [7], WATER [8], JUNK [1], AMMO [1], SILVER [1], LEAD [1], ALUMINUM [1], OIL [1]

Converted Munitions Factory (Exterior and Interior)

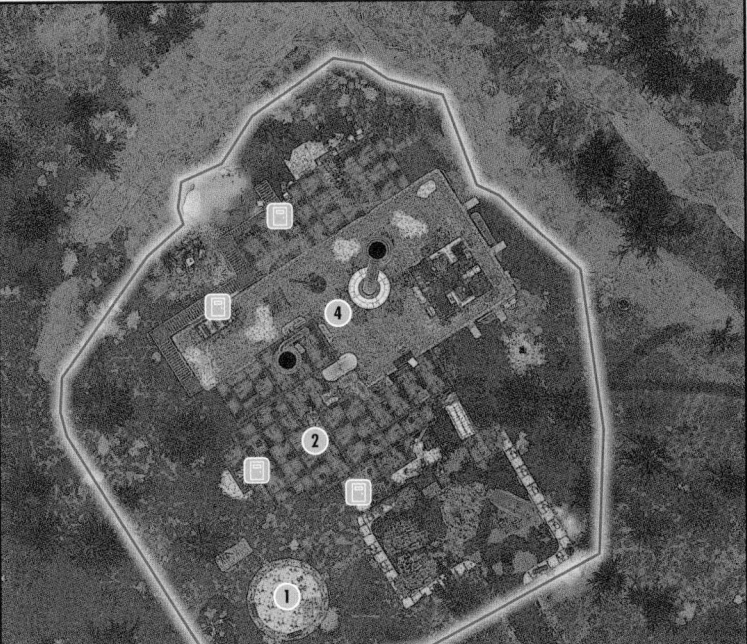

LEGEND

1. VERTIBOT LANDING PAD
2. FACTORY OFFICES
3. SUPERVISOR'S OFFICE
4. FACTORY FLOOR
5. REACTOR ROOM
6. BREAK ROOM
7. EMPTY STORAGE ROOM
8. LOCKED STORAGE

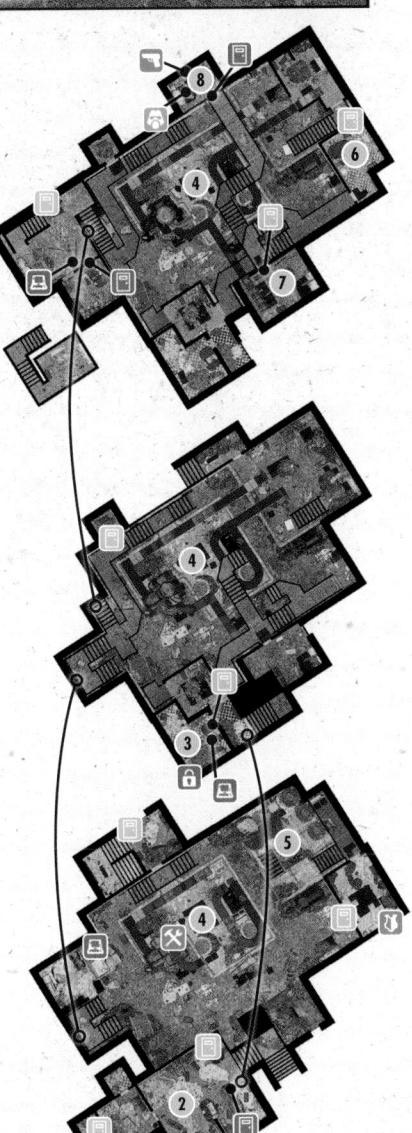

On a remote stretch of Route 98, you'll find the rusting remains of a military munitions location, complete with three repairable gun emplacement turrets and a vertibot landing pad (for that extra airborne defense!). Inside the factory, unlock the door by the stairs (2) to access a small ammo closet. On the upper gantry is a second locked door (1), leading to a storage room with possible Power Armor and a Weapons Workbench. Start the munitions conveyor belts to begin pumping out masses of ammo and a variety of other resources.

03. BAILEY FAMILY CABIN

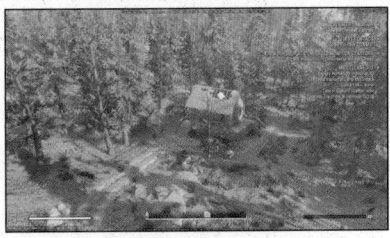

- **COLLECTIBLES:** BOBBLEHEAD, MAGAZINE
- **DANGER:** EXPLOSIVE CANISTER!
- **ITEM:** RECIPE/MOD/PLAN
- **INFO:** EXPECTED ENEMY: SCORCHED; NOTES; SCAVENGE RATING: 2; SIZE: 1; SLEEPING; THREAT LEVEL: 15–99
- **ITEM EXAMPLES:** BEER BOTTLE+, BOBBY PIN BOX, COFFEE CUP, COOKING POT, COTTON YARN, DIRTY ASHTRAY, ENAMEL BUCKET, PIPE WRENCH, PEPPER, SALT, TEDDY BEAR, USED OIL CAN, YELLOW PAINT CAN

This remote wilderness cabin is said to be the final resting of an elderly couple who lived out their last days here. This is a reasonable place to hide away from it all. There's a cabin and metal trailer to loot.

04. FISSURE SITE BETA (FISSURE)

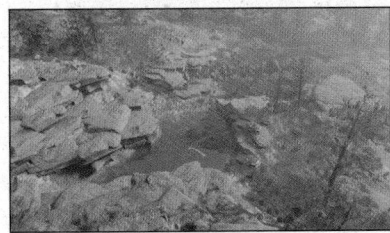

- **DANGER:** LONG DROP! RADIATION!++
- **ITEMS:** HARVESTABLE: BRAIN FUNGUS, DECAYING ULTRACITE
- **INFO:** EXPECTED ENEMY: SCORCHBEAST, SCORCHED; SCAVENGE RATING: 2; SIZE: 1; THREAT LEVEL: 15–99
- **ITEM EXAMPLES:** NOT MUCH!

On the rough and rocky terrain is a horrifying slit in the earth; a gathering of Scorched and a terrifying Scorchbeast appear from this fissure. Avoid unless you're powerful enough!

TRAINING

CRAFTING AND C.A.M.P.ING

INVENTORY

QUESTS

ATLAS

BESTIARY

APPENDICES

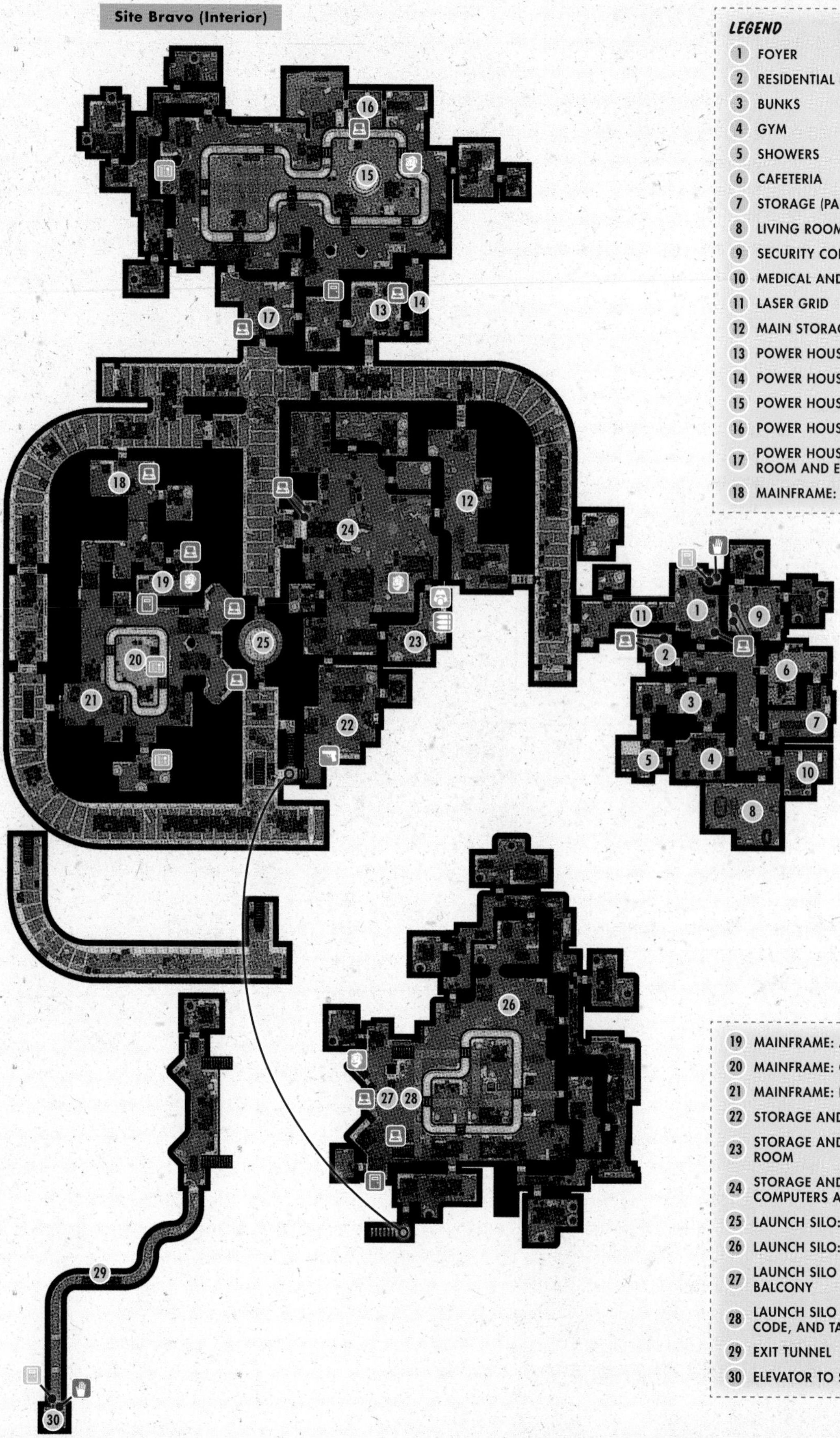

Site Bravo (Interior)

LEGEND

1. FOYER
2. RESIDENTIAL ROOM (BIOMETRICS)
3. BUNKS
4. GYM
5. SHOWERS
6. CAFETERIA
7. STORAGE (PANTRY)
8. LIVING ROOMS AND GAME ROOM
9. SECURITY CONTROL ROOM
10. MEDICAL AND BIOMETRIC SCANNER ROOM
11. LASER GRID
12. MAIN STORAGE CORRIDOR
13. POWER HOUSE: MONITORING ROOM
14. POWER HOUSE: FUMIGATION CORRIDOR
15. POWER HOUSE: REACTOR ROOM
16. POWER HOUSE: REACTOR CONTROL ROOM
17. POWER HOUSE: SECURITY COMMAND ROOM AND EXIT
18. MAINFRAME: ACCESS CONTROL ROOM

19. MAINFRAME: ACCESS CONTROL CORRIDOR
20. MAINFRAME: CENTRAL CHAMBER
21. MAINFRAME: EXIT
22. STORAGE AND FACILITIES: ENTRANCE
23. STORAGE AND FACILITIES: MECHANICAL ROOM
24. STORAGE AND FACILITIES: MAINFRAME COMPUTERS AND EXIT
25. LAUNCH SILO: ENTRANCE
26. LAUNCH SILO: MAIN CHAMBER
27. LAUNCH SILO (UPPER): LAUNCH CONTROL BALCONY
28. LAUNCH SILO (LOWER): LAUNCH KEYCARD, CODE, AND TARGETING COMPUTER
29. EXIT TUNNEL
30. ELEVATOR TO SURFACE

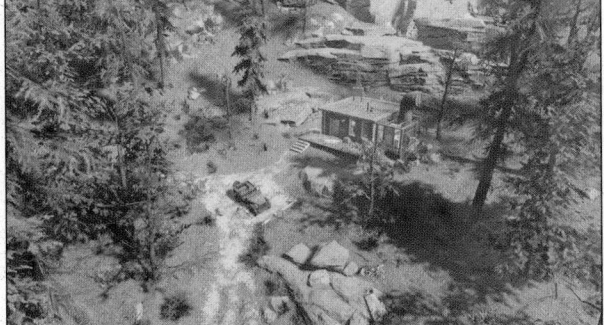

- **COLLECTIBLES:** BOBBLEHEAD (4), MAGAZINE (3), NUKA-CHERRY, POWER ARMOR
- **CRAFTING:** ARMOR (2), POWER ARMOR (2), TINKER'S, WEAPONS (3)
- **DANGER:** EXPLOSIVE CANISTER! OIL!, RADIATION!+++
- **ITEMS:** ARMS AND AMMO++, HEALTH AND CHEMS+, OVERSEER'S CACHE
- **INFO:** EXPECTED ENEMY: ROBOT; QUEST: MISSION: COUNTDOWN BRAVO; SCAVENGE RATING: 4; SIZE: 5; SLEEPING; THREAT LEVEL: 15–99
- **LOCK:** DOOR (3, 3), TERMINAL (3)
- **ITEM EXAMPLES:** ANTIQUE GLOBE, BLUE TABLE LAMP+, BURGUNDY BOTTLE, CLOWN, COFFEE CUP, COOLANT++, CRUSHED RUSTY CANISTER, DIRTY ASHTRAY, DOG TAGS, DUCT TAPE+, ENAMEL BUCKET+, FUMIGUS BLOWTORCH+, FUSE, HAZMAT SUIT+, HOT PLATE+, GLASS JAR, MAINFRAME CORE, MEDICAL LIQUID NITROGEN DISPENSER, MILITARY FATIGUES, MILITARY GRADE CIRCUIT BOARD, MOP+, OFFICE DESK FAN, OLD BIOMETIC ID CARD, PACK OF DUCT TAPE+, PILLOW+, PLASTIC PUMPKIN, POOL BALL+, POOL CUE, PORK N' BEANS, PURIFIED WATER+, RUSTY CANISTER, SCREWDRIVER, SPICES, TIN CAN+, TRIFOLD AMERICAN FLAG, TURPENTINE, TYPEWRITER, UNSTOPPABLE SHINDIG BOARD GAME, SLIDE RULE, USED OIL CAN, WONDERGLUE, WRENCH, YUM YUM DEVILED EGGS

Exterior: One of the three nuclear launch silos is hidden deep below this unassuming brick-walled military hut. Enter to open the Overseer's Cache inside before opening the elevator and using the hand scanner (if the aforementioned quest is active).

Interior: If you've managed to access the scanner as part of the quest, you can finally reach this vast, underground bunker. After fooling the biometric scanner to access the chambers beyond the initial laser grid, you may have to restore power to the reactor, destroy the mainframe, replace the mainframe cores, and defend the section chief robots while they coordinate a possible nuclear strike you (and your cohorts) may be attempting. After the targeting computer is ready, you just need to solve the code and launch that nuke!

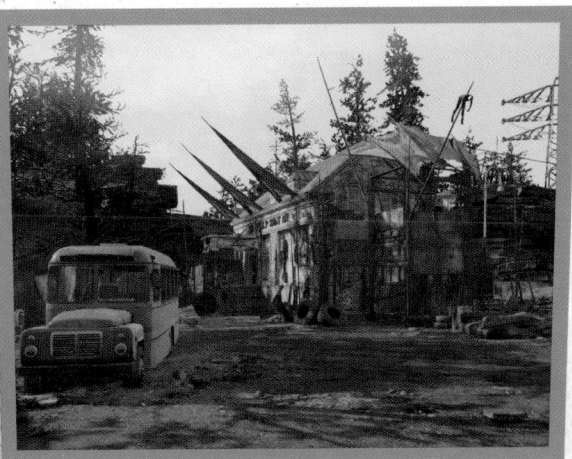

⚡ 06. MONONGAH POWER SUBSTATION MZ-01

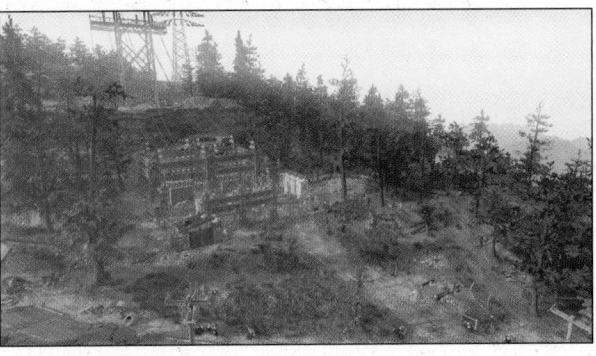

- **DANGER:** EXPLOSIVE CANISTER!
- **ITEM:** HARVESTABLE: WILD CARROT
- **INFO:** C.A.M.P. POWER; EXPECTED ENEMY: SCORCHED; SCAVENGE RATING: 1; SIZE: 1; THREAT LEVEL: 15–99
- **ITEM EXAMPLES:** BALL-PEEN HAMMER, CAN

This run-down substation once provided power to Sunnytop. You can bring it to life again and use the power box to generate energy for your C.A.M.P.

🏚 07. SUNNYTOP STATION

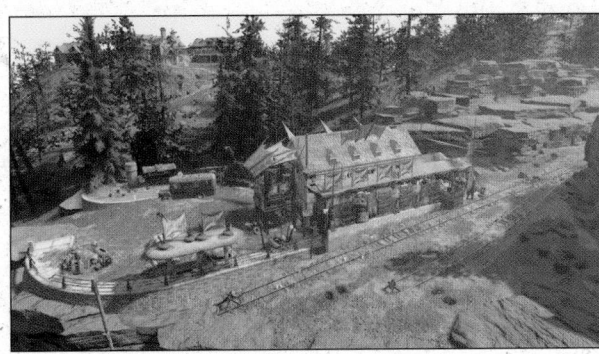

- **CRAFTING:** ARMOR
- **ITEMS:** ARMS AND AMMO; HEALTH AND CHEMS; MY STASH BOX; VENDING MACHINE: AMMUNITION, MEDICAL SUPPLIES
- **INFO:** SCAVENGE RATING: 2; SIZE: 2; SLEEPING; THREAT LEVEL: 15–99; TRADER: VENDOR BOT
- **ITEM EXAMPLES:** ANTIQUE GLOBE, BEER BOTTLE, CRANBERRY MOONSHINE, FIREAXE, LADLE, TEAL ROUNDED VASE, WINE

This was one of the many fortified Raider locations in the Sunnytop complex, and the ramshackle, spiky architecture has been added to a once-idyllic train station exterior. Use this as a base camp when exploring the vicinity, due to the trading and stashing opportunities.

TRAINING

CRAFTING AND C.A.M.P.ING

INVENTORY

QUESTS

ATLAS

BESTIARY

APPENDICES

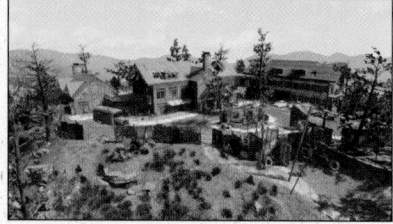

- **COLLECTIBLES:** BOBBLEHEAD (4), HOLOTAPE, MAGAZINE (4), NUKA-CHERRY, POWER ARMOR
- **CRAFTING:** ARMOR, POWER ARMOR, WEAPONS
- **DANGER:** CAN CHIMES! GRENADE! PUNJI BOARD! TRIPWIRE!
- **ITEMS:** ARMS AND AMMO+; HEALTH AND CHEMS+; RECIPE/MOD/PLAN; TRUNK
- **INFO:** EXPECTED ENEMY: IRRADIATED INSECT, SUPER MUTANT; INSTRUMENT; NOTE; SCAVENGE RATING: 4; SIZE: 3; SLEEPING; THREAT LEVEL: 15–99
- **LOCK:** DOOR (C, C, C, KEY), SAFE (2), TERMINAL (1)
- **ITEM EXAMPLES:** ALARM CLOCK, BEER BOTTLE+, BINOCULARS, BLUE TABLE LAMP, BOURBON, BUBBLEGUM, CHESSBOARD, COFFEE CUP, CRAM+, EMPTY WILLOW BARREL VASE, ENAMEL BUCKET, FUSION CORE, GARDEN GNOME, GLASS JAR, GUM DROPS, HAIRBRUSH, MED-X, NEW RIVER RED ALE, NUKA-COLA BOTTLE, PILLOW, PLUNGER, POSTMAN HAT, PURIFIED WATER, RUM, SHORT 10-MM AUTO PISTOL, SKIING OUTFIT HAT, SKI SWORD, SKULL+, SUNNYTOP SKI LANES ROOM 6 KEY, TALL DRINKING GLASS+, TELEPHONE, TIN CANISTER, TOILET PAPER+, WAKEMASTER ALARM CLOCK, WOOD BLOCK+, WOODEN BEER STEIN, YELLOW FEDORA

Sunnytop Ski Lanes (Exterior)

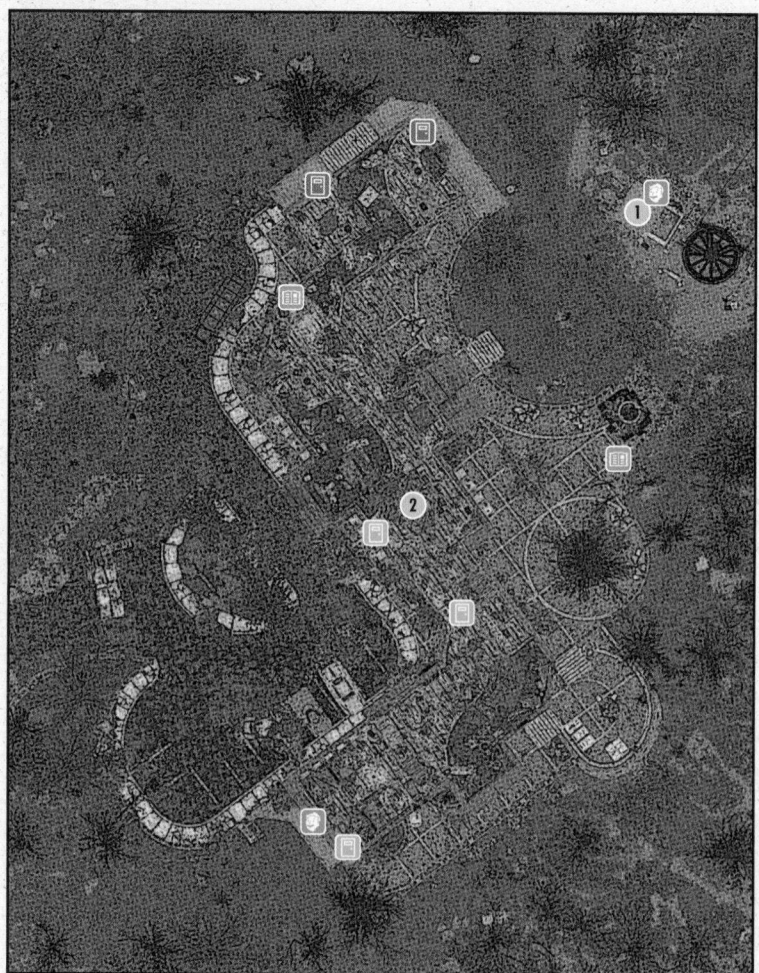

Sunnytop Ski Lanes (Interior)

LEGEND

1. LIFT OPERATOR HUT
2. RECEPTION FOYER
3. ROOM 1
4. ROOM 2
5. ROOM 3
6. DINING AREA AND BAR
7. ROOM 4
8. ROOM 5
9. SKI RENTAL COUNTER
10. MEZZANINE LOUNGE
11. ROOM 6

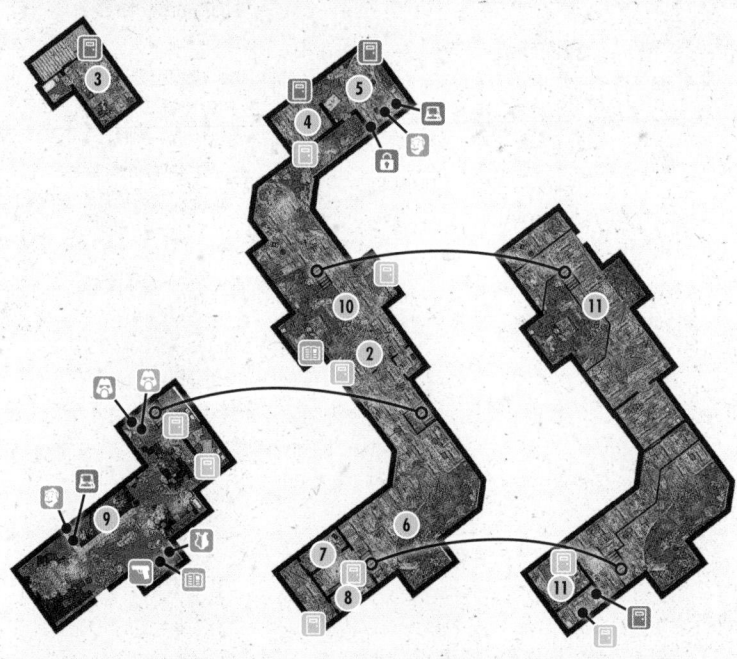

Once a high-class mountaintop ski chalet and hotel, this has changed hands between Raiders and Super Mutants for some time now, and the greenskins seem to be winning. Feel free to mooch around behind the main entrance for an alternate method of entering the three main joined structures, which are spread over three interior floors.

09. SUNNYTOP SKI LANES BASE LODGE

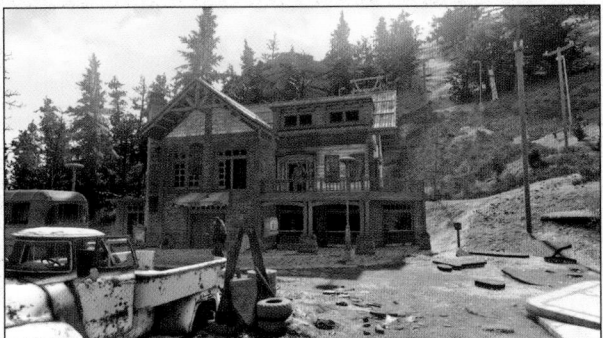

- **COLLECTIBLES:** BOBBLEHEAD (2), MAGAZINE (2), POWER ARMOR
- **DANGER:** PUNJI BOARD! TENSION TRIGGER!
- **ITEMS:** ARMS AND AMMO, HEALTH AND CHEMS
- **INFO:** EXPECTED ENEMY: IRRADIATED INSECT, SCORCHED, SUPER MUTANT; NOTES; SCAVENGE RATING: 3; SIZE: 2; THREAT LEVEL: 15–99
- **ITEM EXAMPLES:** BEER BOTTLE+, BOBBY PIN BOX, BOILED WATER, BURGUNDY BOTTLE, GIDDYUP BUTTERCUP, GLASS JAR, GUM DROPS, HAND CUFFS, NOODLE CUP, PSYCHO, SKI POLE, TELEPHONE, VODKA BOTTLE

This small, green-roofed lodge at the base of the ruined ski lift is usually filled with revolting foes, as well as some choice collectibles. Watch for traps!

10. NORTH MOUNTAIN LOOKOUT

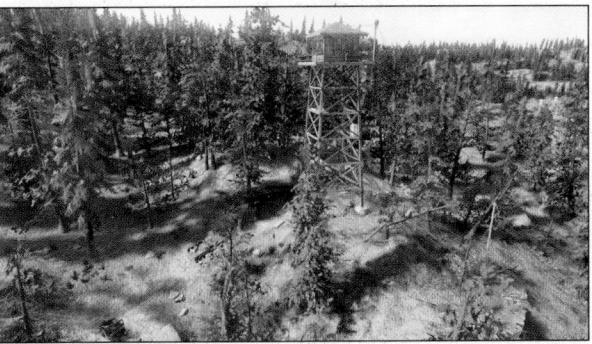

- **DANGER:** LONG DROP!
- **INFO:** NOTES; SCAVENGE RATING: 3; SIZE: 1; SLEEPING BAG, SURVEY AREA; THREAT LEVEL: 15–99
- **ITEM EXAMPLES:** ALARM CLOCK, BINOCULARS, COFFEE POT, COTTON CANDY BITES, CRANBERRY MOONSHINE, ENAMEL BUCKET, FLIP LIGHTER, HALLOWEEN COSTUME SKELETON, HALLOWEEN COSTUME WITCH HAT, GAS CANISTER, OAK HOLLER LAGER, PACK OF CIGARETTES, PLASTIC PUMPKIN, WHISKEY BOTTLE

Need to survey the northern mountains? Then locate this tower on a relatively steep rock slope with light scrub. Check the parked pickup for some minor junk; then scale the tower to its extra-spooky top—there's a Halloween party going on up here!

11. FISSURE SITE SIGMA (FISSURE)

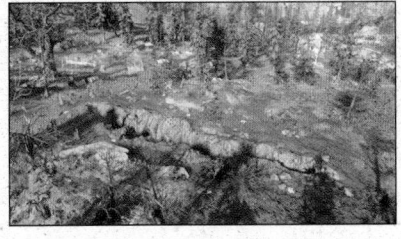

- **DANGER:** LONG DROP! RADIATION!++
- **ITEM:** HARVESTABLE: ULTRACITE
- **INFO:** EXPECTED ENEMY: SCORCHBEAST, SCORCHED; SCAVENGE RATING: 1; SIZE: 1; THREAT LEVEL: 15–99
- **ITEM EXAMPLES:** NOT MUCH!

A large crack in the earth has appeared in the farmland in the neighborhood, close to the Pumpkin House attraction. Exercise extreme caution—there are hordes of Scorched and their winged and monstrous brethren!

12. HOPEWELL CAVE

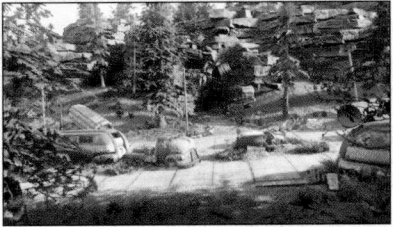

- **COLLECTIBLES:** BOBBLEHEAD, HOLOTAPE, MAGAZINE, POWER ARMOR
- **ITEM:** HARVESTABLE: DEATHCLAW NEST
- **INFO:** EXPECTED ENEMY: DEATHCLAW; SCAVENGE RATING: 2; SIZE: 2; SLEEPING; THREAT LEVEL: 15–99
- **ITEM EXAMPLES:** BLACKWATER BREW BOTTLE, ENAMEL BUCKET, GAS CANISTER, HALLUCINOGEN CANISTER, SKULL

Close to a traffic pileup on the nearby road is a strange cave—all the more eerie if you visit it at night; the glowing fungus causes the cave opening to appear as a large simulacrum of a skull. Inside, expect to need additional verticality to reach some upper ledges. Outside, trek to the top of the hill above the cave to explore a small cemetery.

13. PUMPKIN HOUSE

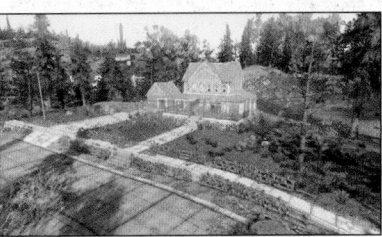

- **CRAFTING:** WEAPONS
- **DANGER:** EXPLOSIVE CANISTER!
- **ITEM:** HEALTH AND CHEMS
- **INFO:** NOTES; QUEST: TRICK OR TREAT?; SCAVENGE RATING: 3; SIZE: 1; SLEEPING; THREAT LEVEL: 15–99
- **ITEM EXAMPLES:** ALARM CLOCK, BOWL, CIGARETTE CARTON, COMBINATION WRENCH, GAS CANISTER, LANTERN, OIL CAN, PAINT CAN, PLASTIC PUMPKIN+, PLASTIC SPOON, SCREWDRIVER, TIN CANISTER, USED OIL CAN, YELLOW TABLE LAMP.

Do you like pumpkins? Not as much as the residents of this abode, who've dressed a Mr. Handy (jack-o'-lantern) up to look like a motorized gourd. You can never have enough pumpkins.

TRAINING

CRAFTING AND C.A.M.P.ING

INVENTORY

QUESTS

ATLAS

BESTIARY

APPENDICES

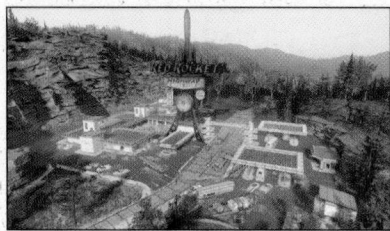

- **COLLECTIBLE:** POWER ARMOR
- **CRAFTING:** COOKING, POWER ARMOR, TINKER, WORKSHOP
- **DANGER:** RADIATION!++

- **ITEMS:** HARVESTABLE: ALUMINUM, JUNK, STEEL, ULTRACITE; HEALTH AND CHEMS; MY STASH BOX (2); VENDING MACHINE: AMMUNITION, MEDICAL SUPPLIES
- **INFO:** EXPECTED ENEMY: VARIES; LANDMARK; QUEST: CLAIM WORKSHOP AT RED ROCKET MEGA STOP; QUEST: WASTE NOT; SCAVENGE RATING: 5 (5+); SIZE: 4; SLEEPING; THREAT LEVEL: 15–99
- **LOCK:** DOOR (1), SAFE (3)
- **ITEM EXAMPLES:** ABRAXO CLEANER, ABRAXO CLEANER INDUSTRIAL GRADE+, BLAMCO BRAND MAC AND CHEESE, BOBBY PIN BOX, BOILED WATER, CANNED DOG FOOD, CIGARETTE CARTON, COFFEE CANISTER, COFFEE CUP+, COOKING PAN, COOLANT, CUTTING BOARD, DIRTY ASHTRAY, DISHRAG, DUCT TAPE+, EXTINGUISHER, FARMHAND CLOTHES, GARDEN GNOME, MILITARY GRADE CIRCUIT BOARD, OFFICE DESK FAN, PORK N' BEANS, PLUNGER+, PORTABLE FUEL TANK, RAT POISON, SCREWDRIVER, SKI SWORD, SOAP, STEW POT+, SUGAR, SUPRATHAW ANTIFREEZE+, TALL DRINKING GLASS+, TIN CANISTER+, TOILET PAPER, WASTE ACID, WHITE PLATE+
- **WORK:** FOOD (5), WATER (8), JUNK (1), ALUMINUM (3), NUCLEAR (1), STEEL (1)

Red Rocket Mega Stop (Exterior)

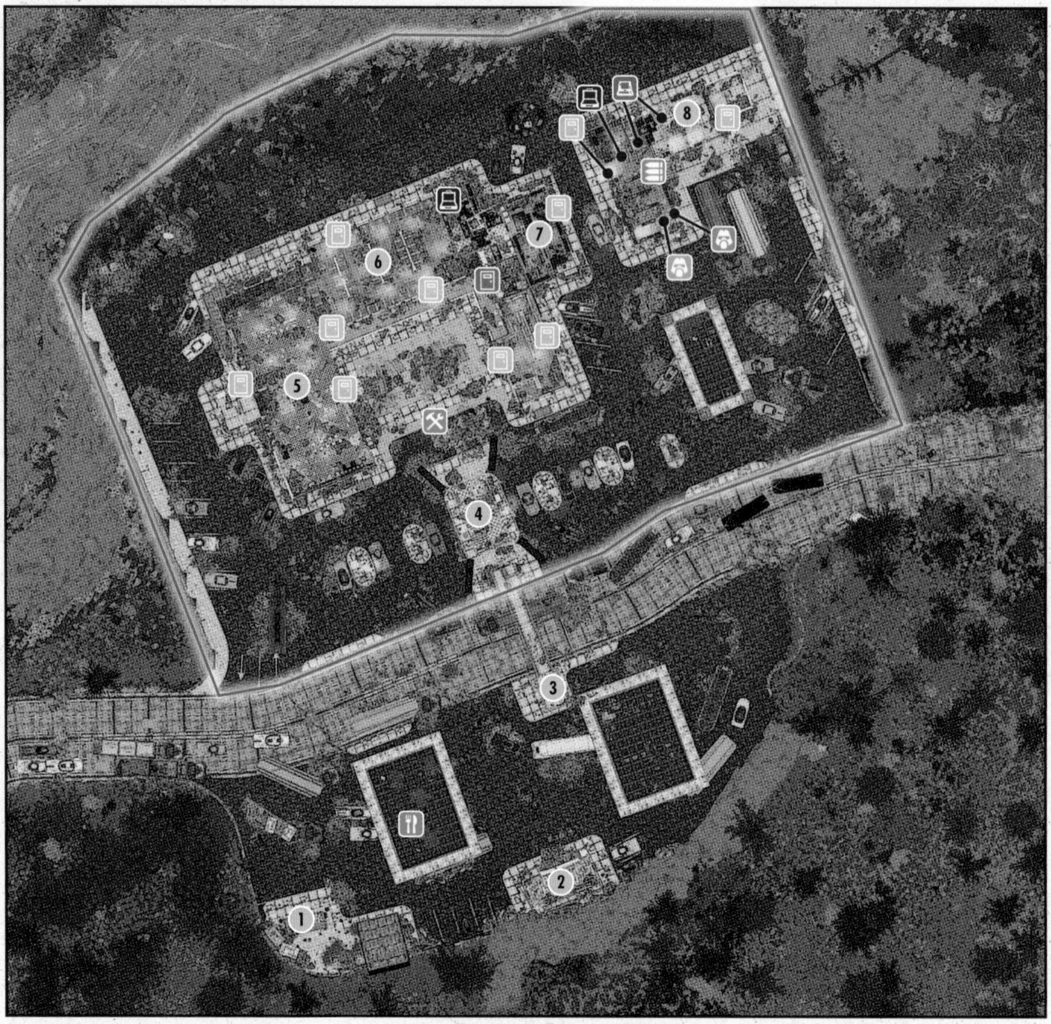

LEGEND

1. BUS STOP
2. RED ROCKET GAS STATION
3. FOOTBRIDGE
4. GAS PUMP STORE
5. RESTROOMS
6. DINER
7. KITCHENS
8. MAINTENANCE, STORAGE, AND SHIPPING

A host of rusting vehicles stand where they were abandoned at this huge Red Rocket Gas Station, diner, and shopping area. Concentrate on the radioactive barrels and patio area at the foot of the giant Red Rocket sign. This is where the workshop is; defend it. Defend, too, the outlying structures (it's easy to build defenses and get onto the low roofs) and scavenge for a multitude of junk.

15. VAULT 94 (VAULT)

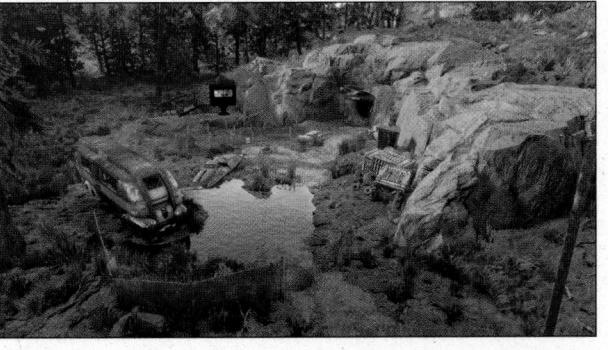

- COLLECTIBLES:
  BOBBLEHEAD,
  CAPS STASH (14),
  MAGAZINE
- ITEMS:
  HARVESTABLE: GIANT
  PITCHER PLANT, WILD
  TATO BLOSSOM;
  HEALTH AND CHEMS
- INFO: SCAVENGE
  RATING: 2; SIZE: 1;
  THREAT LEVEL: 15–99
- ITEM EXAMPLES: COFFEE CUP, HOT PLATE

Vault 94 Entrance (Exterior)

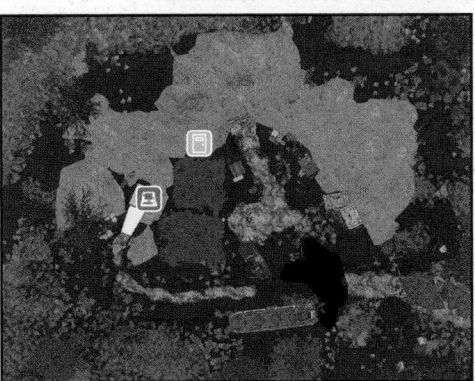

An unassuming cave entrance, close to the rusting remains of a coach, is a clue to a vast subterranean Vault-Tec location, currently sealed (with the possible collectibles inside). You will initially be unable to access the vault via the Vault Access Control Terminal's inner entrance door. Perhaps you could "raid" it at a later date?

16. INGRAM MANSION

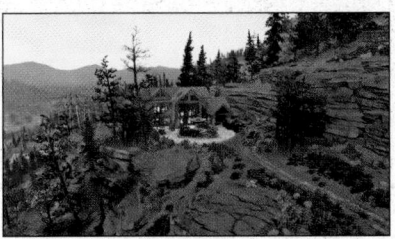

- COLLECTIBLES: BOBBLEHEAD, MAGAZINE
- CRAFTING: WEAPONS
- ITEMS: ARMS AND AMMO; HARVESTABLE:
  FIRECRACKER BERRY, RESIN, WILD CARROT FLOWER;
  HEALTH AND CHEMS; TRUNK
- INFO: EXPECTED ENEMY: ROBOT; SCAVENGE
  RATING: 2; SIZE: 2; SLEEPING; THREAT LEVEL: 15–99
- LOCK: SAFE (1)
- ITEM EXAMPLES: EMPTY TEAL VAULTED VASE,
  GAS CANISTER, OFFICE DESK FAN, PAINT CAN+,
  PEPPER, PIPE BOLT-ACTION PISTOL, PORK N' BEANS,
  SALT, SPICES, WALKING CANE

This mansion sits on a rocky bluff overlooking Morgantown. Its boundary begins at a locked gatehouse (0) with armaments inside. The main lodge needs a lick of paint. You can explore it by stepping through the broken windows.

17. MONONGAH OVERLOOK

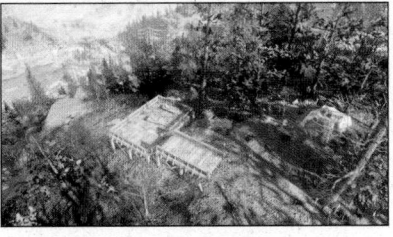

- ITEMS: ARMS AND AMMO; HARVESTABLE:
  BLACKBERRY, WILD CARROT FLOWER
- INFO: EXPECTED ENEMY: SCORCHED, SUPER
  MUTANT, YAO GUAI; NOTES; SCAVENGE RATING: 2;
  SIZE: 2; SLEEPING; THREAT LEVEL: 15–99
- ITEM EXAMPLES: BEER BOTTLE+, BLOWTORCH,
  BONESAW, BOWLING PIN, FASHIONABLE GLASSES,
  GAS CANISTER+, HOT PLATE, MOONSHINE JUG, RAD
  POKER BOARD GAME, SHORT 10-MM AUTO PISTOL,
  WINE BOTTLE

On the winding road atop the mountain mine, expect the remains of a Raider checkpoint, now taken over by some decidedly less savory characters. Close by is the Overlook, offering some tents to check and a wooden deck with impressive vistas across to Grafton lake.

18. MONONGAH MINE

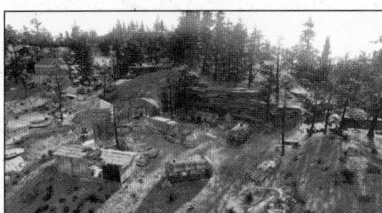

- DANGER: EXPLOSIVE CANISTER!
- ITEMS: ARMS AND AMMO+; HARVESTABLE:
  BLACKBERRY, WILD CARROT FLOWER
- INFO: EXPECTED ENEMY: MOLE MINER, SUPER
  MUTANT; NOTE; SCAVENGE RATING: 3; SIZE: 3;
  SLEEPING; THREAT LEVEL: 15–99
- LOCK: SAFE (2)
- ITEM EXAMPLES: ANTIFREEZE BOTTLE,
  BEER BOTTLE+, BLAST RADIUS BOARD GAME,
  BLOWTORCH, BLUE PAINT, BOWLING PIN,
  DOG BOWL, DOG TAGS, DUCT TAPE, ECONOMY
  WONDERGLUE, GARDEN GNOME, GAS CANISTER+,
  HOT PLATE+, MARKSMAN'S SNIPER RIFLE,
  MOONSHINE JUG, PAINT CAN, PIPE, PLUNGER, RAT
  POISON, STRAW PILLOW, TIN CANISTER+, TOY CAR,
  TUBE FLANGE, USED OIL CAN, WHISKEY BOTTLE,
  YELLOW PAINT

This mine complex was recently taken over and then abandoned by Raiders. Currently, strange other creatures lurk among the roadside fortifications and mine yard. Though there's no interiors to explore, expect to check a road block (near the electrical pylon) by the large "Monongah Mine" sign. Farther up Route 95 is another Raider blockade. The mine consists of a red water tower, various trailers, and a curved roof but its entrance is blocked by fallen rock. Farther up the hill to the east are three boarded-up houses.

19. MONONGAH POWER PLANT

- **COLLECTIBLES:** HOLOTAPE, POWER ARMOR, NUKA-CHERRY
- **CRAFTING:** ARMOR, CHEMISTRY, POWER ARMOR (2), TINKER, WEAPONS (2)
- **DANGER:** LONG DROP! RADIATION!++
- **ITEMS:** ARMS AND AMMO+, HEALTH AND CHEMS+, RECIPE/MOD/PLAN, TRUNK
- **INFO:** EXPECTED ENEMY: ROBOT, SUPER MUTANT; SCAVENGE RATING: 4; SIZE: 5; THREAT LEVEL: 15–99
- **LOCK:** SAFE (2)

- **ITEM EXAMPLES:** ALARM CLOCK, ALUMINUM CANISTER+, ANTIFREEZE BOTTLE, ASHTRAY, BEAKER STAND, BEER BOTTLE+, BLAST RADIUS BOARD GAME, BLOWTORCH, BOBBY PIN BOX, BOURBON BOTTLE, BOWLING BALL, BROOM, CAMERA, CANNED DOG FOOD, CHALK, CHESSBOARD, COFFEE CUP+, COFFEE POT, COMBINATION WRENCH, COOLANT, CRUSHED ORANGE CANISTER, CUTTING BOARD, DANDY BOY APPLES, DESK FAN, DINNER PLATE, DIRTY ASHTRAY, DUCT TAPE, ECONOMY WONDERGLUE, EMPTY MILK BOTTLE, ENAMEL BUCKET+, EXTINGUISHER, FLIP LIGHTER, FUSE, FUSION CORE+++, GAS CANISTER+, HATCHET, HOT PLATE+, INDUSTRIAL LEAGUE BOWLING PIN, LUXOBREW COFFEE POT, OIL CANISTER, MAKESHIFT BATTERY, METAL BUCKET, METAL TUB, MILITARY AMMO BAG, OAK HOLLER LAGER, OIL CAN, OIL CANISTER, PACK OF CIGARETTES, PLUNGER, RAT POISON, RIGHT ARM BONES, SAW, SCREWDRIVER, SUPRATHAW ANTIFREEZE, TELEPHONE, TOASTER, TYPEWRITER, WHISKEY BOTTLE, WONDERGLUE, YELLOW CANISTER

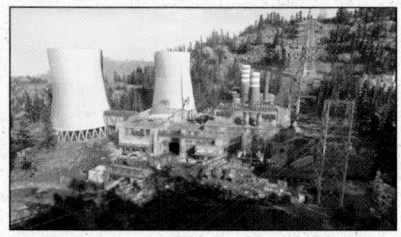

LEGEND

1. MAIN ENTRANCE
2. COOLING TOWER #1
3. COOLING TOWER #2
4. CONTAINER STACKS
5. MAIN POWER PLANT BUILDING
6. PRIMARY LOCATION: MONONGAH POWER PLANT YARD (WORKSHOP)

Monongah Power Plant (Exterior)

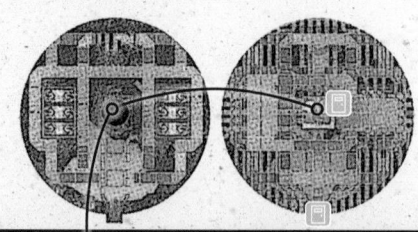

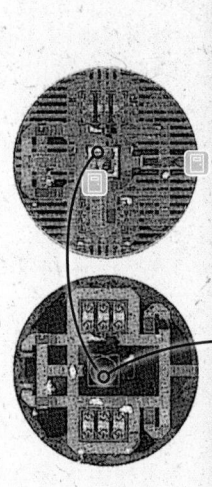

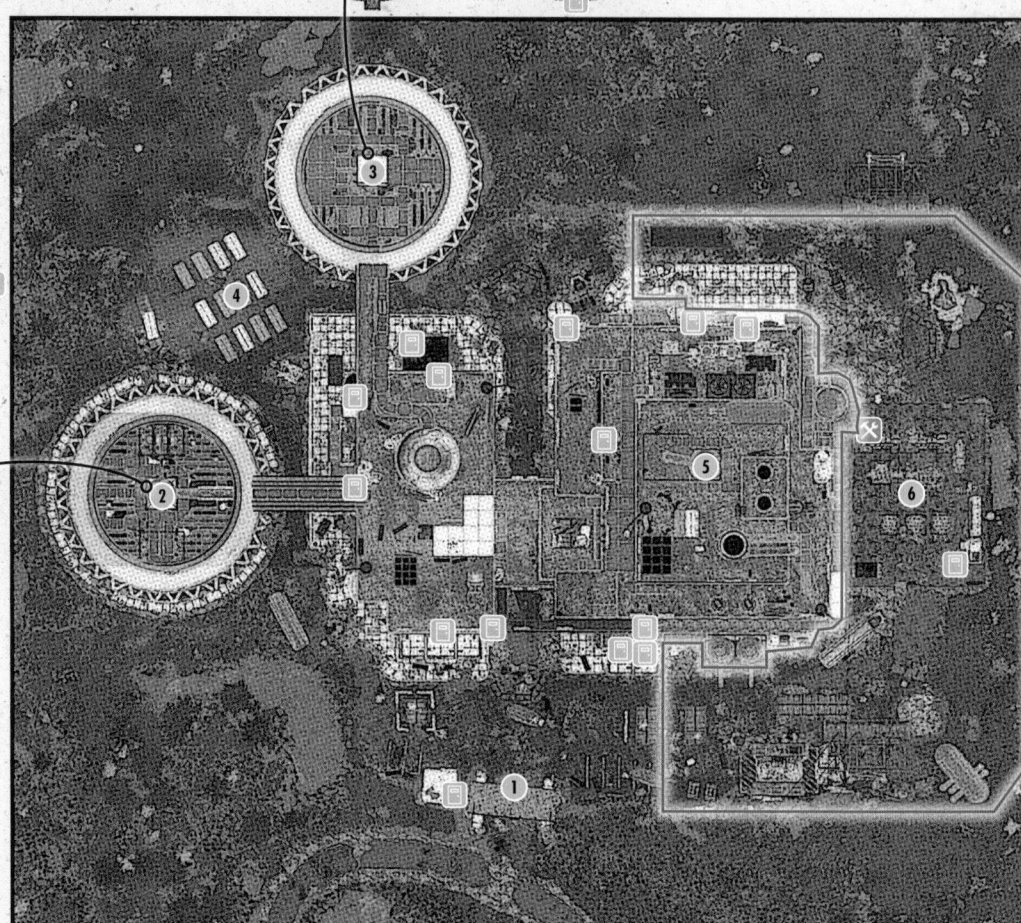

Monongah Power Plant (Interior)

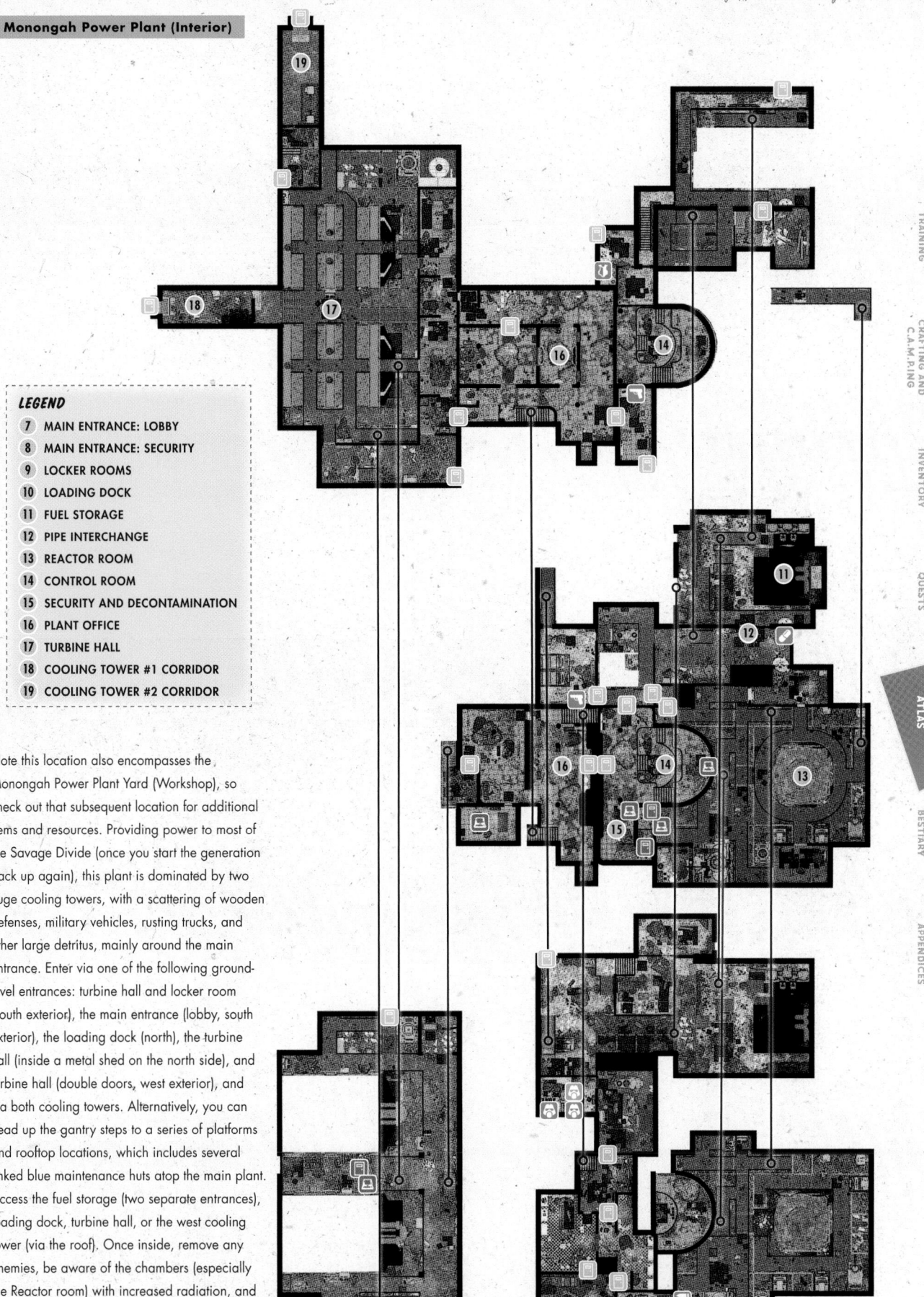

LEGEND

- **7** MAIN ENTRANCE: LOBBY
- **8** MAIN ENTRANCE: SECURITY
- **9** LOCKER ROOMS
- **10** LOADING DOCK
- **11** FUEL STORAGE
- **12** PIPE INTERCHANGE
- **13** REACTOR ROOM
- **14** CONTROL ROOM
- **15** SECURITY AND DECONTAMINATION
- **16** PLANT OFFICE
- **17** TURBINE HALL
- **18** COOLING TOWER #1 CORRIDOR
- **19** COOLING TOWER #2 CORRIDOR

Note this location also encompasses the Monongah Power Plant Yard (Workshop), so check out that subsequent location for additional items and resources. Providing power to most of the Savage Divide (once you start the generation back up again), this plant is dominated by two huge cooling towers, with a scattering of wooden defenses, military vehicles, rusting trucks, and other large detritus, mainly around the main entrance. Enter via one of the following ground-level entrances: turbine hall and locker room (south exterior), the main entrance (lobby, south exterior), the loading dock (north), the turbine hall (inside a metal shed on the north side), and turbine hall (double doors, west exterior), and via both cooling towers. Alternatively, you can head up the gantry steps to a series of platforms and rooftop locations, which includes several linked blue maintenance huts atop the main plant. Access the fuel storage (two separate entrances), loading dock, turbine hall, or the west cooling tower (via the roof). Once inside, remove any enemies, be aware of the chambers (especially the Reactor room) with increased radiation, and claim the quality junk you crave.

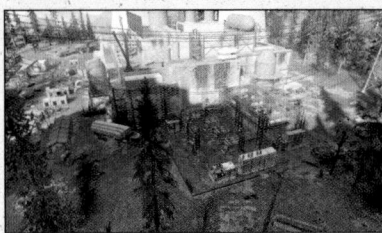

- **CRAFTING:** WORKSHOP
- **DANGER:** RADIATION!+ TURRET!
- **ITEMS:** HARVESTABLE: ACID, FUSION CORE, SILT BEAN, SILVER, URANIUM, WOOD; HEALTH AND CHEMS
- **INFO:** EXPECTED ENEMY: VARIES; QUEST: CLAIM WORKSHOP AT MONONGAH POWER PLANT YARD; SCAVENGE RATING: 3 (5+); SIZE: 4; SLEEPING;

- **THREAT LEVEL:** 15–99.
- **ITEM EXAMPLES:** BEER BOTTLE+, CAMPAIGN HAT, FUSION CORE+++, MILITARY AMMO BAG, OIL CANISTER, PACK OF CIGARETTES, TYPEWRITER+, VOLATILE MATERIALS BOX
- **WORK:** FOOD (8), WATER (9), FUSION CORE (3), SILVER (1), ACID (1), NUCLEAR (1), WOOD (1)

The map for this location is within the perimeter of the Monongah Power Plant (see the red Transformer Yard signs throughout the plant). If you're hankering for Fusion Cores, prepare to claim and defend this workshop, as there's a couple of Fusion Core Processors already within the workshop area, attached to the Monongah Power Box. The workshop itself is on the wire fencing near the power station's substation. Also think about using the gun emplacements too; one is northeast of the workshop.

 21. MONONGAH

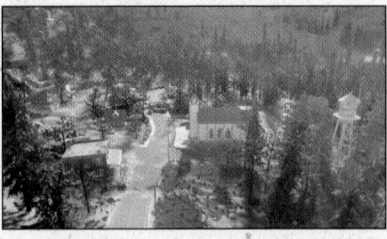

- **ITEM:** ARMS AND AMMO++; HARVESTABLE: ASTER, SOOT FLOWER; HEALTH AND CHEMS++; RECIPE/MOD/PLAN; TRUNK; VENDING MACHINE: AMMUNITION, MEDICAL SUPPLIES
- **INFO:** EXPECTED ENEMY: MOLE MINER, SCORCHED; QUEST: SOMEONE TO TALK TO; SCAVENGE RATING: 4; SIZE: 4; SLEEPING; THREAT LEVEL: 15–99
- **LOCK:** DOOR (1), SAFE (1, 2)
- **ITEM EXAMPLES:** 10-MM PISTOL, ACCIDTOL, BEER BOTTLE++, BLOWTORCH, BOILED WATER+, BONESAW, BROKEN LAMP, CANNED DOG FOOD, CIGAR BOX, CIGARETTE CARTON, COFFEE CUP, COP CAP, COP UNIFORM, DANDY BOY APPLES, ENAMEL BUCKET, FANCY LADS SNACK CAKES, FLOWER POT, GARDEN GNOME, GAS CANISTER+, HANDCUFFS+, INDUSTRIAL SIZE SHORTENING, MICROSCOPE, OFFICE DESK FAN, OIL CANISTER, PATROLMAN SUNGLASSES, PORK N' BEANS, SALISBURY STEAK, SAW, SHORT HUNTING RIFLE, SMALL LEFT ANTLER, STRAIGHT JACKET, SUGAR BOMBS, VAULT-TEC LUNCHBOX, VODKA BOTTLE+

- **COLLECTIBLES:** BOBBLEHEAD, HOLOTAPE, MAGAZINE, NUKA-CHERRY
- **CRAFTING:** CHEMISTRY, COOKING

Monongah (Exterior)

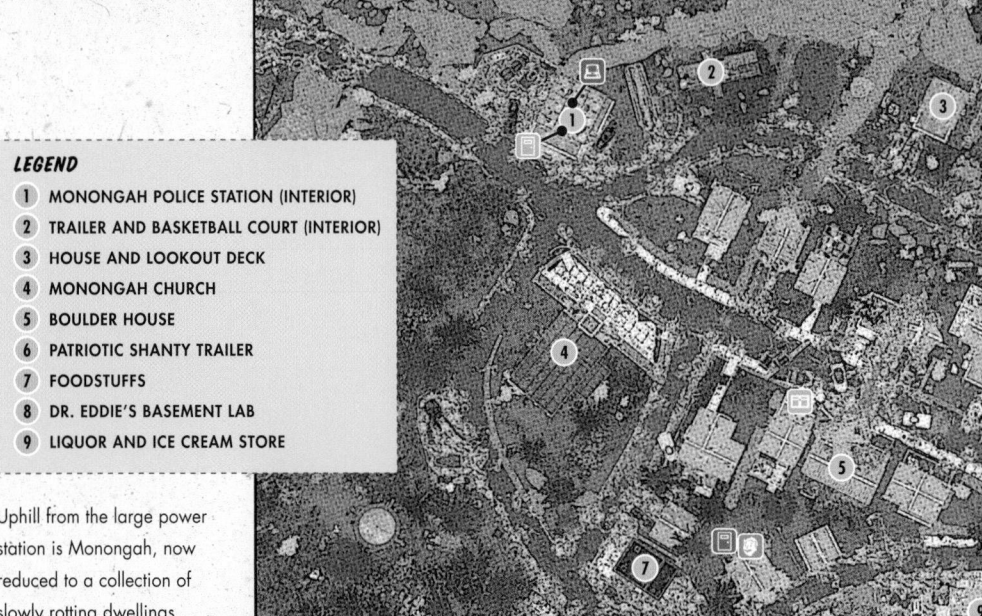

LEGEND
1. MONONGAH POLICE STATION (INTERIOR)
2. TRAILER AND BASKETBALL COURT (INTERIOR)
3. HOUSE AND LOOKOUT DECK
4. MONONGAH CHURCH
5. BOULDER HOUSE
6. PATRIOTIC SHANTY TRAILER
7. FOODSTUFFS
8. DR. EDDIE'S BASEMENT LAB
9. LIQUOR AND ICE CREAM STORE

Uphill from the large power station is Monongah, now reduced to a collection of slowly rotting dwellings. There is evidence of some holdouts, though the large boulders that have recently come crashing down from the mountain above have further damaged this old mining town.

22. OBSERVATORY

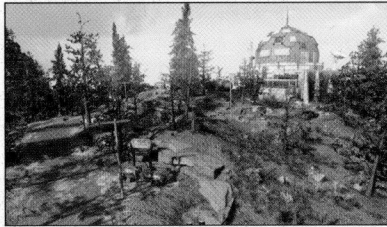

- **COLLECTIBLES:** BOBBLEHEAD, CAPS STASH (8), HOLOTAPE, MAGAZINE, NUKA-CHERRY
- **CRAFTING:** ARMOR, CHEMISTRY (3), WEAPONS (2)
- **ITEMS:** ARMS AND AMMO+, HEALTH AND CHEMS, TRUNK
- **INFO:** EXPECTED ENEMY: ROBOT; LANDMARK; SCAVENGE RATING: 3; SIZE: 4; THREAT LEVEL: 15–99
- **LOCK:** DOOR (0, 0, 1, 1, 2), SAFE (3), TERMINAL (1, 1, 2, 3, 3)
- **ITEM EXAMPLES:** ATLAS UTILITY KEY+, BOBBY PIN BOX, CRYO MINE, DESK FAN, ENAMEL BUCKET, INSTAMASH, OIL CAN, PLASMA MINE, RUM BOTTLE, SECURITY BATON, TACTICAL COMBAT SHOTGUN

LEGEND

1. ACCELERATOR CONTROL ROOM (BASEMENT)
2. SECURITY DESK
3. LOADING BAY
4. ACCESS CONTROL ROOM
5. STORAGE CHAMBER
6. MECHANIC'S WORKROOM
7. ROBOTIC CONTROL ROOM
8. BREAK ROOM
9. MECHANICAL ROOM
10. RESEARCH DATABASE ROOM
11. SCIENTIFIC DIRECTOR'S OFFICE
12. PROTOTYPE DEVELOPMENT LABORATORY
13. WEATHER ANALYSIS ROOM
14. MASTER CONTROL ROOM
15. TELESCOPE AND DOME

Observatory (Exterior)

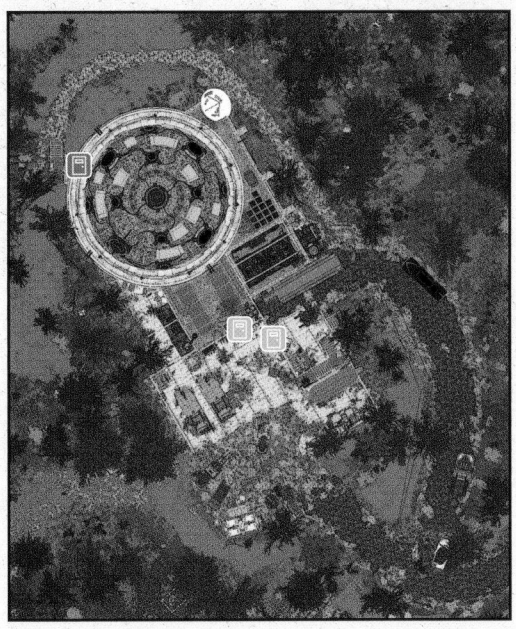

The Atlas Observatory, an atmospheric and astronomic facility, is one of the largest domed telescopes still left standing. It offers loot as well as information on what scientific research was going on before the bombs dropped. Outside, the rocky mountain outcrop upon which the observatory is built offers exceptional views to the west, toward Monongah. There's a small exterior door (2) on the structure's western edge, but the main entrance is on the south side, after navigating an enemy-filled parking lot (or sneaking in via the lower loading dock entrance to the southeast). Inside, the circular structure is somewhat confusing unless you methodically search each chamber, culminating with a check of the giant telescope itself.

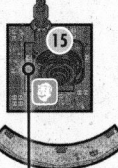

Observatory (Interior)

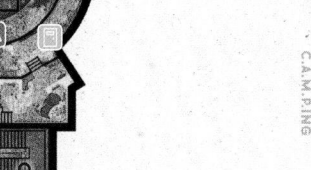

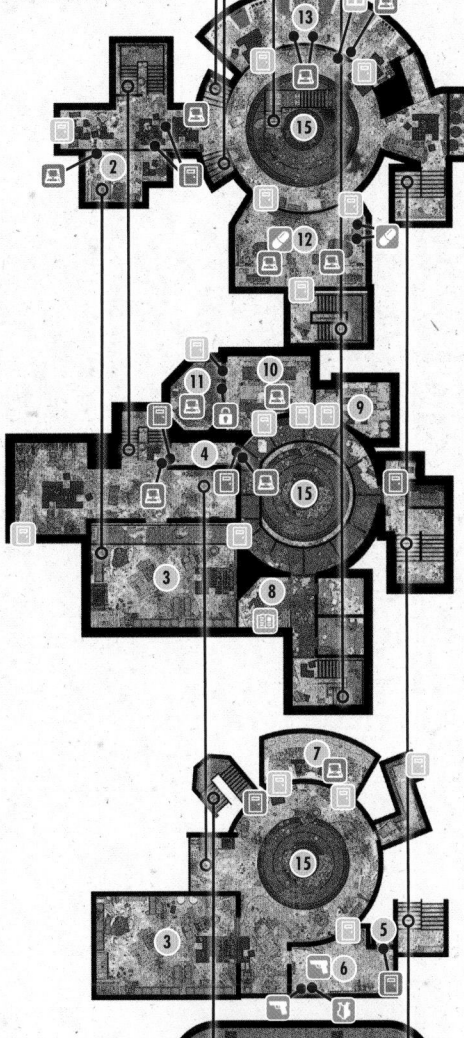

TRAINING

CRAFTING AND C.A.M.P.ING

INVENTORY

QUESTS

ATLAS

BESTIARY

APPENDICES

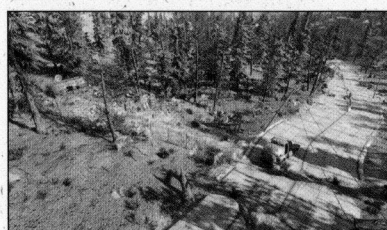

- **COLLECTIBLES:** CAP STASH, POWER ARMOR
- **CRAFTING:** POWER ARMOR
- **DANGER:** TURRET!
- **ITEMS:** ARMS AND AMMO; HARVESTABLE: CORN, WILD GOURD BLOSSOM; HEALTH AND CHEMS
- **INFO:** EXPECTED ENEMY: IRRADIATED INSECT; NOTE; SCAVENGE RATING: 2; SIZE: 1; THREAT LEVEL: 15–99

- **LOCK:** SAFE (1)
- **ITEM EXAMPLES:** CAFETERIA TRAY, COFFEE CUP, COFFEE POT, NUKA-COLA BOTTLE+

This metal caravan is parked at the far end of a small junkyard and is guarded by turrets. Come for the Power Armor Station. Stay for the small collection of skulls?

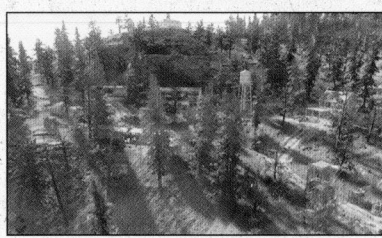 24. SONS OF DANE COMPOUND

- **CRAFTING:** ARMOR, CHEMISTRY (3), COOKING (2), POWER ARMOR, WATER PUMP, WEAPONS.
- **DANGER:** EXPLOSIVE CANISTER!
- **ITEMS:** ARMS AND AMMO++, HEALTH AND CHEMS++, TRUNK
- **INFO:** EXPECTED ENEMY: SUPER MUTANT; INSTRUMENT; SCAVENGE RATING: 4; SIZE: 3; THREAT LEVEL: 15–99
- **LOCK:** DOOR (3)
- **ITEM EXAMPLES:** ABRAXO CLEAN INDUSTRIAL GRADE, BAG OF CEMENT, BEER BOTTLE+++, BINOCULARS, BIRD DECORATION, BLAMCO BRAND MAC AND CHEESE, BOBBY PIN BOX, BOILED WATER+, BROWN BOTTLE++, CREAM, DUCT TAPE, EMPTY WILLOW FLARED VASE, ENAMEL BUCKET, FANCY LADS SNACK CAKES, GLASS JAR+, GLASS PITCHER+, GREASER JACKET AND JEANS, MAGNIFYING GLASS, MAKESHIFT BATTERY, PACK OF CIGARETTES, PAINT POT, PLASMA MINE, PORTABLE FUEL TANK, POTATO CRISPS, ROLLING PIN, SHOT GLASS+, SMALL LEFT ANTLER, STIMPAK, TABLE KNIFE+, TEDDY BEAR, TIN CANISTER+, VODKA BOTTLE+, WINE BOTTLE++, WOOD SAW, YELLOW CANISTER

- **COLLECTIBLES:** BOBBLEHEAD (3), MAGAZINE (3), POWER ARMOR

Sons of Dane Compound (Exterior)

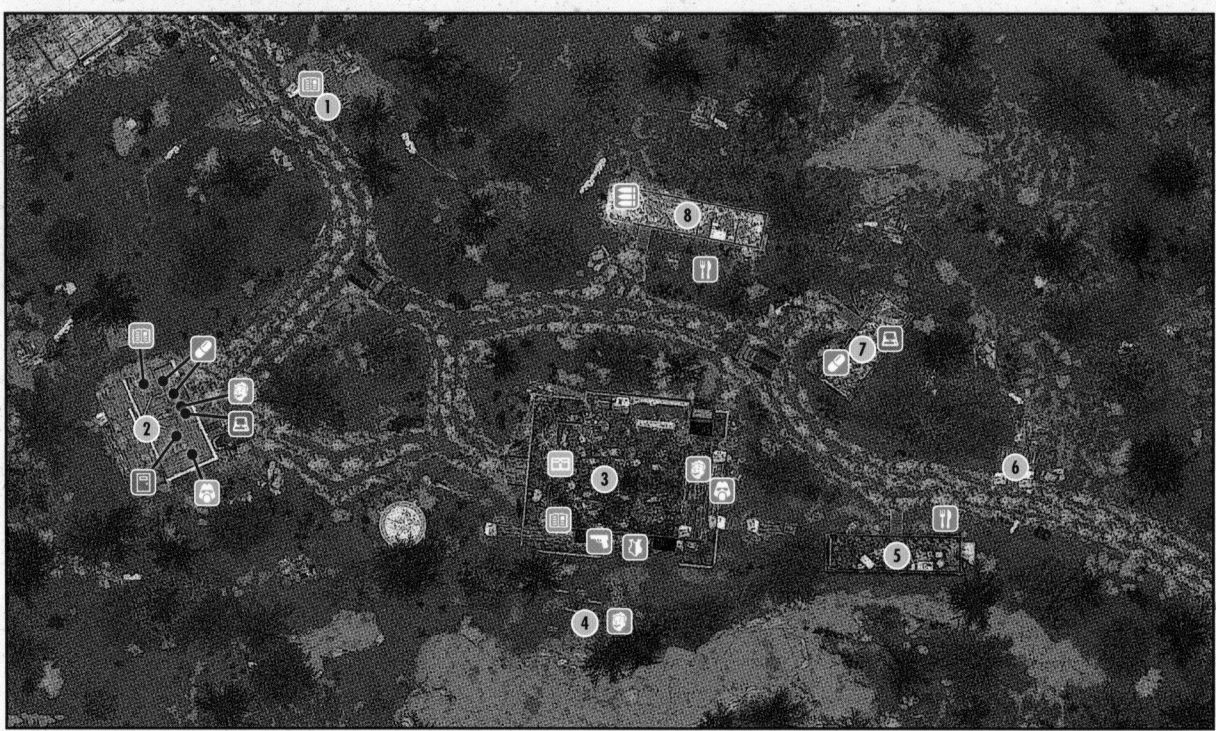

LEGEND
1. GUARD TOWER (NORTH)
2. FADED BLUE FARMHOUSE
3. THE BUCK'S DEN
4. SHOOTING RANGE
5. TRAILER
6. GUARD TOWER (EAST)
7. CHEM TRAILER
8. TINKER'S TRAILER

This small chem-producing compound is ruled over by a Raider offshoot gang. Dane and his cohorts are no longer present, but the place is still dangerous. Check the basement of the faded blue house for a locked security gate (3) behind which may be some Power Armor. There's a whole load of tin canisters and glass bottles at the shooting range, on the hill next to the Buck's Den—Dane's tavern of ill repute.

🗼 25. RELAY TOWER LW-B1-22

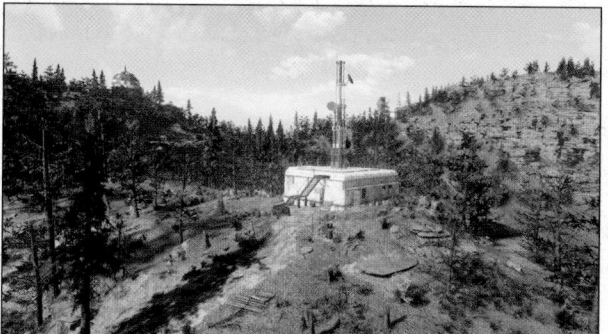

- **COLLECTIBLES:** BOBBLEHEAD, HOLOTAPE, MAGAZINE
- **DANGER:** EXPLOSIVE CANISTER! TRIPWIRE!
- **ITEMS:** ARMS AND AMMO; HARVESTABLE: BLACKBERRY; HEALTH AND CHEMS
- **INFO:** EXPECTED ENEMY: SUPER MUTANT; EVENT: ALWAYS VIGILANT; SCAVENGE RATING: 2; SIZE: 1; THREAT LEVEL: 15–99
- **ITEM EXAMPLES:** ALARM CLOCK, BOILED WATER, FUSION CORE, GAS CANISTER+, NEW RIVER RED ALE, PIPE REVOLVER, SCALPEL

Should you wish to visit one of the mountain summits and access the Emergency Management System Relay Terminal (after repairing it first), then head to this small radio transmitter.

⌂ 26. SYLVIE & SONS LOGGING CAMP

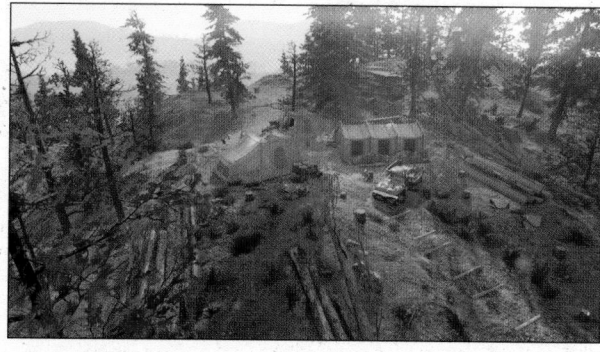

- **COLLECTIBLES:** BOBBLEHEAD (2), MAGAZINE (2)
- **CRAFTING:** COOKING
- **ITEMS:** HARVESTABLE: BLACKBERRY, WOOD++; RECIPE/MOD/PLAN
- **INFO:** EXPECTED ENEMY: IRRADIATED INSECT; SCAVENGE RATING: 2; SIZE: 1; SLEEPING; THREAT LEVEL: 15–99
- **ITEM EXAMPLES:** ALUMINUM CAN, MATERIALS BOX, SUGAR BOMBS, TOMAHAWK, VOLATILE WHISKEY

The mountaintop forest in this area was once cleared and chopped into more manageable stacks of wood, which can now be scavenged, along with other junk items at this tent camp.

ZONE A: SECONDARY LOCATIONS

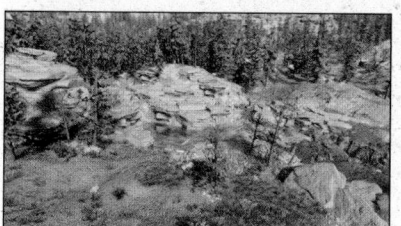

Bailey Family Pond

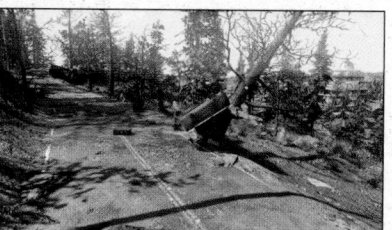

Oil Slick on Route 98

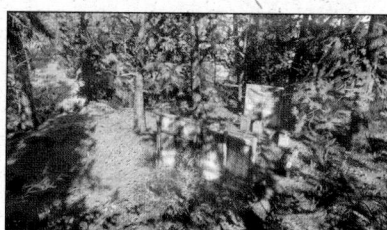

North Mountain Oratory Camp

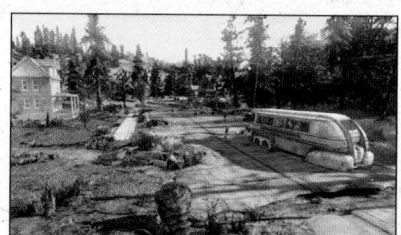

Pumpkin House Neighbors: Plastic Peoples' Bus

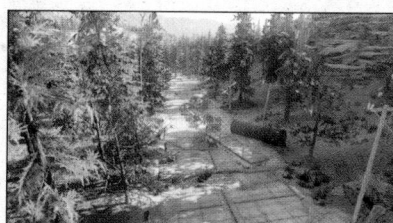

Vehicle Pile-up on I-63

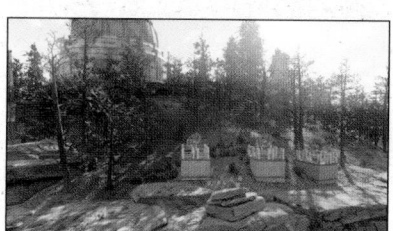

Observatory Silo

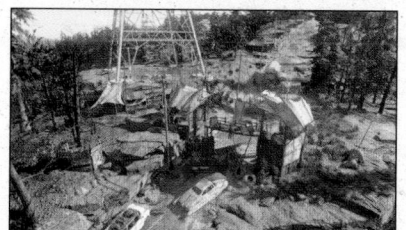

Wreckage Camp and Raider Lookout

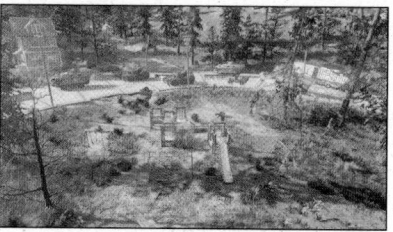

Pumpkin House Playground (and Military Convoy)

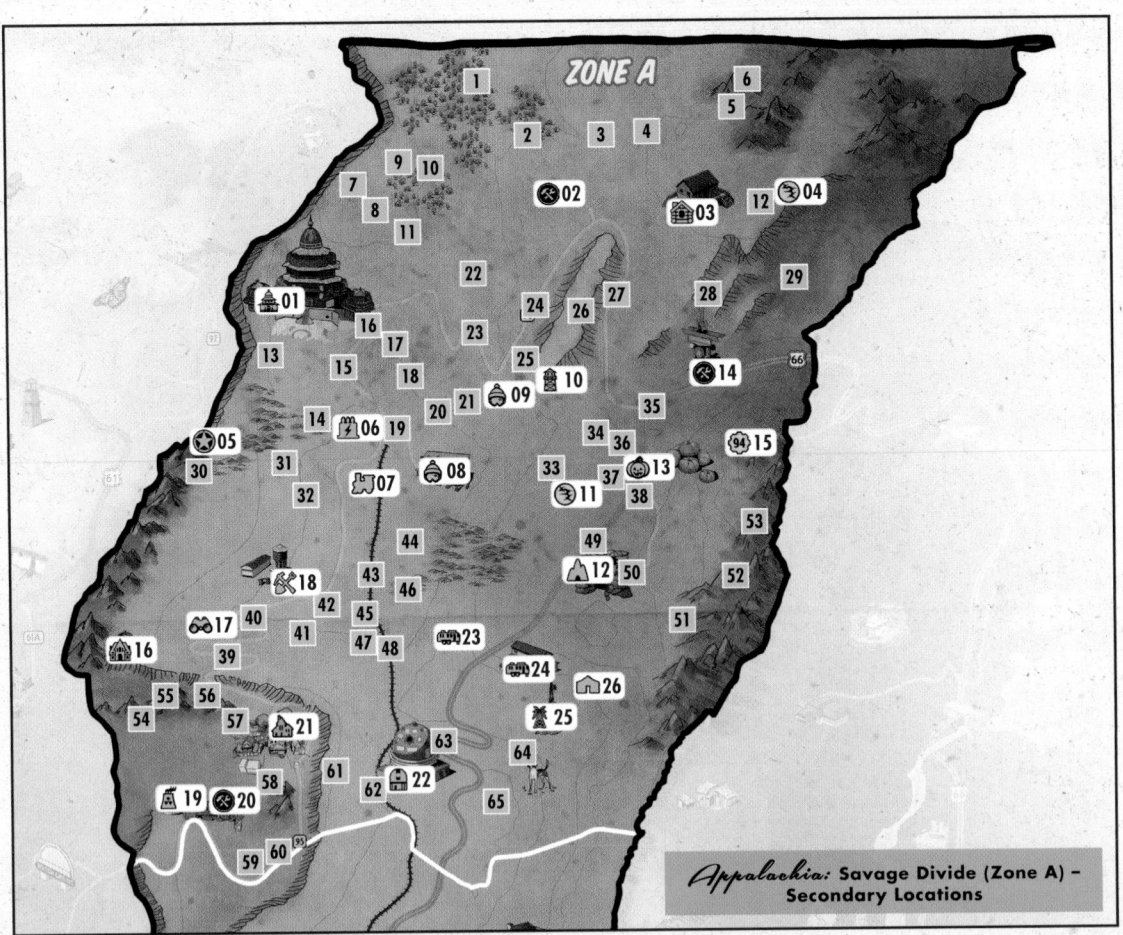

Appalachia: Savage Divide (Zone A) –
Secondary Locations

#	NAME	DESCRIPTION
1	Tent Town at Trail Picnic Spot	There are multiple tents and sleeping bags to check out at this information post along the northern trail.
2	The Hunter's Comeuppance	A wooden deck along the trail, at a small rock outcrop, features a couple of fallen skeletal hunters and a recently culled Yao Guai.
3	Razor Edge Raider Camp	A medium-sized Raider camp, constructed from a trail picnic area north of the Converted Munitions Factory.
4	Rustbucket Shrine	A circular henge of vehicles, with a central car fashioned into a rough throne, possibly for a deranged (and now dead) Raider chief.
5	Cave at Wilderness Edge	A cave opening, good hiding spot, and small interior with three sleeping bags, a cooking station, and some junk to gather.
6	Safe Robbers' Standoff	A pickup parked on a cliff still has a safe on the back; the robbers attempted to settle their differences using blind, ugly violence.
7	Water Purifier Pond and Camp (southeast of Prickett's Fort)	A water purifier sits on a clifftop pond, with two tents and a sleeping bag.
8	Raider's Last Flight	A pistol, ammo, and chems lie next to a dead Raider pilot and her crashed plane.
9	Toxic Junk Dump	A cluster of scrap and junk, some of it radioactive, along with two truck trailers. Pick the lock of one for a chance at Power Armor!
10	Low Foothills Cyclists' Camp	Rugged terrain, two small white tents, and a cooking station on a bluff edge where bikes (and lives) have been discarded.
11	Car Henge	Amid the high mountain forests, someone has erected a circle of half-buried cars. What fresh demonry is this?
12	Bailey Family Pond	A large irradiated pond with a teddy enjoying that tire ring; check the pond bed for a locked safe.

#	NAME	DESCRIPTION
13	Mole Miners' Camp	A steep rocky hill with strewn pipes and debris, and a small collection of junk at the top, manned by the Mole Miners.
14	Hilltop House Ruins	There's still some junk to gather (dinner plates anyone?) at this almost-completely-destroyed home.
15	Pickup Truck Crash (Route 98)	A pickup veered off the sharp corners of the main road, but the real prize is a gravel pit in the vicinity.
16	Oil Slick on Route 98	The road is messy, as a vehicle flipped and struck a pole, oil leaking everywhere.
17	Wreckage Camp and Raider Lookout	Aster flowers grow where Raiders once murdered and strung up their foes. Check this lookout for items, too.
18	Mole Miner Network (North)	Mole Miners have gathered scrap and chimes and have blocked off small mine shafts in this area.
19	Monongah Power Truck Jackknife	There's rusty vehicle parts, tires, and some scattered items outside the substation at the road junction here.
20	Mole Miner Network (South)	Mole Miners have gathered scrap and chimes and have blocked off small mine shafts in this area.
21	Sunnytop Steps	If you're following the hiking trail, check the long deck steps with a "car bed" camp at the bottom of them.
22	Vertibird Crash Site (Converted Minions Factory)	No one survived the crash of this craft, with wings and fuselage everywhere, on mountainous terrain southwest of the factory.
23	Military Checkpoint (Route 98)	A platform, parked vehicles, and a green tent with some loot to gather, on the high forest road.
24	Caution! Fallen Rocks on Route 98	The warning signs are there for a reason; falling rocks have blocked the road, though this is the least of your worries.
25	North Mountain Oratory Camp	Tainted milk? It seems a group of folks all took milk; their skeletal corpses lie bleaching in the sun in this small gathering place.

#	NAME	DESCRIPTION
26	Military Checkpoint (North Route 98)	This tent and road block haven't quite been picked clean yet; check it and the various rusting road vehicles for chems.
27	Roadside T-Bone (Route 98)	A particularly vicious accident involving two vehicles on a remote and sharp corner of the road.
28	Deathclaw Alcove	Corpses and cracked eggs lie under a shallow rock alcove, close to where Deathclaws have been known to prowl.
29	Mole Rat Watering Hole	Someone has been tipping trash into a tiny dirty pond in these remote parts. Check the pond for two bodies and a crate to open.
30	Cultist Barrel Storage	A collection of half-buried barrels below a strange Mothman cultist totem.
31	Cliffside Picnic and Parasols	A cooking station, "beer basketball," and fantastic vistas await if you can reach this remote and rocky picnic.
32	End of the Road (Trailer)	A friend of Vincent's has left a note inside the locked trailer, which had crashed and slid down this hill.
33	Halloween Fright Farm	A small ticket shed and some Halloween-themed farm fields, though the real terror is the nearby fissure.
34	Pumpkin House Neighbors: Glamping Site	Featuring a cooking station, picnic table, and expanded green caravan, welcome to the latest in camping technology.
35	Pumpkin House Playground (and Military Convoy)	Stalled on Interstate 66 is a military convoy, close to a small playground.
36	Pumpkin House Neighbors	A group of dilapidated homes, some without roofs and some with junk to grab in and around them.
37	Pumpkin House Neighbors: Container Cottage	A roofless cottage, with a variety of containers cunningly jammed into it.
38	Pumpkin House Neighbors: Plastic Peoples' School Bus	A yellow school bus filled with passengers of the plastic persuasion.
39	Monongah Switchbacks (Log Truck)	A logging truck has fallen down through the switchback road on a descent from the mine summit.
40	Monongah Mine West Raider Checkpoint	The Raiders' mine dominance used to stretch west to this road checkpoint, which has two lookouts and a hilltop shack with junk to grab.
41	Mine Cart Camp	Another part of the Monongah mine Raider camp complex. There are mine carts here. Climb the rocks to a small white tent, too.
42	Monongah Mine East Raider Checkpoint	A Raider checkpoint with lookouts on both sides of the road, a mattress, ammo, and a hilltop shack to rummage through.
43	Lonely Railroad Shack	This small red shed used to house a variety of workman's items; now these are mostly stolen and the shack fallen into dereliction.
44	The Lovebirds (south of Sunnytop)	A bony groom and his plastic bride are enjoying bathtub relaxation in the back of a pickup, on the rough scree slopes in this area.
45	Railroad Ravine Raider Camp	A railroad gorge between two rock walls is the perfect place for an ambush, which is why Raiders camped here.
46	Top of the Hill Military Camp	A green tent and small satellite dish are on this hillside, which has impressive views in all directions.
47	Vehicle Pileup on I-63	A locked safe, a sealed mine tunnel, a rusting crane, and Raider corpses are in this shanty camp, which has three main structures.
48	Monongah Mine Tower	A massively tall wooden tower that used to dump coal on carriages. Now it's a good landmark when exploring the mine area.
49	Vehicle Pileup on I-63	There are numerous rusting vehicles, including a coach to sleep in, and a locked (3) big-rig full of bikes.
50	Hopewell Cave Graves	A small hilltop cemetery above the cave, with some strangely arranged skulls. Possible cultist activity?

#	NAME	DESCRIPTION
51	East Ridge Hunter's Pickup	There's a Radstag corpse here for the skinning, though the hunter may have been eaten by wolves. Check the cooking station too.
52	Clifftop Vista Cabin	Take a friend to this half-finished cabin with epic views across the Mire; come for the Weapons Workbench, Water Pump, mods, and more!
53	Two Ponds at East Ridge	The remains of a watering hole play area with a picnic table and a river leading down into the Mire.
54	Ingram Guardhouse	A guardhouse on the outskirts of Ingram Manor has some ammo and items to discover both inside and around the small hut.
55	Ingram Overlook Camp	An orange tent, small deck with two picnic tables, and impressive views, and even a Caps Stash to gather on this cliffside camp.
56	Yao Guai Alcove (Monongah)	A shallow alcove below the rock ridge holds carcasses of slain beasts, killed by Yao Guai. Or something worse?
57	Monongah Campground	A tent and barbecue northwest of town, with majestic views of...the power plant.
58	Comms Shed (Monongah)	Strange wiring from the tree and a small shed with a safe (2) in it. Is this anything to do with the nearby basement lab in Monongah?
59	Woodland Outhouse	Northwest of Seneca Rocks Visitor Center is a small outhouse, now a storage shed.
60	Seneca Gardener's Truck	Aster and Wild Carrot Flower grow in the back of this half-buried pickup truck, off the road south of Monongrah.
61	Fisherman's Lookout (west of Observatory)	Raiders with a penchant for fishing managed to scavenge and place the cabin of a boat atop one of their spiky lookouts, on this rock ledge.
62	Observatory Silo	A talo electronics silo, a rusty bike with a skeletal rider, and three smaller satellites; all are on this upper ridge.
63	Observatory Control Point	A small Raider lookout checkpoint on the road, with some minor boxes to loot from.
64	Crashed Prop Plane	A propeller plane took a grooved chunk out of the landscape when it crashed in this remote area.
65	The Yellow Bike Tent	A cyclist has parked their bike at a fallen tent, with a cooking station and Acid to harvest if you peer over the edge of the cliff.

TRAINING

CRAFTING AND C.A.M.P.ING

INVENTORY

QUESTS

ATLAS

BESTIARY

APPENDICES

SAVAGE DIVIDE: ZONE B— CENTRAL MOUNTAINS, PLEASANT VALLEY, AND WHITESPRING

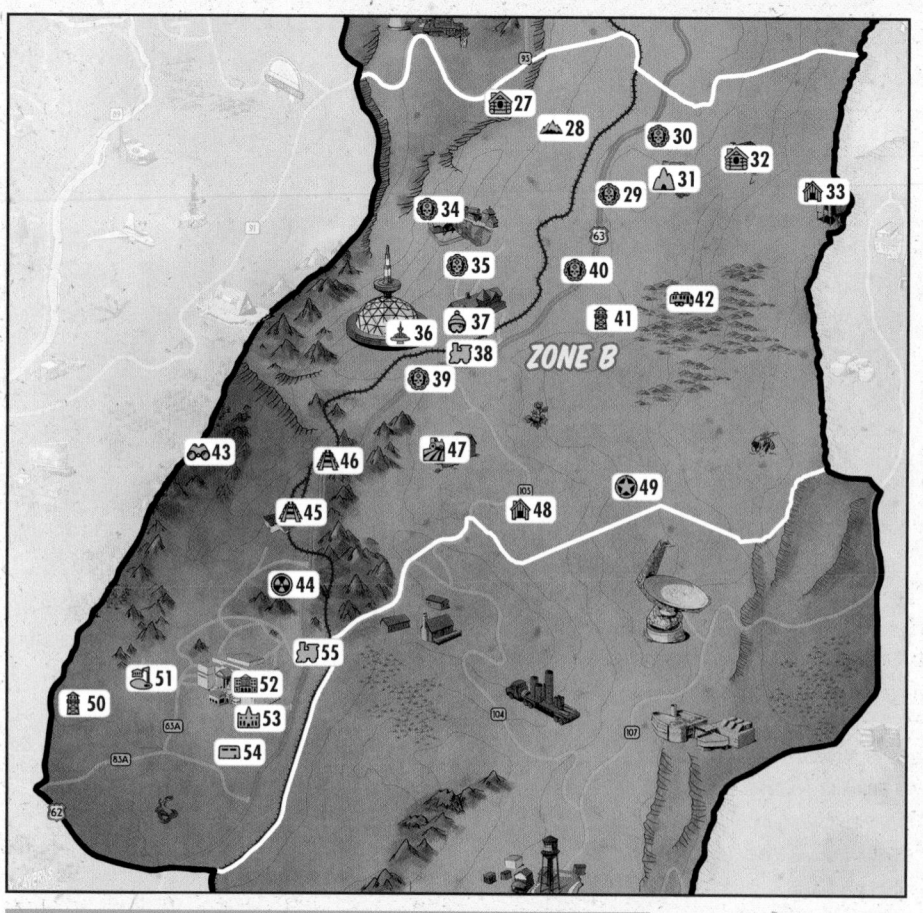

The central part of Savage Divide has a southwestern peninsula stretching to the edge of the Forest and the Ash Heap. Here there are geographical wonders (the Seneca Rocks); cave systems with cryptids (the infamous Wendigo Cave); and a huge ski resort (Pleasant Valley) with cabins, lodges, and the "map thumbtack" known as Top of the World (a landmark so large it can be seen from pretty much every region). Then there are the smaller, but no less bizarre locales: a shack selling strange meat, a chemical disposal site not living up to its name, and a huge derailment with numerous rusting carriages to inspect. But the finely manicured golf course, marble-white grand hotel, and hidden subterranean bunker—part of The Whitespring complex where the nation's greatest minds (and politicians) sought refuge—is perhaps the most intriguing location to attempt to infiltrate.

Appalachia: **Savage Divide (Zone B) – Primary Locations**

WORLD MAP LEGEND

— REGION BOUNDARY   — ZONE BOUNDARY

PRIMARY LOCATIONS

■ BOBBLEHEADS   ■ CAP STASHES   ■ MAGAZINES   ■ POWER ARMOR

				icon	NAME
				27	SENECA ROCKS VISITOR CENTER
				28	SENECA ROCKS
				29	THE SLUDGE HOLE
1		1	1	30	SENECA GANG CAMP
4	1	4	1	31	WENDIGO CAVE
1		1		32	AUTUMN ACRE CABIN
2		2		33	TOXIC LARRY'S MEAT 'N GO
1		1		34	SKULLBONE VANTAGE
2		6	1	35	PLEASANT VALLEY CABINS
3		4		36	TOP OF THE WORLD
3		3		37	PLEASANT VALLEY SKI RESORT
				38	PLEASANT VALLEY STATION
4		2		39	SOUTH CUTTHROAT CAMP
1		2		40	NORTH CUTTHROAT CAMP
				41	CENTRAL MOUNTAIN LOOKOUT

				icon	NAME
1		1		42	YELLOW SANDY'S STILL
1		1	1	43	CLIFFWATCH
1		1		44	SAFE 'N CLEAN DISPOSAL
1		3	1	45	NEW APPALACHIAN CENTRAL TRAINYARD
1		1		46	98 NAR REGIONAL
			1	47	BECKWITH FARM
				48	BIG FRED'S BBQ SHACK
4		3	1	49	SITE ALPHA
				50	WHITESPRING LOOKOUT
3	2	4		51	WHITESPRING GOLF CLUB
	2			52	THE WHITESPRING RESORT
	10			53	WHITESPRING SERVICE ENTRANCE
	2		1	54	THE WHITESPRING BUNKER
				55	WHITESPRING STATION

ZONE B: PRIMARY LOCATIONS

MAP LEGEND
- MY STASH BOX
- OVERSEER'S CACHE
- TRUNK
- TRADER

COLLECTIBLES
- BOBBLEHEAD
- MAGAZINE
- POWER ARMOR

CRAFTING
- ARMOR WORKBENCH
- CHEMISTRY WORKBENCH
- COOKING STATION
- POWER ARMOR STATION
- TINKER'S WORKBENCH
- WEAPONS WORKBENCH
- WORKSHOP WORKBENCH

IMPORTANT
- DOOR/GATE
- LOCKED DOOR/GATE
- SAFE
- SCANNER
- TERMINAL

27. SENECA ROCKS VISITOR CENTER

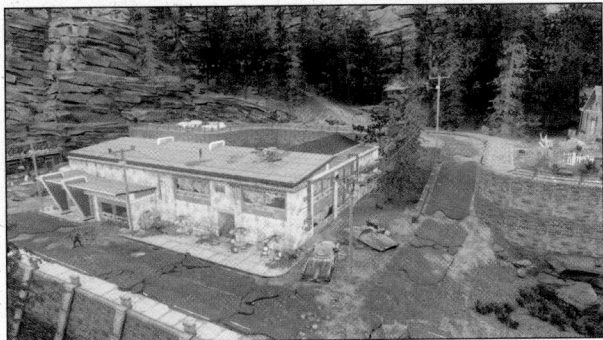

- **COLLECTIBLE:** NUKA-CHERRY+
- **CRAFTING:** COOKING, POWER ARMOR, TINKER, WEAPONS
- **ITEMS:** ARMS AND AMMO, HEALTH AND CHEMS, MY STASH BOX, RECIPE/MOD/PLAN, TRUNK
- **INFO:** EXPECTED ENEMY: GHOUL, IRRADIATED INSECT; SCAVENGE RATING: 3; SIZE: 3; THREAT LEVEL: 15–99
- **ITEM EXAMPLES:** ALUMINUM CAN, BEER BOTTLE+, BOBBY PIN BOX, BOILED WATER+, CAFETERIA TRAY+, CAN+, CARLISLE TYPEWRITER, COFFEE CUP, CRAM, DOLL, FLARE, GLASS PITCHER, METAL BUCKET+, PAINTBRUSH, PAINT CAN, PEPPER, PRE-WAR MONEY+, PURIFIED WATER, SPICES, STIMPAK, SURGICAL TRAY, YELLOW CANISTER, WOOD BLOCK, YUM YUM DEVILED EGGS

A trio of cottages (ransacked but in relatively good shape) and a torn-up cabin sit above a small motel and Red Rocket Gas Station at the foot of the massive Seneca Rocks formation. Utilize the My Stash Box (in the Red Rocket Gas Station) for all your junk-transferring needs.

28. SENECA ROCKS

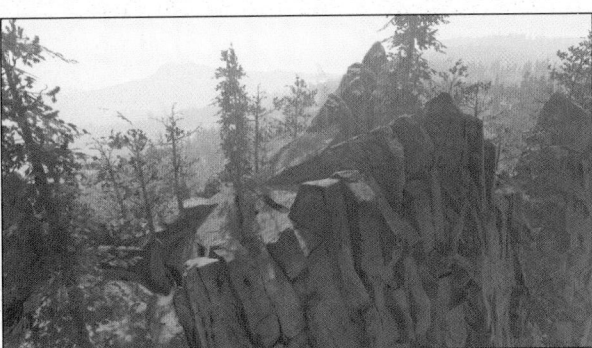

- **INFO:** LANDMARK; SCAVENGE RATING: 1; SIZE: 5; THREAT LEVEL: 15–99

This inaccessible fin-like peak, also known colloquially as "razorback ridge," is a massive mountain of quartzite and cannot be climbed. However, there is a path south of the Visitor Center that cuts up and east toward the railroad and Interstate 63.

29. THE SLUDGE HOLE

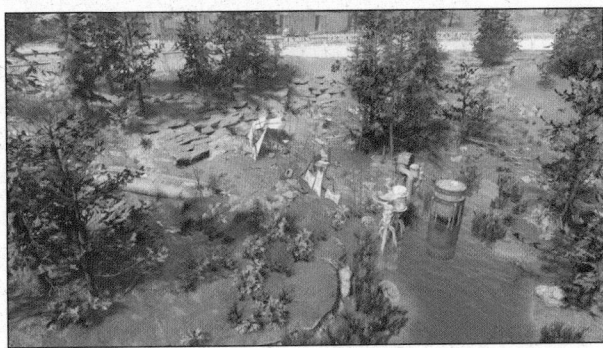

- **CRAFTING:** COOKING.
- **DANGER:** EXPLOSIVE CANISTER! RADIATION!
- **ITEMS:** HARVESTABLE: WOOD PILE; RECIPE/MOD/PLAN; TRUNK
- **INFO:** EXPECTED ENEMY: IRRADIATED ANIMAL; SCAVENGE RATING: 2; SIZE: 1; THREAT LEVEL: 15–99
- **LOCK:** SAFE (X2) (U, U)
- **ITEM EXAMPLES:** ALUMINUM CAN, BLAMCO BRAND MAC AND CHEESE, BOILED WATER++, GAS CANISTER, NUKA-COLA, PURIFIED WATER, VODKA

The delightfully named Sludge Hole is one of the small Raider camps dotted around the vicinity of Pleasant Valley. This one is adjacent to a small toxic lake, with some purification machinery still standing.

TRAINING

CRAFTING AND C.A.M.P.ING

INVENTORY

QUESTS

ATLAS

BESTIARY

APPENDICES

30. SENECA GANG CAMP

- **COLLECTIBLES:** BOBBLEHEAD, MAGAZINE, NUKA-CHERRY, POWER ARMOR
- **CRAFTING:** COOKING (X2)
- **ITEMS:** ARMS AND AMMO; HARVESTABLE: FIRECRACKER BERRY; RECIPE/MOD/
  PLAN; TRUNK
- **INFO:** EXPECTED ENEMY: SUPER MUTANT; SCAVENGE RATING: 3; SIZE: 2;
  SLEEPING; THREAT LEVEL: 15–99
- **LOCK:** SAFE (2)
- **ITEM EXAMPLES:** ALUMINUM CAN, BEER BOTTLE, COFFEE CUP, ENAMEL BUCKET,
  MOP, NUKA-COLA, OVEN MITT, PLUNGER

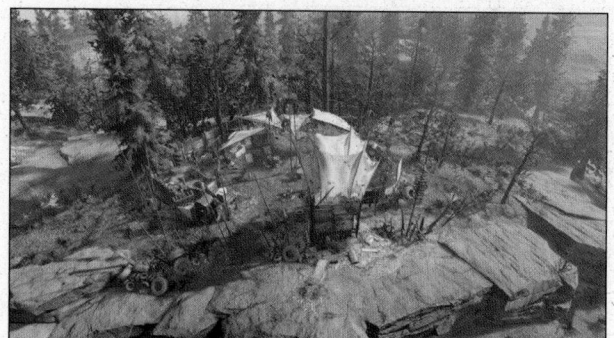

If you enjoy gazing at the Seneca Rocks with human heads on stakes in
the foreground of your photos, then head to this small Raider camp, usually
overrun by a new menace.

31. WENDIGO CAVE

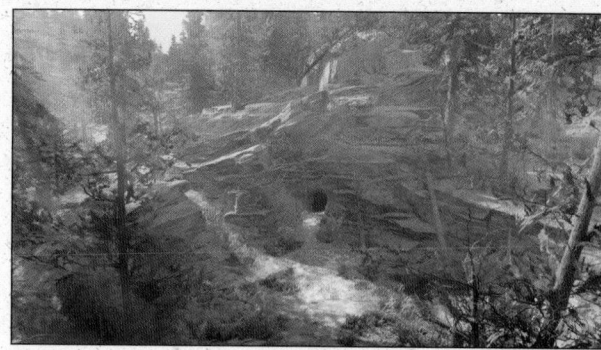

- **COLLECTIBLES:** BOBBLEHEAD (4), CAPS STASH, MAGAZINE (4), POWER ARMOR
- **DANGER:** BONE CHIME! PUNJI BOARD! RADIATION!
- **ITEMS:** ARMS AND AMMO; HARVESTABLE: BRAIN FUNGUS, GLOWING FUNGUS;
  HEALTH AND CHEMS; RECIPE/MOD/PLAN; TRUNK
- **INFO:** EXPECTED ENEMY: GHOUL, IRRADIATED ANIMAL, MIRELURK, WENDIGO;
  NOTE; SCAVENGE RATING: 3; SIZE: 3; THREAT LEVEL: 15–99
- **ITEM EXAMPLES:** BLAMCO BRAND MAC AND CHEESE, COMBAT HELMET, ENAMEL
  BUCKET, FANCY LADS SNACK CAKES+, INSTAMASH, LANTERN, LEFT HAND BONES,
  MACHETE, MELON, MENTATS, METAL TUB, PURIFIED WATER, RAT POISON, RED
  BANDANNA, RIGHT HAND BONES, SUGAR BOMBS, SURGICAL TRAY, TIBIA

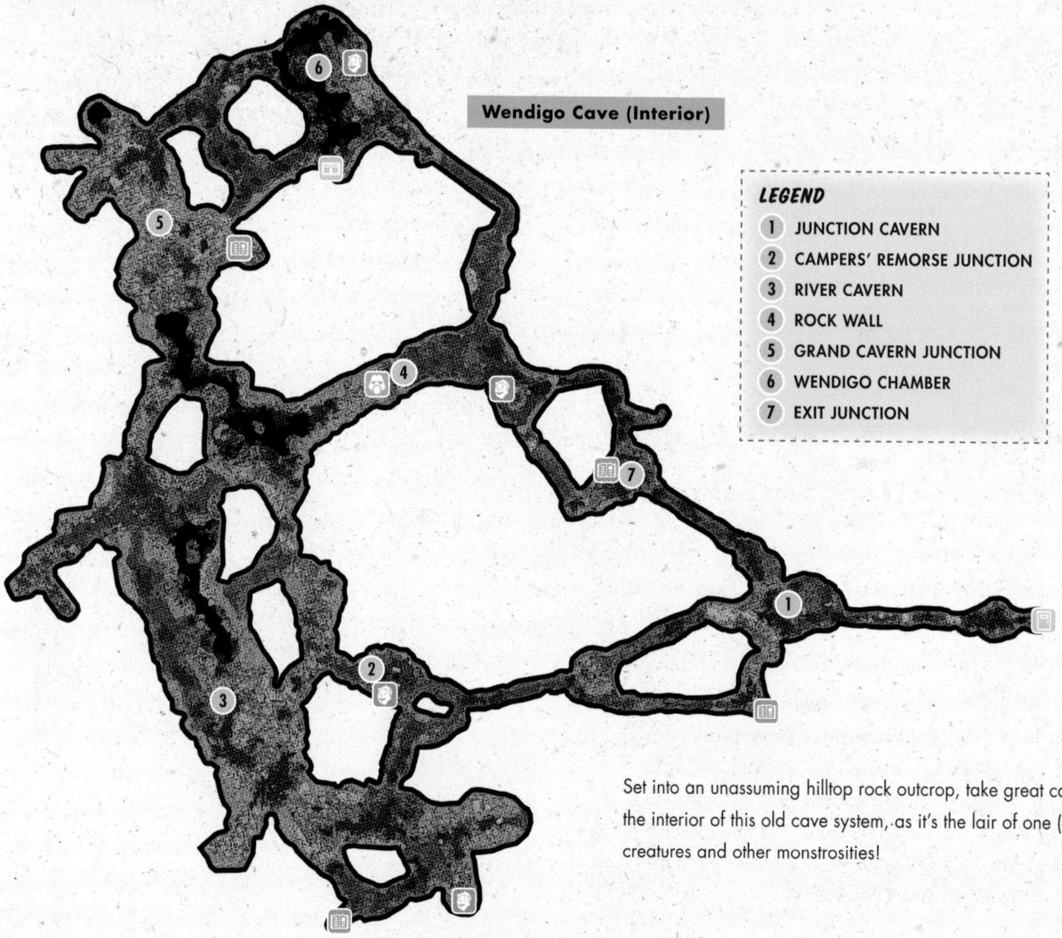

Wendigo Cave (Interior)

LEGEND
1. JUNCTION CAVERN
2. CAMPERS' REMORSE JUNCTION
3. RIVER CAVERN
4. ROCK WALL
5. GRAND CAVERN JUNCTION
6. WENDIGO CHAMBER
7. EXIT JUNCTION

Set into an unassuming hilltop rock outcrop, take great care when exploring
the interior of this old cave system, as it's the lair of one (or more) Wendigo
creatures and other monstrosities!

32. AUTUMN ACRE CABIN

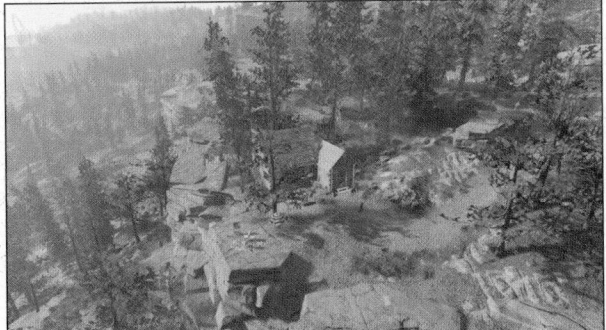

- **COLLECTIBLES:** BOBBLEHEAD, MAGAZINE
- **DANGER:** LONG DROP!
- **ITEMS:** HARVESTABLE: WOOD; RECIPE/MOD/PLAN; TRUNK
- **INFO:** EXPECTED ENEMY: IRRADIATED ANIMAL; NOTE; SCAVENGE RATING: 2; SIZE: 1; SLEEPING; THREAT LEVEL: 15–99
- **ITEM EXAMPLES:** ANTIQUE GLOBE, BLAMCO BRAND MAC AND CHEESE, BOBBY PIN BOX, COFFEE CUP, LANTERN, MOLDY FOOD, PLASTIC PLATE+, SUGAR, TELEPHONE, WINE BOTTLE

If you enjoy incredible vistas, steep rocky terrain, and remote locations, trek to this lone cabin atop a cliff. Remember to approach it from the right direction (heading west to east)!

33. TOXIC LARRY'S MEAT 'N GO

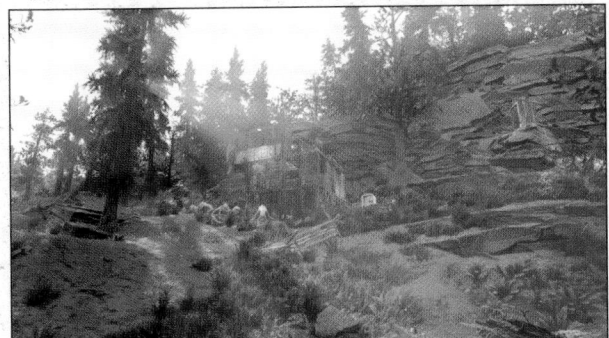

- **COLLECTIBLES:** BOBBLEHEAD (2), MAGAZINE (2)
- **CRAFTING:** COOKING
- **DANGER:** LONG DROP!
- **ITEMS:** ARMS AND AMMO; HARVESTABLE: ASTER, FIRECRACKER BERRY+, WOOD PILE+; HEALTH AND CHEMS; RECIPE/MOD/PLAN; TRUNK
- **INFO:** EXPECTED ENEMY: CRYPTID; SCAVENGE RATING: 4; SIZE: 2; SLEEPING; THREAT LEVEL: 15–99
- **LOCK:** SAFE (3)
- **ITEM EXAMPLES:** BOILED WATER, FUEL TANK++, GAS CANISTER, JAWLESS BRAHMIN SKULL, MILK BOTTLE, MOLE RAT MEAT, MOONSHINE JUG+, SACK HOOD, SQUIRREL BITS, TIN CAN+, WRENCH

On the winding switchback path that runs up from Berkeley Springs (the Mire Region), up west toward Autumn Acre Cabin, there's a smattering of odd or abandoned locations, starting with an empty campsite. Farther up is Toxic Larry's shack. Gather a variety of interesting meat from here. Atop the cliff is a rough deck and outhouse, where Larry collected a large amount of fuel tanks. And jugs. Don't forget to check the outhouse perched away from the main structures; there's a buried safe there (3) to open.

34. SKULLBONE VANTAGE

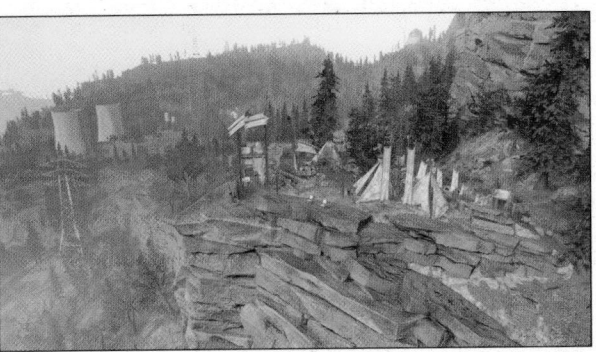

- **COLLECTIBLES:** BOBBLEHEAD, MAGAZINE
- **DANGER:** LONG DROP!
- **ITEMS:** ARMS AND AMMO; HEALTH AND CHEMS; RECIPE/MOD/PLAN; TRUNK
- **INFO:** EXPECTED ENEMY: GHOUL; SCAVENGE RATING: 3; SIZE: 1; SLEEPING; THREAT LEVEL: 15–99
- **ITEM EXAMPLES:** BOILED WATER, CHEF HAT, COFFEE POT, DIRTY ASHTRAY, ENAMEL BUCKET+, MINI NUKE, MOLE RAT HIDE, MR. HANDY FUEL, PRE-WAR MONEY+, SKULL, SPICES, WOODEN SKI

Atop the western edge of the mountains, north of Pleasant Valley, is a small Raider camp with a raised lookout tower, some improvised seating, and body parts strewn and spiked.

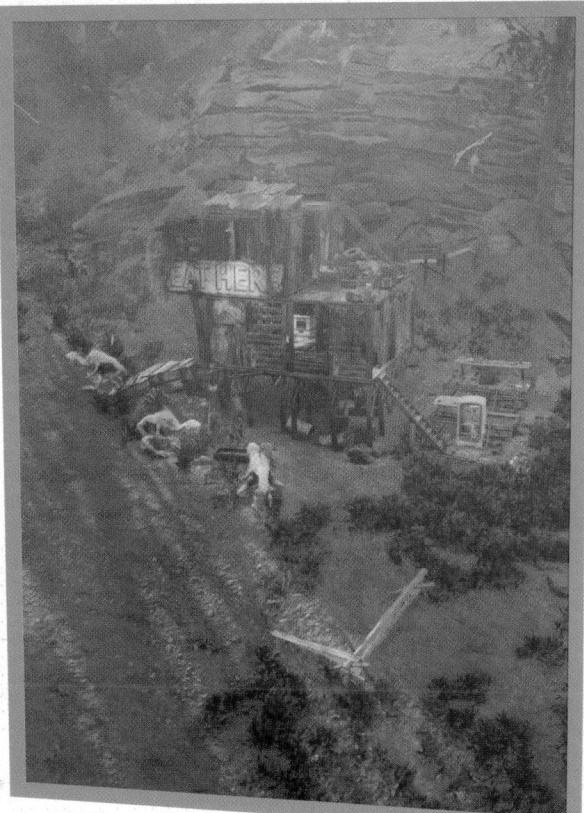

TRAINING

CRAFTING AND C.A.M.P.ING

INVENTORY

QUESTS

ATLAS

BESTIARY

APPENDICES

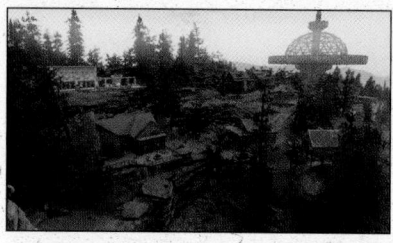

- **COLLECTIBLES:** BOBBLEHEAD (2), HOLOTAPE, MAGAZINE (6), NUKA-CHERRY+, POWER ARMOR
- **CRAFTING:** ARMOR (2), CHEMISTRY, COOKING (3), WEAPONS (2)
- **DANGER:** CAN CHIMES! TRIPWIRE! TURRET!
- **ITEMS:** ARMS AND AMMO+; HARVESTABLE: WOOD PILE; HEALTH AND CHEM++; RECIPE/MOD/PLAN; TRUNK
- **INFO:** EXPECTED ENEMY: IRRADIATED ANIMAL, IRRADIATED INSECT, MOLE MINER; NOTE; SCAVENGE RATING: 5; SIZE: 4; SLEEPING; THREAT LEVEL: 15–99
- **LOCK:** DOOR (0, 0, 1, 3), SAFE (3, 3), TERMINAL (3)
- **ITEM EXAMPLES:** ABRAXO CLEANER, ALARM CLOCK, AUTOPSY BOARD GAME, BEER BOTTLE++, BLAST RADIUS BOARD GAME, BLUE TABLE LAMP+, BOILED WATER+, BROKEN LAMP+, BURGER TRAY, CAFETERIA TRAY, CAMERA+, CATCH THE COMMIE BOARD GAME, CHESSBOARD, CLEAN COFFEE CANISTER, COFFEE CUP+, COOKING POT, COP CAP, CRAM, CUTTING BOARD+, DESK FAN, DINNER PLATE, GLASS PITCHER, HOT PLATE+, LADLE, LOOSE SPRING, OVEN MITT+, PEPPER+, PILLOW+, PLASTIC PUMPKIN, POOL BALL+, POOL CUE, PRE-WAR MONEY, RACK, RAD POKER BOARD GAME, RADAWAY, RED BANDANNA, RUM, SALT+, SAW, SEA CAPTAIN'S HAT, SKI POLE, SKI SWORD, SKIING OUTFIT, SUGAR+, TELEPHONE, TIN CAN+, TOASTER+, TOY ROCKETSHIP, USHANKA HAT, VODKA BOTTLE, WHISKEY, WINE+, WOODEN SKI, WRAPAROUND GOGGLES, YELLOW TABLE LAMP, YUM YUM DEVILED EGGS

LEGEND

1. PRIMARY LOCATION: PLEASANT VALLEY CABINS
2. LOWER ROOFLESS LODGE
3. LOWER GRAND LODGE ("KEEP OUT")
4. LOWER GRAND CHALET (THE ARENA)
5. THE SMALL BAR
6. RAIDER SHANTY TOWN
7. UPPER GRAND CHALET (WITH POOL ROOM)
8. THREE CABIN CLUSTER
9. LONE EAST CABIN
10. RESTAURANT AND LOUNGE
11. PLAYGROUND AND VISTA
12. PRIMARY LOCATION: TOP OF THE WORLD
13. PRIMARY LOCATION: PLEASANT VALLEY SKI RESORT
14. OLD TENT STALL (WEAPONS)
15. OLD TENT STALL (ARMOR)
16. RAIDER BATTLEMENTS
17. PRIMARY LOCATION: TOP OF THE WORLD

Pleasant Valley (Exterior)

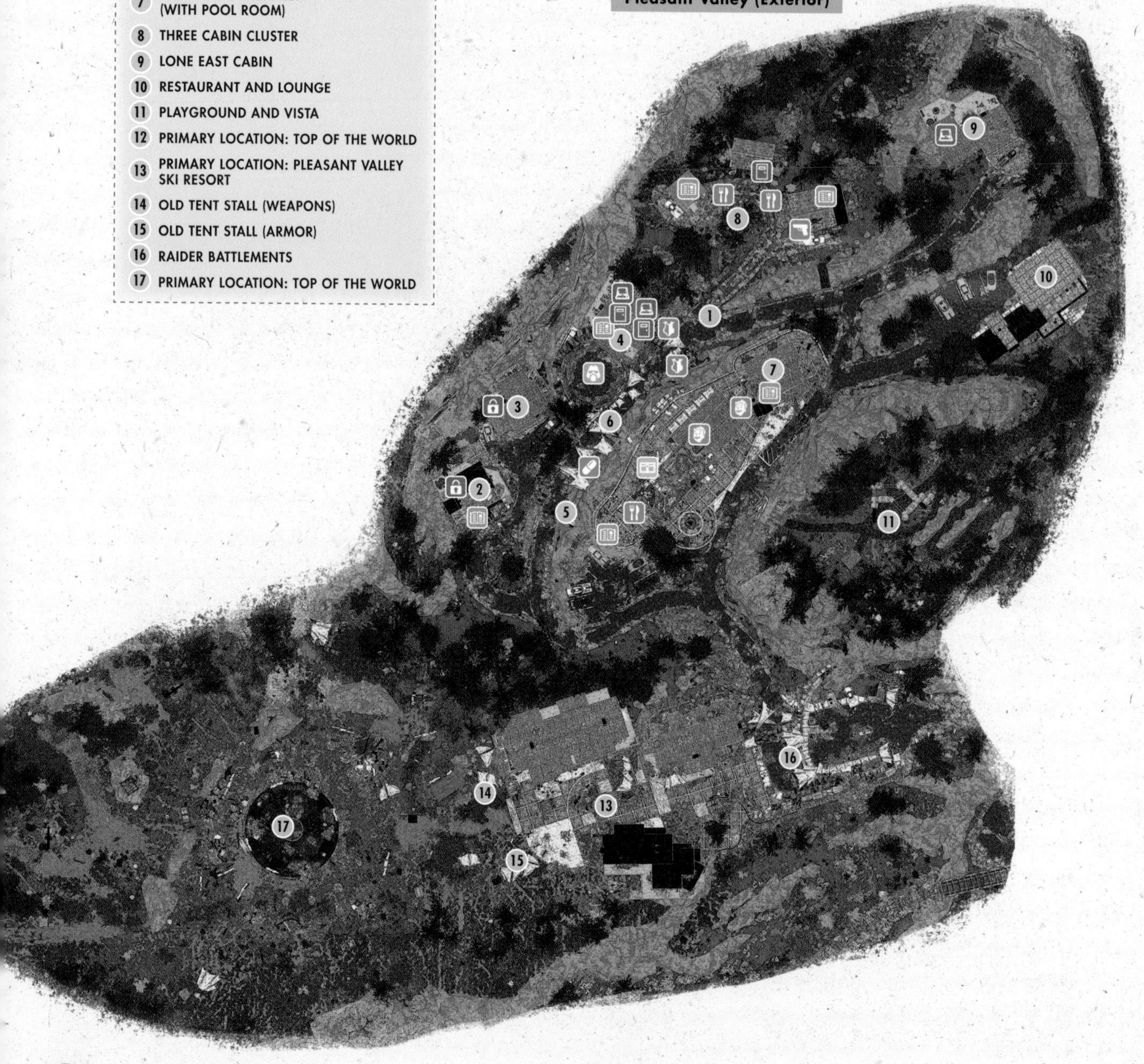

The adjacent map shows the entirety of the Pleasant Valley area, which includes this location, Top of the World, the Ski Resort, and the Station. Though the borders between these locations aren't rigid, in general, anywhere north of the top of the mountain ridge (with the children's playground and lookout point), all the way to the lookout at Skullbone Vantage is this location, while anything south is the Ski Resort.

Expect slight confusion as you orient yourself regarding the numerous medium-sized cabins and lodges in this area. All have a variety of loot (both junk and collectibles) as well as locked doors and safes to pry open. The lower of the ridges features a lodge that Raiders had turned into a brutal arena; Power Armor may be available here, as well as various workbenches and refreshments. Watch for a few traps as you scout around (mainly a turret and a tripwire in the lower grand lodge).

36. TOP OF THE WORLD

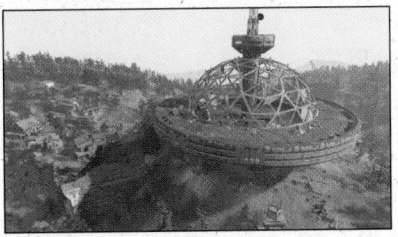

- COLLECTIBLE: BOBBLEHEAD (3), MAGAZINE (4)
- CRAFTING: ARMOR, CHEMISTRY, WEAPONS (2)
- DANGER: LONG DROP! MINES!
- ITEMS: ARMS AND AMMO++, HEALTH AND CHEMS+; OVERSEER'S CACHE; RECIPE/MOD/PLAN; TRUNK
- INFO: EXPECTED ENEMY: IRRADIATED INSECT; INSTRUMENT; LANDMARK; NOTE; QUEST: SIGNAL STRENGTH, THE MISSING LINK; SCAVENGE RATING: 4; SIZE: 4; THREAT LEVEL: 35–99
- LOCK: SAFE (3, 3, 3, 3, 3)
- ITEM EXAMPLES: ALARM CLOCK, ANTIFREEZE BOTTLE, BAG OF CEMENT, BEER+, BEER BOTTLE++, BOILED WATER, BOURBON+, CAFETERIA TRAY+, CASUAL OUTFIT, COFFEE CUP++, COFFEE POT+, COOLANT, DESK FAN, DIRTY ASHTRAY, DUCT TAPE, GLASS PITCHER+, HACKSAW, HOT DOG+, HUNTING RIFLE, OLD POSSUM, OIL CANISTER, ORANGE DRINKING GLASS+, ORANGE PLATE+, PADDED BLUE JACKET, PLASTIC PLATE, PORTABLE FUEL TANK, PURIFIED WATER, RADAWAY, RED PAINT, SAW, SHORT 10-MM PISTOL, SKI POLE, SOAP, SURGICAL MASK, TALL DRINKING GLASS++, TIN CAN, TIN CANISTER, WHITE BOTTLE, WINE, WOODEN SKI, WONDERGLUE, YELLOW PAINT

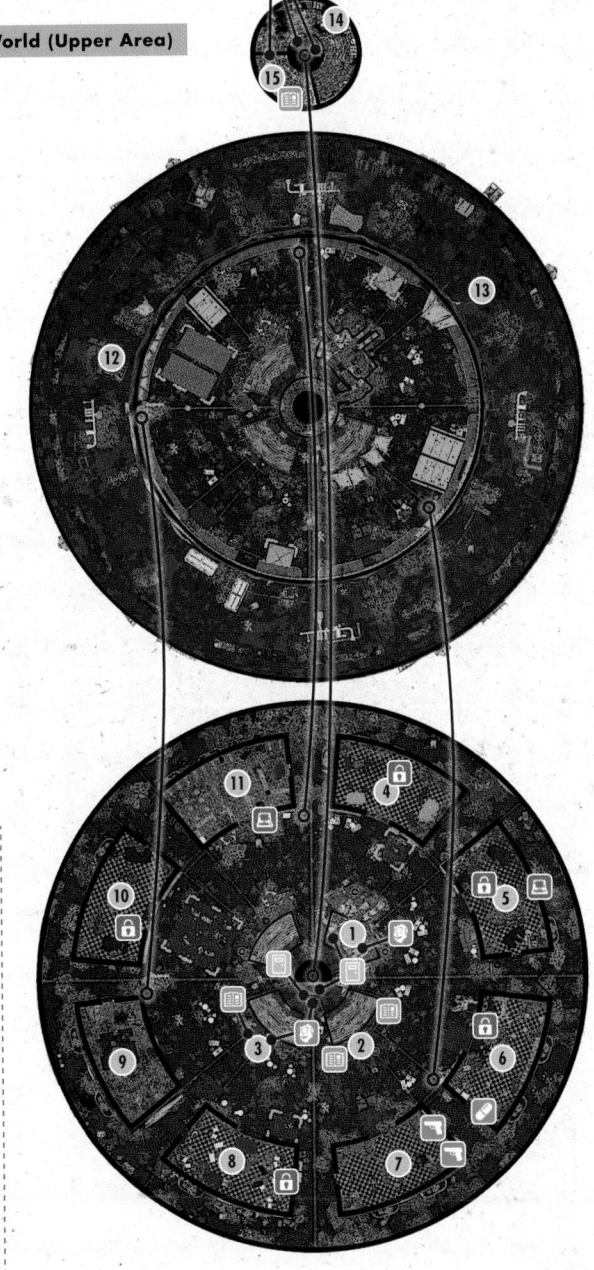

Top of the World (Upper Area)

LEGEND
1. RICKETY STAGE
2. SHACK STALL: WINES
3. SHACK STALL: CLOTHESE
4. PEAK CONDITION
5. DIAMOND DUST
6. MATTERHORN CHOPHOUSE
7. SNOWFLAKE BAUBLES
8. DREAMBOAT YACHTS
9. ICE SCULPTURE ART GALLERY
10. APRES APRES SKI
11. A LA CHEZ BURGER
12. OUTER RUST DECK ROOF: THE BBQ
13. OUTER RUST DECK ROOF: GUITARIST GUARD
14. UPPER DOME: SKY RESTAURANT
15. UPPER DOME: COMPUTER CONTROL

Think of this landmark as a giant red thumbtack in the middle of Savage Divide! The huge, red shopping and eating attraction, seen from across Appalachia, is known as Top of the World. Most recently, Raiders from the cabins and resort have erected small defenses and dropped mines underneath the superstructure, so approach and explore with care.

Take the central elevator up to the shopping center in the sky; however, many of the stores have been significantly repurposed and the whole place now has something of a "shantytown" vibe. Ride the elevator again to a sky restaurant and computer control room, where you can further your quests.

37. PLEASANT VALLEY SKI RESORT

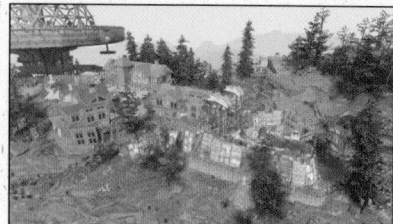

- **COLLECTIBLES:** BOBBLEHEAD (3), HOLOTAPE, MAGAZINE (3)
- **CRAFTING:** ARMOR (2), CHEMISTRY, WEAPONS
- **DANGER:** CAN CHIMES!
- **ITEMS:** ARMS AND AMMO, HEALTH AND CHEMS, RECIPE/MOD/PLAN, TRUNK
- **INFO:** EXPECTED ENEMY: IRRADIATED ANIMAL, IRRADIATED INSECT, MOLE MINER; INSTRUMENT; QUEST: SIGNAL STRENGTH; SCAVENGE RATING: 3; SIZE: 3; SLEEPING; THREAT LEVEL: 15–99; TRADER: VENDOR BOT
- **LOCK:** DOOR (KEY), SAFE (3).
- **ITEM EXAMPLES:** ALUMINUM CAN, BALL-PEEN HAMMER, BOILED WATER, BRAHMIN SKULL, COFFEE CUP+, COFFEE POT, COMBINATION WRENCH, ECONOMY WONDERGLUE, ENAMEL BUCKET+, FANCY LADS SNACK CAKES, GLASS JAR, GREASER JACKET AND JEANS, HANDCUFFS, MOP, NUKA-COLA BOTTLE, OFFICE DESK FAN, PACK OF CIGARETTES, PACK OF DUCT TAPE, RAT POISON, SHORT DOUBLE-BARREL SHOTGUN, SILVER TIE MR. FUZZY, SKIING OUTFIT, SKI SWORD, STEALTH BOY, SUGAR BOMBS, USHANKA HAT, WALKING CANE, WOODEN SKI+

The southern part of Pleasant Valley encompasses a large ski resort building and various Raider reinforcements and blockade structures. See Primary Location: Pleasant Valley Cabins for the full map. Head east to west, and you move through the battlements and into a stone-floored exterior plaza, with three large wooden lodge structures. Of the three, only the interior of the northwest lodge is accessible (though you can gather items from the outside decks of the other two structures). Inside, check the Trading Post for bartering possibilities, as well as a small locked armory in the basement. Then head upstairs across the landing, through the double doors, to the trunk and possible Magazine on the upper (south) deck.

38. PLEASANT VALLEY STATION

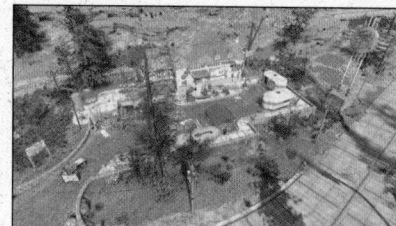

- **CRAFTING:** ARMOR, COOKING (2)
- **ITEMS:** ARMS AND AMMO; MY STASH BOX; VENDING MACHINE: AMMUNITION, MEDICAL SUPPLIES
- **INFO:** ARMS AND AMMO; SCAVENGE RATING: 3; SIZE: 2; SLEEPING; TRADER: VENDOR BOT; THREAT LEVEL: 15–99
- **ITEM EXAMPLES:** BEER BOTTLE+, BLACKWATER BREW BOTTLE, BOILED WATER+, BOURBON, BOWL+, COOKING POT, LADLE, PLASTIC SPOON+, PURIFIED WATER, RUM, WINE+, YELLOW PAINT.

The southeastern edge of Pleasant Valley (Top of the World) is the train station, which is spitting distance from the South Cutthroat Camp and features a "Top of the World" sign. Once used as a food distribution center (before being ransacked by Raiders), this should be your base of operations; trade with the Bot and leave your Stashed items here between explorations around and about.

39. SOUTH CUTTHROAT CAMP

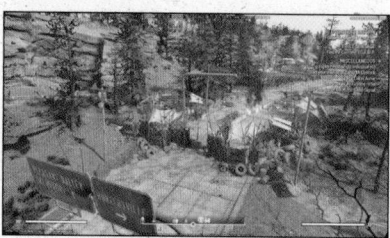

- **COLL:** BOBBLEHEAD (4), MAGAZINE (2)
- **ITEM:** ARMS AND AMMO. TRUNK.
- **INFO:** EXPECTED ENEMY: MOLE MINER, ROBOT, SCORCHED, SUPER MUTANT. SCAVENGE RATING: 3. SIZE: 2. THREAT LEVEL: 15–99.
- **LOCK:** SAFE (X2) (0, 2)
- **ITEM EXAMPLES:** BEER BOTTLE, BOURBON, COMBAT KNIFE, CRAM, ENAMEL BUCKET+, FUEL TANK, GAS CANISTER, METAL BUCKET+, MILK BOTTLE, SKI POLE+, SPICES, TIN CAN, VODKA, WOODEN SKI

Blocking the main arterial road to the south of Top of the World is an old Raider camp, which seems to have had the most rudimentary of trading possibilities, as well as heads on stakes.

40. NORTH CUTTHROAT CAMP

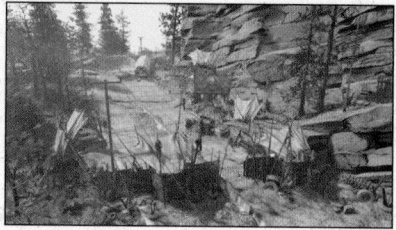

- **COLLECTIBLES:** BOBBLEHEAD, MAGAZINE (2), NUKA-CHERRY
- **CRAFTING:** COOKING, TINKER
- **ITEMS:** ARMS AND AMMO+, HEALTH AND CHEMS, TRUNK
- **INFO:** EXPECTED ENEMY: MOLE MINER, ROBOT, SCORCHED, SUPER MUTANT; SCAVENGE RATING: 3; SIZE: 2; THREAT LEVEL: 15–99
- **ITEM EXAMPLES:** BLOWTORCH, BOBBY PIN BOX, BOILED WATER, CONNECTING ROD, ENAMEL BUCKET, GLASS JAR, HOT PLATE, MAKESHIFT BATTERY, SKI SWORD, SKULL, STRAW PILLOW, TEAPOT, TUBE FLANGE

Highway 63 is completely blocked at this Raider checkpoint, though current threats are usually more robotic in nature. Heads-up: there's a possible Magazine on a plank table and a Bobblehead perched above the Tinker's Workbench, among the various small fortifications that litter either side of the road.

41. CENTRAL MOUNTAIN LOOKOUT

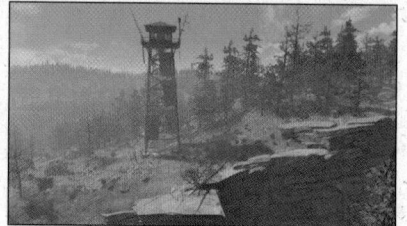

- **COLLECTIBLE:** CAPS STASH
- **DANGER:** LONG DROP! MINES!
- **ITEMS:** ARMS AND AMMO; HARVESTABLE: GLOWING RESIN
- **INFO:** SCAVENGE RATING: 2; SIZE: 1; SURVEY AREA; THREAT LEVEL: 15–99
- **ITEM EXAMPLES:** ALARM CLOCK, BEER BOTTLE, CAPS, CHESSBOARD, MACHETE, PIPE PISTOL, PORTABLE FUEL TANK

Long-dead Raiders have still left some explosive surprises as you climb this tower; beware of mines as you ascend. Two dead Raiders seem to have finished their game of checkers a little prematurely. The views up here are excellent from almost every angle.

42. YELLOW SANDY'S STILL

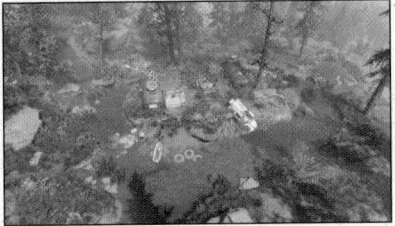

- **COLLECTIBLES:** BOBBLEHEAD, MAGAZINE
- **DANGER:** RADIATION!
- **ITEMS: HARVESTABLE:** BLACKBERRY, WILD CARROT FLOWER
- **INFO: EXPECTED ENEMY:** SCORCHED; SCAVENGE RATING: 2; SIZE: 1; THREAT LEVEL: 15–99
- **LOCK:** SAFE (2)
- **ITEM EXAMPLES:** GARDEN GNOME, GAS CANISTER, MOONSHINE JUG+, PORTABLE FUEL TANK+, TEDDY BEAR, TV DINNER TRAY

On a particularly boggy area of high mountains is a pond (making a natural moat). A moonshiner's fermentation operation is up here as well. Check the one of the two caravans for a possible Magazine, and scavenge the rest of the junk.

43. CLIFFWATCH

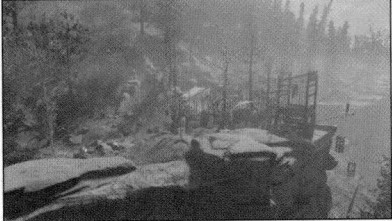

- **COLLECTIBLES:** BOBBLEHEAD, MAGAZINE, POWER ARMOR
- **CRAFTING:** COOKING
- **DANGER:** LONG DROP!
- **ITEM:** ARMS AND AMMO
- **INFO: EXPECTED ENEMY:** SCORCHED, ROBOT; SCAVENGE RATING: 3; SIZE: 1; THREAT LEVEL: 15–99
- **ITEM EXAMPLES:** BOWIE KNIFE, FANCY LADS SNACK CAKES, FRYING PAN, GAS CANISTER+, LANTERN, PORTABLE FUEL TANK, POTATO CRISPS, SQUIRREL BITS, WHISKEY

An old Raider camp offering excellent views of Summersville across the valley to the west. Watch your step; you don't want other Vault Dwellers to rename this location "cliff fall" after a stumble in the wrong direction.

44. SAFE 'N CLEAN DISPOSAL

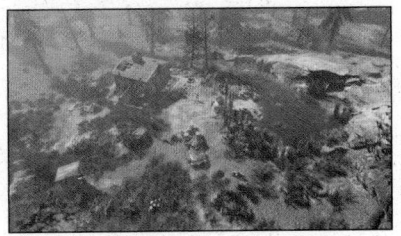

- **COLLECTIBLES:** BOBBLEHEAD, MAGAZINE
- **CRAFTING:** WEAPONS
- **DANGER:** RADIATION!
- **ITEMS: HARVESTABLE:** BLACKBERRY, SILT BEAN, WILD CARROT FLOWER; HEALTH AND CHEMS
- **INFO: EXPECTED ENEMY:** SUPER MUTANT; NOTE; SCAVENGE RATING: 1; SIZE: 2; SLEEPING; THREAT LEVEL: 15–99
- **ITEM EXAMPLES:** ALUMINUM CAN, CAN, CLEAN COFFEE TIN, TIN CAN+, TOILET PAPER, WOOD PILE

You may be shocked to learn that this dumping ground for rusting vehicles is neither safe, nor clean (though there is usually toilet paper in the outhouse). Expect fighting clustered around the small red barn.

45. NEW APPALACHIAN CENTRAL TRAINYARD

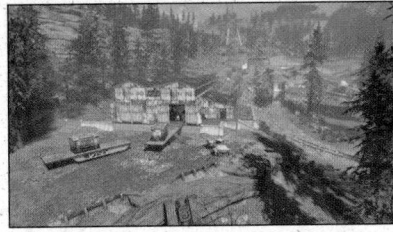

- **COLLECTIBLES:** BOBBLEHEAD, MAGAZINE (3), NUKA-CHERRY, POWER ARMOR
- **CRAFTING:** ARMOR, COOKING, WEAPONS
- **DANGER:** EXPLOSIVE CANISTER! RADIATION!
- **ITEMS: HARVESTABLE:** BLACKBERRY; HEALTH AND CHEMS; TRUNK
- **INFO: EXPECTED ENEMY:** SCORCHED; SCAVENGE RATING: 4; SIZE: 3; SLEEPING; THREAT LEVEL: 15–99
- **LOCK:** DOOR (0), SAFE (0, 0, 1, 1)
- **ITEM EXAMPLES:** ADJUSTABLE WRENCH, ALARM CLOCK, AUTOPSY BOARD GAME, BLUE PAINT, BOILED WATER, BROKEN FEMUR, CAT BOWL+, CIGAR BOX, COTTON YARN, DIRTY POSTMAN HAT, DUCT TAPE, ENAMEL BUCKET, FUEL TANK, GLOBE, GOLD PLATED FLIP LIGHTER, FASCHNACHT MAN MASK, HOOKED PIPE WRENCH, HUFFWARBLER TEAPOT, RIB CAGE AND PELVIS, SHOPPING BASKET, SUGAR, SUGAR BOMBS, TEDDY BEAR, TOILET PAPER, USED OIL CAN, VOLATILE MATERIALS BOX, YELLOW CANISTER

New Appalachian Central Trainyard (Exterior)

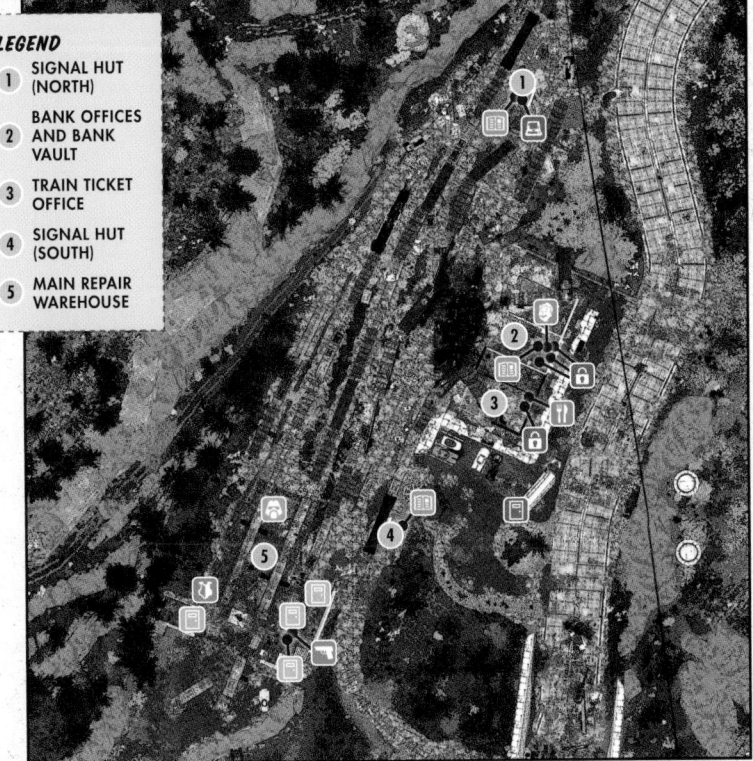

LEGEND
1. SIGNAL HUT (NORTH)
2. BANK OFFICES AND BANK VAULT
3. TRAIN TICKET OFFICE
4. SIGNAL HUT (SOUTH)
5. MAIN REPAIR WAREHOUSE

Dozens of railroad containers and carriages lie in various positions; almost none of them sit on the rusting tracks. Sweep the two signal switch towers, the offices behind the ticket office and bank facades, and the main repair warehouse, along with checking any open carriages for items.

TRAINING

CRAFTING AND C.A.M.P.ING

INVENTORY

QUESTS

ATLAS

BESTIARY

APPENDICES

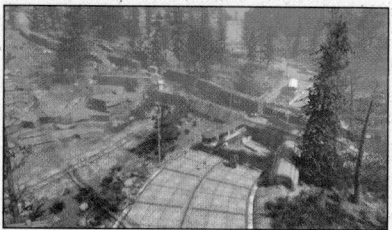

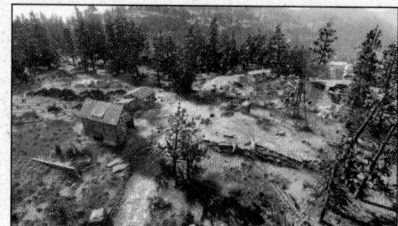

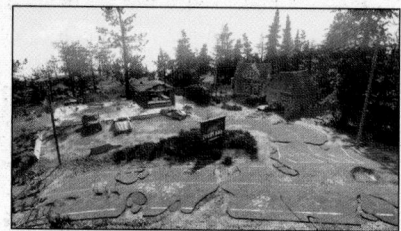

- **COLLECTIBLES:** BOBBLEHEAD, MAGAZINE
- **DANGER:** RADIATION!
- **ITEMS:** ARMS AND AMMO+; HARVESTABLE: BLACKBERRY; TRUNK
- **INFO:** EXPECTED ENEMY: ROBOT; SCAVENGE RATING: 2; SIZE: 3; THREAT LEVEL: 15–99
- **ITEM EXAMPLES:** AMMUNITION

The northern end of the railyard features even more mangled metal: train carriages, including those carrying military supplies; cargo carriages; containers; and road traffic. All of this is snarled up in a large and slowly rusting maze. Check under one of the balanced carriages for a hidey-hole.

- **COLLECTIBLE:** POWER ARMOR
- **CRAFTING:** WEAPONS
- **DANGER:** EXPLOSIVE CANISTER! RADIATION!
- **ITEMS:** ARMS AND AMMO; HARVESTABLE: BLACKBERRY, SOOT FLOWER, WILD CARROT FLOWER; TRUNK
- **INFO:** EXPECTED ENEMY: IRRADIATED ANIMAL, YAO GUAI; SCAVENGE RATING: 1; SIZE: 2; SLEEPING; THREAT LEVEL: 15–99
- **ITEM EXAMPLES:** BAG OF FERTILIZER, BASEBALL HELMET, COFFEE CAN, COFFEE POT, TIN CAN+

The Beckwiths have long since shuffled off this mortal coil, but their farmstead still stands—but only just! There's meager pickings, though the tractor shed has a Weapons Workbench to fiddle with.

- **CRAFTING:** COOKING
- **ITEM:** HARVESTABLE: WILD CARROT FLOWER
- **INFO:** EXPECTED ENEMY: IRRADIATED ANIMAL; SCAVENGE RATING: 1; SIZE: 2; THREAT LEVEL: 15–99
- **ITEM EXAMPLES:** ALUMINUM CAN, CLEAN SALT SHAKER, CLOWN HAT, CUTTING BOARD, DIRTY ASHTRAY, ENAMEL BUCKET, GLASS PITCHER, MAKESHIFT BATTERY, OFFICE DESK FAN, OVEN MITT, PEPPER, RED PLATE, SALT, WHITE BOTTLE.

This was once a must-stop along Route 105, but if you're looking forward to some pork ribs, you might have to make do with squirrel bits. Or worse. The red barn houses the majority of the junk, with two small (and sealed) adjacent cottages nearby.

 49. SITE ALPHA

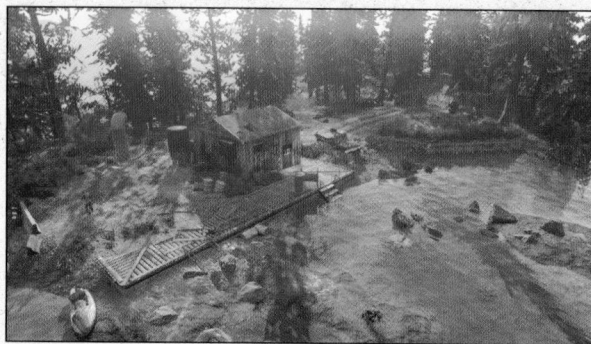

- **COLLECTIBLES:** BOBBLEHEAD (4), MAGAZINE (3), NUKA-CHERRY, POWER ARMOR
- **CRAFTING:** ARMOR (2), POWER ARMOR (2), TINKER'S, WEAPONS (3)
- **DANGER:** EXPLOSIVE CANISTER! OIL! RADIATION!+++
- **ITEMS:** ARMS AND AMMO++, HEALTH AND CHEMS+, OVERSEER'S CACHE
- **INFO:** EXPECTED ENEMY: ROBOT; QUEST: MISSION: COUNTDOWN ALPHA; SCAVENGE RATING: 4; SIZE: 5; SLEEPING; THREAT LEVEL: 15–99
- **LOCK:** DOOR (3, 3), TERMINAL (3)
- **ITEM EXAMPLES:** ANTIQUE GLOBE, BLUE TABLE LAMP+, BURGUNDY BOTTLE, CLOWN, COFFEE CUP, COOLANT++, CRUSHED RUSTY CANISTER, DIRTY ASHTRAY, DOG TAGS, DUCT TAPE+, ENAMEL BUCKET+, FUMIGUS BLOWTORCH+, FUSE, GLASS JAR, HAZMAT SUIT+, HOT PLATE+, MAINFRAME CORE, MEDICAL LIQUID NITROGEN DISPENSER, MILITARY FATIGUES, MILITARY GRADE CIRCUIT BOARD, MOP+, OFFICE DESK FAN, OLD BIOMETIC ID CARD, PACK OF DUCT TAPE+, PILLOW+, PLASTIC PUMPKIN, POOL BALL+, POOL CUE, PORK N' BEANS, PURIFIED WATER+, RUSTY CANISTER, SCREWDRIVER, SPICES, TIN CAN+, TRIFOLD AMERICAN FLAG, TURPENTINE, TYPEWRITER, UNSTOPPABLE SHINDIG BOARD GAME, SLIDE RULE, USED OIL CAN, WONDERGLUE, WRENCH, YUM YUM DEVILED EGGS

Exterior: A small, unassuming shed with a rusty pickup, close to a small pond, gives little indication of the massive military base underneath. Discover the Overseer's Cache here, before entering a door and accessing the elevator using the hand scanner (which you're able to utilize as part of the quest).

Interior: If you've managed to access the scanner as part of the quest, you can finally reach this vast, underground bunker site. After fooling the biometric scanner to access the chambers beyond the initial laser grid, you may have to restore power to the reactor, destroy the mainframe, replace the mainframe cores, and defend the section chief robots while they coordinate a possible nuclear strike you (and your cohorts) may be attempting. After the targeting computer is ready, you just need to solve the code and launch that nuke!

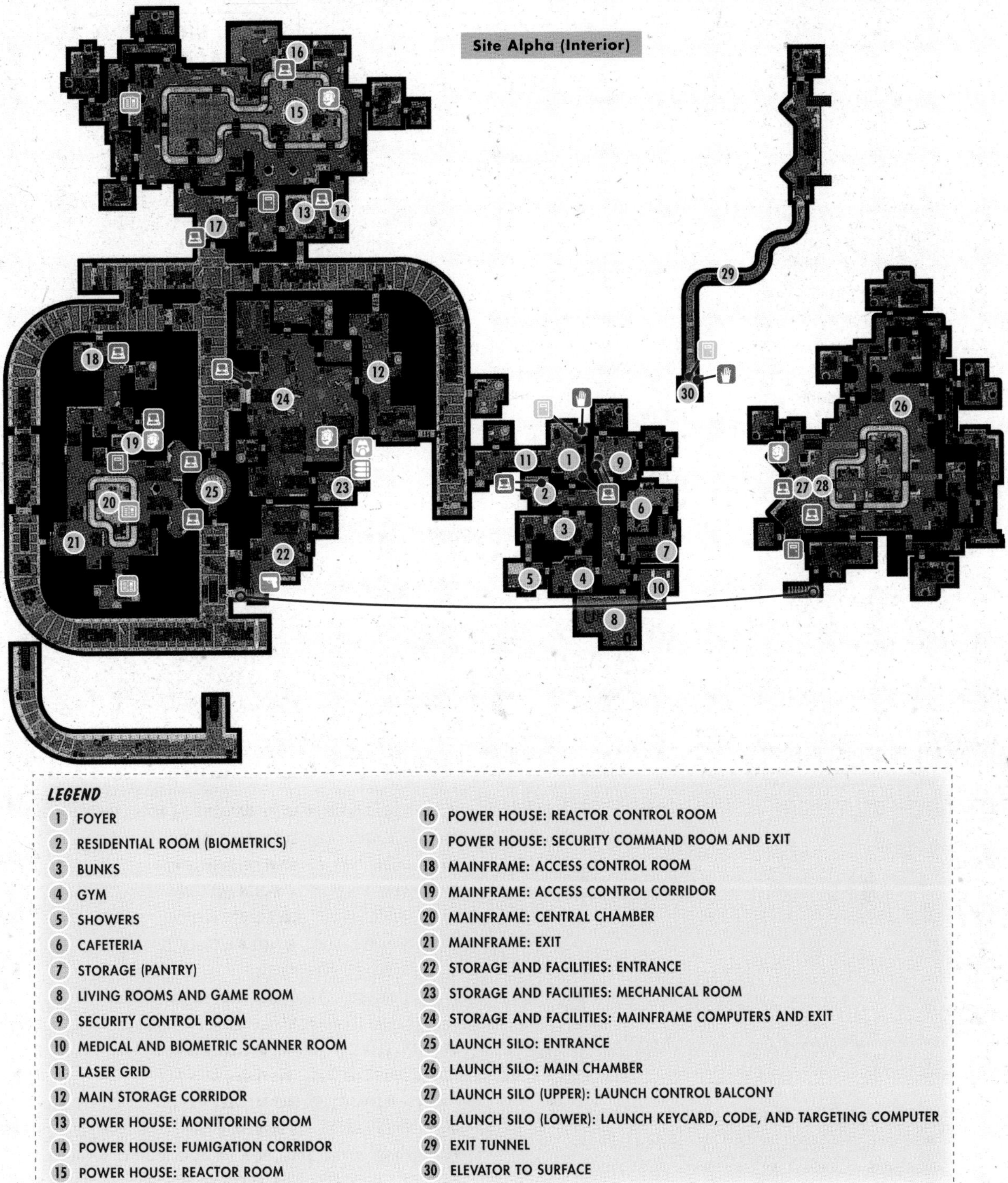

Site Alpha (Interior)

TRAINING

CRAFTING AND C.A.M.P.ING

INVENTORY

QUESTS

ATLAS

BESTIARY

APPENDICES

LEGEND

1. FOYER
2. RESIDENTIAL ROOM (BIOMETRICS)
3. BUNKS
4. GYM
5. SHOWERS
6. CAFETERIA
7. STORAGE (PANTRY)
8. LIVING ROOMS AND GAME ROOM
9. SECURITY CONTROL ROOM
10. MEDICAL AND BIOMETRIC SCANNER ROOM
11. LASER GRID
12. MAIN STORAGE CORRIDOR
13. POWER HOUSE: MONITORING ROOM
14. POWER HOUSE: FUMIGATION CORRIDOR
15. POWER HOUSE: REACTOR ROOM

16. POWER HOUSE: REACTOR CONTROL ROOM
17. POWER HOUSE: SECURITY COMMAND ROOM AND EXIT
18. MAINFRAME: ACCESS CONTROL ROOM
19. MAINFRAME: ACCESS CONTROL CORRIDOR
20. MAINFRAME: CENTRAL CHAMBER
21. MAINFRAME: EXIT
22. STORAGE AND FACILITIES: ENTRANCE
23. STORAGE AND FACILITIES: MECHANICAL ROOM
24. STORAGE AND FACILITIES: MAINFRAME COMPUTERS AND EXIT
25. LAUNCH SILO: ENTRANCE
26. LAUNCH SILO: MAIN CHAMBER
27. LAUNCH SILO (UPPER): LAUNCH CONTROL BALCONY
28. LAUNCH SILO (LOWER): LAUNCH KEYCARD, CODE, AND TARGETING COMPUTER
29. EXIT TUNNEL
30. ELEVATOR TO SURFACE

50. WHITESPRING LOOKOUT

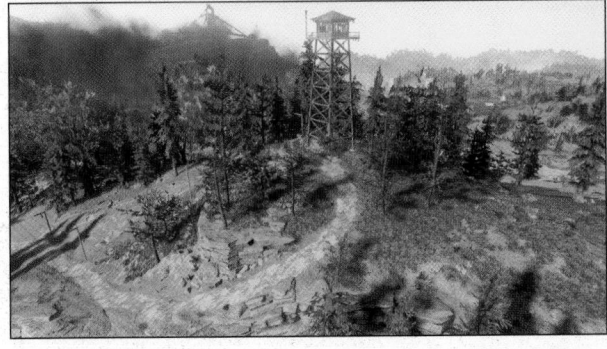

- **DANGER:** CAN CHIMES! LONG DROP!
- **INFO:** EXPECTED ENEMY: GHOUL; INSTRUMENT; SCAVENGE RATING: 1; SIZE: 1; SLEEPING; SURVEY AREA; THREAT LEVEL: 15–99
- **ITEM EXAMPLES:** BINOCULARS, MAKESHIFT BATTERY, NEW FLORAL FLARED VASE, RANGER HAT

The Whitespring maintenance robots don't venture this far west, so expect the lookout tower (and outhouse) to be overgrown. The tower offers excellent 360-degree views.

- **COLLECTIBLES:** BOBBLEHEAD (3), CAPS STASH (2), MAGAZINE (4)
- **DANGER:** RADIATION! TRIPWIRE!
- **ITEMS:** ARMS AND AMMO; HARVESTABLE: RHODODENDRON, SOOT FLOWER; HEALTH AND CHEMS; RECIPE/MOD//PLAN, TRUNK
- **INFO:** EXPECTED ENEMY: IRRADIATED ANIMAL, IRRADIATED INSECT, SCORCHED; SCAVENGE RATING: 4; SIZE: 5; SLEEPING; THREAT LEVEL: 15–99
- **LOCK:** DOOR (S, 0, 1, 1, 1), SAFE (2)
- **ITEM EXAMPLES:** BAG OF FERTILIZER, BATTERED FEDORA, BLUE VISOR, BOURBON, BUMBLEBEAR, CHESSBOARD, CLOWN, COFFEE POT, COLANDER, DIRTY ASHTRAY, FLORAL ROUNDED VASE, GOLF BALL+++, GOLF OUTFIT, GOLF SKIRT, FANCY HAIRBRUSH, FANCY LAD SNACK CAKES, FASHIONABLE GLASSES, GARDEN GNOME, GLASS PITCHER, GOLD WATCH, INDUSTRIAL SIZE SHORTENING, KITCHEN

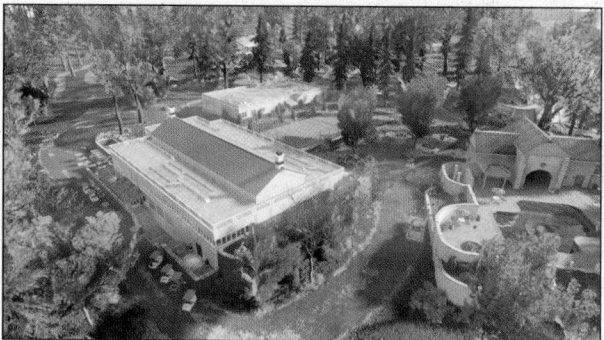

SCALE, LIFE PRESERVER, NOODLE CUP, NUKA-COLA+, NUKA-COLA CUP+, NUKA-COLA CUP PACK+, OLD POSSUM+, ORNAMENTAL VASE, OVEN MITTS, PACK OF CIGARETTES, PLASTIC SPOON, POOL BALL+, POOL CUE, PRE-WAR MONEY+, RAD POKER BOARD GAME, RED PLATE, SEALED CHARLESTON HERALD, SHOVEL, SMALL DRINKING GLASS+, SUGAR, SUGAR BOMBS, TEDDY BEAR, TELEPHONE, TOILET PAPER, TRIFOLD AMERICAN FLAG, UNUSED ENAMEL BUCKET, WHITE TABLE LAMP+, WHISKEY, WINE, WOOD BLOCK

The Whitespring Golf Club (Exterior and Interior)

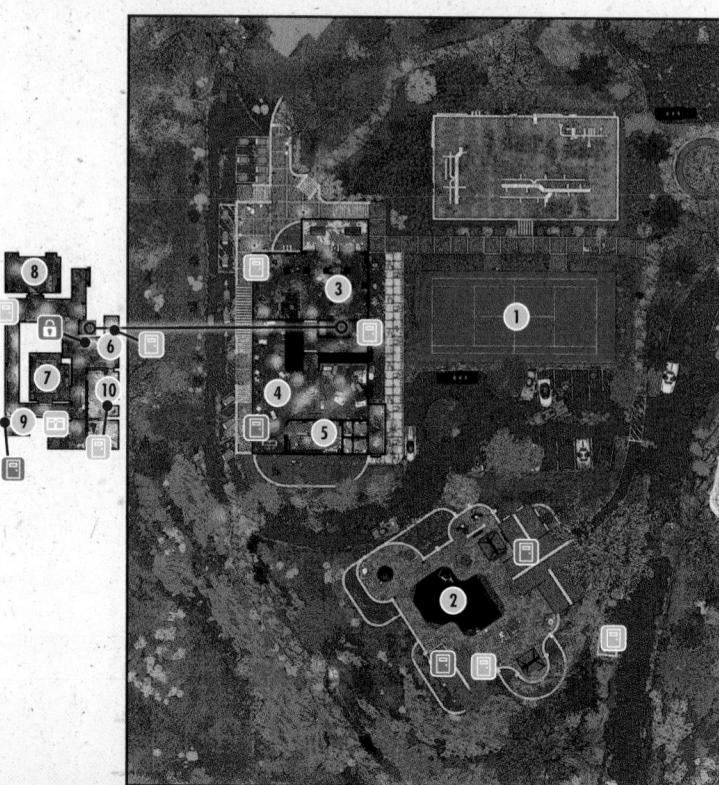

LEGEND

1. TENNIS COURTS AND CLUBHOUSE
2. POOL HOUSE
3. CLUBHOUSE: LOUNGE AND GAME ROOM
4. CLUBHOUSE: RESTAURANT
5. CLUBHOUSE: KITCHENS
6. CLUBHOUSE: CLOAKROOM AND RECEPTION
7. CLUBHOUSE: SMOKING ROOM
8. CLUBHOUSE: STUDY
9. CLUBHOUSE: KITCHENETTE
10. CLUBHOUSE: LOCKER ROOM AND SHOWERS

This is part of The Whitespring Resort, and the exterior map is referenced with that location. Looking amazingly untouched by the ravages of war, this golf club (once popular with politicians and titans of industry) has been kept well manicured by robotic attendants, as the human occupants are looking distinctly emaciated. There's a full 18 holes to explore (with small stone storage huts and a refreshment kiosk to gather loot from), though the main area of interest is the club house (for junk appropriation). The row of white bungalows and Presidential Cottage and Museum along the edge of the location are off-limits unless you have the necessary hand scanner code.

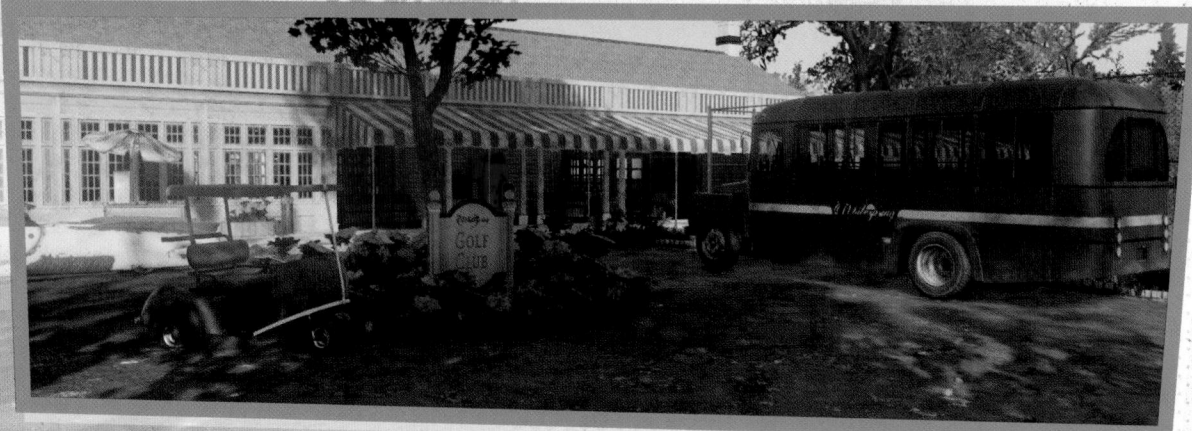

52. THE WHITESPRING RESORT

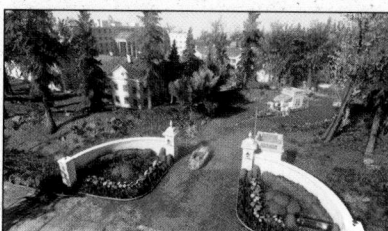

- **COLLECTIBLES:** CAPS STASH (10), HOLOTAPE, NUKA-CHERRY++, NUKA-COLA DARK+, NUKA-GRAPE+, NUKA-ORANGE+, NUKA-COLA QUANTUM+, NUKA-COLA WILD++
- **CRAFTING:** ARMOR (3), CHEMISTRY (2), COOKING (3), POWER ARMOR (3), TINKER'S (5), WEAPONS (3)

- **ITEMS:** ARMS AND AMMO+++; HEALTH AND CHEMS+++; MY STASH BOX (2)
- **INFO:** EXPECTED ENEMY: GHOUL, IRRADIATED INSECT, ROBOT; INSTRUMENT; SCAVENGE RATING: 5+; SIZE: 5; THREAT LEVEL: 15–99; TRADER: ASSAULTRON, PROTECTRON, MR. HANDY ROBOTS
- **LOCK:** DOOR (0, S, S, S, S, S, S, S, S, S, S, S)
- **ITEM EXAMPLES:** ABRAXO CLEANER INDUSTRIAL GRADE+, ALARM CLOCK, ASHTRAY+, BAG OF CEMENT+, BAG OF FERTILIZER+, BINOCULARS, BLAST RADIUS BOARD GAME, BROOM, CAKE PAN, CLOTHES HANGER+++, COFFEE CUP+++, COFFEE POT, DISHRAG, ENAMEL BUCKET, FORMAL OUTFIT, FUEL TANK, GIDDYUP BUTTERCUP+, GLOBE, KITCHEN

SCALES+ NEW FLORAL BUD VASE+++, NEW TEAL FLARED VASE++, PEN, PLASTIC BOWL, PLASTIC SPOON, POTATO CRISPS, MAKESHIFT BATTERY, MR. HANDY FUEL, MOP, NEW RIVER RED ALE, NUKA-COLA+++, NUKA-COLA CUP+, NUKA-COLA CUP PACK, ORANGE BOWL, ORNAMENTAL VASE, PUMPKIN, RAD POKER BOARD GAME, SAUCER+++, SMALL LEFT ANTLER, SOAP+, SUGAR, SUGAR BOMBS, TEACUP+++, TEDDY BEAR++, TOY ALIEN+, TOILET PAPER, TRIFOLD AMERICAN FLAG, VODKA BOTTLE+, WAKEMASTER ALARM CLOCK, WHISKEY BOTTLE+, WINE BOTTLE+, WOOD BLOCK+

The Whitespring Resort (Exterior)

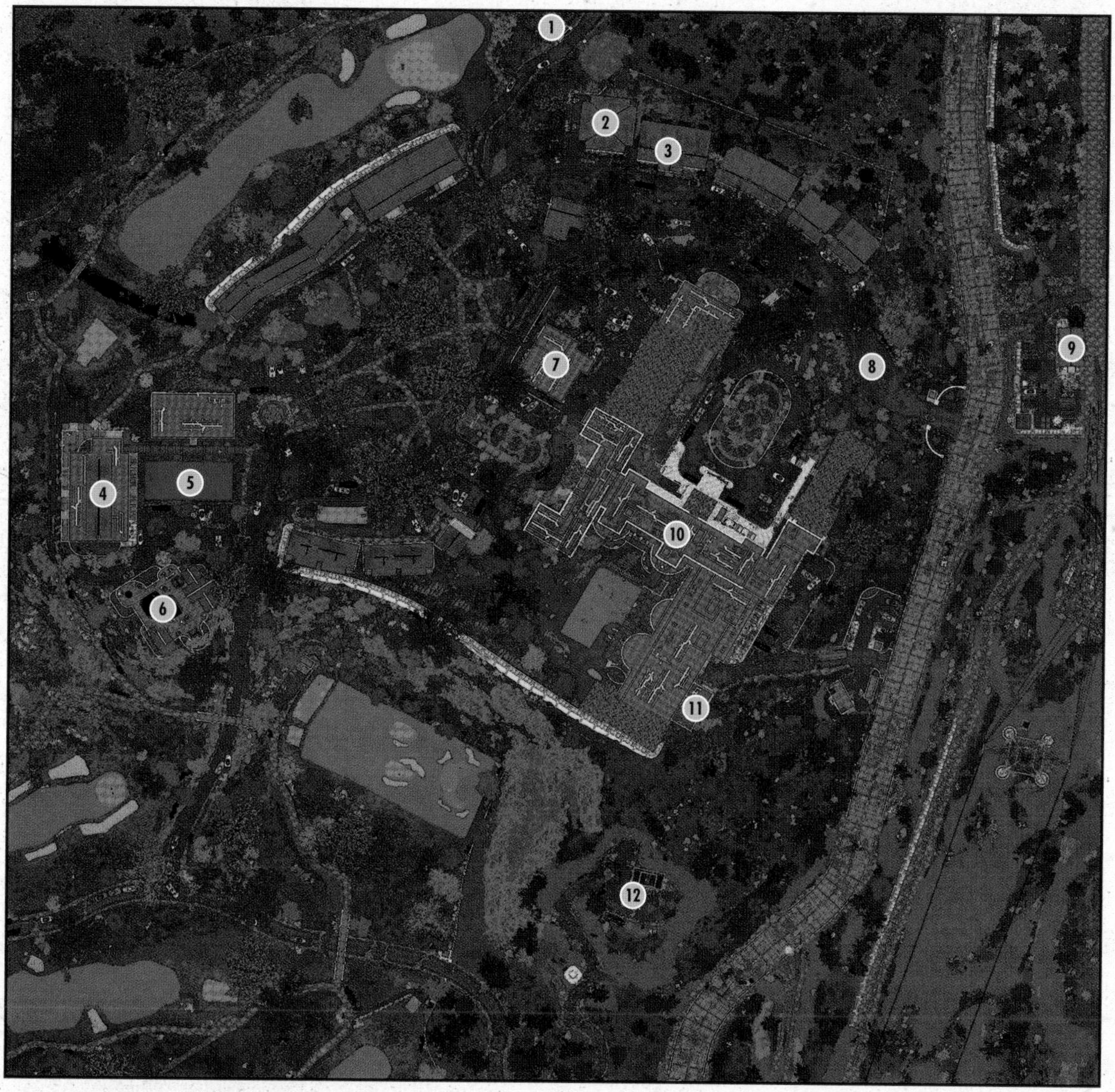

LEGEND

1. SECURITY ENTRANCE: NORTH
2. WHITESPRING PRESIDENTIAL COTTAGE AND MUSEUM
3. WHITESPRING MANSION (AND BUNGALOWS)
4. PRIMARY LOCATION; THE WHITESPRING GOLF CLUB
5. TENNIS COURT
6. POOL HOUSE
7. STAFF QUARTERS (LOUNGE, LAUNDRY, AND STORAGE)
8. SECURITY ENTRANCE: EAST
9. PRIMARY LOCATION: WHITESPRING STATION
10. PRIMARY LOCATION: THE WHITESPRING RESORT
11. PRIMARY LOCATION: THE WHITESPRING SERVICE ENTRANCE
12. PRIMARY LOCATION: THE WHITESPRING BUNKER

Encompassing five primary locations, this lavish resort has received presidents, senators, and many other high-ranking officials in the past—not least because of the large nuclear bunker underneath the main hotel structure. The U-shaped resort hotel has a central entrance and numerous side and other entrances around its perimeter. Other areas of interest around the exterior include formal gardens and a grand double staircase up to the main entrance, a pitch-and-putt area (because you can never have too many golf courses), and a veranda, all with Protectron butlers to take care of the new-departed VIPs' every whim. Also on the property is a small staff lounge, laundry, and garden storage structure.

LEGEND

1. GRAND GREEN FOYER
2. UPPER LOBBY LOUNGE (CHECKERBOARD FLOOR)
3. LOWER LOBBY CONSERVATORY WITH PIANO
4. THE LOBBY BAR
5. THE SMOKING (AND BOARD GAME) ROOM
6. THE BALLROOM
7. THE SODA FOUNTAIN
8. DINING ROOM AND PIANO
9. MEETING CHAMBER

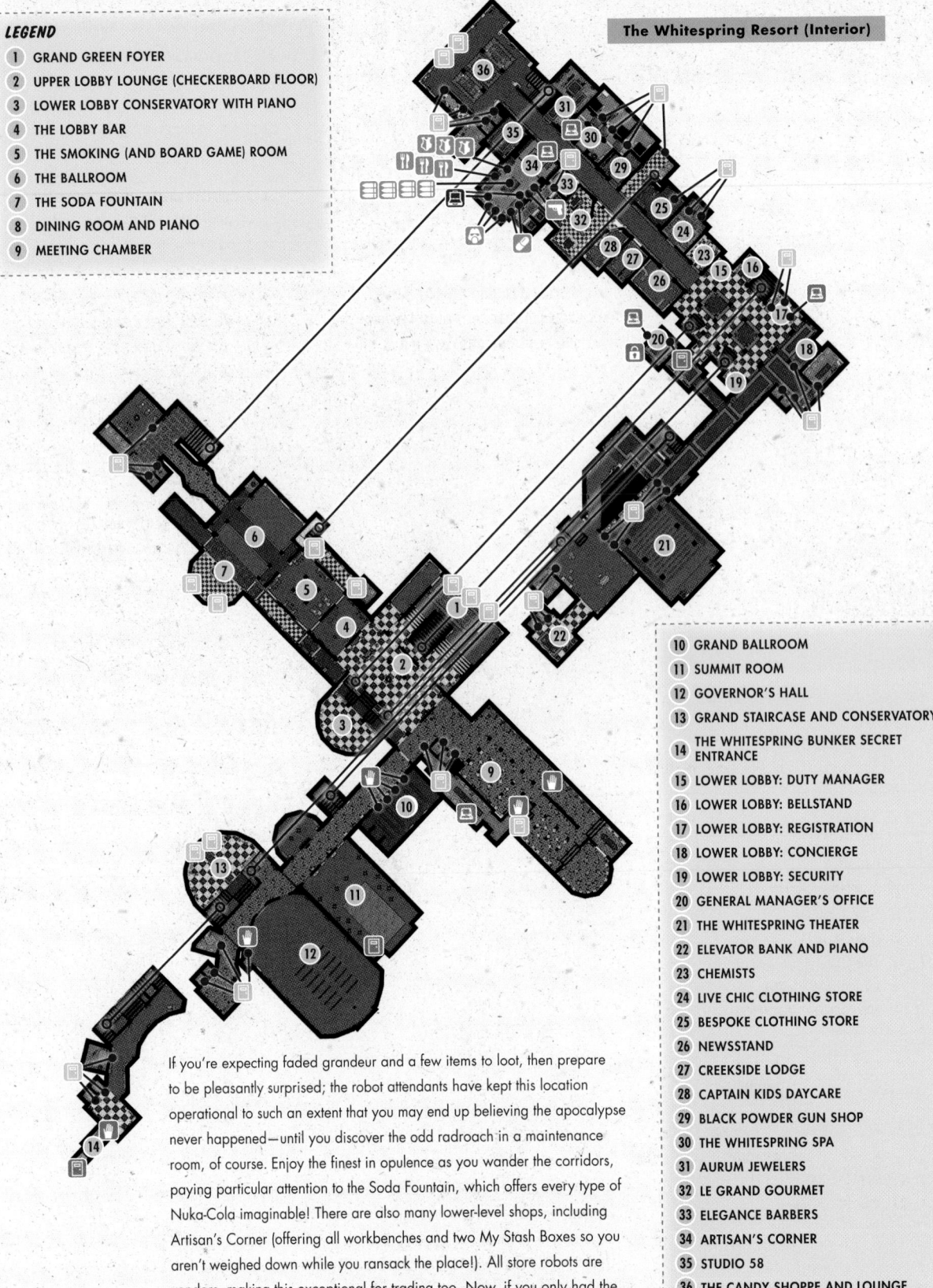

10. GRAND BALLROOM
11. SUMMIT ROOM
12. GOVERNOR'S HALL
13. GRAND STAIRCASE AND CONSERVATORY
14. THE WHITESPRING BUNKER SECRET ENTRANCE
15. LOWER LOBBY: DUTY MANAGER
16. LOWER LOBBY: BELLSTAND
17. LOWER LOBBY: REGISTRATION
18. LOWER LOBBY: CONCIERGE
19. LOWER LOBBY: SECURITY
20. GENERAL MANAGER'S OFFICE
21. THE WHITESPRING THEATER
22. ELEVATOR BANK AND PIANO
23. CHEMISTS
24. LIVE CHIC CLOTHING STORE
25. BESPOKE CLOTHING STORE
26. NEWSSTAND
27. CREEKSIDE LODGE
28. CAPTAIN KIDS DAYCARE
29. BLACK POWDER GUN SHOP
30. THE WHITESPRING SPA
31. AURUM JEWELERS
32. LE GRAND GOURMET
33. ELEGANCE BARBERS
34. ARTISAN'S CORNER
35. STUDIO 58
36. THE CANDY SHOPPE AND LOUNGE

If you're expecting faded grandeur and a few items to loot, then prepare to be pleasantly surprised; the robot attendants have kept this location operational to such an extent that you may end up believing the apocalypse never happened—until you discover the odd radroach in a maintenance room, of course. Enjoy the finest in opulence as you wander the corridors, paying particular attention to the Soda Fountain, which offers every type of Nuka-Cola imaginable! There are also many lower-level shops, including Artisan's Corner (offering all workbenches and two My Stash Boxes so you aren't weighed down while you ransack the place!). All store robots are vendors, making this exceptional for trading too. Now, if you only had the hand scanner to access the hidden entrance into The Whitespring Bunker....

53. THE WHITESPRING SERVICE ENTRANCE

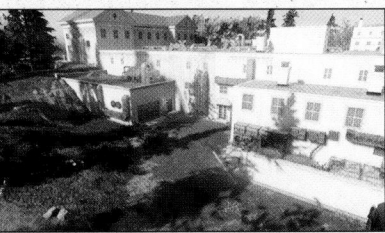

- **COLLECTIBLE: CAPS STASH**
- **LOCK: DOOR (S)**

Attached to the exterior of the main Whitespring Hotel exterior is an unassuming garage and service door. This white-brick structure is actually a secondary entrance and exit to The Whitespring Bunker, though a hand scanner and three laser grids prevent progress.

54. THE WHITESPRING BUNKER

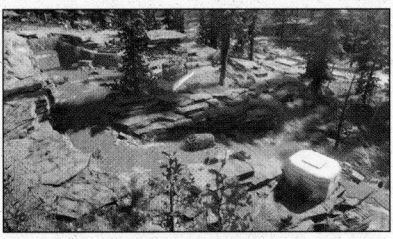

- **COLLECTIBLES: CAPS STASH (2), NUKA-CHERRY**
- **CRAFTING: ARMOR (4), CHEMISTRY (6), COOKING (3), POWER ARMOR (11), TINKER (4), WEAPONS (4)**
- **DANGER: RADIATION!**
- **ITEMS: ARMS AND AMMO; HARVESTABLE: BLACKBERRY; HEALTH AND CHEMS; VENDING MACHINE: DISPENSER, MEDICAL SUPPLIES**

- **INFO: EXPECTED ENEMY: ROBOT; QUEST: THE MOTHERLODE; SCAVENGE RATING: 4; SIZE: 4; THREAT LEVEL: 15–99**
- **LOCK: DOOR (KEY)**
- **ITEM EXAMPLES: BATTERED CLIPBOARD+, CIGAR BOX, COFFEE CUP+, COFFEE POT, CRAM, CUTTING BOARD, DESK FAN, DINNER PLATE, DIRTY ASHTRAY, ENAMEL BUCKET+, GLASS JAR+, GLOBE, HOT PLATE, INDUSTRIAL OIL CANISTER, LEAD PIPE, LIGHTBULB, MR. HANDY FUEL, NEW WILLOW BARREL VASE+, NUKA-COLA BOTTLE, PACK OF CIGARETTES, PACK OF DUCT TAPE, PIPE PISTOL, PORTABLE FUEL TANK, POOL BALL, POOL CUE, RACK, SALT+, SAUCER++, SECURITY BATON, SUGAR, SURGICAL TRAY, TALL BEAKER, TEAPOT, TEACUP++, TELEPHONE+**

The Whitespring Bunker (Interior)

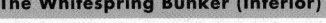

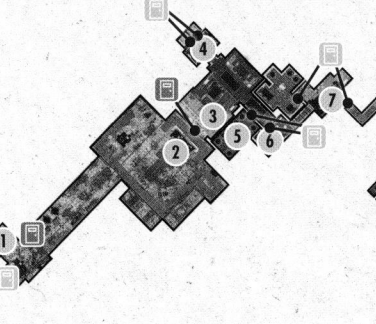

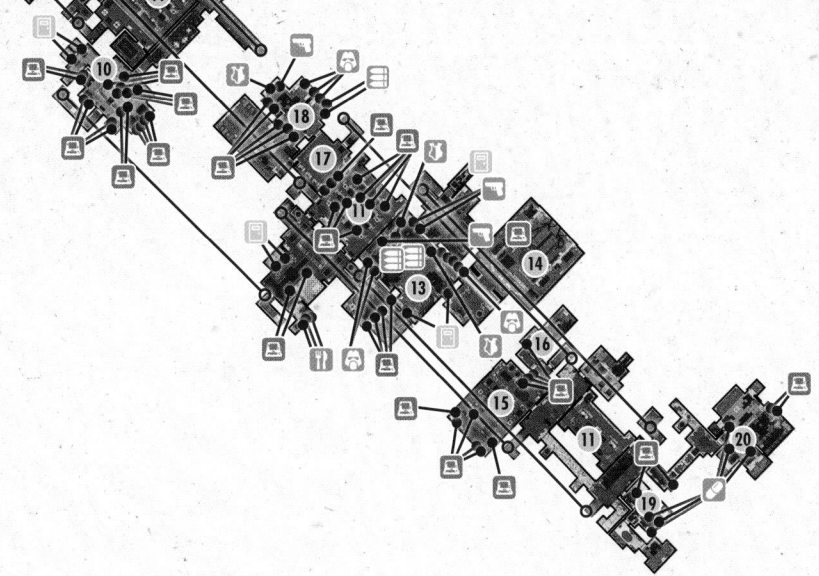

LEGEND

1. OUTER SECURITY OFFICE
2. STORAGE AND VAULT DOOR CONTROLS
3. ENTRANCE
4. ELEVATORS
5. ROBOTICS ROOM
6. INTAKE
7. BUNKER SECURITY
8. ORIENTATION
9. GAME ROOM
10. ADMISSIONS
11. COMMUNICATIONS
12. PRESIDENTIAL ROOMS
13. PRODUCTION
14. ROBOTICS AND REACTOR
15. MILITARY WING: OPERATIONS
16. MILITARY WING: BRIG
17. MILITARY WING: COMMAND
18. MILITARY WING: ARMORY
19. MEDICAL BAY
20. SCIENCE WING

This is part of The Whitespring Resort, and the exterior map is referenced with that location. There are three separate access points: the service entrance, the hidden exit from the military wing into the resort hotel, and the maintenance hut entrance shown on the map. You need an ID card and your best behavior in order to enter this large, well-kept vault (due to the multiple robots that turn hostile if you start shooting). Access the Modus terminals, learn about the different mutated species the geneticists are tracking, and even find a special suit of Power Armor.

TRAINING

CRAFTING AND C.A.M.P.ING

INVENTORY

QUESTS

ATLAS

BESTIARY

APPENDICES

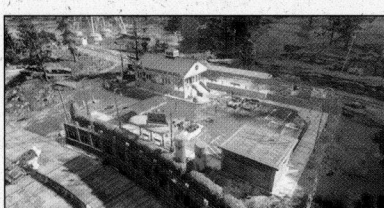

- **COLLECTIBLE:** NUKA-CHERRY
- **CRAFTING:** TINKER'S
- **ITEMS:** ARMS AND AMMO; HEALTH AND CHEMS; MY STASH BOX; VENDING MACHINE: AMMUNITION, MEDICAL SUPPLIES
- **INFO:** SCAVENGE RATING: 2; SIZE: 2; SLEEPING; TRADER: VENDOR BOT; THREAT LEVEL: 15–99
- **ITEM EXAMPLES:** COOKING POT, GLOWING FUNGUS PUREE+, ORNAMENTAL VASE+, PLASTIC SPOON+, PURIFIED WATER, SHOT GLASS, TABLETOP PICTURE FRAME, WHISKEY, WINE

As one might expect, there's a higher standard of workmanship and cleanliness once you pry open the locked door (0) that leads to this station's plush interior. Outside, use the Stash Box and Vendor Bot between missions in and around Whitespring.

ZONE B: SECONDARY LOCATIONS

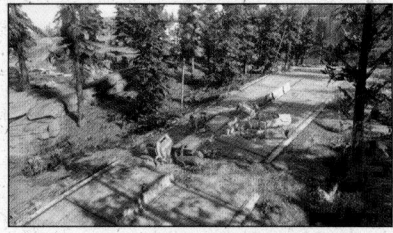
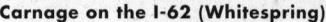

Carnage on the I-62 (Whitespring)

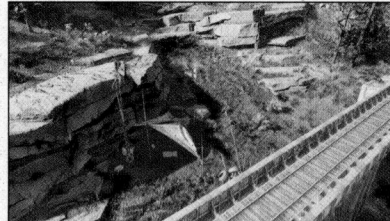

Seneca Skewer

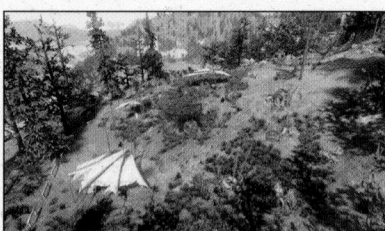

Ski Lift Base Camp

Appalachia: Savage Divide (Zone B) – Secondary Locations

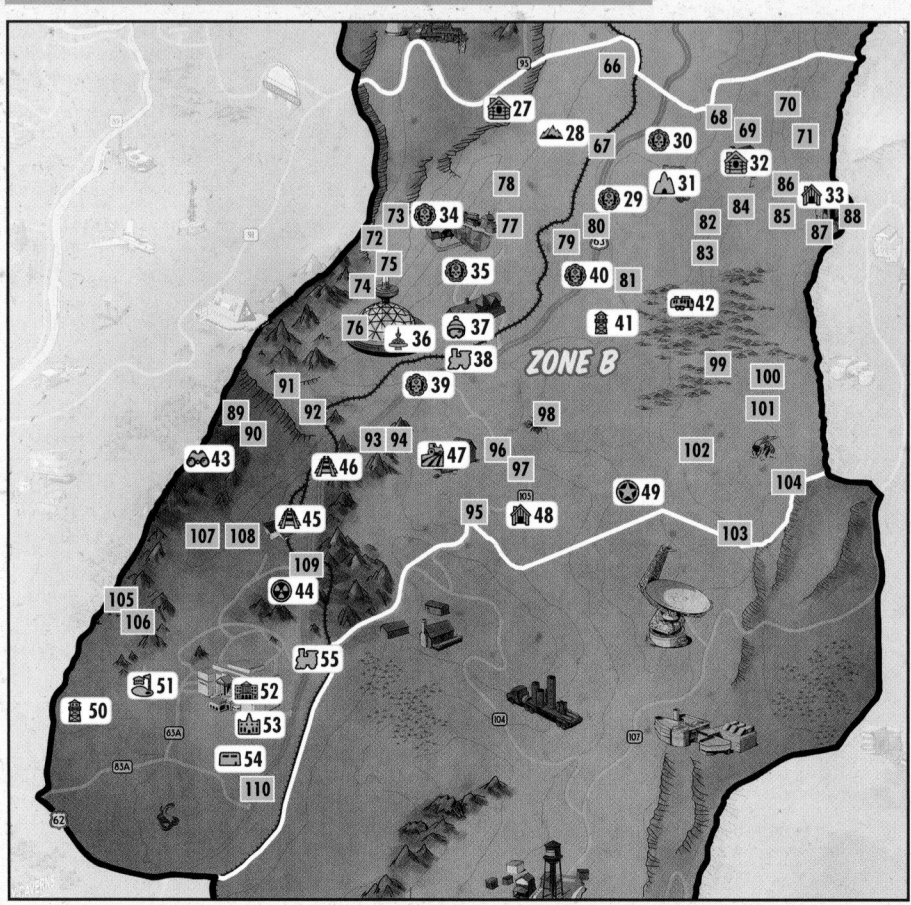

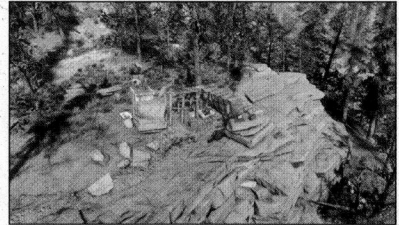

Moonshiner's Overlook

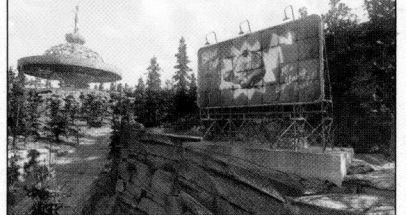
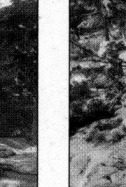

Blue Zip Billboard

Bathtub Garden Camp

#	NAME	DESCRIPTION
66	Gnomes' Allotment	Half-buried pickups are the planters for this carrot and tato garden, tended to by inanimate dwarven folk.
67	Seneca Skewer	An impressive rusty pole with multiple skewered corpses on it, near the red rail bridge.
68	Military Comms Tower Autumn Acre	A small, quest-related comms dish standing on a wood deck at a cliff edge, near a large collection of human cages.
69	Gnomes on the Range	Cousin Ted sits over a trio of gnomes as they inspect some skeletal remains on a rock outcrop.
70	Isolated Outhouse (north of Autumn Acres Cabin)	Plans, two toolboxes, and a skeleton with a crushed skull are all close to a rickety outhouse among the rocks.
71	Autumn Acre Rollover Crash	A military SUV and a cyclist have both succumbed to the elements after crashing down this remote ravine.
72	Picnic Overlook	A cliffside picnic area with stunning views to the west, Silt Beans to nibble on, and a possible Albino Radstag sighting!
73	Rock Outcrop Tarp Camp (west of Skullbone Vantage)	A small, blue tarp tent camp of a woodsman, close to the gondolas.
74	Shenanigan Raider Tower of Power	A monumental windmill on the dirt ski slopes north of Top of the World, with steps and platforms that lead to ammo at the top.
75	Going, Going, Gondola	The remains of the ski lift has its upper anchor point here; check the fallen and hanging gondolas for possible items or sniping positions.
76	Ski Lift Base Camp	A medium-sized camp of rusting red gondolas, below and west of Top of the World.
77	Pleasant Valley Picnic Vista	A good place to stop, admire the view, use the cooking station, and pick up a new sniper rifle.
78	Battle Site	Gore splatters, Hallucigen canisters, and corpses on the rocks on this mountainous cliffside terrain.
79	Walking Trail Picnic Area and Vista	Though the view is still there, the laughing picnic-goers have been replaced by skeletal corpses and slowly rotting junk.
80	Roadkill Raider Spikes	A collection of severed heads on spikes on the way from Interstate 63 to the Sludge Hole.
81	Pond and Raft (Central Mountains)	A settler lies quietly rotting on a small floating raft with a blue tarp sail on a small cliffside pond.
82	Gardener's Shack	Aster, Carrots, Tato, and Wild Carrot Flowers are grown next to a tiny cabin with a sleeping bag, against the rock cliff.
83	Marksman's Trailer	An old military truck pulling a metal trailer has parked up on a rocky bluff. Check the trailer for a Weapons Workbench.
84	The Fishing Spot: Autumn Acres	A small pond with a rickety jetty and some strewn skeletons.
85	Autumn Acre Arch	An interesting geological novelty, a rock arch southeast of Autumn Acres.
86	Moonshiner's Overlook	On the edge of Toxic Larry's, this clifftop platform and small camp has two resident skeletons and some Aster to harvest.
87	Larry's Tent Camp and Switchbacks	Below Larry's meat shack is a steep path up from Berkeley Springs and a campground with Wild Carrot Flower to pick.

#	NAME	DESCRIPTION
88	Copper Load of This!	A selection of Copper Veins on the rocks east of Toxic Larry's Meat 'n Go.
89	Stuck in the Mud	Matters took a turn for the bloody during the rescue of one pickup truck using a winch from another.
90	Cliffwatch Offroader	A rusty vehicle with a skeletal driver has given up the ghost halfway up this mountain. Grab the jug and gas mask before you leave.
91	Cliff Path Duel	On the narrow rock tiers in this rough terrain are two skeletons, both slain in a possible duel, though one has a pickax through his skull.
92	Tent Camp (southwest of Top of the World)	A green tent with a cooking station, wild carrot flowers, and two mattresses to sleep on, under the path of the electrical pylons.
93	Pileup on I-63	An impressive mangle of rust, steel, and skeletal remains on the interstate.
94	Blue Zip Billboard	A billboard above Interstate 63 hides a small camp at its base with items, a cooking station, and a sleeping bag.
95	DUI on Route 105	A crashed car with the driver's skeletal remains next to the moonshine jug that caused the accident.
96	The Broken Bus: Raider Checkpoint	Mangled metal, pieces of vehicles, spikes, and small lookouts, as well as possible Raider Power Armor on the upper roadside rocks.
97	Road Washout (Route 105)	The road is almost completely washed away in places on this high mountain pass.
98	Rotting Rowboat (Acid Pond)	A decaying rowboat moored at a small pond with an Acid deposit beneath the waters.
99	Fallen Tree Camp	Evidence of an amateur's attempt at a camp, with boards nailed against a clifftop tree.
100	Ravine Camp	Two sleeping bags in the back of a pickup, Firecracker berries to gnaw on, and a cooking station; also come to this ravine for the junk.
101	Biker's Grove	One of the dotted rusting trailers in this region, though this one was used by a dirt bike fan. There's a sleeping bag in the trailer.
102	Garden Gnome Party	A couple of skeletons and garden gnomes in a shallow rock fissure.
103	Quiet Time Chem Trailer	A rusty caravan trailer with a cooking and chem station, wooden platform battlements, and some choice junk and blackberries.
104	Bathtub Garden Camp	A gnome seems happy with himself as he guards a bathtub of tato and carrot plants in this small camp against a rock wall.
105	Cliffwatch Target Range	A steep slope and a jug of mountain honey await those seeking target practice down this mountain.
106	The Clifftop Drunkard	A rusty SUV and a skeleton with a scattering of vices sit atop this rocky bluff.
107	Raider Lookout (south of Cliffwatch)	Need to check out Whitespring and cook, sleep, or play the guitar too? Then this is the lookout to look for.
108	Outcrop Camp (northwest of Safe 'n Clean Disposal)	A cooking station, tent, sleeping bag, some tinned coffee, and evidence of Super Mutant human cages.
109	New Appalachian Underpass	A mangle of two coaches and a small Raider checkpoint under the rail bridge.
110	Carnage on the I-62 (Whitespring)	Corpses in various forms of disintegration lie next to mangled vehicles in various forms of disintegration. Come for the junk.

TRAINING

CRAFTING AND C.A.M.P.ING

INVENTORY

QUESTS

ATLAS

BESTIARY

APPENDICES

SAVAGE DIVIDE: ZONE C— SOUTH MOUNTAINS, SUGAR GROVE, AND SPRUCE KNOB

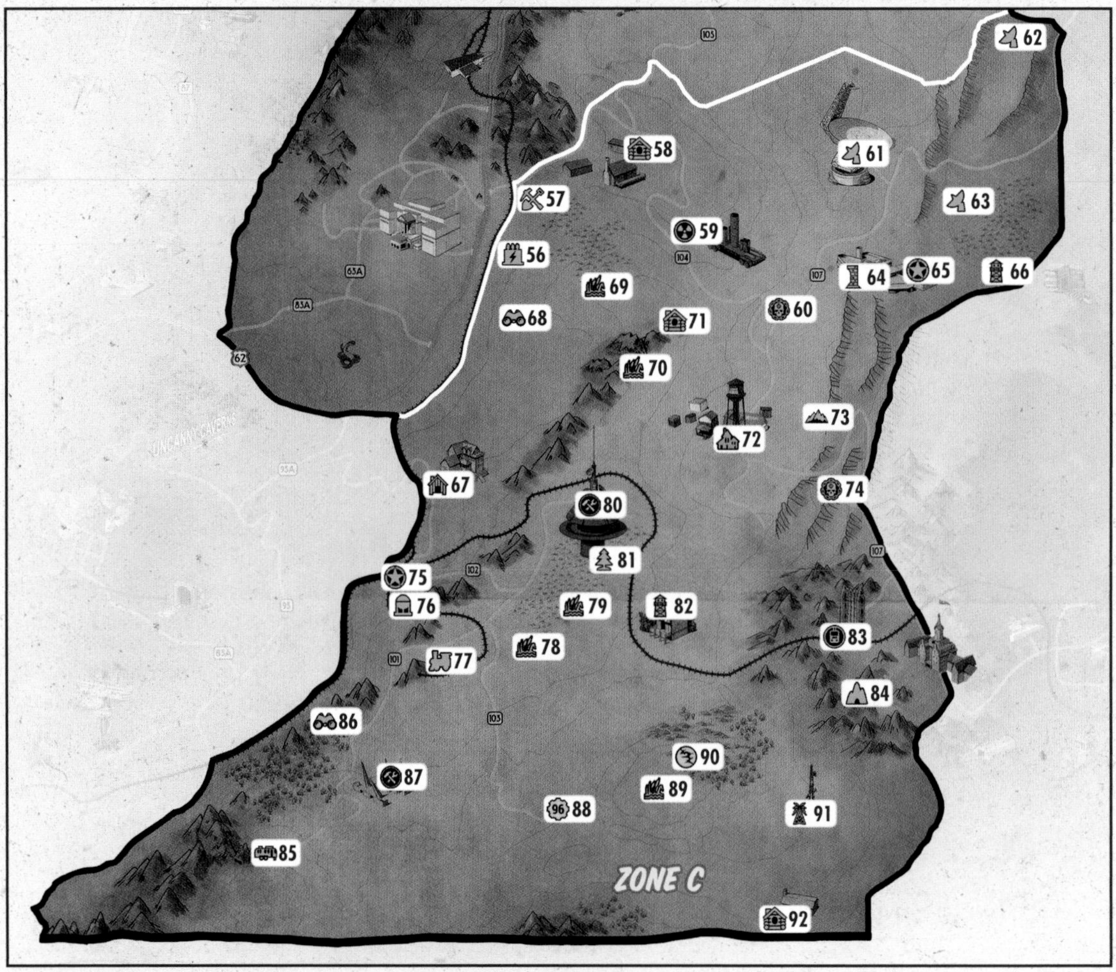

Appalachia: **Savage Divide (Zone C) – Primary Locations**

A giant green thumbtack known as Spruce Knob isn't even the largest landmark in this part of the region; that honor belongs to the National Isolated Radio Array—a dish of epic proportions, though the real prize (if you like holotapes and Caps Stashes) is inside a secondary scientific center to the northeast known as Sugar Grove. Elsewhere there are mines, remote cabins, mountain lakes with only lightly irradiated waters, scattered Raider camps, a natural landmark of razor-sharp rock known as Devil's Backbone, a quaint bed-and-breakfast, and the tallest structure outside of Watoga—a vertigo-inducing monorail monolith close to Cranberry Bog.

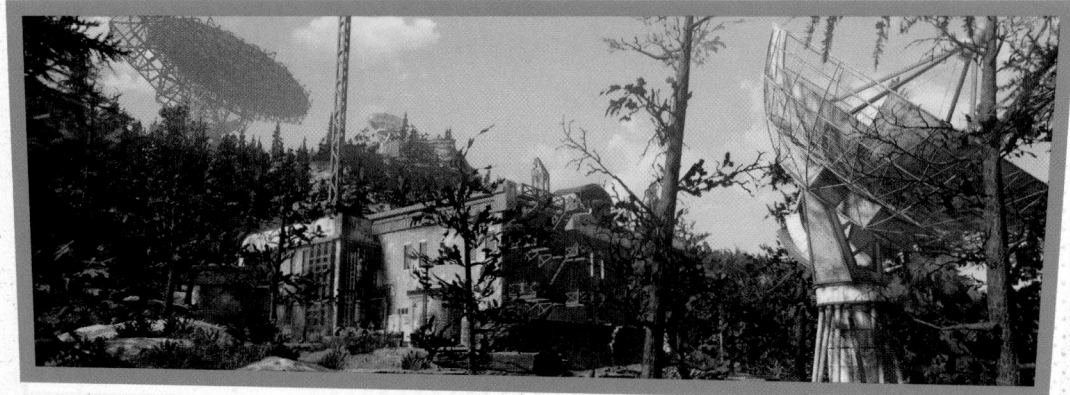

WORLD MAP LEGEND

— REGION BOUNDARY   — ZONE BOUNDARY

■ BOBBLEHEADS   ■ CAP STASHES   ■ MAGAZINES   ■ POWER ARMOR

PRIMARY LOCATIONS

Bobbleheads	Cap Stashes	Magazines	Power Armor	#	NAME
				56	MONONGAH POWER SUBSTATION MZ-02
4		4	1	57	BLACKWATER MINE
2	1	2	1	58	MIDDLE MOUNTAIN CABINS
3		2	1	59	EMMETT MOUNTAIN DISPOSAL SITE
1		1	1	60	RIPPER ALLEY
4		3	1	61	NATIONAL ISOLATED RADIO ARRAY
6	9	6		62	SUGAR GROVE
2		2		63	NATIONAL RADIO ASTRONOMY RESEARCH CENTER
1	7	1		64	WEST TEK RESEARCH CENTER
2		2	1	65	US-13C BIVOUAC
				66	EAST MOUNTAIN LOOKOUT
5		4		67	MOUNTAINSIDE BED & BREAKFAST
		1		68	THE VANTAGE
2		2	2	69	SOLOMON'S POND
		1		70	TWIN LAKES
				71	INVESTIGATOR'S CABIN
2		2	2	72	HUNTERSVILLE
				73	DEVIL'S BACKBONE
1				74	THE FREAK SHOW

Bobbleheads	Cap Stashes	Magazines	Power Armor	#	NAME
4	3	1		75	SITE CHARLIE
1	2			76	R&G PROCESSING SERVICES
		1		77	R&G STATION
				78	SPRUCE KNOB CHANNELS
1	1			79	SPRUCE KNOB LAKE
1	1			80	SPRUCE KNOB
1				81	SPRUCE KNOB CAMPGROUND
				82	SOUTH MOUNTAIN LOOKOUT
				83	MONORAIL ELEVATOR
3	1	1		84	LUCKY HOLE MINE
				85	DENT & SONS CONSTRUCTION
				86	SCENIC OVERLOOK
		1		87	FEDERAL DISPOSAL FIELD HZ-21
				88	VAULT 96
		1		89	LAKE ELOISE
				90	FISSURE SITE GAMMA
1	1			91	RELAY TOWER EL-B1-02
2	2	1		92	JOHNSON'S ACRE

ZONE C: PRIMARY LOCATIONS

MAP LEGEND

MAP LEGEND
- MY STASH BOX
- OVERSEER'S CACHE
- TRUNK
- TRADER

COLLECTIBLES
- BOBBLEHEAD
- MAGAZINE
- POWER ARMOR

CRAFTING
- ARMOR WORKBENCH
- CHEMISTRY WORKBENCH
- COOKING STATION
- POWER ARMOR STATION
- TINKER'S WORKBENCH
- WEAPONS WORKBENCH
- WORKSHOP WORKBENCH

IMPORTANT
- DOOR/GATE
- LOCKED DOOR/GATE
- SAFE
- SCANNER
- TERMINAL

56. MONONGAH POWER SUBSTATION MZ-02

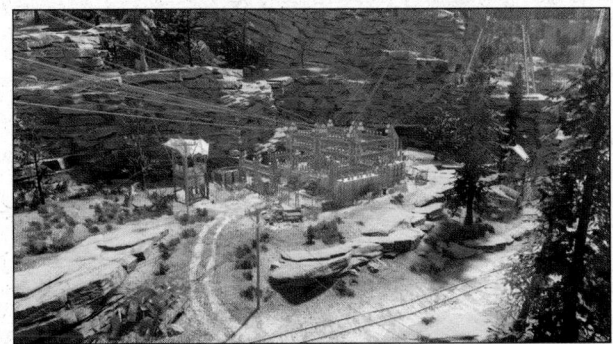

- **ITEMS:** ARMS AND AMMO; HARVESTABLE: BLACKBERRY
- **INFO:** C.A.M.P. POWER; EXPECTED ENEMY: CANINE, GHOUL, MOLE RAT; SCAVENGE RATING: 1; SIZE: 1; THREAT LEVEL: 15–99
- **ITEM EXAMPLES:** MOP, TIN CANISTER, USED OIL CAN

This substation has the added "bonus" of some ramshackle Raider defenses you can clear, though the place doesn't have an overabundance of junk. Restore power to the Monongah Power Plant, and expect to use this to power a C.A.M.P. you may wish to set up.

TRAINING
CRAFTING AND C.A.M.P.ING
INVENTORY
QUESTS
ATLAS
BESTIARY
APPENDICES

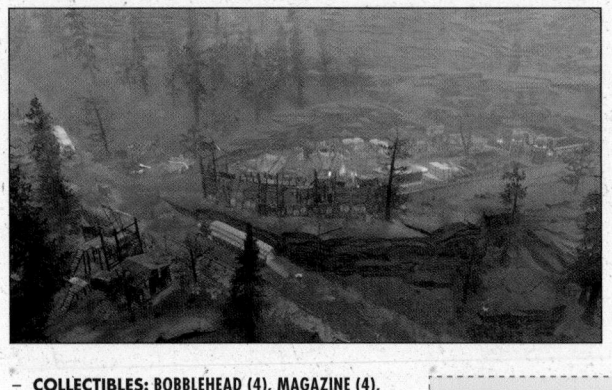

Blackwater Mine (Exterior)

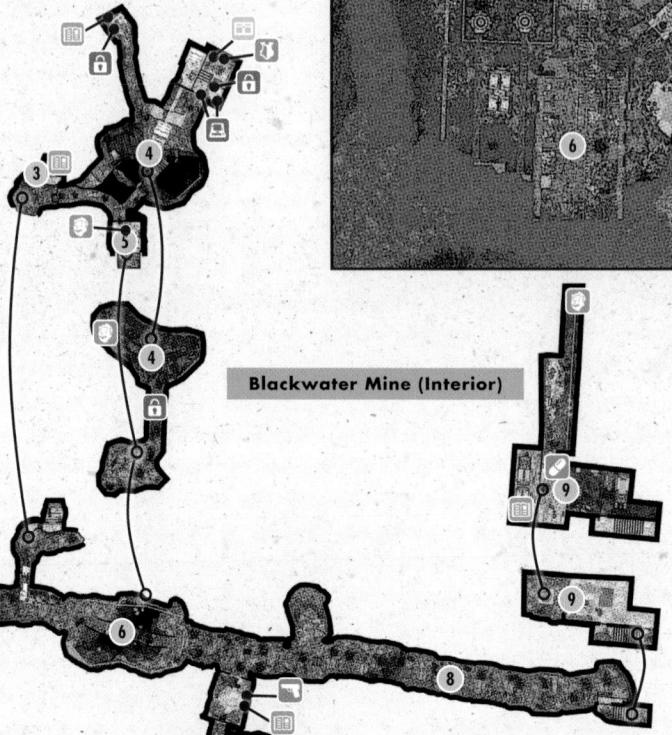

- **COLLECTIBLES:** BOBBLEHEAD (4), MAGAZINE (4), POWER ARMOR
- **CRAFTING:** ARMOR (2), CHEMISTRY (2), COOKING (2), POWER ARMOR, TINKER, WEAPONS (2)
- **DANGER:** EXPLOSIVE CANISTER! RADIATION!
- **ITEMS:** ARMS AND AMMO+; HARVESTABLE: BRAIN FUNGUS; HEALTH AND CHEMS+; TRUNK
- **INFO:** EXPECTED ENEMY: IRRADIATED ANIMAL, MOLE MINER; EVENT: URANIUM FEVER; SCAVENGE RATING: 4; SIZE: 4; SLEEPING; THREAT LEVEL: 15–99
- **LOCK:** DOOR (2), SAFE (1, 2, 2, 3)
- **ITEM EXAMPLES:** BAG OF CEMENT, BLOWTORCH, CARTON OF CIGARETTES, CIGAR BOX, COOLANT++, DIRTY DESKTOP FRAME, DUCT TAPE, EXTINGUISHER, FUEL TANK+, FUSION CORE+, GAS CANISTER++, GOLD PLATED FLIP LIGHTER, HARD HAT+, INSTAMASH, MICROSCOPE, MINING HELMET, MAKESHIFT BATTERY+, METAL BUCKET, OIL CANISTER+, PACK OF CIGARETTES, PILLOW, POTATO CRISPS, PORTABLE FUEL TANK, SHORT HUNTING RIFLE, SOAP, STEEL WORKERS HELMET, TALL DRINKING GLASS, TOILET PAPER+, VOLATILE MATERIALS BOX+, WINE+

LEGEND

1. OLD STORE
2. CONCRETE HUT AND BATTLEMENTS
3. SMALL TRAILERS
4. MECHANIC'S SHED
5. WAREHOUSE STORE
6. MINE WAREHOUSE

Blackwater Mine (Interior)

After being closed due to leaking uranium detected inside the mine structure, this was a shanty camp and Raider stronghold and is now the domain of the odd and dangerous Mole Miners. Check the exterior for signs of a trading location, now reduced to rotting counters and battlements, along with rusting warehouses and the mine entrance. Inside, the mine is partly waterlogged and has more Mole Miners than you might expect. Blackwater Mine exit is just south of Monongah Power Substation MZ-02; look for the hatch in the rocks just east of the railroad tracks overlooking Whitespring.

LEGEND

1. RESTROOM AND DECONTAMINATION
2. ENTRANCE OFFICE
3. WATER SYSTEMS SECURITY ROOM
4. WATERLOGGED CAVERN AND DR. COTTON'S CAVE LABORATORY
5. MINE TUNNEL BRIDGE SECURITY ROOM
6. MINE TUNNEL BRIDGE
7. DRILLING CHAMBERS
8. WATERLOGGED TUNNEL
9. AIR EXTRACTION, GENERATORS AND EXIT TUNNEL

🏠 58. MIDDLE MOUNTAIN CABINS

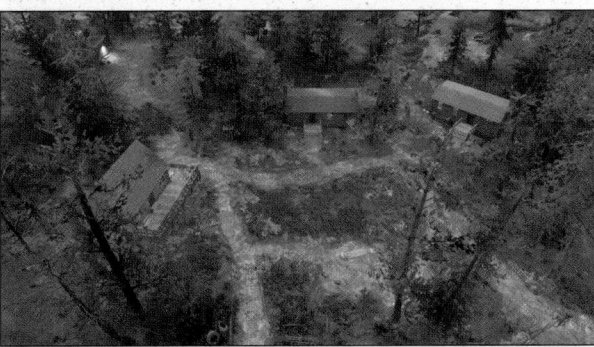

- **COLLECTIBLES:** BOBBLEHEAD (2), CAPS STASH, MAGAZINE (2), POWER ARMOR
- **ITEMS:** ARMS AND AMMO; HARVESTABLE: WILD CARROT FLOWER, WOOD PILE
- **INFO:** EXPECTED ENEMY: CRYPTID, IRRADIATED INSECT; SCAVENGE RATING: 3; SIZE: 2; SLEEPING; THREAT LEVEL: 15–99
- **ITEM EXAMPLES:** BLACKWATER BREW, BLAST RADIUS BOARD GAME, HAIRBRUSH, PICKAXE PILSNER, PILLOW, RED PLATE+, TALL DRINKING GLASS+, TOASTER

Head off route 105 to investigate this trio of scout cabins deep in the remote mountain wilderness. Chat to the Robotron here for more information, and search for some collectibles and junk.

☢ 59. EMMETT MOUNTAIN DISPOSAL SITE

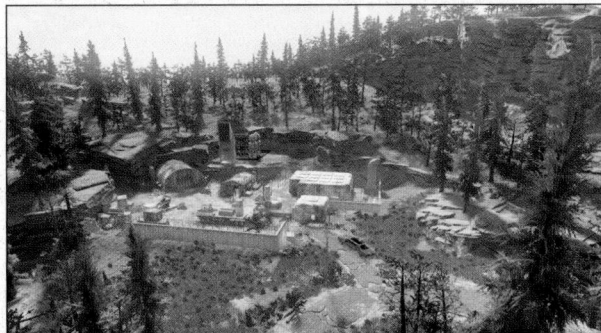

- **COLLECTIBLES:** BOBBLEHEAD (3), MAGAZINE (2), POWER ARMOR
- **CRAFTING:** POWER ARMOR
- **DANGER:** EXPLOSIVE CANISTER! RADIATION!++
- **ITEM:** ARMS AND AMMO
- **INFO:** EXPECTED ENEMY: DEATHCLAW, IRRADIATED INSECT, SCORCHED; SCAVENGE RATING: 3; SIZE: 3; THREAT LEVEL: 15–99
- **LOCK:** DOOR (1)
- **ITEM EXAMPLES:** ABRAXO CLEANER, ALUMINUM SCRAP, BOILED WATER, EXTINGUISHER, FUSION CORE, HAZMAT SUIT+, LOOSE SCREWS, METAL BUCKET, MOP, PURIFIED WATER, SHORT LASER PISTOL, SUGAR, TELEPHONE, TURPENTINE, USED OIL CAN, VOLATILE MATERIALS BOX, WASTE ACID, WONDERGLUE, YELLOW PAINT

Emmett Mountain Disposal Site (Exterior)

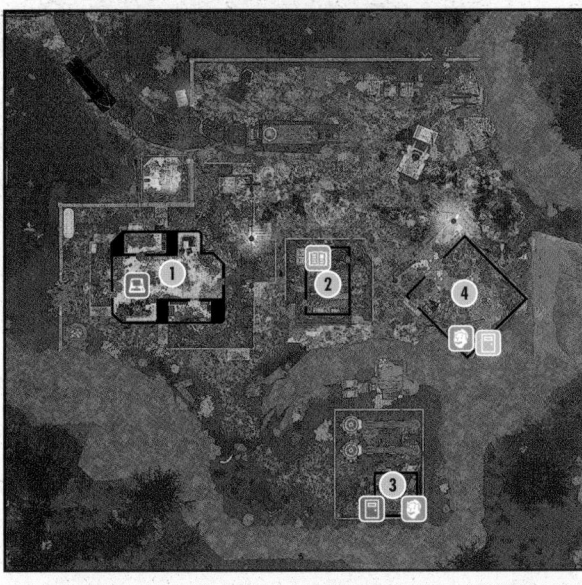

LEGEND
1. OFFICE AND STORAGE
2. WASTE STORAGE SHED
3. MECHANICS SHED
4. HAZARDOUS WASTE MINE ENTRANCE

Emmett Mountain Disposal Site (Interior)

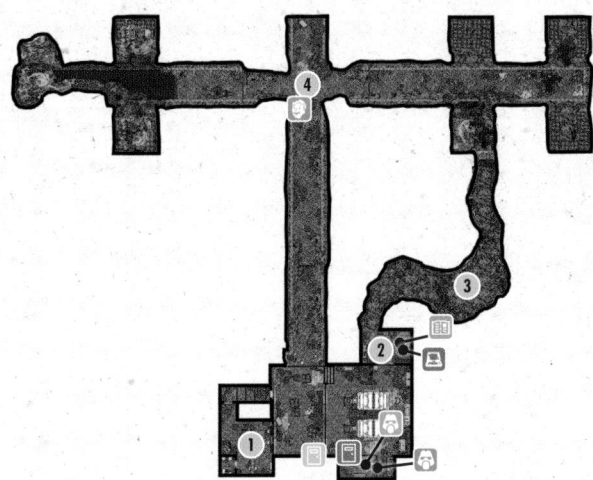

LEGEND
1. LOCKER ROOM AND DECONTAMINATION
2. STORAGE AND OFFICE
3. NATURAL TUNNEL
4. TUNNEL CROSSROADS

Just off the bend in the road on Route 104 is a radioactive dumping ground, ripe for the scavenging (assuming you have the necessary protective gear). The curved-roof mine entrance leads to a couple of mine tunnels, stacked with leaking barrels and toxic water. Find narrower tunnels that all lead to a hole in the security room at the entrance, where you can possibly claim some Power Armor.

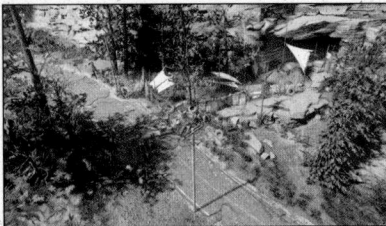

- **COLLECTIBLES:** BOBBLEHEAD, MAGAZINE, POWER ARMOR
- **CRAFTING:** COOKING
- **DANGER:** TENSION TRIGGER!
- **ITEMS:** ARMS AND AMMO, HARVESTABLE: BLACKBERRY

- **INFO:** EXPECTED ENEMY: SCORCHED; SCAVENGE RATING: 2; SIZE: 1; THREAT LEVEL: 15–99
- **ITEM EXAMPLES:** BEER BOTTLE, BOBBY PIN BOX, CRANBERRY MOONSHINE+, FRAG MINE, MOONSHINE JUG, PORTABLE FUEL TANK, TIN CANISTER

Raiders once guarded this uphill stretch of Route 107 leading to and from West Tek Research Center. Now the place offers a few choice scavenging items and perhaps some light reading.

61. NATIONAL ISOLATED RADIO ARRAY

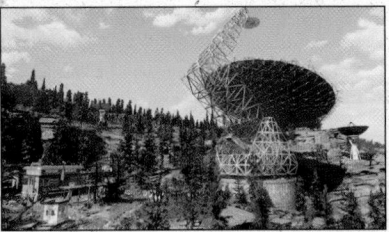

- **COLLECTIBLES:** BOBBLEHEAD (4), CAPS STASH, HOLOTAPE, MAGAZINE (3), POWER ARMOR
- **CRAFTING:** WEAPONS
- **ITEMS:** HARVESTABLE: GLOWING RESIN; HEALTH AND CHEMS
- **INFO:** EXPECTED ENEMY: GHOUL, SUPER MUTANT; SCAVENGE RATING: 4; SIZE: 5; THREAT LEVEL: 15–99
- **LOCK:** DOOR (1, 2, C), SAFE (2)
- **ITEM EXAMPLES:** ABRAXO CLEANER, ALUMINUM CANISTER, ANTIFREEZE BOTTLE+, BAG OF CEMENT, BASEBALL, BOBBY PIN BOX, BOTTLECAP SUNGLASSES, BROKEN LAMP, BURNT BOOK, CIGAR BOX, COFFEE CUP+, COFFEE POT, COOLANT, CRAM, DESK FAN+, DINNER PLATE, DIRTY ASHTRAY, DUCT TAPE, ECONOMY WONDERGLUE, ENAMEL BUCKET, HOT PLATE, MAGNIFYING GLASS, METAL BUCKET, NUKA-COLA BOTTLE, OIL CANISTER, OVEN MITT, PACK OF CIGARETTES, PENCIL, PICKAXE PILSNER, PIPE WRENCH, PLASTIC PUMPKIN++, PLUNGER, PORTABLE FUEL TANK, SAW, TEAL ROUNDED VASE, TELEPHONE+, TUBE FLANGE, TYPEWRITER+, USED OIL CAN+, VODKA, WHISKEY, WONDERGLUE

LEGEND (EXTERIOR)

1. SECURITY HUT (OFFICE PARKING LOT)
2. OFFICE BUILDING
3. SECURITY HUT (MAINTENANCE YARD)
4. MAINTENANCE WAREHOUSE
5. DISH ARRAY CONTROL HUTS
6. GIANT SATELLITE DISH

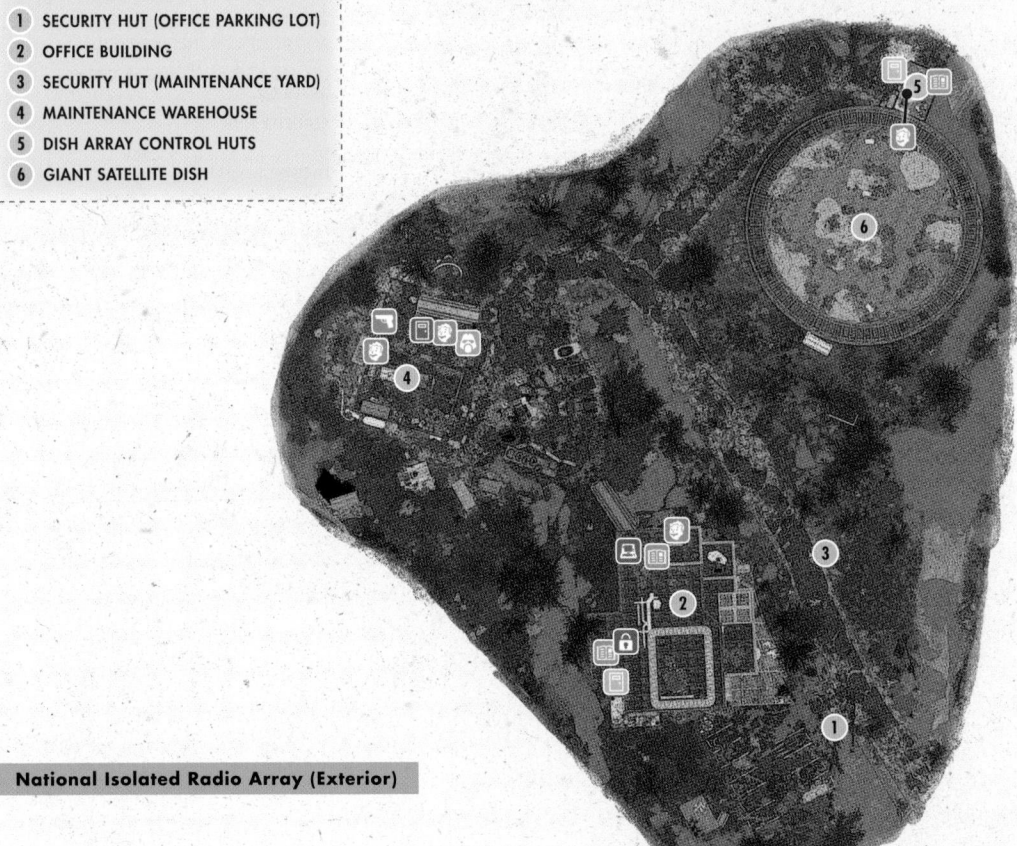

National Isolated Radio Array (Exterior)

The crown jewel in the old National Radio Quiet Zone is the rectangular area of land encompassing this location known as the National Radio Isolated Radio Array. The office building is relatively small, with a main open-plan area and some exterior rooms, including one with a sagging floor that allows you to reach a ground-floor chamber with a chained door. Continue to the maintenance warehouse to gather more junk, and unlock the side room for a possible Power Armor frame. The massive dish array is controlled at a metal stilt hut but is currently offline. Aside from the base, the huge dish is inaccessible.

62. SUGAR GROVE

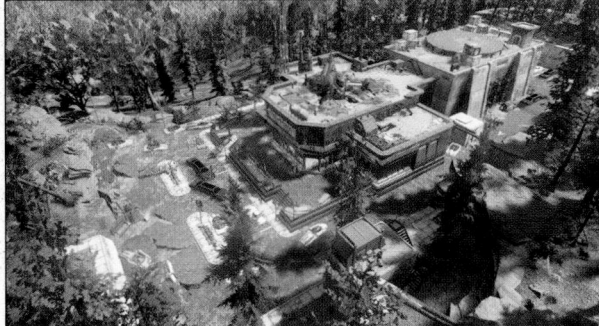

- **COLLECTIBLES:** BOBBLEHEAD (6), CAPS STASH (9), HOLOTAPE+++, MAGAZINE (6)
- **CRAFTING:** ARMOR (2), CHEMISTRY, WEAPONS (2)
- **DANGER:** LONG DROP! TURRET!
- **ITEMS:** ARMS AND AMMO++; HARVESTABLE: BLACKBERRY; HEALTH AND CHEMS; RECIPE/MOD//PLAN; TRUNK; VENDING MACHINE: ARCHIVAL DISPENSER
- **INFO:** EXPECTED ENEMY: IRRADIATED ANIMAL, ROBOT, SUPER MUTANT; SCAVENGE RATING: 5; SIZE: 4; SLEEPING; THREAT LEVEL: 15–99
- **LOCK:** DOOR (KEY, 1, KEY, KEY, KEY), SAFE (2, 2, 2), TERMINAL (KEY)
- **ITEM EXAMPLES:** ASHTRAY, BALL-PEEN HAMMER, BEER BOTTLE, BLANK HOLOTAPE+++, BOILED WATER, CARTON OF CIGARETTES+, COFFEE CUP++, COFFEE POT, CRAM, DETECTIVE CASE FILE, DIRTY ASHTRAY++, DIRTY DESKTOP FRAME+, DOG BOWL, FUEL TANK+, GAS CANISTER+, GLASS PITCHER+, GREASER JACKET AND JEANS, INSTAMASH, KITCHEN SCALES, LAB BOTTLE, MILITARY INTEL OFFICER DRESS HAT, MILITARY FATIGUES, OFFICE DESK FAN++, OIL CANISTER, SHORT AUTOMATIC LASER PISTOL, SUGAR BOMBS, TABLETOP PICTURE FRAME+, TELEPHONE+, TUBE FLANGE, VODKA BOTTLE+, WHISKEY+, WILLOW VAULTED VASE+, YUM YUM DEVILED EGGS

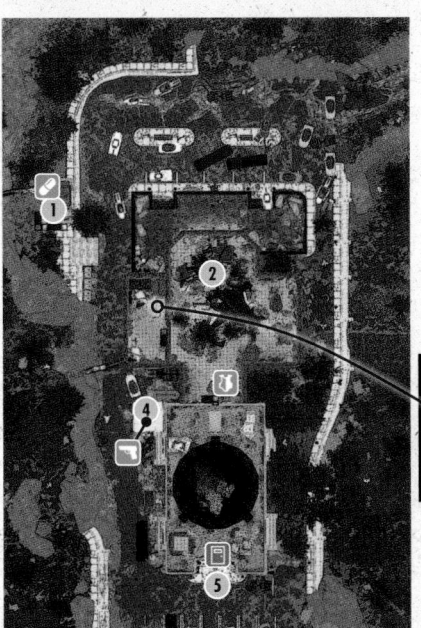

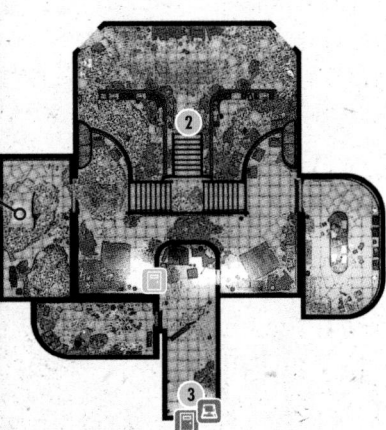

Sugar Grove (Exterior)

LEGEND

1. CONCRETE RADIO COMMS BOOTH
2. SUGAR GROVE FACILITY LOBBY AND ROOF (CRASHED VERTIBIRD)
3. LOCKED ACCESS TO SUGAR GROVE (INTERIOR)
4. SECURITY HUT
5. LOCKED ACCESS TO SECRET FACILITY (ELEVATOR)

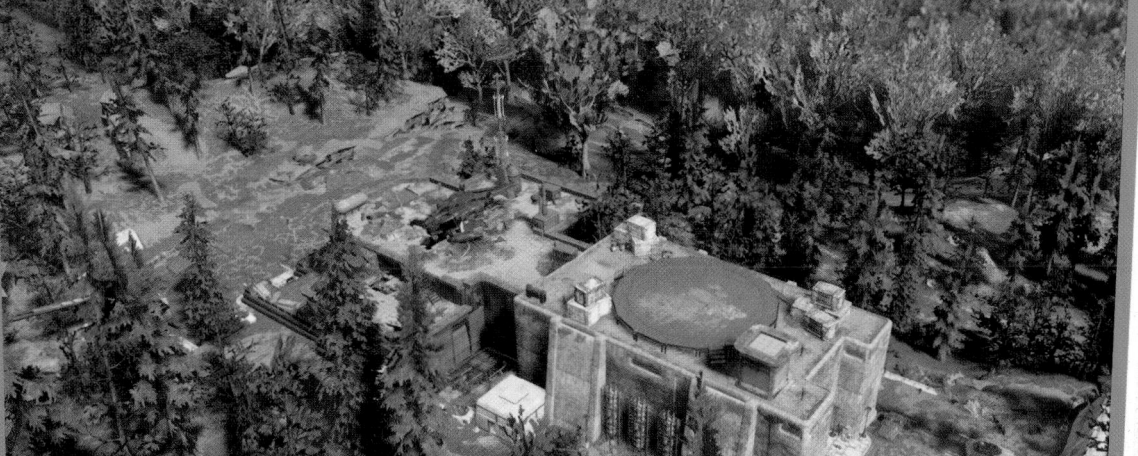

TRAINING

CRAFTING AND C.A.M.P.ING

INVENTORY

QUESTS

ATLAS

BESTIARY

APPENDICES

The Sugar Grove Communications Naval Radio Station was once connected to the other satellite stations in the area. It is now in a shocking state of disrepair, with the weight of a Vertibird compromising the roof, which also has a hole through which you can descend into the interior. To enter the structure, you must access the rear outside elevator or the foyer terminal, both requiring an ID.

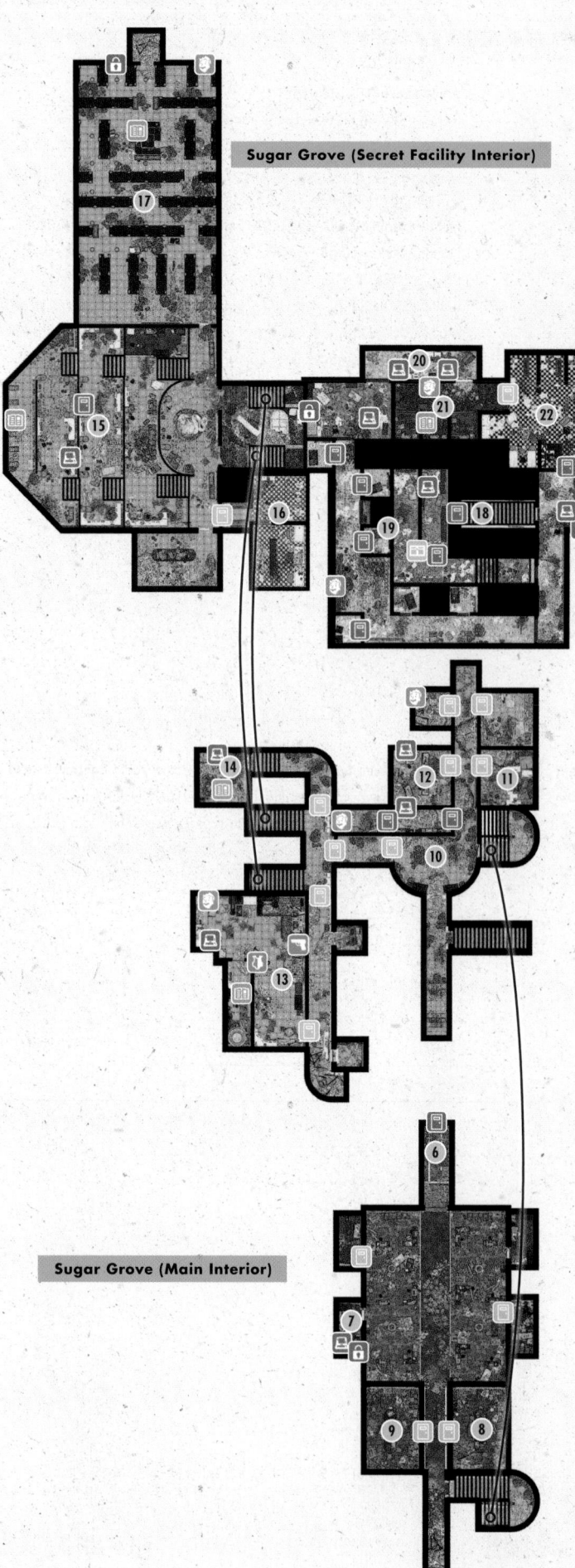

Sugar Grove (Secret Facility Interior)

Sugar Grove (Main Interior)

Inside, the immediate office space appears to have been compromised, and someone was attempting to amass flammable items before lighting the place on fire (this never actually occurred, despite the mess). Explore further to reach a huge mission control room, learn about cryptids, and uncover other secrets (and collectibles) as you go.

Enter the facility using the rear exterior elevator. You have a second door (ID) to access; this leads to a series of cells, an experimentation area, and a small infirmary.

63. NATIONAL RADIO ASTRONOMY RESEARCH CENTER

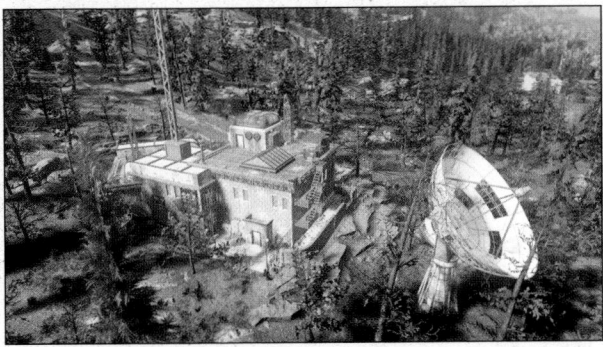

- COLLECTIBLES: BOBBLEHEAD (2), HOLOTAPE, MAGAZINE (2)
- CRAFTING: ARMOR

- **DANGER:** LONG DROP!
- **ITEMS:** HARVESTABLE: BLACKBERRY, WILD CARROT FLOWER; HEALTH AND CHEMS
- **INFO:** EXPECTED ENEMY: IRRADIATED INSECT, SCORCHED; NOTE; SCAVENGE RATING: 3; SIZE: 3; THREAT LEVEL: 15–99
- **LOCK:** DOOR (1, 2), SAFE (0, 1, 2), TERMINAL (2)
- **ITEM EXAMPLES:** ABRAXO CLEANER, ANTIQUE GLOBE, BAYONETED ARMOR-PIERCING PIPE PISTOL, BLUE BANDANNA, CHALK, CIGARETTE CARTON, COFFEE CUP+, COFFEE POT, COLANDER, DIRTY ASHTRAY, DOG BOWL, DUCT TAPE+, ECONOMY WONDERGLUE, FLIP LIGHTER, FUSE+, HARD HAT+, HOT PLATE, LARGE BABY BOTTLE, MENTATS, METAL BUCKET, MILITARY GRADE DUCT TAPE, MOP, NUKA-COLA, OFFICE DESK FAN, PACK OF CIGARETTES, PLUNGER+, PRE-WAR MONEY+, RAD-X, RAT POISON, SALISBURY STEAK, SMALL PICTURE FRAME, TALL DRINKING GLASS+, TEDDY BEAR, TELEPHONE+, TYPEWRITER+, YELLOW TABLE LAMP

National Radio Astronomy Research Center (Interior)

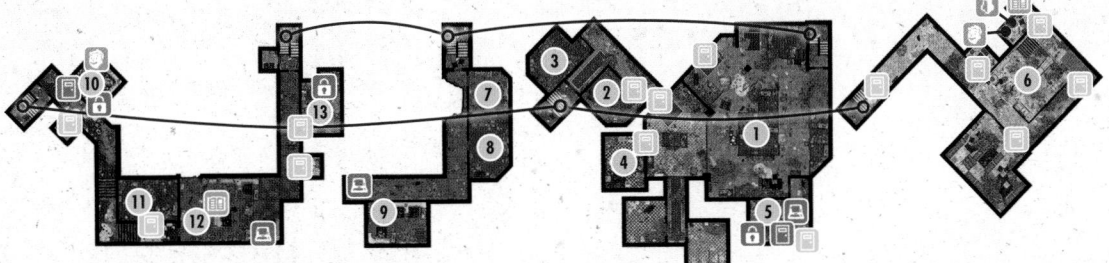

LEGEND

1. OPEN-PLAN OFFICE FLOOR
2. BOOKKEEPING OFFICE
3. OFFICE AND LOUNGE
4. KITCHEN
5. ACCOUNTING OFFICE (LOCKED)
6. BASEMENT AND MACHINE ROOM
7. EXECUTIVE OFFICE
8. CONFERENCE ROOM
9. DATA REVIEW OFFICE
10. MAINTENANCE OFFICE (LOCKED)
11. MEETING ROOM
12. COMMS ROOM
13. FILING ROOM

A small research center is linked to the other radio transmitters and dish arrays dotted around this area. Inside, check the main office pens and balcony offices upstairs to discover some radio anomalies this center had discovered. Also check the ruined basement generator room, accessed via the main stairwell.

TRAINING

CRAFTING AND C.A.M.P.ING

INVENTORY

QUESTS

ATLAS

BESTIARY

APPENDICES

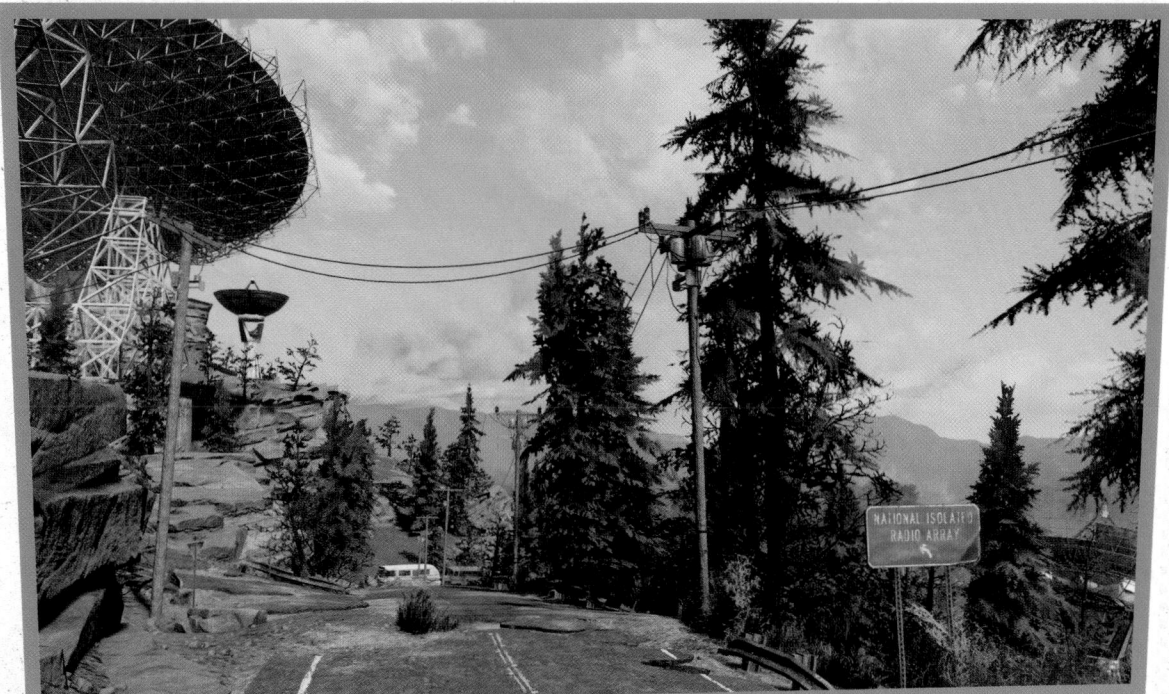

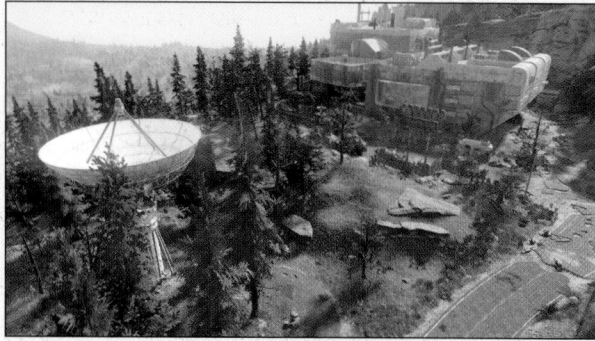

- **COLLECTIBLES:** BOBBLEHEAD, CAPS STASH (7), HOLOTAPE, MAGAZINE, NUKA-CHERRY
- **CRAFTING:** CHEMISTRY (6), COOKING (3), TINKER
- **DANGER:** OIL! RADIATION!
- **ITEMS:** ARMS AND AMMO+; HARVESTABLE: MUTFRUIT PLANT, TATO PLANT; HEALTH AND CHEMS++; TRUNK
- **INFO:** EXPECTED ENEMY: SUPER MUTANT; SCAVENGE RATING: 4; SIZE: 4; SLEEPING; THREAT LEVEL: 15–99
- **LOCK:** SAFE (1, 2, 2, 2, 3), TERMINAL (1, KEY)
- **ITEM EXAMPLES:** ABRAXO CLEANER, ANTIFREEZE BOTTLE, ASHTRAY, BEAKER, BLUE PAINT+, BONE CUTTER, CHEMISTRY JAR, COMBAT HELMET, DAMAGED HAZMAT SUIT, EXTINGUISHER+, FUSION CORE, GAS MASK, INDUSTRIAL OIL CANISTER, LARGE BEAKER+, LEAD PIPE, MEDICAL LIQUID NITROGEN CONTAINER, METAL BEER STEIN, MICROSCOPE, NUKA-COLA BOTTLE, PIPE REVOLVER, PITCHFORK, PORTABLE FUEL TANK, RED PAINT, STIMPAK, TALL DRINKING GLASS, TEDDY BEAR, TELEPHONE, TOXIC GOO+, TURPENTINE, TYPEWRITER, YELLOW PAINT+, YELLOW TABLE LAMP

West Tek Research Center (Exterior)

LEGEND

1. WEST TEK RESEARCH CENTER BUILDING
2. ROOFTOP ART STUDIO

LEGEND

3. SUNKEN FRONT DESK AND LOBBY
4. SECURITY OFFICE AND PROTECTRON PODS
5. LOCKER ROOM AND FUMIGATION
6. CONE VAT JUNCTION ROOM AND STAIRWELL
7. MAINFRAME COMPUTER AND CULTIVATION ROOM
8. VATS CHAMBER
9. RESEARCH STUDY LABORATORY
10. UPPER CONTROL ROOM
11. DISPENSARY LABORATORY
12. RESEARCH WING ENTRANCE
13. RESEARCH ADMIN DESK
14. ADVANCED MUTATIONS LAB
15. RESEARCH AND TESTING LAB
16. SPECIMEN CONTAINMENT LAB
17. MAIN SPECIMEN LAB
18. DECONTAMINATION RESEARCH LAB
19. HOLDING CELL

West Tek Research Center (Interior)

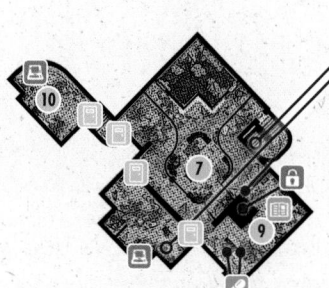

A remote research facility holds several secrets, though some must have been destroyed by the revolting antics of a recent influx of Super Mutants. Still, there's some extra paint (and paintings) to check out on the roof, before you head inside. Explore the mazelike interior to discover just why the Super Mutants are drawn to this particular location.

65. US-13C BIVOUAC

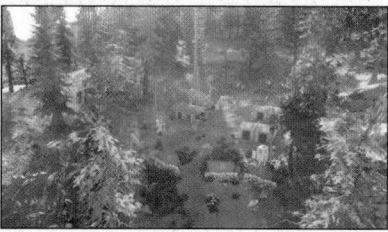

- **COLLECTIBLES:** BOBBLEHEAD (2), MAGAZINE (2), POWER ARMOR
- **CRAFTING:** COOKING, WEAPONS
- **DANGER:** EXPLOSIVE CANISTER!
- **ITEMS:** ARMS AND AMMO; HARVESTABLE: SILT BEAN; HEALTH AND CHEMS
- **INFO:** EXPECTED ENEMY: IRRADIATED ANIMAL, IRRADIATED INSECT; SCAVENGE RATING: 3; SIZE: 1; SLEEPING; THREAT LEVEL: 15–99
- **ITEM EXAMPLES:** ALUMINUM CAN, BEER BOTTLE, COFFEE CUP, HALLUCIGEN GAS CANISTER, MINI NUKE, PILLOW+, PORTABLE FUEL TANK, PURIFIED WATER, RADAWAY, RAD-X

This small military camp just east of the Research Center consists of a cluster of tents, each with a small but helpful variety of items and collectibles. Clear the area when exploring in this vicinity.

66. EAST MOUNTAIN LOOKOUT

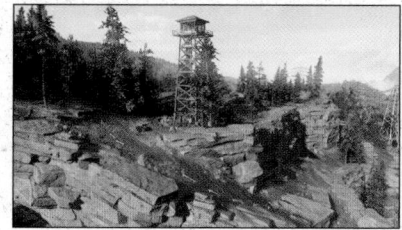

- **CRAFTING:** COOKING (2)
- **DANGER:** LONG DROP!
- **ITEMS:** ARMS AND AMMO; HARVESTABLE: BLOODLEAF, CARROT, CORN, MELON, TATO PLANT, WILD CARROT FLOWER, WILD TATO BLOSSOM; HEALTH AND CHEMS
- **INFO:** EXPECTED ENEMY: IRRADIATED ANIMAL; NOTE; SCAVENGE RATING: 3; SIZE: 1; SLEEPING; SURVEY AREA; THREAT LEVEL: 15–99
- **ITEM EXAMPLES:** ABRAXO CLEANER, ANTIFREEZE, COWBOY HAT, ENAMEL BUCKET, GAS CANISTER, HACKSAW, IV BAG, MELON, RAD POKER BOARD GAME, RED PLATE, SAW, SCISSORS, STEWPOT, YELLOW PLATE

Offering more than just epic views of Cranberry Bog (to the east), some right-minded cowboy had started up a planter garden, giving you access to a wide variety of plants you can cook with.

67. MOUNTAINSIDE BED-AND-BREAKFAST

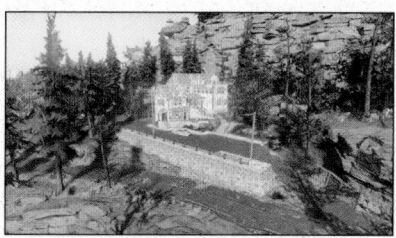

- **INFO:** EXPECTED ENEMY: GHOUL; SCAVENGE RATING: 3; SIZE: 2; THREAT LEVEL: 15–99
- **LOCK:** DOOR (C, 0, 0, 2), SAFE (3)
- **ITEM EXAMPLES:** ABRAXO CLEANER, ANTIFREEZE, BAG OF FERTILIZER, BASEBALL, BINOCULARS, BLAST RADIUS BOARD GAME, BOBBY PIN BOX, BOILED WATER, CHEF HAT, ENAMEL BUCKET, GOLF BALL+, HAIRBRUSH, MR. HANDY FUEL, OFFICE DESK FAN, SHORT PUMP ACTION SHOTGUN, SILVER LOCKET, SUGAR, SUGAR BOMBS, TIN CANISTER, TIN PITCHER, TOOTHBRUSH, TYPEWRITER, WHISKEY BOTTLE, YELLOW PLATE, YELLOW TABLE LAMP
- **COLLECTIBLES:** BOBBLEHEAD (5), HOLOTAPE, MAGAZINE (4)
- **CRAFTING:** TINKER
- **ITEMS:** ARMS AND AMMO; HARVESTABLE: BLACKBERRY, WOOD PILE; HEALTH AND CHEMS; RECIPE/MOD/PLAN; TRUNK

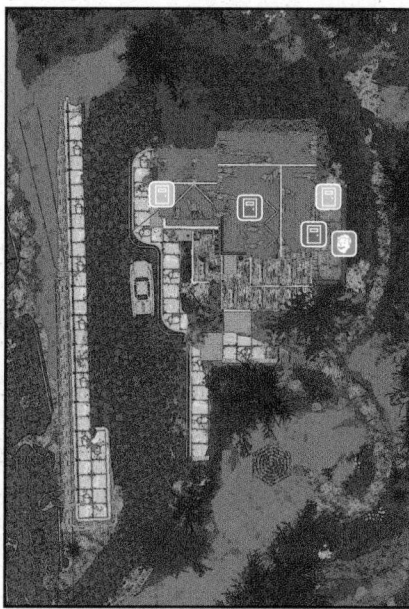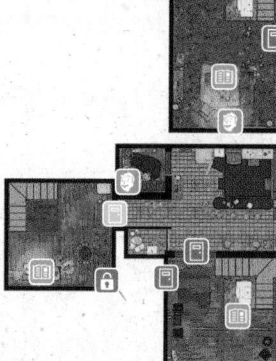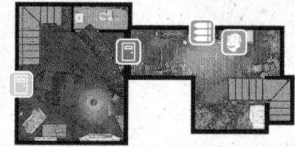

Mountainside Bed-and-Breakfast (Exterior and Interior)

Just above the railroad tracks (and a rusting locomotive) is a yellow-colored Victorian house, once offering wonderful views and delicious home-cooked meals. Now it's a series of enemy-filled chambers, requiring a modicum of unlocking to see everything, including some impressive collectible potential.

68. THE VANTAGE

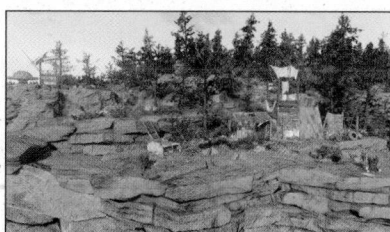

- **COLLECTIBLE:** MAGAZINE
- **CRAFTING:** COOKING
- **DANGER:** LONG DROP!
- **ITEMS:** HARVESTABLE: BLACKBERRY, WILD CARROT FLOWER; HEALTH AND CHEMS
- **INFO:** EXPECTED ENEMY: IRRADIATED ANIMAL; SCAVENGE RATING: 1; SIZE: 1; THREAT LEVEL: 15–99
- **ITEM EXAMPLES:** RAD-X

A small Raider camp consisting of a short tower, with sweeping views of Whitespring and the Ash Heap to the west.

69. SOLOMON'S POND

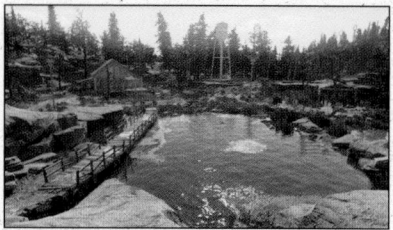

- **COLLECTIBLES:** BOBBLEHEAD, MAGAZINE, NUKA-CHERRY, POWER ARMOR
- **CRAFTING:** CHEMISTRY, ARMOR, POWER ARMOR, TINKER, WEAPONS
- **DANGER:** RADIATION!
- **ITEMS:** ARMS AND AMMO; HARVESTABLE: BLACKBERRY, FIRECRACKER BERRY, WILD CARROT FLOWER; HEALTH AND CHEMS
- **INFO:** EXPECTED ENEMY: GHOUL; SCAVENGE RATING: 2; SIZE: 3; SLEEPING; THREAT LEVEL: 15–99
- **ITEM EXAMPLES:** ABRAXO CLEANER, ALUMINUM CAN, COOKING OIL, COOLANT, FUSE, GOLD PLATED FLIP LIGHTER, GOLF CLUB, SPICES

A closed-off cottage, along with a water tower, a rickety shed, a pond pump, and a metal lean-to all sit close to this lightly irradiated mountaintop pond. Don't come for the meager scavenging opportunities; instead use the variety of workbenches at your disposal.

70. TWIN LAKES

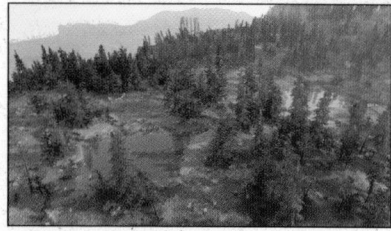

- **COLLECTIBLE:** MAGAZINE
- **DANGER:** RADIATION!+
- **ITEMS:** HARVESTABLE: FIRECRACKER BERRY, LOGS
- **INFO:** EXPECTED ENEMY: IRRADIATED ANIMAL, SUPER MUTANT; NOTES; SCAVENGE RATING: 2; SIZE: 3; THREAT LEVEL: 15–99
- **ITEM EXAMPLES:** BEER BOTTLE, CAMERA, GARDEN GNOME, PROSNAP CAMERA, SWIMSUIT, WONDERGLUE

Scattered about this high mountain watershed lake are several small areas of interest: a dinghy with two plastic flamingos, some junk in the middle of the lake (underwater), a picnic rock on the lake's bank, a gnome with a Prosnap camera, and a skeleton in a rowboat.

71. INVESTIGATOR'S CABIN

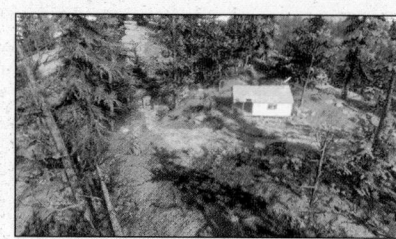

- **CRAFTING:** WATER PUMP
- **ITEMS:** ARMS AND AMMO; HARVESTABLE: GLOWING RESIN; HEALTH AND CHEMS
- **INFO:** EXPECTED ENEMY: IRRADIATED INSECT; NOTES; SCAVENGE RATING: 1; SIZE: 1; THREAT LEVEL: 15–99
- **ITEM EXAMPLES:** ENAMEL BUCKET, MAGNIFYING GLASS, TALL DRINKING GLASS, TOILET PAPER

Find out more about Curtis Wilson at his rusting terminal, within his cabin, on a lonely part of the mountaintop wilderness.

72. HUNTERSVILLE

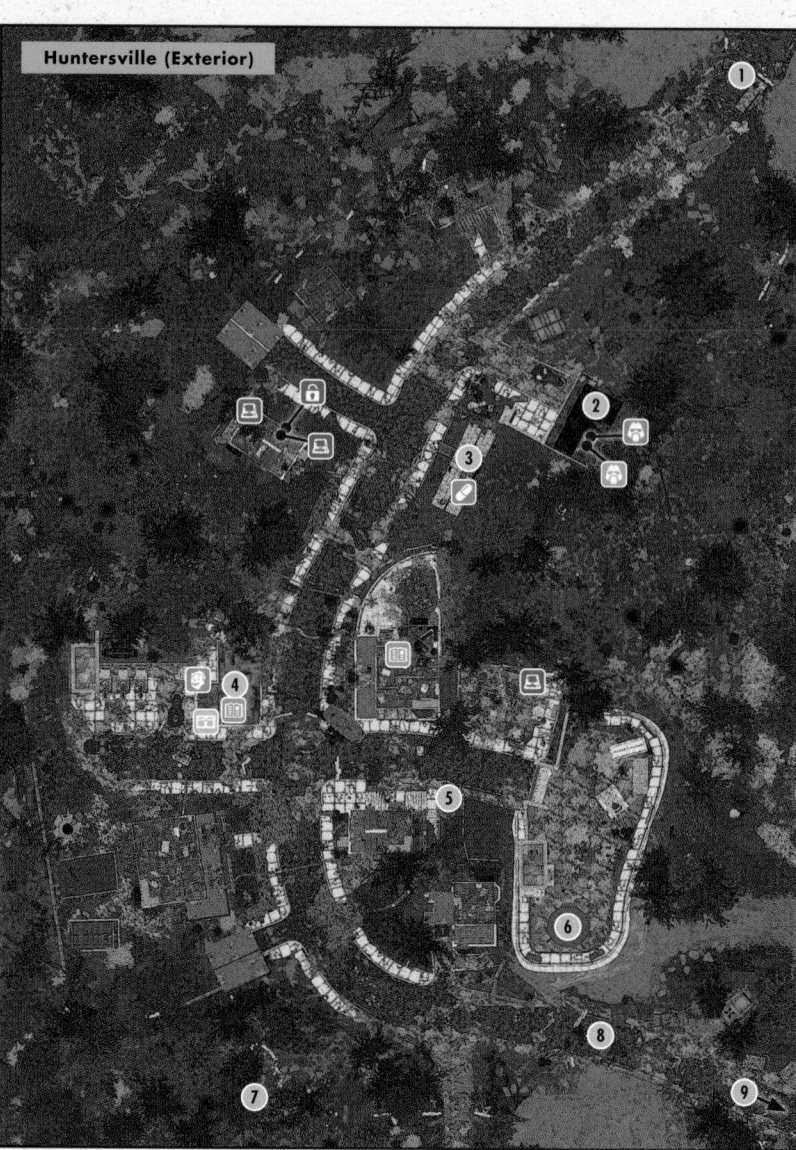

Huntersville (Exterior)

LEGEND

1	MILITARY CHECKPOINT BRIDGE	6	WATER TOWER AND GENERATOR
2	MECHANIC'S GARAGE	7	MINEFIELD
3	CHEM TRAILER	8	MILITARY BLOCKADE
4	HARDWARE STORE	9	BROTHERHOOD OF STEEL GRAVEYARD
5	GNOME OUTHOUSE		

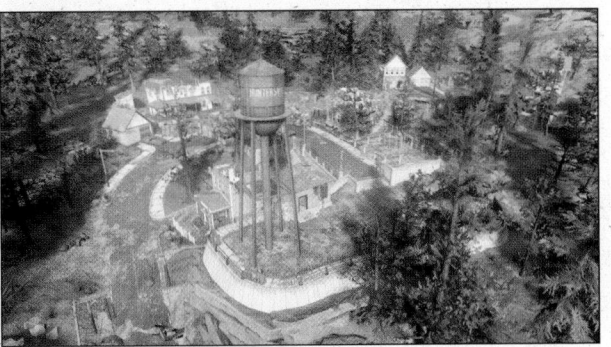

- COLLECTIBLES: BOBBLEHEAD (2), HOLOTAPE, MAGAZINE (2), POWER ARMOR (2)
- CRAFTING: CHEMISTRY, POWER ARMOR
- DANGER: MINES!
- ITEMS: ARMS AND AMMO+; HARVESTABLE: WILD CARROT FLOWER; HEALTH AND CHEMS+; TRUNK
- INFO: EXPECTED ENEMY: SUPER MUTANT; SCAVENGE RATING: 3; SIZE: 4; SLEEPING; THREAT LEVEL: 15–99
- LOCK: SAFE
- ITEM EXAMPLES: ABRAXO CLEANER, BINOCULARS, COFFEE CUP, COOKING POT, DINNER PLATE, FLOWER POT+, FUEL TANK, FUSION CORE, GARDEN GNOME+, GRADUATED CYLINDER, INDUSTRIAL OIL CANISTER, INDUSTRIAL SIZE SHORTENING, INSTAMASH, JANGLES THE MOON MONKEY, PEPPER, SALT, TALL DRINKING GLASS, THIN BEAKER, TUBE FLANGE

Signs of severe and brutal fighting are evident as you visit the small town of Huntersville. The Brotherhood of Steel graveyard, at the southeastern edge of the town threshold (with a dead soldier sporting Power Armor) leads to a military roadblock, evidence that the town was once held by this faction; however, the bloated hanging meat bags reveal a more recent Super Mutant presence.

73. DEVIL'S BACKBONE

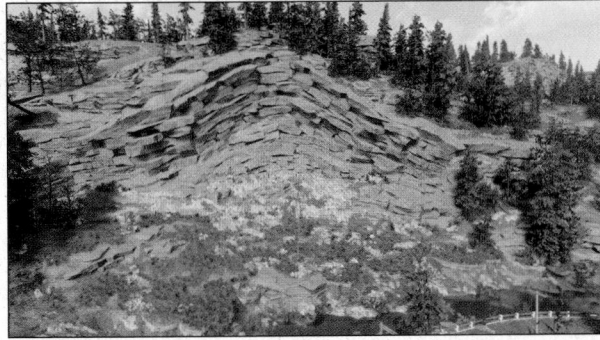

- DANGER: LONG DROP!
- ITEMS: ARMS AND AMMO; HARVESTABLE: WILD CARROT FLOWER; HEALTH AND CHEMS
- INFO: LANDMARK; SCAVENGE RATING: 1; SIZE: 3; THREAT LEVEL: 15–99
- ITEM EXAMPLES: CAMPAIGN HAT, DUCT TAPE, PURIFIED WATER, TEDDY BEAR

This natural arch of Tuscarora sandstone is a local landmark just east of Huntersville. Visible from the remains of a bridge along Route 107, this has a flagpole, some minor camping detritus atop its peak, and a pond below the bridge with the rudimentary graves of two military soldiers.

74. THE FREAK SHOW

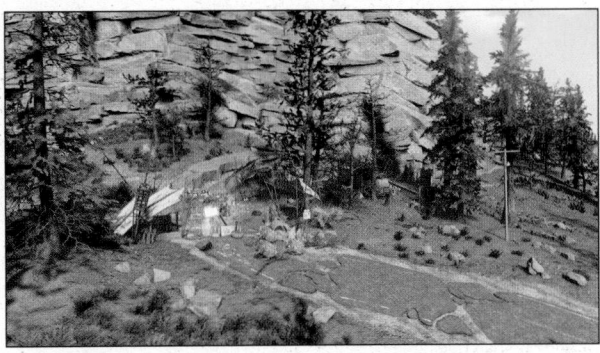

- COLLECTIBLES: CAPS STASH, HOLOTAPE
- DANGER: BONE CHIMES! FLAMETHROWER! MINES! TENSION TRIGGER!
- ITEMS: HARVESTABLE: BLACKBERRY, WILD CARROT FLOWER
- INFO: EXPECTED ENEMY: IRRADIATED ANIMAL, IRRADIATED INSECT; NOTES; SCAVENGE RATING: 2; SIZE: 1; THREAT LEVEL: 15–99
- LOCK: SAFE (TRAP)
- ITEM EXAMPLES: BASEBALL CAP, BOWLING BALL+, BOWLING PIN+, BRAHMIN SKULL, CAP, ENAMEL BUCKET, LARGE BABY BOTTLE, MONGREL DOG MEAT, SMALL BABY BOTTLE, STRAIGHT JACKET

Another derelict roadside Raider camp, on Route 107 offering exceptional views to the southeast, down the mountain all the way to Watoga (in Cranberry Bog Region). The place is booby-trapped and features a revolting selection of what can loosely be described as "carnival attractions."

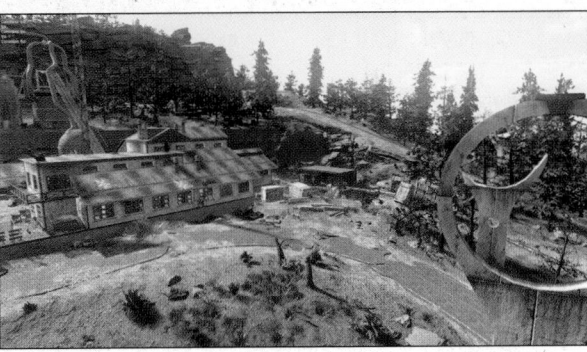 75. SITE CHARLIE

- COLLECTIBLES: BOBBLEHEAD (4), MAGAZINE (3), NUKA-CHERRY, POWER ARMOR
- CRAFTING: ARMOR (2), POWER ARMOR (2), TINKER'S, WEAPONS (3)
- DANGER: EXPLOSIVE CANISTER! OIL! RADIATION!+++
- ITEMS: ARMS AND AMMO++; HEALTH AND CHEMS+; OVERSEER'S CACHE
- INFO: EXPECTED ENEMY: ROBOT; QUEST: MISSION: COUNTDOWN CHARLIE; SCAVENGE RATING: 5; SIZE: 5; SLEEPING; THREAT LEVEL: 15–99
- LOCK: DOOR (3, 3), TERMINAL (3)
- ITEM EXAMPLES: ANTIQUE GLOBE, BLUE TABLE LAMP+, BURGUNDY BOTTLE, CLOWN, COFFEE CUP, COOLANT++, CRUSHED RUSTY CANISTER, DIRTY ASHTRAY, DOG TAGS, DUCT TAPE+, ENAMEL BUCKET+, FUMIGUS BLOWTORCH+, FUSE, GLASS JAR, HAZMAT SUIT+, HOT PLATE+, MAINFRAME CORE, MEDICAL LIQUID NITROGEN DISPENSER, MILITARY FATIGUES, MILITARY GRADE CIRCUIT BOARD, MOP+, OFFICE DESK FAN, OLD BIOMETIC ID CARD, PACK OF DUCT TAPE+, PILLOW+, PLASTIC PUMPKIN, POOL BALL+, POOL CUE, PORK N' BEANS, PURIFIED WATER+, RUSTY CANISTER, SCREWDRIVER, SLIDE RULE, SPICES, TIN CAN+, TRIFOLD AMERICAN FLAG, TURPENTINE, TYPEWRITER, UNSTOPPABLE SHINDIG BOARD GAME, USED OIL CAN, WONDERGLUE, WRENCH, YUM YUM DEVILED EGGS

TRAINING

CRAFTING AND C.A.M.P.ING

INVENTORY

QUESTS

ATLAS

BESTIARY

APPENDICES

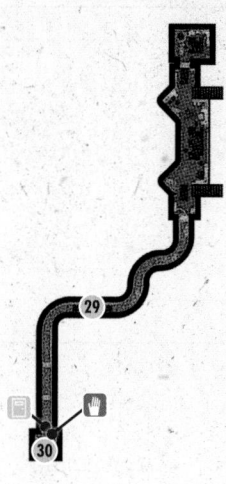

Site Charlie (Interior)

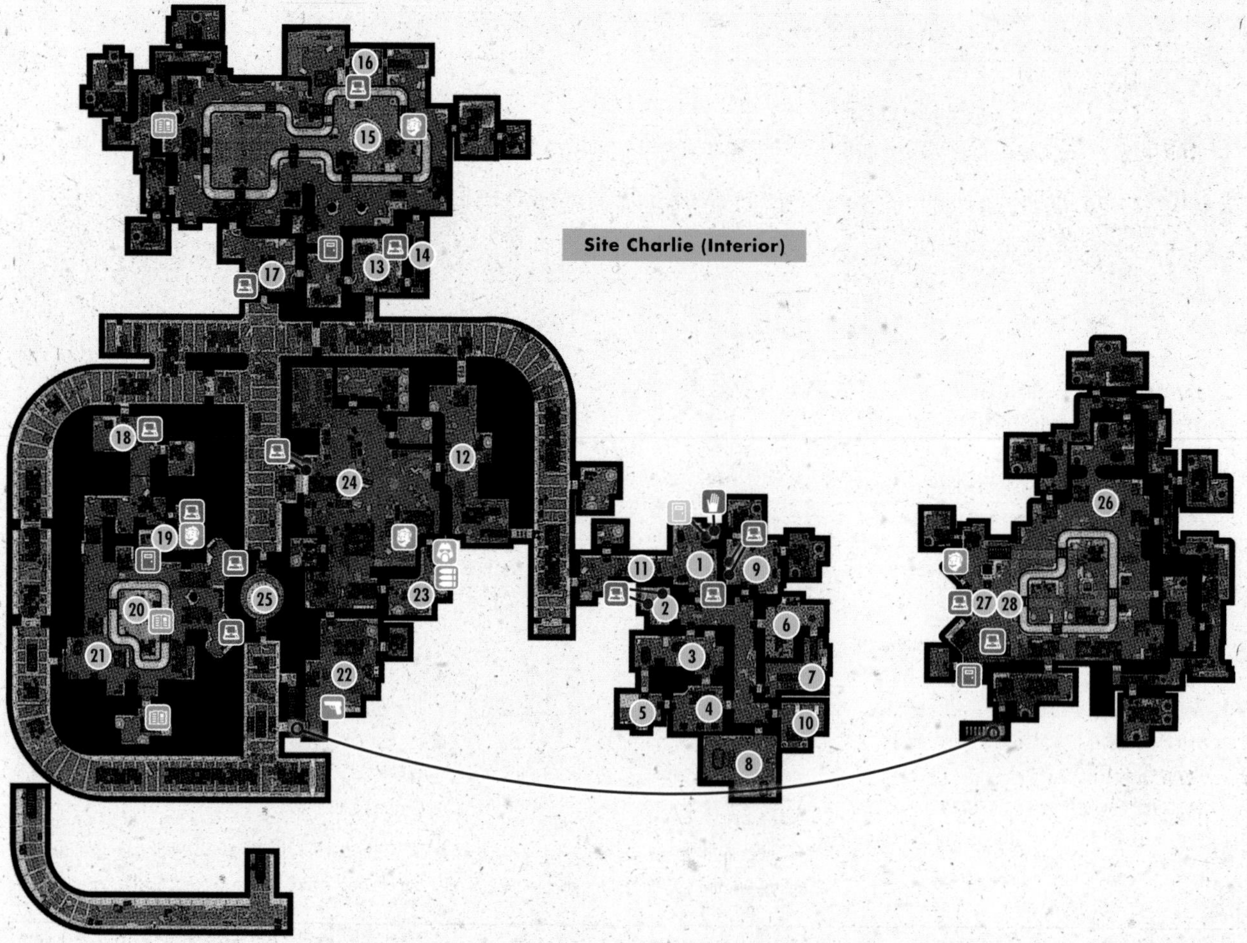

LEGEND

1. FOYER
2. RESIDENTIAL ROOM (BIOMETRICS)
3. BUNKS
4. GYM
5. SHOWERS
6. CAFETERIA
7. STORAGE (PANTRY)
8. LIVING ROOMS AND GAME ROOM
9. SECURITY CONTROL ROOM
10. MEDICAL AND BIOMETRIC SCANNER ROOM
11. LASER GRID
12. MAIN STORAGE CORRIDOR
13. POWER HOUSE: MONITORING ROOM
14. POWER HOUSE: FUMIGATION CORRIDOR
15. POWER HOUSE: REACTOR ROOM
16. POWER HOUSE: REACTOR CONTROL ROOM
17. POWER HOUSE: SECURITY COMMAND ROOM AND EXIT
18. MAINFRAME: ACCESS CONTROL ROOM
19. MAINFRAME: ACCESS CONTROL CORRIDOR
20. MAINFRAME: CENTRAL CHAMBER
21. MAINFRAME: EXIT
22. STORAGE AND FACILITIES: ENTRANCE
23. STORAGE AND FACILITIES: MECHANICAL ROOM
24. STORAGE AND FACILITIES: MAINFRAME COMPUTERS AND EXIT
25. LAUNCH SILO: ENTRANCE
26. LAUNCH SILO: MAIN CHAMBER
27. LAUNCH SILO (UPPER): LAUNCH CONTROL BALCONY
28. LAUNCH SILO (LOWER): LAUNCH KEYCARD, CODE, AND TARGETING COMPUTER
29. EXIT TUNNEL
30. ELEVATOR TO SURFACE

Exterior: The entrance to this sprawling subterranean military installation is hidden inside the R&G Processing Services location (see next entry). Access the hand scanner elevator if the quest is active.

Interior: If you've accessed the scanner as part of the quest, you can finally reach this vast, underground bunker site. After fooling the biometric scanner to access the chambers beyond the initial laser grid, you may have to restore power to the reactor, destroy the mainframe, replace the mainframe cores, and defend the section chief robots while they coordinate a possible nuclear strike you (and your cohorts) may be attempting. After the targeting computer is ready, you just need to solve the code and launch that nuke!

76. R&G PROCESSING SERVICES

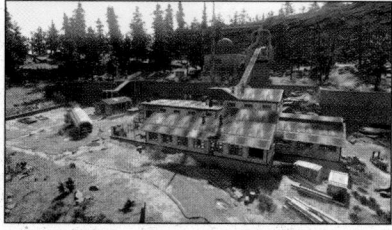

- **COLLECTIBLES:** BOBBLEHEAD, MAGAZINE (2)
- **DANGER:** EXPLOSIVE CANISTER!
- **ITEMS:** ARMS AND AMMO; HEALTH AND CHEMS; OVERSEER'S CACHE
- **INFO:** EXPECTED ENEMY: GHOUL; QUEST: MISSION: COUNTDOWN; SCAVENGE RATING: 3; SIZE: 3; THREAT LEVEL: 15–99
- **LOCK:** ELEVATOR (S); SAFE
- **ITEM EXAMPLES:** ABRAXO CLEANER, ANTIFREEZE, AUTOPSY BOARD GAME, BLOWTORCH, BURGUNDY BOTTLE, CAN, COFFEE CUP+, COFFEE POT, COMBINATION WRENCH, CRUSHED YELLOW CANISTER, DIRTY ASHTRAY, ECONOMY WONDERGLUE, ENAMEL BUCKET, GAS CANISTER, GLOBE, HOT PLATE, ORANGE CANISTER, TORQUE ROD END, USHANKA HAT, WASTE ACID, YELLOW PAINT

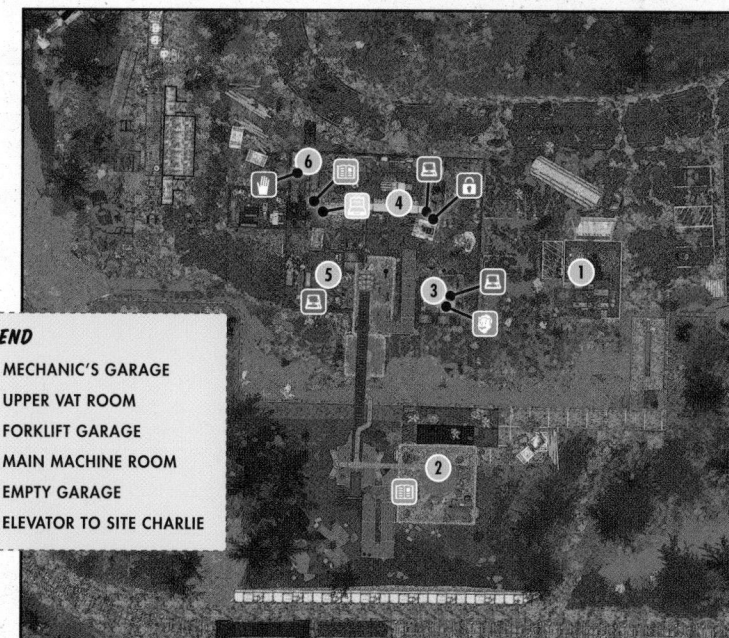

R&G Processing Services (Exterior)

LEGEND
1. MECHANIC'S GARAGE
2. UPPER VAT ROOM
3. FORKLIFT GARAGE
4. MAIN MACHINE ROOM
5. EMPTY GARAGE
6. ELEVATOR TO SITE CHARLIE

Ostensibly a nondescript factory and warehouse location off Route 102, this collection of garages around the main machine room is actually the entrance to the hidden military installation Site Charlie (see previous entry). Be sure you have the (quest-related) hand scanner code if you want to descend to the base!

77. R&G STATION

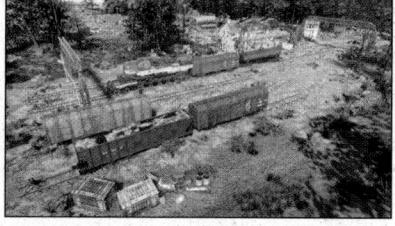

- **COLLECTIBLES:** POWER ARMOR, NUKA-CHERRY
- **DANGER:** MINES!
- **CRAFTING:** WEAPONS
- **ITEMS:** ARMS AND AMMO; HARVESTABLE: WILD CARROT FLOWER; HEALTH AND CHEMS; MY STASH BOX; VENDING MACHINE: AMMUNITION, MEDICAL SUPPLIES
- **INFO:** SCAVENGE RATING: 2; SIZE: 3; TRADER: VENDOR BOT; THREAT LEVEL: 15–99
- **ITEM EXAMPLES:** BATTERED CLIPBOARD, BOILED WATER, CANNED COFFEE, COFFEE CUP+, DIRTY ASHTRAY, PACK OF CIGARETTES, RADAWAY

This company train station is just south of the processing factory sharing the same initials. Check the signal tower and a variety of rusting vehicles in the parking lot behind the station, including the green truck-trailer (1), which may have Power Armor inside. Use this as a base camp when exploring the area, trading and storing items as you return here.

78. SPRUCE KNOB CHANNELS

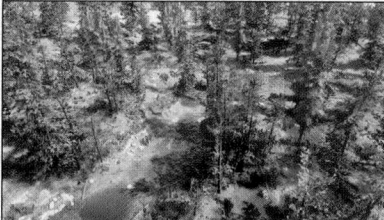

- **DANGER:** RADIATION!
- **ITEMS:** ARMS AND AMMO; HARVESTABLE: BLACKBERRY, BLOODLEAF, GLOWING RESIN; HEALTH AND CHEMS
- **INFO:** EXPECTED ENEMY: IRRADIATED ANIMAL, IRRADIATED INSECT; NOTES; SCAVENGE RATING: 2; SIZE: 3; THREAT LEVEL: 15–99
- **ITEM EXAMPLES:** BEAR TRAP, CRAM, CRUSHED YELLOW CANISTER, ENAMEL BUCKET, GLASS JAR, MAKESHIFT BATTERY, MOONSHINE JUG, PORTABLE FUEL TANK

This wilderness area of lightly irradiated water channels leads to a small lower lake with a derelict cabin nearby. This merges with Spruce Knob Lake to the north.

79. SPRUCE KNOB LAKE

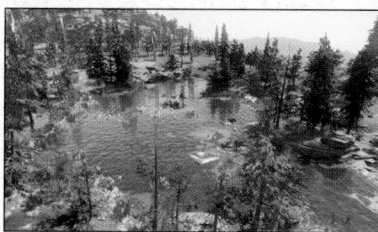

- **COLLECTIBLES:** BOBBLEHEAD, HOLOTAPE, MAGAZINE
- **DANGER:** CAN CHIMES! RADIATION!
- **ITEMS:** ARMS AND AMMO; HARVESTABLE: BLOODLEAF, GLOWING FUNGUS
- **INFO:** EXPECTED ENEMY: IRRADIATED ANIMAL, MIRELURK; NOTE; SCAVENGE RATING: 2; SIZE: 4; SLEEPING; THREAT LEVEL: 15–99
- **ITEM EXAMPLES:** 10-MM AUTO PISTOL, CIGAR BOX, COFFEE CUP, COOKING OIL, DANDY BOY APPLES, FISHERMAN'S HAT, TOILET PAPER, WHISKEY

This merges with Spruce Knob Channels to the south. This lightly irradiated lake is usually swarming with Mirelurks. Check the northern, flat-rock shoreline for a shallow cave opening you can wade into, revealing a small military hideout with scavenging potential. The north docks and picnic area is in disrepair, and the rotting hut yields few items, though there may be some light reading in one of the portable toilets.

80. SPRUCE KNOB (WORKSHOP)

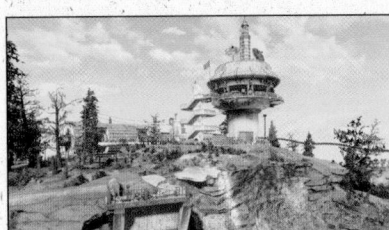

Spruce Knob (Exterior)

- **COLLECTIBLES:** BOBBLEHEAD, MAGAZINE, NUKA-CHERRY
- **CRAFTING:** TINKER, WORKSHOP
- **DANGER:** LONG DROP! RADIATION!
- **ITEMS:** ARMS AND AMMO+; HARVESTABLE: ACID, BLACKBERRY, COPPER, GOLD, WILD CARROT FLOWER; HEALTH AND CHEMS
- **INFO:** EXPECTED ENEMY: VARIES; SCAVENGE RATING: 3 (5+); SIZE: 3; THREAT LEVEL: 15–99

- **ITEM EXAMPLES:** ADJUSTABLE WRENCH, AUTOMATIC LASER PISTOL, BEER BOTTLE++, BOBBY PIN BOX, COFFEE CUP+, DOG TAGS, FUSION CELL, CRACKED GLASS BOWL, DUCT TAPE, GLASS JAR, LIQUOR BOTTLE, MILITARY AMMO BAG, MILITARY FATIGUES, PACK OF CIGARETTES, SEALED CHARLESTON HERALD, SHADELESS TABLE LAMP, TOY ALIEN
- **WORK:** FOOD (4), WATER (4), GOLD (3), COPPER (1), ACID (1)

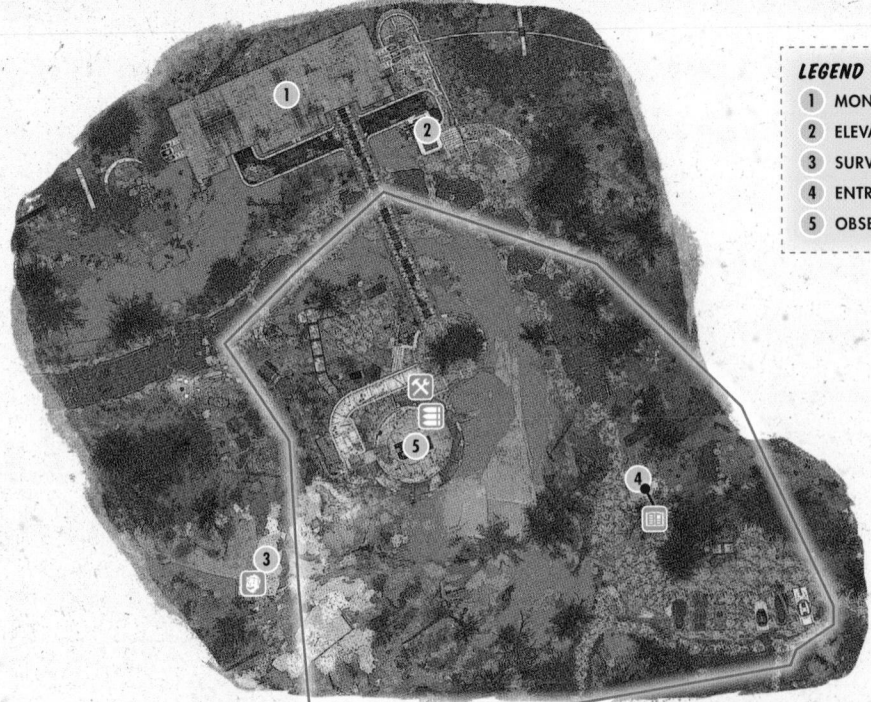

LEGEND
1. MONORAIL STATION
2. ELEVATOR
3. SURVEY MARKER AND VISTA
4. ENTRANCE HUT
5. OBSERVATION TOWER

The name of the highest mountain in the Allegheny Mountains, this alpine horror show of a location features a monorail station, as well as a circular observation tower. Check the geographical survey marker on the southwest ground vista platform for a possible Bobblehead (by the trash can), and inspect a guard hut at the lower road entrance to the southeast for some light reading. The monorail station features a train in atrocious condition but with some junk to grab. The tower requires access from the bridge or the winding exterior stairwell; it offers good junk and a defensive position, with the workshop at its base.

81. SPRUCE KNOB CAMPGROUND

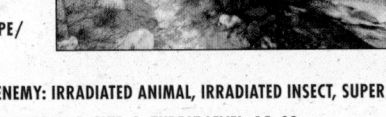

- **COLLECTIBLE:** BOBBLEHEAD
- **CRAFTING:** COOKING
- **ITEMS:** HARVESTABLE: BLACKBERRY; RECIPE/MOD/PLAN
- **INFO:** EXPECTED ENEMY: IRRADIATED ANIMAL, IRRADIATED INSECT, SUPER MUTANT; SCAVENGE RATING: 1; SIZE: 1; THREAT LEVEL: 15–99
- **ITEM EXAMPLES:** SALT

Follow the trail paths from the lake or workshop to reach scattered tent camps under the monorail. Come for the possibility of a Bobblehead.

82. SOUTH MOUNTAIN LOOKOUT

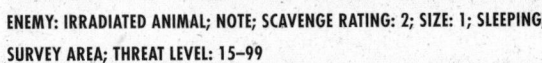
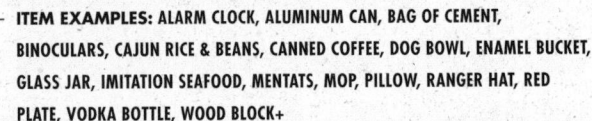

- **DANGER:** LONG DROP! OIL!
- **ITEMS:** ARMS AND AMMO; HARVESTABLE: WILD CARROT FLOWER; HEALTH AND CHEMS
- **INFO:** EXPECTED ENEMY: IRRADIATED ANIMAL; NOTE; SCAVENGE RATING: 2; SIZE: 1; SLEEPING; SURVEY AREA; THREAT LEVEL: 15–99
- **ITEM EXAMPLES:** ALARM CLOCK, ALUMINUM CAN, BAG OF CEMENT, BINOCULARS, CAJUN RICE & BEANS, CANNED COFFEE, DOG BOWL, ENAMEL BUCKET, GLASS JAR, IMITATION SEAFOOD, MENTATS, MOP, PILLOW, RANGER HAT, RED PLATE, VODKA BOTTLE, WOOD BLOCK+

This tower offers views of Spruce Knob, as well as a small hut with a meager pantry; there's more canned goods at the top of the tower, as well as other bric-a-brac.

83. MONORAIL ELEVATOR

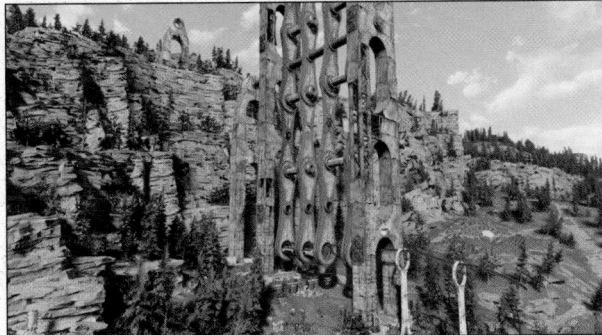

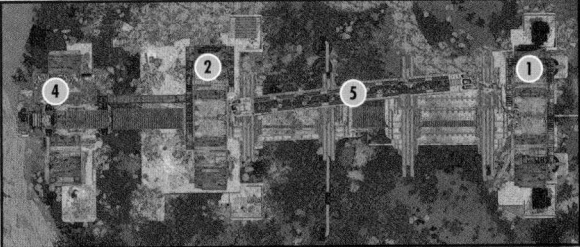

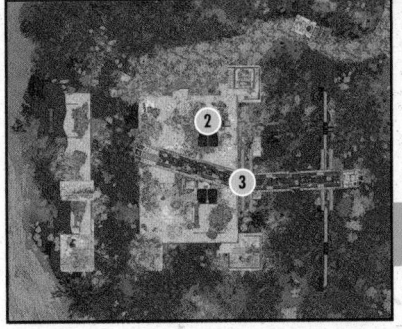

Monorail Elevator (Exterior)

- COLLECTIBLE: NUKA-COLA QUANTUM
- DANGER: LONG DROP!+++
- ITEMS: HARVESTABLE: FIRECRACKER BERRY, WILD CARROT FLOWER; HEALTH AND CHEMS+
- INFO: EXPECTED ENEMY: SCORCHED; LANDMARK; SCAVENGE RATING: 4; SIZE: 3; THREAT LEVEL: 15–99
- ITEM EXAMPLES: BAG OF CEMENT+, BLUE VISOR, CAT BOWL+, COFFEE CUP, COMBINATION WRENCH, CREAM+, ENAMEL BUCKET, EXTINGUISHER, FLIP LIGHTER, FUSION CORE+, GARDEN GNOME, LOOSE SCREWS, MAKESHIFT BATTERY, PACK OF CIGARETTES, SCREWDRIVER, TIN CANISTER, USED OIL CAN, WASTE ACID, WINE, WOOD BLOCK+

LEGEND

1. LOWER ELEVATOR
2. UPPER ELEVATOR
3. FALLEN MONORAIL
4. MID-LEVEL: MAINTENANCE HUT
5. SKY LEVEL MONORAIL CARRIAGES

This gigantic vertical structure is arguably the tallest building in all of Appalachia. It used to serve as a monorail access point and maintenance dock. Now it's a precarious vista where the foolhardy can seek spectacular views and vertigo-inducing maneuvers. The lower (east) tower contains an elevator, while the upper (west) superstructure has a maintenance hut, a fallen monorail, and another elevator. Take the upper elevator to a mid-level gantry and maintenance hut, and take the sky-level stepped gantry up to a stranded monorail with some very precarious planks to traverse! This links to a second gantry and the sky level of the lower elevator, which you can take back down to earth.

84. LUCKY HOLE MINE

- COLLECTIBLES: BOBBLEHEAD (3), MAGAZINE, POWER ARMOR
- CRAFTING: CHEMISTRY, COOKING
- DANGER: CAN CHIMES! RADIATION!
- ITEMS: ARMS AND AMMO; HARVESTABLE: BLACK TITANIUM, WOOD (EXTRACTOR); HEALTH AND CHEMS+; TRUNK
- INFO: EXPECTED ENEMY: GHOUL, IRRADIATED ANIMAL, IRRADIATED INSECT, MOLE MINER; NOTE; SCAVENGE RATING: 4; SIZE: 3; THREAT LEVEL: 15–99
- LOCK: DOOR (1, 1, 2), SAFE (2)
- ITEM EXAMPLES: BEAKER STAND, BEER BOTTLE, BOILED WATER, BOURBON+, BUFFOUT+, CERAMIC BOWL, CHEMISTRY JAR+, COFFEE CUP, COFFEE POT, COOKING POT, DESK FAN, DUCT TAPE, ENAMEL BUCKET+, FLIP LIGHTER, FUSION CORE, GAS CANISTER, GAS MASK+, GLASS JAR+, INSTAMASH, LADLE, LARGE BEAKER, LUCKY HOLE KEY, MENTATS, METAL BUCKET+, MINER'S LAMP, MINING HELMET+, MOUNTAIN HONEY, NEW RIVER RED ALE, NOODLE CUP, OLD POSSUM, PLUNGER, RITUAL MASK, RUSTY CANISTER, SHORT PUMP ACTION SHOTGUN, SKULL, SMALL RIGHT ANTLER, STRAW PILLOW, TALL BEAKER, THIN BEAKER, TOILET PAPER+, TORQUE ROD END+ TYPEWRITER, USED OIL CAN

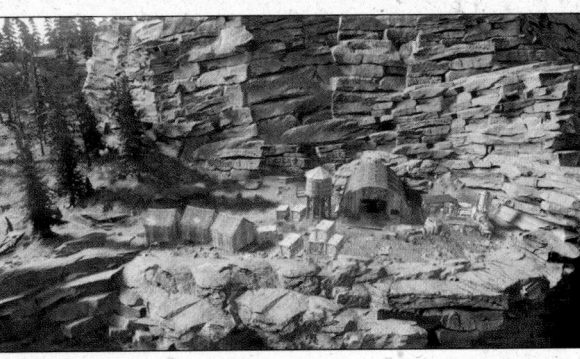

TRAINING · CRAFTING AND C.A.M.P.ING · INVENTORY · QUESTS · ATLAS · BESTIARY · APPENDICES

Lucky Hole Mine (Interior)

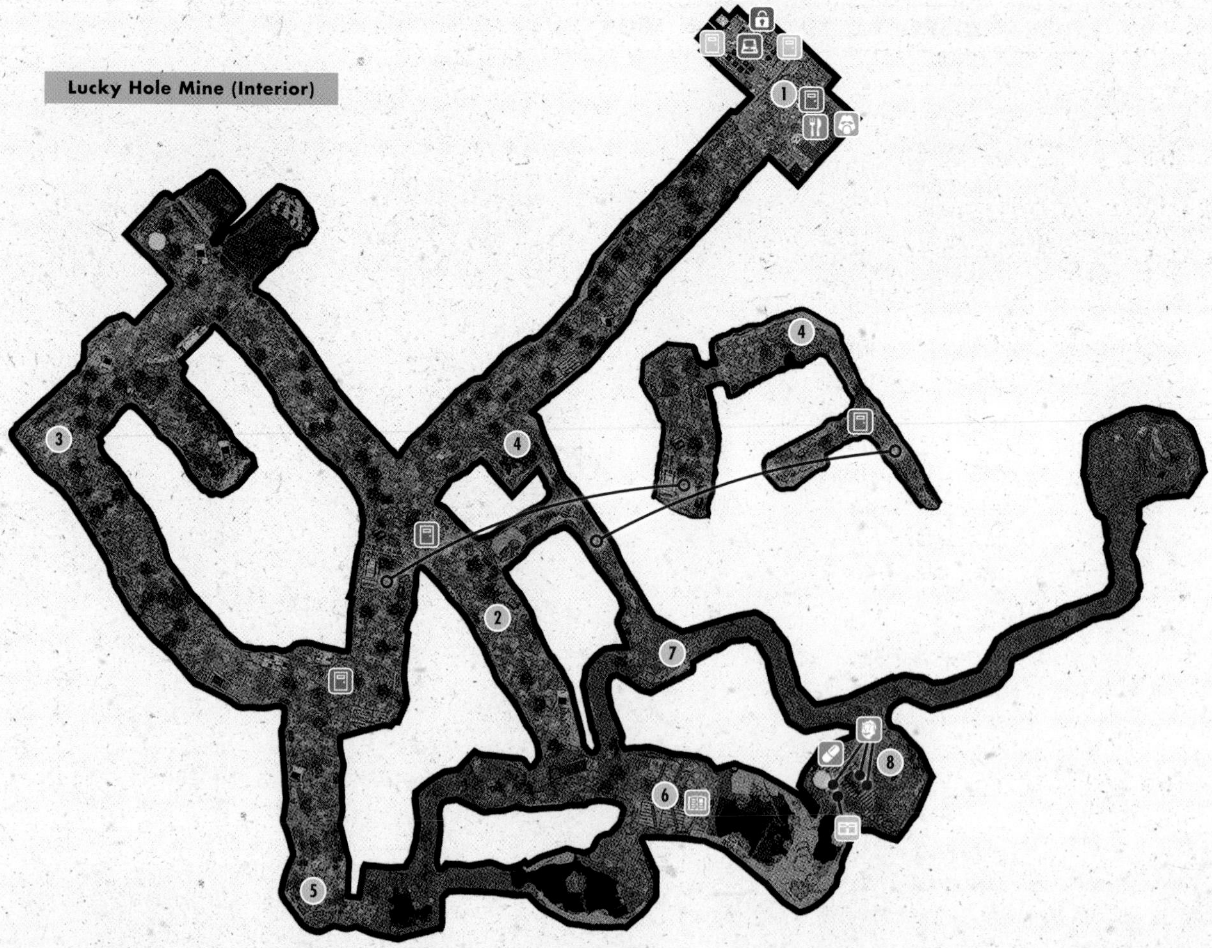

Sitting on a large rock ridge above a small fetid pond are three huts and a warehouse entrance into an old abandoned mine. The single Cultist totem by the water tower at the exterior entrance is but a prelude to the Mothman shrine found deep within the bowels of the earth. Inside, an eerie mine features lit candles and strange, tangled-branched effigies, along with locked doors; find the keys on the corpses of those you kill to advance. There are multiple passages leading to a cultist chapel and a key on the lectern. Don't leave without visiting a well-hidden chemistry laboratory, found by squeezing through a narrow and easily missed tunnel opening. Need a passcode for the locked keypad door inside the mine? It's on a note in one of the three exterior huts.

85. DENT & SONS CONSTRUCTION

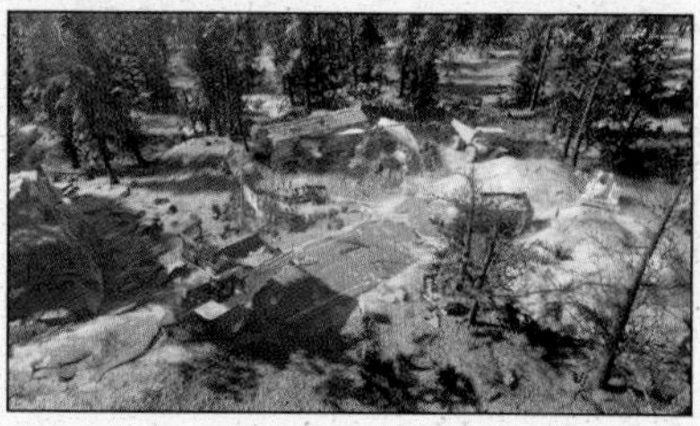

- **CRAFTING:**
  CHEMISTRY, COOKING
- **ITEMS:** ARMS AND
  AMMO, HARVESTABLE:
  BLACKBERRY, HEALTH
  AND CHEMS
- **INFO:** EXPECTED
  ENEMY: IRRADIATED
  INSECT; SCAVENGE RATING: 2; SIZE: 1; THREAT LEVEL: 15–99
- **ITEM EXAMPLES:** BEER BOTTLE+, COFFEE CUP, COFFEE POT, ENAMEL BUCKET,
  MED-X, PICKAXE PILSNER, PSYCHO,

This small construction yard is filled with rusting trucks and other machinery. Most recently, this was a Raider checkpoint into southern parts of The Ash Heap. You find corpses rotting in this makeshift camp.

86. SCENIC OVERLOOK

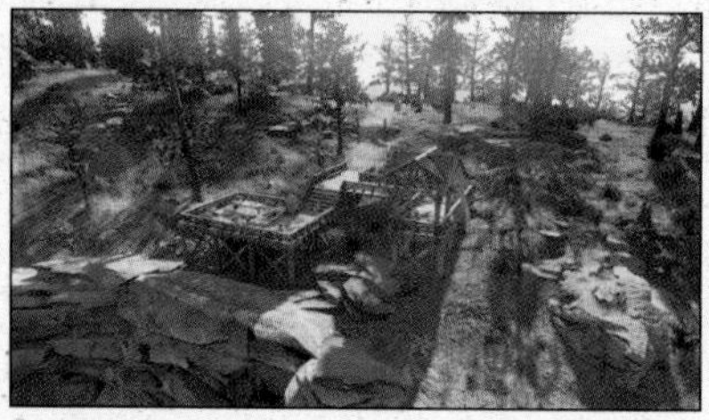

- **DANGER:** LONG
  DROP!
- **ITEMS:** ARMS AND
  AMMO; HARVESTABLE:
  BLACKBERRY
- **INFO:** SCAVENGE
  RATING: 1; SIZE: 1;
  THREAT LEVEL: 15–99
- **ITEM EXAMPLES:** GAS CANISTER

On the high mountains, just off the abandoned vehicles of Route 101, is an impressive vista point offering views of the Ash Heap, as well as the monorail (and inaccessible nuclear missile launch tube cover) below.

87. FEDERAL DISPOSAL FIELD HZ-21 (WORKSHOP)

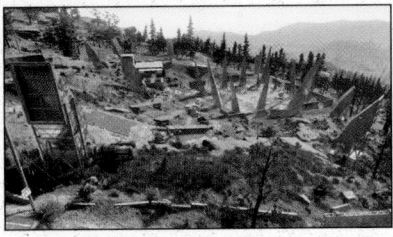

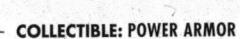

Federal Disposal Site HZ-21 (Exterior)

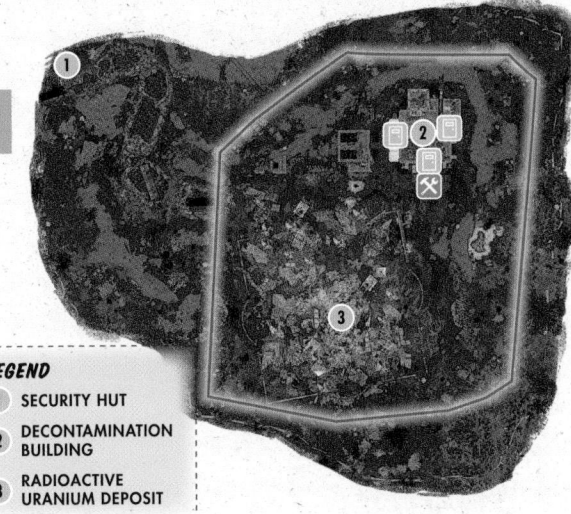

- **COLLECTIBLE:** POWER ARMOR
- **CRAFTING:** POWER ARMOR: WORKSHOP
- **DANGER:** RADIATION!+++
- **ITEMS:** ARMS AND AMMO; HARVESTABLE: ACID, BLACKBERRY, GLOWING RESIN, OIL, URANIUM, WILD CARROT FLOWER; HEALTH AND CHEMS

- **INFO:** EXPECTED ENEMY: VARIES; SCAVENGE RATING: 2(5); SIZE: 3; THREAT LEVEL: 15–99
- **ITEM EXAMPLES:** ABRAXO CLEANER+, HAZMAT SUIT+, RAD-X+, RECON .44 PISTOL.
- **WORK:** FOOD (9), WATER (4), ACID (1), NUCLEAR (3), OIL (1)

LEGEND
1. SECURITY HUT
2. DECONTAMINATION BUILDING
3. RADIOACTIVE URANIUM DEPOSIT

This highly contaminated nuclear disposal site has suffered partial structural collapse, with its center now accessible for uranium resource gathering. Protective clothing is a must; search the decontamination structure for Hazmat or Power Armor. Once you've powered up the Monongah Power Plant, expect this workshop to already have available power, negating the need for your first generator or two. Then get your Nuclear Materials mined, and fast!

88. VAULT 96 (VAULT)

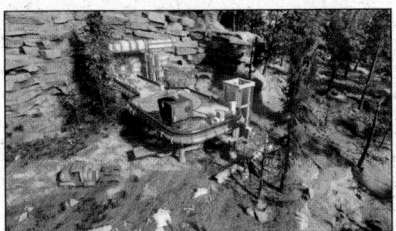

- **INFO:** SCAVENGE RATING: 1; SIZE: 5; THREAT LEVEL: 15–99
- **LOCK:** DOOR (I)
- **ITEM EXAMPLES:** BATTERED CLIPBOARD, BLACK-RIM GLASSES, BOURBON

Set into a large rock outcrop on the divide's southern edge is the entrance to another vault, this one apparently containing cryogenically preserved samples of fauna and genetic data logs for regeneration. Alas, there is no initial method of opening the large "cog" door. Perhaps you can "raid" this location when a special quest becomes active?

89. LAKE ELOISE

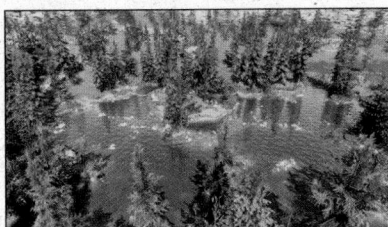

- **COLLECTIBLE:** MAGAZINE
- **DANGER:** RADIATION!
- **ITEM:** HARVESTABLE: BLOODLEAF
- **INFO:** EXPECTED ENEMY: IRRADIATED INSECT, SCORCHED; NOTE; SCAVENGE RATING: 1; SIZE: 3; THREAT LEVEL: 15–99
- **ITEM EXAMPLES:** DOLL, FISHING ROD, YELLOW TABLE LAMP

This lightly irradiated lake features the remains of a pier and a ruined cabin on its eastern banks. There are some rotting walkway bridges to a small campground here too.

90. FISSURE SITE GAMMA (FISSURE)

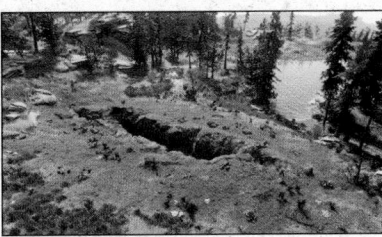

- **DANGER:** LONG DROP! RADIATION!++
- **ITEMS:** HARVESTABLE: BRAIN FUNGUS, ULTRACITE
- **INFO:** EXPECTED ENEMY: SCORCHBEAST, SCORCHED; SCAVENGE RATING: 2; SIZE: 1; THREAT LEVEL: 15–99
- **ITEM EXAMPLES:** NOT MUCH!

Venture too far northeast from the lake, and you'll stumble upon a break in the earth; a gathering of Scorched and a terrifying Scorchbeast appear from this fissure. Avoid unless you're impressively tooled up!

91. RELAY TOWER EL-B1-02

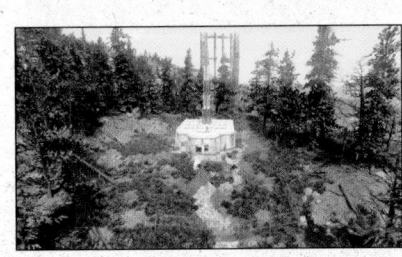

- **COLLECTIBLES:** BOBBLEHEAD, HOLOTAPE, MAGAZINE
- **DANGER:** TURRET!
- **ITEMS:** ARMS AND AMMO; HARVESTABLE: WILD CARROT FLOWER; HEALTH AND CHEMS
- **INFO:** EXPECTED ENEMY: SCORCHED; EVENT: ALWAYS VIGILANT; SCAVENGE RATING: 2; SIZE: 1; THREAT LEVEL: 15–99
- **ITEM EXAMPLES:** BASEBALL BAT, BEER BOTTLE, CHESSBOARD, CRAM, PSYCHO, RECOIL COMPENSATED PIPE BOLT-ACTION RIFLE

In the upper wilderness area, along one of the trails close to the region's southeast edge, is a small transmission tower with laser turret defenses. Check inside for a possible supply drop request.

TRAINING

CRAFTING AND C.A.M.P.ING

INVENTORY

QUESTS

ATLAS

BESTIARY

APPENDICES

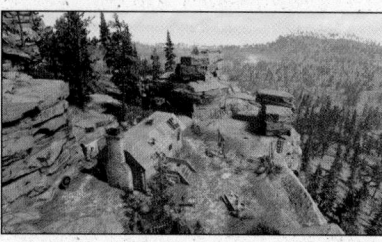

- – **COLLECTIBLES:** BOBBLEHEAD (2), HOLOTAPE, MAGAZINE (2), POWER ARMOR
- – **CRAFTING:** COOKING, WATER PUMP, WEAPONS
- – **DANGER:** LONG DROP!
- – **ITEMS:** ARMS AND AMMO+; HARVESTABLE: WOOD PILE; HEALTH AND CHEMS
- – **INFO:** EXPECTED ENEMY: IRRADIATED ANIMAL; SCAVENGE RATING: 3; SIZE: 2; SLEEPING; THREAT LEVEL: 15–99
- – **ITEM EXAMPLES:** AUTOPSY BOARD GAME, BEAR TRAP, BEER BOTTLE, BINOCULARS, DIRTY ASHTRAY, ENAMEL BUCKET, FLIP LIGHTER, FOX HIDE, GOLD POCKET WATCH, MAKESHIFT BATTERY, MARKSMAN'S SNIPER RIFLE, PEPPER, PUMPKIN PIE, SALT, SPICES, SUGAR, WHISKEY BOTTLE, YELLOW CANISTER.

This cabin was recently turned into a Raider execution camp; there is evidence of torture atop a nearby rock column with possible Power Armor at the top. Check the cabin and the picnic table, and delve into the outhouse for some items of interest.

ZONE C: SECONDARY LOCATIONS

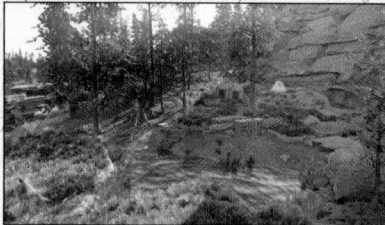

Mountainside Family Pond

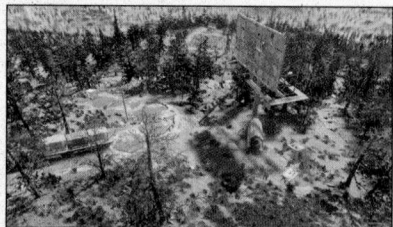

Deep Powder Billboard Camp

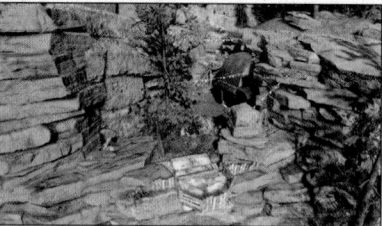

Cheater's Camp

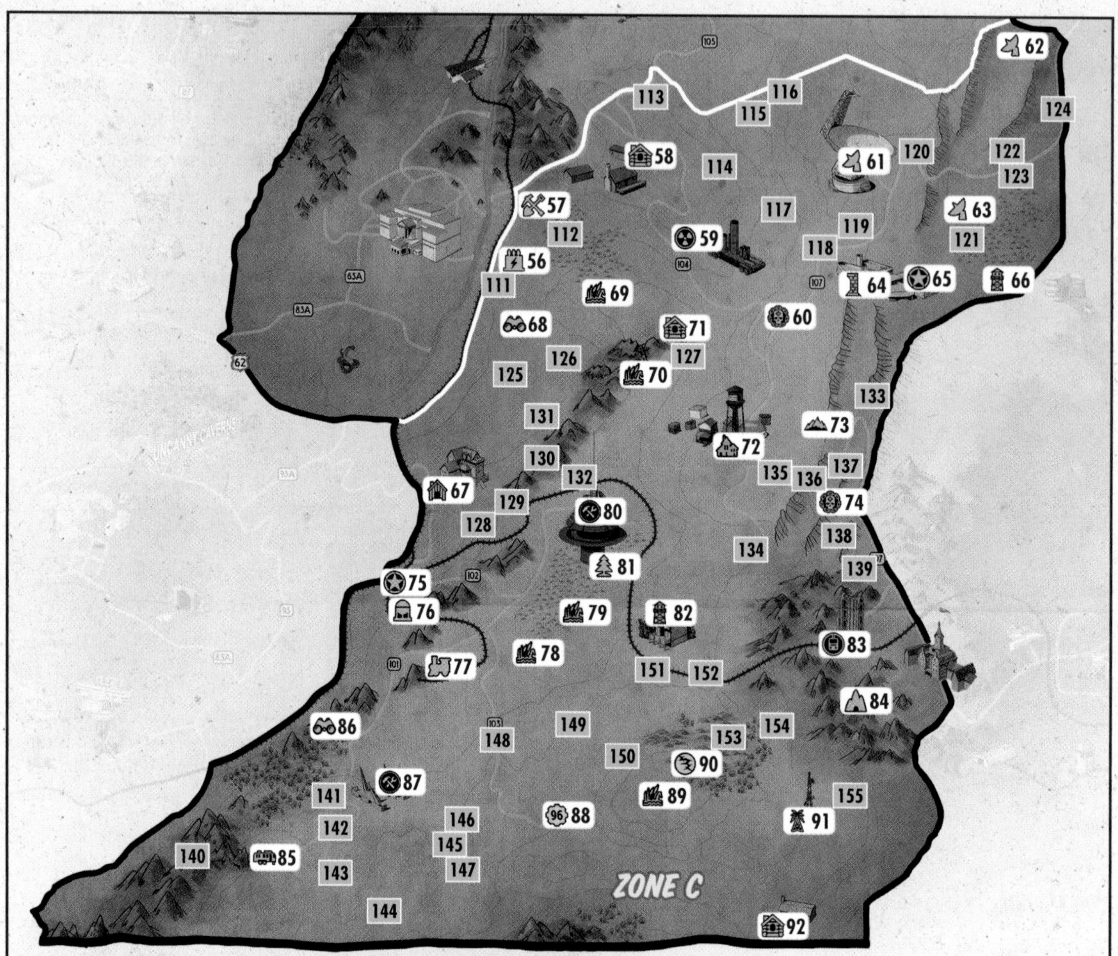

Appalachia: Savage Divide (Zone C) – Secondary Locations

#	NAME	DESCRIPTION
111	Monongah Raider Tower	An shanty tower by the substation with impressive views of The Whitespring Resort to the west, across the tracks.
112	Raider Lookout (Blackwater Mine)	On a rock ridge above the main mine entrance is a Raider sniper tower with a cooking station.
113	Raider Road Lookout (R105)	Expect even more inhumane foes to have commandeered this Raider tower at a sharp hilly road bend.
114	Middle Mountain Lake	A lake with two deck chairs; the pair of fishing folk went skinny-dipping headfirst into the rocks farther along the lake shore.
115	Hunter's Alcove	The hunter has become the decomposed corpse at his favorite rock alcove, overlooking some high mountain ponds.
116	Raider Bridge over the Rapids	If you're having trouble navigating the rock outcrops and mountain lakes, use the rickety wood and rope bridge in this vicinity.
117	Raider Outhouse (and Moat)	On a grassy mountaintop is a locked door (2) to a fridge stocked with Nuka-Cola; there's a trunk here as well.
118	Ripper Alley Bus Crash	Steal from the suitcases of the dead while scavenging this half-buried coach and vehicle; a rock slide seems to have done them in.
119	National Outhouse Gnome Array	A small garden and satellite dish garden manned by miniature men; grab those portable fuel tanks!
120	Traffic Jam on Route 107	A school bus and small coach are stuck on the switchback up to the dish array; check vehicles for goods.
121	Trailhead Picnic Site	Tents, picnic tables, and a disregard for trash; gather what you need from here and stare at the forests from this vantage.
122	Shopping Cart Downhill Race	Someone has set up a shopping cart race between skeletons and gnomes. In the end, the telephone pole won.
123	Duffel Bag Drop-off	Root through some duffel bags among the rusting vehicles and speedboat.
124	Spilled Goods on Route 107	If teal vases are your thing, grab them from the back of the spilled trailer; there's more (and a cooking station) inside the trailer, too.
125	Mountainside Cabin	The low rock cliffs above the railroad is home to a cabin with some junk left by previous scavengers.
126	Solomon's Lower Pond	Southwest of Solomon's Pond is another, smaller pond with Rad barrels and a pickup, pump, scattered items, and a skeletal barbecuer.
127	Twin Lakes Rowboater	The skeletal remains of a rowboater, on his boat with a baseball bat, aground on the lake shore.
128	Mountainside High Wire	A viewing area and a high wire across a deadly plummet; definitely come here for the view and selfie opportunities.
129	Teddy's Fishing Hole	Teddy is knocking back an ale and fishing at this Mirelurk pond, near a sewage outlet and safe (2).
130	Mountainside Family Pond	A green tent with supplies, a smaller white tent, a skeleton fisherman, and one of the best vistas by a pond that there is.
131	Mountainside Hunter's Platform	A small platform with a skeleton, lunch pail, and the possibility of hunting albino Radstags.
132	Amateur Communications (north of Spruce Knob)	A rusting military SUV is parked close to a small boulder with comms equipment built into it and dishes up a tree.
133	Trapper Camp and Amazing Outhouse	A large cliffside Raider camp with tremendous views, sleeping bags for everyone, a cooking station, and a toilet where you can really feel the breeze.
134	Vertibird Crash Site (South Mountain Nuke Crater)	A vertibird has crashed on the rim of a huge crater, which took out a building, according to the debris you'll be wading through.

#	NAME	DESCRIPTION
135	Brotherhood of Steel Graves (Huntersville)	Ad Victorium! Brotherhood of Steel soldiers who gave their lives are buried in this hillside. Come to steal from their graves.
136	Police Roadblock on Route 107	The cops had stopped a car or two on this steep hillside road.
137	Road Bridge Tent	A pickup, canoe, tiny tent, and other detritus to find items in or around, close to the road bridge.
138	Out of Their Gourds (the Domestics)	A family of plastic people are busy harvesting their pumpkins and blackberries.
139	Nuke Crater (South Mountain East)	A large nuke crater with a scientist skeleton sitting on the northern rim.
140	Pinned Peter at Torture Rock	Pinned to a rock and left to die? Not a great way to watch the apocalypse unfold. Still, there's an aluminum deposit nearby.
141	Deep Powder Billboard Camp	A billboard with a cluster of vehicles, sleeping bags, and a cooking station, just off the cluttered road.
142	Dilapidated Shacks (Route 101)	Look for the rusty van, and pause for a quick pitstop to ransack a couple of old sheds (one with a safe) and an outhouse.
143	Dilapidated Farm and Barn	A roofless farmhouse, along with some blackberry, corn, and tato crops and a phosphate deposit, close to a big red barn with ammo and sleeping bags.
144	Cliff Vista: Southwest Savage Divide	A couple of off-road fans drove their vehicles to this cliff, pitched an orange tent, and killed some time...and then themselves.
145	Out-of-the-Way Hut	A narrow wood hut with cooking station, duffel bag, granite to dig up, and a mattress.
146	Miner's Last Stand	The remains of a miner at the base of a cliff with iron veins to harvest.
147	Vertibird Crash Site (South Savage Divide)	One of the pilots of this downed craft managed to erect a blue tarp tent, where you can find the majority of the ammo and other loot.
148	Vault-Tec Delivery Van (Route 103)	A van driver transporting crates to Vault 96 suffered more than a flat tire on the remains of this road.
149	Lunch Pail Vista	Just a lunch pail, a deck chair, a clifftop, and incredible views.
150	Fungus Cave Hidey-hole	A resin-soaked pine tree sits to the right of a small cave entrance, leading to a fungus-filled cave, a sleeping spot, and other loot to purloin.
151	The Marksman's Monorail	Just south of South Mountain Lookout is another monorail pylon you can climb and sleep atop. You can even walk the rail!
152	Monorail Walk	Thought about taking selfies but suffering from vertigo? Then find the cliff branch allowing access to the monorail itself.
153	Cheater's Camp	A rock camp where two gamers seem to be in disagreement. There's a cooking station, blocks, board games, and possible Magazine on the TV.
154	Military Comms Tower Lucky Hole	A small, quest-related comms dish standing on a cliff edge with sandbags around it, near a corpse and a rusty van with explosive canisters inside.
155	Comrade Chubs and Scattered Suitcases	A red teddy bear named Chubs sits by two skeletons; the rest of his bony brethren lie at the bottom of the adjacent cliff, their suitcases ripe for the pillaging.

TRAINING

CRAFTING AND C.A.M.P.ING

INVENTORY

QUESTS

ATLAS

BESTIARY

APPENDICES

REGION 5: THE MIRE

What hellish secrets lie in the dark, forested swamps of this northeastern region? A great many, including a variety of monstrous cryptids— mutated creatures that beggar belief and attack with an animalistic ferocity! In fact, even the more static wildlife has a mind of its own; radiation fallout seems to have caused a shocking growth spurt among the sycamores, maples, and mulberries that populate this region; long, snaking tendrils wrap around and choke anything in their path, be it vehicles, rail carriages, and, shockingly, even an entire town, in the case of Tanagra! Aside from hunting Gulpers, stalking giant Sloths, and wondering just what the hell went on in Braxson's Quality Medical Supplies, what else is there to do? Well, expect several hidden survivalist bunkers, some with more secrets than others. It's also wise to look up; enterprising (but now deceased) folks have spent considerable time elevating their dwellings from the swamp effluent, and you may chance upon a variety of treehouses, some with platforms higher than you may be comfortable climbing!

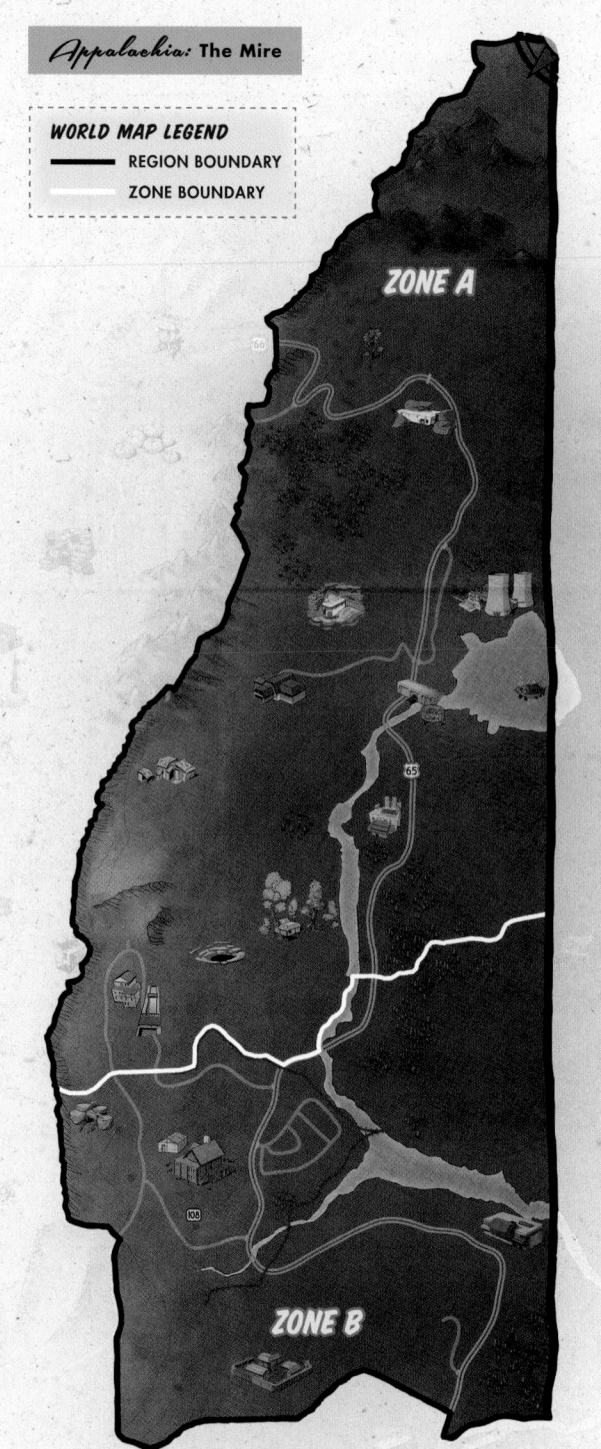

Appalachia: **The Mire**

WORLD MAP LEGEND
— REGION BOUNDARY
— ZONE BOUNDARY

ZONE A

ZONE B

ENEMY THREAT LEVELS

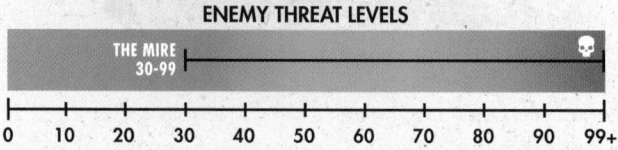

THE MIRE
30-99

| 0 | 10 | 20 | 30 | 40 | 50 | 60 | 70 | 80 | 90 | 99+ |

THE MIRE: ZONE A—
NORTH MIRE, THUNDER MOUNTAIN, AND
BERKELEY SPRINGS

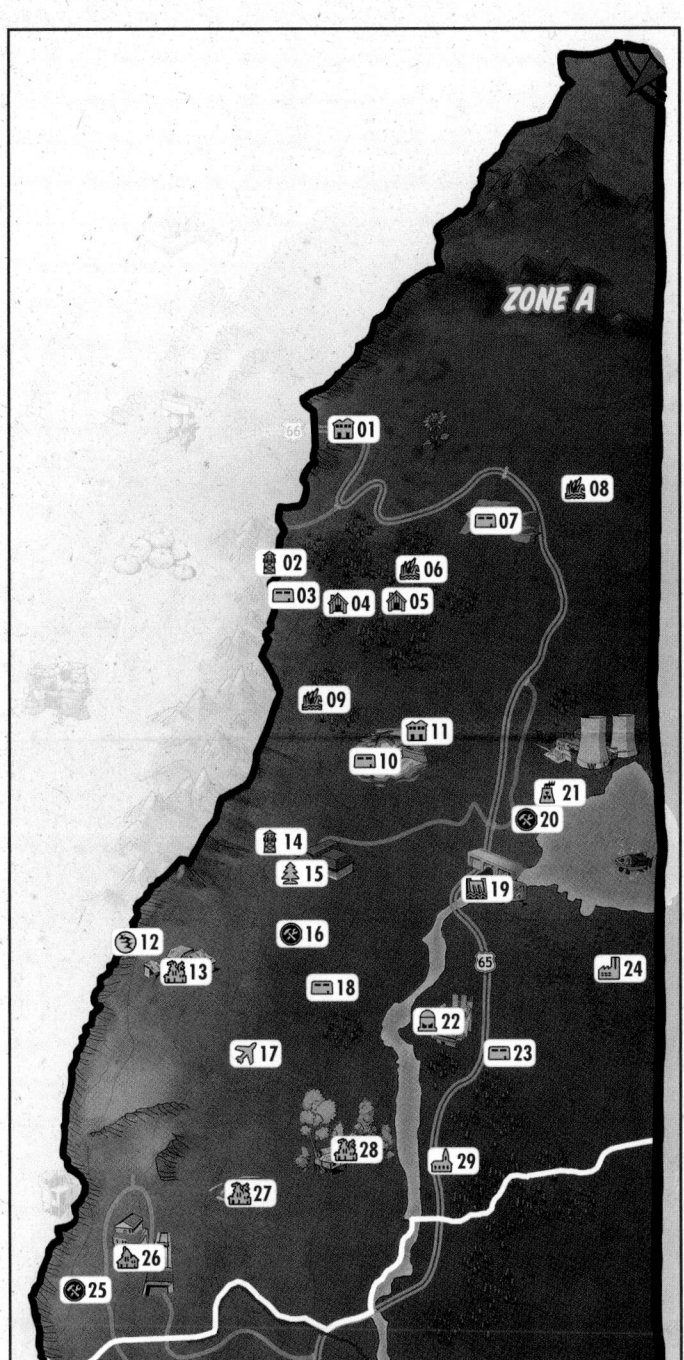

TRAINING

CRAFTING AND C.A.M.P.I.N.G

INVENTORY

QUESTS

ATLAS

BESTIARY

APPENDICES

WORLD MAP LEGEND

━━━ REGION BOUNDARY ━━━ ZONE BOUNDARY

PRIMARY LOCATIONS

				icon	NAME
				01	FREDDY FEAR'S HOUSE OF SCARES
				02	EAST RIDGE LOOKOUT
				03	ABANDONED BUNKER
				04	HUNTER'S SHACK
2		2		05	SOUTHHAMPTON ESTATE
				06	HIGHLAND MARSH
				07	ABBIE'S BUNKER
				08	GNARLED SHALLOWS
				09	GULPER LAGOON
				10	ELLA AMES' BUNKER
				11	EXCELSIOR MODEL HOME
				12	FISSURE SITE OMICRON
2		3		13	MOSSTOWN
				14	DOLLY SODS LOOKOUT
2		2	1	15	DOLLY SODS WILDERNESS
				16	DOLLY SODS CAMPGROUND
				17	CRASHED PLANE
				18	CARSON FAMILY BUNKER
2		2	1	19	CREVASSE DAM
		1		20	THUNDER MT. POWER PLANT YARD
5	1	6	1	21	THUNDER MOUNTAIN POWER PLANT
4	5	3	1	22	DYER CHEMICAL
				23	RALEIGH CLAY'S BUNKER
		1		24	BRAXSON'S QUALITY MEDICAL SUPPLIES
1				25	BERKELEY SPRINGS WEST
2		2		26	BERKELEY SPRINGS
				27	BIG MAW
3		3	1	28	TREEHOUSE VILLAGE
1		1	1	29	HAVEN CHURCH

● BOBBLEHEADS ● CAP STASHES

● MAGAZINES ● POWER ARMOR

Appalachia: **The Mire (Zone A) –
Primary Locations**

The majority of the primary locations exist in this northern part of the Mire, which is dominated by a massive power plant to the east (helpful if you're after Fusion Cores or electricity for power boxes) and the once-quaint but now-ruined town of Berkeley Springs to the southwest, with its grand but decaying mansions and rooftop workshop. Another place to set up a workshop is in the middle of the forest at the Dolly Sods Campground; this is part of a wilderness area with two lodges that offers peace, quiet, and attacks from mutated wildlife or worse. Visit the Dyer Chemical complex if irradiated prizes are more your thing, watch your step at the large hole in the ground known as Big Maw, and tread carefully as you visit the tendril-wrapped Haven Church, especially after dark—those glowing fungi look like eyes, don't they? But what if they *were* eyes...

ZONE A: PRIMARY LOCATIONS

MAP LEGEND

- 🗄 MY STASH BOX
- 🗄 OVERSEER'S CACHE
- 🗄 TRUNK
- ❤ TRADER

COLLECTIBLES

- 🎯 BOBBLEHEAD
- 📖 MAGAZINE
- 🦾 POWER ARMOR

CRAFTING

- 🔧 ARMOR WORKBENCH
- 🧪 CHEMISTRY WORKBENCH
- 🍳 COOKING STATION
- 🦾 POWER ARMOR STATION

- 🔩 TINKER'S WORKBENCH
- 🔫 WEAPONS WORKBENCH
- 🛠 WORKSHOP WORKBENCH

IMPORTANT

- 🚪 DOOR/GATE
- 🔒 LOCKED DOOR/GATE
- 🔐 SAFE
- ✋ SCANNER
- 💻 TERMINAL

🏠 01. FREDDY FEAR'S HOUSE OF SCARES

- **COLLECTIBLES:** HOLOTAPE, NUKA-CHERRY
- **ITEMS:** HEALTH AND CHEMS; RECIPE/MOD/PLAN; TRUNK
- **INFO:** EXPECTED ENEMY: GHOUL; SCAVENGE RATING: 3; SIZE: 2; SLEEPING; THREAT LEVEL: 30–99
- **LOCK:** DOOR (KEY), SAFE (X2), (3, 3)
- **ITEM EXAMPLES:** ALARM CLOCK, CHESSBOARD, COFFEE CUP, CLOWN HAT, CLOWN OUTFIT, CUTTING BOARD, DUCT TAPE, FUEL TANK+, FUSE, INDUSTRIAL OIL CANISTER, MILITARY-GRADE CIRCUIT BOARD; MR. HANDY FIGURINE, PLASTIC BOWL, PRE-WAR MONEY+, SALT, SENSOR MODULE, SUGAR, TALL DRINKING GLASS+, UNSTOPPABLE SHINDIG BOARD GAME

On the edge of the tangled forest is an odd little Halloween store, filled with strange junk. Choose the front, rear, or fire escape entrances, with another entrance on the roof (key). The waffle diner has a floor safe, while the store has one on the wall. Find the Rusted Key (all the way in Toxic Valley!) to enter the rooftop bedroom, which has a collection of board games and military-grade junk.

🗼 02. EAST RIDGE LOOKOUT

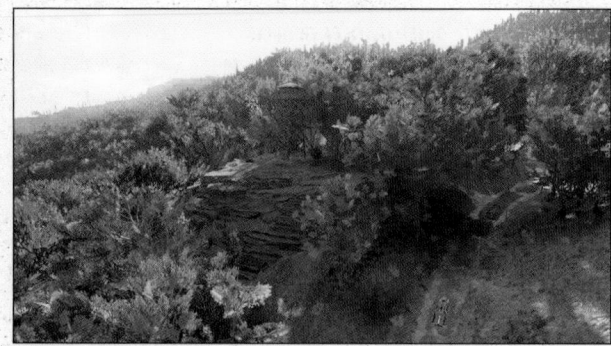

- **DANGER:** LONG DROP!
- **ITEMS:** HARVESTABLE: MUTATED FERN; HEALTH AND CHEMS
- **INFO:** EXPECTED ENEMY: IRRADIATED ANIMAL; LANDMARK; SCAVENGE RATING: 1; SIZE: 1; SURVEY AREA; THREAT LEVEL: 30–99
- **ITEM EXAMPLES:** BINOCULARS, HUNTING RIFLE, LANTERN, NUKA-COLA BOTTLE

This is one of the first places to visit if you're entering the Mire from the north; it offers views across to the east and a pinpointing of new locations.

🗄 03. ABANDONED BUNKER

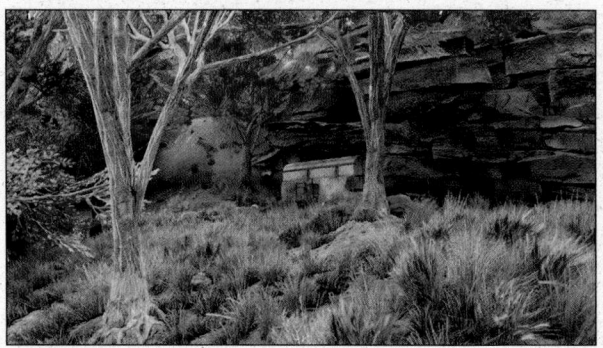

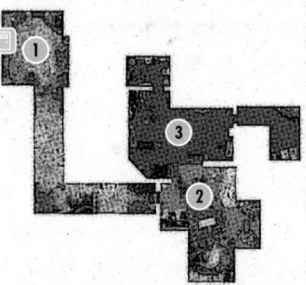

Abandoned Bunker (Interior)

- **DANGER:** RADIATION!
- **ITEMS:** HARVESTABLE: GLOWING FUNGUS; HEALTH AND CHEMS
- **INFO:** EXPECTED ENEMY: IRRADIATED ANIMAL, IRRADIATED INSECT; SCAVENGE RATING: 2; SIZE: 2; THREAT LEVEL: 30–99
- **ITEM EXAMPLES:** ABRAXO CLEANER, BREAD BOX, CATCH THE COMMIE BOARD GAME, DISHRAG, DUCT TAPE, MILITARY-GRADE CIRCUIT BOARD, NUKA-COLA BOTTLE, SCREWDRIVER

LEGEND

1. ENTRANCE
2. KITCHEN
3. WATERLOGGED LIVING QUARTERS

This small, derelict bunker has a few scraps of junk to gather. Inside the unlocked entrance, the main living quarters have flooded.

04. HUNTER'S SHACK

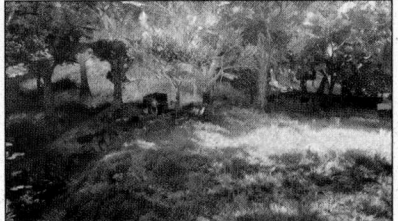

- DANGER: GRENADE!
- ITEM: ARMS AND AMMO
- INFO: EXPECTED ENEMY: IRRADIATED ANIMAL, IRRADIATED INSECT; QUEST: QUEEN OF THE HUNT; SCAVENGE RATING: 2; SIZE: 1; THREAT LEVEL: 30–99
- ITEM EXAMPLES: BEAR TRAP, ENAMEL BUCKET, LANTERN, MICROSCOPE

A hunter named Shelby seems to be out at the moment, but the shack and outhouse she (or he) built is still standing…and is booby-trapped! Check one of the huts for a terminal with Shelby's thoughts on cryptids roaming this region.

05. SOUTHHAMPTON ESTATE

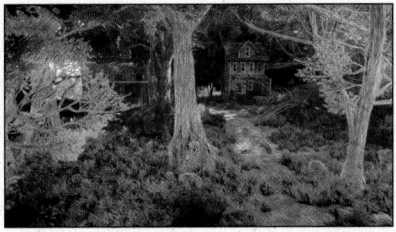

- COLLECTIBLES: BOBBLEHEAD (2), MAGAZINE (2)
- ITEMS: ARMS AND AMMO, HEALTH AND CHEMS
- INFO: EXPECTED ENEMY: IRRADIATED INSECT; SCAVENGE RATING: 2; SIZE: 2; THREAT LEVEL: 30–99
- ITEM EXAMPLES: CANNED DOG FOOD, CHESSBOARD, MILK BOTTLE+, RED BANDANNA, RED PLATE, SUGAR, TYPEWRITER

A house and barn are slowly being choked by swampy tendrils. Check both structures for a modicum of junk, as well as some fine collectible possibilities.

06. HIGHLAND MARSH

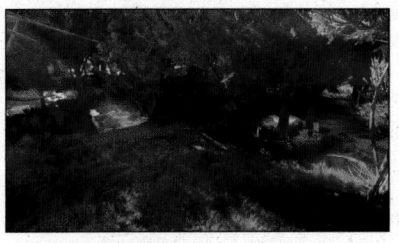

- DANGER: RADIATION!
- ITEMS: ARMS AND AMMO; HARVESTABLE: MIRELURK EGG+
- INFO: EXPECTED ENEMY: MIRELURK; NOTE; SCAVENGE RATING: 1; SIZE: 3; THREAT LEVEL: 30–99
- ITEM EXAMPLES: NOT MUCH!

Stretching from the road (north) to the Southhampton Estate (south) is a woodland marsh, home to a number of Mirelurks. The pickings are slim, unless you're here to collect Mirelurk eggs.

07. ABBIE'S BUNKER

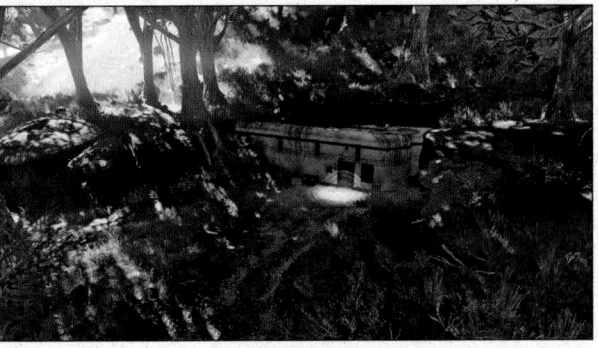

- COLLECTIBLE: CAPS STASH
- CRAFTING: TINKER
- DANGER: EXPLOSIVE CANISTER!
- ITEMS: HARVESTABLE: GLOWING FUNGUS; HEALTH AND CHEMS; OVERSEER'S CACHE.
- INFO: EXPECTED ENEMY: IRRADIATED INSECT; NOTES; QUEST: EARLY WARNINGS, THE MISSING LINK, DEFIANCE HAS FALLEN , COMING TO FRUITION, REASSEMBLY REQUIRED; SCAVENGE RATING: 4; SIZE: 2; THREAT LEVEL: 30–99

- LOCK: SAFE (T), TERMINAL (0)
- ITEM EXAMPLES: ABRAXO CLEANER, BEER BOTTLE+, BLAST RADIUS BOARD GAME, CAKE PAN, COMFY PILLOW, DIRTY ASHTRAY, EMPTY FLORAL VAULTED VASE, GLASS JAR, INDUSTRIAL SIZE SHORTENING, MAKESHIFT BATTERY, METAL BUCKET, MILITARY-GRADE CIRCUIT BOARD, SENSOR MODULE, RAT POISON, WOODEN SPOON

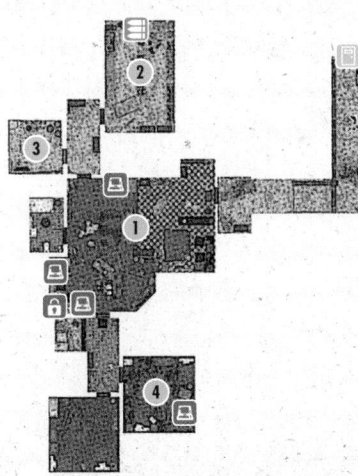

Abbie's Bunker (Interior)

> **LEGEND**
> 1 KITCHEN AND DINING AREA
> 2 STORAGE AREA
> 3 MECHANICAL ROOM
> 4 ABBIE'S BEDROOM

Close to the road but hidden at the bottom of a marshy dell where the fungus glows like orange eyes are the remains of a concrete bunker. The Overseer has been here. Once you unlock the door via the terminal (0), inspect the initial storage area and head downstairs to check the relatively tidy bunker.

08. GNARLED SHADOWS

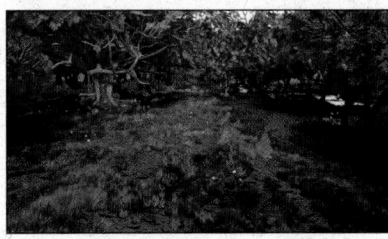

- DANGER: RADIATION!
- ITEMS: ARMS AND AMMO; HARVESTABLE: BLOODLEAF, GLOWING FUNGUS, MUTATED FERN
- INFO: EXPECTED ENEMY: CRYPTID; SCAVENGE RATING: 1; SIZE: 3; THREAT LEVEL: 30–99
- ITEM EXAMPLES: COMBINATION WRENCH, DUCT TAPE, MACHETE, OIL CAN, TIN CANISTER

This gloomy marsh has a dilapidated shed across from a waist-deep wade to a tendril-choked tree enveloping an old pickup. Beware the mutated wildlife that lurk in these parts—usually the odd Angler entities.

TRAINING

CRAFTING AND C.A.M.P.ING

INVENTORY

QUESTS

ATLAS

BESTIARY

APPENDICES

09. GULPER LAGOON

- DANGER:
  RADIATION!
- ITEMS:
  HARVESTABLE:
  BLOODLEAF, MUTATED
  FERN
- INFO: EXPECTED
  ENEMY: CRYPTID;
  SCAVENGE RATING: 1; SIZE: 1; THREAT LEVEL: 30–99
- ITEM EXAMPLES: TOOTHBRUSH

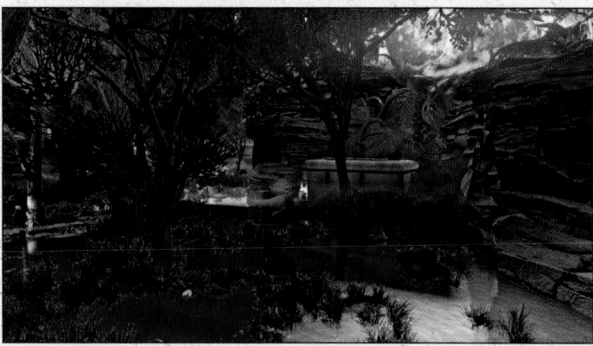

This forested marsh has a small rock pool inhabited by the location's namesakes—giant mutated newt-like foes.

10. ELLA AMES' BUNKER

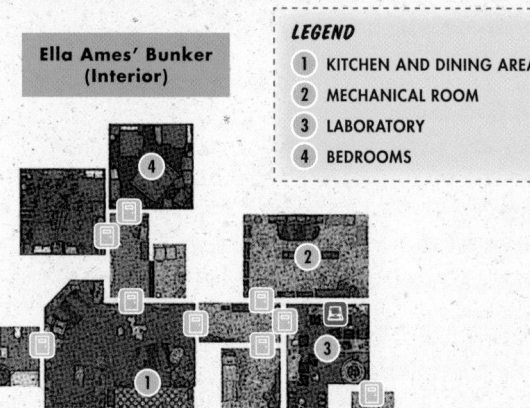

- DANGER: EXPLOSIVE CANISTER! RADIATION!
- ITEMS: HARVESTABLE: BRAIN FUNGUS, GLOWING FUNGUS; HEALTH AND CHEMS+
- INFO: EXPECTED ENEMY: CRYPTID, IRRADIATED ANIMAL, IRRADIATED INSECT; QUEST: AN ORGANIC SOLUTION; SCAVENGE RATING: 4; SIZE: 2; SLEEPING; THREAT LEVEL: 30–99
- ITEM EXAMPLES: ABRAXO CLEANER, ALUMINUM CAN, BEAKER STAND, BEER BOTTLE++, CHESSBOARD, CIGARETTE CARTON, COMFY PILLOW+, DIRTY DESKTOP FRAME+, EMPTY FLORAL VAULTED VASE+, HOT PLATE, MAKESHIFT BATTERY, MICROSCOPE+, SENSOR MODULE, SURGICAL TRAY+, TEA KETTLE, TECH BOX, TEST TUBE RACK+, TIN CAN+, WONDERGLUE

Against a rock outcrop, within dashing distance of the Excelsior Model Home, is the underground laboratory of Ella Ames, an amateur researcher of radiation-protective flowers.

Ella Ames' Bunker (Interior)

LEGEND
1. KITCHEN AND DINING AREA
2. MECHANICAL ROOM
3. LABORATORY
4. BEDROOMS

11. EXCELSIOR MODEL HOME

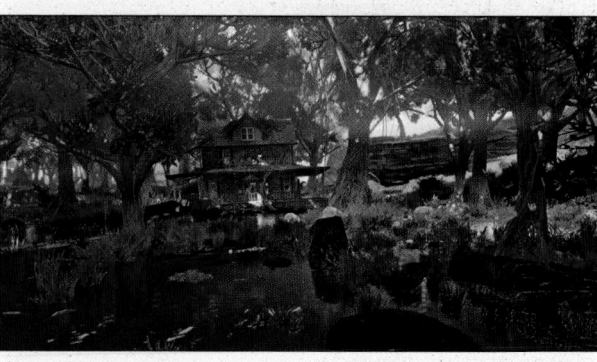

- DANGER: RADIATION!
- ITEMS: HARVESTABLE: BLOODLEAF, RHODODENDRON
- INFO: EXPECTED ENEMY: CRYPTID, GHOUL, ROBOT; NOTE; SCAVENGE RATING: 1; SIZE: 1; THREAT LEVEL: 30–99
- LOCK: SAFE (2)
- ITEM EXAMPLES: CUTTING BOARD, SALISBURY STEAK

This once-magnificent but now sagging mansion is sinking into the Mire at an alarming rate, thanks in part to the root tendrils wrenching the home apart. Be ready for the appearance of an impressively large cryptid, armored in an almost-ironic shell.

12. FISSURE SITE OMICRON (FISSURE)

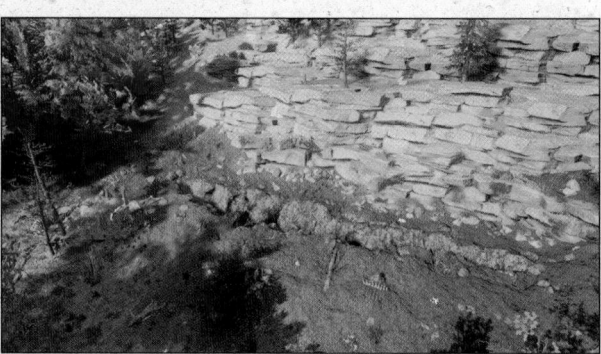

- DANGER: LONG DROP! RADIATION!++
- ITEMS: HARVESTABLE: BRAIN FUNGUS, ULTRACITE
- INFO: EXPECTED ENEMY: SCORCHBEAST, SCORCHED; SCAVENGE RATING: 1; SIZE: 1; THREAT LEVEL: 30–99
- ITEM EXAMPLES: NOT MUCH!

Up the hill in a clearing west of Mosstown is a terrifying fissure site; a horde of Scorched and a dreaded Scorchbeast emerge from the crevasse at the base of a rock outcrop. Avoid unless you're powerful enough!

13. MOSSTOWN

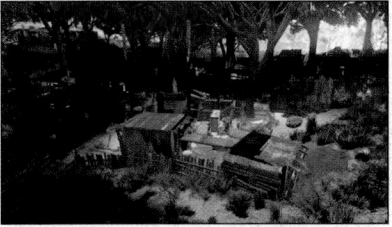

- **COLLECTIBLES:** BOBBLEHEAD (2), MAGAZINE (3)
- **CRAFTING:** ARMOR, CHEMISTRY, COOKING,, TINKER, WEAPONS
- **DANGER:** EXPLOSIVE CANISTER!
- **ITEMS:** HEALTH AND CHEMS; RECIPE/MOD/PLAN; TRUNK
- **INFO:** EXPECTED ENEMY: GHOUL, IRRADIATED ANIMAL; NOTES; SCAVENGE RATING: 4; SIZE: 3; SLEEPING; THREAT LEVEL: 30–99
- **LOCK:** SAFE (X5) (0, 1, 1, 1, 2)
- **ITEM EXAMPLES:** BEER BOTTLE++, BLAMCO BRAND MAC AND CHEESE, BOBBY PIN BOX, BRAHMIN SKULL, BRASS MINER'S LAMP, CRANBERRIES, CRANBERRY MOONSHINE, ELECTRO FUSION, HAIRBRUSH, HIDE BUNDLE, LOOSE SCREWS, MENTATS, PAINT CAN, PROTEST SIGN, RUM BOTTLE, SALT, SUGAR, TALL DRINKING GLASS+++, TYPEWRITER, VODKA

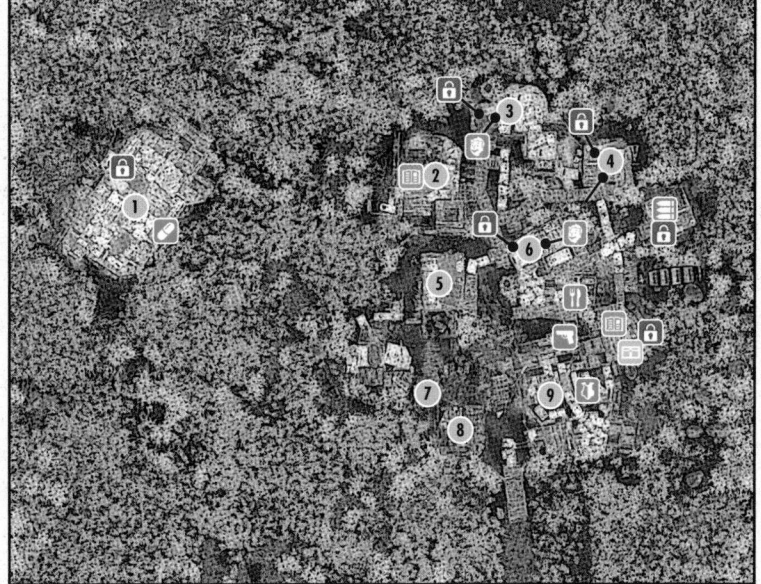

Mosstown (Exterior)

LEGEND

1	LARGE SHACK AND PANTRY	6	WAFFLE SHACK
2	DRUGS SHACK	7	PROPELLER SHED
3	MOTEL SHACK	8	BED SHACK
4	BARBER & DENTIST SHACK	9	THE CIGARETTE CAFE
5	HOT DOG SHACK		

This small maze of interconnecting shack structures was unfortunately built a little too close to a nearby fissure. However, the scavenging potential here is exceptional; just ensure you gather items one shack at a time.

14. DOLLY SODS LOOKOUT

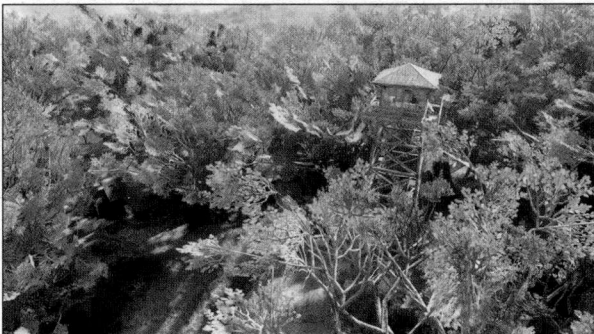

- **CRAFTING:** CHEMISTRY
- **DANGER:** LONG DROP!
- **INFO:** SCAVENGE RATING: 1; SIZE: 1; SURVEY AREA; THREAT LEVEL: 30–99
- **ITEM EXAMPLES:** BOTTLECAP MINE, TATTERED MOE HEAD, TATTERED MOE OUTFIT

Sitting atop a rock plateau on the northwestern edge of the wilderness area is a lookout tower, offering the ability to open up your map and view the forest canopy. Don't leave without the Moe getup!

15. DOLLY SODS WILDERNESS

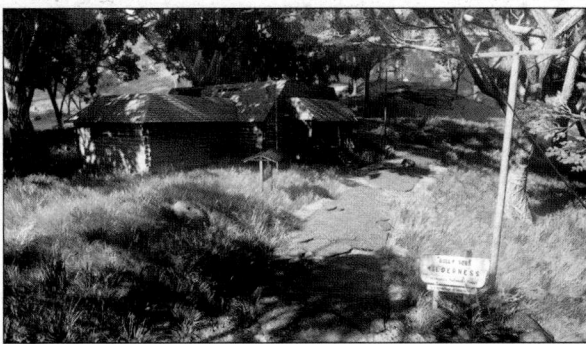

- **COLLECTIBLES:** BOBBLEHEAD (2), MAGAZINE (2), POWER ARMOR
- **CRAFTING:** TINKER
- **ITEMS:** ARMS AND AMMO+; HARVESTABLE: WOOD; HEALTH AND CHEMS
- **INFO:** EXPECTED ENEMY: IRRADIATED INSECT, YAO GUAI; INSTRUMENT; SCAVENGE RATING: 4; SIZE: 3; THREAT LEVEL: 30–99
- **LOCK:** DOOR (2)
- **ITEM EXAMPLES:** ABRAXO CLEANER+, BATTERED CLIPBOARD, BEER BOTTLE++, BOURBON+, CARLISLE TYPEWRITER, JANGLES THE MOON MONKEY, PAPER CUTTER, RABBIT HIDE, SOAP, SWIMSUIT, TEDDY BEAR+

TRAINING

CRAFTING AND C.A.M.P.ING

INVENTORY

QUESTS

ATLAS

BESTIARY

APPENDICES

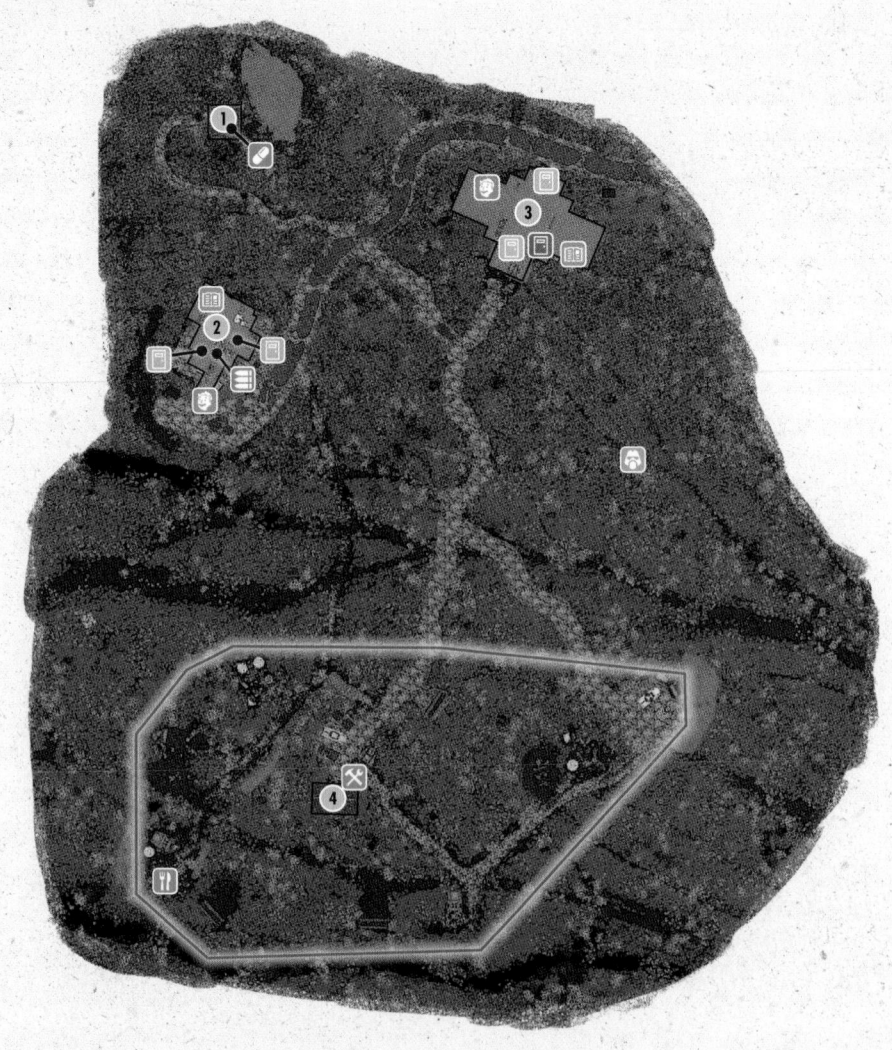

LEGEND

1. PRIMARY LOCATION: DOLLY SODS LOOKOUT
2. WEST LODGE
3. EAST LODGE
4. PRIMARY LOCATION: CAMPGROUND (WORKSHOP)

Named for a Civil War–era soldier and landowner, the tendril trees have taken control of this nature park, which comprises the lookout, wilderness, and campground (workshop) areas. The wilderness area consists of two lodges: one to the east, with a gift shop and a locked armory closest (2), and the other on higher ground to the west.

16. DOLLY SODS CAMPGROUND (WORKSHOP)

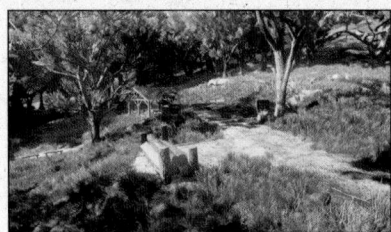

- **CRAFTING: COOKING**
- **ITEMS: HARVESTABLE: WOOD; HEALTH AND CHEMS**
- **INFO: EXPECTED ENEMY: IRRADIATED ANIMAL, GHOUL; SCAVENGE RATING: 2; SIZE: 3; SLEEPING; THREAT LEVEL: 30–99**
- **ITEM EXAMPLES: COFFEE CUP, HOT PLATE, PORTABLE FUEL TANK, NUKA-COLA CUP, TIN CANISTER**
- **WORK: FOOD (9), WATER (7)**

For a map of this workshop area, consult the previous location. This covered picnic area offers some prime food and water resources but little else. Clear the area of foes, checking the four or five small secondary campgrounds with tents and sleeping bags, as well as a small vehicle turnout.

17. CRASHED PLANE

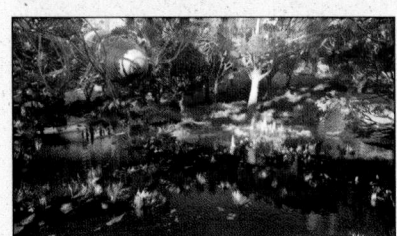

- **DANGER: RADIATION!**
- **ITEM: HARVESTABLE: BRAIN FUNGUS**
- **INFO: EXPECTED ENEMY: SCORCHED; SCAVENGE RATING: 2; SIZE: 2; THREAT LEVEL: 30–99**
- **ITEM EXAMPLES: PICKAXE PILSNER, PILLOW, TOILET PAPER**

Pieces of a Horizon Airlines flight can be found tangled in the mire. Sections are strewn about, with the cockpit gathered up by forest tendrils. Use the ladders to search this interior. Close by is the shell of an old cabin, possibly used by the survivors.

18. CARSON FAMILY BUNKER

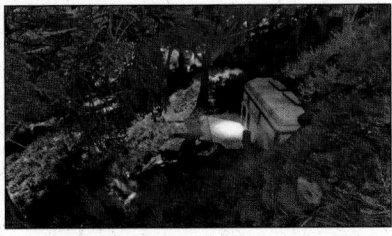

- **ITEMS:** HARVESTABLE: BRAIN FUNGUS, GLOWING FUNGUS; HEALTH AND CHEMS
- **INFO:** EXPECTED ENEMY: IRRADIATED ANIMAL; NOTE; SCAVENGE RATING: 2; SIZE: 2; SLEEPING; THREAT LEVEL: 30–99
- **ITEM EXAMPLES:** COFFEE CUP, DIRTY ASHTRAY, DIRTY DESKTOP FRAME+, GLASS JAR, TOY TRUCK

Carson Family Bunker (Interior)

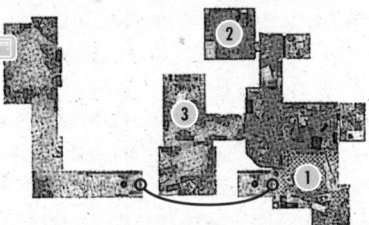

LEGEND
1 BURNED-OUT KITCHEN
2 BEDROOM
3 STORAGE ROOM

South of Dolly Sods Campground, tucked into the forested and marshy slopes, is the concrete remains of an old bunker. The door is unlocked, and the place is in a sorry state. Fire, then moisture have made the kitchen a haven for mold and fungus, and the remaining rooms are mostly picked clean.

19. CREVASSE DAM

- **COLLECTIBLES:** BOBBLEHEAD (2), MAGAZINE (2), POWER ARMOR
- **DANGER:** CAN CHIMES! LONG DROP!
- **ITEMS:** ARMS AND AMMO++, HEALTH AND CHEMS
- **INFO:** EXPECTED ENEMY: IRRADIATED INSECT, MIRELURK; SCAVENGE RATING: 4; SIZE: 3; THREAT LEVEL: 30–99
- **LOCK:** DOOR (0)
- **ITEM EXAMPLES:** ANTIFREEZE BOTTLE, COFFEE CUP, FOLDER, FUEL TANK+, MISSILE LAUNCHER, MUZZLED LASER RIFLE, OAK HOLLER LAGER, PLASTIC PUMPKIN, TYPEWRITER, WONDERGLUE

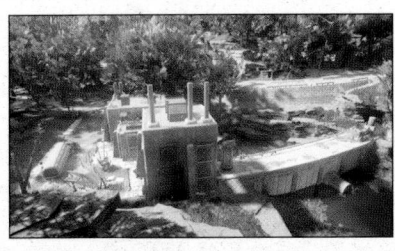

Crevasse Dam (Exterior)

LEGEND
1 DAM WALL
2 MAINTENANCE BUILDING
3 WATER CONTROL STATION

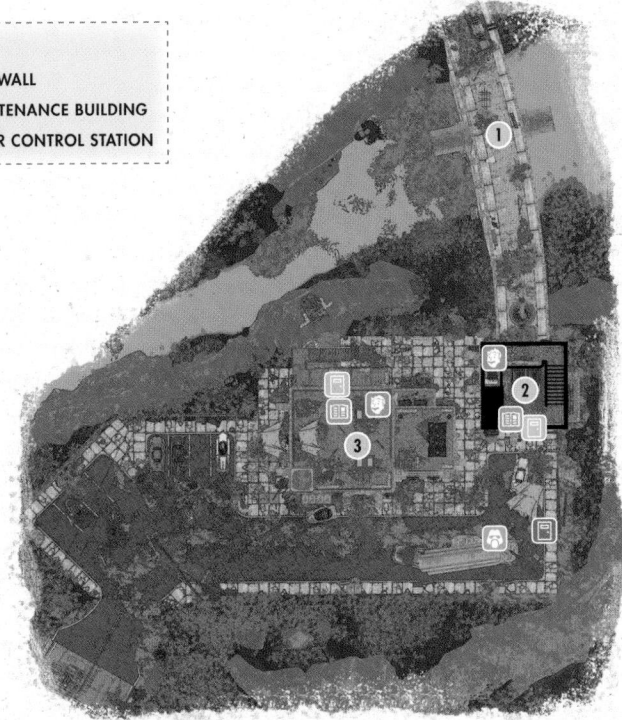

Across from the rusting road vehicles (and mannequin party inside the bus) is the compact Crevasse Dam. It is called this because of the tall rock outcrops and low river you can fall into (and cripple yourself). This bears the signs of being a Raider camp. Unlocking the trailer (0) in the parking lot (using bobby pins or the key from the dead Raider on the roof) confirms this; there may be Raider Power Armor inside!

20. THUNDER MOUNTAIN POWER PLANT YARD (WORKSHOP)

- **COLLECTIBLE:** POWER ARMOR
- **CRAFTING:** COOKING, WORKSHOP
- **DANGER:** RADIATION!+ RADTOAD MINE! TURRET!
- **ITEMS:** HARVESTABLE: CRYSTAL, IRON, STEEL, URANIUM, WOOD; HEALTH AND CHEMS
- **ITEM EXAMPLES:** ABRAXO CLEANER INDUSTRIAL GRADE, ANTIFREEZE BOTTLE, BEER BOTTLE, BOWL, BUNSEN BURNER, CAFETERIA TRAY+, CIGAR BOX, CIGARETTE CARTON, COFFEE CUP, COOLANT, COOLANT CAP, DRILL, ECONOMY WONDERGLUE, ENAMEL BUCKET, FUSE, FUSION CORE+++, GAS MASK WITH GOGGLES, IV BAG, LUXOBREW COFFEE POT, METAL BOX, MICROSCOPE, OIL CANISTER, PACK OF CIGARETTES, RAD-X, SHAPED CHARGE, STEEL WORKER HAT, SUPRATHAW ANTIFREEZE, TALL FLASK
- **WORK:** FOOD [7], WATER [9], FUSION CORE [3], CRYSTAL [1], NUCLEAR [1], STEEL [1], WOOD [1]

- **INFO:** EXPECTED ENEMY: VARIES; QUEST: CLAIM WORKSHOP AT THUNDER MT. POWER PLANT YARD; SCAVENGE RATING: 3 (5+); SIZE: 2; THREAT LEVEL: 30–99

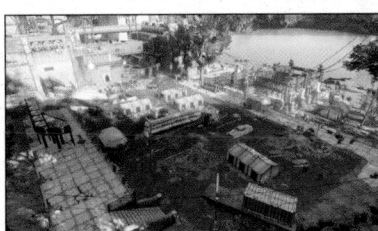

The map for this location is within the perimeter of the Thunder Mountain Power Plant. Find the workshop on the upper yard, where several military tents have been set up. Scour the area for resources, and build your defenses around the ones you wish to keep. Note the two Fusion Core Processors, as well as the power box and gun emplacements you can use (after some possible repair work) to bolster your base.

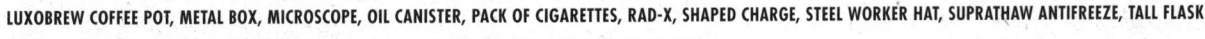

- **COLLECTIBLES:** BOBBLEHEAD (5), CAPS STASH, MAGAZINE (6), NUKA-CHERRY, POWER ARMOR
- **CRAFTING:** CHEMISTRY, POWER ARMOR (2), WEAPONS
- **DANGER:** EXPLOSIVE CANISTER! LONG DROP! RADIATION!++
- **ITEMS:** ARMS AND AMMO++; HARVESTABLE: BRAIN FUNGUS, GLOWING FUNGUS; HEALTH AND CHEMS+; RECIPE/MOD/PLAN
- **INFO:** EXPECTED ENEMY: CRYPTID, IRRADIATED ANIMAL, IRRADIATED INSECT, SCORCHED; SCAVENGE RATING: 5; SIZE: 5; THREAT LEVEL: 30–99
- **LOCK:** DOOR (0), TERMINAL (2)
- **ITEM EXAMPLES:** ABRAXO CLEANER, ABRAXO CLEANER INDUSTRIAL GRADE, ADJUSTABLE WRENCH, ALARM CLOCK, ALUMINUM SCRAP, ANTIFREEZE BOTTLE, BAG OF CEMENT, BLAMCO BRAND MAC AND CHEESE, BLOWTORCH, BOILED WATER, CANNED DOG FOOD, CIGARETTE CARTON, CLEAN BROOM, COOKING OIL, COTTON YARN, CRAM, DAMAGED HAZMAT SUIT, DOLL, DUCT TAPE++, ENAMEL BUCKET+, EXTINGUISHER, FIELD SCRIBE'S HAT, FUSE, GLASS JAR+, HARD HAT, ICE TONGS, INDUSTRIAL SOLVENT+, MECHANIC JUMPSUIT, MEDICAL GOGGLES, METAL BOX, MOP, OIL CAN, PIPE WRENCH, POOL BALL+, RACK, SAW, SHORT AUTOMATIC LASER PISTOL, SUBMACHINE GUN, SUPRATHAW ANTIFREEZE, TONGS, WELDING HELMET, WONDERGLUE

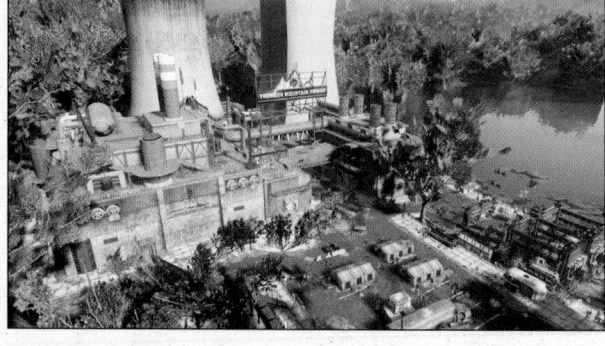

Thunder Mountain Power Plant (Exterior)

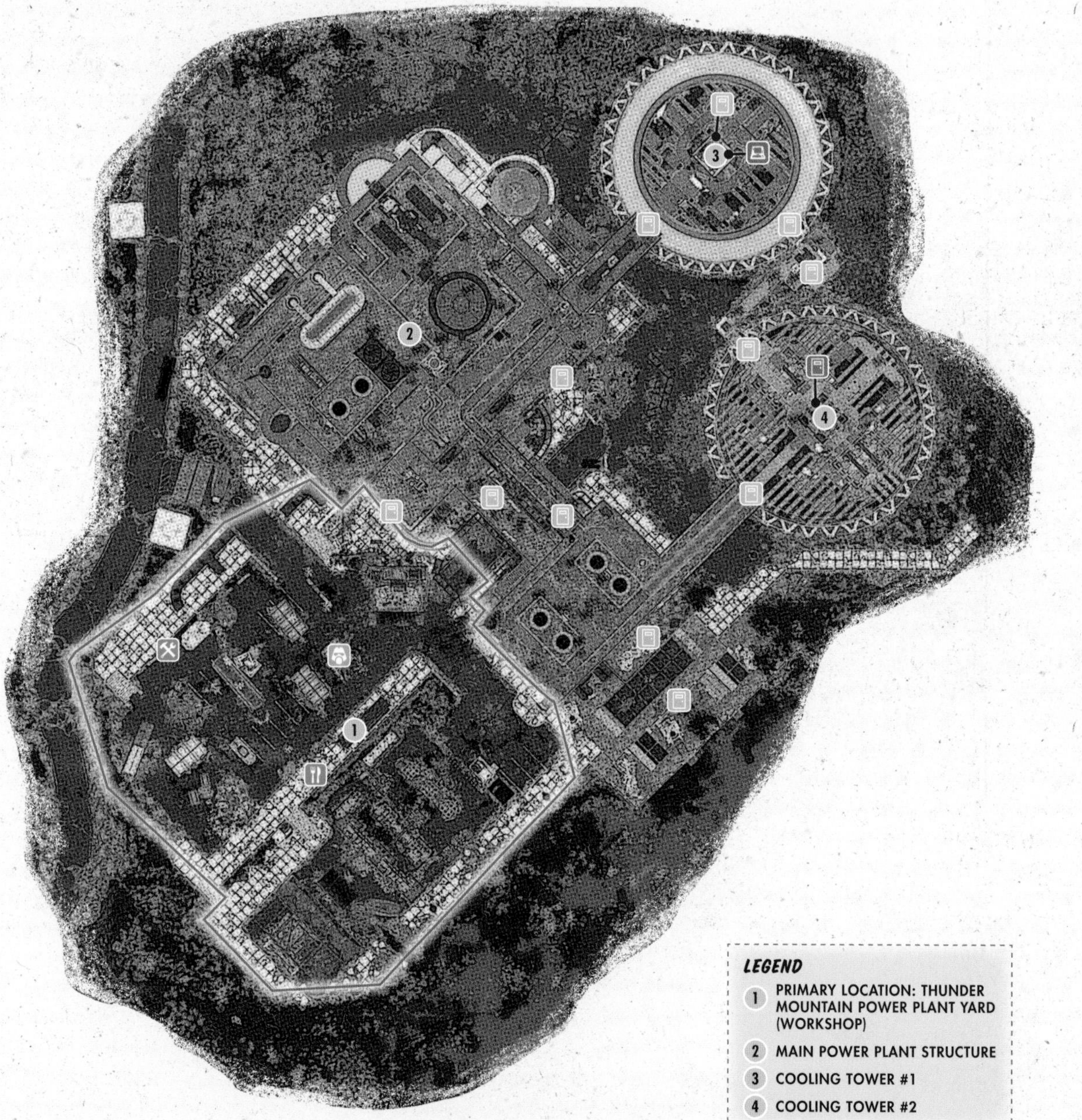

LEGEND

1. PRIMARY LOCATION: THUNDER MOUNTAIN POWER PLANT YARD (WORKSHOP)
2. MAIN POWER PLANT STRUCTURE
3. COOLING TOWER #1
4. COOLING TOWER #2

Thunder Mountain Power Plant (Interior)

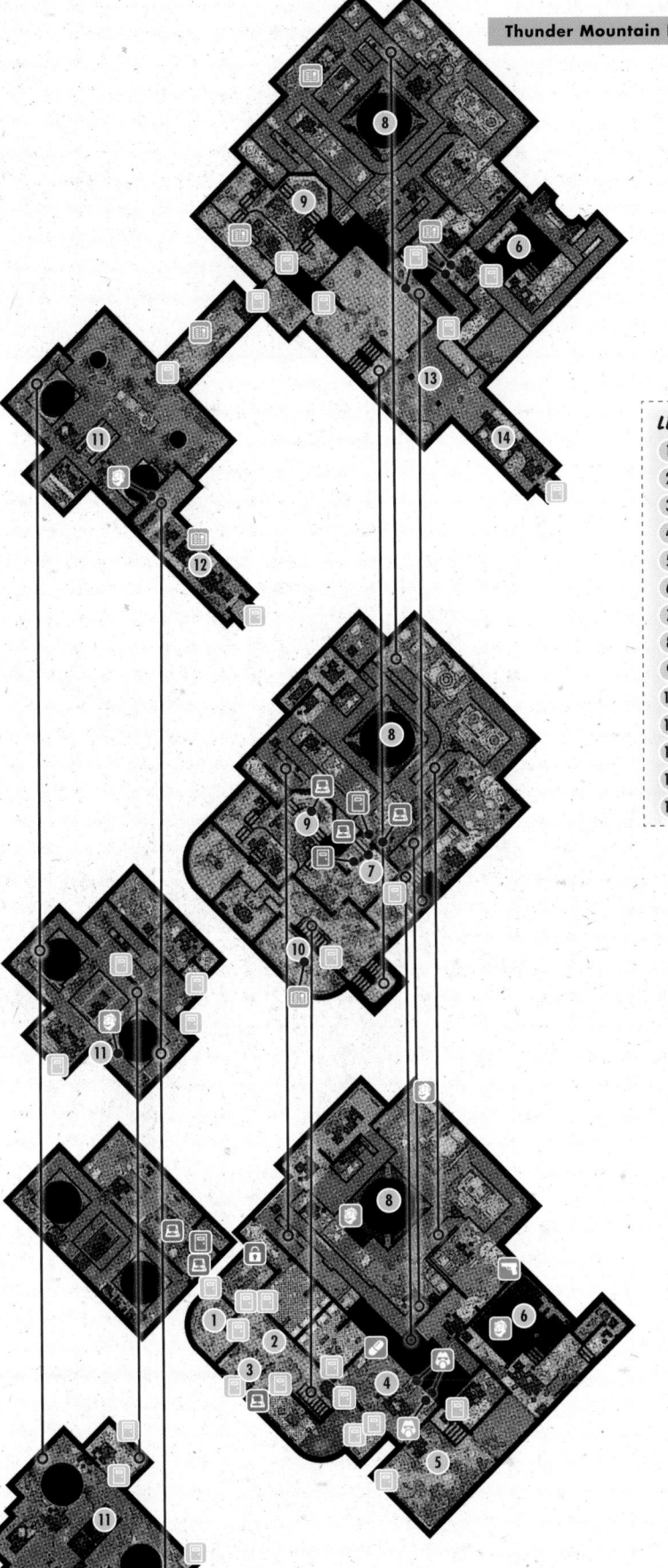

LEGEND

1. SECURITY ENTRANCE
2. MAIN ENTRANCE FOYER
3. LOBBY
4. MECHANICAL BAY
5. LOADING DOCK
6. FUEL STORAGE
7. REACTOR CONTROL AND DECONTAMINATION
8. REACTOR ROOM
9. MASTER CONTROL ROOM
10. CONFERENCE ROOM
11. TURBINE HALL
12. CORRIDOR TO COOLING TOWER #2
13. PIPE INTERCHANGE
14. CORRIDOR TO COOLING TOWER #1

This location also encompasses the Thunder Mountain Power Plant Yard (Workshop), so consult that location for more information on available resources and items. This gigantic power plant usually requires the power to be turned on in order to power other locations in the region. The exterior is dominated by two gigantic cooling towers, with a container area close to the lake (east), as well as a large, tent-filled parking lot (the workshop area). Enter via one of five entrances: security, main entrance (office), loading dock, turbine hall (cooling tower), or turbine hall (lake container area). Once inside, remove any enemy threats. Beware of the chambers (especially the reactor room) with increased radiation threats, and claim the quality junk you need.

TRAINING

CRAFTING AND C.A.M.P.ING

INVENTORY

QUESTS

ATLAS

BESTIARY

APPENDICES

- COLLECTIBLES: BOBBLEHEAD (4), CAPS STASH (5), MAGAZINE (3), POWER ARMOR
- CRAFTING: CHEMISTRY, POWER ARMOR, WEAPONS
- DANGER: EXPLOSIVE CANISTER! RADIATION!++
- ITEMS: ARMS AND AMMO; HARVESTABLE: SOOT FLOWER; HEALTH AND CHEMS+
- INFO: EXPECTED ENEMY: GHOUL, IRRADIATED INSECT, ROBOT; SCAVENGE RATING: 4; SIZE: 5; SLEEPING; THREAT LEVEL: 30–99; TRUNK
- LOCK: DOOR (KEY, KEY, KEY, 1)
- ITEM EXAMPLES: ABRAXO CLEANER, BAG OF CEMENT, BASEBALL CAP, BEAR TRAP, CAP, CHESSBOARD, COFFEE POT, COOLANT, DESK FAN, DIRTY ASHTRAY, DOG TAGS, DUCT TAPE, ENAMEL BUCKET, FUEL TANK, FUSION CORE+, HARD HAT, HAZMAT SUIT, LIFE PRESERVER, METAL BUCKET, MILK BOTTLE, OIL CANISTER, PEPPER, PIPE BOLT-ACTION, PLASTIC SPOON, PRE-WAR MONEY+, RAT POISON, SALT, STEEL WORKER UNIFORM, SUGAR, TIN CANISTER, WELDING GOGGLES, WONDERGLUE

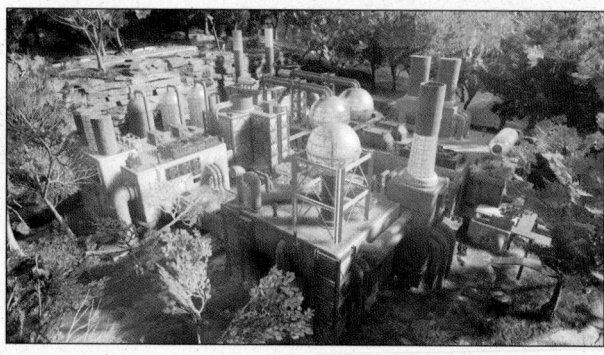

Dyer Chemical (Exterior)

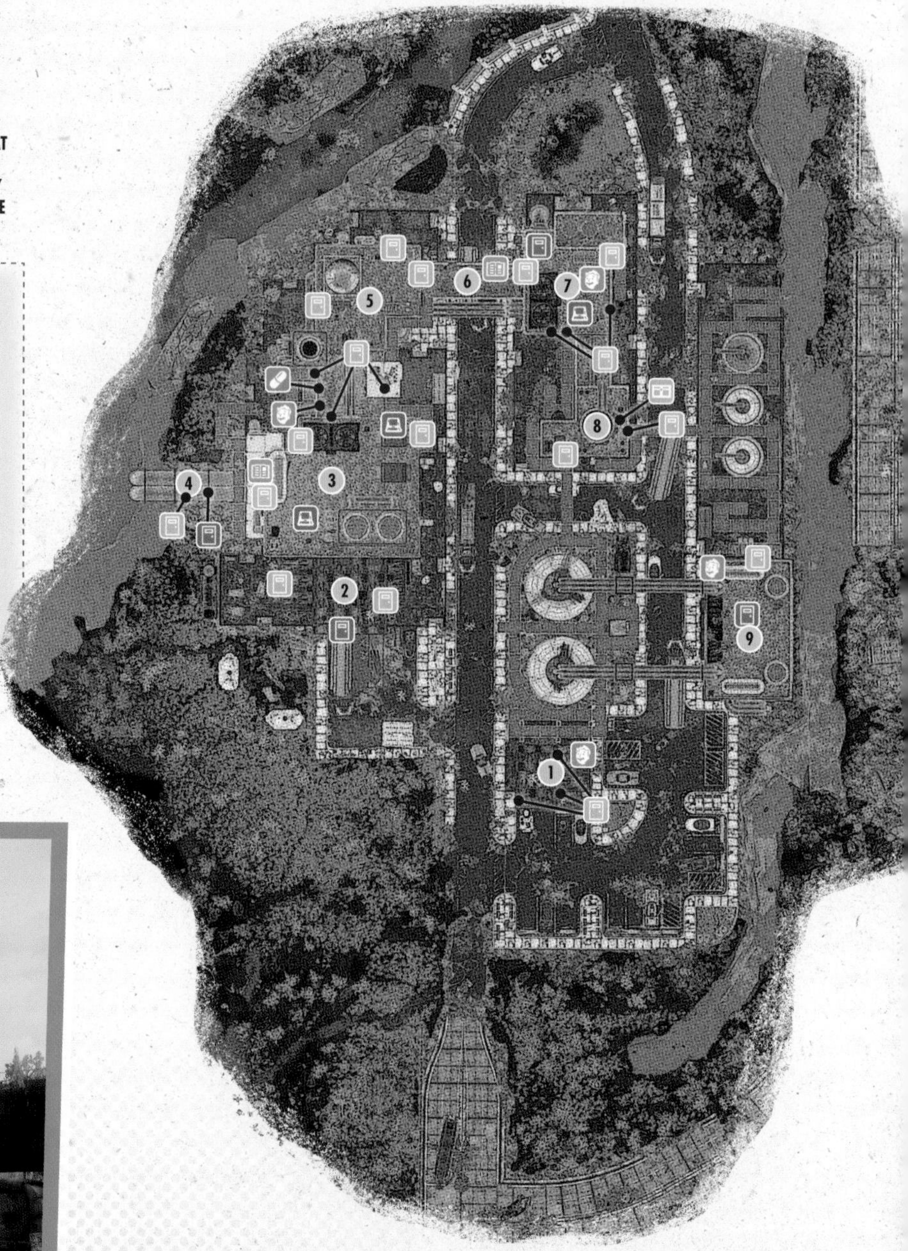

LEGEND

1. "WELCOME" OFFICE AND LOCKER ROOM
2. OFFICE AND UNLOADING WAREHOUSE
3. CHEMICAL MIXING, VATS, AND SUPERVISOR OFFICE
4. EFFLUENT PIPE AND HATCH (SEWER ACCESS)
5. STORAGE WAREHOUSE
6. BRIDGE
7. STATION CONTROL BUILDING (SEWER ACCESS)
8. CENTRAL SERVERS AND CONTROL ROOM
9. SEWER MAINTENANCE BUILDING (SEWER ACCESS)

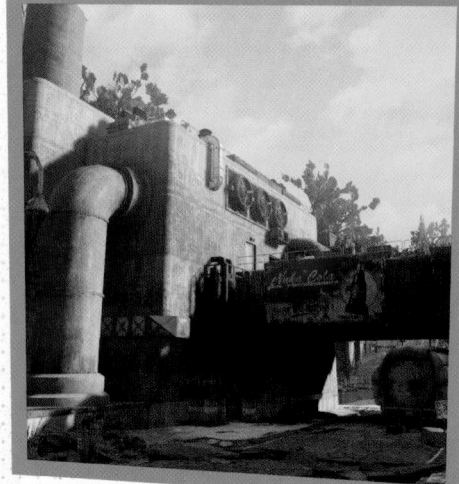

Dyer Chemical: Sewer (Interior)

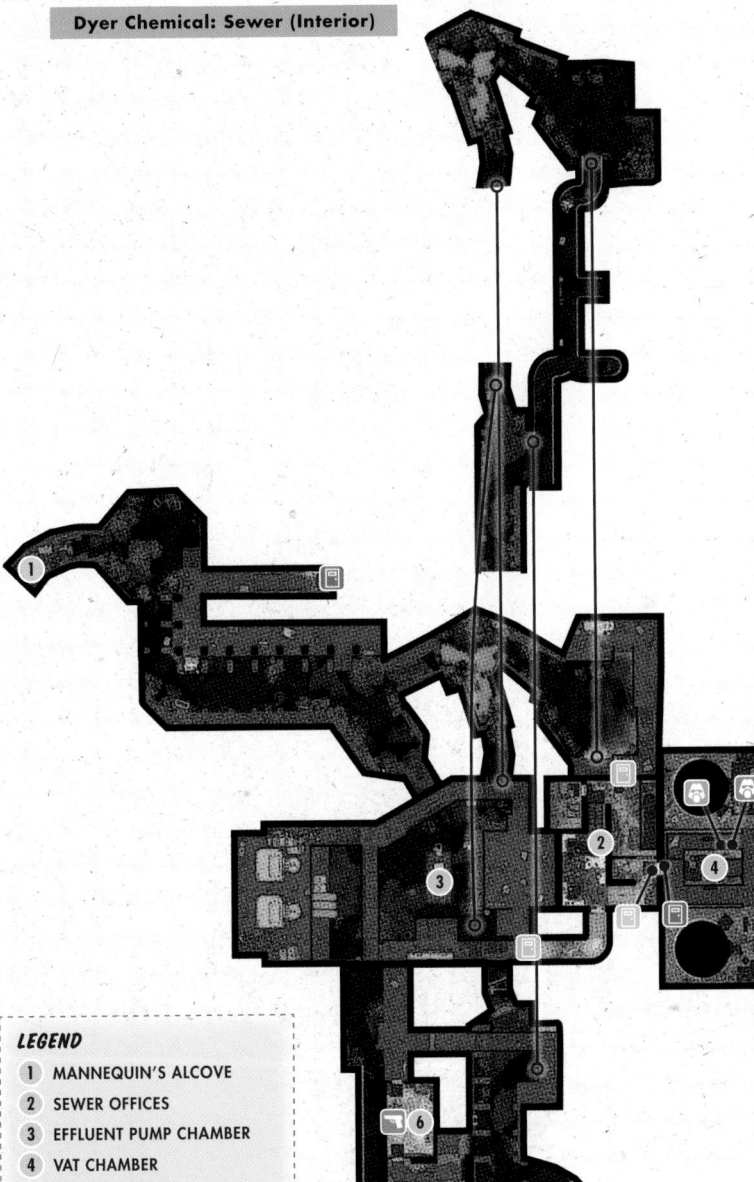

TRAINING

CRAFTING AND
C.A.M.P.ING

INVENTORY

QUESTS

ATLAS

BESTIARY

APPENDICES

23. RALEIGH CLAY'S BUNKER

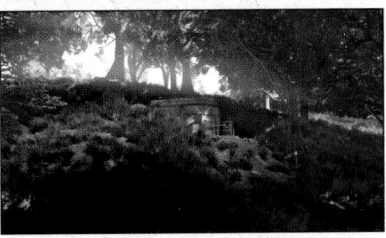

- **CRAFTING:** TINKER
- **DANGER:** EXPLOSIVE CANISTER! RADIATION!++
- **ITEMS: HARVESTABLE:** BRAIN FUNGUS, CARROT PLANTER, CORN PLANTER, GLOWING FUNGUS, GOURD PLANTER, MUTFRUIT PLANTER; HEALTH AND CHEMS; RECIPE/MOD/PLAN
- **INFO: EXPECTED ENEMY:** IRRADIATED ANIMAL, IRRADIATED INSECT; SCAVENGE RATING: 2; SIZE: 2; THREAT LEVEL: 30–99
- **LOCK:** TERMINAL (X2), (1, KEY)
- **ITEM EXAMPLES:** ABRAXO CLEANER INDUSTRIAL GRADE, BEER BOTTLE+, CUTTING BOARD, DIRTY DESKTOP FRAME+, DUCT TAPE, FLOWER POT, HOT PLATE, LANTERN+, PAPER CUTTER, TIN CAN+, TOY TRUCK, TUBE FLANGE, WOOD BLOCK

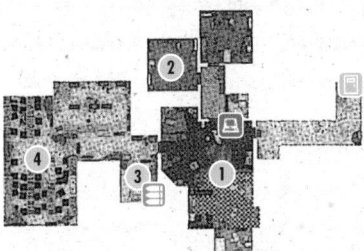

Raleigh Clay's Bunker (Interior)

LEGEND
1. LIVING ROOM AND KITCHEN
2. BEDROOM
3. TINKERER'S STORAGE ROOM
4. HYDROPONIC PLANTING ROOM

LEGEND
1. MANNEQUIN'S ALCOVE
2. SEWER OFFICES
3. EFFLUENT PUMP CHAMBER
4. VAT CHAMBER
5. CORPSE ALCOVE
6. SMALL GENERATOR ROOM
7. HATCH PIPE TUNNELS

Dyer Chemical maintains a large facility along the river, with ample pipes and an extensive sewer system that you can access only with an ID Card. The sprawling facility is on both sides of I-65, with giant vats and facilities structures, mostly automated, but some terminals are still functional. Access the sewer via the outlet pipe or the maintenance facility door. Watch for radiation once you enter, and start fiddling with the pump chamber controls.

Once you have the key to the terminal, you can enter this lair. The descent is worth it, as there's bric-a-brac and a small growing operation, with numerous planters of food to harvest.

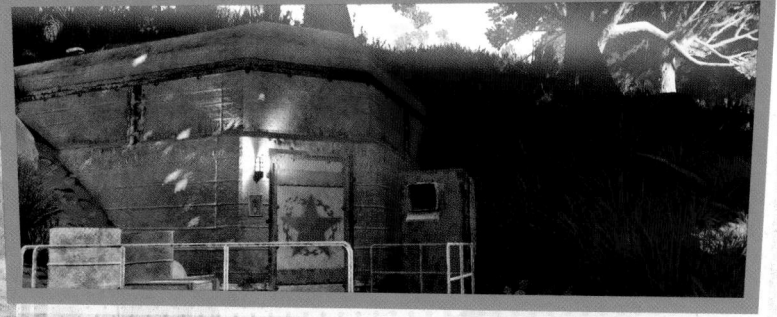

24. BRAXSON'S QUALITY MEDICAL SUPPLIES

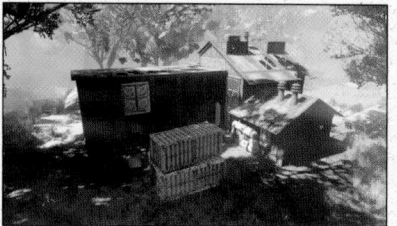

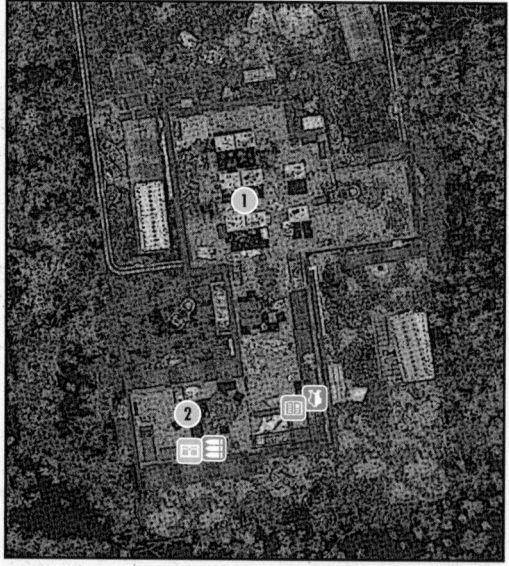

Braxson's Quality Medical Supplies (Exterior and Interior)

LEGEND
1. MEDICAL SUPPLY OFFICE
2. GARAGE STORAGE

- **COLLECTIBLE:** MAGAZINE
- **CRAFTING:** ARMOR, TINKER'S
- **DANGER:** RADIATION!++
- **ITEMS:** HEALTH AND CHEMS, TRUNK
- **INFO:** EXPECTED ENEMY: GHOUL; SCAVENGE RATING: 3; SIZE: 2; THREAT LEVEL: 30–99
- **ITEM EXAMPLES:** ABRAXO CLEANER, DIRTY ASHTRAY, DISHRAG, FUSION CORE, INDUSTRIAL OIL CANISTER, LOOSE SCREWS, LUXOBREW COFFEE POT, PLUNGER, SKULL++, TIBIA, WOOD BUCKET

Someone appears to have abused their knowledge of removing skeletal remains from corpses; the "quality" of the "medical supplies" is now nothing short of grotesque!

 ## 25. BERKELEY SPRINGS WEST (WORKSHOP)

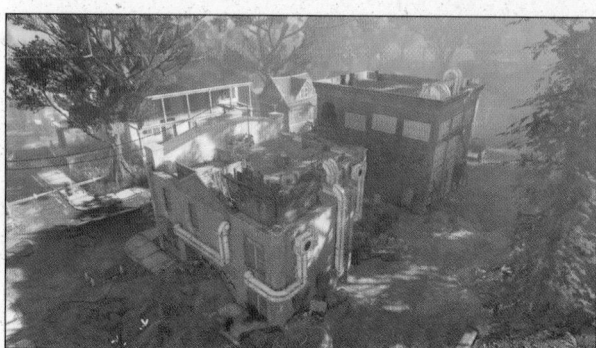

- **COLLECTIBLE:** BOBBLEHEAD
- **CRAFTING:** ARMOR (2), COOKING, WEAPONS, WORKSHOP
- **DANGER:** LONG DROP!
- **ITEMS:** ARMS AND AMMO; HARVESTABLE: ALUMINUM, CORN, CRYSTAL, LEAD, WILD CARROT FLOWER, WILD CORN; HEALTH AND CHEMS
- **INFO:** C.A.M.P. POWER; EXPECTED ENEMY: VARIES; QUEST: CLAIM WORKSHOP AT BERKELEY SPRINGS; SCAVENGE RATING: 2 (5+); SIZE: 3; THREAT LEVEL: 30–99
- **LOCK:** SAFE (2, 2)
- **ITEM EXAMPLES:** ALARM CLOCK, ALUMINUM CANISTER, BATTERED CLIPBOARD, FLOWER POT+, OIL CANISTER, OLD POSSUM BOTTLE, PICKAXE PILSNER, PURIFIED WATER, TEDDY BEAR, TELEPHONE
- **WORK:** FOOD (1), WATER (10), CRYSTAL (1), LEAD (1), ALUMINUM (1)

This location is part of Berkeley Springs. The map can be found at that next location. Set on ground higher than the main part of Berkeley Springs (to the east), this area of town features several relatively intact buildings and a rooftop workshop (accessed via the bookstore interior) that allow you to plan some interesting defenses once you clear the nearby foes. Also note the large amount of water available (hence the name of the location) once the workshop is up and running, and a power box to instantly grant electricity if Thunder Mountain Power Plant is in operation. Also think about setting up cross-fire opportunities from the hotel across the street or flanking foes from the Berkeley Castle (with the stone battlements) to the north.

 ## 26. BERKELEY SPRINGS

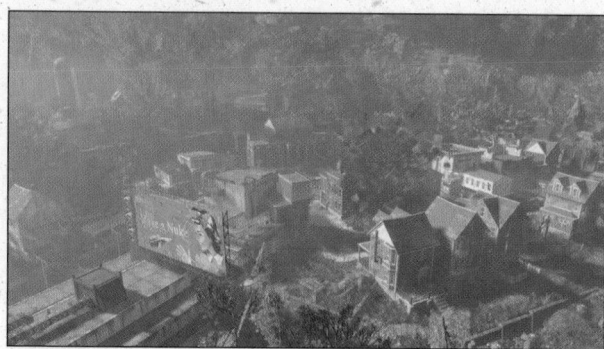

- **COLLECTIBLES:** BOBBLEHEAD (2), HOLOTAPE, MAGAZINE (2)
- **CRAFTING:** WEAPONS
- **DANGER:** LONG DROP! RADIATION! TURRET!
- **ITEMS:** ARMS AND AMMO+; HARVESTABLE: GLOWING RESIN, WILD CARROT FLOWER; HEALTH AND CHEMS; MY STASH BOX; TRUNK; VENDING MACHINE: AMMUNITION, MEDICAL SUPPLIES
- **INFO:** EXPECTED ENEMY: SCORCHED; NOTE; QUEST: PLAY TIME; SCAVENGE RATING: 4; SIZE: 4. SLEEPING; THREAT LEVEL: 30–99
- **LOCK:** DOOR (1, 1, 2, 2), SAFE (2), TERMINAL (2, 2)
- **ITEM EXAMPLES:** ABRAXO CLEANER INDUSTRIAL GRADE, ALARM CLOCK, ANTIFREEZE BOTTLE, BASEBALL BAT, BEER BOTTLE+, BOBBY PIN BOX, BOILED WATER, BOWIE KNIFE, BROKEN LAMP+, CAMERA, CANNED DOG FOOD, COFFEE CUP+, COFFEE POT, COMBINATION WRENCH, COOLANT, CRAM, DESK FAN, DIRTY ASHTRAY+, DOG BOWL+, ECONOMY WONDERGLUE, ENAMEL BUCKET, FASHIONABLE SUNGLASSES, FLIP LIGHTER, FLOWER POT, GUM DROPS, INDUSTRIAL SIZE SHORTENING, LANTERN, NEW RIVER RED ALE, NUKA-COLA, OLD FISHERMAN'S HAT, OLD POSSUM, PILLOW+, PLUNGER, PRE-WAR MONEY, RAW FERTILIZER, RUM, SILVER LOCKET, SOAP+, STIMPAK, SUGAR BOMBS, SUPRATHAW ANTIFREEZE, TEAL BUD VASE, TELEPHONE, TV DINNER TRAY

Atlas of Appalachia – The Mire: Zone A

TRAINING

CRAFTING AND C.A.M.P.ING

INVENTORY

QUESTS

ATLAS

BESTIARY

APPENDICES

Berkeley Springs (Exterior)

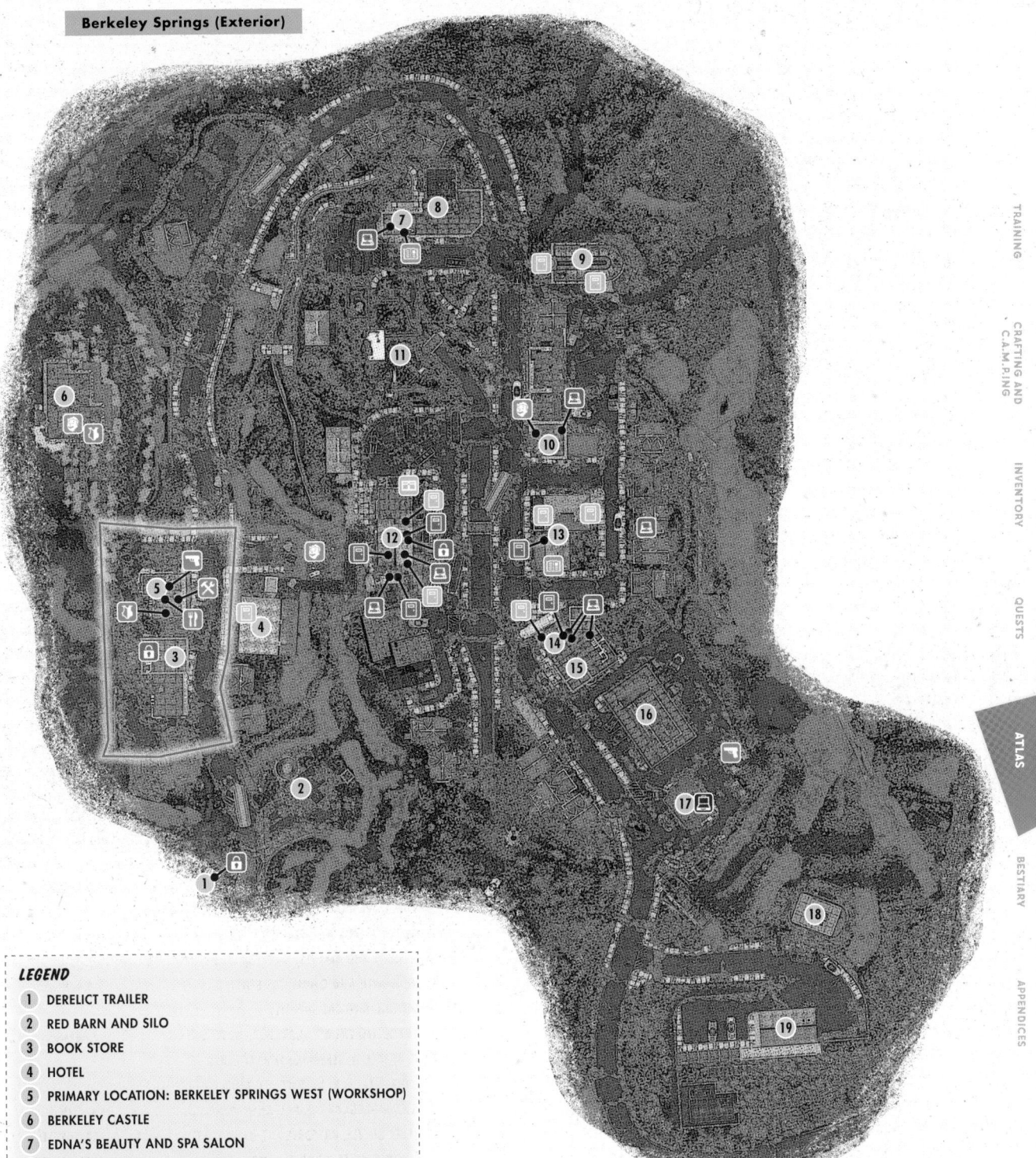

LEGEND

1. DERELICT TRAILER
2. RED BARN AND SILO
3. BOOK STORE
4. HOTEL
5. PRIMARY LOCATION: BERKELEY SPRINGS WEST (WORKSHOP)
6. BERKELEY CASTLE
7. EDNA'S BEAUTY AND SPA SALON
8. ROOFTOP SHANTY HUT (EDNA'S SPA)
9. BERKELEY SPRINGS CHURCH
10. DAVIS FAMILY APARTMENT (ABOVE GRAVIANO'S)
11. PLAYGROUND AND PARK
12. CITY HALL
13. PAIR OF MANSIONS
14. DR. BARNABY'S PHARMACY
15. GUN SHOP (INACCESSIBLE)
16. CLOTHING STORE
17. RED ROCKET GAS STATION
18. ROBCO BOT SHOP
18. OLD MINING STATION

Welcome to America's First Spa! This used to be a quaint tourist attraction, beckoning folk in with tales of mineral waters. Now the ooze that flows through the river has little of the health benefits. The town has a large square and overgrown area close to the once-ornate city hall structure, which has some locked doors to jimmy before you can access the main dwelling's rooftop. Also use the My Stash Box at the Red Rocket Gas Station on the south side of town.

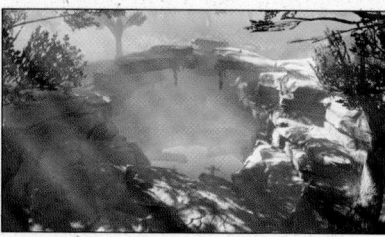

- **CRAFTING:** COOKING
- **DANGER:** RADIATION! RADTOAD MINES!
- **ITEMS:** HARVESTABLE: MUTATED FERN; TRUNK
- **INFO:** EXPECTED ENEMY: CRYPTID, IRRADIATED INSECT; NOTES; SCAVENGE RATING: 1; SIZE: 2; THREAT LEVEL: 30–99
- **ITEM EXAMPLES:** BOILED WATER, FISHING ROD, NEWSBOY CAP, NUKA-COLA BOTTLE

A natural hole in the rock outcrop features a small campground off the nature trail. Platforms lead down to the waterlogged maw bottom, where there's evidence of a cultist altar.

28. TREEHOUSE VILLAGE

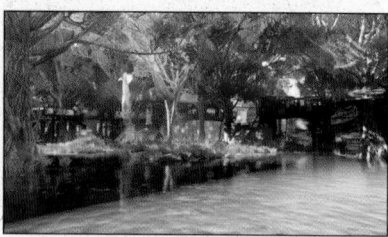

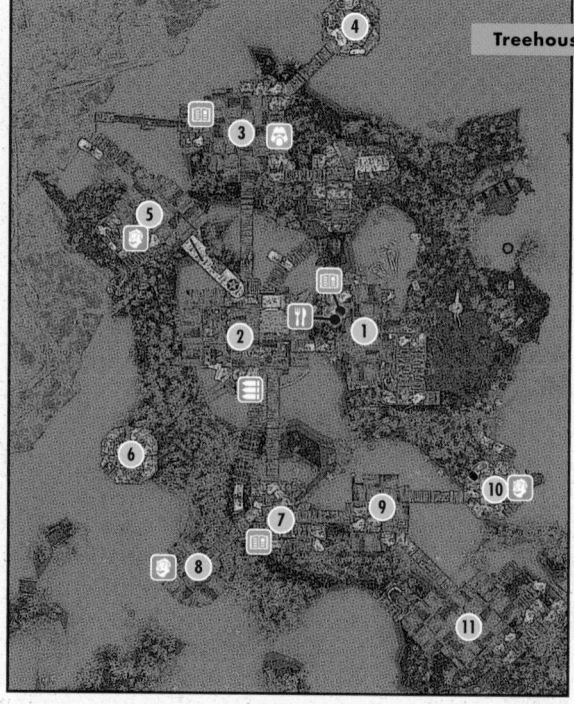

Treehouse Village (Exterior)

LEGEND

1	KITCHEN PLATFORM
2	TINKERER'S PLATFORM
3	LIVING PLATFORM
4	PARTY PLATFORM
5	PLANE WING PLATFORM
6	THE ROPE BRIDGE PLATFORM
7	THE CONNECTING TREE
8	THE BIRDHOUSE BEDROOM
9	THE SECOND KITCHEN PLATFORM
10	THE BAR
11	THE BEAR RUG BEDROOM

- **COLLECTIBLES:** BOBBLEHEAD (3), MAGAZINE (3), POWER ARMOR
- **CRAFTING:** COOKING, TINKER'S
- **DANGER:** CAN CHIMES, RADIATION!+, TRIPWIRE
- **ITEMS:** ARMS AND AMMO+; HARVESTABLE: GLOWING FUNGUS; RECIPE/MOD/PLAN
- **INFO:** EXPECTED ENEMY: CRYPTID; INSTRUMENT SCAVENGE RATING: 3; SIZE: 3; THREAT LEVEL: 30–99
- **ITEM EXAMPLES:** BASEBALL CAP, BEER BOTTLE, BOBBY PIN BOX, BLACKSMITH HAMMER, CHESSBOARD, COMBAT RIFLE, CRAM, FISHING ROD, FUSION CORE, GIDDYUP BUTTERCUP, GLASS JAR, METAL BUCKET, METAL TUB LID, OAK HOLLER LAGER, RUBY TIE MR. FUZZY, SALT, SERRATED MACHETE, SPICES, SUGAR, SUPRATHAW ANTIFREEZE, TATTERED RAGS, WELDING GOGGLES, WOOD BLOCK+

Above the irradiated swamp waters is a baker's dozen platforms, built by survivors before being taken over by Raiders. Now the place is empty, save for the mutated wildlife wading about. Visit and ransack the place as time and radiation-removal chems permit.

29. HAVEN CHURCH

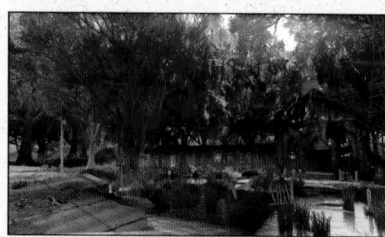

- **COLLECTIBLES:** BOBBLEHEAD, CAPS STASH, MAGAZINE
- **CRAFTING:** CHEMISTRY
- **ITEMS:** HARVESTABLE: BLOODLEAF; HEALTH AND CHEMS; TRUNK
- **INFO:** EXPECTED ENEMY: GHOUL; INSTRUMENT; NOTES; SCAVENGE RATING: 2; SIZE: 2; THREAT LEVEL: 30–99
- **ITEM EXAMPLES:** BURNT BOOK+, INSTAMASH, PASTOR'S VESTMENTS, SALISBURY STEAK, YELLOW TABLE LAMP

The remains of a church and attached school offices are now covered in thick vines and undergrowth. The dilapidation of the structures is even worse inside, partly thanks to "Skig" the Raider.

Haven Church (Exterior)

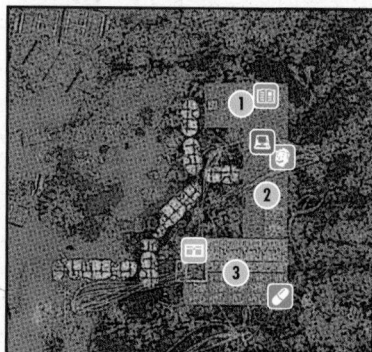

LEGEND

1	SUNDAY SCHOOL ROOM
2	ADMINISTRATION OFFICE
3	CHURCH

ZONE A: SECONDARY LOCATIONS

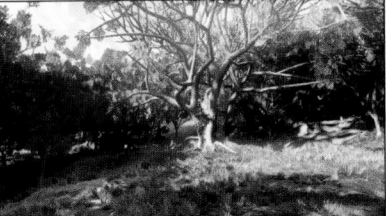

Remote Storage Tangle

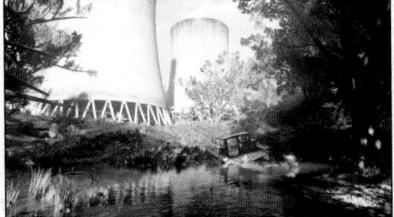

The Faraway Treehouse

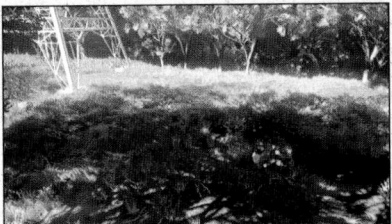

Scupper Boat
(southeast of Thunder Mt. Power Plant)

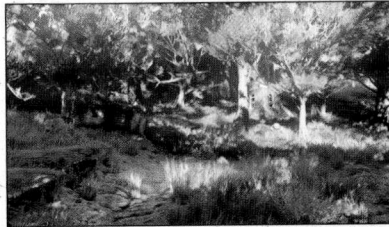

Beehive: East of I-65

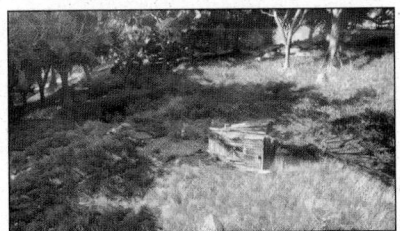

The Swallowed Town

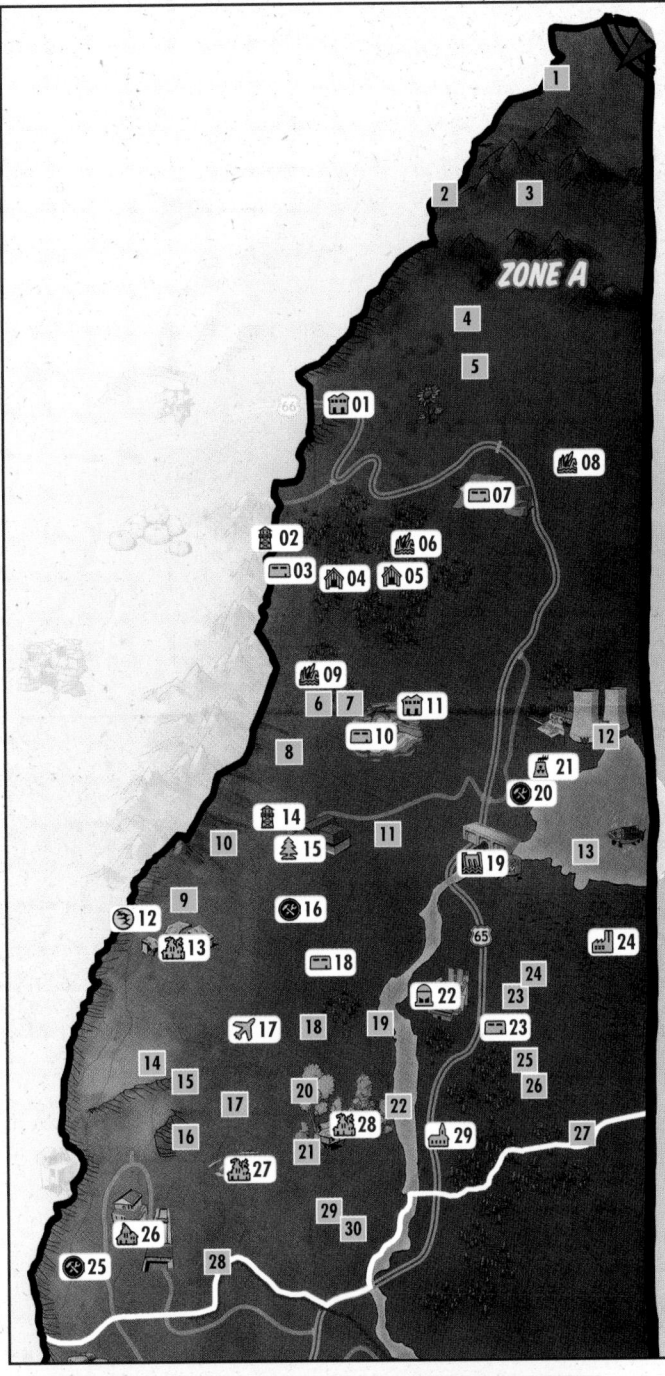

Appalachia: **The Mire (Zone A) – Secondary Locations**

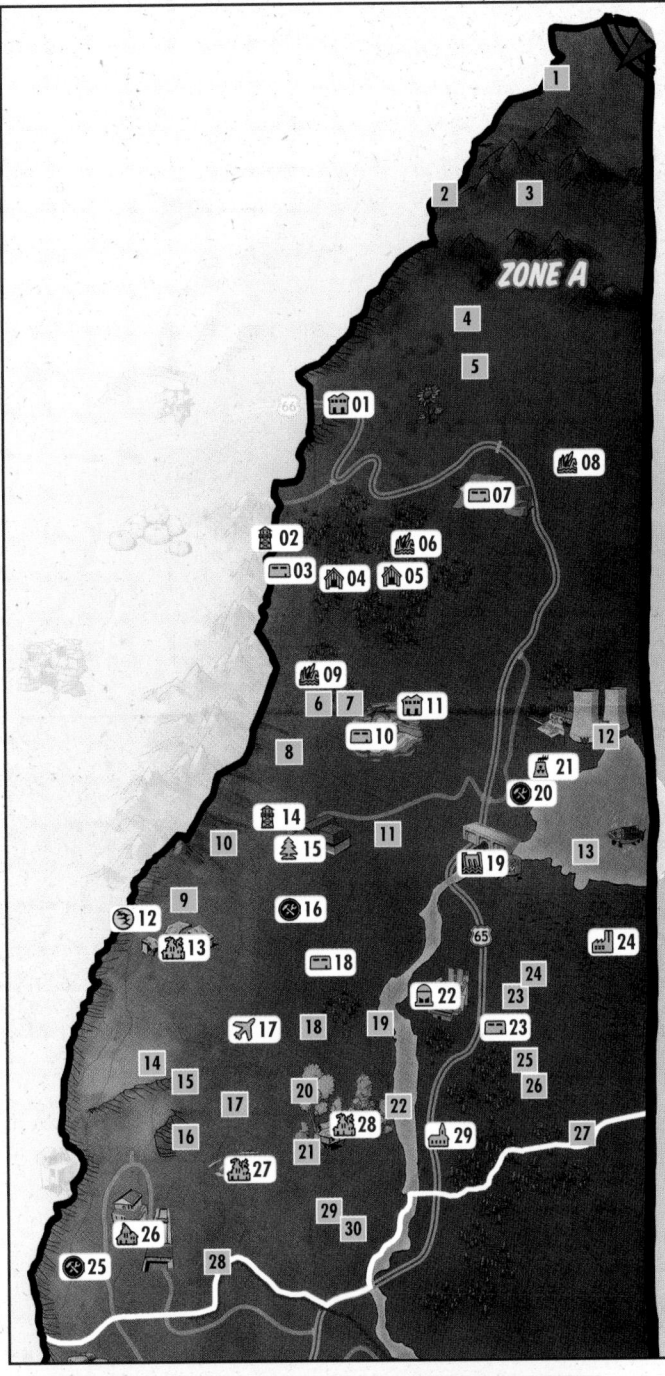

Woodsman's Shack

#	NAME	DESCRIPTION
1	Wilderness Edge Camp	A small camp in a clearing at the very northeastern edge of Appalachia. There's a cooking station and sleeping bags near the rusty SUV.
2	Vertibird Crash Site (Two Bird Marsh)	Two military aircraft have been downed in the far northern part of the Mire.
3	Treehouse High-Dive	In the upper reaches of the Mire, someone has constructed a rickety high-dive, though the pool below is very shallow.
4	Bloatfly Lair (north of Abbie's Bunker)	A humid, rotting mess of animal and human remains in a cave alcove.
5	Remote Storage Tangle	A junk pile, red shed, and a gravel parking lot with tendrils elevating a number of vehicles, including a big-rig cabin into the canopy.
6	The Bike Thief's Shed	A derelict and tendril-tangled structure filled with old bicycles.
7	Stranglemouth Cottage	A strange little dwelling, in a rock alcove with slow tangled roots, some junk to scavenge, and a Tinker's Workbench.
8	The Faraway Treehouse	Though moonface isn't home, there's a mattress and items if you can reach the top of the platforms attached to this tree.
9	The Captured Boater	It seems the tendril-flaying trees of the Mire don't take long to claim their vehicular victims.
10	Dolly Sods' Lost Canoe	A lost and tangled canoe and corpse with an orange tool box, in the dark streams of the west Mire.
11	Tipped Trailer Truck (east of Dolly Sods)	Slowly slipping off the road into a marsh pond, this trailer truck and van have some sealed crates to pry open.
12	Scuppered Boat (southeast of Thunder Mt. Power Plant)	Broken bits of a white boat run aground on the north lake shore are worth inspecting for some minor loot.
13	Biplane Crash (east of Crevasse Dam)	The southern shore of the lake features the remains of a broken plane, with pieces scattered hither and yon.
14	Woodland Trail Outhouse	At the end of a trail is an outhouse with a tin-foil-hatted surprise inside.
15	Tent and Canoe	The remains of a small barbecue camp on a wooded rock ridge in the remote Mire forest.

#	NAME	DESCRIPTION
16	Fairy Ring	A rare natural phenomenon, this circle of glowing fungi grows around a tree trunk.
17	Treehouse Hamlet	This rickety set of tree platforms seems to belong to a lover of hanging meat.
18	Dyer Gulley Waterfall and Tent Camp	The top of the gulley that descends east to the river has a small camp on the rocky outcrop.
19	Dyer Gulley Bottom	Across the brown water from Dyer Chemical is a gulley where waters from uphill flowed down; follow it to see where it goes.
20	Military Comms Tower Treehouse Village	A small, quest-related comms dish situated on a rock bluff near sandbags and military weaponry and junk.
21	Mangled Shed	A red shed has been captured by the tendril growths. Is there more than a lead deposit nearby?
22	Abandoned Swamp Ship	A footlocker, crate, and Bloodleaf plants around a rusting white boat that has run aground can be scavenged.
23	Glowing Fungus Pylon	It's best not to look too closely at what's imprisoned in this large log, covered in glowing fungus, under an electrical pylon.
24	Beehive: East of I-65	Gather honey and try not to get stung at this beehive, stuck on a tendril tree and nearby rock.
25	The Swallowed Town	Several buildings, with interiors to search, have succumbed to the tendrils; descend down the church spire to spot cultist totems and a trunk.
26	Prepper's Pylon Paradise	Unless creatures came and devoured the survivalists, this below-ground pylon paradise was almost hidden; check here for junk and a safe (3).
27	Woodsman's Shack	East of Haven Church is a tin and wood shack with a cooking station and the remains of a settler.
28	Railroad Tent (southeast of Berkeley Springs)	A mattress and tent, a corpse and a radio, a blue rail carriage, and some ammunition to scavenge.
29	Shredded Shed	Something has completely destroyed an old red shed, close to an electrical pylon.
30	Tree Stump Altar	Who has laid out this black bowl and candles on the tree stump? Another mystery of the Mire.

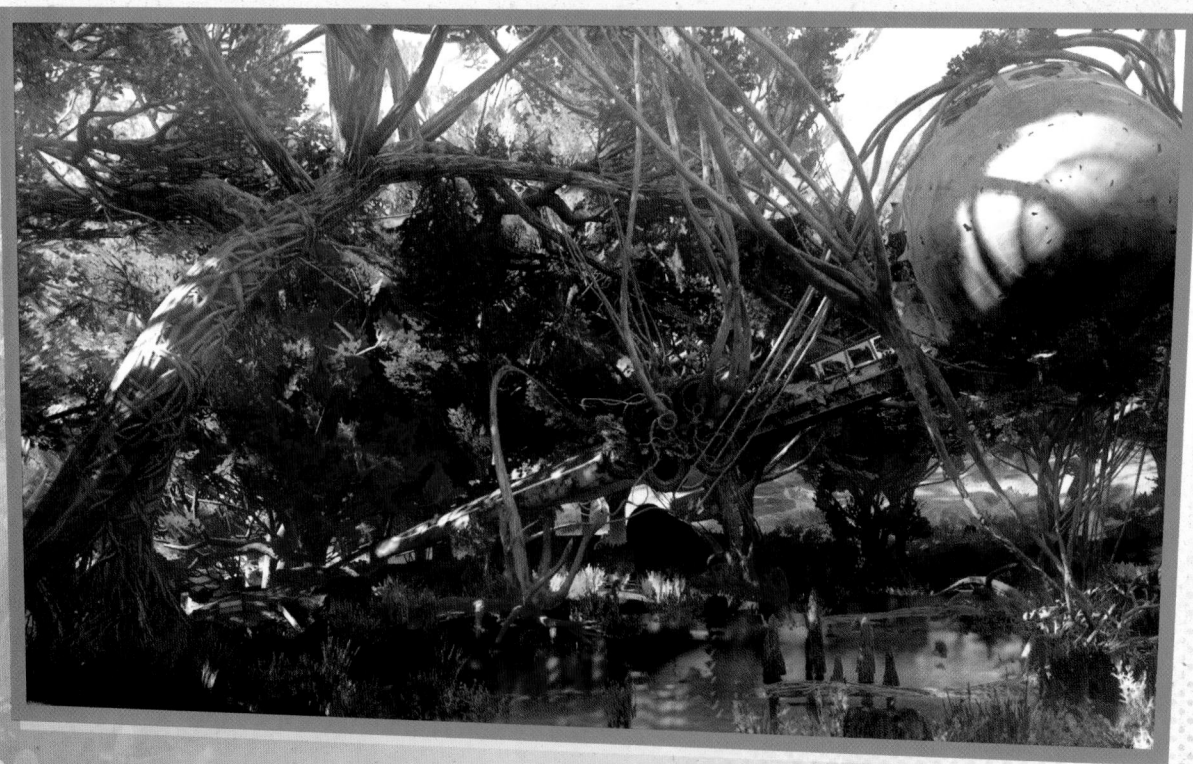

THE MIRE: ZONE B—SOUTH MIRE, HARPERS FERRY, AND TANAGRA TOWN

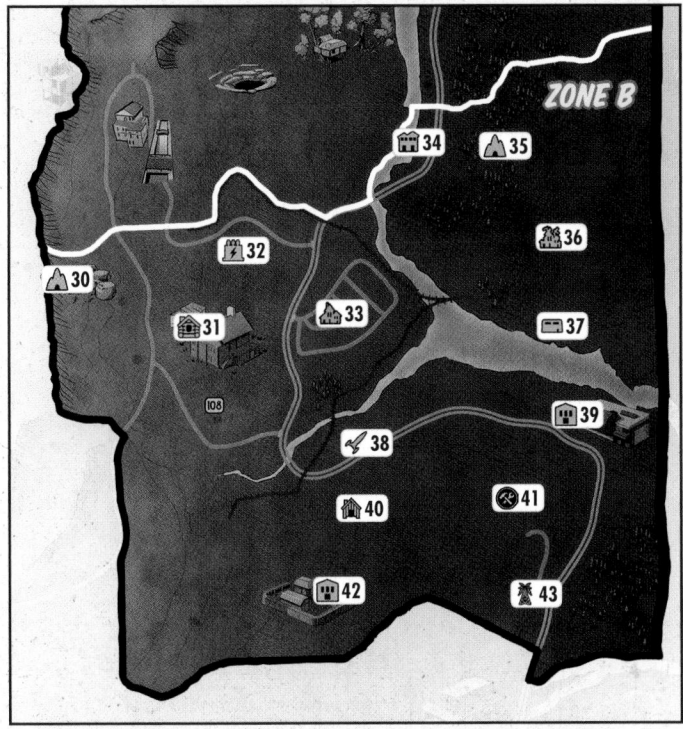

WORLD MAP LEGEND

━━━ REGION BOUNDARY   ━━━ ZONE BOUNDARY

PRIMARY LOCATIONS

				icon	NAME
2		2	1	🏔 30	HAWKE'S REFUGE
1		1	1	🏚 31	SUNDAY BROTHERS' CABIN
				⚡ 32	THUNDER MOUNTAIN SUBSTATION TM-01
				🏛 33	HARPERS FERRY
				🏨 34	SOUTHERN BELLE MOTEL
				🏔 35	ABANDONED WASTE DUMP
1			3	🏚 36	TANAGRA TOWN
				🗄 37	RANSACKED BUNKER
1		1	1	⚔ 38	BIG B'S REST STOP
3		2		🏬 39	VALLEY GALLERIA
4		1		🏚 40	TREETOPS
				☢ 41	DABNEY HOMESTEAD
3		2	1	🏕 42	CAMP VENTURE
				📡 43	KMAX TRANSMISSION

■ BOBBLEHEADS   ■ CAP STASHES
■ MAGAZINES   ■ POWER ARMOR

Appalachia: **The Mire (Zone B) – Primary Locations**

An inhospitable swamp with mountains to the west and boggy terrors to the south, this part of the Mire packs in several truly memorable locations: Big B's Rest Stop, which is helpful, and the remains of the Valley Galleria, a mall that has seen better days but is filled with junk. There is also the historic town of Harpers Ferry, which until recently was a stronghold for the mysterious Free States Faction (in fact, their armory is still intact, if you can get into it!). Those looking to add some height to their exploring would do well to visit Treetops, where a madman has crafted a platform ascent that never seems to stop. But for sheer, mutated magnificence, you must see the wonders of Tanagra, a settlement mangled into a vertical town-sized ball of detritus. Finally, don't leave without continuing to discover the secrets of the Brotherhood of Steel; they had a small base along the southern border.

ZONE B: PRIMARY LOCATIONS

MAP LEGEND

- 📦 MY STASH BOX
- 📋 OVERSEER'S CACHE
- 🗄 TRUNK
- 🤲 TRADER

COLLECTIBLES

- 🧠 BOBBLEHEAD
- 📖 MAGAZINE
- 🦾 POWER ARMOR

CRAFTING

- 🛡 ARMOR WORKBENCH
- 🧪 CHEMISTRY WORKBENCH
- 🍴 COOKING STATION
- 🦾 POWER ARMOR STATION
- 🔧 TINKER'S WORKBENCH
- 🔫 WEAPONS WORKBENCH
- ✖ WORKSHOP WORKBENCH

IMPORTANT

- 🚪 DOOR/GATE
- 🔒 LOCKED DOOR/GATE
- 🔐 SAFE
- ✋ SCANNER
- 🖥 TERMINAL

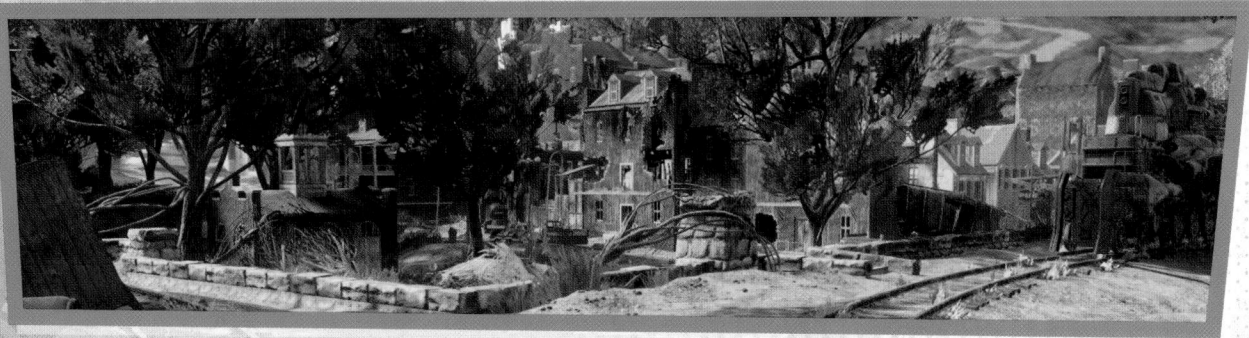

30. HAWKE'S REFUGE

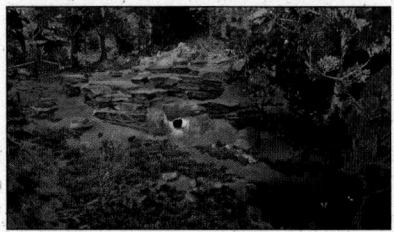

- **COLLECTIBLES:** BOBBLEHEAD (2), MAGAZINE (2), POWER ARMOR
- **CRAFTING:** COOKING
- **DANGER:** CAN CHIMES!
- **ITEMS:** ARMS AND AMMO+; HARVESTABLE: BRAIN FUNGUS, GLOWING FUNGUS; RECIPE/MOD/PLAN
- **INFO:** EXPECTED ENEMY: GHOUL, IRRADIATED ANIMAL, IRRADIATED INSECT; INSTRUMENT; SCAVENGE RATING: 3; SIZE: 2; SLEEPING; THREAT LEVEL: 30–99
- **ITEM EXAMPLES:** BOBBY PIN BOX, CRAM, DUCT TAPE, FUSION CORE, HOT PLATE, LANTERN+, METAL BUCKET, MINI-NUKE, PACK OF CIGARETTES, PLASMA CARTRIDGE, STEALTH BOY, TEDDY BEAR, TIN CAN

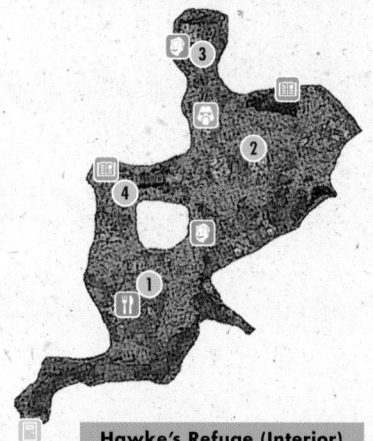

Hawke's Refuge (Interior)

LEGEND
1. COOKING CAMP
2. RED SOFA LAIR
3. SLEEPING ALCOVE (NORTH)
4. MOLE RAT ALCOVE (WEST)

A small clearing in the upper woods features a rocky outcrop with a cave entrance. Inside are two main sections inside a large cavern and an upper alcove, with scattered junk to look out for.

31. SUNDAY BROTHERS' CABIN

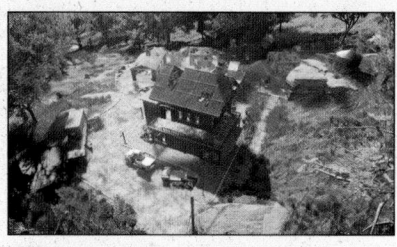

- **COLLECTIBLES:** BOBBLEHEAD, HOLOTAPE, MAGAZINE, POWER ARMOR
- **CRAFTING:** CHEMISTRY, TINKER'S, WEAPONS
- **ITEMS:** ARMS AND AMMO; HARVESTABLE: MUTFRUIT, RAZORGRAIN, RHODODENDRON, WILD CORN; RECIPE/MOD/PLAN
- **INFO:** EXPECTED ENEMY: IRRADIATED ANIMAL; NOTES; SCAVENGE RATING: 3; SIZE: 2; SLEEPING; THREAT LEVEL: 30–99
- **LOCK:** DOOR (1), SAFE (X2) (T, 2)
- **ITEM EXAMPLES:** BAG OF FERTILIZER, BOBBY PIN BOX, BOXING GLOVE, COFFEE MUG, COFFEE TIN, COOKING OIL, ENAMEL BUCKET, FLOWER POT, FUEL TANK, GLASS JAR+, HOT PLATE, MAKESHIFT BATTERY, PILLOW+, TALL DRINKING GLASS+, TIN CAN+, TOASTER, USHANKA HAT, WILLOW VAULTED VASE

Sitting on a flat, rocky outcrop is a lodge-style cabin, a greenhouse, and a mechanic's barn with a floor safe and possible suit of Power Armor. The main building has two main levels and a lower cellar with a locked door (1) leading to a pantry, sleeping area, and storage room with a smattering of junk.

32. THUNDER MOUNTAIN SUBSTATION TM-01

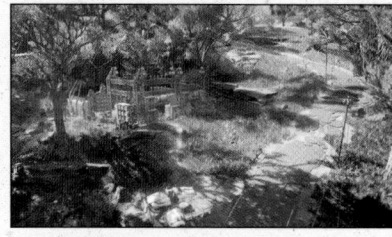

- **DANGER:** RADTOAD MINE!
- **ITEMS:** HARVESTABLE: BRAIN FUNGUS, MUTATED FERN; RECIPE/MOD/PLAN
- **INFO:** C.A.M.P. POWER; EXPECTED ENEMY: IRRADIATED ANIMAL, RADTOAD, TOAD; SCAVENGE RATING: 1; SIZE: 1; THREAT LEVEL: 30–99
- **ITEM EXAMPLES:** NOT MUCH!

Close to the road from Berkeley Springs is a good spot for a C.A.M.P., after you cull the mutated wildlife. Hook up power here, though the power plant may need to be online first.

33. HARPERS FERRY

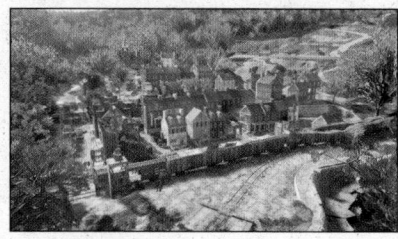

- **COLLECTIBLE:** NUKA-CHERRY
- **CRAFTING:** ARMOR (2), CHEMISTRY, COOKING (3), TINKER'S, WEAPONS (2)
- **DANGER:** FLAMETHROWER! GRENADE! MINE! TENSION TRIGGER! TRIPWIRE! TURRET!
- **ITEMS:** ARMS AND AMMO+++; HARVESTABLE: RHODODENDRON; HEALTH AND CHEMS+++; RECIPE/MOD/PLAN; TRUNK
- **INFO:** EXPECTED ENEMY: SCORCHED, SUPER MUTANT; INSTRUMENT; NOTE; QUEST: TRACKING UNKNOWNS; SCAVENGE RATING: 5; SIZE: 5; SLEEPING; THREAT LEVEL: 30–99; TRADING: VENDOR BOT
- **LOCK:** DOOR (2, 3, 3, 3, 3), SAFE (U), TERMINAL (0, 1)
- **ITEM EXAMPLES:** ABRAXO CLEANER, ALARM CLOCK+, ANTIFREEZE BOTTLE, ANTIQUE GLOBE, ASSAULT RIFLE, BAG OF CEMENT, BALL-PEEN HAMMER, BEER BOTTLE+, BEER HAT, BLACK POWDER PISTOL, BLACKSMITH HAMMER, BLAST RADIUS BOARD GAME, BOILED WATER+, BONE CUTTER, BOWIE KNIFE, BROKEN LAMP+, CANNED DOG FOOD, CHALK, CLAW HAMMER, CRAM, CRYOGENIC GRENADE, DANDY BOY APPLES, DESK FAN, DESKTOP DIRTY FRAME+, EMPTY TEAL ROUNDED VASE, ENAMEL BUCKET, FANCY LADS SNACK CAKES, GAS CANISTER, GLASS PITCHER, GUM DROPS, HOT PLATE, INDUSTRIAL SIZE SHORTENING, IV BAG, LARGE BABY BOTTLE, METAL BUCKET, MICROSCOPE, MISSILE LAUNCHER, MONGREL DOG MEAT, NUKA-COLA BOTTLE, OAK HOLLER LAGER, PASTOR'S VESTMENTS, PORK N' BEANS, POTATO CRISPS, RADAWAY+, RED BANDANNA, SUGAR BOMBS+, TABLE SPOON, TALL FLASK, TEDDY BEAR, TEST TUBE, TEST TUBE RACK, TIN CANISTER+, TOY ALIEN, TYPEWRITER+, VODKA BOTTLE, YUM YUM DEVILED EGGS

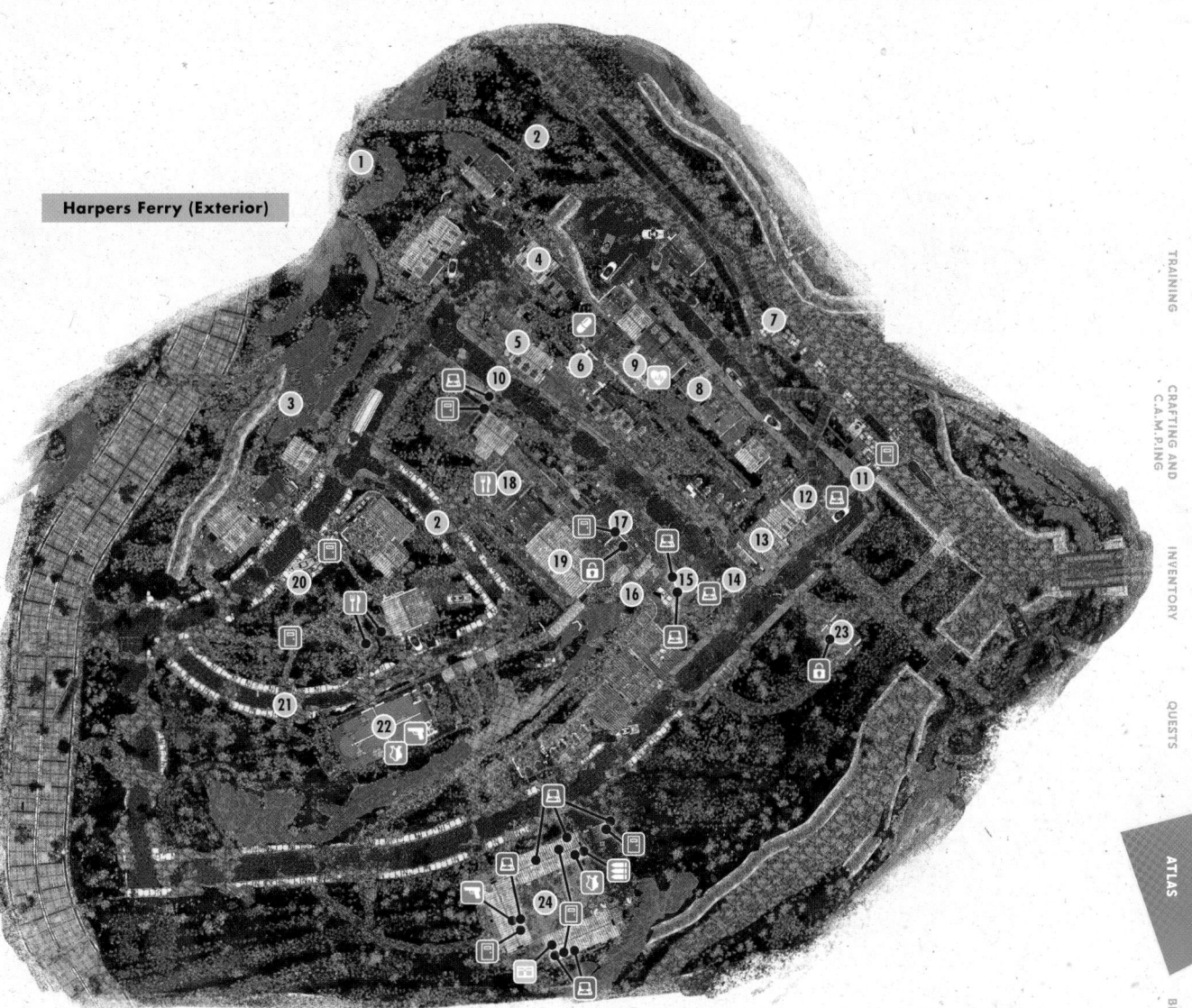

Harpers Ferry (Exterior)

TRAINING

CRAFTING AND C.A.M.P.ING

INVENTORY

QUESTS

ATLAS

BESTIARY

APPENDICES

LEGEND

1. NORTHWEST DECK LOOKOUT
2. NORTH DECK LOOKOUT
3. WEST LOOKOUT
4. TOWNHOME: RED BRICK (NORTH) (INTERIOR)
5. TOWNHOMES: SHENANDOAH ST (NORTH) (INTERIORS)
6. NORTH ALLEY BARRICADE
7. NORTHEAST RAILROAD BARRICADE
8. TOWNHOME 326 (INTERIOR)

9. TRADING POST
10. NORTH GATE
11. EAST GATE
12. TOWNHOME 394 (INTERIOR)
13. TOWNHOME 398: VOTING MACHINES (INTERIOR)
14. SOUTH GATE
15. HOME 126: CLINIC (INTERIOR)
16. STONE ACCESS STEPS

17. TOWNHOMES 118-124: RUINED OFFICES (INTERIORS)
18. TOWNHOME 106: OFFICES (INTERIOR)
19. TOWNHOME 114: OFFICES AND APARTMENT (INTERIOR)
20. WEST BARRICADES
21. WEST GATE
22. HARPERS FERRY CHURCH
23. JOHN BROWN'S FORT (THE ENGINE HOUSE)
24. HARPERS FERRY ARMORY

A once-beautiful historic town, Harpers Ferry is set on the hillside, with large rocky outcrops and two lookouts along the settlement's northwestern edge. The place was once a base of operations for the clandestine faction known as the Free States. Even now, the inner part of the settlement is extremely well fortified, with a number of "gates," most with a locked door (3) that prevents less-competent trespassers from entering. Use the stone steps on the south side or the gap in the middle of the railroad barricade to the east. Once inside, beware of traps and several turrets, both at the church (the main Free States structure aside from the clinic) and at the locked armory just outside town. If you know the terminal code to get in you can maneuver through a trap-filled building and secure some choice weaponry.

34. SOUTHERN BELLE MOTEL

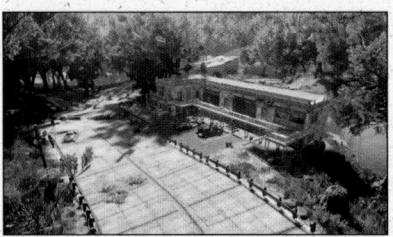

- **INFO:** EXPECTED ENEMY: GHOUL; QUEST: IDLE EXPLOSIVES; SCAVENGE RATING: 2; SIZE: 1; THREAT LEVEL: 30–99
- **LOCK:** DOOR (0)
- **ITEM EXAMPLES:** ABRAXO CLEANER, COFFEE POT, EXTINGUISHER, HOT PLATE, MOP, SEALED WONDERGLUE, SOAP, TOASTER+, USED OIL CAN

Though faded, this garish blue roadside motel still stands apart from the dreary surroundings it sits in. The place is mostly boarded up, save for a locked door (0) along the upper balcony leading to a toaster-filled storage closet.

35. ABANDONED WASTE DUMP

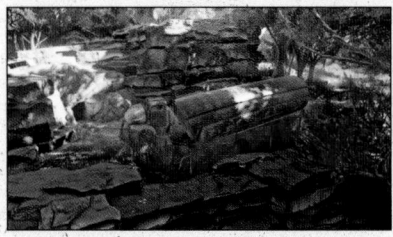

- **COLLECTIBLE:** HOLOTAPE
- **CRAFTING:** CHEMISTRY
- **DANGER:** EXPLOSIVE CANISTER! RADIOACTIVE!++
- **ITEMS:** HARVESTABLE: BRAIN FUNGUS, GLOWING FUNGUS, SOOT FLOWER; HEALTH AND CHEMS; RECIPE/MOD/PLAN
- **INFO:** EXPECTED ENEMY: DEATHCLAW; NOTE; QUEST: BUNKER BUSTER, ONE OF US; SCAVENGE RATING: 3; SIZE: 4; SLEEPING; THREAT LEVEL: 30–99
- **LOCK:** DOOR (KEY), SAFE (0), TERMINAL (3)
- **ITEM EXAMPLES:** ABRAXO CLEANER INDUSTRIAL GRADE, ALARM CLOCK, ALUMINUM CANISTER, ASHTRAY, BEAKER STAND, BOURBON, BUNSEN BURNER, CAN, COFFEE POT, DIRTY DESKTOP FRAME, EMPTY PAINT POT, EMPTY WILLOW BUD VASE, EMPTY WILLOW FLARED VASE, GLASS BEAKER, HOT PLATE+, HUNTING RIFLE, METAL BUCKET, PENCIL, RAT POISON, TOILET PAPER

This initially appears to be an unassuming (but highly radioactive) dumping area with a rusty trailer and abandoned containers. However, it leads into a dangerous cavern interior, with two elevators. One allows access to an exterior exit (due east of the location marker), while the other leads to the Blackwell Bunker, which can be further explored and pillaged if you can turn off the laser grid.

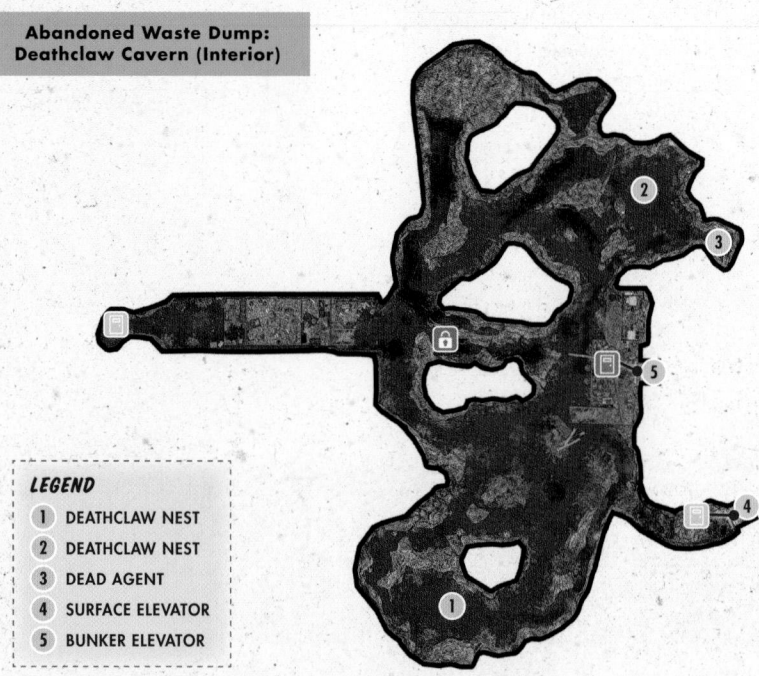

Abandoned Waste Dump: Deathclaw Cavern (Interior)

LEGEND
1. DEATHCLAW NEST
2. DEATHCLAW NEST
3. DEAD AGENT
4. SURFACE ELEVATOR
5. BUNKER ELEVATOR

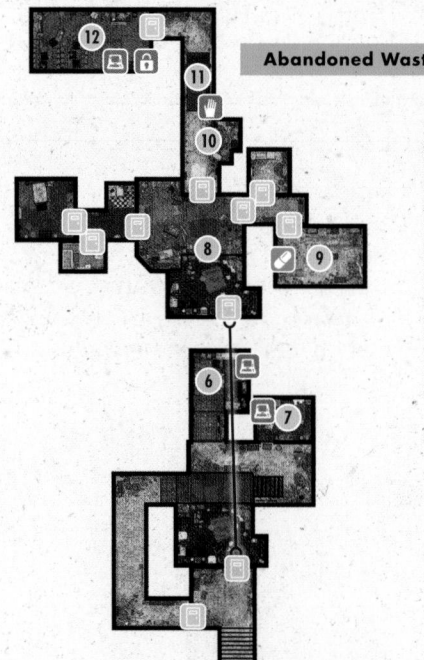

Abandoned Waste Dump: Blackwell Bunker (Interior)

LEGEND
6. SECURITY ROOM
7. JUDY'S BEDROOM
8. KITCHEN AND LIVING ROOM
9. LABORATORY
10. LAUNDRY ROOM AND CIRCUIT BREAKER
11. LASER GRID
12. SAM'S OFFICE

36. TANAGRA TOWN

- **COLLECTIBLES:** BOBBLEHEAD, MAGAZINE (3)
- **CRAFTING:** ARMOR, CHEMISTRY, COOKING, WEAPONS
- **DANGER:** LONG DROP!+++
- **ITEMS:** ARMS AND AMMO; HARVESTABLE: BRAIN FUNGUS, GLOWING FUNGUS, SOOT FLOWER; HEALTH AND CHEMS+; RECIPE/MOD/PLAN; TRUNK
- **INFO:** EXPECTED ENEMY: CRYPTID, GHOUL, IRRADIATED INSECT, MIRELURK; NOTE; SCAVENGE RATING: 4; SIZE: 4; THREAT LEVEL: 30–99

- **ITEM EXAMPLES:** ALARM CLOCK, BROWN BOTTLE, CLOWN, DESK FAN, DIRTY ASHTRAY, DUCT TAPE, FISHING ROD, FLOWER POT, GIDDYUP BUTTERCUP, KITCHEN SCALES, LEAD PIPE, MEDICAL LIQUID NITROGEN DISPENSER, METAL BUCKET, MICROSCOPE, OIL CANISTER, OVEN MITT, PLUNGER, RABBIT HIDE, SMALL LEFT ANTLER, SPICES, SUPATHAW ANTIFREEZE, SURGICAL TRAY, SURVEYOR OUTFIT, T-SHIRT AND SLACKS, TEDDY BEAR, UNSTOPPABLE SHINDIG BOARD GAME, WONDERGLUE

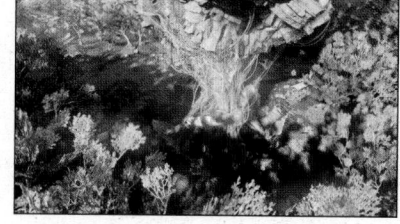

Perhaps nothing in the Mire is as terrifying as the force of a mutated Mother Nature: The woods have gathered the entire settlement of Tanagra and strangled it into a gigantic trunk shaped with various vehicles, homes, and other elements, forming a horrifyingly beautiful "tree." Check the buildings that survived the tendril menace before crossing a log onto a snared school bus. Head up the outside and then enter the structure, before going to the eventual top! If you haven't found the red Industrial Trunk, then you haven't climbed high enough! If you haven't spotted the odd stone face, then you haven't explored deep enough!

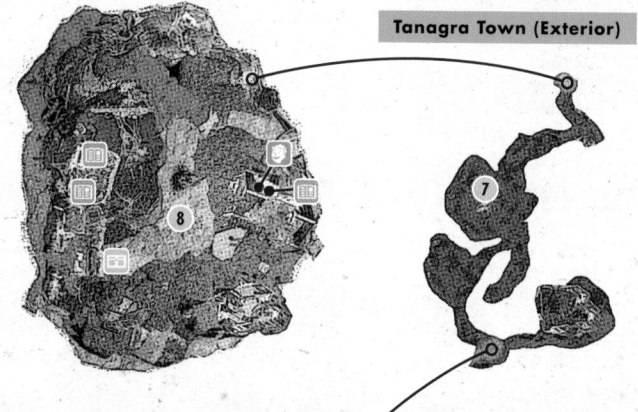

Tanagra Town (Exterior)

LEGEND

1. MONITORING LABORATORY
2. METAL SHEDS
3. TANAGRA BUS STOP
4. WOODEN SHED
5. TENDRILLED HOME
6. TANAGRA TOWER
7. THE FACE
8. TANAGRA TOWER (TREETOP FINISH)

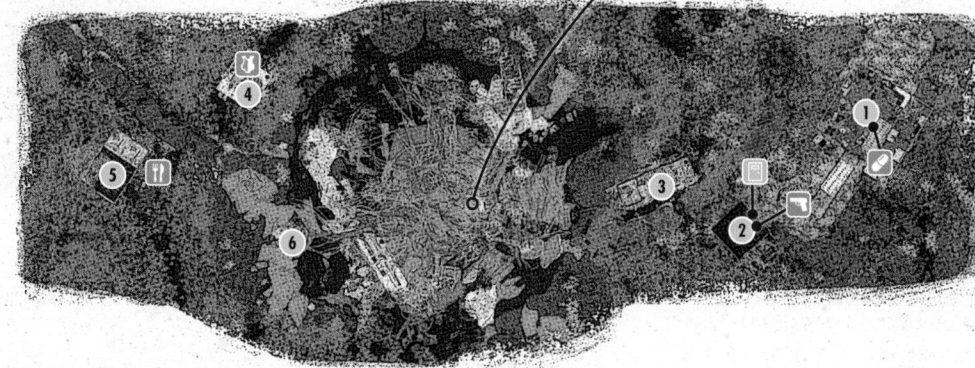

37. RANSACKED BUNKER

- **ITEMS:** HARVESTABLE: GLOWING FUNGUS, RHODODENDRON; HEALTH AND CHEMS
- **INFO:** EXPECTED ENEMY: IRRADIATED INSECT; SCAVENGE RATING: 4; SIZE: 2; THREAT LEVEL: 30–99
- **ITEM EXAMPLES:** 25-LB WEIGHT, ACCORDION, ADJUSTABLE WRENCH, ALUMINUM CAN+, BAG OF CEMENT, BEER BOTTLE+, BLAST RADIUS BOARD GAME, DIRTY DESKTOP FRAME+, DUCT TAPE+, ECONOMY WONDERGLUE, EMPTY PAINT CAN, FUEL TANK, FUSE+, GAS CANISTER, GREASER JACKET AND JEANS, GREEN BANDANNA, GLASS JAR+, LANTERN+, MAKESHIFT BATTERY, TOILET PAPER, UNSTOPPABLE SHINDIG BOARD GAME, USED OIL CAN+

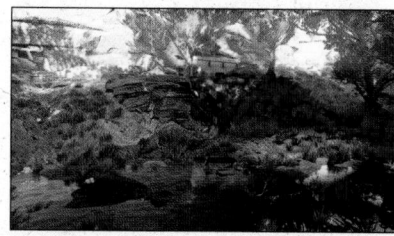

At the base of a stacked rock cliff, on the river's north side, is a Free States bunker. Though there are only two interior chambers, each is so well stocked with junk that some believe the location was named to throw off scavengers.

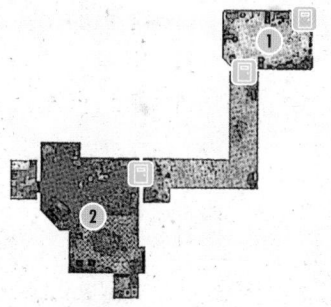

Ransacked Bunker (Interior)

LEGEND

1. STORAGE ROOM
2. KITCHEN AND LIVING AREA

38. BIG B'S REST STOP

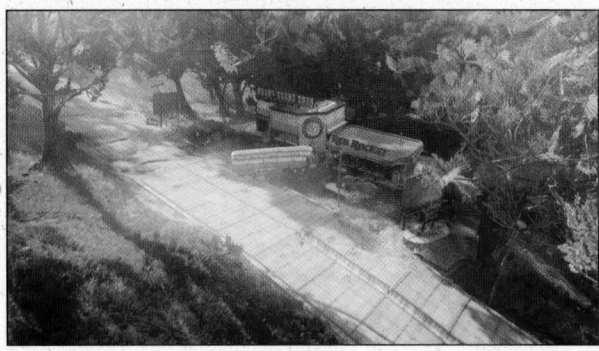

- **COLLECTIBLES:** BOBBLEHEAD, CAPS STASH, MAGAZINE, POWER ARMOR
- **CRAFTING:** ARMOR, COOKING, POWER ARMOR
- **ITEMS:** ARMS AND AMMO, HEALTH AND CHEMS, MY STASH BOX
- **INFO:** EXPECTED ENEMY: SCORCHED; SCAVENGE RATING: 3; SIZE: 2; SLEEPING; THREAT LEVEL: 30–99
- **LOCK:** SAFE (1)
- **ITEM EXAMPLES:** BEER BOTTLE, BOBBY PIN BOX, CAFETERIA TRAY, COFFEE CUP+, COMBAT SNIPER RIFLE, EMPTY PAINT CAN, INDUSTRIAL SIZE SHORTENING, MILK BOTTLE, RED PLATE+, SPICES, SUGAR, TIN CAN+

Use this old gas station and attached Super Duper Mini-Mart as base camp for offloading items, as well as a place to gather a variety of junk and some choice collectibles. Check the roof of the Super Duper Mini-Mart for some sniper goods.

39. VALLEY GALLERIA

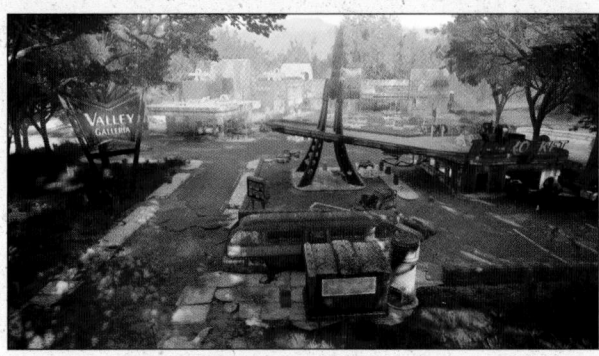

- **INFO:** EXPECTED ENEMY: ROBOT, SCORCHED; INSTRUMENT; SCAVENGE RATING: 5; SIZE: 4; SLEEPING; THREAT LEVEL: 35–99
- **LOCK:** DOOR (2), SAFE (2, 2), TERMINAL (1)
- **ITEM EXAMPLES:** ADJUSTABLE WRENCH, BANDAGE SCISSORS, BASEBALL+, BASEBALL BAT, BASEBALL GLOVE, BASKETBALL+, BEER BOTTLE++, BONE CUTTER, BOWL+, BREAD BOX, BROOM, BURNT BOOK, CAFETERIA TRAY++, CAKE TIN, CAT BOWL, CLOTHES HANGER, COFFEE CUP++, COFFEE POT, COLANDER, COOKING POT, COTTON YARN+, COVERED SAUCEPAN, CRAM, DINNER PLATE+, DIRTY ASHTRAY, DUCT TAPE, EMPTY PAINT CAN, ENAMEL BUCKET+, GLASS PITCHER+, HOT PLATE, KITCHEN SCALE+, LIGHTBULB+, MARKSMAN'S SNIPER RIFLE, METAL BUCKET, NUKA-COLA CUP AND STRAW+, OIL CANISTER, PLUNGER+, POTATO CRISPS, PRE-WAR MONEY, SALISBURY STEAK, SCREWDRIVER, SURGICAL TRAY, TALL DRINKING GLASS+, TIN CAN+, TELEPHONE+, TOY ALIEN, TOY CAR, TOY ROCKETSHIP, TYPEWRITER, USED OIL CAN, WHITE PLATE, WOOD BLOCK+, YELLOW TABLE LAMP+, YUM YUM DEVILED EGGS

- **COLLECTIBLES:** BOBBLEHEAD (3), HOLOTAPE, MAGAZINE (2)
- **DANGER:** GRENADE! RADIATION!
- **ITEMS:** ARMS AND AMMO; HARVESTABLE: BRAIN FUNGUS, GLOWING FUNGUS, RHODODENDRON, SOOT FLOWER, WILD CARROT FLOWER; HEALTH AND CHEMS; MY STASH BOX; RECIPE/MOD/PLAN; TRUNK

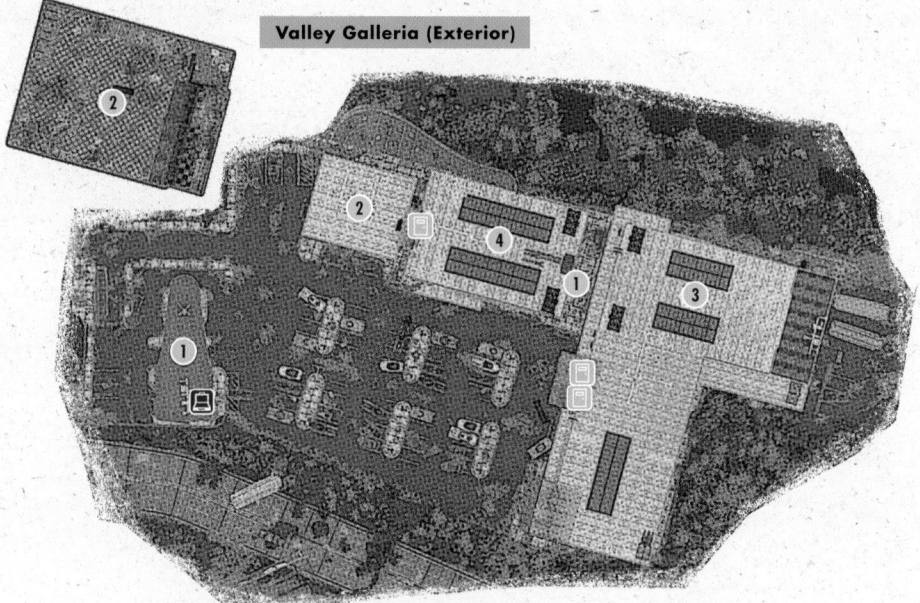

Valley Galleria (Exterior)

LEGEND
1. RED ROCKET GAS STATION
2. WESTSIDE RESTAURANT
3. VALLEY GALLERIA (MAIN)
4. VALLEY GALLERIA (SIDE)

Valley Galleria (Interior)

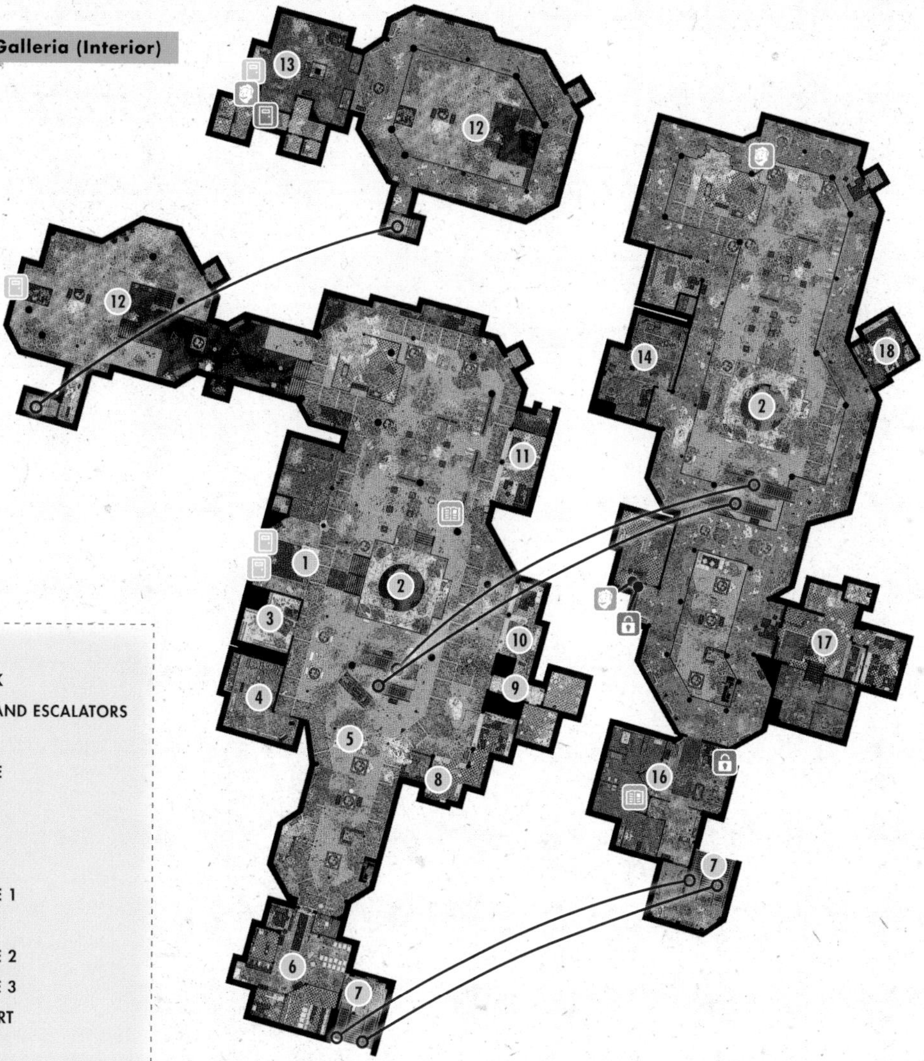

LEGEND

1. INFORMATION DESK
2. MAIN FORECOURT AND ESCALATORS
3. TOY SHOP
4. ELECTRONICS STORE
5. COFFEE STALL
6. DEPARTMENT STORE
7. ESCALATORS
8. FOOD COURT STORE 1
9. RESTROOMS
10. FOOD COURT STORE 2
11. FOOD COURT STORE 3
12. FLOODED FORECOURT
13. VALLEY'S BOUTIQUE
14. BOOK SHOP
15. BIG STEVE'S SPORTING GOODS
16. HOUSEWARES
17. LITTLE ITALY RESTAURANT
18. UPSTAIRS DINER

Those shoppers craving a five-finger discount are in luck; there's still quite a collection of junk lying around this derelict shopping mall, spread over two floors with an exterior parking lot filled with rusting vehicles and a Red Rocket Gas Station (where you can store items from your haul). Inside, work your way methodically through every store, grabbing what you need and fending off attacks as you go. Watch the flooded area near the side entrance; it's slightly radioactive.

40. TREETOPS

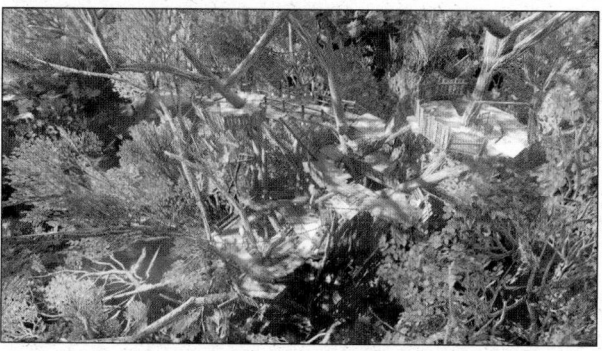

- **COLLECTIBLES:** BOBBLEHEAD (4), MAGAZINE
- **CRAFTING:** ARMOR, COOKING (X2)
- **DANGER:** LONG DROP!
- **ITEMS:** ARMS AND AMMO; HARVESTABLE: WOOD; RECIPE/MOD/PLAN; TRUNK
- **INFO:** EXPECTED ENEMY: CRYPTID; INSTRUMENT; NOTES; SCAVENGE RATING: 5; SIZE: 3; SLEEPING; THREAT LEVEL: 30–99
- **ITEM EXAMPLES:** ALARM CLOCK, ALUMINUM CANISTER, BLAST RADIUS BOARDGAME, BLUE PAINT, BLOWTORCH, BOBBY PIN BOX, BOWLING PIN+, CAT BOWL, GARDEN GNOME, GAS CANISTER, HONEY JAR, MAKESHIFT BATTERY+, METAL TUB, MOLE RAT HIDE+, MR. HANDY FUEL, SCREWDRIVER+, SUPRATHAW ANTIFREEZE, TEA KETTLE, TYPEWRITER, USHANKA HAT, WELDING GOGGLES, WOOD BLOCK+

Aside from the danger of falling, there are no drawbacks from scaling this precarious, junk-filled series of tree platforms. Keep going until you reach the trunk, and don't look down!

41. DABNEY HOMESTEAD (WORKSHOP)

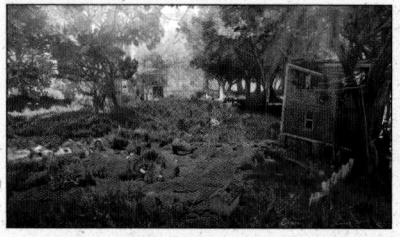

- **CRAFTING:** WATER PUMP, WEAPONS, WORKSHOP
- **ITEMS:** HARVESTABLE: COPPER DEPOSIT, GINSENG ROOT, PHOSPHATE, WOOD
- **INFO:** EXPECTED ENEMY: VARIES; QUEST: CLAIM WORKSHOP AT DABNEY HOMESTEAD; SCAVENGE RATING: 2(5); SIZE: 2; SLEEPING; THREAT LEVEL: 30-99
- **LOCK:** SAFE (3)
- **ITEM EXAMPLES:** BEER BOTTLE, DUCT TAPE, FLIP LIGHTER, METAL BUCKET, MR. HANDY FUEL, PLUNGER, RAT POISON, TOILET PAPER, TURPENTINE
- **WORK:** FOOD (6), WATER (8), FERTILIZER (1), JUNK (1), COPPER (3), CONCRETE (1), WOOD (1)

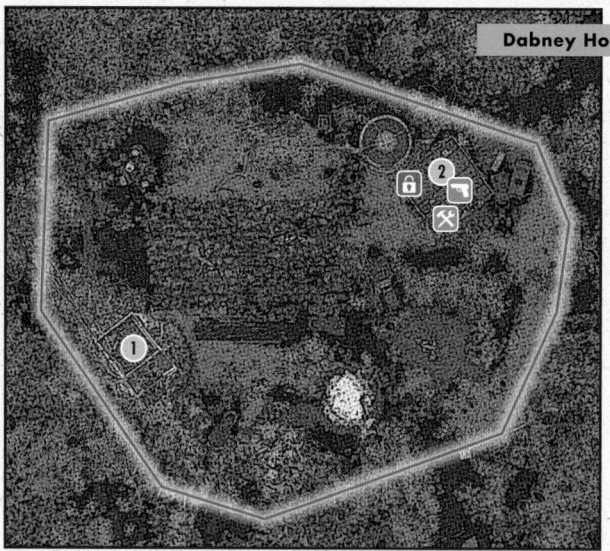

Dabney Homestead (Exterior)

LEGEND
1. RUINED DABNEY HOME
2. DILAPIDATED RED BARN

Close to the Valley Galleria but still far enough away to be a good defendable asset, this workshop area consists of two derelict structures: the barn and a roofless house. The barn has a lot more useful junk than the house. Clear the area of foes, and start mining those resources!

42. CAMP VENTURE

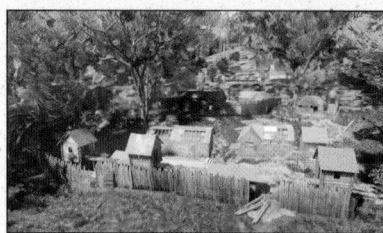

- **COLLECTIBLES:** BOBBLEHEAD (3), HOLOTAPE, MAGAZINE (2), NUKA-CHERRY, POWER ARMOR
- **CRAFTING:** ARMOR, CHEMISTRY, POWER ARMOR (2), TINKER, WEAPONS (2)
- **DANGER:** EXPLOSIVE CANISTER!
- **ITEMS:** ARMS AND AMMO++; HEALTH AND CHEMS+; OVERSEER'S CACHE; RECIPE/MOD/PLAN; TRUNK; VENDING MACHINE: AMMUNITION
- **INFO:** EXPECTED ENEMY: GHOUL; NOTE; SCAVENGE RATING: 4; SIZE: 3; THREAT LEVEL: 30-99
- **LOCK:** DOOR (3, 3, KEY), TERMINAL (PASS)
- **ITEM EXAMPLES:** ABRAXO CLEANER, BEER BOTTLE+, BLASTING CAPS BOX, COOLANT, COTTON YARN, DIRTY ASHTRAY, DISHRAG, DUCT TAPE, ENAMEL BUCKET, FUEL TANK, FUSE, GOLD PLATED FLIP LIGHTER, HOT PLATE, LIGHTBULB, MAKESHIFT BATTERY, MILITARY AMMO BAG, MILITARY FATIGUES, MILITARY GRADE CIRCUIT BOARD+, MISSILE LAUNCHER, MR. HANDY FUEL, NUKA-COLA CUP, OIL CANISTER, PACK OF CIGARETTES, SOAP, STRAW PILLOW+, SYRINGER AMMO, TOILET PAPER, TURPENTINE, VOLATILE MATERIALS BOX, YELLOW PLATE

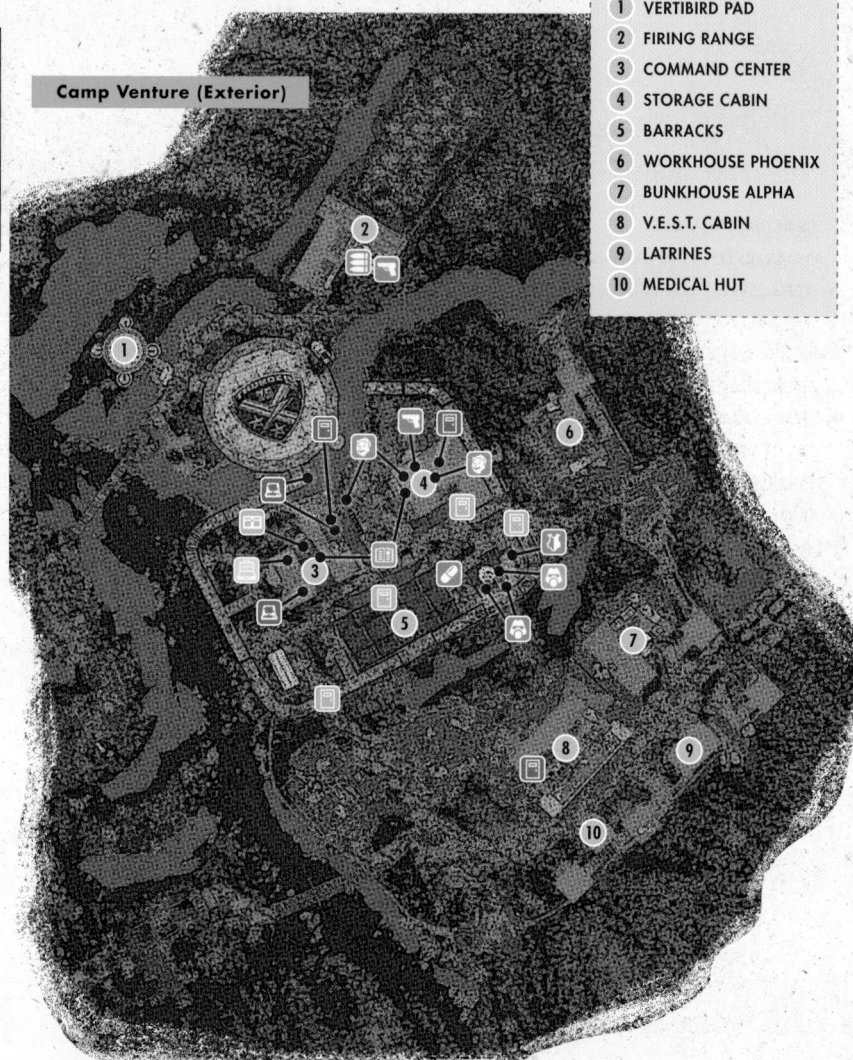

Camp Venture (Exterior)

LEGEND
1. VERTIBIRD PAD
2. FIRING RANGE
3. COMMAND CENTER
4. STORAGE CABIN
5. BARRACKS
6. WORKHOUSE PHOENIX
7. BUNKHOUSE ALPHA
8. V.E.S.T. CABIN
9. LATRINES
10. MEDICAL HUT

ZONE B: SECONDARY LOCATIONS

A hillside adventure fort on three tiered rock outcrops surrounded by woodland, this old wilderness adventure area was recently commandeered by the Brotherhood of Steel, who reinforced the defenses. At the top is a firing range and landing pad within the upper battlements; use the exterior terminal at the pad to summon a Cargobot during the quest. The main, reinforced Brotherhood cabins (including a storage cabin, which has high-quality junk, and the command center) are within a strong defensive wall in the middle of the camp. The old rickety camp structures are mainly confined to the lower area, which includes the V.E.S.T. (Virginia Endurance and Survival Training) Cabin; check behind a propped-up door to find a basement with a locked (3) door and the command center terminal password: Inside is more information about the Brotherhood, as well as an Overseer's Cache and Trunk.

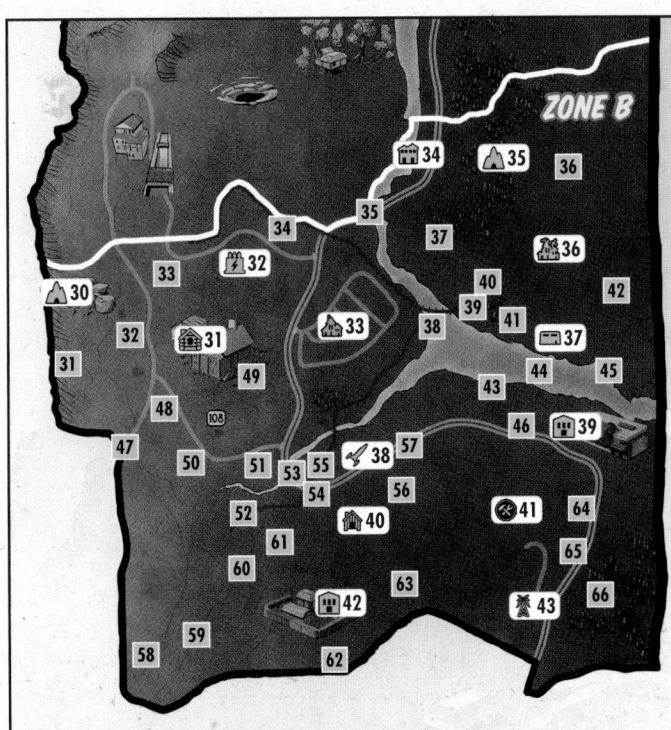

Appalachia: **The Mire (Zone B) – Secondary Locations**

🌴 43. KMAX TRANSMISSION

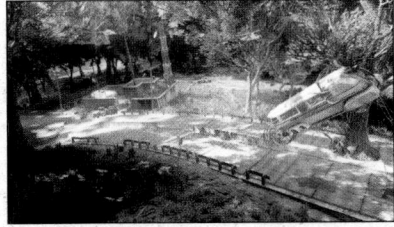

- **CRAFTING:** WEAPONS
- **DANGER:** EXPLOSIVE CANISTER!
- **ITEM:** HARVESTABLE: MUTATED FERN
- **INFO:** EXPECTED ENEMY: GHOUL; SCAVENGE RATING: 3; SIZE: 1; THREAT LEVEL: 30–99
- **LOCK:** DOOR (KEY)
- **ITEM EXAMPLES:** ASHTRAY, BOBBY PIN BOX, BOX OF SAN FRANCISCO SUNLIGHTS, CAMERA, ENHANCED TARGETING CARD, FLIP LIGHTER, GAS CANISTER, PAINT CAN, TIN CAN, TIN CANISTER, TUBE FLANGE, USED OIL CAN

Close to a bus suspended above the road by forest tendrils is the remains of an old radio station. Use the Broadcast Station Key to access the small station interior, where you find junk-filled detritus and a talk-show terminal.

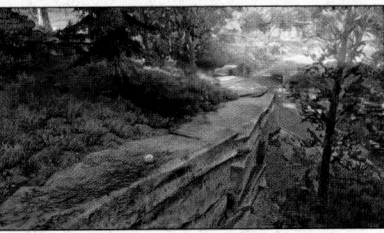

Aluminum and Beers

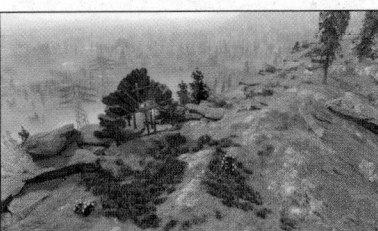

East Mountain Arch

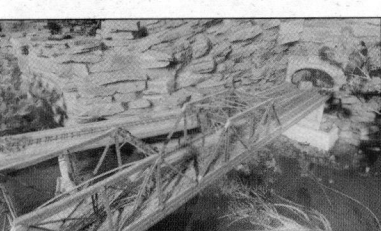

Harpers Ferry Tunnel Camp

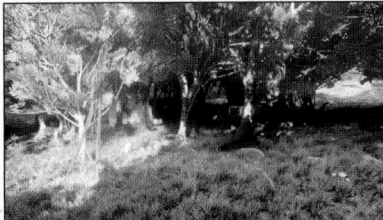

Derelict Hamlet

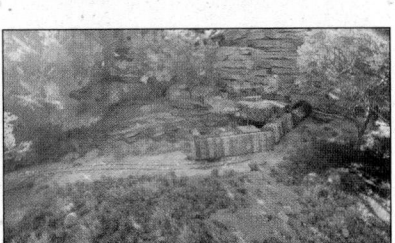

End of the Line

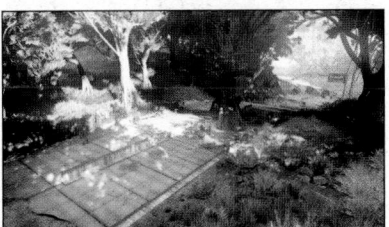

Treehouse on I-65

TRAINING
CRAFTING AND C.A.M.P.ING
INVENTORY
QUESTS
ATLAS
BESTIARY
APPENDICES

#	NAME	DESCRIPTION
31	Barrel Burial	Someone was paid stacks of cash to bury some barrels at the edge of the Mire. The prewar money is still there, as useless as the skeleton.
32	Woodland Ramp	A plant tendril appears to have caught a hapless dirt biker in midair, at this rickety rock ramp.
33	Aluminum and Beers	A rock outcrop with a deck chair and cooler on it, above an aluminum deposit.
34	Thunder Mountain Deathclaw Nest	A ruined blue carriage by the train tracks and a Deathclaw nest. Can the clawed beasts be far away?
35	Under the I-65 Bridge	Giant holes in the road bridge and a coach in the Mire below.
36	Abandoned Waste Dump Exit	An elevator exit shrouded in bushes allows you to leave after exploring the waste dump to the west.
37	Gully Shack (west of Tanagra Town)	Whoever last used this shack was a fan of purified water, radios, cats, and other junk. Worth a pitstop.
38	Carriage Crash	East of Harpers Ferry, cargo carriages are strewn about, some caught and held by tough tendrils, close to the rail bridge.
39	Harpers Ferry Tunnel Camp	A medium-sized camp built into the bridge and blocked rail tunnel, with a Chemistry Workbench and a small lab inside a tunnel carriage.
40	Tanagra Town: West Outskirts	A prelude to the horror of Tanagra itself, this is a home and two outbuildings (and Weapons Workbench) taken over by plant life.
41	Military Comms Tower Tanagra	A small, quest-related comms dish standing atop a rock bluff with platforms and ladders up from the tunnel camp.
42	The Remains of Murphy and Kelly	Two settlers are slumped against a tree near a first aid kit, deep into the marshes.
43	River Treehouse	Want precarious platform ascending, mattress sleeping, and irradiated waters? Then this is the place for a junk hunt.
44	The Strangled Canoeist (and Quantum Bear)	Foul play befell the corpse on the tangled canoe in this part of the river.
45	The Aquatic Outhouse (Valley Galleria)	Running short on toilet paper? Check the safe atop the tendril stump in the middle of the river, near a skeleton raft.
46	Tank Guardian	A rusting military tank (and vicious Assaultron) is parked next to the Red Rocket Gas Station in the Galleria parking lot.
47	Biker's Truck (Route 107)	A pickup with beers and bikes, stalled out on the road.
48	Plastic People's Camp (R108)	A meeting in the woods with mannequins, close to a trap-filled camp with sleeping and cooking available.

#	NAME	DESCRIPTION
49	Sunday Brothers' Coach Camp	A couple of coaches have been turned into a compact camp with cooking and armor stations as well as junk to gather.
50	Pylon Tent Camp	Food, a sleeping bag, and a tent are under an electrical pylon on the edge of the Mire.
51	The Mechanic's Metal Shack	A curved-roof metal shack with wire fencing surrounding it. Inside is a safe (1), an Armor Workbench, and junk to scavenge.
52	End of the Line	There's quite a large shanty camp at the blocked railroad tunnel, with a banjo, sleeping bag, junk, carriages, and shacks to find.
53	Under the I-65 Bridge (west of Treetops)	While Deathclaws prowl the road bridge, inspect the river underneath for a bony fan of chems.
54	Railroad Bridge Strangle	Rusting train carriages sit marooned on the broken tracks, with a locked safe (2) on one of the blue carriages on the bridge.
55	Train Tendril Derailment	Rusting rail carriages are flung about on this stretch of track, which includes a steamer trunk.
56	Rock Overhang at Treetops	Northeast of Treetops is a rocky outcrop, with an alcove, a sleeping bag, and some food to gather.
57	Strangled Roadway (Route 65)	Tendrils from mutated trees are pulling a van (and its skeletal passengers) into its depths. Come for the spectacle, and the Brain Fungus.
58	East Mountain Arch	An arch of large cut boulders placed into an arch by unknown hands. This is a great cliff from which to view the Mire and Bog.
59	Tinkerer's Truck	Armor and Tinker's Workbenches as well as junk are available in this compact and well-designed truck and workshop, with a safe (1) to unlock.
60	The Witch's Picnic	A witch and her three sisters have finished a picnic, but not recently. They're lounging atop a rocky bluff in the forest.
61	Boulder Outcrop Camp	A long-departed survivalist managed to drag an ornate dresser and a locked safe into a camp set into this upper rock circle.
62	Military Vehicle Wreckage (Camp Venture)	A military APC and two SUVs are being gobbled up by the tendril roots investing this region.
63	Derelict Hamlet	This cluster of four sagging buildings in the marsh forest has a surprising number of choice items to grab.
64	Traffic Jam (Route 65)	There is a collection of rusting vehicles and some minor defenses to hide behind on the road to Valley Galleria.
65	Treehouse on I-65	The power of mutated tree life continues to astound, as a tree has ripped through the tarmac and now supports a camp platform.
66	Sniper's Treehouse	There's likely to be a very special sniper rifle at the top of the tendril tree platform.

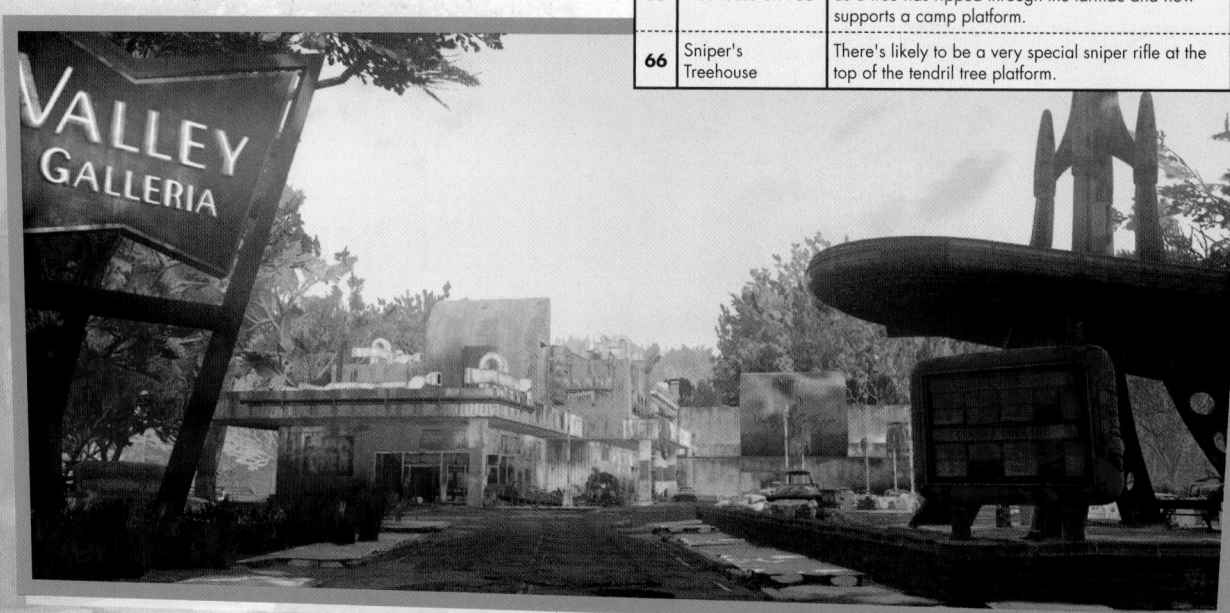

REGION 6: CRANBERRY BOG

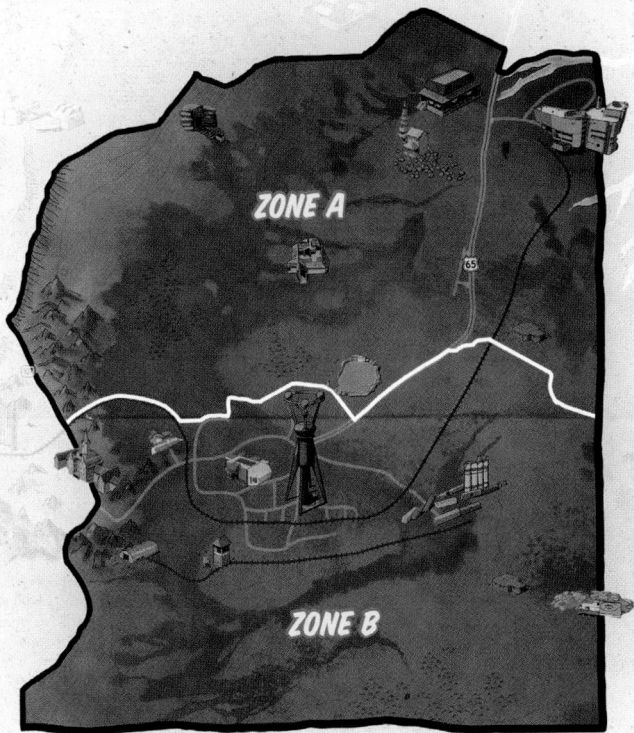

ZONE A

ZONE B

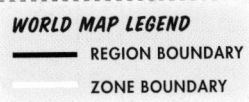

Appalachia: **Cranberry Bog**

WORLD MAP LEGEND
— REGION BOUNDARY
— ZONE BOUNDARY

This is a delightfully named region, but one that belies the high-level horrors that await those attempting to navigate the wetlands that encompass the southeastern parts of Appalachia. You'll be seeing more than red as you visit the dilapidated farms, groves of huge and possibly carnivorous Sundew plants (now bigger than a house), and radiation-soaked, water-filled quarries interspersed by small Brotherhood of Steel forward operation camps. These are the only places that may offer a chance to rest (as many have their own turret defenses you can utilize). Use the web of bog channels that crisscross this entire region, which consists of narrow grooves cut into the bog that aren't quite shallow enough to climb out of (except at certain junctions); though these passageways are confining, they can reveal their own share of secrets, including a tunnel that runs under the main highway from Watoga to the Abandoned Bog Town. Aside from Fort Defiance, there is an old asylum now recently commandeered by the Brotherhood of Steel. The dominant location in these parts is the city of Watoga, where an attempt was made to automate every aspect of life but is now a wild west of rogue robots, looming skyscrapers, and Scorchbeast nests.

ENEMY THREAT LEVELS

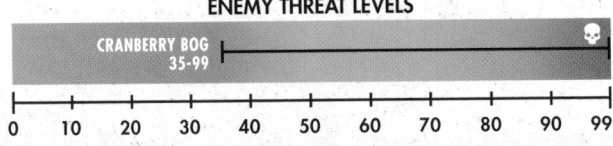

| CRANBERRY BOG 35-99 | | | | | | | | | | ☠ |

| 0 | 10 | 20 | 30 | 40 | 50 | 60 | 70 | 80 | 90 | 99+ |

TRAINING

CRAFTING AND C.A.M.P.ING

INVENTORY

QUESTS

ATLAS

BESTIARY

APPENDICES

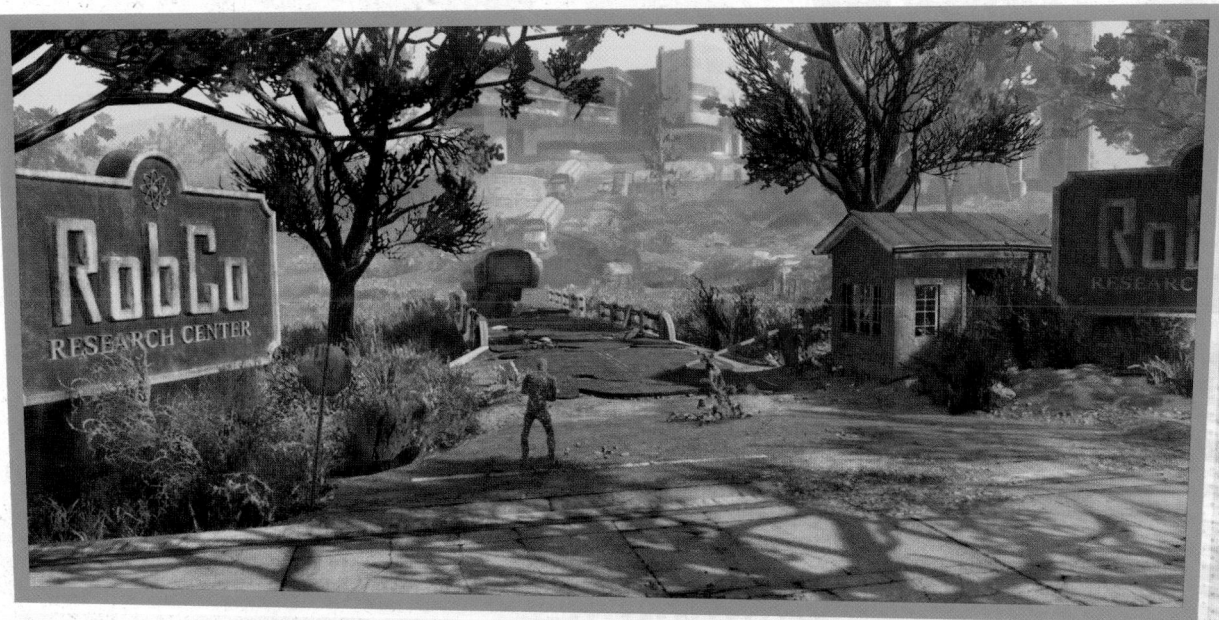

CRANBERRY BOG: ZONE A—NORTH BOG, ROBCO RESEARCH CENTER, AND ABANDONED BOG TOWN

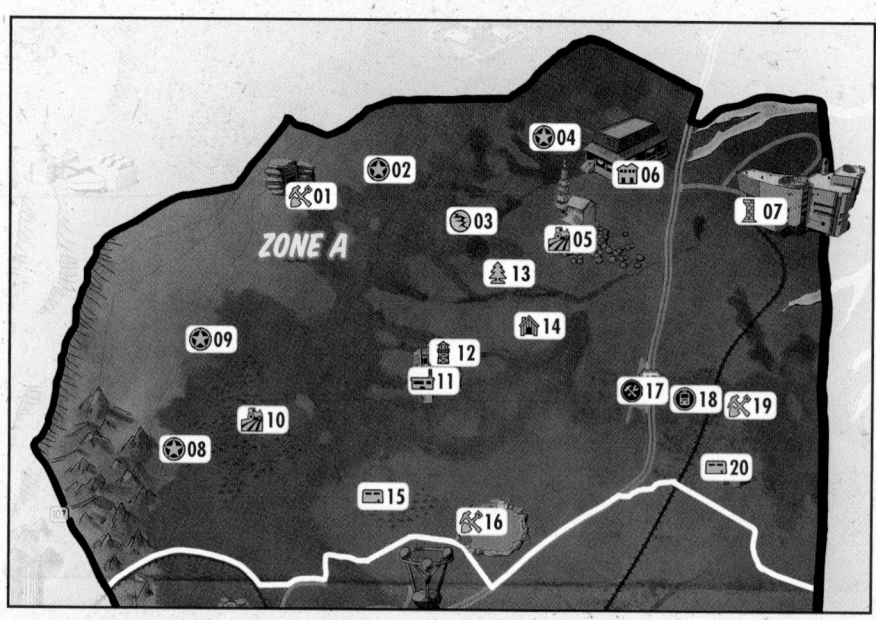

The northern part of Cranberry Bog is a bit more sparsely populated, offering a few forward-operating bases now abandoned by the defeated Brotherhood of Steel. There is also evidence that this region was once a rich farmland. Visit the remains of the cranberry farm over at Mac's; ogle the gardens of the General's Steakhouse, then head inside to gather more than just Salisbury steaks; and uncover secrets within the RobCo Research Center. Check every inch of the Bootlegger's Shack (both high and low), and spend some quality time in the Abandoned Bog Town, which has a great deal of scavenging potential and the only workshop in this region. There is also a My Stash Box and secret tunnels all the way to Watoga!

Appalachia: **Cranberry Bog (Zone A) – Primary Locations**

WORLD MAP LEGEND

— REGION BOUNDARY — ZONE BOUNDARY

■ BOBBLEHEADS ■ CAP STASHES ■ MAGAZINES ■ POWER ARMOR

PRIMARY LOCATIONS

				icon	NAME
4		4	1	01	KERWOOD MINE
1			1	02	FIREBASE MAJOR
				03	FISSURE SITE
		1	1	04	FIREBASE LT
1			1	05	MAC'S FARM
2	4	2	1	06	THE GENERAL'S STEAKHOUSE
3		3	1	07	ROBCO RESEARCH CENTER
1			1	08	THE THORN
1			1	09	FORWARD STATION ALPHA
				10	SUPERIOR SUNSET FARM

				icon	NAME
1		1		11	RANGER DISTRICT OFFICE
1				12	RANGER LOOKOUT
				13	CREEKSIDE SUNDEW GROVE
2		2	1	14	BOOTLEGGER'S SHACK
		1		15	DROP SITE G3
1		1	1	16	QUARRY X3
				17	ABANDONED BOG TOWN
1		2		18	PYLON V-13
1		1		19	OLD MOLD QUARRY
		1		20	DROP SITE C2

ZONE A: PRIMARY LOCATIONS

MAP LEGEND

- MY STASH BOX
- OVERSEER'S CACHE
- TRUNK
- TRADER

COLLECTIBLES
- BOBBLEHEAD
- MAGAZINE
- POWER ARMOR

CRAFTING
- ARMOR WORKBENCH
- CHEMISTRY WORKBENCH
- COOKING STATION
- POWER ARMOR STATION
- TINKER'S WORKBENCH
- WEAPONS WORKBENCH
- WORKSHOP WORKBENCH

IMPORTANT
- DOOR/GATE
- LOCKED DOOR/GATE
- SAFE
- SCANNER
- TERMINAL

⚒ 01. KERWOOD MINE

- **COLLECTIBLES:** BOBBLEHEAD (4), HOLOTAPE, MAGAZINE (4), POWER ARMOR
- **DANGER:** EXPLOSIVE CANISTER! RADIATION!+
- **ITEMS:** ARMS AND AMMO; HARVESTABLE: BRAIN FUNGUS, GLOWING FUNGUS, WOOD PILE; HEALTH AND CHEMS+; RECIPE/MOD/PLAN; TRUNK
- **INFO:** EXPECTED ENEMY: GHOUL, IRRADIATED INSECT, WENDIGO; SCAVENGE RATING: 3; SIZE: 4; SLEEPING; THREAT LEVEL: 35–99
- **LOCK:** DOOR (1, KEY), SAFE (2), TERMINAL (2)

- **ITEM EXAMPLES:** ALARM CLOCK, BLASTING CAPS BOX+, BOURBON, BRASS MINER'S LAMP, COFFEE CUP, COFFEE POT, CRANBERRY MOONSHINE, FIRE AXE, FUSION CORE, HAZMAT SUIT, KERWOOD MINE KEY, LANTERN+, PILLOW, PLASMA GRENADE, PORTABLE FUEL TANK, RADAWAY+, SPICES, SUGAR BOMBS, TEDDY BEAR, TIN CAN, UNUSED ENAMEL BUCKET, USED OIL CAN, VOLATILE MATERIALS BOX, WHISKEY BOTTLE

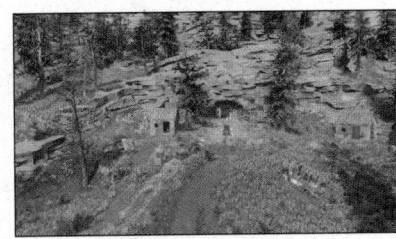

LEGEND
1. RAISED PLATFORM AND GENERATORS
2. MINE SHAFT
3. MACHINERY CAVERN
4. SLAG HEAP CAVERN
5. JUNCTION CAVERN
6. BACK TUNNEL

Kerwood Mine (Interior)

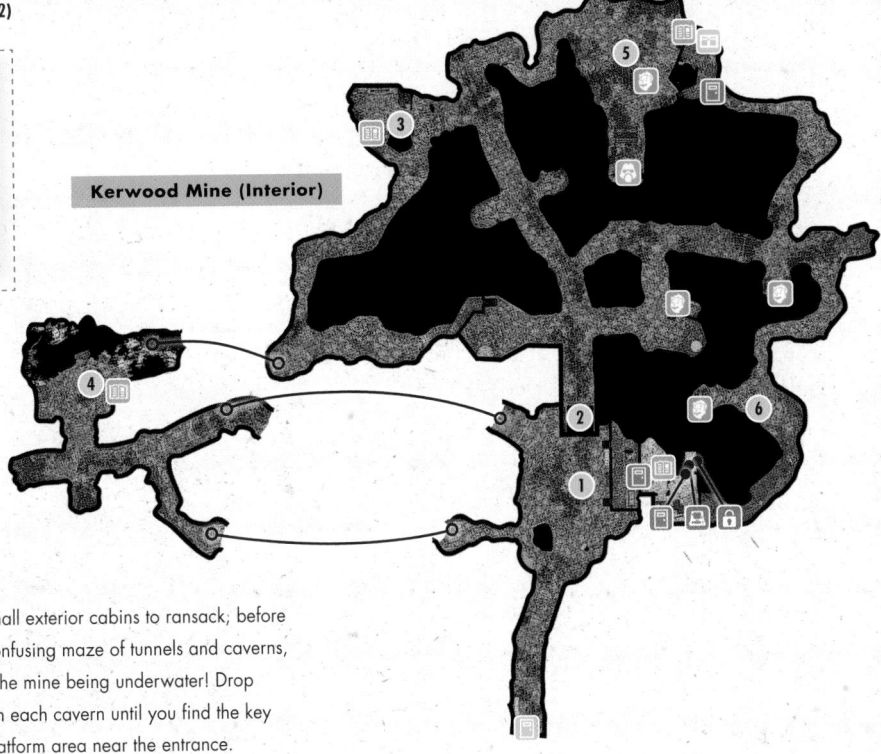

This highly dangerous location has three small exterior cabins to ransack; before you enter the mine itself. The interior is a confusing maze of tunnels and caverns, made all the more problematic due to half the mine being underwater! Drop down the shaft, and swim your way through each cavern until you find the key that opens the double doors at the initial platform area near the entrance.

★ 02. FIREBASE MAJOR

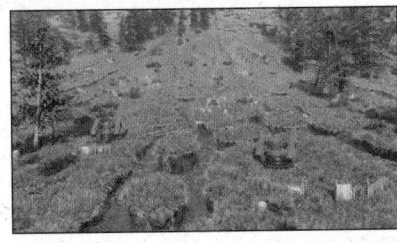

- **COLLECTIBLES:** BOBBLEHEAD, POWER ARMOR
- **CRAFTING:** COOKING
- **ITEMS:** ARMS AND AMMO; HARVESTABLE: DISEASED CRANBERRY; HEALTH AND CHEMS
- **INFO:** EXPECTED ENEMY: IRRADIATED ANIMAL; SCAVENGE RATING: 2; SIZE: 1; SLEEPING; THREAT LEVEL: 35–99

- **ITEM EXAMPLES:** ASSAULT RIFLE, CRANBERRY MOONSHINE, GAS CANISTER, HALLUCIGEN GAS CANISTER, MILITARY AMMO BAG, MINI NUKE, SALISBURY STEAK, WHISKEY BOTTLE

A small Brotherhood of Steel forward operations base is located on the northwestern edge of the Bog. The tent and scattered barriers have a small quantity of impressive loot to scavenge.

🐟 03. FISSURE SITE (FISSURE)

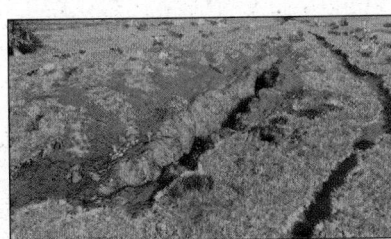

- **DANGER:** LONG DROP! RADIATION!++
- **ITEM:** HARVESTABLE: ULTRACITE
- **INFO:** EXPECTED ENEMY: SCORCHBEAST, SCORCHED; SCAVENGE RATING: 1; SIZE: 1; THREAT LEVEL: 3–99
- **ITEM EXAMPLES:** NOT MUCH!

Cut into the earth on the soft, boggy terrain is a terrible crevasse; a group of Scorched clustered around their queen. Avoid unless you're powerful enough!

TRAINING

CRAFTING AND C.A.M.P.ING

INVENTORY

QUESTS

ATLAS

BESTIARY

APPENDICES

04. FIREBASE LT

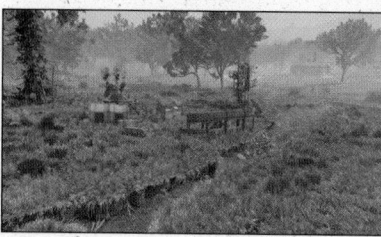

- **COLLECTIBLES:** MAGAZINE, POWER ARMOR
- **CRAFTING:** WEAPONS
- **DANGER:** TURRET!
- **ITEMS:** ARMS AND AMMO; HARVESTABLE: DISEASED CRANBERRY; HEALTH AND CHEMS
- **INFO:** EXPECTED ENEMY: ROBOT; SCAVENGE RATING: 2; SIZE: 1; SLEEPING; THREAT LEVEL: 35–99

- **ITEM EXAMPLES:** 10-MM AUTO PISTOL, ADJUSTABLE WRENCH, ARMY HELMET, CAMPAIGN HAT, CAN, DISHRAG, FRAGMENTATION GRENADE, GAS CANISTER, HALLUCIGEN GAS CANISTER, INDUSTRIAL OIL CANISTER, PURIFIED WATER, RAD-X, SCREWDRIVER, STEALTH BOY, WONDERGLUE

If you're planning on C.A.M.P.ing close by and need the extra firepower, repair one of the two automated surface-to-air missile turrets at this small tent base. Otherwise, come here for the scavenging (and Power Armor) potential.

05. MAC'S FARM

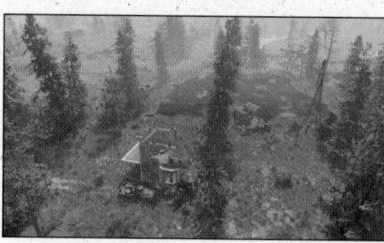

- **COLLECTIBLES:** BOBBLEHEAD, MAGAZINE
- **CRAFTING:** COOKING STATION, WATER PUMP
- **DANGER:** RADIATION!
- **ITEMS:** HARVESTABLE: CRANBERRY, DISEASED CRANBERRY, WILD CARROT FLOWER

- **INFO:** EXPECTED ENEMY: IRRADIATED ANIMAL; SCAVENGE RATING: 2; SIZE: 1; SLEEPING; THREAT LEVEL: 35–99
- **ITEM EXAMPLES:** COFFEE CUP, COOKING POT, DISHRAG, FIRECRACKER BERRY, GLASS JAR++, LADLE, METAL TUB, MOONSHINE JUG+, SUGAR

This tiny cranberry farm has a home lacking its roof and a shed in even worse repair. Wade into the lightly irradiated bog pond to pick some less-diseased cranberries.

06. THE GENERAL'S STEAKHOUSE

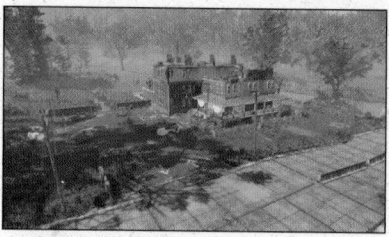

- **DANGER:** TOO MANY GNOMES!
- **ITEMS:** HARVESTABLE: CARROT, TATO PLANT, WILD CORN, WILD MELON BLOSSOM; HEALTH AND CHEMS+; TRUNK (2); VENDING MACHINE: MEDICINAL SUPPLIES
- **INFO:** EXPECTED ENEMY: IRRADIATED INSECT, SUPER MUTANT; NOTE; QUEST: SEARCH GENERAL'S STEAKHOUSE FOR SUPPLIES; SCAVENGE RATING: 5; SIZE: 3; THREAT LEVEL: 35–99
- **LOCK:** DOOR (C, C, C), SAFE (2)

- **COLLECTIBLES:** BOBBLEHEAD (2), CAPS STASH (4), MAGAZINE (2), POWER ARMOR
- **CRAFTING:** ARMOR, COOKING

- **ITEM EXAMPLES:** ABRAXO CLEANER+, BAG OF CEMENT+, BEER BOTTLE+++, BOILED WATER, BOURBON BOTTLE, CAN, CIGAR BOX, COVERED SAUCEPAN, DINNER PLATE+, DIRTY ASHTRAY, DIRTY POSTMAN HAT, EMPTY WILLOW ROUNDED VASE+, FEATHER DUSTER, FUSION CORE, GARDEN GNOME++, GLASS PITCHER+, GREASER JACKET AND JEANS, LADLE, MAKESHIFT BATTERY, METAL BUCKET+, MOONSHINE JUG, NOODLE CUP+, OVEN MITT, PATCHED THREE-PIECE SUIT, PEPPER+, PURIFIED WATER, RIB CAGE, SALISBURY STEAK+, SALT+, SPICES, SUGAR, SUPRATHAW ANTIFREEZE, VODKA BOTTLE, YELLOW TABLE LAMP

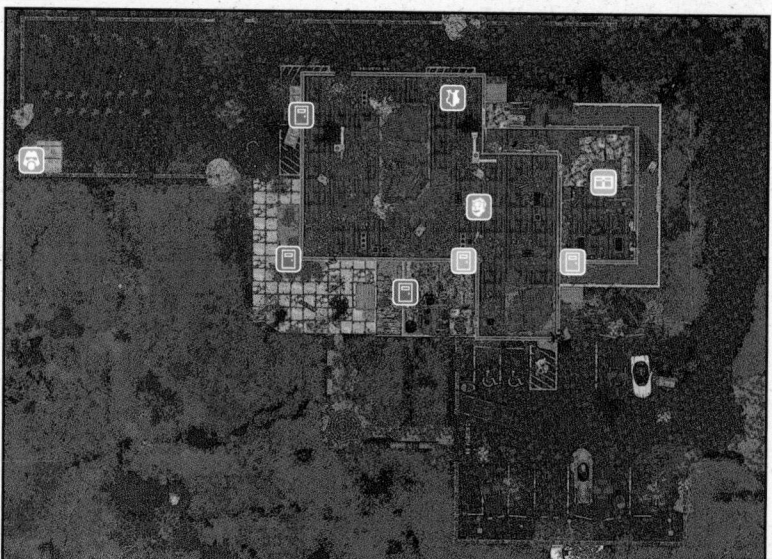

The General's Steakhouse
(Exterior and Interior)

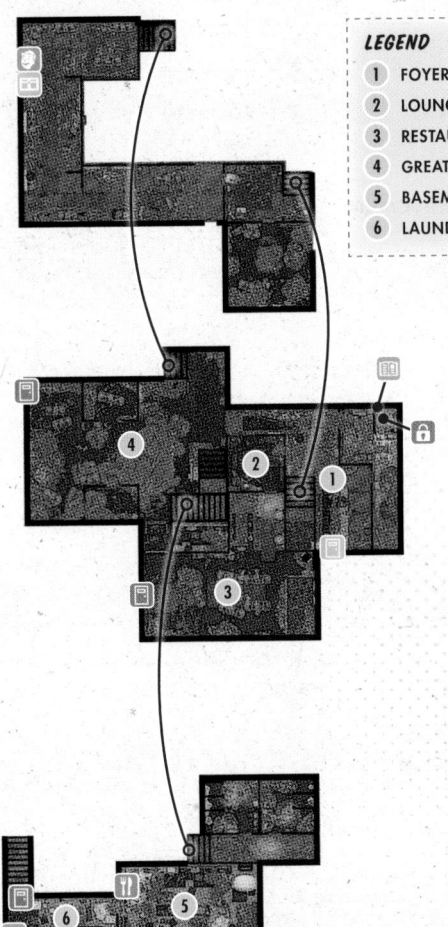

LEGEND

1. FOYER
2. LOUNGE
3. RESTAURANT
4. GREAT DINING HALL
5. BASEMENT KITCHEN
6. LAUNDRY ROOM

There's much to enjoy at this steakhouse, providing you can clear the interior of fiendish foes. Expect a good number of harvestable plants, recipes, and garden gnomes. Enter via the red front door; all other exterior doors are chained from the inside.

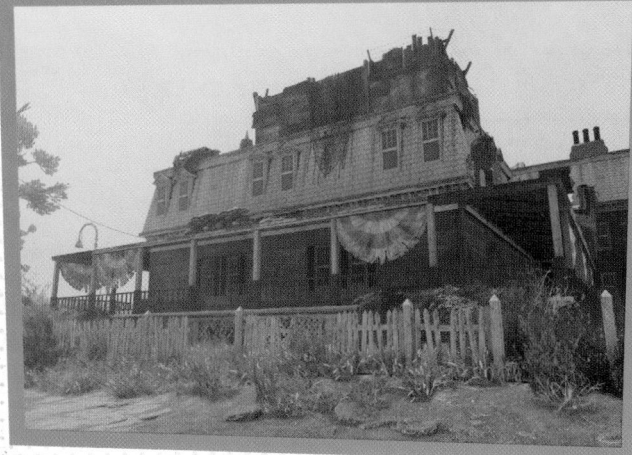

07. ROBCO RESEARCH CENTER

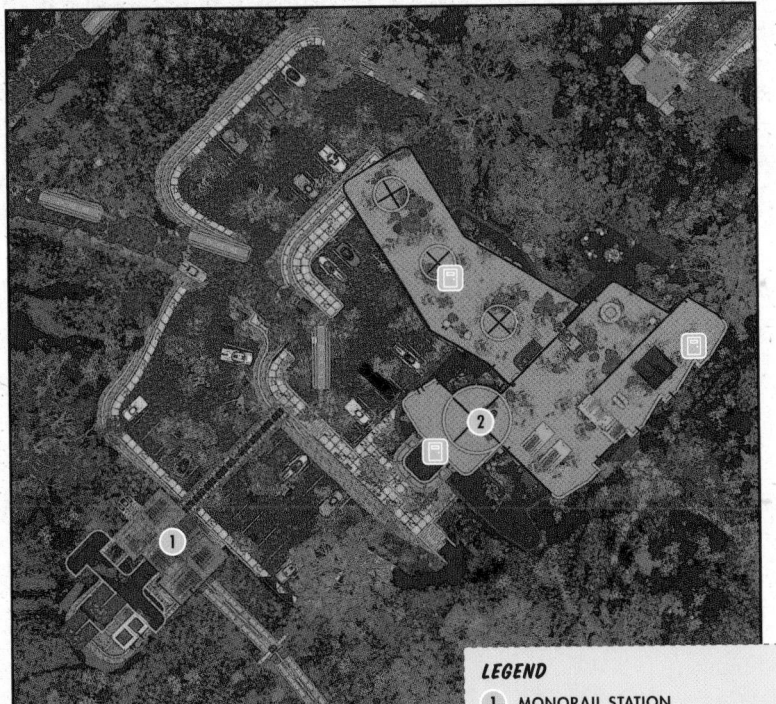

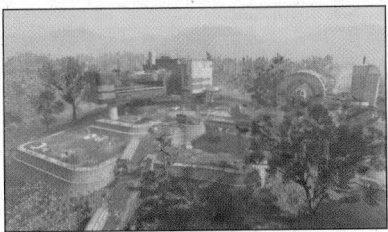

- **COLLECTIBLES:** BOBBLEHEAD (3), MAGAZINE (3), NUKA-CHERRY, POWER ARMOR
- **CRAFTING:** POWER ARMOR (3), WEAPONS
- **DANGER:** EXPLOSIVE CANISTER! PUNJI BOARD! LONG DROP!
- **ITEMS:** ARMS AND AMMO; HARVESTABLE: GIANT PITCHER PLANT, MUTATED FERN; HEALTH AND CHEMS; RECIPE/MOD/PLAN; TRUNK
- **INFO:** EXPECTED ENEMY: IRRADIATED INSECT, ROBOT, SCORCHED; SCAVENGE RATING: 5; SIZE: 4; THREAT LEVEL: 35–99
- **LOCK:** DOOR (KEY, 1, 2, 3), SAFE (3)

LEGEND

1. MONORAIL STATION
2. ROBCO RESEARCH CENTER (INTERIOR)

RobCo Research Center (Exterior)

- **ITEM EXAMPLES:** 2-MM ELECTROMAGNETIC CARTRIDGE, ABRAXO CLEANER, ALARM CLOCK, ASSAULT RIFLE, BATTERED FEDORA, BLOWTORCH, CIRCUITS, COFFEE CUP+, COMBINATION WRENCH, DIRTY ASHTRAY, DIRTY BLACK SUIT, DIRTY DESKTOP FRAME, ECONOMY WONDERGLUE, ENAMEL BUCKET+, FUSION CORE+, GAS CANISTER, GLASS PITCHER, HAZMAT SUIT, HH-3A CAPACITOR, HIGH-POWERED MAGNET, HOT DOG, INDUSTRIAL OIL CANISTER, MAKESHIFT BATTERY+, MICROSCOPE+, MILITARY GRADE CIRCUIT BOARD+, MOP, MR. HANDY MODEL, NUKA-COLA BOTTLE+, OIL CANISTER, PACK OF CIGARETTES, PEPPER, PLASTIC BOWL+, PLASTIC SPOON, PROTECTRON MODEL, SALT, SCREWDRIVER, SENSOR MODULE, SKULL, SOAP, SPICES, STEALTH BOY, SUGAR BOMBS, SURGICAL TRAY+, SUSPENDERS AND SLACKS, TALL DRINKING GLASS+, TALL FLASK, TELEPHONE+, TOILET PAPER+, TYPEWRITER, USED OIL CAN, VODKA, WELDING GOGGLES, YELLOW TABLE LAMP

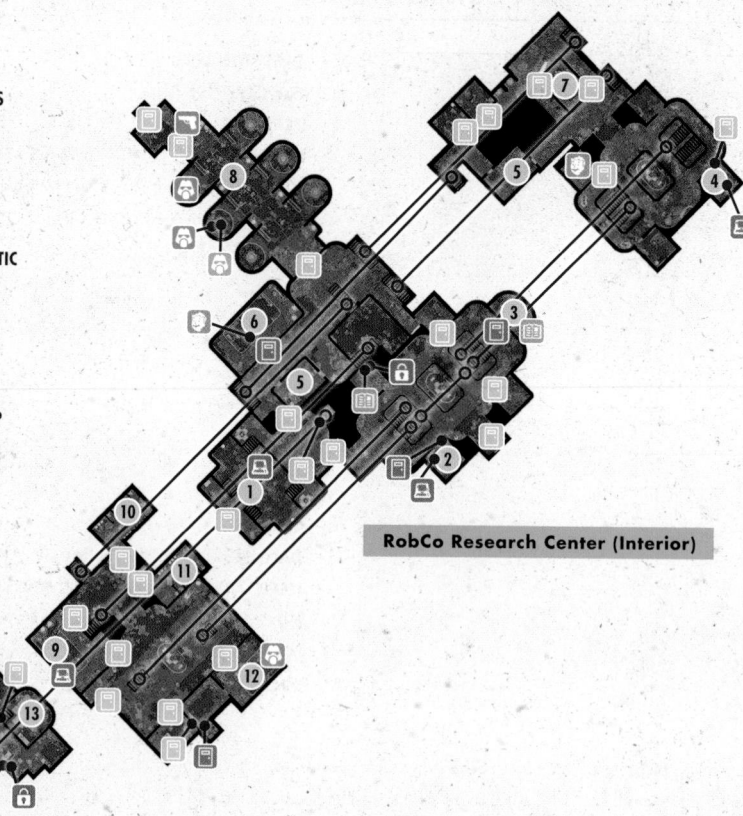

RobCo Research Center (Interior)

The major supplier of automatons in Appalachia has their headquarters here. Green trucks and trailers sit on the entrance road, their contents mostly scavenged. The forecourt and dilapidated monorail station (complete with waiting tram) bears the signs of recent Super Mutant and Raider activity, and Brotherhood of Steel corpses still litter the ground. Explore inside via the main entrance (the black door between the two lamps), the rear door, or the elevator.

LEGEND

1. SUNKEN FOYER AND RECEPTION
2. FACILITIES MANAGEMENT: LOCKED OFFICE
3. FACILITIES MANAGEMENT: LOCKED CONFERENCE ROOM
4. FACILITIES MANAGEMENT: HR OFFICE
5. RESEARCH WING: KITCHEN AND DINING
6. RESEARCH WING: LOCKED LABORATORY
7. RESEARCH WING: QUALITY CONTROL
8. ROBOTICS TECHNOLOGY FACILITY
9. BASEMENT: ROBOBRAIN ASSEMBLY
10. BASEMENT: RESTROOMS (MALE)
11. BASEMENT: RESTROOMS (FEMALE)
12. BASEMENT: ROBOBRAIN R&D
13. UPPER LABORATORY

With a wealth of robotics parts and other high-value junk, this is a must-explore interior: an abandoned facility set out over two main levels, with an upper laboratory accessible via the foyer elevator.

08. THE THORN

- **COLLECTIBLES:** BOBBLEHEAD, MAGAZINE
- **CRAFTING:** COOKING
- **DANGER:** TURRET!
- **ITEMS:** ARMS AND AMMO; HARVESTABLE: MUTATED FERN; HEALTH AND CHEMS
- **INFO:** EXPECTED ENEMY: IRRADIATED ANIMAL; SCAVENGE RATING: 1; SIZE: 1; SLEEPING; THREAT LEVEL: 35–99
- **ITEM EXAMPLES:** BLASTING CAPS BOX, DUCT TAPE, MILITARY AMMO BAG, PURIFIED WATER, SCREWDRIVER, TIN CAN

This small Brotherhood of Steel base consists of a single tent, turret, missile turret, and meager pickings to scavenge. A Brotherhood corpse reveals evidence of recent battles at this location.

09. FORWARD STATION ALPHA

- **COLLECTIBLES:** BOBBLEHEAD, MAGAZINE
- **CRAFTING:** COOKING
- **DANGER:** TURRET!
- **ITEMS:** ARMS AND AMMO; HARVESTABLE: DISEASED CRANBERRY, SOOT FLOWER, WILD CARROT FLOWER; HEALTH AND CHEMS
- **INFO:** EXPECTED ENEMY: MIRELURK; SCAVENGE RATING: 2; SIZE: 1; SLEEPING; THREAT LEVEL: 35–99
- **ITEM EXAMPLES:** BEER, BUFFOUT, COFFEE CUP, GAS CANISTER+, HALLUCIGEN GAS CANISTER+, PURIFIED WATER, SALT, SHORT ASSAULT RIFLE, TIN CAN

A compact Brotherhood of Steel base, with only the missile turrets still active in the general vicinity. Check the small gantry and two tents for a modest supply of quality junk.

10. SUPERIOR SUNSET FARM

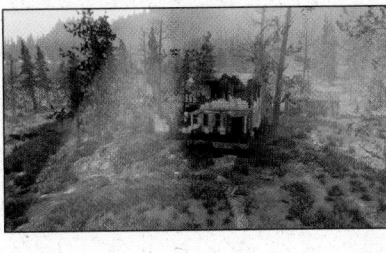

- CRAFTING: ARMOR
- DANGER: RADIATION!
- ITEMS: HARVESTABLE: BRAIN FUNGUS, DISEASED CRANBERRY, GIANT PITCHER PLANT, MUTATED FERN, SCORCHBEAST GUANO PILE; RECIPE/MOD/PLAN
- INFO: EXPECTED ENEMY: SCORCHED; SCAVENGE RATING: 2; SIZE: 2; THREAT LEVEL: 35–99

- LOCK: SAFE (0, 0)
- ITEM EXAMPLES: ABRAXO CLEANER, ADJUSTABLE WRENCH, ALARM CLOCK, CAN+, CANNED DOG FOOD, CAT BOWL, ECONOMY WONDERGLUE, ENAMEL BUCKET, FANCY HAIRBRUSH, FRYING PAN, GAS CANISTER, MOONSHINE JUG, RAT POISON, SKULL, SMALL ANTLER+, STRAW PILLOW, TALL DRINKING GLASS, TEA KETTLE, TOOTHPASTE

Adjacent to the bog channels running throughout this region, the farmhouse lacks a roof but features two locked safes to find. There's a small storage shed to pillage, too.

11. RANGER DISTRICT OFFICE

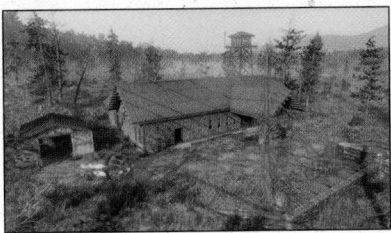

- COLLECTIBLES: BOBBLEHEAD, MAGAZINE
- CRAFTING: ARMOR
- DANGER: RADIATION!
- ITEMS: ARMS AND AMMO, HEALTH AND CHEMS+, TRUNK
- INFO: EXPECTED ENEMY: GHOUL, IRRADIATED ANIMAL; SCAVENGE RATING: 3; SIZE: 3; THREAT LEVEL: 35–99
- LOCK: SAFE (3)

- ITEM EXAMPLES: ABRAXO CLEANER, BANDAGE SCISSORS, BINOCULARS, BOBBY PIN BOX, CAT BOWL, CHEMISTRY JAR, COFFEE CUP, DOG BOWL, GARDEN GNOME, HEAVY LEAD PIPE, MEDICAL LIQUID NITROGEN DISPENSER, MILK BOTTLE, OIL CAN, ORANGE MENTATS, PLUNGER, RABBIT HIDE, RANGER HAT+, RANGER OUTFIT, SAW, SURGICAL TRAY+, TELEPHONE, TOMAHAWK, VASE, YELLOW PLATE

Scattered picnic areas around a large lodge welcomed visitors to the Kanawha County Ranger Station and offices. The place is in relatively good shape, despite the interior ransacking. Check both the outbuildings and the station interior for junk, and look for evidence the rangers were studying the abnormal animals in the vicinity.

12. RANGER LOOKOUT

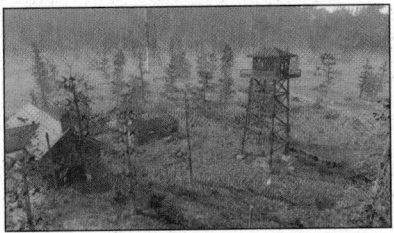

- COLLECTIBLE: BOBBLEHEAD
- INFO: EXPECTED ENEMY: IRRADIATED ANIMAL; SCAVENGE RATING: 1; SIZE: 1; SLEEPING; SURVEY AREA; THREAT LEVEL: 35–99
- ITEM EXAMPLES: BATTERED CLIPBOARD, BINOCULARS, PACK OF CIGARETTES, RANGER OUTFIT

Head to the outskirts of the Ranger Station compound, and scale the lookout tower to survey the immediate area. The items to scavenge are minor, though there's a Bobblehead opportunity.

13. CREEKSIDE SUNDEW GROVE

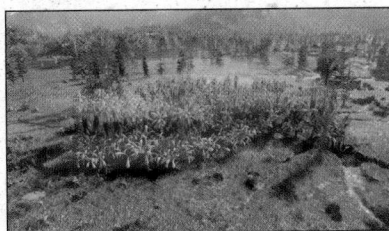

- ITEMS: HARVESTABLE: BRAIN FUNGUS, CRANBERRY, GIANT PITCHER PLANT
- INFO: EXPECTED ENEMY: GULPER, IRRADIATED ANIMAL, MIRELURK; SCAVENGE RATING: 1; SIZE: 2; THREAT LEVEL: 35–99

A grove of drosera plants (giant, carnivorous mutant specimens) are rapidly taking over this part of the bog. Weave through the channels below the plants, checking for harvest items and fending off the more violent wildlife.

14. BOOTLEGGER'S SHACK

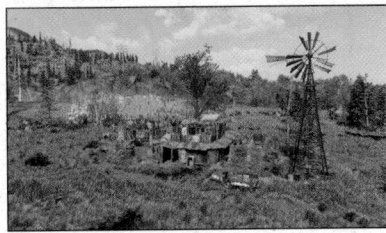

- COLLECTIBLES: BOBBLEHEAD (2), MAGAZINE (2), POWER ARMOR
- CRAFTING: ARMOR, CHEMISTRY (3), COOKING, WEAPONS
- DANGER: RADIATION!
- ITEMS: ARMS AND AMMO, HEALTH AND CHEMS, RECIPE/MOD/PLAN
- INFO: EXPECTED ENEMY: IRRADIATED INSECT. NOTE. SCAVENGE RATING: 3. SIZE: 2. THREAT LEVEL: 35-99.
- ITEM EXAMPLES: ABRAXO CLEANER, ALUMINUM CANISTER+, BAG OF FERTILIZER+, LAB BOTTLE+, LARGE BEAKER+, MOONSHINE JUG+, OIL CANISTER, NUKA-COLA BOTTLE, RAD-X, SUGAR, THIN BEAKER+, TV DINNER TRAY, TYPEWRITER, WINE

This shanty shack is two stories, with a rudimentary and rickety defensive wall, with clusters of radioactive barrels to avoid. Come for the small collection of lab beakers and other junk items, as well as some light reading materials. Don't leave without investigating the impressive (but small) hidden cellar chem lab!

TRAINING

CRAFTING AND C.A.M.P.ING

INVENTORY

QUESTS

ATLAS

BESTIARY

APPENDICES

15. DROP SITE G3

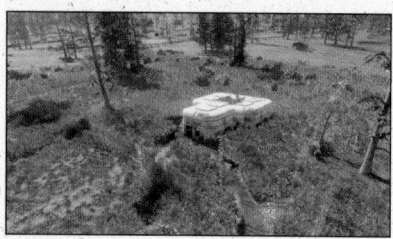

- **COLLECTIBLE: MAGAZINE**
- **DANGER: RADIATION!++**
- **ITEMS: HARVESTABLE: ULTRACITE; HEALTH AND CHEMS**
- **INFO: EXPECTED ENEMY: GHOUL; SCAVENGE RATING: 2; SIZE: 1; THREAT LEVEL: 35–99**
- **ITEM EXAMPLES: MAKESHIFT BATTERY, RADAWAY**

A sagging metal hut with toxic water may be enough to deter most visitors to this small drop site. But check the roof for a skeleton and check the interior for a rare Ultracite Vein.

16. QUARRY X3

- **COLLECTIBLES: BOBBLEHEAD, MAGAZINE, NUKA-CHERRY, POWER ARMOR**
- **CRAFTING: WEAPONS**
- **DANGER: RADIATION!**
- **ITEMS: ARMS AND AMMO, HEALTH AND CHEMS, TRUNK**
- **INFO: EXPECTED ENEMY: GHOUL, MIRELURK; SCAVENGE RATING: 3; SIZE: 3; THREAT LEVEL: 35–99**
- **ITEM EXAMPLES: BALL-PEEN HAMMER, BLASTING CAPS BOX++, BOILED WATER, CAN+, CAT BOWL, COFFEE CUP, COFFEE POT, DESK FAN, ENAMEL BUCKET, GAS CANISTER, LANTERN, MOP, PAINT CAN+, WALKING CANE, WONDERGLUE**

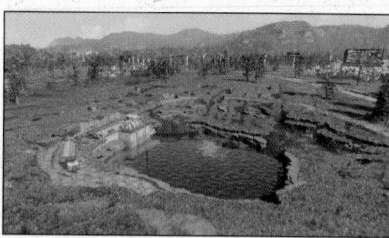

A waterlogged quarry, complete with a (blocked) underwater tunnel entrance and a trunk to swim to (in the pond's northeast area) has its fill of foes, as well as numerous metal-based junk.

17. ABANDONED BOG TOWN (WORKSHOP)

Abandoned Bog Town (Exterior)

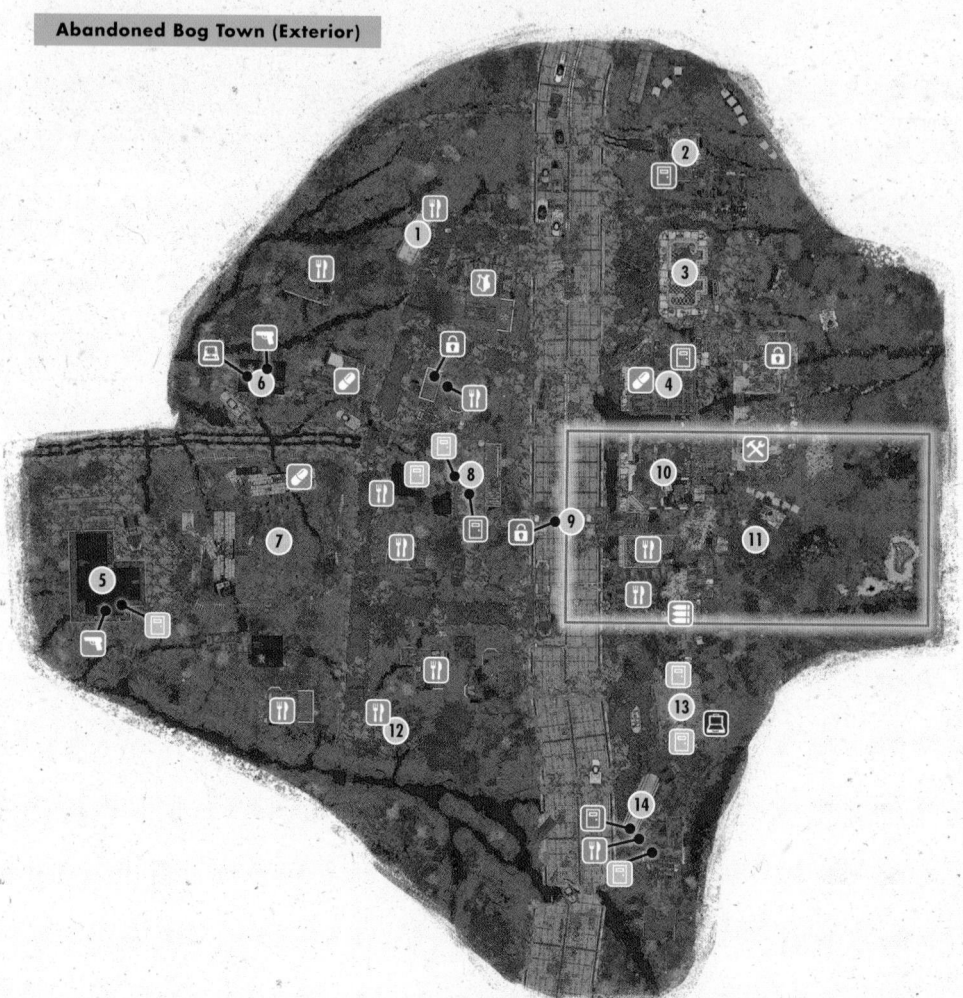

LEGEND

1. BUS STOP
2. LOCKED CONDEMNED HOUSE
3. CONDEMNED DINER
4. SHANTY ROOFTOP MYCOLOGY LAB
5. CONDEMNED WAREHOUSE
6. SABOTEUR'S TRAILER
7. BURNT-OUT CHEM TRAILERS
8. POLICE STATION
9. RAIDER BLOCKADE
10. BRICK OFFICE BUILDING
11. SHANTY SHEDS AND WORKSHOP
12. BOOBY-TRAPPED CARAVAN
13. CONDEMNED RED ROCKET GAS STATION
14. LOCKED TRUCK TRAILER

- **COLLECTIBLES:** HOLOTAPE, NUKA-CHERRY++, NUKA-COLA QUANTUM
- **CRAFTING:** ARMOR, CHEMISTRY (2), COOKING (9), TINKER, WATER PUMP (2), WEAPONS (2), WORKSHOP
- **DANGER:** OIL! LONG DROP! TRIPWIRE! SWING TRAP!
- **ITEMS:** ARMS AND AMMO++; HARVESTABLE: ACID, GIANT PITCHER PLANT, GOLD, GRAVEL PIT, OIL, SILVER, WILD CARROT FLOWER, WOOD PILE; HEALTH AND CHEMS++; MY STASH BOX; RECIPE/MOD/PLAN
- **INFO:** EXPECTED ENEMY: CRYPTID, IRRADIATED INSECT; POWER; NOTE; SCAVENGE RATING: 5 (5+); SIZE: 5; SLEEPING; THREAT LEVEL: 35–99
- **LOCK:** DOOR (C, 0, 1, 3), SAFE (2, 2, 3)
- **ITEM EXAMPLES:** 50-CAL MACHINE GUN, ACETONE CANISTER, ALUMINUM CAN+, ANTIFREEZE BOTTLE, ATOMIC ROLLER BALL+, BAG OF FERTILIZER+, BALL-PEEN HAMMER, BEAR TRAP+, BLACK-RIM GLASSES, BLUE PAINT+, BLUE TABLE LAMP, BOBBY PIN BOX, BOILED WATER++, BRAHMIN HIDE, BROKEN LAMP, BUBBLEGUM, CAT BOWL, CIGARETTE CARTON, CLOWN+, COFFEE CUP++, COFFEE POT+, COOKING PAN, COOLANT, COP HAT, COP UNIFORM, CRUSHED YELLOW CANISTER, CULTIST BLADE, ENAMEL BUCKET+, FANCY LAD SNACK CAKES, GAS CANISTER+, GLASS JAR, GUITAR SWORD, HANDCUFFS+, HATCHET, HOT PLATE, HUNTING RIFLE, INDUSTRIAL SIZE SHORTENING, INSTAMASH, LARGE LEFT ANTLER, LOOSE SCREWS, MAKESHIFT BATTERY, MECHANIC JUMPSUIT, MENTATS, MUZZLED LASER RIFLE, NEW RIVER RED ALE, OIL CANISTER+, PILLOW, POLICE JAIL KEY, PORK N' BEANS, POWER FIST, PROTECTRON MODEL, SALISBURY STEAK, SCREWDRIVER, SHOPPING BASKET, SUGAR BOMBS, TELEPHONE+, TIN CAN, TYPEWRITER+, USED OIL CAN, WINE, YARDSTICK, YELLOW PAINT+, YUM YUM DEVILED EGGS
- **WORK:** FOOD (7), WATER (3), SILVER (1), GOLD (1), ACID (1), CONCRETE (3), OIL (1)

Bog Town was built on unstable earth even before the bombs dropped, and the area became even more uninhabitable. The west side of town features a variety of condemned homes, trailers, and garages, separated by a Raider fortification along the main road. The workshop, the main office building, the remains of the main street, the gas station and diner, and a large, low-lying shantytown are on the eastern side, where you should build your defense. The unfinished brick office building has a Thunder Mountain Power Box (if the power plant is operational) to attach electrical wires to.

18. PYLON V-13

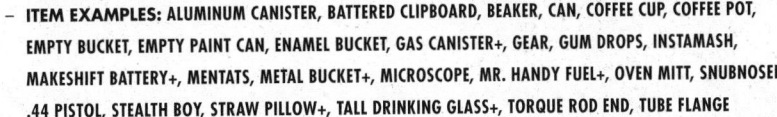

- **COLLECTIBLES:** BOBBLEHEAD, HOLOTAPE, MAGAZINE (2)
- **CRAFTING:** WEAPONS
- **DANGER:** EXPLOSIVE CANISTER! LONG DROP! TESLA ARC!
- **ITEMS:** HARVESTABLE: ACID; ARMS AND AMMO; DISEASED CRANBERRY; HEALTH AND CHEMS; RECIPE/MOD/PLAN; TRUNK
- **INFO:** EXPECTED ENEMY: SCORCHED; SCAVENGE RATING: 3; SIZE: 2; SLEEPING; THREAT LEVEL: 35–99
- **ITEM EXAMPLES:** ALUMINUM CANISTER, BATTERED CLIPBOARD, BEAKER, CAN, COFFEE CUP, COFFEE POT, EMPTY BUCKET, EMPTY PAINT CAN, ENAMEL BUCKET, GAS CANISTER+, GEAR, GUM DROPS, INSTAMASH, MAKESHIFT BATTERY+, MENTATS, METAL BUCKET+, MICROSCOPE, MR. HANDY FUEL+, OVEN MITT, SNUBNOSED .44 PISTOL, STEALTH BOY, STRAW PILLOW+, TALL DRINKING GLASS+, TORQUE ROD END, TUBE FLANGE

A scientist of some repute has constructed an electrical scientific experiment (an inter-dimensional time traveling portal) at the front end of a suspended monorail tram. To test it out, you must climb the pylon the tram is stopped at. Watch your step: the place is rickety!

19. OLD MOLD QUARRY

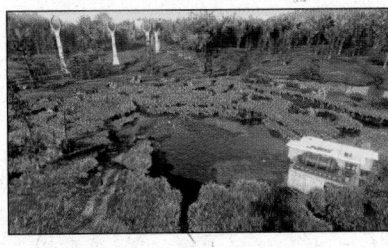

- **COLLECTIBLES:** BOBBLEHEAD, MAGAZINE
- **CRAFTING:** WEAPONS
- **DANGER:** RADIATION!
- **INFO:** EXPECTED ENEMY: GHOUL; SCAVENGE RATING: 2; SIZE: 3; THREAT LEVEL: 35–99
- **ITEM EXAMPLES:** BLASTING CAPS BOX, CRAM, DIRTY ASHTRAY, HARD HAT, HIGH-POWERED MAGNET, FLIP LIGHTER, PACK OF CIGARETTES, RUSTY CANISTER, STEALTH BOY

This waterlogged quarry once belonged to the AMS corporation. Now a metal maintenance shed is accessible, where the majority of the junk is located. You may also wish to brave waterborne diseases and dive into the quarry, where you can open a few crates.

20. DROP SITE C2

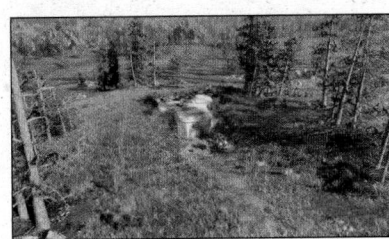

- **COLLECTIBLE:** MAGAZINE
- **DANGER:** RADIATION!++
- **ITEMS:** HARVESTABLE: DISEASED CRANBERRY; HEALTH AND CHEMS
- **INFO:** EXPECTED ENEMY: IRRADIATED ANIMAL; SCAVENGE RATING: 1; SIZE: 1; THREAT LEVEL: 35–99
- **ITEM EXAMPLES:** BATTERED CLIPBOARD, EXTINGUISHER, HAZMAT SUIT, PACK OF CIGARETTES

Poor drainage and broken pumps have caused this site to flood with irradiated water; bring protective clothing before wading into this small hut to secure some possible reading materials and meager provisions.

TRAINING
CRAFTING AND C.A.M.P.ING
INVENTORY
QUESTS
ATLAS
BESTIARY
APPENDICES

#	NAME	DESCRIPTION
1	Mountainside Plane Crash	There were no survivors in this light plane disaster, with one wing stuck in a pine tree above the main fuselage.
2	East Mountain Hunter's Shack	You're greeted by a gnome and bear rug at this still-idyllic wood shack, with items and a great view to the east.
3	Kerwood Shack	A shack on the side of a rock outcrop, with a small lookout deck and skeleton. There's a sleeping bag inside.
4	Bog Channel Beaver Dam	Expect a nest of vicious mutated beavers at this log dam.
5	Trash Camp (edge of the Bog)	Looking more like a collection of debris than a camp, this sleeping bag and lean-to tent still has junk to scavenge.
6	Cranberry Rad Hole: Firebase LT	A deadly hole of luminous radiation; watch your step or you'll dissolve in this horrific muck!
7	Cranberry Island (General's Steakhouse)	Gather beer, cranberries, and the contents of a locked safe (3) on a rowboat moored at this small island.
8	Marsh Cottage (northeast of General's Steakhouse)	A trailer has been wrenched in half by creeping root tendrils. Loot the place, as well as the phosphate deposite outside the dwelling.
9	Biker's Rock Alcove	Among the scree slopes and boulders is a camp within the rocks; a white tent and a smattering of items are yours for the taking.
10	Bog Channel Military Stash	Brain Fungus, rusty military SUVs, and scattered crates below in the Bog Channels.
11	Bog Channel: Tunnel of Horrors	Close to the rusting military SUV, the bog channel turns into a tunnel where multiple coffins and corpses are oozing out from the walls.
12	Bog Channel Log Bridge and Alcove	Beer, a bike, and a corpse; hide here and use this boggy area as an ambush point.
13	Bog Channel: Teddy Fear's Picnic	A council of Teddy Fear and his gnome bodyguards are sitting around a table in the bog here. Is the Hallucigen canister leaking?
14	Vertibird Crash Site (Bog Wilderness)	A vertibird is sinking into the bog; come and get the ammo here.
15	Black Titanium Bog Channel	The bog channels west of the Ranger District Office include a Black Titanium deposit.
16	Bog Channel Turret Camp	Expect a couple of turrets in this bog camp, where a few military skeletons recline near a small orange tent and some crates to loot.
17	Sunk Truck	Half-buried in the soggy road is a dump truck, filled with radioactive barrels, now a growing ground for fungus.
18	Bog Channel Beaver Tunnel	Expect human bones and vicious mutated wildlife as you head through this short bog tunnel.
19	Military Comms Tower Kerwood	A small, quest-related comms dish standing in the middle of a bog.
20	Bog Channel Bridge and Advance Comms	You may need to venture aboveground at this road bridge; vehicles are blocking the bog channel underneath.
21	Cranberry Rad Hole: Bootlegger Shack	A deadly hole of disgusting irradiated magma, easy to slip into and impossible to escape from.
22	Bootlegger's Bridge and Dam	Effective damming has led to the bog channels in this area being a little more wet than normal.

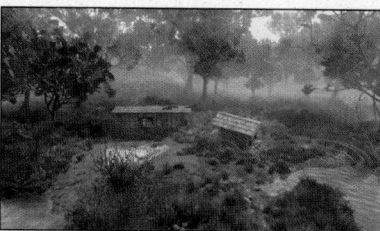

Marsh Cottage (northeast of General's Steakhouse)

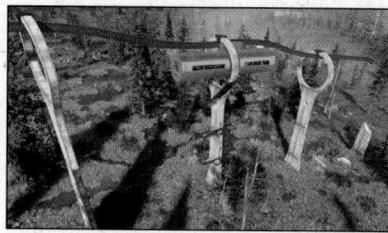

Monorail Pylon: Stranded Carriage

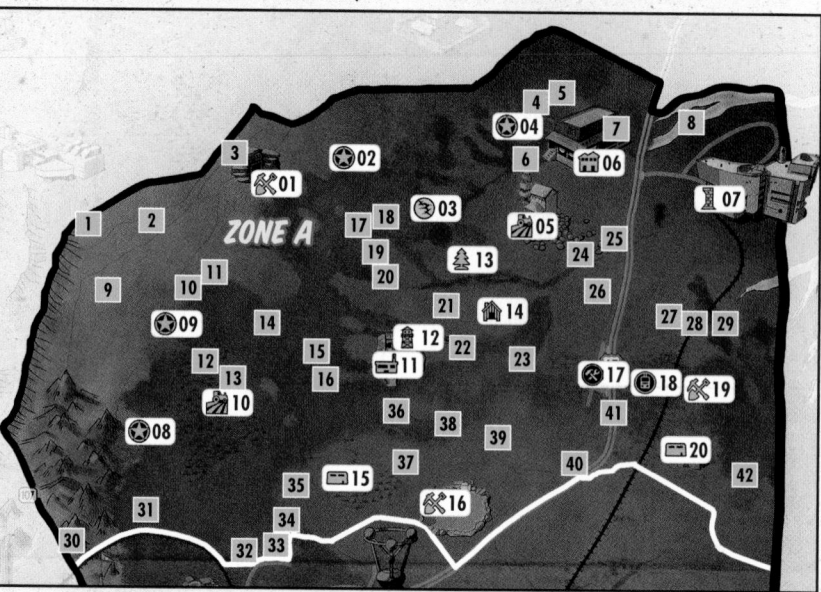

Appalachia: **Cranberry Bog (Zone A) – Secondary Locations**

#	NAME	DESCRIPTION
23	Traffic Jam (Rural Bog Road)	A cop car, a pickup, a motor boat, and other vehicles are slowly rusting in this humid marsh hell.
24	Cranberry Rad Hole: Mac's Farm	A deadly hole of yellow gunk that's straightforward to plunge into but tricky to extract yourself from.
25	Mac's Hidden Stash	A Caps Stash, floor safe, writing desk, and more are hidden underground, by a bog channel at the interstate.
26	Red Wood Garage	The rotting remains of a mechanic's garage and store, mostly picked clean and exposed to the elements.
27	Cranberry Rad Hole: North of Pylon V-13	A deadly hole of yellow radioactive filth, north of Pylon V-13 and close to a second pylon platform.
28	Pylon V-12	A monorail pylon with a rickety platform staircase leading to a great sniper's nest.
29	Monorail Camp	A fallen monorail, dragged by unknown hands, is now a half-sunken camp filled with junk and grotesque foes.
30	Crumbling Monorail Monoliths	The row of dilapidated monorail towers hide more than fallen masonry; there's a junk pile to harvest here.
31	Monorail Pylon: Stranded Carriage	A monorail carriage is stuck atop a pylon with a rusting gantry staircase to reach it. This is a good sniping point, but don't get trapped!
32	Bot Stop (North Watoga)	If you wish to access the Bot Stop Terminals just outside (northwest of) Watoga, RobCo has constructed one here.

#	NAME	DESCRIPTION
33	Truck Parking Lot	A small parking lot with dump trucks and other rusting vehicles; dumpster-dive to secure some choice junk.
34	Upturned Boat (Bog Channel)	An upturned rowboat in the bog channel holds a few scattered items around it.
35	Derelict Bog Home	Four shards of walls and a pond is all that's left of a home. Nearby is a shattered shed.
36	Bog Channel Short Tunnel	There's a sleeping bag, duffel bag, and rusty shopping cart in this hiding spot under the main boggy ground.
37	Bog Channel Tunnel	East of Drop Site G3 are bog channels and a corrugated metal tunnel with a skeleton, duffel bag, and minor items to scavenge.
38	Bog Channel Shelter	Glowing Fungus, a Mini Nuke, and a Stealth Boy are just some of the items to scavenge under this blue tarp bog shelter.
39	Cranberry Rad Hole: Quarry X3	A deadly hole of highly radioactive grime; swimming in it is highly discouraged.
40	Bog Town Shed	A strong gust of wind is likely to blow this dilapidated shed over, so get here quick to snag junk from the pile and inside the structure.
41	Bog Channel: Labyrinth (Bog Town exit)	Head here to access (or appear from) a lengthy, subterranean bog tunnel that runs under the freeway from here to Watoga, with six possible exits along the route.
42	Bog Channel: Tiny Camp	A gray tent and sinking rusty vehicle; the corpse of a settler who couldn't hack it.

CRANBERRY BOG: ZONE B — SOUTH BOG AND WATOGA

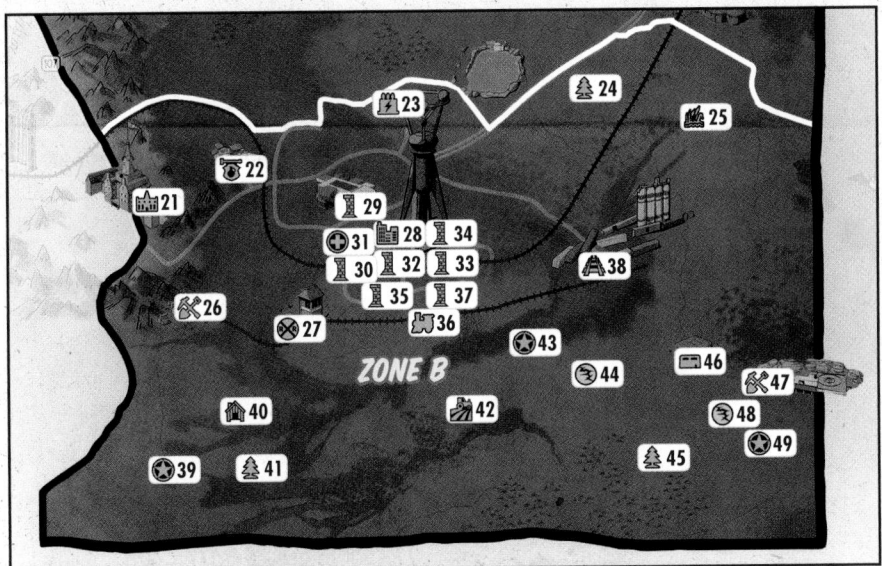

Appalachia: **Cranberry Bog (Zone B) – Primary Locations**

From the very northwestern edge of this zone (the imposing Allegheny Asylum, now known as Fort Defiance), to the southeastern corner (the infamous and incredibly dangerous Glassed Cavern, where you uncover the final secrets), this is perhaps the most dangerous part of Appalachia: The threat level is the highest you'll encounter, and you might very well end your days scrambling to exit the radioactive mess within the Flooded Trainyard or lose your footing and fall from a tall building within the city of Watoga (the landmark city within this zone). Indeed, Watoga is a place more dangerous than most, with robots and other high-level entities to battle. You also find evidence of the machinations of the AMS Corporation, and a maze of structures offer both vertical and horizontal exploration antics.

WORLD MAP LEGEND

— REGION BOUNDARY   — ZONE BOUNDARY

■ BOBBLEHEADS   ■ CAP STASHES   ■ MAGAZINES   ■ POWER ARMOR

PRIMARY LOCATIONS

■	■	■	■	icon	NAME
1		1	4	21	FORT DEFIANCE
2	1	2	1	22	APPALACHIAN ANTIQUES
				23	THUNDER MOUNTAIN SUBSTATION TM-02
				24	VEILED SUNDEW GROVE
1		1		25	CRANBERRY GLADE
			1	26	BIG BEND TUNNEL EAST
1				27	NAR REPAIR YARD
		2	1	28	WATOGA
3	1	3	2	29	WATOGA CIVIC CENTER
2		3	1	30	WATOGA TRANSIT HUB
3	1	2	2	31	WATOGA EMERGENCY SERVICES
2	1	2	1	32	WATOGA MUNICIPAL CENTER
1		1	2	33	AMS CORPORATE HEADQUARTERS
1		2	1	34	WATOGA SHOPPING PLAZA
1		1		35	WATOGA ESTATES

■	■	■	■	icon	NAME
				36	WATOGA STATION
5	1	5	1	37	WATOGA HIGH SCHOOL
1		1		38	FLOODED TRAINYARD
1			1	39	FIREBASE HANCOCK
3		2	1	40	LOST HOME
				41	SPARSE SUNDEW GROVE
1		1		42	SUNRISE FARM
1		1	2	43	SURVEY CAMP ALPHA
				44	FISSURE SITE
				45	OVERGROWN SUNDEW GROVE
1			2	46	DROP SITE V9
	2		2	47	GLASSED CAVERN
				48	FISSURE SITE PRIME
2		2	1	49	FORWARD STATION DELTA

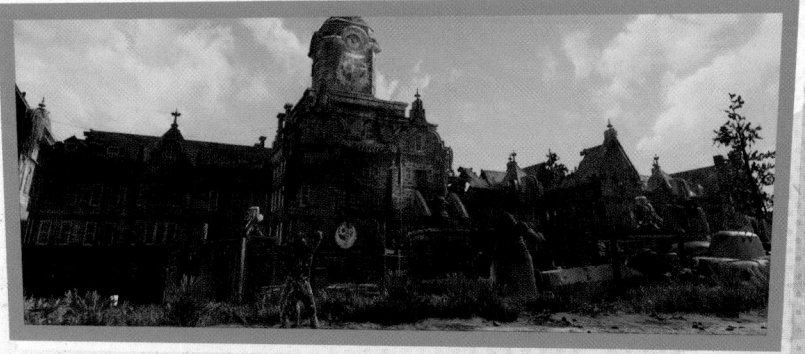

ZONE B: PRIMARY LOCATIONS

MAP LEGEND

- MY STASH BOX
- OVERSEER'S CACHE
- TRUNK
- TRADER

COLLECTIBLES

- BOBBLEHEAD
- MAGAZINE
- POWER ARMOR

CRAFTING

- ARMOR WORKBENCH
- CHEMISTRY WORKBENCH
- COOKING STATION
- POWER ARMOR STATION
- TINKER'S WORKBENCH
- WEAPONS WORKBENCH
- WORKSHOP WORKBENCH

IMPORTANT

- DOOR/GATE
- LOCKED DOOR/GATE
- SAFE
- SCANNER
- TERMINAL

21. FORT DEFIANCE

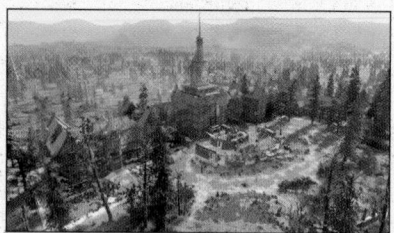

- **INFO:** EXPECTED ENEMY: GHOUL, IRRADIATED ANIMAL, IRRADIATED INSECT, SCORCHED; NOTE; QUEST: DEFIANCE HAS FALLEN, RECRUITMENT BLUES, BELLY OF THE BEAST; SCAVENGE RATING: 5+; SIZE: 5; SLEEPING; THREAT LEVEL: 35–99
- **LOCK:** DOOR (0, 1, 1, 2, 2, 2), SAFE (0, 0), TERMINAL (KEY)
- **ITEM EXAMPLES:** ABRAXO CLEANER+, ABRAXO CLEANER INDUSTRIAL GRADE+, ACETONE CONTAINER, ADJUSTABLE WRENCH, ARMY HELMET, ASYLUM WORKER HAT BLUE/PINK/RED/WEATHERED/YELLOW, ASYLUM WORKER UNIFORM WHITE DIRTY, AUTOPSY BOARD GAME, BAG OF FERTILIZER, BASKETBALL, BINOCULARS, BLAMCO BRAND MAC AND CHEESE, BLUE TABLE LAMP, BOBBY PIN BOX, BOILED WATER, BRAHMIN SKULL, BROKEN LAMP, CARLISLE TYPEWRITER+, CHALK, CHEMISTRY JAR+, CLOTHES HANGER, COFFEE CUP++, CRAM, DANDY BOY APPLES, DIRTY ASHTRAY, DOLL, DUCT TAPE, ECONOMY WONDERGLUE+, ENAMEL BUCKET++, EXCESS ADHESIVE, FASCHNACHT MAN MASK, FLASK, GARDEN GNOME, GLASS JAR, GOLD PLATED FLIP LIGHTER, GUM DROPS, HALLUCIGEN GAS CANISTER+, HOT DOG, HOT PLATE, JANGLES THE MOON MONKEY, KITCHEN SCALES, LAB BOTTLE+, LARGE BEAKER, MAKESHIFT BATTERY, MARKSMAN SNIPER RIFLE, MICROSCOPE+, MILITARY AMMO BAG, MINI NUKE, MOP, NUKA-COLA, OFFICE DESK FAN, PACK OF CIGARETTES, PACK OF DUCT TAPE+, PEN, PERFECTLY PRESERVED PIE, PILLOW+, PLASTIC PLATE+, POOL BALL+, POOL CUE, PORK N' BEANS, PROSNAP CAMERA, PROSPECTOR'S HAT, SHOT GLASS, SOAP, STRAIGHT JACKET+, SURGICAL TRAY+, TALL DRINKING GLASS, TALL FLASK, TOILET PAPER+, TOY ROCKETSHIP, VODKA BOTTLE, WAKEMASTER ALARM CLOCK, WALKING CANE, WHISKEY BOTTLE, WINE BOTTLE, WOOD BLOCK++

- **COLLECTIBLES:** BOBBLEHEAD, HOLOTAPE, MAGAZINE, NUKA-CHERRY, POWER ARMOR (4)
- **CRAFTING:** CHEMISTRY (2), COOKING (3), POWER ARMOR (2), TINKER, WEAPONS (2)
- **DANGER:** TURRET!
- **ITEMS:** ARMS AND AMMO+++; HARVESTABLE: BRAIN FUNGUS, GLOWING FUNGUS, SCORCHBEAST GUANO PILE, WILD CARROT FLOWER; HEALTH AND CHEMS++; RECIPE/MOD/PLAN; OVERSEER'S CACHE

Fort Defiance (Exterior)

LEGEND

1. SECURITY HUT
2. BROTHERHOOD OF STEEL DEFENSES

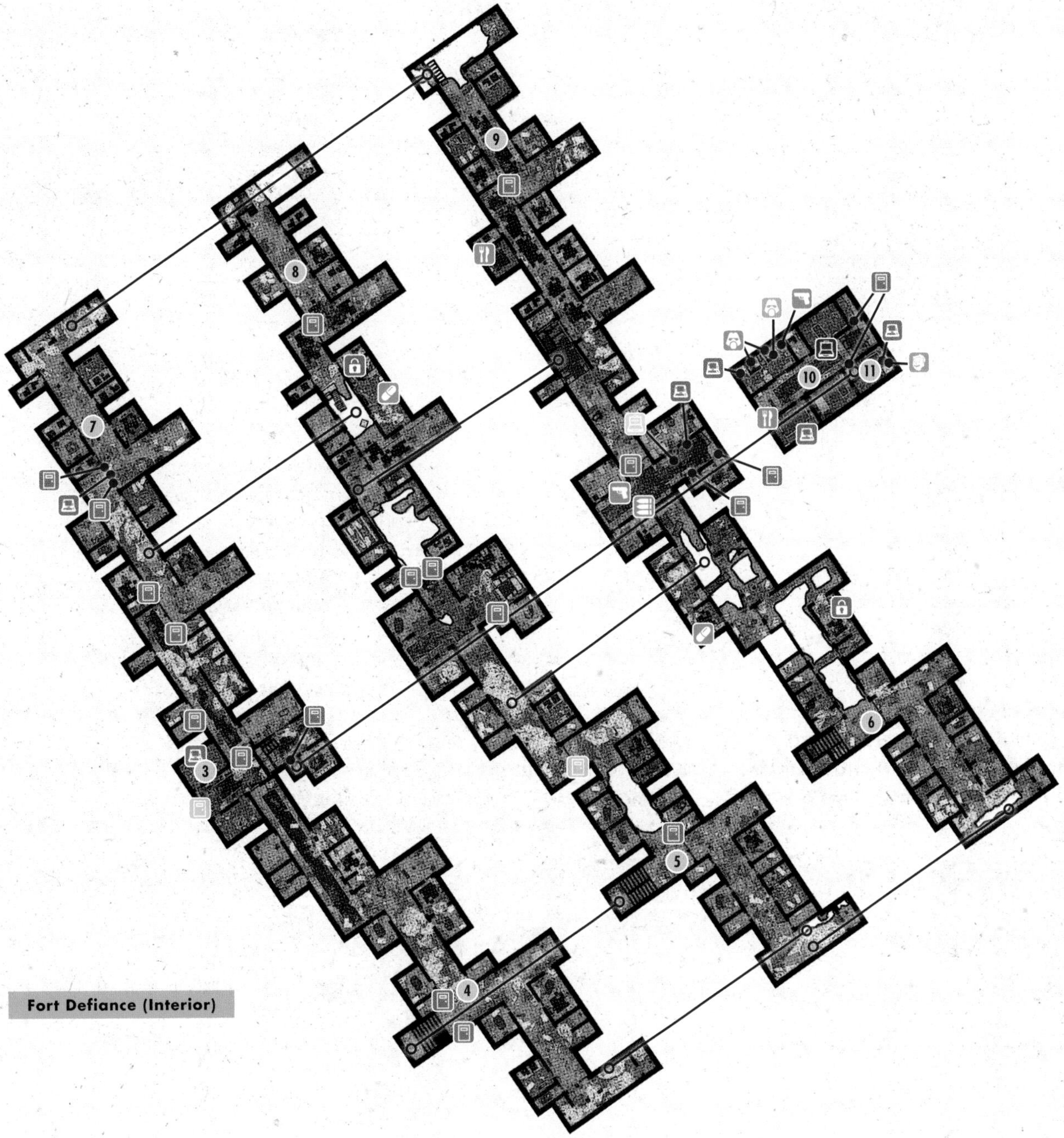

Fort Defiance (Interior)

Known historically as the Allegheny Asylum until it was commandeered (and subsequently lost) by the Brotherhood of Steel, this sprawling and imposing Gothic structure is dilapidated, though the outer defenses are still operational (including surface-to-air missile launchers and a sonic generator). Aside from the odd sprawled skeleton and a good view of Cranberry Bog, the rest of the exterior is relatively sedate. Check the main doors to find two possible Brotherhood of Steel corpses clad in Power Armor.

Inside the asylum, expect a lengthy and confusing trek through a multitude of ruined cells, rooms, offices, and sagging floors, which have given way to treacherous gaps the farther up you go. When you've powered up the doors and returned to the security doors near the entrance, you can investigate the Brotherhood of Steel wing of the fortification and finally reveal its base of operations.

LEGEND

3 DESILVA'S OFFICE
4 FLOOR 1: ASYLUM CELLS
5 FLOOR 2: ASYLUM CELLS AND OFFICE
6 FLOOR 3: ASYLUM CELLS, BATHS, OFFICES AND BREAK ROOM
7 FLOOR 1: BOS WING: OFFICES, CELLS AND STORAGE
8 FLOOR 2: BOS WING: GANTRY STEPS, CELLS, DESTROYED FLOORS
9 FLOOR 3: BOS WING: CAGES, BARRACKS, WORKBENCHES, ARMORY
10 TOP FLOOR: BOS HIDEOUT: BREAK ROOM, POWER ARMOR ROOM.
11 TOP FLOOR: BOS HIDEOUT: PALADIN TAGGERDY'S OFFICE

TRAINING

CRAFTING AND C.A.M.P.ING

INVENTORY

QUESTS

ATLAS

BESTIARY

APPENDICES

22. APPALACHIAN ANTIQUES

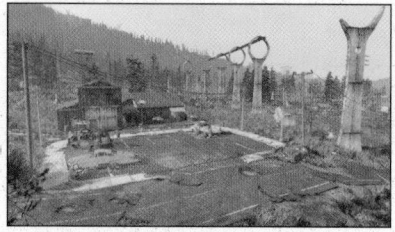

- **COLLECTIBLES:** BOBBLEHEAD (2), CAPS STASH, HOLOTAPE, MAGAZINE (2), POWER ARMOR
- **ITEMS:** ARMS AND AMMO; HARVESTABLE: WILD CARROT FLOWER; HEALTH AND CHEMS
- **INFO:** EXPECTED ENEMY: IRRADIATED ANIMAL; SCAVENGE RATING: 4; SIZE: 2; SLEEPING; THREAT LEVEL: 35–99
- **ITEM EXAMPLES:** ARMY HELMET, ASHTRAY, BROTHERHOOD LAB COAT, CANNED DOG FOOD, CIGARETTE CARTON, CRYSTAL LIQUOR DECANTER, CUTTING BOARD, DESK FAN, DOG COLLAR, DOLL, ECONOMY WONDERGLUE, GAS CANISTER+, FLIP LIGHTER, FOX HIDE, FUSE, HOT PLATE, LIGHTHOUSE SOUVENIR, MEDICAL LIQUID NITROGEN DISPENSER, OVEN MITT, PURIFIED WATER, RADAWAY (DILUTED), SALISBURY STEAK, SILVER TABLE SPOON, SUGAR, SUPER SLEDGE, TEA CUP, TEAPOT, TACTICAL COMBAT SHOTGUN, TELEPHONE, VACUUM TUBE

A veritable treasure trove of junk is available throughout this two-level store, with a few scraps in the dilapidated red shed out back. The Brotherhood of Steel have been here recently; learn more about their activities, and take a Power Armor frame if it's available.

23. THUNDER MOUNTAIN SUBSTATION TM-02

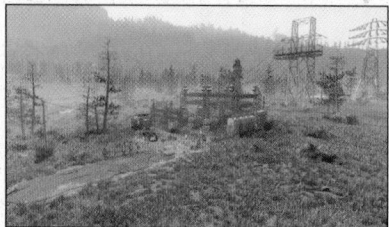

- **ITEM:** HARVESTABLE: GLOWING FUNGUS
- **INFO:** C.A.M.P. POWER; EXPECTED ENEMY: DEATHCLAW, IRRADIATED INSECT, RADANT; SCAVENGE RATING: 1; SIZE: 2; THREAT LEVEL: 35–99
- **ITEM EXAMPLES:** NOT MUCH!

This substation provides some of the power for Watoga, if you've managed to restore power to Thunder Mountain Power Plant (in the Mire). Feel free to attach wires to the power box to generate juice for your own camp.

24. VEILED SUNDEW GROVE

- **ITEMS:** HARVESTABLE: CRANBERRY, GLOWING FUNGUS
- **DANGER:** RADIATION!
- **INFO:** EXPECTED ENEMY: GULPER, IRRADIATED ANIMAL; SCAVENGE RATING: 1; SIZE: 2; THREAT LEVEL: 35–99

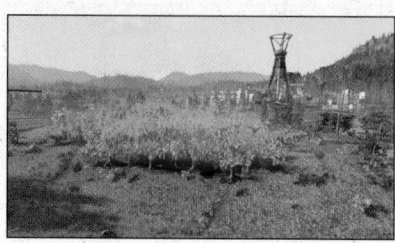

A large cluster of carnivorous drosera plants is flourishing in this part of the Bog. Weave through the channels below the plants, checking for harvest items and fending off the more violent wildlife.

25. CRANBERRY GLADE

- **COLLECTIBLES:** BOBBLEHEAD, MAGAZINE
- **CRAFTING:** COOKING
- **DANGER:** RADIATION!
- **ITEMS:** ARMS AND AMMO; HARVESTABLE: CRANBERRY, GRAVEL; MUTATED FERN; RECIPE/ MOD/PLAN
- **INFO:** EXPECTED ENEMY: GHOUL; INSTRUMENT; SCAVENGE RATING: 2; SIZE: 3; THREAT LEVEL: 35–99
- **ITEM EXAMPLES:** ACCORDION, BATTERED FEDORA, BEER, CRANBERRY, FANCY LADS SNACK CAKES, STEEL GUITAR, TRIGGERMAN BOWLER, TRUMPET

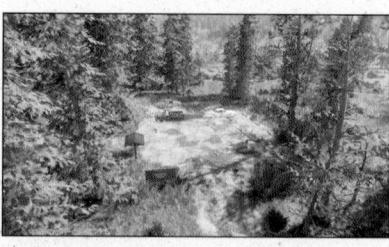

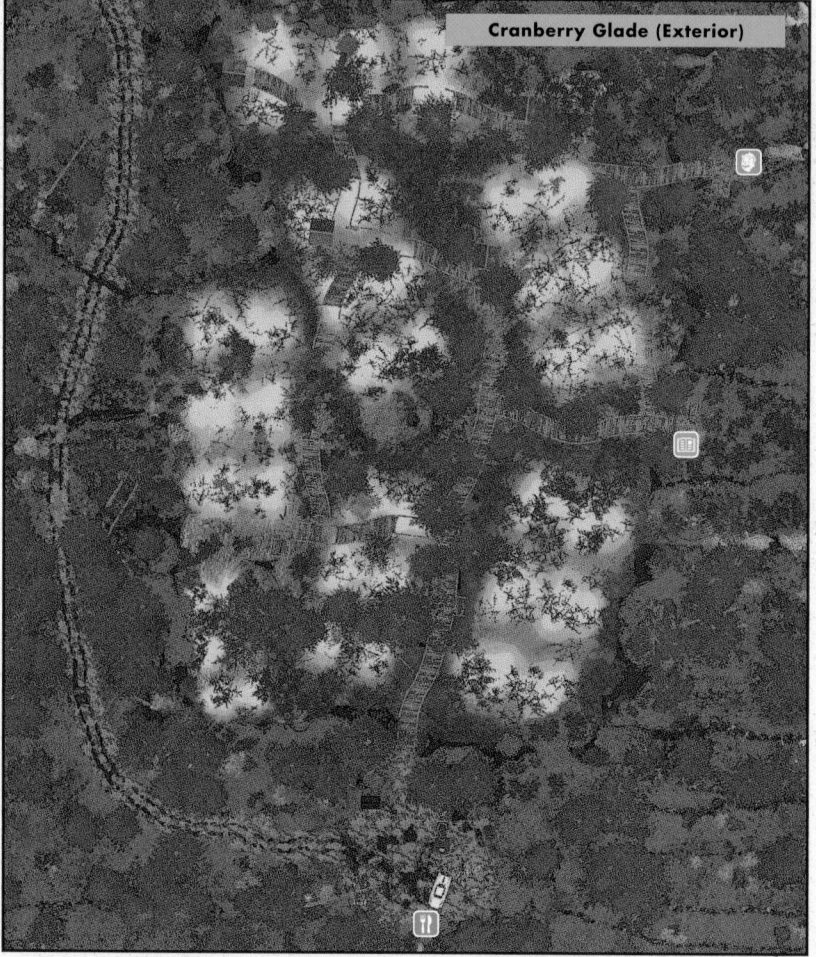

Cranberry Glade (Exterior)

This natural glade of boggy ground where cranberries still grow is now lightly irradiated. Find a small gravel pit and cooking area in the parking lot, and seek out a stranded musicians' coach if you can find it in the mist.

26. BIG BEND TUNNEL EAST

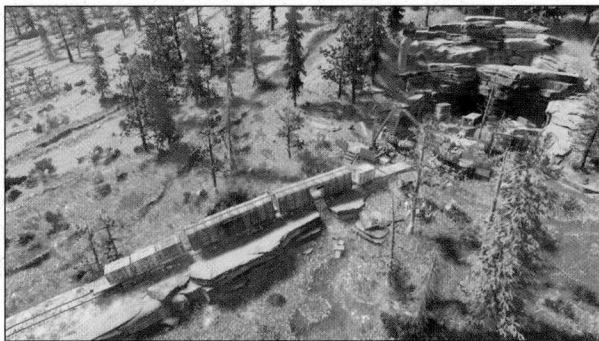

- **COLLECTIBLE:** POWER ARMOR
- **CRAFTING:** ARMOR, COOKING, POWER ARMOR (2), WEAPONS
- **DANGER:** EXPLOSIVE CANISTER!
- **ITEMS:** ARMS AND AMMO++, HEALTH AND CHEMS
- **INFO:** EXPECTED ENEMY: SCORCHED; NOTE; QUEST: SEARCH BIG BEND TUNNEL FOR SURVIVORS; SCAVENGE RATING: 3; SIZE: 2(5); SLEEPING; THREAT LEVEL: 35–99
- **LOCK:** SECURITY GATE (1)
- **ITEM EXAMPLES:** ABRAXO CLEANER, ALUMINUM CANISTER, AUTOMATIC COMBAT RIFLE, BALL-PEEN HAMMER, BOILED WATER, BROOM, CAN, CANNED DOG FOOD, DOG BOWL, ECONOMY WONDERGLUE, GAS CANISTER, LANTERN, MAKESHIFT BATTERY, METAL BUCKET+, MISSILE LAUNCHER, PILLOW+, SENSOR MODULE, SHOT GLASS, TUBE FLANGE, VOLATILE MATERIALS BOX

This is the entrance and exit into the Big Bend Tunnel, with a long interior and western exit over in the Ash Heap (where the main map is annotated). This details the exterior of the tunnel entrance within Cranberry Bog, which was a Brotherhood staging point.

27. NAR REPAIR YARD

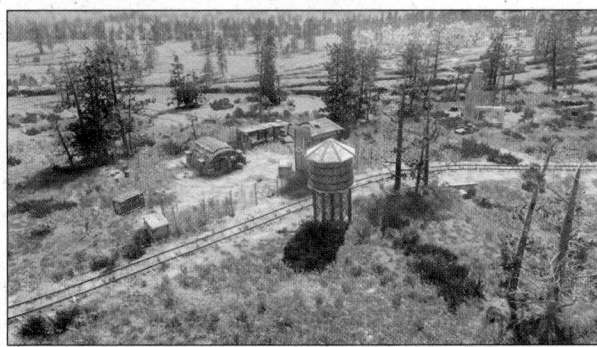

- **COLLECTIBLE:** BOBBLEHEAD
- **CRAFTING:** ARMOR
- **DANGER:** RADIATION!
- **ITEMS:** HARVESTABLE: CRANBERRY, DISEASED CRANBERRY
- **INFO:** EXPECTED ENEMY: SUPER MUTANT; SCAVENGE RATING: 2; SIZE: 2; THREAT LEVEL: 35–99
- **LOCK:** SAFE (2)
- **ITEM EXAMPLES:** BALL-PEEN HAMMER, BOBBY PIN BOX, GLASS JAR, METAL TUB, ORANGE CANISTER, PAINT CAN, SCREWDRIVER, TRILBY HAT, TURPENTINE, USED OIL CAN, WHISKEY BOTTLE, YELLOW CANISTER

This small yard has a signal tower and a curved-roof mechanic's shed. It offers a few choice bits of junk and a possible fracas on the very edge of Watoga township.

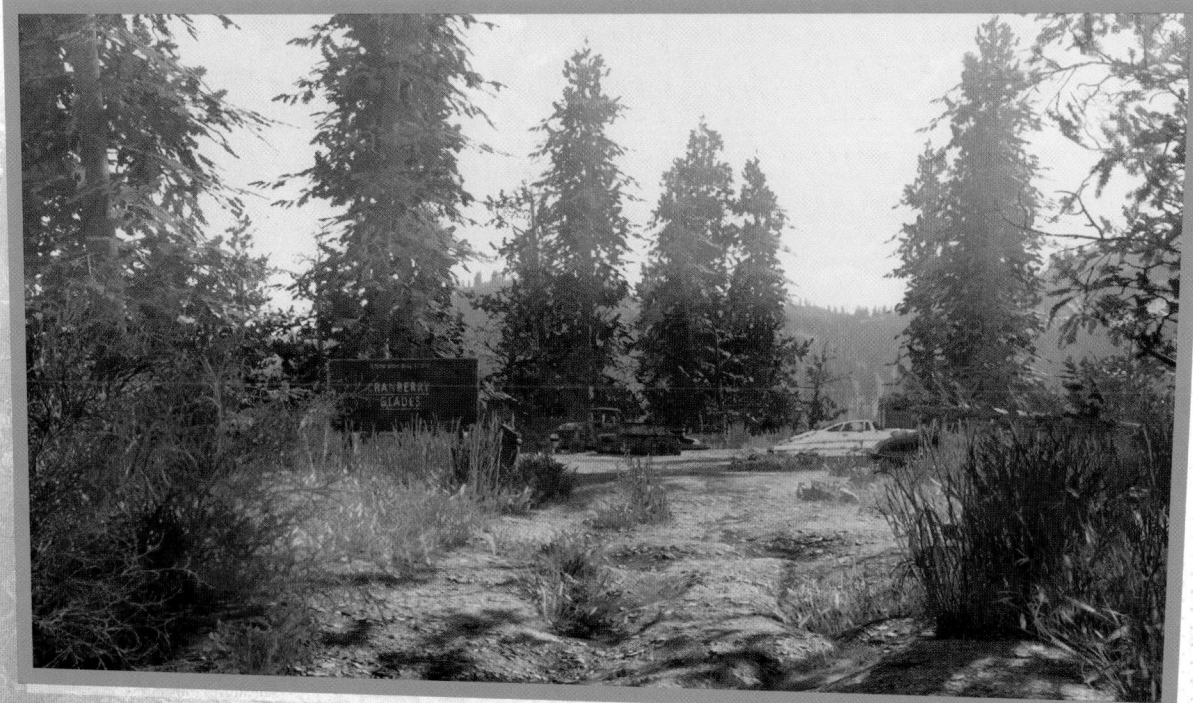

TRAINING

CRAFTING AND C.A.M.P.ING

INVENTORY

QUESTS

ATLAS

BESTIARY

APPENDICES

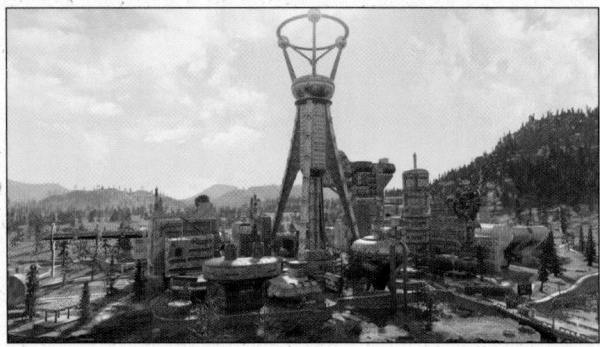

- **COLLECTIBLE: MAGAZINE (2)**
- **INFO: EXPECTED ENEMY: ROBOT; SCAVENGE RATING: 5+++; SIZE: 5+++; THREAT LEVEL: 35–99**

This area was built at the site of an old ghost town. The titans of industry and robotics crafted this shining new center of commerce to be the jewel of southeast Appalachia—a fully autonomous city, where robots catered to your every whim. As the more cynical detractors pointed out at the time, there was likely to be a downside if these robots were to ever malfunction. Now Watoga is abandoned aside from a sizable mechanical population. Exercise extreme caution as you explore the rusting towers of the Cranberry Bog Capital; emotionless automatons and extremely long drops are just the start of the threats that abound in these parts!

Watoga (Exterior)

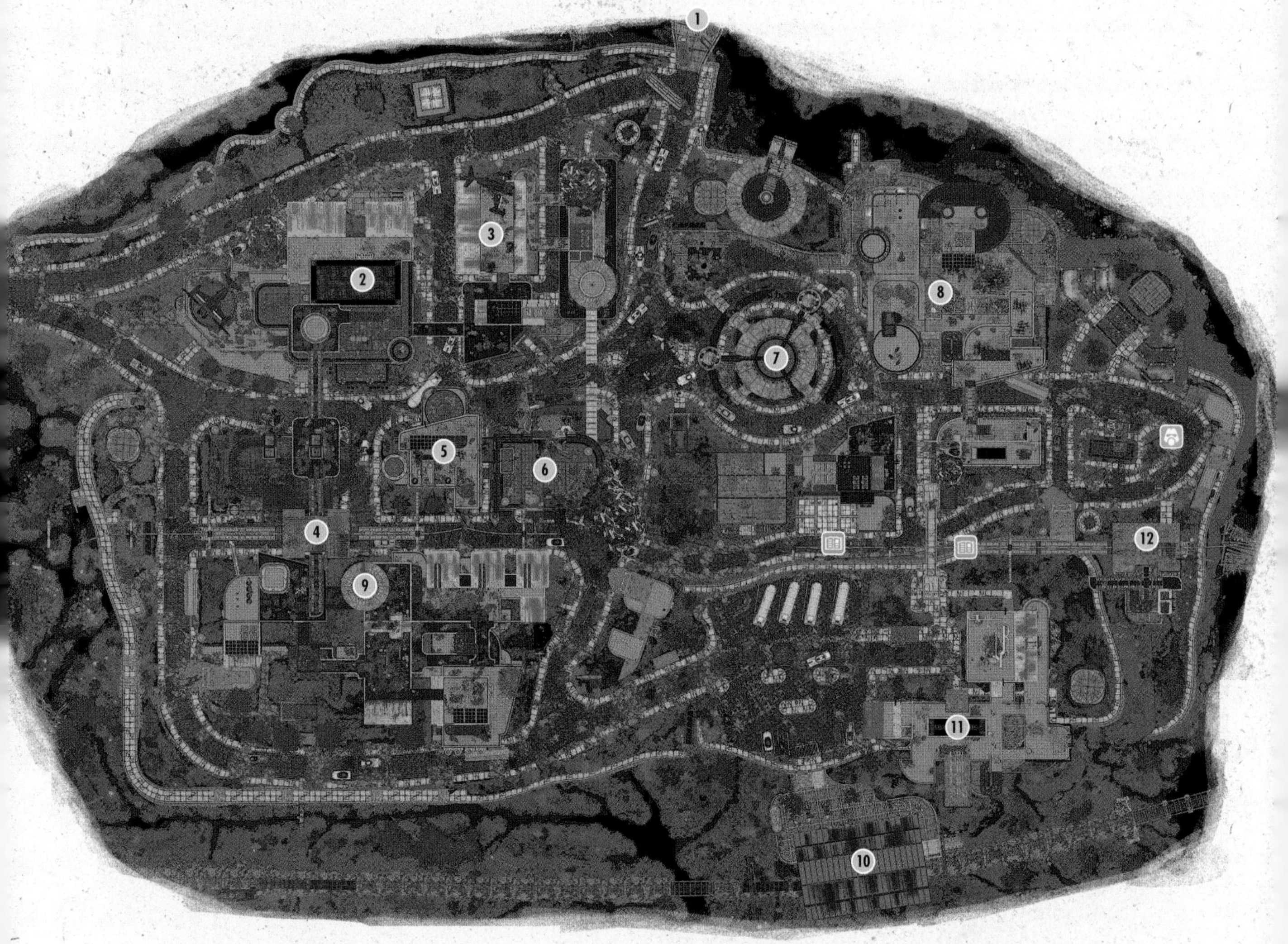

LEGEND

1. MAIN HIGHWAY ENTRANCE
2. PRIMARY LOCATION: WATOGA CIVIC CENTER
3. WATOGA TOWERS
4. PRIMARY LOCATION: WATOGA TRANSIT HUB
5. PRIMARY LOCATION: WATOGA EMERGENCY SERVICES
6. PRIMARY LOCATION: WATOGA MUNICIPAL CENTER
7. PRIMARY LOCATION: AMS CORPORATE HEADQUARTERS
8. PRIMARY LOCATION: WATOGA SHOPPING PLAZA
9. PRIMARY LOCATION: WATOGA ESTATES
10. PRIMARY LOCATION: WATOGA STATION
11. PRIMARY LOCATION: WATOGA HIGH SCHOOL
12. MONORAIL STATION

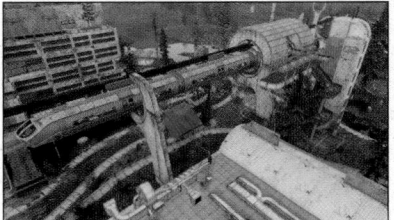

Watoga Towers

The city of Watoga encompasses this and the next nine primary locations, all within a low boundary wall that, at least for now, is keeping the Bog at bay. Therefore, information regarding

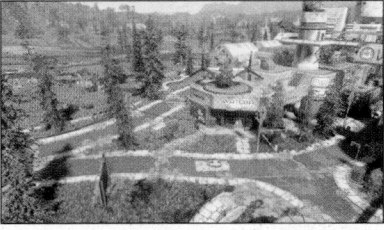

Monorail Station

The largest of these is Watoga Towers, an inaccessible residential structure with balcony access from the ground and roof access from the Civic Center, on the city's northern side. The other minor

Crafting, Dangers, Items, certain Information, Locked interactions, and Item Examples have been specified for individual locales.

area is in the southeastern part of the city (just east of the high school); check a monorail station, which includes a tram still hanging from its rail and a possible Magazine to gather near the front of the vehicle.

29. WATOGA CIVIC CENTER

- **COLLECTIBLES:** BOBBLEHEAD (3), CAPS STASH, HOLOTAPE, MAGAZINE (3), NUKA-CHERRY, POWER ARMOR (2)
- **DANGER:** LONG DROP!
- **ITEMS:** ARMS AND AMMO+; HARVESTABLE: SCORCHBEAST GUANO PILE; HEALTH AND CHEMS++; RECIPE/MOD/PLAN; TRUNK
- **INFO:** EXPECTED ENEMY: ROBOT, SCORCHED; SCAVENGE RATING: 5; SIZE: 5; THREAT LEVEL: 35–99
- **LOCK:** DOOR (1, 1, 1, 2, KEY), SAFE (0, 1, 2, 2), TERMINAL (1)

- **ITEM EXAMPLES:** ABRAXO CLEAN INDUSTRIAL GRADE, ANTIFREEZE BOTTLE, ASSAULT RIFLE, BEER BOTTLE+, BROKEN LAMP, BUFFOUT, CAMPAIGN HAT, CANNED DOG FOOD, CIVIC CENTER BOOTH KEY, COOKING OIL, COOKING POT+, CRAM+, DANDY BOY APPLES, EMPTY FLORAL BARREL VASE, ENAMEL BUCKET+, FRYING PAN, GARDEN GNOME+, HALLUCIGEN GAS CANISTER+, HOT PLATE, JANGLES THE MOON MONKEY, LARGE BABY BOTTLE, LIGHTBULB, MILITARY AMMO BAG, MINI NUKE, MISSILE, MISSILE LAUNCHER, MOP, NUKA-COLA CUP+++, NUKA-COLA CUP PACK, OVEN MITT+, PACK OF DUCT TAPE, PICKAXE PILSNER, PLUNGER, PORK N' BEANS+, POTATO CRISPS+, PROSNAP CAMERA, RUM, SALT SHAKER+, SOAP+, SPATULA+, STEW POT, TALL DRINKING GLASS+, TEA CUP, TEDDY BEAR+, TOASTER, TOY TRUCK, TV DINNER TRAY+, VODKA

Watoga Civic Center (Exterior)

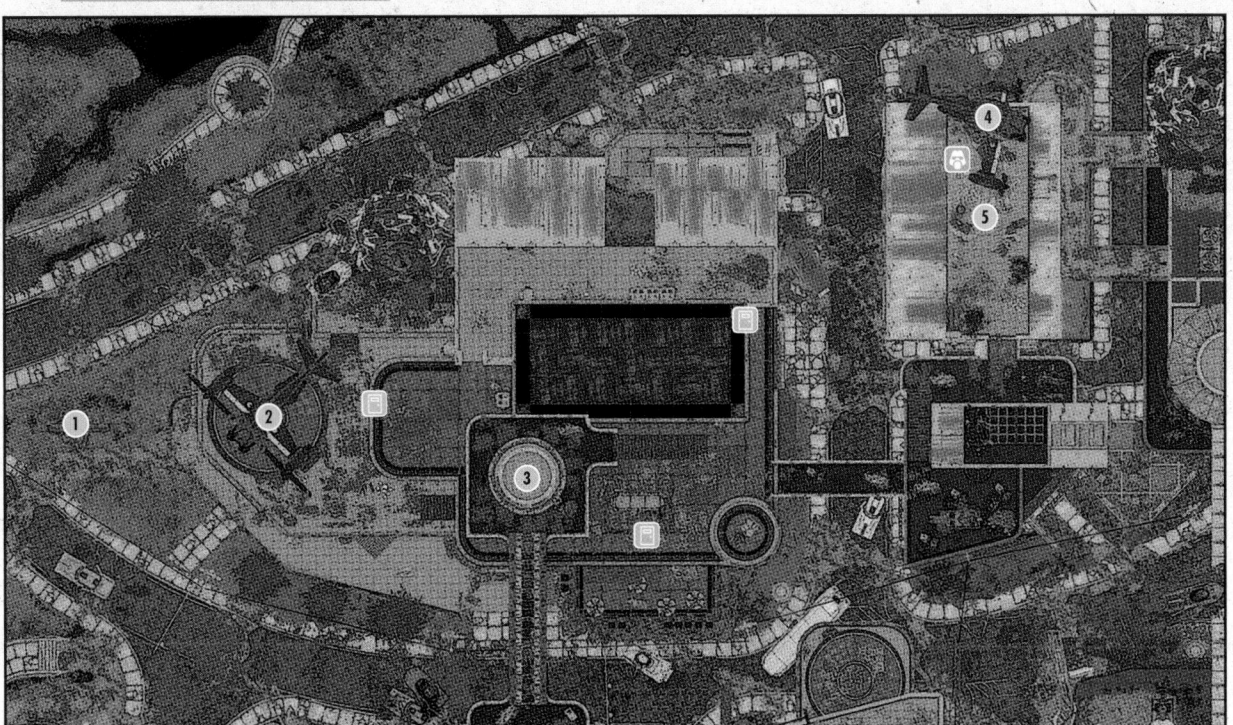

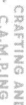

LEGEND

1. CIVIC CENTER SIGN
2. VERTIBIRD AND HELIPAD (ROOF)
3. CIVIC CENTER
4. CRASHED VERTIBIRD (WATOGA TOWERS ROOF)
5. WATOGA TOWERS (ROOF)

TRAINING

CRAFTING AND C.A.M.P.ING

INVENTORY

QUESTS

ATLAS

BESTIARY

APPENDICES

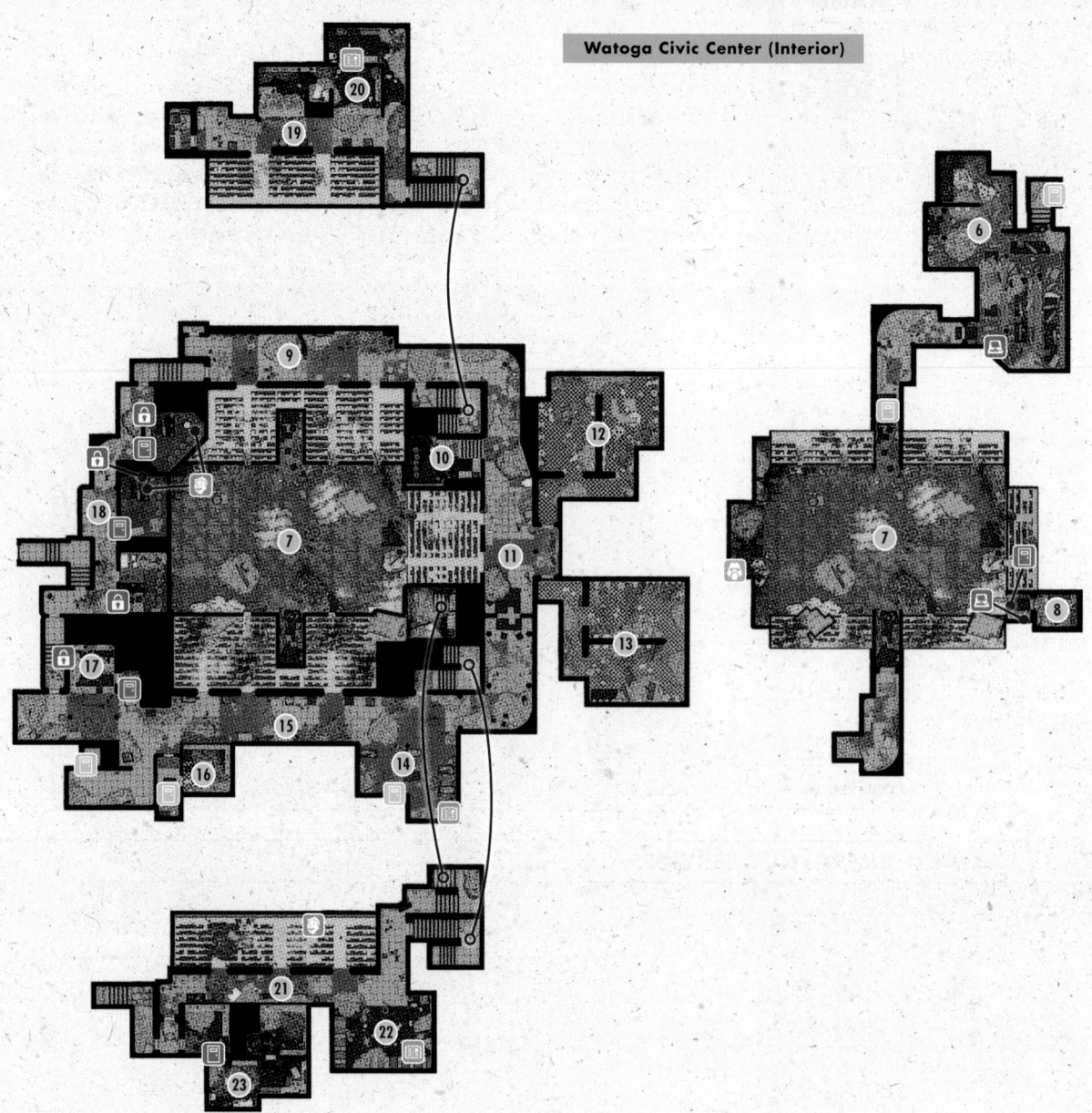

LEGEND

6	LOCKER ROOM	**12**	RESTROOMS (FEMALE)	**18**	VIP ROOMS 1, 2, 3
7	STADIUM FLOOR	**13**	RESTROOMS (MALE)	**19**	"B" LEVEL SEATING (NORTH)
8	LOCKED STORAGE ROOM	**14**	CAFETERIA (TO EXTERIOR BALCONY)	**20**	UPPER KITCHENS (NORTH)
9	"A" LEVEL BALCONY AND SEATING (NORTH)	**15**	"A" LEVEL BALCONY AND SEATING (SOUTH)	**21**	"B" LEVEL SEATING (SOUTH)
10	"S" LEVEL SEATING	**16**	KITCHEN	**22**	UPPER CAFETERIA (SOUTH)
11	"A" LEVEL BALCONY AND SEATING (EAST)	**17**	LOCKED CONFECTIONERY STAND	**23**	UPPER KITCHENS (SOUTH)

The large green, orange and white structure to the northwest of the city is the Civic Center. Check for the entrance (ground level) and a fire escape to the rooftops on the eastern side of the structure. This leads to the Civic Center rooftop (with an elevator from inside the center you can access), where you can inspect a landed Vertibird and a giant Scorchbeast nest (a huge lump of mud and detritus close to the Vertibird). From the roof, you can also access the walkway and elevator to the monorail bridge and the Watoga Transit Hub. Head east along the roof to reach a walkway to the adjacent apartment block (only the roof here is accessible) with another parked Vertibird.

Inside, you can fully explore a large stadium with a wooden floor in the center, surrounded by seating on all sides. You can go up three additional levels, including locked VIP areas and three separate kitchens! There's a wealth of items to gather here, so be sure to learn your exits.

30. WATOGA TRANSIT HUB

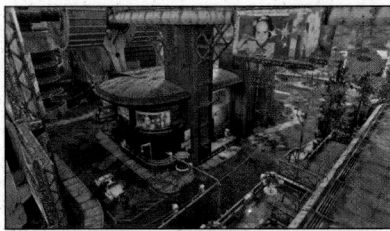

- **COLLECTIBLES:** BOBBLEHEAD (2), MAGAZINE (3), POWER ARMOR
- **DANGER:** LONG DROP!
- **ITEMS:** ARMS AND AMMO; HEALTH AND CHEMS; RECIPE/MOD/PLAN
- **INFO:** EXPECTED ENEMY: ROBOT; NOTE; SCAVENGE RATING: 3; SIZE: 3; SLEEPING; THREAT LEVEL: 35–99
- **LOCK:** DOOR (3), TERMINAL (3)
- **ITEM EXAMPLES:** BOILED WATER, BOURBON, BUFFOUT, CANNED DOG FOOD, CRAM, EXTINGUISHER, FUSION CORE, MINI NUKE, MUZZLED LASER RIFLE, NOODLE CUP, PACK OF CIGARETTES, POTATO CRISPS, RADAWAY, SALISBURY STEAK, SEALED CHARLESTON HERALD, YUM YUM DEVILED EGGS

Watoga Transit Hub (Exterior)

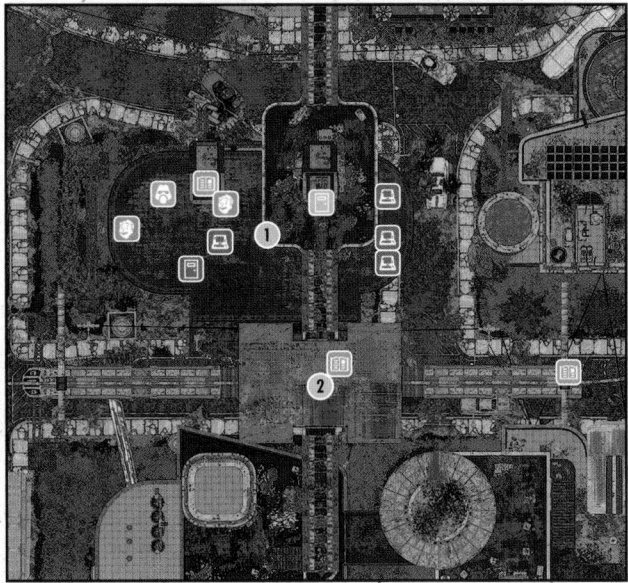

This monorail hub (top) and bus line (ground) allows monorail bridge access to and from the Civic Center (to the north), to the roof of Watoga Estates (to the south), and to an elevator to and from the ground-level lobby and monorail station. If you want to explore the monorail tram, there's one parked at the station. Watch those open doors leading to a death plummet! The lobby is accessible from the north or south streets or the elevator (to and from the roof). Hack or unlock the door to the generator closet for some choice items and possible power armor.

LEGEND
1. TRANSIT HUB LOBBY AND ELEVATOR
2. MONORAIL STATION

31. WATOGA EMERGENCY SERVICES

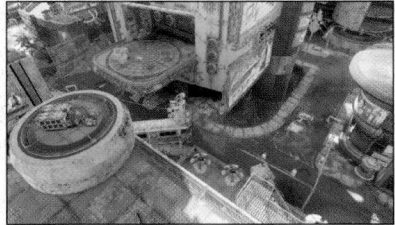

Watoga Emergency Services (Exterior)

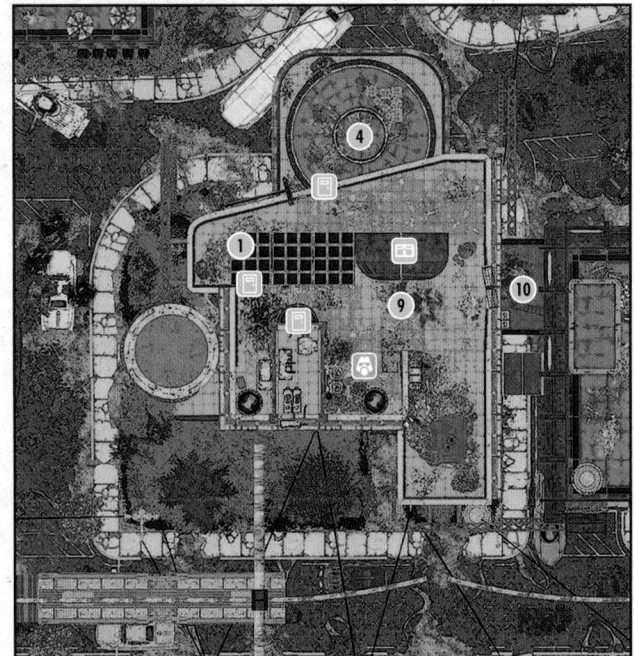

- **COLLECTIBLES:** BOBBLEHEAD (3), CAPS STASH, MAGAZINE (2), POWER ARMOR (2)
- **DANGER:** LONG DROP!
- **ITEMS:** ARMS AND AMMO; HEALTH AND CHEMS+++; RECIPE/MOD/PLAN; TRUNK
- **INFO:** EXPECTED ENEMY: ROBOT, SCORCHED; QUEST: COP A SQUATTER; SCAVENGE RATING: 4; SIZE: 4; THREAT LEVEL: 35–99
- **LOCK:** DOOR (2, 2)
- **ITEM EXAMPLES:** BANDAGE SCISSORS, BEER, BLOOD PACK, BOILED WATER, BONE CUTTER, CANNED DOG FOOD, COP HAT, CRAM, DANDY BOY APPLES, DUCT TAPE, ENAMEL BUCKET, GAS CANISTER+, GUMDROPS, LAB BOTTLE, MEDICAL LIQUID NITROGEN DISPENSER, MENTATS+, MICROSCOPE, MINI NUKE, MOP, PATROLMAN SUNGLASSES, PLUNGER, PSYCHO, PURIFIED WATER, RAD-X+, RADAWAY+, RADAWAY (DILUTED), STIMPAK, SUGAR BOMBS, SURGICAL TRAY, TALL FLASK, TEST TUBE RACK, TOILET PAPER+, USED OIL CAN, WHISKEY, WINE

LEGEND
1. EXTERIOR LOBBY AND ELEVATOR
4. HELIPAD PLATFORM (FROM INTERIOR)
9. ROOF (FROM INTERIOR)
10. SKELETAL REMAINS (FROM INTERIOR)

TRAINING

CRAFTING AND C.A.M.P.ING

INVENTORY

QUESTS

ATLAS

BESTIARY

APPENDICES

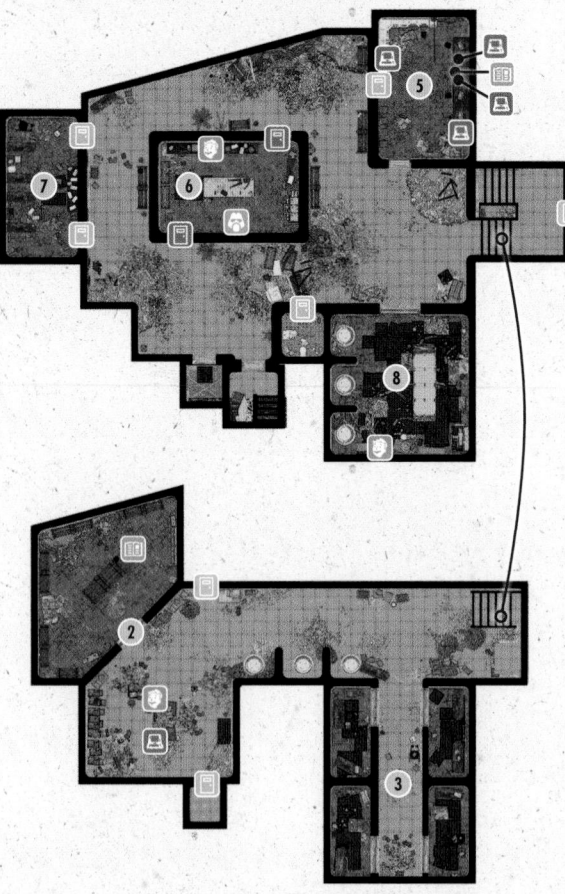

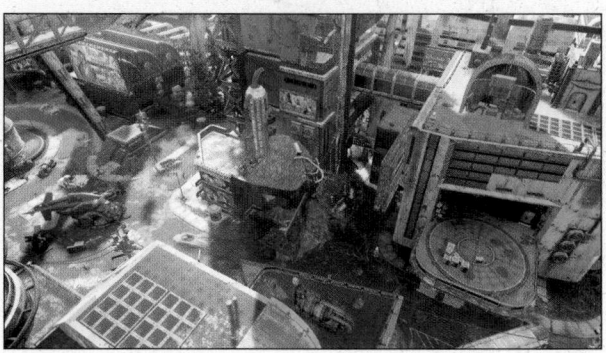

- **COLLECTIBLES:** BOBBLEHEAD (2), CAPS STASH, MAGAZINE (2), NUKA-CHERRY, POWER ARMOR
- **DANGER:** LONG DROP!
- **ITEMS:** ARMS AND AMMO+; HARVESTABLE: GLOWING FUNGUS; HEALTH AND CHEMS; TRUNK
- **INFO:** EXPECTED ENEMY: ROBOT, SCORCHED; NOTE; QUEST: MAYOR FOR A DAY, REACH THE MAYOR'S OFFICE; SCAVENGE RATING: 4; SIZE: 4; THREAT LEVEL: 35–99
- **LOCK:** SAFE (2, 2, 2, 2, KEY), TERMINAL (2, 2)
- **ITEM EXAMPLES:** 10-MM PISTOL, ABRAXO CLEANER, ABRAXO CLEANER INDUSTRIAL GRADE, ANTIQUE GLOBE, BLOW TORCH, BOBBY PIN BOX, BROKEN LAMP, COFFEE CUP, COFFEE POT, CRYSTAL LIQUOR DECANTER, DIRTY ASHTRAY+, DOLL, DUCT TAPE+, GARDEN GNOME, GAS CANISTER, HOT PLATE, JANGLES AND MOON MONKEY, LARGE BABY BOTTLE, MAGNIFYING GLASS, MOP, NEWSBOY CAP, OFFICE DESK FAN+, PLASTIC PUMPKIN+, PLUNGER, PRE-WAR MONEY+, RECON .44 PISTOL, RIB CAGE AND PELVIS, RUM BOTTLE, SHORT PUMP ACTION SHOTGUN, TALL DRINKING GLASS+, TEAL VAULTED VASE, TEDDY BEAR+, TELEPHONE+, TOY ALIEN, TYPEWRITER+, VACUUM TUBE, VASE

LEGEND

- **2** RECEPTION AND WAITING ROOM
- **3** PATIENT EXAMINATION ROOMS (LOWER)
- **5** EMERGENCY REPORT ROOM
- **6** LOCKED LABORATORY
- **7** PATIENT EXAMINATION ROOMS (UPPER) [8] SERVER ROOM

This primarily green structure has a relatively small ground-level footprint, with a small reception lobby leading to an elevator. Inside, there's access to the initial floor of patient rooms and an exterior helipad. Head to the upper floor to discover a report room, a server and protectron pod chamber, and a locked (2) laboratory where a pair of Brotherhood of Steel soldiers have succumbed to their wounds. One is clad in Power Armor, and there's another possible suit on the roof (accessed from this interior level), along with a trunk and a good view from the middle of Watoga.

Watoga Municipal Center (Exterior)

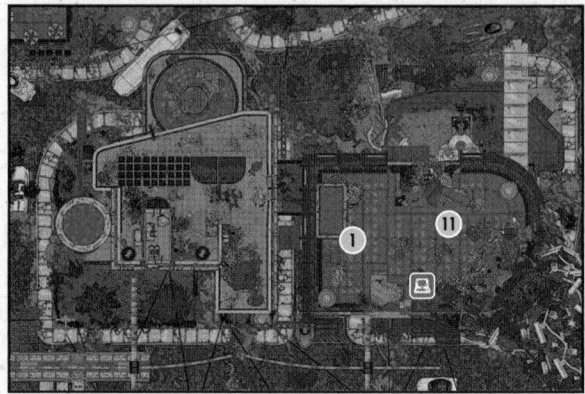

LEGEND

- **1** EXTERIOR AND FOYER
- **11** ROOF AND RUINED OFFICES (FROM INTERIOR)

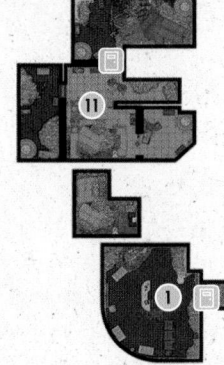

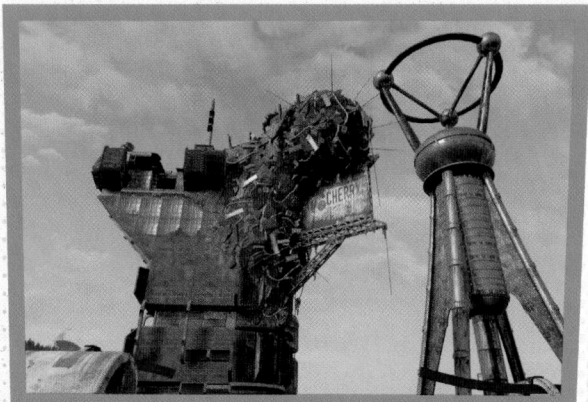

Watoga Municipal Center (Interior)

LEGEND

- **2** VISITOR FOYER
- **3** RESTROOMS
- **4** INFORMATION OFFICE
- **5** COMPLAINTS ARCHIVE OFFICE
- **6** EXECUTIVE OFFICE
- **7** COURTROOM
- **8** OFFICIAL'S OFFICE (LOCKED)
- **9** WASTEBASKET OFFICE
- **10** MAYOR'S OFFICE

On the corner of RobCo Boulevard and Innovation West Street is the second-tallest building in town, offering access to the local government offices. Not surprisingly, the place is condemned. Access the interior via the elevator in the once-plush lobby. Use the stairs to reach the upper offices surrounding the main foyer; then ascend to the executive level, with an office, a courtroom (avoid falling into the hole in the floor), and the locked senator's office (2).

Head to a door via the fallen ceiling in the courtroom to reach the upper offices interior. Here, there's an office full of wastebaskets; a large lobby; an elevator to the roof; and the mayor's office, where you can contact Maia (the computer) while you check the corpse of the dead mayor.

Access the roof via the executive office-level elevator. Here you find a Scorchbeast nest of dirt, scrap, and detritus (which you can climb for the ultimate selfie!), as well as a long drop to your death. Exploration into some extremely "open-plan" maintenance offices is possible only from here.

33. AMS CORPORATE HEADQUARTERS

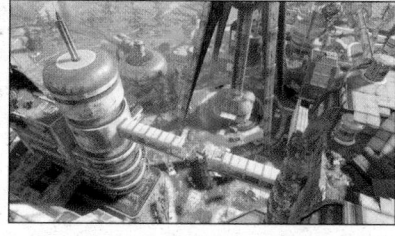

- **ITEM EXAMPLES:** ABRAXO CLEANER, ASHTRAY+++, BEAKER+, BEAKER STAND, BOILED WATER, BUNSEN BURNER, CARTON OF CIGARETTES, COMBAT KNIFE, DIRTY ASHTRAY, ENAMEL BUCKET, EYEBOT MODEL, FRAGMENTATION MINE, FRAMED LIGHTHOUSE PHOTO, FUSION CORE, HAZMAT SUIT, METAL BUCKET, MICROSCOPE, MOP, MR. HANDY MODEL, OIL CANISTER, PEPPER, PLUNGER+, PRE-WAR MONEY+, PROTECTRON MODEL, RAD-X+, RAW FERTILIZER, SALT, SECURITY BATON, SKULL, SURGICAL MASK, TOILET PAPER+, TYPEWRITER, ULTRACITE SCRAP+, UNDAMAGED AMERICAN FLAG, WILLOW VAULTED VASE

- **COLLECTIBLES:** BOBBLEHEAD, MAGAZINE, POWER ARMOR (2)
- **DANGER:** LONG DROP! TURRET!
- **ITEMS:** ARMS AND AMMO; HARVESTABLE: GLOWING FUNGUS; HEALTH AND CHEMS
- **INFO:** EXPECTED ENEMY: ROBOT; LANDMARK; NOTE; SCAVENGE RATING: 4; SIZE: 4; THREAT LEVEL: 35–99
- **LOCK:** DOOR (2), SAFE (1, 2, 3), TERMINAL (1, 1, 1)

AMS Corporate Headquarters: (Exterior)

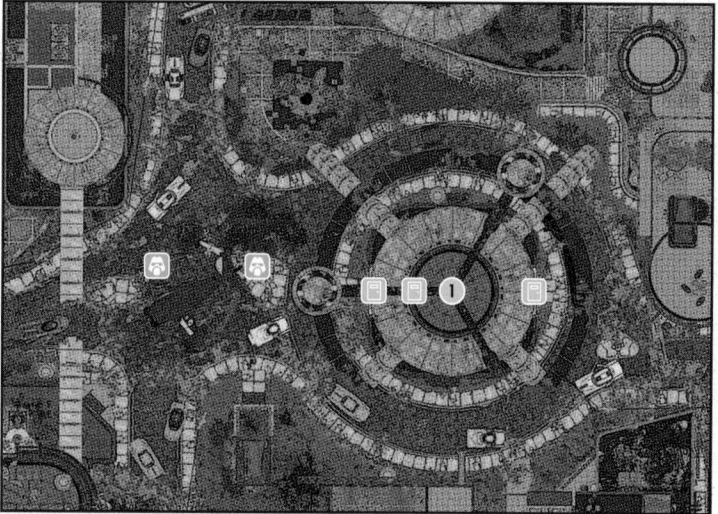

LEGEND

- **1** AMS BUILDING: CIRCULAR LOBBY

TRAINING

CRAFTING AND C.A.M.P.ING

INVENTORY

QUESTS

ATLAS

BESTIARY

APPENDICES

Towering over all other skyscrapers in Watoga is the AMS building, with its distinctive structure and extensive interior to explore. Before heading inside, check the crashed Vertibird in the main town square junction outside for two possible Power Armor suits (one is a frame, while the other still has a Brotherhood of Steel soldier corpse inside). Pick any of the three ground-level doors through which to enter the headquarters foyer, and then use the elevator.

Inside, there are numerous cylindrical elevators that used to allow travel throughout the building; many are now inaccessible and blocked. With terminal access, you can reach the AMS Headquarters Third Floor, and begin your exploration. The Top Floor elevator is used during your exit. Note the large "3" and "T" above the elevators you'll be using. All others are inaccessible.

AMS Corporate Headquarters: Third and Top Floors (Interior)

LEGEND
1 CIRCULAR LOBBY AND ELEVATOR
2 FORECOURT AND SECURITY BALCONY
3 CAGE
4 HYDRAULIC PRESS ROOM
5 FURNACE ROOM
6 PROTECTRON PODS AND SUBJECT 43
7 STORAGE
8 CAGE CONTROL ROOM
9 LABORATORY
10 BOOKKEEPING
11 GENERATOR ROOM
12 BREAK ROOM AND BALCONY
13 ANIMAL HOLDING OFFICE AND CHAMBER
14 RESTROOMS
15 FACILITIES OFFICE AND GENERATORS
16 UPPER GENERATOR ROOM
17 CEO'S OFFICE
18 DATA PROCESSING OFFICE
19 DATA MONITORING (EXECUTIVE LEVEL)

You can head to the third or top floors and work your way up or down to the other floor; the various rooms, experimentation chambers, and laboratory rooms all reveal the unpleasant animal testing this corporation was attempting, including the creation of a freakish two-headed bull! Continue to explore to gather some impressive loot, including rare Ultracite scrap.

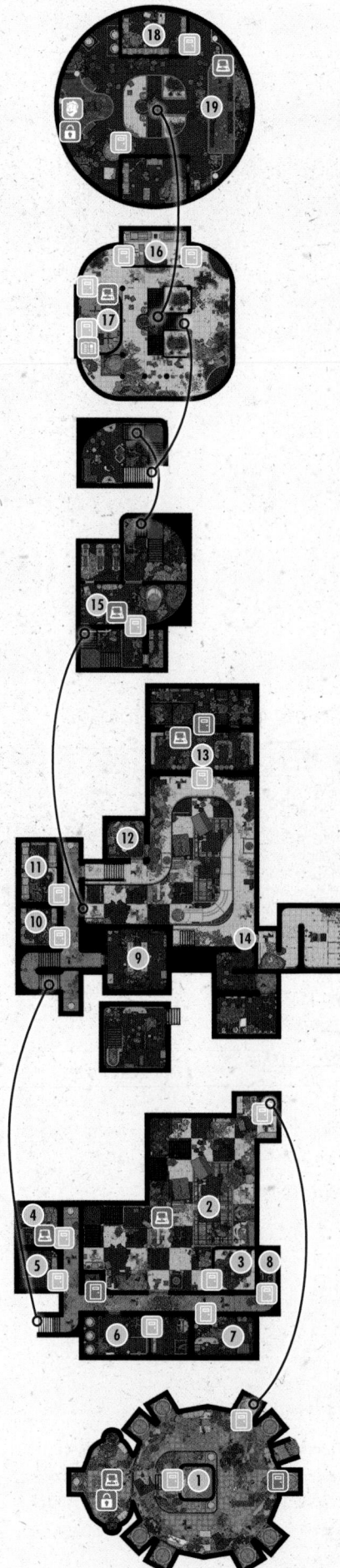

34. WATOGA SHOPPING PLAZA

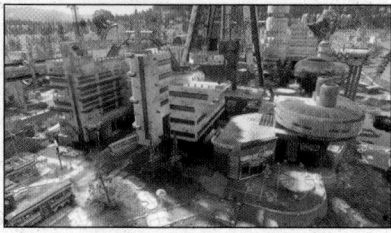

- **COLLECTIBLES:** BOBBLEHEAD, HOLOTAPE, MAGAZINE (2), NUKA-CHERRY, POWER ARMOR
- **CRAFTING:** COOKING
- **DANGER:** EXPLOSIVE CANISTER!
- **ITEMS:** ARMS AND AMMO; RECIPE/MOD/PLAN
- **INFO:** EXPECTED ENEMY: ROBOT; INSTRUMENT; SCAVENGE RATING: 3; SIZE: 4; THREAT LEVEL: 35–99; TRADER: VENDOR BOT
- **LOCK:** SAFE (2)
- **ITEM EXAMPLES:** BAG OF FERTILIZER, BLAMCO BRAND MAC AND CHEESE, BLOWTORCH, BOTTLECAP SUNGLASSES, BROOM, BURNT MANTA-MAN COMIC, CHEF HAT, CLOTHES HANGER, COFFEE CUP+, COFFEE POT+, DANDY BOY APPLES, ECONOMY WONDERGLUE, FANCY LADS SNACK CAKES, GARDEN GNOME, GAS CANISTER, GLASS PITCHER, HAIRBRUSH, HOT PLATE, INSTAMASH+, LIGHTBULB, MARKSMAN'S SNIPER RIFLE, MICROSCOPE, MOP, NUKA-COLA, NUKA-COLA BOTTLE+, PACK OF CIGARETTES, PURIFIED WATER, RED PLATE, SALT, SHOPPING BASKET, SHOT GLASS, SPICES, SUGAR, SUGAR BOMBS+, TALL DRINKING GLASS, WONDERGLUE

The northeastern part of Watoga is taken up by a large shopping plaza, featuring all the latest wares and the latest in automated purchases! That is, of course, until the bombs dropped: Now the place has mostly been picked clean, though the Responders did set up a trading post here.

SUPER-DUPER MART

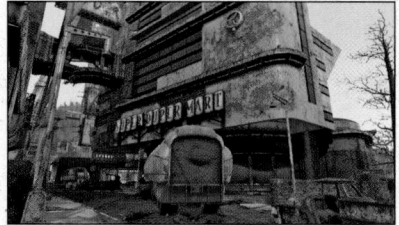

With a "spooky sale" going on right now, this Responder Trading Post is also a great place to barter with the Vendor Bot, one of the few automatons that isn't trying to kill you. Although "everything must go!" it seems most of it has; come here for the junk scraps.

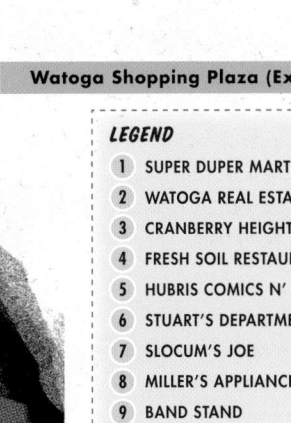

Watoga Shopping Plaza (Exterior)

LEGEND

1. SUPER DUPER MART
2. WATOGA REAL ESTATE
3. CRANBERRY HEIGHTS
4. FRESH SOIL RESTAURANT
5. HUBRIS COMICS N' TOYS
6. STUART'S DEPARTMENT STORE
7. SLOCUM'S JOE
8. MILLER'S APPLIANCES
9. BAND STAND
10. DRUMLIN DINER

WATOGA REAL ESTATE AND CRANBERRY HEIGHTS

The real estate offices and the Cranberry Heights apartments across the street (to the south) are linked via a bridge (above) and elevators (inside each office). Take either elevator bank to the roof to explore: There's a (revolting and toxic) pool, walkways, and staircases down to a balcony area and an elevator down to either office.

FRESH SOIL RESTAURANT

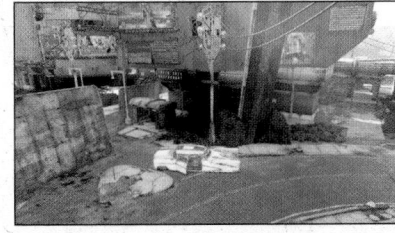

Across the road (south) of the Watoga Real Estate office is an organic restaurant. This is fully boarded up and inaccessible.

HUBRIS COMICS 'N' TOYS

Unfortunately, all the cool comics have been left smoldering, leaving little for you to hunt for, aside from a Bobblehead and holotape inside this store.

STUART'S DEPARTMENT STORE

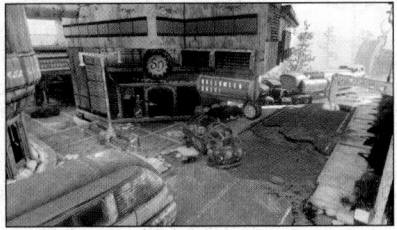

Next door to Hubris Comics is a clothing store that's been picked clean a while ago; there's little more than clothes hangers here.

SLOCUM'S JOE

There's no coffee on the boil anymore, but there's some reasonable tinned food to scavenge, as well as a possible Magazine in the rack.

MILLER'S APPLIANCES

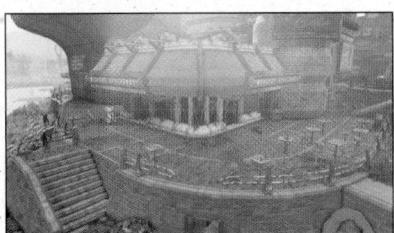

This store is full of useless washing machines, TVs, and fridges. You have better scavenging potential outside, grabbing the bottles on the cafe tables by the small jetty.

BANDSTAND

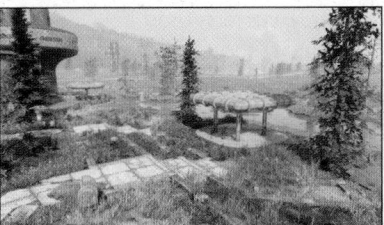

On the grassy area just north of the shopping plaza is a small bandstand with enough musical instruments for four.

DRUMLIN DINER

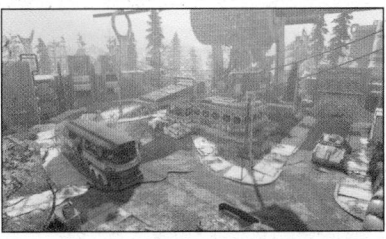

Need some bottles, condiments, and glasses to complete your junk collection? Come here, but also check outside on the sidewalk corner to the east for a possible suit of Power Armor.

TRAINING

CRAFTING AND C.A.M.P.ING

INVENTORY

QUESTS

ATLAS

BESTIARY

APPENDICES

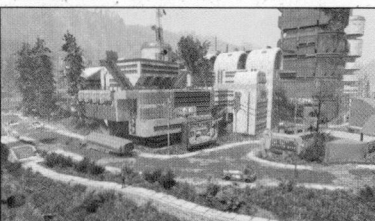

- **COLLECTIBLES:** BOBBLEHEAD, MAGAZINE
- **DANGER:** LONG DROP! RADIATION!
- **ITEMS:** RECIPE/MOD/PLAN; TRUNK
- **INFO:** EXPECTED ENEMY: ROBOT; SCAVENGE RATING: 2; SIZE: 4; THREAT LEVEL: 35–99
- **LOCK:** SAFE (2, 3)
- **ITEM EXAMPLES:** BEER BOTTLE, BLACKWATER BREW, BLAMCO BRAND MAC AND CHEESE, BREAD BIN, COFFEE CUP+, COFFEE POT, DESK FAN, DRINKING GLASS, EMPTY TEAL ROUNDED VASE, GLASS PITCHER, NAPKIN, NOODLE CUP, SHOT GLASS, TELEPHONE

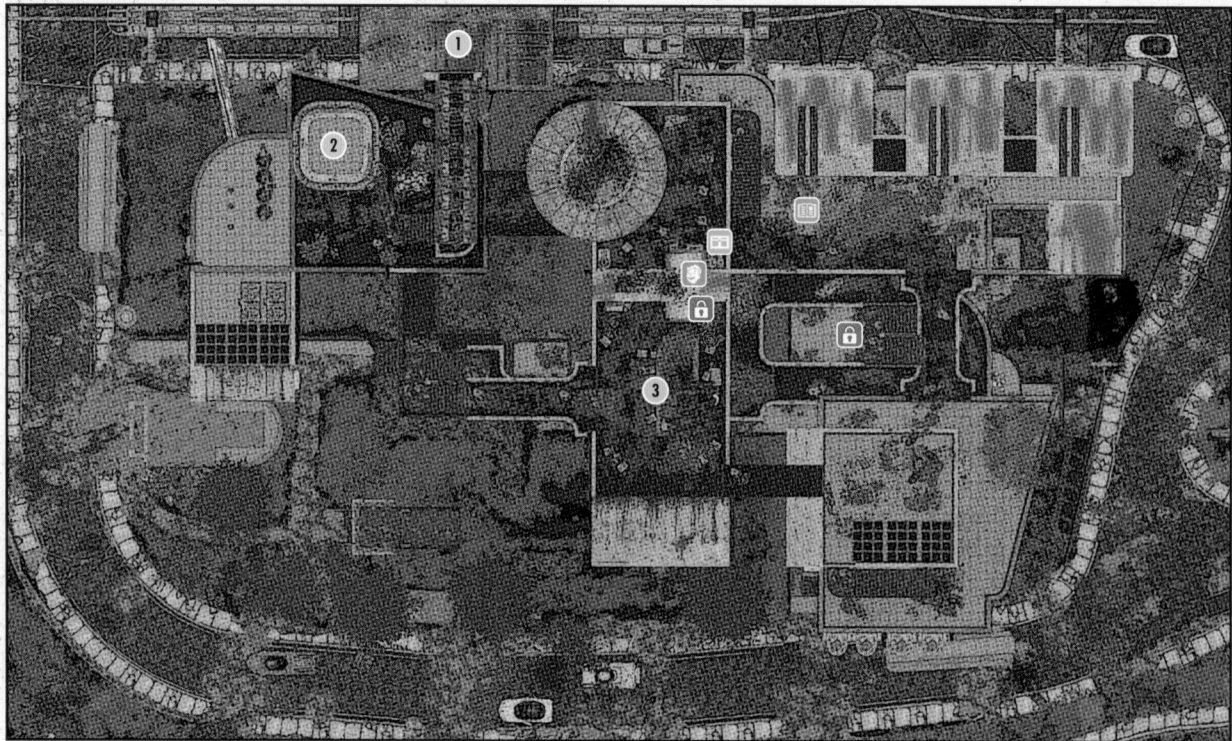

Watoga Estates (Exterior)

LEGEND

1. PRIMARY LOCATION: WATOGA TRANSIT HUB
2. WATOGA ESTATES OFFICE
3. POOL AND BAR

The majority of the residents of Watoga live in this large housing complex. Aside from the lobby, no interiors are accessible (so check the Watoga map for a visual on this predominantly white set of structures), though you are able to access the roof, with its walkways, stairs, a small set of cafe tables, and a once-swanky pool and bar area. Farther west is access to the transit hub (via ground or upper walkway). Otherwise, check the exterior grounds and structures for loot, and use the roof to your advantage should combat occur.

36. WATOGA STATION

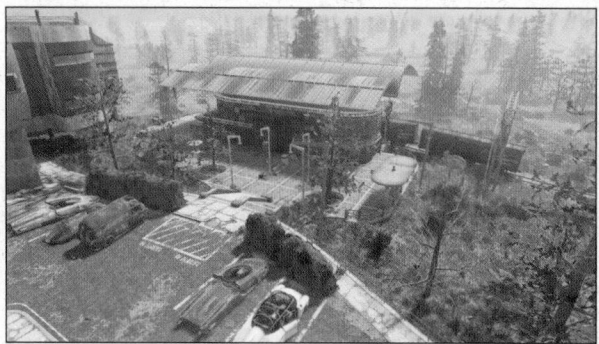

- **CRAFTING:** TINKER'S
- **ITEMS:** HARVESTABLE: MUTATED FERN; HEALTH AND CHEMS+; MY STASH BOX; VENDING MACHINE: AMMUNITION, MEDICAL SUPPLIES
- **INFO:** EXPECTED ENEMY: ROBOT; SCAVENGE RATING: 3; SIZE: 2; SLEEPING; THREAT LEVEL: 35–99; TRADER: VENDOR BOT
- **ITEM EXAMPLES:** BEER BOTTLE+, BOBBY PIN BOX, CREAM, DUCT TAPE, FUSE, GARDEN GNOME, GAS CANISTER, IMITATION SEAFOOD, INSTAMASH, MACHETE, MONGREL DOG MEAT, OAK HOLLER LAGER, TACTICAL ARMOR PIERCING PIPE PISTOL, VODKA BOTTLE

Compared to most train stations, this features a more modern and automated architecture and is close to the high school. Feel free to use this as a "base camp" (due to the My Stash Box) if you're exploring Watoga, and note the map on the wall inside the station shows some of the other available stations across Appalachia.

37. WATOGA HIGH SCHOOL

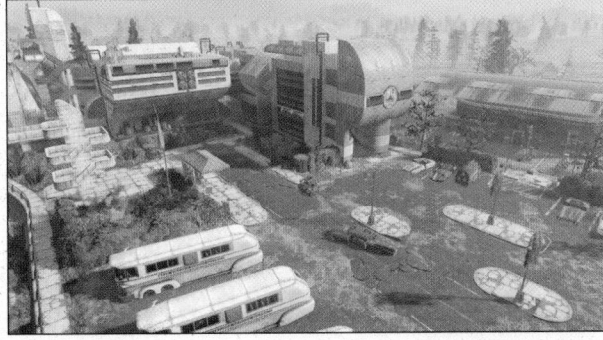

Watoga High School offered the latest in technological learning before the bombs dropped. Now it is little more than a rusting shell, despite having some intact classrooms and a still-impressive auditorium. Enter via the lobby, the auditorium, or the roof access doors. Scour the parking lot (checking the radioactive school bus for a possible collectible), and use the exterior stairwell near the train station to reach the roof for some additional items, including a possible Power Armor frame. Also check out a tent and sleeping area.

- **COLLECTIBLES:** BOBBLEHEAD (5), CAPS STASH, MAGAZINE (5), NUKA-CHERRY, NUKA-COLA QUANTUM, POWER ARMOR
- **CRAFTING:** CHEMISTRY (2), COOKING
- **DANGER:** LONG DROP! RADIOACTIVE!
- **ITEMS:** ARMS AND AMMO+; HEALTH AND CHEMS+; RECIPE/MOD/PLAN; VENDING MACHINE: TOKEN DISPENSER
- **INFO:** EXPECTED ENEMY: ROBOT; INSTRUMENT; NOTE; SCAVENGE RATING: 5+; SIZE: 4; THREAT LEVEL: 35–99
- **LOCK:** DOOR (1), SAFE (3), TERMINAL (2)
- **ITEM EXAMPLES:** ABRAXO CLEANER, BINOCULARS, BIRD DECORATION, BLACK DRINKING GLASS++, BLUE PAINT, BOILED WATER+, BURNT TEXTBOOK++, BUTTERCHURN STICK, CANNED DOG FOOD, CLOTHES HANGER, CRAM, ENAMEL BUCKET, ENHANCED TARGETING CARD, FASHIONABLE SUNGLASSES, FOLDER, GARDEN GNOME, GLASS PITCHER, GLOBE+, HOT DOG, HOUSE TEAPOT, INDUSTRIAL SOLVENT, KICKBALL, MAGNIFYING GLASS, MENTATS, MICROSCOPE, NAPKIN++, NUKA-COLA CUP, NUKA-COLA BOTTLE, OFFICE DESK FAN, OIL CANISTER, ORANGE BOWL++, ORANGE DRINKING GLASS+++, OVEN MITT, PAINTBRUSH, PLASTIC FORK++, PLASTIC KNIFE++, PLASTIC PLATE+++, PLASTIC SPOON++, PLUNGER, PORK N' BEANS, POTATO CRISPS, PURIFIED WATER, RAD POKER BOARD GAME, RUM, SCREWDRIVER, SILT BEAN SOUP, SPICES, SUGAR BOMBS, SWEET MUTFRUIT TEA, TALL DRINKING GLASS, TALL FLASK+, TEAL VAULTED VASE, TEDDY BEAR+, TELEPHONE, TEST TUBE RACK, TOILET PAPER+, TOY ALIEN, TV DINNER TRAY++, TYPEWRITER, VAULT-TEC LUNCHBOX, VEGETABLE MEDLEY SOUP, VODKA, WAKEMASTER ALARM CLOCK, WHITE BOTTLE, WINE, YELLOW PAINT

Watoga High School (Exterior)

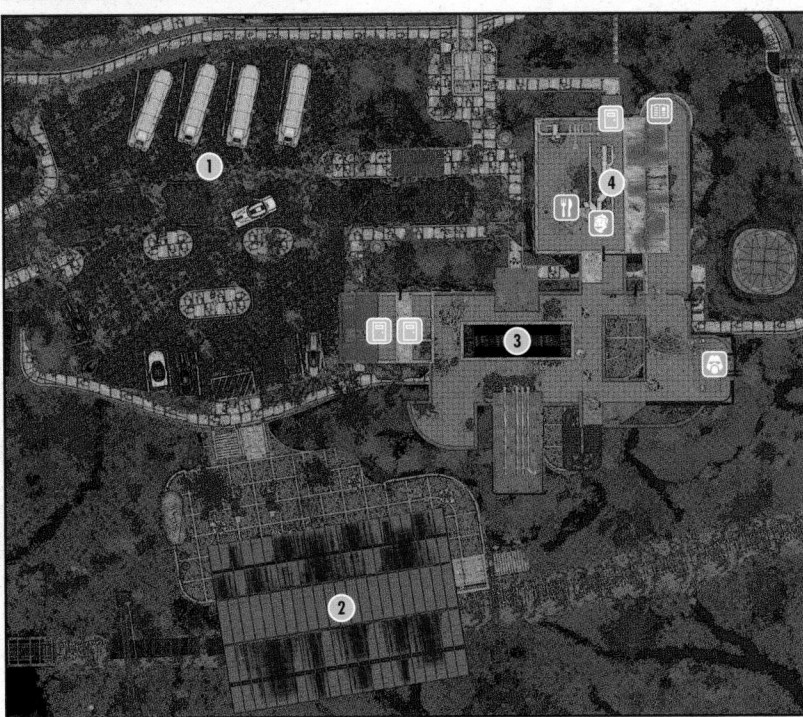

LEGEND
1. SCHOOL BUSES AND PARKING LOT
2. WATOGA STATION
3. WATOGA HIGH SCHOOL (MAIN BUILDING)
4. WATOGA HIGH SCHOOL (AUDITORIUM)

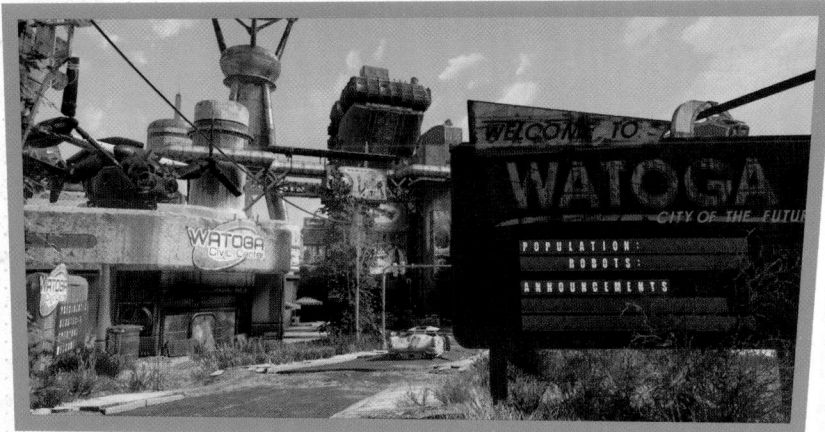

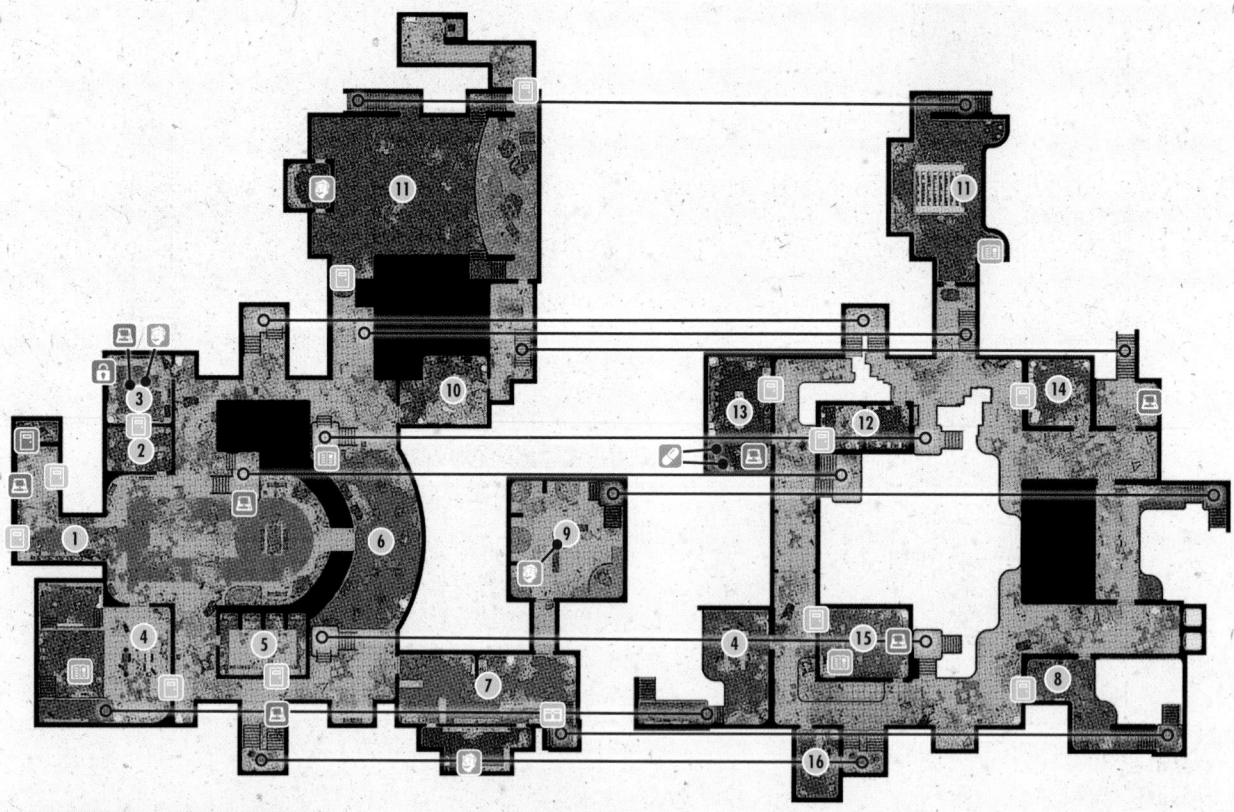

Watoga High School (Interior)

Inside, the school planners had thoughtfully included a sign above each door to indicate which room you're entering. This allows you to quickly explore and gather loot. The majority of the school is set out over two floors, along with a stairwell leading to the roof.

LEGEND

1	LOBBY	**7**	CAFETERIA	**13**	SCIENCE
2	OFFICE	**8**	UPPER CAFETERIA	**14**	BREAK ROOM
3	HEADMASTER'S OFFICE	**9**	ART STUDIO	**15**	HISTORY
4	LIBRARY	**10**	WARDROBE	**16**	LOCKERS
5	CS LAB	**11**	THEATER (AUDITORIUM)		
6	DINING AREA	**12**	RESTROOMS		

---

 38. FLOODED TRAINYARD

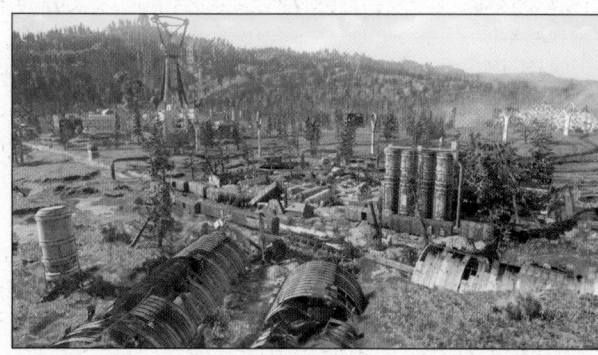

- **COLLECTIBLES:** BOBBLEHEAD, HOLOTAPE, MAGAZINE
- **CRAFTING:** ARMOR, COOKING (2), POWER ARMOR (2)
- **DANGER:** PUNJI BOARD! OIL! RADIATION!++
- **ITEMS:** ARMS AND AMMO++; HARVESTABLE: GRAVEL PIT; HEALTH AND CHEMS; RECIPE/MOD/PLAN
- **INFO:** EXPECTED ENEMY: IRRADIATED ANIMAL, IRRADIATED INSECT; SCAVENGE RATING: 4; SIZE: 3; THREAT LEVEL: 35–99
- **LOCK:** DOOR (0), SAFE (2, 2, 3)
- **ITEM EXAMPLES:** ALUMINUM CANISTER, ANTIFREEZE BOTTLE+, BOBBY PIN BOX, BOILED WATER+, CANNED CRYOGENIC GRENADE, CHESSBOARD, CIGARETTE CARTON, COFFEE CUP, COOLAND CAP, CRUSHED YELLOW CANISTER, DANDY BOY APPLES, DIRTY ASHTRAY, DOG MEAT, DUCT TAPE, EXTINGUISHER, FARMHAND CLOTHES, FUEL, GAS CANISTER+, GLASS JAR, LOOSE SPRING, MASONRY HAMMER, METAL BUCKET+, MINER'S LAMP, MINING HELMET, OIL CANISTER+, ORANGE CANISTER, PACK OF CIGARETTES, PEN, PILLOW, PORK N' BEANS, POTATO CRISPS, RADIO JAMMER, RADSTAG HIDE, RADSTAG HIDE OUTFIT, RAT POISON, SALT, SAW, SCREWDRIVER, SMALL LEFT ANTLER, TEDDY BEAR, TIN CAN+, TONGS, TORQUE ROD END, TURPENTINE, VODKA BOTTLE

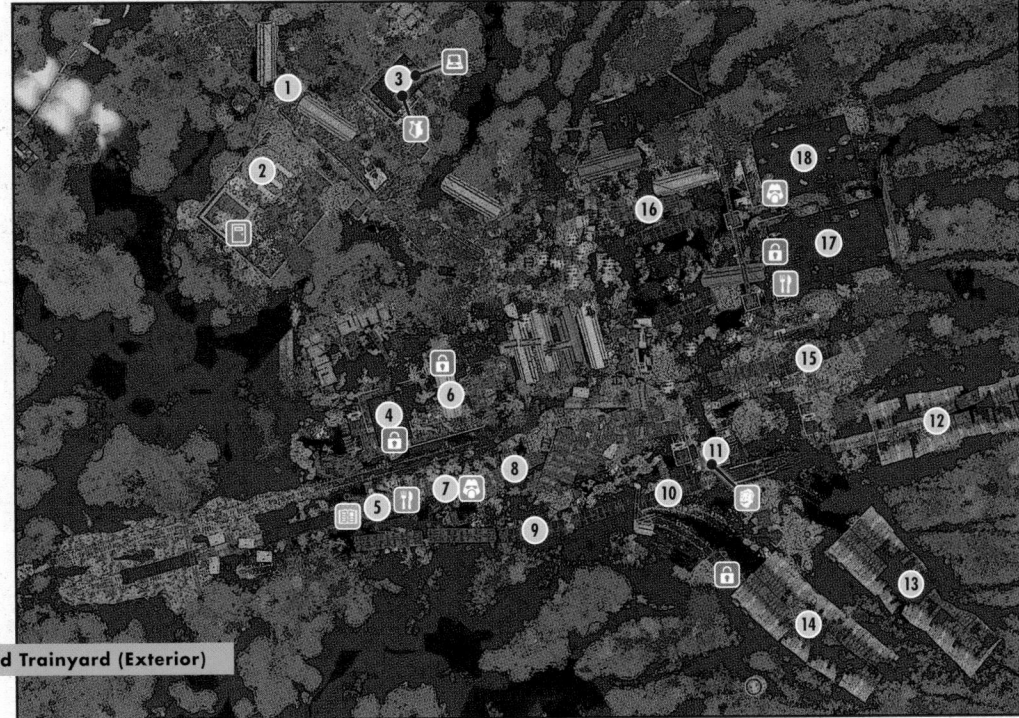

Flooded Trainyard (Exterior)

LEGEND

1 TRUCK TRAILERS	**7** POWER ARMOR STATION CARRIAGE	**13** MUD HANGAR
2 TORTURE HUT AND GENERATORS	**8** OPEN CARRIAGE (ANTIFREEZE BOTTLES)	**14** OPEN CARRIAGES HANGAR
3 MECHANIC'S GARAGE	**9** OPEN CARRIAGE (CHEM DESK)	**15** OPEN CARRIAGE (EAST)
4 GARAGE WITH SAFE	**10** OPEN CARRIAGE (WOOD GANG PLANK)	**16** OPEN CARRIAGE (HALF-SUBMERGED)
5 OPEN CARRIAGE	**11** SIGNAL TOWER	**17** TRAINYARD WAREHOUSE (ACCESS VIA ROOF)
6 TRUCK TRAILER WITH SAFE	**12** EAST HANGAR	**18** TRAINYARD WAREHOUSE (OPEN)

The road to the east of Watoga is in particular need of repair, but that's nothing compared to the mire of effluent and radiation seeping into every nook and cranny of the main trainyard in this area. Take protective clothing so you aren't constantly swallowing Rad-reducing chems and so you can use the number of workbenches and loot the open carriages.

---

39. FIREBASE HANCOCK

- **COLLECTIBLES:** BOBBLEHEAD, NUKA-CHERRY, POWER ARMOR
- **CRAFTING:** COOKING
- **DANGER:** TURRET!
- **ITEMS:** ARMS AND AMMO; HEALTH AND CHEMS; RECIPE/MOD/PLAN
- **INFO:** EXPECTED ENEMY: MOLE MINER; SCAVENGE RATING: 3; SIZE: 1; SLEEPING; THREAT LEVEL: 35–99
- **ITEM EXAMPLES:** ABRAXO CLEANER, ARMY HELMET, BINOCULARS, BOWIE KNIFE, CAN, DANDY BOY APPLES, DUCT TAPE, FRAGMENTATION GRENADE, FRAGMENTATION MINE, METAL BUCKET, MILITARY AMMO BAG, MILITARY GRADE DUCT TAPE, MINI NUKE, TOILET PAPER, TOOTHPASTE

A small Brotherhood of Steel set of defenses, including automated surface-to-air missile turrets, have been comprised. Remove threats and scour the gantry defenses and two huts for items you can use.

---

40. LOST HOME

- **COLLECTIBLES:** BOBBLEHEAD (3), HOLOTAPE, MAGAZINE (2), POWER ARMOR
- **CRAFTING:** ARMOR, COOKING (2)
- **DANGER:** TRIPWIRE!
- **ITEMS:** ARMS AND AMMO; HARVESTABLE: BRAIN FUNGUS, DISEASED CRANBERRY; HEALTH AND CHEMS
- **INFO:** EXPECTED ENEMY: IRRADIATED ANIMAL; SCAVENGE RATING: 3; SIZE: 2; SLEEPING; THREAT LEVEL: 35–99
- **ITEM EXAMPLES:** ALARM CLOCK, ASHTRAY, BROKEN DOLL, CHESSBOARD, COTTON YARN, DOG BOWL, EMPTY PAINT CAN, FOX HIDE, FUSION CORE, GLASS JAR+, LANTERN, MINI NUKE, NEW TOY CAR, OAK HOLLER LAGER BOTTLE, PIPE REVOLVER, RUM BOTTLE, SMALL LEFT ANTLER, SMALL PILLOW, SOUVENIR TEDDY BEAR, TIN PITCHER, TURPENTINE

Hidden in the bog channels is a shanty dwelling consisting of two small wooden outer hovels and a larger main shack, with a possible Power Armor on the roof. There's plenty of collectibles and a good amount of junk, making the journey well worth it.

TRAINING

CRAFTING AND C.A.M.P.ING

INVENTORY

QUESTS

ATLAS

BESTIARY

APPENDICES

41. SPARSE SUNDEW GROVE

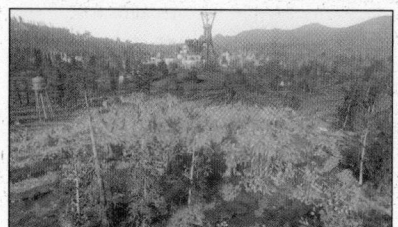

- **ITEMS: HARVESTABLE: GLOWING FUNGUS**
- **DANGER: RADIATION!**
- **INFO: EXPECTED ENEMY: GHOUL, IRRADIATED ANIMAL; SCAVENGE RATING: 1; SIZE: 2; THREAT LEVEL: 35–99**

Don't look too closely at the skeletons within the trunks of these massive carnivorous drosera plants; instead wander the bog channels, searching out scraps of items and removing foes.

42. SUNRISE FARM

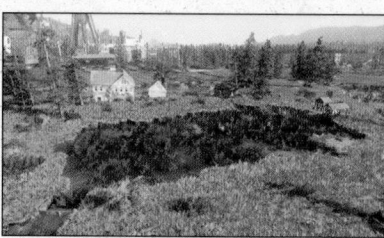

- **COLLECTIBLES: BOBBLEHEAD, MAGAZINE**
- **CRAFTING: CHEMISTRY**
- **DANGER: RADIATION!**
- **ITEMS: HARVESTABLE: CRANBERRY, DISEASED CRANBERRY; HEALTH AND CHEMS**
- **INFO: EXPECTED ENEMY: IRRADIATED ANIMAL; SCAVENGE RATING: 3; SIZE: 3; SLEEPING; THREAT LEVEL: 35–99**
- **ITEM EXAMPLES: ABRAXO CLEANER INDUSTRIAL GRADE, ALARM CLOCK, BEER BOTTLE, BOBBY PIN BOX, BOILED WATER, CAKE PAN, DISHRAG, DUCT TAPE, FUSE, GLASS JAR+++, MOONSHINE JUG, MOUNTAIN HONEY, OIL CAN, PEPPER, PILLOW, PORK N' BEANS, RAW FERTILIZER, SALISBURY STEAK, SOAP, SUGAR, WHISKEY, YUM YUM DEVILED EGGS**

The natural beauty of this small farmstead is somewhat lessened, as it's full of mud. However, it still has a surprising amount of junk to gather. Check the shed for a huge number of glass jars and a small cranberry pond, with a tiny shed on an equally small jetty.

43. SURVEY CAMP ALPHA

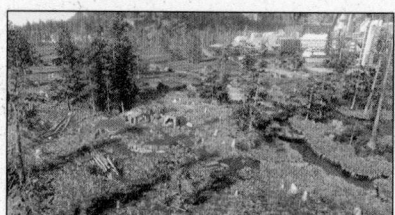

- **COLLECTIBLES: BOBBLEHEAD, MAGAZINE, NUKA-CHERRY, POWER ARMOR (2)**
- **CRAFTING: COOKING, POWER ARMOR**
- **ITEMS: ARMS AND AMMO; HARVESTABLE: BRAIN FUNGUS**
- **INFO: EXPECTED ENEMY: IRRADIATED ANIMALS; SCAVENGE RATING: 2; SIZE: 1; SLEEPING; THREAT LEVEL: 35–99**
- **ITEM EXAMPLES: ADJUSTABLE WRENCH, CANNED DOG FOOD, ENAMEL BUCKET, FUEL TANK, METAL TUB, MILITARY AMMO BAG, OIL CANISTER, PURIFIED WATER, SPICES, STEALTH BOY, TURPENTINE, VOLATILE MATERIALS BOX**

This Brotherhood of Steel camp has meager defenses, two tents, and a Power Armor Station, along with the possibility of two Power Armor frames to scavenge (one from a fallen soldier).

44. FISSURE SITE (FISSURE)

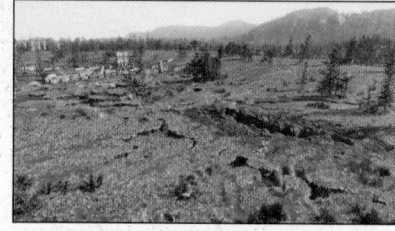

- **DANGER: LONG DROP! RADIATION!++**
- **ITEMS: HARVESTABLE: ULTRACITE, SCORCHBEAST GUANO PILE**
- **INFO: EXPECTED ENEMY: SCORCHBEAST, SCORCHED; SCAVENGE RATING: 1; SIZE: 1; THREAT LEVEL: 35–99**
- **ITEM EXAMPLES: NOT MUCH!**

Watch your wandering in this part of the Bog, as you may reach a split in the earth, where swarms of Scorched are congregating near a Scorchbeast. Battle here only if you have the mettle!

45. OVERGROWN SUNDEW GROVE

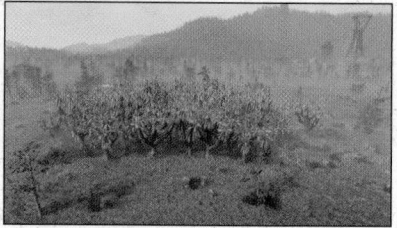

- **ITEMS: HARVESTABLE: CRANBERRY, GLOWING FUNGUS; RECIPE/MOD/PLAN**
- **DANGER: RADIATION!**
- **INFO: EXPECTED ENEMY: IRRADIATED ANIMAL, SUPER MUTANT; SCAVENGE RATING: 1; SIZE: 2; THREAT LEVEL: 35–99**
- **ITEM EXAMPLES: NOT MUCH!**

This copse of carnivorous drosera plants have swallowed up a small outbuilding or two, adding to the confusion as you attempt to navigate and check the area for items (mainly cranberry plants).

46. DROP SITE V9

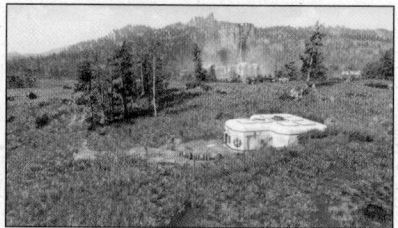

- **COLLECTIBLES: BOBBLEHEAD, POWER ARMOR (2)**
- **CRAFTING: COOKING**
- **ITEMS: HARVESTABLE: SCORCHBEAST GUANO PILE; HEALTH AND CHEMS**
- **INFO: EXPECTED ENEMY: SCORCHED; SCAVENGE RATING: 3; SIZE: 1; THREAT LEVEL: 35–99**
- **LOCK: SAFE (3)**
- **ITEM EXAMPLES: BATTERED CLIPBOARD, CIGARETTE+, CIGARETTE CARTON+, FUSION CORE, GLASS JAR, HIGH-POWERED MAGNET, MINI NUKE, PACK OF CIGARETTES, PIPE WRENCH, PURIFIED WATER, SCREWDRIVER, SKULL, STEALTH BOY, TRIFOLD AMERICAN FLAG, VACUUM TUBE**

Until recently, this small metal structure was held by the Brotherhood of Steel, and their transponder is still on the roof. Unlike the other drop sites, this isn't filled with radioactive water—instead it has a variety of high-quality junk pieces.

47. GLASSED CAVERN

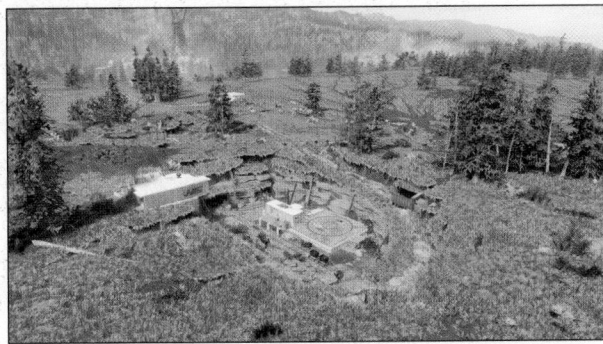

- **LOCK:** DOOR (0, 2, 3)
- **ITEM EXAMPLES:** ABRAXO CLEANER, ALUMINUM CANISTER, AUTOMATIC ASSAULT RIFLE, BAG OF CEMENT+, BEER BOTTLE, BINOCULARS, BRASS MINER'S LAMP+, BUNSEN BURNER, COFFEE CUP, COFFEE POT, ECONOMY WONDERGLUE, ENAMEL BUCKET, EXTINGUISHER+, FUEL TANK, FUSION CORE, GAS CANISTER, GLASS JAR, GRADUATED CYLINDER, HARD HAT++, HOT DOG, HOT PLATE, INDUSTRIAL OIL CANISTER, KITCHEN SCALES, LAB BOTTLE+, LEFT ARM BONES, LIGHTBULB, MAKESHIFT BATTERY, MINER HAT, MINER'S LAMP+, MINER UNIFORM, MINING HELMET, NEW RIVER RED ALE, NUKA-COLA BOTTLE, NUKA-COLA CUP, OFFICE DESK FAN, OIL CAN, OIL CANISTER, PICKAXE, PIPE WRENCH, PLUNGER, PORTABLE FUEL TANK, RAD-X+, SKULL, SURGICAL TRAY, TEDDY BEAR+, TOILET PAPER+, VODKA BOTTLE+, WAKEMASTER ALARM CLOCK, WOOD BLOCK+, YELLOW CANISTER

- **COLLECTIBLES:** CAPS STASH (2), HOLOTAPE, NUKA-CHERRY, POWER ARMOR (2)
- **CRAFTING:** COOKING
- **DANGER:** EXPLOSIVE CANISTER! RADIATION!+
- **ITEMS:** ARMS AND AMMO; HARVESTABLE: GIANT PITCHER PLANT, GLOWING FUNGUS, ULTRACITE; HEALTH AND CHEMS++; TRUNK
- **INFO:** EXPECTED ENEMY: MIRELURK, SCORCHBEAST, SCORCHED; QUEST: BELLY OF THE BEAST; SCAVENGE RATING: 4; SIZE: 4; THREAT LEVEL: 35–99

Glassed Cavern (Interior)

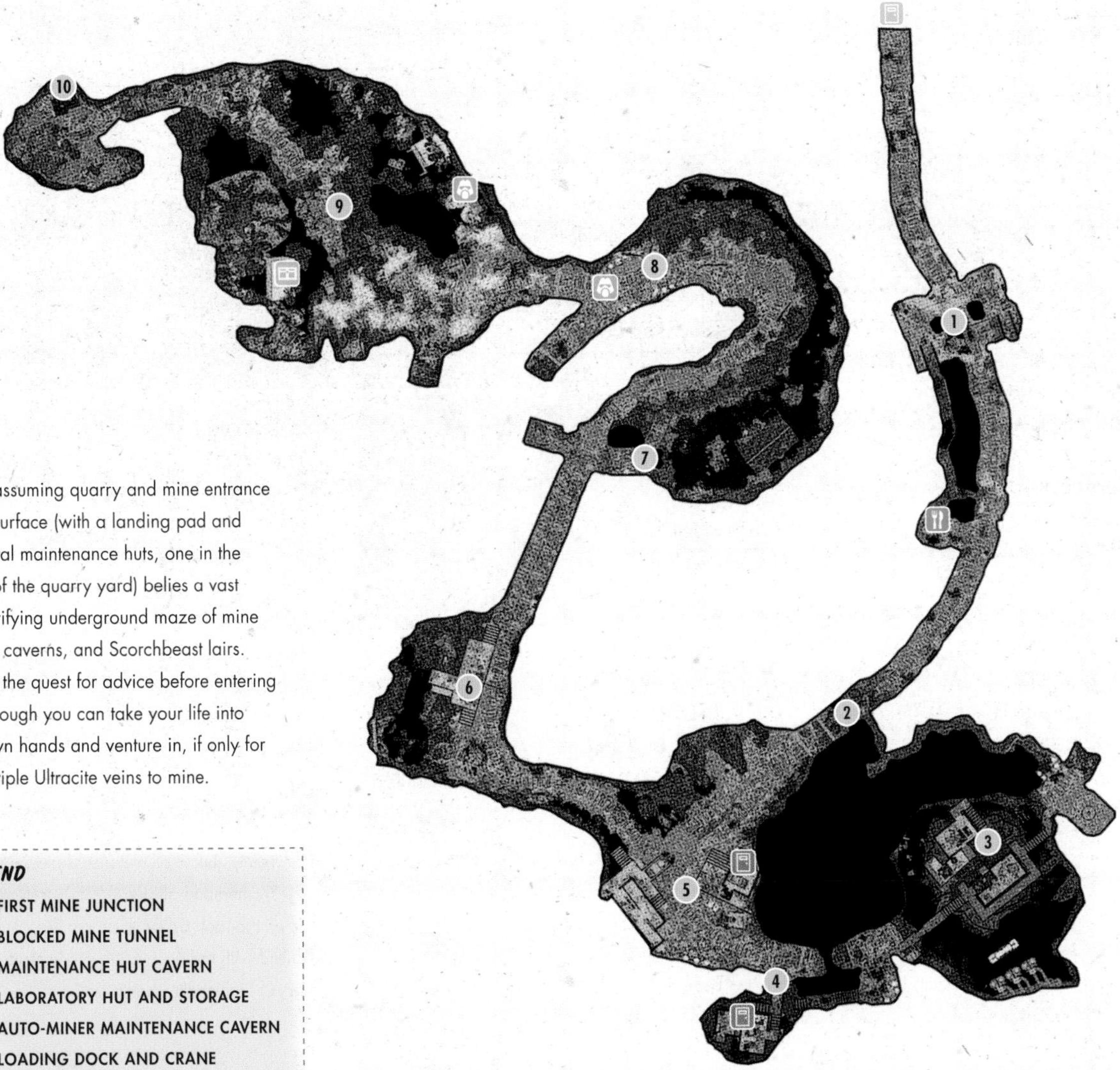

This unassuming quarry and mine entrance on the surface (with a landing pad and two metal maintenance huts, one in the center of the quarry yard) belies a vast and terrifying underground maze of mine tunnels, caverns, and Scorchbeast lairs. Consult the quest for advice before entering here, though you can take your life into your own hands and venture in, if only for the multiple Ultracite veins to mine.

LEGEND
1. FIRST MINE JUNCTION
2. BLOCKED MINE TUNNEL
3. MAINTENANCE HUT CAVERN
4. LABORATORY HUT AND STORAGE
5. AUTO-MINER MAINTENANCE CAVERN
6. LOADING DOCK AND CRANE
7. STORAGE AND WATERLOGGED SHELTER
8. MINE TRACKS JUNCTION
9. GRAND SCORCHBEAST CAVERN
10. MINE ELEVATOR

48. FISSURE SITE PRIME (FISSURE)

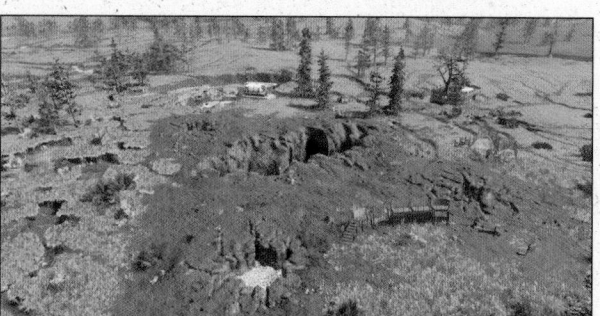

- **DANGER:** LONG DROP! RADIATION!++
- **ITEMS:** HARVESTABLE: GIANT PITCHER PLANT, SCORCHBEAST GUANO PILE, ULTRACITE
- **INFO:** EXPECTED ENEMY: SCORCHBEAST, SCORCHED; SCAVENGE RATING: 1; SIZE: 1; THREAT LEVEL: 35–99
- **ITEM EXAMPLES:** NOT MUCH!

Face extreme hardships as you navigate this area, close to the infamous Glassed Cavern. Close by is this slit in the earth, where a horde of Scorched and a Scorchbeast are lurking. Fight here with friends or superior aggression.

49. FORWARD STATION DELTA

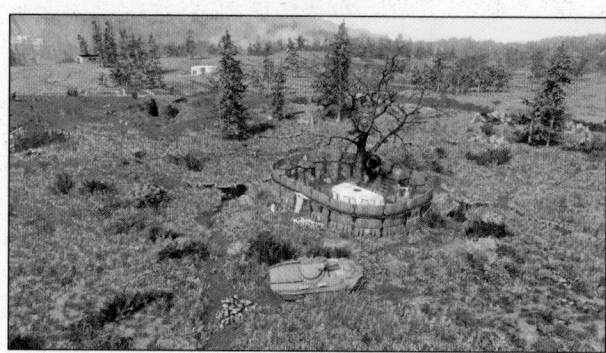

- **COLLECTIBLES:** BOBBLEHEAD (2), HOLOTAPE, MAGAZINE (2), POWER ARMOR
- **CRAFTING:** COOKING, POWER ARMOR
- **DANGER:** RADIATION!
- **ITEMS:** ARMS AND AMMO+; HARVESTABLE: DISEASED CRANBERRY, GIANT PITCHER PLANT; RECIPE/MOD/PLAN
- **INFO:** EXPECTED ENEMY: GHOUL, IRRADIATED ANIMAL; SCAVENGE RATING: 3; SIZE: 1; SLEEPING; THREAT LEVEL: 35–99
- **ITEM EXAMPLES:** 10-MM AUTO PISTOL, ARMY HELMET, BINOCULARS, BOBBY PIN BOX, FUSION CORE+, MILITARY AMMO BAG, MILITARY GRADE DUCT TAPE, PEPPER, SALT, SHORT PUMP ACTION SHOTGUN, SPICES, SUGAR, WINE BOTTLE

This small operating base marks the last stand for a group of Brotherhood of Steel soldiers whose corpses are still inside the small defensive structure.

ZONE B: SECONDARY LOCATIONS

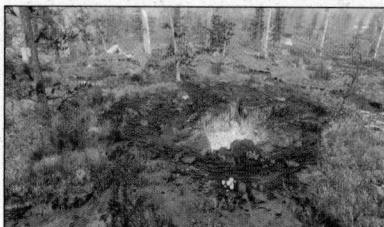

Cranberry Rad Hole: Appalachian Antiques

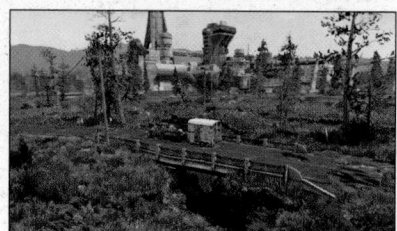

Bog Channel: Buttercup Bridge

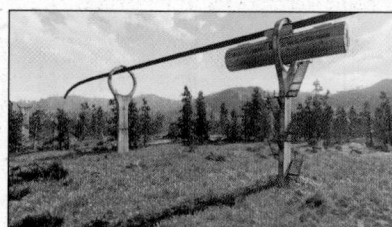

Marooned Monorail

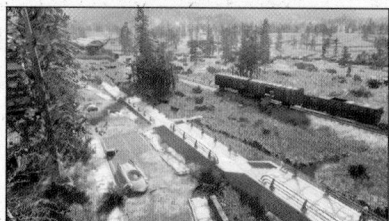

Bog Channel Bridge (South Watoga and Rail Carriages)

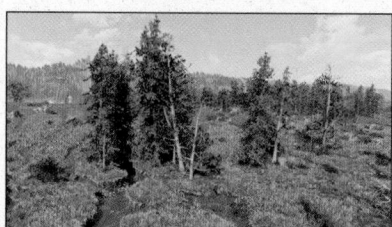

Bog Channel: Fungus Tunnel and Woods

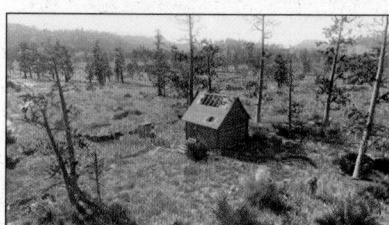

The Poet's Cottage

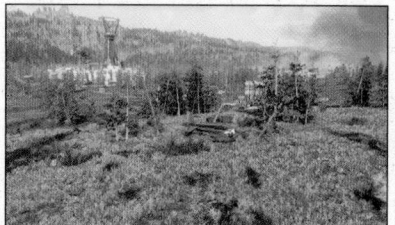

Vertibird Crash Site (Drop Site V9)

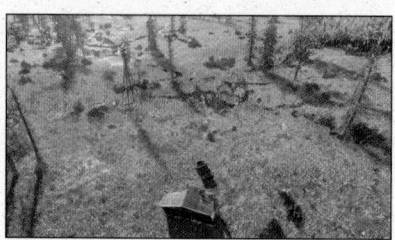

Bog Channel: Tarberry Cottage

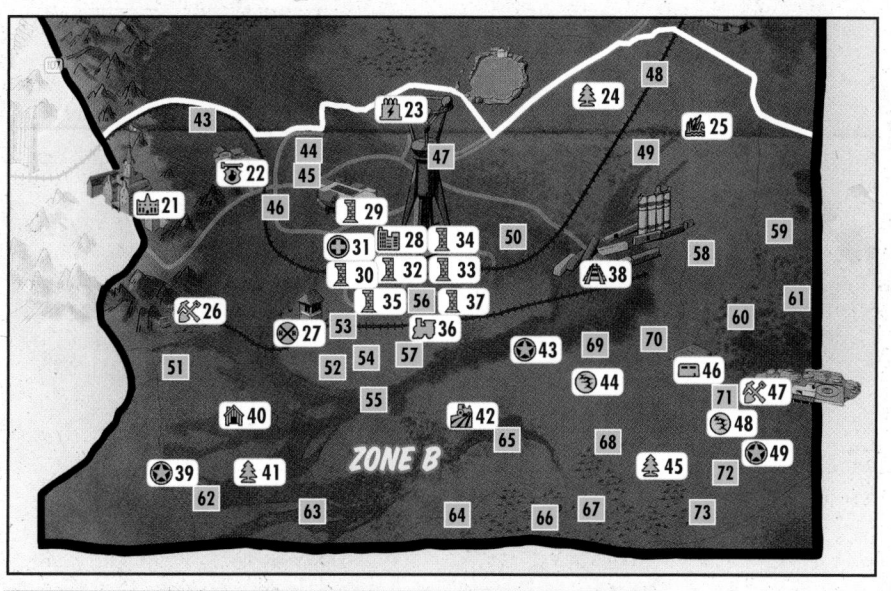

#	NAME	DESCRIPTION
43	Cranberry Rad Hole: Appalachian Antiques	A deadly hole of miasmic muck that's easy to fall into but impossible to escape from.
44	Bog Channel Nest	An L-shaped "nest" with logs on top; one of many places to hide from foes (or humans) before striking back.
45	Bog Channel: Buttercup Bridge	It seems Jangles is driving a number of Giddyup Buttercups but has been stranded on this road bridge.
46	Brotherhood of Steel Bridge Transponder JZ-3	This Brotherhood of Steel checkpoint has a transponder, but the paladins are missing; they're not even under the bridge.
47	Bog Channel: Labyrinth (Watoga exit)	Head here to access (or appear from) a lengthy, subterranean bog tunnel that runs under the freeway from here to the Abandoned Bog Town, with six possible exits along the route.
48	Marooned Monorail	A rusting staircase wrapped around a pylon leads up into a stranded monorail carriage with some loot to pick through.
49	Cranberry Rad Hole: Cranberry Glade	A deadly hole of yellow ooze that's difficult to extricate yourself from.
50	Bog Channel Dam	Use this tangle of branches and mud as a landmark when exploring the maze of channels east of Watoga.
51	Bog Channel Corpse Cave	Look below ground for a small bog cave lined with corpses and a couple of boxes to open.
52	Cranberry Rad Hole: NAR Repair Yard	A deadly hole of molten liquid, bubbling up like a fissure crack. Drop in and die.
53	Bog Channel Bridge (South Watoga and Rail Carriages)	A bridge allowing access into the south side of Watoga, and carriages with junk to gather from.
54	Military Comms Tower Watoga	A small, quest-related comms dish standing in the middle of a bog, near a spiky shelter.
55	Bog Channel: Forlorn Farmhouse	A bog channel is literally splitting a farmhouse in two, revealing silver veins and a safe (2). There's a place to sleep, too.
56	Watoga Radioactive School Bus	One of the buses parked in the school yard at Watoga High School is irradiated, with items to grab inside.
57	Bog Bridge and Streambeds	A small log dam, a bridge, and stream channels to allow the sneakier a means of heading to and from Watoga.

#	NAME	DESCRIPTION
58	Fungus Fun at the Panda Tree	A couple of imported Chinese pandas are stuck up a fungus tree. Hallucigen gas may be involved.
59	Bog Channel Fungus Tunnel and Woods	Bones and Glowing Fungus are found under this copse of tired-looking trees.
60	Cranberry Rad Hole: Drop Site V9	A deadly hole of irradiated death that's simple to slip into but much trickier to ascend up from.
61	Bog Channel Alcove	Look for the large tire at the entrance to this small alcove with a skeleton and some chems to snag.
62	Vertibird Crash Site (East of Firebase Hancock)	A vertibird didn't quite make it to the nearby Firebase and crash-landed in the bog channel to the east.
63	Cranberry Rad Hole: Sparse Sundew Grove	A deadly hole of glowing yellow lava, which spells doom for those traipsing about the bog without proper care.
64	Cranberry Rad Hole: South of Sunrise Field	A deadly hole of Scorchbeast-friendly molten magma; step into here and you don't step out again.
65	Bog Channel Settler Camp (southeast of Sunrise Field)	A fallen tree with a blue tarp on it, a sleeping bag, a cooking station, and a sense of despair; that's the Bog Channel life!
66	The Poet's Cottage	A skeleton with an unfinished poem lies in the outhouse. The nearby cottage has additional items and sleeping for at least four.
67	Bog Channel Beaver Pond	A shallow pool of logs with trees surrounding it.
68	Bog Channel Copse	Occasionally while exploring bog channels, you run into tunnels around a copse of trees. Check here for a Mini Nuke and more.
69	Bog Channel Mirelurk Alcove	If you're exploring the channels here, fend off the mutated wildlife to find a small alcove with ammo and a duffel bag.
70	Vertibird Crash Site (Drop Site V9)	A Brotherhood of Steel vertibird has hit the bog close to a drop site. There are no survivors. But there are some scavengeable items.
71	Tiny Camp	There's little but a small tent and lunch pail, but this tiny camp is worth finding if only for the holotape contained there.
72	Cranberry Rad Hole: Forward Station Delta	A deadly hole of glowing molten goo, offering instant death to those careless enough to fall into it.
73	Bog Channel: Tarberry Cottage	A cottage ripped apart by a bog channel beneath it. Find a safe (2) and a toaster in a bath.

Bestiary

ENEMY ENCOUNTERS

Appalachia has one of the most diverse ecosystems seen in a *Fallout* title to date. Step from one region to another and you'll deal with new creatures, new enemies, new climates, and new dangers. Even if you were to visit the same location twice, odds are you'd find new creatures, and some enemies are so rare that you may only see them once or twice during your entire journey.

How, then, are you supposed to know the best way to tackle enemies if you're not sure if you'll meet them more than once? We're so glad you asked.

THIS CHAPTER COVERS THE ANIMALS, ROBOTS, AND HUMANOID ENEMIES STREWN ABOUT APPALACHIA. AS YOU LEVEL UP, SO DO YOUR ENEMIES, INHERITING NEW STRENGTH AND OFTEN NEW LOOKS. DON'T WORRY. WE'VE COVERED ALL OF THOSE TOO. READ ON TO LEARN ABOUT EVERY ENEMY TYPE YOU CAN EXPECT TO FIND, ALONG WITH THEIR DIFFERENT FORMS THAT YOU'LL SEE AS YOU LEVEL UP.

ANGLERS

Anglers aren't fast, per se, but their stride allows them to glide over terrain with little resistance. They fight exclusively with melee, but their resistances and aggressive natures make them hard to kill.

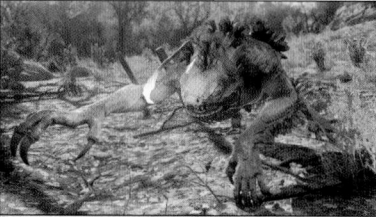

ANGLER (LVL 15)

- BASE HEALTH: 350
- DAMAGE RESISTANCE: 150
- ENERGY RESISTANCE: 125
- RADIATION RESISTANCE: 350

GLOWING ANGLER (LVL 25)

- BASE HEALTH: 525
- DAMAGE RESISTANCE: 150
- ENERGY RESISTANCE: 125
- RADIATION RESISTANCE: 350

ALBINO ANGLER (LVL 37)

- BASE HEALTH: 650
- DAMAGE RESISTANCE: 150
- ENERGY RESISTANCE: 125
- RADIATION RESISTANCE: 350

VENOMOUS ANGLER (LVL 51)

- BASE HEALTH: 900
- DAMAGE RESISTANCE: 150
- ENERGY RESISTANCE: 125
- RADIATION RESISTANCE: 350

ASSAULTRONS

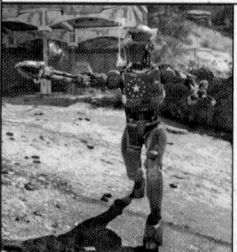

Assaultrons are highly aggressive attackers that will pursue their targets until they've blended them into people juice. Aside from trying to grind their victims up with their claw hands, some Assaultrons also fire lasers from their hands, and some even have the ability to cloak themselves, making them almost invisible. They are also capable of firing a massive, powerful laser, which they charge as they attack you. If their heads look like they're completely engulfed in flames, duck and take cover. They are about to fire their super-laser and you don't want to be anywhere near it when it goes off.

ASSAULTRON (LVL 10)

- BASE HEALTH: 230
- DAMAGE RESISTANCE: 60
- ENERGY RESISTANCE: 30
- RADIATION RESISTANCE: 60

ASSAULTRON INVADER (LVL 36)

- BASE HEALTH: 1,100
- DAMAGE RESISTANCE: 130
- ENERGY RESISTANCE: 75
- RADIATION RESISTANCE: 130

ASSAULTRON (LVL 24)

- BASE HEALTH: 660
- DAMAGE RESISTANCE: 130
- ENERGY RESISTANCE: 75
- RADIATION RESISTANCE: 130

ASSAULTRON DOMINATOR (LVL 46)

- BASE HEALTH: 1,550
- DAMAGE RESISTANCE: 130
- ENERGY RESISTANCE: 75
- RADIATION RESISTANCE: 130

BEE SWARMS

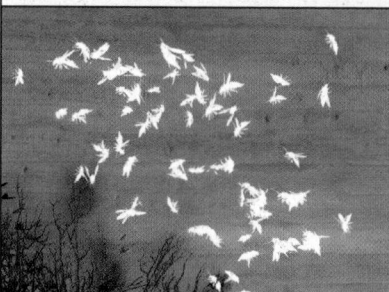

More of a nuisance than a terrifying foe, Bee Swarms come from Honey Beasts and beehives. They can be incredibly difficult to kill with ballistic guns, but explosive, energy, and melee weapons all make short work of them.

BEE SWARM (LVL 16)

- BASE HEALTH: 50
- DAMAGE RESISTANCE: 5
- ENERGY RESISTANCE: 5
- RADIATION RESISTANCE: 5

BEE SWARM (LVL 6)

- BASE HEALTH: 20
- DAMAGE RESISTANCE: 5
- ENERGY RESISTANCE: 5
- RADIATION RESISTANCE: 5

BEE SWARM (LVL 26)

- BASE HEALTH: 80
- DAMAGE RESISTANCE: 5
- ENERGY RESISTANCE: 5
- RADIATION RESISTANCE: 5

BEE SWARM (LVL 36)

- **BASE HEALTH:** 100
- **DAMAGE RESISTANCE:** 5
- **ENERGY RESISTANCE:** 5
- **RADIATION RESISTANCE:** 5

BEE SWARM (LVL 46)

- **BASE HEALTH:** 130
- **DAMAGE RESISTANCE:** 5
- **ENERGY RESISTANCE:** 5
- **RADIATION RESISTANCE:** 5

BEE SWARM (LVL 56)

- **BASE HEALTH:** 150
- **DAMAGE RESISTANCE:** 5
- **ENERGY RESISTANCE:** 5
- **RADIATION RESISTANCE:** 5

BEHEMOTHS

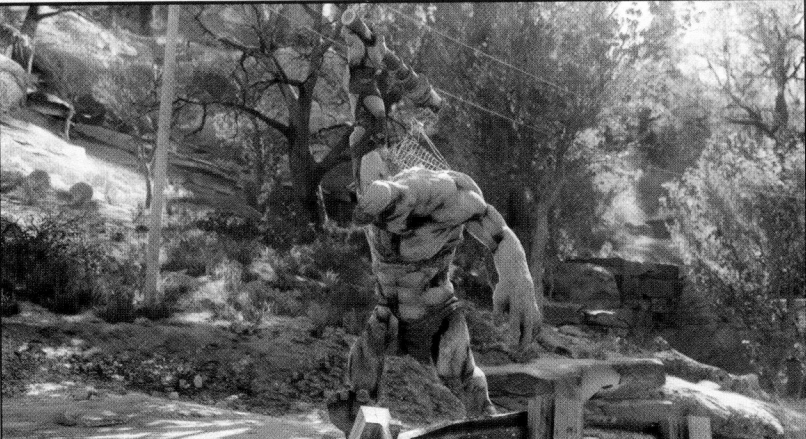

Overwhelmingly big and powerful, Behemoths are never to be taken lightly. As melee-based enemies, their long legs and arms help them close gaps quicker than most enemies. If it's anywhere near you, run fast and hard. It primarily attacks by slamming its mace down in front of it, but if you approach its side, it will stomp on the ground, damaging anything near it. Get far enough away and it will throw projectiles at you. Nowhere is safe when a Behemoth is around, so get as far away as possible.

BEHEMOTH (LVL 50)

- **BASE HEALTH:** 3,700
- **DAMAGE RESISTANCE:** 150
- **ENERGY RESISTANCE:** 100
- **RADIATION RESISTANCE:** 150

EPIC BEHEMOTH (LVL 80)

- **BASE HEALTH:** 4,025
- **DAMAGE RESISTANCE:** 250
- **ENERGY RESISTANCE:** 200
- **RADIATION RESISTANCE:** 250

GLOWING BEHEMOTH (LVL 65)

- **BASE HEALTH:** 3,850
- **DAMAGE RESISTANCE:** 250
- **ENERGY RESISTANCE:** 200
- **RADIATION RESISTANCE:** 250

ANCIENT BEHEMOTH (LVL 95)

- **BASE HEALTH:** 4,175
- **DAMAGE RESISTANCE:** 250
- **ENERGY RESISTANCE:** 200
- **RADIATION RESISTANCE:** 250

BLOATFLIES

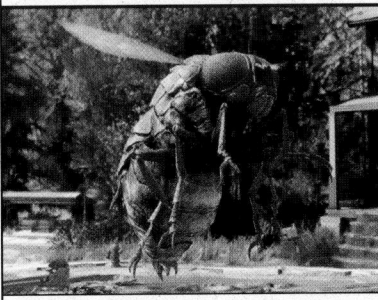

All the irritation of an actual fly, but with the added bonuses of being giant and shooting stingers. Bloatflies aren't hard to kill, but they sure can be hard to see and hit. They don't deal a lot of damage, nor can they take a lot. If you want to end the fight quickly, just activate V.A.T.S. and zap 'em.

BLOATFLY (LVL 1)

- **BASE HEALTH:** 20
- **DAMAGE RESISTANCE:** 15
- **ENERGY RESISTANCE:** 15
- **RADIATION RESISTANCE:** 15

BLACK BLOATFLY (LVL 9)

- **BASE HEALTH:** 20
- **DAMAGE RESISTANCE:** 15
- **ENERGY RESISTANCE:** 15
- **RADIATION RESISTANCE:** 15

FESTERING BLOATFLY (LVL 17)

- **BASE HEALTH:** 75
- **DAMAGE RESISTANCE:** 15
- **ENERGY RESISTANCE:** 15
- **RADIATION RESISTANCE:** 15

GLOWING BLOATFLY (LVL 27)

- **BASE HEALTH:** 75
- **DAMAGE RESISTANCE:** 15
- **ENERGY RESISTANCE:** 15
- **RADIATION RESISTANCE:** 15

BLOODBUGS

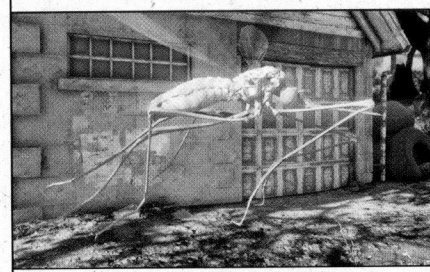

Bloodbugs scratch, sting, and bite, but what does it all really mean? They don't deal a lot of damage and they are killed by very little damage in return. Sometimes you meet a creature that's trying its little heart out for little gain and you have to ask yourself, "Why?" Hit it with a bat and end this existential crisis.

BLOODBUG HATCHLING (LVL 2)

- **BASE HEALTH:** 30
- **DAMAGE RESISTANCE:** 1
- **ENERGY RESISTANCE:** 1
- **RADIATION RESISTANCE:** 1

BLOODBUG (LVL 10)

- **BASE HEALTH:** 40
- **DAMAGE RESISTANCE:** 15
- **ENERGY RESISTANCE:** 15
- **RADIATION RESISTANCE:** 15

RED WIDOW BLOODBUG (LVL 18)

- **BASE HEALTH:** 140
- **DAMAGE RESISTANCE:** 15
- **ENERGY RESISTANCE:** 15
- **RADIATION RESISTANCE:** 15

INFECTED BLOODBUG (LVL 26)

- **BASE HEALTH:** 170
- **DAMAGE RESISTANCE:** 25
- **ENERGY RESISTANCE:** 25
- **RADIATION RESISTANCE:** 25

GLOWING BLOODBUG (LVL 34)

- **BASE HEALTH:** 180
- **DAMAGE RESISTANCE:** 25
- **ENERGY RESISTANCE:** 25
- **RADIATION RESISTANCE:** 25

VAMPIRIC BLOODBUG (LVL 42)

- **BASE HEALTH:** 250
- **DAMAGE RESISTANCE:** 25
- **ENERGY RESISTANCE:** 25
- **RADIATION RESISTANCE:** 25

TRAINING

CRAFTING AND C.A.M.P.ING

INVENTORY

QUESTS

ATLAS

BESTIARY

APPENDICES

CARGOBOTS

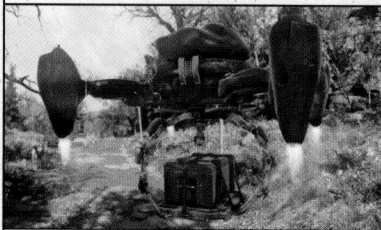

Cargobots don't attack, but they are usually worth shooting down if you spot one. They frequently carry precious cargo like supply drops and keycards for the nuclear silo locations.

CARGOBOT (LVL 15)

- BASE HEALTH: 1,450
- DAMAGE RESISTANCE: 135
- ENERGY RESISTANCE: 135
- RADIATION RESISTANCE: 135

CARGOBOT (LVL 25)

- BASE HEALTH: 2,225
- DAMAGE RESISTANCE: 135
- ENERGY RESISTANCE: 135
- RADIATION RESISTANCE: 135

CARGOBOT (LVL 35)

- BASE HEALTH: 2,750
- DAMAGE RESISTANCE: 135
- ENERGY RESISTANCE: 135
- RADIATION RESISTANCE: 135

CAVE CRICKETS

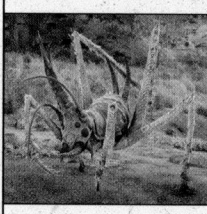

Typically found in the Mire, Cave Crickets are more creepy than they are dangerous. Can their melee attacks hurt you? Of course! But it's damage you can take without breaking a sweat. Just be warned: They have high Damage Resistance, which makes it nearly impossible to kill them quickly without an energy weapon in hand.

CAVE CRICKET (LVL 30)

- BASE HEALTH: 350
- DAMAGE RESISTANCE: 115
- ENERGY RESISTANCE: 250
- RADIATION RESISTANCE: 250

CAVE CRICKET HUNTER (LVL 38)

- BASE HEALTH: 425
- DAMAGE RESISTANCE: 115
- ENERGY RESISTANCE: 250
- RADIATION RESISTANCE: 250

CAVE CRICKET PIERCER (LVL 46)

- BASE HEALTH: 600
- DAMAGE RESISTANCE: 115
- ENERGY RESISTANCE: 250
- RADIATION RESISTANCE: 250

GLOWING CAVE CRICKET (LVL 60)

- BASE HEALTH: 800
- DAMAGE RESISTANCE: 115
- ENERGY RESISTANCE: 250
- RADIATION RESISTANCE: 250

DEATHCLAWS

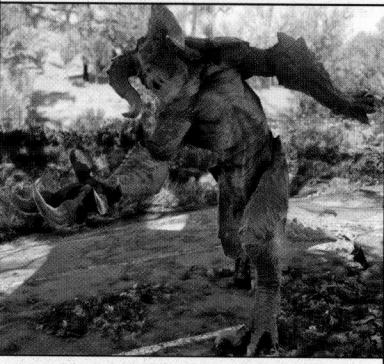

As scary as they are powerful, Deathclaws are the kings of beasts across the whole of Appalachia. If you see one, avoid it unless you have specific reason to kill one. They are fast and their claws will make you regret even facing them in the first place. Try to keep an obstacle between you and it, or climb on top of something it can't climb.

DEATHCLAW (LVL 21)

- BASE HEALTH: 625
- DAMAGE RESISTANCE: 150
- ENERGY RESISTANCE: 150
- RADIATION RESISTANCE: 150

ALPHA DEATHCLAW (LVL 31)

- BASE HEALTH: 850
- DAMAGE RESISTANCE: 150
- ENERGY RESISTANCE: 150
- RADIATION RESISTANCE: 150

GLOWING DEATHCLAW (LVL 41)

- BASE HEALTH: 1,050
- DAMAGE RESISTANCE: 150
- ENERGY RESISTANCE: 150
- RADIATION RESISTANCE: 150

DEATHCLAW MATRIARCH (LVL 51)

- BASE HEALTH: 1,150
- DAMAGE RESISTANCE: 300
- ENERGY RESISTANCE: 300
- RADIATION RESISTANCE: 300

SAVAGE DEATHCLAW (LVL 61)

- BASE HEALTH: 1,300
- DAMAGE RESISTANCE: 300
- ENERGY RESISTANCE: 300
- RADIATION RESISTANCE: 300

ALBINO DEATHCLAW (LVL 71)

- BASE HEALTH: 1,450
- DAMAGE RESISTANCE: 300
- ENERGY RESISTANCE: 300
- RADIATION RESISTANCE: 300

CHAMELEON DEATHCLAW (LVL 81)

- BASE HEALTH: 1575
- DAMAGE RESISTANCE: 300
- ENERGY RESISTANCE: 300
- RADIATION RESISTANCE: 300

MYTHIC DEATHCLAW (LVL 91)

- BASE HEALTH: 1,725
- DAMAGE RESISTANCE: 300
- ENERGY RESISTANCE: 300
- RADIATION RESISTANCE: 300

EYEBOTS

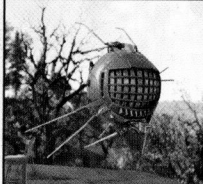

Eyebots aren't typically hostile toward Vault Dwellers. In fact, aside from attacking the local, violent wildlife, some Eyebots will actually reveal locations to you as they fly by. If you do end up fighting one, it will drop with a few attacks from any weapon.

EYEBOT (LVL 1)

- BASE HEALTH: 20
- DAMAGE RESISTANCE: 10
- ENERGY RESISTANCE: 10
- RADIATION RESISTANCE: 10

FERAL GHOULS

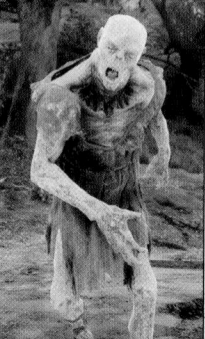

Feral Ghouls are highly aggressive, persistent, and some of the fastest creatures in Appalachia. Once they decide to attack you, they'll chase you down no matter where you go. Their attacks only involve them swatting you with their hands, but don't take them lightly. They typically attack in groups; if you're not careful, they'll surround you and turn you into a bloody mess.

To deal with them, your best bet is to give them the same aggression they showed you. Pull out your most powerful weapon and take them out as they approach. The only other option is to get on top of something they can't climb and pick them off from there.

FERAL GHOUL (LVL 3)

- BASE HEALTH: 35
- DAMAGE RESISTANCE: 10
- ENERGY RESISTANCE: 20
- RADIATION RESISTANCE: 1,000

FERAL GHOUL ROAMER (9)

- BASE HEALTH: 40
- DAMAGE RESISTANCE: 10
- ENERGY RESISTANCE: 20
- RADIATION RESISTANCE: 1,000

FERAL GHOUL STALKER (LVL 15)

- BASE HEALTH: 80
- DAMAGE RESISTANCE: 85
- ENERGY RESISTANCE: 140
- RADIATION RESISTANCE: 1,000

FERAL GHOUL REAVER (22)

- BASE HEALTH: 90
- DAMAGE RESISTANCE: 85
- ENERGY RESISTANCE: 140
- RADIATION RESISTANCE: 1,000

WITHERED FERAL GHOUL (LVL 32)

- BASE HEALTH: 125
- DAMAGE RESISTANCE: 85
- ENERGY RESISTANCE: 140
- RADIATION RESISTANCE: 1,000

GANGRENOUS FERAL GHOUL (LVL 42)

- BASE HEALTH: 150
- DAMAGE RESISTANCE: 85
- ENERGY RESISTANCE: 140
- RADIATION RESISTANCE: 1,000

ROTTING FERAL GHOUL (LVL 52)

- BASE HEALTH: 200
- DAMAGE RESISTANCE: 85
- ENERGY RESISTANCE: 140
- RADIATION RESISTANCE: 1,000

CHARRED FERAL GHOUL (LVL 62)

- BASE HEALTH: 300
- DAMAGE RESISTANCE: 85
- ENERGY RESISTANCE: 140
- RADIATION RESISTANCE: 1,000

FOG CRAWLERS

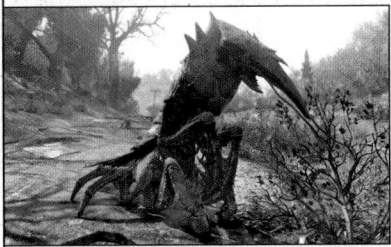

Fog Crawlers are very slow melee-focused enemies with high resistances. You'll have a hard time killing them with weaker weapons, but you can easily avoid them by sprinting. If they appear in groups with other monsters, you might be in for some trouble. But on their own they pose little threat to anything but your patience.

FOG CRAWLER (LVL 27)

- BASE HEALTH: 975
- DAMAGE RESISTANCE: 100
- ENERGY RESISTANCE: 100
- RADIATION RESISTANCE: 100

GLOWING FOG CRAWLER (LVL 39)

- BASE HEALTH: 1,200
- DAMAGE RESISTANCE: 100
- ENERGY RESISTANCE: 100
- RADIATION RESISTANCE: 100

SKULKING FOG CRAWLER (LVL 51)

- BASE HEALTH: 1,575
- DAMAGE RESISTANCE: 125
- ENERGY RESISTANCE: 100
- RADIATION RESISTANCE: 125

DISEASED FOG CRAWLER (LVL 63)

- BASE HEALTH: 1,775
- DAMAGE RESISTANCE: 125
- ENERGY RESISTANCE: 100
- RADIATION RESISTANCE: 125

ENRAGED FOG CRAWLER (LVL 75)

- BASE HEALTH: 1,975
- DAMAGE RESISTANCE: 125
- ENERGY RESISTANCE: 100
- RADIATION RESISTANCE: 125

GLOWING ONES

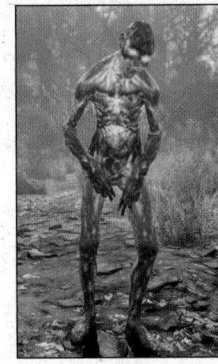

Glowing Ones are an irradiated version of Feral Ghouls. They attack in the same fashion but with the added threat of increasing the Rads of anyone they stand near. Take them out quickly and keep your distance if you want to avoid losing you max HP to their radiation.

GLOWING ONE (LVL 22)

- BASE HEALTH: 690
- DAMAGE RESISTANCE: 115
- ENERGY RESISTANCE: 230
- RADIATION RESISTANCE: 1,000

PUTRID GLOWING ONE (LVL 40)

- BASE HEALTH: 1,150
- DAMAGE RESISTANCE: 115
- ENERGY RESISTANCE: 230
- RADIATION RESISTANCE: 1,000

BLOATED GLOWING ONE (LVL 58)

- BASE HEALTH: 1,625
- DAMAGE RESISTANCE: 115
- ENERGY RESISTANCE: 230
- RADIATION RESISTANCE: 1,000

GULPERS

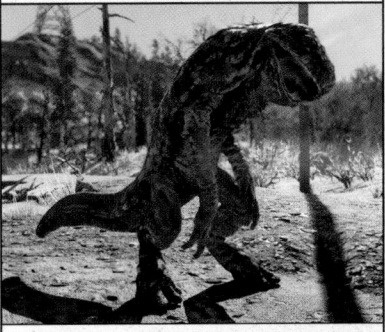

Gulpers aren't the brightest bulbs of the bunch, but they are slippery little devils. They'll chase you down and give you a quick nibble from their tiny, sharp teeth. Even if you're sprinting, they'll catch up with you. You best bet is to either get on top of something they can't climb, or take them down directly. Run and they'll get you—always remember that.

GULPER NEWT (LVL 10)

- BASE HEALTH: 250
- DAMAGE RESISTANCE: 30
- ENERGY RESISTANCE: 30
- RADIATION RESISTANCE: 250

GULPER (LVL 22)

- BASE HEALTH: 750
- DAMAGE RESISTANCE: 90
- ENERGY RESISTANCE: 90
- RADIATION RESISTANCE: 250

GLOWING GULPER (LVL 34)

- BASE HEALTH: 1,025
- DAMAGE RESISTANCE: 90
- ENERGY RESISTANCE: 90
- RADIATION RESISTANCE: 250

GULPER DEVOURER (LVL 46)

- BASE HEALTH: 1,800
- DAMAGE RESISTANCE: 90
- ENERGY RESISTANCE: 90
- RADIATION RESISTANCE: 250

TRAINING

CRAFTING AND C.A.M.P.ING

INVENTORY

QUESTS

ATLAS

BESTIARY

APPENDICES

HERMIT CRABS

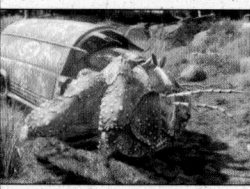

Hermit Crabs are gigantic, van-wearing crustaceans with Rad-infected claws and resistance to just about anything under the sun. They are hard to outrun, but they have a hard time getting through tight spaces—use those to your advantage. If you want to have any hope of killing them, you must target their bodies and not the car attached to their backs; shooting that will yield no results.

They don't have many attacks, but they hit hard and are insanely persistent. Find a space they can't climb through, like a house or a van, and attack from there. Taking them on directly will cost you a lot more than it's worth.

ALPHA HERMIT CRAB (LVL 31)

- **BASE HEALTH:** 850
- **DAMAGE RESISTANCE:** 150
- **ENERGY RESISTANCE:** 100
- **RADIATION RESISTANCE:** 150

GLOWING HERMIT CRAB (LVL 41)

- **BASE HEALTH:** 1,050
- **DAMAGE RESISTANCE:** 150
- **ENERGY RESISTANCE:** 100
- **RADIATION RESISTANCE:** 150

SAVAGE HERMIT CRAB (LVL 51)

- **BASE HEALTH:** 1,475
- **DAMAGE RESISTANCE:** 150
- **ENERGY RESISTANCE:** 100
- **RADIATION RESISTANCE:** 150

GIANT HERMIT CRAB (LVL 21)

- **BASE HEALTH:** 625
- **DAMAGE RESISTANCE:** 150
- **ENERGY RESISTANCE:** 100
- **RADIATION RESISTANCE:** 150

ALBINO HERMIT CRAB (LVL 61)

- **BASE HEALTH:** 1,650
- **DAMAGE RESISTANCE:** 150
- **ENERGY RESISTANCE:** 100
- **RADIATION RESISTANCE:** 150

LIBERATORS

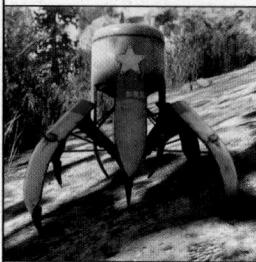

Liberators aren't particularly strong on their own, but their agility, small size, and numbers often make them a fearsome enemy. You'll have to avoid laser and melee attacks, so don't be afraid to hop behind cover if things start getting hot. Use V.A.T.S. to cut their numbers down quickly. The fewer of them there are, the less damage potential they possess.

LIBERATOR MK 0 (LVL 5)

- **BASE HEALTH:** 25
- **DAMAGE RESISTANCE:** 10
- **ENERGY RESISTANCE:** 10
- **RADIATION RESISTANCE:** 10

LIBERATOR MK I (LVL 10)

- **BASE HEALTH:** 30
- **DAMAGE RESISTANCE:** 10
- **ENERGY RESISTANCE:** 10
- **RADIATION RESISTANCE:** 10

LIBERATOR MK II (LVL 18)

- **BASE HEALTH:** 100
- **DAMAGE RESISTANCE:** 10
- **ENERGY RESISTANCE:** 10
- **RADIATION RESISTANCE:** 10

LIBERATOR MK III (LVL 30)

- **BASE HEALTH:** 150
- **DAMAGE RESISTANCE:** 10
- **ENERGY RESISTANCE:** 10
- **RADIATION RESISTANCE:** 10

LIBERATOR MK IV (LVL 42)

- **BASE HEALTH:** 200
- **DAMAGE RESISTANCE:** 10
- **ENERGY RESISTANCE:** 10
- **RADIATION RESISTANCE:** 10

LIBERATOR MK V (LVL 54)

- **BASE HEALTH:** 300
- **DAMAGE RESISTANCE:** 10
- **ENERGY RESISTANCE:** 10
- **RADIATION RESISTANCE:** 10

HONEY BEASTS

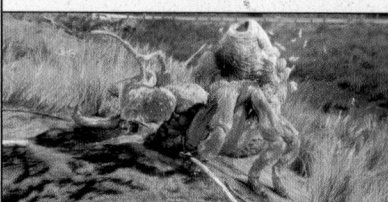

Honey Beasts are slow, but they are resilient. They aren't particularly deadly, but you definitely don't want them anywhere near you. When they are close to enemies, they release Bee Swarms from the hive on their backs. It can be really easy to get locked in a cycle of trying to kill Bee Swarms, rather than taking the Honey Beast on directly. Attack and kill them at a distance and they'll never get the chance to let a Bee Swarm free.

PUTRIFIED HONEY BEAST (LVL 26)

- **BASE HEALTH:** 620
- **DAMAGE RESISTANCE:** 100
- **ENERGY RESISTANCE:** 100
- **RADIATION RESISTANCE:** 250

RAGING HONEY BEAST (LVL 36)

- **BASE HEALTH:** 700
- **DAMAGE RESISTANCE:** 125
- **ENERGY RESISTANCE:** 125
- **RADIATION RESISTANCE:** 250

GLOWING HONEY BEAST (LVL 46)

- **BASE HEALTH:** 900
- **DAMAGE RESISTANCE:** 150
- **ENERGY RESISTANCE:** 150
- **RADIATION RESISTANCE:** 250

HONEY BEAST (LVL 16)

- **BASE HEALTH:** 450
- **DAMAGE RESISTANCE:** 75
- **ENERGY RESISTANCE:** 75
- **RADIATION RESISTANCE:** 250

ULTRACITE HONEY BEAST (LVL 56)

- **BASE HEALTH:** 1,050
- **DAMAGE RESISTANCE:** 175
- **ENERGY RESISTANCE:** 175
- **RADIATION RESISTANCE:** 250

MEGA SLOTHS

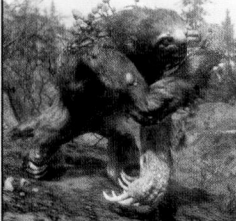

Mega Sloths might look intimidating at first glance, but they are very surmountable. They aren't fast, but you allow them to get in close, they'll swipe at you with their giant claws or shake poison spores from their backs, dealing poison damage over time. If you keep your distance, they'll pelt you with rocks. Keep your distance and strafe to avoid getting pelted by the rocks. If it can't hit you, it can't hurt you. Pull out a powerful gun and give it hell.

MEGA SLOTH (LVL 30)

- **BASE HEALTH:** 775
- **DAMAGE RESISTANCE:** 200
- **ENERGY RESISTANCE:** 150
- **RADIATION RESISTANCE:** 250

PONDEROUS MEGA SLOTH (LVL 40)

- **BASE HEALTH:** 975
- **DAMAGE RESISTANCE:** 200
- **ENERGY RESISTANCE:** 150
- **RADIATION RESISTANCE:** 250

SCORCHED MEGA SLOTH (LVL 50)

- **BASE HEALTH:** 1,500
- **DAMAGE RESISTANCE:** 200
- **ENERGY RESISTANCE:** 150
- **RADIATION RESISTANCE:** 250

MIRELURKS

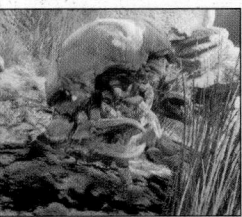

Mirelurks primarily follow the same rules of engagement: shoot their bodies, not the shell on their backs. Don't try to circle them (they are actually quite fast and can easily keep up with their foe) and keep your distance. If you can follow these rules, you'll have little trouble with these pesky sea spiders.

SOFTSHELL MIRELURK (LVL 5)

- **BASE HEALTH:** 35
- **DAMAGE RESISTANCE:** 45
- **ENERGY RESISTANCE:** 40
- **RADIATION RESISTANCE:** 200

MIRELURK (LVL 12)

- **BASE HEALTH:** 50
- **DAMAGE RESISTANCE:** 90
- **ENERGY RESISTANCE:** 90
- **RADIATION RESISTANCE:** 250

MIRELURK RAZORCLAW (LVL 18)

- **BASE HEALTH:** 160
- **DAMAGE RESISTANCE:** 90
- **ENERGY RESISTANCE:** 90
- **RADIATION RESISTANCE:** 250

MIRELURK KILLCLAW (LVL 26)

- **BASE HEALTH:** 250
- **DAMAGE RESISTANCE:** 90
- **ENERGY RESISTANCE:** 90
- **RADIATION RESISTANCE:** 250

GLOWING MIRELURK (LVL 34)

- **BASE HEALTH:** 275
- **DAMAGE RESISTANCE:** 90
- **ENERGY RESISTANCE:** 90
- **RADIATION RESISTANCE:** 250

BLOODRAGE MIRELURK (LVL 42)

- **BASE HEALTH:** 350
- **DAMAGE RESISTANCE:** 303
- **ENERGY RESISTANCE:** 290
- **RADIATION RESISTANCE:** 250

MIRELURK HUNTERS

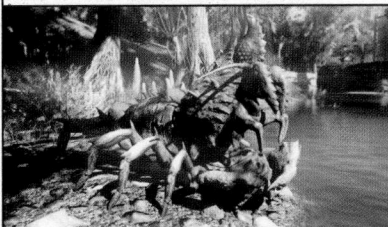

Hunters don't have the same back protection that normal Mirelurks have. Instead they rely on spitting projectiles and speed to take down their foes. Keep your distance and circle them while shooting to make quick work of any Hunters you meet.

MIRELURK HUNTER (LVL 24)

- **BASE HEALTH:** 275
- **DAMAGE RESISTANCE:** 90
- **ENERGY RESISTANCE:** 90
- **RADIATION RESISTANCE:** 250

GLOWING MIRELURK HUNTER (LVL 34)

- **BASE HEALTH:** 375
- **DAMAGE RESISTANCE:** 90
- **ENERGY RESISTANCE:** 90
- **RADIATION RESISTANCE:** 250

ALBINO MIRELURK HUNTER (LVL 46)

- **BASE HEALTH:** 650
- **DAMAGE RESISTANCE:** 90
- **ENERGY RESISTANCE:** 90
- **RADIATION RESISTANCE:** 250

MIRELURK KINGS

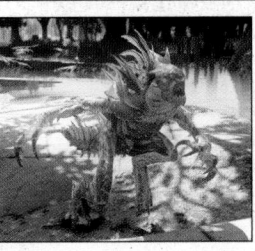

Extremely resistant to energy weapons, Mirelurk Kings can be a real bear to take down. They aren't particularly fast, and unlike their smaller offspring, they can't keep up with an enemy that is circle-strafing them. They shoot projectiles and can turn invisible, reappearing only when they are ready to strike your blind side. They can take a whole lot of effort and focus to defeat, but they can definitely be defeated.

MIRELURK KING (LVL 30)

- **BASE HEALTH:** 1,275
- **DAMAGE RESISTANCE:** 50
- **ENERGY RESISTANCE:** 75
- **RADIATION RESISTANCE:** 250

MIRELURK DEEP KING (LVL 40)

- **BASE HEALTH:** 1,575
- **DAMAGE RESISTANCE:** 50
- **ENERGY RESISTANCE:** 75
- **RADIATION RESISTANCE:** 250

GLOWING MIRELURK KING (LVL 50)

- **BASE HEALTH:** 2,200
- **DAMAGE RESISTANCE:** 140
- **ENERGY RESISTANCE:** 350
- **RADIATION RESISTANCE: IMMUNE**

MIRELURK QUEENS

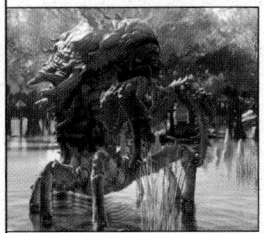

Mirelurk Queens are giant and fast, and their poisonous spit is truly deadly. They are hard to avoid and hard to kill. Your best bet is to get as far away as possible and attack from a distance. Their spit can travel long distances and is fired in a volley, rather than one shot at a time. They also birth Mirelurk Spawn to help aid them in taking down their prey. Mirelurk Queens are truly dangerous; tread carefully.

MIRELURK QUEEN (LVL 20)

- **BASE HEALTH:** 2,125
- **DAMAGE RESISTANCE:** 150
- **ENERGY RESISTANCE:** 100
- **RADIATION RESISTANCE:** 150

MIRELURK QUEEN (LVL 35)

- **BASE HEALTH:** 2,650
- **DAMAGE RESISTANCE:** 150
- **ENERGY RESISTANCE:** 100
- **RADIATION RESISTANCE:** 150

MIRELURK QUEEN (LVL 50)

- **BASE HEALTH:** 3,725
- **DAMAGE RESISTANCE:** 150
- **ENERGY RESISTANCE:** 100
- **RADIATION RESISTANCE:** 150

MIRELURK SPAWN

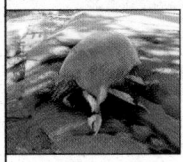

Not intimidating on their own, Mirelurk Spawn are slow and easy to kill. They are only truly dangerous when spawned by a Mirelurk Queen; the combination of fighting both the Spawn and the Queen makes for one challenging fight.

MIRELURK SPAWN (LVL 1)

- **BASE HEALTH:** 25
- **DAMAGE RESISTANCE:** 5
- **ENERGY RESISTANCE:** 5
- **RADIATION RESISTANCE:** 5

MOLE MINERS

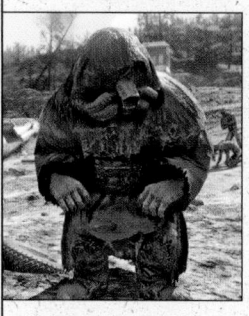

Mole Miners are a soldier-type enemy like Scorched and Super Mutants. They brandish melee weapons and guns and are rarely ever found alone. They have high resistances but aren't particularly fast. You'll find them at any mine in Appalachia and the Ash Heap.

FAMISHED MOLE MINER (LVL 2)

- **BASE HEALTH:** 40
- **DAMAGE RESISTANCE:** 50
- **ENERGY RESISTANCE:** 25
- **RADIATION RESISTANCE:** 250

TIRED MOLE MINER (LVL 4)

- **BASE HEALTH:** 45
- **DAMAGE RESISTANCE:** 50
- **ENERGY RESISTANCE:** 25
- **RADIATION RESISTANCE:** 250

MOLE MINER LABORER (LVL 8)

- **BASE HEALTH:** 50
- **DAMAGE RESISTANCE:** 50
- **ENERGY RESISTANCE:** 25
- **RADIATION RESISTANCE:** 250

MOLE MINER (LVL 14)

- **BASE HEALTH:** 225
- **DAMAGE RESISTANCE:** 50
- **ENERGY RESISTANCE:** 25
- **RADIATION RESISTANCE:** 250

ANGRY MOLE MINER (LVL 22)

- **BASE HEALTH:** 250
- **DAMAGE RESISTANCE:** 100
- **ENERGY RESISTANCE:** 75
- **RADIATION RESISTANCE:** 250

MOLE MINER SUPERVISOR (LVL 30)

- **BASE HEALTH:** 325
- **DAMAGE RESISTANCE:** 100
- **ENERGY RESISTANCE:** 75
- **RADIATION RESISTANCE:** 250

FURIOUS MOLE MINER BATTLER (LVL 40)

- **BASE HEALTH:** 400
- **DAMAGE RESISTANCE:** 100
- **ENERGY RESISTANCE:** 75
- **RADIATION RESISTANCE:** 250

MOLE RATS

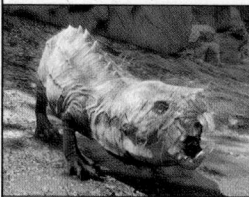

These pests are so irritating you'll be praying for another bomb to drop in the off chance it removes them from the face of the planet. They may not be powerful, they may not have many attacks, but dang it they are persistent and like to attack in groups. They'll bury themselves underground, then pop up right next to you. They are also quite small, making them harder to hit than most enemies. If you see one, turn on V.A.T.S. and send it to the great molehill in the sky. You'll be doing us all a favor.

MOLE RAT (LVL 1)

- **BASE HEALTH:** 15
- **DAMAGE RESISTANCE:** 5
- **ENERGY RESISTANCE:** 5
- **RADIATION RESISTANCE:** 5

GLOWING MOLE RAT (LVL 14)

- **BASE HEALTH:** 65
- **DAMAGE RESISTANCE:** 5
- **ENERGY RESISTANCE:** 5
- **RADIATION RESISTANCE:** 5

RABID MOLE RAT (LVL 7)

- **BASE HEALTH:** 45
- **DAMAGE RESISTANCE:** 5
- **ENERGY RESISTANCE:** 5
- **RADIATION RESISTANCE:** 5

MOLE RAT BROOD MOTHER (LVL 21)

- **BASE HEALTH:** 175
- **DAMAGE RESISTANCE:** 10
- **ENERGY RESISTANCE:** 10
- **RADIATION RESISTANCE:** 10

MONGRELS

Mongrels are fodder enemies. They aren't fast, they don't hit hard, and they don't have much health. They attack very similarly to Mole Rats, but slower and without the ability to bury themselves. A few hits from anything is all it takes to take one down.

WILD MONGREL (LVL 3)

- **BASE HEALTH:** 35
- **DAMAGE RESISTANCE:** 10
- **ENERGY RESISTANCE:** 10
- **RADIATION RESISTANCE:** 10

RABID MONGREL (LVL 40)

- **BASE HEALTH:** 250
- **DAMAGE RESISTANCE:** 15
- **ENERGY RESISTANCE:** 15
- **RADIATION RESISTANCE:** 15

VICIOUS MONGREL (LVL 12)

- **BASE HEALTH:** 50
- **DAMAGE RESISTANCE:** 10
- **ENERGY RESISTANCE:** 10
- **RADIATION RESISTANCE:** 10

GLOWING MONGREL (LVL 50)

- **BASE HEALTH:** 350
- **DAMAGE RESISTANCE:** 20
- **ENERGY RESISTANCE:** 20
- **RADIATION RESISTANCE:** 20

FERAL MONGREL (LVL 20)

- **BASE HEALTH:** 150
- **DAMAGE RESISTANCE:** 15
- **ENERGY RESISTANCE:** 15
- **RADIATION RESISTANCE:** 15

ALPHA GLOWING MONGREL (LVL 60)

- **BASE HEALTH:** 750
- **DAMAGE RESISTANCE:** 20
- **ENERGY RESISTANCE:** 20
- **RADIATION RESISTANCE:** 20

ALBINO MONGREL (LVL 30)

- **BASE HEALTH:** 200
- **DAMAGE RESISTANCE:** 15
- **ENERGY RESISTANCE:** 15
- **RADIATION RESISTANCE:** 15

MR. HANDIES

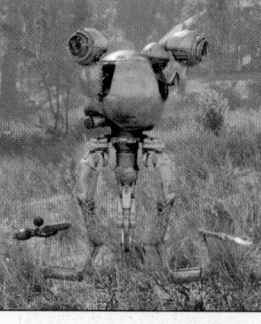

Mr. Handy can be hard to get away from, but it doesn't have enough health to truly be a threat. It mostly attacks with melee strikes, but it can also pull out a pretty mean flamethrower if you're out of its reach. If you see a Mr. Handy coming for you, don't run. Pull out any weapon and hit it a few times to send it to the scrapyard.

MR. FARMHAND (LVL 1)

- **BASE HEALTH:** 35
- **DAMAGE RESISTANCE:** 10
- **ENERGY RESISTANCE:** 5
- **RADIATION RESISTANCE:** 10

MR. HANDY (LVL 8)

- **BASE HEALTH:** 35
- **DAMAGE RESISTANCE:** 10
- **ENERGY RESISTANCE:** 5
- **RADIATION RESISTANCE:** 10

PRISON MARSHAL (LVL 14)

- **BASE HEALTH:** 55
- **DAMAGE RESISTANCE:** 10
- **ENERGY RESISTANCE:** 5
- **RADIATION RESISTANCE:** 10

MR. GUTSIES

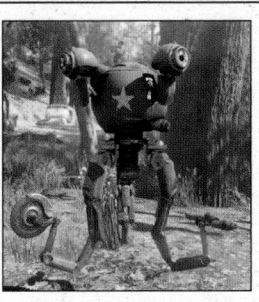

This is Mr. Handy's meaner, tankier cousin. There aren't many differences between Mr. Handy and Mr. Gutsy, aside from resistances, but be prepared to deal with Mr. Gutsy's much more robust arsenal. Each Gutsy can come with a variety of weapons, but they'll mostly rely on lasers and ballistic weapons to take you down.

LIEUTENANT GUTSY (LVL 32)

— **BASE HEALTH:** 350
— **DAMAGE RESISTANCE:** 110
— **ENERGY RESISTANCE:** 100
— **RADIATION RESISTANCE:** 110

MAJOR GUTSY (LVL 40)

— **BASE HEALTH:** 425
— **DAMAGE RESISTANCE:** 110
— **ENERGY RESISTANCE:** 100
— **RADIATION RESISTANCE:** 110

MR. GUTSY (LVL 22)

— **BASE HEALTH:** 280
— **DAMAGE RESISTANCE:** 80
— **ENERGY RESISTANCE:** 70
— **RADIATION RESISTANCE:** 80

COLONEL GUTSY (LVL 47)

— **BASE HEALTH:** 600
— **DAMAGE RESISTANCE:** 110
— **ENERGY RESISTANCE:** 100
— **RADIATION RESISTANCE:** 110

MUTANT HOUNDS

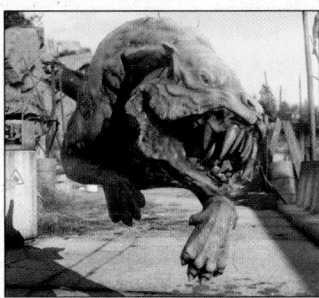

Mutant Hounds are rarely seen away from the sides of their Super Mutant masters. They aren't terribly difficult to fight by themselves, but they do add a good bit of pressure to any Super Mutant encounter. They do little more than chase and bite, but they have decent resilience, which makes for a good distraction in the middle of a chaotic battle.

MUTANT HOUND (LVL 8)

— **BASE HEALTH:** 35
— **DAMAGE RESISTANCE:** 15
— **ENERGY RESISTANCE:** 10
— **RADIATION RESISTANCE:** 15

GLOWING MUTANT HOUND (LVL 28)

— **BASE HEALTH:** 150
— **DAMAGE RESISTANCE:** 40
— **ENERGY RESISTANCE:** 30
— **RADIATION RESISTANCE:** 40

PROTECTRONS

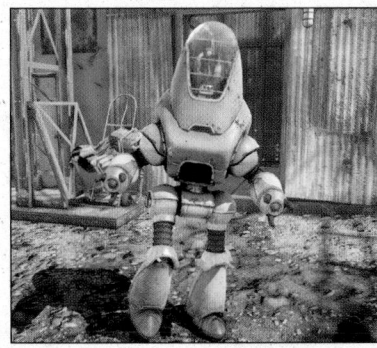

PROTECTRON WATCHER (LVL 14)

— **DAMAGE RESISTANCE:** 25
— **ENERGY RESISTANCE:** 15
— **RADIATION RESISTANCE:** 15

PROTECTRON GUARDIAN (LVL 26)

— **DAMAGE RESISTANCE:** 75
— **ENERGY RESISTANCE:** 50
— **RADIATION RESISTANCE:** 75

PROTECTRON DEFENDER (LVL 36)

— **DAMAGE RESISTANCE:** 75
— **ENERGY RESISTANCE:** 50
— **RADIATION RESISTANCE:** 75

Protectrons aren't very threatening. Sure, they shoot lasers, but those lasers hardly do damage and they can't take much of a beating. Aim for their head dome and they'll drop like a busted toaster in a garbage can.

PROTECTRON (LVL 5)

— **DAMAGE RESISTANCE:** 25
— **ENERGY RESISTANCE:** 15
— **RADIATION RESISTANCE:** 15

PROTECTRON SENTINEL (LVL 46)

— **DAMAGE RESISTANCE:** 125
— **ENERGY RESISTANCE:** 100
— **RADIATION RESISTANCE:** 125

RAD ANTS

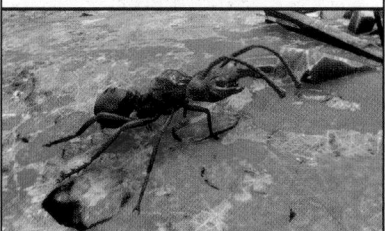

Rad Ants aren't particularly dangerous. They aren't very fast and their only attack strategy is to chase and bite. Even in large numbers, they are still very manageable. Just watch your toes and you'll be just fine.

SMALL FORAGER ANT (LVL 1)

— **BASE HEALTH:** 35
— **DAMAGE RESISTANCE:** 10
— **ENERGY RESISTANCE:** 20
— **RADIATION RESISTANCE:** 250

SMALL SOLDIER ANT (LVL 4)

— **BASE HEALTH:** 40
— **DAMAGE RESISTANCE:** 10
— **ENERGY RESISTANCE:** 20
— **RADIATION RESISTANCE:** 250

SMALL GLOWING ANT (LVL 8)

— **BASE HEALTH:** 50
— **DAMAGE RESISTANCE:** 10
— **ENERGY RESISTANCE:** 20
— **RADIATION RESISTANCE:** 250

FORAGER ANT (LVL 12)

— **BASE HEALTH:** 65
— **DAMAGE RESISTANCE:** 10
— **ENERGY RESISTANCE:** 20
— **RADIATION RESISTANCE:** 250

SOLDIER ANT (LVL 16)

— **BASE HEALTH:** 95
— **DAMAGE RESISTANCE:** 40
— **ENERGY RESISTANCE:** 50
— **RADIATION RESISTANCE:** 250

GLOWING ANT (LVL 20)

— **BASE HEALTH:** 110
— **DAMAGE RESISTANCE:** 40
— **ENERGY RESISTANCE:** 50
— **RADIATION RESISTANCE:** 250

OVERGROWN FORAGER ANT (LVL 24)

— **BASE HEALTH:** 120
— **DAMAGE RESISTANCE:** 50
— **ENERGY RESISTANCE:** 60
— **RADIATION RESISTANCE:** 250

OVERGROWN SOLDIER ANT (LVL 28)

— **BASE HEALTH:** 130
— **DAMAGE RESISTANCE:** 50
— **ENERGY RESISTANCE:** 60
— **RADIATION RESISTANCE:** 250

OVERGROWN GLOWING ANT (LVL 32)

— **BASE HEALTH:** 150
— **DAMAGE RESISTANCE:** 50
— **ENERGY RESISTANCE:** 60
— **RADIATION RESISTANCE:** 250

TRAINING

CRAFTING AND C.A.M.P.ING

INVENTORY

QUESTS

ATLAS

BESTIARY

APPENDICES

RAD ROACHES

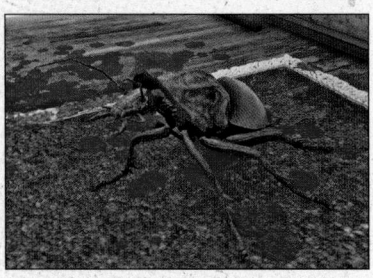

Rad Roaches are hardly a threat. In fact, you're more likely to die from a heart attack when one of these things unexpectedly falls from the ceiling than you are to die from their attacks. Just listen for the telltale nasty bug noise they make to know when they're near; then stomp them back to the Stone Age.

RAD ROACH (LVL 1)

- **BASE HEALTH:** 20
- **DAMAGE RESISTANCE:** 5
- **ENERGY RESISTANCE:** 5
- **RADIATION RESISTANCE:** 250

GLOWING RAD ROACH (LVL 5)

- **BASE HEALTH:** 30
- **DAMAGE RESISTANCE:** 5
- **ENERGY RESISTANCE:** 5
- **RADIATION RESISTANCE:** 250

RADROACH (LVL 10)

- **BASE HEALTH:** 35
- **DAMAGE RESISTANCE:** 5
- **ENERGY RESISTANCE:** 5:
- **RADIATION RESISTANCE:** 250

RAD STAGS

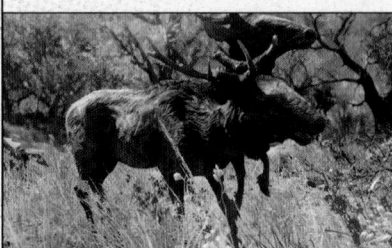

Rad Stags are mostly nonhostile, but some of them will attack you with little warning (i.e., Erratic, Rabid, Devolved, and Glowing Rad Stags). They aren't very strong, nor are they fast, but they do have delicious meat that's worth pursuing them for.

RADSTAG YEARLING (LVL 1)

- **DAMAGE RESISTANCE:** 10
- **ENERGY RESISTANCE:** 20
- **RADIATION RESISTANCE:** 250

RADSTAG DOE (LVL 4)

- **DAMAGE RESISTANCE:** 10
- **ENERGY RESISTANCE:** 20
- **RADIATION RESISTANCE:** 250

RADSTAG (LVL 10)

- **DAMAGE RESISTANCE:** 30
- **ENERGY RESISTANCE:** 40
- **RADIATION RESISTANCE:** 250

ERRATIC RADSTAG DOE (LVL 12)

- **DAMAGE RESISTANCE:** 30
- **ENERGY RESISTANCE:** 40
- **RADIATION RESISTANCE:** 250

ALBINO RADSTAG (LVL 16)

- **DAMAGE RESISTANCE:** 90
- **ENERGY RESISTANCE:** 50
- **RADIATION RESISTANCE:** 250

ERRATIC RADSTAG (LVL 21)

- **DAMAGE RESISTANCE:** 90
- **ENERGY RESISTANCE:** 50
- **RADIATION RESISTANCE:** 250

RABID RADSTAG (LVL 24)

- **DAMAGE RESISTANCE:** 90
- **ENERGY RESISTANCE:** 50
- **RADIATION RESISTANCE:** 250

DEVOLVED RADSTAG DOE (LVL 26)

- **DAMAGE RESISTANCE:** 110
- **ENERGY RESISTANCE:** 60
- **RADIATION RESISTANCE:** 250

GLOWING RADSTAG (LVL 32)

- **DAMAGE RESISTANCE:** 110
- **ENERGY RESISTANCE:** 60
- **RADIATION RESISTANCE:** 250

DEVOLVED RADSTAG (LVL 40)

- **DAMAGE RESISTANCE:** 130
- **ENERGY RESISTANCE:** 70
- **RADIATION RESISTANCE:** 250

RAD TOADS

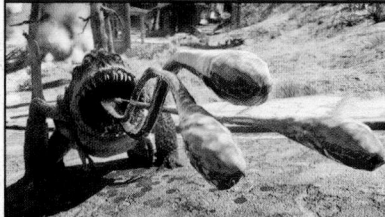

Rad Toads look more like creatures from some dark, forgotten dimension than anything actually resembling a toad. Their attacks also match their terrifying appearance. Whipping you with their three tongues, biting you with their gnarled teeth, or leaving exploding egg mines all over the ground to make escape more dangerous, the Rad Toad is not a creature to ignore. Thankfully they are painfully slow, so get some distance and erase these abominations from your realm.

RAD TOAD (LVL 5)

- **BASE HEALTH:** 60
- **DAMAGE RESISTANCE:** 25
- **ENERGY RESISTANCE:** 25
- **RADIATION RESISTANCE:** 250

PARASITIC RAD TOAD (LVL 18)

- **BASE HEALTH:** 150
- **DAMAGE RESISTANCE:** 100
- **ENERGY RESISTANCE:** 100
- **RADIATION RESISTANCE:** 250

GLOWING RAD TOAD (LVL 28)

- **BASE HEALTH:** 225
- **DAMAGE RESISTANCE:** 100
- **ENERGY RESISTANCE:** 100
- **RADIATION RESISTANCE:** 250

ALBINO RAD TOAD (LVL 40)

- **BASE HEALTH:** 250
- **DAMAGE RESISTANCE:** 150
- **ENERGY RESISTANCE:** 150
- **RADIATION RESISTANCE:** 250

SCORCHED RAD TOAD (LVL 50)

- **BASE HEALTH:** 350
- **DAMAGE RESISTANCE:** 150
- **ENERGY RESISTANCE:** 150
- **RADIATION RESISTANCE:** 250

RADRATS

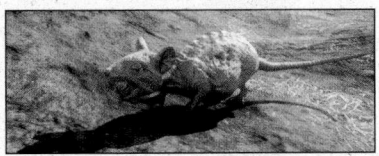

Radrats are pests more than actual threats. They aren't very fast and their only means of offense is biting with its two giant teeth. It's not a very dangerous enemy, but it can be a massive pain to land hits on. We suggest using V.A.T.S. the second you see this enemy to take it out swiftly.

MANGY RADRAT PUP (LVL 4)

- **BASE HEALTH:** 35
- **DAMAGE RESISTANCE:** 10
- **ENERGY RESISTANCE:** 20
- **RADIATION RESISTANCE:** 250

MANGY RADRAT (LVL 16)

- **BASE HEALTH:** 100
- **DAMAGE RESISTANCE:** 40
- **ENERGY RESISTANCE:** 50
- **RADIATION RESISTANCE:** 250

RADRAT (LVL 8)

- **BASE HEALTH:** 45
- **DAMAGE RESISTANCE:** 10
- **ENERGY RESISTANCE:** 20
- **RADIATION RESISTANCE:** 250

INFECTED RADRAT (LVL 20)

- **BASE HEALTH:** 120
- **DAMAGE RESISTANCE:** 40
- **ENERGY RESISTANCE:** 50
- **RADIATION RESISTANCE:** 250

RADRAT PUP (LVL 1)

- **BASE HEALTH:** 30
- **DAMAGE RESISTANCE:** 10
- **ENERGY RESISTANCE:** 20
- **RADIATION RESISTANCE:** 250

INFECTED RADRAT PUP (LVL 12)

- **BASE HEALTH:** 55
- **DAMAGE RESISTANCE:** 10
- **ENERGY RESISTANCE:** 20
- **RADIATION RESISTANCE:** 250

GLOWING PLAGUED RADRAT (LVL 25)

- **BASE HEALTH:** 150
- **DAMAGE RESISTANCE:** 40
- **ENERGY RESISTANCE:** 50
- **RADIATION RESISTANCE:** 250

RADSCORPIONS

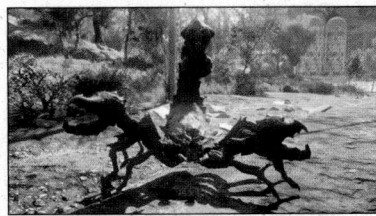

Radscorpions are resilient and aggressive. They attack exclusively with melee attacks, but they are fast enough and hard enough to kill that they can reach you before you can kill them, unless you're packing some serious firepower. Their stinger hits you with a burst of Rads, while their pincers are quick and painful. Get somewhere high to avoid taking damage from this thing.

RADSCORPION (LVL 14)

- **BASE HEALTH:** 150
- **DAMAGE RESISTANCE:** 50
- **ENERGY RESISTANCE:** 35
- **RADIATION RESISTANCE:** 350

ALBINO RADSCORPION (LVL 38)

- **BASE HEALTH:** 650
- **DAMAGE RESISTANCE:** 150
- **ENERGY RESISTANCE:** 125
- **RADIATION RESISTANCE:** 350

RADSCORPION HUNTER (LVL 22)

- **BASE HEALTH:** 390
- **DAMAGE RESISTANCE:** 150
- **ENERGY RESISTANCE:** 125
- **RADIATION RESISTANCE:** 350

RADSCORPION STALKER (LVL 46)

- **BASE HEALTH:** 900
- **DAMAGE RESISTANCE:** 150
- **ENERGY RESISTANCE:** 125
- **RADIATION RESISTANCE:** 350

GLOWING RADSCORPION (LVL 30)

- **BASE HEALTH:** 525
- **DAMAGE RESISTANCE:** 150
- **ENERGY RESISTANCE:** 125
- **RADIATION RESISTANCE:** 350

RADSCORPION PREDATOR (LVL 54)

- **BASE HEALTH:** 900
- **DAMAGE RESISTANCE:** 150
- **ENERGY RESISTANCE:** 125
- **RADIATION RESISTANCE:** 350

DEATHSKULL RADSCORPION (LVL 64)

- **BASE HEALTH:** 1,100
- **DAMAGE RESISTANCE:** 150
- **ENERGY RESISTANCE:** 125
- **RADIATION RESISTANCE:** 350

ROBOBRAINS

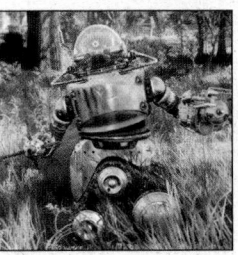

Robobrains are the army knife of killer robots. They attack with ballistic projectiles and electrical bursts, and they like to pepper the field with smoke bombs, making it significantly harder to track them. They keep their distance and don't move very fast, making cover easier to use and more beneficial to hide behind. They are very durable, but if you aim for the brain they are named for, you'll have them decommissioned in moments flat.

ROBOBRAIN (LVL 30)

- **BASE HEALTH:** 325
- **DAMAGE RESISTANCE:** 135
- **ENERGY RESISTANCE:** 70
- **RADIATION RESISTANCE:** 135

ROBOBRAIN SENTRY (LVL 35)

- **BASE HEALTH:** 400
- **DAMAGE RESISTANCE:** 135
- **ENERGY RESISTANCE:** 70
- **RADIATION RESISTANCE:** 135

ROBOBRAIN TACTICIAN (LVL 40)

- **BASE HEALTH:** 425
- **DAMAGE RESISTANCE:** 135
- **ENERGY RESISTANCE:** 70
- **RADIATION RESISTANCE:** 135

ROBOBRAIN WAR MIND (LVL 45)

- **BASE HEALTH:** 450
- **DAMAGE RESISTANCE:** 135
- **ENERGY RESISTANCE:** 70
- **RADIATION RESISTANCE:** 135

ROBOBRAIN DEVASTATOR (LVL 50)

- **BASE HEALTH:** 600
- **DAMAGE RESISTANCE:** 175
- **ENERGY RESISTANCE:** 100
- **RADIATION RESISTANCE:** 175

TRAINING

CRAFTING AND C.A.M.P.ING

INVENTORY

QUESTS

ATLAS

BESTIARY

APPENDICES

SCORCHBEASTS

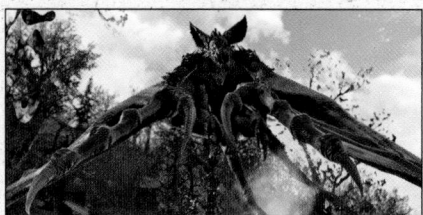

Scorchbeasts are devastating, flying death machines who never leave home without an entourage of Scorched to back them up. Their primary method of attack involves them shooting sonic beams of energy from their mouths while they hover in the air. They'll also fly overhead and dust the surrounding area with irradiated dust, which will fill up your Rads faster than you can sprout a new digit.

Once on the ground, Scorchbeasts become significantly easier to deal with. They'll still shoot sonic beams, but you'll have a much better idea of where they're headed. If you get in too close, it will swat you with a deadly melee attack. If it covers its face with its wings, run as far away as you can. Moments later the Scorchbeast will unleash a powerful explosion of energy around its body.

Scorchbeasts are no joke; never take them lightly (or one-on-one). If you don't have a team with you, stay away from fissure sites and duck and cover if you see one fly overhead. Finally, if you're in a flat area with little cover, avoid challenging them altogether. If you have no place to hide, you have no hope to win.

SCORCHBEAST (LVL 50)
– **BASE HEALTH:** 3,700
– **DAMAGE RESISTANCE:** 125
– **ENERGY RESISTANCE:** 125
– **RADIATION RESISTANCE:** 125

SCORCHBEAST (LVL 65)
– **BASE HEALTH:** 3,800
– **DAMAGE RESISTANCE:** 150
– **ENERGY RESISTANCE:** 150
– **RADIATION RESISTANCE:** 150

SCORCHBEAST (LVL 80)
– **BASE HEALTH:** 3,900
– **DAMAGE RESISTANCE:** 200
– **ENERGY RESISTANCE:** 200
– **RADIATION RESISTANCE:** 200

SCORCHBEAST QUEENS

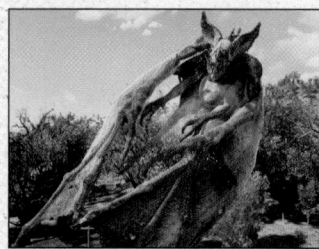

The queen of the Scorched and undisputed ruler of the skies, the Scorchbeast Queen is everything a Scorchbeast is and then some. On top of the standard Scorchbeast moves, the Queen attacks with its freezing gale winds. It will blanket the field with pockets of deep cold and can shoot out freezing bursts of cold toward anyone on the ground. Once on the ground, it will behave like the Scorchbeasts you know and love. Queens are powerful and nearly indestructible. Expect to do a lot of prepping and planning if you and your team hope to survive the encounter.

SCORCHBEAST QUEEN (LVL 95)
– **BASE HEALTH:** 32, 767
– **DAMAGE RESISTANCE:** 300
– **ENERGY RESISTANCE:** 300
– **RADIATION RESISTANCE:** 300

THE SCORCHED

Scorched come in many flavors and are never seen outside of a group. They aren't hard to kill and are easily beaten with basic tactics: kill the melee enemies first, then take on the gun-toting Scorched from behind cover. The difficulty that comes with fighting Scorched is entirely based on what weapons they carry, how many of them there are, and what level each of them is.

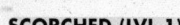

SCORCHED BELIEVER (LVL 14)
– **BASE HEALTH:** 60
– **DAMAGE RESISTANCE:** 5
– **ENERGY RESISTANCE:** 20
– **RADIATION RESISTANCE:** 150

SCORCHED LEADER (LVL 47)
– **BASE HEALTH:** 200
– **DAMAGE RESISTANCE:** 85
– **ENERGY RESISTANCE:** 100
– **RADIATION RESISTANCE:** 150

SCORCHED ZEALOT (LVL 23)
– **BASE HEALTH:** 125
– **DAMAGE RESISTANCE:** 40
– **ENERGY RESISTANCE:** 65
– **RADIATION RESISTANCE:** 150

SCORCHED CONTROLLER (LVL 54)
– **BASE HEALTH:** 225
– **DAMAGE RESISTANCE:** 85
– **ENERGY RESISTANCE:** 100
– **RADIATION RESISTANCE:** 150

SCORCHED (LVL 1)
– **BASE HEALTH:** 35
– **DAMAGE RESISTANCE:** 5
– **ENERGY RESISTANCE:** 20
– **RADIATION RESISTANCE:** 150

SCORCHED WARRIOR (LVL 32)
– **BASE HEALTH:** 145
– **DAMAGE RESISTANCE:** 40
– **ENERGY RESISTANCE:** 65
– **RADIATION RESISTANCE:** 150

SCORCHED CHAMPION (LVL 62)
– **BASE HEALTH:** 250
– **DAMAGE RESISTANCE:** 85
– **ENERGY RESISTANCE:** 100
– **RADIATION RESISTANCE:** 150

SCORCHED WANDERER (LVL 6)
– **BASE HEALTH:** 50
– **DAMAGE RESISTANCE:** 5
– **ENERGY RESISTANCE:** 20
– **RADIATION RESISTANCE:** 150

SCORCHED BERSERKER (LVL 40)
– **BASE HEALTH:** 185
– **DAMAGE RESISTANCE:** 40
– **ENERGY RESISTANCE:** 65
– **RADIATION RESISTANCE:** 150

SCORCHED CONQUEROR (LVL 68)
– **BASE HEALTH:** 300
– **DAMAGE RESISTANCE:** 85
– **ENERGY RESISTANCE:** 100
– **RADIATION RESISTANCE:** 150

SENTRY BOTS

These robots are walking arsenals of deadly weaponry. To make matters worse, they have high resistances and are relentless in their pursuit of their prey. Don't try to face one down if you like living. Use mines, get behind cover, and do NOT let one box you into a corner. Its miniguns will shred you in moments, as will its melee attacks.

If you manage to defeat one, loot it quickly and run like hell! After about 60 seconds the Sentry Bot's remains will detonate, creating a massive explosion where it used to stand.

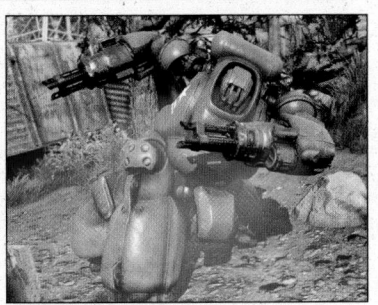

SIEGE BREAKER SENTRY BOT (LVL 40)
- BASE HEALTH: 1,075
- DAMAGE RESISTANCE: 135
- ENERGY RESISTANCE: 70
- RADIATION RESISTANCE: 135

ANNIHILATOR SENTRY BOT (LVL 50)
- BASE HEALTH: 1,550
- DAMAGE RESISTANCE: 135
- ENERGY RESISTANCE: 70
- RADIATION RESISTANCE: 135

SENTRY BOT (LVL 30)
- BASE HEALTH: 875
- DAMAGE RESISTANCE: 135
- ENERGY RESISTANCE: 70
- RADIATION RESISTANCE: 135

ANNIHILATOR SENTRY BOT MK. II (LVL 60)
- BASE HEALTH: 1,725
- DAMAGE RESISTANCE: 135
- ENERGY RESISTANCE: 70
- RADIATION RESISTANCE: 135

STINGWINGS

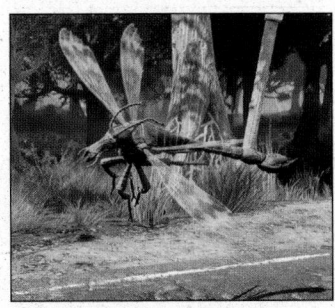

Sting Wings don't have a lot of health, but they can be a real pain to kill. They tend to use stick-and-move tactics over a direct assault. Expect them to fly in, stab you with their stinger, then fly away before you can retaliate. You can try to practice your marksmanship skills to take them out, but we suggest immediately using V.A.T.S. to swiftly take them out.

STINGWING SKIMMER (LVL 30)
- BASE HEALTH: 150
- DAMAGE RESISTANCE: 40
- ENERGY RESISTANCE: 60
- RADIATION RESISTANCE: 1,000

GLOWING STINGWING (LVL 42)
- BASE HEALTH: 175
- DAMAGE RESISTANCE: 50
- ENERGY RESISTANCE: 75
- RADIATION RESISTANCE: 1,000

STINGWING (LVL 10)
- BASE HEALTH: 40
- DAMAGE RESISTANCE: 20
- ENERGY RESISTANCE: 30
- RADIATION RESISTANCE: 1,000

STINGWING DARTER (LVL 18)
- BASE HEALTH: 125
- DAMAGE RESISTANCE: 30
- ENERGY RESISTANCE: 45
- RADIATION RESISTANCE: 1,000

STINGWING CHASER (LVL 54)
- BASE HEALTH: 225
- DAMAGE RESISTANCE: 60
- ENERGY RESISTANCE: 90
- RADIATION RESISTANCE: 1,000

SUPER MUTANTS

Super Mutants are formidable foes—anyone who's played a past *Fallout* game knows that. They are battle-hardened soldiers that attack with every kind of implement of destruction. Deal with them as you would any soldier: take cover, avoid their attacks, and return attacks of your own. They are formidable in large groups and should never be underestimated.

SUPER MUTANT (LVL 5)
- BASE HEALTH: 80
- DAMAGE RESISTANCE: 10
- ENERGY RESISTANCE: 35
- RADIATION RESISTANCE: 10

SUPER MUTANT (LVL 10)
- BASE HEALTH: 160
- DAMAGE RESISTANCE: 10
- ENERGY RESISTANCE: 5
- RADIATION RESISTANCE: 10

SUPER MUTANT SKIRMISHER (LVL 16)
- BASE HEALTH: 300
- DAMAGE RESISTANCE: 50
- ENERGY RESISTANCE: 25
- RADIATION RESISTANCE: 50

SUPER MUTANT BRUTE (LVL 22)
- BASE HEALTH: 350
- DAMAGE RESISTANCE: 50
- ENERGY RESISTANCE: 25
- RADIATION RESISTANCE: 50

SUPER MUTANT ENFORCER (LVL 28)
- BASE HEALTH: 375
- DAMAGE RESISTANCE: 100
- ENERGY RESISTANCE: 50
- RADIATION RESISTANCE: 100

SUPER MUTANT BUTCHER (LVL 35)
- BASE HEALTH: 475
- DAMAGE RESISTANCE: 100
- ENERGY RESISTANCE: 50
- RADIATION RESISTANCE: 100

SUPER MUTANT MASTER (LVL 42)
- BASE HEALTH: 500
- DAMAGE RESISTANCE: 100
- ENERGY RESISTANCE: 50
- RADIATION RESISTANCE: 100

SUPER MUTANT OVERLORD (LVL 48)
- BASE HEALTH: 725
- DAMAGE RESISTANCE: 100
- ENERGY RESISTANCE: 50
- RADIATION RESISTANCE: 100

SUPER MUTANT PRIMUS (LVL 59)
- BASE HEALTH: 750
- DAMAGE RESISTANCE: 135
- ENERGY RESISTANCE: 80
- RADIATION RESISTANCE: 135

SUPER MUTANT WARLORD (LVL 68)
- BASE HEALTH: 950
- DAMAGE RESISTANCE: 135
- ENERGY RESISTANCE: 80
- RADIATION RESISTANCE: 135

TICKS

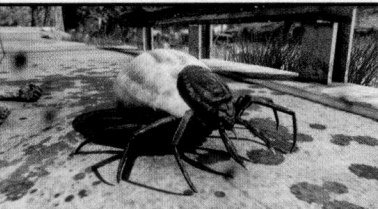

Ticks are hoppy little bloodsuckers that are hard to shake. If they are able to attack you a handful of times, they'll swell with blood, which will cause them to slow down. Unfortunately they can use this blood as an irradiating projectile, which also has the consequence of shrinking them back to size, allowing them to attack at their normal speed.

There's little you can do to avoid Ticks, so it's best to just go on the offense and attack them before they can attack you.

TICK (LVL 1)

- BASE HEALTH: 25
- DAMAGE RESISTANCE: 5
- ENERGY RESISTANCE: 5
- RADIATION RESISTANCE: 250

FOUL TICK (LVL 8)

- BASE HEALTH: 30
- DAMAGE RESISTANCE: 5
- ENERGY RESISTANCE: 5
- RADIATION RESISTANCE: 250

WRETCHED TICK (LVL 16)

- BASE HEALTH: 100
- DAMAGE RESISTANCE: 5
- ENERGY RESISTANCE: 5
- RADIATION RESISTANCE: 250

VILE TICK (LVL 26)

- BASE HEALTH: 150
- DAMAGE RESISTANCE: 5
- ENERGY RESISTANCE: 5
- RADIATION RESISTANCE: 250

SCORCHED TICK (LVL 35)

- BASE HEALTH: 200
- DAMAGE RESISTANCE: 5
- ENERGY RESISTANCE: 5
- RADIATION RESISTANCE: 250

VERTIBOTS

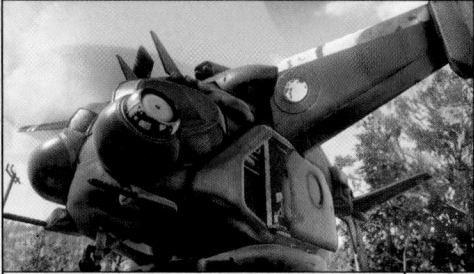

Vertibots are typically found escorting Cargobots. They aren't terribly difficult to destroy if you have cover to hide behind; being in the open is a completely different story. They are resilient to ballistic attacks, so rely on Explosive and Energy damage to take them down quickly.

VERTIBOT (LVL 20)

- BASE HEALTH: 650
- DAMAGE RESISTANCE: 135
- ENERGY RESISTANCE: 135
- RADIATION RESISTANCE: 135

VERTIBOT (LVL 30)

- BASE HEALTH: 875
- DAMAGE RESISTANCE: 135
- ENERGY RESISTANCE: 135
- RADIATION RESISTANCE: 135

VERTIBOT (LVL 40)

- BASE HEALTH: 1,100
- DAMAGE RESISTANCE: 135
- ENERGY RESISTANCE: 135
- RADIATION RESISTANCE: 135

VERTIBOT (LVL 50)

- BASE HEALTH: 1,550
- DAMAGE RESISTANCE: 135
- ENERGY RESISTANCE: 135
- RADIATION RESISTANCE: 135

WOLVES

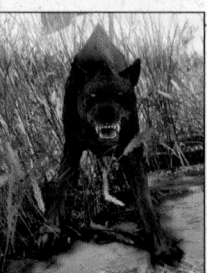

Wolves are simple creatures and aren't particularly dangerous. They tend to attack in packs and can whittle your health down little by little as they each attack from all sides. Their main method of attack is to charge up and bite, which you can easily avoid by staying on the move. Their Resistances are incredibly low, so taking them out is a breeze.

FERAL WOLF (LVL 20)

- BASE HEALTH: 350
- DAMAGE RESISTANCE: 15
- ENERGY RESISTANCE: 15
- RADIATION RESISTANCE: 15

GREY WOLF (LVL 30)

- BASE HEALTH: 450
- DAMAGE RESISTANCE: 15
- ENERGY RESISTANCE: 15
- RADIATION RESISTANCE: 15

RABID WOLF (LVL 40)

- BASE HEALTH: 500
- DAMAGE RESISTANCE: 20
- ENERGY RESISTANCE: 20
- RADIATION RESISTANCE: 20

VICIOUS WOLF (LVL 10)

- BASE HEALTH: 110
- DAMAGE RESISTANCE: 10
- ENERGY RESISTANCE: 10
- RADIATION RESISTANCE: 10

GLOWING WOLF (LVL 50)

- BASE HEALTH: 750
- DAMAGE RESISTANCE: 20
- ENERGY RESISTANCE: 20
- RADIATION RESISTANCE: 20

YAO GUAIS

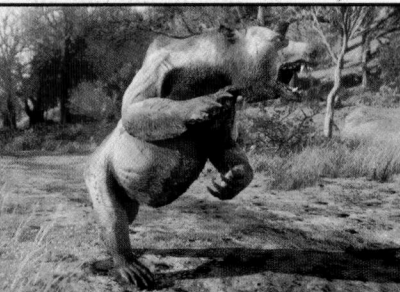

Yao Guai aren't combat experts, but that is of little importance when you consider how near-indestructible they are. Their main method of attack is to charge and swipe you with their claws until you die. They hit hard and are relentless, but if you can get an object between you and them (or get on top of something they can't climb, like a car) they can be pretty easy to manipulate.

YAO GUAI (LVL 26)

- BASE HEALTH: 600
- DAMAGE RESISTANCE: 100
- ENERGY RESISTANCE: 100
- RADIATION RESISTANCE: 250

SHAGGY YAO GUAI (LVL 36)

- BASE HEALTH: 750
- DAMAGE RESISTANCE: 100
- ENERGY RESISTANCE: 100
- RADIATION RESISTANCE: 250

STUNTED YAO GUAI (LVL 16)

- BASE HEALTH: 400
- DAMAGE RESISTANCE: 100
- ENERGY RESISTANCE: 100
- RADIATION RESISTANCE: 250

YAO GUAI GHOUL (LVL 31)

- BASE HEALTH: 625
- DAMAGE RESISTANCE: 100
- ENERGY RESISTANCE: 100
- RADIATION RESISTANCE: 250

IRRADIATED YAO GUAI (LVL 46)

- BASE HEALTH: 775
- DAMAGE RESISTANCE: 100
- ENERGY RESISTANCE: 100
- RADIATION RESISTANCE: 250

GLOWING YAO GUAI (LVL 46)

- BASE HEALTH: 1,100
- DAMAGE RESISTANCE: 100
- ENERGY RESISTANCE: 100
- RADIATION RESISTANCE: 250

ALBINO YAO GUAI (LVL 56)

- BASE HEALTH: 1,275
- DAMAGE RESISTANCE: 100
- ENERGY RESISTANCE: 100
- RADIATION RESISTANCE: 250

RABID YAO GUAI (LVL 66)

- BASE HEALTH: 1,300
- DAMAGE RESISTANCE: 150
- ENERGY RESISTANCE: 150
- RADIATION RESISTANCE: 250

DUSKY YAO GUAI (LVL 76)

- BASE HEALTH: 1,475
- DAMAGE RESISTANCE: 150
- ENERGY RESISTANCE: 150
- RADIATION RESISTANCE: 250

MACHINE-GUN TURRET MK SERIES

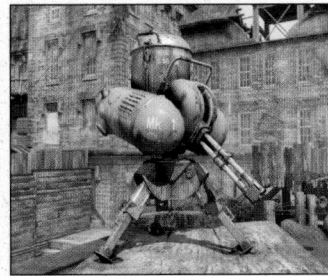

The Machine-Gun Turret MK I is rarely hostile to humans. In fact, these turrets are usually used to defend areas from hostile creature attacks. They can be endlessly repaired, provided you have the components to do so, and they can be a major help in situations that require you to hold down a position.

MACHINE-GUN TURRET MK I (LVL 6)

- BASE HEALTH: 110
- DAMAGE RESISTANCE: 5
- ENERGY RESISTANCE: 5
- RADIATION RESISTANCE: 5

MACHINE-GUN TURRET MK III (LVL 16)

- BASE HEALTH: 300
- DAMAGE RESISTANCE: 15
- ENERGY RESISTANCE: 15
- RADIATION RESISTANCE: 15

MACHINE-GUN TURRET MK V (LVL 28)

- BASE HEALTH: 375
- DAMAGE RESISTANCE: 25
- ENERGY RESISTANCE: 25
- RADIATION RESISTANCE: 25

MACHINE-GUN TURRET MK VII (LVL 40)

- BASE HEALTH: 500
- DAMAGE RESISTANCE: 25
- ENERGY RESISTANCE: 25
- RADIATION RESISTANCE: 25

ASAM TURRETS

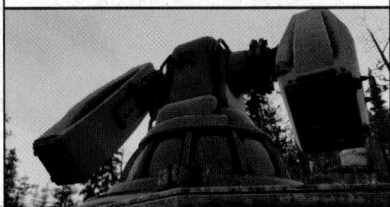

Automated Surface to Air Missile Turrets (ASAM Turrets) aren't hostile unless you shoot them by mistake (or on purpose; we're not here to judge). They are usually seen in military camps and can be utilized to shoot down Scorchbeasts that are roaming the skies.

If you do agitate one, simply find cover, wait for it to fire a volley of missiles, then pop up and get a few rounds into it. Repeat this process until you dismantle it.

ASAM TURRET

- BASE HEALTH: 200
- DAMAGE RESISTANCE: 20
- ENERGY RESISTANCE: 10
- RADIATION RESISTANCE: 0

WALL-MOUNTED TURRETS

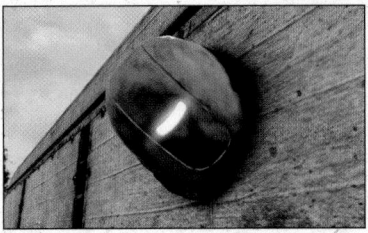

Wall-Mounted Turrets are like bees: one of them is painful but relatively harmless; get attacked by several at once, however, and you're be in a world of trouble. They are easily destroyed so long as you don't just stand in front of them soaking up damage while trying to dismantle them.

LASER TURRET (LVL 16)

- BASE HEALTH: 225
- DAMAGE RESISTANCE: 5
- ENERGY RESISTANCE: 5
- RADIATION RESISTANCE: 5

MACHINE-GUN TURRET (LVL 28)

- BASE HEALTH: 250
- DAMAGE RESISTANCE: 10
- ENERGY RESISTANCE: 10
- RADIATION RESISTANCE: 10

LASER TURRET (LVL 40)

- BASE HEALTH: 300
- DAMAGE RESISTANCE: 10
- ENERGY RESISTANCE: 10
- RADIATION RESISTANCE: 10

LASER TURRET (LVL 1)

- BASE HEALTH: 50
- DAMAGE RESISTANCE: 5
- ENERGY RESISTANCE: 5
- RADIATION RESISTANCE: 5

LASER TURRET (LVL 50)

- BASE HEALTH: 450
- DAMAGE RESISTANCE: 10
- ENERGY RESISTANCE: 10
- RADIATION RESISTANCE: 10

MACHINE-GUN TURRET (LVL 7)

- BASE HEALTH: 50
- DAMAGE RESISTANCE: 5
- ENERGY RESISTANCE: 5
- RADIATION RESISTANCE: 5

LASER TURRET (LVL 60)

- BASE HEALTH: 500
- DAMAGE RESISTANCE: 10
- ENERGY RESISTANCE: 10
- RADIATION RESISTANCE: 10

TRAINING

CRAFTING AND C.A.M.P.ING

INVENTORY

QUESTS

ATLAS

BESTIARY

APPENDICES

NONHOSTILE CRITTERS

These sweet, innocent creatures mean no harm to anyone. They are a reminder that even at the end of the world, there are still creatures who only care for peace. They also taste delicious! Hunt 'em, gut 'em, and throw 'em on the grill! It's dog eat dog out here! Or maybe human eat cat is more appropriate... Either way, get out there and fetch you some delicious meat—except from the Cargobot. Don't eat that. That's a robot. You don't want that in your mouth.

BEAVERS
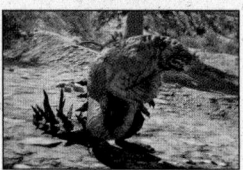

FOXES
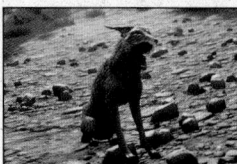

OWLETS
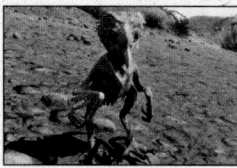

BRAHMIN
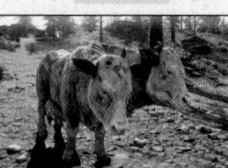

FROGS
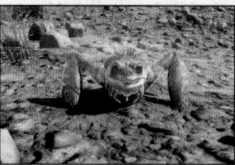

RABBITS
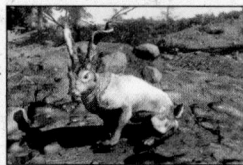

CHICKENS
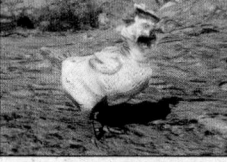

HOUSE CATS
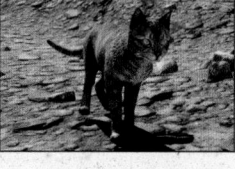

SQUIRRELS
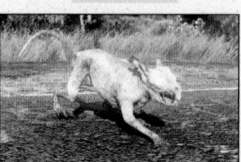

FIREFLIES
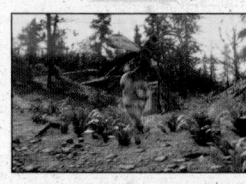

OPOSSUMS
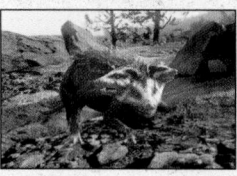

GRAFTON MONSTER

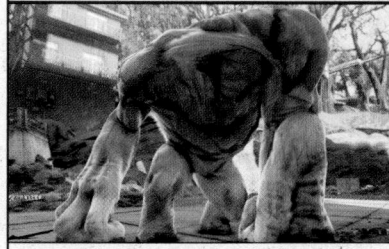

The Grafton Monster is a bulky, hulking white mass of power. It soaks up damage like a plant soaks up the sun and it can hit like a wrecking ball. Your first visit to Charleston will almost certainly put you face-to-face with one of these deadly beasts. Keep your distance at all costs if you want to make it out in one piece.

GRAFTON MONSTER (LVL 10)

- **DAMAGE RESISTANCE:** 150
- **ENERGY RESISTANCE:** 25
- **RADIATION RESISTANCE:** IMMUNE
- **POISON RESISTANCE:** 100

ENRAGED GRAFTON MONSTER (LVL 30)

- **DAMAGE RESISTANCE:** 200
- **ENERGY RESISTANCE:** 50
- **RADIATION RESISTANCE:** IMMUNE
- **POISON RESISTANCE:** 100

PARASITIC GRAFTON MONSTER (LVL 40)

- **DAMAGE RESISTANCE:** 250
- **ENERGY RESISTANCE:** 100
- **RADIATION RESISTANCE:** IMMUNE
- **POISON RESISTANCE:** 100

SCORCHED GRAFTON MONSTER (LVL 50)

- **DAMAGE RESISTANCE:** 435
- **ENERGY RESISTANCE:** 250
- **RADIATION RESISTANCE:** IMMUNE
- **POISON RESISTANCE:** 100

CRYPTIDS

Appalachia is no stranger to myths about strange and deadly creatures. Unfortunately, some of those myths are true. We list all the Cryptids in Appalachia here. These creatures are often elusive, particularly strange, and are almost certainly deadly. Keep a watchful eye out for them; Lord knows they'll be watching out for you.

FLATWOODS MONSTER ENCOUNTERS

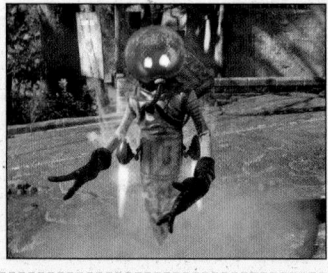

This rather elusive, floating, alien-like creature is named after one of the first towns you'll visit on your adventures through Appalachia. If you stumble upon it in the wild, odds are it will disappear before you can even get a shot off.

Encounter it again and it will almost certainly challenge you to a fight. Regularly check the town it's named after and you might just surprise it instead of the other way around.

FLATWOODS MONSTER (LVL 30)

- **BASE HEALTH:** 850
- **DAMAGE RESISTANCE:** 150
- **ENERGY RESISTANCE:** 250
- **RADIATION RESISTANCE:** 250

FABLED FLATWOODS MONSTER (LVL 40)

- **BASE HEALTH:** 1,050
- **DAMAGE RESISTANCE:** 150
- **ENERGY RESISTANCE:** 250
- **RADIATION RESISTANCE:** 250

MYTHICAL FLATWOODS MONSTER (LVL 50)

- **BASE HEALTH:** 1,475
- **DAMAGE RESISTANCE:** 150
- **ENERGY RESISTANCE:** 250
- **RADIATION RESISTANCE:** 250

MOTHMAN ENCOUNTERS

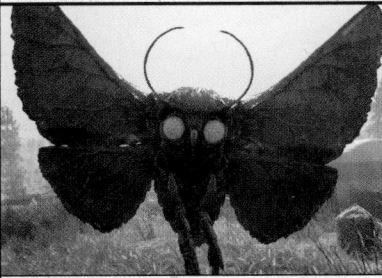

The Mothman is definitely one of the creepier enemies in the game, but it's surprisingly not that hard to fight. It has a lot of resistance and it teleports around the map, but it only has two attacks, both of which are easy to avoid.

Its primary attack comes while it flutters in the air. It will continuously fire out projectiles until it teleports again. To avoid these, just sidestep them. They are hard to see and fast, but sidestepping will avoid them entirely.

Its second attack is a large discharge of energy around its body. If you see it curl its wings around itself, back off and you'll be fine. The rest of the fight is simply dealing enough damage to defeat it.

MOTHMAN (LVL 35)

- **BASE HEALTH:** 1,050
- **DAMAGE RESISTANCE:** 150
- **ENERGY RESISTANCE:** 150
- **RADIATION RESISTANCE:** 150

DREAD MOTHMAN (LVL 45)

- **BASE HEALTH:** 1,100
- **DAMAGE RESISTANCE:** 250
- **ENERGY RESISTANCE:** 250
- **RADIATION RESISTANCE:** 250

ALBINO MOTHMAN (LVL 55)

- **BASE HEALTH:** 1,550
- **DAMAGE RESISTANCE:** 250
- **ENERGY RESISTANCE:** 250
- **RADIATION RESISTANCE:** 250

GLOWING MOTHMAN (LVL 65)

- **BASE HEALTH:** 1,700
- **DAMAGE RESISTANCE:** 250
- **ENERGY RESISTANCE:** 250
- **RADIATION RESISTANCE:** 250

SNALLYGASTERS

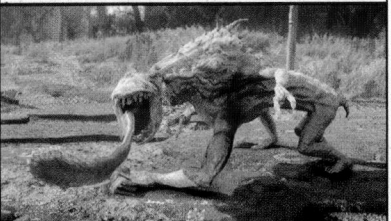

Snallygasters aren't particularly aggressive, but they are quick when it comes to chasing down prey. They are primarily melee attackers, but they can also spit out projectiles to damage from a distance. They have high Damage Resistance, so stick to Energy weapons to take them down quickly.

NASCENT SNALLYGASTER (LVL 14)

- **BASE HEALTH:** 525
- **DAMAGE RESISTANCE:** 50
- **ENERGY RESISTANCE:** 50
- **RADIATION RESISTANCE:** 50

SNALLYGASTER (LVL 22)

- **BASE HEALTH:** 575
- **DAMAGE RESISTANCE:** 50
- **ENERGY RESISTANCE:** 50
- **RADIATION RESISTANCE:** 50

FETID SNALLYGASTER (LVL 30)

- **BASE HEALTH:** 600
- **DAMAGE RESISTANCE:** 150
- **ENERGY RESISTANCE:** 150
- **RADIATION RESISTANCE:** 150

BLOODY SNALLYGASTER (LVL 38)

- **BASE HEALTH:** 650
- **DAMAGE RESISTANCE:** 150
- **ENERGY RESISTANCE:** 150
- **RADIATION RESISTANCE:** 150

GLOWING SNALLYGASTER (LVL 46)

- **BASE HEALTH:** 700
- **DAMAGE RESISTANCE:** 300
- **ENERGY RESISTANCE:** 300
- **RADIATION RESISTANCE:** 300

ULTRACITE SNALLYGASTER (LVL 54)

- **BASE HEALTH:** 700
- **DAMAGE RESISTANCE:** 300
- **ENERGY RESISTANCE:** 300
- **RADIATION RESISTANCE;** 300

WENDIGOS

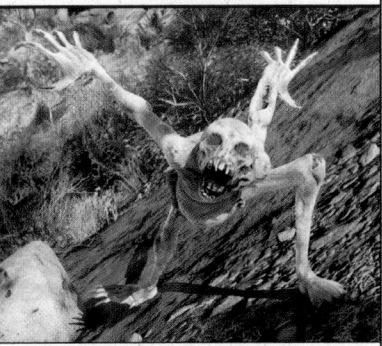

Wendigos are fast, powerful, and terrifying. Their method of attack is to charge you relentlessly and swing their long, powerful claws at you. If you stay at a distance from one long enough, it will stick its hand in its mouth, then belt out an ear-shattering roar, which will damage you if you're anywhere near it.

The simplest strategy for taking out a Wendigo is to run, get some distance, then shoot. Staying still will work in the Wendigo's favor more than yours. Putting an object between you and the Wendigo, or climbing on top of something it can't climb, can turn the tides in your favor, but you'll have to constantly be prepared to avoid its roar.

WENDIGO (LVL 22)

- **BASE HEALTH:** 390
- **DAMAGE RESISTANCE:** 150
- **ENERGY RESISTANCE:** 100
- **RADIATION RESISTANCE: IMMUNE**

RAVENOUS WENDIGO (LVL 32)

- **BASE HEALTH:** 525
- **DAMAGE RESISTANCE:** 200
- **ENERGY RESISTANCE:** 150
- **RADIATION RESISTANCE: IMMUNE**

GLOWING WENDIGO (LVL 42)

- **BASE HEALTH:** 650
- **DAMAGE RESISTANCE:** 250
- **ENERGY RESISTANCE:** 200
- **RADIATION RESISTANCE: IMMUNE**

SCORCHED WENDIGO (LVL 52)

- **BASE HEALTH:** 900
- **DAMAGE RESISTANCE:** 150
- **ENERGY RESISTANCE:** 125
- **RADIATION RESISTANCE:** 350

ZETAN ALIENS

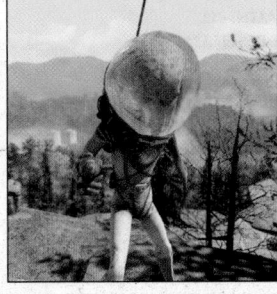

The Zetan Alien isn't much for combat, which is probably good considering how hard it is to find one. It will simply shoot at you with its Alien Blaster until you give it a proper Earth welcome. Kill it to collect the Alien Blaster and ammunition.

ALIEN (LVL 1)

- **BASE HEALTH:** 40
- **DAMAGE RESISTANCE:** 50
- **ENERGY RESISTANCE:** 100
- **RADIATION RESISTANCE:** 250

ALIEN LIEUTENANT (LVL 32)

- **BASE HEALTH:** 300
- **DAMAGE RESISTANCE:** 50
- **ENERGY RESISTANCE:** 100
- **RADIATION RESISTANCE:** 250

ALIEN CAPTAIN (LVL 42)

- **BASE HEALTH:** 375
- **DAMAGE RESISTANCE:** 50
- **ENERGY RESISTANCE:** 100
- **RADIATION RESISTANCE:** 250

ALIEN STAR ADMIRAL (LVL 52)

- **BASE HEALTH:** 550
- **DAMAGE RESISTANCE:** 50
- **ENERGY RESISTANCE:** 100
- **RADIATION RESISTANCE:** 250

TRAINING

CRAFTING AND C.A.M.P.ING

INVENTORY

QUESTS

ATLAS

BESTIARY

APPENDICES

Appendices

ACHIEVEMENTS

QUEST RELATED

NAME	ACHIEVEMENT POINTS	TROPHY POINTS	DESCRIPTION
Reclamation Day!	10	15	Leave Vault 76.
First Contact	10	15	Complete "First Contact."
Final Departure	20	15	Complete "Final Departure."
Second Helpings	20	15	Complete "Second Helpings."
Into the Fire	20	30	Complete "Into the Fire."
Recruitment Blues	20	15	Complete "Recruitment Blues."
Heart of the Enemy	30	30	Complete "Heart of the Enemy."
Key to the Past	10	30	Complete "Key to the Past."
Coming to Fruition	10	15	Complete "Coming to Fruition."
Bunker Buster	10	15	Complete "Bunker Buster." Gain access to The Whitespring
One of Us	10	15	Complete "One of Us." MODUS considers you a member of the Enclave.
Officer on Deck	30	30	Complete "Officer on Deck."
I Am Become Death	50	90	Complete "I Am Become Death." Launch a Nuke.
Personal Matters	20	15	Complete "Personal Matters."
Queen of the Hunt	10	15	Complete "Queen of the Hunt."
The Mistress of Mystery	20	30	Complete "The Mistress of Mystery."

SURVIVAL RELATED

NAME	ACHIEVEMENT POINTS	TROPHY POINTS	DESCRIPTION
Happy C.A.M.P.er	10	15	Build a C.A.M.P.
We Must Rebuild	10	15	Build 20 C.A.M.P. Items.
Appalachian HOA	20	30	Build 100 C.A.M.P. Items.
A Fighting Chance	10	15	Craft a Weapon.
Monet of Murder	30	30	Mod 50 Weapons.
Second Skin	10	15	Craft 5 Pieces of Armor.
Junker Funk	10	15	Gather 200 Pieces of Junk.

MULTIPLAYER RELATED

NAME	ACHIEVEMENT POINTS	TROPHY POINTS	DESCRIPTION
Never Go It Alone!	15	15	Join 20 Teams.
Field Medic	20	15	Revive 20 Fallen Players.
Bounty Hunter	20	15	Kill a Wanted Player.
Kill or Be Killed	10	15	Kill Another Player.
Good Grief!	20	15	Kill 20 Players.
Breach and Clear	20	15	Win the "Breach and Clear" Event.
Monster Mash	20	15	Win the "Monster Mash" Event.
Scorched Earth	30	30	Win the "Scorched Earth" Event.

MISCELLANEOUS

NAME	ACHIEVEMENT POINTS	TROPHY POINTS	DESCRIPTION
Tested Mettle	30	15	Complete 5 Challenges.
A Real Challenger	20	15	Complete 20 Challenges.
Moneybags	20	15	Possess 10,000 Caps.
Retro Now	10	15	Play a Holotape Game.
Ground Zero	30	30	Be at Ground Zero of a Nuclear Blast.

EXPLORATION RELATED

NAME	ACHIEVEMENT POINTS	TROPHY POINTS	DESCRIPTION
Ain't He the Cutest?	10	15	Collect a Bobblehead.
Shwag	20	30	Collect 10 Bobbleheads.
LITerally	20	15	Read 20 Magazines.
Code Cruncher	30	30	Hack 50 Terminals.
Gimme Gimme!	30	30	Pick 50 Locks.
Photo Bomber	10	15	Take 20 Photos.
Pioneer Scout	40	30	Discover 100 Locations.
Giant Slayer	20	15	Kill 5 Giant Creatures; includes Behemoths, Mirelurk Queens, Scorchbeasts.
Pest Control	20	15	Kill 300 Creatures.

LEVEL RELATED

NAME	ACHIEVEMENT POINTS	TROPHY POINTS	DESCRIPTION
Wild West Virginian	10	15	Reach Level 10.
Appalachian Trailblazer	25	15	Reach Level 25.
American Hero	50	30	Reach Level 50.
Fallout Forever	30	30	Reach Level 100.
Perked Up	20	15	Fully Rank Up One Perk.

BOBBLEHEADS, POWER ARMOR, AND MAGAZINES

APPENDIX: BOBBLEHEAD LOCATIONS

Not strictly limited edition, there are 20 different Bobbleheads available to find across all six Regions of Appalachia. Sadly, these have already been taken out of the packaging. But they do bestow a fancy improvement for a limited time. The following are "known" locations where Bobbleheads have been spotted. They may not appear (this is random), or may have already been taken by other players, so keep checking on each location.

REGION 1: THE FOREST

#	PRIMARY LOCATION NAME	BOBBLEHEAD LOCATION DESCRIPTION
ZONE A: VAULT 76 AND FLATWOODS		
7	Landview Lighthouse	On the desk in the upstairs bedroom between the typewriter and Lighthouse Keeper's Terminal, inside the faded yellow house near the lighthouse.
7	Landview Lighthouse	On the white brick window sill, at the highest gantry platform inside the lighthouse, before the lamp chamber is reached (inside the lighthouse tower).
8	Alpine River Cabins	On top of the corner bunk bed, inside the southeast cabin.
8	Alpine River Cabins	On the floor under the corner bunk bed, inside the south cabin with the bear rug.
9	Wixon Homestead	On a barrel, on the south wall of the curve-roofed hay barn and garage, just right of the metal shelving.
15	Vault-Tec Agricultural Research Center	In or on the open rusty fridge, one of three in the western corner of the hydroponics room (lower level) with the flower pots, opposite a fertilizer hatch, left of the wood door (interior).
15	Vault-Tec Agricultural Research Center	In the urinal, inside the men's restroom, by the stairwell (interior).
15	Vault-Tec Agricultural Research Center	In the filing cabinet tray with the office desk fan, on the floor in front of the empty filing cabinets, in the upper (east side) filing office (interior).
15	Vault-Tec Agricultural Research Center	On the corner of the metal desk with the destroyed terminal, just left of the empty filing cabinets, on the dry part of the basement laboratory level (interior).
ZONE B: NORTHWEST FOREST AND POINT PLEASANT		
17	WV Lumber Co.	On the edge of the roof, in the waste bin, or just inside the structure with the "protect your hands" poster; in the partly ruined maintenance garage next to the stacked squared-off lumber.
17	WV Lumber Co.	On the raised area by an upturned filing cabinet and first aid box, inside the red barn storage warehouse.
18	Darling Sister's Lab	On the roof of the "welkcom" metal caravan trailer, by the gramophone and banjo.
19	Groves Family Cabin	On top of the bunk bed, in the southeast corner, inside the cabin with the trunk and American flag.
20	Aaronholt Homestead	Under the baby's crib, in the southwest corner of the upstairs bedroom, inside the pale blue/gray cottage.
20	Aaronholt Homestead	Behind the bookcase, in the southeast corner of the burgundy bedroom of the main (white) farmhouse (with the red star on the porch wall).
20	Aaronholt Homestead	At the foot of the wood and metal stud wall, behind and right of the Power Armor, left of the tool cabinet, in the silo garage.
21	Tyler County Fairgrounds	On or below the two token machines, in the open corrugated metal sheds by the "Hoop Shots" games, on the south side of the grounds.
21	Tyler County Fairgrounds	On the metal shelving with the Nuka-Cherry and Nuka-Cola bottles, below the blue-and-white awning, at the base of the huge, rusty, Nuka-Cola bottle.

#	PRIMARY LOCATION NAME	BOBBLEHEAD LOCATION DESCRIPTION
21	Tyler County Fairgrounds	On the long table with the pumpkins and scarecrow, inside the large warehouse with the Tinker's Workbench in it (and lots of pumpkins).
23	Deathclaw Island	On top of the small covered bench on the north bank of the island. It may have fallen to the ground near the bench.
28	Marigold Pavilion	In the attic area with the sagging floor, by the vertical support pole between the two mattress beds, inside the pavilion.
29	Hunter's Ridge	On the corner of the wooden sub-floor attached to the roof of the northeast treehouse shack near the living tree trunk, with the mattress and metal bucket. It could have fallen onto the shack floor.
ZONE C: MORGANTOWN AND EASTERN FOREST		
33	Morgantown Trainyard	On the table by the ham radio and Supervisor's Safe (Key), in the tall tower above the main trainyard warehouse.
35	Morgantown Airport	On the narrow wall shelf, on the interior (southwest corner) wall of the Responder laboratory hangar.
36	Morgantown High School	On a tall bookshelf to the right of a wall clock, in the locked (2) blue-checkered-wallpaper office, inside the school.
36	Morgantown High School	On a toilet, in a closed stall inside the boys' restroom, inside the school.
36	Morgantown High School	On a cinder block near a basketball hoop (without a pole), on the upper storage roof of the southwest interior of the gymnasium (the roof of the interior corner kitchen with the trunk). Access by leaping from the stands.
37	Portside Pub	Sitting on a group of rusting AC units, on top of the roof, in the north corner of the structure, near the safe (exterior).
38	Mama Dolce's Food Processing	In the underground Fujiniya Intelligence Base, on a small wooden side cabinet shelf, by the door in the northeast corner of the dormitory.
38	Mama Dolce's Food Processing	In the underground Fujiniya Intelligence Base, on a metal shelf against the interior wall of the laboratory chamber (between a ladder and Protectron pod).
38	Mama Dolce's Food Processing	In the underground Fujiniya Intelligence Base, on or below one of the linked computer and phone terminals in the southwest corner near an orange tool box and fallen Chinese flag.
38	Mama Dolce's Food Processing	In the underground Fujiniya Intelligence Base, on top of a mainframe computer, in the sunken southwestern corner of the main processing chamber, near the huge cylinder.
39	Vault-Tec University	Behind the filing box on the filing cabinets, in the office with the clock and arched window, inside Room 203 (Office of the Dean) beyond the hole in the wall (interior).
39	Vault-Tec University	On or near the black mirror and sink, in the shower room northwest of the gym area of the simulation vault (interior).
39	Vault-Tec University	Inside the upper refrigerator, part of the cafeteria counter inside the simulation vault (interior).
40	Grafton Dam	On the metal typewriter desk, in the first interior blue gantry hut office on the top floor.
42	Gauley Mine	In the left locker, in the southwest corner of the locker room (with the hole in the wall), just south of the mine entrance, inside the mine.

TRAINING

CRAFTING AND C.A.M.P.ING

INVENTORY

QUESTS

ATLAS

BESTIARY

APPENDICES

#	PRIMARY LOCATION NAME	BOBBLEHEAD LOCATION DESCRIPTION
42	Gauley Mine	Atop a ceiling mine support, in the mine junction shack, at the end of the first mine tunnel, inside the mine.
42	Gauley Mine	On the top edge of the blackened wall AC unit with the light above it, on the northwest concrete wall of the main generator and gantry chamber.
43	Arktos Pharma	On the floor between one of the Protein Sequencer Terminals and collection chamber, in the Protein Sequencing laboratory, inside the building.
44	Greg's Mine Supply	On the wooden desk with Greg's Terminal, in the upstairs interior of the Mine Supply store, near a bed and trunk.
45	Bolton Greens	In the baby pram, by the playground near the green bench, outside the mansion.
45	Bolton Greens	On the concrete steps with the ammo box, on top of the roof of the mansion.
45	Bolton Greens	On the floor near a golf bag, in the narrow golf course reception office, accessed via the locked door off the kitchen.
45	Bolton Greens	On an ornate side table, on the north mezzanine balcony, inside the mansion.
45	Bolton Greens	On or near the small round table with the two burgundy chairs, in the western corner of the upstairs bunk bed room with the large brick fireplace.
47	New River Gorge Resort	North across Interstate 59, after completing the adventure course in the woods (or using enhanced jumping), inside the top platform of the adventure tower (exterior).
48	Sutton	On the roof of the Liquor Store, hidden behind (and at the foot of) two barrels with tongs and an enamel bucket on them; access the exterior via other rooftops, not the inside of the Liquor Store.
48	Sutton	In the rectangular wicker basket atop the white locker, in front of the green "You've got Vim!" poster, in the Tinkerer's cellar, inside The Overseer's Childhood Home on the north side of town (interior).
52	Horizon's Rest	On a small metal table next to a safe (1) and jail key, inside the highest metal hut, attached to the electrical pylon.
52	Horizon's Rest	On the floor just behind one of the cockpit seats, in the nose section of the crashed plane.
53	Relay Tower HN-B1-12	On the small mainframe computer bank, on the red wrist rest, in the southern corner of the interior hut.
55	Tygart Water Treatment	On the small wooden crate near the two mattresses, in the middle of the upper Raider base defensive wall (southeast side).

ZONE D: SOUTHWEST FOREST

#	PRIMARY LOCATION NAME	BOBBLEHEAD LOCATION DESCRIPTION
60	Ohio River Adventures	On the boat computer, inside the cabin in the fishing boat mooring off the dock.
63	Silva Homestead	On the long ornate dresser behind the small vase, along the northwest wall of the bedroom (without the mattress), upstairs inside the gray, roadside farmhouse building.
63	Silva Homestead	On the metal desk by the Arktos Pharma Terminal, inside the red silo barn close to the electrical pylon, on the hillside pasture.
67	Lewis & Sons Farming Supply	On the floor, or balanced on the engine adjacent to the Power Armor Station, inside the large metal tractor barn, on the southeast side of the location.
67	Lewis & Sons Farming Supply	Behind or on the two corner barrels, on the upstairs balcony of the large metal tractor barn, on the southeast side of the location.
67	Lewis & Sons Farming Supply	On the ground or corner counter, by the blue cash register, inside the greenhouse.
68	Kanawha Nuka-Cola Plant	In an open locker, in the small concrete stairwell and locker room between the two largest chambers inside the plant.
68	Kanawha Nuka-Cola Plant	On a metal shelf, in the locked (1) large storage pantry, inside the Snackability R&D laboratory, upper floor interior.
68	Kanawha Nuka-Cola Plant	On a section of mainframe computer, in the blue maintenance hut attached to the ceiling of the sunken loading dock (interior). This is only accessible via the locked hatch (3) on the roof by the orange-and-white metal trailer.
71	The Giant Teapot	On the shelf of the counter, below the blue cash register, inside the Red Rocket Gas Station.
71	The Giant Teapot	By the toilet, in the upstairs bathroom of the Gift Shop with the red painted wood siding.
72	Poseidon Energy Plant WV-06	At the end of the giant T-shaped horizontal pipes that enter the first of the two cooling towers, near a chem-addled skeleton; access via the gantry stairs on the northeast side of the main building.

#	PRIMARY LOCATION NAME	BOBBLEHEAD LOCATION DESCRIPTION
72	Poseidon Energy Plant WV-06	Inside a crate at the very end of the catwalks that circle around the smokestacks on the uppermost roof of the energy plant.
72	Poseidon Energy Plant WV-06	On the west corner of the expansion cooling tower roof, by a skeleton slumped against the tower, with chems scattered about. Enhanced jumping may be required to reach this location.
72	Poseidon Energy Plant WV-06	In the largest pool in the Fuel Storage chamber, on an underwater girder (interior).
72	Poseidon Energy Plant WV-06	In the Reactor Room, on the south side girders (with Cap Stashes), supporting the top of the reactor near the ceiling; carefully jump from the computer bank on the highest gantry to eventually reach it.

ZONE E: CHARLESTON AND SURROUNDINGS

#	PRIMARY LOCATION NAME	BOBBLEHEAD LOCATION DESCRIPTION
76	Charleston Railyard	On the corner table in the narrow filing cabinet office, in the upper brick office building (with the Mr. Handy billboard on top of it), just south of the bridge connecting the road (main entrance) to the main unloading rooftop.
78	AVR Medical Center	On top of the entrance lobby ceiling light (the western of the two), near a draped skeleton; access it via shooting it or leaping from the upper broken balcony to the northwest.
78	AVR Medical Center	On the metal desk with the terminal by the door, in the office on the eastern level 2 balcony, above the massive basement hole and cafeteria area.
78	AVR Medical Center	Third floor, south side office, accessed via a hole in the wall; on a wooden and metal cabinet in the northeast corner alcove of the office.
78	AVR Medical Center	Near or on the terminal shell in the southwest corner of the upper lab room with the Chemistry Station in it, and the large hole in the floor.
79	Hornwright Industrial Headquarters	On the metal counter half hidden by a wooden crate, in the south corner of the reactor lab room, on Floor 03 of the interior.
79	Hornwright Industrial Headquarters	In the tiny leg alcove of the red mainframe computer by the circular Protectron calibration pad, in the southern part of the lowest sunken floor area of the External Connection System Chamber.
79	Hornwright Industrial Headquarters	In the tiny foot alcove of the jutting part of the red mainframe computer, in the northwest computer room overlooking the Sub-Level Basement, inside the basement level.
82	Charleston Capitol Building	On the judge's table with the American flag on the back wall, in the first courtroom through the doorway marked "State Courthouse".
85	Summersville Docks	On the rickety shelf, or fallen to the ground inside the small red storage shed, in the northwest corner (with the dinghy propped up against it, and flagpole adjacent).
85	Summersville Docks	On the metal shelf below the metal tub, among other junk, on the west wall of the fish store shack, in the southwest corner.
85	Summersville Docks	On the dry lakebed just below the northeast boathouse, by the scuppered red fishing boat.
89	Burdette Manor	Lying on the floor near the flattened side door on the western side of the manor, just outside.
89	Burdette Manor	On the rock cliff between the edge of the property and the dry lake, on a narrow ledge halfway down, below the cluster of Soot Flowers.
91	Overlook Cabin	On the ground, just outside the broken windows on the northern side of the cabin, by the pool table and game room (exterior).
91	Overlook Cabin	On the rock cliff between the edge of the property and the dry lake, on a narrow ledge halfway down, on the north edge just beyond the low stone driveway wall and blue car.
92	Riverside Manor	On top of the tall dresser, along the west wall of the corner bedroom, second floor (interior).
92	Riverside Manor	In the bureau outside the master bedroom, second floor (interior).
93	Torrance House	On the eastern crenelations, in the corner of the roof, just east of the skeletal couple embracing, and "Hubba Hubba" wood blocks.
93	Torrance House	On the top of the corner of the stone perimeter wall of the hedge maze.
94	Hornwright Summer Villa	On top of the garden gazebo, near the greenhouse.

REGION 2: TOXIC VALLEY

#	PRIMARY LOCATION NAME	BOBBLEHEAD LOCATION DESCRIPTION
1	The Crosshair	On the rusting human cage (turned sideways) at the back of the cave alcove, by a small light-blue cooler, near the tire and spikes.
1	The Crosshair	On wooden crates just left of the Armor Workbench, on the northeastern alcove part of the camp, just beyond the Radstag hanging pole.
2	Clancy Manor	On a wood board between one of the sets of two dormer windows, on the exterior (back side) roof of the manor.
3	Cobbleton Farm	On the central apex of the roof with the four different-colored sheets attached to it; this may fall to the center of the shack below.
4	Lady Janet's Soft Serve	Either on the blue metal window sill, or the broken trailer roof apex, near the locked safe (1) at the northwest end of the ice cream trailer.
7	Becker Farm	On the bedside drawer with the hat and radio on it, south corner of the bedroom, inside the white house by the bridge.
7	Becker Farm	On or below the metal table right of the Industrial Trunk, opposite the safe (1), upstairs in the roofless white farmhouse south of the aerosolizer.
10	Eastern Regional Penitentiary	By a Caps Stash, by the two small chimneys, in the southeast corner of the roof of the penitentiary building (exterior).
10	Eastern Regional Penitentiary	On the corner of the mainframe computer bank, inside the south (middle) watchtower (above the main entrance), on the roof of the penitentiary (exterior).
10	Eastern Regional Penitentiary	On the dirt ground near the rock outcrop, outside the perimeter of the location, just right of the huge hole in the wall, below the north watchtower (exterior).
10	Eastern Regional Penitentiary	On top of the locked safe (0), in the cell with the two barrels, inside Cell Block B, upper level, by the crumbling floor.

#	PRIMARY LOCATION NAME	BOBBLEHEAD LOCATION DESCRIPTION
13	Wavy Willard's Water Park	On, in, or near the open lockers under the "L" in the "Lockers" sign, in the raised and covered locker room area of the Wavy Waves swimming pool area of the water park (exterior).
13	Wavy Willard's Water Park	On the workman's wall board, above the Armor Workbench, inside the Employees Only maintenance garage, beyond the fence at the deep end of the swimming pool.
13	Wavy Willard's Water Park	On the metal shelving on the raised wood platform camp, inside the mouth of Wavy Willard (the crocodile), in the Crocolossus Mountain ride.
13	Wavy Willard's Water Park	On the toolbox sitting on the metal shelving, on the opposite wall to the fusion core generator, in the flooded basement maintenance room under the park.
14	Willard Corporate Housing	On the metal desk by the ruined terminal, in the trailer just north of the roundabout and cooking station.
18	Kiddie Corner Cabins	On the desk inside the ruined trailer, just north of the roundabout and cooking station.
19	Black Bear Lodge	On the metal desk, above the green footlocker, near the door, in the Huntmaster's basement office, inside the lodge.
22	Pioneer Scout Camp	On the edge of a picnic table in the upper dining area of the mess hall (interior).
22	Pioneer Scout Camp	On top of the adventure tower (not the lookout tower), accessed via the log ramp and rickety wood platforms attached to the tower (exterior).
26	Philippi Battlefield Cemetery	On the shelf below the wooden counter (far left end), inside the wooden museum structure.

TRAINING

CRAFTING AND C.A.M.P.ING

INVENTORY

QUESTS

ATLAS

BESTIARY

APPENDICES

#	PRIMARY LOCATION NAME	BOBBLEHEAD LOCATION DESCRIPTION
ZONE A: BECKLEY AND MOUNT BLAIR		
1	Camden Park	On the small ride cart with the skeleton, on the tracks just below the "Minor Miner Zone" sign.
1	Camden Park	On the file box between the two filing cabinets, behind the desk with the terminal on it, in metal employees-only warehouse.
1	Camden Park	On the rollercoaster "hut", at the summit of the first ascent, just above a crashed rollercoaster train (that's halfway up the track), on The Widow Maker ride.
1	Camden Park	On the barrel by the green plastic outhouse, at the ruined Raider stall, on the north side of the camp in the middle of The Widow Maker ride.
4	Relay Tower HG-B7-09	On the roof of the hut, at the base of the tower mast, by the skeletal remains of the worker.
6	Belching Betty	On top of the tool box (one of two) inside the white-and-orange trailer, inside the mine at the shaft and stairwell (at the side of the railroad tracks, near the Chemistry Station).
6	Belching Betty	On the inside corner shelving in the storage and locker room midway down the main shaft steps.
6	Belching Betty	By the body of firefighter Rita Wilcox, on a metal table by a mainframe computer between the two light-blue generators in the main cavern generator room.
6	Belching Betty	On the end of a horizontal metal rod, in a tunnel alcove in the long conveyor belt room, before the exit.
7	The Rusty Pick	Behind Mick Flanagan's terminal, on the metal desk, inside the cellar workbench room, just before the locked (2) double doors (interior).
7	The Rusty Pick	Behind an overturned, half-buried barrel near pallets and containers in netting, in the dead-end cavern at the end of the tunnel (with the rough barrel-and-wood table in the middle) (interior).
10	Beckley	On a small green card table, on the upper defensive Raider wall, south side, in the middle of town.
10	Beckley	On the inside of the "C" shape of the air conditioning duct, on the roof of the inaccessible store just south of the gas station, on the east side of town; access this via the rooftops of the taller structures to the west.
11	Sal's Grinders	On the desk by Sal's personal terminal, in the large upstairs bedroom with the trunk (interior).
11	Sal's Grinders	On the roof of the (inaccessible) gun shop attached to Sal's Grinders, with other junk and detritus, near the hole from inside the Sal's Grinders upstairs building (exterior).
16	Mount Blair Trainyard	Northwest area; halfway down the narrow coal conveyor belt running from the Abandoned Mine Shaft Elaine area into the trainyard, just east of the long blue metal hut platform.
16	Mount Blair Trainyard	On the southern edge of the roof, at the foot of the large chimney on the western trainyard (large concrete structure) roof, between the two concrete rooftop extractor fans.
16	Mount Blair Trainyard	On the northeastern corner of the eastern trainyard roof, near the small corner chevron plate, on the exterior corner of the locked (2) roof maintenance hut.
16	Mount Blair Trainyard	On a girder holding the large L-shaped coal pipe attached to the huge bulbous white metal tower, above the coal carriages east of the yard building; access via enhanced jumps, careful pipe walking, or explosive weaponry.
17	Mount Blair	On the oval table inside the west trailer, near the large bulldozer warehouse southeast of the gigantic bucket wheel excavator.
17	Mount Blair	In the basement (ID card needed) of one of the bulldozer garages, through the barred door, on or near the tall tool cabinet near the explosive canisters and metal shelving.
19	Rollins Work Camp	Tucked under the winch cables on the roof of the huge bucket excavator, accessed via the rust-red gantry.

#	PRIMARY LOCATION NAME	BOBBLEHEAD LOCATION DESCRIPTION
ZONE B: LEWISBURG, WELCH, AND GARRAHAN MINING		
21	The Burning Mine	On the blue conveyor end attached to the yellow machinery, at the lower end of the sloping coal conveyor belt, in the huge tiered chamber, inside the mine.
21	The Burning Mine	On a metal shelf behind the fusion core generator, on the western side of the large room with the gantry platform, large blue piston machinery, metal stairs, and two conveyor belts.
21	The Burning Mine	Inside the yellow and metal crate trolley, on the tiered rock area with the burning coal, halfway down the large smoke-filled room with the generators at the bottom and metal gantry steps and shaft structure at the top (and small tunnel entrances at the top).
21	The Burning Mine	On top of the metal mainframe computer in the upper break room with the jukebox, in the room with the two yellow generators, where the coring takes place.
22	Widow's Perch	At the very end of the plank linking the shack to the top of the billboard, on the top middle edge of the billboard itself, at the foot of the opposite fence post to the radio.
25	Uncanny Caverns	On or around the Nuka-Cola machine on the wood deck, just right of audio tour #1.
25	Uncanny Caverns	On the rocks above the sprawled skeleton near the lantern and liquor bottles; the small cave at audio tour #6.
25	Uncanny Caverns	On the rocks by a small patch of Glowing Fungus and skeletal remains, across from the "cold deep" water, southeast of the audio switch for tour #7 (wooden deck bridge).
25	Uncanny Caverns	On the horizontal "crease" part of the cave wall, left of the two sleeping bags, right of the cooking station, in the cave with the trunk, part of audio tour #8.
27	Bastion Park	On the ground by the bench with the two skeletons on it, near the flagpole, on the north (cliff) side of the park.
27	Bastion Park	Inside the school bus, second seat on the right from the driver's seat. The bus is parked next to the fountain.
31	Lewisburg	On the crate acting as a side table, in the "rooftop living room" on top of the two-level white brick building, in the east-central block of the rooftop garden area of town.
31	Lewisburg	On or near the writing desk, in the upper interior of the Visitor Center, close to the restroom door.
34	Big Bend Tunnel West	On a filing cabinet, behind the metal counter with the wire wall and locked door, in the central mine warehouse (accessed via the key), in the middle of the tunnel interior.
40	AMS Testing Site	At the south warehouse, on the south-middle edge of the arched roof, on the ground near the fusion core generator outside, or behind the two concrete barriers near the Power Armor Station.
42	Red Rocket Filling Station	On the southeast corner of the roof of the filling station; attempt to reach via the cylinders and trailers; enhanced jumping may be needed.
44	Hornwright Testing Site #03	On the small light blue mainframe computer at the end of the gantry.
46	Striker Row	On the dashboard radio, inside the rusting coach/tent near the tire piles.
46	Striker Row	On the metal desk, inside the blue-and-white metal trailer, at the top of the location by a trunk and tarp-covered sitting area.
50	Garrahan Mining Headquarters	On the white shelf, in the southeast corner of the CEO's office, inside the headquarters.

REGION 4: SAVAGE DIVIDE

#	PRIMARY LOCATION NAME	BOBBLEHEAD LOCATION DESCRIPTION
ZONE A: NORTH MOUNTAINS, SUNNYTOP, AND MONONGAH		
1	Palace of the Winding Path	On top of or below (underwater) one of the two gigantic vats, in the basement with the generator and gantry.
3	Bailey Family Cabin	On the metal shelving, two shelves down from the teddy bear, inside the rusting metal caravan.
5	Site Bravo	In the Reactor Area, on top of plywood, on some large green crates, on the northeast side of the main room.
5	Site Bravo	In the Operations Center, on some metal crates, in a side room to your left, just past the first laser grid, under the painting of the mountain and lake.
5	Site Bravo	In the Storage Area's main room, on the inside corner of the shelves just outside the door to the room with the Tinker's Workbench.
5	Site Bravo	In the Control Room, on the upper-level platform, on top of the tall consoles just outside the Launch Control Chief's room.
8	Sunnytop Ski Lanes	On the rusting human cages with the skeleton draped on them, on the green tin roof porch of the side (southeast) building, on the southwest exterior side of that building (access via the smashed window from bedroom #6).
8	Sunnytop Ski Lanes	On the ornate dresser with the skull and locked Guest Terminal (1), to the right of the large stone fireplace, in guest room #2.
8	Sunnytop Ski Lanes	On the corner of the counter shelving, to the right of Vincent Fried's Terminal, southwest end of the ski rental counter, facing the lockers.
8	Sunnytop Ski Lanes	On the corner of the computer bank, inside the tiny lift operator hut, by the ski gondola line.
9	Sunnytop Ski Lanes Base Lodge	On or under the counter with the lockers behind them, below (and near) a blue cash register, in the northwest corner window overlooking the parking lot.
9	Sunnytop Ski Lanes Base Lodge	On the white corner computer bank (with the ham radio on it), in the southwest corner of the upper balcony mezzanine, next to the terminal in the white wooden wall alcove.
12	Hopewell Cave	On the triangular hole directly above the cave entrance; access with enhanced jumping or explosive weaponry.
16	Ingram Mansion	On the mantle of the stone fireplace, just left of the trunk, at the western end of the mansion, in the master bedroom.
21	Monongah	Among the junk (mini-nuke, baseball bat) on the wooden crate pile behind the security gate (1) attached to the brick cottage near the center of town.
22	Observatory	On top of the viewing lens, in the huge domed telescope chamber (interior).
24	Sons of Dane Compound	On the desk by Dane Roger's Terminal on the upstairs landing, inside the faded blue farmhouse.
24	Sons of Dane Compound	On the right side of the left cinder block section, at the shooting range south of The Buck's Den (exterior).
24	Sons of Dane Compound	On the amplifier under the stairs, on the left side of the stage with the instruments, east wall of The Buck's Den.
25	Relay Tower LW-B1-22	In the locker to the right of the computer bank, on the northwest wall of the interior, inside the hut.
26	Sylvie & Sons Logging Camp	On the cardboard box and wood crates at the back of the large green tent just to the left of the rusting pickup truck.
26	Sylvie & Sons Logging Camp	On the metal containers with the rounded corners, at the back of the small green tent with the rusting dirt bike propped up next to it.
ZONE B: CENTRAL MOUNTAINS, PLEASANT VALLEY, AND WHITESPRING		
30	Seneca Gang Camp	On the small painted dresser behind the faded red trunk, by the red seat with the corpse on it, near the safe (1) on the south side of the camp.
31	Wendigo Cave	In the cave alcove with the spike floor trap board, two sleeping bags, and skeletons, inside the cave interior.
31	Wendigo Cave	In the watery junction cavern with the rock column, between two skeletons, open first aid boxes, and some revolting offal, in a small blue tray container, inside the cave interior.
31	Wendigo Cave	At the foot of a rock column, by some Canned Dog Food, near a skeleton in the junction cavern of the cave interior.

#	PRIMARY LOCATION NAME	BOBBLEHEAD LOCATION DESCRIPTION
31	Wendigo Cave	By the chained skeleton with the red bandana, below the shaft of light in the rubble-filled alcove with the metal box, inside the cave interior.
32	Autumn Acre Cabin	On the small writing table, next to a coffee mug, by the restroom doorway, inside the cabin.
33	Toxic Larry's Meat 'n Go	On the top of the oven, inside the main shack, near and under the hanging meats.
33	Toxic Larry's Meat 'n Go	Near the ruined metal shelf with the gas canister, on the roof of the main shack by the spit-roast cooking station.
34	Skullbone Vantage	On the leather couch, at the top of the cliffside tower.
35	Pleasant Valley Cabins	Above the Raider shanty town, on the low roof connecting the first two chalets, close to (and above) a bus stop, on a ham radio sitting on a crate under a black-and-white umbrella.
35	Pleasant Valley Cabins	Above the Raider shanty town, on the upper floor of the chalet with parts of its roof missing, on the floor by a short book cabinet, by the pool table.
36	Top of the World	On or below the TV stand opposite the sofa, inside the central elevator column (south side), in the middle of the giant shopping platform (interior).
36	Top of the World	On or near the amplifier on the tin stage (with instruments) northeast of the central elevator column (upper interior).
36	Top of the World	On the wooden shelf with the gramophone on it, behind the rickety shop counter west of the central elevator column (interior).
37	Pleasant Valley Ski Resort	On the red ski gondola, atop the Raider defensive wall, on the eastern corner of the defenses.
37	Pleasant Valley Ski Resort	On the shelf with the three teddy bears, inside the main lodge at the Responder Trading Post, next to the Vendor Bot and counter.
37	Pleasant Valley Ski Resort	On the desk with the ruined terminal and holotape, in the Employees Only office, on the hallway inside the main lodge, close to the Trading Post.
39	South Cutthroat Camp	On the ledge of the red ski gondola toilet, with the "Caution Wet Floor" sign outside it, on the north edge of the road.
39	South Cutthroat Camp	On the small side table, just left of the burgundy sofa "car throne" seat, on the north side of the road.
39	South Cutthroat Camp	On top of the burgundy "car throne" chair, near the trunk on the south side of the road.
39	South Cutthroat Camp	In the tall glass cabinet, on the right side of the storefront on the south side of the road.
40	North Cutthroat Camp	On the floor below (tire pile) or the low wall of the checkpoint tower attached to the large Raider skull billboard.
42	Yellow Sandy's Still	On the wooden connecting 2x4s hammered into the tree by the east metal trailer, on the roof of the trailer by the tree and the green road sign (used as a platform).
43	Cliffwatch	On the lower of the two platforms of the main lookout, behind the wooden steps, near the metal bucket and sleeping bag.
44	Safe 'n Clean Disposal	Sitting on the seat next to the skeleton driving the small yellow bulldozer, by the fetid pond.
45	New Appalachian Central Trainyard	On the wooden desk with the typewriter, eastern side (with windows), inside the dull red-wallpapered interior, in the upstairs part of the half-demolished bank building.
46	98 NAR Regional	On the small book cabinet near the bed, inside the overturned military carriage lying on top of two other carriages; accessed via the opening underneath.
49	Site Alpha	In the Reactor Area, on top of some plywood, on some large green crates, on the northeast side of the main room.
49	Site Alpha	In the Operations Center, on some metal crates, in a side room to your left, just past the first laser grid, under the painting of the mountain and lake.
49	Site Alpha	In the Storage Area's main room, on the inside corner of the shelves just outside the door to the room with the Tinker's Workbench.
49	Site Alpha	In the Control Room, on the upper-level platform, on top of the tall consoles just outside the Launch Control Chief's room.

#	PRIMARY LOCATION NAME	BOBBLEHEAD LOCATION DESCRIPTION
51	The Whitespring Golf Club	Inside the clubhouse, on the lower level, in one of the trophy case windows in the hallway with the snack bar at one end.
51	The Whitespring Golf Club	Inside the clubhouse, on the lower level, on a shelf under the counter at the far left end of the shoe-shine counter in the men's locker room.
52	The Whitespring Resort	On the side table in the children's bedroom, on the second floor of The Whitespring Presidential Cottage and Museum.

ZONE C: SOUTH MOUNTAINS, SUGAR GROVE, AND SPRUCE KNOB

#	PRIMARY LOCATION NAME	BOBBLEHEAD LOCATION DESCRIPTION
57	Blackwater Mine	On the middle chimney, on the roof of the curve-roofed warehouse with the mine entrance inside. This is on the exterior roof, and may require projectiles or enhancing jumping to access.
57	Blackwater Mine	Underwater, at the bottom of the vertical cavern with the metal gantry and generator at the top.
57	Blackwater Mine	On the metal desk with the ammo, in the tiny computer room with a view of the mine shaft, a short tunnel away from the vertical cavern.
57	Blackwater Mine	On the horizontal metal bar, in the dead-end alcove to the right of the exit ladder, behind the two chevron blockades.
58	Middle Mountain Cabins	On the desk with the Pioneer Scout Terminal, between the bunk beds, in the center (south) cabin.
58	Middle Mountain Cabins	On the mantle of the fireplace, on the northwest side of the right (southwest) cabin.
59	Emmett Mountain Disposal Site	Hidden on the ground behind three corroding metal barrels, in the small locked (1) metal garage, inside the upper fenced exterior area with the two large, blue, vertical processing units.
59	Emmett Mountain Disposal Site	Inside the right sink, in the south corner of the curve-roofed warehouse, just right of the mine entrance door.
59	Emmett Mountain Disposal Site	On the orange forklift with the radioactive barrels, at the interior mine junction, at the southeast end of the initial mine tunnel.
60	Ripper Alley	Up the hill off the road, by a human spine on a rock alcove with strewn bones and candles, near the small lookout and possible Power Armor frame.
61	National Isolated Radio Array	By the suicidal skeleton slumped on the northern edge of the roof of the Office Building; access it via the roof of the crashed red big rig trailer.
61	National Isolated Radio Array	On or near the metal shelving, in the northwest corner of the mezzanine upstairs balcony inside the maintenance warehouse (with the two flagpoles outside).
61	National Isolated Radio Array	On the work surface counter, against the wall of the locked (2) maintenance warehouse side room (where a Power Armor frame may be available).
61	National Isolated Radio Array	On top of, or on the floor near the small central mainframe computer island, inside the dish array control hut at the foot of the dish (with the flagpole outside).
62	Sugar Grove	In the green wall cabinet, in the northwest corner of the Advanced Research Laboratory, opposite the collection of blank holotapes, in the upper floor with the window.
62	Sugar Grove	Behind the upturned orange cylindrical cabinet on the desk, inside the small storage room; the last room on the right if heading north at the bottom of the stairs on the lower level.
62	Sugar Grove	On the far metal desk, in the curved corner of the narrow reception and security room, locked with a door (1) and terminal, off the lower lobby, en route to the mission control room.
62	Sugar Grove	On or at the foot of the mainframe computer, in the northeast corner of The Archives.
62	Sugar Grove	On the wooden table, in the green wallpapered cognitive programming room (with the three televisions), in the Secret Facility basement.
62	Sugar Grove	On the wooden crates by the wall, near the two blue barrels, in the southwest corner of the Secret Facility, close to a security door and metal shelving.
63	National Radio Astronomy Research Center	On the mainframe computer in the locked (1) office with the locked safe (1), at the top of the brick stairwell.
63	National Radio Astronomy Research Center	On the tall tool case, in the small room with the Armor Workbench and giant wall fan, adjacent to the ruined generator basement room.
64	West Tek Research Center	On a small mainframe computer sill, next to a beaker of Toxic Goo, near the yellow machinery, just inside the Dispensary Lab.
65	US-13C Bivouac	On the wood crates at the front (left side) of the green tent with tarp entrance (south), just left of the telephone pole.
65	US-13C Bivouac	On the curved metal containers, at the back of the green tent, southwest area, just right of the telephone pole.
67	Mountainside Bed & Breakfast	On or near the metal shelf with the ladder leaning on it, inside the kitchen pantry, inside the house.
67	Mountainside Bed & Breakfast	On the reception desk just behind the Comment Terminal, in the locked (2) foyer area of the house.
67	Mountainside Bed & Breakfast	On top of the television, in the upstairs landing living room with the board games, green carpet, and dark red furniture, inside the house.
67	Mountainside Bed & Breakfast	On or near the washing machine, by the Tinker's Workbench in the chained basement room, inside the house.
67	Mountainside Bed & Breakfast	On the upper deck fence or floor, near the trunk, outside the locked (0) door, once the house has been explored; outside the house.
69	Solomon's Pond	On top of the tin roof of the workbench structure, with the Chemistry and Tinker's Workbenches underneath.
72	Huntersville	On the edge of the broken attic floor, above the upper bedroom, inside the half-destroyed house with the red star, red roof, and light blue siding (with a locked (1) terminal, and Gail Meyer's Terminal).
72	Huntersville	Perched above the Plumbing sign near the collapsed roof, at the back of the Hardware store.
75	Site Charlie	In the Reactor Area, on top of some plywood, on some large green crates, on the northeast side of the main room.
75	Site Charlie	In the Operations Center, on some metal crates, in a side room to your left, just past the first laser grid, under the painting of the mountain and lake.
75	Site Charlie	In the Storage Area's main room, on the inside corner of the shelves just outside the door to the room with the Tinker's Workbench.
75	Site Charlie	In the Control Room, on the upper-level platform, on top of the tall consoles just outside the Launch Control Chief's room.
76	R&G Processing Services	On the green wall cabinet, southeast corner of the double garage with the orange forklift in it, next to the gantry ramp.
79	Spruce Knob Lake	Inside the military hideout cave on the north shore of the lake, on or near the rock shelf above the stilt platform with the sleeping bag on it.
80	Spruce Knob	On or near the circular geographical survey marker, at the vista point southwest of the observation tower.
81	Spruce Knob Campground	On or under the small green table next to the cooking station, below the monorail pylon (exterior).
84	Lucky Hole Mine	On the bottom lip of the chalkboard, in the hidden chem laboratory inside the mine.
84	Lucky Hole Mine	On the metal table with the beakers, right of the chalkboard, in the hidden chem laboratory inside the mine.
84	Lucky Hole Mine	On the mainframe computer bank with the large blue cylinder behind it, right of the trunk, in the hidden chem laboratory.
91	Relay Tower EL-B1-02	On the metal desk next to the maintenance personnel terminal, against the central pillar, inside the hut.
92	Johnson's Acre	In the "effluent hole" of the outhouse.
92	Johnson's Acre	By the corner of the broken wood crate with the skeleton inside, near the tire and detritus pile, on the top of the tall rock promontory with the three dead skeletons (and possible Power Armor frame), east of the cabin.

REGION 5: THE MIRE

#	PRIMARY LOCATION NAME	BOBBLEHEAD LOCATION DESCRIPTION
	**ZONE A: NORTH MIRE, THUNDER MOUNTAIN, AND BERKELEY SPRINGS**	
5	Southhampton Estate	On the right side of the bed headboard, in the upstairs bedroom, inside the tendril-infested farmhouse.
5	Southhampton Estate	On the small metal table, in the northeast corner of the upper balcony area, inside the tendril-infested red barn.
13	Mosstown	On the cube-shaped metal work surface with the oven mitts, inside the Waffle shack, in the middle of the location.
13	Mosstown	On the metal desk with the typewriter, inside the Motel shack, in the northwest corner of the location.
15	Dolly Sods Wilderness	West lodge building, inside (after climbing the stairs by the red star and American flag) in the upstairs bunk bedroom, on the left of the two dressers along the south wall.
15	Dolly Sods Wilderness	South lodge, inside in the gift shop, on the lowest shelf of the metal counter with the green cash register on it, in front of the wall with the Nuka-Cola clock and poster.
19	Crevasse Dam	Enter via the west entrance of the main building (with the Can Chimes), open the first door ahead and to the left, enter the office and workroom, and check the sink in the northeast corner.
19	Crevasse Dam	In the mainframe computer alcove, on the concrete balcony with the sandbags, on the upper part of the large pump room, inside the secondary building.
21	Thunder Mountain Power Plant	At the right end, atop the black mainframe computer on the wall marked "Turbine Hall", at corner of the corridor from Cooling Tower #2 (interior).
21	Thunder Mountain Power Plant	On an explosives box, under the toxic water, in the flooded base of the giant fuel storage room (interior).
21	Thunder Mountain Power Plant	In the toxic water, under the middle of five submerged trolley carts carrying yellow radiation barrels, in the flooded bottom of the smaller Fuel Storage room with the gantry ramp (below the large open red warehouse doors and "Reactor" sign).
21	Thunder Mountain Power Plant	In the small section of rusting hatch pipe, right in the northwestern corner of the Reactor Room.
21	Thunder Mountain Power Plant	On the corner (light blue) mainframe computer bank, at the foot of the reactor, south side of the Reactor Room.
22	Dyer Chemical	On the ground in the northeast corner, by the empty filing cabinet, across from the trapped Caps Stash, in the "welcome" office off the locker room, on the south side of the facility.
22	Dyer Chemical	At the bottom of an open filing cabinet, part of a cluster of cabinets in a blue gantry maintenance hut with two giant pipes on the east wall, in the northwestern upper storage warehouse area.
22	Dyer Chemical	In the southwest corner, at the base of a vertical steel girder and metal work surface, inside the main storage area, just left of the Chemistry Station and Nuka-Cola machine.
22	Dyer Chemical	In a small blue tray-crate (with other trays) in the northwest upper-level corner, left of the top of the gantry stairs, above the locked door to the sewers, in the Sewer Maintenance Building.
25	Berkeley Springs West	On the ornate table, inside the ruined upper chamber (exposed to the outside) in the castle mansion, accessed via the scaffolding.

#	PRIMARY LOCATION NAME	BOBBLEHEAD LOCATION DESCRIPTION
26	Berkeley Springs	On a small, two-shelf table with a bottle on it, outside on the tiered rock outcrop, below the hotel and behind city hall, near the white wooden steps and bathtub.
26	Berkeley Springs	On the television stand, in the southwest corner of the blue wallpapered apartment above Graviano's Italian Eatery (access via the roof).
28	Treehouse Village	In the fridge, on the Bar platform, east side of the village.
28	Treehouse Village	Behind the support post, near the sleeping bag and dark red sofa, in the platform shack with the two birdhouses in it.
28	Treehouse Village	Behind the metal crate with the ammo crate on top of it, near the blue rocket ship rug, in the plane wing platform, north west side of the village.
29	Haven Church	On the desk next to Skig's Terminal, in the hallway office.
	**ZONE B: SOUTH MIRE, HARPERS FERRY, AND TANAGRA TOWN**	
30	Hawke's Refuge	In a cardboard box, by a wooden wall section (and orange tool box) and Can Chimes, as on the way into the second cavern, on the upper level.
30	Hawke's Refuge	Near a half-buried Nuka-Cola crate, in the cave alcove camp with the sleeping bag, in the northwest end of the refuge.
31	Sunday Brothers' Cabin	At the base of the small weathervane cupola, on the roof of the large red barn.
36	Tanagra Town	On the headboard of the master bedroom bed, in the collapsed dark gray house with the moonshine still in the bathtub and the Giddyup Buttercup on the main floor, at the summit of the massive town tangle.
38	Big B's Rest Stop	Under the mattress bed, on the roof of the Super Duper Mart building, below the "R" of the sign.
39	Valley Galleria	In the display case above the wall safe, on the left side of Big Steve's Sporting Goods (upon entering), in the alcove area behind the main display cases.
39	Valley Galleria	On the long metal light fixture (ceiling height), in the small corridor of the locked (2) and trapped (grenades) changing rooms, inside Valley's Boutique.
39	Valley Galleria	On the wheelchair between the tree and trash can, on the upper balcony in the northwestern corner of the Galleria (interior).
40	Treetops	By the sleeping bag, orange tool cabinet, and small side dresser, east of the bowling pins.
40	Treetops	In the center of the bowling pins.
40	Treetops	On the tiny platform with the red Garden Gnome, south of the bowling pins.
40	Treetops	On the small writing desk with the typewriter and tea kettle, near a traffic cone, on the platform with the rugs and wood blocks.
42	Camp Venture	Between the two small chimneys on the roof of the Brotherhood of Steel Storage Cabin (with the locked (key) security gate inside) (exterior).
42	Camp Venture	On the floor between the metal work table (left) and the Weapons Workbench (right), inside the Storage Cabin (with the locked (key) security gate) (interior).
42	Camp Venture	Hidden in the grass between two green plastic barrels, near the latched containers by the low gantry ramp up to the Command Center door (3).

TRAINING

CRAFTING AND C.A.M.P.ING

INVENTORY

QUESTS

ATLAS

BESTIARY

APPENDICES

#	PRIMARY LOCATION NAME	BOBBLEHEAD LOCATION DESCRIPTION
	**ZONE A: NORTH BOG, ROBCO RESEARCH CENTER, AND ABANDONED BOG TOWN**	
1	Kerwood Mine	Near a support strut and wooden crate (1), in a mine alcove before you descend into the water, close to a junction with an explosive canister (mine interior).
1	Kerwood Mine	Near a support strut and ammo box, in a small dead-end alcove, southeast of the main mine tracks, just above the cave-in that blocks the track tunnel (mine interior).
1	Kerwood Mine	Inside the "effluent hole", inside a green plastic outhouse, underwater on the metal platform, in the flooded cavern with the huge yellow extractor fan on the ceiling (mine interior).
1	Kerwood Mine	Hidden with the wood crate, explosive canister, yellow crate trolley, and netted crates, close to an orange forklift, southwest of the red trunk, in the Junction Cavern (mine interior).
2	Firebase Major	Inside the green tent, by the sleeping bag.
5	Mac's Farm	On a wooden barrel, inside the muddy ruined moonshine barn by the cranberry pond.
6	The General's Steakhouse	On the shelf of the short bookcase, just right of the trunk, in the upper balcony area, in the northwest corner of the main interior restaurant area.
6	The General's Steakhouse	On a small crate with a green suitcase and barrel, in the middle of the roof (exterior).
7	RobCo Research Center	Under the red wrist sill of a mainframe computer, at the south end of the locked laboratory, in the research wing (ground floor interior).
7	RobCo Research Center	In the bottom desk shelf under the terminal, in the office just left of the Protectron pod, on the western side of upper curved balcony chamber.
7	RobCo Research Center	In the south corner, by the locked safe (3), to the right of the elevator, in the upper laboratory area.
8	The Thorn	By the green footlocker and wood crate, at the back of the green tent.
9	Forward Station Alpha	On the metal shelf, in the rear-left corner of the green tent.
11	Ranger District Office	Near Ranger Simon's Terminal, on the filing cabinet or the floor, near the locked safe (3) in the northwest office.
12	Ranger Lookout	On or below the desk at the top of the lookout tower.
14	Bootlegger's Shack	Behind the wooden crates in the northwest corner, just left of the Armor Workbench.
14	Bootlegger's Shack	Under the shack, on the workman's tool board, by the restroom in the chem lab.
16	Quarry X3	On the metal desk inside the orange-and-white metal caravan with the flag outside.
18	Pylon V-13	On a yellow tub, in the monorail cockpit, in the monorail suspended from the rails.
19	Old Mold Quarry	On the filing cabinet by the central desk, inside the metal maintenance hut with the Weapons Workbench in it.
	**ZONE B: SOUTH BOG AND WATOGA**	
21	Fort Defiance	In the top floor BoS base of operations, on the writing desk, inside the eastern corner office with the terminal.
22	Appalachian Antiques	On the very edge of the roof of the main structure, above the wind chimes (northeast edge of the premises); also check the area below where the pallets are.
22	Appalachian Antiques	At the right corner (foot) of the bed, near the white suitcase, in the mezzanine bedroom inside the antique shop.
25	Cranberry Glade	On the corner of the decking with the duffle bag, in the far eastern corner of the location.
27	NAR Repair Yard	On the filing cabinet by the locked safe (2) in the signal tower.
29	Watoga Civic Center	On the front balcony row, between seat section B3 and B4, upper area inside the Civic Center (interior).
29	Watoga Civic Center	On the bar stool by the safe, in the middle locked (key) VIP suite, upper area inside the Civic Center (interior).

#	PRIMARY LOCATION NAME	BOBBLEHEAD LOCATION DESCRIPTION
29	Watoga Civic Center	On the tall ashtray right of the cigarette machine, in the north VIP suite, upper area inside the Civic Center (interior).
30	Watoga Transit Hub	In the Hub lobby (ground level), on the far left side of the main reception desk with the locked (3) Front Desk Terminal on it.
30	Watoga Transit Hub	On the desk with the ruined terminal, in the locked (3) generator closet that may have a Power Armor frame in it, off the lobby room.
31	Watoga Emergency Services	On the counter, or the lower shelf of the L-shaped reception desk, across from the waiting room and elevators on either side of the desk (interior).
31	Watoga Emergency Services	On the narrow metal shelf below the "Protect Your Hands!" poster, right of the Protectron pod, in the server room (interior).
31	Watoga Emergency Services	On the metal counter along the north wall of the locked (2) laboratory with the Brotherhood of Steel corpses inside.
32	Watoga Municipal Center	On the desk with the terminal (2), in the small office on the second level balcony, northeast side (interior), close to the elevator and stairwell.
32	Watoga Municipal Center	Sitting on the blade of the ceiling fan, above the desk with the suitcase, in the Senator's locked (2) office.
33	AMS Corporate Headquarters	On a small ornate desk next to a typewriter and slumped skeleton, on the west conference table area near a safe, in the Executive Level floor of the building's interior.
34	Watoga Shopping Plaza	On a low counter, shelf, or the ground below the blue cash register inside the Hubris Comics & Toys store.
35	Watoga Estates	On the top shelf by the coffee machine, near the trunk at the roof bar, left of the "condemned" door and sign, opposite the jukebox, near the swimming pool (exterior).
37	Watoga High School	On the curved desk, to the left of the Headmaster's Terminal (2), inside the Headmaster's Office (interior).
37	Watoga High School	In the fridge, in the kitchen adjacent to the cafeteria (interior).
37	Watoga High School	On one of the long wooden art tables, in the Art Studio (ground floor, interior).
37	Watoga High School	On the long desk with the green chair and destroyed terminal, in the Director's Office behind the seating in the auditorium (interior).
37	Watoga High School	On the air conditioning duct, adjacent to the rooftop tent and sleeping bags camp, in the middle of the roof (exterior).
38	Flooded Trainyard	On the file box, by the desk inside the signal tower, near the rusting crane and locomotive.
39	Firebase Hancock	On or in the narrow locker, inside the western white-and-orange trailer caravan with the BoS flagpole by it.
40	Lost Home	On the southern corner of the corrugated roof, on or near the blue tray container (one of two possible Bobbleheads in this tray), by the green card table and two deck chairs (sniper's area), exterior.
40	Lost Home	On the southern corner of the corrugated roof, on or near the blue tray container (one of two possible Bobbleheads in this tray), by the green card table and two deck chairs (sniper's area), exterior.
40	Lost Home	In the small wood box with the paint box and "animal control" chem box, in the southern corner shanty house with the dark red couch and cooking pot.
42	Sunrise Farm	On the bedside table, in the green-wallpapered master bedroom, southwest corner, upstairs in the main farmhouse (interior).
43	Survey Camp Alpha	On the wood crates at the back of the tent to the right of the Power Armor Station.
46	Drop Site V9	On the metal work surface with the lamp on it, just beyond the security gate (entrance inside the metal hut).
49	Forward Station Delta	Hidden between the small wood crates and tool box, to the right of the Power Armor Station.
49	Forward Station Delta	On the gantry balcony with the skeleton, at the base of the BoS flagpole.

APPENDIX: POWER ARMOR LOCATIONS

Though not quite as numerous as Bobbleheads and Magazines, Appalachia has a large number of Power Armor Frames, with attached Armor sections on each suit. Each also comes with a Fusion Core. The following are "known" locations where Power Armor has been spotted. They may not appear (this is random), or may have already been taken by other players, so keep checking on each location. If the description begins with the word "Raider", the Power Armor is likely to be of Raider quality, and lower level, though this is not guaranteed.

REGION 1: THE FOREST

#	PRIMARY LOCATION NAME	POWER ARMOR LOCATION DESCRIPTION
ZONE B: NORTHWEST FOREST AND POINT PLEASANT		
17	WV Lumber Co.	Inside one of the two Power Armor Stations, in the large metal warehouse, near the interior stairs, facing an ice and Nuka-Cola machine.
20	Aaronholt Homestead	Inside the shed by the three silos, in the Power Armor Station.
26	Black Mountain Ordnance Works	Inside one of the locked dome interiors (key), northeast of the works site (Nuka-Cola Power Armor).
27	Point Pleasant	Raider: In the power armor station, in the garage below the ruined bridge, at street level.
ZONE C: MORGANTOWN AND EASTERN FOREST		
31	Gorge Junkyard	Raider: Inside the locked green trailer (3) amid the junk, in the yard itself.
33	Morgantown Trainyard	Inside the "USA Star" green carriage with the crane above it, on the east side (and outside) of the main warehouse.
38	Mama Dolce's Food Processing	In the Power Armor Station, inside the booby-trapped warehouse, southwest of the Food Processing building.
38	Mama Dolce's Food Processing	In the secret Fujiniya Intelligence Base, in the locked (ID) Armory Closet, by the Main Processing room.
40	Grafton Dam	In the Power Armor Station, inside the metal storage shed, in the parking lot outside the main Dam building.
43	Arktos Pharma	In the Power Armor Station behind the Security Gate, in the vertipod Loading Dock, in the upper floor interior area.
ZONE D: SOUTHWEST FOREST		
63	Silva Homestead	In the Power Armor Station, inside the silo barn with the tractors, hay, and two Weapons Workbenches.
65	New River Gorge Bridge - West	Raider: In the Power Armor Station, in the locked (key) storage area below the start of the west span of the bridge.
67	Lewis & Sons Farming Supply	Left of the stairs, in the Power Armor Station, inside the tractor barn warehouse.
68	Kanawha Nuka-Cola Plant	In the Power Armor Station, in the sunken Loading Dock chamber, inside the plant.
72	Poseidon Energy Plant WV-06	Inside the locked Security Gate closet (2), in the basement workroom, adjacent to a Tinker's Workbench and Power Armor Station.
ZONE E: CHARLESTON AND SURROUNDINGS		
79	Hornwright Industrial Headquarters	At the bottom of the basement stairs, in the alcove next to two Docking Station Vending Machines.
83	Wade Airport	Raider: Inside the locked (2) and booby-trapped (plasma mine) blue trailer, on the southwestern corner of the runway.
83	Wade Airport	In the corner of the last curve-roofed hangar before the end of the runway, on the north side of the airport, near the ruined fuselage.

REGION 2: TOXIC VALLEY

#	PRIMARY LOCATION NAME	POWER ARMOR LOCATION DESCRIPTION
1	The Crosshair	Raider: Standing in the narrow alcove, just above the cooking station.
10	Eastern Regional Penitentiary	Standing in the Power Armor Station, inside the mechanic's warehouse in the middle of the prison yard.
15	Clarksburg	Raider: In the upper mechanic's room, next to a green trunk chest, in the small engine repair shop (brick tower), accessed via the roof and fire escape steps.
19	Black Bear Lodge	Inside the exterior small red barn with the fallen tree on it, standing between a barrel and chevron road sign.
27	Crashed Space Station	Raider: Southeast, on the upper edge of the crater, standing outside a compact lookout shack (with a Jangles the Moon Monkey inside).

REGION 3: THE ASH HEAP

#	PRIMARY LOCATION NAME	POWER ARMOR LOCATION DESCRIPTION
ZONE A: BECKLEY AND MOUNT BLAIR		
1	Camden Park	Raider: In the Power Armor Station, in the Raider camp within the rollercoaster.
6	Belching Betty	Inside the small concrete hut with the Fire Marshall Protectron, near the mine entrance.
7	The Rusty Pick	Raider: Behind the locked double doors (2) at the east end of the mine tunnel (interior).
10	Beckley	Standing by the military APC, on the south side of the central Raider wall.
15	Abandoned Mine Shaft Elaine	In the Power Armor Station, outside (east side of) the curve-roofed locker room structure.
16	Mount Blair Trainyard	In the Power Armor Station by the Tinker's Workbench, next to the entrance door (ground floor, with the green metal stairs on the outside above the doorway) on the south side of the main building.
17	Mount Blair	By the rusting pickup, inside the large, double-garage warehouse with the bulldozer parked inside.
19	Rollins Work Camp	Outside, in a Power Armor Station attached to the outer exterior of the southwest orange-and-white trailer hut.
ZONE B: LEWISBURG, WELCH, AND GARRAHAN MINING		
21	The Burning Mine	Mine interior, inner entrance room, by the huge red door, across from the Weapons Workbench.
34	Big Bend Tunnel West	Halfway between Lewisburg Station and Big Bend Tunnel West, outside a derailed military carriage.
34	Big Bend Tunnel West	In a Power Armor Station inside the warehouse; part of the locked interior in the center of the Big Bend Tunnel interior.
40	AMS Testing Site	Inside the large curve-roofed warehouse, in the corner Power Armor Station.
42	Red Rocket Filling Station	In the Power Armor Station, outside by the wire fence behind the station and two huge red fuel tanks.
46	Striker Row	Standing near robot parts, in a rock alcove near two chevron road barriers, across from (southeast of) the upper tarp, caravan, and flag.
50	Garrahan Mining Headquarters	In the "Testing Control and Assessment" area, with the terminals, laboratory equipment, and ceiling wiring; across from a Tinker's Workbench.
50	Garrahan Mining Headquarters	Armor Piece: In the "Testing Control and Assessment" area, with the terminals, laboratory equipment, and ceiling wiring; on the main laboratory table.
50	Garrahan Mining Headquarters	Armor Piece: In the "Testing Control and Assessment" area, with the terminals, laboratory equipment, and ceiling wiring; on the main laboratory table.
50	Garrahan Mining Headquarters	Armor Piece: In the "Testing Control and Assessment" area, with the terminals and laboratory equipment, spilled out of the overturned yellow crate trolley, between the Armor and Weapons Workbenches.
50	Garrahan Mining Headquarters	Excavator: Reward for completing Quest: Miner Miracles.

TRAINING

CRAFTING AND C.A.M.P.ING

INVENTORY

QUESTS

ATLAS

BESTIARY

APPENDICES

REGION 4: SAVAGE DIVIDE

#	PRIMARY LOCATION NAME	POWER ARMOR LOCATION DESCRIPTION
ZONE A: NORTH MOUNTAINS, SUNNYTOP, AND MONONGAH		
05	Site Bravo	In the Storage Area, near the Tinker's Workbench.
ZONE B: CENTRAL MOUNTAINS, PLEASANT VALLEY, AND WHITESPRING		
30	Seneca Gang Camp	Raider: Close to the cooking station, standing on metal flooring by a yellow machine.
31	Wendigo Cave	Raider: Between two corpses, at the foot of the "stepped" tunnel before the step you can only descend from.
35	Pleasant Valley Cabins	Raider: In the middle of the makeshift Raider "arena", part of one of the lodges in the Raider shanty town.
43	Cliffwatch	Raider: Standing at the foot of a skull spike, below the Raider tower, just outside the defense wall, on the cliff edge.
45	New Appalachian Central Trainyard	Standing outside the ramp of the "USA Star" carriage, inside the main warehouse.
47	Beckwith Farm	Raider: East of the farm, on the rock outcrop at a small Raider blockade along Route 105.
49	Site Alpha	In the Storage Area, near the Tinker's Workbench.
ZONE C: SOUTH MOUNTAINS, SUGAR GROVE, AND SPRUCE KNOB		
57	Blackwater Mine	Raider: In the Power Armor Station (exterior), at the doorway to the small metal mechanic's garage, adjacent to the two large blue pump cylinders.
58	Middle Mountain Cabins	Raider: Standing outside of the middle cabin, just left of the entrance steps and heads on stakes.
59	Emmett Mountain Disposal Site	In a Power Armor Station, in the locked (2) security area of the generator room, near the entrance to the disposal site mine (interior).
60	Ripper Alley	Raider: Up the hill off the road in a rock alcove with strewn bones and candles, standing next to a small lookout.
61	National Isolated Radio Array	Inside the locked (2) side area of the large metal warehouse with the two flags on either side of it, and blue big-rig trailer nearby.
65	US-13C Bivouac	In the exterior tent camp, inside the tent with the three blue barrels outside it.
69	Solomon's Pond	Standing in a Power Armor Station, next to the blue pond pump machinery, on a concrete base.
72	Huntersville	A fallen Brotherhood of Steel soldier, in the grass by the Brotherhood of Steel roadside graveyard, southeast of Huntersville.
72	Huntersville	Outside, in a Power Armor Station behind the metal garage, near the low military wall and two Super Mutant hanging cages.
75	Site Charlie	In the Storage Area, near the Tinker's Workbench.
77	R&G Station	Inside the locked (1) green truck trailer near the signal tower, behind the station.
84	Lucky Hole Mine	Behind the chained door, at the interior entrance area of the mine. Drop down from the gap above near the sleeping bag to reach it.
87	Federal Disposal Field HZ-21	Raider: Inside the main concrete facility building, in the cage room, in the Power Armor Station.
92	Johnson's Acre	Raider: On the high rock promontory with the three skeletons, roughly east of the cabin.

REGION 5: THE MIRE

#	PRIMARY LOCATION NAME	POWER ARMOR LOCATION DESCRIPTION
ZONE A: NORTH MIRE, THUNDER MOUNTAIN AND BERKELEY SPRINGS		
15	Dolly Sods Wilderness	Southeast of the lodge with the rusty pickup outside it; close to a tree and tree stump, near the remains of a concrete block campfire; in the woods.
19	Crevasse Dam	Raider: Inside the locked (2) green truck trailer, in the unloading road area by both buildings.
20	Thunder Mountain Power Plant Yard	Armor Piece: On a table inside one of the tents outside the power plant.
21	Thunder Mountain Power Plant	In the right Power Armor Station, in the connecting room with the two concrete pillars near the Loading Dock area.
22	Dyer Chemical	In the Sewers interior area, in the Power Armor Station at the base of the large vat (exit) room, leading to the Sewer Maintenance Facility structure.
28	Treehouse Village	Raider: On the eastern edge of the living room platform, close to a small (inaccessible) distillery.
ZONE B: SOUTH MIRE, HARPERS FERRY, AND TANAGRA TOWN		
30	Hawke's Refuge	Raider: On the connecting wood platform northwest of the main initial cavern.
31	Sunday Brothers' Cabin	Standing in the wooden barn with all the workbenches.
38	Big B's Rest Stop	In the Power Armor Station, outside and around the back of the Red Rocket Gas Station.
42	Camp Venture	Standing on the Brotherhood of Steel plate, by the two Power Armor Stations, close to the middle of the base.

REGION 6: CRANBERRY BOG

#	PRIMARY LOCATION NAME	POWER ARMOR LOCATION DESCRIPTION
ZONE A: NORTH BOG, ROBCO RESEARCH CENTER, AND ABANDONED BOG TOWN		
1	Kerwood Mine	Inside the mine, in the mine junction cavern, standing in ankle-deep water at the short, dead-end mine tunnel south of the Industrial Trunk.
2	Firebase Major	Outside the tent, between the rusting off-road vehicle and tire-and-wire wall.
4	Firebase LT	Standing outside the east tent, between the back of the tent and the low defensive wall.
6	The General's Steakhouse	In the Gnome-filled metal garden shed, at the far end of the outside allotment area near the river.
7	RobCo Research Center	In one of the curved alcoves, in a Power Armor Station, inside the large Robotics Technology Facility RB-2851 chamber (interior).
14	Bootlegger's Shack	Raider: Standing by the rusting truck cab along the inside of the wooden west perimeter wall.
16	Quarry X3	Standing outside, by the lamppost next to the orange-and-white trailer hut.
ZONE B: SOUTH BOG AND WATOGA		
21	Fort Defiance	A fallen Brotherhood of Steel soldier, to the left of the main entrance, outside by the defenses.
21	Fort Defiance	A fallen Brotherhood of Steel soldier, on the steps of the main entrance, outside by the defenses.
21	Fort Defiance	A fallen Brotherhood of Steel soldier, slumped on the defensive wall near the vertibird tail, at the edge of the outside defenses.
21	Fort Defiance	Inside the Power Armor Station, on the Brotherhood of Steel upper floor (accessed via Laser Grid and Elevator).
22	Appalachian Antiques	Inside the tiny, exterior front porch, between the two white chairs.
26	Big Bend Tunnel East	Outside the tunnel entrance, in the right Power Armor Station, under the tarp tent, by the two half-buried barrels.
29	Watoga Civic Center	On a wooden board in the western alcove, ground floor court between the two Brotherhood of Steel flags, inside the Civic Center.

#	PRIMARY LOCATION NAME	POWER ARMOR LOCATION DESCRIPTION
29	Watoga Civic Center	Standing by the vertibird, on the roof of the residential tower building just east of the Civic Center (exterior).
30	Watoga Transit Hub	Inside the locked (3) generator room and armory, behind and left of the information desk.
31	Watoga Emergency Services	A fallen Brotherhood of Steel soldier, inside the locked (2) laboratory (interior).
31	Watoga Emergency Services	On the roof (exterior), between barrels and crates, around the corner (to the right) from the elevator.
33	AMS Corporate Headquarters	A fallen Brotherhood of Steel soldier, slumped by the broken vertibird wing, in the main road junction, outside the Headquarters building (exterior).
33	AMS Corporate Headquarters	Standing by the crashed vertibird, in the main road junction, outside the Headquarters building (exterior).
34	Watoga Shopping Plaza	Standing on the cracked corner sidewalk, just east of the Drumlin Diner, near the blue aeration wall (exterior).
37	Watoga High School	On the roof, in the southeast corner; accessed via the exterior stairs.
39	Firebase Hancock	Standing between the two orange-and-white trailer huts, by the defensive battlements.

#	PRIMARY LOCATION NAME	POWER ARMOR LOCATION DESCRIPTION
40	Lost Home	Standing on the roof of the edge of the western shack, next to the sleeping bag (also on the roof).
43	Survey Camp Alpha	Standing in the Power Armor Station, under the tarp.
43	Survey Camp Alpha	A fallen Brotherhood of Steel soldier, slumped on the low defensive wall.
46	Drop Site V9	Standing by the low concrete defenses, outside the concrete hut, near the fallen Brotherhood of Steel soldier.
46	Drop Site V9	A fallen Brotherhood of Steel soldier, at the entrance to the concrete hut.
47	Glassed Cavern	A fallen Brotherhood of Steel soldier, at the entrance to the main Scorchbeast cavern, as the railroad tracks split.
47	Glassed Cavern	A fallen Brotherhood of Steel soldier, on ruined metal stairs, at the right side of the entrance to the main Scorchbeast cavern.
49	Forward Station Delta	Inside the Power Armor Station to the right of the metal steps.

APPENDIX: MAGAZINE LOCATIONS

There are 12 different magazine publications for you to gather, including one set with a free holotape game you simply must attempt! The following are "known" locations where Magazines have been spotted. They may not appear (this is random), or may have already been taken by other players, so keep checking on each location.

REGION 1: THE FOREST

#	PRIMARY LOCATION NAME	MAGAZINE LOCATION DESCRIPTION
ZONE A: VAULT 76 AND FLATWOODS		
1	Vault 76	RobCo Fun! Magazine, on the bedside computer terminal table, with Nuka Tapper Holotape Game.
4	Twin Pine Cabins	Vertical, between two metal barrels, at the entrance corner of the lower cabin with the green trunk inside it.
7	Landview Lighthouse	On the dining table with the chair stacked on it, inside the white Lighthouse Keeper's house (interior).
7	Landview Lighthouse	On the picnic table, in the covered picnic area south of the lighthouse (exterior).
8	Alpine River Cabins	On the bottom bunk bed to the right of the bear rug, inside the south cabin (interior).
8	Alpine River Cabins	On the small circular metal table in the treehouse to the south of the cabins, next to the terminal that controls the "spooky" effects.
9	Wixon Homestead	On the small ornate upstairs table, in the middle of the east wall in the bedroom, inside the farmhouse.
15	Vault-Tec Agricultural Research Center	On the cardboard boxes sitting on the sofa, by the sleeping bag in the office with Macfadden's Terminal in it; upstairs and southwest of the stairwell, in the Research Center (interior).
15	Vault-Tec Agricultural Research Center	On or around the shelf in the northwest corner of the small storage room (blue wallpaper), between the ruined conference room (hole in the wall) and the filing room (across the hallway), in the Research Center (interior).
15	Vault-Tec Agricultural Research Center	On the desk with the destroyed terminal and telephone, northeast corner of the filing office, left of the propped "atom" picture, upstairs inside the center (interior).
15	Vault-Tec Agricultural Research Center	On the large sink and wire shelving, in the southwest washroom area of the basement laboratory of the Research Center (not in the flooded area) (interior).
ZONE B: NORTHWEST FOREST AND POINT PLEASANT		
17	WV Lumber Co.	On the large, rough wood dining table adjacent to the stairwell, in the large interior chamber of the lumber mill with the table saw.
17	WV Lumber Co.	On the metal desk with the skeletal parts on it, at the back (raised) area of the mechanic's metal garage with the Chemistry Station in it, east side of the yard.

#	PRIMARY LOCATION NAME	MAGAZINE LOCATION DESCRIPTION
18	Darling Sister's Lab	Vertically placed, behind the picture frame leaning against the wall, to the right of the bed near a standing lamp in the northwest corner, inside the cabin on the west side, by the cliff, with the weathervane on the roof.
19	Groves Family Cabin	On or below the bottom bunk of the bunk bed outside the northwest cabin with the lockers inside it. The bed is on the side of the cabin near the small allotment of crops (exterior).
20	Aaronholt Homestead	On the top shelf of the tall bookcase, south corner of the master bedroom, upstairs in the faded blue farmhouse with the red star on the porch wall (interior).
20	Aaronholt Homestead	In the enamel bucket by the red wheelbarrow, right of the Weapons Workbench (and Power Armor Station), inside the metal silo barn (interior).
21	Tyler County Fairgrounds	On top of one of the two wood barrels, in the long, empty metal hay barn with the metal audience chairs outside; east side of the grounds.
21	Tyler County Fairgrounds	In the second-to-left green outhouse toilet (the middle cluster of three sets of outhouses), southwest area of the grounds, close to the "Apples, Hotdogs" stall.
21	Tyler County Fairgrounds	On the bottom of the metal shelving with the Toy Rocketships on it, in the "prize booth" stall with the green-and-white tent top, west side of the grounds.
23	Deathclaw Island	Near a possible Caps Stash, on the muddy Deathclaw burrow hole, in the middle of the island.
24	Transmission Station 1AT-U03	On or below the metal shelving just right of the red trunk, east corner of the locked concrete transmission hut (interior).
28	Marigold Pavilion	In the attic area with the sagging floor, between the dirty bed and the toy truck, inside the pavilion.
29	Hunter's Ridge	Under the sofa, on the floor of the northeast treehouse shack near the living tree trunk, with the mattress and metal bucket. It could have fallen onto the shack floor.
ZONE C: MORGANTOWN AND EASTERN FOREST		
33	Morgantown Trainyard	On or around the wood crates stored on the metal upstairs gantry of the storage warehouse, northeast balcony with the bed, above the main warehouse entrance.

#	PRIMARY LOCATION NAME	MAGAZINE LOCATION DESCRIPTION
33	Morgantown Trainyard	On the wooden box in the eastern corner, left of the black mainframe, inside the supervisor's tower above the open warehouse door.
35	Morgantown Airport	Inside the terminal building, on the low side table, north wall between the airport seating, opposite the kitchen and food stall (interior).
35	Morgantown Airport	On the counter near the hot plate and coffee pot, at the top of the airport control tower.
36	Morgantown High School	In the last locker on the left (with the door propped next to it), under the wall clock near the chained door, at the far end of the girls' restroom (interior).
36	Morgantown High School	Between the two broken terminals on the table in the southeast corner of the library with the checkered floor (interior).
36	Morgantown High School	On the metal desk with the locked terminal (2), in the middle of the upstairs interior by the short (but wide) set of steps. The office has a red door with "Happy Halloween" bunting above it (interior).
37	Portside Pub	Behind the wood board, against the northeast wall, right of the hat stand and exit doorway, on the upper balcony eating area (interior).
38	Mama Dolce's Food Processing	In the underground Fujiniya Intelligence Base, on the shelf of the metal shelving trolley, in the raised area near the dead potted plant, in the laboratory (southern end).
38	Mama Dolce's Food Processing	In the underground Fujiniya Intelligence Base, on top of the metal shelf trolley between two stretchers, along the south wall of the infirmary and laboratory room.
38	Mama Dolce's Food Processing	In the underground Fujiniya Intelligence Base, on the southwest lower bunk with the skeleton on it, right of the Chinese flagpole, inside the dormitory.
38	Mama Dolce's Food Processing	In the underground Fujiniya Intelligence Base, on the square lab table along the window shutter wall of the kitchen, north side of the base.
39	Vault-Tec University	On the circular wood table with the white leather chairs, by a reclining skeleton, in the blue wallpaper lounge; Room 204.
39	Vault-Tec University	On the teacher's desk with the Globe on it, in the Classroom inside the Simulation Vault (interior).
39	Vault-Tec University	On the square table by the counter, in the cafeteria of the Simulation Vault (interior).
40	Grafton Dam	Just outside the piece of large pipe made into a hidey-hole camp, on the roof of the concrete rooms, below the gantry maintenance huts (interior).
42	Gauley Mine	On the work surface with drawers, left of the locked safe (1), on the roof of the entrance area, inside the mine (interior).
42	Gauley Mine	On the open locker in the upper western corner just left of the gantry steps, inside the large gantry platform and generator room inside the mine (interior).
43	Arktos Pharma	On a wooden crate, with other crates on the top of the large rusting container shelf, under the fallen concrete ceiling (used as a foot ramp), in the large loading bay (interior).
43	Arktos Pharma	On the curved desk, to the right of the Arktos Pharma Terminal, on the right side of the top balcony, near the trunk, in the Cargobot Control chamber (interior).
44	Greg's Mine Supply	On the coffee table in the living room of the house with the rusting van parked outside it, northwest of (and across the road from) the Mine Supply store.
45	Bolton Greens	Near the telephone on or under the main reception counter, in the entrance foyer by the pram and bicycle, and pair of double doors (interior).
45	Bolton Greens	On the shelf of the last counter, by the light blue waste bin, under the window of the golf course reception passage accessed via the kitchens (interior).
45	Bolton Greens	On the lower bunk bed closest to the sofa, cabinet, and fireplace along the west wall, opposite the trunk, in the upstairs bedroom (interior).
48	Sutton	Wedged halfway under the baseboard between the sink and toilet, in the restroom with the fallen door, in the junk-filled Tinkerer's basement (opposite the Tinker's Workbench), inside The Overseer's Childhood Home, north side of town (interior).

#	PRIMARY LOCATION NAME	MAGAZINE LOCATION DESCRIPTION
48	Sutton	Vertical, between the three cardboard boxes and plunger, on the ornate console, under the faded blue-and-white-striped tent tarp, on the roof due north of the church, on top of the Pharmacy building, with tree-trunk access from the railroad tracks to the east (exterior).
52	Horizon's Rest	On or around the metal shelf near the single airplane seat, on the north side of the electrical pylon platforms, at the bottom of the steps, near a covered fuselage walkway onto the rock outcrop.
52	Horizon's Rest	On the side cabinet with the open chem box, behind the three dark red plane seats, at the table on the kitchen platform attached to the electrical pylon.
52	Horizon's Rest	On the TV cabinet, inside the fuselage (southwest side) of the cockpit section of the airplane.
53	Relay Tower HN-B1-12	On top of the mainframe computer terminal attached to the central pillar, facing southwest (if looking at the middle pillar), northeast side of the interior concrete hut, with the metal shelving to the left of the mainframe.
55	Tygart Water Treatment	On or around the square metal table with the radio under it, eastern corner of the Raider construction, in the upper (main) part of the treatment defenses area.
57	Camp McClintock	On the metal work counter, to the right of the Overseer's Cache, below the "Support Our Troops!" poster, on the north wall, ground level inside the main military building.
	ZONE D: SOUTHWEST FOREST	
60	Ohio River Adventures	On or below the wooden counter with the blue scales and cash register on it, by the white door and "Radioactive Roundup" poster, around the corner from the Weapons Workbench.
61	Kanawha County Cemetery	Inside the church, left side pew third from the front (if facing the cultist totem).
63	Silva Homestead	On or around the sideboard with the green lamp on it, northwest wall of the dining room, ground floor of the gray farmhouse (interior).
63	Silva Homestead	On the bottom metal shelf, between the two Weapons Workbenches, inside the large curve-roofed storage barn.
67	Lewis & Sons Farming Supply	On or around the metal counter on the balcony (southeast corner), on the upper part of the tractor barn.
67	Lewis & Sons Farming Supply	On the green metalwork counter with the drawers, inside the remains of the half-demolished small red barn.
67	Lewis & Sons Farming Supply	On the L-shaped counter attached to the small saloon doors, part of the cash register counter, inside the greenhouse.
68	Kanawha Nuka-Cola Plant	On a small wood crate next to a tool chest, on a gantry that can only be reached by climbing on the yellow crate-lifting machine in the middle of the sunken loading dock; west wall near the large doorway (interior).
68	Kanawha Nuka-Cola Plant	Vertical, half-hidden behind the white mainframe computer bank (right edge), inside the security corridor, near the ladder to the roof (interior).
68	Kanawha Nuka-Cola Plant	On the green work counter with the drawers and two fusion cores on it, inside the security mesh walled area with the mattress, through the security gate (2) in the generator room with the Weapons Workbench.
69	Camp Adams	In the small Wood Pile, against the exterior back wall of the cabin with the bear statue outside it (with the trunk inside), northeast part of the camp.
71	The Giant Teapot	Inside the small blue container tray, at the foot of the shelving; enter using the door to the right of the Nuka-Cola machine, and turn left, to check for the magazine.
71	The Giant Teapot	In, around, or behind the open blue fridge on the south curved wall, inside the Giant Teapot.
72	Poseidon Energy Plant WV-06	On the small filing cabinet, left of the metal desk with the broken terminal inside the small blue maintenance hut, on the northeastern gantry platforms and stairs facing the cooling towers (exterior).
72	Poseidon Energy Plant WV-06	Propped up against the radio, by the "Teddy Bears' Picnic" scenic anomaly, on the northwestern edge of the main plant roof's highest level, behind the smokestacks.

#	PRIMARY LOCATION NAME	MAGAZINE LOCATION DESCRIPTION
72	Poseidon Energy Plant WV-06	On the yellow diagnostic cart, near the two gigantic fans on the section of the main plant roof just above the front entrance.
72	Poseidon Energy Plant WV-06	Vertical, between the consoles and the machinery, inside the maintenance room in the center of cooling tower #1.
72	Poseidon Energy Plant WV-06	Behind some boxes, on the bottom shelf in the locker room near the reactor room (interior).
72	Poseidon Energy Plant WV-06	On the lowest shelf of the metal shelves near the overturned cart in the basement locker room (interior).
72	Poseidon Energy Plant WV-06	On the desk in the Plant Manager's office, near the windows overlooking the turbine hall (interior).
72	Poseidon Energy Plant WV-06	On the table, on the top-most gantry platform in the Reactor Room.

ZONE E: CHARLESTON AND SURROUNDINGS

#	PRIMARY LOCATION NAME	MAGAZINE LOCATION DESCRIPTION
76	Charleston Railyard	In the open corner locker in the last linked blue maintenance hut attached to the ceiling of the main yard building interior.
78	AVR Medical Center	On the coffee table in the ruined office with the hole in the wall adjacent to the two booths (head through the door to the left of the U-shaped reception desk, at the south reception lobby).
78	AVR Medical Center	On the desk by the door, inside the office (with the red sofa and two large mushroom lamps), off the balcony with the microfilm unit on it, north side second level, overlooking the main entrance lobby.
78	AVR Medical Center	On the desk with the ruined terminal farthest away from the door, in the office with the hole in the floor, with three dumped microfilm machines and standing lamp on the balcony outside the office, east side upper level.
79	Hornwright Industrial Headquarters	On or around the wood desk (no terminal) with the red wastebasket, on Level 05, behind the inaccessible door, accessed via the hole in the conference room wall, via the duct ramp.
79	Hornwright Industrial Headquarters	On the shelf of the CEO's curved desk, in balcony office with the CEO's Terminal (3), part of the executive level (interior).
79	Hornwright Industrial Headquarters	On the seat by the terminal sitting on the green metal L-shaped desk attached to the mainframe in the north balcony corner of the Sub-Level (interior).
82	Charleston Capitol Building	On the metal desk by the terminal, northwest corner of the large filing and archive office, in the basement, through the double doors adjacent to the Food Court (interior).

#	PRIMARY LOCATION NAME	MAGAZINE LOCATION DESCRIPTION
85	Summersville Docks	On the broken bookcase, bottom shelf, in the small red storage shed with the rusty pickup outside, towards the southwest end of the docks, by the parking lot.
85	Summersville Docks	On the bottom of the metal shelf, end of the right side railing of the southeast boat dock, above the dry lake.
85	Summersville Docks	Inside the broken opening of the white overturned boat, by the wooden block also under the boat, half-buried at the side of the southeast boathouse, near a rusting red buoy.
89	Burdette Manor	Beneath the Nuka-Cola wooden crate, in the north corner of the kitchen.
89	Burdette Manor	Behind the cardboard box, on the low shelf of the small table in the eastern corner, near a moving dolly, across from the red trunk, in the attic area of the mansion.
91	Overlook Cabin	Vertical, behind the radiator (right side) along the south side wall of the upstairs landing, just left of the ornate cabinet, right of the doorway marked "exit" (interior).
91	Overlook Cabin	Under the boiler, by the yellow trolley container full of debris, south corner of the storage basement (interior).
92	Riverside Manor	Vertical, between the washing machine and suitcase, in the small laundry room close to the south exit onto the back porch (interior).
92	Riverside Manor	Bottom left, lowest bookcase shelf, in the northeast corner of the library, next to the dark red leather sofa, with an upturned coffee table in front of it (interior).
92	Riverside Manor	In the open green footlocker at the foot of the bed in the corner bedroom, second floor (interior).
92	Riverside Manor	On the wooden desk, by the guest room terminal, in the northwest corner of the upstairs dormitory (interior).
93	Torrance House	Tucked halfway under the yellow metal trolley container full of debris, on the stone deck with the child's tricycle, and the wood blocks spelling out "REDRUM", near the "Caution Wet Paint" sign, on the southwest side of the mansion (exterior).
93	Torrance House	Behind the three large paintings (the front one is of water lilies) propped against the east wall of the octagonal room with the ornate furniture (and large desk in the middle) (interior).
94	Hornwright Summer Villa	Vertical, down the side of the yellowing, rusty fridge and east corner wall, in the kitchenette area and apartment, through the storage room above the double garage (interior).
94	Hornwright Summer Villa	Under the stack of wine barrel casks, along the northwest wall of the basement interior (right side of the cask stack).

REGION 2: TOXIC VALLEY

#	PRIMARY LOCATION NAME	MAGAZINE LOCATION DESCRIPTION
1	The Crosshair	On the wood sheet atop the short lookout defensive platform with the chems, just inside and right of the entrance to the Raider camp.
1	The Crosshair	On the wood floor by the sleeping bag, near the Weapons Workbench, under the taller lookout tower, southeast end of the Raider camp.
2	Clancy Manor	On the narrow shelf of the low side cabinet, next to the locked safe (1), on the west wall of the upper living area (west side), in the room where part of the walls are makeshift wood (interior).
3	Cobbleton Farm	On, behind, or near the tall tool cabinet (1), in the middle of the interior northwest wall, to the right of the wooden steps (interior).
4	Lady Janet's Soft Serve	Wedged behind the locked safe (0) in the northwest corner of the ice cream trailer (interior), across from the bathtub.
7	Becker Farm	On the old writing desk, between the two ornate dressers, on the ground level of the roofless white farmhouse.
10	Eastern Regional Penitentiary	On the L-shaped counter in the Intake room, in the center of the Penitentiary (interior).
10	Eastern Regional Penitentiary	On the desk in the Cell Block B Security Office, near the dining hall (interior).

#	PRIMARY LOCATION NAME	MAGAZINE LOCATION DESCRIPTION
10	Eastern Regional Penitentiary	Slipped down between the dryer and the concrete pillar, on the north side of the laundry room, opposite the stacks of washing machines inside the penitentiary (interior).
10	Eastern Regional Penitentiary	On the bedside table in Warden Brennan's bedroom, on the second floor of the Penitentiary's main building, near the Warden mainframe (interior).
10	Eastern Regional Penitentiary	On the lectern shelf, in the remains of the chapel, in the prison yard.
10	Eastern Regional Penitentiary	On a low shelf with a broken lamp, in the visitation trailer with the grill in front of it, in the prison yard.
10	Eastern Regional Penitentiary	In the outhouse with the door, behind the chapel, in the prison yard.
13	Wavy Willard's Water Park	On or below the circular metal table on the raised wood platform camp, inside the mouth of the crocodile, in the Crocolossus Mountain ride.
13	Wavy Willard's Water Park	On the small metal table with the foldable ends, by the wood crates and step ladder, on the southwest wall of the flooded basement generator chamber.
14	Willard Corporate Housing	On the half-buried green golf cart, on the park logo roundabout in the middle of the trailer park.
18	Kiddie Corner Cabins	On the dresser in the small green bunk bedroom, inside the cabin with the green door (interior).

#	PRIMARY LOCATION NAME	MAGAZINE LOCATION DESCRIPTION
18	Kiddie Corner Cabins	On the outhouse seat, in the outhouse between two of the cabins.
19	Black Bear Lodge	By the wooden crate, in an alcove close to the sleeping bag and duffle bag, in the ruined attic section of the lodge, with the long tree trunk lying up against it. Jump through the hole in the roof at the other end of the lodge, near the bed with two mattresses, to reach it.
22	Pioneer Scout Camp	In the small box under the green bunk bed, southeast corner of cabin A02 (interior).

#	PRIMARY LOCATION NAME	MAGAZINE LOCATION DESCRIPTION
22	Pioneer Scout Camp	At the foot of the outhouse, right of the Weapons Workbench, at the Scout Camp shooting range.
26	Philippi Battlefield Cemetery	On the floor by the display cabinet, southwest corner of the Civil War museum, upstairs (interior).
28	Knife Edge	On the green card table with the gas mask and ammo box, on the top platform of the central tower.

REGION 3: THE ASH HEAP

#	PRIMARY LOCATION NAME	MAGAZINE LOCATION DESCRIPTION
	ZONE A: BECKLEY AND MOUNT BLAIR	
1	Camden Park	On the deck, by the fallen metal magazine carousel by the ice cream sign, under the boarded-up ice cream stall, south of the "Sugar Heaps" Trading Post.
1	Camden Park	In the green plastic outhouse, at the ruined Raider stall, on the north side of the camp in the middle of The Widow Maker ride.
1	Camden Park	On the seat next to the Checker Tie Mr. Fuzzy, on the penultimate cart of the stalled rollercoaster train (the horizontal train, not the vertical one near the hut), on The Widow Maker ride.
4	Relay Tower HG-B7-09	On or below the open locker against the north wall, inside the concrete hut, left of the doorway, near an ammo crate (interior).
6	Belching Betty	On top of the mainframe computer, northwest corner of the second metal maintenance office above the interior mine tracks.
6	Belching Betty	Below the orange tool case sitting on the mainframe computer, on the earth between the computer and a wooden crate, opposite the Chemistry Station, above the rail tracks and main shaft.
6	Belching Betty	Near the wastebasket and two filing cabinets, on the windowed wall of the blue metal maintenance hut with the trunk and the Garrahan Mining logo on it, in the main cavern just after the shaft stairway descent.
6	Belching Betty	Around the back of the giant boiler machine, with the Tinker's Workbench at the front of the boiler, in the room with the fusion core generator, in the mesh walled area, west end of the main generator cabin after the shaft and stairwell descent.
7	The Rusty Pick	By the toilet in the middle stall, in the women's restroom, inside the tavern (interior).
7	The Rusty Pick	Tucked halfway under the metal and yellow machine with the levers, left of the rope-rock blocks, southwest wall of the dead-end cavern with the pallet and barrel table, at the end of the tunnel (interior).
10	Beckley	On the toilet, in the locked (0) restroom on the north side of the gas station and store, on the east side of town.
10	Beckley	Among the planks and rubble near a sofa and small metal blue cooler, on a ruined rooftop accessed via debris, on the building with the Nuka-Cherry sign on the brickwork, north end of town near the water tower (exterior).
11	Sal's Grinders	On the metal shelf, right of the sink in the south corner of the men's restroom, across from the kitchen on the ground floor (interior).
13	Nicholson's End	On or around the toilet inside the northwest trailer (the one with the roof platform attached to it that reaches the trailer to the south, with the Super Mutant cauldron hanging from the platform).
16	Mount Blair Trainyard	Vertically, between the two filing cabinets on the west wall of the office up the initial gantry steps, south side of the east concrete yard structure (with the yellow fan clamped to the south wall outside, near the flagpole).
16	Mount Blair Trainyard	Vertically, behind the tall green work cabinet with the two blue tray containers (and Mini Nuke on top of it), northwestern corner of the upstairs balcony area; in the large metal storage warehouse, west side of the trainyard.
16	Mount Blair Trainyard	On the small green chair, on the wood sheet platform, southwest corner of the roof of the east of the two large concrete yard structures.

#	PRIMARY LOCATION NAME	MAGAZINE LOCATION DESCRIPTION
17	Mount Blair	On the surprisingly clean and modern toilet, in the wrecked trailer northwest of the main excavator (workshop), near the three rusting trucks and the fire truck (exterior).
17	Mount Blair	In the basement (ID card needed) of one of the bulldozer garages, through the barred door, above the alarm clock on the wall shelf of the work counter (east wall of the storage room).
19	Rollins Work Camp	At the very back, on the roof of the huge bucket excavator, accessed via the rust-red gantry.
	ZONE B: LEWISBURG, WELCH, AND GARRAHAN MINING	
21	The Burning Mine	On the passenger seat of the yellow mine buggy half-buried in molten slag, across from the yellow-and-blue sloping mine conveyor belt, in the tiered, large cavern (below the Tinker's Workbench).
21	The Burning Mine	In the sink, on the right side of the small wooden deck along the eastern rock wall of the trio of blue piston conveyor belts, in the chamber with the gantry and stairs down the middle.
21	The Burning Mine	On the wooden table, right of a small wood crate, with other wood crates, against a rock wall, near a parked coal buggy, just left (west) of two half-buried white metal generators, in the large cavern with the metal steps to the south.
21	The Burning Mine	On a low wood crate, one of three stacked at the corner of two large metal cargo containers, a barrel, and other debris, near a yellow forklift, at the bottom of the tiered cavern where the coal conveyor belt ends.
22	Widow's Perch	Behind the cinder block and thin wood board, near the broom and protest sign, across from the mattress and small blue-frame painting on the wall, in the lower shack just before you exit to the billboard.
25	Uncanny Caverns	On the magazine carousel, west corner of the gift shop, just left of the massive hole in the exterior wall.
25	Uncanny Caverns	In the right display case, under the "Uncanny Caverns" poster, northwest wall behind the curved reception and transaction desk of the main entrance structure (across the bridge).
25	Uncanny Caverns	By the sleeping bag, corpse, and duffle bag, near the cooking station, in the small cave with the moonshine still and traps, audio tour #4.
25	Uncanny Caverns	Between the two sleeping bags near the radio, in the cavern with the cooking station, green trunk, and audio tour #8.
27	Bastion Park	On the floor of the right-side seating towards the back of the school bus parked between the playground and the fountain.
27	Bastion Park	On the rear passenger seat of the rusting car, parked with other vehicles in the eastern rear of the park, near the second school bus.
30	Pleasant Hills Cemetery	In, around, or behind the large, completely burned safe housing with the smaller, regular-sized locked safe (3) within it, inside the tiny mausoleum.
31	Lewisburg	On the rubble-filled diner counter, near the crushed skeleton, inside the restaurant (interior).
31	Lewisburg	On the small green card table to the right of the green trunk, inside the storage attic of the Visitor Center, accessed via the rooftop garden (near the small greenhouse, southeast corner).

#	PRIMARY LOCATION NAME	MAGAZINE LOCATION DESCRIPTION
34	Big Bend Tunnel West	On the metal desk in the window alcove across from an orange tool case, in the middle of the upper stilted maintenance cabins above the train tracks, in the main maintenance "middle" of the tunnel; access via the locked double doors.
40	AMS Testing Site	Behind the metal worker cabinet counter, by the trunk in the west alcove of the large curve-roofed maintenance warehouse and garage (interior).
42	Red Rocket Filling Station	Vertical, in the slit gap between the two green work cabinets with drawer (one has a tool box on it), on the raised concrete part of the metal maintenance garage (interior).

#	PRIMARY LOCATION NAME	MAGAZINE LOCATION DESCRIPTION
46	Striker Row	On the speaker with the "Danger" sign on it, right of the microphone (if looking uphill to the southeast), on the small wood stage, near the amplifier and below the sealed mine entrance.
46	Striker Row	On the low mesh table by the cooking station, next to the rusting military vehicle and log with axe in it, surrounded by tents.
50	Garrahan Mining Headquarters	In the "Testing Control and Assessment" area, with the terminals, laboratory equipment, and ceiling wiring, on the counter between the two Power Armor Stations.

REGION 4: SAVAGE DIVIDE

#	PRIMARY LOCATION NAME	MAGAZINE LOCATION DESCRIPTION
	ZONE A: NORTH MOUNTAINS, SUNNYTOP, AND MONONGAH	
1	Palace of the Winding Path	On or under the red couch with the ornate wood back and arms, northwest corner of the balcony area, just right of the two bright red chairs, top floor (interior).
3	Bailey Family Cabin	On the low coffee table, inside the cabin, near the chair, sofa, and TV (interior).
5	Site Bravo	In the Reactor Area, on a desk with a broken terminal and a clown on it, on the far west wall of the main room.
5	Site Bravo	In the Operations Center, on a desk with a broken terminal, in the lowered area in the center of the main room.
5	Site Bravo	In the Operations Center, on a desk in a small room with three fabricator pods, just off the main room.
8	Sunnytop Ski Lanes	On the round table with the black-and-white parasol on it, by the curved perimeter stone wall overlooking the view to the east, with a broken tree trunk and a hot tub nearby (exterior).
8	Sunnytop Ski Lanes	On the deck by the Raider corpse draped across the white wood recliner, on the outside raised wood deck to the northwest, attached to the main lodge, just above the parked gray bus (exterior).
8	Sunnytop Ski Lanes	By the Raider corpse collapsed back in the chair, left of the main stone fireplace alcove with the Red Garden Gnome and two human cages on it, in the fireplace alcove with the large dark red sofa, southwest wall of the main lodge interior, opposite the double doors' rear entrance (interior).
8	Sunnytop Ski Lanes	By the Raider corpse, near the crates and barrels in the southeast alcove, between the Armor and Weapons Workbenches, opposite the ski rental counter, inside the main lodge structure (lower floor).
9	Sunnytop Ski Lanes Base Lodge	Behind or around the small stacked wood crates, blue barrel, and pallet, on the green tin roof deck, on the east side of the lodge exterior.
9	Sunnytop Ski Lanes Base Lodge	On the red table, just right of the large stone fireplace (with the mounted Yao Guai head above it), under the wooden upstairs balcony mezzanine (interior).
12	Hopewell Cave	In the overturned small blue tray container, by the burned-out campfire and sleeping bag, inside the cave.
16	Ingram Mansion	On the low side coffee table in the living room with the two green couches and wicker rug, inside the mansion.
16	Ingram Mansion	On the small painted side dresser at the far end of the upstairs balcony hallway (eastern end of the mansion).
21	Monongah	On the upturned Nuka-Cola wooden crate, on the lookout deck, behind and north of the gray cottage, north rock outcrop, on the edge of town.
22	Observatory	On the low coffee table by the L-shaped couch, in the remains of the break room, south of the main circular chamber (interior).
24	Sons of Dane Compound	On top of, or on the ground below, the large lookout tower near the road, northwestern entrance into the compound.
24	Sons of Dane Compound	On the small trolley with the microscope on it, left of the Chemistry Station, in the chem lab basement of the faded blue farmhouse (interior).

#	PRIMARY LOCATION NAME	MAGAZINE LOCATION DESCRIPTION
24	Sons of Dane Compound	On the picnic table, southwest corner of The Buck's Den (on the right when walking in using the main entrance) (interior).
25	Relay Tower LW-B1-22	On the top of the mainframe computer bank (right side), near the lamp, on the computer attached to the large concrete central pillar; northwest if looking at the middle pillar (southeast side of the room).
26	Sylvie & Sons Logging Camp	On the stack of small wood crates with the rusty dirtbike propped up against them, outside the smaller of the two green tents (exterior).
26	Sylvie & Sons Logging Camp	On the stack of curved metal crates, near the radio, inside the larger of the two green tents (interior).
	ZONE B: CENTRAL MOUNTAINS, PLEASANT VALLEY, AND WHITESPRING	
30	Seneca Gang Camp	On the red seat by the dead Raider, next to the faded red trunk, by the red seat with the corpse on it, near the safe (1) on the south side of the camp.
31	Wendigo Cave	By the skeleton with the cooler, in the tiny alcove (west), in the upper part of the main cavern, above the river.
31	Wendigo Cave	By the skull and headless skeleton, near a small pond of dirty water and an ammo box, northwest wall in a small connecting cavern with narrow tunnels to the northwest, north, and southeast.
31	Wendigo Cave	Among the pile of bloody human bones, southeast alcove in one of the main junction caverns with the rock column.
31	Wendigo Cave	By the headless skeleton with the first aid kit and Rad-X, in the small southeast cave alcove with the orange tool box and wicker basket nearby, off the narrow east-west tunnel with the Bone Chimes.
32	Autumn Acre Cabin	On the sideboard by the log pile and antique globe, right of the large stone fireplace, inside the cabin (interior).
33	Toxic Larry's Meat 'n Go	On the headboard shelf of the bed with the red trunk on it, near the mannequin in the shack's upstairs bedroom with the Mothman poster on the wall (interior).
33	Toxic Larry's Meat 'n Go	On the seat of the outhouse, on the rocks roughly north of the main shack structure.
34	Skullbone Vantage	On the tiny, distressed side table, jammed next to the red sofa with two sprawled Raider corpses on it, part of the "car sofa", right of the lookout tower (if looking north).
35	Pleasant Valley Cabins	On the headboard of the double-mattress bed, in the first ruined lodge structure (if approaching from the east), with the planks onto the roof of the coach, near the bus stop (interior, but no roof).
35	Pleasant Valley Cabins	On the lectern, on the stone patio, southwest end of the upper lodge area, with the multiple seats around the lectern, which is flanked by two red ornate chairs (exterior).
35	Pleasant Valley Cabins	On the mattress in the room with the rug, off the room with the three terminals and green carpet, inside the lodge attached to the Raider arena, accessed via the exterior deck (interior).
35	Pleasant Valley Cabins	On the low side table between two red bar stools with backs, above scattered beer bottles, on the deck of the southwestern, faded blue shiplap mansion, lower area (exterior).

#	PRIMARY LOCATION NAME	MAGAZINE LOCATION DESCRIPTION
35	Pleasant Valley Cabins	On the coffee table with the two Cafeteria Trays, by the blue couch under the Brahmin wall mount heads, inside the yellow door and curtained cabin (interior).
35	Pleasant Valley Cabins	On the metal table below the Raider corpse, in the bunk bed cabin with half a red front door, northwest cabin in the group of three, next to the rusty yellow pickup (interior).
36	Top of the World	On the rickety shop counter by the blue cash register, in the stall with the gramophone behind it, west of the central elevator column (interior).
36	Top of the World	On the small low coffee table, right side of the stall with the three stools (one fallen), the pink cash register, and the large (living) tree to the left of it (the tree is in the middle between two stalls).
36	Top of the World	On the magazine carousel by the fallen stool, at one corner of the shanty stall with the large (living) tree to the right of it (the tree is in the middle between two stalls). The stall has a lighthouse painting and a Raider skull board under its tarp; south of the central elevator column (interior).
36	Top of the World	On the small curved side table to the left of the white leather sofa, along the perimeter curved wall of the control room with Madigan's Corpse hanging in the cage (and Rose the Robot), top level (interior).
37	Pleasant Valley Ski Resort	On the small round white metal table, on the deck by the yellow chair, east side of the upper deck, northwest "Trading Post" lodge; access via the double doors, from the interior upstairs hallway (exterior).
37	Pleasant Valley Ski Resort	On the left barrel (the other barrel has a white vodka bottle on it), on the deck of the north lodge (next to the lodge with the Trading Post inside) (exterior).
37	Pleasant Valley Ski Resort	On the small round white metal table, on the deck by the yellow chair, south side upper deck of the south lodge; access via the dead hedge, eaves of the porch, and ladder on the eastern side of the lodge (exterior).
39	South Cutthroat Camp	On a cinder block, on the ground by the gondola seating and wood steps to the road defenses, west part of the camp.
39	South Cutthroat Camp	In the main glass cabinet, in the middle of the storefront on the south side of the road.
40	North Cutthroat Camp	South end of the camp, by the North Highway 63 sign, on or around the toilet with the cymbals monkey sitting on it.
40	North Cutthroat Camp	On, below, or around the "tea party" plank table with two severed heads enjoying a nice cup of tea, next to the red trunk, to the side of the billboard lookout.
42	Yellow Sandy's Still	On the small green card table with the TV Dinner Tray, inside the east rusty caravan trailer with the Nuka-Cola machine inside it.
43	Cliffwatch	On or near the sheet of wood with the Mountain Honey, knife, and decapitated head, set on cinder blocks near a safe, on the south side of the camp.
44	Safe 'n Clean Disposal	On the metal shelving by the sleeping bag, in the middle of the small red barn.
45	New Appalachian Central Trainyard	On the small metal desk with the ham radio, in the signal tower by the red water tower, east of the main trainyard warehouse.
45	New Appalachian Central Trainyard	On the table, inside the bank vault.
45	New Appalachian Central Trainyard	On the table by the Switch-Operator's Terminal, in the signal tower north of the trainyard and bank buildings.
46	98 NAR Regional	On or below the spotted couch, inside the overturned military carriage lying on top of two other carriages; accessed via the opening underneath.
49	Site Alpha	In the Reactor Area, on a desk with a broken terminal and a clown on it, on the far west wall of the main room.
49	Site Alpha	In the Operations Center, on a desk with a broken terminal, in the lowered area in the center of the main room.
49	Site Alpha	In the Operations Center, on a desk in a small room with three fabricator pods, just off the main room.
51	The Whitespring Golf Club	On the circular metal table, upstairs front deck, of the white mansion house, north of the main resort, just east of the Club entrance road and security hut.

#	PRIMARY LOCATION NAME	MAGAZINE LOCATION DESCRIPTION
51	The Whitespring Golf Club	In the Clubhouse, on the upper level, in the men's room near the can chimes, between the wastebasket and the sink cabinet.
51	The Whitespring Golf Club	In the Clubhouse, on the lower level, on the cardboard boxes in the Employees Only closet near the shoe-shine counter.
51	The Whitespring Golf Club	In the Clubhouse, on the lower level, in the lounge in the men's locker room, on the bottom shelf of the northeast bookshelves.
	ZONE C: SOUTH MOUNTAINS, SUGAR GROVE, AND SPRUCE KNOB	
57	Blackwater Mine	Below the metal shelving, by a pipe, right of three radioactive barrels and a safe (3), in Dr. Cotton's tiny cave laboratory, off the vertical waterlogged cavern (interior).
57	Blackwater Mine	In the tiny, locked (1) security closet, off the narrow tunnels connecting the main mine tunnel to the vertical waterlogged cavern, close to some red steel tunnel buttressing (into the main tunnel) (interior).
57	Blackwater Mine	Behind the low, short metal counter to the right of the Weapons Workbench, on the east wall of the concrete store room off the drilling chambers (interior).
57	Blackwater Mine	On the sleeping bag, which is under a mattress bed, in the fan extraction and machine room with the large circular pipe hole in the floor (grate is to the side of it), opposite the Chemistry Station, after the swim.
58	Middle Mountain Cabins	In the outhouse, southeast area, between the left and middle cabins (if facing southeast).
58	Middle Mountain Cabins	On the small metal work counter below the wall tool board, inside the tiny tool shed uphill and east of the three main cabins.
59	Emmett Mountain Disposal Site	On the radioactive yellow barrel, inside the barrel storage garage with the parked orange forklift and more barrels outside, to the right of the curve-roofed disposal site entrance structure (exterior).
59	Emmett Mountain Disposal Site	On the metal desk next to the Disposal Terminal, in the storage room with the hole in the eastern corner wall, just southeast of the double doors from the large generator room (interior).
60	Ripper Alley	On the floor of the short lookout, near the cinder block, accessed via the short ladder, close to the road, with a rusty car on the other (road) side of the defenses.
61	National Isolated Radio Array	On the metal desk with the Bottlecap Sunglasses and Teal Rounded Vase, in the northwest upper office with the red trailer protruding through the outer wall, in the Office Building (interior).
61	National Isolated Radio Array	On the ornate bureau, in the southwest corner of the upstairs office, with the dead potted tree outside the door, on the west side of the Office Building (interior).
61	National Isolated Radio Array	On the metal desk by the destroyed terminal, eastern corner (left of the red machinery), inside the dish array control hut at the foot of the dish (with the flagpole outside).
62	Sugar Grove	On the half-buried curio cabinet, left of the Project Director's Terminal, in the upper office with a window overlooking the mission control room, with the Archive Dispenser Vending Machine in the southwest corner.
62	Sugar Grove	On the yellow machinery, inside the security mesh walled area of the Advanced Research Laboratory, near the collection of blank holotapes, in the upper floor with the window.
62	Sugar Grove	On the small round table with the Lunch Pail on it, near the Nuka-Cola machine, on the north stepped side of the Mission Control room.
62	Sugar Grove	Vertical, jammed between two cardboard boxes, in the center of the shelves of boxes at the foot of the huge map screen, in the Mission Control room.
62	Sugar Grove	Below the red wrist rest shelf, at the central mainframe computer in the middle of The Archives.
62	Sugar Grove	Poking out of the small side table shelf, in the green wallpapered cognitive programming room (with the three televisions), in the Secret Facility basement.
63	National Radio Astronomy Research Center	On top of the L-shaped mainframe computer near the large hole in the wall and floor, inside the top floor Communications Office (interior).

#	PRIMARY LOCATION NAME	MAGAZINE LOCATION DESCRIPTION
63	National Radio Astronomy Research Center	On the green work cabinet wall shelf or counter, near the yellow alarm clock, in the small room with the Armor Workbench and giant wall fan, adjacent to the ruined generator basement room.
64	West Tek Research Center	On the large laboratory table with the dark work surface and two microscopes with display cases attached to them, off the larger lab room with the hole in the wall, eastern side of the balcony level.
65	US-13C Bivouac	Below the bed with the skeleton on it, right side of the tent. The tent is to the right of the telephone pole and small comms dish.
65	US-13C Bivouac	Next to the sleeping bag, front left corner of the tent, adjacent to the three blue barrels just outside the tent entrance.
67	Mountainside Bed & Breakfast	On the metal desk next to the broken terminal and empty filing cabinet, in the southwest corner of the landing area, in the green wallpaper area of the lower extension, west of the kitchen, inside the house.
67	Mountainside Bed & Breakfast	On or below the low coffee table by the staircase, across from the reception desk and the Comment Terminal, in the locked (2) foyer area of the house.
67	Mountainside Bed & Breakfast	On or below the desk fan, on or near the reception desk by the Comment Terminal, in the locked (2) foyer area of the house.
67	Mountainside Bed & Breakfast	On the coffee table, in the upstairs landing living room with the board games, green carpet, and dark red furniture, inside the house.
68	The Vantage	Balanced on the steel girder, just below and outside the wood fence at the top of the lookout tower, in the corner where the ammo box and duffle bag are (or among the box and bag) (exterior).
69	Solomon's Pond	On the ground behind the three large wood crates, near the sleeping bag, between the two doorways on the southeast side of the red barn with the canoe resting on it (interior).
70	Twin Lakes	On the red-and-white checkered picnic rug, by the skeleton and swimsuit, on the rock bank, close to the north side of the lake.
72	Huntersville	Under the bed hanging off the edge of the destroyed upper floor, in the roofless home in the middle of town, with the green propane tank visible next to the blown-out kitchen.

#	PRIMARY LOCATION NAME	MAGAZINE LOCATION DESCRIPTION
72	Huntersville	On the curved counter to the left of the blue cash register, inside the Hardware store.
75	Site Charlie	In the Reactor Area, on a desk with a broken terminal and a clown on it, on the far west wall of the main room.
75	Site Charlie	In the Operations Center, on a desk with a broken terminal, in the lowered area in the center of the main room.
75	Site Charlie	In the Operations Center, on a desk in a small room with three fabricator pods, just off the main room.
76	R&G Processing Services	In the yellow container trolley, against the west wall, inside the upper concrete structure with the giant vat inside it, just right of the open security mesh wall with the green work cabinets (interior).
76	R&G Processing Services	Tucked halfway under the cardboard box, just left of the Overseer's Cache, lowest metal shelf inside the main storage and machine warehouse, close to the elevator down into Site Charlie.
79	Spruce Knob Lake	In the open plastic green outhouse (one of two), on the back side of the small dockside hut, northeast shore of the lake.
80	Spruce Knob	On or around the desk inside the security hut, on the lower southeast fenced entrance, below the cliff Spruce Knob is positioned on.
84	Lucky Hole Mine	On the lectern at the main cultist altar with the pews, in the dead-end tunnel at the end of the mine (interior).
89	Lake Eloise	In the far northeast part of the wilderness area (northeast of the Fissure Site), inside the Gaming Enthusiasts' Camp, on the TV behind the wood blocks spelling "CHEATER", on the rocks.
91	Relay Tower EL-B1-02	On top of the light blue mainframe computer unit, southwest corner of the concrete tower hut (interior).
92	Johnson's Acre	On the hearth of the large stone fireplace, west end of the cabin (interior).
92	Johnson's Acre	On the picnic table by the tire and barrel, outside and south of the cabin (exterior).

TRAINING
CRAFTING AND C.A.M.P.ING
INVENTORY
QUESTS
ATLAS
BESTIARY
APPENDICES

#	PRIMARY LOCATION NAME	MAGAZINE LOCATION DESCRIPTION
	ZONE A: NORTH MIRE, THUNDER MOUNTAIN, AND BERKELEY SPRINGS	
5	Southhampton Estate	On the kitchen sink counter, ground level of the tendril-filled faded blue farmhouse.
5	Southhampton Estate	On the ruined metal shelf, on the lean-to entrance into the red barn.
13	Mosstown	On or below the magazine carousel, close to the red trunk and locked safe (2), on the east side of the shanty town, close to the Cappy Nuka boat.
13	Mosstown	On the low coffee table between the gray and dark red couches, inside the "Drugs" shack, by the green plastic outhouses, northwest side of town.
13	Mosstown	On the corner of the wood shelf with the mirror and scissors on it, near the red chair, inside the "Barber & Dentist" shack, north side of town.
15	Dolly Sods Wilderness	On or around the toilet, in the northwest restroom, ground floor inside the west lodge building.
15	Dolly Sods Wilderness	On the magazine carousel, by the deep red sofa, along the south wall of the large living room with the piano, inside the south lodge.
19	Crevasse Dam	In the wastebasket, in the corner of the concrete balcony on the north side of the upper area inside the main building, close to the Supervisor Terminal, by the shelving with the plastic pumpkin (interior).
19	Crevasse Dam	On the second metal shelf above the Acetone Canister, by the blue machinery on the ground floor of the pump chamber (southwest corner) (interior).
21	Thunder Mountain Power Plant	On or below the large conference table with the Office Desk Fan on it, upstairs and northeast of the entrance lobby, with stairs outside the room (interior).
21	Thunder Mountain Power Plant	On or below the small computer bank, left side of the filing cabinets along the southwest wall of a connecting corridor to the Main Plant, right of the window, with the double door marked "Turbine Hall" at the northeast end (interior).
21	Thunder Mountain Power Plant	On the shelf of the green metal wall cabinet, south corner adjacent to the metal door and wall clock, in the small connecting room (with three exits) between the gantry stairwell and door marked "Pipe Interchange, Cooling Tower #1", and the smaller Fuel Storage chamber with gantries and the flooded floor (interior).
21	Thunder Mountain Power Plant	On the white table with the orange tool box, along the northwest wall in the corridor connecting the Turbine Hall to Cooling Tower #2 (interior).
21	Thunder Mountain Power Plant	On the second-to-bottom shelf of the green metal work shelf, pointed at the southwest wall (by the perimeter wall), along the gantry with two sets of large wall extractor fans on either side, in the Reactor Room (interior).
21	Thunder Mountain Power Plant	In the wastebasket, right of the small black computer bank, south upper corner of the tiered-floor Master Control chamber (interior).
22	Dyer Chemical	In the middle locker along the wall of lockers, in the metal maintenance hut corridor (with the small mainframe computer at one end), on the western side of the facility, above the large sewer pipes with the hatch.
22	Dyer Chemical	On the small wood crate with the ammo crate, by the blue machinery and vertical pipe cluster, upper floor, southwest corner of the sewer maintenance building, east side of the facility (interior).
22	Dyer Chemical	Inside one of the two yellow trolley carts by the explosive canister, on the concrete bridge spanning both sides of the facility, above the road (exterior).
24	Braxson's Quality Medical Supplies	Dropped vertically between the right side of the Armor Workbench and the two lockers, by the exit door, under the gantry corner and stairs, in the southeast part of the premises (interior).

#	PRIMARY LOCATION NAME	MAGAZINE LOCATION DESCRIPTION
26	Berkeley Springs	On the side table between the two comfy dark red chairs (one with a skeleton on it), in the upstairs spa area across from the elevator in the Beauty and Spa Salon (access via the hole in the roof or by entering the spa).
26	Berkeley Springs	On the metal office desk, in the southwest corner of the upper level office, in the brick mansion (one of a pair) in the middle of town. The mansion has two large yellow fans on the side of the structure, near a traffic light post (interior).
28	Treehouse Village	On the car seat by the orange tool box, near the two shopping carts, on the connecting junction platform with the red barrel on it.
28	Treehouse Village	On the wood sheet floor with the fallen mannequin and metal tub lid, on the outside balcony with the red barrel and gray couch, outside the dining platform shack (near the small generator) with the table and yellow barbecue, and the doorless fridge.
28	Treehouse Village	On or near the corner of the dark red couch, on the outside balcony with the wood barrel and small generator, attached to the eastern edge of the living room platform, close to a small (inaccessible) distillery.
29	Haven Church	On the front-left (northeast) school desk, in the school room.
	ZONE B: SOUTH MIRE, HARPERS FERRY, AND TANAGRA TOWN	
30	Hawke's Refuge	On a small refuse pile in the small dead-end alcove due southwest of the red couch with the blue rug on it, back towards the entrance but on the lower ground level (interior).
30	Hawke's Refuge	At the base of the rock wall, due north of the red couch with the blue rug on it, across a small pond of dirty water, in the main cavern (interior).
31	Sunday Brothers' Cabin	Under the bunk bed, in the northwest corner of the small, red-wallpapered bedroom at the south end of the upstairs balcony, inside the main lodge cabin (interior).
36	Tanagra Town	On the metal desk, by the steel support, one of the only bits of this schoolhouse still standing, in the completely open-air and mostly demolished schoolhouse, at the top of the tendril tower (exterior).
36	Tanagra Town	On one of the school desks that have slid across to the north (lower) side of the schoolhouse floor, in the completely open-air and mostly demolished schoolhouse, at the top of the tendril tower (exterior).
36	Tanagra Town	On the shelf of the headboard of the master bedroom bed, in the collapsed dark gray house with the moonshine still in the bathtub and the Giddyup Buttercup on the main floor, at the summit of the massive town tangle.
38	Big B's Rest Stop	Vertically, on the floor between the red striped northeast wall, and the counter with the coffee machine on it; close to a stepladder, inside the Super Duper Mart.
39	Valley Galleria	On or under the booth diner table below the plastic pumpkin on the attached low wall, close to a support pillar and green trash can; east side of the food court, ground level.
39	Valley Galleria	On the formal, oval-shaped dining table, lit by a ceiling light, in the red-ceiling Housewares (furniture) store, upper level, south side.
40	Treetops	On the tiny side dresser by the birdhouse, above the two mattresses, at almost the very top of the treehouse platform ascent.
42	Camp Venture	Below the shelf trolley jutting out from the southwest wall (under the green metal work cabinet), left of the Weapons Workbench inside the locked (key) security gate armory area of the Storage Cabin (interior).
42	Camp Venture	On the metal shelf trolley by the central steel support, in the middle of the Command Center (3), by the "star" trunk and the Overseer's Cache (interior).

REGION 6: CRANBERRY BOG

#	PRIMARY LOCATION NAME	MAGAZINE LOCATION DESCRIPTION
	ZONE A: NORTH BOG, ROBCO RESEARCH CENTER, AND ABANDONED BOG TOWN	
1	Kerwood Mine	On the earth by the toppled metal shelving, near a Nuka-Cola bottle and a large central metal and rock shaft column, close to a tool box in the junction cavern with the "Eye Protection" poster (cave interior).
1	Kerwood Mine	On the left (northeast) side of the slag heap, near an explosive canister, in the waterlogged chamber linking the underwater area to the destroyed mine tracks (cave interior).
1	Kerwood Mine	On a metal table with a lantern, by the explosive canisters, left of the red trunk, in the Junction Cavern (mine interior).
1	Kerwood Mine	On the blue mainframe computer bank along the wall of the monitoring room with the locked double doors (key), accessed when leaving the mine, close to the fusion core generator (on the other side of the door).
4	Firebase LT	On the mattress of the rear bed, inside the large tent (northeast), to the right of the gun emplacement.
5	Mac's Farm	On the plank-and-two-barrels table, in what's left of the living room, in the half-destroyed farmhouse.
6	The General's Steakhouse	Vertical, behind a filing cabinet, by the ground safe in the filing cabinet office with three possible Caps Stashes, in the northeast corner of the interior.
6	The General's Steakhouse	On, near, or under the washing machine and sink, left of the chained double doors, in the laundry room off the main basement kitchens (interior).
7	RobCo Research Center	On the fancy table with the dead plant, right (southeast) side of the locked (3) double door office room with the two skeletons on chairs, northeast area of the center (interior).
7	RobCo Research Center	On the screen of the microfilm unit, on the floor next to the locked safe (3), north corner of the filing office, only accessible by dropping down from the office directly above it (the one on the balcony with the Protectron pod to the right of it, while facing west) (interior).
7	RobCo Research Center	On the metal desk, in the west corner to the left of the trunk, in the upper laboratory area (interior).
8	The Thorn	On the gray defense barrier with the Brotherhood of Steel insignia, the wood spikes in front of the barrier, and the missile launcher to the side of it (exterior).
9	Forward Station Alpha	On the mattress of the rear bed, inside the gray tent, south of the cooking station.
11	Ranger District Office	On the low coffee table in front of the stone fireplace, eastern end of the lodge office (interior).
14	Bootlegger's Shack	On the metal desk with the typewriter on it, left of the filing cabinet, along the west interior wall of the shack (interior).
14	Bootlegger's Shack	On the small table next to the deck chair, on the north side of the shack room, with views of the Creekside Sundew Grove.
15	Drop Site G3	On the right side shelf of the metal counter below the first aid box, just through the open security gate, inside the flooded concrete hut.
16	Quarry X3	On the middle metal shelf, left of the orange tool box, left of the Nuka-Cola machine, southwest corner of the curve-roofed warehouse.
18	Pylon V-13	On the mattress, in the connecting part of the suspended monorail carriage, left side (if moving north), half a carriage north of the top of the exterior pylon steps.
18	Pylon V-13	On the plank with the sleeping bag, inside the suspended monorail carriage, just left of the TV and small satellite dish, across from the skeleton draped on the seat.
19	Old Mold Quarry	On the bed of the rusting pickup truck, northwest of the main concrete and metal maintenance pump building, on the road ramp.
20	Drop Site C2	On the metal counter, just through the security gate, inside the flooded concrete hut.
	ZONE B: SOUTH BOG AND WATOGA	
21	Fort Defiance	In the top floor BoS base of operations, on the ornate side cabinet, in the game room with the pool table, just right of the laser grid.
22	Appalachian Antiques	On the shelf (far left side) under the cash register counter, under the office fan (interior).
22	Appalachian Antiques	By the sleeping bag in the small, dilapidated outside shed.
25	Cranberry Glade	On the thin wood bench, on the deck in the southeast corner of the glade.
28	Watoga	On the seat just to the right of the entrance, inside the coach (not any of the nearby school buses) parked on the road northeast of Watoga High School.

#	PRIMARY LOCATION NAME	MAGAZINE LOCATION DESCRIPTION
28	Watoga	On the suspended monorail tram, at the front left side just before the driver's controls at the front of the tram. The tram is suspended at Watoga station, southeast corner of the city, west of Watoga High School.
29	Watoga Civic Center	On or around the diner table, in the corner booth (southeast corner) of the lower cafeteria area, left of the double-door exit to Appalachia, southeast from the "A3" sign (interior).
29	Watoga Civic Center	On the diner table, in the third booth from the southeast corner, in the upstairs cafeteria area, across from the "B4" sign (interior).
29	Watoga Civic Center	On or near the corner of the kitchen counter, in the small kitchen (with the three ovens) along the north side of the upper area, across from (north of) the "B5" sign (interior).
30	Watoga Transit Hub	On the back seat near the pram, in the coach parked just outside the Transit Hub lobby, on the road. It's the rear of the two coaches.
30	Watoga Transit Hub	On the last seat inside the monorail carriage, east end of the tram suspended on the rail. The tram is parked at the Transit station.
30	Watoga Transit Hub	In the rubble at the bottom of the elevator shaft, by a corpse, northwest corner of the Transit Hub lobby, behind the reception desks and lockers.
31	Watoga Emergency Services	On the second table from the left, by the Emergency Report Terminal, east wall inside the Report office; first room to the north at the top of the stairs, with the mainframe in the opposite corner (interior).
31	Watoga Emergency Services	On the metal magazine carousel, by the uncomfortable red bench seating, in the waiting room across from the reception desk, near the Helipad elevator, across from the main elevator (interior).
32	Watoga Municipal Center	On the short wood bookshelf under the window, right of the desk and wall safe (2), in the narrow Complaints Archive office, upper level, west side of the interior.
32	Watoga Municipal Center	On the metal desk with the microphone and broken terminal, in the small announcement office, southwest side of the upper level (office has windows onto the balcony with the clock) accessed via the corridor with the lockers (interior).
33	AMS Corporate Headquarters	On the floor by the toilet and newspaper, in the restroom off the CEO Kilson's office, upper executive level (interior).
34	Watoga Shopping Plaza	On the circular table with the yellow plate, near the jukebox, inside Slocum Joe's.
34	Watoga Shopping Plaza	On the yellow magazine rack shelf, right of the coffee counter, inside Slocum Joe's.
35	Watoga Estates	On the small circular white metal table with the black-and-white parasol, by the two circular red chairs, near an overturned pram, by the "condemned" door and exterior staircase; lower balcony area (exterior).
37	Watoga High School	Behind the toilet where the Bubblegum Teddy Bear and Garden Gnome are up to mischief, on the northeast corner of the roof, above the entrance to the Auditorium (exterior).
37	Watoga High School	On the low shelf of the long curved wood book check-out desk, on the lower level of the Library (interior).
37	Watoga High School	On the wooden dining table with the black-and-orange place settings, northwest corner of the cafeteria, below the staircase (interior).
37	Watoga High School	On the wooden school desk, in the southwest corner of the History classroom (upper level) (interior).
37	Watoga High School	On the small gray speaker, on the balcony with the stool and stage lights, south side (upper balcony) of the Auditorium (interior).
38	Flooded Trainyard	On the sheet of wood and cinder block table, inside the green USA carriage, on the railroad to the south, near the metal garage and black-and-white parasol.
40	Lost Home	Under the dark red sofa, in the northwest corner of the shack with the bear trap on the table; the northeast shack.
40	Lost Home	On the green chair, around the dining table inside the lone shack in the southern part of the settlement (across the bog channel).
42	Sunrise Farm	On the ornate dresser in the small bunk bed room with the hole in the wall, directly across the landing (through two doors) at the top of the stairs, inside the main sagging farmhouse structure (interior).
43	Survey Camp Alpha	On the small green card table with the army helmet, on the left side of the entrance inside the right green tent (if looking west).
49	Forward Station Delta	On the table inside the orange-and-white metal caravan hut, opposite the Power Armor Station and gantry steps.
49	Forward Station Delta	On the gantry balcony with the skeleton, at the base of the BoS flagpole.

Fallout 76

WRITTEN BY DAVID S.J. HODGSON AND GARITT ROCHA

MAPS BY LOREN GILLILAND

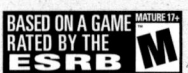
CREDITS

Publishing Manager
Shaida Boroumand

Book Designer
In Color Design:
Targa Funk and
Mark Bernard

Cover Designer
Melissa Jenee Smith

Production
Beth Guzman

Copy Editor
Carrie Andrews

Contributors
Michael Owen,
Christina LaRoche,
Julia Mascardo, and
Ben Connor

PRIMA GAMES STAFF

Publisher
Mark Hughes

Licensing
Paul Giacomotto

Digital Publisher
Julie Asbury

Marketing Manager
Jeff Barton

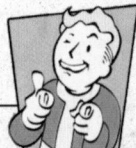

ACKNOWLEDGMENTS

Prima Games would like to thank all our friends at Bethesda Game Studios for the invaluable help, support, and feedback on the production of this guide. Special thanks to:

- JEFF ALBERTSON
- SAM BERNSTEIN
- BRANDON BISHOP
- ASHLEY CHENG
- SHANNON CORWIN
- CHRIS GORSKI
- PATRICK HARRISON
- CHRISTOPHER KRIETZ

- MICHAEL KOCHIS
- JASON LITTLE
- BRAD MARTIN
- WES MCMILLAN
- MARCIA MITNICK
- PHILIP NELSON
- PARIS NOURMOHAMMADI

- MICHAEL SHEARER
- PHIL SPEER
- RYAN TALJONICK
- KEVIN WATTS
- SPENCER WEISSER
- CODY WHARTON
- JESSICA WILLIAMS

DAVID S. J. HODGSON

Adventuring throughout Appalachia wouldn't have been possible without the help and steadfast support of the *Fallout 76* team at Bethesda; Todd, Pete, Emil, Jeff, the good folks in the QA and IT departments, Mike and Jess, and everyone who helped make this guide possible (and for the use of the SimTek 5000). A polite round of applause to Garitt and his work ethic; a co-author of this caliber is a rare find indeed. Exceptional cartographical prowess was exhibited by Loren, and thanks also to the screenshot-wrangling techniques of Michael. Thanks to Shaida and all at Prima for their patience and help during my extended exploration of West Virginia. Thank you to my loving wife Melanie; Mum, Dad, and Ian; Loki; The Moon Wiring Club, Laibach, Kraftwerk, The Benningtons; and V for Friedrich Wilhelm Von Junst, Who wrote a book that drove him most mad, It killed him, his best friend, and lots of other men. Which ultimately is just kind of sad.

GARITT ROCHA

I want to give a special thanks (in no particular order) to Cody, Mike, Luke, Todd, Patrick, Paris, Jess, David, Cheryl, Sam, Wes, and everyone else who took the time to answer our endless avalanche of questions. We genuinely, unquestionably, without a doubt couldn't have made this book without your help. You put up with our constant requests, you adjusted your schedules to give us more time and never once made us feel anything other than welcome. It was an absolute pleasure working with all of you and I can only hope that I'll get the chance to do it again in the future. Thank you.